COMPANION CD-ROM

Recipe Screen

- **Resize recipes, perform metric conversions, show recipe notes, variations and more!**
- **View photos by clicking on the image tab and add your own photos by simply clicking on Add Image Link.**

Nutritional Information:

- **The software allows you to view the important nutritional information for each recipe.**
- **Nutritional information calculates automatically for modified and new recipes!**

Shopping List:

- **The software creates shipping lists automatically from recipe ingredients.**
- **Generate a master shopping list from multiple recipes!**

PROFESSIONAL
COOKING
FOR CANADIAN CHEFS

Photography

by

J. Gerard Smith

WILEY

JOHN WILEY & SONS, INC.

Featuring recipes from

LE CORDON BLEU®
ACADÉMIE D'ART CULINAIRE DE PARIS · 1895

PROFESSIONAL
COOKING

FOR CANADIAN CHEFS

Sixth Edition

WAYNE GISSLEN

With a foreword by André J. Cointreau, *President, Le Cordon Bleu*®

Published by John Wiley & Sons, Inc., Hoboken, New Jersey
Published simultaneously in Canada

For general information on our other products and services or for technical support, please contact our Customer Care Department within the United States at (800) 762-2974, outside the United States at (317) 572-3993 or fax (317) 572-4002.

Wiley also publishes its books in a variety of electronic formats. Some content that appears in print may not be available in electronic books. For more information about Wiley products, visit our web site at www.wiley.com.

Library of Congress Cataloging-in-Publication Data:

Gisslen, Wayne, 1946-
  Professional cooking for Canadian chefs / by Wayne Gisslen; featuring recipes from Le Cordon Bleu, l'Art Culinaire, Paris? 1895.– 6th ed.
      p.   cm.
  Includes bibliographical references and index.
  ISBN-13: 978-0-471-66377-5 (cloth)
  ISBN-10: 0-471-66377-8 (cloth)
  1. Quantity cookery. 2. Food service. II. Title.
  TX820.G543 2006
  641.5'7—dc22
                                                    2005035524

Printed in the United States of America

10 9 8 7 6 5 4 3 2

This

book

is

dedicated

to

the many Chef Instructors preparing a new generation of culinary professionals.

Contents

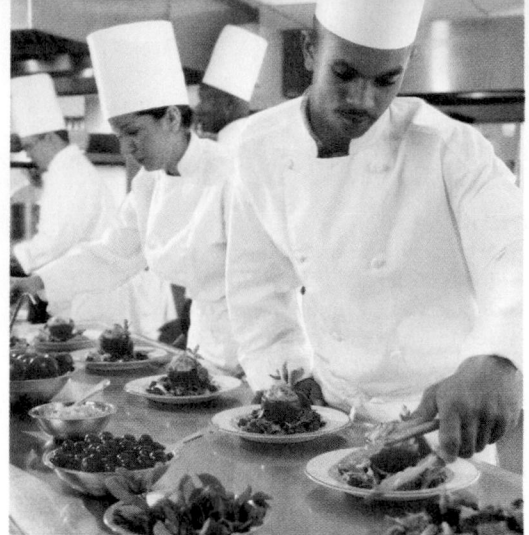

Recipe Contents   xii

About Le Cordon Bleu   xxiv

Foreword   xxv

Preface   xxvi

Acknowledgments   xxix

CHAPTER 1 THE FOOD SERVICE INDUSTRY   2

A History of Modern Food Service   4
  Sidebar: Two Important Cookbooks   6
  Sidebar: Caterina de Medici   8
The Organization of Modern Kitchens   8
Standards of Professionalism   11

CHAPTER 2 SANITATION AND SAFETY   14

Sanitation   16
  Food Hazards   16
  Personal Hygiene   25
  Food Storage   26
  Food Handling and Preparation   28
  Cleaning and Sanitizing Equipment   30
  Rodent and Insect Control   32
  Setting Up a System for Food Safety   32
Safety   35
  The Safe Workplace   35
  Preventing Cuts   35
  Preventing Burns   36
  Preventing Fires   36
  **Preventing Injuries from Machines and
    Equipment**   37
  Preventing Falls   37
  Preventing Strains and Injuries from Lifting   38

CHAPTER 3 TOOLS AND EQUIPMENT   40

Introduction to Quantity Food Equipment   42
Cooking Equipment   43
Processing Equipment   50
Holding and Storage Equipment   52
Pots, Pans, and Containers   53
Measuring Devices   56
Knives, Hand Tools, and Small Equipment   57

CHAPTER 4 BASIC COOKING PRINCIPLES   62

Heat and Food   64
  Effects of Heat on Foods   64
  Heat Transfer   66
  Cooking Times   67
Cooking Methods   68
  Moist-Heat Methods   68
  Dry-Heat Methods   70
  Dry-Heat Methods Using Fat   72
  Microwave Cooking   74
  Summary of Cooking Terms   75
Building Flavor   76
  Building Flavor Profiles   76
    Sidebar: Classic Flavoring Combinations   78
  Seasoning and Flavoring Ingredients   78
  Using Herbs and Spices   84

CHAPTER 5 MENUS, RECIPES, AND COST MANAGEMENT   86

Menu Forms and Functions   88
Building the Menu   90
The Written Recipe   95
Measurement   99
Converting Recipes   103
Food Cost Calculations   107
Controlling Food Costs   112

CHAPTER 6 NUTRITION   116

Nutrients   118
    Sidebar: calories and Calories   119
    Sidebar: Essential Fatty Acids   121
    Sidebar: More Chemistry: Lipoproteins   122
    Sidebar: Phytochemicals   122
The Balanced Diet   122
Cooking Healthful Meals   125

CHAPTER 7 MISE EN PLACE   128

Planning and Organizing Production   130
Using the Knife   133
Preliminary Cooking and Flavoring   140
Preparation for Frying   142
Handling Convenience Foods   144

CHAPTER 8 STOCKS AND SAUCES   148

Stocks   150
    Ingredients   150
    Procedures   153
    Reductions and Glazes   158
    Convenience Bases   159
Sauces   159
    Understanding Sauces   160
    Roux   161
    Other Thickening Agents   164
    Finishing Techniques   166
    Sauce Families   167
    Production   171
        Sidebar: Gastrique   174
        Sidebar: Thai Curries   194

CHAPTER 9 SOUPS   204

Understanding Soups   206
    Classification of Soups   206
    Service of Soups   207
Clear Soups   209
    Broths   209
    Consommé   210
    Vegetable Soups   214
    Other Clear Soups   217
Thick Soups   221
    Cream Soups   221
    Purée Soups   229
    Bisques   237
    Chowders   238
Specialty Soups and National Soups   241

CHAPTER 10 UNDERSTANDING
        MEATS AND GAME   256

Composition, Structure, and Basic Quality Factors   258
    Composition   258
    Structure   259
    Inspection and Grading   260
    Aging   261
Understanding the Basic Cuts   262
    Sidebar: IMPS/NAMP Classifications   262
    Available Forms: Carcasses, Partial Carcasses,
        Primals, and Fabricated Cuts   263
    Sidebar: Meat-Cutting Terminology   267
    Bone Structure   267
    Beef, Lamb, Veal, and Pork Cuts   268
    Selecting Meats for Your Operation   270
Cooking and Handling Meats   271
    Tenderness and Appropriate Cooking
        Methods   271
        Sidebar: Milk-Fed, Grain-Fed, or Grass-Fed   272
    Doneness   275
    Cooking Variety Meats   278
    Game and Specialty Meats   281
        Sidebar: Bone Structure of Game   282
        Sidebar: Hanging Game   283
    Storage of Meats   284

CHAPTER 11 COOKING MEATS AND GAME   286

Roasting and Baking   288
Broiling, Grilling, and Pan-Broiling   305
Sautéing, Pan-Frying, and Griddling   313
Simmering   324
Braising   331

CHAPTER 12 UNDERSTANDING POULTRY
        AND GAME BIRDS   350

Composition and Structure   352
Inspection and Grading   354
Classification and Market Forms   354
Handling and Storage   358
Doneness   358
Trussing Methods   359
Cutting Up Chicken   360

CHAPTER 13 COOKING POULTRY
AND GAME BIRDS 364

Roasting and Baking 366
Broiling and Grilling 376
Sidebar:Tandoori Chicken 381
Sautéing, Pan-Frying, and Deep-Frying 383
Sidebar:Teriyaki 396
Simmering and Poaching 399
Sidebar: Cooking Styles in Chinese Dishes 407
Sidebar: Mole Poblano 409
Braising 410
Sidebar: Confit of Duck and Goose 422
Dressings and Stuffings 423

CHAPTER 14 UNDERSTANDING FISH
AND SHELLFISH 426

Fin Fish 428
Composition and Structure 428
Special Problems in Cooking Fish 428
Cutting Fish 429
Varieties and Characteristics 432
Handling and Storage 439
Shellfish 441
Mollusks 441
Cephalopods 446
Crustaceans 447
Miscellaneous Seafood 454

CHAPTER 15 COOKING FISH
AND SHELLFISH 456

Baking 458
Broiling and Grilling 464
Sidebar: Escabeche 467
Sautéing and Pan-Frying 470
Deep-Frying 479
Sidebar: Tempura 481
Poaching and Simmering 482
Sidebar: Cuisson 483
Steaming and Mixed Cooking Techniques 492
Seafood Served Raw 498
Sidebar: Sushi—A Japanese Classic 501

CHAPTER 16 UNDERSTANDING
VEGETABLES 504

Controlling Quality Changes During Cooking 506
Controlling Texture Changes 506
Controlling Flavor Changes 507
Controlling Color Changes 508
Controlling Nutrient Losses 510
General Rules of Vegetable Cookery 511
Standards of Quality in Cooked Vegetables 512
Handling Vegetables 512
Fresh Vegetables 512
Processed Vegetables 536
Production and Holding Problems in Quantity
Cooking 539
Storage 540

CHAPTER 17 COOKING VEGETABLES 542

Boiling and Steaming 544
Sautéing and Pan-Frying 556
Braising 559
Baking 565
Broiling and Grilling 573
Deep-Frying 575

CHAPTER 18 POTATOES 580

Understanding Potatoes 582
Cooking Potatoes 585

CHAPTER 19 LEGUMES, GRAINS, PASTA,
AND OTHER STARCHES 606

Dried Legumes 608
Grains 617
Pasta, Noodles, and Dumplings 635
Sidebar: Singapore Noodles 650

CHAPTER 20 COOKING FOR
VEGETARIAN DIETS 654

Understanding Vegetarian Diets 656
Sidebar: Amino Acids 658
Menus for Vegetarian Diets 658
Sidebar: Enchiladas 666

CHAPTER 21 SALADS AND SALAD
         DRESSINGS 672

Salads 674
   Types of Salads 674
   Ingredients 675
   Arrangement and Presentation 684
   Recipes and Techniques 686
Salad Dressings 720
   Ingredients 720
      Sidebar: Balsamico Tradizionale
         (Traditional Balsamic Vinegar) 721
   Emulsions in Salad Dressings 722
   Oil and Vinegar Dressings 723
   Emulsified Dressings 726
   Other Dressings 730

CHAPTER 22 SANDWICHES 734

   Breads 736
   Spreads 736
   Fillings 737
   Types of Sandwiches 738
      Sidebar: Panini 740
   Making Sandwiches 740
      Sidebar: Associazione Verace Pizza Napoletana 753

CHAPTER 23 HORS D'OEUVRES 754

   Serving Hors d'Oeuvres 756
   Canapés 756
      Sidebar: "Outside the Work" 757
   Cocktails 760
   Relishes 760
   Dips 761
   Miscellaneous Hors d'Oeuvres 763
      Sidebar: Spanish Tapas Traditions 765

CHAPTER 24 BREAKFAST PREPARATION 784

Eggs 786
   Understanding Eggs 786
   Cooking Eggs 790
Breakfast Breads, Cereals, and Meats 800
   Pancakes and Waffles 800
   French Toast 802
   Cereals 804
   Breakfast Meats 804

CHAPTER 25 DAIRY AND BEVERAGES 806

Dairy Products 808
   Milk and Cream 808
   Butter 810
   Cheese 811
Coffee and Tea 819
   Coffee 819
   Tea 822

CHAPTER 26 SAUSAGES AND
         CURED FOODS 824

Curing and Smoking 826
Sausages 831

CHAPTER 27 PÂTÉS, TERRINES, AND
         OTHER COLD FOODS 846

The Handling and Service of Cold Dishes 848
Aspic and Chaud-Froid 849
Special Forcemeat Dishes 854
Terrines Based on Mousselines 863
Terrines and Other Molds with Gelatin 865
Foie Gras, Liver Terrines, and Rillettes 871

CHAPTER 28 FOOD PRESENTATION
         AND GARNISH 876

Hot Food Presentation 878
   Fundamentals of Plating 878
   Garnish 882
Cold Food Presentation and Buffet Service 884
   Buffet Arrangement and Appearance 885
   Cold Platter Presentation 887
   Hot Foods for Buffets 889

CHAPTER 29 BAKESHOP PRODUCTION:
         BASIC PRINCIPLES
         AND INGREDIENTS 890

Basic Principles of Baking 892
   Formulas and Measurement 892
   Mixing and Gluten Development 895
   The Baking Process 896
   Staling 896
Ingredients 897
   Flours, Meals, and Starches 897
   Fats 899
   Sugars 900
   Liquids 902
   Eggs 903
   Leavening Agents 903
   Salt, Flavorings, and Spices 905

CHAPTER 30 YEAST PRODUCTS 908

Understanding Yeast Products 910
  Yeast Product Types 910
  Mixing Methods 910
  Steps in Yeast Dough Production 911
Dough Formulas and Techniques 916
  Bread and Roll Formulas 916
  Rolled-In Doughs: Danish Pastry and Croissants 920
  Makeup Techniques 924

CHAPTER 31 QUICK BREADS 930

Mixing and Production Methods 932
  Types of Dough 932
  Gluten Development in Quick Breads 932
  The Biscuit Method 933
  Makeup of Biscuits 933
  The Muffin Method 933
  Summary: Biscuit and Muffin Methods 934
Formulas 935

CHAPTER 32 CAKES AND ICINGS 938

Understanding Cake-Making 940
  Basic Mixing Methods 940
  Cake Formula Types 942
  Scaling and Panning 943
  Baking and Cooling 944
  Altitude Adjustments 946
Cake Formulas 948
  Creaming Method 948
  Two-Stage Method 950
  Foaming Methods 951
Icings: Production and Application 953
  Producing and Handling Basic Types 953
  Assembling and Icing Cakes 958

CHAPTER 33 COOKIES 962

  Cookie Characteristics and Their Causes 964
  Mixing Methods 965
  Types and Makeup Methods 966
  Panning, Baking, and Cooling 968

CHAPTER 34 PIES AND PASTRIES 976

Pies 978
  Pie Doughs 978
  Assembly and Baking 982
  Fillings 984
Pastries, Meringues, and Fruit Desserts 992
  Puff Pastry 992
  Éclair Paste 997
  Meringues 999
  Fruit Desserts 1001

CHAPTER 35 CREAMS, CUSTARDS, PUDDINGS, FROZEN DESSERTS, AND SAUCES 1004

  Sugar Cooking 1006
  Basic Custards and Creams 1007
  Puddings 1010
  Bavarians, Chiffons, Mousses, and Soufflés 1013
  Frozen Desserts 1021
  Dessert Sauces 1023

APPENDIX 1 METRIC CONVERSION FACTORS 1026

APPENDIX 2 STANDARD CAN SIZES 1026

APPENDIX 3 APPROXIMATE WEIGHT-VOLUME EQUIVALENTS OF DRY FOODS 1027

APPENDIX 4 KITCHEN MATH EXERCISES—METRIC VERSIONS 1028

APPENDIX 5 EGGS AND SAFETY 1030

  Bibliography 1031
  Glossary 1033
  U.S.–U.K. Cooking Vocabulary 1040
  French-English Cooking Vocabulary 1041
  Subject Index 1047
  Recipe Index 1050

Recipe Contents

♥ = heart smart recipes
Blue type indicates recipes that were developed by
    Le Cordon Bleu.
V = vegetarian recipes

CHAPTER 8 STOCKS AND SAUCES

♥ Basic White Stock   155
    Vegetable Stock   155
♥ Basic Brown Stock   157
♥ Fish Fumet   158
V Béchamel Sauce   171
    Light Béchamel   171
    Heavy Béchamel   171
Small Sauces   171
    Cream Sauce   171
    Mornay Sauce   171
    Mornay Sauce for Glazing or Gratinéeing   171
    Cheddar Cheese Sauce   171
    Mustard Sauce   171
    Soubise Sauce   171
    Tomatoed Soubise Sauce   171
    Nantua Sauce   171
♥ Velouté Sauce (Veal, Chicken, or Fish)   172
White Wine Sauce   172
Suprême Sauce   172
Allemande Sauce   173
Small Sauces   173
    Poulette   173
    Aurora   173
    Hungarian   173
    Ivory or Albufera   173
    Curry   173
    Mushroom   173
    Bercy   173
    Herb   173
    Normandy   173
    Anchovy   173
    Shrimp   173
    Venetian   173
    Horseradish   173
♥ Brown Sauce or Espagnole   174
♥ Fond Lié or Jus Lié   174
♥ Demi-glace   175
Small Sauces   175
    Bordelaise   175

Marchand de Vin (Wine Merchant)   175
    Robert   175
    Charcutière   175
    Chasseur   175
    Diable (Deviled)   175
    Madeira   175
    Perigueux   175
    Poîvrade   175
    Port Wine   175
    Italian Sauce   175
    Mushroom   175
    Bercy   175
    Piquante   175
    Lyonnaise   175
    Bigarade   175
♥ Tomato Sauce I   176
    Tomato Sauce II (Vegetarian)   176
Tomato Sauce III   176
Small Sauces   176
    Portugaise (Portuguese)   176
    Spanish   176
    Creole   176
V Fresh Tomato Coulis with Garlic   177
V Maître d'Hotel Butter   179
    Anchovy Butter   179
    Garlic Butter   179
    Escargot (Snail) Butter   179
    Shrimp Butter   179
    Mustard Butter   179
    Herb Butter   179
    Scallion or Shallot Butter   179
    Curry Butter   179
V Beurre Blanc   180
    Herbed Butter Sauce   180
    Beurre Rouge (Red Butter Sauce)   180
Red Wine Butter Sauce for Fish   180
V Hollandaise Sauce I   182
V Hollandaise Sauce II   182
V Small Sauces   183
    Maltaise   183
    Mousseline   183
V Béarnaise Sauce   183
Small Sauces   183
    Foyot   183
    Choron   183
♥ V Mushroom Jus   188

❤ Bell Pepper Coulis 189
        Bell Pepper and Tomato Coulis 189
❤ V Sweet Corn and Chile Purée 189
V White Bean Purée 189
Chipotle Cream Sauce 190
        Herb Cream Sauce 190
❤ V Salsa Verde Cocida 190
        Salsa Roja 190
        Tomato Broth for Chiles Rellenos 190
❤ V Salsa Cruda 191
❤ Ancho Sauce 191
V Chimichurri Sauce 191
V Vegetable Caper Relish 192
❤ V Tomato Raisin Chutney 192
❤ V Pineapple Chutney 193
❤ V Cucumber Raita 193
❤ Nuoc Cham (Vietnamese Dipping Sauce) 193
Thai Red Curry Sauce 194
        Thai Green Curry Sauce 194
V Red Curry Paste 194
V Green Curry Paste 195
V Indonesian Peanut Sauce 195
❤ Dashi 195
        Vegetarian Dashi 195
❤ V Yakitori Sauce 196
❤ Ponzu Sauce 196
V Sesame Miso Sauce 196
White Wine Cream Sauce for Fish 197
Yogurt Sour Cream Sauce 197
V Sauce Vierge 197
Port Wine Sauce 198
❤ V Applesauce 198
❤ V Barbecue Sauce 198
❤ Chili Barbecue Sauce 199
V Soy Barbecue Sauce 199
❤ V Fruit Salsa 199
V Shallot Oil 200
        Ginger Oil, Horseradish Oil, or Garlic Oil 200
        Lemon or Orange Oil 200
        Rosemary Oil, Sage Oil, Thyme Oil, or Oregano Oil 200
        Cinnamon Oil, Cumin Oil, Curry Oil, Ginger Oil, or Paprika Oil 200
        Basil Oil, Parsley Oil, Chervil Oil, or Cilantro Oil 200
Tartar Sauce 200
        Rémoulade Sauce 200
V Aioli I 201
V Horseradish Sauce (Sauce Raifort) 201
❤ Cocktail Sauce 201
❤ V Mignonette Sauce 202
❤ V Lime and Ginger Chutney 202
❤ V Fig Compote 202

CHAPTER 9 SOUPS

❤ Beef Broth 210
❤ Consommé 212
        Double Consommé 213
        Chicken Consommé 213
        Cold Jellied Consommé 213

Consommé Madrilène 213
Essence of Celery Consommé 213
Consommé au Porto 213
Consommé au Sherry 213
Garnished Consommés 213
        Consommé Brunoise 213
        Consommé Julienne 213
        Consommé Printanière 213
        Consommé Paysanne 213
        Consommé with Pearl Tapioca 213
        Consommé Vermicelli 213
❤ Chicken and Celery Consommé 214
Clear Vegetable Soup 215
        Vegetable Rice Soup 215
        Chicken Vegetable Rice Soup 215
        Vegetable Beef Soup 215
        Vegetable Beef Barley Soup 215
Piquant Vegetable Soup with Chickpeas 216
        Piquant Vegetable Soup with Roasted Garlic 216
❤ Mushroom Barley Soup 216
❤ Chicken Noodle Soup 217
        Beef Noodle Soup 217
        Chicken or Beef Noodle Soup with Vegetables 217
❤ Brunswick Soup 217
Chicken Tomato Bouillon with Pesto 218
        Chicken Tomato Bouillon with Rice 218
        Cold Chicken Tomato Bouillon 218
Oxtail Soup 219
Asian-Style Shrimp Soup with Egg Flowers 220
Cream of Celery Soup (Cream Soup Method 1) 223
        Cream of Asparagus 223
        Cream of Broccoli 223
        Cream of Carrot 223
        Cream of Cauliflower 223
        Cream of Corn 223
        Cream of Cucumber 223
        Cream of Mushroom 223
        Cream of Pea 223
        Cream of Spinach 223
        Cream of Watercress 223
        Cream of Chicken 223
        Cold Cream Soups 223
Cream of Mushroom Soup (Cream Soup Method 2) 224
        Cream of Asparagus 224
        Cream of Broccoli 224
        Cream of Carrot 224
        Cream of Cauliflower 224
        Cream of Celery 224
        Cream of Corn 224
        Cream of Cucumber 224
        Cream of Green Pea 224
        Cream of Spinach 224
        Cream of Watercress 224
        Cream of Chicken 224
Cream of Broccoli Soup (Cream Soup Method 3) 225
Cream of Tomato Soup 226
Wild Rice and Mushroom Soup 227
Wisconsin Cheddar and Broccoli Soup 228
Purée of Green Pea Soup with Mint Cream 229
Purée of Carrot Soup (Potage Crècy) 230

Purée of Cauliflower Soup (Purée Dubarry) 230
Purée of Celery or Celery Root Soup 230
Purée of Jerusalem Artichoke Soup 230
Purée of Potato Soup (Potage Parmentier) 230
Purée of Potato and Leek Soup 230
Purée of Turnip Soup 230
Purée of Watercress Soup 230
Purée of Mixed Vegetable Soup 230
Potage Solferino 230
Purée of Split Pea Soup 231
Purée of White Bean Soup 231
Purée of Yellow Split Pea Soup 231
Purée of Lentil Soup 231
Purée of Kidney Bean Soup 231
Purée of Black Bean Soup 231
Purée Mongole 231
Nonpuréed Bean Soups 231
Butternut Squash Soup with Caramelized Apples 232
Purée of Spring Vegetable Soup 233
Potage Cressonière (Watercress Soup) 233
Navy Bean Soup 234
Apple and Parsnip Soup with
Floating Calvados Cream 234
Potato and Leek Soup with Sorrel 235
Spicy Black Bean Soup 235
Chilled Leek and Potato Soup with Shrimp and Fennel
Salad 236
Vichyssoise 236
Shrimp Bisque 237
Lobster Bisque 237
Potato Chowder 238
Corn Chowder 238
Corn and Crab Chowder with Basil 239
New England Clam Chowder 240
Manhattan Clam Chowder 240
New England Fish Chowder 240
French Onion Soup Gratinée 241
Roasted Garlic Soup with Black Olive Crostini 242
Viennese-Style Vegetable Broth 242
Borscht 243
Cold Borscht 243
Gulyas 243
Seafood Gumbo 244
Chicken and Andouille Gumbo 244
Pho Bo (Vietnamese Beef and Rice Noodle Soup) 245
Chinese Hot and Sour Soup 246
♥ Chilled Tomato and Basil Soup 247
V Ecuadorian Quinoa and Peanut Soup 247
Tortilla Soup 248
Summer Vegetable and Smoked Tomato Soup 249
V Red Lentil and Apricot Soup 249
♥ Japanese Clear Soup with Shrimp 250
Miso Soup 250
Caldo Verde 251
Lightly Saffroned Mussel Soup 251
Velouté Agnes Sorel (Chicken and Leek Soup) 252
Zuppa di Ceci e Riso (Italian Chickpea and
Rice Soup) 252
Minestrone 253
Scotch Broth 253
V Gazpacho 254
♥ V Chilled Melon and Mint Soup 255

CHAPTER 11 COOKING MEATS AND GAME

Roast Rib of Beef au Jus 291
Roast Rib-Eye Roll, Top Round, Sirloin, or Strip
Loin 291
Roast Beef with Gravy 291
♥ Roast Beef Gravy 292
Jus Lié 292
Roast Loin of Pork with Sage and Apples 293
Roast Loin or Rack of Veal with Sage and
Apples 293
Roast Stuffed Shoulder of Lamb 294
Roast Boneless Shoulder of Lamb 294
Roast Leg of Lamb 294
Roast Leg of Lamb Boulangère 294
Roast Rack of Lamb 296
Rack of Lamb aux Primeurs (with Spring
Vegetables) 296
Rack of Lamb Persillé 296
Persillade 296
Smoke-Roasted Pork Shoulder 298
Smoke-Roasted Shoulder of Boar 298
V Spice Rub I 298
Barbecued Spareribs 299
V Spice Rub II 299
Roast Pork Tenderloin with Leeks and Whole-Grain
Mustard 300
Roasted Loin of Pork with Ginger 300
Baked Pork Chops with Prune Stuffing 301
Glazed Ham with Cider Sauce 302
Ham with Brown Cider Sauce 302
Fruit-Glazed Ham 302
Home-Style Meatloaf 303
Home-Style All-Beef Meatloaf 303
Italian-Style Meatloaf 303
Salisbury Steak 303
Baked Meatballs 303
Loin or Rack of Venison Grand Veneur 304
Leg of Venison Grand Veneur 304
Red Wine Marinade for Game 304
Roast Loin of Rabbit with Risotto 305
Broiled Strip Loin Steak Maître d'Hôtel 307
Broiled Lamb Chops 307
London Broil 308
Teriyaki-Style London Broil 308
Beef Fajitas 309
Broiled Smoked Pork Chop with Flageolet Beans and
Wilted Arugula 309
Grilled Marinated Pork Tenderloin with Sweet Potato
Purée and Warm Chipotle Salsa 310
Grilled Chopped Lamb "Steaks" with Rosemary and
Pine Nuts 311
Grilled Chopped Beef "Steaks" with Marjoram 311
Shish Kebab 311
Broiled Lamb Kidneys with Bacon 312
Grilled Venison with Lime Butter 312
Grilled Loin of Elk 312
Breaded Veal Cutlets 315
Veal Cutlet Sauté Gruyère 315
Schnitzel à la Holstein 315
Veal Cutlet Viennese Style (Wiener Schnitzel) 315

Veal Parmigiana   315
Veal Cordon Bleu   315
Breaded Pork Cutlets   315
Veal Scaloppine alla Marsala   316
Veal Scaloppine with Sherry   316
Veal Scaloppine with Lemon   316
Veal Scaloppine à la Crème   316
Veal Scaloppine with Mushrooms and
    Cream   316
Tournedos Vert-Pré   317
Tournedos Béarnaise   317
Tournedos Bordelaise   317
Tournedos Chasseur   317
Tournedos Rossini   317
Pork Chops Charcutière   318
Pork Chops Robert   318
Pork Chops Piquante   318
Veal Chops   318
Thai Green Curry of Pork with Vegetables   318
Entrecôte Sauté Bordelaise (Sirloin Steak with Red Wine
    and Shallot Sauce)   319
Côte de Veau Grandmère (Veal Chops with Bacon,
    Mushrooms, and Onions)   319
Lamb Medallions with Thyme and Garlic Cream   320
Fillet of Lamb with Mint and Cilantro Jus   321
Calf's Liver Lyonnaise   321
Medallions of Venison Poîvrade with Cassis   322
Medallions of Boar Poîvrade with Cassis   322
Sautéed Veal Sweetbreads with Shiitake Mushrooms and
    Port Wine Sauce   322
Stir-Fried Beef with Green Peppers   323
Costolette di Vitello Ripiene alla Valdostana   323
Costolette alla Milanese   323
Simmered Fresh Beef Brisket ("Boiled Beef")   325
Simmered Pork Shoulder with Cabbage   325
New England Boiled Dinner   325
Blanquette of Veal   326
Blanquette of Lamb   326
Blanquette of Pork   326
Irish Lamb Stew   327
Tripes à la Mode de Caen   327
Pearl Balls   328
Fried Pork Balls   328
Wontons   328
Shredded Pork (Carnitas)   328
Picadillo   328
Shortcut Picadillo   328
Dillkött   329
Dillkött på Lamm   329
Lamb Tagine with Chickpeas   329
Poached Beef Tenderloin with Beef Short Rib Ravioli in
    Morel Consommé   330
Beef Pot Roast   334
Braised Beef Jardinière   334
Braised Lamb Shoulder   334
Braised Short Ribs   335
Swiss Steak   335
Swiss Steaks in Tomato Sauce   335
Swiss Steaks with Sour Cream   335
Swiss Steaks in Red Wine Sauce   335
Braised Oxtails   335
Braised Lamb Shanks   335

Beef Stew   336
Beef Stew with Red Wine   336
Boeuf Bourguignon   336
Navarin of Lamb (Brown Lamb Stew)   336
Brown Veal Stew   336
Brown Veal Stew with White Wine   336
Beef Pot Pie   336
Boeuf à la Mode   337
Beef Stew with Carrots   337
Lombatine di Maiale alla Napoletana   338
Pollo con Peperoni all'Abruzzese   338
Chile con Carne   339
Chili with Beans   339
Game Chili   339
Texas Red   339
Texas Short Ribs   339
Braised Beef with Ancho Chiles   340
Braised Pork Loin with Olives   341
Daube d'Agneau Provençale
    (Braised Lamb Provençale)   342
Veal Fricassée   342
Pork Fricassée   342
Veal Shank with Orange   343
Hungarian Goulash (Veal, Beef, or Pork)   344
Rabbit with Mustard   344
Sauerbraten   345
Sauerbraten with Sour Cream Gravy   345
Braised Sweetbreads   346
Swedish Meatballs   346
Veal Curry with Mangoes and Cashews   347
Lamb Curry   347
Saltimbocca alla Romana   348
Carbonnade à la Flamande   348

CHAPTER 13 COOKING POULTRY AND GAME BIRDS

Baked Chicken   367
Baked Herbed Chicken   367
Baked Rosemary Chicken   367
Baked Chicken Parmesan   367
Roast Chicken with Natural Gravy   368
Roast Herbed Chicken   368
Roast Chicken with Gravy   368
Roast Chicken with Cream Gravy   368
Roast Turkey with Giblet Gravy   370
Roast Capons and Large Chickens   370
Roast Turkey, Chicken, or Capon with
    Cream Gravy   370
Roast Duckling with Caramelized Apples   372
Duckling in Paprika   373
Herb-Roasted Squab   373
Smoke-Roasted Spiced Chicken Breasts with
    Fruit Salsa   374
Quail Baked with Prosciutto and Herbs   375
Broiled Chicken   377
Broiled Chicken, Quantity Method   377
Broiled Rock Cornish Game Hen   377
Broiled Tarragon Chicken   377
Chicken Paillard with Grilled Vegetables   377
Broiled Poussin or Cornish Hens with Mustard Crust   378
Grilled Spiced Squab with Couscous and Fig Compote   379

Grilled Spiced Cornish Hen   379
Grilled Chicken with Garlic and Ginger   380
   Southwestern Grilled Chicken   380
   Spicy Barbecue-Style Grilled Chicken   380
   Grilled Chicken, Oriental Style   380
   Grilled Chicken Marinated in
      Yogurt and Spices   380
Grilled Quail Marinated in Soy Barbecue Sauce   381
Grilled Ostrich or Emu with Adobo Spices   381
Grilled Spiced Turkey Burger   382
Pan-Fried Chicken   384
   Country-Style Fried Chicken   384
Sautéed Boneless Breast of Chicken with
   Mushroom Sauce   385
Deep-Fried Chicken   386
   Fried Chicken Maryland   386
   Fried Chicken Breast Strips   386
Turkey Scaloppine with Shiitake Mushrooms and
   Roasted Shallots   387
Quail with Balsamic Glaze   388
Quail with Creole Spices   389
Sautéed Chicken with Tomatoes and Mushrooms   390
Tangerine-Marinated Breast of Duck   391
Sautéed Chicken Breasts with Lemon Grass and
   Three Peppers   392
Chicken Pojarski Princesse   393
Goujons of Chicken in Salad with Sesame Seeds   394
Chicken Stir-Fry with Walnuts   395
Chicken Teriyaki   396
Chicken Breasts Parmesan   397
Vietnamese Stir-Fried Chicken with Chile   398
"Boiled" Fowl   400
   Simmered Chicken or Turkey   400
Poached Chicken Breast Princesse   401
   Poached Chicken Breast Florentine   401
Chicken or Turkey Pot Pie   402
   Chicken or Turkey Stew   402
Chicken Blanquette I   403
   Chicken Blanquette II   403
   Chicken Blanquette à l'Ancienne
      (Ancient Style)   403
   Chicken Blanquette Brunoise   403
   Chicken Blanquette Argenteuil   403
Stuffed Chicken Breasts Doria   404
Chicken Stew with Sorrel   405
Oyako Donburi   406
   Tendon   406
Red-Cooked Chicken   407
Tea-Smoked Duck   408
   Crispy Duck   408
Mole Poblano de Pollo or de Guajolote   409
Chicken Fricassée   410
   Chicken Fricassée with Tarragon   410
   Chicken Fricassée à l'Indienne   410
   Fricassée of Turkey Wings   410
   Veal Fricassée   410
   Pork Fricassée   410
   Fricassée à l'Ancienne   410
   Fricassée Brunoise   410
   Fricassée Argenteuil   410
Chicken Chasseur   411
   Chicken Bercy   411

Chicken Portugaise   411
Chicken Hongroise   411
Braised Duckling with Sauerkraut   412
   Braised Duckling with Cabbage   412
Paprika Chicken   413
Poulet Sauté Basquaise (Basque-Style Chicken)   414
Poulet Sauté au Vinaigre (Lyonnaise-Style Chicken with
   Tomatoes and Vinegar)   414
Pheasant en Cocotte   415
Fricassée de Volaille Vallée d'Auge (Fricassée of Chicken
   with Apples and Cider)   416
Chicken en Cocotte with Côte du Rhône   417
Ballotine de Poulet Grandmère (Stuffed Boneless
   Chicken Legs with Mushrooms, Onion, and
   Bacon)   418
Salmis of Partridge   419
Coq au Vin   420
Arroz con Pollo (Spanish Rice with Chicken)   421
Duck Confit   422
Basic Bread Dressing   424
   Sausage Dressing   424
   Chestnut Dressing   424
   Mushroom Dressing   424
   Giblet Dressing   424
   Cornbread Dressing   424

CHAPTER 15 COOKING FISH AND SHELLFISH

Baked Cod Fillets Portugaise   459
Baked Fish with Tomatoes and Mushrooms   460
   Baked Fish à la Menagère   460
Baked Stuffed Mackerel   461
Baked Clams Oreganata   461
Smoke-Roasted Salmon Fillet with Pepper Salad   462
Roasted Monkfish Wrapped in Prosciutto   463
Baked Oysters with Balsamic Vinegar, Arugula, and
   Pine Nuts   463
Broiled Fish Steaks Maître d'Hotel   465
Grilled Tuna with Sauce Vierge and Spinach   465
Grilled Mahi-mahi with Fruit Salsa   466
Broiled Mako Shark Steaks with Browned Garlic
   Vinaigrette   466
Broiled Salmon in Escabeche   467
Broiled Lobster   468
   Broiled Rock Lobster Tail   468
Broiled Shrimp, Scampi Style   469
   Shrimp Brochettes   469
   Broiled Scallops   469
   Broiled Fish Fillets or Steaks with
      Garlic Butter   469
Oysters Casino   470
   Clams Casino   470
Fillets of Sole Meunière   472
   Fillets of Fish Doré   472
   Trout Meunière   472
   Fish Sauté Amandine   472
   Fish Sauté Grenobloise   472
   Sautéed Soft-Shell Crabs   472
Sautéed Scallops with Tomato, Garlic, and Parsley   473
   Sautéed Shrimp   473
Escalope of Salmon with Sorrel   473

Salmon with an Almond Crust   474
Crab Cakes with Roasted Pepper Rémoulade   474
Cornmeal-Crusted Soft-Shell Crabs with Cornmeal
    Pancakes and Roasted Tomatoes   475
Peppered Haddock with Garlic Whipped Potatoes and
    Parsley Sauce   475
        Peppered Haddock with
            Purée of Flageolet Beans   475
Spicy Shrimp or Scallop Sauté   476
Shrimp and Cucumber in Thai Red Curry   477
Skate with Caper Butter   477
Pan-Fried Catfish with Shrimp Etouffée   478
Fried Breaded Fish Fillets   479
        Fried Breaded Scallops   479
        Fried Breaded Shrimp   479
        Fried Oysters or Clams   479
Cod Cakes   480
        Salmon or Tuna Cakes   480
Deep-Fried Calamari with Spicy Tomato Sauce and
    Aioli   480
Shrimp and Vegetable Tempura   481
Court Bouillon for Fish   484
♥ Poached Whole Fish   485
        Poached Fish Steaks   485
        "Boiled" Shellfish (Lobster, Crab, Shrimp)   485
Sole Vin Blanc (Poached Fillets of Sole in
    White Wine Sauce)   486
        Glazed Poached Fish   487
        Poached Fish Bonne Femme   487
        Poached Fish Dugléré   487
        Poached Fish Mornay   487
        Poached Fish Florentine   487
        Seafood à la Nage   487
Poached Fingers of Salmon and Turbot with Saffron and
    Julienne of Vegetables   488
Poached Salmon with Lentils in Cream   488
Pesce con Salsa Verde   489
Sole Fillets Steamed in Beaujolais   489
Bourride of Monkfish   490
Zuppa di Vongole   491
        Zuppa di Cozze   491
        Zuppa di Frutti di Mare   491
        Zuppa di Pesce   491
Lobster à l'Americaine   493
        Lobster Newburg   493
        Shrimp à l'Americaine or Shrimp Newburg   493
Moules Marinière (Steamed Mussels)   494
        Steamed Mussels (without wine)   494
        Mussels in Cream   494
Mackerel en Papillote   495
Steamed Sea Bass with Garlic and Ginger   496
Seafood Newburg   496
        Seafood Curry   496
Fisherman's Stew   497
Seafood Casserole au Gratin   498
        Salmon or Tuna Casserole   498
Tartar of Sea Bass and Salmon   499
♥ V Sushi Rice   500
        Nigirizushi (Finger Sushi)   500
        Kappa-maki (Cucumber Roll)   500
        Tekka-maki (Tuna Roll)   500
        Chirashizushi (Scatter Sushi)   500

Scallop Seviche   502
Tuna Carpaccio with Sheep's Milk Cheese   503

CHAPTER 17 COOKING VEGETABLES

V Peas, Carrots, and Pearl Onions with
    Tarragon Butter   546
        Buttered Vegetables   546
        Herbed Vegetables   546
        Amandine   546
        Hollandaise   546
        Polonaise   546
V Puréed Butternut Squash   547
        Mashed Rutabagas or Yellow Turnips   547
V Creamed Spinach   547
        Creamed Vegetables   547
V Broccoli Mornay   548
        Broccoli with Cheddar Cheese Sauce   548
♥ V Vegetable Tagliatelle   548
V Cauliflower au Gratin   549
V Green Beans Basquaise   549
V Mixed Vegetables with Herbs   550
Green Beans with Sesame Dressing   550
        Sesame Miso Dressing   550
Green Beans with Roasted Peppers and Bacon   551
        Green Beans with Pecans and
            Browned Shallots   551
♥ V Compote of Carrots and Onions   551
Collards with Ham   552
Brussels Sprouts Paysanne   552
V Artichokes Gribiche   553
V Artichokes Clamart   553
♥ V Glazed Root Vegetables   554
V Glazed Carrots (Carrots Vichy)   554
Spinaci alla Romana   555
        Spinaci alla Piemontese   555
♥ V Cipolline in Agrodolce   555
Pan-Fried Eggplant with Tomato Sauce   557
        Pan-Fried Eggplant Creole   557
        Eggplant Parmigiana   557
V Zucchini Sauté Provençale   557
        Shredded Zucchini with Shallots   557
        Zucchini with Tomatoes   557
        Zucchini with Cream   557
V Sautéed Mushrooms   558
        Creamed Mushrooms   558
        Duxelles   558
V Corn with Poblanos   558
        Gratin of Corn and Poblanos   558
        Corn and Poblanos in Cream   558
Stir-Fried Mixed Vegetables   559
Braised Red Cabbage   560
        Braised Green or White Cabbage   560
♥ Sauerkraut   561
♥ V Fresh Sauerkraut   561
Peas à la Française   562
Braised Celery   562
        Braised Celery Hearts   562
        Braised Celery with Brown Sauce   562
        Braised Celery Root   562
        Braised Lettuce   562

V Carrots with Orange and Cumin 563
    Carrot Purée with Orange and Cumin 563
V Ratatouille 563
Eggplant, Sichuan Style 564
Lecsó (Hungary) 564
Gratin of Fennel 565
❤ V Baked Acorn Squash 566
    Gingered Squash 566
    Puréed Squash 566
V Roasted Winter Vegetables 567
    Roasted Onions 567
    Roasted Summer Vegetables 567
V Roasted Garlic 567
❤ V Glazed Sweet Potatoes 568
V Spinach Timbales 568
Southwestern Corn and Pinto Bean Gratin 569
V Provençale Vegetables Confit 569
V Eggplants Bayaldi 570
V Tomato and Zucchini Tian 571
V Elote con Queso 571
Moussaka 572
V Broiled Tomato Slices 573
    Herbed Broiled Tomatoes 573
    Parmesan Broiled Tomatoes 573
V Grilled Vegetable Medley 574
V Grilled Vegetable Kebabs 574
V Onion Rings 576
    Beer Batter 576
    Buttermilk Batter 576
    Other Fried Vegetables 576
V Celery Leaf Fritters 576
V Pea Fritters with Sesame 577
V Vegetable Fritters 577
    Fruit Fritters 577
Chiles Rellenos 578

CHAPTER 18 POTATOES

❤ V Boiled Potatoes (Pommes Natures) 586
    Steamed Potatoes (Pommes Vapeurs) 586
    Parsley Potatoes 586
    New Potatoes 586
    Creamed Potatoes 586
Hungarian Potatoes 587
    Bouillon Potatoes 587
V Colcannon 587
V Potato and Eggplant Stew with Cilantro 588
V Mashed or Whipped Potatoes 589
    Garlic Mashed Potatoes 589
    Ancho Mashed Potatoes 589
V Duchesse Potatoes 590
❤ V Baked Potatoes 592
V Stuffed Baked Potatoes 593
    Macaire Potatoes 593
❤ V Oven Roast Potatoes 593
V Roasted New Potatoes with Herbs and Garlic 594
V Gratin Dauphinoise I 594
V Gratin Dauphinoise II 595
    Savoyarde Potatoes 595
V Scalloped Potatoes 595
    Scalloped Potatoes with Onions 595
    Scalloped Potatoes with Cheese 595
    Scalloped Potatoes with Ham 595
Boulangère Potatoes 596
V Potatoes au Gratin 596
V Anna Potatoes 597
    Voisin Potatoes 597
V Hashed Brown Potatoes 598
    Roesti Potatoes 598
    Lyonnaise Hashed Browns 598
V Rissolé or Cocotte Potatoes 599
    Parisienne and Noisette Potatoes 599
    Château Potatoes 599
V Lyonnaise Potatoes 599
    Home Fries or American Fries 599
    Potatoes O'Brien 599
V Potato Pancakes 600
V Potatoes with Chickpeas and Chiles 601
V French Fries 603
    Pont-Neuf Potatoes 603
    Allumette Potatoes (Shoestring or Matchstick
        Potatoes) 603
    Straw Potatoes 603
    Steakhouse Fries 603
    Potato Chips 603
    Waffle or Gaufrette Potatoes 603
V Potato Croquettes 604
    Berny Potatoes 604
    Dauphine Potatoes 604
    Lorette Potatoes 604
V Potato Croquettes with Peppers 605

CHAPTER 19 LEGUMES, GRAINS, PASTA, AND OTHER STARCHES

Baked Beans, New England Style 611
    Michigan Baked Beans 611
Frijoles de la Olla (Mexican Pinto Beans) 611
    Frijoles Refritos 611
    Vegetarian Pinto Beans 611
White Beans, Bretonne Style 612
V Black Bean Cakes with Salsa 612
Lentils in Cream 613
V Purée of Flageolet Beans with Garlic 613
    Flageolet Beans with Wilted Arugula 613
Pasta e Fagioli 614
❤ Hoppin' John 615
V Masoor Dal (Red Lentils with Spices) 615
V Cranberry Beans with Asparagus 616
V Chickpeas in Spicy Tomato Sauce 617
❤ V Boiled and Steamed Rice 622
Rice Pilaf 625
    Tomato Pilaf 625
    Spanish Rice 625
    Turkish Pilaf 625
    Cracked Wheat Pilaf 625
    Orzo Pilaf 625
    Barley Pilaf 625
Risotto alla Parmigiana 626
    Risotto Milanese 626
    Risotto with Mushrooms 626
    Risi Bisi 626

Basic Fried Rice   628
♥ Bulgur Pilaf with Lemon   628
Arroz à la Mexicana   629
    Arroz Verde   629
Barley with Wild Mushrooms and Ham   629
V Wheatberries with Pecans and Poblanos   630
    Brown Rice, Barley, Farro, or Cracked Wheat
        with Pecans and Poblanos   630
Paella   631
♥ V Polenta   632
    Polenta con Sugo di Pomodoro   632
    Polenta con Salsicce   632
    Polenta al Burro e Formaggio   632
    Polenta Fritta or Grigliata   632
    Polenta Grassa   632
    Polenta Pasticciata   632
V Grits with Cheddar Cheese   633
V Farrotto with Pecorino Cheese   634
Kasha Pilaf with Egg   634
V Tomato Sauce for Pasta   639
    Meat Sauce   639
    Tomato Cream Sauce   639
    Tomato Sauce with Sausage   639
    Tomato Sauce with Sausage and Eggplant   639
    Tomato Sauce with Ham and Rosemary   639
V Fresh Egg Pasta   640
    Spinach Pasta   640
    Other Colored Pastas   640
    Whole-Wheat Pasta   640
    Buckwheat Pasta   640
V Ravioli with Cheese Filling   641
V Fettuccine Alfredo   642
    Fettuccine with Vegetables I
        (Fettuccine Primavera)   642
    Fettuccine with Vegetables II   642
    Fettuccine with Seafood   642
    Fettuccine with Gorgonzola   642
♥ Spaghettini Puttanesca   643
Linguine with White Clam Sauce   643
V Pesto (Fresh Basil Sauce)   644
Baked Lasagne   644
V Vegetable Ravioli in Lemon Grass Broth   645
Rigatoni or Penne with Sausage and Clams   646
    Rigatoni or Penne with Sausage, Peppers, and
        Tomatoes   646
V Macaroni and Cheese   646
Fettuccine with Chiles and Grilled Chicken   647
V Pizzoccheri   648
V Whole Wheat Maltagliate with Porcini and Peas   649
Rice Sticks, Singapore Style   650
V Potato Dumplings   651
V Spaetzle   651
V Potato Gnocchi with Tomato Sauce   652

CHAPTER 20 COOKING FOR VEGETARIAN DIETS

V Yellow Split Pea and Vegetable Curry with Spiced Rice
    and Cucumber Raita   663
    Vegan Vegetable and Split Pea Curry   663
V Noodle Bowl with Stir-Fried Vegetables, Tofu, and
    Peanuts   664

V Zucchini and Eggplant Lasagne   665
V Pinto Bean Enchiladas   666
V Three-Bean Chili with Tostaditas   667
V Red Rice, Spinach with Tofu Dressing, and Eggplant
    Dengaku   668
V Vietnamese Vegetable Pancakes   669
V Winter Vegetable Gratin with Feta Cheese and
    Bulgur Pilaf   670
V Falafel   671

CHAPTER 21 SALADS AND SALAD DRESSINGS

♥ V Mixed Green Salad   688
Spinach Salad   688
Caesar Salad (Method 1)   689
    Caesar Salad (Method 2)   689
    Grilled Chicken Caesar   689
♥ V Garden Salad   690
Coleslaw   691
    Mixed Cabbage Slaw   691
    Carrot Coleslaw   691
    Garden Slaw   691
    Coleslaw with Fruit   691
V Salad of Mixed Cabbage and Apples   692
V Basque-Style Pepper Salad   692
♥ V Cucumber Salad with Dill and Yogurt   693
V White Bean Salad   693
V Mushrooms à la Grecque   694
Carrot Salad   695
    Carrot Raisin Salad   695
    Carrot Pineapple Salad   695
    Carrot Celery Salad   695
    Celery Salad   695
Pacific Rim Salad with Beef   696
Mixed Vegetable Salad with Pasta   697
V Heirloom Tomato Salad   697
    Insalata Caprese   697
Vegetable Chopped Salad with Kidney Beans and
    Provolone   698
V Mixed Bean Salad with Olives and Tomatoes   698
V Quinoa Salad with Bell Peppers   699
V Panzanella   699
V Lentil Salad   700
Broccoli, Prosciutto, and Sunflower Salad   700
V Tabouli   701
V Wheatberry Salad with Mint   701
Macedoine of Vegetables Mayonnaise   703
Chicken or Turkey Salad   703
    Egg Salad   703
    Tuna or Salmon Salad   703
Potato Salad   704
V French Potato Salad   705
    Hot German Potato Salad   705
Dilled Shrimp Salad   705
    Crab or Lobster Salad   705
    Crab, Shrimp, or Lobster Louis   705
    Rice and Shrimp Salad   705
    Curried Rice Salad with Shrimp   705
Waldorf Salad   706
V Arugula, Citrus, and Fennel Salad   707
♥ Thai Papaya and Mango Salad   707

Chef's Salad   708
V Rohkostsalatteller (German Vegetable Salad)   709
V Roasted Beet Salad with Gorgonzola   710
Salade Niçoise   711
Chicken Breast Salad with Walnuts and
   Blue Cheese   712
Salad of Seared Sea Scallops with
   Oriental Vinaigrette   713
Chicory and Smoked Chicken Salad with
   Mustard Vinaigrette   713
Salad of Belgian Endive, Scallops, and Walnuts   714
V Warm Goat Cheese Salad   714
Stuffed Tomatoes Chinoise   715
Taco Salad   716
Jellied Fruit Salad   718
♥ Basic Flavored Gelatin with Fruit   719
V Basic Vinaigrette   723
      Mustard Vinaigrette   723
      Herbed Vinaigrette   723
      Lemon Vinaigrette   723
      Balsamic Vinaigrette   723
      Italian Dressing   723
      Piquante Dressing   723
      Chiffonade Dressing   723
      Avocado Dressing   723
      Blue Cheese or Roquefort Dressing   723
V Walnut Herb Vinaigrette   724
V Sauce Gribiche   724
American French or Tomato French Dressing   725
V Oriental Vinaigrette   725
Reduced-Fat Vinaigrette   726
♥ V Fat-Free Vinaigrette   726
      Fat-Free Roasted Garlic Vinaigrette   726
V Mayonnaise   728
Mayonnaise-Based Dressings   728
      Thousand Island Dressing   728
      Louis Dressing   728
      Russian Dressing   728
      Chantilly Dressing   728
      Blue Cheese Dressing   728
      Ranch Dressing   728
      Aioli II   728
Caesar Dressing   729
V Emulsified French Dressing   729
Sour Cream Fruit Salad Dressing   730
      Yogurt Fruit Salad Dressing   730
♥ V Cooked Salad Dressing   730
♥ Honey Lemon Dressing   731
      Honey Cream Dressing   731
      Honey Lime Dressing   731
♥ V Fruit Salad Dressing   731
♥ V Low-Fat Buttermilk Yogurt Dressing   732

CHAPTER 22 SANDWICHES

California Burger   742
      California Cheeseburger   742
      Cheeseburger (plain)   742
      Cheeseburger with Bacon   742
      California Cheeseburger Deluxe   742
Submarine Sandwich   743

Club Sandwich   743
      Bacon, Lettuce, and Tomato
         Sandwich (BLT)   743
V Grilled Cheese Sandwich   744
      Grilled Ham and Swiss Sandwich   744
      Grilled Cheese and Bacon Sandwich   744
Reuben Sandwich   744
Monte Cristo Sandwich   745
Barbecued Pork or Beef Sandwich   745
Turkey BLT Wrap   746
V Vegetarian Wrap with White Beans   746
V Falafel and Roasted Vegetables in Pita   747
      Traditional Falafel in Pita   747
♥ V Tahini Yogurt Dressing   747
Southwestern Grilled Salmon Sandwich   748
♥ V Chili Marinade   748
Smoked Ham and Taleggio Panino   749
V Eggplant, Roasted Pepper, and Fontina Panino   750
V Grilled Vegetable Sandwich with Goat Cheese
      and Sun-Dried Tomatoes   750
V Grilled Portobello and Boursin Sandwich   751
Grilled Chicken Aioli Sandwich with Tomato
      and Avocado   751
      Grilled Portobello and Tomato Sandwich   751
V Pizza Margherita   752
      Pizza Marinara   752

CHAPTER 23 HORS D'OEUVRES

Blue Cheese Dip   761
      Cheddar Cheese Dip   761
      Garlic Cheese Dip   761
      Bacon Cheese Dip   761
      Cheese and Chile Dip   761
V Romesco   762
V Hummus (Chickpea Dip)   762
      Babaganouj   762
V Guacamole   763
      Sour Cream Avocado Dip   763
V Spinach Boreks   766
V Stuffed Mushrooms with Cheese   767
Smoked Salmon Rolls   767
Fried Chicken Wings   768
V Eggplant Caviar   768
♥ Prosciutto and Melon Balls   769
♥ Apple Slices with Curried Chicken and Mango   769
Smoked Chicken Purses with Sun-Dried Tomatoes   770
V Crêpes   770
Chicken Satay   771
Beef Teriyaki Skewers   771
Smoked Salmon and Trout Logs on Pumpernickel   772
Prosciutto, Blue Cheese, and Walnut Parcels   772
Cucumber Roundels with Smoked Trout Pâté   773
Feuilleté Chorizo   773
Crab Beignets with Lime and Ginger Chutney   774
Mushrooms Stuffed with Tapenade   774
Deviled Eggs   775
V Miniature Gougère Puffs   775
Egg Rolls or Spring Rolls   776
Chicken Liver Pâté   778
V Black Bean Quesadillas   778

Brandade de Morue (France)   779
V Bruschetta (Basic)   780
    Bruschetta with Tomato and Basil   780
    Bruschetta with Parmesan Cheese   780
    Bruschetta with White Beans
      and Prosciutto   780
Spicy Meat Empanadas   781
    Empanadas with Roasted Poblanos
      and Cheese   781
V Cauliflower Pakoras   782

CHAPTER 24 BREAKFAST PREPARATION

Eggs Benedict   791
    Eggs Florentine   791
    Eggs Bombay   791
V Huevos Rancheros   793
V Summer Squash, Spinach, and Leek Frittata   797
V Cheese Soufflé   798
    Spinach Soufflé   798
    Spinach and Ham Soufflé   798
    Mushroom Soufflé   798
    Other Vegetable Soufflés   798
    Salmon Soufflé   798
V Quiche au Fromage (Cheese Tart)   799
    Quiche Lorraine   799
    Onion Quiche   799
    Spinach Quiche   799
    Mushroom Quiche   799
    Seafood Quiche   799
V Buttermilk Pancakes   801
V Waffles   801
❤ Buckwheat Pancakes   802
V Cinnamon Raisin French Toast   803

CHAPTER 25 DAIRY AND BEVERAGES

V Welsh Rabbit   817
V Sirniki (Russian Fried Cheese Cakes)   817
V Swiss Fondue   818
V Cheese Wafers   818
    Cheese Straws   818

CHAPTER 26 SAUSAGES AND CURED FOODS

Gravlax   829
Smoked Salmon   830
Smoked Trout   830
Smoked Duck   831
    Smoked Turkey or Chicken   831
V Quatre épices I   839
V Quatre épices II   839
Pork Sausage   839
    Toulouse Sausage   839
    Crêpinettes   839
French Garlic Sausage   840
Hot Italian Sausage   840
    Mild Italian Sausage   840
    Spicy Garlic Sausage   840
Veal or Beef Sausage   840

Venison Sausage   840
Fresh Bratwurst   841
Lamb Sausage   841
    Herbed Lamb Sausage   841
Duck Sausage   841
Boudin Blanc (White Sausage)   842
Mortadella   843
    Bologna   843
Cajun-Style Sausage   844
    Andouille   844
Smoked Garlic Sausage   845
    Cured Garlic Sausage   845

CHAPTER 27 PÂTÉS, TERRINES, AND OTHER COLD FOODS

Classic Chaud-Froid   851
Mayonnaise Chaud-Froid   851
Basic Pork Forcemeat   856
    Veal Forcemeat   856
    Chicken Forcemeat I   856
    Chicken Forcemeat II   856
    Duck, Pheasant, or Game Forcemeat   856
Pâté Pastry (Pâte à Pâté)   857
Veal and Ham Terrine   861
    Veal and Ham Terrine with Foie Gras   861
    Veal and Tongue Terrine   861
    Rabbit Terrine   861
    Game Terrine   861
    Duck Terrine   861
    Country Terrine   861
Chicken Galantine   862
Basic Mousseline Forcemeat   863
Terrine of Vegetables with Chicken Mousseline   864
    Seafood Terrine with Vegetables   864
Jambon Persillé (Parslied Ham in Aspic)   866
❤ Terrine of Vegetables and Chicken in Aspic   867
    Terrine of Vegetables with Foie Gras
      in Aspic   867
❤ Lentil and Leek Terrine with Smoked Turkey
    and Prosciutto   868
Tricolor Vegetable Terrine   869
Ham Mousse   870
Mousse of Foie Gras   870
Terrine of Foie Gras   873
Chicken Liver Terrine   874
Rillettes of Salmon, Haddock, or Finnan Haddie   874
Rillettes of Pork   875
    Rillettes of Duck, Goose, Rabbit,
      Turkey, or Chicken   875

CHAPTER 30 YEAST PRODUCTS

❤ V Hard Rolls   916
❤ V Soft Rolls   916
❤ V French Bread   917
❤ V White Pan Bread   917
    Whole Wheat Bread   917
❤ V Rye Bread and Rolls   918
❤ V Focaccia   918

Rosemary Focaccia   918
Olive Focaccia   918
V Brioche   919
V Sweet Roll Dough   919
Raised Doughnuts   919
V Danish Pastry   920
V Croissants   920
❤ V Cinnamon Sugar   922
V Streusel or Crumb Topping   922
Nut Streusel   922
❤ V Clear Glaze for Coffee Cakes and Danish   922
❤ V Date, Prune, or Apricot Filling   923
V Almond Filling   923
V Cheese Filling   923

CHAPTER 31 QUICK BREADS

V Biscuits   935
Buttermilk Biscuits   935
Cheese Biscuits   935
Currant Biscuits   935
Herb Biscuits   935
V Banana Bread   935
V Plain Muffins   936
Raisin Spice Muffins   936
Date Nut Muffins   936
Blueberry Muffins   936
Whole Wheat Muffins   936
Corn Muffins   936
Bran Muffins   936
Crumb Coffee Cake   936
V Popovers   936
V Corn Bread, Muffins, or Sticks   937
V Orange Nut Bread   937

CHAPTER 32 CAKES AND ICINGS

V Yellow Butter Cake   948
V Brown Sugar Spice Cake   948
Carrot Nut Cake   948
V Chocolate Butter Cake   949
V Old-Fashioned Pound Cake   949
Raisin Pound Cake   949
Chocolate Pound Cake   949
Marble Pound Cake   949
V White Cake   950
Yellow Cake   950
V Devil's Food Cake   950
V Sponge Cake (Genoise)   951
Chocolate Genoise   951
Sponge Roll or Jelly Roll   951
V Milk and Butter Sponge   951
❤ V Jelly Roll Sponge   952
V Yellow Chiffon Cake   952
Chocolate Chiffon Cake   952
❤ V Angel Food Cake   952
Chocolate Angel Food Cake   952
V Simple Buttercream   954
Decorator's Buttercream   954
Cream Cheese Icing   954

V Meringue-Type Buttercream   954
V French Buttercream   955
Chocolate Buttercream   955
Coffee Buttercream   955
❤ V Flat Icing   956
V Caramel Fudge Icing   956
V Quick White Fudge Icing   956
Quick Chocolate Fudge Icing   956
V Cocoa Fudge Icing   957
Vanilla Fudge Icing   957

CHAPTER 33 COOKIES

V Chocolate Chip Cookies   969
Brown Sugar Nut Cookies   969
V Oatmeal Raisin Cookies   969
V Tea Cookies   970
Almond Tea Cookies   970
Sandwich-Type Cookies   970
Chocolate Tea Cookies   970
V Ladyfingers   970
V Coconut Macaroons (Meringue Type)   971
V Sugar Cookies   971
Rolled Brown Sugar Cookies   971
Rolled Chocolate Cookies   971
V Shortbread Cookies   971
V Cinnamon Cookies   972
Chocolate Cinnamon Cookies   972
V Raisin Spice Bars   972
V Peanut Butter Cookies   973
V Icebox Cookies   973
Butterscotch Icebox Cookies   973
Chocolate Icebox Cookies   973
Nut Icebox Cookies   973
V Brownies   974
Butterscotch Brownies or Blondies   974
V Almond Biscotti   975

CHAPTER 34 PIES AND PASTRIES

V Flaky Pie Dough   980
V Mealy Pie Dough   980
Graham Cracker Crust   981
V Short Dough   981
❤ V Apple Pie Filling (Canned Fruit)   986
Dutch Apple Pie Filling   986
Cherry Pie Filling   986
Peach Pie Filling   986
Pineapple Pie Filling   986
❤ V Blueberry Pie Filling (Frozen Fruit)   987
Apple Pie Filling   987
Cherry Pie Filling   987
❤ V Fresh Strawberry Pie Filling   987
❤ V Rhubarb Pie Filling   988
Fresh Apple Pie Filling   988
❤ V Raisin Pie Filling   988
❤ V Old-Fashioned Apple Pie Filling   989
❤ V Custard Pie Filling   990
Coconut Custard Pie Filling   990
❤ V Pumpkin Pie Filling   991

Sweet Potato Pie Filling   991
Squash Pie Filling   991
V Pecan Pie Filling   991
V Puff Pastry   993
V Blitz Puff Pastry   995
V Éclair Paste or Pâte à Choux   998
♥ V Meringue   1000
V Fruit Cobbler   1001
V Apple Betty   1001
V Apple Crisp   1002
Peach, Cherry, or Rhubarb Crisp   1002
♥ V Poached Pears   1002
Pears in Wine   1002
Poached Peaches   1002
Peaches in Wine   1002
Raspberry or Cherry Gratin   1003

CHAPTER 35 CREAMS, CUSTARDS, PUDDINGS,
FROZEN DESSERTS, AND SAUCES

V Crème Anglaise (Vanilla Custard Sauce)   1008
Chocolate Crème Anglaise   1008
V Vanilla Pastry Cream   1009
Chocolate Pastry Cream   1009
Coffee Pastry Cream   1009
Vanilla Cream Pie Filling   1009
Coconut Cream Pie Filling   1009
Banana Cream Pie Filling   1009
Chocolate Cream Pie Filling I   1009
Chocolate Cream Pie Filling II   1009
Butterscotch Cream Pie Filling   1009
Lemon Pie Filling   1009
Vanilla Pudding   1009
Coconut Pudding   1009
Banana Cream Pudding   1009
Chocolate Pudding I and II   1009
Butterscotch Pudding   1009

V Baked Custard   1010
Crème Caramel   1010
V Blancmange, English Style   1011
V Rice Pudding   1012
Raisin Rice Pudding   1012
V Bread and Butter Pudding   1012
Cabinet Pudding   1012
Bavarian Cream   1015
Chocolate Bavarian Cream   1015
Coffee Bavarian Cream   1015
Strawberry Bavarian Cream   1015
Raspberry Bavarian Cream   1015
♥ Strawberry Chiffon Dessert or Pie Filling   1016
Raspberry Chiffon Dessert or Pie Filling   1016
Pineapple Chiffon Dessert or Pie Filling   1016
Frozen Strawberry or Raspberry Mousse   1016
♥ Chocolate Chiffon Dessert or Pie Filling   1017
Chocolate Cream Chiffon Pie Filling   1017
♥ Lemon Chiffon Dessert or Pie Filling   1018
Lime Chiffon Dessert or Pie Filling   1018
Orange Chiffon Dessert or Pie Filling   1018
Frozen Lemon Mousse   1018
♥ Pumpkin Chiffon Dessert or Pie Filling   1019
Pumpkin Cream Chiffon   1019
V Vanilla Soufflé   1020
Chocolate Soufflé   1020
Lemon Soufflé   1020
Liqueur Soufflé   1020
Coffee Soufflé   1020
V Chocolate Mousse   1021
V Chocolate Sauce   1024
V Caramel Sauce   1024
Hot Caramel Sauce   1024
Clear Caramel Sauce   1024

About Le Cordon Bleu

With more than 25 schools on five continents and a student body made up of over seventy different nationalities, Le Cordon Bleu is well known and highly regarded throughout the gastronomic world. Le Cordon Bleu and its master chefs are renowned for their tradition of excellence in the culinary arts and hospitality management, and are committed to furthering the appreciation of fine food and fine living. Already involved in consulting and the promotion of a variety of culinary products, Le Cordon Bleu has successfully developed partnerships worldwide with major hospitality and culinary institutions, professional organisations and with the cruise industry.

Le Cordon Bleu Addresses

Le Cordon Bleu Paris
8, rue Léon Delhomme
75015 Paris
France
Phone: 33-1-53-68-22-50
Fax: 33-1-48-56-03-96
Email: paris@cordonbleu.edu

Le Cordon Bleu Ottawa
453 Laurier Avenue East
Ottawa, Ontario
K1N 6R4 Canada
Phone: 1 613 236-CHEF (2433)
Fax: 1 613 236 2460
Toll-free: 1 888 289-6302
Email: ottawa@cordonbleu.edu

Le Cordon Bleu Yokohama
2-18-1, Takashima, Nishi-Ku
Yokohama-Shi Kanagawa
Japan
Phone: 81 45 440 4720
Fax: 81 45 440 4722
E-mail: tokyo@cordonbleu.edu

**Le Cordon Bleu, Inc.,
corporate office**
40 Enterprise Ave
Secaucus, New Jersey 07094
USA
Phone 1-201 617 5221
Fax: 1-201 617 1914
Toll-free: 1 800 457 2433 (CHEF)
Email: info@cordonbleu.edu

Le Cordon Bleu London
114 Marylebone Lane
London, W1U 2HH
United Kingdom
Phone: 44 20 7935 3503
Fax: 44 20 7935 7621
Email: london@cordonbleu.edu

Le Cordon Bleu Tokyo
Roob-1, 28-13 Sarugaku-Cho
Daikanyama, Shibuya-Ku
Tokyo 150-0033
Japan
Phone: 81 3 5489 0141
Fax: 81 3 5489 0145
E-mail: tokyo@cordonbleu.edu

Le Cordon Bleu Kobe
The 45th 6F, 45 Harima-cho
Chuo-Ku, Kobe-shi
Hyogo 650-0036
Japan
Phone: 81 78 393 8221
Fax: 81 78 393 8222
E-mail: kobe@cordonbleu.edu

Le Cordon Bleu Australia
Days Road, Regency Park
South Australia 5010
Australia
Phone: 61 8 8346 3700
Fax: 61 8 8346 3755
Email: australia@cordonbleu.edu

Le Cordon Bleu Peru
Av. Nunez de Balboa 530
Miraflores, Lima 18
Peru
Phone 51 1 242 8222
Fax: 51 1 242 9209
E-mail: info@cordonbleu.edu

Le Cordon Bleu Liban
Rectorat B.P. 446
USEK University – Kaslik
Jounieh
Lebanon
Phone: 961 9640 664/665
Fax: 961 9642 333
E-mail: liban@cordonbleu.edu

Le Cordon Bleu Mexico
Universidad Anahuac del Sur
Avenida de las Torres #131, Col.
Olivar de los Padres
C.P. 01780
Del Alvaro Obregon, Mexico D.F.
Phone: 52 55 5628 8800
Fax: 52 55 5628 8837
E-mail: mexico@cordonbleu.edu

www.cordonbleu.edu
info@cordonbleu.edu

US School Locations

Arizona
Scottsdale Culinary Institute
8100 E. Camelback Road
Scottsdale, Arizona 85251
Tel: (480) 990 3773

California
California Culinary Academy
625 Polk Street
San Francisco, California 94102
Tel: (415) 771 3500

California School of Culinary Arts
521 East Green Street
Pasadena, California 91101
Tel: (626) 403 8490

Florida
Le Cordon Bleu College of Culinary
Arts—Miami
3221 Enterprise Way
Miramar, FL 33025
Tel: (954) 438 8882

Orlando Culinary Academy
8511 Commodity Circle
Orlando, Florida 32819
Tel: (407) 888 4000

Georgia
Le Cordon Bleu College of
Culinary Arts – Atlanta
1957 Lakeside Parkway, Suite 515
Tucker, Georgia 30084
Tel: (770) 938 4711

Illinois
Culinary & Hospitality Institute
of Chicago
361 West Chestnut
Chicago, Illinois 60610
Tel: (312) 944 0882

Minnesota
Le Cordon Bleu College of Culinary
Arts—Minneapolis/St. Paul
1440 Northland Drive
Mendota Heights, Minnesota 55120
Tel: (651) 905 3400

Nevada
Le Cordon Bleu College of
Culinary Arts—Las Vegas
1451 Center Crossing Road
Las Vegas, Nevada 89144
Tel: (702) 365 7690

New Hampshire
Atlantic Culinary Academy
23 Cataract Avenue
Dover, New Hampshire 03820
Tel: (603) 742 1234

Oregon
Western Culinary Institute
921 SW Morrison Street Suite 400
Portland, Oregon 97205
Tel: (800) 848-3202

Pennsylvania
Pennsylvania Culinary Institute
71 Liberty Avenue
Pittsburgh, Pennsylvania 15222
Tel: (412) 566 2433

Texas
Texas Culinary Academy
11400 Burnet Road Suite 2100
Austin, Texas 78758
Tel: (512) 837 2665

www.lecordonbleuschoolsusa.com

Foreword

Le Cordon Bleu was delighted to work once again with author Wayne Gisslen on the sixth edition of *Professional Cooking*. This continued collaboration underlines the importance of French culinary technique at the service of the gastronomic world. It has always been the philosophy of Le Cordon Bleu that, through mastering and understanding French culinary techniques, processes, and methods, students gain the tools and confidence with which to create their own style. Le Cordon Bleu envisions the sixth edition of *Professional Cooking* as continuing to be an indispensable culinary tool that balances tradition with cutting-edge innovation.

Founded in Paris in 1895, Le Cordon Bleu today has become a network of over twenty-six schools and programs in fifteen countries and has more students worldwide than any other culinary education provider. Le Cordon Bleu maintains close relations with the culinary industry, and benefits from its international recognition, setting the standard of excellence. Known for classical French cuisine, Le Cordon Bleu continues to teach long-celebrated culinary traditions while creating a balanced, harmonious, and flavorsome repertoire of contemporary and international cuisines.

Le Cordon Bleu's authority on culinary techniques, training, and development are recognized and supported by noted establishments including the Ministry of Tourism of Shanghai, China, and the government of Australia. Le Cordon Bleu also provides training in the French culinary arts to many organizations, including chefs of the Club Managers Association of America and Radisson Seven Seas Cruises.

Each year Le Cordon Bleu master chefs pass on their knowledge and experience to a student body of over fifty nationalities, and share their expertise and craft at a variety of annual festivals and culinary events around the world. Selected for their skill and professional experience, our chefs hail from Michelin-starred restaurants and top hotel kitchens, and are winners of numerous international competitions. With more than 75 master chefs worldwide, our students are exposed to a variety of styles, tastes, and philosophies that make for a unique learning experience. Through the combined talents of our chefs, Le Cordon Bleu is the only culinary school to operate a CAA/AAA Five Diamond restaurant in North America.

Through its expansion worldwide, Le Cordon Bleu has responded to the growing needs of the hospitality industry through the establishment of cutting-edge management programs that reflect the same level of excellence as our culinary programs. Le Cordon Bleu has created Diploma, Bachelors, and Masters degrees in direct response to industry demands.

Professional Cooking has been a mainstay in North American universities, community colleges, and culinary schools. It has been used to train hundreds of thousands of chefs and cooks, many of whom continue to use the book in their kitchens. Created by the talented Wayne Gisslen, the text teaches, through its clear writing style, precise photography, and recipes, first to understand and then to perform—presenting a no-nonsense view of the workings of a professional kitchen.

Wayne Gisslen has balanced his practical knowledge with a clean, pedagogical and consistent approach to make this a reference for a lifetime. *Professional Cooking*'s flexible format is the reason why we consider it to be the best textbook for promoting good theory and practice, and it has the adaptability to be used all over the world. For Le Cordon Bleu this is a necessary tool for any kitchen, at work or at home. In the sixth edition of *Professional Cooking*, Le Cordon Bleu chefs and Wayne Gisslen unite once again to combine their knowledge and experience resulting in a definitive text and reference book.

ANDRÉ J. COINTREAU
President and CEO
Le Cordon Bleu International

Preface

This new edition of *Professional Cooking for Canadian Chefs* is the most extensively revised yet, including content specifically of interest to Canadian readers. Canadian cooks and chefs are rightly proud of their local food products and of a grading and inspection system with a sterling record of promoting and protecting food safety.

Professional Cooking for Canadian Chefs contains new information in virtually every chapter. At the same time, the book has retained the core material that has made this text the standard reference and learning tool in its field for more than 20 years. The fifth edition introduced a new and modern design that made the text not only more appealing to the eye, but also easier to use. The range of new material in this sixth edition, added to that modern design, now makes this the most comprehensive and most useful culinary arts text to date.

WHAT'S NEW

Many important additions have been made to *Professional Cooking for Canadian Chefs* to make it even more useful and versatile. These changes have been made, in large part, in response to input from instructors, students, and other readers. Communication from readers has always been valuable in helping the text adapt to the evolving needs of users. Among the most important additions and changes are the following:

- Updated information on Canadian inspection and grading of meat, poultry, seafood, dairy products, and eggs.

- A new chapter devoted to vegetarianism and cooking for the various types of vegetarian diets has been added. In addition, recipes suitable for a vegetarian diet are indicated by a symbol throughout the book. Further information on the use of this symbol is on page 661.

- New information on topics ranging from nutritional information to the cultural backgrounds of new recipes from international cuisines has been added in sidebars throughout the text.

- Coverage of the history of modern food service has been expanded.

- Concepts of flavor building and flavor profiles have been added to the discussion of basic cooking principles.

- The information on menus, recipes, and cost management is now its own chapter.

- Now in a dedicated chapter, nutrition information has been updated to incorporate new nutritional guidelines as well as the new food pyramid.

- The vegetable chapters have been expanded and revised to incorporate ingredients and preparations that have become mainstream in more recent years.

- The information on potatoes and cooking them is now its own chapter, and cooking with legumes, grains, pastas, and other starches is covered separately.

- Breakfast preparation and dairy and beverages are now found in their own dedicated chapters.

- The chapter on food presentation and garnish has been revised to reflect current ideas on plating and presenting finished recipes.

- Recipes from various international and regional cuisines are now integrated throughout the book.

- More than 100 new recipes have been added, bringing the book's total to about 1,200.

- Many new photographs have been added to all sections of the book, illustrating even more clearly the techniques and procedures necessary in the modern kitchen. New identification photos of key ingredients are also included.

- This red logo indicates recipes I have developed and tested.

- This blue logo indicates recipes that were developed and tested by Le Cordon Bleu.

THE RECIPES

The recipes in this book are planned and organized to reinforce the basic skills the student is learning. In each case, specific recipes follow a discussion of theories, guidelines, and general procedures applicable to a defined category of foods and/or cooking methods. Students are encouraged, by means of recipe variations, to see how they can apply these procedures to other ingredients, and to see the similarities and differences among preparations.

Attention to the basics has always been the hallmark of the text. Because the purpose of the text is to teach fundamental cooking techniques, it is important to illustrate these techniques—and to allow the student to experience them—with fundamental, straightforward recipes that reveal the connection between general theory and specific application in the most direct way. Many new recipes have been added to this edition to provide updates and alternatives that will achieve these goals.

While basic preparations illustrating fundamental principles are the core of the recipe collection, the book builds on these primary techniques to include more advanced styles of preparation. More challenging recipes, including many new to this edition, enable readers to refine their techniques and to prepare dishes of increasing sophistication. The more than 90 recipes developed and tested by the chefs of Le Cordon Bleu, which first appeared here in a previous edition, help immeasurably to enrich the learning experience of students. These recipes are regularly used by Le Cordon Bleu chefs on five continents to train students for work in the kitchens of the finest restaurants in the world.

What makes a dish feel modern is as much a matter of presentation as it is of ingredients or recipe instructions. How an item, along with its garnish and sauce, is plated can make it look rustic or elegant, simple or elaborate, traditional or modern. Photographs accompanying the recipes illustrate a variety of preparations and plating styles. As the photographs show, a simple item such as a sautéed chicken breast can be as stylish as a complicated dish requiring exotic or expensive ingredients.

Readers are urged to study Chapter 5, "Menus, Recipes, and Cost Management," before actually proceeding with any of the recipes. This will help them know how to use the recipes in this book as well as understand the structure and limitations of the many recipes they will be using in their careers.

While every culinary program has different requirements, the recipes in this book should be adaptable to any purpose. Most major recipes are written for 24 or 25 portions, a quantity that can be converted easily to higher or lower yields if necessary. Those recipes requiring more costly ingredients, those that are generally made to order, or those that are more complex are written for smaller yields, such as 10, 12, or 16 portions. In addition, variations often indicate ingredient substitutions so the recipes will fit different budgetary requirements and different local or regional tastes.

NUTRITIONAL INFORMATION

Cooks and chefs are increasingly aware of the importance of learning to prepare healthful foods. To support this effort, nutritional analyses have been included for each main recipe. These analyses were done using the software program Genesis R&D 6.00, which calculates nutrients based on ingredients. It is important to realize that the actual nutrients in a prepared dish will vary depending on many factors, just as the taste, texture, and appearance of a dish will vary depending on the skill of the cook and the quality of the ingredients. The following factors should also be taken into account when reading the nutritional analyses:

- Where a portion size is indicated in the recipe, the analysis is per portion. Where there is no portion size, such as for stock and sauce recipes as well as most of the recipes in the baking chapters, the analysis is usually per ounce; for most hors d'oeuvre recipes, analysis is per piece.

- The following ingredients are not included in the analyses: ingredients listed "to taste" or "as needed"; ingredients in sachets and bouquets garnis; optional ingredients; garnishes such as parsley sprigs.

- Stocks are adjusted for removal of bones, mirepoix, and other ingredients that are strained out.

- Ingredients in mirepoix are not included, except for a small amount of sodium.

- If there is a range for an ingredient quantity, the smaller number was used for analysis.

- Adjustments are made for recipes in which the food is degreased or the fat is skimmed off. The amount of fat remaining will vary depending on how thoroughly the item is degreased.

- Fat has been added for pan-fried and deep-fried foods based on a percentage of the total weight. The amount of fat actually absorbed will vary depending on the temperature of the fat, the cooking time, and the surface area of the food.

- For marinated foods, 10 percent of the marinade is included in the analysis, unless the marinade is used to make a sauce, in which case all the marinade is, of course, included.

- The amount of fat used for sautéing has been estimated for the analysis.

- The numbers for each nutrient are rounded off according to FDA rounding rules for food labeling.

- The "(% cal.)" information following the fat content in each analysis refers to percentage of calories from fat and is required to determine whether or not a recipe can be labeled as low in fat. It can't be used to determine percentage of fat in the total diet.

To help you become more aware of the fat content of various dishes, those dishes that are especially low in fat are designated by a special symbol to the right of the recipe title. *Low in fat* means, according to FDA labeling laws, that the food contains 3 grams of fat or less per reference amount (or serving size indicated in the analysis) if the reference amount is greater than 30 grams (about 1 ounce). If the reference amount is 30 grams or less, the fat content must also be 3 grams of fat or less per 50 grams of the food. This is to prevent making foods sound low in fat just by making the portion size smaller. Main-dish items and meals must contain 3 grams of fat or less per 100 grams, and not more than 30 percent of calories from fat.

GOALS AND ORGANIZATION OF THIS BOOK

This book has a dual goal: *understanding*—that is, an understanding of cooking theory, of how to cook—and *performing*—that is, the mastery of a set of manual skills and the ability to apply them to a wide range of cooking styles and products.

The current revision retains the book's basic structure and organization, which created the flexibility that has made *Professional Cooking for Canadian Chefs* adaptable to nearly any course of study. The basic cooking methods (dry-heat methods, moist-heat methods, and so on) are introduced early on. Then, within each of the main cooking chapters, the material is arranged by cooking method.

Thus, for those curricula that are organized by cooking method, it is a simple matter to select the appropriate sections—for example, moist-heat methods—from the meat, poultry, fish, and vegetable chapters. At the same time, the arrangement of the chapters by product type enables the instructor to emphasize how the basic cooking methods differ as they are applied to different products.

The new *Professional Cooking for Canadian Chefs* focuses, as did the earlier editions, on the development of flexible skills, which are essential for success in a cooking career. Modern food service is evolving rapidly. There is a tremendous variety of establishments on the scene today, from the executive dining room to the school cafeteria, from the simplest short-order coffee shop to the most exclusive restaurant or club, from kitchens that make extensive use of convenience foods to those that use only fresh produce. The graduate who understands the workings of foods and the interplay of ingredients, cooking methods, cost factors, and other elements can function successfully in any type of food service operation.

THE ROLE OF THE CHEF-INSTRUCTOR

No textbook, of course, can substitute for practical kitchen experience. Furthermore, a book cannot replace an experienced chef-instructor who can give practical demonstrations, supervise students' work, answer questions, and give advice and assistance as the need arises. Every instructor has had unique experience and has developed special techniques and procedures. Many chefs, in fact, disagree with one another on a number of points. Although this book presents methods and recipes that are widely used and accepted, many instructors will prefer procedures that differ from some of those explained in this text, and they may wish to supplement the recipes in this book with some of their own. Throughout the book, the instructor's input is encouraged. Exposure to a variety of recipes and techniques can only enrich the students' education and enhance the depth of their experience.

FEATURES

Pronunciation Guides and Glossaries

Much kitchen terminology is taken from French. Phonetic guides are included for difficult words, giving the approximate pronunciation using English sounds. (Exact rendering is impossible in many cases, because French has a number of sounds that don't exist in English.) Because food workers must be able to communicate with each other, definitions of terms introduced in the text are summarized in the glossaries at the end of the book. Additionally, vocabularies from Le Cordon Bleu enable readers to move smoothly between North American, British, and French terminology.

Illustrations

More than 175 new, clear, concise, full-color photographs illustrate basic manual techniques, shown from the point of view of the person performing them. Additional photographs illustrate hundreds of ingredients and finished dishes.

Format

This book is designed to be readable and useful. The format emphasizes and highlights key points in bold type, italics, and numbered sequences, so basic information can be located and reviewed at a glance.

Realistic Procedures

Although supported by discussions of cooking theory, procedures given here are based on actual practices in the industry. Attention is given not just to quantity production but also to the special problems of cooking to order. Presentation and service of the finished product are considered in detail, as is pre-preparation, or mise en place—so essential to the organization of a working restaurant. At the same time, the major emphasis is on quality, too often neglected in the quest for convenience.

Even a book as large as this one cannot possibly contain all a cook needs to know. Other information is included if it has a direct bearing on kitchen and bakeshop work. More specialized information, such as stewarding and managerial skills, has to be omitted. Finally, although much of what we talk about is strongly influenced by the cooking of other nations, especially France, the practices discussed are those of North American food service.

CD-ROM

The CD-ROM, designed to complement the book, accompanies the academic edition of this book and utilizes Wiley CulinarE-Companion™, a professional-level software program used in the food service industry. The CD-ROM contains all of the recipes from this book, plus a range of useful features that make them easy to adapt and manipulate to suit individual needs:

- Add, edit, modify, and print recipes, portion sizes, or yield and create shopping lists.
- Search recipes by main ingredient, meal, and cuisine type.
- Resize recipes in U.S. or metric measurements.
- Perform metric conversions instantly.
- Calculate nutritional analyses of recipes in FDA format, and update nutritional analysis if an ingredient is changed.

Supplements

To enhance mastery of the material in *Professional Cooking for Canadian Chefs*, the following student and instructor supplements are available:

The *Study Guide* (0-470-04171-4) contains review materials, practice problems, and exercises. (Answers to questions are included in the Instructor's Manual.)

The *Instructor's Manual with Study Guide Solutions* includes teaching suggestions and test questions. The test questions are also available in electronic form on a CD-ROM and on our website, available to course instructors upon request.

WebCT and Blackboard on-line courses are available for this book. Visit www.wiley.com/college and click on Technology Solutions for more information, or contact your Wiley representative.

The newly updated and revised website contains information for the student and instructor, and is available at http://www.wiley.com/canada/gisslen.

Acknowledgments

Photographer Jim Smith has been my partner in these texts for 25 years. His hundreds of photographs are an indispensable part of *Professional Cooking for Canadian Chefs* and valuable teaching tools. I can never thank him enough. Thanks also to Anne Smith for all her support and assistance through the years, and to Ryan Basten for his work in Jim's studio.

During a long and productive session of photography and recipe testing for this edition, I was fortunate to have the expert assistance of Chef-Instructors Rick Forpahl and David Eisenreich of Hennepin Technical College, Chef-Instructor Gil Gaitan of Le Cordon Bleu, Myros Billy, Rose Scaramuzza, Jeff Bieniek, Jason Riedel, Jessica Entzel, Jane Jost, Liz McCormick, Stephanie O'Connor, Steve Goldschmidt, Martina Cameron, and Jennifer Peck. My wife Meg assisted our kitchen crew and, in addition, helped with my research for many of the text revisions. I am grateful to one and all for their help. They were a pleasure to work with.

The fourth edition of *Professional Cooking* saw the beginning of Le Cordon Bleu's participation in the development of this text, a participation that continued with the third and fourth editions of *Professional Baking* and with the fifth and now the sixth edition of *Professional Cooking for Canadian Chefs*. My deepest gratitude goes to André J. Cointreau, president of Le Cordon Bleu, and to chefs Patrick Lebouc, Patrick Terrien, Michel Cliché, MOF, Jean-Claude Boucheret, Gregory Steneck, and Andrew Males.

Christin Loudon, who calculated nutritional analyses in the fourth and fifth editions, has again contributed her expertise and culinary understanding to provide analyses for the new recipes in this edition, for which I thank her most warmly. I would also like to thank Drew Appleby, whose expertly written test questions form an important part of the support materials for this text.

Because the best ingredients are essential to good cooking, I would like to extend a special thanks to Jay and Jane Bunting of Wayzata Bay Spice Company and Blue River Gourmet for helping me obtain high-quality seasonings for recipe testing, and to Jay Flattum, owner of Lofton Ridge Deer and Bison Farm, for supplying specialty meats at a moment's notice. In addition, a warm thank-you goes to Larry DeVries, Chef-Instructor at Crocus Plains Regional Secondary School, Brandon, Manitoba, for his continuing support, counsel, and friendship.

The list of culinary and hospitality professionals who have provided support, guidance, advice, and constructive criticism for all six editions of this book has grown so long that it isn't possible to mention everyone in these paragraphs. I can only hope I have not omitted many of them in the list of reviewers that follows. I would also like to thank all those unnamed individuals who have corresponded with me over the years to point out errors and to offer suggestions.

Wiley CulinarE-Companion™ would not have been a part of this new edition without a team effort. Thank you to Lisa Brefere and Brad Barnes for their consultation every step of the way in designing and developing the new software. I am also grateful to the beta testers who took time to test the program: Patrick Beach, Tom Beckman, Amy Carter, Steve Cornelius, Ross Headlee, Susan Hendee, Anne Jachim, John Kane, James Paul, Mario Ramsay, Robert Salzmann, Jeremy Sledge, Will Thornton.

Finally, I would like to thank everyone at John Wiley & Sons who worked so hard on this project: Jennifer Mazurkie, Brent Savage, Fred Bernardi, Diana Cisek, Julie Kerr, Tzviya Siegman, Lynne Marsala, Nick Lewis, Michael Mukhoyan, Alexey Zhukov, Vladimir Karpukhin, Pavel Ivchenkov, Maxim Mukhoyan, Oleg Solovyov, Sergey Semin, Mauna Eichner and Lee Fukui, and especially my editor and friend, Melissa Oliver.

Contributors

I would like to thank the following contributors for their valuable input and feedback for this edition of *Professional Cooking for Canadian Chefs.*

Roy W. Blundell	LaSalle College
Tom Hummel	Liaison College
Brian Clafton	Liaison College
Roger Maurer	George Brown College
Bill Gregorash	Confederation College
Hal V. Trask	Saskatchewan Institute of Applied Science and Technology
David Hawey	Sir Sanford Fleming College
Alan E. Fleming	Algonquin College
Jean-Guy Robichaud	Cambrian College
Fred German	Saskatchewan Institute of Applied Science and Technology
Norman Brownlee	Northern Alberta Institute of Technology

Reviewers

I would like to acknowledge the following instructors who have contributed to this book over six editions by suggesting revisions and additions, and answering survey questions.

George Akau
Clark College
Vancouver, WA

Erik Anderson
Camosun College
Victoria, British Columbia

Angela M. Anderson
Miami Dade Community
    College
Miami, FL

Robert Anderson
Des Moines Area
    Community College
Ankeny, IA

Alan Argulski
Genesee Community College
Batavia, NY

Kirk Bachman
Le Cordon Bleu Schools
North America
Hoffman Estates, IL

Moses Ball
Atlantic Vocational-Technical
    Center
Coconut Creek, FL

Carl A. Behnke
Purdue University
West Lafayette, IN

Joseph L. Belvedere Jr.
Paul Smith's College
Paul Smiths, NY

Perry Bentley
Okanagan University College
Kelowna, British Columbia

Claire A. Berg
Brookdale Community College
Howell, NJ

Nancy Berkoff
Los Angeles Trade Technical
    College
Los Angeles, CA

Leslie Bilderback
California School of
    Culinary Arts
South Pasadena, CA

George Bissonette
Pikes Peak Community College
Colorado Springs, CO

Peter Blakeman
George Brown College
Toronto, Ontario

LeRoy Blanchard
Los Angeles Trade
    Technical College
Los Angeles, CA

Roy Blundell
College Lasalle
Montreal, Quebec

Pete Bordi
Penn State University
University Park, PA

Kenneth P. Bourgoin
Valencia Community College
Orlando, FL

Roy Butterworth
New Brunswick Community
    College
Moncton, New Brunswick

Alfredo Cabaccingan
Kapiolani Community College
Honolulu, HI

Harska Chacko
University of New Orleans
New Orleans, LA

Daniel Charna
Ashland College
Ashland, OH

Albert D. Cipryk
Niagara College
Niagara Falls, Ontario

Jesse Clemons
State Technical Institute at
Memphis
Memphis, TN

Alec O. Cline
American Culinary
Federation, Inc.
Redwood City, CA

Michael M. Collins
San Jacinto College
Pasadena, TX

Randall Colman
Sullivan County Community
College
Loch Sheldrake, NY

Steven Cornelius
Sinclair Community College
Dayton, OH

Mike Costello
St. Cloud Area Vocational-
Technical Institute
St. Cloud, MN

Chris Cutler
Georgian College
Barrie, Ontario

William J. Daly
State University of New York
at Cobleskill
Cobleskill, NY

Juanita M. Decker
Waukesha County Technical
Institute
Pewaukee, WI

Bob Demers
Niagara College
Niagara Falls, Ontario

Larry DeVries
Brandon School District
Brandon, Manitoba

Marian Dobbins
Tucson, AZ

Brendan Dolan
Atlantic Culinary Academy
Dover, NH

Bob Dowden
Nova Scotia Community
College
Kentville, Nova Scotia

Dominique and Cindy Duby
DC Duby School
Richmond, British Columbia

Dale Dunham
Oklahoma State University
Okmulgee, OK

Michael Durrer
Algonquin College
Nepean, Ontario

Michael A. Elliott
Liason College
Toronto, Ontario

Evan Enowitz
Grossmont College
El Cajon, CA

Daniel Esposito
Canadore College
North Bay, Ontario

Guy Ethier
Canadian Federation of Chefs
and Cooks
Surrey, British Columbia

Mark Facklam
The Cooking and Hospitality
Institute of Chicago
Chicago, IL

Fred T. Faria
Johnson and Wales University
Providence, RI

Alan Fleming
Algonquin College
Ottawa, Ontario

Robyn L. Flipse
Brooksdale Community
College
Lincroft, NJ

Sandra Flowerday
Educational Consultant
Charlotte, MI

Sandra Foley
Gogebic Community College
Ironwood, MI

Willard L. Geach
Long Beach City College
Long Beach, CA

Joan W. Geerken
State University of New York
at Cobleskill
Cobleskill, NY

Dave Gibson
Niagara College
Niagara Falls, Ontario

Gilles Godin
Nova Scotia Community
College
Stellarton, Nova Scotia

James Goering
El Centro College
Dallas, TX

Jeff Graves
Purdue University
West Lafayette, IN

Michael Graves
Atlantic Culinary
Dover, NH

Nancy Graves
University of Houston
Houston, TX

Juliet Groux
West Liberty State College
West Liberty, WV

Robert Harrington
Nichols State University
Thibodaux, LA

Robert S. Haynes
Lambton College
Sarnia, Ontario

John D. Hedley
Los Angeles Trade-Technical
College
Los Angeles, CA

Rosemary L. Hedlund
Des Moines Area Community
College
Ankeny, IA

Iris Helveston
State of Florida Department
of Education
Tampa, FL

Maynard G. Hemmah
Moorhead Area Vocational-
Technical Institute
Moorhead, MN

Margaret A. Howard
Sheridan Vocational-Technical
Center
Hollywood, FL

Russ Hudson
North Island College
Courtenay, British Columbia

Lynn Huffman
Texas Tech University
Lubbock, TX

Anne L. Jachim
Moraine Valley Community
College
Palos Hills, IL

Daniel K. Jeatran
Milwaukee Area Technical
College
Milwaukee, WI

Frank F. Johnson Jr.
University of South Florida
Tampa, FL

Roosevelt Johnson
Sidney North Colver
Vocational-Technical
Institute
New Orleans, LA

Todd Jones
Mattatuck Community College
Waterbury, CT

Mike Jung
Hennepin Technical Center
Brooklyn Park, MN

Sandy Kapoor
Cal Poly Pomona
Pomona, CA

Tom King
Cabrillo College
Aptos, CA

Suzanne Little, M.S., R.D.
San Jacinto College
Pasadena, TX

Shirley Lotze
Western Wisconsin Technical
Institute
LaCrosse, WI

Robert M. Lyna
Southern Maine Vocational-
Technical Institute
South Portland, ME

George Macht
College of DuPage
Glen Ellyn, IL

Merle Maerz
Selkirk College
Nelson, British Columbia

Sylvia Marple
University of New Hampshire
Durham, NH

Valeria S. Mason
State Department of Education
Gainesville, FL

John McDonald
St. Augustine Technical Center
St. Augustine, FL

Terence F. McDonough
Erie Community College
Buffalo, NY

Marcia W. McDowell
Monroe Community College
Rochester, NY

Linda McDuffie
North Seattle Community
College
Seattle, WA

Robert McLean
The Fay School
Southboro, MA

Ann Miglio
Williamsport Area Community
College
Williamsport, PA

Harold O. Mishoe
Southern Maine Vocational-
Technical Institute
South Portland, ME

Ken W. Myers
University of Minnesota-
Crookston
Crookston, MN

Kathy Niemann
Portland State University
Portland, OR

William T. Norvell
William Rainey Harper College
Palatine, IL

Andrew Ormiston
Brandon, Manitoba

Gary Page
Grand Valley State College
Allendale, MI

Michael Palmer
Western Culinary Institute
Portland, OR

Philip Panzarino
New York City Technical
College
Brooklyn, NY

Jayne Pearson
Manchester Community
College
Manchester, CT

Richard Petrello
Withlacoochee Vocational-
Technical Center
Inverness, FL

William F. Petsch
Pinellas Vocational Technical
Institute
Clearwater, FL

Michael PiccZinino
Shasta College
Redding, CA

Tony Rechsteiner
Northern Lights College
Dawson Creek, British
Columbia

John Reimers
Red River College
Winnipeg, Manitoba

Larry Richardson
Hinds Junior College-Jackson
Branch
Jackson, MI

Neil Rittenaur
North Dakota State College
of Science
Wahpeton, ND

Hubert E. Robert
Holyoke Community College
Holyoke, PA

Richard Roberts
Wake Technical Community
College
Raleigh, NC

Vance Roux
Delgado Community College
New Orleans, LA

Ricardo G. Saenz
Renton Vocational-Technical
Institute
Renton, WA

Robert R. Santos
Maui Community College
Kahului, HI

Frank Schellings
Diablo Valley College
Pleasant Hill, CA

David Schneider
Macomb Community College
Mt. Clemens, MI

Charlotte Schwyn
Delta College
Stockton, CA

Roy John Sharp
Portland Community College
Portland, OR

Settimio Sicoli
Vancouver Community
College
Vancouver, British Columbia

Diane Sinkinson
Cape Fear Community College
Wilmington, NC

Norman C. Smith
Sir Sanford Fleming College
Peterborough, Ontario

Reuel J. Smith
Truckee Meadows Community
College
Reno, NV

William Sprowl
Mt. San Jacinto College
San Jacinto, CA

Nancy S. Steryous
St. Petersburg Vocational-
Technical Institute
St. Petersburg, FL

Siegfried Stober
Joliet Junior College
Joliet, IL

Peter Sugameli
Wayne Community College
Detroit, MI

Julia Sullivan
Copiah-Lincoln Junior College
Wesson, MI

William Thornton
St. Phillips College
San Antonio, TX

Sheila A. Tillman
Asheville-Buncombe Technical
Community College
Asheville, NC

S.W. (Stan) Townsend
Northern Alberta Institute of
Technology
Edmonton, Alberta

Robin W. Turner
State University of New York at
Delhi
Delhi, NY

Jerry L. Vincent
Johnson County Community
College
Overland Park, KS

Barbara Vredeveld
Iowa Western Community
College
Council Bluffs, IA

D. Michael Wallace
North Island College
Courtenay, British Columbia

R.G. Werth
Asheville-Buncombe Technical
Community College
Asheville, NC

Eberhard Werthman
St. Paul Technical College
St. Paul, MN

J. William White
Pinellas County School System
St. Petersburg, FL

Doris Wilkes
Florida Hospitality Education
Program
The Florida State University
Tallahassee, FL

Wes J. Wilkinson
Lambton College
Sarnia, Ontario

Ronald S. Wolf
Florida Community College
Jacksonville, FL

Ron Wong
Northern Alberta Institute of
Technology
Edmonton, Alberta

Tony Wood
Hospitality Industry Education
Advisory Committee
Surrey, British Columbia

Ronald Zabkiewicz
South Technical Education
Center
Boynton Beach, FL

Mike Zema
Elgin Community College
Elgin, IL

Ronald Zwerger
Elgin Community College
Elgin, IL

PROFESSIONAL
COOKING

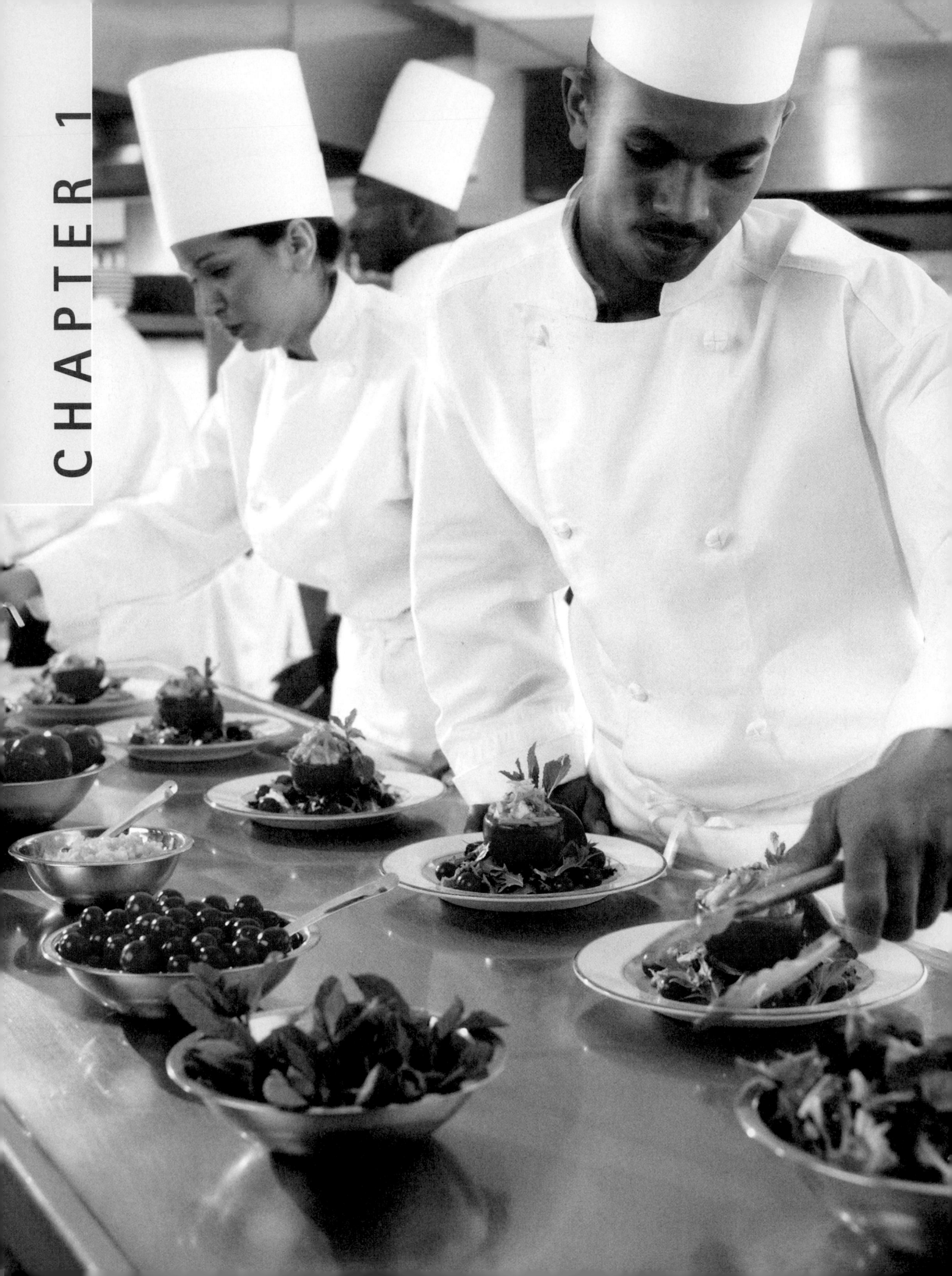

CHAPTER 1

The Food Service Industry

This is an exciting time to begin a career in food service. Interest in dining and curiosity about new foods are greater than ever. More new restaurants open every year. Many restaurants are busy every night, and restaurant chains number among the nation's largest corporations. The chef, once considered a domestic servant, is now respected as an artist and skilled craftsperson.

The growth of the food service industry creates a demand for thousands of skilled people every year. Many people are attracted by a career that is challenging and exciting and, above all, provides the chance to find real satisfaction in doing a job well.

Unfortunately, many people see only the glamorous side of food service and fail to understand that this is a tiny part of the picture. The public does not often see the years of training, the long hours, and the tremendous pressures that lie behind every success.

Before you start your practical studies, covered in later chapters, it is good to know a little about the profession you are entering. This chapter gives you a brief overview of modern food service, including how it got to where it is today and where it is headed.

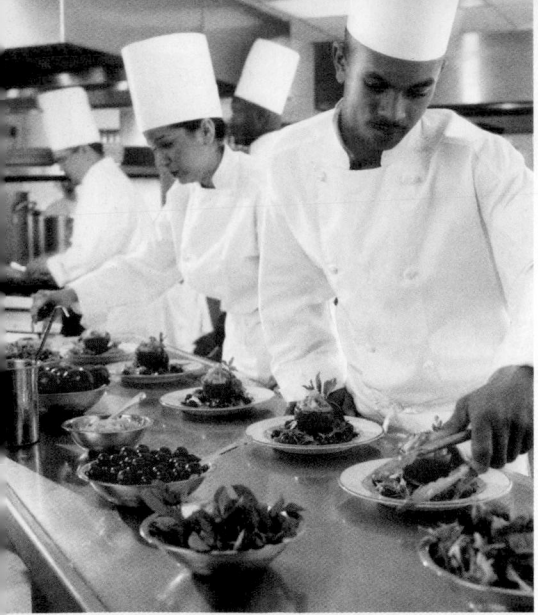

A HISTORY OF MODERN FOOD SERVICE

The value of history is that it helps us understand the present and the future. In food service, knowledge of our professional heritage helps us see why we do things as we do, how our cooking techniques have been developed and refined, and how we can continue to develop and innovate in the years ahead.

An important lesson of history is that the way we cook now is the result of the work done by countless chefs over hundreds of years. Cooking is as much science as it is art. Cooking techniques are not based on arbitrary rules that some chefs made up long ago. Rather, they are based on an understanding of how different foods react when heated in various ways, when combined in various proportions, and so on. The chefs who have come before us have already done much of this work so we don't have to.

This doesn't mean there is no room for innovation and experimentation or that we should never challenge old ideas. But it does mean a lot of knowledge has been collected over the years, and we would be smart to take advantage of what has already been learned. Furthermore, how can we challenge old ideas unless we know what those old ideas are? Knowledge is the best starting point for innovation.

THE ORIGINS OF CLASSICAL AND MODERN CUISINE

Quantity cookery has existed for thousands of years, as long as there have been large groups of people to feed, such as armies. But modern food service is said to have begun shortly after the middle of the eighteenth century. At this time, food production in France was controlled by guilds. Caterers, pastry makers, roasters, and pork butchers held licenses to prepare specific items. An innkeeper, in order to serve a meal to guests, had to buy the various menu items from those operations that were licensed to provide them. Guests had little or no choice and simply ate what was available for that meal.

In 1765, a Parisian named Boulanger began advertising on his shop sign that he served soups, which he called *restaurants* or *restoratives*. (Literally, the word means "fortifying.") According to the story, one of the dishes he served was sheep's feet in a cream sauce. The guild of stew makers challenged him in court, but Boulanger won by claiming he didn't stew the feet *in* the sauce but served them *with* the sauce. In challenging the rules of the guilds, Boulanger unwittingly changed the course of food service history.

The new developments in food service received a great stimulus as a result of the French Revolution, beginning in 1789. Before this time, the great chefs were employed in the houses of the French nobility. With the revolution and the end of the monarchy, many chefs, suddenly out of work, opened restaurants in and around Paris to support themselves. Furthermore, the revolutionary government abolished the guilds. Restaurants and inns could serve dinners reflecting the talent and creativity of their own chefs, rather than being forced to rely on licensed caterers to supply their food. At the start of the French Revolution, there were about 50 restaurants in Paris. Ten years later there were about 500.

Another important invention that changed the organization of kitchens in the eighteenth century was the stove, or *potager*, which gave cooks a more practical and controllable heat source than an open fire. Soon commercial kitchens became divided into three departments: the rotisserie, under the control of the meat chef or *rôtisseur*, the oven, under the control of the pastry chef or *pâtissier*, and the stove, run by the cook or *cuisinier*. The meat chef and pastry chef reported to the cuisinier, who was also known as *chef de cuisine*, which means "head of the kitchen."

CARÊME

All the changes that took place in the world of cooking during the 1700s led to, for the first time, a difference between home cooking and professional cooking. One way we can try to understand this difference is to look at the work of the greatest chef of the pe-

After reading this chapter, you should be able to

1. **Name and describe four major developments that have significantly changed the food service industry in the twentieth century.**

2. **Identify seven major stations in a classical kitchen.**

3. **Explain how the size and type of an operation influence the organization of the modern kitchen.**

4. **Identify and describe three skill levels of food production personnel.**

5. **Identify eight behaviorial characteristics that food service workers should develop and maintain to achieve the highest standards of professionalism.**

riod following the French Revolution, Marie-Antoine Carême (1784–1833). As a young man, Carême learned all the branches of cooking quickly, and he dedicated his career to refining and organizing culinary techniques. His many books contain the first systematic account of cooking principles, recipes, and menu making.

At a time when the interesting advances in cooking were happening in restaurants, Carême worked as a chef to wealthy patrons, kings, and heads of state. He was perhaps the first real celebrity chef, and he became famous as the creator of elaborate, elegant display pieces and pastries, the ancestors of our modern wedding cakes, sugar sculptures, and ice and tallow carvings. But it was Carême's practical and theoretical work as an author and an inventor of recipes that was responsible, to a large extent, for bringing cooking out of the Middle Ages and into the modern period.

Carême emphasized procedure and order. His goal was to create more lightness and simplicity. The complex cuisine of the aristocracy—called *Grande Cuisine*—was still not much different from that of the Middle Ages and was anything but simple and light. Carême's efforts were a great step toward modern simplicity. The methods explained in his books were complex, but his aim was pure results. He added seasonings and other ingredients not so much to add new flavors but to highlight the flavors of the main ingredients. His sauces were designed to enhance, not cover up, the food being sauced. Carême was a thoughtful chef, and, whenever he changed a classic recipe, he was careful to explain his reasons for doing so.

Beginning with Carême, a style of cooking developed that can truly be called international, because the same principles are still used by professional cooks around the world. Older styles of cooking, as well as much of today's home cooking, are based on tradition. In other words, a cook makes a dish a certain way because that is how it always has been done. On the other hand, in Carême's *Grande Cuisine*, and in professional cooking ever since, a cook makes a dish a certain way because the principles and methods of cooking show it is the best way to get the desired results. For example, for hundreds of years, cooks boiled meats before roasting them on a rotisserie in front of the fire. But when chefs began thinking and experimenting rather than just accepting the tradition of boiling meat before roasting, they realized that either braising the meat or roasting it from the raw state were better options.

Marie-Antoine Carême
L'Art de la Cuisine Française au Dix-Neuvième Siècle.
Paris: L'auteur, 1833–1844. Courtesy of the Rare Manuscript Collections, Cornell University Library.

ESCOFFIER

Georges-Auguste Escoffier (1847–1935), the greatest chef of his time, is still today revered by chefs and gourmets as the father of twentieth-century cookery. His two main contributions were (1) the simplification of classical cuisine and the classical menu, and (2) the reorganization of the kitchen.

Escoffier rejected what he called the "general confusion" of the old menus, in which sheer quantity seemed to be the most important factor. Instead, he called for order and diversity and emphasized the careful selection of one or two dishes per course, dishes that followed one another harmoniously and delighted the taste with their delicacy and simplicity.

Escoffier's books and recipes are still important reference works for professional chefs. The basic cooking methods and preparations we study today are based on Escoffier's work. His book *Le Guide Culinaire*, which is still widely used, arranges recipes in a simple system based on main ingredient and cooking method, greatly simplifying the more complex system handed down from Carême. Learning classical cooking, according to Escoffier, begins with learning a relatively few basic procedures and understanding basic ingredients.

Escoffier's second major achievement, the reorganization of the kitchen, resulted in a streamlined workplace that was better suited to turning out the simplified dishes and menus he instituted. The system of organization he established is still in use today, especially in large hotels and full-service restaurants, as we discuss later in this chapter.

MODERN TECHNOLOGY

Today's kitchens look much different from those of Escoffier's day, even though our basic cooking principles are the same. Also, the dishes we eat have gradually changed due to the innovations and creativity of modern chefs. The process of simplification and refinement, to which Carême and Escoffier made monumental contributions, is still ongoing, adapting classical cooking to modern conditions and tastes.

Before we discuss the changes in cooking styles that took place in the twentieth century, let's look at some of the developments in technology that affected cooking.

Development of New Equipment

We take for granted such basic equipment as gas and electric ranges and ovens and electric refrigerators. But even these essential tools did not exist until fairly recently. The easily controlled heat of modern cooking equipment, as well as motorized food cutters, mixers, and other processing equipment, has greatly simplified food production.

Research and technology continue to produce sophisticated tools for the kitchen. Some of these products, such as tilting skillets and steam-jacketed kettles, can do many jobs and are popular in many kitchens. Others can perform specialized tasks rapidly and efficiently, but their usefulness depends on volume because they are designed to do only a few jobs.

Modern equipment has enabled many food service operations to change their production methods. With sophisticated cooling, freezing, and heating equipment, it is possible to prepare some foods further in advance and in larger quantities. Some large multiunit operations prepare food for all their units in a central commissary. The food is prepared in quantity, packaged, chilled or frozen, then heated or cooked to order in the individual units.

Development and Availability of New Food Products

Modern refrigeration and rapid transportation caused revolutionary changes in eating habits. For the first time, fresh foods of all kinds—meats, fish, vegetables, and fruits—became available throughout the year. Exotic delicacies can now be shipped from anywhere in the world and arrive fresh and in peak condition.

The development of preservation techniques—not just refrigeration but also freezing, canning, freeze-drying, vacuum-packing, and irradiation—increased the availability of most foods and made affordable some that were once rare and expensive.

Techniques of food preservation have had another effect. It is now possible to do some or most of the preparation and processing of foods before shipping rather than in the food service operation itself. Thus, convenience foods have come into being. Convenience foods continue to account for an increasing share of the total food market.

Some developments in food science and agriculture are controversial. Irradiation, mentioned above, caused much controversy when it was introduced because it exposes foods to radioactivity to rid them of organisms that cause spoilage and disease. Scientists say, however, that no traces of radioactivity remain in the foods, and the procedure has become more widely used.

A more controversial technique is genetic engineering, which involves artificially changing the gene structure of a food to give it some desirable trait, such as resistance to disease, drought, or insect damage. Reactions by cooks and the public to this and other developments have changed the way many chefs think about food and menus.

Sanitary and Nutritional Awareness

The development of the sciences of microbiology and nutrition had a great impact on food service. One hundred years ago, there was little understanding of the causes of food poisoning and food spoilage. Food handling practices have come a long way since Escoffier's day.

Also, little knowledge of nutritional principles was available until fairly recently. Today, nutrition is an important part of a cook's training. Customers are also more knowledgeable and therefore more likely to demand healthful, well-balanced menus. Unfortunately, nutrition science is constantly shifting. Diets considered healthful one year become eating patterns to be avoided a few years later. Fad diets come and go, and chefs often struggle to keep their menus current. It is more important than ever for cooks to keep up to date with the latest nutritional understanding.

COOKING IN THE TWENTIETH AND TWENTY-FIRST CENTURIES

All these developments have helped change cooking styles, menus, and eating habits. The evolution of cuisine that has been going on for hundreds of years continues.

Changes occur not only because of technological developments, such as those just described, but also because of our reactions to culinary traditions.

Two opposing forces can be seen at work throughout the history of cooking. One is the urge to simplify, to eliminate complexity and ornamentation, and instead to emphasize the plain, natural tastes of basic, fresh ingredients. The other is the urge to invent, to highlight the creativity of the chef, with an accent on fancier, more complicated presentations and procedures. Both these forces are valid and healthy; they continually refresh and renew the art of cooking.

A generation after Escoffier, the most influential chef in the middle of the twentieth century was Fernand Point (1897–1955). Working quietly and steadily in his restaurant, La Pyramide, in Vienne, France, Point simplified and lightened classical cuisine. He was a perfectionist who sometimes worked on a dish for years before he felt it was good enough to put on his menu. "I am not hard to please," he said. "I'm satisfied with the very best." Point insisted that every meal should be "a little marvel."

Point's influence extended well beyond his own life. Many of his apprentices, such as Paul Bocuse, Jean and Pierre Troisgros, and Alain Chapel, went on to become some of the greatest stars of modern cooking. They, along with other chefs in their generation, became best known in the 1960s and early 1970s for a style of cooking called **nouvelle cuisine**. Reacting to what they saw as a heavy, stodgy, overly complicated classical cuisine, these chefs took Point's lighter approach even further. They rejected many traditional principles, such as a dependence on flour to thicken sauces, and instead urged simpler, more natural flavors and preparations, with lighter sauces and seasonings and shorter cooking times. In traditional classical cuisine, many dishes were plated in the dining room by waiters. Nouvelle cuisine, however, placed a great deal of emphasis on artful plating presentations done by the chef in the kitchen.

Very quickly, however, this "simpler" style became extravagant and complicated, famous for strange combinations of foods and fussy, ornate arrangements and designs. By the 1980s, nouvelle cuisine was the subject of jokes. Still, the best achievements of nouvelle cuisine have taken a permanent place in the classical tradition. Meanwhile, many of its excesses have been forgotten. It is probably fair to say that most of the best new ideas and the lasting accomplishments were those of classically trained chefs with a solid grounding in the basics.

New Emphasis on Ingredients

Advances in agriculture and food preservation have had disadvantages as well as advantages. Everyone is familiar with hard, tasteless fruits and vegetables that were developed to ship well and last long, without regard for eating quality. Many people, including chefs, began to question not only the flavor but also the health value and the environmental effects of genetically engineered foods, of produce raised with chemical pesticides and fertilizers, and of animals raised with antibiotics and other drugs and hormones.

A landmark event in the history of modern North American cooking was the opening of Alice Waters's restaurant Chez Panisse in Berkeley, California, in 1971. Waters's philosophy is that good food depends on good ingredients, so she set about finding dependable sources of the best-quality vegetables, fruits, and meats, and preparing them in the simplest ways. Over the next decades, many chefs and restaurateurs followed her lead, seeking out the best seasonal, locally grown, organically raised food products. A few years later, Larry Forgione picked up the banner of local ingredients and local cuisine in his New York City restaurant An American Place. Other chefs quickly followed suit, and soon chefs across the continent made names for themselves and their restaurants at least in part by emphasizing good-quality local ingredients. Half a century ago, nearly all the most respected chefs working in the United States and Canada were European-born. Today, the movement begun by the pioneering quality-oriented chefs of the 1970s and 1980s has fostered a great number of creative North American–born chefs who are among the most respected in the world.

The public has benefited greatly from these efforts. Today, in supermarkets as well as in restaurants, a much greater variety of high-quality foods is available than there was 40 or 50 years ago. Many chefs have modified their cooking styles to highlight the natural flavors and textures of their ingredients, and their menus are often simpler now for this reason.

International Influences

After the middle of the twentieth century, as travel became easier and as immigrants arrived in Europe and North America from around the world, awareness of and taste for

CATERINA DE MEDICI

The Medicis were a powerful Italian family that ruled Florence from the fourteenth to the sixteenth century and provided, in addition to the rulers of Florence, three popes and two queens of France.

Until recently, the accepted and often-told story is that when Caterina de Medici went to France in 1533 to marry the future King Henry II, she brought with her a staff of cooks as part of her household. This introduction of Italian cooking practices into France supposedly changed and modernized the cooking not only of France but of all of Western Europe. According to this story, Caterina and her Italian cooks should be credited with fostering modern cuisine.

When cookbooks and other culinary writings of the period are examined, however, it appears that French cooking doesn't begin to modernize until at least a century later. During the hundred years after Caterina's arrival in France, no new, important cookbooks were written. There is no sign of a revolution in cooking. In fact, banquet menus that survive from the period

(continues next page)

regional dishes grew. Chefs became more knowledgeable not only about the traditional cuisines of other parts of Europe but about those of Asia, Latin America, and elsewhere. Many of the most creative chefs have been inspired by these cuisines and use some of their techniques and ingredients. For example, many North American and French chefs, looking for ways to make their cooking lighter and more elegant, have found ideas in the cuisine of Japan. In the southwestern United States, a number of chefs have transformed Mexican influences into an elegant and original cooking style. Throughout North America, traditional dishes and regional specialties combine the cooking traditions of immigrant settlers and the indigenous ingredients of a bountiful land. For many years, critics often argued that menus in most North American restaurants offered the same monotonous, mediocre food. In recent decades, however, American and Canadian cooks have rediscovered traditional North American dishes.

The use of ingredients and techniques from more than one regional, or international, cuisine in a single dish is known as **fusion cuisine**. Early attempts to prepare fusion cuisine often produced poor results because the dishes were not true to any one culture and were too mixed up. This was especially true in the 1980s, when the idea of fusion cuisine was new. Cooks often combined ingredients and techniques without a good feeling for how they would work together. The result was sometimes a jumbled mess. But chefs who have taken the time to study in depth the cuisines and cultures they borrow from have brought new excitement to cooking and to restaurant menus.

Today chefs make good use of all the ingredients and techniques available to them. It is almost second nature to give extra depth to the braising liquid for a beef pot roast by adding Mexican ancho peppers, for example, or to include Thai basil and lemon grass in a seafood salad. In the recipe sections of this book, classic dishes from many regions of the world are included among more familiar recipes from home. To help you understand these recipes and the cuisines they come from, background information accompanies many of them.

Cooking and cooking styles continue to change. Technology continues to make rapid advances in our industry, and men and women are needed who can adapt to these changes and respond to new challenges. Although automation and convenience foods will no doubt grow in importance, imaginative chefs who can create new dishes and develop new techniques and styles will always be needed, as will skilled cooks who can apply both old and new techniques to produce high-quality foods in all kinds of facilities, from restaurants and hotels to schools and hospitals.

THE ORGANIZATION OF MODERN KITCHENS

THE BASIS OF KITCHEN ORGANIZATION

The purpose of kitchen organization is to assign or allocate tasks so they can be done efficiently and properly and so all workers know what their responsibilities are.

The way a kitchen is organized depends on several factors.

1. **The menu.**
   The kinds of dishes to be produced obviously determine the jobs that need to be done. The menu is, in fact, the basis of the entire operation. Because of its importance, we devote a whole chapter to a study of the menu (Chapter 5).

2. **The type of establishment.**
   The major types of food service establishments are as follows:

   - Hotels
   - Institutional kitchens
       Schools
       Hospitals, nursing homes, and other health-care institutions
       Employee lunchrooms
       Airline catering
       Military food service
       Correctional institutions

- Catering and banquet services
- Fast-food restaurants
- Carry-out or take-out food facilities
- Full-service restaurants

3. **The size of the operation (the number of customers and the volume of food served).**
4. **The physical facilities, including the equipment in use.**

THE CLASSICAL BRIGADE

As you learned earlier in this chapter, one of Escoffier's important achievements was the reorganization of the kitchen. This reorganization divided the kitchen into departments, or stations, based on the kinds of foods produced. A station chef was placed in charge of each department. In a small operation, the station chef may be the only worker in the department. But in a large kitchen, each station chef might have several assistants.

This system, with many variations, is still used today, especially in large hotels with traditional kinds of food service. The major positions are as follows:

1. The *chef* is the person in charge of the kitchen. In large establishments, this person has the title of **executive chef**. The executive chef is a manager who is responsible for all aspects of food production, including menu planning, purchasing, costing, planning work schedules, hiring, and training.

2. If a food service operation is large, with many departments (for example, a formal dining room, a casual dining room, and a catering department), or if it has several units in different locations, each kitchen may have a **chef de cuisine**. The chef de cuisine reports to the executive chef.

3. The **sous chef** (*soo* shef) is directly in charge of production and works as the assistant to the executive chef or chef de cuisine. (The word "sous" is French for "under.") Because the executive chef's responsibilities may require a great deal of time in the office, the sous chef takes command of the actual production and the minute-by-minute supervision of the staff.

4. The **station chefs**, or *chefs de partie*, are in charge of particular areas of production. The following are the most important station chefs.

   - The *sauce chef*, or **saucier** (so-see-*ay*), prepares sauces, stews, and hot hors d'oeuvres, and sautés foods to order. This is usually the highest position of all the stations.

   - The *fish cook*, or **poissonier** (pwah-so-*nyay*), prepares fish dishes. In some kitchens, this station is handled by the saucier.

   - The *vegetable cook*, or **entremetier** (awn-truh-met-*yay*), prepares vegetables, soups, starches, and eggs. Large kitchens may divide these duties among the vegetable cook, the fry cook, and the soup cook.

   - The *roast cook*, or **rôtisseur** (ro-tee-*sur*), prepares roasted and braised meats and their gravies and broils meats and other items to order. A large kitchen may have a separate *broiler cook*, or **grillardin** (gree-ar-*dan*), to handle the broiled items. The broiler cook may also prepare deep-fried meats and fish.

   - The *pantry chef*, or **garde manger** (gard-mawn-*zhay*), is responsible for cold foods, including salads and dressings, pâtés, cold hors d'oeuvres, and buffet items.

   - The *pastry chef*, or **pâtissier** (pa-tees-*syay*), prepares pastries and desserts.

   - The *relief cook*, *swing cook*, or **tournant** (toor-*nawn*), replaces other station heads.

   - The **expediter**, or **aboyeur** (ah-bwa-yer), accepts orders from waiters and passes them on to the cooks on the line. The expediter also calls for orders to be finished and plated at the proper time and inspects each plate before passing it to the dining room staff. In many restaurants, this position is taken by the head chef or the sous chef.

5. *Cooks* and *assistants* in each station or department help with the duties assigned to them. For example, the assistant vegetable cook may wash, peel, and trim vegetables. With experience, assistants may be promoted to station cooks and then to station chefs.

are not much different from menus of the Middle Ages.

Banquets during the Middle Ages were like huge sit-down buffets. For each course, the table was loaded with large quantities of meats, poultry, and fish dishes, usually heavily spiced, and an assortment of side dishes and sweets. Diners generally ate only what they could reach. The course was then removed, and another course, also meats and side dishes, was loaded onto the table. Again, each person ate only a fraction of the dishes present, depending on what was within reach.

The modern idea of a menu in which everyone at the table eats the same dishes in the same order does not appear until the 1700s.

So it is not historically accurate to give the Italian princess Caterina credit for modernizing French cuisine. On the other hand, it is fair to say that she and her offspring brought more refined manners and elegance to European dining rooms. Italian innovations included the use of the fork as well as greater cleanliness in general. An additional Italian contribution was the invention of sophisticated pastries and desserts.

MODERN KITCHEN ORGANIZATION

As you can see, only a large establishment needs a staff like the classical brigade just described. In fact, some large hotels have even larger staffs, with other positions such as separate day and night sous chefs, assistant chef, banquet chef, butcher, baker, and so on.

Most modern operations, on the other hand, are smaller than this. The size of the classical brigade may be reduced simply by combining two or more positions where the workload allows it. For example, the *second cook* may combine the duties of the sauce cook, fish cook, soup cook, and vegetable cook.

A typical medium-size operation may employ a chef, a second cook, a broiler cook, a pantry cook, and a few cooks' helpers.

A working chef is in charge of operations that are not large enough to have an executive chef. In addition to being in charge of the kitchen, the working chef also handles one of the production stations. For example, he or she may handle the sauté station, plate foods during service, and help on other stations when needed.

Small kitchens may have only a chef, one or two cooks, and perhaps one or two assistants to handle simple jobs such as washing and peeling vegetables. Cooks who prepare or finish hot à la carte items during service in a restaurant may be known as line cooks. Line cooks are said to be on the hot line, or simply on the line.

In many small operations, the short-order cook is the backbone of the kitchen during service time. This cook may handle the broiler, deep fryer, griddle, sandwich production, and even some sautéed items. In other words, the short-order cook's responsibility is the preparation of foods that are quickly prepared to order.

By contrast, establishments such as school cafeterias may do no cooking to order at all. Stations and assignments are based on the requirements of quantity preparation rather than cooking to order.

SKILL LEVELS

The preceding discussion is necessarily general because there are so many kinds of kitchen organizations. Titles vary also. The responsibilities of the worker called the *second cook*, for example, are not necessarily the same in every establishment. Escoffier's standardized system has evolved in many directions.

One title that is often misunderstood and much abused is *chef*. The general public tends to refer to anyone with a white hat as a chef, and people who like to cook for guests in their homes refer to themselves as amateur chefs.

Strictly speaking, the term *chef* is reserved for one who is *in charge of a kitchen* or a part of a kitchen. The word *chef* is French for "chief" or "head." Studying this book will not make you a chef. The title must be earned by experience not only in preparing food but also in managing a staff and in planning production. New cooks who want to advance in their careers know they must always use the word *chef* with respect.

Skills required of food production personnel vary not only with the job level but also with the establishment and the kind of food prepared. The director of a hospital kitchen and the head chef in a luxury restaurant need different skills. The skills needed by a short-order cook in a coffee shop are not exactly the same as those needed by a production worker in a school cafeteria. Nevertheless, we can group skills into three general categories.

1. **Supervisory.**

   The head of a food service kitchen, whether called *executive chef, head chef, working chef,* or *dietary director*, must have management and supervisory skills as well as a thorough knowledge of food production. Leadership positions require an individual who understands organizing and motivating people, planning menus and production procedures, controlling costs and managing budgets, and purchasing food supplies and equipment. Even if he or she does no cooking at all, the chef must be an experienced cook in order to schedule production, instruct workers, and control quality. Above all, the chef must be able to work well with people, even under extreme pressure.

2. **Skilled and technical.**

   While the chef is the head of an establishment, the cooks are the backbone. These workers carry out the actual food production. Thus, they must have knowledge of and experience in cooking techniques, at least for the dishes made in their own department. In addition, they must be able to function well with their fellow workers and to coordinate with other departments. Food production is a team activity.

3. **Entry level.**
   Entry-level jobs in food service usually require no particular skills or experience. Workers in these jobs are assigned such work as washing vegetables and preparing salad greens. As their knowledge and experience increase, they may be given more complex tasks and eventually become skilled cooks. Many executive chefs began their careers as pot washers who got a chance to peel potatoes when the pot sink was empty.

Beginning in an entry-level position and working one's way up with experience is the traditional method of advancing in a food service career. Today, however, many cooks are graduates of culinary schools and programs. But even with such an education, many new graduates begin at entry-level positions. This is as it should be and certainly should not be seen as discouragement. Schools teach general cooking knowledge, while every food service establishment requires specific skills, according to its own menu and its own procedures. Experience as well as theoretical knowledge is needed to be able to adapt to real-life working situations. However, students who have studied and learned well should be able to work their way up more rapidly than the beginners with no knowledge at all.

STANDARDS OF PROFESSIONALISM

What does it take to be a good food service worker?

The emphasis of a food service education is on learning a set of skills. But in many ways, *attitudes are more important than skills* because a good attitude will help you not only learn skills but also persevere and overcome the many difficulties you will face.

The successful food service worker follows an unwritten code of behavior and set of attitudes we call *professionalism.* Let's look at some of the qualities a professional must have.

POSITIVE ATTITUDE TOWARD THE JOB

In order to be a good professional cook, you have to like cooking and want to do it well. Being serious about your work doesn't mean you can't enjoy it. But the enjoyment comes from the satisfaction of doing your job well and making everything run smoothly.

Every experienced chef knows the stimulation of the rush. When it's the busiest time of the evening, the orders are coming in so fast you can hardly keep track of them, and every split second counts—then, when everyone digs in and works together and everything clicks, there's real excitement in the air. But this excitement comes only when you work for it.

A cook with a positive attitude works quickly, efficiently, neatly, and safely. Professionals have pride in their work and want to make sure it is something to be proud of.

Pride in your work and in your profession is important, but humility is important too, especially when you are starting out. Sometimes new culinary school graduates arrive on the job thinking they know everything. Remember that learning to cook and learning to manage a kitchen is a lifelong process and that you are not yet qualified to be executive chef.

The importance of a professional attitude begins even before you start your first job. The standard advice for a successful job interview applies to cooks as well as to office professionals: Dress and behave not for the group you belong to but for the group you want to join. Arrive neat, clean, appropriately dressed, and on time. Get noticed for the right reasons. Carry this attitude through every day on the job.

STAYING POWER

Food service requires physical and mental stamina, good health, and a willingness to work hard. It is hard work. The pressure can be intense and the hours long and grueling. You may be working evenings and weekends when everyone else is playing. And the work can be monotonous. You might think it's drudgery to hand-shape two or three dozen dinner rolls for your baking class, but wait until you get that great job in the big hotel and are told to make 3,000 canapés for a party.

Overcoming these difficulties requires a sense of responsibility and a dedication to your profession, to your coworkers, and to your customers or clients. Dedication also means staying with a job and not hopping from kitchen to kitchen every few months. Sticking with a job at least a year or two shows prospective employers you are serious about your work and can be relied on.

ABILITY TO WORK WITH PEOPLE

Few of you will work in an establishment so small that you are the only person on the staff. Food service work is teamwork, and it's essential to be able to work well on a team and to cooperate with your fellow workers. You can't afford to let ego problems, petty jealousy, departmental rivalries, or feelings about other people get in the way of doing the job well. In the old days, many chefs were famous for their temper tantrums. Fortunately, self-control is more valued today.

EAGERNESS TO LEARN

There is more to learn about cooking than you will learn in a lifetime. The greatest chefs in the world are the first to admit they have more to learn, and they keep working, experimenting, and studying. The food service industry is changing so rapidly that it is vital to be open to new ideas. No matter how good your techniques are, you might learn an even better way.

Continue to study and read. Seek extra work that gives you the opportunity to learn from people with more experience. For example, if you are working on the hot line in a restaurant, ask the pastry chef if you could come in early, on your own time, to help out and, in the process, gain new knowledge and experience.

Many culinary schools and programs have continuing education programs that can help you add new skills. Professional associations such as the American Culinary Federation (ACF) and the International Association of Culinary Professionals (IACP) provide opportunities for learning as well as for making contacts with other professionals.

A FULL RANGE OF SKILLS

Most people who become professional cooks do so because they like to cook. This is an important motivation, but it is also important to develop and maintain other skills that are necessary for the profession. To be successful, a cook must understand and manage food cost and other financial matters, manage and maintain proper inventories, deal with purveyors, and understand personnel management.

EXPERIENCE

One of our most respected chefs said, "You don't really know how to cook a dish until you have done it a thousand times."

There is no substitute for years of experience. Studying cooking principles in books and in schools can get your career off to a running start. You may learn more about basic cooking theories from your chef instructors than you could in several years of working your way up from washing vegetables. But if you want to become an accomplished cook, you need practice, practice, and more practice. A diploma does not make you a chef.

DEDICATION TO QUALITY

Many people think only a special category of food can be called *gourmet food*. It's hard to say exactly what that is. Apparently, the only thing so-called gourmet foods have in common is high price.

The only distinction worth making is between well-prepared food and poorly prepared food. There is good roast duckling à l'orange and there is bad roast duckling à l'orange. There are good hamburgers and French fries, and there are bad hamburgers and French fries.

Whether you work in a top restaurant, a fast-food restaurant, a college cafeteria, or a catering house, you can do your job well, or not. The choice is yours.

High quality doesn't necessarily mean high price. It costs no more to cook green beans properly than to overcook them. But in order to produce high-quality food, you must want to. It is not enough to simply know how.

GOOD UNDERSTANDING OF THE BASICS

Experimentation and innovation in cooking are the order of the day. Brilliant chefs are breaking old boundaries and inventing dishes that would have been unthinkable years ago. There seems to be no limit to what can be tried.

However, the chefs who seem to be most revolutionary are the first to insist on the importance of solid grounding in basic techniques and in the classic methods practiced since Escoffier's day. In order to innovate, you have to know where to begin.

For the beginner, knowing the basics will help you take better advantage of your experience. When you watch a practiced cook at work, you will understand better what you are seeing and will know what questions to ask. In order to play great music on the piano, you first have to learn to play scales and exercises.

That's what this book is about. It's not a course in French cooking or American cooking or gourmet cooking or coffee shop cooking. It's a course in the basics. When you finish the book, you will not know everything. But you should be ready to take good advantage of the many rewarding years of food service experience ahead of you.

■ TERMS FOR REVIEW

Marie-Antoine Carême	chef de cuisine	rôtisseur	aboyeur
Georges-Auguste Escoffier	sous chef	grillardin	working chef
nouvelle cuisine	station chef	garde manger	line cook
fusion cuisine	saucier	pâtissier	short-order cook
chef	poissonier	tournant	professionalism
executive chef	entremetier	expediter	

■ QUESTIONS FOR DISCUSSION

1. Escoffier is sometimes called the father of modern food service. What were his most important accomplishments?

2. Discuss several ways in which modern technology has changed the food service industry.

3. Discuss how an emphasis on high-quality ingredients beginning in the late twentieth century has influenced cooks and cooking styles.

4. What is fusion cuisine? Discuss how successful chefs make use of international influences.

5. What is the purpose of kitchen organization? Is the classical system of organization developed by Escoffier the best one for all types of kitchens? Why or why not?

6. True or false: A cook in charge of the sauce and sauté station in a large hotel needs to have supervisory skills as well as cooking skills. Explain your answer.

7. True or false: If a culinary arts student in a professional school studies hard, works diligently, gets top grades, and shows real dedication, he or she will be qualified to be a chef upon graduation. Explain your answer.

2

Sanitation and Safety

In the last chapter, we talked about professionalism in food service. Professionalism is an attitude that reflects pride in the quality of your work. One of the most important ways of demonstrating professional pride is in the area of sanitation and safety. Pride in quality is reflected in your appearance and work habits. Poor hygiene, poor grooming and personal care, and sloppy work habits are nothing to be proud of.

Even more important, poor sanitation and safety can cost a lot of money. Poor food handling procedures and unclean kitchens cause illness, unhappy customers, and even fines, summonses, and lawsuits. Food spoilage raises food costs. Poor kitchen safety results in injuries, medical bills, and workdays lost. Finally, poor sanitation and safety habits show lack of respect for your customers, for your fellow workers, and for yourself.

In this chapter you will study the causes of food-borne diseases and kitchen injuries, and you will learn ways of preventing them. Prevention, of course, is the most important thing to learn. It is not as important to be able to recite the names of disease-causing bacteria as it is to be able to prevent their growth in food.

SANITATION

Rules of personal hygiene and sanitary food handling were not invented just to make your life difficult. There are good reasons for all of them. Instead of starting this chapter with lists of rules, we first talk about the causes of food-borne diseases. Then, when we get to the rules, you will understand why they are important. This will make them easier to remember and to practice.

The rules presented in this chapter are only basic guidelines. Local health departments have more detailed regulations. *All food service operators are responsible for knowing the health department regulations in their own city and state.*

The information presented here is practical as well as theoretical. It should not merely be learned but should be put to use systematically. One effective system food service establishments can use to ensure food safety is the Hazard Analysis Critical Control Point (HACCP) system. This practical program identifies possible danger points and sets up procedures for corrective action. HACCP is introduced later in this chapter.

After reading this chapter, you should be able to

1. **Describe steps to prevent food poisoning and food-borne diseases in the following areas: personal hygiene; food handling and storage techniques; cleaning and sanitizing techniques; and pest control.**

2. **Demonstrate safe workplace habits that prevent injuries from the following: cuts, burns, operation of machinery and equipment, and lifting.**

3. **Identify safe workplace habits that minimize the likelihood of fires and falls.**

FOOD HAZARDS

Preventing food-borne illness is one of the most important challenges facing every food service worker. In order to prevent illness, a food worker must understand the sources of food-borne disease.

Most food-borne illness is the result of eating food that has been contaminated. To say that a food is contaminated means it contains harmful substances that were not present originally in the food. In other words, contaminated food is food that is not pure. In this section we first discuss the various substances that can contaminate food and cause illness. Afterward, we consider how these substances get into food to contaminate it and how food workers can prevent contamination and avoid serving contaminated food.

Any substance in food that can cause illness or injury is called a hazard. Food hazards are of three types:

1. Biological hazards
2. Chemical hazards
3. Physical hazards

Notice it was said that *most* food-borne illness is caused by eating food that has been contaminated with foreign substances. Some illness is caused not by contaminants but by substances that occur naturally in foods. These include plant toxins (*toxin* means "poison") that occur naturally in some foods, such as the chemicals in poisonous mushrooms, and also certain natural food components to which some people are allergic. This section considers all these kinds of food hazards.

PATHOGENS

The most important kind of biological hazards to consider are microorganisms. A microorganism is a tiny, usually single-celled organism that can be seen only with a microscope. A microorganism that can cause disease is called a pathogen. Although these organisms sometimes occur in clusters large enough to be seen with the naked eye, they are not usually visible. This is one reason why they can be so dangerous. Just because food looks good doesn't mean it is safe.

Four kinds of microorganisms can contaminate food and cause illness:

1. Bacteria
2. Viruses
3. Fungi
4. Parasites

Most food-borne diseases are caused by bacteria, so most of our attention in this chapter is focused on them, but the other types can be dangerous as well. Many of the measures we take to protect food from bacteria also help prevent the other three kinds of microorganisms.

Bacteria

Bacteria are everywhere—in the air, in the water, in the ground, on our food, on our skin, inside our bodies. Scientists have various ways of classifying and describing these bacteria. As food workers, we are interested in a way of classifying them that may be less scientific but is more practical to our work.

1. **Harmless bacteria.**
   Most bacteria fall into this category. They are neither helpful nor harmful to us. We are not concerned with them in food sanitation.

2. **Beneficial bacteria.**
   These bacteria are helpful to us. For example, many live in the intestinal tract, where they fight harmful bacteria, aid the digestion of food, and produce certain nutrients. In food production, bacteria make possible the manufacture of many foods, including cheese, yogurt, and sauerkraut.

3. **Undesirable bacteria.**
   These are the bacteria that are responsible for food spoilage. They cause souring, putrefying, and decomposition. These bacteria may or may not cause disease, but they offer a built-in safety factor: They announce their presence by means of sour odors, sticky or slimy surfaces, and discoloration. As long as we use common sense and follow the rule that says "when in doubt, throw it out," we are relatively safe from these bacteria.
   We are concerned with these bacteria for two reasons:
   - Food spoilage costs money.
   - Food spoilage is a sign of improper food handling and storage. This means the next kind of bacteria is probably present.

4. **Disease-causing bacter**ia, or pathogens.
   These are the bacteria that cause most food-borne illness, the bacteria we are most concerned with.

Pathogens do not necessarily leave detectable odors or tastes in food. In other words, you can't tell if food is contaminated by smelling, tasting, or looking at it. The only way to protect food against pathogenic bacteria is to use proper hygiene and sanitary food handling and storage techniques.

Each kind of bacterial pathogen causes disease in one of three ways:

1. *Intoxications* are caused by poisons (toxins) the bacteria produce while they are growing in the food. It is these poisons, not the bacteria themselves, that cause the diseases.

2. *Infections* are caused by bacteria (or other organisms) that get into the intestinal system and attack the body. Disease is caused by the bacteria as they multiply in the body.

3. *Toxin-mediated infections* are also caused by bacteria that get into the body and grow. Disease is caused by poisons the bacteria produce as they grow and multiply. Most food-borne diseases are toxin-mediated infections.

Bacterial Growth

Bacteria multiply by splitting in half. Under ideal conditions for growth, they can double in number every 15 to 30 minutes. This means that one single bacterium could multiply to a million in less than 6 hours!

Conditions for Growth

1. **Food.**
   Bacteria require some kind of food in order to grow. They like many of the foods we do. Foods with sufficient amounts of proteins are best for bacterial growth.

These include meats, poultry, fish, dairy products, and eggs, as well as some grains and vegetables.

2. **Moisture.**
    Bacteria require water in order to absorb food. Dry foods do not support bacterial growth. Foods with a very high salt or sugar content are also relatively safe, because these ingredients make the bacteria unable to use the moisture present.

3. **Temperature.**
    Bacteria grow best at warm temperatures. *Temperatures between 41°F and 135°F (5°C and 57°C) promote the growth of disease-causing bacteria.* This temperature range is called the **Food Danger Zone.**

4. **Acidity or alkalinity.**
    In general, disease-producing bacteria like a neutral environment, neither too acidic nor too alkaline. The acidity or alkalinity of a substance is indicated by a measurement called *pH*. The scale ranges from 0 (strongly acidic) to 14 (strongly alkaline). A pH of 7 is neutral. Pure water has a pH of 7.

5. **Oxygen.**
    Some bacteria require oxygen to grow. These are called aerobic. Some bacteria are anaerobic, which means they can grow only if there is no air present, such as in metal cans. Botulism, one of the most dangerous forms of food poisoning, is caused by anaerobic bacteria. A third category of bacteria can grow either with oxygen or without it. These bacteria are called facultative. Most bacteria in food that cause disease are facultative.

6. **Time.**
    When bacteria are introduced to a new environment, they need time to adjust to their surroundings before they start growing. This time is called the lag phase. If other conditions are good, the lag phase may last about 1 hour or somewhat longer.

    If it weren't for the lag phase, there would be much more food-borne disease than there is. This time delay makes it possible to have foods at room temperature *for very short periods* in order to work on them.

Potentially Hazardous Foods

Foods that provide a good environment for the growth of disease-causing microorganisms are called **potentially hazardous foods.** Looking back at our list of conditions for growth of bacteria, we can see that protein foods with sufficient moisture and neutral pH are the most likely to host bacteria that cause disease. Of the conditions in the list, the one over which we have the most control is *temperature*.

Potentially hazardous foods fall into two general categories, plus three specific items that do not fit into these categories. All these foods, plus any foods prepared with any of them, are potentially hazardous:

1. Any food derived from animals, or any food containing animal products, including meat, poultry, fish, shellfish, eggs, and dairy products.

2. Any food derived from plants that has been cooked, partially cooked, or otherwise heat-treated. This category includes not only cooked vegetables but also such items as cooked pasta, cooked rice, and tofu (soybean curd).

3. Raw seed sprouts.

4. Sliced melons (because the edible flesh can be contaminated by organisms on the rind exterior, which has been in contact with soil).

5. Garlic and oil mixtures (because the oil seals the garlic from the air, fostering the growth of anaerobic bacteria, as explained above).

    Foods that are not potentially hazardous include dried or dehydrated foods, foods that are strongly acidic, and commercially processed foods that are still in their original unopened, sealed containers.

Locomotion

Bacteria can move from place to place in only one way: They must be carried. They can't move on their own.

Foods can become contaminated by any of the following means:

Hands	Air
Coughs and sneezes	Water
Other foods	Insects
Equipment and utensils	Rats and mice

Protection Against Bacteria

Because we know how and why bacteria grow, we should be able to keep them from growing. Because we know how bacteria get from place to place, we should know how to keep them from getting into our food.

There are three basic principles of food protection against bacteria. These principles are the reasons behind nearly all the sanitation techniques we discuss in the rest of this chapter.

1. **Keep bacteria from spreading.**
   Don't let food touch anything that may contain disease-producing bacteria, and protect food from bacteria in the air.

2. **Stop bacteria from growing.**
   Take away the conditions that encourage bacteria to grow. In the kitchen, our best weapon is temperature. *The most effective way to prevent bacterial growth is to keep foods below 41°F (5°C) or above 135°F (57°C).* These temperatures won't necessarily kill bacteria; they'll just slow down their growth greatly.

3. **Kill bacteria.**
   Most disease-causing bacteria are killed if they are subjected to a temperature of 170°F (77°C) for 30 seconds or higher temperatures for shorter times. This enables us to make food safe by cooking and to sanitize dishes and equipment with heat. The term *sanitize* means to kill disease-causing bacteria.

   Certain chemicals also kill bacteria. These may be used for sanitizing equipment.

Bacterial Diseases

Table 2.1 describes some of the most common bacterial diseases. For each disease, pay particular attention to the way it is spread, the foods involved, and the means of prevention. General practices and procedures for prevention of food-borne diseases are discussed in a later section.

Viruses

Viruses are even smaller than bacteria. They consist of genetic material surrounded by a protein layer. Unlike bacteria, they can't reproduce or multiply unless they are inside a living cell, but they can be carried on almost any surface and can survive for days or even months. Viruses are inactive or dormant until they enter a living cell. Then they use that cell to make more viruses and release them into the organism. The new viruses can then enter new cells and continue to multiply.

Because viruses do not multiply in food like bacteria, food-borne viral diseases are usually caused by contamination from people, food contact surfaces, or, in the case of seafood, contaminated water.

Table 2.2 identifies the most important food-borne viral diseases.

Parasites

Parasites are organisms that can survive only by living on or inside another organism. The organism a parasite lives in and takes nourishment from is called the *host*. Parasites may pass from one host organism to another and complete a different stage of their life cycle in each organism. Human parasites are generally transmitted to them from animal hosts.

Human parasites are usually very small, and although they may be microscopic, they are larger than bacteria. They can usually be killed by proper cooking or by freezing.

The most important diseases caused by human parasites transmitted by food are found in Table 2.3.

Table 2.1
Bacterial Diseases

Bacteria Disease	Cause/Characteristics	Source of Bacteria	Foods Usually Involved	Prevention
Botulism	Caused by toxins produced by the bacterium *Clostridium botulinum*, botulism attacks the nervous system and is usually *fatal*, even if only a small amount of poisoned food is eaten. The bacteria are anaerobic (do not grow in air) and do not grow in high-acid foods. Most outbreaks are caused by improper canning techniques. The toxin (although not the bacteria) is destroyed by boiling (212°F/100°C) for 20 minutes.	soil on vegetables and other foods	home-canned, low-acid vegetables (very rare in commercially canned foods)	Use only commercially canned foods. Discard *without tasting* any bulged or damaged cans or foods with off odors.
Staphylococcal Food Poisoning (Staph)	Caused by toxins produced in foods by the bacterium *Staphylococcus aureus*, staph is probably the most common food poisoning, characterized by nausea, vomiting, stomach cramps, diarrhea, and prostration.	usually food workers	custards and desserts made with dairy products, potato salad, protein salads, ham, hollandaise sauce, and many other high-protein foods	Practice good hygiene and work habits. Do not handle foods if you have an illness or infection. Clean and sanitize all equipment. Keep foods below 41°F (5°C) or above 135°F (57°C).
Escherichia coli	This bacterium causes severe illness, either as an intoxication or an infection. Severe abdominal pain, nausea, vomiting, diarrhea, and other symptoms result from E. coli intoxication. As an infection, E. coli causes intestinal inflammation and bloody diarrhea. While the illness normally lasts from one to three days, in some cases it can lead to long-term illness.	intestinal tracts of humans and some animals, especially cattle; contaminated water	raw or undercooked red meats, unpasteurized dairy products, sometimes fish from contaminated water, prepared foods such as mashed potatoes and cream pies	Cook foods, including red meats, thoroughly; avoid cross-contamination. Practice good hygiene.
Salmonella	The food infection caused by salmonella bacteria exhibits symptoms similar to those of staph poisoning, though the disease may last longer. Most poultry carry this bacterium.	contaminated meats and poultry; fecal contamination by food workers	meats, poultry, eggs, poultry stuffings, gravies, raw foods, and shellfish from polluted waters	Practice good personal hygiene, proper food storage and handling, and insect and rodent control. Wash hands and sanitize all equipment and cutting surfaces after handling raw poultry. Use certified shellfish.
Clostridium perfringens	This is another infection characterized by nausea, cramps, stomach pain, and diarrhea. The bacteria are hard to destroy because they are not always killed by cooking.	soil, fresh meats, human carriers	meats and poultry, reheated or unrefrigerated gravies and sauces	Keep foods hot (above 135°F/57°C) or cold (below 41°F/5°C).
Streptococcal (Strep) Infections	The symptoms of this disease are fever and sore throat.	coughs, sneezes, infected food workers	any food contaminated by coughs, sneezes, or infected food workers, then	Do not handle food if you are infected. Protect displayed food (salad bars,

Bacteria Disease	Cause/Characteristics	Source of Bacteria	Foods Usually Involved	Prevention
Streptococcal (Strep) Infections (*continued*)			served without further cooking	pastry carts, etc.) from customers' sneezes and coughs.
Shigellosis	Caused by various species of *Shigella* bacteria. The symptoms of this disease are diarrhea, abdominal pain, fever, nausea, vomiting, cramps, chills, and dehydration. The illness can last 4 to 7 days or longer if not treated.	human intestinal tract, flies, and water contaminated by feces	salads and other raw or cold cooked foods, dairy products, poultry	Good personal hygiene. Good sanitary food handling practices. Control flies, Use foods from sanitary sources.
Listeriosis	Caused by *Listeria monocytogenes* bacteria. This disease has many symptoms, including nausea, vomiting, diarrhea, headache, fever, chills, backache, and inflammation of the tissues around the brain and spinal cord. It can cause spontaneous abortion in pregnant women. The disease may not appear for days or even several months after the contaminated food is eaten, and it can last indefinitely if not treated properly. May be fatal in people with poor immune systems.	soil, water, and damp environments; carried in intestinal tracts of humans and animals, particularly poultry	unpasteurized dairy products; raw vegetables and meats; seafood; ready-to-eat foods that have been contaminated and then not cooked further	Use good food handling practices to avoid cross-contamination; use pasteurized dairy products; keep facilities clean and dry.
Bacillus cereus Gastroenteritis	Caused by *Bacillus cereus*. Symptoms include nausea, vomiting, diarrhea, and stomach cramps or pain. This disease usually lasts less than a day.	soil and dust, grains, and cereals	grains and starches, including pastries and foods with starch thickeners; meats, milk, vegetables, and fish	Temperature control: cook foods to proper internal temperatures; chill foods quickly and properly.
Camphylobacteriosis	Caused by *Camphylobacter jejuni*. This disease usually lasts 2 to 5 days, or up to 10 days, and causes diarrhea, fever, nausea, vomiting, abdominal pain, muscle pain, and headache.	meat and dairy animals and poultry	unpasteurized dairy products; raw poultry; contaminated water	Cook foods to proper internal temperatures; use pasteurized dairy products; safe food handling practices to avoid cross-contamination; avoid using contaminated water.
Vibrio Gastroenteritis and Septicemia	Caused by two species of *Vibrio* bacteria. Symptoms include diarrhea, nausea, vomiting, stomach cramps, and headache. Severe cases of the disease can involve chills, fever, sores on skin, decreased blood pressure, and septicemia (blood poisoning). The illness lasts from 1 to 8 days and can be fatal in people with poor immune systems.	shellfish, especially from the Gulf of Mexico	raw or undercooked shellfish	Avoid eating raw or undercooked shellfish; avoid cross-contamination.
Yersiniosis	Caused by the bacteria *Yersinia enterocolitica*. The disease lasts from a few days to several weeks and is characterized by fever and severe abdominal pain and sometimes headache, sore throat, vomiting, and diarrhea.	domestic pigs, soil, contaminated water, rodents	meats, especially pork; fish, oysters, unpasteurized milk, tofu, untreated water	Cook meats, especially pork, to proper internal temperatures; avoid cross-contamination; proper sanitation procedures and food handling; avoid contaminated water.

Table 2.2
Viruses

Virus	Cause/Characteristics	Source of Contamination	Foods Usually Involved	Prevention
Hepatitis A	This is a severe disease that can last for many months.	contaminated water or ice, shellfish from polluted waters, raw fruits and vegetables, milk and milk products, infected food workers	shellfish eaten raw, any food contaminated by an infected person	Practice good health and hygiene. Use only certified shellfish from safe waters.
Norwalk Virus Gastro-enteritis	This disease affects the digestive tract, causing nausea, vomiting, stomach cramps, diarrhea, and fever.	human intestinal tract, contaminated water	water, shellfish from polluted waters, raw vegetables and fruits	Practice good health and hygiene. Use only certified shellfish from safe waters. Use sanitary, chlorinated water. Cook foods to safe internal temperatures.
Rotovirus Gastro-enteritis	The symptoms of this disease are vomiting and diarrhea, abdominal pain, and mild fever. Around the world, rotovirus infections are the leading cause of digestive disease in infants and children. The illness lasts from 4 to 8 days.	human intestinal tract and contaminated water	water and ice, raw and cold prepared foods, such as salads	Practice good health and hygiene. Use sanitary, chlorinated water. Cook foods to safe internal temperatures.

Fungi

Molds and yeasts are examples of fungi. These organisms are associated primarily with food spoilage rather than food-borne disease. Most molds and yeasts, even those that cause spoilage, are not dangerous to most human beings. Some, in fact, are beneficial, and are responsible for the veining in blue cheese and the fermentation of bread dough, for example.

Some molds, however, produce toxins that can cause allergic reactions and severe disease in those people who are susceptible. For example, certain molds produce a toxin called *aflatoxin* in such foods as peanuts and other nuts, corn, cottonseed, and milk. This toxin can cause serious liver disease in some people.

Other Biological Hazards

In addition to the biological hazards associated with bacteria and other organisms, discussed in the preceding section, some hazards occur naturally in foods and are not the result of contamination. These hazards include plant toxins, seafood toxins, and allergens.

Plant Toxins

Put simply, some plants are naturally poisonous to human beings. The only way to avoid plant toxins is to avoid the plants in which they occur, as well as products made with those plants. In some cases, the toxins can be transferred in milk from cows that have eaten the plant (such as jimsonweed and snakeroot) or in honey from bees that have gathered nectar from the plants (such as mountain laurel).

The best-known plant toxins are those found in certain wild mushrooms. There are many kinds of poisonous mushrooms, and eating them causes symptoms that range from mild intestinal discomfort to painful death. Some mushroom toxins attack the nervous system, some attack and destroy the digestive system, and some attack other internal organs.

Other toxic plants to avoid are rhubarb leaves, water hemlock, apricot kernels, and nightshade.

Table 2.3
Parasites

Parasite	Cause/Characteristics	Source of Contamination	Foods Usually Involved	Prevention
Trichinosis	This disease is often mistaken for the flu at first, but it can last for a year or more. It is caused by a tiny worm that becomes embedded in the muscles of pigs.	infected pork from hogs that ate unprocessed garbage. Modern farming practices have eliminated most, but not all, of this problem.	pork products	Trichinosis organisms are killed if held at a temperature of 137°F (58°C) for 10 seconds. To be safe, cook all pork products to an internal temperature of at least 150°F (65°C). Some authorities recommend a higher temperature (165°F/74°C). Canadian pork is considered to be free of trichinosis and does not need to be cooked to these temperatures.
Anisakiasis	Like trichinosis, this disease is caused by a tiny roundworm. Symptoms are tingling sensation in the throat, vomiting up worms, abdominal pain, nausea.	ocean fish, especially bottom-feeding fish	raw or undercooked fish, such as cod, haddock, fluke, herring, flounder, monkfish, and salmon	Cook fish properly. Fish to be eaten raw should be frozen at −4°F (−20°C) or lower for 7 days or 31°F (−1°C) or lower for 15 hours in a blast freezer.
Giardiasis	This disease is caused by a protozoan (a type of single-celled organism) that gets into the intestinal tract. Symptoms include fatigue, nausea, intestinal gas, cramps, feeling of weakness, and weight loss. Symptoms usually last 1 to 2 weeks, but the human host may be infectious for months.	domestic pets; wild animals, especially bears and beavers; human intestinal tracts	water and ice; salads and other raw vegetables	Use sanitary water supplies; practice good personal hygiene; wash raw produce well.
Toxoplasmosis	Like giardiasis, this disease is caused by a protozoan. A human host sometimes shows no symptoms, but the disease can cause enlarged lymph nodes, severe muscle pain and headaches, and skin rash. Pregnant women and people with poor immune systems are most severely affected.	animal feces, mammals, birds	raw or undercooked contaminated meat	Good personal hygiene; cook meats to proper internal temperatures.
Cyclosporiasis	Another disease caused by a protozoan. Symptoms include diarrhea, weight loss, appetite loss, intestinal gas, cramps, nausea, vomiting, muscle aches, and fatigue. May last a few days to more than a month and may recur every month or two.	contaminated water, human intestinal tract	water, ocean fish, raw vegetables and fruits, and unpasteurized milk	Good personal hygiene. Use safe water supplies. Wash produce properly.
Intestinal Cryptosporidiosis	Caused by a protozoan. This disease may last 4 days to 3 weeks. The host may have no symptoms or may have severe diarrhea. Can be long-lasting and very severe, even fatal, in people with poor immune systems.	intestinal tracts of humans and livestock; water contaminated by runoff from farms or slaughterhouses	water, raw vegetables and fruits, and milk	Good personal hygiene; wash produce properly; use safe water supplies.

Seafood Toxins

Some toxins occur in fish or shellfish that have eaten a kind of algae that contains the toxins. Because these toxins are not destroyed by cooking, the only method of protection against them is to purchase fish and shellfish from approved suppliers who can certify that the seafood comes from safe water.

Some fish naturally contain toxins. The best-known fish toxin is the one present in pufferfish, known in Japanese as fugu. Raw fugu is considered a delicacy in Japan, but it must be prepared only by certified chefs who have been trained to remove the glands that produce the toxin without breaking them so they don't contaminate the flesh of the fish. This toxin attacks the nervous system and can be fatal.

Some other species of fish, such as moray eels, contain natural toxins and should be avoided.

Allergens

An allergen is a substance that causes an allergic reaction. Allergens affect only some people, and these people are said to be *allergic* to that specific substance. Not all allergens are biological hazards, but the most important ones are, so we discuss them together in this section.

Allergic reactions to food may occur as soon as the food is eaten or, in some cases, merely touched, or they may not occur until hours after the food is eaten. Common symptoms of allergic reaction to foods include itching, rash or hives, shortness of breath, tightness in the throat, and swelling of the eyes and face. In severe cases, allergic reactions may lead to unconsciousness or death.

Foods to which some people are allergic include wheat products, soy products, peanuts and other nuts, eggs, milk and dairy products, fish, and shellfish. Nonbiological allergens include food additives such as nitrites, used in cured meats, and monosodium glutamate (MSG), often used in Asian foods.

Because these products are common and are perfectly safe for most people, it is difficult to avoid serving them. For the sake of people who are sensitive to these foods, food service personnel, especially all dining room staff, must be well informed of the ingredients in all menu items and be able to inform customers as needed. If any staff member does not know, when asked by a customer, if a food might contain an allergen, that employee should tell the customer so and then find someone who does know or else urge the customer to order a different item.

CHEMICAL AND PHYSICAL HAZARDS

Some kinds of chemical poisoning are caused by the use of defective or improper equipment or equipment that has been handled improperly. The following toxins (except lead) create symptoms that show themselves very quickly, usually within 30 minutes of eating poisoned food. By contrast, symptoms of lead poisoning can take years to appear. To prevent these diseases, do not use the materials that cause them.

1. **Antimony.**
   Caused by storing or cooking acid foods in chipped gray enamelware.

2. **Cadmium.**
   Caused by cadmium-plated ice cube trays or containers.

3. **Cyanide.**
   Caused by silver polish containing cyanide.

4. **Lead.**
   Caused by lead water pipes, solder containing lead, or utensils containing lead.

5. **Copper.**
   Caused by unclean or corroded copper utensils, acid foods cooked in unlined copper utensils, or carbonated beverages in contact with copper tubing.

6. **Zinc.**
   Caused by cooking foods in zinc-plated (galvanized) utensils.

Other chemical contamination can result from exposure of foods to chemicals used in commercial food service establishments. Examples include cleaning compounds, polishing compounds, and insecticides. Prevent contamination by keeping these items physically separated from foods. Do not use them around food. Label all containers properly. Rinse cleaned equipment thoroughly.

Physical contamination is contamination of food with objects that may not be toxic but may cause injury or discomfort. Examples include pieces of glass from a broken container, metal shavings from an improperly opened can, stones from poorly sorted dried beans, soil from poorly washed vegetables, insects or insect parts, and hair. Proper food handling is necessary to avoid physical contamination.

PERSONAL HYGIENE

Earlier in this chapter, we said that most food-borne disease is caused by bacteria. Now we change that statement slightly to say that *most food-borne disease is caused by bacteria spread by food workers*.

At the beginning of this chapter, we defined *contamination* as harmful substances not present originally in the food. Some contamination occurs before we receive the food, which means that proper purchasing and receiving procedures are important parts of a sanitation program. But most food contamination occurs as a result of **cross-contamination**, which may be defined as the transferring of hazardous substances, mainly microorganisms, to a food from another food or another surface, such as equipment, worktables, or hands. Some examples of situations in which cross-contamination can occur include the following:

- Mixing contaminated leftovers with a freshly cooked batch of food.
- Handling ready-to-eat foods with unclean hands. Handling several types of foods without washing hands in between.
- Cutting raw chicken, then using the same cutting board, unsanitized, to cut vegetables.
- Placing ready-to-eat foods on a lower refrigerator shelf and allowing juices from raw fish or meat to drip onto them from an upper shelf.
- Wiping down work surfaces with a soiled cloth.

For the food worker, the first step in preventing food-borne disease is good personal hygiene. Even when we are healthy, we have bacteria all over our skin and in our nose and mouth. Some of these bacteria, if given the chance to grow in food, will make people ill.

1. Do not work with food if you have any communicable disease or infection.
2. Bathe or shower daily.
3. Wear clean uniforms and aprons.
4. Keep hair neat and clean. Always wear a hat or hairnet.
5. Keep mustaches and beards trimmed and clean. Better yet, be clean-shaven.
6. Wash hands and exposed parts of arms before work and as often as necessary during work, including:
   - After eating, drinking, or smoking.
   - After using the toilet.
   - After touching or handling anything that may be contaminated with bacteria.
7. Cover coughs and sneezes, then wash hands.
8. Keep your hands away from your face, eyes, hair, and arms.
9. Keep fingernails clean and short. Do not wear nail polish.
10. Do not smoke or chew gum while on duty.
11. Cover cuts or sores with clean bandages.
12. Do not sit on worktables.

Procedure for Washing Hands

1. Wet your hands with hot running water. Use water as hot as you can comfortably stand, but at least 100°F (38°C).
2. Apply enough soap to make a good lather.
3. Rub hands together thoroughly for 20 seconds or longer, washing not only the hands but the wrists and the lower part of the forearms.
4. Using a nail brush, clean beneath the fingernails and between the fingers.
5. Rinse hands well under hot running water. If possible, use a clean paper towel to turn off the water to avoid contaminating the hands by contact with soiled faucets.
6. Dry hands with clean single-use paper towels or a warm-air hand dryer.

USE OF GLOVES

If used correctly, gloves can help protect foods against cross-contamination. If used incorrectly, however, they can spread contamination just as easily as bare hands. Health departments in some localities require the use of some kind of barrier between hands and any foods that are ready to eat—that is, foods that will be served without further cooking. Gloves, tongs, and other serving implements, and bakery or deli tissue can serve as barriers. To be sure gloves are used correctly, observe the following guidelines.

Guidelines for Using Disposable Gloves

1. Wash hands before putting on gloves or when changing to another pair. Gloves are not a substitute for proper handwashing.
2. Remove and discard gloves, wash hands, and change to a clean pair of gloves after handling one food item and before starting work on another. In particular, never to fail to change gloves after handling raw meat, poultry, or seafood. Gloves are for single use only. Remember that the purpose of using gloves is to avoid cross-contamination.
3. Change to a clean pair of gloves whenever gloves become torn, soiled, or contaminated by contact with an unsanitary surface.

FOOD STORAGE

The following rules of safe food storage have two purposes:

1. To prevent contamination of foods
2. To prevent growth of bacteria that may already be in foods

Temperature control is an important part of food storage. Perishable foods must be kept out of the Food Danger Zone—41°F to 135°F (5°C to 57°C)—as much as possible, because these temperatures support bacterial growth. See Figure 2.1 for a chart of important temperatures.

THE FOUR-HOUR RULE

Food is handled in many stages between the time it is received and the time it is finally served. This progression, called the flow of food, is discussed further in a later section. During each stage, food might be allowed to remain in the Food Danger Zone for a time. To protect food and keep it safe, follow the four-hour rule: Do not let food remain in the Food Danger Zone for a cumulative total of more than 4 hours between receiving and serving.

For example, imagine a food that is left on the loading dock for 30 minutes before being put into cold storage, removed from storage and left on the worktable for an hour before being prepared, and finally cooked at a low temperature so that it takes 3 hours to reach a safe internal temperature (see p. 29). This food has spent a total of 4½ hours in the danger zone and should be considered unsafe.

RECEIVING

1. Safe food handling begins the moment food is unloaded from the delivery truck. In fact, it begins even earlier than this, with the selection of good, reputable suppliers. Keep the receiving area clean and well lit.

2. Inspect all deliveries. Try to schedule deliveries during non-peak hours to allow proper time to inspect the items. For the same reason, try to schedule deliveries so they arrive one at a time.

3. Reject shipments or parts of shipments that are damaged or not at the proper temperature. Frozen foods should show no signs of having been thawed and refrozen.

4. Label all items with the delivery date or a use-by date.

5. Transfer items immediately to proper storage.

DRY FOOD STORAGE

Dry food storage pertains to those foods not likely to support bacterial growth in their normal state. These foods include

> Flour
>
> Sugar and salt
>
> Cereals, rice, and other grains
>
> Dried beans and peas
>
> Ready-prepared cereals
>
> Breads and crackers
>
> Oils and shortenings
>
> Canned and bottled foods (unopened)

1. Store dry foods in a cool, dry place, off the floor, away from the wall, and not under a sewer line.

2. Keep all containers tightly closed to protect from insects, rodents, and dust. Dry foods can be contaminated, even if they don't need refrigeration.

FREEZER STORAGE

1. Keep frozen foods at 0°F (−18°C) or lower.

2. Keep all frozen foods tightly wrapped or packaged to prevent freezer burn.

3. Label and date all items.

4. Thaw frozen foods properly. Do not thaw at room temperature, because the surface temperature will go above 41°F (5°C) before the inside is thawed, resulting in bacterial growth. These methods may be used:
   - In refrigerator
   - Under cold running water
   - In a microwave oven, if the item is to be cooked or served immediately

REFRIGERATOR STORAGE

1. Keep all perishable foods properly refrigerated. Note that the lower limit of the Food Danger Zone (41°F/5°C) is only the upper limit for refrigerator storage. Most foods keep even better at lower temperatures. The major exception is fresh fruits and vegetables, which are not considered potentially hazardous foods. See Table 2.4 for preferred storage temperatures for various foods.

2. Do not crowd refrigerators. Leave space between items so cold air can circulate.

3. Keep refrigerator doors shut except when removing or putting in foods.

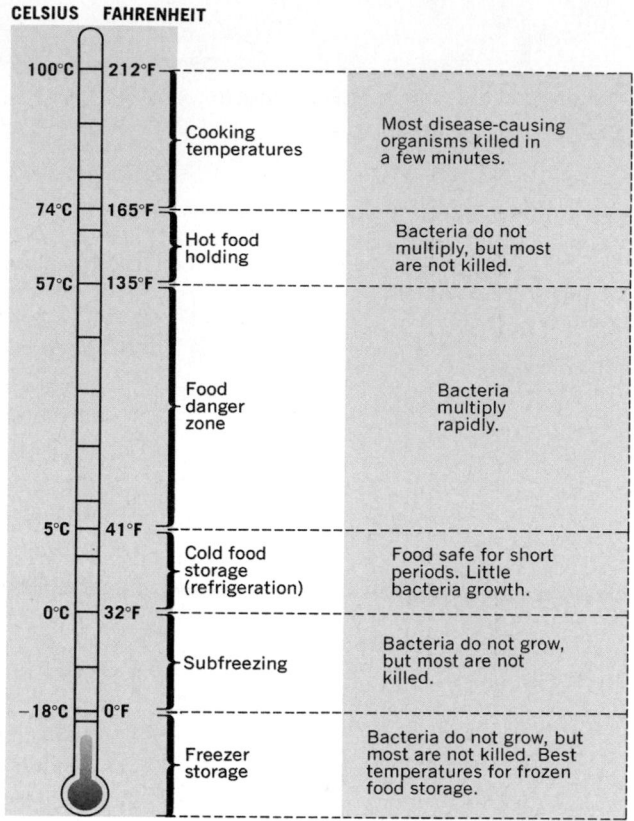

Figure 2.1
Important temperatures in sanitation and food protection.

Table 2.4
Food Storage Temperatures

Raw vegetables and fruits (see note)	40°–45°F	4°–7°C
Eggs	38°–40°F	3°–4°C
Milk and cream	36°–40°F	2°–4°C
Poultry and meat	32°–36°F	0°–2°C
Fish and seafood	30°–34°F	-1°–1°C

Note: Potatoes, onions, and winter squash are best held at cool temperatures (50°–65°F or 10°–18°C).

4. Keep shelves and interiors of refrigerators clean.
5. Store raw and cooked items separately if possible.
6. If raw and cooked foods must be kept in the same refrigerator, keep cooked foods above raw foods. If cooked foods are kept below raw foods, they can become contaminated by drips and spills. Then, if they are not to be cooked again before serving, they may be hazardous.
7. Keep refrigerated foods wrapped or covered and in sanitary containers.
8. Do not let any unsanitary surface, such as the bottoms of other containers, touch any food.
9. Chill foods as quickly as possible over ice or in a cold-water bath before placing in the refrigerator. A gallon of stock placed in a refrigerator hot off the stove may take 10 hours to go below 41°F (5°C), giving bacteria plenty of time to grow.
10. When holding foods such as protein salads in a cold bain-marie or refrigerated table for service, do not heap the food above the level of the container. The food above this level will not stay cold enough.

HOT FOOD HOLDING

1. To keep foods hot for service, use steam tables or other equipment that will keep all parts of all foods above 135°F (57°C) at all times.
2. Keep foods covered.
3. Bring foods to holding temperature as quickly as possible by using ovens, steamers, range-top pots and pans, or other cooking equipment. Do not warm cold foods by placing them directly in the steam table. They will take too long to heat, and bacteria will have time to grow.
4. Do not let ready-to-eat foods come in contact with any contaminated surface.

FOOD HANDLING AND PREPARATION

We face two major sanitation problems when handling and preparing food. The first is *cross-contamination*, which is defined on page 25.

The second problem is that, while we are working on it, food is usually at a temperature between 41°F and 135°F (5°C to 57°C), or in the Food Danger Zone. The lag phase of bacteria growth (p. 18) helps us a little but, to be safe, we must keep foods out of the danger zone whenever possible.

1. Start with clean, wholesome foods from reputable purveyors. Whenever applicable, buy government-inspected meats, poultry, fish, dairy, and egg products.
2. Handle foods as little as possible. Use tongs, spatulas, or other utensils instead of hands when practical.
3. Use clean, sanitized equipment and worktables.
4. Clean and sanitize cutting surfaces and equipment after handling raw poultry, meat, fish, or eggs and before working on another food.
5. Clean as you go. Don't wait until the end of the workday.
6. Wash raw fruits and vegetables thoroughly.
7. When bringing foods out of refrigeration, do not bring out more than you can process in 1 hour.

8. Keep foods covered unless in immediate use.

9. Limit the time that foods spend in the Food Danger Zone. Observe the four-hour rule (p. 26).

10. Cook foods to Minimum Safe Internal Temperatures (see next section).

11. Taste foods properly. With a ladle or other serving implement, transfer a small amount of the food to a small dish. Then taste this sample using a clean spoon. After tasting, do not use either the dish or the spoon again. Send them to the warewashing station or, if using disposables, discard them.

12. Boil leftover gravies, sauces, soups, and vegetables before serving.

13. Don't mix leftovers with freshly prepared foods.

14. Chill all ingredients for protein salads and potato salads *before* combining.

15. Cool and chill foods quickly and correctly, as explained in the following section. Chill custards, cream fillings, and other hazardous foods as quickly as possible by pouring them into shallow, sanitized pans, covering them, and refrigerating. Do not stack the pans.

MINIMUM SAFE INTERNAL TEMPERATURES

Minimum Safe Internal Temperature is the internal temperature for a given food product at which microorganisms are killed. The product must be held at that temperature for a specified amount of time for the food to be considered safe. See Table 2.5.

Be sure to measure internal temperatures in at least two or three places, always inserting the thermometer into the thickest part of the food. Use sanitary thermometers that are accurate to within 2°F or 1°C.

Table 2.5
Minimum Safe Internal Temperatures

Product	Temperature and Time
Fish; seafood; veal; lamb; mutton; pork; pork roasts and cured pork (e.g., ham); raw shell eggs for immediate service (Exceptions: any fish and meat mentioned below)	145°F (63°C) for 15 seconds
Ground beef, ratites (e.g., ostrich, emu); injected meats; ground fish or ground meat (e.g., pork, beef); raw eggs not prepared for immediate service; inspected game animals	155°F (68°C) for 15 seconds
Poultry; wild game; stuffed fish; stuffed meat; stuffed pasta; stuffed poultry; stuffed ratites (ostrich, emu); stuffing containing fish, meat, poultry, or ratites; any dish containing previously cooked foods	165°F (74°C) for 15 seconds
All raw animal foods cooked in a microwave	165°F (74°C). Rotate or stir the food midway through cooking process, cover to retain moisture, and let stand covered for two minutes following cooking to allow post-cooking heat to rise.
Whole beef roasts, pork roasts, and ham	Any of the following combinations of time and temperature: 130°F (54°C) for 112 minutes 131°F (56°C) for 89 minutes 133°F (57°C) for 56 minutes 135°F (57°C) for 36 minutes 136°F (58°C) for 28 minutes 138°F (59°C) for 18 minutes 140°F (60°C) for 12 minutes 142°F (61°C) for 8 minutes 144°F (62°C) for 5 minutes 145°F (63°C) for 4 minutes

COOLING PROCEDURES

If cooked foods are not to be served immediately or kept hot for service, they must be cooled quickly so they do not spend too much time in the Food Danger Zone. The rate at which foods cool depends on their total volume in relation to how much surface area they have to transfer heat away. In other words, a large batch of food cools more slowly because it has less surface area per unit of volume. One of the hazards of cooking foods in large volumes is cooling them so slowly that they spend too much time in the Food Danger Zone.

To help gauge the time you may safely take to cool large volumes of food, use either the two-stage cooling method or the one-stage cooling method.

For the two-stage cooling method, cool foods from 135°F (57°C) to 70°F (21°C) in no more than 2 hours, and then from 70°F (21°C) to below 41°F (5°C) within an additional 4 hours, for a total cooling time of no more than 6 hours. The temperature range between 70°F (21°C) and 125°F (52°C) is the most dangerous part of the Food Danger Zone. This method ensures that the food spends a minimum time in that temperature range. If food has not cooled to 70°F (21°C) within 2 hours, it must be reheated to 165°F (74°C) and held at that temperature for at least 15 seconds and then cooled again.

For the one-stage cooling method, cool foods to below 41°F (5°C) in no more than 4 hours. If the food does not reach this temperature in 4 hours, it must be reheated to 165°F (74°C) and held at that temperature for at least 15 seconds and then cooled again.

Guidelines for Cooling Foods

1. Never put hot foods directly into the cooler. Not only will they cool too slowly but also they will raise the temperature of other foods in the cooler.

2. If they are available, use quick-chill units or blast chillers to cool foods quickly before transferring them to cold storage.

3. Use ice-water baths to bring down temperatures of hot foods quickly.

4. Stir foods as they are cooling to redistribute the heat and help them cool more quickly.

5. Divide large batches into smaller batches. This increases the amount of surface area for the volume of food and helps it cool more quickly. Pouring foods into flat, shallow pans also increases surface area and cooling speed.

CLEANING AND SANITIZING EQUIPMENT

Cleaning means removing visible soil. *Sanitizing* means killing disease-causing bacteria. Two ways of killing bacteria are by *heat* and by *chemicals*.

MANUAL DISHWASHING

Figure 2.2 shows the setup of a three-compartment sink for washing dishes, glassware, and eating utensils by hand.

Procedure for Manual Dishwashing

1. Scrape and rinse.

   The purpose of this step is to keep the wash water cleaner longer.

2. Wash.

   Use warm water at 110°F to 120°F (43°C to 49°C) and a good detergent. Scrub well with a brush to remove all traces of soil and grease.

3. Rinse.

   Use clean, warm water to rinse off detergent. Change the water frequently, or use running water with an overflow, as in Figure 2.2.

4. Sanitize.

   Place utensils in a rack and immerse in hot water at 171°F (77°C) for 30 seconds. (A gas or electric heating element is needed to hold water at this temperature.)

5. Drain and air dry.

   Do not towel dry. This may recontaminate utensils. Do not touch food contact surfaces of sanitized dishes, glasses, and silverware.

Figure 2.2
Setup of three-compartment sink for manual dishwashing.

MECHANICAL DISHWASHING

The steps in washing dishes by machine are the same as in the hand method, except that the machine does the washing, rinsing, and sanitizing.

WASHING KITCHEN UTENSILS AND EQUIPMENT

1. Use the same three-compartment sink setup and procedure as for manual dishwashing.
2. Do not use scouring powder or steel wool. These may make scratches where bacteria can hide. Also, pieces of steel wool break off and can remain in the pan and thus get into food.
3. Utensils with baked-on foods should be scraped and rinsed, soaked in the first compartment to loosen the baked-on food, and then scraped and rinsed again.
4. Kitchen equipment may be sanitized with *chemical disinfectants* instead of heat. Use an approved disinfectant, and follow the instructions on the label.

Procedure for Mechanical Dishwashing

1. Scrape and rinse.
2. Rack dishes so the dishwasher spray will strike all surfaces.
3. Run the dishwasher for a full cycle.
4. Sanitizing temperatures:
   180°F (82°C) for machines that sanitize by heat
   120°F (49°C) for machines that sanitize by chemical disinfectant
5. Air dry and inspect dishes. Do not touch food contact surfaces.

CLEANING AND SANITIZING STATIONARY EQUIPMENT AND WORK SURFACES

1. Unplug electric equipment before cleaning. You could seriously injure yourself if you accidentally hit the power switch while you are cleaning a piece of equipment.
2. Disassemble equipment when possible. (This obviously doesn't apply to such equipment as worktables.) All immersible parts should be cleaned and sanitized like kitchen utensils.
3. Wash all food contact surfaces, using a detergent solution and clean cloths.
4. Sanitize all surfaces with a double-strength sanitizing solution and with clean cloths used only for this purpose.
5. Allow to air dry.
6. Reassemble equipment.

RODENT AND INSECT CONTROL

Rats, mice, flies, and cockroaches can spread disease by contaminating food and food contact surfaces. Any sign of rodent or insect infestation is usually considered a serious violation of health codes.

There are four basic methods of pest control. We start with the most important and most effective.

BUILD THEM OUT

1. Block all possible rodent entrances, including structural defects in the building.
2. Put screens on all windows and doors.
3. Make sure all doors are self-closing, or install fly fans or air curtains.
4. Inspect incoming supplies for signs of insect infestation.

ELIMINATE HARBORAGE AND BREEDING PLACES

1. Repair holes and all other structural defects in walls and floors.
2. Eliminate narrow spaces between and behind equipment, counters, and other fixtures, and hollow spaces made by false bottoms in counters, cabinets, and so on.
3. Store food and supplies off the floor.
4. Seal all cracks and crevices. Repair loose tiles, wall coverings, and so on.
5. Remove all fly-breeding places inside and out: garbage, manure, and general filth.

ELIMINATE FOOD SUPPLIES

1. Keep all foods tightly covered or wrapped.
2. Keep garbage containers tightly covered, and use metal (rat-proof) garbage cans.
3. Clean up all spilled food.
4. General sanitation: Keep floors, walls, and equipment clean.

EXTERMINATE

Hire a qualified, licensed exterminator who knows how to use poisons, insecticides, and traps. Most poisons should not be used in a food production operation, so it's better not to do the job yourself.

Extermination is a temporary solution only. For permanent freedom from rodents and insects, you must rely on the other methods of control.

SETTING UP A SYSTEM FOR FOOD SAFETY

Once you have learned the information in the first part of this chapter, you must apply it in the kitchen.

Many food service operations have designed food safety systems that enable food workers to keep a close check on food items whenever there is a risk of contamination or of the growth of pathogens. In the most effective systems, nothing is left to chance. At each stage of food production and storage, workers refer to written guidelines that explain what to look for and what action to take if the standards are not met. Having written guidelines helps everyone avoid costly mistakes.

THE HACCP SYSTEM

One effective food safety system is called the *Hazard Analysis Critical Control Point* system, or **HACCP**. Versions of this system have been widely adopted throughout the food service industry.

The following discussion is a brief introduction to the basic concepts of HACCP. For a more detailed explanation, you may refer to other published material listed in the Bibliography (pp. 1031–1032). The discussion below is based on information presented in those books.

The Steps of the HACCP System

The purpose of HACCP is to identify, monitor, and control dangers of food contamination. It is a system of seven steps:

1. Assess hazards.
2. Identify critical control points (CCPs).
3. Set up standards or limits for critical control points.
4. Set up procedures for monitoring critical control points.
5. Establish corrective actions.
6. Set up a recordkeeping system.
7. Verify that the system is working.

These steps are the basis of the following discussion.

The Flow of Food

HACCP begins with a concept called the **flow of food**. This term refers to the movement of food through a food service operation, from receiving through the various stages of storage, preparation, and service, until it gets to the final consumer.

The flow of food is different for each item being prepared. Some menu items involve many steps. For example, a luncheon dish of creamed chicken and vegetables over rice might have the following steps:

Receiving raw ingredients (chicken, vegetables, cream, rice, etc.)

Storing raw ingredients

Preparing ingredients (washing, cutting, trimming, etc.)

Cooking

Holding and serving

Cooling and storing leftovers

Reheating, holding, and storing leftovers

Even the simplest items undergo several steps. For example, a cake that is bought already prepared from a commercial baker and served as dessert will go through at least the following steps on its way to the customer:

Receiving   Storing   Serving

Hazards and Critical Control Points

At each of these steps, as foods flow through the operation, risks can lead to dangerous conditions, which are called *hazards*. These hazards can be divided into three categories:

1. *Contamination*, such as cross-contamination from a soiled cutting surface, torn packaging that permits insect infestation, working on food without washing hands, spilling cleaning chemicals on food.

2. *Growth of bacteria and other pathogens* due to such conditions as inadequate refrigeration or storage, and holding hot foods below 135°F (57°C).

3. *Survival of pathogens or the continued presence of toxins*, usually because of inadequate cooking or heating or inadequate sanitizing of equipment and surfaces.

Note that these hazards correspond to the sanitation techniques discussed on page19 (keep bacteria from spreading, stop bacteria from growing, kill bacteria). The important difference is that the hazards addressed by HACCP include chemical and other hazards in addition to disease-causing organisms. Naturally, however, most of the hazards we are concerned with are those that affect *potentially hazardous foods* (see page 18).

At each step where there is a risk of one of these hazards, it is possible to take action that eliminates the hazard or reduces it to a minimum. These steps are called **critical control points**, or CCPs. In simple language, setting up an HACCP system starts with reviewing the flow of food to figure out where something might go wrong, then deciding what can be done about it. In the language of HACCP, these steps are called *assessing the hazards* and *identifying critical control points*.

Setting Standards and Following Procedures

The next step in designing an HACCP food safety system is setting up procedures for critical control points. At each critical control point, food workers need to know what standards must be met, what procedures to follow to meet the standards, and what to do if they aren't met. To reduce the chances for making mistakes, these standards and procedures are written out. Whenever possible, they should be included in the operation's recipes. In Chapter 5, you will see how CCPs are incorporated into a standardized recipe.

Some procedures are general and include the sanitation rules discussed earlier in this chapter. For example: Wash hands before handling food and after handling raw foods; hold foods above 135°F (57°C) or below 41°F (5°C). Others apply to specific items. For example: Cook a beef roast to an internal temperature of at least 145°F (63°C) and ensure that it stays at that temperature for at least 3 minutes. The Minimum Safe Internal Temperatures discussed on page 29 are an important part of the standards of a HACCP system.

Careful observation is needed to know when standards are met. This often involves measuring. The only way to know, for example, that a roast has reached the required internal temperature is to measure it, using a clean, sanitized thermometer.

Managers must ensure that all employees are trained to follow procedures and have the equipment needed to do the job.

Once these procedures are developed, additional steps in setting up an HACCP system are important to ensure that the system is effective: monitoring critical control points, taking corrective action if procedures are not followed, keeping records of all aspects of the system, and verifying that the system is working.

As this brief introduction to HACCP implies, establishing such a system to control all aspects of food production requires more information than this chapter has space for. Refer to the Bibliography for more detailed information.

LEARNING MORE ABOUT FOOD SAFETY

It is important for you to understand that food safety and sanitation is a large and complex topic. The first half of this chapter is only an introduction to the study of food safety. To advance in a food service career, you will be required to demonstrate a detailed knowledge of the subject well beyond what can be presented in such a short space. Entire textbooks are devoted to kitchen sanitation and safety. Many organizations, including local and regional health departments and organizations such as the National Restaurant Association (in the United States), sponsor training programs leading to certificates of competency in food safety. Food service employees in supervisory positions in the United States may be required to hold such a certificate by state or local law. In Canada, many provinces have their own safety regulations, and food service operators should be familiar with these as well as with federal regulations. The health and safety of your clientele depend on your diligent study.

SAFETY

Kitchen work is usually considered a relatively safe occupation, at least in comparison with many industrial jobs. Nevertheless, the kitchen has many hazards. Minor injuries from cuts and burns are common, and more serious injuries are all too possible. The quantity of hot equipment and powerful machinery, combined with the busy, sometimes frantic pace, make it important for everyone to work carefully and with constant attention to the rules of safety.

In the United States, the Occupational Safety and Health Administration (OSHA) established sets of rules governing workplace safety. Employers are required to follow these rules and guidelines. In Canada, information on comparable legislation, both national and provincial, is provided by the Canadian Centre for Occupational Health and Safety (CCOHS).

THE SAFE WORKPLACE

Most of this section is concerned with ways workers can prevent certain kinds of accidents, such as cuts, burns, and falls. However, it is much easier to develop and practice habits that prevent accidents if safety is built into the workplace.

The management of a food service operation must see to it that the structure and equipment have necessary safety features.

1. Structure, equipment, and electric wiring in good repair
2. Adequate lighting on work surfaces and in corridors
3. Nonslip floors
4. Clearly marked exits
5. Equipment supplied with necessary safety devices
6. Heat-activated fire extinguishers over cooking equipment, especially deep fryers
7. Conveniently located emergency equipment, such as fire extinguishers, fire blankets, and first-aid kits
8. Clearly posted emergency telephone numbers
9. Clearly posted emergency procedures, including the Heimlich maneuver for victims of choking. One or more employees should have received formal training in this procedure. In addition, it is a good idea to train one or more employees in cardiopulmonary resuscitation (CPR).
10. Smooth traffic patterns to avoid collisions between workers

PREVENTING CUTS

1. Keep knives sharp. A sharp knife is safer than a dull one because it requires less pressure and is less likely to slip.
2. Use a cutting board. Do not cut against a metal surface. Place a damp towel under the board to keep it from slipping.
3. Pay attention to your work when using a knife or cutting equipment.
4. Cut away from yourself and other workers.
5. Use knives only for cutting, not for such jobs as opening bottles.
6. Don't try to catch a falling knife. Step back and let it fall.
7. Don't put knives in a sink, under water, or any other place where they can't be seen.

8. Clean knives carefully, with the sharp edge away from you.

9. Store knives in a safe place, such as a rack, when not in use.

10. Carry knives properly. Hold the knife beside you, point down, with the sharp edge back and away from you. Don't swing your arm. Whenever possible, carry knives in a sheath. Warn people when you are walking past them with a knife in hand.

11. Keep breakable items, such as dishes and glassware, out of the food production area.

12. Don't put breakable items in the pot sink.

13. Sweep up—don't pick up—broken glass.

14. Discard chipped or cracked dishes and glasses.

15. Use special containers for broken dishes and glasses. Don't throw them in with other garbage.

16. If there is broken glass in the sink, drain the sink before trying to take out the glass.

17. Remove all nails and staples when opening crates and cartons, and dispose of them.

PREVENTING BURNS

1. Always assume a pot handle is hot. Don't just grab it with your bare hand.

2. Use dry pads or towels to handle hot pans. Wet ones will create steam, which can burn you.

3. Keep pan handles out of the aisle so people won't bump into them. Also, keep handles away from the open flames of gas burners.

4. Don't fill pans so full that they are likely to spill hot foods.

5. Get help when moving heavy containers of hot food.

6. Open lids away from you to let steam escape safely.

7. Use care when opening compartment steamers.

8. Make sure gas is well vented before trying to light ovens or pilot lights. Strike matches before turning on the gas. Also, strike matches away from your body.

9. Wear long sleeves and a double-breasted jacket to protect yourself from spilled or spattered hot foods or fat. Also, wear sturdy leather shoes with closed toes.

10. Dry foods before putting them in frying fat, or hot fat may splatter on you.

11. When placing foods in hot fat, let them fall away from you so fat will not splash on you.

12. Keep liquids away from the deep fryer. If a liquid were spilled into the fryer, the sudden rush of steam could spray hot fat on anyone nearby.

13. Always warn people when you are walking behind them with hot pans or when you are walking behind someone who is working with hot items.

14. Warn service people about hot plates.

PREVENTING FIRES

1. Know where fire extinguishers are located and how to use them.

2. Use the right kind of fire extinguisher. There are three classes of fires, and fire extinguishers should be labeled according to the kind of fire for which they can be used.

- **Class A** fires: wood, paper, cloth, ordinary combustibles
- **Class B** fires: burning liquids, such as grease, oil, gasoline, solvents
- **Class C** fires: switches, motors, electrical equipment, and so forth

Never use water or a Class A fire extinguisher on a grease fire or electrical fire. You will only spread the fire.

3. Keep a supply of salt or baking soda handy to put out fires on rangetops.

4. Keep hoods and other equipment free from grease buildup.

5. Don't leave hot fat unattended on the range.

6. Smoke only in designated areas. Do not leave burning cigarettes unattended.

7. If a fire alarm sounds and if you have time, turn off all gas and electric appliances before leaving the building.

8. Keep fire doors closed.

9. Keep exits free from obstacles.

10. Establish and post a plan for emergency evacuation, clearly identifying routes and exits. The plan should include procedures for evacuating customers and other non-employees.

PREVENTING INJURIES FROM MACHINES AND EQUIPMENT

1. Do not use any equipment unless you understand its operation.

2. Use all guards and safety devices on equipment. Set slicing machines at zero (blade closed) when not in use.

3. Don't touch or remove food from any kind of equipment while it is running, not even with a spoon or spatula.

4. Unplug electric equipment before disassembling or cleaning.

5. Make sure the switch is off before plugging in equipment.

6. Do not touch or handle electric equipment, including switches, if your hands are wet or if you are standing in water.

7. Wear properly fitting clothing and tuck in apron strings to avoid getting them caught in machinery.

8. Use equipment only for the purpose intended.

9. Stack pots and other equipment properly on pot racks so they are stable and not likely to fall.

PREVENTING FALLS

1. Clean up spills immediately.

2. Throw salt on a slippery spot to make it less slippery while a mop is being fetched.

3. Keep aisles and stairs clear and unobstructed.

4. Don't carry objects too big to see over.

5. Walk, don't run.

6. Use a safe ladder, not chairs or piles of boxes, to reach high shelves or to clean high equipment.

PREVENTING STRAINS AND INJURIES FROM LIFTING

1. Lift with the leg muscles, not the back. Figure 2.3 shows proper lifting technique.
2. Don't turn or twist your back while lifting, and make sure your footing is secure.
3. Use a cart to move heavy objects long distances, or get help.

Figure 2.3
Proper lifting technique.

(a) Squat on one knee, then lift with the leg muscles.

(b) Do not bend over and lift with the back.

■ TERMS FOR REVIEW

sanitation	aerobic	salmonella	Minimum Safe Internal
contaminated	anaerobic	*E. coli*	Temperature
hazard	facultative	parasite	two-stage cooling method
microorganism	lag phase	trichinosis	one-stage cooling method
pathogen	potentially hazardous food	allergen	HACCP
bacteria	sanitize	physical contamination	flow of food
intoxication	botulism	cross-contamination	critical control point
infection	staph	four-hour rule	Class A, B, and C fires
Food Danger Zone			

■ QUESTIONS FOR DISCUSSION

1. True or false: Holding food in a steam table above 135°F (57°C) kills disease-causing bacteria and eliminates the problem of food poisoning. Explain your answer.

2. True or false: Canning foods eliminates air so disease-causing bacteria can't grow. Explain your answer.

3. Which of the following foods can become contaminated by disease-causing organisms?

Chocolate éclairs	Dinner rolls
Potato salad	Shrimp cocktail
Roast beef	After-dinner mints
Lettuce	Saltine crackers
Turkey sandwich	Rice pudding

4. How often should you wash your hands when working on food?

5. Why is temperature control one of the most effective weapons against bacterial growth? What are some important temperatures to remember?

6. What is the importance of cleaning and sanitizing equipment and cutting boards immediately after working on raw poultry?

7. You are making egg salad, and you have just cooked the eggs. What step do you take before chopping the eggs and mixing them with the other ingredients? Why?

8. Is it possible for a dish to be clean but not sanitized? Sanitized but not clean?

9. Explain the concepts of *hazards* and *critical control points*. Give at least three examples of each.

10. What are the three general categories of potentially hazardous foods? Give examples of each category. Give examples of foods that are not potentially hazardous.

11. True or false: The lower limit of the Food Danger Zone is the proper refrigeration temperature for perishable foods. Discuss.

12. What are the seven steps of HACCP?

CHAPTER 3
Tools and Equipment

Thorough knowledge of equipment is essential for success in the kitchen. Few food service operations depend on nothing more than a range and an oven, an assortment of pots and pans, and knives and other hand tools. Modern technology continues to develop more and more specialized and technically advanced tools to reduce kitchen labor.

Much of this equipment is so complex or so sophisticated that only firsthand instruction and practice will teach you how to operate it effectively and safely. Other items, especially hand tools, are simple and need no explanation but require much practice to develop good manual skills.

A vast array of specialized equipment is available for today's kitchens. It would take a large book, not just a short chapter, to describe all of the many items you will come in contact with in your career—items such as pasta machines, crêpe machines, burger formers, breading machines, cookie droppers, beverage machines, Greek gyro broilers, doughnut glazers, conveyor fryers, and so on. In this technological age, nearly every year brings new tools to simplify various tasks.

This chapter introduces you to the most commonly used equipment in food service kitchens. It cannot, in this short space, serve as an operating manual for every model of every machine you will use. It cannot take the place of demonstration by your instructor and of actual experience.

After reading this chapter, you should be able to identify the do's and don'ts associated with the safe and efficient use of standard kitchen equipment; processing equipment; holding and storage equipment; measuring devices; and knives, hand tools, and small equipment.

INTRODUCTION TO QUANTITY FOOD EQUIPMENT

Before we look at specific items, we must first consider points relating to the use of equipment in general.

FOOD EQUIPMENT CAN BE DANGEROUS

Modern cooking and food processing equipment has an extraordinary capacity to burn, cut, smash, mangle, and amputate parts of the tender human body. This may sound like a harsh way to begin a chapter, but the intent is not to intimidate you or scare you but to inspire a healthy respect for the importance of proper safety and operating procedures.

Never use a piece of equipment until you are thoroughly familiar with its operation and all its features. You must also learn how to know when a machine is not operating correctly. When this happens, shut it down immediately and report the malfunction to a supervisor.

NOT ALL MODELS ARE ALIKE

Each manufacturer introduces slight variations on the basic equipment. While all convection ovens operate on the same basic principle, each model is slightly different, if only in the location of the switches. It is important to study the operating manual supplied with each item or to be taught by someone who already knows that item well and has operated it.

CLEANING IS PART OF THE OPERATING PROCEDURE

Thorough, regular cleaning of all equipment is essential. Most large equipment can be partially disassembled for cleaning. Again, every model is slightly different. Operating manuals should describe these procedures in detail. If a manual is not available, you must get the information from someone who knows the equipment.

When purchasing equipment, look for models that have been tested and certified by recognized agencies that certify products and write standards for food, water, air, and consumer goods. Three prominent agencies are NSF International (www.nsf.org; formerly the National Sanitation Foundation) and CSA International (www.csa-international.org; formerly Canadian Standards Association), and Underwriter Laboratory (www.ul.com). These three agencies are recognized internationally. Products meeting their testing requirements are labeled or marked accordingly. (Figure 3.1). Criteria govern such factors as design and construction (for example, sealed joints and seams), materials used (for example, nontoxic materials, smooth and easily cleanable surfaces), and performance testing.

Figure 3.1
NSF International certification mark.
Courtesy NSF International.

The CSA International logo.
Courtesy of the Canadian Standard Association.

The Underwriters Laboratory logo.
Reproduced with permission of Underwriters Laboratory, Inc.

CONSERVE ENERGY

At one time, it was standard procedure for the chef to turn on the ovens and ranges first thing in the morning and keep them on all day. Today, high energy costs have made such practices expensive. Fortunately, modern equipment takes less time to heat.

Know the preheating time for all your cooking equipment so you don't need to turn it on before necessary. Plan production so that equipment that requires a lot of energy is not on for long periods when not in use.

YOUR HANDS ARE YOUR BEST TOOLS

Machines are intended to be labor-saving devices. However, the usefulness of specialized processing equipment often depends on the volume of food it handles. It takes less time for a cook to slice a few pounds of onions by hand than to set up a slicing attachment, pass the onions through it, and break down and clean the equipment. This is why it is important to develop good manual skills.

COOKING EQUIPMENT

RANGETOPS

The range is still the most important piece of cooking equipment in the kitchen, even though many of its functions have been taken over by other tools such as steamers, steam kettles, tilting skillets, and ovens.

Types of Cooktops

1. **Open elements** (burners), either electric coils or gas flames. These tops are the fastest to heat and can be turned off after short use. However, cooktop space is limited to one pot per burner.
2. **Flattop** or **hot top** (lightweight). Burners covered with steel plate. More cook space is available. Top supports moderately heavy weights.
3. **Heavy-duty flattop.** Burners covered with heavy cast steel. The top supports many heavy pots. A thick top requires longer preheating. Set burners for different levels, and adjust cooking heat by moving pots to different spots on the top.
4. **Induction cooktops.** A fairly new type of rangetop, the induction cooktop is slowly making its way into commercial kitchens. The top itself does not become hot. Rather, it works by magnetically agitating the molecules in steel or iron cookware so the cookware becomes hot. As a result, much less energy is used and the kitchen stays cooler, because only the pots and pans and their contents become hot. There are no hot surfaces or open flames. Also, no warm-up is required. The top can be turned instantly on or off. Small, easily portable induction burners are available. These are useful for off-premise catering operations, for buffet service, and even for tableside heating and cooking. The disadvantage of this cooktop is that only iron or steel pots can be used. Traditional aluminum or copper cookware will not work. Some manufacturers of cookware have responded to the new demand by producing pots and pans made of aluminum sandwiched between layers of stainless steel. In this way, the good heat-conducting qualities of aluminum are preserved as well as adapted to this new technology.

Open-burner gas range with griddle
Courtesy of Vulcan Hart Company.

Do's and Don'ts

1. Make sure gas pilots are lit before turning on burners. If burners do not light, turn off gas and allow the gas to ventilate before trying again to light pilots or burners.
2. Adjust air intake so gas flames are blue with a white tip for maximum heat.

Flat-top range
Courtesy of Vulcan Hart Company.

3. Do not keep flat-top ranges on high heat unless items are being cooked over them. Damage to tops could result.

OVENS

The oven and the rangetop are the two workhorses of the traditional kitchen, which is why they are so often found in the same unit. Ovens are enclosed spaces in which food is heated, usually by hot air or, in some newer kinds of ovens, by microwaves or infrared radiation.

In addition to roasting and baking, ovens can do many of the jobs normally done on the rangetop. Many foods can be simmered, stewed, braised, or poached in the oven, freeing the rangetop and the chef's attention for other tasks.

There are many kinds of ovens beyond those discussed here, but they are often for specialty or high-volume uses. These include **conveyor ovens**, which carry foods through the oven on a steel conveyor belt; **holding ovens** or warmers, which are designed to hold many types of foods at serving temperatures for extended periods without drying out or overcooking (this category includes ovens that also cook the food, then automatically switch to holding temperature); and high-volume **roll-in ovens**, with large doors into which one can roll carts loaded with trays of food.

Conventional Ovens

Conventional ovens operate simply by heating air in an enclosed space. The most common ovens are part of the range unit, although separate oven units or ovens as part of a broiler unit are also available. **Stack ovens** are units that consist of individual shelves or decks arranged one above the other. Pans are placed directly on the oven deck rather than on wire shelves. Temperatures are adjustable for each deck.

Stack or deck ovens
Copyright Blodgett Corporation.

Do's and Don'ts

Many of these points apply to other types of ovens as well.

1. Preheat ovens thoroughly, but no longer than necessary, to avoid excess energy use.
2. To avoid high energy loss and interruption of cooking, do not open the door more often than necessary.
3. Space items well to allow for heat circulation.
4. Be sure the pilot light is on before turning on gas ovens.

Convection Ovens

Convection ovens contain fans that circulate the air and distribute the heat rapidly throughout the interior. Because of the forced air, foods cook more quickly at lower temperatures. Also, shelves can be placed closer together than in conventional ovens without blocking the heat flow.

Convection oven
Courtesy of Vulcan Hart Company.

Do's and Don'ts

1. For most products, set the temperature 25°F to 50°F (15°C to 30°C) lower than you would a conventional oven. Check manufacturer's recommendations.
2. Watch cooking times closely. The forced heat cooks foods more quickly and tends to dry out some foods excessively if they are overcooked. Roasts shrink more than they do in conventional ovens.
3. Many convection oven models should not be operated with the blower switch off, as the motor may burn out.
4. The forced air of a convection oven may deform soft items. Cake batters, for example, develop ripples. Check manufacturer's recommendations.

Revolving Ovens

Revolving ovens, also called **reel ovens**, are large chambers containing many shelves or trays on an attachment like a Ferris wheel. This oven eliminates the problem of hot

spots or uneven baking because the mechanism rotates the foods throughout the oven.
Revolving ovens are used in bakeshops and in high-volume operations.

Slow-Cook-and-Hold Ovens

The traditional oven is nothing more than a heated box equipped with a thermostat. Some modern ovens have more sophisticated features, such as computerized electronic controls and special probes that sense when a roast is done and tell the oven to switch from cooking temperature to holding temperature.

Many of these ovens are designed to be especially useful for low-temperature roasting (see p. 288). The sensitive controls make it possible to cook at steady, reliable temperatures of 200°F (95°C) or lower and to hold foods at 140°F (60°C) for long periods. Large cuts of meat take many hours to roast at a low temperature like 200°F (95°C). By setting the controls in advance, the operator can even let meats roast overnight, unattended.

These ovens are available as convection ovens and as regular stationary-air ovens.

Combination Steamer Ovens

The **combination steamer oven**, also called a *combi oven*, is a relatively new kind that can be operated in three modes: as a convection oven, as a convection steamer (see p. 49), and, with both functions on at once, as a high-humidity oven. Injecting moisture into an oven while roasting meats can help to reduce shrinkage and drying.

Combination steamer oven
Courtesy of Vulcan Hart Company.

Barbecue Ovens or Smoke Ovens

Barbecue ovens are like conventional ovens, but with one important difference: They produce wood smoke, which surrounds the food and adds flavor while it bakes or roasts. Special woods such as hickory, mesquite, or fruit woods such as apple or cherry must be added to the smoke-producing part of the oven according to the manufacturer's instructions. This device is usually nothing more complicated than an electric heating element that heats small blocks or chips of the wood so they are hot enough to smoke but not hot enough to burst into flame.

Depending on the model, various cooking features are available. Thus, ovens may have smokeless roast/bake cycles, cold-smoke cycles (with the smoke element on but the oven off), holding cycles, and broiling capabilities.

A barbecue oven that uses wood smoke should not be confused with a smoker, used for making hot-smoked and cold-smoked foods, as discussed in Chapter 26. The interior of a smoker is shown on page 837.

Infrared or Reconstituting Ovens

Infrared units contain quartz tubes or plates that generate intense infrared heat. These ovens are used primarily for reconstituting frozen foods. They bring large quantities of foods to serving temperature in a short time. The heat is even and controllable.

Wood-burning Ovens

Ancient ovens were made of heavy masonry, brick, or clay and heated by building a wood fire inside them. In this type of oven, the brick absorbs the intense heat of the fire and cooks foods long after the fire has gone out and the ashes removed. Items such as breads and pizzas are baked directly on the floor of the oven, just as in modern deck ovens. Wood-burning ovens have once again come into fairly wide use, mostly in specialty restaurants that feature roasted meats, pizzas, and similar items. The foods absorb some of the appealing wood-smoke flavors and aromas.

Because a traditional wood-burning oven lacks a temperature control knob, some experience is needed to produce consistent quality baked foods. During the firing of the oven, a wood fire is built directly on the hearth inside the oven. The flue and the door are kept open to allow the smoke to escape. After the fire is stopped, the ashes and embers are swept out. The door and flue are closed to allow the heat to equalize inside the dome of the oven. Initial temperatures inside the oven at this point may be as high as 850°F (450°C). Pizza can be baked at this temperature. For meats and breads, the oven is left to stand until the temperature gradually drops to the desired range. Alternatively, a fire can be kept going in the back of the oven while foods are roasted to-

Microwave oven
Courtesy of Vulcan Hart Company.

ward the front, with the flue kept open.

Combination ovens, also available, are more controllable. These can be fired by gas alone, by wood alone, or by gas and wood together.

Microwave Ovens

In these ovens, special tubes generate microwave radiation, which creates heat inside the food. Microwave cooking is discussed in detail in Chapter 4.

BROILERS AND SALAMANDERS

Broilers are sometimes called **overhead broilers** to avoid confusing them with grills. Overhead broilers generate heat from above, and food items are placed on a grate beneath the heat source. Broiling is a favorite way of preparing steaks, chops, chicken, and many other items.

Heavy-duty broilers produce very high heat and consume vast quantities of energy. Some broilers are said to go as high as 2,000°F (1,100°C) at the burner.

Foods must be watched closely to avoid burning. Cooking temperature is adjusted by raising or lowering the grate that holds the food.

Heavy-duty broiler
Courtesy of Vulcan Hart Company.

Salamander (above range)
Courtesy of Vulcan Hart Company.

Salamanders are small broilers used primarily for browning or glazing the tops of some items. They may also be used for broiling small quantities during off-peak hours. Salamanders are usually mounted above the range, as illustrated in the photo. In addition, the photo of an open-burner gas range on page 43 shows a salamander under the griddle.

GRILLS

Gas grill
Courtesy of Vulcan Hart Company.

Grills are used for the same cooking operations as broilers, except the heat source is below the grid that holds the food rather than above it. Many people like grilled foods because of their charcoal taste, which is created by smoke from meat fats that drip into the heat source.

Although smoke from meat fats creates the taste people associate with grilled foods, actual wood-smoke flavors such as hickory or mesquite can be added to foods if those woods are burned in the grill under the food. In order to do this, you must use a grill designed to burn such fuels.

Types

Many grill models are in use. The major differences in operation among them are due to the difference in heat source—gas, electricity, or charcoal.

To operate, set areas of the grill to different temperatures and place foods in the areas with the appropriate cooking temperature. Keep grills clean, as the high temperatures can easily start grease fires.

GRIDDLES

Griddles are flat, smooth, heated surfaces on which food is cooked directly. Pancakes, French toast, hamburgers and other meats, eggs, and potato items are the foods most frequently cooked on a griddle. Griddles are available as separate units or as part of a rangetop.

Clean griddle surfaces after every use so they will cook at peak efficiency. Polish with a griddle stone or griddle cloth until the surface shines. Follow the grain of the metal to avoid scratching.

Condition griddles after each cleaning or before each use to create a nonstick surface and to prevent rusting. Procedure: Spread a thin film of oil over the surface and heat to 400°F (200°C). Wipe clean and repeat until griddle has a smooth, nonstick finish.

ROTISSERIES

Rotisserie broilers cook meats and other foods by turning them slowly in front of electric- or gas-powered heating elements. Even though classical cooking theory categorizes spit-cooking as roasting, these cookers are more closely related to broilers in that the foods are cooked by the infrared heat of the elements.

Although they are especially suitable for chicken and other poultry, rotisseries can be used to cook any meat or other food that can be held on a spit or in any of various attachments or accessories.

Both enclosed (ovenlike) rotisseries and open or unclosed units are available. Small units hold about 8 chickens, and sizes range all the way to very large models that can hold as many as 70 chickens.

Because the heating elements are on the side (or sometimes above), the fats and juices don't drip into the flames as they do with grills. Drip pans catch juices, which can be used for basting or gravy making.

DEEP FRYERS

A deep fryer has only one use: to cook foods in hot fat. Yet because of the popularity of fried foods, this function is an important one.

Standard deep fryers are powered by either gas or electricity and have thermostatic controls that maintain fat at preset temperatures.

Automatic fryers remove food from the fat automatically after a preset time.

Pressure fryers are covered fry kettles that fry foods under pressure. Foods cook faster, even at a lower fat temperature.

Do's and Don'ts

Frying procedures and the care of frying fat are discussed in detail in Chapter 4. The following points relate to the operation of the equipment.

1. When filling kettles with solid fats, set the thermostat at 250°F (120°C) until the fat has melted enough to cover the heating elements.
2. Keep kettles filled to the fill line.
3. Make sure the drain valve is shut before adding fat to the empty kettle.
4. Check the accuracy of the thermostat regularly by reading the fat temperature with a thermometer.

Deep fryers
Courtesy of Vulcan Hart Company.

Cleaning

Cleaning procedures differ greatly depending on the model. Here is a general procedure.

1. Shut off the power.
2. Drain the fat through a filter into a dry container (unless you are discarding it). Be sure the container is large enough to hold all the fat before you start.
3. Flush food particles from sides and bottom of the kettle with some of the hot fat.
4. Wash the kettle with a mild detergent solution. If the kettle is not removable, turn on the fryer and bring the detergent solution almost to a boil (beware of foaming over). Scrub with a stiff brush.
5. Drain and rinse thoroughly with clean water.
6. Dry the kettle, heating elements, and baskets thoroughly.
7. Refill with strained or fresh fat.

TILTING SKILLET

The tilting skillet, also known as the **tilting brazier** and **tilting fry pan**, is a versatile and efficient piece of equipment. It can be used as a griddle, fry pan, brazier, stewpot, stockpot, steamer, and bain-marie or steam table.

The tilting skillet is a large, shallow, flat-bottomed pot. To look at it another way, it is a griddle with 6-inch-high sides and a cover. It has a tilting mechanism that enables liquids to be poured out of it. Power may be gas or electric.

Clean the skillet immediately after each use, before food has time to dry on. Add water, turn on the skillet to heat it, and scrub thoroughly.

STEAM-JACKETED KETTLES

Steam-jacketed kettles, or **steam kettles**, are sometimes thought of as stockpots that are heated not just on the bottom but on the sides as well. This comparison is only partly accurate. Steam kettles heat much more quickly and have more uniform and controllable heat than pots on the range.

Types

Steam kettles range in capacity from 2 gallons to over 100 gallons. Some large institutional kettles hold 4,000 gallons. **Tilt** or **trunnion kettles** can be tilted for emptying, either by turning a wheel or by pulling a lever. **Nontilt kettles** are emptied by a spigot and drain on the bottom. Heat is controlled by regulating the steam flow or by adjusting

Tilting skillet
Courtesy of Vulcan Hart Company.

Small tile (trunnion) kettle
Courtesy of Vulcan Hart Company.

Large floor-model steam kettle
Courtesy of Vulcan Hart Company.

the thermostat. Steam may be from an outside source or self-generated. *Exercise caution when operating all steam equipment. Steam can cause serious burns.*

Clean immediately after use to avoid food drying on surfaces. Disassemble the spigot and drain, and clean with a bottle brush.

STEAM COOKERS

Steam cookers are ideal for cooking vegetables and many other foods rapidly and with minimum loss of nutrients and flavor. For this reason, they are becoming more common in both large and small kitchens.

Types

Pressure steamers cook foods under a pressure of 15 pounds per square inch (high-pressure steamers) or 4 to 6 pounds per square inch (low-pressure steamers). They are operated by a timer, which shuts the equipment off after a preset time. The door cannot be opened until the pressure returns to zero.

Pressureless or **convection steamers** do not operate under pressure. Jets of steam are directed at the food to speed the heat transfer, just as the fan in a convection oven speeds cooking. The door can be opened any time during cooking.

All steamers hold standard-size counter pans (12 x 20 inches or 325 x 530 mm) or fractions thereof. Their capacity varies from one to many pans.

Steamer operation varies greatly, depending on the model. Check operating manuals and be sure you understand a particular model well before attempting to operate it.

Caution is important with all steam equipment because of the danger of severe burns.

Pressure steamer
Courtesy of Vulcan Hart Company.

Convection steamer
Courtesy of Vulcan Hart Company.

PROCESSING EQUIPMENT

MIXERS

Vertical mixers are important and versatile tools for many kinds of food mixing and processing jobs, both in the bakeshop and in the kitchen.

Types

Bench-model mixers range in capacity from 5 to 20 quarts (5 to 20 L). Floor models are available as large as 140 quarts (133 L). Adaptor rings enable several bowl sizes to be used on one machine. Most mixers have three operating speeds.

Agitator Attachments

There are three main mixing attachments, plus some specialized ones. The **paddle** is a flat blade used for general mixing. The **wire whip** is used for such tasks as beating cream and eggs and making mayonnaise. The **dough arm** is used for mixing and kneading yeast doughs.

Small table-model mixer
Courtesy of Hobart Corporation.

Mixer attachments: (left) whip, (center) paddle, (right) dough arm
Courtesy of Hobart Corporation.

Do's and Don'ts

1. Make sure the bowl and the mixing attachment are firmly in place before turning on the machine.
2. Make sure you are using the right size attachment for the bowl. Using a 40-quart paddle with a 30-quart bowl, for example, could cause serious damage. Sizes in quarts are marked on the sides of large bowls and on the tops of attachments.
3. Turn off the machine before scraping down the bowl or inserting a spoon, scraper, or hand into the bowl. Mixer motors are powerful and can cause serious injury.
4. Turn off the machine before changing speeds.

Large floor-model mixer
Courtesy of Hobart Corporation.

FOOD CUTTER

The food cutter or food chopper, familiarly known as the **buffalo chopper**, is a common piece of equipment used for general food chopping. A variety of attachments (described in the next section) makes it a versatile tool.

General Operation

Food is placed in a rotating bowl, which carries the food to a pair of knives that are spinning rapidly under a cover. The fineness of the cut depends on how long the food is left in the machine.

Food chopper
Courtesy of Hobart Corporation.

Do's and Don'ts

1. Always make sure the machine is completely assembled before use.
2. Close the cover lock knob, or the machine will not turn on.
3. Never reach under the bowl cover while the machine is running.
4. For uniform chopping, place the food in the bowl all at one time.
5. Keep the knives sharp. Dull knives will bruise food rather than cut it cleanly.

ATTACHMENTS FOR MIXERS AND FOOD CHOPPERS

The following are the most common of the many attachments designed to fit both the food chopper and the vertical mixer.

1. The **food grinder** is used mostly for grinding meats, although other moist foods may be ground also. Food is forced through a feed tube into a screw, which pushes the food through holes in a plate, where it is cut by a rotating blade. The size of the holes regulates the fineness of the grind.

    Make sure the rotating blade is attached properly, cutting edge out, when assembling the grinder.

2. The **slicer/shredder** consists of a hopper and a lever that feeds the food onto a rotating disk or plate. The plate cuts or shreds the food and drops it into a receiving container. The slicing plate may be adjusted to cut various thicknesses.

3. The **dicer** attachment forces foods through a grid-type blade that cuts them into perfect dice. Blades of different sizes may be used.

Grinder attachment (on separate motor)
Courtesy of Hobart Corporation.

SLICER

The slicer is a valuable machine because it slices foods more evenly and uniformly than can be done by hand. Thus it is valuable for portion control and for reducing cutting loss.

Types

Most modern slicers have blades set at an angle. Slices fall away from these blades with less breaking and folding than from vertical blades.

    With manual machines, the operator must move the carriage back and forth to slice the food. Automatic machines move the carriage with an electric motor.

Slicer/shredder attachment
Courtesy of Hobart Corporation.

Do's and Don'ts

1. Be sure the machine is properly assembled before using.
2. Always use the end weight to press the food against the blade. This protects the hand from serious cuts and provides a more even pressure on the food, resulting in more uniform slices.
3. Set the thickness control knob at zero when the machine is not in use or is being cleaned.
4. Always unplug the machine before dismantling and cleaning.
5. Keep the blade sharp with the sharpening stones provided with the slicer.

VERTICAL CUTTER/MIXER

The vertical cutter/mixer (VCM) is like a large, powerful, high-speed blender. It is used to chop and mix large quantities of foods rapidly. It can also be used for puréeing (soups, for example) and for mixing liquids.

Slicer
Courtesy of Hobart Corporation.

Food processor
Courtesy of Hobart Corporation.

Types

VCMs range in size from 15 to 80 quarts (liters). The small models have a hand-operated mixing baffle, which moves the foods into the blades. Larger machines have automatic baffles.

Do's and Don'ts

1. Watch processing times closely. Chopping times are so short that an extra second can make cabbage soup out of coleslaw.
2. Make sure the machine is properly assembled before use.
3. After turning the machine off, allow the blades to come to a full stop before opening the cover.
4. Keep the blades sharp. Dull blades bruise food.

FOOD PROCESSOR

Food processors were used in commercial kitchens long before home models were introduced. Professional models are two to four times larger than the largest home models. They consist of a motor in a heavy base, topped by a cylindrical workbowl containing an S-shaped blade. Processors are used to chop or purée foods, including raw or cooked meats, and to mix or emulsify such items as sauces and flavored butters. With special disk attachments in place of the standard blade, they can also slice, shred, and julienne solid foods such as vegetables.

In basic design, a food processor is similar to a vertical cutter/mixer. The same do's and don'ts should be observed.

BLENDER

Like the VCM and the food processor, a blender consists of a motor in a base, topped by a container with a spinning blade. Because the blender's container is tall and narrow, it is more suited for mixing and puréeing liquids than for chopping solid foods, however. In the commercial kitchen, the blender is used to mix, purée, and emulsify liquids such as soups, sauces, and batters. It is also used in bars and coffeehouses to prepare certain drinks.

Blender motors may have from 2 to 10 or more speeds. The containers are made of stainless steel, glass, or plastic. The blade assembly at the base of the container can be disassembled for thorough cleaning.

IMMERSION BLENDER

An immersion blender, also called a **stick blender** or **burr mixer**, consists of the blade of a blender, protected by a guard, at the bottom end of a long wand or shaft that has a motor at the top. Using an immersion blender, the cook can purée or mix hot or cold foods in any container without transferring them to a blender jar. This makes it possible to blend hot foods in their cooking pots. The largest stick blenders are long enough to be used to purée foods in large steam kettles.

HOLDING AND STORAGE EQUIPMENT

HOT FOOD HOLDING EQUIPMENT

Several types of equipment are used to keep food hot for service. This equipment is designed to hold foods above 135˚F (57˚C) in order to prevent the growth of bacteria that can cause disease. Because food continues to cook at these temperatures, it should be held for as short a time as possible.

1. **Steam tables** are standard holding equipment for serving lines. Standard-size counter pans or hotel pans are used as inserts to hold the foods. Flat or domed covers may be used to cover the foods.

    Check water levels in steam tables periodically to make sure they don't go dry. Electrically heated counters that operate dry—without steam—are also available.

2. A **bain-marie** is a hot-water bath. Containers of foods are set on a rack in a shallow container of water, which is heated by electricity, gas, or steam. The bain-marie is used more in the production area, while the steam table is used in the service area.

3. **Overhead infrared lamps** are used in service areas to keep plated food warm before it is picked up by the service staff. They are also used for keeping large roasts warm.

    Foods dry out quickly under holding lamps. This is a disadvantage for almost all foods except French fries and other deep-fried foods, which lose their crispness if they are kept moist.

Steam table
Courtesy of Hobart Corporation.

COLD FOOD STORAGE EQUIPMENT

The quality of the food you serve depends to a great degree on refrigeration equipment. By keeping foods cold, usually below 41°F (5°C), the refrigerator (known in the trade as the *cooler* or the *box*) guards against spoilage and bacterial growth.

Freezers are used to hold foods for longer times, or to store foods purchased in frozen form.

There are so many sizes, models, and designs of refrigeration equipment that it would be futile to try to describe them all here.

To enable refrigerators and freezers to work at top efficiency, observe the following rules:

1. Place items far enough apart and away from the inside walls of refrigerators so cold air can circulate. Freezers, on the other hand, work most efficiently when they are full.

2. Keep the door closed as much as possible. When storing or removing an item, do it quickly and shut the door.

3. Keep stored foods well wrapped or covered to prevent drying and transfer of odors. Meats are an exception to this rule (see p. 284).

4. Keep refrigerators spotlessly clean.

POTS, PANS, AND CONTAINERS

METALS AND CONDUCTIVITY

A good cooking utensil distributes heat evenly and uniformly. A poor cooking utensil develops hot spots that are likely to burn or scorch the food being cooked. Two factors affect a pan's ability to cook evenly:

1. *Thickness of the metal.* A heavy-gauge pot cooks more evenly than one made of thin metal. Thickness is most important on the bottom.

2. *Kind of metal.* Different metals have different conductivity, which means the speed at which they transfer or disperse heat. The following materials are used for cooking equipment:

    *   *Aluminum* is used for most cooking utensils in food service kitchens. It is a good conductor, and its light weight makes pots and pans easy to handle. Because it is a relatively soft metal, it should not be banged around or abused.

        Do not use aluminum for storage or for long cooking of strong acids because it reacts chemically with many foods. Also, it tends to discolor light-colored foods such as sauces, especially if they are stirred or beaten with a metal spoon or whip.

        Pans made of *anodized aluminum*, sold under such brand names as Calphalon, have surfaces that are harder and more corrosion-resistant than regular aluminum pans. Although this is not, strictly speaking, a nonstick finish, it is less porous than untreated aluminum, so foods are less likely to stick. Also, it is more resistant to acids than regular aluminum, and it will not discolor light-colored foods. Its disadvantages are that it is more expensive than and not quite as durable as standard aluminum.

    *   *Copper,* the best heat conductor of all, was once widely used for cooking utensils. However, it is extremely expensive and requires a great deal of care. In addition, it is very heavy. Today it is used mostly for show, although a few high-end restaurants use it for cooking as well.

        Copper reacts chemically with many foods to create poisonous compounds, so copper pans must be lined with another metal, such as tin or stainless steel.

    *   *Stainless steel* is a poor heat conductor. Cooking pots and pans made of it tend to scorch foods easily because the heat does not disperse throughout the pan quickly and evenly. Stainless steel is ideal for storage containers because it does not react with foods as aluminum does. It is also used for low-temperature cooking or holding equipment, such as steamer pans and counter pans, where scorching or hot spots are not a problem.

        Stainless-steel pots and pans are available with a heavy layer of copper or aluminum bonded to the bottom. Heavy aluminum pans may also be lined with stainless steel on the inside, or on both the inside and outside. This feature gives the advantages of stainless steel (its hardness, durability, nonreactivity with acid foods, and nondiscoloration of light sauces) with the heat-conducting qualities of copper or aluminum. These pans are usually expensive.

    *   *Cast iron* is a favorite material with many chefs because of its ability to distribute heat evenly and to maintain high temperatures for long periods. It is used in griddles and heavy skillets. Cast iron cracks easily if dropped. It rusts quickly unless kept properly conditioned (see p. 795) and dry.

    *   *Porcelain enamel-lined pans* should not be used. In fact, they are forbidden by some health departments. They scratch and chip easily, providing good hiding places for bacteria. Also, certain kinds of gray enamel can cause food poisoning if chipped.

    *   *Nonstick plastic-type coatings,* known by brand names including Teflon and Silverstone, provide a slippery finish, but one that requires a lot of care because it is easily scratched. Do not use metal spoons or spatulas with this equipment. Many chefs keep a set of nonstick egg pans and use them for no other purpose.

        Because more customers are requesting low-fat foods, nonstick coatings are increasing in popularity. They enable cooks to sauté foods with little or no added fat.

    *   *Glass and earthenware* have limited use in commercial kitchens because they are very breakable. They are poor conductors of heat but are resistant to corrosion and food acids.

POTS AND PANS AND THEIR USES

1. **Stockpot.**
   A large, deep, straight-sided pot for preparing stocks and simmering large quantities of liquids. Stockpots with spigots allow liquid to be drained off without disturbing the solid contents or lifting the pot. Sizes: 8 to 200 quarts (liters).

2. **Saucepot.**
   A round pot of medium depth. Similar to a stockpot but shallower, making stirring or mixing easier. Used for soups, sauces, and other liquids. Sizes: 6 to 60 quarts (liters).

3. **Brazier.**
   A round, broad, shallow, heavy-duty pot with straight sides. Used for browning, braising, and stewing meats. Sizes: 11 to 30 quarts (liters).

Saucepan

4. **Saucepan.**
   Similar to a small, shallow, light saucepot, but with one long handle instead of two loop handles. May have straight or slanted sides. Used for general range-top cooking. Sizes: 1½ to 15 quarts (liters).

5. **Sauté pan, straight-sided.**
   Similar to a shallow, straight-sided saucepan, but heavier. Used for browning, sautéing, and frying. Because of its broad surface area, the sauté pan is used for cooking sauces and other liquids when rapid reduction is required. Sizes: 2½ to 5 inches (65 to 130 mm) deep; 6 to 16 inches (160 to 400 mm) in diameter.

6. **Sauté pan, slope-sided.**
   Also called *fry pan*. Used for general sautéing and frying of meats, fish, vegetables, and eggs. The sloping sides allow the cook to flip and toss items without using a spatula, and they make it easier to get at the food when a spatula is used. Sizes: 6 to 14 inches (160 to 360 mm) top diameter.

7. **Cast-iron skillet.**
   Very heavy, thick-bottomed fry pan. Used for pan frying when steady, even heat is desired.

   Cast-iron skillet

8. **Double boiler.**
   A pot with two sections. The lower section, similar to a stockpot, holds boiling water. The upper section holds foods that must be cooked at low temperatures and cannot be cooked over direct heat. Size of top section: 4 to 36 quarts (liters).

9. **Sheet pan or bun pan.**
   A shallow rectangular pan (1 inch/25 mm deep) for baking cakes, rolls, and cookies, and for baking or broiling certain meats and fish. Sizes: full pan, 18 x 26 inches (46 x 66 cm); half pan, 18 x 13 inches (46 x 33 cm).

Bake pan

10. **Bake pan.**
    A rectangular pan about 2 inches (50 mm) deep. Used for general baking. Available in a variety of sizes.

11. **Roasting pan.**
    A large rectangular pan, deeper and heavier than a bake pan. Used for roasting meats and poultry.

12. **Hotel pan, also called counter pan, steam table pan, or service pan.**
    A rectangular pan, usually made of stainless steel. Designed to hold foods in service counters. Also used for baking, steaming, and subsequent serving. Also used for storage. Standard size: 12 x 20 inches. Fractions of this size (½, ⅓, etc.) are also available. Standard depth: 2½ inches (65 mm). Deeper sizes are also available. (Standard metric pan is 325 x 530 mm.)

13. **Bain-marie insert, usually called simply bain-marie.**
    A tall, cylindrical stainless-steel container. Used for storage and for holding foods in a bain-marie (water bath). Sizes: 1 to 36 quarts (liters).

Stockpot   **Stockpot with spigot**

Saucepot   **Brazier**

Straight-sided sauté pan

Slope-sided sauté pan

Double boiler

Sheet pan

Roasting pan

Hotel pan

Bain-marie inserts

14. Stainless-steel bowl.
A round-bottomed bowl. Used for mixing, whipping, and producing hollandaise, mayonnaise, whipped cream, and egg white foams. Round construction enables whip to reach all areas. Available in many sizes.

MEASURING DEVICES

The following equipment is discussed in terms of U.S. measurements. Comparable items in metric units are also available.

1. **Scales.** Most recipe ingredients are measured by weight, so accurate scales are very important. **Portion scales** are used for measuring ingredients as well as for portioning products for service. The baker's **balance scale** is discussed in Chapter 29.

Portion scale

2. **Volume measures** used for liquids have lips for easy pouring. Sizes are pints, quarts, half-gallons, and gallons. Each size is marked off into fourths by ridges on the sides.

3. **Measuring cups** are available in 1-, ½-, ⅓-, and ¼-cup sizes. They can be used for both liquid and dry measures.

4. **Measuring spoons** are used for measuring very small volumes: 1 tablespoon, 1 teaspoon, ½ teaspoon, and ¼ teaspoon. They are used most often for spices and seasonings.

Liquid volume measure

5. **Ladles** are used for measuring and portioning liquids. The size, in ounces, is stamped on the handle.

6. **Scoops** come in standard sizes and have a lever for mechanical release. They are used for portioning soft solid foods. Scoop sizes are listed in Table 3.1. The number of the scoop indicates the number of level scoopfuls per quart. In actual use, a rounded scoopful is often more practical than a level scoopful, so exact weights will vary.

Ladles

Scoop

7. **Thermometers** measure temperatures. There are many kinds for many purposes.

- A **meat thermometer** indicates internal temperature of meats. It is inserted before cooking and left in the product during cooking.

- An **instant-read thermometer** gives readings within a few seconds of being inserted in a food product. It reads from 0°F to 220°F. Many chefs carry these in their jacket pocket like a pen, ready whenever needed. Instant-read thermometers must not be left in meats during roasting, or they will be damaged.

- **Fat thermometers** and **candy thermometers** test temperatures of frying fats and sugar syrups. They read up to 400°F.

- Special thermometers are used to test the accuracy of oven, refrigerator, and freezer thermostats.

Instant-read thermometers

Meat thermometer

Table 3.1
Scoop Sizes

| Scoop Number | U.S. Measure | | Metric Measure | |
	Volume	Approximate Weight	Volume	Approximate Weight
6	⅔ cup	5 oz	160 mL	140 g
8	½ cup	4 oz	120 mL	110 g
10	3 fl oz	3–3½ oz	90 mL	85–100 g
12	⅓ cup	2½–3 oz	80 mL	70–85 g
16	¼ cup	2–2½ oz	60 mL	60–70 g
20	1½ fl oz	1¾ oz	45 mL	50 g
24	1⅓ fl oz	1⅓ oz	40 mL	40 g
30	1 fl oz	1 oz	30 mL	30 g
40	0.8 fl oz	0.8 oz	24 mL	23 g
60	½ fl oz	½ oz	15 mL	15 g

Note: Weights vary greatly with different foods, depending on how compact they are. Best practice is to weigh a scoopful of an item before proceeding with portioning.

KNIVES, HAND TOOLS, AND SMALL EQUIPMENT

KNIFE MATERIALS

The metal that a knife blade is made of is an important consideration, as the metal must be able to take and hold a very fine edge.

1. **Carbon steel** was for many years the traditional favorite because it can be honed to an extremely sharp edge. Its disadvantages are that it corrodes and discolors easily, especially when used with acid foods and onions. Also, it discolors some foods (such as hard-cooked eggs) and may leave a metallic taste. Because of these disadvantages, it has given way to high-carbon stainless steel (described in item 3 below), which is now the preferred material for the best knives.

2. **Traditional stainless-steel alloys** will not rust or corrode, but they are much harder to sharpen than carbon steel. Stainless steel is used mostly for low-cost, lightweight knives.

3. **High-carbon stainless steel** is a relatively new alloy that combines the best aspects of carbon steel and stainless steel. It takes an edge almost as well as carbon steel, and it will not rust, corrode, or discolor. Knives made of this material are highly prized and relatively expensive.

KNIFE HANDLES

The **tang** is the portion of the metal blade that is inside the handle. The highest-quality, most durable knives have a **full tang**, which means that the tang runs the *full length* of the handle.

KNIVES AND THEIR USES

French knife or chef's knife

Santoku knife or Japanese cook's knife

Utility knife

Boning knife

Slicer

Butcher knife

Scimitar

Oyster knife

Clam knife

Vegetable peeler

Steel

1. **French knife or chef's knife.**
   Most frequently used knife in the kitchen, for general-purpose chopping, slicing, dicing, and so on. The blade is wide at the heel and tapers to a point. Blade length of 10 inches (260 mm) is most popular for general work. Larger knives are for heavy cutting and chopping. Smaller blades are for more delicate work.

   This is your most important tool, so you must learn to handle it and care for it well. Chapter 7 explains its use in detail.

2. **Santoku knife or Japanese cook's knife.**
   A wide-bladed knife that is becoming increasingly popular as a substitute for the traditional chef's knife. Blades are usually 5 inches (13 cm) or 7 inches (18 cm) long.

3. **Utility knife or salad knife.**
   A narrow, pointed knife 6 to 8 inches (160 to 200 mm) long. Used mostly for pantry work, cutting and preparing lettuce, fruits, and so on. Also useful for carving roast chicken and duck.

4. **Paring knife.**
   A small pointed blade 2 to 4 inches (50 to 100 mm) long. Used for trimming and paring vegetables and fruits.

   Paring knife

5. **Boning knife.**
   A thin, pointed blade about 6 inches (160 mm) long. Used for boning raw meats and poultry. Stiff blades are used for heavier work. Flexible blades are used for lighter work and for filleting fish.

6. **Slicer.**
   A long, slender, flexible blade up to 14 inches (360 mm) long. Used for carving and slicing cooked meats.

7. **Serrated slicer.**
   Like a slicer, but with a serrated edge. Used for cutting breads, cakes, and similar items.

   Serrated slicer

8. **Butcher knife.**
   A heavy, broad, slightly curved blade. Used for cutting, sectioning, and trimming raw meats in the butcher shop.

9. **Scimitar or steak knife.**
   A curved, pointed blade. Used for accurate cutting of steaks.

10. **Cleaver.**
    A very heavy, broad blade. Used for cutting through bones.

11. **Oyster knife.**
    A short, rigid, blunt knife with a dull edge. Used for opening oysters.

    Cleaver

12. **Clam knife.**
    A short, rigid, broad-bladed knife with a slight edge. Used for opening clams.

13. **Vegetable peeler.**
    A short tool with a slotted, swiveling blade. Used for peeling vegetables and fruits.

14. **Steel.**
    Not a knife, but an essential part of the knife kit. Used for truing and maintaining knife edges (not for sharpening them – see Chapter 7).

15. **Cutting board.**
    An important partner to the knife. Hardwood boards are favored by many chefs. Hard rubber or plastic boards are thought to be more sanitary, but there is some evidence that bacteria survive longer on plastic and rubber than on wood. Cutting boards must be kept very clean.

Note: In some communities, wooden boards are prohibited by health regulations.

HAND TOOLS AND SMALL EQUIPMENT

1. **Ball cutter, melon ball scoop, or parisienne knife.**
   The blade is a small, cup-shaped half-sphere. Used for cutting fruits and vegetables into small balls.

Ball cutter

2. **Cook's fork.**
   A heavy, two-pronged fork with a long handle. Used for lifting and turning meats and other items. Must be strong enough to hold heavy loads.

Cook's fork

3. **Straight spatula or palette knife.**
   A long, flexible blade with a rounded end. Used mostly for spreading icing on cakes and for mixing and bowl scraping.

Straight Spatula

4. **Sandwich spreader.**
   A short, stubby spatula. Used for spreading fillings and spreads on sandwiches.

Sandwich spreader

5. **Offset spatula.**
   A broad blade, bent to keep the hand off hot surfaces. Used for turning and lifting eggs, pancakes, and meats on griddles, grills, sheet pans, and so on. Also used as a scraper to clean benches and griddles.

Offset spatula

6. **Rubber spatula or scraper.**
   A broad, flexible rubber or plastic tip on a long handle. Used to scrape bowls and pans. Also used for folding in egg foams or whipped cream.

Rubber spatula

7. **Pie server.**
   A wedge-shaped offset spatula. Used for lifting pie wedges from pan.

Pie server

8. **Bench scraper or dough knife.**
   A broad, stiff piece of metal with a wooden handle on one edge. Used to cut pieces of dough and to scrape workbenches.

Bench scraper

9. **Pastry wheel or wheel knife.**
   A round, rotating blade on a handle. Used for cutting rolled-out doughs and pastry and baked pizza.

Pastry wheel

10. **Spoons: solid, slotted, and perforated.**
    Large stainless-steel spoons that hold about 3 ounces (90 mL). Used for stirring, mixing, and serving. Slotted and perforated spoons are used when liquid must be drained from solids.

Spoons: slotted, perforated, solid

11. **Skimmer.**
    A perforated disk, slightly cupped, on a long handle. Used for skimming froth from liquids and for removing solid pieces from soups, stocks, and other liquids.

Skimmer

12. **Tongs.**
    Spring-type or scissors-type tools used to pick up and handle foods.

Tongs

13. **Wire whip.**
    Loops of stainless-steel wire fastened to a handle. There are two kinds of whips:

    - Heavy whips are straight, stiff, and have relatively few wires. Used for general mixing, stirring, and beating, especially heavy liquids.

    - Balloon whips or piano-wire whips have many flexible wires. Used for whipping eggs, cream, and hollandaise, and for mixing thinner liquids.

Wire whip

Chinois

14. **China cap.**

    A cone-shaped strainer. Used for straining stocks, soups, sauces, and other liquids. Pointed shape allows the cook to drain liquids through a relatively small opening.

China cap

15. **Fine china cap or chinois (shee-nwah).**

    A china cap with very fine mesh. Used when great clarity or smoothness is required in a liquid.

16. **Strainer.**

    A round-bottomed, cup-shaped tool made of screen-type mesh or perforated metal. Used for straining pasta, vegetables, and so on.

Strainer

17. **Sieve.**

    A screen-type mesh supported in a round metal frame. Used for sifting flour and other dry ingredients.

Sieve

Colander

18. **Colander.**

    A large perforated bowl made of stainless steel or aluminum. Used to drain washed or cooked vegetables, salad greens, pasta, and other foods.

19. **Food mill.**

    A tool with a hand-turned blade that forces foods through a perforated disk. Interchangeable disks produce different coarseness or fineness. Used for puréeing foods.

Food mill

Box grater

20. **Grater.**

    A four-sided metal box with grids of varying sizes. Used for shredding and grating vegetables, cheese, citrus rinds, and other foods.

Zester

21. **Zester.**

    A small hand tool used for removing the colored part of citrus peels in thin strips.

22. **Channel knife.**

    A small hand tool used mostly in decorative work.

Channel knife

23. Mandoline.

A manual slicing implement consisting of blades fitted in a flat metal or wood framework. Folding legs position the mandoline on the worktable at a 45-degree angle for use. Levers allow the blades to be adjusted to control the thickness of the slices. A traditional mandoline has a flat blade and a serrated blade. Additional blades can be used in combination with the flat blade to cut julienne and batonnet. The serrated blade is used to cut gaufrette or waffle slices.

For safest use, a detachable guard is also supplied. The guard holds the food and allows it to be sliced without getting the fingers near the blades.

Mandolin

Pastry bag and tubes

24. Pastry bag and tubes.

Cone-shaped cloths or plastic bags with an open end that can be fitted with metal tubes or tips of various shapes and sizes. Used for shaping and decorating with items such as cake icing, whipped cream, duchesse potatoes, and soft dough.

25. Pastry brush.

Used to brush items with egg wash, glaze, etc.

Pastry brush

26. Can opener.

Heavy-duty can openers are mounted on the edge of the workbench. They must be carefully cleaned and sanitized every day to prevent contamination of foods. Replace worn blades, which can leave metal shavings in the food.

Can opener

CHAPTER 4

Basic Cooking Principles

No written recipe can be 100 percent accurate. No matter how carefully a recipe is written, the judgment of the cook is still the most important factor in making a preparation turn out well. A cook's judgment is based on experience, on an understanding of the raw materials available, and on knowledge of basic cooking principles.

This chapter deals with basic principles. You will learn about what happens to food when it is heated, about how food is cooked by different cooking methods, and about rules of seasoning and flavoring. It is important to understand the theories so you can successfully put them into practice in the kitchen.

HEAT AND FOOD

To cook food means to heat it in order to make certain changes in it. Skillful cooks know exactly what changes they want to make and what they have to do to get them right. To learn these cooking skills, it is important for you to know why foods behave as they do when heated. For this, you have to study the theory.

Perhaps not all the parts in this section will make sense to you at first. But they should become clearer to you after you have thought about them in relation to specific techniques, as demonstrated by your instructor. Later in your studies, when you are learning about cooking meats, fish, vegetables, and other foods, review this section from time to time. Not only will you understand it better, but it should also help you make more sense of the procedures you are learning and practicing.

After reading this chapter, you should be able to

1. **Name the most important components of foods and describe what happens to them when they are cooked.**

2. **Name and describe three ways in which heat is transferred to food in order to cook it.**

3. **List three factors that affect cooking times.**

4. **Explain the differences between moist-heat cooking methods, dry-heat cooking methods, and dry-heat cooking methods using fat.**

5. **Describe each basic cooking method used in the commercial kitchen.**

6. **Identify the five properties that determine the quality of a deep-fried product.**

7. **Explain the difference between a seasoning and a flavoring ingredient and give examples of each.**

8. **Identify appropriate times for adding seasoning ingredients to the cooking process in order to achieve optimal results.**

9. **Identify appropriate times for adding flavoring ingredients to the cooking process in order to achieve optimal results.**

10. **List eleven guidelines for using herbs and spices in cooking.**

EFFECTS OF HEAT ON FOODS

Foods are composed of proteins, fats, carbohydrates, and water, plus small amounts of other compounds such as minerals (including salt), vitamins, pigments (coloring agents), and flavor elements. It is important to understand how these components react when heated or mixed with other foods. You will then be better equipped to correct cooking faults when they occur and to anticipate the effects of changing cooking methods, cooking temperatures, or ingredient proportions.

In other words, when you know why foods behave as they do, you can understand how to get them to behave as you want them to.

The following discussion is concerned with the physical and chemical reactions that affect the components of food. The nutritional aspects of these components are discussed in Chapter 6.

CARBOHYDRATES

1. Starches and sugars are carbohydrates. Both compounds are present in foods in many forms. They are found in fruits, vegetables, grains, beans, and nuts. Meats and fish also contain a small amount of carbohydrate.

2. For the cook, the two most important changes in carbohydrates caused by heat are caramelization and gelatinization.

   • Caramelization is the browning of sugars. The browning of sautéed vegetables and the golden color of bread crust are forms of caramelization.

   • Gelatinization occurs when starches absorb water and swell. This is a major principle in the thickening of sauces and in the production of breads and pastries.

   Acids inhibit gelatinization. A sauce thickened with flour or starch will be thinner if it contains acid.

FRUIT AND VEGETABLE FIBER

1. Fiber is the name for a group of complex substances that give structure and firmness to plants. Fiber cannot be digested.

2. The softening of fruits and vegetables in cooking is, in part, the breaking down of fiber.

3. Sugar makes fiber firmer. Fruit cooked with sugar keeps its shape better than fruit cooked without sugar.

4. Baking soda (and other alkalis) makes fiber softer. Vegetables should not be cooked with baking soda because they become mushy and lose vitamins.

PROTEINS

1. Protein is a major component of meats, poultry, fish, eggs, milk, and milk products. It is present in smaller amounts in nuts, beans, and grains.

2. Coagulation. Proteins consist of long chains of components called amino acids. These chains normally form tight coils. As proteins are heated, the coils gradually unwind. At this point, the protein is said to be **denatured**.

   For the cook, the important fact about denaturing is that, when the protein coils unwind, they become attracted to each other and form bonds. This bonding is called coagulation. The coagulated proteins form a solid network of these bonds and become firm. As the temperature increases, the proteins shrink, become firmer, and lose more moisture. Exposure of proteins to excessive heat toughens them and makes them dry. Most proteins complete coagulation or are cooked at 160°F to 185°F (71°C to 85°C).

3. Many protein foods, such as meats, contain small quantities of carbohydrates. When proteins are heated to about 310°F (154°C), the amino acids in the protein chains react with carbohydrate molecules and undergo a complex chemical reaction. The result is that they turn brown and develop richer flavors. This reaction is called the **Maillard reaction**. It is what happens when meat browns. Because of the high temperature required for this reaction, the Maillard reaction takes place only on the dry surface. Because of its water content, the interior of the meat cannot get this hot.

4. Connective tissues are special proteins that are present in meats. Meats with a great deal of connective tissue are tough, but some connective tissues are dissolved when cooked slowly with moisture. Cooking tough meats properly, therefore, makes them more tender. These techniques are explained in Chapter 10.

5. *Acids*, such as lemon juice, vinegar, and tomato products, do two things to proteins:
   - They speed coagulation.
   - They help dissolve some connective tissues.

FATS

1. Fats are present in meats, poultry, fish, eggs, milk products, nuts, whole grains, and, to a lesser extent, vegetables and fruits. Fats are also important as cooking mediums, as for frying.

2. Fats can be either solid or liquid at room temperature. Liquid fats are called oils. When solid fats are heated, they melt, or change from solid to liquid. The melting point of solid fats varies.

3. When fats are heated, they begin to break down. When hot enough, they deteriorate rapidly and begin to smoke. The temperature at which this happens is called the **smoke point**, and it varies by type of fat. A stable fat—one with a high smoke point—is an important consideration in deep-fat frying.

4. Many flavor compounds dissolve in fat, so fats are important carriers of flavor. When fats melt and are lost from food, some flavors, as well as some vitamins, are lost with them.

5. For the functions of fats in baked goods, see page 899.

MINERALS, VITAMINS, PIGMENTS, AND FLAVOR COMPONENTS

1. Minerals and vitamins are important to the nutritional quality of the food. Pigments and flavor components are important to a food's appearance and taste and may determine whether the food is appetizing enough to eat. So it is important to preserve all these elements.

2. Some of these components are soluble in water, and others are soluble in fats. All of these components may be leached out, or dissolved away, from foods during cooking.

3. Vitamins and pigments may also be destroyed by heat, by long cooking, and by other elements present during cooking.

4. It is important, then, to select cooking methods that preserve, as much as possible, a food's nutrients, taste, and appearance. This is addressed whenever cooking techniques are explained in the remainder of this book.

WATER

1. Nearly all foods contain water. Dried foods may contain as little as a fraction of 1 percent water, but fresh meats, fish, vegetables, and fruits consist mostly of water.

2. Water exists in three states, solid (ice), liquid, and gas (water vapor or steam). At sea level, pure liquid water becomes solid, or freezes, at 32°F (0°C) and turns to steam at 212°F (100°C). When water molecules turn to steam and energetically escape into the atmosphere, water is said to be boiling.

3. Water can also turn from liquid to gas at lower temperatures. When water turns to gas at any temperature, the process is called evaporation. Evaporation happens more slowly the lower the temperature is. Evaporation is responsible for the drying of foods. The drying of food surfaces as they are cooked enables them to be browned.

4. Many minerals and other compounds dissolve in water, so water can be a carrier of flavor and of nutritional value.

5. When water carries dissolved compounds, such as salt or sugar, its freezing point is lowered and its boiling point is raised.

HEAT TRANSFER

In order for food to be cooked, heat must be transferred from a heat source (such as a gas flame or an electric element) to and through the food. Understanding the ways in which heat is transferred and the speed at which it is transferred helps the cook control the cooking process.

Heat is transferred in three ways: conduction, convection, and radiation. It is important to remember that, during a cooking process, more than one of these methods of transfer may be happening at the same time. For example, food on a grill may be heated by conduction from the hot metal grill, by convection from hot air rising from the burner or charcoal, and by radiation from the glowing burner or coals.

CONDUCTION

Conduction occurs in two ways:

1. When heat moves directly from one item to something touching it—for example, from the top of the range to a soup pot placed on it, from the pot to the broth inside, and from the broth to the solid food items in it.

2. When heat moves from one part of something to an adjacent part of the same item—for example, from the exterior of a roast to the interior, or from a sauté pan to its handle.

Different materials conduct heat at different speeds. Heat moves rapidly through copper and aluminum, more slowly in stainless steel, more slowly yet in glass and porcelain. Air is a poor conductor of heat.

CONVECTION

Convection occurs when heat is spread by the movement of air, steam, or liquid (including hot fat). There are two kinds of convection:

1. **Natural.**
   Hot liquids and gases rise while cooler ones sink. Thus, in any oven, kettle of liquid, or deep-fat fryer a constant, natural circulation distributes heat.

2. **Mechanical.**
   In convection ovens and convection steamers, fans speed the circulation of heat. Thus, heat is transferred more quickly to the food, and the food cooks faster.

   Stirring is a form of mechanical convection. Thick liquids cannot circulate as quickly as thin ones, so the rate of natural convection is slower. This explains, in part, why it is so easy to scorch thick soups and sauces. The heat is not carried away from the bottom of the pan quickly enough, so it stays concentrated on the bottom and scorches the food. Stirring redistributes the heat and helps prevent this. (Using heavy pots made of a material that conducts heat well also helps prevent scorching because the pot conducts the heat more quickly and evenly across the bottom and up the sides.)
   Convection is the process that carries the heat from the heat source to the food. Once the carrier of the heat (air or liquid) comes in contact with the food, the heat is transferred from the carrier to the food by conduction.

RADIATION

Radiation occurs when energy is transferred by waves from a source to the food. The waves themselves are not actually heat energy but are changed into heat energy when they strike the food being cooked. (Light waves, radio waves, and x-rays are examples of radiation not used for cooking.)
Two kinds of radiation are used in the kitchen:

1. **Infrared.**
   Broiling is the most familiar example of infrared cooking. In a broiler, an electric element or a ceramic element heated by a gas flame becomes so hot that it gives off infrared radiation, which cooks the food. High-intensity infrared ovens are designed to heat food rapidly.

2. **Microwave.**
   In microwave cooking, the radiation generated by the oven penetrates partway into the food, where it agitates the molecules of water. The friction this agitation causes creates heat, which cooks the food.

   - Because microwave radiation affects only water molecules, a completely waterless material will not heat in a microwave oven. Plates become hot only when heat is *conducted* to them by hot foods.

   - Because most microwaves penetrate no more than about 2 inches (50 mm) into foods, heat is transferred to the center of large pieces of food by *conduction*, just as in roasting.

   Cooking with microwaves is discussed in more detail later in this chapter.

COOKING TIMES

It takes time to heat a food to a desired temperature, the temperature at which a food is "done" (meaning the desired changes have taken place). This time is affected by three factors:

1. **Cooking temperature.**
   This means the temperature of the air in the oven, the fat in the fryer, the surface of a griddle, or the liquid in which a food is cooking.

2. **The speed of heat transfer.**
   Different cooking methods transfer heat at different rates, as shown by these examples:
   Air is a poor conductor of heat, while steam is much more efficient. A jet of steam (212°F/100°C) will easily burn your hand, but you can safely reach into an

oven at 500˚F (260˚C).This is why it takes longer to bake potatoes than to steam them.

　　A convection oven cooks faster than a conventional oven, even if both are set at the same temperature.The forced air movement transfers heat more rapidly.

3. **Size, temperature, and individual characteristics of the food.**
   For example:

   A small beef roast cooks faster than a large one.

   A chilled steak takes longer to broil than one at room temperature.

   Fish items generally cook more quickly than meats.

　　Because there are so many variables, it is difficult or even impossible to determine exact cooking times in most recipes. Individual ovens, fryers, and steamers, for example, may transfer heat more or less efficiently or have different recovery times. Roasting charts that give cooking times for various cuts of meat can be used only as guidelines, and the cook must use his or her judgment to make the final determination of doneness. Cooking times are discussed again in the next chapter.

COOKING METHODS

Cooking methods are classified as moist heat or dry heat.

　　Moist-heat methods are those in which the heat is conducted to the food product by water or water-based liquids such as stock and sauces, or by steam.

　　Dry-heat methods are those in which the heat is conducted without moisture—that is, by hot air, hot metal, radiation, or hot fat.We usually divide dry-heat methods into two categories: without fat and with fat.

　　Different cooking methods are suited to different kinds of foods. For example, some meats are high in connective tissue and will be tough unless this tissue is broken down slowly by moist heat. Other meats are low in connective tissue and are naturally tender. They are at their best and juiciest when cooked with dry heat to a rare or medium-done stage.

　　Many other factors must be considered when choosing cooking methods for meats, fish, and vegetables, such as the flavor and appearance imparted by browning, the flavor imparted by fats, and the firmness or delicacy of the product.These factors are discussed in later chapters with respect to individual foods.

　　The basic cooking methods are summarized here.Their practical application to foods is discussed in detail in the remainder of the book and reinforced by your instructors' demonstrations and your own experience and practice.

MOIST-HEAT METHODS

POACH, SIMMER, AND BOIL

Poaching, simmering, and boiling all mean cooking a food in water or a seasoned or flavored liquid.The temperature of the liquid determines the method.

1. To boil means to cook in a liquid that is bubbling rapidly and is greatly agitated. Water boils at 212˚F (100˚C) at sea level. No matter how high the burner is turned, the temperature of the liquid will go no higher.

   　　Boiling is generally reserved for vegetables and starches.The high temperature toughens the proteins of meats, fish, and eggs, and the rapid bubbling breaks up delicate foods.

2. To simmer means to cook in a liquid that is bubbling gently at a temperature of about 185°F to 205°F (85°C to 96°C).

    Most foods cooked in a liquid are simmered. The higher temperatures and intense agitation of boiling are detrimental to most foods. The word *boiled* is sometimes used as a menu term, as when simmered fresh beef is called "boiled beef."

3. To poach means to cook in a liquid, usually a small amount, that is hot but not actually bubbling. Temperature is about 160°F to 180°F (71°C to 82°C).

    Poaching is used to cook delicate foods such as fish and eggs out of the shell. It is also used to partially cook foods such as variety meats in order to eliminate undesirable flavors and to firm the product before final cooking.

4. A rule of thumb: Whether a food is to be simmered or boiled, the liquid is often brought to a full boil at first. This compensates for the lowering of the temperature when the food items are added. The heat is then adjusted to maintain a steady temperature.

5. To blanch means to cook an item partially and briefly, usually in water but sometimes by other methods (as when French fries are blanched in deep fat).

    There are two ways of blanching in water:

    - Place the item in cold water, bring to a boil, and simmer briefly. Cool the item by plunging it into cold water.
      Purpose: to dissolve out blood, salt, or impurities from meats and bones.

    - Place the item in rapidly boiling water and return the water to the boil. Remove the item and cool in cold water.
      Purpose: to set the color and destroy harmful enzymes in vegetables, or to loosen the skins of tomatoes, peaches, and similar items for easier peeling.

6. Altitude note: The boiling point of water decreases as altitude above sea level is increased. At 5,000 feet (1,500 meters) above sea level, water boils at about 203°F (95°C). Thus, it takes longer to boil foods to doneness at high altitudes because the temperature is lower.

STEAM

To steam means to cook foods by exposing them directly to steam.

1. In quantity cooking, steaming is usually done in special steam cookers, which are designed to accept standard-size pans. Steaming can also be done on a rack above boiling water. This method is more cumbersome, however, and is used only occasionally in food service. Cooking in a steam-jacketed kettle is not steaming because the steam does not actually touch the food.

2. The term *steaming* also refers to cooking an item tightly wrapped or in a covered pan so that it cooks in the steam formed by its own moisture. This method is used in cooking items en papillote, meaning wrapped in parchment paper (or foil). "Baked" potatoes wrapped in foil are actually steamed.

3. Steam at normal pressure is 212°F (100°C), the same as boiling water. However, it carries much more heat than boiling water and cooks foods very rapidly. Cooking times must be carefully controlled to avoid overcooking.

4. A *pressure steamer* is a steam cooker that holds in steam under pressure. The temperature of the steam then goes higher than 212°F (100°C), as the following chart shows:

Pressure	Steam Temperature
5 psi (pounds per square inch)	227°F (106°C)
10 psi	240°F (116°C)
15 psi	250°F (121°C)

    Because of these temperatures, pressure steaming is an extremely rapid method of cooking and must be carefully controlled and timed.

5. Steaming is widely used for vegetables. It cooks them rapidly, without agitation, and minimizes the dissolving away of nutrients that occurs when vegetables are boiled.

BRAISE

To braise means to cook covered in a small amount of liquid, usually after preliminary browning. In almost all cases, the liquid is served with the product as a sauce.

Braising is sometimes referred to as a *combination cooking method* because the product is first browned, using dry heat, before it is cooked with a liquid. Nevertheless, in most cases, moist heat is responsible for most of the cooking process, and the browning may be thought of as a preliminary technique. The purpose of the browning step is not so much to cook the item as to develop color and flavor.

Some references describe braising and stewing as two different cooking methods. The term *braising* is used for large cuts of meat, and *stewing* is used for smaller items. In this book, however, we use the term *braising* for both methods because the basic procedure in both cases is the same—first browning with dry heat, then cooking with moist heat. (Note that the term *stewing* is also used for simmering in a small amount of liquid without preliminary browning.)

1. Braised meats are usually browned first using a dry-heat method such as panfrying. This gives a desirable appearance and flavor to the product and sauce.

2. Braising also refers to cooking some vegetables, such as lettuce or cabbage, at low temperature in a small amount of liquid without first browning in fat, or with only a light preliminary sautéing.

3. Foods being braised are usually not completely covered by the cooking liquid. The top of the product is actually cooked by the steam held in the covered pot. Pot roasts, for example, are cooked in liquid that covers the item by one-third to two-thirds. The exact amount depends on how much sauce is needed for service. This method yields a flavorful, concentrated sauce.

4. In some preparations, especially of poultry and fish, no liquid is added. This is still considered braising because steam is trapped by the cover and the item cooks in its own moisture and in the moisture of other ingredients, such as vegetables.

5. Braising may be done on the range or in the oven. Oven-braising has three major advantages:

    • Uniform cooking. The heat strikes the braising pot on all sides, not just the bottom.

    • Less attention required. Foods braise at a low, steady temperature without having to be checked constantly.

    • Range space is free for other purposes.

DRY-HEAT METHODS

ROAST AND BAKE

To roast and to bake both mean to cook foods by surrounding them with hot, dry air, usually in an oven. Cooking on a spit in front of an open fire may also be considered roasting.

The term *roasting* usually applies to meats and poultry. The term *baking* usually applies to breads, pastries, vegetables, and fish. It is a more general term than roasting, although, in practice, there is little or no difference in actual technique, and the terms are often interchangeable (except for breads and pastries).

Please note, however, that it has recently become fashionable on menus to apply the term *roasted* to a wide variety of foods, including meats, poultry, fish, and vegetables that are not actually baked or roasted but rather sautéed, fried, or braised. One restaurant even labeled steamed vegetables as "roasted baby vegetables."

1. Cooking *uncovered* is essential to roasting. Covering holds in steam, changing the process from dry-heat to moist-heat cooking, such as braising or steaming.

2. Meat is usually roasted on a rack (or, if it is a rib roast, on its own natural rack of bones). The rack prevents the meat from simmering in its own juices and fat. It also allows hot air to circulate around the product.

3. When roasting in a conventional oven, the cook should allow for uneven temperatures by occasionally changing the position of the product. The back of the oven is often hotter because heat is lost at the door.

4. To **barbecue** means to cook with dry heat created by the burning of hardwood or by the hot coals of this wood. In other words, barbecuing is a roasting or grilling technique requiring a wood fire.

   Authentic, traditional barbecue is done in wood-burning ovens or pits, but these are not practical for the average restaurant that wants to add barbecued items to the menu. So today, most barbecuing is done in specially designed smoke ovens or cookers. In principle, these units work like regular ovens, except that they also have a device that heats small pieces of hardwood to produce smoke. Foods should be suspended in the ovens or placed on racks so the smoke can contact all surfaces.

   Technically, the foods cooked in these units cannot be said to be barbecued, as the heat is created by electric or gas burners. But because of the wood smoke, the results can be nearly identical.

5. **Smoke-roasting** is a procedure done on top of the stove in a closed container, using wood chips to make smoke. Use this procedure for small, tender, quick-cooking items such as fish fillets, tender meat and poultry pieces, and some vegetables.

   To smoke-roast, place a layer of fine hardwood chips or shavings on the bottom of a hotel pan (see Figure 4.1). Disposable pans may be used for light smoking. Place a rack in the pan over the chips and lay the seasoned food items on the rack. Cover tightly with a second hotel pan or with aluminum foil. Place on the cooktop (making sure the ventilating hood is on!) over moderate heat. Smoke will begin rising from the wood chips. After about five minutes, remove the food items from the smoke-roaster and, if necessary, complete the cooking in the oven. Leaving the food in the smoke too long will result in a strong, bitter taste.

**Figure 4.1
Rangetop smoke-roasting**

(a) Place hardwood chips or sawdust in a disposable hotel pan. Place over moderately high heat and heat until the wood begins to smoke.

(b) Place the items to be cooked on a rack and set the rack over the chips so that the food is not touching the chips. Cover tightly with another pan and cook for desired time.

BROIL

To **broil** means to cook with radiant heat from above.

Note: The terms *broiling*, *grilling*, and *griddling* are sometimes confused. Grilling (see below) is often called *broiling*, and griddling is called *grilling*. This book uses the terms that refer to the equipment used. Thus, broiling is done in a broiler, grilling on a grill, and griddling on a griddle.

1. Broiling is a rapid, high-heat cooking method used mainly for tender meats, poultry, fish, and a few vegetable items.

2. Note the following rules of broiling:

   - *Turn heat on full.* Cooking temperature is regulated by moving the rack nearer to or farther from the heat source.

   - *Use lower heat for larger, thicker items and for items to be cooked well done.* Use higher heat for thinner pieces and for items to be cooked rare. This is done so the inside and outside are cooked to the desired degree at the same time. It takes practice and experience to cook foods of different thickness to the right degree of doneness inside with the desired amount of surface browning.

   - *Preheat the broiler.* This helps sear the product quickly, and the hot broiler will make the desired grill marks on the food.

   - Foods may be dipped in oil to prevent sticking and to minimize drying. (This may not be necessary if the food is high in fat.) Care should be taken, as too much oil on a hot broiler grate may cause a fire.

   - Turn foods over only once, to cook from both sides and to avoid unnecessary handling.

3. A low-intensity broiler called a *salamander* is used for browning or melting the top of some items before service.

GRILL, GRIDDLE, AND PAN-BROIL

Grilling, griddling, and pan-broiling are all dry-heat cooking methods that use heat from below.

1. **Grilling** is done on an open grid over a heat source, which may be charcoal, an electric element, or a gas-heated element. Cooking temperature is regulated by moving the items to hotter or cooler places on the grill. Grilled meats should be turned to achieve desired grill marks, just as in broiling.

2. **Griddling** is done on a solid cooking surface called a griddle, with or without small amounts of fat to prevent sticking. The temperature is adjustable and much lower (around 350°F/177°C) than on a grill. In addition to meats, items such as eggs and pancakes are cooked on a griddle.

    Grooved griddles have a solid top with raised ridges. They are designed to cook like grills but to create less smoke. Meats cooked on a grooved griddle do not have the charcoal-grilled flavor imparted by smoke from burning fats.

3. **Pan-broiling** is like griddling except that it is done in a sauté pan or skillet instead of on a griddle surface. Fat must be poured off as it accumulates, or the process becomes pan-frying. No liquid is added, and the pan is not covered, or else the item would steam.

DRY-HEAT METHODS USING FAT

SAUTÉ

To **sauté** means to cook quickly in a small amount of fat.

1. The French word *sauter* means "to jump," referring to the action of tossing small pieces of food in a sauté pan (see Figure 17.1). However, larger foods, such as slices of meat and pieces of chicken, are sautéed without actually being tossed in the pan.

2. Note these two important principles:
    *   Preheat the pan before adding the food to be sautéed. The food must start cooking at high heat, or it will begin to simmer in its own juices.
    *   Do not overcrowd the pan. Doing so lowers the temperature too much, and again the food begins to simmer in its own juices.

3. Meats to be sautéed are often dusted with flour to prevent sticking and to help achieve uniform browning.

4. After a food is sautéed, a liquid such as wine or stock is often swirled in the pan to dissolve browned bits of food sticking to the bottom. This is called **deglazing**. The liquid becomes part of a sauce served with the sautéed items.

5. Stir-frying is a variation of sautéing. See pages 313–314 for a discussion.

PAN-FRY

To **pan-fry** means to cook in a moderate amount of fat in a pan over moderate heat.

1. Pan-frying is similar to sautéing except that more fat is used and the cooking time is longer. The method is used for larger pieces of food, such as chops and chicken pieces, and the items are not tossed by flipping the pan, as they often are in sautéing.

2. Pan-frying is usually done over lower heat than sautéing because of the larger size of the pieces being cooked.

3. The amount of fat depends on the food being cooked. Only a small amount is used for eggs, for example, while as much as 1 inch (2.5 cm) or more may be used for pan-fried chicken.

4. Most foods must be turned at least once for even cooking. Some larger foods may be removed from the pan and finished in the oven to prevent excessive surface browning. This method of finishing in the oven is also used to simplify production when large quantities of foods must be pan-fried.

DEEP-FRY

To **deep-fry** means to cook a food submerged in hot fat. Quality in a deep-fried product is characterized by the following properties:

Minimum fat absorption

Minimum moisture loss (that is, not overcooked)

Attractive golden color

Crisp surface or coating

No off flavors imparted by the frying fat

Many foods are dipped in a breading or batter before frying. This forms a protective coating between food and fat and helps give the product crispness, color, and flavor. Obviously, the quality of the breading or batter affects the quality of the finished product (see Chapter 7, pp. 142–144).

Guidelines for Deep-Frying

1. Fry at proper temperatures.

    Most foods are fried at 350°F to 375°F (175°C to 190°C). Excessive greasiness in fried foods is usually caused by frying at too low a temperature.

2. Don't overload the baskets.

    Doing so greatly lowers the fat temperature.

3. Use good-quality fat.

    The best fat for frying has a high smoke point (the temperature at which the fat begins to smoke and to break down rapidly).

4. Replace about 15 to 20 percent of the fat with fresh fat after each daily use.

    This extends frying life.

5. Discard spent fat.

    Old fat loses frying ability, browns excessively, and imparts off flavors.

6. Avoid frying strong- and mild-flavored foods in the same fat, if possible.

    French fries should not taste like fried fish.

7. Fry as close to service as possible.

    Do not leave foods in the basket above the fry kettle, and do not hold under heat lamps for more than a few minutes. The foods' moisture quickly makes the breading or coating soggy.

8. Protect fat from its enemies:

    Heat. **Turn fryer off or to a lower holding temperature (200°F to 250°F/95°C to 120°C) when not in use.**

    Oxygen. **Keep fat covered between services, and try to aerate the fat as little as possible when filtering.**

    Water. **Remove excess moisture from foods before frying. Dry baskets and kettle thoroughly after cleaning. Keep liquids away from the fryer to prevent accidental spills.**

    Salt. **Never salt foods over the fat.**

    Food particles. **Shake loose crumbs off breaded items before placing over fat. Skim and strain fat frequently.**

    Detergent. **Rinse baskets and kettle well after cleaning.**

Pressure Frying

Pressure frying means deep-frying in a special covered fryer that traps steam given off by the foods being cooked and increases the pressure inside the kettle.

In a standard fryer, even though the fat may be at 350°F (175°C), the temperature inside the food will not rise above 212°F (100°C), the boiling point of water. Just as in a pressure steamer, a pressure fryer raises this temperature and cooks the food more quickly without excessive surface browning. At the same time, the fat temperature can be lower, 325°F (165°C) or less.

Pressure frying requires accurate timing because the product cannot be seen while it is cooking.

MICROWAVE COOKING

Microwave cooking refers to the use of a specific tool rather than to a basic dry-heat or moist-heat cooking method. The microwave oven is used mostly for heating prepared foods and for thawing raw or cooked items. However, it can be used for primary cooking as well.

Microwave oven models range in power from about 500 watts up to about 2,000 watts. The higher the wattage, the more intense the energy the oven puts out and the faster it heats foods. Most models have switches that allow you to cook at different power levels.

One of the most important advantages of the microwave oven in à la carte cooking is that it enables you to heat individual portions of many foods to order quickly and evenly. Instead of keeping such foods as stews hot in the steam table, where they gradually become overcooked, you can keep them refrigerated (either in bulk or in individual portions) and reheat each order as needed. This is perhaps the main reason why most restaurants have one or more microwave ovens, even though they may not use them for primary cooking.

Because the microwave oven is a unique tool in food service, the cook should observe the following special points regarding its use:

1. Small items will not brown in a standard microwave. Large roasts may brown somewhat from the heat generated in the item itself. Some models have browning elements that use conventional heat.

2. Watch timing carefully. Overcooking is the most common error in microwave use. High energy levels cook small items very rapidly.

3. Large items should be turned once or twice for even cooking.

4. An on/off cycle is often used for large items to allow time for heat to be conducted to the interior.

5. If your equipment has a defrost cycle (which switches the oven to lower power), use this cycle rather than full power to thaw frozen foods. Lower power enables the item to thaw more evenly, with less danger of partially cooking it. If your oven does not have this feature, use an on/off cycle.

6. Sliced, cooked meats and other items that are likely to dry out in the microwave should be protected either by wrapping them loosely in plastic or wax paper or by covering them with a sauce or gravy.

7. Because microwaves act only on water molecules, foods with high water content, such as vegetables, heat faster than denser, drier foods, such as cooked meats.

8. Foods at the edge of a dish or plate heat faster than foods in the center. This is because they are hit by rays bouncing off the walls of the oven as well as by rays directly from the energy source. Therefore:

    • Depress the center of casseroles so the food is not as thick there as at the edges. This will help it heat more evenly.

    • When you are heating several foods at once on a plate, put the moist, quick-heating items like vegetables in the center and the denser, slower-heating items at the edges.

9. Because microwaves do not penetrate metal, aluminum foil and other metals shield foods from the radiant energy. For example, a potato wrapped in foil will not cook in a microwave oven.

    With older machines, it was a general rule not to put any metal in the oven, as the radiation could bounce off the metal and damage the magnetron (the oven's generator). With newer machines, it is possible to heat foods in foil pans and to shield certain parts of the food by covering them with pieces of foil so they do not overheat. Follow the procedures recommended by the manufacturer.

Because microwaves cook so rapidly, they will not break down the connective tissues of less tender meats. Slow, moist cooking is necessary for dissolving these connective tissues.

The more food placed in a microwave at once, the longer the cooking time. Thus, the primary advantage of microwave cooking—speed—is lost with large roasts and other large quantities.

SUMMARY OF COOKING TERMS

The following is an alphabetical list of terms that describe ways of applying heat to foods. Basic cooking methods described earlier are included, as well as more specific applications of these basic methods.

bake. To cook foods by surrounding them with hot, dry air. Similar to *roast*, but the term *bake* usually applies to breads, pastries, vegetables, and fish.

barbecue. (1) To cook with dry heat created by the burning of hardwood or by the hot coals of this wood. (2) Loosely, to cook over hot coals, such as on a grill or spit, often with a seasoned marinade or basting sauce.

blanch. To cook an item partially and very briefly in boiling water or in hot fat. Usually a pre-preparation technique, as to loosen peels of vegetables, fruits, and nuts, to partially cook French fries or other foods before service, to prepare for freezing, or to remove undesirable flavors.

boil. To cook in water or other liquid that is bubbling rapidly, about 212°F (100°C) at sea level and at normal pressure.

braise. (1) To cook covered in a small amount of liquid, usually after preliminary browning. (2) To cook certain vegetables slowly in a small amount of liquid without preliminary browning.

broil. To cook with radiant heat from above.

deep-fry. To cook submerged in hot fat.

deglaze. To swirl a liquid in a sauté pan, roast pan, or other pan to dissolve cooked particles of food remaining on the bottom.

dry-heat cooking methods. Methods in which heat is conducted to foods without the use of moisture.

fry. To cook in hot fat.

glaze. To give shine to the surface of a food by applying a sauce, aspic, sugar, or icing, and/or by browning or melting under a broiler or salamander or in an oven.

griddle. To cook on a flat, solid cooking surface called a *griddle*.

grill. To cook on an open grid over a heat source.

moist-heat cooking methods. Methods in which heat is conducted to foods by water or other liquid (except fat) or by steam.

pan-broil. To cook uncovered in a skillet or sauté pan without fat.

pan-fry. To cook in a moderate amount of fat in an uncovered pan.

(en) papillote. Wrapped in paper (or sometimes foil) for cooking so the enclosed food is steamed in its own moisture.

parboil. To cook partially in a boiling or simmering liquid.

parcook. To cook partially by any method.

poach. To cook gently in water or other liquid that is hot but not actually bubbling, about 160°F to 180°F (71°C to 82°C).

reduce. To cook by simmering or boiling until the quantity of liquid is decreased, often to concentrate flavors.

roast. To cook foods by surrounding them with hot, dry air in an oven or on a spit in front of an open fire.

sauté. To cook quickly in a small amount of fat, usually while mixing or tossing the foods by occasionally flipping the pan.

sear. To brown the surface of a food quickly at a high temperature.

simmer. To cook in water or other liquid that is bubbling gently, about 185°F to 205°F (85°C to 96°C).

smoke-roasting. To cook with dry heat in the presence of smoke, as on a rack over wood chips in a covered pan.

steam. To cook by direct contact with steam.

stew. To simmer or braise a food or foods in a small amount of liquid, which is usually served with the food as a sauce.

stir-fry. To cook quickly in a small amount of fat by tossing cut-up foods in a wok or pan with spatulas or similar implements. Similar to sauté, except that the pan is stationary.

sweat. To cook slowly in fat without browning, sometimes under a cover.

BUILDING FLAVOR

People eat because they enjoy the flavors of good food, not just because they must fill their stomachs to stay alive. Appearance, texture, and nutrition are important, too, but good taste is the first mark of good cooking. Enhancement and adjustment of flavors is one of a cook's most critical tasks, one requiring experience and judgment.

The most important flavors of a given preparation are those of its main ingredients. A grilled beef tenderloin steak should taste like beef, green beans should taste like green beans, tomato soup should taste primarily of tomato. Plain, unseasoned foods, however, usually taste a little bland and one-dimensional, so it is the cook's job to add interest by combining ingredients to build depth of flavor. The harmony of ingredient flavors and aromas the cook creates by combining ingredients skillfully is sometimes called a **flavor profile**.

BUILDING FLAVOR PROFILES

Foods offer complex experiences for the senses. When composing a new dish, a cook must first of all understand that more than just taste should be considered. The senses of sight, smell, taste, and touch all come into play. The fifth sense, hearing, also plays a role, as when we react to the sizzle of a steak or the crunch of a potato chip, but this sense is less of a concern for the cook than the other four. Consider how we perceive these characteristics of a dish:

- Appearance (color and color contrast, shape, shine, arrangement on the plate)
- Aroma
- Taste
- Mouth feel (texture, moistness or dryness, softness or crispness) and temperature

All of these factors are important to making a dish appealing to the diner. The discussion in this section, however, is concerned mostly with aroma and taste. Why not just taste? Taste buds on the tongue perceive only four basic sensations: salty, sweet, bitter, and sour. What we think of as flavor is a combination of taste and aroma. When the sense of smell is lacking, such as when you have a cold, foods seem to have little flavor.

The flavors in a dish can be thought of as primary flavors and supporting, or secondary, flavors. The primary flavors are the flavors of the main ingredients. For example, the **primary flavor** in blanquette of veal (p. 326) is veal; the primary flavors in calf's liver lyonnaise (p. 321) are liver and onions; and the primary flavors in Irish lamb stew (p. 327) are lamb, onions, leeks, and potatoes. These are the flavors that predominate. When you taste each of these dishes, the first tastes you encounter are the main ingredients. Other flavors, which we can call **supporting flavors**, support and enhance the primary flavors of the main ingredients.

Examining how a flavor profile is built in a single classic and fairly simple recipe can help you begin to understand some of the general principles involved.

An Example of Flavor Building

Let's look more closely at the recipe for blanquette of veal mentioned above. Veal, by itself, does not have a strong or pronounced flavor. Unlike meats such as beef or venison, veal has a mild, subtle flavor. In this recipe, the veal is simmered, so the flavor is even milder than it would be if the meat were browned by roasting, sautéing, or braising. For this reason, when choosing seasonings and other supporting flavors, we want to avoid strong flavors that will mask the delicate flavor of the veal. Using white veal stock as a cooking medium reinforces and strengthens the primary flavor. We could use water, but the result would be a less flavorful dish. Brown stock would be too strong for our purpose and would completely change the character of the dish. White chicken stock might be an acceptable substitute, but it wouldn't reinforce the veal flavor as well. The onion and bouquet garni are added to the stock to give it more depth and fullness of flavor.

Continuing to the finishing ingredients, we find roux, a cream-and-egg liaison, lemon juice, nutmeg, and white pepper. The roux functions as a thickener and contributes primarily to texture, although the butter in the roux also gives some richness to the flavor. The liaison is used for both texture and flavor, adding richness and creaminess. The cream and the simmered veal are a classic marriage of flavors that work well together in many dishes. However, too much richness, combined with the mildness of the veal, can make a dish cloying. The acidity of the lemon juice cuts through the richness of the cream and egg yolks, gives a more balanced flavor, and perks up the taste buds. Just enough lemon is used to balance the richness of the cream and egg, not so much as to make the dish taste lemony. Finally, the smallest amount of nutmeg and white pepper gives a pleasing complexity to the finished taste without adding identifiable flavors. If one of the first things you taste is nutmeg, then too much nutmeg has been used.

If the dish is well composed, all of these flavors, primary and supporting, combine to form a complex but unified whole that we identify as the taste of veal blanquette.

GENERAL CONCEPTS IN FLAVOR BUILDING

There are no fixed rules for combining flavors, but the example just discussed suggests some general principles. When you are developing or modifying a recipe, think about the following points.

Every ingredient should have a purpose. Start with the main ingredients, and then think about what will work with them. Continue to build the flavor, using just the ingredients you need.

Ingredients can work together by harmonizing or by contrasting. In the example above, the rich taste of the liaison and the mild taste of the veal harmonize. The tartness of the lemon, on the other hand, contrasts with the cream.

When two ingredients contrast, be sure they balance. For example, add just enough lemon juice to the blanquette to balance the cream, not too much or too little.

Consider not only the components of the single recipe but also other items that will be served with it on the plate. For example, think of how we use lemon to balance the richness or fattiness of the cream in the blanquette. We can use the same idea to balance the fattiness of a pork pâté or sausage by serving it with a tart mustard or chutney on the side. In other words, think of building the flavor profile of the entire plate. Plan sauces, accompaniments, and garnishes to balance, enhance, and contrast with the main item and with each other, just as the flavors in an individual recipe do.

Simplicity and Complexity

Simpler is usually better. Some cooks mistakenly think that adding more ingredients is always preferable to adding fewer. But the more flavors you combine, the harder you have to work to balance them all. Further, the more competing flavors you have, the more you have to take care that the primary flavors of the main ingredients don't get lost.

This is true whether you are planning the ingredients in a single recipe or the components on a plate. Some cooks are tempted to put too many things on a plate. When you have a meat item perched on layers of three or four vegetables and starches, with additional garnishes and two or three sauces, the result is often a confused jumble.

It would be incorrect, however, to say that simpler is *always* better. Classic dishes from many of the world's regions have complex flavor profiles. Look through any collection of recipes from India, China, or Mexico, and you will find dishes that use a large number of spices and other flavoring ingredients. The recipe for mole poblano on page 409 is an example. When these dishes work, all the ingredients blend well. In a good curry, for example, it is difficult, if not impossible, to taste each of the individual spices.

Classic Flavor Profiles

How do you know what flavors work together? Perhaps the best place to start is to study traditional recipes from around the world as well as from the classical cuisine passed down to us through Escoffier. These are dishes that have stood the test of time. We know the flavor combinations work because they have been used over and over for decades or even centuries.

We have already seen some classic flavor combinations in our discussion of veal blanquette. The pairing of white meat, cream, and lemon, with a hint of nutmeg, is a quartet of flavors that you will find repeatedly in classic and regional dishes.

International or ethnic dishes provide other examples. In northern India, many dishes are based on a mixture of onion, garlic, and fresh ginger puréed together and fried in a little oil. Studying these recipes suggests to us that these three flavors might be used together in new dishes as well. Similarly, the combination of ginger and soy sauce from Japan, paprika and cured ham from Spain, garlic, tomato, and parsley from Provence, and olives and anchovies from around the Mediterranean are all successful flavor mixtures that we learn to use when we study classic dishes.

For chefs who want to create their own dishes, studying classic recipes is a good place to start.

CLASSIC FLAVORING COMBINATIONS

These are just a few of the many traditional flavoring combinations from around the world. Keep in mind that, although only one or two combinations are given for each country or region mentioned, they are not the only combinations used there. These are merely examples to stimulate your thinking.

Sour cream, paprika, caraway (Hungary)

Sour cream or mustard, dill (Scandinavia)

Caraway, onion, vinegar (Germany)

Apples, apple cider or apple brandy, cream (France—Normandy)

Shallot, garlic, parsley (France—Burgundy)

Tomato, basil, olive oil (Italy)

Olive oil, garlic, anchovy (Italy)

Lemon, oregano (Greece)

Cinnamon, nuts, honey (eastern and southern Mediterranean, Middle East)

Ginger, onion, garlic (India)

Fish sauce (nam pla), lemon grass, chiles (Thailand)

Ginger, soy sauce (Japan)

Soy sauce, sake or mirin, dried bonito (Japan)

Ginger, garlic, scallion (China)

SEASONING AND FLAVORING INGREDIENTS

The preceding discussion of flavor building concerns all ingredients that add flavor to or change the flavor of a dish. These include the primary ingredients and the supporting or secondary ingredients. The remainder of this chapter is concerned primarily with herbs and spices as well as common flavoring ingredients such as onion, garlic, and mustard.

To repeat the most important concept of flavoring, the main ingredients are the primary sources of flavor. Use good-quality main ingredients, handle all foods with care, and employ correct cooking procedures. Remember that herbs and spices play only a supporting role. Badly prepared foods can't be rescued by a last-minute addition of herbs and spices.

Although chefs do not always use the terms this way, it might be said that there is a difference between seasoning and flavoring. Seasoning means enhancing the natural flavor of a food without significantly changing its flavor. Salt is the most important seasoning ingredient. Flavoring means adding a new flavor to a food, thus changing or modifying the original flavor.

The difference between seasoning and flavoring is often one of degree. For example, salt is usually used only to season, not to flavor. But in the case of potato chips or pretzels, the salt is so predominant that it can be considered an added flavoring. On the other hand, nutmeg is normally used for its distinctive flavor, but just a dash can perk up the flavor of a cream sauce without being detectable to most people.

SEASONING

1. The most important time for seasoning liquid foods is ~~at the end of the cooking process~~.

    The last step in most recipes, whether written or not, is "adjust the seasoning." This means you have to first taste and evaluate the product. Then you must decide what should be done, if anything, to improve the taste. Often, a little salt in a stew or a dash of fresh lemon juice in a sauce is enough.

    The ability to evaluate and correct flavors takes experience, and it is one of the most important skills a cook can develop.

2. ~~Salt and other seasonings are also added at the beginning of cooking~~, particularly for larger pieces of food, when seasonings added at the end would not be absorbed or blended in but just sit on the surface.

3. Adding some of the seasoning during the cooking process also aids in evaluating the flavor along the way.

4. Do not add much seasoning if it will be concentrated during cooking, as when a liquid is reduced.

FLAVORING

Flavoring ingredients can be added at the beginning, middle, or end, depending on the cooking time, the cooking process, and the flavoring ingredient.

1. ~~Only a few flavorings can be added successfully at the end of cooking~~. These include fresh (not dried) herbs, sherry or flamed brandy, and condiments like prepared mustard and Worcestershire sauce.

2. Most flavorings need heat to release their flavors and time for the flavors to blend. Whole spices take longest. Ground spices release flavors more quickly and thus don't require as long a cooking time.

3. Too much cooking results in loss of flavor. Most flavors, whether in spices or in main ingredients, are **volatile**, which means they evaporate when heated. That is why you can smell food cooking.

We can conclude that herbs and spices should cook with the foods long enough to release their flavors but not so long that their flavors are lost. If cooking times are short, you can generally add spices and herbs at the beginning or middle of cooking time. If cooking times are long, it is usually better to add them in the middle or toward the end of cooking time.

Note: Food safety experts recommend adding dried spices and herbs at least 30 minutes before the end of cooking so any microorganisms they might carry will be destroyed.

COMMON SEASONING AND FLAVORING INGREDIENTS

Any food product can be used as a flavoring ingredient, even meat (as when crumbled bacon is added to sautéed potatoes or diced ham is included in a mirepoix). Sauces, which are complex preparations containing many flavoring ingredients, are themselves used as flavorings for meat, fish, vegetables, and desserts.

We obviously cannot treat all possible flavoring ingredients here, but we discuss some of the most important as follows. A survey of herbs and spices is provided in Table 4.1 on pages 80–82. Ingredients used primarily in the bakeshop are discussed in Chapter 29.

Table 4.1
Herbs and Spices

Product	Market Forms	Description	Examples of Use
Allspice	Whole, ground	Small brown berry; flavor resembles blend of cinnamon, cloves, and nutmeg	Sausages and braised meats, poached fish, stewed fruits, pies, puddings
Anise seed	Whole, ground	Small seed; licorice flavor	Cookies, pastries, breads
Basil	Crushed leaves	Aromatic leaf; member of mint family	Tomatoes and tomato dishes, pesto (Italian basil sauce), egg dishes, lamb chops, eggplant, peas, squash
Bay leaf	Whole	Stiff, dark green, oblong leaves; pungent aroma	One of the most important herbs for stocks, sauces, stews, braised meats
Caraway seed	Whole	Dark brown, curved seeds; familiar rye bread seasoning	Rye bread, cabbage, sauerkraut, pork, cheese spreads, Eastern European dishes
Cardamom	Whole pod, ground seed	Tiny brown seeds inside white or green pod; sweet and aromatic; expensive	Pickling, Danish pastries, curries
Cayenne (red pepper)	Ground	Ground form of hot red pepper; looks like paprika but is extremely hot	In small amounts in many sauces, soups, meat, fish, egg, and cheese dishes (see p. 82)
Celery seed	Whole, ground, ground mixed with salt (celery salt)	Tiny brown seeds with strong celery flavor	Salads, coleslaw, salad dressings, tomato products
Chervil	Crushed leaves	Herb with mild flavor of parsley and tarragon	Soups, salads, sauces, egg and cheese dishes
Chili powder	Ground blend	Blend of spices including cumin, chili peppers, oregano, garlic	Chili and other Mexican dishes, egg dishes, appetizers, ground meat
Chive	Fresh, dried, frozen	Grasslike herb with onion flavor	Salads, egg and cheese dishes, fish, soups
Cilantro (fresh coriander, Chinese parsley)	Fresh leaves	The plant that produces coriander seeds; delicate texture; assertive, herbaceous aroma and flavor; leaves resemble flat parsley	Widely used in Asian and Southwestern cooking and in dishes with various ethnic influences
Cinnamon	Sticks, ground	Aromatic bark of cinnamon or cassia tree	Pastries, breads, desserts, cooked fruits, ham, sweet potatoes, hot beverages
Clove	Whole, ground	Dried flower buds of a tropical tree; pungent, sweet flavor	Whole: marinades, stocks, sauces, braised meats, ham, pickling Ground: cakes, pastries, fruits
Coriander	Whole, ground	Round, light brown, hollow seed, slightly sweet, musty flavor	Pickling, sausage, pork, curried dishes, gingerbread
Cumin seed	Whole, ground	Small seed resembling caraway, but lighter in color	Ingredient of curry and chili powders, sausages and meats, egg and cheese dishes
Curry powder	Ground blend	A mixture of 16 to 20 spices, including red pepper, turmeric, cumin, coriander, ginger, cloves, cinnamon, black pepper; brands vary greatly in flavor and hotness	Curried dishes, eggs, vegetables, fish, soups, rice
Dill	Crushed leaves (called *dill weed*), whole seed	Herb and seed with familiar dill pickle flavor; seed is more pungent than the herb	Seed: pickling, sauerkraut, soups Herb: salads, cheese dishes, fish and shellfish, some vegetables

Product	Market Forms	Description	Examples of Use
Epazote	Fresh and dried leaves	A pungent herb with coarse-textured leaves	Used in Mexican cooking; often cooked with beans
Fennel	Whole seed	Greenish-brown seeds similar in flavor to anise, but larger in size	Italian sausage, tomato sauce, fish
Garlic	Fresh: whole bulbs; dried: granulated, powder, and mixed with salt	Strong, aromatic member of onion family; fresh bulbs composed of many small cloves	Wide variety of foods
Ginger	Whole, ground (also fresh and candied or crystallized)	Light brown, knobby root of ginger plant	Baked goods and desserts, fruits, curried dishes, braised meats; fresh in Chinese and other Asian dishes
Juniper berry	Whole	Slightly soft, purple berries with piney flavor; principal flavoring of gin	Marinades, game dishes, sauerkraut
Lemon grass	Fresh stalks	A tropical grass with a slightly bulbous base and an aroma of lemon	Used in Southeast Asian dishes and in dishes influenced by Asian cuisine
Mace	Whole (blade), ground	Orange outer covering of nutmeg; similar flavor, but milder	Baked goods, desserts, fruits, sausages, pork, fish, spinach, squash, other vegetables
Marjoram	Crushed leaves	Gray-green herb with pleasant aroma and slightly minty flavor, similar to oregano, but much milder	Pâtés and ground meats, braised meats, sauces, roast lamb, poultry and poultry stuffings
Mint	Leaves	Aromatic herb with familiar cool flavor; two varieties: spearmint and peppermint	Lamb, fruits, tea and fruit beverages, peas, carrots, potatoes
Mustard seed	Whole, ground (also prepared mustard; see p. 83)	Very pungent seed in two varieties: white or yellow and brown—brown is stronger	Cheese and egg dishes, pickling, meats, sauces and gravies
Nutmeg	Whole, ground	Sweet, aromatic kernel of nutmeg fruit	Soups, cream sauces, chicken, veal, many vegetables (spinach, mushrooms, squash, potatoes), desserts, custards, breads, pastries
Oregano	Leaves, ground	Pungent herb known as the "pizza herb"	Italian and Mexican dishes, tomato products
Paprika	Ground	Ground form of a dried, sweet red pepper. Spanish variety is brighter in color, mild in flavor; Hungarian is darker and more pungent	Spanish: used (or overused) primarily as garnish on light-colored foods; Hungarian: goulash, braised meats and poultry, sauces
Parsley	Fresh: whole sprigs, in bunches; dried: in flakes	Most widely used herb; dark green curly or flat leaves with delicate, sweet flavor	Almost all foods
Pepper, black and white	Whole (pepper-corns); ground fine, medium, or coarse	Small black or creamy white hard berry; pungent flavor and aroma	Most widely used spice (see p. 82)
Pepper, red	(see Cayenne)		
Peppercorn, pink	Whole	Bright pink, dried seed or berry; pungent, floral taste; unrelated to black pepper	Limited uses in meat, poultry, and fish dishes; sauce garnish; used in peppercorn mixtures

Product	Market Forms	Description	Examples of Use
Poppy seed	Whole	Tiny blue-black seeds with faint but distinctive flavor	Garnish for breads and rolls, buttered noodles; ground: in pastry fillings
Rosemary	Whole	Light-green leaves resembling pine needles	Lamb, braised meats and poultry, soups, tomato and meat sauces
Saffron	Whole (thread)	Red stigma of saffron crocus; gives bright-yellow color to foods; mild, distinctive flavor; very expensive	Should be steeped in hot liquid before use. Rice dishes, poultry, seafood, bouillabaisse, baked goods
Sage	Whole, rubbed (finer consistency than whole leaves), ground	Pungent gray-green herb with fuzzy leaves	Pork, poultry, stuffings, sausage, beans, tomatoes
Savory	Crushed leaves	Fragrant herb of mint family; summer savory is preferred to winter	Many meat, poultry, fish, egg, and vegetable dishes
Sesame seed	Whole (hulled or unhulled)	Small yellowish seed with nutlike taste; familiar hamburger bun garnish; high oil content	Bread and roll garnish
Sichuan peppercorn	Whole	Brown seed pod, usually partially opened; spicy, peppery flavor, but unrelated to black peppercorns	Spicy meat and poultry dishes
Star anise	Whole or broken	Dried, star-shaped seed pod, with an aniselike flavor (but unrelated to anise) but more aromatic	Braised Chinese dishes
Tarragon	Crushed leaves	Delicate green herb with flavor that is both minty and licoricelike	Béarnaise sauce, tarragon vinegar, chicken, fish, salads and dressings, eggs
Thyme	Crushed leaves, ground	Tiny brownish-green leaves; very aromatic	One of the most important and versatile of herbs; stocks, soups, sauces, meats, poultry, tomatoes
Turmeric	Ground	Intense yellow root of ginger family; mild but distinctive peppery flavor	A basic ingredient of curry powder; pickles, relishes, salads, eggs, rice

Basil

Chervil

Chives

1. *Salt* is the most important seasoning ingredient. Don't use too much. You can always add more, but you can't take it out.

2. *Pepper* comes in three forms: white, black, and green. All three are actually the same berry, but processed differently. (Black pepper is picked unripe; white is ripened and the hull is removed; green peppercorns are picked unripe and preserved before their color darkens.)

    • Whole and crushed *black pepper* is used primarily in seasoning and flavoring stocks and sauces and, sometimes, red meats. Ground black pepper is used in the dining room by the customer.

    • Ground *white pepper* is more important as a seasoning in the food service kitchen. Its flavor is slightly different from that of black pepper, and it blends well (in small quantities) with many foods. Its white color makes it visually undetectable in light-colored foods.

    • *Green peppercorns* are fairly expensive and are used in special recipes, primarily in luxury restaurants. The types packed in water, brine, or vinegar (those in water and in brine have better flavor) are soft. Wet-pack peppercorns are perishable. Water-packed peppercorns will keep only a few days in the refrigerator after they are opened, while the others will keep longer. Dried green peppercorns are also available.

3. *Red pepper* or *cayenne* is completely unrelated to black and white pepper. It belongs to the same family as paprika and fresh sweet bell peppers. Used in tiny

Garlic chives

Cilantro

Dill

Epazote

Regular ginger and green ginger

Lemon grass

amounts, it gives a spicy hotness to sauces and soups without actually altering the flavor. In larger amounts, it gives both heat and flavor to many spicy foods, such as those of Mexico and India.

4. *Lemon juice* is an important seasoning, particularly for enlivening the flavor of sauces and soups.

5. *Fresh herbs* are almost always superior to dried herbs. They should be used whenever cost and availability permit. Not long ago, the only fresh herbs generally available in many areas of North America were parsley, chives, and sometimes mint and dill. Now, however, most herbs are available fresh. The accompanying photos illustrate the most commonly used fresh herbs as well as some unusual fresh flavoring ingredients.

6. *Onion, garlic, shallots,* and other members of the onion family, as well as carrots and celery, are used as flavorings in virtually all stations of the kitchen and even in the bakeshop. Try to avoid the use of dried onion and garlic products, except as a component of spice blends. They have less flavor, and the fresh product is always available.

7. *Wine, brandy,* and other alcoholic beverages are used to flavor sauces, soups, and many entrées. Brandy should be boiled or flamed to eliminate the high percentage of alcohol, which would be unpleasant in the finished dish. Table wines usually need some cooking or reduction (either separately or with other ingredients) to produce the desired flavors. Fortified wines like sherry and Madeira, on the other hand, may be added as flavorings at the end of cooking.

Marjoram

8. *Prepared mustard* is a blend of ground mustard seed, vinegar, and other spices. It is used to flavor meats, sauces, and salad dressings and as a table condiment. For most cooking purposes, European styles such as Dijon (French) or Dusseldorf (German) work best, while the bright yellow American ballpark style is more appropriate as a table condiment than as a cooking ingredient. A coarse, grainy style is sometimes called for in specialty recipes.

9. Grated *lemon* and *orange rind* is used in sauces, meats, and poultry (as in duckling à l'orange) as well as in the bakeshop. Only the colored outer portion, called the *zest*, which contains the flavorful oils, is used. The white pith is bitter.

Mint

10. *MSG*, or *monosodium glutamate*, is a flavor enhancer widely used in Asian cooking. MSG doesn't actually change the flavor of foods but acts on the taste buds. It has a bad reputation for causing chest pains and headaches in some individuals.

Oregano

Tarragon

Sage

Parsley, curly

Thyme

Rosemary

Parsley, flat

USING HERBS AND SPICES

DEFINITIONS

Herbs are the leaves of certain plants that usually grow in temperate climates.

Spices are the buds, fruits, flowers, bark, seeds, and roots of plants and trees, many of which grow in tropical climates.

The distinction is often confusing, but it is not as important to know which flavorings are spices and which are herbs as it is to use them skillfully.

Guidelines for Using Herbs and Spices

1. Be familiar with each spice's aroma, flavor, and effect on food. Looking at a spice chart, including the one in this book, is no substitute for familiarity with the actual product.

2. Store dried herbs and spices in a cool place, tightly covered, in opaque containers. Heat, light, and moisture cause herbs and spices to deteriorate rapidly.

3. Don't use stale spices and herbs, and don't buy more than you can use in about six months. Whole spices keep longer than ground, but both lose much flavor after six months.

4. Be cautious after you have replaced old spices. The fresher products are more potent, so the amount you used before might now be too much.

5. Use good-quality spices and herbs. It doesn't pay to economize here. The difference in cost is only a fraction of a cent per portion.

6. Whole spices take longer to release flavors than ground spices, so allow for adequate cooking time.

7. Whole herbs and spices for flavoring a liquid are tied loosely in a piece of cheesecloth (called a sachet) for easy removal.

8. When in doubt, add less than you think you need. You can always add more, but it's hard to remove what you've already added.

9. Except in dishes like curry or chili, spices should not dominate. Often, they should not even be evident. If you can taste the nutmeg in the creamed spinach, there's probably too much nutmeg.

10. Herbs and spices added to uncooked foods such as salads and dressings need several hours for flavors to be released and blended.

11. Taste foods before serving, whenever possible. How else can you adjust the seasoning?

Table 4.1 is not a substitute for familiarity with the actual products. Eventually, you should be able to identify any spice on your shelf by aroma, taste, and appearance without looking at the label. The accompanying photos illustrate a number of whole spices.

Top row, left to right: black peppercorns, green peppercorns, pink peppercorns. Bottom row, left to right: white peppercorns, Sichuan peppercorns.

Top row, left to right: cloves, nutmeg, allspice, cinnamon sticks. Bottom row, left to right: juniper berries, cardamom, saffron, star anise.

Top row, left to right: celery seed, dill seed, coriander seed, caraway seed. Bottom row, left to right: fennel seed, cumin seed, anise seed.

■ TERMS FOR REVIEW

caramelization	infrared	bake	deglaze
gelatinization	microwave	barbecue	flavor profile
fiber	boil	smoke-roast	primary flavor
coagulation	simmer	broil	supporting flavor
denature	poach	grill	seasoning
Maillard reaction	blanch	griddle	flavoring
connective tissues	steam	pan-broil	volatile
smoke point	en papillote	sauté	herb
conduction	braise	pan-fry	spice
convection	stew	deep-fry	
radiation	roast	pressure fry	

■ QUESTIONS FOR DISCUSSION

1. Your broiler cook has just broiled a codfish fillet that turned out dry, rubbery, and shrunken. Explain what happened to it.

2. Why might adding some tomato product to a beef stew help make the meat more tender?

3. You are roasting a large quantity of ducklings and must use both your conventional ovens and your convection oven. You set all the ovens at the same temperature, but find the ducklings in the convection oven are done first. Why did this happen?

4. Arrange the following cooking methods in three groups, depending on whether they are moist-heat methods, dry-heat methods without fat, or dry-heat methods with fat: braising, roasting, deep-frying, sautéing, poaching, steaming, broiling, pressure frying, grilling, simmering.

5. What are some advantages of braising a pan of Swiss steaks in the oven instead of on the range?

6. A cook in your restaurant is roasting several pans of chickens. He thinks they are browning too fast, and he covers the pans with foil to keep the chickens from browning much more. What is wrong with this?

7. You are sautéing beef tenderloin tips for stroganoff, and you suddenly find that the meat is simmering in liquid rather than sautéing. What did you do wrong?

8. Your customers complain that your French fries are too greasy and soggy. How can you correct the problem?

9. Describe the difference between primary flavor and supporting flavor. Select a favorite recipe and explain the function of each ingredient, indicating which are primary flavors and which are secondary flavors.

10. What is meant by the phrase "adjust the seasoning"?

11. What is wrong with adding whole caraway seed to a portion of goulash just before serving?

5 Menus, Recipes, and Cost Management

A menu is a list of dishes served or available to be served at a meal. But a menu is also more than this. It is an important management tool. Nearly every aspect of the operation of a food service business depends on the menu. In fact, it is fair to say that the menu is the single most important document in the business. Purchasing, production, sales, cost accounting, labor management, even the kitchen layout and equipment selection of a new facility—all are based on the menu.

Recipes can be said to be the building blocks of the menu. Each item on the menu can be represented by the recipe or the procedure for preparing it. Therefore, recipes, like menus, are important management tools. They indicate ingredients to be purchased and stored, and they give measuring and preparation instructions to the kitchen staff.

In addition, recipes are important tools for the cook because they are a means of recording and passing along essential information. Learning to cook without being able to consult recipes would be like learning to play the piano without using written music.

This chapter discusses menus and recipes as they are used in commercial kitchens. How do we construct a menu that builds sales by offering the best choices to the customer and that also promotes efficiency and productivity? How do we read and understand recipes? How do we measure ingredients and portions, convert recipes to different yields, and calculate food cost with the aid of written recipes?

MENU FORMS AND FUNCTIONS

Menus must be planned for the people eating the food. This sounds like a simple rule, but it is frequently forgotten. You must never forget that the customer is the main reason for being in business.

This rule means that, in most operations, the taste and preferences of the cooks or chefs are of little importance when planning the menu. True, some of the most famous restaurants exist primarily as showcases for the chef's own artistry, but these are only a small percentage of all food service establishments. Instead, the taste and preferences of the clientele must be given top priority if the business is to succeed. The kind of clientele the business serves influences the form the menu takes.

THE CLIENTELE

Type of Institution

Each kind of operation has a different menu because each serves the needs of a different clientele.

> *Hotels* must provide a variety of services for their guests, from budget-minded tourists to businesspeople on expense accounts, from quick breakfast and sandwich counters to elegant dining rooms and banquet halls.
>
> *Hospitals* must satisfy the dietary needs of the patients.
>
> *Schools* must consider the ages of the students and their tastes and nutritional needs.
>
> *Employee food services* need menus that offer substantial but quickly served reasonably priced food for working customers.
>
> *Catering and banquet operations* depend on menus that are easily prepared for large numbers but that are lavish enough for parties and special occasions.
>
> *Fast-food and take-out quick-service operations* require limited menus featuring inexpensive, easily prepared, easily served foods for people in a hurry.
>
> *Full-service restaurants* range from simple neighborhood diners to expensive, elegant restaurants. Menus, of course, must be planned according to the customers' needs. Trying to institute a menu of high-priced, luxurious foods in a café situated in a working-class neighborhood will probably not succeed.

Customer Preferences

Even facilities with captive audiences, such as school cafeterias and hospital kitchens, must produce food that is appealing to their customers and in sufficient variety to keep them from getting bored with the same old things. Grumbling about the food is a favorite sport among students, but at least it can be kept to a minimum.

Restaurants have an even harder job because their customers don't just grumble if they don't like the selections. They don't come back. People are becoming more and more interested in trying unfamiliar foods, especially ethnic foods. Nevertheless, tastes vary by region, by neighborhood, by age group, and by social and ethnic background. Foods enjoyed by some people are completely rejected by others.

Prices must be kept in line with the customers' ability and willingness to pay. Prices, of course, place limits on what foods can be offered.

KIND OF MEAL

Menus vary not only by kind of operations but by meal as well.

Breakfast

Breakfast menus are fairly standard within any one country. In North America, for example, a restaurant has to offer the usual selection of fruits, juices, eggs, cereals, breads,

After reading this chapter, you should be able to

1. Explain how the makeup of a menu depends on the type of meal and on the institution using it.

2. Describe the differences between static and cycle menus, and between à la carte and table d'hôte menus.

3. List in order of their usual service the various courses that might appear in modern menus.

4. Devise balanced menus that contain an adequate variety of foods and that can be efficiently and economically prepared.

5. Describe the problems and limitations of written recipes and the importance of using judgment when you cook.

6. Discuss the structure and functions of standardized recipes.

7. Use and understand the recipes in this book to practice basic cooking techniques.

8. Measure ingredients and portions.

9. Use metric measurements.

10. Convert recipes to higher or lower yields.

11. Perform yield-cost analysis.

12. Calculate raw food costs.

pancakes, waffles, breakfast meats, and regional specialties because this is what customers want and expect. In addition, featuring one or two unusual items on the menu—such as an English muffin topped with creamed crabmeat and a poached egg, a special kind of country ham, or an assortment of freshly made fruit sauces or syrups for the pancakes and waffles—often attracts additional customers. Breakfast menus must feature foods that can be prepared quickly and can be eaten in a hurry.

Lunch

The following factors are important to consider when planning lunch menus.

1. **Speed.**
   Like breakfast customers, luncheon diners are usually in a hurry. They are generally working people who have a limited time to eat. Foods must be prepared quickly and be easy to serve and eat. Sandwiches, soups, and salads are important items on many lunch menus.

2. **Simplicity.**
   Menu selections are fewer, and fewer courses are served. In many cases, customers select only one course. Luncheon specials—combinations of two or three items, such as soup and a sandwich or omelet and salad, offered at a single price—satisfy the need for simplicity and speed.

3. **Variety.**
   In spite of the shortness of the menu and the simplicity of the selections, luncheon menus must have variety. This is because many customers eat at the same restaurant several times a week or even every day. In order to keep the menu short, many operations offer several luncheon specials every day, so there is always something new on the menu.

Dinner

Dinner is usually the main meal and is eaten in a more leisurely fashion than either breakfast or lunch. Of course, some people are in a hurry in the evening, too, but, in general, people come to a restaurant to relax over a substantial meal. Dinner menus offer more selections and more courses. Not surprisingly, prices and check averages are also higher than at lunch.

TYPES OF MENUS

Static and Cycle Menus

A static menu is one that offers the same dishes every day. These menus are used in restaurants and other establishments where the clientele changes daily or where enough items are listed on the menu to offer sufficient variety. A static menu may be in place indefinitely, or it may change at regular intervals, such as every season, every month, or even every week.

Some restaurants use a menu that is part static and part variable. This means they have a basic menu of foods prepared every day, plus daily specials to offer variety without putting too much strain on the kitchen. The daily specials may take advantage of seasonal produce and other occasionally available foods the chef or purchaser finds in the wholesale market.

A cycle menu is one that changes every day for a certain period; after this period, the daily menus repeat in the same order. For example, a seven-day cycle menu has a different menu every day for a week and repeats each week. This kind of menu is used in such operations as schools and hospitals, where the number of choices must be kept small. The cycle menu is a way of offering variety.

À la Carte and Table d'Hôte

An à la carte menu (Figure 5.1) is one in which each individual item is listed separately, with its own price. The customer makes selections from the various courses and side dishes to make up a meal. (Note: The term *à la carte* is also used to refer to cooking to order, as opposed to cooking ahead in large batches.)

Appetizers

SOUP OF THE DAY
MARKET

PIADINA SERVED WITH ROASTED FRUIT, SAGE HONEY AND ARTISAN BLUE CHEESE
$10.50

BISTRO HOUSE SALAD WITH BABY GREENS, BALSAMIC VINAIGRETTE AND MANCHEGO
$7.00

STAR PRAIRIE SMOKED TROUT SALAD WITH BIBB LETTUCE AND
WARM HORSERADISH/CREME FRAICHE DRESSING
$10.50

CLASSIC CAESAR SALAD WITH BABY ROMAINE, PARMESAN AND SEMOLINA CROUTONS
$6.50
WITH OIL-PACKED SPANISH ANCHOVIES ADD $2

SASHIMI OF TUNA SERVED ON BABY ARUGULA, PICKLED PINEAPPLE AND FRESH MINT
$12.50

BISTRO CALAMARI WITH THAI DIPPING SAUCE
$8.00

JP'S RUSTIC PIZZA WITH APPLEWOOD SMOKED BACON,
CASHEW/CURRANT PESTO AND PECORINO-ROMANO
$11.00

PIZZA WITH SAN MARZANO TOMATO SAUCE, BASIL AND HOUSE-MADE MOZZARELLA
$10.50

PIZZA OF THE DAY
MARKET

SEARED MINNESOTA FOIE GRAS SERVED WITH CARAMELIZED SHALLOTS AND QUINCE CONFIT
$15.00

SIDES

YUKON GOLD POTATO PURÉE $4.50 OR STEAMED JASMINE RICE $3.50

POMMES FRITES WITH SMOKED PAPRIKA OR VEGETABLE OF THE DAY
$4.50

BOWL OF OLIVES
$3.50

SPLIT PLATE CHARGE $1.00

Entrées

HOUSE-MADE FETTUCINI TOSSED WITH CHICKEN CONFIT,
ORGANIC BROCCOLI, HARISSA AND PARMESAN
$18.50

POTATO GNOCCHI WITH ORGANIC GREEN BEANS,
TOASTED HAZELNUT CREME FRAICHE, AND CHIVE OIL
$17.50

CARNAROLI RISOTTO WITH WILD MUSHROOMS, SWEET ONIONS AND GREMOLATA
$22.50

PAN-SEARED GROUPER SERVED ON YUKON GOLD POTATO PURÉE WITH
BROWN BUTTER SPINACH AND BLOOD ORANGE RELISH
$27.50

WILD ACRES DUCK CONFIT RAVIOLI TOSSED WITH AN APPLE CIDER
DEMI-GLACE, SHAVED APPLE AND FRIED SAGE
$19.50

SEARED RIB-EYE RUBBED WITH GREEN THAI CURRY AND SERVED WITH
HOUSE-PICKLED PINEAPPLE, JICAMA AND RED ONION SALAD
$28.50

PAN-ROASTED VENISON STEAK ON YUKON GOLD POTATO PURÉE WITH
ROASTED BRUSSEL SPROUTS AND A CRANBERRY RED WINE REDUCTION
$32.50

BONE-IN PORK TENDERLOIN BRAISED WITH APPLE, ONION AND SWEET CURRY,
SERVED WITH GOLDEN RAISIN-RED BELL PEPPER RELISH
$24.50

SLOW-ROASTED DUCK BREAST AND CONFIT OF DUCK LEG WITH
SPINACH/MANGO SALAD AND ORANGE-MISO VINAIGRETTE
$28.50

ENTRÉE OF THE DAY
MARKET

Figure 5.1
An example of an à la carte menu from a fine-dining restaurant.
Courtesy of JP American Bistro, Minneapolis, MN

Table d'hôte (tobble dote) originally meant a fixed menu with no choices—like a meal you would be served if you were invited to someone's home for dinner. Banquet menus are familiar examples of this kind of menu. The term has also come to mean a menu that offers a selection of complete meals at set prices. In other words, a customer may choose from among several selections, each of which includes an entrée and side dishes plus other courses, such as appetizer, salad, and dessert. Each full meal selection has a single package price.

Many restaurants use a combination of à la carte and table d'hôte selections. For example, a steak house may include salad, potato, vegetable, and beverage with the entrée choice, while additional dishes like appetizers and desserts may be offered at extra cost.

Closely related to the table d'hôte menu is the **prix fixe** (pree fix), meaning "fixed price," menu. On a pure prix fixe menu, only one price is given. Each guest may choose one selection from each course offered, and the total meal costs the single price indicated. Often, on such menus, a few items featuring costly ingredients carry an extra charge, called a *supplement*. The supplement is usually indicated in parentheses after the listing. It is best to limit the number of supplements as much as possible. Too many extra charges on a prix fixe menu can leave customers frustrated and angry.

A special variety of the prix fixe menu sometimes used in fine restaurants is the **tasting menu**, also known by its French name, *menu dégustation*. A tasting menu (Figure 5.2) is offered in addition to the regular menu and gives patrons a chance to try a larger number of the chef's creations. The menu may feature 5 or 6 or even as many as 10 or 12 individual courses served in small portions. Because of the complexity of service, a restaurant may require that the tasting menu can be served only if everyone at the table orders it. Tasting menus may change daily, depending on the chef's choices and the availability of ingredients.

BUILDING THE MENU

A **course** is a food or group of foods served at one time or intended to be eaten at the same time. In a restaurant, the courses are normally served in sequence, allowing enough time for each to be eaten before the next is served. In a cafeteria, the customers may select all their courses at once—appetizer, salad, main dish and vegetables, and dessert, for example—but eat them in a particular order.

In the following pages, we discuss the principles that apply to planning the courses that make up a menu. The main purpose of these principles is to lend variety and interest to a meal. They are not arbitrary rules you must follow for no reason.

THE CLASSICAL MENU

Today's menus are descendants of elaborate banquet menus served in the nineteenth and early twentieth centuries. These menus had 12 or more courses, and the sequence in which they were served was well established by tradition.

The following sequence of courses is typical of one that may have been served at a great banquet early in the twentieth century.

1. **Cold hors d'oeuvre**
   small, savory appetizers

2. **Soup**
   clear soup, thick soup, or broth

3. **Hot hors d'oeuvre**
   small, hot appetizers

4. **Fish**
   any seafood item

5. **Main course or pièce de resistance**
   a large cut of roasted or braised meat, usually beef, lamb, or venison, with elaborate vegetable garnishes

6. **Hot entrée**
   individual portions of meat or poultry, broiled, braised, or pan-fried, etc.

7. **Cold entrée**
   cold meats, poultry, fish, pâté, and so on

8. **Sorbet**
   a light ice or sherbet, sometimes made of wine, to refresh the appetite before the next course

9. **Roast**
   usually roasted poultry, accompanied by or followed by a salad

10. **Vegetable**
    usually a special vegetable preparation, such as artichokes or asparagus, or a more unusual vegetable such as cardoons

11. **Sweet**
    what we call *dessert*—cakes and tarts, pudding, soufflés, etc.

12. **Dessert**
    fruit and cheese and, sometimes, small cookies or petits fours

Figure 5.2
An example of two tasting menus from a fine-dining restaurant
Gramercy Tavern, New York, NY

MODERN MENUS: COURSES AND ARRANGEMENT

Such extensive classical menus are rarely served today. Even grand, elegant banquets comprising many courses are usually shorter than the menu we just described. However, if you study that menu, you will be able to see the basic pattern of modern menus hiding amid all those courses.

The main dish is the centerpiece of the modern meal. If the meal consists of only one dish, it is considered the main course, even if it is a salad or a bowl of soup. There is usually only one main course, although large banquets may still have more than one, such as a poultry dish followed by a meat dish.

One or more dishes may be served before the main dish. These are usually light in character so the customer is not satiated before the main course.

Study the following outline of the modern menu and compare it to the classical menu. The notes that follow explain several aspects that may be puzzling. Then, in the next sections, we discuss how to select specific dishes for each course to arrive at a balanced menu.

The Modern Menu

First courses	Appetizer
	Soup
	(Fish)
	Salad
Main dish	Meat, poultry, or fish
	Vegetable accompaniment
Dessert dishes	Salad
	Fruits and cheeses
	Sweets

Notes

- Appetizer, soup, and salad are the three courses usually served before the main course. One, two, or all three of them may be served, and they are usually served in this order. Thus, meals may have the following courses:

Appetizer	Soup	Salad
Main dish	Main dish	Main dish

Appetizer	Soup	Appetizer
Soup	Salad	Salad
Main dish	Main dish	Main dish

Appetizer
Soup
Salad
Main dish

- A fish course is sometimes included in more formal dinners, after appetizer and soup courses. It should be a relatively small portion, and the main dish should not also be fish.

- Salads may be served either before or after the main course (but not both). In more traditional meals, they are served after the main course to refresh the appetite before the cheese and sweet courses. Serving the salad before the main course is a comparatively recent development.

- Sometimes, one or more of the first courses are served at the same time as the main dish, possibly on the same plate. This is especially popular on luncheon menus, where quick service is desired. Thus, you will find soup and sandwich combinations, salad and omelet combinations, and so on.

- If both cheese and sweets are served for dessert, they may come in either order. English menus have cheese after the sweets, while French menus generally place the sweets last.

VARIETY AND BALANCE

Balancing a menu means providing enough variety and contrast for the meal to hold interest from the first course to the last. To balance a menu, you must develop a feeling for which foods complement each other or provide pleasing contrasts. And you must avoid repeating flavors and textures as much as possible.

These principles apply whether you are planning a banquet menu, where the diners have no choices; a school cafeteria menu, where students have only a few choices; or a large à la carte menu, where customers have many choices.

Of course, with an à la carte menu, the customers' own choices determine how balanced their meals are. There's nothing wrong with listing a creamed dish among the appetizers and another creamed dish among the main dishes. But you should offer enough choices so customers can easily select balanced meals if they desire. In other words, if half the appetizers and half the entrée selections are served in a cream sauce, you're not offering enough variety.

The following factors must be considered in balancing a menu.

1. **Flavors.**
   Don't repeat foods with the same or similar tastes. This applies to any predominant flavor, whether of the main ingredient, of the spices, of the sauce, and so on. For example:

   • Don't serve broiled tomato halves with the main dish if the appetizer has a tomato sauce.

   • Don't serve both a spicy, garlicky appetizer and a spicy, garlicky main dish. On the other hand, don't make everything too bland.

   • Unless you operate a specialty restaurant like a steak house or a seafood restaurant, balance the menu among meats (beef, pork, lamb, veal), poultry, and fish.

   • Acid or tart foods are often served as accompaniments to fatty foods because they help cut the fatty taste. This is why applesauce and pork, mint sauce and lamb, and orange sauce and duckling are such classic combinations.

2. **Textures.**
   Texture refers to the softness or firmness of foods, their feel in the mouth, whether or not they are served with sauces, and so on. Don't repeat foods with the same or similar texture. For example:

   • Serve a clear soup instead of a thick soup if the main course is served with a cream sauce. On the other hand, a cream soup goes well before a simple sautéed or broiled item.

   • Don't serve too many mashed or puréed foods unless you are running a baby-food restaurant.

   • Don't serve too many heavy, starchy items.

3. **Appearance.**
   Serve foods with a variety of colors and shapes. Colorful vegetables are especially valuable for livening up the appearance of meats, poultry, fish, and starches, which tend to be mostly white or brown. (Creating attractive food is discussed in Chapter 28.)

4. **Nutrients.**
   The importance of a nutritionally balanced menu is obvious in the case of menus for hospitals and nursing homes, for example. But even à la carte menus in restaurants should provide enough nutritional variety to allow customers to select nutritionally balanced meals. Dietary health and nutrition are considered in detail in Chapter 6.

   There are so many possible combinations of foods that it is impossible to give rules that cover all of them. Besides, creative chefs are continually experimenting with new combinations, breaking old rules, and coming up with exciting menus. Years of experience, however, are required to develop this kind of creativity and a feel for what makes certain combinations work. In the meantime, pay close attention to the principles discussed.

KITCHEN CAPABILITIES AND AVAILABILITY OF FOODS

Physical conditions place limitations on your menu. Depending on your equipment, your labor force, and the foods available to you, certain items will be inconvenient, difficult, or even impossible to serve.

Equipment Limitations

Know the capacities of your equipment and plan menus accordingly. If your broiler capacity is 200 steaks an hour and you plan a banquet menu for 400 people that features broiled shrimp as an appetizer and broiled steaks as a main course, you're in big trouble.

Spread the workload evenly among your equipment. If you have ovens, a broiler, and a fryer, balance the roasted and braised items, the broiled items, and the fried items. Don't let the broiler stand idle while orders are backed up at the deep fryer. Also, using a variety of cooking methods adds variety of taste and texture to the menu.

Personnel Limitations

Spread the workload evenly among the workers. As with equipment, you don't want the fry cook to have more than he or she can handle, while the broiler cook has little to do.

Spread the workload throughout the day. Balance the cooked-to-order items against the cooked-ahead items so you don't have to do everything at the last minute.

Offer items the cooks are able to prepare. Don't put items on the menu that are above the skill level of the staff.

Availability of Foods

Use foods in season. Foods out of season are expensive and often low in quality, and their supply is undependable. Don't put asparagus on the menu if you can't get good asparagus.

Use locally available foods. Fresh seafood is an obvious example of a food that is hard to get in some regions unless you—and your customers—are willing to pay premium prices.

MENUS AND COST CONTROL

Food costs are a major part of the expenses of any food service operation. You can't afford to throw away food any more than you can afford to throw away money. Total utilization of foods must be planned into menus. Whether or not this is done can make or break an operation.

Cost control requires not only planning but also careful arithmetic. See pages 107–112 for a discussion of kitchen mathematics as well as other factors in cost control, including the role of the menu.

MENU TERMINOLOGY AND ACCURACY

After you have selected the items you want to include on your menu, you are then faced with the problem of what to call them. Decades ago, when the classical cuisine of Escoffier was the normal offering in fine restaurants, a standard terminology existed. Everyone knew what was meant by Tournedos Chasseur, Suprême de Volaille Orly, and Sole Nantua, and these terms meant the same dish on any menu. Today, however, there is little standardization. Chefs feel obliged to give as much information on their menus as possible in order to describe their dishes adequately to their customers. As a result, one often sees menu descriptions that list almost every ingredient in a dish, including what farms the ingredients came from.

It is probably better to give too much information than too little. The important thing is to provide enough information so the customer will understand the basic character of the dish and not have any unpleasant surprises. An alternative to writing everything out on the menu is to educate the serving staff so they know the dishes well enough to fill in any missing details for the customer.

The menu is a sales tool, so it is understandable to try to make every dish sound as appealing as possible. Accurate and truthful descriptions, however, are required. Giving misleading names to menu items is not only dishonest and unfair to the customer, it is actually illegal in some localities that have adopted truth-in-menu laws, and you can be prosecuted for fraud. Furthermore, customers who feel confused or cheated may not come back.

Calling something chicken salad if it is made with turkey, veal cutlet if it is made with pork, or whipped cream if it is actually artificial whipped topping is such obvious mislabeling that it can hardly be accidental. However, some kinds of menu inaccuracies result not from intentional deception but from simple misunderstanding. In particular, look out for these types of labeling problems:

1. **Point of origin.**
   If your menu lists "Maine lobsters," they must be from Maine. Roquefort dressing must be made with Roquefort cheese from Roquefort, France. Idaho potatoes must be from Idaho. On the other hand, generally accepted names or names that indicate type rather than origin can be used. For example: Swiss cheese, French bread, Swedish meatballs.

2. **Grade or quality.**

    U.S. Choice and Canada A are names of grades, and you'd better be using those grades if you say you are. Incidentally, the word *prime* in "prime rib" indicates a cut, not a grade. But if you say "U.S. Prime Rib," you are talking about a grade.

3. **Cooking method.**

    A menu item described as "grilled" or "roasted" should be cooked by the method indicated. Billing a pan-fried item as "roasted" because it sounds better on the menu misrepresents the item and risks disappointing the customer.

4. **"Fresh."**

    If you call something fresh, it must be fresh, not frozen, canned, or dried. There is no such thing as "fresh frozen."

5. **"Imported."**

    An item labeled imported must come from outside the country.

6. **"Homemade."**

    The word homemade means the item was made on the premises. Adding a few fresh carrots to canned vegetable soup does not make it homemade.

7. **"Organic."**

    For a food to be labeled organic, it must be raised without the use of hormones, antibiotics, synthetic pesticides, irradiated components, genetically modified organisms, or reprocessed sewage. In some countries, including the United States, the use of the word *organic* on labels is defined by law (p. 512).

8. **Size or portion.**

    If you indicate a portion size on the menu, be sure you serve that size (within allowable tolerances). A "10-ounce steak" must weigh at least 10 ounces before cooking (9½ ounces would be within allowable tolerance). "Jumbo shrimp" are not just big shrimp. They are a specific size.

    Here are other examples of common violations:

    Listing "maple syrup" and serving maple-flavored syrup.

    Listing a product, such as a carbonated beverage, by brand name and serving another brand.

    Listing "butter" and serving margarine.

    Listing coffee or breakfast cereal "with cream" and serving milk.

    Listing "ground round" and serving other ground beef.

    Finally, please use a dictionary. Unfortunately, it is common to see menus full of misspellings. These errors reflect poorly on the restaurant. Customers may think that if you don't care enough even to spell words on the menu correctly, you may not care enough to cook the food correctly either.

THE WRITTEN RECIPE

A recipe is a set of instructions for producing a certain dish. In order to duplicate a desired preparation, it is necessary to have a precise record of the ingredients, their amounts, and the way in which they are combined and cooked. This is the purpose of a recipe.

In spite of their importance, written recipes have many limitations. No matter how detailed a recipe may be, it assumes you already have certain knowledge—that you understand the terminology it uses, for example, and that you know how to measure ingredients.

THE USES AND LIMITATIONS OF RECIPES

Many people believe that learning to cook means simply learning recipes. Knowledgeable cooks, on the other hand, are able to prepare food without written recipes, if they have to, because they have a good understanding of basic principles and techniques. A recipe is a way of applying basic techniques to specific ingredients.

If you have read Chapter 4, or have even casually leafed through this book, you know it is not just a book of recipes. Although there are hundreds of recipes in this book, they take up a relatively small part of it. Your main concern is learning techniques and procedures you can apply to any recipe.

The main purpose of learning basic cooking principles is not to be able to cook without recipes, however, but to understand the recipes you use. As we said in the beginning of this chapter, every recipe assumes you have certain knowledge that enables you to understand the instructions and follow them correctly.

Some recipes supply very little information, and some supply a great deal. But no matter how detailed it is, a written recipe can't tell you everything, and some judgment by the cook is always required. There are several reasons for this:

1. **Food products are not uniform.**
    Food ingredients are natural products, so they are not uniform like machine bolts, ballpoint pens, and typing paper. One tomato may be riper than another, one carrot more tender or sweeter than another, one oyster saltier than another. Such variations may affect how the ingredients are handled, how long they are cooked, what proportions are needed, and how much seasoning is required.

2. **Kitchens do not have the same equipment.**
    Different pans distribute heat at different rates. Different broilers heat to different temperatures. Liquid evaporates from wide pots faster than from tall, narrow ones, and so on.

3. **It is impossible to give exact instructions for many processes.**
    How do you set the burner if the instructions say "Cook over medium heat"? How thick is a "thick" sauce? How long do you broil a rare steak?

The difference between an experienced cook and a beginning cook is the ability to make judgments about these variables.

STANDARDIZED RECIPES

1. **Definition.**
    A **standardized recipe** is a set of instructions describing the way a particular establishment prepares a particular dish. In other words, it is a customized recipe developed by an operation for the use of its own cooks, using its own equipment, to be served to its own patrons.

2. **The structure of a standardized recipe.**
    Recipe formats differ from operation to operation, but nearly all of them try to include as much precise information as possible. The following details may be listed:

    *   Name of the recipe.
    *   Yield, including total yield, number of portions, and portion size.
    *   Ingredients and exact amounts, listed in order of use.
    *   Equipment needed, including measuring equipment, pan sizes, portioning equipment, and so on.
    *   Directions for preparing the dish. Directions are kept as simple as possible.
    *   Preparation and cooking times.
    *   Directions for portioning, plating, and garnishing.
    *   Directions for breaking down the station, cleaning up, and storing leftovers.

3. **The function of standardized recipes.**
    An operation's own recipes are used to control production. They do this in two ways:

    *   They control quality. Standardized recipes are detailed and specific. This is to ensure that the product is the same every time it is made and served, no matter who cooks it.
    *   They control quantity. First, they indicate precise quantities for every ingredient and how they are to be measured. Second, they indicate exact yields and portion sizes, and how the portions are to be measured and served.

4. **The limitations of standardized recipes.**
Standardized recipes have the same problems as all recipes—the problems we discussed earlier regarding variations in foods, equipment, and vagueness of instructions. These problems can be reduced by writing the recipe carefully, but they cannot be eliminated. Even if an operation uses good standardized recipes, a new employee making a dish for the first time will usually require supervision to make sure he or she interprets the instructions the same way as the rest of the staff. These limitations don't invalidate standardized recipes. If anything, they make exact directions even more important. But they do mean that experience and knowledge are still very important.

Table 5.1 gives an example of a standardized recipe based on a recipe in this book. Compare and note the differences between this recipe and the recipe on page 397, an instructional recipe (explained in the following section). In particular, note the following differences:

- There are no metric units. Because this recipe is designed for a single kitchen in the United States, only one set of measurements is needed.

- The procedure appears below the ingredients rather than in a column to the right. An operation can choose any recipe format, but the operation using this recipe wants to emphasize collecting and measuring all ingredients before beginning to cook.

- The recipe includes Critical Control Points. The operation using this recipe has established a HACCP system. Food safety instructions are included as part of the standardized recipe. (Read or review the section on HACCP, pp. 33–34, if necessary.)

INSTRUCTIONAL RECIPES

The recipes in this book are *not* standardized recipes. Remember that a standardized recipe is custom-made for a particular operation. The recipes in this book are obviously not.

The purpose of a standardized recipe is to direct and control the production of a particular food item. Directions must be as complete and exact as possible.

The purpose of the instructional recipes in this book is to teach basic cooking techniques. They provide an opportunity for you to practice, with specific ingredients, the general procedures you have learned.

If you glance at any of the recipes in this book, you will see that they do not contain all the features of a standardized recipe, as described in the previous section. In particular, you will see the following differences:

1. **Instructions for preparation.**
In most cases, recipes in this book follow a discussion of a basic procedure. The recipes are examples of the general procedure, and they give you experience in applying what you have learned. The information you are given in the recipe instructions is intended primarily to encourage you to think and to learn a technique, not just to turn out a product. You should consult your instructor when you have a question about a procedure.

2. **Variations and optional ingredients.**
Many recipes are followed by variations. These are actually whole recipes given in abbreviated terms. It is possible to write them out as separate, full-length recipes. (You are encouraged to do this before preparing a variation, as a learning experience.)

Giving recipes as variations rather than as separate recipes encourages you to see the patterns behind each. Again, you are learning techniques, not just recipes. You develop a lot more understanding of what you are doing if you see Spanish rice and Turkish pilaf, for example, or coconut cream pie and chocolate pudding as variations of the same basic techniques rather than as separate, unrelated recipes.

Your instructors may have their own variations, or they may wish to make changes in the basic recipes in order to teach you certain points. Unlike standardized recipes, instructional recipes are not engraved in stone.

Table 5.1
Chicken Breasts Parmesan

Portion size: 1 chicken breast, 4 oz   Total yield: 12 portions

Quantity	Ingredients	Equipment
4 oz	Flour	2 half-size hotel pans
1¼ tsp	Salt	one 2-qt stainless-steel bowl
½ tsp	Ground white pepper	1 wire whip
5	Whole eggs, size large	1 meat mallet
3½ oz	Grated parmesan cheese	four 12-in. sauté pans
1½ oz	Whole milk	1-oz ladle
12	Boneless, skinless chicken breasts, 4 oz each	tongs
4 oz	Clarified butter	plastic wrap
		instant-read thermometer, sanitized

■ P r o c e d u r e

Advance Prep:

CCP   1.   Collect and measure all ingredients. *Refrigerate eggs, cheese, milk, and chicken at 40°F or lower until needed.*

2.   Collect all equipment.

3.   Place the flour in the hotel pan. Season with the salt and white pepper.

4.   Break the eggs into the stainless-steel bowl and discard the shells. Beat with the wire whip until foamy. Add the grated cheese and milk. Mix in with the whip.

CCP   5.   *Cover the bowl with plastic wrap and refrigerate at below 40°F until needed.*

6.   Flatten the chicken breasts lightly with the meat mallet until ½ in. thick. Place the breasts in a hotel pan.

CCP   *Cover with plastic wrap. Refrigerate at below 40°F until ready to cook.*

CCP   7.   *Clean and sanitize the mallet and the work surface. Wash hands thoroughly.*

Cooking:

8.   Place one of the sauté pans over moderate heat. Allow to heat 2 minutes.

9.   Measure 1 oz clarified butter into the pan.

CCP   10.   One at a time, dip 3 chicken breasts in the seasoned flour until completely coated on both sides. Shake off excess. Dip in the egg mixture. Coat both sides completely. *Return remaining chicken and egg mixture to refrigerator.*

CCP   11.   Place the 3 breasts in the sauté pan. *Wash hands after handling the raw chicken and before handling cooked food.*

CCP   12.   Cook the chicken over moderate heat until golden brown on the bottom. Using the tongs, turn over and continue to cook *until the chicken reaches an internal temperature of 165°–170°F. Test internal temperature with sanitized instant-read thermometer.*

CCP   13.   Repeat with the remaining chicken breasts, using clean sauté pans. *If your work is interrupted before completion, cover and refrigerate chicken and egg mixture.*

CCP   14.   *If the chicken is not served immediately, hold in a heated holding cabinet to maintain internal temperature of 145°F.*

CCP   15.   *Discard leftover egg mixture and seasoned flour. Do not use for any other products. Clean and sanitize all equipment.*

COOKING WITH JUDGMENT

When you make a recipe for the first time, you should apply your knowledge and thinking about the recipe in relation to the skills you have. In particular, you should determine the following points:

1.   **What are the basic cooking methods?**
When you read the recipe for Sauerbraten (p. 345), you will quickly figure out that the cooking method used is braising (even if the word *braise* is never used in the recipe). Then you should review in your mind everything you know about basic braising procedures.

2.   **What are the characteristics of the ingredients?**
If the sauerbraten recipe calls for bottom round of beef, for example, you should ask yourself, "What do I know about bottom round? Is it lean or fatty? Tough or tender? How do these traits affect cooking?"

3. **What are the functions of the ingredients?**

What does the vinegar do in the sauerbraten recipe? What about the vegetables? The gingersnaps?

When you have gained more experience, you will be able to easily answer these questions. You will know what ingredients contribute to flavor, to texture, or to body, and how they do it.

4. **What are the cooking times?**

Most of the recipes in this book do not give cooking times, except as general guidelines to help you plan production. This is because cooking times are too variable to be stated exactly.

Instead, you will learn how to test for doneness by observing changes in the product. You must be able to judge when a product has reached the right temperature, the proper texture or consistency, or the desired taste.

When you learn to cook with judgment, you will be able to cook with most recipes, even poorly written ones. You will be able to see what might be wrong with a new recipe before you try it and to make adjustments in it. You will know how to substitute ingredients or use different equipment. You will even be able to create new recipes.

Remember we said that some recipes supply very little information and depend largely on the cook's knowledge. With enough experience, you will even be able to cook from recipes like the following, a complete recipe for Fillets of Sole Bercy, quoted in its entirety from *Le Répertoire de la Cuisine*, a favorite book used by chefs in classical French cooking: "Poached with shallots and chopped parsley, white wine and fish stock. Reduce the stock, add butter, and coat the fish, glaze."

MEASUREMENT

Many restaurants budget a profit of 10 percent or less. This means that a sandwich selling for $3.00 makes a profit of only 30 cents. If the cook happens to put a half-ounce too much meat in the sandwich, the operation is probably losing money on it. No wonder so many restaurants go out of business.

Careful measurement is one of the most important parts of food production. It is important for consistent quality each time a recipe is prepared and served. And it is important for cost controls.

There are two important kinds of measurement in the kitchen:

1. Ingredient measurement
2. Portion measurement, or portion control

INGREDIENT MEASUREMENT

Weight

Weighing is the most accurate method of measuring ingredients. It is the method used for most solid ingredients.

Accurate scales are necessary for weighing. Small portion scales are often used in the kitchen because of their convenience. Balance scales are used in the bakeshop (see p. 893 for procedure).

Procedure for Weighing Ingredients on a Portion Scale

1. Place receiving container, if any, on the scale.
2. Set the scale so that it reads zero.
3. Add the item being weighed to the container (or place on scale, if no container is used) until the scale reads desired weight.

To be able to weigh ingredients, you must observe the difference between AP (as purchased) weight and EP (edible portion) weight.

AP weight is the weight of the item as purchased, before any trimming is done.

EP weight is the weight after all inedible or nonservable parts are trimmed off.

Recipes sometimes specify which weight they are referring to. When they don't, you must judge from the instructions.

1. If a recipe calls for "2 lb potatoes" and the first instruction is "scrub, peel, and eye the potatoes," then you know that AP weight is called for.

2. If the recipe calls for "2 lb peeled, diced potatoes," then you know that EP weight is called for. You will need more than 2 lb AP.

Volume

Volume measures are used for liquids. Measuring a liquid by volume is usually faster than weighing it, and accuracy is good.

Solid ingredients are usually not measured by volume because they cannot usually be measured accurately by this method. One pint of chopped onions will vary considerably in weight, depending on how large or small the onions are cut and whether the volume measure is filled loosely or packed.

Dry ingredients such as flour or sugar are usually weighed in the bakeshop. However, they are sometimes measured by volume in the kitchen, when speed is more important than accuracy. To measure dry ingredients by volume, fill a dry-volume measure until the ingredient is mounded over the top. Then level it off with a spatula or other straightedge.

Very small quantities, such as ¼ teaspoon salt, are measured by volume when the amount is too small to weigh.

Count

Measuring ingredients by count is done in these circumstances:

1. When units are in fairly standard sizes. *Examples*: 6 large eggs for a pancake batter; 8 parsley stems for a stock.

2. When serving portions are determined by numbers of units. *Examples*: 1 baked apple per portion; 6 fried shrimp per portion.

PORTION CONTROL

Portion control is the measurement of portions to ensure that the correct amount of an item is served. In order for portion control to be carried out, cooks and service personnel must be aware of proper portion sizes. These facts are usually indicated on the house recipes and on the working menu used in the kitchen and service area.

Portion Control in Preparation

Portion control actually begins with the measuring of ingredients. If this is not done correctly, then the yield of the recipe will be thrown off.

When portions are determined by count—1 hamburger patty, 2 tomato slices, 1 wedge of pie—then the units must be measured or cut according to instructions: 4 ounces of meat per patty; ¼-inch slices of "5 x 6" tomatoes; 8 equal edges per pie.

Portion Control in Plating and Service

Portioning for service may be done by the cook, as in a short-order restaurant, or by the service personnel, as in a cafeteria. The following tools and techniques are used.

1. **Count.**
   Examples: 1 slice of ham per order; 5 shrimp per order. This is accurate if cutting and other prep work have been done correctly.

2. **Weight.**
   Example: 4 ounces of sliced ham per order. A portion scale must be at the serving station for this method of portion control.

3. **Volume.**
   Ladles, scoops, and kitchen spoons come in standard sizes and are used for portioning. The exact size of the ladle or scoop must be determined in advance and indicated on service instructions.

   Kitchen spoons, either solid or perforated, are not as accurate for portioning but are often used for convenience and speed. You must be able to judge by eye how full to fill the spoon (rounded, heaped, etc.). Check a spoonful on a portion scale from time to time to make sure you are being consistent.

4. **Even division.**
   Examples: cutting a pie into 8 equal wedges; cutting a pan of lasagne 4 by 6 to make 24 equal portions.

5. **Standard fill.**
   Standard-size dishes, cups, or glasses are filled to a given level, as judged by eye. Example: a glass of orange juice. This is actually a form of volume measure.

UNITS OF MEASURE

The system of measurement used in the United States is complicated. Even when people have used the system all their lives, they still sometimes have trouble remembering things like how many fluid ounces are in a quart or how many feet are in a mile.

Table 5.2 lists abbreviations used in this book. Table 5.3 lists equivalents among the units of measure used in the kitchen. You should memorize these thoroughly so you don't have to lose time making simple calculations.

THE METRIC SYSTEM

The United States is the only major country that uses the complex system of measurement we have just described. In Canada, this system is also used, at least part of the time, although the metric system has been introduced. Other countries use a much simpler system called the **metric system**. It is possible that someday the metric system may be used in U.S. kitchens. Even if this never happens, it is useful, in this age of international influences on cooking, to be able to read and use recipes from around the world. So it is a good idea to become familiar with the metric system.

Basic Units

In the metric system, there is one basic unit for each type of measurement:

> The **gram** is the basic unit of weight.
>
> The **liter** is the basic unit of volume.
>
> The **meter** is the basic unit of length.
>
> The **degree Celsius** is the basic unit of temperature.

Larger or smaller units are made simply by multiplying or dividing by 10, 100, 1000, and so on. These divisions are expressed by *prefixes*. The ones you will need to know are:

> **kilo-** (kill-o) = 1,000
>
> **deci-** (dess-i) = 1/10
>
> **centi-** (sent-i) = 1/100
>
> **milli-** (mill-i) = 1/1,000

Once you know these basic units, there is no longer any need for complicated tables like Table 5.3. Table 5.4 summarizes the metric units you will need to know in the kitchen. (Note: The prefix deci- is rarely used in Canada, although the deciliter is a regularly used unit of volume in Europe.)

Converting to Metric

Most people think that the metric system is much harder to learn than it really is. This is because they think about metric units in terms of U.S. units. They read that there are

Table 5.2	
Abbreviations of U.S. Units in This Book	
pound	lb
ounce	oz
gallon	gal
quart	qt
pint	pt
cup	cup (abbreviation not used)
fluid ounce	fl. oz or oz
tablespoon	tbsp
teaspoon	tsp
inch	in.

Table 5.3	
Units of Measure—U.S. System	
Weight	
1 pound	= 16 ounces
Volume	
1 gallon	= 4 quarts
1 quart	= 2 pints or 4 cups or 32 (fluid) ounces
1 pint	= 2 cups or 16 (fluid) ounces
1 cup	= 8 (fluid) ounces
1 (fluid) ounce	= 2 tablespoons
1 tablespoon	= 3 teaspoons
Length	
1 foot	= 12 inches

Note: One fluid ounce (usually called simply *ounce*) of water weighs 1 ounce. One pint of water weighs 1 pound.

Table 5.4
Metric Units

Basic Units		
Quantity	**Unit**	**Abbreviation**
weight	gram	g
volume	liter	L
length	meter	m
temperature	degree Celsius	°C
Divisions and Multiples		
Prefix/Example	**Meaning**	**Abbreviation**
kilo-	1,000	k
kilogram	1,000 grams	kg
deci-	1/10	d
deciliter	0.1 liter	dL
centi-	1/100	c
centimeter	0.01 meter	cm
milli-	1/1,000	m
millimeter	0.001 meter	mm

28.35 grams in an ounce, and they are immediately convinced that they will never be able to learn metrics.

Do not worry about being able to convert between U.S. and metric units. This is a very important point to remember, especially if you think that the metric system might be hard to learn.

The reason for this is simple. You will usually be working in either one system or the other. You will rarely, if ever, have to convert from one to the other. (An exception might be if you have equipment based on one system but want to use a recipe written in the other.) If U.S. kitchens change to the metric system, everyone will use scales that measure in grams and kilograms, volume measures that measure in liters and deciliters, and thermometers that indicate degrees Celsius. And everyone will use recipes that indicate these units. No one will have to worry about how many grams are in an ounce. All one will have to remember is the information in Table 5.4.

To become accustomed to working in metric units, it is helpful to have a feel for how large the units are. The following equivalents may be used to help you visualize metric units. They are not exact conversion factors. (When you need exact conversion factors, see Appendix 1.)

A *kilogram* is slightly more than 2 pounds.

A *gram* is about 1/30 ounce. (1/2 teaspoon flour weighs a little less than 1 gram.)

A *liter* is slightly more than 1 quart.

A *deciliter* (100 milliliters) is slightly less than 1/2 cup.

A *centiliter* (10 milliliters) is about 2 teaspoons.

A *meter* is slightly more than 3 feet.

A *centimeter* is about 3/8 inch.

0°C is the freezing point of water (32°F).

100°C is the boiling point of water (212°F).

An increase or decrease of *1 degree Celsius* is equivalent to about 2 degrees Fahrenheit.

Metric Recipes

Many recipe writers in the United States print exact metric equivalents in their recipes. As a result, you will see recipes calling for 454 grams of potatoes, 28.35 grams of butter, or a baking temperature of 191°C. No wonder many Americans are afraid of the metric system!

Kitchens in countries that use the metric system do not work with such impractical numbers, any more than cooks in the United States normally use figures like 1 lb 1¼ oz potatoes, 2.19 oz butter, or a baking temperature of 348°F. That would defeat the purpose of the metric system, which is to be simple and practical. If you have a chance to look at a French cookbook, you will see nice, even numbers like 1 kg, 200 g, and 4 dL. (Note that the metric abbreviations used in this book are consistent with common usage in Canada. Abbreviations used in Europe are somewhat different, such as lowercase *l* instead of uppercase *L* for liter.)

The metric equivalents in the recipes in this book are rounded off. What's more, they are not always rounded off in the same way. In some places, you may see 1 pound rounded off to 500 grams, in other places to 450 grams. The object is to keep the proportions and the total yield as close as possible while arriving at practical measurements. Unfortunately, it is not always possible to keep the proportions exactly the same because the U.S. system is not decimal-based like the metric system. In some cases, the metric quantities may produce slightly different results due to these varying proportions, but these differences are small. If you have U.S. equipment, use the U.S. units, and if you have metric equipment, use the metric units. You should rarely have to worry about converting between the two.

CONVERTING RECIPES

Unless you are working in an operation that uses only its own standardized recipes, you will frequently be required to convert recipes to different quantities. For example, you may have a recipe for 50 portions of Swiss steak but need only 25 portions.

Converting recipes is an important technique. It is a skill you will probably need to use many times in this book. There is no "best" yield to write recipes for, as every operation, every school, and every individual has different needs.

Nearly everyone instinctively can double a recipe or cut it in half. It seems more complicated, though, to change a recipe from 10 to 18 portions, say, or from 50 to 35. Actually,

Procedure for Converting Total Yield

1. **Divide the desired yield by the recipe yield:**

   $$\frac{\text{new yield}}{\text{old yield}} = \text{conversion factor}$$

2. **Multiply each ingredient quantity by the conversion factor:**

   conversion factor $\times$ old quantity = new quantity

   In order to do this in the U.S. system, you usually have to convert all weights to ounces and all volumes to fluid ounces. (This is not necessary in the metric system.)

   Example 1: You have a recipe for 10 portions of Broccoli Mornay requiring 3 lb AP broccoli and 2½ cups Mornay Sauce. Convert to 15 portions.

   $$\frac{\text{new yield}}{\text{old yield}} = \frac{15}{10} = 1.5$$

   Broccoli: 3 lb = 48 oz

   48 oz $\times$ 1.5 = 72 oz = 4 lb 8 oz

   Sauce: 2½ cups = 20 fl. oz

   20 fl. oz $\times$ 1.5 = 30 fl. oz = 3¾ cups

   Example 2: You have a recipe for 10 portions of Broccoli Mornay requiring 1,500 grams AP broccoli and 600 mL Mornay Sauce. Convert to 15 portions.

   $$\frac{\text{new yield}}{\text{old yield}} = \frac{15}{10} = 1.5$$

   Broccoli: 1500 g $\times$ 1.5 = 2250 g

   Sauce: 600 mL $\times$ 1.5 = 900 mL

Procedure for Changing Portion Sizes

If your recipe yields, let's say, 20 portions, 4 ounces each, and you need 30 portions, 5 ounces each, you must add a few extra steps to the conversion process.

1. **Determine total yield of the recipe by multiplying the number of portions by the portion size:**

   portions $\times$ portion size = total yield (old)

2. **Determine the total yield you desire by multiplying the desired number of portions by the desired portion size:**

   desired portions $\times$ desired portion size = total yield (new)

3. **Divide desired yield by recipe yield to get the conversion factor:**

   $$\frac{\text{total yield (new)}}{\text{total yield (old)}} = \text{conversion factor}$$

4. **Multiply each ingredient by the conversion factor:**

   conversion factor $\times$ old quantity = new quantity

   Note: The conversion factor may sometimes turn out to be 1. In these cases, the total yield is obviously the same, and the recipe does not need to be changed.

the principle is exactly the same: You multiply each ingredient by a number called a **conversion factor**, as on the previous page.

In order to make these procedures clearer, let's work through the conversion of a full recipe to give you practice with the equations. The following examples are in the U.S. system of measures. For metric examples, see Appendix 4, page 1028.

In the first column that follows is a list of ingredients for a sautéed beef dish. As you can see, the quantities given in the second column are enough to make eight portions at 8 ounces each.

Beef tenderloin tips and mushrooms à la crème
Portions: 8
Portion size: 8 oz

Butter	2 oz
Onions	4 oz
Flour	1 tbsp
Mushrooms	½ lb
Beef tenderloin	2½ lb
White wine	½ cup
Prepared mustard	2 tsp
Brown sauce	1½ pt
Heavy cream	1 cup
Salt	to taste
Pepper	to taste

Let's say we need 18 portions instead of 8. To find the conversion factor, we divide the new yield by the old yield:

$$\frac{\text{new yield}}{\text{old yield}} = \frac{18}{8} = 2.25$$

To convert the recipe to 18 portions, we simply multiply each ingredient quantity by this conversion factor of 2.25.

First, to make this easier, we should change pounds to ounces and cups, pints, and quarts to fluid ounces, using the figures in Table 5.2. For example, to change the measurement for beef tenderloin to ounces, multiply 2½ (the weight in pounds) by 16 (the number of ounces in a pound) to get 40 ounces.

The equivalents we need for this recipe are as follows:

½ lb equals 8 ounces

2½ pounds equals 40 ounces

½ cup equals 4 fluid ounces

1½ pints equals 24 fluid ounces

In Example 1, page 105, we have substituted these equivalent quantities. Then we have multiplied all the ingredient quantities by the conversion factor to get the quantities that we need for 18 portions. Check through all the calculations to make sure you follow them. The quantities for salt and pepper will still, of course, be indicated as "to taste."

Now let's suppose we want to find the quantities needed to give us 40 portions, 6 ounces each. Because the portion size changes, we must use the second procedure explained previously. First, to find the total yield of the old recipe, we multiply the number of portions by the portion size:

8 (portions) x 8 oz = 64 oz

Do the same calculation for the desired yield:

40 (portions) x 6 oz = 240 oz

When we divide the new yield by the old yield (240 divided by 64), we arrive at a conversion factor of 3.75. In Example 2, we have done the conversions using the new factor of 3.75.

Example 1

Ingredient	Quantity	Times	Conversion Factor	Equals	New Quantity
Butter	2 oz	x	2.25	=	4.5 oz
Onions	4 oz	x	2.25	=	9 oz
Flour	1 tbsp	x	2.25	=	2.25 tbsp *or* 2 tbsp plus ¾ tsp
Mushrooms	8 oz	x	2.25	=	18 oz *or* 1 lb 2 oz
Beef tenderloin	40 oz	x	2.25	=	90 oz *or* 5 lb 10 oz
White wine	4 fl oz	x	2.25	=	9 fl. oz
Prepared mustard	2 tsp	x	2.25	=	4½ tsp *or* 1½ tbsp
Brown sauce	24 fl oz	x	2.25	=	54 fl oz *or* 3 pt plus 6 fl oz
Heavy cream	8 fl oz	x	2.25	=	18 fl oz *or* 2¼ cups

Example 2

Ingredient	Quantity	Times	Conversion Factor	Equals	New Quantity
Butter	2 oz	x	3.75	=	7.5 oz
Onions	4 oz	x	3.75	=	15 oz
Flour	1 tbsp	x	3.75	=	3.75 tbsp *or* 3 tbsp plus 2¼ tsp
Mushrooms	8 oz	x	3.75	=	30 oz *or* 1 lb 14 oz
Beef tenderloin	40 oz	x	3.75	=	150 oz *or* 9 lb 6 oz
White wine	4 fl oz	x	3.75	=	15 fl. oz
Prepared mustard	2 tsp	x	3.75	=	7½ tsp *or* 2½ tbsp
Brown sauce	24 fl oz	x	3.75	=	90 fl oz *or* 5 pt plus 10 fl oz
Heavy cream	8 fl oz	x	3.75	=	30 fl oz *or* 3¾ cups

PROBLEMS IN CONVERTING RECIPES

For the most part, these conversion procedures work well. But when you make some very large conversions—from 10 to 400 portions, for example, or from 500 to 6—you may encounter problems.

For example, you may have to make major equipment changes, like from a 2-quart saucepot to a large steam kettle. Consequently, you have to adjust your techniques and, sometimes, even ingredients. Evaporation rates may be different, thickening agents may need increasing or decreasing, seasonings and spices may have to be cut back. Or sometimes quantities may be too large or too small to mix properly.

This is one more example of the importance of cooking with judgment. Experienced chefs develop a feel for these problems over the years. When you make such adjustments on converted recipes, be sure to make a note of them for future reference.

Although there are no fixed rules you can learn for these adjustments, it is possible to list the most common types of problems encountered so that you can be on the alert for them when making recipe conversions. In general, most of the pitfalls fall into one of the following categories.

Measuring

This is most often a problem when you are expanding small recipes, such as when you want to take a consumer recipe for four portions and adapt it to a high-volume operation such as a large cafeteria. Many such recipes use volume measures for both solids and liquids. As we explained earlier, volume measurement of solids is inaccurate. Of course, small inaccuracies can become large ones when a recipe is multiplied. Therefore, it is important to be cautious and to test carefully when you are converting a recipe that uses volume measures for solid ingredients.

This problem is largely avoided when all solids are measured by weight. But such items as spices and seasonings may be too small to be measured accurately by weight. For this reason, it is usually a good idea to cut back on spices and salt in a converted recipe. You can always add more if you taste the product and decide it needs more seasoning.

Surface and Volume

If you have studied geometry, you may remember that a cube with a volume of 1 cubic foot has a top surface area of 1 square foot. But if you double the volume of the cube, the top surface area is not doubled but is in fact only about 1½ times as large.

What in the world, you ask, does this have to do with cooking? Consider the following example.

Suppose you have a good recipe for a half-gallon of cream soup, which you normally make in a small soup pot. You want to make 16 gallons of the soup, so you multiply all ingredients by a conversion factor of 32 and make the soup in a steam kettle. To your surprise, not only do you end up with more soup than you expected, but it turns out rather thin and watery. What happened?

Your converted recipe has 32 times as much volume to start, but the amount of surface area has not increased nearly as much. Because the ratio of surface area to volume is less, there is less evaporation. This means that there is less reduction and less thickening, and the flavors are not as concentrated. To correct this problem, you would have to use less stock, and preferably a stock that is more concentrated.

Suppose instead that you made the expanded recipe in a tilting skillet. In this case, there is so much surface area that the liquid would evaporate very quickly, resulting in an overly thickened and overly seasoned soup.

Differences in surface area and volume can cause other problems as well. Food service operations have to be more careful than home cooks do about food spoilage and the Food Danger Zone (Chapter 2), because large volumes of food cool down and heat up much more slowly than small volumes do.

For the same reason, a home baker worries about keeping a bread dough warm so that it will ferment, but a commercial baker worries about keeping a dough cool enough so that it doesn't ferment too fast. This is because a large batch of dough has so much volume in comparison with its surface area that it tends to retain heat rather than cool down quickly to room temperature.

Equipment

When you change the size of a recipe, you must often change the equipment, too. This change often means that the recipe does not work in the same way. Cooks must be able to use their judgment to anticipate these problems and to modify their procedures to avoid them. The example just given, of cooking a large batch of soup in a steam kettle or in a tilting skillet, is among the kinds of problems that can arise when you change cooking utensils.

Other problems can arise because of mixers or other processing equipment. For example, if you break down a salad dressing recipe to make only a small quantity, you might find there is so little liquid in the mixing machine that the beaters don't blend the ingredients properly.

Or you might have a recipe for a muffin batter that you usually make in small quantities and mix the batter by hand. When you increase the recipe greatly, you find you have too much to do by hand. Therefore, you use a mixer but keep the mixing time the same. Because the mixer does the job so efficiently, you overmix the batter and end up with poor-quality muffins.

Many mixing and stirring jobs can be done only by hand. This is easy with small quantities but difficult with large batches. The result is often an inferior product. On the other hand, some handmade products are better if they are done in large batches. It is hard, for example, to make a very small batch of puff pastry because the dough cannot be rolled and folded properly.

Time

Some people make the mistake of thinking that if you double a recipe, you must also double the cooking time. That this is an error can be shown by a simple example. Assume that it takes 15 minutes to cook a steak in a broiler. If you put two steaks in the broiler, it still takes 15 minutes to cook them, not 30 minutes.

If all other things are equal, cooking times stay the same when a recipe is converted. Problems arise, however, because all other things are not always equal. For example, a large pot of liquid takes longer to bring to a boil than a small pot. Therefore, the total cooking time is longer.

On the other hand, a big kettle of vegetable soup that you are making ahead for tomorrow's lunch takes longer to cool than a small pot. Meanwhile, the vegetables continue to cook in the retained heat during the cooling. In order to avoid overcooking, you may need to undercook the large batch slightly.

In cases where the cooking time must be increased, you sometimes might find that you have to increase the amount of herbs and spices. This is because the flavors are volatile (see p. 79), and more flavor is lost because of the increased cooking time. (Another answer to this problem is to add the spices later.)

Changing recipe sizes can affect not only cooking times but also mixing times. The best way to avoid this problem is to rely not on printed cooking and mixing times but on your own judgment and skills to tell you when a product is properly cooked or properly blended.

Recipe Problems

Many recipes have flaws, either in the quantities or types of ingredients or in the cooking procedures. When the item is made in small quantities, these flaws may not be noticeable, or the cook may almost unconsciously or automatically make adjustments during production. When the recipe is multiplied, however, the flaws may suddenly become apparent and the product quality lower. The only solution here is to carefully test recipes and to have a good understanding of basic cooking principles.

FOOD COST CALCULATIONS

Food service operations are businesses. This means that someone in the operation has to worry about budgets, cost accounting, bills, and profits. Usually this is the job of the manager, while the cook takes care of food production.

The cooks have a great deal of responsibility for food cost controls, however. They must always be conscious of accurate measurement, portion control, and careful processing, cooking, and handling of foods to avoid excess trimming loss, shrinkage, and waste.

The manager, on the other hand, is concerned with determining budgets, calculating profits and expenses, and so on. We cannot deal with these subjects here, as this is a book about food preparation. But you may encounter them later in your studies or in your career.

Every cook should understand three areas of cost accounting, however: doing yield analyses, calculating raw food cost or portion cost, and using food cost percentages.

FOOD COST PERCENTAGES

An individual operation's food cost percentage is usually determined by the budget. The chef is interested in this figure because it tells him or her whether the menu prices and the costs for each item are in line.

The **food cost percentage** of a menu item equals the raw food cost or portion cost divided by the menu price:

$$\text{percentage} = \frac{\text{food cost}}{\text{menu price}}$$

You can use this figure in two ways:

1. If you know the menu price and want to see what your food cost should be in order to be within the budget, multiply the menu price by the percentage:

    food cost = menu price x percentage

    Example: Menu price is $6.75 and food cost percentage is 35%.

    35% = 0.35
    6.75 x 0.35 = $2.36

2. If you know the food cost and want to determine what the menu price should be at a particular percentage, divide the cost by the percentage:

$$menu\ price = \frac{food\ cost}{percentage}$$

Example: Food cost is $1.60 and food cost percentage is 40%.

$$\frac{\$1.60}{40\%} = \frac{\$1.60}{0.40} = \$4.00$$

YIELD COST ANALYSIS

In order to calculate portion costs of recipes, you must first determine the costs of your ingredients. For many ingredients, this is relatively easy. You just look at your invoices or at price lists from your purveyors.

Many recipes, however, specify trimmed weight rather than the weight you actually pay for. For example, a stew might call for 2 pounds of sliced onions. Let's say that you pay 24 cents a pound for onions, and to get 2 pounds of sliced onions, you need 2¼ pounds of untrimmed onions. In order to calculate the cost of the recipe correctly, you have to figure out what you actually paid for the onions. In this case, the true cost is 54 cents (2¼ lb x $.24 per lb), not 48 cents (2 lb x $.24 per lb).

The following are two frequently used abbreviations that you must understand:

- AP stands for **as purchased**. This means the untrimmed quantity, in the same form in which it is purchased. This is the amount you pay for.

- EP stands for **edible portion**. This means the raw, uncooked quantity after all trimming is done. This is the quantity you actually cook.

In the case of fruits and vegetables, the best way to determine AP quantities for use in costing recipes is to make a note of them when you are preparing the item. Tables of

---

Table 5.5
Raw Yield Test Form

Item .... Test number .... Date ....

Purveyor .... Price per pound .... Total cost ....

AP weight (1) .... Lb price (2) .... Total cost (3) ....

Trim, salvage, and waste:

Item	Weight	Value/lb	Total Value (lb x value)
(4)	....	....	_____
(5)	....	....	_____
(6)	....	....	_____
(7)	....	....	_____
(8)	....	....	_____
(9)	....	....	_____
(10)	....	....	_____

Total Weight (4 thru 10)   (11) _____   Total Value (4 thru 10)   (12) _____

Total yield of item (13) ....

Net cost (3 minus 12)   (14) _____

Cost per lb (14 divided by 13)   (15) _____

Percentage of increase (15 divided by 2)   (16) _____

vegetable and fruit trimming yields in Chapters 16 and 19 will also help you. (Chapter 16 explains how to use these figures.)

In the case of ingredients such as meats and fish, figuring the cost can be a little more complicated. If you buy precut portion-controlled steaks or fish fillets and use them just as you receive them, your AP and EP costs are the same. But if you buy whole loins of beef or whole fish and cut them yourself, you have to do a yield cost analysis in order to determine your actual costs.

The examples discussed in the remainder of this chapter use U.S. measures. For metric examples, see Appendix 4, pages 1028–1029.

Raw Yield Test

Suppose you work in a restaurant that serves veal scaloppine. The restaurant buys whole legs of veal. It is your job to bone out the veal, trim off all fat and connective tissue, separate the muscles at the seams, and cut the large pieces into scaloppine.

A typical whole leg of veal might weigh 30 pounds and cost $5.00 a pound for a total cost of $150.00. After finishing your trimming and cutting, you find you have 18 pounds of veal scallopine. How do you figure the cost per pound of this meat?

The simplest example would be if you threw away all the trimmings, bones, and scrap meat. Then you would know that your 18 pounds of veal cost you $150.00. Dividing $150 by 18 pounds gives you a cost per pound of $8.33.

But in your restaurant, you don't throw away the trimmings. You make stock with the bones, grind up the small trimmings for meatballs, use the larger trimmings for veal stew, and sell the fat to the fat collector who picks up all your waste fat once a week. Now you must do a **yield test** to figure your costs.

Table 5.5 shows a typical form that you might use for a yield test. For simplification, the blanks in the form are of two types. The dotted lines are to be filled in by reading your invoices and by taking the weights from your actual yield test. The solid lines are to be filled in by doing calculations.

Table 5.6
Completed Raw Yield Test Form

Item	veal leg to scaloppine	Test number	3	Date	6/5/02
Purveyor	ABC Meats	Price per pound	$5.00	Total cost	$150
AP weight (1)	30 lb	Lb price (2)	$5.00	Total cost (3)	$150

Trim, salvage, and waste:

	Item	Weight	Value/lb	Total Value (lb x value)
(4)	fat	2½ lb	$ .12	$ .30
(5)	bone	3 lb 5 oz	$ .38	$1.26
(6)	ground veal	2 lb 2 oz	$4.89	$10.39
(7)	stew meat	3 lb	$5.29	$15.87
(8)	unusable trim	14 oz	0	0
(9)	cutting loss	3 oz	0	0
(10)				
	Total Weight (4 thru 10) (11)	12 lb	Total Value (4 thru 10) (12)	$27.82

Total yield of item (13) .... 18 lb

Net cost (3 minus 12) (14) _____ $122.18

Cost per lb (14 divided by 13) (15) _____ $6.79

Percentage of increase (15 divided by 2) (16) _____ 1.36 (136%)

Note that in Table 5.6, the form has been filled in with the results of a yield test on a leg of veal. We go through the form step by step.

The executive chef in this restaurant fills out the first two lines based on the invoice, gives you the form, and requests you to do the test. You fill out the rest of the form, beginning with blank 1 on the third line. You proceed as follows:

1. Weigh the whole leg of veal and enter the weight in blank 1. Copy the price per pound and total cost from line 2 to blanks 2 and 3.

    Note that blank 3 can also be arrived at by multiplying the weight by the price per pound. However, suppose the veal were left in the cooler for several more days and dried out a bit. The weight then might be 29½ pounds. By multiplying 29.5 by $5.00, you would get a total cost of $147.50. But because the price you paid was actually $150, it is important to use that figure and not fill in the blank by multiplying.

2. Break down the veal into all its component parts and record the weights of the trim and waste, starting in blank 4. In this case, there are only six items: fat, bones, small meat scraps for grinding, meat for stew, unusable waste, and cutting loss.

    Record the weight of the finished scaloppine in blank 13.

    What is **cutting loss**? This is not something you can actually weigh. However, there is always some loss of weight due to particles of meat and fat sticking to the cutting board, to drying, and to other factors. So when you add up all your weights, you find that they total less than 30 pounds. To determine cutting loss, add up blanks 4 through 8 and blank 13. Subtract this total from line 1.

3. Enter the values per pound of the trim, salvage, and waste on lines 4 through 10. In this case, these numbers are given to you by the executive chef from the invoices.

    •   The fat collector pays 12 cents a pound for waste fat.

    •   When you have to buy extra bones for your stockpot, you have to pay 38 cents a pound for them, so this is their value to you. This is also the figure you use when you cost out your stock recipe. If you didn't make stock and threw out the bones, you'd enter zero in this blank.

    •   Similarly, the values entered for ground veal and stew meat are the prices you'd have to pay if you bought them.

    •   Unusable trim and cutting loss have no value, so you enter zero.

4. Calculate the total value of each item on lines 4 through 10 by multiplying the weight by the value per pound. Note that this particular form tells you how to do all the calculations.

5. Add the weights in lines 4 through 10 and enter the total in blank 11. Add the total values in lines 4 through 10 and enter this figure in blank 12.

6. Subtract the total value of all the trim (blank 12) from the price you paid for the veal (blank 3). This gives you the net cost of your 18 pounds of scaloppine.

7. To find the cost per pound of the scaloppine, divide the net cost (blank 14) by the weight (blank 13). This is the figure you will use in costing recipes for veal scaloppine.

8. The percentage of increase in the last line is determined by dividing the net cost per pound (blank 15) by the price per pound of the whole leg (blank 2). This figure can be used as follows:

    Suppose next week you buy another leg of veal from the same purveyor, but the price has gone up to $5.29. Instead of doing another yield test, you can simply multiply this new price by the percentage of increase ($5.29 times 1.36), to get a new cost per pound of $7.19.

Cooked Yield Test

Earlier we introduced two important abbreviations, AP (as purchased) and EP (edible portion). A third expression sometimes used is **AS**, meaning **as served**. When foods such as fruits are served raw, AS may be the same as EP. But if the food is cooked, these weights are different.

In the case of the veal scaloppine, your recipe portions, and therefore your portion costs, are based on raw weight. For example, your scaloppine recipe might call for 5½ ounces of raw meat per portion.

Table 5.7
Cooked Yield Test Form

Item .... Test number .... Date ....

AP price per lb ....

Cooking temperature ....

Net raw weight (1) .... Net cost per lb (2) ....

Total net cost (3) ....

Weight as served (4) ....

Cooked cost per lb (3 divided by 4)   (5) ....

Shrinkage (1 minus 4)   (6) ....

Percentage of shrinkage (6 divided by 1)   (7) ....

Total percentage of cost increase (5 divided by AP price per lb)   (8) ....

Table 5.8
Completed Cooked Yield Test Form

Item .... roast fresh ham .... Test number .... 2 .... Date ... 6/5/02 ....

AP price per lb .... $3.49 ....

Cooking temperature .... 325° ....

Net raw weight (1) .... 12 lb .... Net cost per lb (2) .... $3.93 ....

Total net cost (3) .... $47.16 ....

Weight as served (4) .... 8 lb 4 oz ....

Cooked cost per lb (3 divided by 4)   (5) ...... $5.72 ....

Shrinkage (1 minus 4)   (6) .... 3¾ lb ....

Percentage of shrinkage (6 divided by 1)   (7) .... 31% ....

Total percentage of cost increase (5 divided by AP price per lb)   (8) .... 164% ....

In some cases, on the other hand, your portions may be based on cooked weight. This is most often true of roasts. For example, let's say you buy whole fresh hams, bone and trim them, and serve them as roasts, allowing 6 ounces of sliced, cooked meat per portion. To arrive at your cost, you will have to do a cooked yield test, as illustrated by Tables 5.7 and 5.8. (This form may be printed on the same sheet of paper as the raw yield test form so the operation can have a complete cost analysis on one form.)

This form has been filled in with the results of a cooked yield test done on a roast, boneless fresh ham. Let's assume that this same ham has already had a raw yield test done on it.

The first half of the form, through blank 3, is filled in before the test starts. The numbers for blanks 1, 2, and 3 are taken from the raw yield test form, but you should double-check the net raw weight by weighing the item again before roasting.

Enter the total weight of cooked ham served in blank 4. You arrive at this figure by recording the total number of portions served and multiplying this number by the portion size. Let's say that 22 portions are served at 6 ounces each. This gives us a total of 132 ounces (22 x 6), or 8¼ pounds.

You might be tempted to simply weigh the whole roast after cooking and trimming. Remember, though, that there will be some waste—crumbs on the slicer or cutting board, spillage of juices, and so on. It is more accurate to record the weight you actually sell.

If this had been a bone-in roast, you would have another reason to carve the meat before weighing, because you could not include the weight of the bone in your as-served figure.

Example: Costing a Recipe
Item: Baked Rice

Ingredient	Amount	Recipe Quantity	Price	Total
Rice, long grain	4 lb	4 lb	$0.62/lb	$2.48
Butter	12 oz	0.75 lb	1.97/lb	1.48
Onions	1 lb	1.2 lb	0.36/lb	0.43
Chicken stock	4 qt	4 qt	0.25/qt	1.00
Salt	1 oz	1/16 lb	0.15/lb	0.01
			Total cost	$5.40
			Number of portions	50
			Cost per portion	$0.11

Note: Cost of chicken stock is determined by costing out the operation's recipe for chicken stock.

The remaining blanks on the form are determined by doing the calculations, just as you would do the calculations for the raw yield test.

PORTION COSTS

Portion cost, or *raw food cost*, is the total cost of all the ingredients in a recipe divided by the number of portions served:

$$\text{portion cost} = \frac{\text{cost of ingredients}}{\text{number of portions}}$$

Here we cost out a sample recipe to show you how the procedure works. First, note the following points and keep them in mind when you are calculating portion costs. Many errors in costing are caused by forgetting one of these points.

1. Costs must be based on AP (as purchased) amounts, even though recipes often give EP (edible portion) quantities. These terms are explained in the preceding section.

2. Include *everything*. That means the lemon wedge and parsley garnish for the fish fillet, the cream and sugar that go with the coffee, and the oil that was used for pan-frying the eggplant. These are sometimes called **hidden costs**.

    Seasonings and spices are a typical example of hidden costs that are difficult to calculate. Some operations add up the cost of all seasonings used in a year and divide that by the total food cost to get a percentage. This percentage is added to each item. For example, if the cost of an item is $2.00 and the seasoning cost percentage is 5 percent, the total cost is $2.00 plus 5 percent of $2.00, or $2.10.

    Other hidden costs can be calculated in the same way. For example, you could figure out your cost percentage for frying fat and add the percentage to all deep-fried foods.

    Some restaurants take an arbitrary figure for all hidden costs, usually from 8 to 12 percent, and add this to all menu items.

3. Record the number of portions *actually served*, not just the number the recipe is intended to serve. If the roast shrank more than you expected during cooking, or if you dropped a piece of cake on the floor, those costs still have to be covered.

Procedure for Calculating Portion Cost

1. List ingredients and quantities of recipe as prepared.

2. Convert the recipe quantities to AP (as purchased) quantities.

3. Determine the price of each ingredient (from invoices, price lists, etc.). The units in this step and in step 2 must be the same in order for you to do the calculation.

4. Calculate the total cost of each ingredient by multiplying the price per unit by the number of units needed.

5. Add the ingredient costs to get the total recipe cost.

6. Divide the total cost by the number of portions served to get the cost per portion.

CONTROLLING FOOD COSTS

Calculating food costs is a critical part of the business of selling and serving food. The preceding section explains the basic mathematics of determining these costs. But cost control is much more than calculating costs based on written recipes. Cost control begins with menu planning and encompasses every phase of the operation from purchasing to service.

MENU PLANNING

A well-planned menu takes care to utilize ingredients efficiently and in a way that avoids waste. When writing a menu, consider the following guidelines for total utilization of foods.

1. **Use all edible trim.**
    Unless you use only portion-controlled meats, poultry, and fish and only frozen and canned vegetables, you will have edible trim. You can either throw it away and call it a loss, or you can use it and make money on it.
    Plan recipes that utilize these trimmings and put them on the menu. For example:

    *   Use small meat scraps for soups, chopped meat, pâtés, creamed dishes, croquettes.
    *   Use larger meat trimmings for soups, stews, braised items.
    *   Use bones for stocks and soups.
    *   Use vegetable trimmings for purées, soups, stews, stocks, fillings for omelets and crêpes.
    *   Use day-old breads for stuffings, breading, French toast, croutons, meat extender.

2. **Don't add an item to the menu unless you can use the trimmings.**
    This is really the same as the preceding item, looking from the opposite angle. In other words, don't put rissolé potatoes on your menu unless you also plan to serve an item that uses the trimmings, such as whipped potatoes or croquettes.

3. **Plan production to avoid leftovers.**
    The best way to use leftovers is not to create them in the first place. Handling food twice—once as a fresh item and once as a leftover—is more expensive and time-consuming than handling it once, and it almost always results in loss of quality. Limited menus—that is, with fewer selections—decrease the likelihood of leftovers.

4. **Plan ahead for use of leftovers.**
    Careful planning of production can keep leftovers to a minimum. But some leftovers are almost inevitable, and it's better for your costs to use them than to throw them out.
    Whenever you put an item on the menu that could become a leftover, you should have a recipe ready that will use it. This is better than being surprised with leftovers that you don't know what to do with.
    For example, if you served roast chicken for dinner one day, you might plan on chicken salad for a luncheon special the next day.
    Remember to handle all leftovers according to proper sanitary procedures.

5. **Avoid minimum-use perishable ingredients.**
    Minimum-use ingredients are those that are used in one or two items on your menu. For example, an operation might serve chicken breast topped with sautéed mushrooms but not use mushrooms in any other item. When the ingredient is perishable, the result is a high percentage of spoilage or waste.
    This situation can be remedied in any of three ways.

    *   Change the recipe to eliminate the minimum-use ingredient.
    *   Eliminate the item from the menu.
    *   Add other items to the menu using the ingredient.

    Be careful not to unbalance the menu, however, by using an ingredient in too many dishes. Try to avoid both extremes.

PURCHASING

Managing Inventory

Par stock is the inventory of goods that an operation must have on hand to continue operating between deliveries. It is important to maintain a proper par stock to avoid running out of essential items. On the other hand, it is costly to maintain a larger inventory than necessary. This is partly because part of your operating cash is tied up in unused inventory. Secondly, excessive inventory of perishable items can lead to spoilage and thus to loss. Accurate forecasting of future business, based on careful study of past business, is key to managing inventory and establishing par stock.

Write specifications for each item purchased carefully so that the item is described accurately. Compare price and quality offered by several vendors in order to get the best quality for the best price. Order from up-to-date quotes and price lists.

RECEIVING

Pay careful attention to receiving procedures:

- Schedule receipts so an employee can devote full attention to checking the shipment without being rushed. Try to schedule deliveries so they don't arrive at the same time. If the employee receiving the goods has kitchen duties as well, schedule deliveries during off hours so there is adequate time to check the shipments.

- Check the delivery immediately, while the driver is there. Don't allow the driver to unload the shipment and depart, leaving the order on the loading dock.

- Compare the delivery invoice to the order forms to make sure the right goods are delivered.

- Compare the delivery invoice to the actual goods received, to make sure you have received everything you are paying for. A scale should be present at the receiving entrance so items can be checked for proper weight.
    Check the delivery for quality:

    - Check the temperature of refrigerated goods.

    - Check the temperature of frozen goods, and check for signs of thawing and refreezing.

    - Check all perishables for freshness.

    - Check all containers and packaging for damage.

- Immediately transfer all goods to proper storage.

STORING

Proper storage is essential to avoid spoilage and loss of food items. The basic principles of storing dry foods, refrigerated foods, and frozen foods are detailed in Chapter 2 (see pp. 26–28). In addition, storage of specific categories of foods, including meats, poultry, seafood, produce, and dairy products, is included in the discussions of each category of food. Consult the index for further reference.

MEASURING

As discussed earlier in this chapter, the concept of measurement applies to two principle areas: measurement of ingredients in recipe preparation, and measurement of portions to be served, also known as portion control. The fundamentals of both types of measurement are explained earlier in this chapter (see pp. 99–101) and need not be repeated here.

Measurement is an indispensable part of good kitchen procedures. Think of measurement as part of your basic cooking procedures, not as something separate. All cooking procedures, including measuring, combine to help control food costs, because proper cooking procedures help avoid waste due to improperly prepared foods. For example, lack of attention at the grill station often results in meats returned by the customer for being overcooked. Having to discard and replace badly cooked foods greatly increases food cost.

SERVING

All the cook's attention to measurement and portion control goes for nothing if a server drops the plate on the way to the dining room. A well-trained serving staff is an important part of controlling food costs. Serving staff must be trained in serving techniques and in portion control for those items, such as desserts or salads, that they are responsible for plating. Servers must understand the menu well so they can explain each item to customers and avoid returned dishes. The chef often may wish to sell more of some items than others as part of inventory and cost control, so serving staff must also be trained to be effective but pleasant salespeople. The demands made on the service personnel can best be met when the chef and the service manager cooperate in their training.

■ TERMS FOR REVIEW

static menu	homemade	liter	as purchased (AP)
cycle menu	organic	meter	edible portion (EP)
à la carte	recipe	degree Celsius	yield test
table d'hôte	standardized recipe	kilo-	cutting loss
prix fixe	AP weight	deci-	as served (AS)
tasting menu	EP weight	centi-	portion cost
course	portion control	milli-	hidden cost
fresh	metric system	conversion factor	minimum-use ingredient
imported	gram	food cost percentage	par stock

■ QUESTIONS FOR DISCUSSION

1. What role is played by the chef's favorite dishes when a menu is written?

2. What are the main differences among breakfast, lunch, and dinner menus?

3. Which of the following are most likely to have static menus?

   Fast-food restaurant   Army mess

   High school cafeteria   French restaurant

   Employee lunchroom

4. The following menus are made up of dishes prepared from recipes in this book. Evaluate each for variety and balance.

Clear vegetable soup	Cream of mushroom soup
Green salad with French dressing	Waldorf salad
Chicken fricassée	Veal scaloppine à la crème
Cauliflower au gratin	Broccoli mornay
	Rice pilaf

Scotch broth	Oxtail soup
Cucumber and tomato salad	Coleslaw
Roast rack of lamb with spring vegetables	Beef pot roast
	Braised green cabbage
	Bouillon potatoes

Oysters casino	Gazpacho
Vichyssoise	Tomato and avocado salad
Broiled steak	Chicken Pojarski
Baked potato	Baked acorn squash
Buttered green beans	Duchesse potatoes

5. What is the best solution to the problem of using up leftovers? What is the next best solution?

6. What are some reasons written recipes can't be 100 percent exact and must depend on the cook's judgment? Select two or three recipes (from this book or any other) and try to determine where they depend on the cook's judgment.

7. What is the purpose of a standardized recipe?

8. What are the three basic ways of measuring ingredients? Which method is used for most solid ingredients, and why?

9. What is the first step in portion control? List four other techniques in portion control.

10. Make the following conversions in the U.S. system of measurement:

    3½ pounds = _____ ounces

    6 cups = _____ pints

    8½ quarts = _____ fluid ounces

    ¾ cup = _____ tablespoons

    46 ounces = _____ pounds

    2½ gallons = _____ fluid ounces

    5 pounds 5 ounces divided by 2 = _____

    10 teaspoons = _____ fluid ounces

11. Make the following conversions in the metric system:

    1.4 kilograms = _____ grams

    53 deciliters = _____ liters

    15 centimeters = _____ millimeters

    2,590 grams = _____ kilograms

    4.6 liters = _____ deciliters

    220 centiliters = _____ deciliters

12. Turn to the recipe for Swedish Meatballs on page 346. Convert it to yield 35 portions.

13. Discuss the main types of problems you may face when converting recipe yields.

14. What is the difference between AP weight and EP weight? Explain how these terms are related to calculating costs per portion of menu items.

15. The following problems are calculations with food cost percentages, portion cost, and menu price. For each problem, two of these figures are given. Find the third.

	Food cost percentage	Portion cost	Menu price
a.	_____	$1.24	$4.95
b.	40%	_____	$2.50
c.	30%	$2.85	_____

Courtesy of the U.S. Department of Agriculture

CHAPTER 6

Nutrition

Menu planners must have a basic understanding of nutrition because the human body requires a variety of foods in order to function and be healthy.

The food service worker's responsibility to provide nutritious food and well-balanced menus depends, in part, on the operation. School and hospital food services must, of course, plan menus carefully to meet basic nutritional needs. A qualified dietitian is usually required in such establishments.

The obligations of restaurateurs are more subtle. Because they are in business to sell food, they must offer foods that will attract customers. People who plan menus are as concerned with presenting attractive, flavorful foods as they are with serving nutritious foods. Also, if the menu is à la carte, there is no way to ensure that a customer will order items that make up a nutritionally balanced meal.

But restaurateurs do have an obligation to offer a choice. That is, menus should be planned so customers can order well-balanced meals if they desire. People are becoming more concerned with fitness and health, so a nutritiously balanced menu may even help attract customers.

MyPyramid
STEPS TO A HEALTHIER YOU
MyPyramid.gov

GRAINS   VEGETABLES   FRUITS   MILK   MEAT & BEANS

After reading this chapter, you should be able to

1. List and describe the six categories of nutrients, explain their functions in the body, and name some food sources of each.

2. Define the term *calorie* and describe the relationship between calories and weight gain.

3. List and describe the eight guidelines for maintaining a healthful diet.

4. Describe ways that cooks can incorporate nutrition principles into their cooking and their menu construction.

NUTRIENTS

Nutrients are certain chemical compounds that are present in foods and that fulfill one or more of the following functions:

- Supply energy for body functions.
- Build and replace cells that make up body tissues.
- Regulate body processes.

There are six categories of nutrients:

- Carbohydrates
- Fats
- Proteins
- Vitamins
- Minerals
- Water

CALORIES

The **calorie** is a unit of measurement of energy. It is defined as the amount of heat needed to raise the temperature of 1 kilogram of water by 1°C.

Remember that one of the functions of nutrients is to supply energy to the body. The calorie is used to measure how much energy certain foods supply for these functions. In our overfed society, calories have come to be viewed as something to be avoided. Nevertheless, without sufficient food energy, we could not live.

Carbohydrates, proteins, and fats can be used by the body to supply energy.

1 gram of carbohydrate supplies 4 calories

1 gram of protein supplies 4 calories

1 gram of fat supplies 9 calories

There is a direct connection between calorie intake, physical activity, and weight gain. Simply put, if you consume more calories than you burn, you gain weight. If you consume fewer calories than you burn, you lose weight. All the diet schemes and fashions in the world—at least the ones that are medically sound—can be reduced to this. In other words, losing weight is possible only by eating fewer calories, by burning more calories through exercise, or, preferably, by both.

In order to lose weight while maintaining good nutrition and health, one should avoid **empty calories** as much as possible and eat primarily foods of high **nutrient density**. Empty calorie foods are those that provide few nutrients per calorie. Refined sugars and starches are examples of empty calories. Foods of high nutrient density are those that have relatively many nutrients per calorie. Fruits, vegetables, and whole grains are examples of foods with high nutrient density.

KINDS OF NUTRIENTS AND THEIR IMPORTANCE

Each of the nutrients listed has certain characteristics and functions in the body. These are discussed below in general terms. For a summary of individual nutrients and the foods in which they are found, see Table 6.1.

Many fad diets emphasize either the good or the bad qualities of one particular nutrient. For example, a particular weight loss diet may advise eating mostly protein foods and eliminating carbohydrates as much as possible. However, because all nutrients are essential, such diets can lead to nutritional imbalances. Thus, it is necessary to understand the function and importance of all nutrients.

The amount of each nutrient needed daily varies from person to person, depending on such factors as age, sex, general health, and level of activity.

Carbohydrates

Carbohydrates are compounds consisting of carbon, hydrogen, and oxygen atoms bound together in chains of varying lengths.

Sugars are simple carbohydrates. Simple sugars, such as glucose, are small compounds containing 6 carbon atoms. Table sugar, or sucrose, is a larger sugar molecule with 12 carbon atoms. Sugars are found in sweets and, to a lesser extent, in fruits and vegetables.

Starches are complex carbohydrates consisting of long chains of simple sugars bound together. They are found in such foods as grains, bread, peas and beans, and many vegetables and fruits.

Carbohydrates are the body's most important source of food energy. Fats and proteins can also be burned for energy, but the body uses carbohydrates first. If no carbohydrates are available, the body then burns fat. However, if fats are burned with no carbohydrates present, toxic compounds called **ketone bodies** are produced. If too many ketone bodies accumulate, a condition called **ketosis** develops, and the blood becomes unable to carry oxygen properly. The result can be fatal. Thus, one of the important functions of carbohydrates is to help the body burn fat properly. About 50 to 100 grams of carbohydrates are needed every day to prevent ketosis.

Most authorities believe that complex carbohydrates, especially those from whole grains and unrefined foods, are better for you than simple carbohydrates. This is partly because starchy foods also have many other nutrients, while sweets have few other nutrients. Also, there is some evidence that a lot of sugar in the diet may contribute to heart and circulatory diseases. Simple sugars and refined starches are primary sources of empty calories.

Another reason that carbohydrates from whole grains and unrefined foods are preferable to those from refined sugars and starches is that these unrefined foods are sources of fiber. The term **fiber** refers to a group of carbohydrates that cannot be absorbed and used by the body. Therefore, fiber supplies no food energy. However, it is important for the proper functioning of the intestinal tract and the elimination of body waste. In addition, there is evidence that sufficient dietary fiber helps prevent some kinds of cancers and helps decrease cholesterol in the blood. Fruits and vegetables, especially raw, and whole grains supply dietary fiber.

Fiber can be classified as either soluble or insoluble. Soluble fiber absorbs water and forms a kind of gel. It is found inside and between plant cells. Insoluble fiber also absorbs water, but less, and forms bulk in the intestines. It is found in cell walls and other structural parts of plants.

Fats

Fats supply energy to the body in highly concentrated form. Also, some fatty acids are necessary for regulating certain body functions. Third, fats act as carriers of fat-soluble vitamins (vitamins A, D, E, and K). Because of these important functions, it is necessary to have some fats in the diet.

Fats may be classified as saturated, monounsaturated, or polyunsaturated. These terms reflect chemical differences in the composition of fats. Cooks do not need to know the chemical structure of fats, but they should understand their nutritional characteristics and the foods in which they are found. Many foods contain a combination of these three types, with one type predominating.

Saturated fats are solid at room temperature. Animal products—meats, poultry, fish, eggs, dairy products—and solid shortenings are the major source of saturated fats. Tropical oils such as coconut oil and palm kernel oil are also rich in saturated fats. Health experts believe these fats contribute significantly to heart disease and other health problems.

Polyunsaturated fats and monounsaturated fats are liquid at room temperature.

CALORIES AND CALORIES

In scientific terminology, the amount of heat needed to raise the temperature of 1 kilogram of water by 1°C is called a *kilocalorie*, sometimes written *Calorie* (with a capital C) and abbreviated *kcal*. When written with a small *c*, the term *calorie* refers to a unit of energy measurement that is only 1,000th as large—the amount of heat needed to raise the temperature of 1 *gram* of water by 1°C.

Nevertheless, in discussions of nutrition, the word *calorie* is commonly substituted for *kilocalorie*. Just remember that when you see *calorie* in connection with food, the real meaning is *Calorie* (or *kilocalorie*).

Table 6.1
Major Nutrients

Nutrient	Major Dietary Sources		Functions in the Body
Carbohydrates	Grains (including breads and pasta) Dried beans	Potatoes Corn Sugar	Major source of energy (calories) for all body functions. Necessary for proper utilization of fats. Unrefined carbohydrates supply fiber, important for proper waste elimination.
Fats	Meats, poultry, and fish Dairy products Eggs	Cooking fats and shortening Salad dressings	Supply food energy (calories). Supply essential fatty acids. Carry fat-soluble vitamins.
Proteins	Meats, poultry, and fish Milk and cheese Eggs	Dried beans and peas Nuts	Major building material of all body tissues. Supply energy (calories). Help make up enzymes and hormones, which regulate body functions.
Vitamin A	Liver Butter and cream Egg yolks	Green and yellow vegetables and fruits	Helps skin and mucous membranes resist infection. Promotes healthy eyes and makes night vision possible.
Thiamin (Vitamin B_1)	Pork Whole grains and fortified grains	Nuts Legumes Green vegetables	Needed for utilization of carbohydrates for energy. Promotes normal appetite and healthy nervous system. Prevents beriberi.
Riboflavin (Vitamin B_2)	Organ meats Milk products	Whole grains and fortified grains	Needed for utilization of carbohydrates and other nutrients. Promotes healthy skin and eyes.
Niacin (a B vitamin)	Liver Meat, poultry, and fish	Legumes	Needed for utilization of energy foods. Promotes healthy nervous system, skin, and digestion. Prevents pellagra.
Vitamin B_{12}	Most animal and dairy products		Promotes healthy blood and nervous system.
Vitamin C (ascorbic acid)	Citrus fruits Tomatoes Potatoes Dark green leafy vegetables	Peppers, cabbage, and broccoli Cantaloupe Berries	Strengthens body tissues. Promotes healing and resistance to infection. Prevents scurvy.
Vitamin D	Fortified milk products	Formed in skin when exposed to sunlight	Necessary for utilization of calcium and phosphorus to promote healthy bones, teeth, and muscle tissue.
Vitamin E	Unsaturated fats (vegetable oils, nuts, whole grains, etc.)		Protects other nutrients.
Calcium	Milk products Leafy vegetables	Canned fish with bones	Forms bones and teeth. Necessary for healthy muscles and nerves.
Iron	Liver and red meat Raisins and prunes Egg yolks	Leafy vegetables Dried beans Whole grains	Needed for formation of red blood cells.

Although too much of any kind of fat is unhealthy, these fats are considered more healthful than saturated fats. Polyunsaturated fats are found in vegetable oils such as corn oil, safflower oil, sunflower oil, and cottonseed oil. High levels of monounsaturated fats are found in olive oil and canola oil. Both kinds of unsaturated fats are also found in other plant products as well, including whole grains, nuts, and some fruits and vegetables.

One group of saturated fats of special concern is trans fats. These fats occur naturally in small amounts only. Most of the trans fats in our diets are from manufactured fats subjected to a process called *hydrogenation*. *Hydrogenated fats* are fats that are changed from liquid to solid by adding hydrogen atoms to the fat molecules. This is the process used to make products such as solid shortening and margarine. Trans fats are of concern because they limit the body's ability to rid itself of cholesterol that builds up on the walls of arteries (see sidebar, p. 122).

Fats are members of a group of compounds called lipids. Another lipid found in the body is cholesterol, a fatty substance that has been closely linked with heart disease because it collects on the walls of arteries and blocks the flow of blood to the heart and other vital organs. It is found only in animal products and is especially high in egg yolks, butterfat, and organ meats such as liver and brains. In addition, the human body can manufacture its own cholesterol, so not all the cholesterol in the blood is necessarily from foods. Although some cholesterol is necessary for body functions, it is not considered a nutrient because the body is able to manufacture all the cholesterol it needs. Experts generally agree it is best to keep the cholesterol in the diet as low as possible.

Recent research has suggested that monounsaturated fat may actually lower the levels of the most harmful kinds of cholesterol in the body. This may explain the relatively low incidence of heart disease in Mediterranean regions, where olive oil is the most widely used fat. This research has helped popularize the use of olive oil in other parts of the world, especially in North America.

Remember, however, that *too much fat of any kind is bad for the health*. Do not make the mistake of thinking that monounsaturated fats are good for you and can be used in excess.

Proteins

Proteins are known as the building blocks of the body. They are essential for growth, for building body tissues, and for basic body functions. They can also be used for energy if the diet does not contain enough carbohydrates and fats.

Proteins consist of substances called *amino acids*. The body is able to manufacture many of them, but there are nine amino acids it cannot manufacture and must get from foods. A food protein that contains all nine essential amino acids is called a complete protein. Meats, poultry, fish, eggs, and dairy products contain complete proteins.

Proteins that lack one or more of these essential amino acids are called *incomplete proteins*. Foods high in incomplete proteins include nuts, grains, and dried beans and other legumes. Foods that, *if eaten together*, supply all the amino acids are called complementary proteins. For example, cornmeal tortillas topped with chili beans supply complete protein because the corn supplies the amino acids lacking in the beans. Beans and rice is another example of a food combination supplying complementary proteins.

Complementary proteins are especially of interest to vegetarians, especially vegans, and are discussed in more detail in Chapter 20.

The average adult needs about 50 to 60 grams of protein a day. For most North Americans, getting enough protein daily is not a problem; most get about twice as much as they need. Greatly excessive protein in the diet can lead to a variety of health problems, including kidney and liver damage.

Vitamins

Vitamins are present in foods in extremely small quantities, but they are essential for regulating body functions. Unlike proteins, fats, and carbohydrates, they supply no energy, but some of them must be present in order for energy to be utilized in the body. Also, lack of certain vitamins causes *deficiency diseases*.

Vitamins are classified as *water soluble* and *fat soluble*. The water-soluble vitamins (the B vitamins and vitamin C) are not stored in the body and must be eaten every day. Foods containing these vitamins should be handled so the vitamins are not dissolved into the cooking water and lost (as discussed in Chapter 16).

ESSENTIAL FATTY ACIDS

Fats are made up of smaller compounds called *fatty acids*. Two of these are called essential fatty acids because they cannot be made by the body. The essential fatty acids are *linoleic acid* and *alpha-linolenic acid*. Linoleic acid is a member of a group of compounds called *omega-6 fatty acids* (the term refers to its chemical structure). It is found in vegetable oils and is usually abundant in North American diets.

Alpha-linolenic acid is a member of the group of omega-3 fatty acids. The body can change alpha-linolenic acid into other omega-3 fatty acids called DHA and EPA. These are all important nutrients that play vital roles in growth, in the immune system, in proper eyesight, and in cell structure. Alpha-linolenic acid is found in certain vegetable oils. DHA and EPA, in addition to being made by the body, are also found in some fatty fish such as salmon, mackerel, tuna, and sardines. Unlike omega-6 fatty acids, omega-3 acids are not usually abundant in North American diets, so it is important to be aware of foods that supply them.

Fat-soluble vitamins (A, D, E, and K) can be stored in the body, so they do not need to be eaten every day as long as the total amount eaten over time is sufficient. Consuming too much of a fat-soluble vitamin daily, as sometimes happens when people take too many vitamin supplements, can result in toxic levels of the vitamin stored in the tissues.

More detail about individual vitamins, their functions, and their sources, can be found in Table 6.1.

Minerals

Minerals, like vitamins, are consumed in very small quantities and are essential for regulating certain body processes. Minerals that must be consumed in relatively large amounts—more than 100 milligrams daily—are called **major minerals**. These include calcium, chloride, magnesium, phosphorus, sulfur, sodium, and potassium. Minerals that must be present in smaller amounts are called **trace minerals**. These include chromium, copper, fluoride, iodine, iron, manganese, molybdenum, selenium, and zinc. Less is known about the functions of some of the trace minerals. It is important to understand, however, that although small quantities are needed by the body, too much of any of them can be harmful.

Sodium, a component of table salt, is well known as a health problem. Too much sodium is thought to contribute to high blood pressure. Health authorities try to convince people to reduce the sodium in their diets, primarily by salting foods less.

Water

The adult human body is 50 to 60 percent water by weight. Water plays a role in all the body's functions, including metabolism and other cell functions, digestion, delivery of nutrients, removal of waste, temperature regulation, and lubrication and cushioning of joints and tissues.

Water forms a large part of most of the food we eat and all the beverages we drink. The body is good at regulating its own water content and tells us when we need more by making us feel thirsty. This signal should not be ignored. Even better is to drink enough fluids to *prevent* feeling thirsty. Required daily water intake varies greatly from person to person, depending on age, level of activity, and environmental factors such as heat. The common recommendation of 8 glasses of water a day is not enough for some people, such as athletes and others who exercise strenuously, and is too much for others, such as older, sedentary adults.

THE BALANCED DIET

In order to stay healthy, we must consume a varied diet that contains all the essential nutrients. In addition, we must limit our intake of foods that can be harmful in large quantities. Although researchers still have much to learn about nutrition and our knowledge is constantly changing, there is strong evidence about what good eating patterns are. According to government health agencies, the following guidelines are suggested for maintaining a healthful diet. It should be noted that these are only general recommendations for people who are already healthy and want to stay that way. They are not necessarily for those who need special diets because of disease or other abnormal conditions.

1. **Getting Adequate Nutrients Within Calorie Needs**
   The greater the variety of nutrient-dense foods and beverages within and among the basic food groups we consume, the more likely we are to get all the nutrients we need. Choosing nutrient-dense foods and avoiding empty calories is necessary in order for us to get adequate nutrition without consuming too many calories in the process. Choose foods that limit the intake of saturated and trans fats, cholesterol, added sugars, salt, and alcohol.

2. **Managing Weight**
   To maintain a healthy body weight, balance the calories you consume with the calories you burn. People who are greatly overweight are more likely to develop

MORE CHEMISTRY: LIPOPROTEINS

Lipoproteins are combinations of protein and fat that carry cholesterol and fat through the bloodstream. Two of these compounds are of concern to us. *Low-density lipoprotein* (LDL) is the most important carrier of cholesterol. Although it performs a needed function, if too much of it is present it deposits excess cholesterol inside arteries, blocking the flow of blood. High-density lipoprotein (HDL), on the other hand, helps remove cholesterol from the blood and eliminate it from the body. Consequently, HDL is seen as a major preventer of heart disease.

Certain saturated fats called *trans fats* (see text) are considered especially bad in the diet because they apparently interfere with the action of HDL and thus raise cholesterol levels in the blood.

PHYTOCHEMICALS

A phytochemical is any of several hundred compounds that are found in foods in tiny amounts and may help reduce the chance of cancer or heart disease. The list of phytochemicals includes flavonoids, isoflavonoids, phenols, lycopene, indoles, dithiolthiones, and sulforaphane. These chemicals are not yet well understood, and research is continuing. Phytochemicals are found most abundantly in whole grains, fruits, and vegetables.

certain chronic diseases, such as high blood pressure, heart disease, and stroke. People who consume more calories than they burn off will gain weight.

To prevent gradual weight gain, make small decreases in the calories you consume and increase your physical activity. Rather than depending on crash diets, it is usually better to lose weight slowly and gradually, to develop better habits of eating, and to increase physical activity. To get all the nutrients you need while cutting down on calories, cut down on foods that are high in calories but low in nutrients, especially fat and fatty foods, sugar and sweets, and alcohol.

3. **Engaging in Physical Activity**

Engaging in regular physical activity promotes health, psychological well-being, and a healthy body weight. For general health and reducing the risk of chronic diseases, getting at least 30 minutes of moderately vigorous exercise every day is desirable, and more and longer vigorous exercise can be even more beneficial. In order to avoid gaining weight, adults should try to get 60 minutes of exercise most days, while at the same time not consuming too many calories. For those who wish to lose weight gradually, try to get 60 to 90 minutes of exercise most days, again while limiting calorie intake.

4. **Selecting from the Right Food Groups**

Fruits, vegetables, whole grains, and low-fat or fat-free milk and milk products are the foods with the highest nutrient density. These foods should be strongly emphasized in a healthy diet. In particular, someone who consumes 2,000 calories a day should try to eat the following daily:

- 2 cups (4 servings) of fruit, selecting from a variety of fruits.

- 2½ cups (5 servings) of vegetables, selected from as many of the basic vegetable groups as possible: dark green vegetables, orange vegetables, legumes, starchy vegetables, and others.

- 3 servings of whole grains.

- 3 cups of fat-free or low-fat milk or its equivalent in other dairy products, such as yogurt and cheese.

In the United States, these food groups, along with others including meats, poultry, and fish, form what is known as the **food guide pyramid**. Figure 6.1(a) shows the standard pyramid developed by the United States Department of Agriculture (USDA). Although it reflects the pyramid shape of earlier versions of the food guide, the current diagram is only a generalized symbol of healthful eating patterns, with a stick figure climbing stairs to represent physical exercise. Each colored stripe represents one of the basic five food groups: grains, vegetables, fruits, milk, and meat and beans. A thin stripe between fruits and milk represents oils. The thickness of each stripe represents the relative proportion of each group to include in the diet. The image contains no information on portions and portion sizes. Instead, it is intended to refer consumers to resources such as the website www.mypyramid.gov, where different pyramids can be customized based on age, sex, and level of activity.

Canadian nutrition experts have devised the "Food Guide to Healthy Eating," usually referred to as the **food rainbow** because of its format (Figure 6.1e). The number of daily servings of each group, as well as information about standard portion sizes, is indicated in the Canadian rainbow.

Figure 6.1a
Food guide pyramid.

Figure 6.1b
The traditional healthy Mediterranean diet pyramid.
© 2000 Oldways Preservation & Exchange Trust. www.oldwayspt.org.

Figure 6.1c
The traditional healthy Asian diet pyramid.
© 2000 Oldways Preservation & Exchange Trust. www.oldwayspt.org.

Figure 6.1d
The traditional healthy Latin American diet pyramid.
© 2000 Oldways Preservation & Exchange Trust. www.oldwayspt.org.

Figure 6.1e
The Canadian food rainbow.

5. **Manage Consumption of Fats**

   Keep total fat intake between 20 and 35 percent of calories, with most fats coming from sources of polyunsaturated and monounsaturated fatty acids, such as fish, nuts, and vegetable oils. This means that for a diet of 2,000 calories daily, calories from fat should be between 400 and 700.

   Why not lower than 20 percent? Remember that some fatty acids are essential nutrients, and fats also carry fat-soluble vitamins. Consuming less fat than 20 percent of daily calories could be unhealthy.

   Keep consumption of saturated fats, especially trans fats, as low as possible. Consume less than 10 percent of calories from saturated fatty acids.

   Consume less than 300 mg of cholesterol per day.

   When selecting and preparing meat, poultry, dry beans, and milk or milk products, make choices that are lean, low-fat, or fat-free.

   Remember: High fat intake, especially of saturated fats and cholesterol, is associated with such conditions as heart disease and high blood pressure. Although other factors contribute to these diseases, such as heredity and smoking, following this dietary recommendation should increase the chances of staying healthy.

6. **Manage Consumption of Carbohydrates**

   Choose fiber-rich fruits, vegetables, and whole grains. These foods are the sources of the most healthful carbohydrates. Avoid prepared foods high in added sugars.

   Reducing refined sugars and starches in the diet has the added benefit of helping reduce tooth decay.

7. **Manage Consumption of Sodium and Potassium**

   Consume less than 2,300 mg (approximately 1 tsp or 5 mL of salt) of sodium per day. Sodium, as noted earlier, appears to contribute to high blood pressure. For people who already have high blood pressure, it is especially important to cut down on sodium in the diet. The best ways to do this are to decrease the use of salt in the kitchen and at the table and to limit the intake of prepared foods that are high in salt, such as potato chips, salted nuts, pretzels, pickled foods, cured meats, and salty condiments like soy sauce.

   Reduce the harmful effects of sodium by eating potassium-rich foods, such as fruits and vegetables.

8. **Manage Consumption of Alcoholic Beverages**

   People who choose to drink alcoholic beverages should do so sensibly and in moderation—defined as the consumption of up to one drink per day for women and up to two drinks per day for men.

   Alcoholic beverages are high in calories while providing few other nutrients. Heavy drinking may cause a variety of serious diseases. Moderate drinking—one or two drinks a day—appears to do little harm and may, in fact, be of some benefit.

   Many people, including children and adolescents, pregnant and lactating women, people taking medications that interact with alcohol, and people with certain medical conditions, should avoid alcohol completely. In addition, alcoholic beverages should be avoided by people engaging in activities that require attention, skill, or coordination, such as driving or operating machinery.

COOKING HEALTHFUL MEALS

Restaurateurs and chefs are becoming more and more attentive to people's health and diet concerns. Many of them are reexamining their menus, modifying their cooking practices, and adding new, healthful items to their menus. Some have developed new menus that are specially planned to follow as closely as possible the eight recommendations listed above.

An increased health consciousness has affected the way we think about food and the way we cook. Professional cooks are making their foods more healthful in several ways:

1. **Using less fat in cooking.**
   Cooking methods that require no added fat, such as simmering, poaching, baking, steaming, and grilling, can be considered the most healthful.

   For sautéing, nonstick pans are becoming more widely used because little or no fat is needed. With regular pans, one can be careful to use as little fat as possible.

   Grilling is popular because it can be done without first coating the food with fat. If this is done, however, one must be careful not to let the food dry out.

   Using less fat in cooking also means using ingredients with less fat. Excess external fat can be trimmed from meats and poultry. Low-fat sauces, such as salsas and vegetable purées, can often be used instead of high-fat sauces. Recipes can often be modified so that quantities of high-fat ingredients, such as butter, cheese, and bacon, are reduced.

2. **Using unsaturated fats.**
   When you do use fats, try to substitute monounsaturated fats, such as olive oil or canola oil, for saturated fats when appropriate.

3. **Emphasizing flavor.**
   Taste is the most important factor in preparing nutritious food. The most vitamin-packed dish does no one any good if it is uneaten because it doesn't taste good. Preparing flavorful foods requires knowledge of the principles of cooking. You can't rely simply on nutritional information.

   Rely more on the natural flavors of foods and less on salt and other additives that should be decreased in the diet.

4. **Using the freshest, highest-quality foods possible.**
   In order to prepare delicious foods with little or no added salt and with less reliance on high-fat, high-sodium sauces and condiments, it is important to use high-quality natural ingredients at their peak of flavor. Healthful cooking means letting the true flavors of foods dominate.

   To enhance natural flavors without added salt, cooks are using more fresh herbs, hot seasonings such as chilies, ginger, and pepper, and flavorful ingredients like garlic, browned onions, and flavored vinegars.

5. **Storing foods properly.**
   Foods in storage lose nutrients as they age. The loss of nutrients can be slowed, however, by proper storage. This applies particularly to proper refrigeration. For each category of perishable food discussed in this book, pay close attention to how the foods should be stored.

6. **Modifying portion sizes.**
   It is not necessary to feature huge slabs of meat to serve satisfying meals. Smaller portions of well-trimmed meat, poultry, or fish, nicely balanced on the plate with an assortment of attractive fresh vegetables and complex carbohydrates, are likely to be more healthful.

   Sauces often get the blame for adding calories to a meal, but if a sauce is flavorful, you don't need much. Make a better sauce and serve less of it. Also, if a sauce isn't too thick, it won't cling as heavily to the food, and a little will go farther.

7. **Giving customers a healthful choice.**
   Offer a menu with a variety of foods so customers can choose a well-balanced meal suited to their needs and desires. It's not necessary to cook only "diet food," but a menu that offers French fries as the only available starch is not well balanced.

   Place more emphasis on fruits, vegetables, and whole grains. Offer a menu with choices from all the groups in the USDA food pyramid or the Canadian rainbow, with a variety of choices from the bottom half of the pyramid or the outer rings of the rainbow.

   Be flexible in the kitchen. A good chef should be willing to modify menu items to meet dietary requirements and to satisfy special requests from his or her customers.

8. **Training the dining room staff.**
   Some restaurants offer special "spa menus" in addition to their regular menus, or they highlight "healthy" items with a special symbol. Unfortunately, this approach may suggest to some people that the highlighted menu items are boring "health

food," while the other menu items are unhealthful because they aren't flagged. Consequently, many chefs prefer to train their dining room personnel to answer customers' questions about the menu and to offer suggestions when asked.

9. **Using nutritional information.**
    Study the nutritional content of foods in order to plan healthful menus. Many publications are available that list the nutritional content of common food items. Some restaurants have even hired registered dietitians to analyze their menus and give advice on how to make their food more healthful.

    Hiring a dietitian is, of course, not practical for every operation. On the other hand, a basic awareness of nutrition helps every professional minimize the fat, cholesterol, and sodium in and maximize the nutritional content and balance of the foods they serve.

■ TERMS FOR REVIEW

calorie	soluble fiber	omega-3 fatty acid	cholesterol
empty calorie	insoluble fiber	trans fat	complete protein
nutrient density	saturated fat	lipoprotein	complementary protein
carbohydrate	polyunsaturated fat	LDL	vitamin
ketone body	monounsaturated fat	HDL	major mineral
ketosis	essential fatty acid	lipid	trace mineral
fiber			

■ QUESTIONS FOR DISCUSSION

1. Describe the difference between foods with empty calories and foods with high nutrient density. Give examples of foods in each category.

2. Why are unrefined carbohydrates more healthful than refined starches and sugars?

3. Why is it necessary to have some fat in the diet?

4. Which vitamins are water soluble? Which are fat soluble? Which of the two groups is more important to include in the diet every day? Why?

5. According to the recommendations of government health agencies, which food groups should we consume more of than we now do, on average? Which foods should we consume less of?

6. Discuss and compare the healthful or unhealthful qualities of saturated fats, polyunsaturated fats, and monounsaturated fats. Give examples of each type.

7. What are some ways that you, as a cook, can reduce the fat and sodium content of your menu offerings?

8. How can you ensure a nutritionally balanced menu without actually calculating the nutrient content of every item?

Mise en Place

To be successful in the food service industry, cooks need more than the ability to prepare delicious, attractive, and nutritious foods. They also must have a talent for organization and efficiency. In every kitchen, a great many tasks must be completed over a given time and by a limited number of workers. No matter when these tasks are done, they all must come together at one crucial point: service time. Only if advance preparation is done thoroughly and systematically will service go smoothly.

Good chefs take pride in the thoroughness and quality of their advance preparation, or mise en place (meez-on-plahss). This French term, meaning "everything put in place," has become almost a professional password in North American kitchens because food service professionals understand its importance to the success of the establishment.

This chapter deals with the basic concepts of mise en place as well as specific operations that are normally part of the mise en place.

PLANNING AND ORGANIZING PRODUCTION

Even on the simplest level, pre-preparation is necessary. If you prepare only one short recipe, you must first:

- Assemble your tools.
- Assemble your ingredients.
- Wash, trim, cut, prepare, and measure your raw materials.
- Prepare your equipment (preheat oven, line baking sheets, etc.).

Only then can you begin the actual preparation.

When many items are to be prepared in a commercial kitchen, the situation is much more complex. Dealing with this complexity is the basis of kitchen organization.

THE PROBLEM

Every food service operation faces a basic conflict between two unavoidable facts:

1. There is far too much work to do in a kitchen to leave until the last minute, so some work must be done ahead.

2. Most foods are at their best quality immediately after preparation, and they deteriorate as they are held.

THE SOLUTION

To address this conflict, the chef must plan the pre-preparation carefully. Planning generally follows these steps:

1. **Break down each menu item into its stages of production.**
   Turn to any recipe in this book. Note that the procedures are divided into a sequence of steps that must be done in a certain order to make a finished product.

2. **Determine which stages may be done in advance.**

   - The first step of every recipe, written or not, is always part of advance preparation: *assembling and preparing the ingredients.* This includes cleaning and cutting produce, cutting and trimming meats, and preparing breadings and batters for frying.

   - Succeeding steps of a recipe may be done in advance *if the foods can then be held without loss of quality*.

   - Final cooking should be done as close as possible to service for maximum freshness.

   Frequently, separate parts of a recipe, such as a sauce or a stuffing, are prepared in advance, and the dish is assembled at the last minute.

   In general, items cooked by dry-heat methods, such as broiled steaks, sautéed fish, and French-fried potatoes, do not hold well. Large roasts are an important exception to this rule. Items cooked by moist heat, such as braised beef, soups, and stews, are usually better suited to reheating or holding in a steam table. Very delicate items should always be freshly cooked.

3. **Determine the best way to hold each item at its final stage of pre-preparation.** *Holding temperature* **is the temperature at which a product is kept for service or for storage. Holding temperatures for all potentially hazardous foods must be outside the Food Danger Zone.**

   - Sauces and soups are frequently kept hot, above 135°F (57°C), for service in steam tables or other holding equipment. Foods such as vegetables, however, should be kept hot only for short periods because they quickly become overcooked.

   - Refrigerator temperatures, below 41°F (5°C), are best for preserving the

After reading this chapter, you should be able to

1. Define *mise en place* and explain why care must be taken in its planning.

2. Describe five general steps used in planning mise en place.

3. Explain the difference in preparation requirements for set meal service and extended meal service.

4. List five guidelines to observe when sharpening a chef's knife.

5. Demonstrate major cutting techniques required in food preparation.

6. Describe basic precooking and marinating procedures.

7. Set up and use a standard breading station.

8. Define *convenience foods* in the context of mise en place and list eight guidelines for their use.

quality of most foods, especially perishable meats, fish, and vegetables, before final cooking or reheating.

4. **Determine how long it takes to prepare each stage of each recipe. Plan a production schedule beginning with the preparations that take the longest.** Many operations can be carried on at once because they don't all require your complete attention the full time. It may take 6 to 8 hours to make a stock, but you don't have to stand and watch it all that time.

5. **Examine recipes to see if they might be revised for better efficiency and quality as served.**
   For example:

   - Instead of preparing a full batch of green peas and holding them for service in the steam table, you might blanch and chill them, then heat portions to order in a sauté pan, steamer, or microwave oven.

   - Instead of holding a large batch of veal scaloppine in mushroom sauce in the steam table, you might prepare and hold the sauce, sauté the veal to order, combine the meat with a portion of the sauce, and serve fresh from the pan.

   Caution: Unless you are in charge of the kitchen, do not change a recipe without authorization from your supervisor.

THE GOAL

The goal of pre-preparation is to do as much work in advance as possible *without loss of quality*. Then, at service time, all energy can be used for finishing each item immediately before serving, with the utmost attention to quality and freshness.

Many preparation techniques in common use are designed for the convenience of the cooks at the expense of quality. Remember, quality should always take highest priority.

ADAPTING PREPARATION TO STYLE OF SERVICE

The way you plan production and do your mise en place depends in large part on the style of meal service. The following discussion of **set meal service** and **extended meal service** illustrates the basic differences.

Set Meal Service

- All customers eat at one time.
- Often called *quantity cooking* because large batches are prepared in advance.
- Examples: school cafeterias, banquets, employee dining rooms.

The traditional method of set meal preparation, still widely used, is to prepare the entire quantity of each item in a single large batch and to keep it hot for the duration of the meal service. This method has two major disadvantages:

- Deterioration of quality due to long holding.
- Large quantities of leftovers.

Modern high-speed equipment, such as pressure steamers, convection ovens, infrared ovens, and microwave ovens, make possible a system called *small-batch cooking*. Needed quantities are divided into smaller batches, placed in pans ready for final cooking or heating, and then cooked only as needed. The advantages of this system are as follows:

- Fresher food, because it is not held as long.
- Fewer leftovers, because servings not needed are not cooked.

Small-batch cooking also accommodates items prepared in advance and frozen or chilled for storage.

Figure 7.1
When sharpening a knife, hold the blade at a 20-degree angle to the stone.

Figure 7.2
Using a sharpening stone.

(a) Hold the knife firmly. Start with the tip of the knife against the stone as shown, and hold the edge against the stone at a 20-degree angle. Use the guiding hand to keep an even pressure on the blade.

(b) Start to draw the knife over the stone. Press very gently on the blade.

(c) Keep the motion smooth, using even, light pressure.

(d) Draw the knife across the stone all the way to the heel of the blade.

Extended Meal Service

- Customers eat at different times.
- Often called *à la carte cooking* because customers usually select items from a written menu (*carte* in French).
- Examples: restaurants, short-order counters.

Individual items are cooked to order rather than cooked ahead, but pre-preparation is extensive, down to the final cooking stage.

The short-order cook, for example, must have everything ready to go: cold meats, tomatoes and other sandwich ingredients sliced and arranged, spreads prepared and ready, hamburger patties shaped, garnishes prepared, and so on. If the cook has to stop during service to do any of these things, orders will back up and service will fall behind.

A steak that takes 10 minutes to broil may be cut and trimmed in advance, but broiling should be started 10 minutes before it is to be served.

Obviously, if the last step in a recipe is to braise the item for 1½ hours, one cannot wait until an order comes in before beginning to braise. An experienced cook can estimate closely how many orders will be needed during the meal period and prepare a batch that, ideally, will finish braising just when service begins.

Note the differences in these two methods for Chicken Chasseur. In both cases, the final product is chicken in a brown sauce with mushrooms, shallots, white wine, and tomatoes.

1. **Quantity method—Chicken Chasseur:**

    Brown chicken in fat; remove.

    Sauté shallots and mushrooms in same fat.

    Add flour to make a roux.

    Add white wine, tomatoes, brown stock, seasonings; simmer until thickened.

    Add chicken; braise until done.

2. **À la carte method—Chicken Chasseur:**

    Prepare Sauce Chasseur in advance; hold in bain-marie.

    For each order:

    Brown chicken in sauté pan; finish cooking in oven.

    Deglaze pan with white wine; reduce.

    Add one portion of sauce; add chicken and simmer briefly; serve.

MISE EN PLACE: THE REQUIRED TASKS

Up to this point, we have discussed planning the production schedule. Our planning helps us determine what tasks we must do before beginning the final cooking during the meal service period. Chefs refer to performing these preliminary tasks as "doing the mise en place." In many restaurants, especially large ones, the mise en place is extensive. It includes the preparation of stocks, sauces, breadings, and batters as well as the cutting and trimming of all the meat, poultry, fish, and vegetables the chef expects will be needed during the meal service. A large part of a cook's workday is spent doing mise en place. This means that a large part of learning how to cook is learning how to do mise en place. In fact, a large part of this book is devoted to these tasks of preparation. There are many more such tasks than can be included in a single chapter.

The remainder of this chapter discusses the most basic and general skills required for a mise en place. The most basic of these are knife skills. Fundamentals such as how to hold the chef's knife, how to maintain a sharp edge, and how to make basic cuts are illustrated. More specific techniques required for individual food products are explained in appropriate chapters later in the book. For example, vegetable trimming techniques are discussed in the first vegetable chapter, methods for cutting chicken in the first poultry chapter.

USING THE KNIFE

Many kinds of laborsaving tools are available for cutting, chopping, and slicing fresh foods. Chapter 3 lists the basic kinds.

The chef's knife or French knife, however, is still the cook's most important and versatile cutting tool. The knife is more precise than a machine. Unless you are cutting a large quantity, the knife can even be faster. Cleaning a large machine takes time.

To get the best use out of your knife, *you must learn to keep it sharp and to handle it properly*.

KEEPING A SHARP EDGE

The Sharpening Stone

A stone is the best tool for sharpening a chef's knife. The best electric sharpeners do an excellent job of sharpening chef's knives, but many models wear away too much of your expensive knife without making a good edge. You may not be lucky enough to have ready use of a good electric sharpener, so it is important to know how to sharpen a knife on a stone.

Follow these guidelines:

1. Hold the blade at a constant 20-degree angle to the stone, as shown in Figure 7.1.
2. Make light, even strokes, the same number on each side of the blade.
3. Sharpen in one direction only to get a regular, uniform edge.
4. Do not oversharpen.
5. Finish with a few strokes on the steel (see next section), then wipe the blade clean.

Figure 7.2 illustrates one of several sharpening methods. There are other good ones, too, and your instructor may prefer a method not illustrated here.

The Steel

This tool is used not to sharpen the edge but to *true the edge* (to perfect it, or to smooth out irregularities) and to *maintain the edge* (to keep it sharp as it is used).

Observe these guidelines for using the steel:

1. Hold the blade at a constant 20-degree angle to the steel, just as when using the stone (Figure 7.2). A smaller angle will be ineffective. A larger one will dull the edge.
2. Make light strokes. Do not grind the knife against the steel.
3. Make even, regular strokes. Alternate each stroke, first on one side of the blade, then on the other.
4. Use no more than five or six strokes on each side of the blade. Too much steeling can actually dull the blade.
5. Use the steel often. Then you will rarely have to sharpen the knife on the stone.

Figure 7.3 illustrates one of several steeling methods. This one is popular, but several others are equally correct. Carefully observe your instructors' demonstrations of their preferred methods.

HANDLING THE KNIFE

The Grip

A proper grip gives you maximum control over the knife, increases your cutting accuracy and speed, prevents slipping, and lessens the chance of an accident. The type of grip you use depends, in part, on the job you are doing and the size of the knife.

The grip illustrated in Figure 7.4 is one of the most frequently used for general cutting and slicing. Many chefs feel that grasping the blade with the thumb and forefinger in this manner gives them greatest control.

Figure 7.3
Using a steel.

(a) Hold the steel and the knife away from your body. With the knife in a vertical position and at a 20-degree angle to the steel, touch the steel with the heel of the blade.

(b) Pass the knife lightly along the steel, bringing the blade down in a smooth arc.

(c) Complete the movement. Do not strike the guard of the steel with the tip of the blade.

(d, e, f) Repeat the motion on the other side of the steel.

Figure 7.4
Grasping the blade of the knife between the thumb and forefinger gives the worker good control over the blade.

Figure 7.5
The position of the guiding hand, which holds the item being cut or sliced and also guides the blade, from two points of view.

Holding the knife may feel awkward at first, but practice will make it seem natural. Watch your instructors demonstrate the grips they use, then practice under their supervision.

The Guiding Hand

While one hand controls the knife, the other hand controls the product being cut. Proper positioning of the hand achieves three goals:

1. **Hold the item being cut.**
   In Figure 7.5, the item is held firmly so it will not slip.

2. **Guide the knife.**
   Note that the knife blade slides against the fingers. The position of the hand controls the cut.

3. **Protect the hand from cuts.**
   Fingertips are curled under, out of the way of the blade.

BASIC CUTS AND SHAPES

Cutting food products into uniform shapes and sizes is important for two reasons:

1. It ensures even cooking.

2. It enhances the appearance of the product.

   Figure 7.6 shows common shapes, with their names and dimensions. The following terms describe other cutting techniques:

   Chop: to cut into irregularly shaped pieces.

   Concasser (con-cass-say): to chop coarsely.

   Mince: to chop into very fine pieces.

   Emincer (em-man-say): to cut into very thin slices (does not mean "to mince").

   Shred: to cut into thin strips, either with the coarse blade of a grater (manual or power) or with a chef's knife.

	Tourné: 2 in. long × ³⁄₄ in. diameter, with 7 sides, and flat-ended.		**Rondelle:** round or bias-round cuts, varied diameter or thickness.
	Large dice: ³⁄₄ in. × ³⁄₄ in.× ³⁄₄ in. (2 cm × 2 cm × 2 cm).		**Paysanne:** ¹⁄₂ in. × ¹⁄₂ in. × ¹⁄₈ in. (round, square, or rectangular).
	Medium dice: ¹⁄₂ in. × ¹⁄₂ in. × ¹⁄₂ in. (12 mm × 12 mm × 12 mm).		**Batonnet:** ¹⁄₄ in. × ¹⁄₄ in. × 2¹⁄₂–3 in. (6 mm × 6 mm × 6–7.5 mm).
	Small dice: ¹⁄₄ in. × ¹⁄₄ in. × ¹⁄₄ in. (6 mm × 6 mm × 6 mm).		
	Brunoise: ¹⁄₈ in. × ¹⁄₈ in. × ¹⁄₈ in. (3 mm × 3 mm × 3 mm).		**Julienne:** ¹⁄₈ in. × ¹⁄₈ in. × 2¹⁄₂ in. (3 mm × 3 mm × 6 mm).
	Fine brunoise: ¹⁄₁₆ in. × ¹⁄₁₆ in. × ¹⁄₁₆ in.		**Fine julienne:** 2 in. long × ¹⁄₁₆ in. × ¹⁄₁₆ in.

Figure 7.6
Basic cuts and shapes.
(a) Tourné: 2 in. long x ³⁄₄ in. diameter, with 7 sides, and flat-ended (5 cm x 2 cm).
(b) Large dice: ³⁄₄ in. x ³⁄₄ in. x ³⁄₄ in. (2 cm x 2 cm x 2 cm).
(c) Medium dice: ¹⁄₂ in. x ¹⁄₂ in. x ¹⁄₂ in. (12 mm x 12 mm x 12 mm).
(d) Small dice: ¹⁄₄ in. x ¹⁄₄ in. x ¹⁄₄ in. (6 mm x 6 mm x 6 mm).
(e) Brunoise (broon-wahz): ¹⁄₈ in. x ¹⁄₈ in. x ¹⁄₈ in. (3 mm x 3 mm x 3 mm).
(f) Fine brunoise: ¹⁄₁₆ in. x ¹⁄₁₆ in. x ¹⁄₁₆ in. (1.5 mm x 1.5 mm x 1.5 mm).
(g) Rondelle: round or bias-round cuts, varied diameter or thickness.
(h) Paysanne: ¹⁄₂ in. x ¹⁄₂ in. x ¹⁄₈ in. (12 mm x 12 mm x 3 mm; round, square, or rectangular).
(i) Batonnet: ¹⁄₄ in. x ¹⁄₄ in. x 2¹⁄₂–3 in. (6 mm x 6 mm x 6–7.5 cm).
(j) Julienne (or allumette potatoes): ¹⁄₈ in. x ¹⁄₈ in. x 2¹⁄₂ in. (3 mm x 3 mm x 6 cm).
(k) Fine julienne: 2 in. long x ¹⁄₁₆ in. x ¹⁄₁₆ in. (1.5 mm x 1.5 mm x 5 cm).

CUTTING TECHNIQUES

Different parts of the blade are appropriate for different purposes, as shown in Figure 7.7. (*Note*: Prying off bottle caps is not a function of any part of the knife.)

Figure 7.7
Using different parts of the knife blade.

(a) The tip of the knife, where the blade is thinnest and narrowest, is used for delicate work and small items.

(b) The center of the blade is used for most general work.

(c) The heel of the knife is used for heavy or coarse work, especially when greater force is required.

1. **Slicing.**

   Two basic slicing techniques are illustrated in Figures 7.8 and 7.9. When carrots and similar items are cut into round slices as shown, the cut is called **rondelle**.

Figure 7.8
Slicing technique 1.

(a) Start the knife at a sharp angle, with the tip of the knife on the cutting board.

(b) Move the knife forward and down to slice through the carrot.

(c) Finish the cut with the knife against the board. For the second slice, raise the heel of the knife and pull it backward, but be sure the tip always stays on the board.

Figure 7.9
Slicing technique 2.

a) Start the blade at a 45-degree angle, with the tip on the cucumber against the fingers of the guiding hand.

(b, c) Slice downward and forward through the item.

2. **Cutting dice, brunoise, batonnet, allumette, and julienne.**
Figure 7.10 shows the steps in dicing a product, using a potato to illustrate. Note in Figure 7.10c that the process of cutting dice first requires that you cut stick shapes, such as batonnet. Thus, this illustration demonstrates the method used to cut not only dice and brunoise (fine dice) but also batonnet, allumette, and julienne.

Figure 7.10
Dicing a potato.

(a) Square off the peeled, eyed potato by cutting a slice from all sides. Use the trimmings for mashed potatoes or soup.

(b) Cut the potato into even slices of the desired thickness. Here we are making a ¼-in. dice, so the slices are ¼ in. thick (metric equivalent: 6 mm).

(c) Stack the slices and again slice across the stack in even ¼-in. slices. You now have batonnet potatoes, slightly smaller than regular French fries. Slices ⅛ in. thick would give you allumette potatoes.

(d) Looking from this angle shows how the slices have been stacked up.

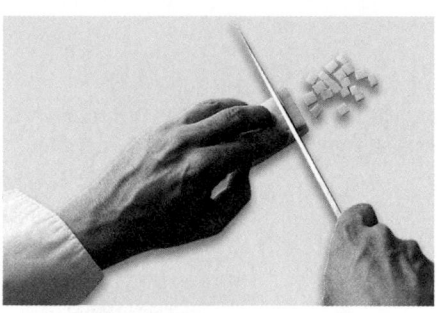

(e) Pile the batonnets together and cut across in slices ¼ in. apart. You now have perfect ¼-in. dice.

3. **Cutting paysanne.**
Paysanne are thin square, or roughly square, cuts. The procedure begins the same as for cutting medium dice. However, in the last step, cut the ½-inch (12 mm) -thick sticks into thin slices rather than into dice. Figure 7.11 illustrates.

4. **Cutting lozenges.**
This is a diamond-shape cut, as illustrated in Figure 7.12.

Figure 7.11
Cut the vegetable into sticks ½ inch (12 mm) square. To cut the sticks into paysanne, cut them crosswise into thin slices.

Figure 7.12
To cut lozenges, first cut the vegetable into thin slices, then cut these slices lengthwise into strips about ⅛ inch (1 cm) wide. Cut the strips at an angle to form diamond shapes.

5. Dicing an onion.

Dicing an onion presents a special problem for cutting because its form is in layers, not a solid piece. This technique is illustrated in Figure 7.13.

Figure 7.13
Dicing an onion.

(a) Cut the peeled onion in half lengthwise, through the root end. Place one half on the cutting board, cut side down.

(b) With the root end away from you, make a series of vertical lengthwise cuts. Do not cut through the root end. The closer together you make the cuts, the smaller the dice will be.

(c) Holding the onion carefully at the top, make a few horizontal cuts toward but not through the root end, which is holding the onion together.

(d) Finally, slice across the onion to separate it into dice. Again, the closer together the cuts, the smaller the dice.

(e) Continue making slices almost to the root end. The root end may be rough cut for mirepoix, to be used for stocks, sauces, and roasts.

6. Chopping mirepoix.

Mirepoix is a mixture of coarsely chopped vegetables, primarily onions, carrots, and celery, used to flavor stocks, gravies, sauces, and other items, as explained in Chapter 8. Because mirepoix is not served but is almost always strained out of the product before finishing, neatness of cut is not important. The products are cut roughly into pieces of approximately uniform size—small pieces if cooking time is to short, larger pieces for longer cooking times. Figure 7.14 illustrates mirepoix ingredients being cut.

7. Chopping herbs.

This chopping technique is used to cut a product when no specific shape is needed. Figure 7.15 illustrates chopping parsley.

In the case of chives and scallions, a more regular cut is used, similar to the slicing cut used for larger items like carrots. Figure 7.16 illustrates this procedure.

Figure 7.14
To chop mirepoix, cut onions, celery, and carrots roughly into pieces of approximately equal size. The exact size depends on what the mirepoix is to be used for.

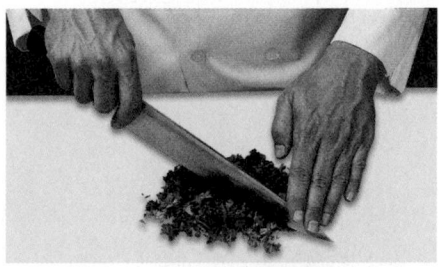

Figure 7.15
Chopping with a French knife. Holding the tip of the knife against the cutting board, rock the knife rapidly up and down. At the same time, gradually move the knife sideways across the product on the board so the cuts pass through all parts of the pile of food. After several cuts, redistribute the pile and begin again. Continue until the product is chopped as fine as you want.

Figure 7.16
Stack chives and cut crosswise into very thin slices.

8. **Cutting parisienne.**

Cuts made with a ball cutter are perhaps most often used for potatoes. Potatoes cut into large balls (about 1⅓ inch or 3 cm) are called **parisienne**. When cut into smaller balls (about ⅞ inch or 2.5 cm), they are called **noisette**. Of course, other solid vegetables, such as turnips, as well as many fruits, can be cut the same way. The procedure is illustrated in Figure 7.17.

Figure 7.17
Cutting parisienne potatoes.

(a) Place the ball cutter against the potato as shown.

(b) With the thumb, press the cutter firmly into the potato as far as it will go.

(c) Lift the handle of the cutter outward, twist the cutter around, and remove the ball.

9. **Cutting tournéed vegetables.**

To tourné a vegetable is to cut it into a neat seven-sided oval shape, as illustrated in Figure 7.18. Many root vegetables, such as carrots and turnips, are cut this way. When potatoes are tournéed, they are named according to their size. **Cocotte** potatoes are about 1½ inches (4 cm) long. **Château** potatoes are about 2 inches (5 cm) long.

Figure 7.18
Tournéing potatoes and other root vegetables.

(a) Cut the potatoes roughly into pieces slightly larger than the final size desired. Cut off the top and bottom of each piece so they are flat and parallel.

(b) Hold the potato between the thumb and forefinger and place the paring knife against the top edge as shown and the thumb of the cutting hand firmly against the potato. Your hand should be far enough up on the blade to maintain steady control.

(c) Cut downward toward your thumb with a curving movement of the blade.

(d) Turn the potato slightly (one-seventh of a full turn, to be exact) and repeat the motion.

(e) The finished product. If perfectly done, the potato has seven sides (but customers rarely count them).

10. Peeling grapefruit.

This technique, as shown in Figure 7.19, can also be used for peeling yellow turnips or other round vegetables and fruits with heavy peels.

Figure 7.19
Peeling a grapefruit.

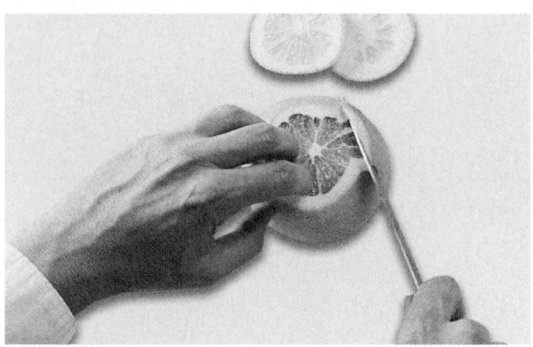

(a) Cut off the ends of the grapefruit and turn it on a flat end so it is stable. Slice off a section of the peel, following the contour of the grapefruit.

(b) Make sure the cut is deep enough to remove the peel but not so deep as to waste the product.

(c) Continue making slices around the grapefruit until all the peel is removed.

(d) Slice or section the fruit. (Squeeze the remaining pulp for juice.)

11. Chiffonade.

This term refers to cutting leaves into fine shreds. It is applied most often to lettuce and sorrel. To cut chiffonade, remove the heavy leaf ribs, roll the leaves into a tight cylinder, and then slice the cylinder crosswise into thin shreds, as shown in Figure 7.20.

Figure 7.20
Cutting a chiffonade of sorrel.

(a) Roll the leaves into a cylinder.

(b) Cut crosswise into thin strips or shreds.

12. Cutting citrus zest.
With a paring knife, cut strips from the citrus peel, removing only the colored part, not the white part below it. Then, with a chef's knife, cut the zest into thin strips or julienne, as shown in Figure 7.21b. An alternative method is to use a citrus zester, as shown in Figure 7.21c.

Figure 7.21
Cutting citrus zest.

(a) Use a paring knife to cut thin strips from the peel, being careful to cut only the outer colored part, not the inner white pith.

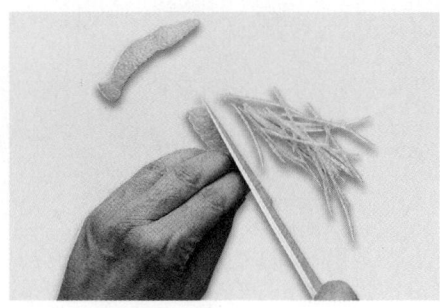

(b) Cut the strips of peel into julienne.

(c) Alternatively, draw a zesting tool over the fruit to cut thin strips of zest.

PRELIMINARY COOKING AND FLAVORING

Advance preparation often requires certain precooking and flavoring of ingredients to make them ready for use in the finished recipe.

On the most obvious level, if a recipe for chicken salad calls for cooked, diced chicken, you must first cook the chicken before you can proceed with the recipe. A complete cooking procedure, in such a case, is part of the mise en place or pre-preparation.

BLANCHING AND PARCOOKING

Partial cooking is a significant part of advance preparation. It requires a degree of culinary skill and judgment to determine when and how much cooking is necessary or desirable.

Partial cooking may be done by any moist-heat or dry-heat method. Those commonly used are simmering or boiling (parboiling), steaming, and deep-frying (especially for potatoes). The term blanching may mean any of these methods, but it usually implies *very brief* cooking.

There are four main reasons for blanching or parcooking:

1. **To increase holding quality.**
    Heating helps preserve foods by:

    •   Destroying bacteria that cause spoilage.

    •   Destroying enzymes that discolor foods (as when potatoes turn brown) and help them deteriorate.

2. **To save time.**
    It takes less time to finish parboiled vegetables for service than it does to finish raw vegetables. Large batches of foods may be blanched and chilled, and individual portions then finished to order.

    Items such as roast duck, which take too long to cook completely to order, are often roasted half to three-quarters done, and then finished as the orders are received.

3. **To remove undesirable flavors.**
   Some variety meats and certain strong-flavored vegetables, such as rutabaga, are sometimes blanched to make them milder and more acceptable to the customer.

4. **To enable the product to be processed further.**
   For example, vegetables and fruits such as tomatoes and peaches, as well as some nuts, are blanched to loosen the skins for peeling.

   Sweetbreads are blanched so they are firm enough for slicing and breading or other kinds of handling.

MARINATING

To **marinate** means to soak a food product in a seasoned liquid in order to:

1. Flavor the product.
2. Tenderize the product.

The tenderizing effect of the acids in the marinade is relatively small. It is still essential to match the proper cut of meat with the proper cooking techniques for greatest tenderness.

The marinade can also serve as the cooking medium and become part of the sauce. Vegetable marinades, called *vinaigrettes*, are served cold with the vegetables as salads or hors d'oeuvres, without further cooking or processing.

Marinades have three categories of ingredients:

1. **Oil.**
   Oil helps preserve the meat's moisture. Sometimes it is omitted, especially for long marinations, when the oil would only float on top, out of contact with the product being marinated.

   Tasteless vegetable oils are used when a neutral flavor is required. Specialty oils, such as olive oil, are used to add flavor to the item being marinated.

2. **Acid from vinegar, lemon juice, wine.**
   Acid helps tenderize protein foods.

   It carries flavors (its own and dissolved flavors from spices and herbs).

   Use caution when employing strong acids, such as vinegar and lemon juice. A marinade that is too acidic will partially coagulate the protein of the meat, making it seem partially cooked. When the meat is then cooked, its texture will not be as desirable. Strong acids can be used in marinades if they are used in small quantities or if the meat is marinated for only a few hours.

3. **Flavorings—spices, herbs, vegetables.**
   A wide choice is available, depending on the purpose.

   Whole spices release flavors more slowly, so they are more suitable for long marinations.

Kinds of Marinades

1. **Cooked.**
   Used when long keeping quality is important. Modern refrigeration has made cooked marinades less widely used. An advantage of cooked marinades is that spices release more flavor into the marinade when it is cooked.

2. **Raw.**
   Most widely used for long marination under refrigeration. For example, see the recipe for Sauerbraten (p. 345). Figure 7.22 shows meat in a raw marinade.

Figure 7.22
Beef chuck in a raw marinade of red wine, wine vinegar, spices, and aromatic vegetables.

Figure 7.23
Applying a dry rub to a rack of spareribs.

3. **Instant.**
The range of flavors and purposes is wide. Used for marinating a few minutes up to several hours or overnight. For example, see the recipe for London Broil (p. 308).

4. **Dry.**
A dry marinade, also called a *dry rub* or a *spice rub*, is a mixture of salt, spices, and herbs that is rubbed or patted onto the surface of a meat, poultry, or fish item. In some cases, a little oil or a moist ingredient such as crushed garlic is mixed with the spices to make a paste. The item is then refrigerated to allow it time to absorb the flavors. The rub may be left on the item or scraped off before cooking. This technique is widely used for barbecued meats. For an example of a dry marinade, see page 374. Figure 7.23 shows a dry rub being applied to a large cut of meat.
Dry marinades are an effective way to flavor meats. Naturally, because a dry marinade usually doesn't contain an acid, you can't expect it to produce the slight tenderizing effects of liquid marinades containing acids.

Guidelines for Marinating

1. Marinate under refrigeration (unless product is to be cooked for only a few minutes).
2. Remember: The thicker the product, the longer it takes for the marinade to penetrate.
3. Use an acid-resistant container, such as stainless steel, glass, crockery, or some plastics.
4. Tie spices in a cheesecloth bag (sachet) if easy removal is important.
5. Cover product completely with marinade. When marinating small items for a short time, you may use less liquid, but you must then turn the product frequently for even penetration.

PREPARATION FOR FRYING

Most foods to be deep-fried, with the major exception of potatoes, are first given a protective coating of breading or batter. This coating serves four purposes:

1. It helps retain moisture and flavor in the product.
2. It protects the fat against the moisture and salt in the food, which speed deterioration of frying fat.
3. It protects the food from absorbing too much fat.
4. It gives crispness, flavor, and good appearance to the product.

BREADING

Breading means coating a product with bread crumbs or other crumbs or meal before deep-frying, pan-frying, or sautéing. The most widely used method for applying these coatings is called the **Standard Breading Procedure**.

The Three Stages of the Standard Breading Procedure

1. **Flour.**
Helps the breading stick to the product.

2. **Egg wash.**
A mixture of eggs and liquid, usually milk or water. More eggs give greater binding power but increase the cost. A small quantity of oil is occasionally added to the egg wash.

3. **Crumbs.**

Combine with the egg wash to create a crisp, golden coating when fried. Fine, dry bread crumbs are most often used and give good results. Also popular are Japanese-style dry bread crumbs called **panko** (Japanese for "bread crumbs"). These coarser crumbs give a pleasing texture to fried items. Other products used are fresh bread crumbs, crushed corn flakes or other cereal, cracker meal, and cornmeal.

For small items like scallops and oysters, breading may be done with the aid of a series of wire baskets placed in the flour, wash, and crumbs, instead of by hand. The procedure is the same except the baskets are used to lift and shake small quantities of the product and to transfer them to the next basket.

To keep one hand dry during breading, use your right hand (if you are right-handed; if left-handed, reverse the procedure) only for handling the flour and crumbs. Use your other hand for handling the product when it is wet.

Procedure for Making Bread Crumbs

1. For fresh bread crumbs, use bread that is one or two days old. If the bread is fresh, its moisture content will make it difficult to process into crumbs without making gummy wads of bread. For dry bread crumbs, lightly toast the bread in a warm oven until the bread is dry but not browned. Do not use stale bread, which has an off flavor.

2. Trim off crusts to make crumbs of a uniform light color.

3. Cut or tear the bread into smaller pieces.

4. Depending on the quantity, place the pieces in a food processor or a vertical cutter/mixer. Process until the crumbs are of the desired fineness.

5. For dry bread crumbs of uniform size, pass the processed crumbs through a sieve (also called a *tamis*). See page 60.

Procedure for Proper Breading

Figure 7.24 illustrates a station setup for the Standard Breading Procedure.

1. Dry the product to get a thin, even coating of flour.

2. Season the product—or, for greater efficiency, season the flour (step 3). Do not season the crumbs. The presence of salt in contact with the frying fat helps break down the fat and shorten its life.

3. Dip the product in flour to coat evenly. Shake off excess.

4. Dip in egg wash to coat completely. Remove. Let excess drain off so the crumb coating will be even.

5. Dip in bread crumbs. Cover with crumbs and press gently on product. Make sure it is coated completely. Remove. Carefully shake off excess.

6. Fry immediately or hold for service.

7. To hold for later service, place in a single layer on a pan or rack and refrigerate. Do not hold very moist items, such as raw clams or oysters. The breading will quickly become soggy.

8. Strain egg wash and sift flour and crumbs as often as necessary to remove lumps.

Figure 7.24
Setup of station for standard breading procedures. Right-handed cooks work from left to right. Left-handed cooks work from right to left.

DREDGING WITH FLOUR

Purpose

The purpose of dredging is to give a thin, even coating of flour to a product.

Meats to be sautéed or pan-fried are often dredged with flour to give them an even, brown color and to prevent sticking.

Vegetables such as sticks of zucchini are sometimes coated only in flour before deep-frying to give them a light golden color and a very thin coating.

Procedure

Follow steps 1 to 3 of the Standard Breading Procedure (p. 142).

BATTERS

Batters are semiliquid mixtures containing flour or other starch. They are used in deep-frying to give a crisp, flavorful, golden brown coating. There are many formulas and variations for batters.

1. Many liquids are used, including milk, water, or beer.
2. Eggs may or may not be used.
3. Thicker batters make thicker coatings. Too thick a batter makes a heavy, unpalatable coating.
4. Leavenings are frequently used to give a lighter product. These may be:
   • Baking powder
   • Beaten egg whites
   • Carbonation from beer or seltzer used in the batter

Three recipes for basic, typical batters are given in the recipe for Deep-Fried Onion Rings (p. 576). These batters may be used on a wide variety of products.

HANDLING CONVENIENCE FOODS

Convenience foods play an increasingly prominent role in the food service industry. Their use has become so important that no student of professional cooking can afford to be without knowledge of them.

A convenience food may be defined as *any product that has been partially or completely prepared or processed by a manufacturer.* In other words, when you buy a convenience product, you are having the manufacturer do some or all of your preparation for you.

Of course, you must pay for this service, as reflected in the price of the product. Although buying the convenience product will likely cost you more than buying the raw materials, you save in increased kitchen efficiency. As you remember from Chapter 5, labor costs as well as food costs must be figured into your menu prices.

Processed foods for restaurants and institutions range from partially prepared items that can be used as components in your recipes, such as frozen fish fillets, peeled potatoes, concentrated stock bases, and frozen puff pastry dough, to fully prepared items that need only be reconstituted or served as is, such as frozen prepared entrées and frozen pies and pastries. Some items, like frozen French fries, have wide acceptance, while other more fully prepared foods continue to be resisted by both customer and operator.

Guidelines for Handling Convenience Foods

1. Handle with the same care you give fresh, raw ingredients.

   Most loss of quality in convenience foods comes from assuming they are damage-proof and can be treated haphazardly.

2. Examine as soon as received.

   Particularly, check frozen foods—with a thermometer—to make sure they have not thawed in transit. Put away at once.

3. Store properly.

   Frozen foods must be held at 0°F (–18°C) or lower. Check your freezer with a thermometer regularly. Refrigerated foods must stay chilled, below 41°F (5°C), to slow spoilage. Shelf-stable foods (dry products, canned goods, etc.) are shelf-stable only when stored properly, in a cool, dry place, tightly sealed.

4. Know the shelf life of each product.

   Nothing will keep forever, not even convenience foods. (Some, like peeled potatoes, are even more perishable than unprocessed ingredients.) Rotate stock according to the first in, first out principle. And don't stock more than necessary.

5. Defrost frozen foods properly.

   Ideally, defrost in a tempering box set at 28°F to 30°F (–2°C to –1°C) or, lacking that, in the refrigerator at 41°F (5°C) or lower. This takes advance planning and timing, because large items take several days to thaw.

   If you are short of time, the second-best way to defrost foods is under cold, running water, in the original wrapper.

   Never defrost at room temperature or in warm water. The high temperatures encourage bacterial growth and spoilage.

   Do not refreeze thawed foods. Quality will greatly deteriorate.

   Certain foods, like frozen French fries and some individual-portion prepared entrées, are designed to be cooked without thawing.

6. Know how and to what extent the product has been prepared.

   Partially cooked foods need less heating in final preparation than do raw foods. Some cooks prepare frozen, cooked crab legs, for example, as though they were raw, but by the time the customer receives them, they are overcooked, dry, and tasteless. Frozen vegetables, for a second example, have been blanched and often need only to be heated briefly.

   Manufacturers are happy to give full directions and serving suggestions for their products. At least you should read the package directions.

7. Use proper cooking methods.

   Be flexible. Much modern equipment has been designed especially for convenience foods. Don't restrict yourself to conventional ranges and ovens if compartment steamers, convection ovens, or microwave ovens might do a better job more efficiently.

8. Treat convenience foods as though you, not the manufacturer, did the pre-preparation.

   Make the most of your opportunity to use creativity and to serve the best quality you can. Your final preparation, plating, and garnish should be as careful as though you made it from scratch.

In general, the more completely a product has been prepared by the manufacturer, the less it will reflect the individuality of the food service operator—and the less opportunity the cooks have to give it their own character and quality.

Is a stock made from scratch better than a product made from a convenience base? Most quality-conscious chefs would probably answer "Yes!" But the correct answer is, "Not if the homemade stock is poorly made." No matter what products you use, there is no substitute for quality and care. The fresh product is potentially the best, but not if it is badly stored or handled. Convenience foods also need proper handling to maintain their quality.

The key to understanding and handling convenience foods is considering them as normal products with part of the pre-prep completed rather than as totally different kinds of products unlike your normal raw materials. *Convenience products are not a substitute for culinary knowledge and skill.* They should be a tool for the good cook rather than a crutch for the bad cook. It takes as much understanding of basic cooking principles to handle convenience products as it does fresh, raw ingredients, particularly if you want the convenience product to taste as much like the fresh as possible.

■ TERMS FOR REVIEW

mise en place	shred	julienne	marinate
holding temperatures	rondelle	paysanne	Standard Breading
set meal service	small dice	parisienne	Procedure
extended meal service	medium dice	noisette	panko
chop	large dice	cocotte	batter
concasser	brunoise	château	convenience food
mince	batonnet	chiffonade	
emincer	allumette	blanch	

■ QUESTIONS FOR DISCUSSION

1. How does preparation differ for set meal service and extended meal service?

2. It has been said that à la carte cooking, or cooking to order, is nothing more than small-batch cooking carried to its extreme. Based on what you know about pre-preparation, what do you think this statement means?

3. Why is it important to learn to cut foods accurately and uniformly?

4. Name six basic vegetable cuts and give their dimensions.

5. Give six examples of foods that might be blanched or par-cooked during pre-preparation, and give a reason for each.

6. Describe in detail how to set up a breading station and how to use it to bread veal cutlets.

7. The manager of the restaurant in which you are a cook has decided to try using frozen, breaded shrimp instead of having you bread shrimp by hand, but she is worried about customer acceptance and asks for your help. How will you handle the new product?

CHAPTER 8

Stocks and Sauces

The importance of stocks in the kitchen is indicated by the French word for stock: fond, meaning "foundation" or "base." In classical cuisine, the ability to prepare good stocks is the most basic of all skills because so much of the work of the entire kitchen depends on them. A good stock is the foundation of soups, sauces, and most braised foods and stews.

In modern kitchens, stocks have lost much of the importance they once had. In the first place, increased reliance on portion-controlled meats has made bones for stock a rarity in most establishments. Second, making stocks requires extra labor, which most restaurants today aren't able to provide. Finally, more food today is served without sauces, so stocks aren't seen to be quite as necessary.

Nevertheless, the finest cuisine still depends on soups and sauces based on high-quality stocks, so stock-making remains an essential skill that you should learn early in your training. Stocks and sauces are almost never served by themselves but are components of many other preparations. You will need to refer to this chapter in connection with many other subjects.

STOCKS

The preparation of stocks has been simplified in many ways since the days of Escoffier, although this does not mean that it demands less care or skill. Few chefs today bother to tie vegetables for a stock into a bundle, for example. They're going to be strained out anyway. The number and variety of ingredients is usually not as great as it once was. Nor is it common to cook stocks for as many hours as were once thought necessary. All these details are taken up one by one in this section.

A **stock** may be defined as a clear, thin (that is, unthickened) liquid flavored by soluble substances extracted from meat, poultry, and fish, and their bones, and from vegetables and seasonings. Our objective in preparing stocks is to select the proper ingredients and then to extract the flavors we want—in other words, to combine the correct ingredients with the correct procedure.

After reading this chapter, you should be able to

1. **Prepare basic mirepoix.**
2. **Flavor liquids using a sachet or spice bag.**
3. **Prepare white veal or beef stocks, chicken stock, fish stock, and brown stock.**
4. **Cool and store stocks correctly.**
5. **Prepare meat, chicken, and fish glazes.**
6. **Evaluate the quality of convenience bases and use convenience bases.**
7. **Explain the functions of sauces and list five qualities that a sauce adds to food.**
8. **Prepare white, blond, and brown roux and use them to thicken liquids.**
9. **Prepare and use beurre manié.**
10. **Thicken liquids with cornstarch and other starches.**
11. **Prepare and use egg yolk and cream liaison.**
12. **Finish a sauce with raw butter (monter au beurre).**
13. **Prepare the five leading sauces: béchamel, velouté, brown sauce or espagnole, tomato, and hollandaise.**
14. **Prepare small sauces from leading sauces.**
15. **Identify and prepare five simple butter sauces.**
16. **Prepare compound butters and list their uses.**
17. **Prepare pan gravies.**
18. **Prepare miscellaneous hot and cold sauces.**

INGREDIENTS

BONES

Bones are the major ingredient of stocks (except water, of course). Most of the flavor and body of stocks are derived from the bones of beef, veal, chicken, fish, and, occasionally, lamb, pork, ham, and game. (Vegetable stocks, an exception, draw their flavor entirely from vegetables; see p. 153.)

The kinds of bones used determine the kind of stock.

Chicken stock, of course, is made from chicken bones.

White stock is made from beef or veal bones or a combination of the two. Chicken bones or even pork bones are sometimes added in small quantity.

Brown stock is made from beef or veal bones that have been browned in an oven.

Fish stock is made from fish bones and trimmings left over after filleting. Bones from lean white fish give the best stock. Fat fish are not normally used. The term *fumet* is often used for a flavorful fish stock, especially one made with wine. See the note at the beginning of the recipe for Fish Fumet (p. 158).

Lamb, game, turkey, and other stocks have specialized uses.

In Chapter 4, we discussed a group of proteins called *connective tissue*. Remember that some of these proteins are dissolved when cooked with slow, moist heat. Chapter 10, "Understanding Meats," offers more information about these substances. There are two basic facts you should learn and understand:

1. When certain connective tissues (called *collagen*) break down, they form *gelatin*. This gives body to a stock, an important feature of its quality. A well-made stock thickens or even solidifies when chilled.

2. *Cartilage* is the best source of gelatin in bones. Younger animals have more cartilage in their skeletons. As they become older, this hardens into solid bone, which is harder to dissolve into stocks. *Knuckle bones*, on the joints of major bones, have a lot of cartilage and are valued in stock-making. Neck bones and shank bones are also used a great deal.

Cut large bones into pieces about 3 inches (8 centimeters) long. This exposes more surface area and aids extraction. Also, the bones are easier to handle.

MEAT

Because of its cost, meat is rarely used in stock making anymore. (Exception: Chicken hearts and gizzards are often used in chicken stock.)

Occasionally, a broth is produced as a result of simmering meat or poultry, as when fowl is cooked for dishes like creamed chicken. This broth can then be used like a stock. However, the chicken is considered the object of the game in this case. The broth is just a byproduct.

In this book, we use the word **broth** to mean a flavorful liquid obtained from the simmering of meats and/or vegetables.

MIREPOIX

Aromatic vegetables are the second most important contributors of flavor to stocks. (In the case of vegetable stocks, they are the most important.)

Mirepoix (meer-pwah) is a combination of onions, carrots, and celery. It is a basic flavoring preparation that is used in all areas of cooking, not only for flavoring stocks but also for sauces, soups, meats, poultry, fish, and vegetables. (The classical mirepoix of decades ago contained a wider variety of ingredients, sometimes including ham or bacon, leeks and other vegetables, and one or more fresh herbs. The modern version is considerably simplified.)

Learn the proportions in Table 8.1 well. Mirepoix is a basic preparation you will need throughout your career.

A *white mirepoix*, made without carrots, is used when it is necessary to keep the stock as colorless as possible. Mushroom trimmings may be added to white mirepoix. When cost permits, it is a good idea to include leeks in the mirepoix in place of part of the onions in a white mirepoix. They give an excellent flavor.

In vegetable stocks, a variety of vegetables is used in addition to or in place of the traditional mirepoix; see page 153 for a brief discussion.

Table 8.1 Mirepoix		
To Make:	**1 Pound**	**400 Grams**
Onions	8 oz	200 g
Celery	4 oz	100 g
Carrots	4 oz	100 g

Cutting Mirepoix

Chop the vegetables coarsely into pieces of relatively uniform size. As mirepoix is rarely served, it is not usually necessary to cut it neatly.

The size depends on how long the mirepoix will cook. If it will cook a long time, as for beef stock, cut the vegetables into large pieces (1 to 2 inches [3 to 5 cm]). Cutting into small pieces is necessary for releasing flavors in a short time, as when used for fish stock.

ACID PRODUCTS

Acids, as noted in Chapter 4 (p. 65), help dissolve connective tissues. Thus, they are sometimes used in stock making to extract flavor and body from bones.

Tomato products contribute flavor and some acid to brown stocks. They are not used for white stocks because they would give an undesirable color. Similarly, when making brown stocks, be careful not to add too much tomato, because this may make the stock cloudy.

Wine is occasionally used, especially for fish stocks. Its flavor contribution is probably more important than its acidity.

SCRAPS AND LEFTOVERS

In some kitchens, a stockpot is kept going all day, and various scraps are constantly being thrown in. This may or may not be a good idea.

Scraps may be used in stocks if they are *clean, wholesome, and appropriate to the stock being made*. If done correctly, stock-making is a good way of utilizing trimmings that would otherwise be thrown out. It is better to save trimmings and use them in a planned way than to throw them into the stock randomly.

A *stockpot is not a garbage disposal*. The final product is only as good as the ingredients and the care that go into it.

SEASONINGS AND SPICES

Salt is usually not added when making stocks. Stocks are never used as is but are reduced, concentrated, and combined with other ingredients. If salt were added, it might

Figure 8.1
To make a sachet, place the spices and herbs in the center of a square of clean cheesecloth. Draw the corners together and tie with a length of twine. For making stock, use a piece of twine long enough to be tied to the handle of the stockpot for easy removal.

Figure 8.2
Tie the herbs and aromatic vegetables for a bouquet garni in a bundle. To tie small herbs securely, enclose them between the two halves of leek.

become too concentrated. Some chefs salt stocks very lightly because they feel it aids in extracting flavor.

Herbs and spices should be used only lightly. They should never dominate a stock or have a pronounced flavor.

Herbs and spices are usually tied in a cheesecloth bag called a **sachet** (sa-shay; French for "bag"). The sachet (Figure 8.1) is tied by a string to the handle of the stockpot so it can be removed easily at any time.

A **bouquet garni** is an assortment of fresh herbs and other aromatic ingredients tied in a bundle with string. A basic bouquet garni contains pieces of leek and celery, thyme sprigs, bay leaf, and parsley stems (see Figure 8.2). The ingredients can be changed to suit different recipes. Escoffier includes only parsley, thyme, and bay leaf in the classic bouquet garni.

The following seasonings, in varying quantities, are commonly used for stocks:

Thyme

Bay leaves

Peppercorns

Parsley stems

Cloves, whole

Garlic (optional)

INGREDIENT PROPORTIONS

The proportions in Tables 8.2, 8.3, and 8.4 are basic, effective, and widely used, but they are not an ironclad rule. Nearly every chef uses some variations.

Many cooks use ratios to help them remember the basic proportions, as follows:

Bones—50 percent

Mirepoix—10 percent

Water—100 percent

Table 8.2
White Stock (Including Chicken Stock)

To Make:	1 Gallon	4 Liters
Bones	5–6 lb	2.5–3 kg
Mirepoix	1 lb	500 g
Water	5–6 qt	5–6 L
Sachet	1	1

Table 8.3
Brown Stock

To Make:	1 Gallon	4 Liters
Bones	5–6 lb	2.5–3 kg
Mirepoix	1 lb	500 g
Tomato product	8 oz	250 g
Water	5–6 qt	5–6 L
Sachet	1	1

Table 8.4
Fish Stock

To Make:	1 Gallon	4 Liters
Bones	4–6 lb	2–3 kg
Mirepoix	8 oz	250 g
Water	1 gal	4 L
White wine	8 fl oz	250 mL
Sachet	1	1

INGREDIENTS FOR VEGETABLE STOCKS

Vegetable stocks, made without any animal products, play an important role in vegetarian cooking and are also used in more traditional kitchens in response to customers' requests for light, healthful dishes. The basic ingredients for vegetable stocks are vegetables, herbs and spices, water, and, sometimes, wine.

Ingredients and proportions can vary greatly. If you want a particular flavor to predominate, use a larger quantity of that vegetable. For example, if you want a broth tasting primarily of asparagus, use a large quantity of asparagus to make it, with smaller quantities of more neutral vegetables (like onion and celery) to round out the flavor. For a more neutral, all-purpose vegetable stock, avoid strong-flavored vegetables and use more balanced proportions of the various ingredients.

Here are a few additional guidelines for making vegetable stocks or broths:

1. Starchy vegetables such as potatoes, sweet potatoes, and winter squash make a stock cloudy. Use them only if clarity is not important.

2. Some vegetables, especially strong-flavored ones, are best avoided. Brussels sprouts, cauliflower, and artichokes can overwhelm a stock with a strong flavor or odor. Dark green leafy vegetables, especially spinach, develop an unpleasant flavor when cooked for a long time. Beets turn a stock red.

3. Cook long enough to extract flavors but not so long that flavors are lost. Best cooking times are 30 to 45 minutes.

4. Sweating the vegetables in a small amount of oil before adding water gives them a mellower flavor, but this step can be omitted. Butter can be used if it is not necessary to avoid all animal products.

PROCEDURES

Making stock may seem, at first glance, to be a simple procedure. However, many steps are involved, each with a rather complicated set of reasons. If you are to be successful at making consistently good stocks, you must understand not only what to do but also why you are doing it.

The following outlines give procedures for making basic stocks as well as the reasons for every step. After learning these procedures and checking with your instructors for any modifications or variations they may have, you will be able to turn to the individual recipes, where the steps are given again, but without explanations.

BLANCHING BONES

In Chapter 4, we discussed proteins coagulating when heated. Many proteins dissolve in cold water but solidify into small particles or into froth or scum when heated. It is these particles that make a stock cloudy. Much of the technique of stock-making involves avoiding cloudiness to produce a clear stock.

The purpose of blanching bones is to rid them of some of the impurities that cause cloudiness. The bones of *young animals*, especially veal and chicken, are highest in blood and other impurities that cloud and discolor stocks.

Chefs disagree on the importance of blanching. Many feel it is needed to produce clear white stocks. Others feel blanching causes valuable flavors to be lost. Fish bones, at any rate, are not blanched because of their short cooking time.

Procedure for Blanching Bones

1. Rinse bones in cold water.

   This washes off blood and other impurities from the surface. It is especially important if the bones are not strictly fresh.

2. Place bones in a stockpot or steam-jacketed kettle and cover with cold water.

   Impurities dissolve more readily in cold water. Hot water retards extraction.

3. Bring the water to a boil.

   As the water heats, impurities solidify (coagulate) and rise to the surface as scum.

4. Drain the bones and rinse them well.

   The bones are now ready for the stockpot.

PREPARING WHITE STOCKS

A good white stock has rich, full flavor, good body, clarity, and little or no color. Chicken stocks may have a light yellow color.

Procedure for Preparing White Stocks

1. Cut the bones into pieces, 3 to 4 inches (8 to 10 cm) long.

   This exposes more surface area and helps extraction. A meat saw is used to cut heavy veal and beef bones. Fish and chicken bones don't need to be cut, but whole carcasses should be chopped for more convenient handling.

2. Rinse the bones in cold water. (If desired, chicken, veal, or beef bones may be blanched.)

   This removes some impurities that cloud the stock or, if the bones are old, give an off taste.

3. Place bones in a stockpot or steam-jacketed kettle and add cold water to cover.

   Starting in cold water speeds extraction. Starting in hot water delays it because many proteins are soluble in cold water but not in hot.

4. Bring water to a boil, and then reduce to a simmer. Skim the scum that comes to the surface, using a skimmer or perforated spoon.

   Skimming is important for a clear stock because the scum (which is fat and coagulated protein) will cloud the stock if it is broken up and mixed back into the liquid.

5. Add the chopped mirepoix and the herbs and spices.

   Remember, the size to which you cut mirepoix depends on how long it is to be cooked.

6. Do not let the stock boil. Keep it at a low simmer.

   Boiling makes the stock cloudy because it breaks solids into tiny particles that get mixed into the stock.

7. Skim the surface as often as necessary during cooking.

8. Keep the water level above the bones. Add more water if the stock reduces below this level.

   Bones cooked while exposed to air will turn dark and thus darken or discolor the stock. Also, they do not release flavor into the water if the water doesn't touch them.

9. Simmer for recommended length of time:

   Beef and veal bones—6 to 8 hours

   Chicken bones—3 to 4 hours

   Fish bones—30 to 45 minutes

   Most modern chefs do not simmer stocks as long as earlier generations of chefs did. It is true that longer cooking extracts more gelatin, but gelatin isn't the only factor in a good stock. Flavors begin to break down or degenerate over time. The above times are felt to be the best for obtaining full flavor while still getting a good portion of gelatin into the stock.

10. Skim the surface and strain off the stock through a china cap lined with several layers of cheesecloth.

    Adding a little cold water to the stock before skimming stops the cooking and brings more fat and impurities to the surface.

11. Cool the stock as quickly as possible, as follows:

    - Set the pot in a sink with blocks, a rack, or some other object under it. This is called venting. It allows cold water to flow under the pot as well as around it.
    - Run cold water into the sink, but not higher than the level of the stock or the pot will become unsteady. An overflow pipe keeps the water level right and allows for constant circulation of cold water (see Figure 8.3).
    - Stir the pot occasionally so all the stock cools evenly. Hang a ladle in the pot so you can give it a quick stir whenever you pass the sink without actually taking extra time to do it.

    Cooling stock quickly and properly is important. Improperly cooled stock can spoil in 6 to 8 hours because it is a good breeding ground for bacteria that cause food-borne disease and spoilage.

    Do not set the hot stock in the walk-in or, worse yet, the reach-in. All that heat and steam will overload the refrigerator and may damage other perishables as well as the equipment.

12. When cool, refrigerate the stock in covered containers. Stock will keep 2 to 3 days if properly refrigerated. Stock can also be frozen and will keep for several months.

Figure 8.3
Setup for cooling stocks in a cold water bath

Basic White Stock

Yield: 2 gal (8 L)

U.S.	Metric	Ingredients
10–12 lb	5–6 kg	Bones: chicken, veal, or beef
10–12 qt	10–12 L	Water, cold
		Mirepoix:
1 lb	500 g	Onion, chopped
8 oz	250 g	Carrot, chopped (optional)
8 oz	250 g	Celery, chopped
		Sachet:
1	1	Dried bay leaf
¼ tsp	1 mL	Dried thyme
¼ tsp	1 mL	Peppercorns
6–8	6–8	Parsley stems
2	2	Whole cloves

Per 1 ounce:
Calories, 1; Protein, .1 g; Fat, 0 g (0% cal.); Cholesterol, 1 mg;
Carbohydrates, 0 g; Fiber, 0 g; Sodium, 2 mg.

■ P r o c e d u r e

1. Review instructions for stock preparation (pp. 153–154).
2. If beef or veal bones are whole, cut them into pieces, 3–4 in. (8–10 cm) long, with a meat saw. Rinse the bones in cold water.
3. Blanch the bones: Place them in a stockpot, cover with cold water, and bring to a boil. Drain and rinse.
4. Place the bones in the stockpot and cover with cold water.
   Bring to a boil, reduce heat to simmer, and skim the scum carefully.
5. Add the mirepoix and sachet ingredients (tied in cheesecloth).
6. Simmer for required length of time, skimming the surface as often as necessary.

   Beef and veal: 6–8 hours

   Chicken: 3–4 hours

   Add water if necessary to keep bones covered.
7. Strain through a china cap lined with several layers of cheesecloth.
8. Cool the stock, vented, in a cold water bath, and refrigerate.

V A R I A T I O N S

Prepare white lamb stock, turkey stock, and ham stock according to the basic procedure, substituting the appropriate bones.

Vegetable Stock
Omit the bones. Reduce the water to 9 qt (9 L). Add the following ingredients: ½ oz (15 g) garlic, chopped; 8 oz (250 g) leeks; 4 oz (125 g) mushrooms, sliced; 4 oz (125 g) turnip, sliced; 2 oz (60 g) fennel, sliced. Sweat the onion, garlic, leek, and turnip in 1½ fl oz (45 mL) olive oil before adding the remaining ingredients. Cook the stock 30–45 minutes.

PREPARING BROWN STOCKS

The difference between brown stocks and white stocks is that the bones and mirepoix are browned for the brown stock. This causes a few complications, as you will see. Otherwise, the procedure is essentially the same.

Two methods for browning are given below.

Procedure for Preparing Brown Stocks

1. Cut the bones into pieces, 3 to 4 inches (8 to 10 cm) long, as for white stock. Veal and/or beef bones are used for brown stock.

2. Do not wash or blanch the bones. The moisture would hinder browning.

3. Place the bones in a roasting pan in one layer and brown in a hot oven at 375°F (190°C) or higher. The bones must be well browned to color the stock sufficiently. This takes over an hour. Some chefs prefer to oil the bones lightly before browning.

4. When the bones are well browned, remove them from the pan and place them in a stockpot. Cover with cold water and bring to a simmer.

5. Drain and reserve the fat from the roasting pan. Deglaze the pan by adding water and stirring over heat until all the brown drippings are dissolved or loosened. Add to stockpot.

6. While the stock is getting started, place the mirepoix in the roasting pan with some of the reserved fat and brown the vegetables well in the oven. (See alternative procedure below.)

7. When the water in the stockpot comes to a simmer, skim and continue as for white stock.

8. Add the browned vegetables and the tomato product to the stockpot. If desired, they may be held out until 2 to 3 hours before the end of the cooking time.

9. Continue as for white stock.

Figure 8.4
Preparing brown stock.

(a) Roast the bones in a moderately hot oven until well browned.

(b) Place the bones in a stockpot and add the appropriate amount of water.

(c) While the bones are beginning to simmer, brown the mirepoix, using the same roasting pan set on top of the stove or in the oven. Add the browned mirepoix to the stockpot.

(d) Deglaze the roasting pan with water. Add the liquid to the stockpot.

(e) This stock has simmered slowly for 8 hours. Note that the sachet is tied to the handle of the pot with twine for easy removal.

(f) Strain the stock through a china cap lined with cheesecloth.

Alternative Procedure

The mirepoix may be browned with the bones. When the bones are half browned, add the mirepoix to the pan and continue roasting until bones and vegetables are browned. Tomato may be added toward the end of browning time, but exercise caution, as tomato purée burns easily.

Some chefs use this method because it eliminates some steps. Others prefer to brown the mirepoix separately so it can be added to the stock later in the cooking time.

REMOUILLAGE

Remouillage is a stock made from bones that have already been used once to make stock. The literal meaning of the French term is "rewetting." Because not all possible flavor and gelatin is extracted from bones when making a stock, making a remouillage allows the chef to extract a little more value from the bones. The resulting liquid will not be as clear or flavorful as the original stock, but it does have some uses. A remouillage can be used for soups, for braised dishes, and in place of water for making stocks. It can also be reduced to a glaze and used for enriching sauces, soups, and braising liquids.

To make a remouillage, discard the mirepoix and herb sachet after draining a finished stock. Add fresh mirepoix and sachet to the bones, cover with fresh cold water, and simmer about 4 hours. Drain and cool as for regular stock.

 ## Basic Brown Stock

Yield: 2 gal (8 L)

U.S.	Metric	Ingredients
10–12 lb	5–6 kg	Bones: veal or beef
10–12 qt	10–12 L	Water, cold
		Mirepoix:
1 lb	500 g	Onion, chopped
8 oz	250 g	Carrot, chopped
8 oz	250 g	Celery, chopped
1 lb	500 g	Tomatoes or tomato purée
		Sachet:
1	1	Bay leaf
¼ tsp	1 mL	Dried thyme
¼ tsp	1 mL	Peppercorns
6–8	6–8	Parsley stems
2	2	Whole cloves

Per 1 ounce:
Calories, 2; Protein, .2 g; Fat, .1 g (43% cal.); Cholesterol, 1 mg; Carbohydrates, .1 g; Fiber, 0 g; Sodium, 2 mg.

■ Procedure

1. Review instructions for stock preparation (p. 156).
2. If bones are whole, cut into pieces, 3–4 inches (8–10 cm) long, with a meat saw.
3. Place the bones in a roasting pan in a hot oven (400°F/200°C) and brown them well.
4. Remove bones from pan and place in a stockpot. Cover with water and bring to a simmer. Skim and let stock continue to simmer.
5. Drain and reserve the fat in the roasting pan. Deglaze the pan with water and add to stockpot.
6. Toss the mirepoix with some of the reserved fat and brown well in the oven.
7. Add the browned mirepoix, the tomato product, and the sachet to the stockpot.
8. Continue to simmer for a total cooking time of 6–8 hours, skimming the surface as necessary. Add water as needed to keep bones covered.
9. Strain through a china cap lined with several layers of cheesecloth.
10. Cool the stock, vented, in a cold-water bath, and refrigerate.

VARIATIONS

Prepare brown lamb stock and game stock according to the basic procedure, substituting the appropriate bones.

Fish Fumet

Fish stock may be made according to the same recipe as white stock. The following method yields a slightly more flavorful stock due to the preliminary sweating of mirepoix and bones in the butter and to the addition of wine.

Yield: 1 gal (4 L)

U.S.	Metric	Ingredients
1 oz	30 g	Butter
		Mirepoix:
4 oz	125 g	Onion, chopped fine
2 oz	60 g	Celery, chopped fine
2 oz	60 g	Carrot, chopped fine (optional)
2 oz	60 g	Mushroom trimmings (optional)
4–6 lb	2–3 kg	Bones from lean fish
8 fl oz	250 mL	White wine (dry)
		Sachet:
½	½	Bay leaf
¼ tsp	1 mL	Peppercorns
6–8	6–8	Parsley stems
1	1	Whole clove
1 gal	4 L	Water, cold

Per 1 ounce:
Calories, 4; Protein, .4 g; Fat, .2 g (36% cal.); Cholesterol, .5 mg;
Carbohydrates, .1 g; Fiber, 0 g; Sodium, 3 mg.

■ P r o c e d u r e

1. Butter the bottom of a heavy stockpot or saucepot. Place the mirepoix in the bottom of the pot and the bones over the top of it. Cover the bones loosely with a round of brown paper or parchment.

2. Set the pot over low heat and cook slowly for about 5 minutes, until the bones are opaque and begin to exude juices.

3. Add the wine, bring to a simmer, then add the sachet and water to cover.

4. Bring to a simmer again, skim, and let simmer for 30–45 minutes.

5. Strain through a china cap lined with several layers of cheesecloth.

6. Cool, vented, in a cold-water bath, and refrigerate.

REDUCTIONS AND GLAZES

Stocks are concentrated by boiling or simmering them to evaporate part of the water. This is called making a **reduction** or *reducing*.

Reduction is an important technique in sauce-making and in many other areas of cooking because it produces a more flavorful product by concentrating it. A reduced stock also has more body because the gelatin is concentrated.

WHAT ARE GLAZES?

A **glaze**—or, in French, *glace* (glahss)—is a stock that is reduced until it coats the back of a spoon. It is so concentrated—reduced by three-fourths or more—that it is solid and rubbery when refrigerated.

Glazes are used as flavorings in sauce-making and in some meat, poultry, fish, and vegetable preparations. Only small amounts are needed because they are so concentrated.

Glazes diluted to original strength do not taste like the stocks they were made from. The long cooking changes the flavors somewhat.

KINDS OF GLAZES

1. Meat glaze, or **glace de viande** (glahss duh vee awnd)—made from brown stock.

2. Chicken glaze, or *glace de volaille* (voh lye)—made from chicken stock.

3. Fish glaze, or *glace de poisson* (pwah sohn)—made from fish stock.

Procedure for Preparing Glazes

1. Reduce the stock over moderate heat.
2. Skim the surface frequently.
3. When reduced by half to two-thirds, strain into a smaller, heavy saucepan and continue to reduce over lower heat until it is syrupy and coats a spoon.
4. Pour into containers, cool, cover, and refrigerate.
5. Glazes will keep for several weeks or longer if properly stored. They may also be frozen.

CONVENIENCE BASES

The cost, both in time and materials, of making stocks in modern kitchens has led to the widespread use of concentrated convenience products known as bases. These are diluted with water to make flavored liquids similar to stocks.

Glazes can be considered bases and, in fact, they are the original bases, used long before today's manufacturers started producing convenience products.

JUDGING QUALITY

Bases vary greatly in quality. The best ones are composed mainly of meat extracts. These are perishable products and must be refrigerated.

Many bases are made primarily from salt, however—an expensive way to buy salt, we might add. *Read the list of ingredients.* Avoid products that list salt first. The best way to judge the quality of a base is to dilute it and compare its flavor to that of a well-made stock.

USING BASES

Bases can be improved with little labor by simmering the diluted or made-up product for a short time with some mirepoix, a sachet, and a few bones or meat trimmings if possible. This helps give a fresher, more natural taste to a highly processed product.

Bases are also added to stocks to supplement them when only a small quantity of stock is on hand.

Bases are sometimes added to weak stocks to give them more flavor, but this is not as good a practice as making the stock properly in the first place.

Using bases requires taste and judgment, just as other areas of cookery do. If used without care and restraint, bases can detract from the quality of your cooking. But, used carefully, they can be a valuable tool in some situations. Always taste and evaluate as you cook.

There is no substitute for a well-made stock. But it is also true that a good base may be better than a poorly made stock. It all depends on the skills you are learning now.

SAUCES

Like stocks, sauces have lost some of the importance they once had in commercial kitchens—except, of course, in the best restaurants serving what may be considered luxury cuisine. Some of this decline is due to changes in eating habits and to increased labor costs.

However, much of the change is due to misunderstanding. How many times have you heard someone say, "I don't go for all those sauces all over everything. I like good, simple food." No doubt this person puts ketchup—a sweetened tomato sauce—on hamburgers, gravy on mashed potatoes, and tartar sauce on fried fish.

The misunderstandings arise from poorly made sauces. No one likes thick, pasty cream sauces on vegetables or oversalted but otherwise flavorless brown sauces gumming up their meat. But just because some cooks make bad sauces is no reason to reject all sauce cookery.

In fact, many chefs believe good sauces are the pinnacle of all cooking, both in the skill they require and in the interest and excitement they can give to food. Very often, the most memorable part of a really fine meal is the sauce that enhances the meat or fish.

A sauce works like a seasoning. It enhances and accents the flavor of the food; it should not dominate or hide the food.

A good cook knows that sauces are as valuable as salt and pepper. A simple grilled steak is made even better when it has an added touch, something as simple as a slice of seasoned butter melting on it or as refined as a spoonful of béarnaise sauce.

No matter where you work, sauce-making techniques are basic skills you will need in all your cooking. Croquettes, soufflés, and mousses have sauces as their base, nearly all braised foods are served with sauces made of their cooking liquids, and basic pan gravies, favorites everywhere, are made with the same techniques as the classic sauces.

UNDERSTANDING SAUCES

THE FUNCTIONS OF SAUCES

A **sauce** may be defined as a flavorful liquid, usually thickened, that is used to season, flavor, and enhance other foods.

A sauce adds the following qualities to foods:

Moistness	Appearance (color and shine)
Flavor	Interest and appetite appeal
Richness	

THE STRUCTURE OF SAUCES

The major sauces we consider here are made of three kinds of ingredients.

1. A liquid, the body of the sauce
2. A thickening agent
3. Additional seasoning and flavoring ingredients

To understand sauce-making, you must first learn how to prepare these components and then how to combine them into finished sauces.

Liquid

A liquid ingredient provides the body or base of most sauces. Most classic sauces are built on one of five liquids or bases. The resulting sauces are called leading sauces or mother sauces.

White stock (chicken, veal, or fish)—for velouté sauces

Brown stock—for brown sauce or espagnole (ess pahn yohl)

Milk—for béchamel

Tomato plus stock—for tomato sauce

Clarified butter—for hollandaise

The most frequently used sauces are based on stock. The quality of these sauces depends on the stock-making skills you learned in the previous section.

Thickening Agents

A sauce must be thick enough to cling lightly to the food. Otherwise, it will just run off and lie in a puddle in the plate. This doesn't mean it has to be heavy and pasty.

Starches are still the most commonly used thickening agents, although they are used less often than in the past. We discuss starches and other thickening agents in detail below.

Other Flavoring Ingredients

Although the liquid that makes up the bulk of the sauce provides the basic flavor, other ingredients are added to make variations on the basic themes and to give a finished character to the sauces.

Adding specified flavoring ingredients to basic sauces is the key to the whole catalog of classic sauces. Most of the hundreds of sauces listed in the standard repertoires are made by adding one or more flavoring ingredients to one of the five basic sauces or leading sauces.

As in all of cooking, sauce-making is largely a matter of learning a few building blocks and then building with them.

ROUX

STARCHES AS THICKENERS

1. Starches are the most common and most useful thickeners for sauce-making. Flour is the principal starch used. Others available to the chef include cornstarch, arrowroot, waxy maize, instant or pregelatinized starch, bread crumbs, and other vegetable and grain products like potato starch and rice flour. These are discussed later.

2. Starches thicken by *gelatinization*, which, as discussed in Chapter 4, is the process by which starch granules absorb water and swell to many times their original size.

   Another important point made in Chapter 4 is that acids inhibit gelatinization. Whenever possible, do not add acid ingredients to sauces until the starch has fully gelatinized.

3. Starch granules must be separated before heating in liquid to avoid lumping. If granules are not separated, lumping occurs because the starch on the outside of the lump quickly gelatinizes into a coating that prevents the liquid from reaching the starch inside.

   Starch granules are separated in two ways:

   - *Mixing the starch with fat.* This is the principle of the roux, which we discuss now, and of *beurre manié*, which is discussed in the next section.
   - *Mixing the starch with a cold liquid.* This is the principle used for starches such as cornstarch. It can also be used with flour, but as we note later, the result is an inferior sauce. A mixture of raw starch and cold liquid is called **slurry**.

ROUX INGREDIENTS

Roux (roo) is a cooked mixture of equal parts by weight of fat and flour.

Fat

The cooking fats employed for making roux are as follows:

Clarified butter is preferred for the finest sauces because of its flavor. The butter is clarified (p. 178) because the moisture content of whole butter tends to gelatinize some of the starch and makes the roux hard to work.

Margarine is widely used in place of butter because of its lower cost. However, its flavor is inferior to butter, so it does not make as fine a sauce. The quality of margarine varies from brand to brand.

Animal fats, such as chicken fat, beef drippings, and lard, are used when their flavor is appropriate to the sauce. Thus, chicken fat can be used for chicken velouté, and beef drippings can be used for beef gravy. When properly used, animal fats can enhance the flavor of a sauce.

Vegetable oil and *shortening* can be used for roux but, because they add no flavor, they are not preferred. Solid shortening also has the disadvantage of having a high melting point, which gives it an unpleasant fuzzy feeling in the mouth. It is best reserved for the bakeshop and the fry kettle.

Today, roux-thickened sauces are often condemned for health reasons because of the fat content of the roux. It should be remembered, however, that when a roux-bound velouté or brown sauce is properly made, most of the fat is released and skimmed off before the sauce is served.

Flour

The thickening power of flour depends, in part, on its starch content. Bread flour has less starch and more protein than cake flour. Eight parts (such as ounces or grams) of cake flour has the same thickening power as 10 parts of bread flour.

Bread flour frequently is used for general cooking purposes in commercial kitchens even though it has less thickening power than cake flour or pastry flour. Most sauce recipes in this book, as well as in other books, are based on bread flour or on all-purpose flour, which has similar thickening power. Proportions of roux to liquid must be adjusted if another flour is used.

Flour is sometimes browned dry in the oven for use in brown roux. A heavily browned flour has only one-third the thickening power of unbrowned flour.

In addition to starch, wheat flour also contains proteins and other components. As a roux-thickened sauce is simmered, these components rise to the surface as scum. They then can be skimmed off. Sauces are generally simmered for a time even after the starch is completely gelatinized so these "impurities" can be cooked off. This improves the texture, gloss, and clarity of a sauce. When a high-protein flour such as bread flour is used in a roux, the sauce must be cooked longer and skimmed more often to achieve good clarity.

Ingredient Proportions

Correct amounts of fat and flour—*equal parts by weight*—are important to a good roux. There must be enough fat to coat all the starch granules, but not too much. In fact, Escoffier called for even less fat than our standard proportions (8 parts fat to 9 parts flour).

A good roux is stiff, not runny or pourable. A roux with too much fat is called a slack roux. Excess fat not only increases the cost of the roux unnecessarily, but the excess fat rises to the top of the sauce, where it either is skimmed off or makes the sauce look greasy.

PREPARING ROUX

A roux must be cooked so that the finished sauce does not have the raw, starchy taste of flour. The three kinds of roux differ in how much they are cooked.

White roux is cooked for just a few minutes, just enough to cook out the raw taste. Cooking is stopped as soon as the roux has a frothy, chalky, slightly gritty appearance, before it has begun to color. White roux is used for béchamel and other white sauces based on milk. In spite of its name, white roux is actually a pale yellow, because it is made from butter and (usually) unbleached flour. Figure 8.5 illustrates the production of white roux.

Blond roux, or pale roux, is cooked a little longer, just until the roux begins to change to a slightly darker color. Cooking must then be stopped. Blond roux is used for veloutés, sauces based on white stocks. The sauces have a pale ivory color.

Brown roux is cooked until it takes on a light-brown color and a nutty aroma. Cooking must take place over low heat so the roux browns evenly without scorching. For a deeper brown roux, the flour may be browned in an oven before adding to the fat. A heavily browned roux has only about one-third the thickening power of white roux, but it contributes flavor and color to brown sauces.

Figure 8.5
Cooking white roux.

Basic Procedure for Making All Roux

1. Melt fat.
2. Add correct amount of flour and stir until fat and flour are thoroughly mixed.
3. Cook to required degree for white, blond, or brown roux.

Cooking is done in a saucepan on top of the stove, and the roux is stirred for even cooking. Use low heat for brown roux, moderate heat for white or blond roux. Large quantities may be baked in an oven. Some restaurants make up batches large enough to last for several days or a week.

INCORPORATING THE ROUX

Combining the roux and liquid to obtain a smooth, lump-free sauce is a skill that takes practice to master. It's a good idea to practice the various techniques with water, under the guidance of your instructor, so you understand what you are doing before you start working with valuable stocks.

General Principles

Liquid may be added to roux, or roux may be added to liquid.

The liquid may be hot or cooled, but not ice cold. A very cold liquid will solidify the fat in the roux.

The roux may be warm or cold, but not sizzling hot. Adding a hot liquid to a very hot roux causes spattering and, possibly, lumps.

Within these general guidelines, there is room for a number of variations. Two of them are described here. Because successful use of roux is largely a matter of experience, you are advised to profit from your instructors' experience when they demonstrate these techniques or whichever methods they prefer.

Equipment note: Stainless-steel pans are best for white sauces. Whipping in an aluminum pan makes the sauce gray.

Procedures for Incorporating Roux

Method 1: Adding Liquid to Roux

This method is used when a roux is made up specifically for the sauce, gravy, or soup being prepared.

1. Use a heavy saucepot to prevent scorching either the roux or the sauce.
2. When the roux is made, remove the pan from the fire for a few minutes to cool slightly.
3. Slowly pour in the liquid, all the while beating vigorously with a wire whip to prevent lumps from forming.

   If the liquid is hot (such as simmering milk for béchamel sauce), you will have to beat especially well, because the starch will gelatinize quickly.

   If the liquid is cool, you can add a quantity of it, beat to dissolve the roux, then add the remainder of the liquid, hot or cool.
4. Bring the liquid to a boil, continuing to beat well. The roux does not reach its full thickening power until near the boiling point.
5. Simmer the sauce, stirring from time to time, until all the starchy taste of the flour has been cooked out.

   This will take at least 10 minutes, but the flavor and consistency of the sauce will improve if it is cooked longer. Many chefs feel that 20 minutes of simmering is a bare minimum. Others cook some sauces for an hour or longer.
6. When the sauce is finished, it may be kept hot in a bain-marie or cooled for later use. Either way, it should be covered or have a thin film of butter melted onto the top to prevent a skin from forming.

Method 2: Adding the Roux to the Liquid

Many restaurants make up large batches of roux to last all day or even all week. This method may be used in these situations.

1. Bring the liquid to a simmer in a heavy pot.
2. Add a small quantity of roux and beat vigorously with a whip to break up all lumps.
3. Continue to beat small quantities into the simmering liquid until the desired consistency is reached. Remember that roux must simmer for a time to thicken completely, so do not add roux too quickly or you risk overthickening the sauce.
4. Continue to simmer until the roux is cooked out and no starchy taste remains.
5. If the sauce is to simmer a long time, underthicken it because it will thicken as it reduces.

PROPORTIONS OF ROUX TO LIQUID

Table 8.5 indicates the quantities of roux needed to thicken 1 gallon or 4 liters of liquid to thin, medium, and thick consistencies.

Table 8.5 **Roux Proportions in Sauces**				
Sauce	**Butter**	**Flour**	**Roux**	**Liquid**
Thin or light	6 oz/190 g	6 oz/190 g	12 oz/375 g	1 gal/4 L
Medium	8 oz/250 g	8 oz/250 g	1 lb/500 g	1 gal/4 L
Thick or heavy	12 oz/375 g	12 oz/375 g	1½ lb/750 g	1 gal/4 L

How thick is a thick sauce? Obviously, these are not precise, scientific terms that can be defined easily. Experience can be the only teacher in this case. This is another good reason to practice with roux and water, so you can, with experience, produce the exact consistency you want.

You also have available the techniques of dilution and reduction to adjust the consistency of a sauce (see p. 166), and you will learn how to use beurre manié and other thickening agents.

OTHER THICKENING AGENTS

STARCHES

1. **Beurre manié** (burr mahnyay) is a mixture of equal parts soft, raw butter and flour worked together to form a smooth paste. It is used for quick thickening at the end of cooking to finish a sauce. The raw butter adds flavor and gives a sheen to the sauce when it melts.

   To use, drop very small pieces into a simmering sauce and stir with a whip until smooth. Repeat until desired consistency is reached. Simmer just a few minutes more to cook the flour, and then remove from the fire.

2. **Whitewash** is a thin mixture of flour and cold water. Sauces made with whitewash have neither as good a flavor nor as fine a texture as those made with roux. *Whitewash is not recommended for use.*

3. *Cornstarch* produces a sauce that is almost clear, with a glossy texture.

   To use, mix with cold water or other cold liquid until smooth. Stir into the hot liquid. Bring to a boil and simmer until the liquid turns clear and there is no starchy taste. Do not boil for a long period or the starch may break down and the liquid become thin. Sauces thickened with cornstarch may thin out if held on the steam table for long periods. Cornstarch is used extensively in sweet sauces to accompany certain meats as well as in desserts and dessert sauces. It has roughly twice the thickening power of flour.

4. *Arrowroot* is used like cornstarch, but it gives an even clearer sauce. Its use is limited by its high cost. Nevertheless, because of its quality, it is the preferred starch for thickening jus lié. It is less likely than cornstarch to break down when heated for a long time.

5. *Waxy maize* is used for sauces that are to be frozen. Flour and other starches break down and lose their thickening power when frozen. Waxy maize does not. It is handled like cornstarch.

6. *Pregelatinized or instant starches* have been cooked, or gelatinized, and then redried. Thus, they can thicken a cold liquid without heating. These starches are rarely used in sauce-making but are frequently used in the bakeshop.

7. *Bread crumbs* and other crumbs will thicken a liquid quickly because they have already been cooked, like instant starches. Bread crumbs may be used when smoothness of texture is not desired. A common example is the use of gingersnap crumbs to thicken sauerbraten gravy.

8. *Vegetable purées, ground nuts, and other solids* can also be used. A simple tomato sauce is basically a seasoned vegetable purée. The sauce gets its texture from the thickness of the main ingredient. No additional thickener is needed.

Using this same principle, we can add body or texture to sauces by adding a smooth vegetable purée, or by puréeing mirepoix or other vegetables with the sauce. Other puréed or finely ground ingredients, such as ground nuts, add texture as well as flavor to a sauce.

EGG YOLK AND CREAM LIAISON

In classical cooking, a *liaison* is a mixture of egg yolks and cream, used to enrich and lightly thicken a sauce or other liquid. Egg yolks have the power to thicken a sauce slightly due to the coagulation of egg proteins when heated.

Caution must be used when thickening with egg yolks because of the danger of curdling. This happens when the proteins coagulate too much and separate from the liquid.

Pure egg yolks coagulate at about 140°F to 158°F (60°C to 70°C). For this reason, they are beaten with heavy cream before use. This raises their curdling temperature to 180°F – 185°F (82°C – 85°C). (Note that this is still well below the boiling point.) The heavy cream also adds thickness and flavor to the sauce.

Egg yolks have only slight thickening power. The liaison is used primarily to give richness of flavor and smoothness of texture to a sauce and only secondarily to give a slight thickening. Also, because of the instability of the egg yolks, it is used only as a finishing technique. Incorporating a liaison is illustrated in Figure 8.6.

Figure 8.6
Adding a liaison to a sauce.

(a) Slowly stir a little of the hot sauce (chicken velouté, in this picture) into the mixture of cream and egg yolks to warm it and dilute it.

(b) Stir the tempered liaison back into the remaining sauce.

Procedure for Using a Liaison

1. Beat together the egg yolks and cream in a stainless-steel bowl. Normal proportions are 2 to 3 parts cream to 1 part egg yolks.

2. Very slowly add a little of the hot liquid to the liaison, beating constantly. This is known as *tempering*.

3. Off the heat, add the warmed, diluted liaison to the rest of the sauce, stirring well as you pour it in.

4. Return the sauce to low heat to warm it gently, but do not heat it higher than 180°F (82°C) or it will curdle. In no circumstances should it boil.

5. Hold for service above 140°F (69°C) for sanitation reasons, but lower than 180°F (82°C).

EGG YOLK EMULSIFICATION

Egg yolks are used as the thickening agent for hollandaise and related sauces, but in this case the principle is entirely different. The entire procedure is discussed in detail when we get to the hollandaise family of sauces, page 180.

REDUCTION

Simmering a sauce to evaporate some of the water thickens the sauce because only the water evaporates, not the solids. As the solids become more concentrated, the sauce becomes thicker. This technique has always been important for finishing sauces (see the next section). It has become more important as a basic thickening technique as modern chefs use less starch for thickening.

Use caution when reducing stock-based sauces. If such a sauce is reduced too much, the concentration of gelatin may give it a gluey or sticky texture, and it will congeal quickly on plates. Also, the sauce may have a heavily cooked taste that is not as appealing as the fresher, livelier taste of a stock that has not been cooked as much.

FINISHING TECHNIQUES

Remember that the three basic elements of a finished sauce are a liquid, a thickening agent, and additional seasoning and flavoring ingredients. We have discussed in detail how liquids are combined with thickening agents to make the basic sauces. In the next section, we look at the way families of sauces are built on these bases by the addition of flavoring ingredients.

Sauces may be modified or added to in a great many ways. Among these methods are a number of basic techniques that are used over and over again for making sauces. Before we study the structure of the sauce families, it will be helpful to look at these basic finishing techniques.

REDUCTION

1. **Using reduction to concentrate basic flavors.**
    If we simmer a sauce for a long time, some of the water evaporates. The sauce becomes more concentrated, and the resulting product is more flavorful. This is the same technique used when making glazes from stocks. Some reduction takes place in nearly all sauces, depending on how long they are simmered.

2. **Using reduction to adjust textures.**
    Concentrating a sauce by reduction also thickens it because only the water evaporates, not the roux or other solids. A skilled sauce chef uses both reduction and dilution to give a sauce the precise texture sought. If a sauce is too thin, it may be simmered until it reaches desired thickness. Or the chef may add a large quantity of stock or other liquid to a thickened sauce to thin it out greatly, then simmer it again until it is reduced to just the right consistency. By doing this, the chef also gives more flavor to the sauce.

3. **Using reduction to add new flavors.**
    If we can add a liquid to a sauce, then reduce it to concentrate it, why can't we reduce a liquid first and then add it to a sauce?

    In fact, this is one of the most important techniques in sauce-making. We have already mentioned that glazes—reduced stocks—are used to flavor sauces. Reductions of other liquids, especially red and white wines, are used a great deal in this way.

    Skip ahead to the recipe for Bordelaise Sauce (p. 175). Note how the red wine is cooked down with shallots, pepper, and herbs to one-fourth its original volume. Not only is the flavor of the wine concentrated but the flavor from the other spices is extracted. This reduction is a powerful flavoring agent that gives bordelaise sauce its distinctive taste. Reduction allows you to add a great deal of flavor to a sauce without adding much liquid.

Terminology

To reduce by one-half means to cook away one-half of the volume so that half is left.

To reduce by three-fourths means to cook away three-fourths of the volume so that only one-fourth is left.

To reduce **au sec** (oh seck) means to reduce until dry or nearly dry.

STRAINING

If you have learned how to use a roux properly, you should be able to make a smooth, lump-free sauce. However, to bring a sauce's texture to perfection, to create the velvety smoothness that is important to a good sauce, straining is necessary. Even a slight graininess that you can't see can still be felt on your tongue.

Straining through a china cap lined with several layers of cheesecloth is effective. Very fine sieves are also available for straining sauces. Straining is usually done before final seasoning.

DEGLAZING

To **deglaze** means to swirl a liquid in a sauté pan or other pan to dissolve cooked particles of food remaining on the bottom.

This term was discussed in relation to the basic technique of sautéing in Chapter 4 and again in connection with the production of brown stock. It is also an important technique for finishing sauces that accompany sautéed items.

A liquid such as wine or stock is used to deglaze a sauté pan and then is reduced by one-half or three-fourths. This reduction, with the added flavor of the pan drippings, is then added to the sauce that is served with the item.

ENRICHING WITH BUTTER AND CREAM

1. **Liaison.**
   In addition to being a thickening agent, a liaison of egg yolks and cream is used to finish a sauce by giving it extra richness and smoothness.

2. **Heavy cream.**
   Heavy cream has long been used to give flavor and richness to sauces. The most obvious example is adding cream to basic béchamel sauce to make cream sauce.

3. **Butter.**
   A useful enriching technique, both in classical and in modern cooking, is called *finishing with butter*, or **monter au beurre** (mohn tay oh burr).

   To finish a sauce with butter, simply add a few pieces of softened butter to the hot sauce and swirl it in until it melts. The sauce should then be served immediately; if it is allowed to stand, the butter may separate.

   Finishing a sauce with butter gives it a little extra shine and smoothness as well as adding to it the rich, fresh taste of raw butter.

SEASONING

Whether or not a sauce is to be given a final enrichment of liaison, cream, or butter, it must be checked carefully for seasonings before serving. Remember that the last step in any recipe, whether written or not, is "adjust the seasonings."

1. *Salt* is the most important seasoning for sauces. *Lemon juice* is also important. These two seasonings emphasize the flavors that are already there by stimulating the taste buds. *Cayenne* and *white pepper* are perhaps third and fourth in importance.

2. *Sherry* and *Madeira* are frequently used as final flavorings. These wines are added at the end of cooking (unlike red and white table wines, which must be cooked in a sauce) because their flavors are easily evaporated by heat.

SAUCE FAMILIES

LEADING SAUCES

One more time, let's look at the three basic building blocks of sauce cookery, this time from a slightly different angle.

liquid + thickening agent = leading sauce
leading sauce + additional flavorings = small sauce

We have talked about five basic liquids for sauces: milk, white stock, brown stock, tomato purée (plus stock), and clarified butter. From these we get our five **leading sauces**, also known as *mother sauces*, as shown in Chart 8.1.

Chart 8.1 **The Leading Sauces**		
Liquid	**Thickening Agent**	**Leading Sauce**
milk	+ white roux	= béchamel sauce
white stock (veal chicken, fish)	+ white or blond roux	= velouté (veal velouté, chicken velouté, fish velouté)
brown stock	+ brown roux	= brown sauce or espagnole
tomato plus stock	+ (optional roux)	= tomato sauce
butter	+ egg yolks	= hollandaise

Note: Roux is not used in all tomato sauces, as tomato purée is naturally thick.

To these five sauces, we add one more: **fond lié** (fone lee ay), meaning "thickened stock." It is sometimes used in place of espagnole.

brown stock + arrowroot or cornstarch = fond lié

You should understand that these charts are a bit oversimplified. Most of these sauces have a few other ingredients for flavoring. Yet knowing this basic structure is the key to making sauces.

SMALL SAUCES

The major leading sauces—béchamel; veal, chicken, and fish veloutés; and espagnole—are rarely used by themselves as sauces. They are more important as the bases for other sauces, called **small sauces**. Tomato sauce and hollandaise are used as they are, but they, too, are important as bases for small sauces.

Let's expand our sauce family chart one more generation to include examples of the small sauces in order to show the relationships (see Chart 8.2).

Chart 8.2 is probably a little more complicated than you expected because of the extra arrows and the extra category of secondary leading sauces. These are relatively easy to explain.

1. **Secondary leading white sauces.**
    These three sauces—allemande, suprême, and white wine—are really finished sauces, like other small sauces. But they are used so often to build other small sauces that they rate a special category.

    For example, to make suprême sauce, you add cream to chicken velouté.

    To make Albufera sauce, you can add meat glaze (glace de viande) to your suprême sauce. Or, if you don't have suprême sauce, you can make it by adding both cream and meat glaze to chicken velouté. This is why there are two sets of arrows in the chart.

    Allemande, suprême, and white wine sauces are also known as the *main small sauces*. If the concept of secondary leading white sauces seems confusing at first, you may simply think of them as small sauces. The important thing is to understand how the sauces are derived.

2. **Demi-glace.**
    *   **Demi-glace** is defined as half brown sauce plus half brown stock, reduced by half. Most chefs prefer demi-glace to espagnole as a base for small sauces because of its more concentrated, more fully developed flavor.
        Note: It is possible to make small sauces directly from espagnole, but they will not be as fine.
    *   Some modern chefs feel that espagnole is too heavy for modern tastes and that lighter sauces are required. These chefs prepare demi-glace from fond lié by reducing it with mirepoix, white wine, and seasonings, or by simply reducing by half a flavorful brown stock. In other words, demi-glace may be

Chart 8.2
The Small Sauces

Basic Ingredient	Leading Sauce	Secondary Leading Sauce	Small Sauce
White Sauces			
Milk ⟶	Béchamel ⟶		Cream, Mornay, Cheddar Cheese, Nantua, Soubise, Mustard
White Veal Stock ⟶	Veal Velouté ⟶	Allemande ⟶	Poulette, Aurora, Hungarian, Curry
Chicken Stock ⟶	Chicken Velouté ⟶	Suprême ⟶	Mushroom, Albufera or Ivory, Hungarian, Curry
Fish Stock ⟶	Fish Velouté ⟶	White Wine Sauce ⟶	Normandy, Bercy, Mushroom, Herb
Brown Sauces			
Brown Stock ⟶	Espagnole ⟶ / Fond Lié ⟶	Demi-glace, Demi-glace, Demi-glace ⟶	Bordelaise, Robert, Charcutière, Chasseur, Deviled (Diable), Lyonnaise, Madeira, Périgueux, Piquante, Mushroom, Bercy
Red Sauces			
Tomato plus stock ⟶	Tomato Sauce ⟶		Creole, Portuguese, Spanish
Butter Sauces			
Butter ⟶ *clarified*	Hollandaise ⟶		Maltaise, Mousseline
	Béarnaise ⟶		Choron, Foyot

considered a well-flavored brown stock, reduced by half (*demi* means "half"), thickened with roux or other starch or left unthickened (except by natural gelatin).

3. **Small sauces listed twice.**

Notice, for example, that mushroom sauce is listed under both chicken velouté and fish velouté. This means you should use the stock of the product you are serving with the sauce. Mushroom sauce for chicken should be made with chicken velouté, for fish, with fish velouté. To be even more confusing, mushroom sauce is also made with brown sauce. Bercy sauce is also made as both a white and a brown sauce. These are considered unrelated sauces that happen to have the same name.

4. **Hollandaise and béarnaise.**

These are essentially two variations of the same kind of sauce, with different flavorings. Each has its own small family of small sauces.

STANDARDS OF QUALITY FOR SAUCES

1. **Consistency and body.**

Smooth, with no lumps.

Not too thick or pasty, but thick enough to coat the food lightly.

2. **Flavor.**

Distinctive but well-balanced flavor.

Proper degree of seasoning.

No starchy taste.

The flavor should be selected to enhance or complement the food (such as suprême sauce with chicken or white wine sauce with fish) or to provide a pleasing contrast (such as a béarnaise sauce with grilled beef or raisin sauce with ham).

3. **Appearance.**

Smooth, with a good shine.

Good color for its type (rich, deep brown for brown sauce, pale ivory for velouté, white—not gray—for cream sauce).

OTHER SAUCES

As usual, not everything fits into one package. Beyond the five major sauce families, a number of other preparations don't follow these basic patterns. We encounter these later in the chapter.

These other preparations include these groups:

Simple and compound butters, including simple browned butter as well as butter combined with different flavorings.

Pan gravies, or sauces made with the pan drippings of the meat or poultry they are served with.

Miscellaneous hot sauces, which are not made like any of the five basic sauces. These include such items as raisin sauce (for ham) and sour cream sauce.

Miscellaneous cold sauces include not only sauces for meats, like Cumberland sauce and horseradish sauce, but also vinaigrettes, mayonnaise, and their variations, covered in Chapter 21.

MODERN SAUCES

Most of the emphasis in this chapter is on techniques for producing classic sauces. It is a mistake to argue that these sauces are not important and that modern sauce-making is entirely different. Modern sauces still depend on the basic classical techniques, even though the emphasis may have changed. For example, a chef in a modern kitchen may prepare a sauce for a sautéed meat item at the last minute by deglazing a sauté pan with a little wine, adding some reduced brown stock, and finishing the sauce by swirling in a little butter. As you can see, these are all techniques used in the production of classical sauces. Learning to make classical sauces is an important foundation for learning modern cooking.

While many of the recipes in this book, especially the traditional ones, incorporate sauces prepared in advance, many of the others, especially the more modern ones, incorporate sauces made at the last minute.

PRODUCTION

BÉCHAMEL

The classic version of the standard white sauce, béchamel, was made with lean veal and herbs and spices simmered with the sauce for an hour or with white veal stock added to the sauce and then reduced. This is rarely done today.

Nevertheless, the plain béchamel used today—simply milk and roux—can be improved by simmering the sauce with onion and spices. These may be omitted, of course, but the sauce will have less flavor.

 ## Béchamel Sauce

Yield: 1 gal (4 L)

U.S.	Metric	Ingredients
		Roux:
8 oz	250 g	Clarified butter
8 oz	250 g	Bread flour
1 gal	4 L	Milk
1	1	Bay leaf, small
1	1	Small whole onion, peeled
1	1	Whole clove
to taste	to taste	Salt
to taste	to taste	Nutmeg
to taste	to taste	White pepper

Per 1 ounce:
Calories, 40; Protein, 1 g; Fat, 3 g (63% cal.); Cholesterol, 10 mg; Carbohydrates, 3 g; Fiber 0 g; Sodium, 30 mg.

■ Procedure

1. Review instructions for making and incorporating roux (p. 163).
2. Heat the butter in a heavy saucepot over low heat. Add the flour and make a white roux. Cool the roux slightly.
3. In another saucepan, scald the milk. Gradually add it to the roux, beating constantly.
4. Bring the sauce to a boil, stirring constantly. Reduce heat to a simmer.
5. Stick the bay leaf to the onion with the clove and add to the sauce. Simmer at least 15 minutes or, if possible, for 30 minutes or more. Stir occasionally while cooking.
6. Adjust the consistency with more hot milk, if necessary.
7. Season very lightly with salt, nutmeg, and white pepper. Spice flavors should not dominate.
8. Strain the sauce through a china cap lined with cheesecloth. Cover or spread melted butter on surface to prevent skin formation. Keep hot in a bain-marie, or cool in a cold-water bath for later use.

V A R I A T I O N S

Light Béchamel
Use 12 oz (375 g) roux.

Heavy Béchamel
Use 1½ lb (750 g) roux.

Small Sauces

For each of the following sauces, add the ingredients indicated to *1 qt (1 L) béchamel sauce*. Season to taste.

Cream Sauce
4–8 fl oz (125–250 mL) heavy cream, heated or tempered

Mornay Sauce
4 oz (125 g) grated Gruyère cheese and 2 oz (60 g) parmesan, stirred in until just melted. Finish, off heat, with 2 oz (60 g) raw butter. Thin out with a little hot milk, if necessary, or use a stock or broth appropriate for the dish being prepared.

Mornay Sauce for Glazing or Gratinéeing
Finish Mornay Sauce with liaison of 2 egg yolks and 2 fl oz (60 mL) heavy cream.

Cheddar Cheese Sauce
8 oz (250 g) cheddar cheese, ½ tsp (2 mL) dry mustard, 2 tsp (10 mL) Worcestershire sauce

Mustard Sauce
4 oz (125 g) prepared mustard

Soubise Sauce
1 lb (500 g) onions, finely diced, cooked slowly in 2 oz (60 g) butter without browning. Simmer with sauce 15 minutes and force through a fine sieve.

Tomatoed Soubise Sauce
Add 1 pt (500 mL) thick tomato purée to 1 qt (1 L) soubise sauce

Nantua Sauce
6 oz (175 g) Shrimp Butter (p. 179), 4 fl oz (125 mL) heavy cream (*Note:* Classic Nantua sauce is made with crayfish, not readily available in many regions.)

VELOUTÉ

The three velouté sauces are the bases of many variations. Instructions for the small sauces indicate which of the three to use. If more than one is given, the choice depends on what you are serving it with.

Note: In North America, chicken velouté is used much more often than veal velouté. Many of the sauces at one time made with veal stock are now made with chicken stock.

 ## Velouté Sauce (Veal, Chicken, or Fish)

Yield: 2 qt (2L)

U.S.	Metric	Ingredients
		Roux:
4 oz	125 g	Clarified butter
4 oz	125 g	Bread flour
2½ qt	2.5 L	White stock, hot (veal, chicken, or fish)

Per 1 ounce:
Calories, 25; Protein, 0 g; Fat 2 g (82% cal.); Cholesterol, 5 mg; Carbohydrates, 1 g; Fiber, 0 g; Sodium, 20 mg.

VARIATION

Heat the butter for the roux in a heavy saucepot. Add 1 oz (30 g) each onion, leek, and celery. Sweat until soft. Do not brown. Add the flour to make a roux. Continue with step 3 in the procedure.

■ Procedure

1. Review instructions for making and incorporating roux (p. 163).
2. Heat the butter in a heavy saucepot over low heat. Add the flour and make a blond roux. Cool the roux slightly.
3. Gradually add the hot stock to the roux, beating constantly. Bring to a boil, stirring constantly. Reduce heat to a simmer.
4. Simmer the sauce very slowly for 1 hour. Stir occasionally, and skim the surface when necessary. Add more stock if needed to adjust consistency.
5. Do not season velouté, as it is not used as is but as an ingredient in other preparations.
6. Strain through a china cap lined with cheesecloth. Cover or spread melted butter on surface to prevent skin formation. Keep hot in a bain-marie, or cool in a cold-water bath for later use.

 ## White Wine Sauce

Yield: 2 qt (2 L)

U.S.	Metric	Ingredients
8 fl oz	250 mL	White wine (dry)
2 qt	2 L	Fish velouté
8 fl oz	250 mL	Heavy cream, hot
2 oz	60 g	Butter
to taste	to taste	Salt
to taste	to taste	White pepper
to taste	to taste	Lemon juice

Per 1 ounce:
Calories, 45; Protein, 0 g; Fat, 4 g (85% cal.); Cholesterol, 10 mg; Carbohydrates, 1 g; Fiber, 0 g; Sodium, 30 mg.

■ Procedure

1. Reduce the wine by half in a saucepan.
2. Add the velouté and simmer until reduced to desired consistency.
3. Slowly stir in the hot (or tempered) cream.
4. Remove from heat and swirl in the raw butter, cut into pieces.
5. Season to taste with salt, white pepper, and a few drops of lemon juice.
6. Strain through cheesecloth.

VARIATION

Instead of adding the hot or tempered heavy cream, make a liaison with 5 egg yolks and 8 fl oz (250 mL) cold heavy cream. Incorporate the liaison using the procedure on page 165. Then continue with step 4 in the recipe.

 ## Suprême Sauce

Yield: 2 qt (2 L)

U.S.	Metric	Ingredients
2 qt	2 L	Chicken velouté
1 pt	500 mL	Heavy cream
2 oz	60 g	Butter
to taste	to taste	Salt
to taste	to taste	White pepper
to taste	to taste	Lemon juice

Per 1 ounce:
Calories, 50; Protein, 1 g; Fat, 5 g (79% cal.); Cholesterol, 20 mg; Carbohydrates, 2 g; Fiber, 0 g; Sodium, 30 mg.

■ Procedure

1. Place the velouté in a saucepan and simmer over moderate heat until reduced by about one-fourth. Stir occasionally.
2. Pour the cream into a stainless-steel bowl and temper it by slowly stirring in a little of the hot sauce. Stir this mixture slowly back into the sauce in the pan and return the sauce just to a simmer.
3. Swirl in the raw butter, cut into pieces. Season to taste with salt, white pepper, and a few drops of lemon juice.
4. Strain through cheesecloth.

Allemande Sauce

Yield: 2 qt (2 L)

U.S.	Metric	Ingredients
2 qt	2 L	Veal velouté (see note)
		Liaison:
4	4	Egg yolks
8 fl oz	250 mL	Heavy cream
½ fl oz	15 mL	Lemon juice
to taste	to taste	Salt
to taste	to taste	White pepper

Per 1 ounce:
Calories, 40; Protein, 1 g; Fat, 3.5 g (72% cal.); Cholesterol, 25 mg; Carbohydrates, 2 g; Fiber, 0 g; Sodium, 20 mg.

■ P r o c e d u r e

1. Review instructions for incorporating a liaison (p. 165).
2. Place the velouté in a saucepan and simmer a few minutes over moderate heat until slightly reduced.
3. Beat the egg yolks and cream together in a stainless-steel bowl.
4. Temper the liaison by slowly beating in about one-third of the hot sauce. Then slowly stir this mixture back into the sauce in the pan.
5. Reheat to just below simmering. Do not boil.
6. Add lemon juice, salt, and white pepper to taste and strain through cheesecloth.

Note: Allemande sauce, strictly speaking, should be made with veal velouté. However, as a chicken velouté is much more common in North America, allemande sauce and the small sauces derived from it are often made with chicken velouté.

Small Sauces

For each of the following sauces, add the listed ingredients to 1 qt (1 L) *veal, chicken, or fish velouté, suprême sauce, allemande sauce,* or *white wine sauce* as indicated. Season the sauce to taste.

Poulette
Simmer 8 oz (250 g) white mushrooms or mushroom trimmings with velouté when making *allemande*. Make allemande, strain. Finish with 2 tbsp (30 mL) chopped parsley and lemon juice to taste.

Aurora
Add 6 oz (175 g) tomato purée to 1 qt (1 L) *veal or chicken velouté, suprême sauce, or allemande sauce.*

Hungarian
Sweat 2 oz (60 g) minced onion and 1 tbsp (15 mL) paprika in 1 oz (25 g) butter until soft. Add ½ cup (100 mL) white wine and reduce by half. Add 1 qt (1 L) *veal or chicken velouté*, simmer 10 minutes, and strain.

Ivory or Albufera
Add 2 oz (60 g) meat glaze (glace de viande) to 1 qt (1 L) *suprême sauce.*

Curry
Cook 4 oz (125 g) mirepoix, cut brunoise, in 1 oz (25 g) butter until tender but not brown. Add 1 tbsp (15 mL) curry powder, 1 crushed garlic clove, pinch dried thyme, ½ bay leaf, and 2–4 parsley stems and cook another minute. Add 1 qt (1 L) *veal, chicken, or fish velouté.* Simmer 20 minutes, add ½ cup (125 mL) cream, strain, and season with salt and lemon juice.

Mushroom
Sauté 4 oz (125 g) sliced mushrooms in 1 oz (25 g) butter, adding 1 tbsp (15 mL) lemon juice to keep them white. Add to *suprême, allemande, or white wine sauce* or to appropriate velouté.

Bercy
Reduce by two-thirds 2 oz (60 g) chopped shallots and ½ cup (125 mL) white wine. Add 1 qt (1 L) *fish velouté*, reduce slightly, and finish with 2 oz (60 g) raw butter, 2 tbsp (30 mL) chopped parsley, and lemon juice to taste.

Herb
To *white wine sauce* add chopped parsley, chives, and tarragon to taste.

Normandy
To 1 qt (1 L) *fish velouté* add 4 oz (125 mL) mushroom cooking liquid (or 4 oz/125 g mushroom trimmings) and 4 oz (125 mL) oyster liquid or fish fumet. Reduce by one-third. Finish with a liaison of 4 egg yolks and 1 cup (250 mL) cream. Strain and swirl in 3 oz (75 g) raw butter.

Anchovy
Follow the instructions for Normandy sauce but, in place of the raw butter used to finish the sauce, substitute 6 oz (175 g) anchovy butter.

Shrimp
To 1 qt (1 L) *white wine sauce*, add 4 oz (125 g) shrimp butter and a dash of cayenne. If desired, garnish with 4 oz (125 g) diced, cooked shrimp.

Venetian
Combine ½ cup (125 mL) each white wine and tarragon vinegar, ½ oz (15 g) chopped shallots, and 2 tsp (10 mL) chopped fresh chervil. Reduce by two-thirds. Add 1 qt (1 L) *white wine sauce* and simmer 2–3 minutes. Strain. Add fresh tarragon to taste.

Horseradish
Add 2 oz (60 g) drained horseradish, ½ cup (125 mL) heavy cream, and 2 tsp (10 mL) dry mustard dissolved in 1 fl oz (30 mL) vinegar to 1 qt (1 L) *velouté* made with beef or veal stock or broth from Boiled Beef (p. 325).

GASTRIQUE

A classic technique to add a balanced sweet-sour accent to a sauce is to add a **gastrique**, which is caramelized sugar dissolved in vinegar. For example, a gastrique gives necessary sweetness and acidity to sauce bigarade, the classic orange sauce served with roast duck.

A quantity of gastrique can be made in advance, stored, and used as needed. Heat 4 oz (120 g) sugar until it melts and then caramelizes to a light golden brown. Let cool briefly. Add 3 fl oz (90 mL) wine vinegar and simmer until the caramel is dissolved.

ESPAGNOLE OR BROWN SAUCE

As one glance at the procedure for making espagnole will tell you, this sauce is more complicated than béchamel or velouté. Because it is the starting point for the hearty, flavorful sauces that accompany red meats, it is necessary to give it extra flavor and richness with mirepoix. Some chefs even add more browned bones and cook the sauce as long as a stock.

Note how the roux is made in the espagnole recipe. Though mirepoix is also cooked in the fat, the basic principle is the same as when you make a simple roux in a separate pot.

Fond Lié

In its simplest form, fond lié, or jus lié, is a brown stock thickened lightly with arrowroot or cornstarch. Its quality can be improved, however, by applying the technique used for making espagnole. That is, reduce brown stock with browned mirepoix and tomato purée or tomato paste. Then thicken with a starch slurry and strain. You can use the same ratio of stock to mirepoix as for espagnole.

 ## Brown Sauce or Espagnole

Yield: 1 gal (4 L)

U.S.	Metric	Ingredients
		Mirepoix:
1 lb	500 g	Onions, medium dice
8 oz	250 g	Carrots, medium dice
8 oz	250 g	Celery, medium dice
8 oz	250 g	Butter
8 oz	250 g	Bread flour
6 qt	6 L	Brown stock
8 oz	250 g	Tomato purée
		Sachet:
½	½	Bay leaf
¼ tsp	1 mL	Thyme
6–8	6–8	Parsley stems

Per 1 ounce:
Calories, 25; Protein, 1 g; Fat, 1.5 g (53% cal); Cholesterol, 5 mg; Carbohydrates, 2 g; Fiber, 0 g; Sodium, 20 mg.

■ Procedure

1. Sauté the mirepoix in the butter until well browned.
2. Add the flour and stir to make the roux. Continue to cook until the roux is browned.
3. Gradually stir in the brown stock and tomato purée, stirring constantly until the mixture comes to a boil.
4. Reduce heat to simmer and skim the surface. Add the sachet and let simmer for about 2 hours, until the sauce is reduced to 1 gal (4 L). Skim as often as necessary.
5. Strain through a china cap lined with several layers of cheesecloth. Press on the mirepoix gently to extract their juices.
6. Cover or spread melted butter on surface to prevent skin formation. Keep hot in a bain-marie, or cool in a cold-water bath for later use.

 ## Fond Lié or Jus Lié

Yield: 1 qt (1 L)

U.S.	Metric	Ingredients
1 qt	1 L	Brown stock
1 oz	30 g	Cornstarch or arrowroot

Per 1 ounce:
Calories, 5; Protein, 0 g; Fat 0 g (0% cal.); Cholesterol, 0 mg; Carbohydrates, 1 g; Fiber; 0 g; Sodium, 0 mg.

■ Procedure

1. Bring the stock to a boil in a saucepan. Reduce heat to a simmer.
2. Dissolve the starch in a small amount of cold stock or water. Stir it into the simmering stock.
3. Simmer until thickened and clear.

VARIATION

For added flavor, the stock can be reduced with browned mirepoix and tomato (as for espagnole) before being thickened. Browned bones may also be added.

Demi-Glace

Yield:1 gal (4 L)

U.S.	Metric	Ingredients
1 gal	4 L	Brown sauce
1 gal	4 L	Brown stock

Per 1 ounce:
Calories 25; Protein, 1 g; Fat 1.5 g (53% cal.); Cholesterol, 5 mg;
Carbohydrates, 2 g; Fiber, 0 g; Sodium, 20 mg.

■ Procedure

1. Combine the sauce and stock in a saucepan and simmer until reduced by half.

2. Strain through a chinois (fine china cap) or a regular china cap lined with cheesecloth. Cover to prevent a skin from forming. Keep hot in a bain-marie, or cool in a cold-water bath for later use.

Small Sauces

For each of the following sauces, add the listed ingredients to 1 qt (1 L) demi-glace, as indicated.

Bordelaise
Reduce by three-fourths 1 cup (250 mL) dry red wine, 2 oz (60 g) chopped shallots, ¼ tsp (1 mL) crushed peppercorns, a pinch of dried thyme, and ½ bay leaf. Add 1 qt (1 L) demi-glace, simmer 15 to 20 minutes, and strain. Swirl in 2 oz (60 g) raw butter, cut in pieces. Garnish with diced or sliced beef marrow, poached in salted water.

Marchand de Vin (Wine Merchant)
Reduce 6 fl oz (200 mL) red wine and 2 oz (60 g) chopped shallots by three-fourths. Add 1 qt (1 L) demi-glace, simmer, and strain.

Robert
Cook 4 oz (125 g) chopped onion in butter without browning. Add 1 cup (250 mL) white wine and reduce by two-thirds. Add 1 qt (1 L) demi-glace and simmer 10 minutes. Strain and add 2 tsp (10 mL) dry mustard and a pinch of sugar dissolved in a little lemon juice.

Charcutière
Garnish Robert sauce with sour pickles, cut julienne.

Chasseur
Sauté 6 oz (175 g) sliced mushrooms and 2 oz (60 g) minced shallots in 2 oz (60 g) butter. Add 1 cup (250 mL) white wine and reduce by three-fourths. Add 1 qt (1 L) demi-glace and 8 oz (250 g) diced tomato. Simmer 5 minutes and add 2 tsp (10 mL) chopped parsley.

Diable (Deviled)
Reduce by two-thirds 8 fl oz (250 mL) white wine, 4 oz (125 g) chopped shallots, ½ tsp (2 mL) crushed peppercorns. Add 1 qt (1 L) demi-glace and simmer 20 minutes. Season with cayenne to taste and strain.

Madeira
Reduce 1 qt (1 L) demi-glace by about ½ cup (100 mL). Add 3 to 4 fl oz (100 mL) Madeira wine.

Perigueux
Garnish Madeira sauce with finely diced truffle.

Poîvrade
Brown 1 lb (500 g) mirepoix in butter. Add 4 fl oz (125 mL) red wine and 1½ pt (750 mL) Red Wine Marinade for Game (p. 304) and reduce by one-half. Add 1 qt (1 L) demi-glace and reduce by one-third over low heat. Add ½ tsp (2 mL) crushed peppercorns and simmer 10 minutes. Strain.

Port Wine
Follow instructions for Madeira sauce, but use port wine instead of Madeira.

Italian Sauce
Sauté 1 lb (500 g) finely chopped mushrooms and ½ oz (15 g) minced shallots in 2 oz (60 g) butter until all moisture is evaporated. Add 1 cup (250 mL) white wine and reduce by half. Add 1 oz (30 g) tomato paste and 1 qt (1 L) demi-glace and simmer 10 minutes. Add 2 tbsp (30 mL) chopped parsley.

Mushroom
Sauté 8 oz (250 g) sliced mushrooms and 1 oz (30 g) minced shallots in 2 oz (60 g) butter until browned. Add 1 qt (1 L) demi-glace and simmer about 10 minutes. Add 2 oz (60 mL) sherry and a few drops of lemon juice.

Bercy
Reduce by three-fourths 1 cup (250 mL) dry white wine and 4 oz (125 g) chopped shallots. Add 1 qt (1 L) demi-glace and simmer 10 minutes.

Piquante
Reduce by two-thirds 4 oz (125 g) minced shallots, 4 fl oz (125 mL) wine vinegar, and 4 fl oz (125 mL) white wine. Add 1 qt (1 L) demi-glace and simmer until slightly reduced. Add 2 oz (60 g) capers, 2 oz (60 g) sour pickles, cut brunoise, 1 tbsp (15 mL) chopped parsley, and ½ tsp (2 mL) dried tarragon.

Lyonnaise
Sauté 4 oz (125 g) onions in 2 oz (60 g) butter until slightly browned. Add ½ cup (125 mL) white wine vinegar and reduce by half. Add 1 qt (1 L) demi-glace and simmer 10 minutes.

Bigarade
Prepare a gastrique (p. 174) from 6 oz (180 g) sugar and 4 fl oz (125 mL) wine vinegar. Add 8 fl oz (250 mL) orange juice, 3 fl oz (90 mL) lemon juice, 1 qt (1 L) demi-glace, and, if available, the juices from a roast duck. Simmer and reduce to desired consistency. Garnish with blanched julienne of orange zest.

TOMATO SAUCE

Classical tomato sauce, as explained by Escoffier, is made with a roux, but this is rarely done in modern kitchens. The texture of the puréed tomatoes is sufficient to give the sauce the proper texture, even when no starch thickener is used.

This type of sauce may be referred to as a **coulis** (koo-lee). This French term means, in modern kitchens, a purée of vegetables or fruits, used as a sauce. A recipe for another coulis, of sweet peppers, is found on page 189.

Three main techniques are used to purée vegetables and other ingredients for coulis:

1. Puréeing the product in a food processor or blender
2. Passing the product through a food mill
3. Forcing the product through a fine sieve

Of these three methods, the third, forcing through a fine sieve, usually makes the smoothest purée, but it is also the most time-consuming. If you want a smooth purée but the product is difficult to force through a sieve, you can use one of the other methods first, then pass the purée through the sieve to make it smoother.

 ## Tomato Sauce I

Yield: 1 gal (4 L)

U.S.	Metric	Ingredients
4 oz	125 g	Salt pork
8 oz	250 g	Onion, medium dice
8 oz	250 g	Carrots, medium dice
4 qt	4 L	Tomatoes, canned or fresh, coarsely chopped
2 qt	2 L	Tomato purée, canned
1 lb	500 g	Ham bones or browned pork bones
		Sachet:
2 cloves	2 cloves	Garlic, crushed
1	1	Bay leaf
¼ tsp	1 mL	Dried thyme
¼ tsp	1 mL	Dried rosemary
¼ tsp	1 mL	Peppercorns, crushed
to taste	to taste	Salt
to taste	to taste	Sugar

Per 1 ounce:
Calories, 20; Protein, 1 g; Fat, 1 g (35% cal.); Cholesterol, 0 mg; Carbohydrates, 3 g; Fiber, 1 g; Sodium, 120 mg.

■ P r o c e d u r e

1. Render the salt pork in a heavy saucepot, but do not brown it.
2. Add the onion and carrots and sauté until slightly softened, but do not brown.
3. Add the tomatoes and their juice, the tomato purée, bones, and sachet. Bring to a boil, reduce heat, and simmer over very low heat (see note) for 1½–2 hours, until reduced to desired consistency.
4. Remove sachet and bones. Strain sauce or pass it through a food mill.
5. Adjust the seasoning with salt and a little sugar.

V A R I A T I O N

Tomato Sauce II (Vegetarian)
Omit the salt pork. Sweat the vegetables in 2 fl oz (60 mL) olive oil. Omit the bones.

Note: Tomato sauce scorches easily, so heat must be very low. The sauce may be cooked in a slow oven (300°F/150°C), loosely covered, to reduce the danger of scorching.

Tomato Sauce III

See Tomato Sauce for Pasta, page 639.

Small Sauces

For each of the following sauces, add the listed ingredients to 1 qt (1 L) tomato sauce, as indicated.

Portugaise (Portuguese)
Sauté 4 oz (125 g) onions, cut brunoise, in 1 fl oz (30 mL) oil. Add 1 lb (500 g) tomato concassé (see p. 533) and 1 tsp (5 mL) crushed garlic. Simmer until reduced by about one-third. Add 1 qt (1 L) tomato sauce, adjust seasonings, and add 2–4 tbsp (30–60 mL) chopped parsley.

Spanish
Lightly sauté in oil without browning 6 oz (175 g) onion, small dice; 4 oz (125 g) green bell pepper, small dice; and 1 clove garlic, chopped fine. Add 4 oz (125 g) sliced mushrooms and sauté. Add 1 qt (1 L) tomato sauce, and season to taste with salt, pepper, and hot red pepper sauce.

Creole
Sauté in oil 4 oz (125 g) onion, small dice; 4 oz (125 g) celery, sliced; 2 oz (60 g) green bell pepper, small dice; 1 tsp (5 mL) chopped garlic. Add 1 qt (1 L) tomato sauce, 1 bay leaf, pinch dried thyme, and ½ tsp (2 mL) grated lemon rind. Simmer 15 minutes. Remove bay leaf and season to taste with salt, pepper, and cayenne.

Fresh Tomato Coulis with Garlic

Yield: 1 pt (500 mL)

U.S.	Metric	Ingredients
3 oz	90 g	Shallots, chopped fine
6	6	Garlic cloves, chopped fine
2 fl oz	60 mL	Olive oil
1 lb 8 oz	750 g	Tomatoes, peeled, seeded, and chopped
to taste	to taste	Salt
to taste	to taste	White pepper

■ P r o c e d u r e

1. Sweat the shallots and garlic in olive oil until soft.
2. Add the tomatoes and cook until excess liquid has cooked out and the sauce is thick.
3. Season to taste.

Per 1 ounce:
Calories, 45; Protein 1 g; Fat, 3.5 g (66% cal.); Cholesterol, 0 mg;
Carbohydrates, 3 g; Fiber,1 g; Sodium, 5 mg.

BUTTER SAUCES

The fifth leading sauce is hollandaise. Hollandaise and its cousin, béarnaise, are unlike the sauces we have been studying because their major ingredient is not stock or milk but butter.

Before tackling the complexities of hollandaise, we first look at simpler butter preparations used as sauces.

1. **Melted butter.**
   This is the simplest butter preparation of all, and one of the most widely used, especially as a dressing for vegetables.
   Unsalted or sweet butter has the freshest taste and is ideal for all sauce-making.

2. **Clarified butter.**
   Butter consists of butterfat, water, and milk solids. Clarified butter is purified butterfat, with water and milk solids removed (see Figure 8.7). It is necessary for many cooking operations. Clarified butter is used in sautéing because the milk solids of unclarified butter would burn at such high temperatures. It is used in making hollandaise because the water of unclarified butter would change the consistency of the sauce.

3. **Brown butter.**
   Known as **beurre noisette** (burr nwah zett) in French, this is whole melted butter that has been heated until it turns light brown and gives off a nutty aroma. It is usually prepared at the last minute and served over fish, white meats, eggs, and vegetables.
   Care must be taken not to burn the butter, as the heat of the pan will continue to brown it even after it is removed from the fire.

4. **Black butter.**
   Black butter, or *beurre noir* (burr nwahr), is made like brown butter but heated until it is a little darker, and it is flavored with a few drops of vinegar. Capers, chopped parsley, or both are sometimes added.
   To avoid dangerous spattering of the vinegar in the hot butter, many chefs pour the butter over the food item, then deglaze the pan with the vinegar and pour that over the item.

5. **Meunière butter.**
   This is served with fish cooked à la Meunière (see p. 470). Brown butter is seasoned with lemon juice and poured over the fish, which has been sprinkled with chopped parsley.
   As in the case of black butter, dangerous spattering can result when moisture is added to hot butter. To avoid this, cooks often sprinkle the lemon juice directly on the fish before pouring on the brown butter.

Procedure for Clarifying Butter

Method 1

1. Melt the butter in a heavy saucepan over moderate heat.
2. Skim the froth from the surface.
3. Carefully pour off the clear melted butter into another container, leaving the milky liquid at the bottom of the saucepan.

Method 2

1. Melt the butter in a heavy saucepan over moderate heat.
2. Skim the froth from the surface.
3. Leave the pan on the heat and continue to skim the froth from the surface at intervals. The water in the bottom will boil and gradually evaporate.
4. When the butter looks clear and no longer forms a scum on top, strain off the butter through cheesecloth into another container.

You will need 1¼ lb (625 g) raw butter to make 1 lb (500 g) clarified butter; 1 lb (500 g) raw butter yields 12 to 13 oz (about 400 g) clarified butter.

Figure 8.7
Clarifying butter.

(a) Skim the foam from the top of the melted butter.

(b) Ladle off the clear, melted fat.

(c) Continue until only the milky liquid remains in the bottom of the pan.

6. **Compound butters.**

   Compound butters are made by softening raw butter and mixing it with various flavoring ingredients. The mixture is then rolled into a cylinder in waxed paper.

   Compound butters have two main uses:

   - Slices of the firm butter are placed on hot grilled items at service time. The butter melts over the item and sauces it.

   - Small portions are swirled into sauces to finish them and give them a desired flavor.

   Easy as they are to make, compound butters can transform a plain broiled steak into a truly special dish.

   The favorite compound butter for steaks is maître d'hôtel (may truh doh tel) butter. Variations are given after the recipe (p. 179).

7. **Beurre blanc.**

   Beurre blanc (burr blon) is a sauce made by whipping a large quantity of raw butter into a small quantity of a flavorful reduction of white wine and vinegar so that the butter melts and forms an emulsion with the reduction. The technique is basically the same as monter au beurre (p. 167) except that the proportion of butter to liquid is much greater.

   Beurre blanc can be made quickly and easily by adding cold butter all at once and whipping vigorously over moderately high heat. The temperature of the butter keeps the sauce cool enough to prevent it from separating. Be sure to remove it from the heat before all the butter is melted, and continue whipping. It is better to remove the sauce from the heat too soon rather than too late because it can always be rewarmed slightly if necessary. Figure 8.8 illustrates this procedure.

   Some chefs prefer to use low heat and add the butter a little at a time in order to reduce the chance of overheating and breaking the sauce. The process takes a little longer, but the result is the same.

Beurre blanc should be held at a warm, not a hot, temperature and stirred or whipped from time to time so the fat and water do not separate. For more stable mixtures of fat and water—called *emulsions*—see the discussion of hollandaise beginning on page 180.

Figure 8.8
Preparing beurre blanc.

(a) Reduce the liquids (usually wine and vinegar) with chopped shallots.

(b) Whip in the raw butter just until the butter is melted and forms a smooth sauce.

(c) Leave in the shallots or strain them out. Strained beurre blanc has a light, smooth, creamy texture.

Butter-Enriched Sauces

As already noted, the technique for making beurre blanc is the same as *monter au beurre*, except that the proportion of butter is much higher. This same technique can be used to finish a great variety of sauces, usually white sauces, although brown sauces can be finished the same way.

To improvise a butter-enriched version of a classic white sauce, refer to the sauce variations on page 173. In place of the 1 qt (1 L) velouté or other white sauce base, substitute 1 pt (500 mL) concentrated white stock. Combine with the flavoring ingredients indicated in the variation. Reduce to a slightly syrupy consistency. Whip in 8 oz (250 g) raw butter and strain.

Many other sauces for sautéed meat, poultry, or fish items can be improvised using the same technique. Deglaze the sauté pan with wine, stock, or other liquid, add desired flavoring ingredients, reduce, and finish by whipping in a generous quantity of raw butter. Season and strain.

 ## Maître d'Hôtel Butter

Yield: about 1 lb (500 g)

U.S.	Metric	Ingredients
1 lb	500 g	Butter
¼ cup	60 mL	Chopped parsley
1½ fl oz	50 mL	Lemon juice
pinch	pinch	White pepper

Per 1 ounce:
Calories, 45; Protein 1 g; Fat, 3.5 g (66% cal.); Cholesterol, 0 mg;
Carbohydrates, 3 g; Fiber, 1 g; Sodium, 5 mg.

■ **P r o c e d u r e**

1. Using a mixer with the paddle attachment, beat the butter at low speed until it is smooth and creamy.

2. Add the remaining ingredients and beat slowly until completely mixed.

3. Roll the butter into a cylinder about 1 in. (2½ cm) thick in a sheet of parchment or waxed paper. Chill until firm.

4. To serve, cut slices ¼ in. (½ cm) thick and place on broiled or grilled items just before service.

V A R I A T I O N S

For each kind of seasoned butter, add to 1 lb (500 g) butter the listed ingredients instead of the parsley, lemon juice, and pepper.

Anchovy Butter
2 oz (60 g) anchovy fillets, mashed to paste

Garlic Butter
1 oz (30 g) garlic, mashed to a paste (see p. 523)

Escargot (Snail) Butter
Garlic butter plus ½ cup (125 mL) chopped parsley, salt, white pepper

Shrimp Butter
½ lb (250 g) cooked shrimp and shells, ground very fine. Force shrimp butter through a fine sieve to remove pieces of shell.

Mustard Butter
3–4 oz (100 g) Dijon-style mustard

Herb Butter
Chopped fresh herbs to taste

Scallion or Shallot Butter
2 oz (60 g) minced scallions or shallots

Curry Butter
4–6 tsp (20–30 mL) curry powder heated gently with 1 oz (30 g) butter, then cooled.

Beurre Blanc

Yield: 1 pt (500 mL)

U.S.	Metric	Ingredients
8 fl oz	250 mL	Dry white wine
1½ fl oz	50 mL	White wine vinegar
1 oz	30 g	Shallots, chopped
1 lb	500 g	Cold butter
to taste	to taste	Salt

Per 1 ounce:
Calories, 210; Protein, 0 g; Fat, 23 g (94% cal.); Cholesterol, 60 mg;
Carbohydrates, 1 g; Fiber, 0 g; Sodium, 240 mg.

■ P r o c e d u r e

1. Combine the wine, vinegar, and shallots in a saucepan. Reduce until about 1 oz (30 mL) liquid remains.

2. Cut the butter into small pieces.

3. Add the butter to the hot reduction. Set the pan over moderately high heat and whip vigorously. When the butter is nearly all melted and incorporated, remove from the heat and continue to whip until smooth.

4. Season to taste. The shallots may be left in the sauce or strained out.

5. Hold the sauce in a warm, not hot, place until served. Stir or whip it from time to time.

V A R I A T I O N S

Herbed Butter Sauce
Add your choice of chopped fresh herbs to the finished beurre blanc, or use an herbed compound butter instead of the plain raw butter to make beurre blanc.

Beurre Rouge (Red Butter Sauce)
Use dry red wine instead of white wine to make the reduction. For good color, use a young, bright red wine.

 Red Wine Butter Sauce for Fish

Yield: 1 pt 4 oz (600 mL)

U.S.	Metric	Ingredients
1 qt	1 L	Red wine
3½ oz	100 g	Shallots, chopped fine
7 fl oz	200 mL	Fish stock
1 lb	500 g	Cold butter
to taste	to taste	Salt
to taste	to taste	White pepper

Per 1 ounce:
Calories, 200; Protein, 0 g; Fat, 18 g (81% cal.); Cholesterol, 50 mg;
Carbohydrates, 2 g; Fiber, 0 g; Sodium, 190 mg.

■ P r o c e d u r e

1. Combine the red wine and shallots in a saucepan. Reduce until almost completely evaporated.

2. Add the fish stock. Reduce by two-thirds.

3. Cut the butter into small pieces.

4. Add the butter to the hot reduction. Set the pan over moderately high heat and whip vigorously. When the butter is nearly all incorporated, remove from the heat and continue to whip until smooth.

5. Season to taste. The shallots may be left in the sauce or strained out.

HOLLANDAISE AND BÉARNAISE

Hollandaise is considered an egg-thickened sauce, but the egg doesn't thicken by coagulation as it does in a liaison or in a custard sauce. Instead, it works by emulsification.

An **emulsion** is a uniform mixture of two unmixable liquids. In the case of hollandaise, the two liquids are melted butter and water (including the water in the lemon juice or the vinegar reduction). The two stay mixed and thick because the butter is beaten into tiny droplets and the egg yolks hold the droplets apart. You will encounter emulsion again when you prepare mayonnaise and other salad dressings in Chapter 21.

Two recipes for hollandaise are given. The first is the classic version, flavored with lemon and a vinegar reduction (see Figure 8.9). The second, flavored with just lemon juice, is used more often today because it is quicker and easier.

Holding Hollandaise Sauce

Hollandaise sauce, as well as other sauces in this family, poses a special safety problem. It must be kept warm for service, but it must be held below 140°F (60°C) so the eggs

Figure 8.9
Making hollandaise sauce.

(a) Combine the egg yolks and reduction in a stainless-steel bowl.

(b) Whip over a hot-water bath.

(c) Continue to whip over hot water until thick and light.

(d) Very slowly whip in the butter. (Set the bowl in a saucepan lined with a kitchen towel to hold it steady.)

(e) The finished sauce should be thick but pourable.

Guidelines for Preparing Hollandaise and Béarnaise

Students tend to be afraid of hollandaise because it has a reputation for being difficult to make. True, precautions are necessary to avoid overcooking the eggs and for getting the right consistency. But if you follow the instructions in the recipe carefully and keep in mind these guidelines, you should have no trouble.

Many of these rules have one object in common: Don't overcook the egg yolks, or they will lose their ability to emulsify.

1. Cool the reduction before adding the yolks, or they will overcook.

2. Use the freshest eggs possible for the best emulsification.

   For safety, pasteurized eggs are recommended (see pp. 788 and 1030).

3. Beat the yolks over hot water.

   An experienced cook is able to beat them over direct heat, if care is taken, without making scrambled eggs. Until you have gained some confidence, it is safer to use a hot-water bain-marie.

4. Use a round-bottomed stainless-steel bowl.

   The whip must be able to reach all the eggs to beat them evenly. Also, stainless steel will not discolor the sauce or give it a metallic flavor.

5. Have the butter warm but not hot, or it may overcook the eggs. If it is too cool, it might solidify.

6. Add the butter slowly at first.

   The yolks can only absorb a little at a time. Add a few drops at first and beat in thoroughly before adding more. If you add butter faster than it can be absorbed, the emulsion may break.

7. Don't add more butter than the egg yolks can hold.

   Remember this standard proportion:

   6 egg yolks per pound (450 g) of clarified butter

8. Broken or curdled hollandaise can be rescued.

   First, try adding a teaspoon of cold water and beating vigorously. If this doesn't work, start over with a couple of egg yolks and repeat the procedure from step 6 in the recipe, adding the broken sauce as you would the butter.

don't curdle. Unfortunately, bacteria grow quickly in this temperature range. Therefore, extra care must be taken to avoid food-borne diseases.

The following sanitation procedures must be observed to avoid the danger of food poisoning:

1. Make sure all equipment is perfectly clean.
2. Hold sauce no longer than 1½ hours. Make only enough to serve in this time, and discard any that is left over.
3. Never mix an old batch of sauce with a new batch.
4. Never hold hollandaise or béarnaise—or any other acid product—in aluminum. Use stainless-steel containers.

 ## Hollandaise Sauce I

Yield: 1 qt (1 L)

U.S.	Metric	Ingredients
2½ lb	1125 g	Butter
¼ tsp	1 mL	Peppercorns, crushed
¼ tsp	1 mL	Salt
6 fl oz	175 mL	White vinegar or wine vinegar
4 fl oz	120 mL	Water, cold
12	12	Egg yolks (see note after Hollandaise II)
2–4 tbsp	30–60 mL	Lemon juice
to taste	to taste	Salt
to taste	to taste	Cayenne

Per 1 ounce:
Calories, 280; Protein, 1 g; Fat, 31 g (99% cal.); Cholesterol, 155 mg; Carbohydrates, 0 g; Fiber, 0 g; Sodium, 310 mg.

■ P r o c e d u r e

1. Review the guidelines for preparing hollandaise and béarnaise (p. 181).
2. Clarify the butter (see p. 178). You should have about *2 lb (900 g) clarified butter*. Keep the butter warm but not hot.
3. Combine the peppercorns, salt, and vinegar in a saucepan and reduce until nearly dry (*au sec*). Remove from heat and add the cold water.
4. Pass the diluted reduction through a fine strainer into a stainless-steel bowl. Use a clean rubber spatula to make sure you transfer all the flavoring material to the bowl.
5. Add the egg yolks to the bowl and beat well.
6. Hold the bowl over a hot-water bath and continue to beat the yolks until they are thickened and creamy.
7. Remove the bowl from the heat. Using a ladle, slowly and gradually beat in the warm clarified butter. Add the butter drop by drop at first. If the sauce becomes too thick to beat before all the butter is added, beat in a little of the lemon juice.
8. When all the butter has been added, beat in lemon juice to taste and adjust seasoning with salt and cayenne. If necessary, thin the sauce with a few drops of warm water.
9. Strain through cheesecloth if necessary and keep warm (not hot) for service. Hold no longer than 1½ hours (see above).

 ## Hollandaise Sauce II

Yield: 1 qt (1 L)

U.S.	Metric	Ingredients
2½ lb	1125 g	Butter
12	12	Egg yolks (see note)
2 fl oz	60 mL	Water, cold
3 fl oz	100 mL	Lemon juice
to taste	to taste	Salt
to taste	to taste	Cayenne

Per 1 ounce:
Calories, 280; Protein, 1 g; Fat, 31 g (99% cal.); Cholesterol, 155 mg; Carbohydrates, 0 g; Fiber, 0 g; Sodium, 300 mg.

Note: For safety, pasteurized eggs are recommended.

■ P r o c e d u r e

1. Review the guidelines for preparing hollandaise and béarnaise (p. 181).
2. Clarify the butter (see p. 178). You should have about *2 lb (900 g) clarified butter*. Keep the butter warm but not hot.
3. Place the egg yolks and cold water in a stainless-steel bowl and beat well. Beat in a few drops of lemon juice.
4. Hold the bowl over a hot-water bath and continue to beat until the yolks are thickened and creamy.
5. Remove the bowl from the heat. Using a ladle, slowly and gradually beat in the warm butter. Add the butter drop by drop at first. If the sauce becomes too thick to beat before all the butter is added, beat in a little of the lemon juice.
6. When all the butter has been added, beat in lemon juice to taste and adjust seasoning with salt and cayenne. If necessary, thin the sauce with a few drops of warm water.
7. Keep warm (not hot) for service. Hold no longer than 1½ hours (see above).

Small Sauces

Maltaise	Mousseline
To 1 qt (1 L) hollandaise add 2–4 fl oz (60–125 mL) orange juice (from blood oranges, if possible) and 2 tsp (10 mL) grated orange rind. Serve with asparagus.	Whip 1 cup (250 mL) heavy cream until stiff and fold into 1 qt (1 L) hollandaise.

 ## Béarnaise Sauce

Yield: 1 qt (1 L)

U.S.	Metric	Ingredients	■ P r o c e d u r e
2½lb	1125 g	Butter	1. Review the guidelines for preparing hollandaise and béarnaise (p. 181). 2. Clarify the butter (see p. 178). You should have about *2 lb (900 g) clarified butter*. Keep the butter warm but not hot.
2 oz	60 g	Shallots, chopped	3. Combine the shallots, vinegar, tarragon, and peppercorns in a saucepan and reduce by three-fourths. Remove from the heat and cool slightly.
1 cup	250 mL	White wine vinegar	4. To make it easier to beat with a wire whip, it is best now to transfer this reduction to a stainless-steel bowl. Use a clean rubber spatula to make sure you get it all. Let the reduction cool a little.
2 tsp	10 mL	Dried tarragon	
1 tsp	5 mL	Peppercorns, crushed	5. Add the egg yolks to the bowl and beat well.
12	12	Egg yolks (see note)	6. Hold the bowl over a hot-water bath and continue to beat the yolks until they are thickened and creamy. 7. Remove the bowl from the heat. Using a ladle, slowly and gradually beat in the warm clarified butter. Add the butter drop by drop at first. If the sauce becomes too thick to beat before all the butter is added, beat in a little lemon juice or warm water. 8. Strain the sauce through cheesecloth.
to taste	to taste	Salt	9. Season to taste with salt, cayenne, and a few drops of lemon juice. Mix in the parsley and tarragon.
to taste	to taste	Cayenne	
to taste	to taste	Lemon juice	10. Keep warm (not hot) for service. Hold no longer than 1½ hours (see p. 182).
2 tbsp	30 mL	Chopped parsley	
1 tsp	5 mL	Dried tarragon	

Per 1 ounce:
Calories, 280; Protein, 1 g; Fat, 31 g (97% cal.); Cholesterol, 155 mg; Carbohydrates, 1 g; Fiber, 0 g; Sodium, 300 mg.

Note: For safety, pasteurized eggs are recommended.

Small Sauces

Foyot	Choron
Add 2 oz (60 g) melted meat glaze (glace de viande) to 1 qt (1 L) béarnaise.	Add 2 oz (60 g) tomato paste to 1 qt (1 L) béarnaise.

PAN GRAVIES AND OTHER INTEGRAL SAUCES

An **integral sauce** is a sauce based on the juices released during the cooking of a meat, poultry, fish, or vegetable item. Most of the sauces we have discussed so far are not integral sauces. That is, they are made separately from and independently of the items they are served with. An integral sauce, on the other hand, can't be made separately, because it incorporates cooking juices from the item it is served with.

Basic Procedure for Making Pan Gravy

Method 2 has fewer steps, but Method 1 is actually quicker for large quantities and gives greater control over final consistency.

Method 1

1. Remove the roast from the roasting pan.

   If you have not added mirepoix to the pan during roasting, you can do so now.

2. Clarify the fat.

   Set the roasting pan over high heat and cook until all the moisture has evaporated, leaving only the fat, mirepoix, and the brown (caramelized) drippings. Pour off and save the fat.

3. Deglaze the pan.

   Pour stock or other liquid into the roasting pan. Stir over heat until caramelized drippings are dissolved.

4. Combine with stock and simmer.

   Pour the deglazing liquid, plus mirepoix, into a large pot with desired amount of stock. Simmer until mirepoix is well cooked. Skim the surface well to remove fat and scum.

5. Make a roux or, alternatively, a slurry of arrowroot or cornstarch and water.

   For roux, measure enough of the fat from step 2 to make the correct amount of roux for the volume of gravy. Make a blond or brown roux, as desired. For starch slurry, see page 161.

6. Thicken the gravy with the roux or starch slurry.

7. Strain.

8. Adjust seasonings.

Method 2

1. Remove the roast from the roasting pan.

2. Clarify the fat.

3. Add flour to the roasting pan and make a roux.

4. Add stock. Stir until thickened and the pan is deglazed.

5. Strain. Skim excess fat.

6. Adjust consistency, if necessary, with more stock or more roux.

7. Season.

The most important technique required for integral sauces is deglazing (see pp. 72 and 167). Juices released by sautéed and roasted meats are reduced and caramelized in the bottom of the pan during cooking. Deglazing dissolves these caramelized juices and incorporates them into the desired sauce. For the simplest example, if you sauté a chicken breast and then deglaze the sauté pan with a little stock and season the resulting liquid, you end up with an integral sauce that can be served with the chicken.

The most basic and familiar integral sauces are pan gravy and jus. Pan gravy is a sauce made with juices or drippings of the meat or poultry with which it is being served. Standard pan gravies are similar to brown sauces. Instead of being made with espagnole or demi-glace as a base, however, they are made from pan drippings plus roux plus stock or water and, sometimes, milk or cream.

Jus (zhoo) refers to unthickened juices from a roast. When the roast is served with these clear, natural juices, it is said to be served au jus (oh zhoo), meaning "with juice." Stock is usually added to the pan juices to obtain enough quantity to serve.

The preparation of both pan gravy and jus are properly part of meat cookery, and recipes and detailed procedures are included in the meat and poultry chapters. Similarly, recipes for all integral sauces are included as part of the meat, fish, or vegetable in the appropriate chapters.

The principal recipes are on page 292 (Roast Beef Gravy) and page 370 (Roast Turkey with Giblet Gravy). Gravy-making is also incorporated in the recipes for Roast Stuffed Shoulder of Lamb (p. 294), Roast Loin of Pork with Sage and Apples (p. 293), and Roast Chicken with Natural Gravy (p. 368).

Now that you have studied sauce-making in detail, read the general procedure for making pan gravies on page 184 so you can see how similar it is to making brown sauce and how the same techniques you have just learned are applied to a different product.

MODERN SAUCES

As suggested in the introduction to this chapter, sauce-making has changed a great deal since Escoffier's day. Although our basic methods for making many of the sauces in the modern kitchen are derived from classical cuisine, details have changed. Perhaps the most important change is that chefs rely less on roux for thickening a sauce, while reduction has become more important to give sauces body (see p. 166). When starches are used, they are often purer starches such as arrowroot.

Chefs have also been influenced by other cuisines, such as those of Asia and Latin America, and have borrowed ingredients and procedures from many countries and regions to give variety to their repertoire of sauces.

Because of the ongoing experimentation and development of new sauces, it is difficult to classify and define them exactly, the way Escoffier did in the last century. We can, however, describe general groups that many of today's popular sauces fall into. The remaining recipes in this chapter include examples of these types of sauces.

A number of other popular sauces, such as barbecue sauce, that don't fit into any of the categories described in the following sections, are included in this chapter. Other sauce recipes are included elsewhere in this book, often as components of other recipes. Among the more important of these are vinaigrette and mayonnaise variations. These are traditionally used as salad dressings but are also used as sauces for meat, seafood, and vegetable items.

The following recipes from other chapters appear on the pages indicated.

Roast Beef Gravy, page 292

Jus Lié, page 292

Tomato Sauce for Pasta, with variations, page 639

Pesto, page 644

Mole Poblano, page 409

Salsa Verde, page 489

Basic Vinaigrette and variations, page 723

American French Dressing, page 725

Oriental Vinaigrette, page 725

Mayonnaise and variations, page 728

Broths and Jus

Beginning with the introduction of nouvelle cuisine in the 1970s, chefs looked for ways to eliminate starch thickeners in sauces in order to make them lighter. The technique of reduction to concentrate a sauce has been the most important tool in this effort. Reduction hasn't been a cure-all, however. First, some of the fresher, lighter flavors of a sauce are lost when a liquid is subjected to the long cooking required for reduction. In addition, reduced sauces sometimes become so gelatinous that they solidify when they cool—not an appetizing result.

Nevertheless, we have become accustomed to sauces that do not cling thickly to the meat, poultry, or seafood. Sauces, often in smaller quantities, are served under or around the item as often as over the top of it, perhaps even more often. Some chefs have gone to the extreme of serving the item in a little broth in place of a sauce. This technique has long been popular with seafood, as in the case of Seafood à la Nage (p. 487), but it is becoming more common with meat as well. The result is often something like a garnished consommé (pp. 212–213), but with very little consommé and a full portion of meat and garnish. The recipe on page 330 is an example.

For a broth to work well as a substitute for a sauce, it should be well flavored and aromatic. Taste the broth and reduce it as necessary to concentrate the flavor, and check the seasonings carefully.

Procedure for Making a Meat Jus

1. Cut trimmings of the desired meat or poultry product into small pieces. Place them in a heavy pot over moderate heat.

2. Cook until well browned on all sides. Some liquid will be released from the meat. If the trimmings begin to simmer in these juices instead of browning, just let them continue to cook until the liquid has evaporated and browned on the bottom of the pot.

3. Deglaze with a small quantity of white wine or stock. Continue to cook until the liquid is reduced and the juices again caramelize on the bottom.

4. Add enough stock to cover the meat. Stir to dissolve the caramelized juices on the bottom of the pot. Simmer until the liquid is completely reduced and caramelized.

5. Again add enough stock to cover the meat. Stir to dissolve the caramelized juices. Simmer 10 to 15 minutes. Strain and degrease.

A jus is very much like a broth except that it is usually more concentrated, although still unthickened. The term *jus* is usually used in two ways:

1. The unthickened, natural juices resulting from a roast. This is the more traditional meaning of jus (see p. 184). To make a traditional jus, the drippings of a roast are deglazed with stock or other liquid, reduced slightly, seasoned, strained, and served unthickened.
   To make a meat jus without a roast, follow the procedure above.

2. An unthickened liquid carrying the concentrated flavor of a specific ingredient. This type of jus is often made from vegetables and is sometimes called an *essence*. To make a vegetable essence, the vegetable is simmered with a stock or broth until the liquid is concentrated and flavorful. The recipe for Mushroom Jus (p. 188, also called *mushroom essence*) is an example of this type of preparation.

Purées

Vegetable purées have long been used as sauces. Tomato sauce is the classic example. However, nearly any vegetable can be puréed and used as a sauce, provided that it is flavorful, properly seasoned, and of an appropriate consistency or thickness. A vegetable purée is sometimes called a *coulis*.

Purées of starchy vegetables, such as squash or dried beans, may need to be thinned with stock, broth, or water. Even potato purée is sometimes thinned and used as a sauce, usually enriched with a little raw butter stirred in. In addition, potato and other thick purées are used as thickeners for other sauces.

Some vegetables, such as asparagus, make a watery purée. These purées can be reduced to thicken them, but be careful not to lose the fresh vegetable taste and color. This should especially be avoided in the case of green vegetables, which quickly lose their color (see p. 509). Although thin vegetable purées may be thickened with a starch, it is more common to leave them thin or to bind them lightly by finishing them with raw butter (monter au beurre, p. 167) or reducing them with a little cream until they have the desired consistency.

Cream Reductions

In the era of nouvelle cuisine, sauces based on reduced cream became a popular substitute for roux-thickened white sauces. When heavy cream is reduced, it thickens slightly. A common fault with cream reduction sauces is reducing the cream too much, giving it a heavy texture. If it is reduced beyond this point, it is likely to break, and the butterfat will separate. For an appealing, light texture, reduce the cream until it is about two-thirds of its original volume.

A reduced cream sauce is a mixture of reduced cream and a concentrated, flavorful stock. White stock is most often used, although brown cream sauces may also be prepared using brown stock. For good results, the stock should be reduced by about three-fourths. Flavored sauces can be made by reducing the stock with flavoring ingredients, as in the recipe for Chipotle Cream Sauce on page 190.

Two methods are possible:

1. Reducing the cream to the desired consistency and then adding it to the stock reduction.

2. Adding fresh cream to the stock reduction and reducing the mixture to the desired consistency.

Many chefs feel the first method is more controllable. See the following procedure:

Procedure for Making a Cream Reduction Sauce

1. Reduce white stock or brown stock by about three-fourths, or until it is concentrated and flavorful.

2. Measure the reduction. For each pint (500 mL) reduction, measure about 1½ pints (750 mL) heavy cream.

3. Place the cream in a heavy saucepan over moderate heat and reduce until lightly thickened, or until reduced by about one-third. Stir from time to time with a whip.

4. Bring the stock reduction to a simmer in a saucepan. Stir in the reduced cream.

5. Check the consistency. Thicken, if necessary, by reducing further, or thin with additional heavy cream.

6. Season and strain.

Salsas, Relishes, and Chutneys

It is said that, in the United States, salsa has become even more popular than ketchup. The salsa referred to is, of course, the Mexican mixture of chopped tomatoes, onions, chiles, herbs, and other ingredients. *Salsa* is actually the Spanish and the Italian word for "sauce," so the word refers to many types of preparations, both raw and cooked, not just this one Mexican relish. Nevertheless, in English-speaking countries, the word salsa usually refers to a mixture of raw or cooked chopped vegetables, herbs, and, occasionally, fruits.

Salsas are easily improvised. Select a suitable mixture of vegetables, fruits, or both, and chop coarsely or finely, as desired. Mix with appropriate chopped fresh herbs and season to taste. Salt draws juices out of the ingredients to provide moisture for the mixture. Add citrus juice or vinegar if the mixture is lacking in acidity. Acidity should balance any sweetness from fruits because salsas are usually intended for savory dishes, not desserts.

The words *relish* and *chutney* have no exact definitions. One meaning of *relish* is any raw or pickled vegetable used as an appetizer (see p. 760). For example, a dish of celery sticks, carrot sticks, and olives is sometimes called a *relish dish*, for many years a traditional appetizer in steakhouses and other restaurants. As used in a discussion of sauces, a relish is a mixture of chopped vegetables (and sometimes fruits), at least one of which has been pickled in vinegar or a salt solution. By this definition, a salsa may be considered to be a type of relish, especially if it contains an acid such as vinegar or citrus juice.

The word chutney originated in India, where it refers to several types of spicy condiments or relishes, including strongly spiced sweet-and-sour cooked fruit or vegetable mixtures, as well as raw or partially cooked mixtures of chopped herbs or vegetables, also spicy and often containing chiles. Almost all chutneys contain an acid ingredient. Western cooks have been especially inspired by the sweet-and-sour types of chutney, so when the word *chutney* appears on a menu, it usually refers to a cooked fruit or vegetable condiment that is sweet, spicy, and tangy.

Several examples of salsas, relishes, and chutneys are included in this chapter.

Asian Sauces

Sauces from many Asian cuisines, including Japanese, Thai, Vietnamese, and Indian, have entered the Western cook's repertoire in recent years. Asia is, of course, a huge continent, and it would take years of study to become familiar with all its varied cooking traditions. This chapter can only begin that familiarization process by providing a selection of popular recipes with sidebars containing background information on ingredients and techniques.

Incidentally, Chinese cuisines have relatively few standalone sauces. Sauces in stir-fried dishes, for example, are made as part of the cooking process by adding liquids and thickeners to the meat and vegetables as they cook. Ready-made condiments such as oyster sauce and hoisin sauce are also used.

When adopting Asian-style sauces into Western cuisine, cooks should have some familiarity with the regional cuisine they are borrowing from and how the sauces are used in that cuisine. Unless the cook is careful, mixing Asian-style sauces with Western dishes can have strange results.

Flavored Oils

Flavored oils make a light, interesting alternative to vinaigrettes and other sauces when used to dress a wide variety of dishes. They are especially suitable for simple steamed, sautéed, or grilled items, but they can be used with cold foods as well. When used as a sauce, the oil is usually drizzled around or, sometimes, over the item on the plate. A tablespoon (15 mL) or so per portion is often enough.

The simplest way to flavor an oil is simply to put some of the flavoring ingredient in the oil and let it stand until the oil has taken on enough of the flavor. For most flavorings, however, this is not the best way to extract the most flavor. The flavoring ingredient may need some kind of preparation before adding it to the oil. For example, dry spices develop more flavor if they are first heated gently with a little bit of the oil.

Refrigerating flavored oils is recommended. As you will recall from Chapter 2, botulism is caused by a kind of bacteria that grows in the absence of air. Because oil prevents air from reaching the flavoring ingredients, if any botulism bacteria are present in the flavorings (especially possible with fresh, raw roots), those bacteria could grow while covered with oil if not refrigerated.

The following procedure outlines the basic method for making flavored oils, depending on the type of ingredients. Unless otherwise indicated, use a mild or flavorless oil, such as safflower, canola, corn, or grapeseed. In some cases, as with garlic, the flavoring goes well with olive oil, but usually the goal is to have the pure taste of the flavoring ingredient unmasked by the flavor of the oil.

Procedure for Making Flavored Oils

1. **Prepare the flavoring ingredient in one of the following ways:**

   Chop fresh roots (such as horseradish, garlic, shallots, ginger, garlic) or strong herbs (fresh rosemary, sage, thyme, oregano) by hand or in a food processor.

   Grate citrus zests.

   Blanch tender herbs (parsley, basil, tarragon, chervil, cilantro) in boiling water for 10 seconds. Drain immediately and refresh under cold water. Dry well.

   Gently heat dried, ground spices (cinnamon, cumin, curry powder, ginger, mustard, paprika) in a small amount of oil just until they start to give off an aroma.

2. **Place the flavoring ingredient in a jar or other closable container. Add oil.**

3. **Close the jar and shake it well. Let stand 30 minutes at room temperature, then refrigerate.**

4. **The oil is ready to use as soon as it has taken on the desired flavor, which may be as soon as one hour, depending on the ingredient. After two days, strain the oil through a chinois lined with a paper coffee filter. Store in the refrigerator.**

 ## Mushroom Jus

Yield: 2 qt (2 L)

U.S.	Metric	Ingredients
3 lb	1.5 kg	Mushrooms, cleaned, coarsely chopped
2 gal	8 L	Water
2 gal	8 L	Water
2 gal	8 L	Water

Per 1 ounce:
Calories, 5; Protein, 1 g; Fat, 0 g (0% cal.); Cholesterol, 0 mg; Carbohydrates, 1 g; Fiber, 0 g; Sodium, 0 mg.

■ P r o c e d u r e

1. Place the mushrooms and the first quantity of water in a stockpot.
2. Bring to a boil. Reduce the heat to a rapid simmer and cook until most of the liquid has evaporated.
3. Add the second quantity of water and repeat the reduction process.
4. Add the third quantity of water. Reduce by three-quarters.
5. Strain through a china cap lined with cheesecloth, pressing on the mushrooms to extract as much liquid as possible.
6. To use or to finish as a sauce, see Variations.

V A R I A T I O N S

The jus can be used as is, seasoned with salt and pepper. A small amount of arrowroot or other starch may be used to bind the sauce lightly. Alternatively, finish by enriching with cream (see p. 186 for information on cream reductions) or butter (see p. 179). The jus can also be added as a flavoring ingredient to meat or poultry broths and to demi-glace, and it can be used as a deglazing liquid.

Bell Pepper Coulis

Yield: 2½ pt (1.25 L)

U.S.	Metric	Ingredients
4 lb	2 kg	Red or yellow bell peppers
2 fl oz	60 mL	Olive oil
2 oz	60 g	Shallots, chopped
4 fl oz	125 mL	Chicken stock, vegetable stock, or water
1–4 fl oz	30–125 mL	Additional stock or water
to taste	to taste	Salt
to taste	to taste	White pepper

Per 1 ounce:
Calories, 25; Protein, 0 g; Fat, 1.5 g (53% cal.); Cholesterol, 0 mg; Carbohydrates, 3 g; Fiber, 1 g; Sodium, 0 mg.

■ Procedure

1. Split the peppers in half lengthwise. Remove the cores, seeds, and membranes. Chop the peppers coarsely.
2. Heat the olive oil in a saucepot over low heat.
3. Add the shallots and peppers. Cover and sweat over low heat until the vegetables are soft, about 20 minutes.
4. Add the stock or water. Simmer 2–3 minutes.
5. Purée the vegetables and liquid in a blender, then pass through a strainer.
6. Adjust the texture by adding water or stock to thin it.
7. Add salt and white pepper to taste.

VARIATION

Bell Pepper and Tomato Coulis.
Combine bell pepper coulis with an equal volume of tomato purée.

Sweet Corn and Chile Purée

Yield: approximately 1 pt (500 mL)

U.S.	Metric	Ingredients
1 fl oz	30 mL	Vegetable oil
4 oz	125 g	Onion, chopped fine
2	2	Garlic cloves, chopped fine
2	2	Serrano chiles, seeded and chopped
1 lb	500 g	Sweet corn, fresh or frozen
4 oz	125 g	Water
to taste	to taste	Salt

Per 1 ounce:
Calories 50; Protein, 1 g; Fat, 2 g (36% cal.); Cholesterol, 0 mg; Carbohydrates, 7 g; Fiber, 1 g; Sodium, 5 mg.

■ Procedure

1. Heat the oil in a sauté pan.
2. Add the onion, garlic, and chiles. Sauté over moderate heat until the onion is soft but not brown.
3. Add the corn. Cook, stirring a few times, until the corn is hot.
4. Add the water. Simmer about 3 minutes.
5. Transfer the mixture to a food processor and purée until the mixture is fairly smooth.
6. Adjust the texture as necessary by adding additional water or by returning to the pan and reducing slightly. The desired texture may vary, depending on the sauce's use. For the smoothest texture, pass the sauce through a food mill. This reduces the yield to about 13-14 fl oz (405-435 mL).
7. Add salt to taste.

White Bean Purée

Yield: 1½ pt (750 mL)

U.S.	Metric	Ingredients
1 lb	500 g	Cooked white beans, such as navy or cannellini
2	2	Garlic cloves, mashed to a paste
4 tsp	20 mL	Tomato paste
1 fl oz	30 mL	Lemon juice
4 tsp	20 mL	Paprika
½ tsp, or to taste	2 mL	Cayenne
4 fl oz	125 mL	Water
4 fl oz	125 mL	Olive oil
to taste	to taste	Salt

Per 1 ounce:
Calories, 70; Protein, 2 g; Fat, 5 g (58% cal.); Cholesterol, 0 mg; Carbohydrates, 6 g; Fiber, 2 g; Sodium, 10 mg.

■ Procedure

1. Combine the beans, garlic, tomato paste, lemon juice, paprika, cayenne, and water in a food processor. Process to a smooth paste.
2. With the processor running, pour in the olive oil in a thin stream.
3. The resulting purée should have the consistency of a moderately thickened sauce. If it is too thick, mix in a little more water.
4. Season to taste with salt.

Chipotle Cream Sauce

Yield: 12 fl oz (375 mL)

U.S.	Metric	Ingredients
1 qt	1 L	Brown stock
2	2	Whole, dried chipotle chiles
12 fl oz	375 mL	Heavy cream
to taste	to taste	Salt
to taste	to taste	White pepper

Per 1 ounce:
Calories, 110; Protein, 1 g; Fat, 11 g (93% cal.); Cholesterol, 45 mg;
Carbohydrates, 0 g; Fiber, 1 g; Sodium, 20 mg.

■ Procedure

1. Combine the stock and chiles in a saucepot.
2. Bring to a slow simmer. Simmer until reduced by three-fourths.
3. While the stock is reducing, place the cream in a second saucepot and reduce by one-third.
4. Stir the reduced cream into the reduced stock. If necessary, adjust the consistency of the sauce by reducing a little more to thicken or adding fresh cream to thin. The sauce should be about the thickness of heavy cream. The consistency will depend on the gelatin content of the stock and the fat content of the cream.
5. Season to taste with salt and white pepper.
6. Strain. Discard the chiles.

VARIATIONS

White stock, chicken stock, or vegetable stock may be substituted for the brown stock.

Herb Cream Sauce
Use white stock or chicken stock instead of brown stock. Omit the chiles. Add chopped fresh herbs (such as parsley, tarragon, chervil, basil) as desired to the sauce after straining.

Salsa Verde Cocida

Yield: 1 qt (1 L)

U.S.	Metric	Ingredients
4	4	13-oz (368-g) cans whole tomatillos (Mexican green tomatoes)
2 oz	60 g	Onion, chopped
4	4	Garlic cloves, chopped
2–4 oz	60–125 g	Green chiles, such as jalapeño or serrano, canned or fresh
1 oz	30 g	Fresh cilantro leaves (optional)
1 fl oz	30 mL	Oil
to taste	to taste	Salt

Per 1 ounce:
Calories, 25; Protein, 2 g; Fat, 1 g (27% cal.); Cholesterol, 0 mg;
Carbohydrates, 4 g; Fiber, 1 g; Sodium, 55 mg.

■ Procedure

1. Drain the tomatillos.
2. Combine the tomatillos, onion, garlic, chiles, and cilantro in a blender. Blend to a smooth purée.
3. Heat the oil in a large saucepan. Add the purée and cook 4–5 minutes, until slightly thickened.
4. Season to taste with salt.

VARIATIONS

Salsa Roja
Substitute 2 lb (1 kg) red, ripe tomatoes, peeled, or canned red tomatoes for the tomatillos. The onion may be included or omitted to create slightly different flavors.

Tomato Broth for Chiles Rellenos
Prepare as for Salsa Roja, using the onion but omitting the chiles and cilantro. After step 3, add 3 pt (1.5 L) pork stock (including the cooking liquid from making picadillo (p. 328) for the filling for the chiles) and/or chicken stock. Also, add a sachet containing 6 whole cloves, 10 peppercorns, 2 bay leaves, and 1 small cinnamon stick. Simmer until slightly thickened to the consistency of a thick broth or thin sauce.

Salsa Cruda

Yield: 1 qt (1 L)

U.S.	Metric	Ingredients
1 lb 4 oz	600 g	Fresh tomatoes
6 oz	175 g	Fresh green chiles, such as jalapeño or serrano
6 oz	175 g	Onion
½–1 oz	15–30 g	Fresh cilantro leaves, chopped
1 tbsp	15 mL	Lime juice or vinegar
2–4 fl oz	60–125 mL	Water or tomato juice, cold
1½ tsp	7 mL	Salt

Per 1 ounce:
Calories, 10; Protein, 0 g; Fat, 0 g (0% cal.); Cholesterol, 0 mg;
Carbohydrates, 2 g; Fiber, 0 g; Sodium, 110 mg.

■ **P r o c e d u r e**

1. Chop the tomatoes fine. (You may peel them, but it is not necessary.)
2. Remove the stem end of the chiles. Chop the chiles fine.
3. Mince the onion.
4. Mix together the tomato, chiles, onion, cilantro, and lime juice or vinegar. Dilute with water or tomato juice to make a thick, chunky sauce.
5. Add salt to taste.

This sauce is used as a table condiment with many dishes, including eggs, broiled meats, tacos, tortillas, and beans. It is best if used within a few hours.

Ancho Sauce

Yield: about 1½ pt (750 mL)

U.S.	Metric	Ingredients
8	8	Dried ancho chiles
2 oz	60 g	Onion, chopped
3	3	Garlic cloves, chopped
1 tsp	5mL	Ground cumin
½ tsp	2 mL	Dried oregano
1 pt	500 mL	Water or chicken stock
1 fl oz	30 mL	Oil
to taste	to taste	Salt

Per 1 ounce:
Calories, 30; Protein, 1 g; Fat, 1.5 g (46% cal.); Cholesterol, 0 mg;
Carbohydrates, 3 g; Fiber, 1 g; Sodium, 5 mg.

■ **P r o c e d u r e**

1. Toast the chiles lightly in a dry skillet, until softened. Split them open. Remove and discard the seeds and core.
2. Soak the chiles for about 30 minutes in enough hot water to cover. Drain.
3. Combine the chiles, onion, garlic, cumin, oregano, and water or stock in a blender. Blend to a smooth purée.
4. Heat the oil in a saucepan and add the chile purée. Simmer 2–3 minutes.
5. Season to taste with salt.

V A R I A T I O N

Blend 8 oz (250 g) chopped tomato with the chiles in step 3.

Chimichurri Sauce

Yield: 1 pt (500 mL)

U.S.	Metric	Ingredients
6 fl oz	180 mL	Lemon juice
8 fl oz	240 mL	Olive oil
2 oz	60 g	Chopped parsley
1½ oz	45 g	Onion, chopped fine
1 tbsp	15 mL	Finely chopped garlic
1 tbsp	15 mL	Red pepper flakes
to taste	to taste	Salt
to taste	to taste	Pepper

Per 1 ounce:
Calories, 130; Protein, 0 g; Fat, 14 g (94% cal.); Cholesterol, 0 mg;
Carbohydrates, 2 g; Fiber, 0 g; Sodium, 0 mg.

■ **P r o c e d u r e**

1. Combine all ingredients and mix well.
2. Serve as a sauce for grilled meats.

Vegetable Caper Relish

Yield: about 1 lb (480 g)

U.S.	Metric	Ingredients
1 fl oz	30 mL	Olive oil
2 oz	60 g	Carrots, cut brunoise
4 oz	120 g	Zucchini (outside part only, without the seeds), cut brunoise
2 oz	60 g	Fennel, cut brunoise
1 oz	30 g	Shallots, cut brunoise
3 oz	90 g	Red pepper, roasted and peeled (p. 529), cut brunoise
2 oz	60 g	Cucumber, peeled, seeded cut brunoise
1 oz	30 g	Capers, small, drained
2 fl oz	60 mL	Wine vinegar
to taste	to taste	Salt

■ Procedure

1. Heat the olive oil in a sauté pan over low heat.
2. Add the carrots, zucchini, fennel, and shallots. Sweat just until the vegetables soften slightly.
3. In a bowl, combine the sweated vegetables with the red pepper, cucumber, capers, and vinegar. Mix well.
4. Season to taste with salt.
5. Refrigerate several hours or overnight before serving.

Per 1 ounce:
Calories, 25; Protein, 0 g; Fat, 2 g (69% cal.); Cholesterol, 0 mg;
Carbohydrates, 2 g; Fiber, 0 g; Sodium, 55 mg.

Tomato Raisin Chutney

Yield: 1¼ pt (625 mL)

U.S.	Metric	Ingredients
2 lb 8 oz	1.2 kg	Tomatoes, fresh (see note)
2 oz	60 g	Garlic, coarsely chopped
1 oz	30 g	Fresh ginger root, peeled, coarsely chopped
4 fl oz	120 g	Red wine vinegar
6 fl oz	180 g	Red wine vinegar
8 oz	240 g	Sugar
1 tsp	5 mL	Salt
2 tbsp	30 mL	Chopped hot green chiles
1½ oz	45 g	Golden raisins

■ Procedure

1. Blanch the tomatoes in boiling water for 10 seconds to loosen the skins. Peel and trim them.
2. Cut the tomatoes into quarters.
3. Combine the garlic, ginger, and first quantity of vinegar in a blender and blend until smooth.
4. Combine the tomatoes, garlic mixture, second quantity of vinegar, sugar, and salt in a stainless-steel saucepan.
5. Bring the mixture to a boil, stirring to dissolve the sugar.
6. Cook at a slow simmer, stirring occasionally, until the mixture becomes thick. There should be about 1½ pints (750 mL)
7. Add the chiles and raisins. Simmer another 5 to 10 minutes. Remove from heat and cool.
8. Taste and add additional salt if necessary.

Per 1 ounce:
Calories, 70; Protein, 1 g; Fat, 0 g (0% cal.); Cholesterol, 0 mg;
Carbohydrates, 17 g; Fiber, 1 g; Sodium, 125 mg.

Note: If good-quality ripe tomatoes are not available, substitute 2 lb (900 g) canned tomatoes with their juice.

Pineapple Chutney

Yield: 14 oz (440 g)

U.S.	Metric	Ingredients
4 fl oz	125 mL	Wine vinegar
1½ oz	45 g	Sugar
1 lb	500 g	Pineapple, fresh, cut into ¼-inch (6-mm) dice
1	1	Jalapeño chile, seeded and chopped fine
½ oz	15 g	Fresh ginger root, peeled and grated
½ tsp	2 mL	Ground cumin
¼ tsp	1 mL	Ground cardamom
½ tsp	2 mL	Cinnamon
¼ tsp	1 mL	White pepper

■ Procedure

1. Combine the vinegar and sugar in a stainless-steel saucepan large enough to hold the pineapple. Bring to a simmer, stir, and simmer until the sugar is dissolved.
2. Add the pineapple to the vinegar mixture. Simmer until the fruit has softened.
3. Strain. Return the juices to the pan and set the pineapple aside.
4. Add the chile, ginger, and spices to the juices in the pan. Simmer until reduced and syrupy.
5. Mix the spiced juices with the drained pineapple.
6. Refrigerate.

VARIATIONS

Other fruit, such as peaches, pears, or mangoes, may be prepared the same way.

Per 1 ounce:
Calories, 30; Protein, 0 g; Fat, 0 g (0% cal.); Cholesterol, 0 mg; Carbohydrates, 8 g; Fiber, 1 g; Sodium, 0 mg.

 ## Cucumber Raita

Yield: 1½ pt (750 mL)

U.S.	Metric	Ingredients
½ tsp	2 mL	Cumin seed
8 oz	250 g	Cucumber
1 pt	500 mL	Plain yogurt
1 tsp	5 mL	Salt
⅛ tsp	1 mL	Black pepper
⅛–¼ tsp	1–2 mL	Cayenne

■ Procedure

1. In a small, dry skillet over moderate heat, toast the cumin seeds until they are aromatic and turn a slightly darker shade of brown. Remove from the heat and grind in a spice grinder.
2. Peel and grate the cucumbers coarsely.
3. Place the yogurt in a bowl and whip until smooth.
4. Add the ground cumin, grated cucumber, salt, pepper, and cayenne. Mix well.

Per 1 ounce:
Calories, 15; Protein, 1 g; Fat, 1 g (53% cal.); Cholesterol, 0 mg; Carbohydrates, 1 g; Fiber, 0 g; Sodium, 105 mg.

 ## Nuoc Cham (Vietnamese Dipping Sauce)

Yield: 15 fl oz (450 mL)

U.S.	Metric	Ingredients
2	2	Garlic cloves, chopped
2–4	2–4	Fresh Thai chiles, seeded and chopped
3 tbsp	45 mL	Sugar
4 fl oz	125 mL	Lime juice
4 fl oz	125 mL	Nuoc nam (Vietnamese fish sauce) or nam pla (Thai fish sauce)
4 fl oz	125 mL	Water
1 oz	30 g	Carrot, cut fine julienne

■ Procedure

1. Pound the garlic, chiles, and sugar in a mortar to make a paste.
2. Place the garlic paste in a bowl and mix in the lime juice, stirring until the sugar is dissolved.
3. Add the remaining ingredients and mix well.

Per 1 ounce:
Calories, 20; Protein, 1 g; Fat, 0 g (0% cal.); Cholesterol, 0 mg; Carbohydrates, 4 g; Fiber, 0 g; Sodium, 740 mg.

Thai Red Curry Sauce

Yield: 18 fl oz (550 mL)

U.S.	Metric	Ingredients
1 fl oz	30 mL	Vegetable oil
1½ oz	45 mL	Red curry paste (see sidebar)
2 fl oz	60 mL	Water or stock
14 fl oz	410 mL	Coconut milk, canned, unsweetened
1½ oz	45 mL	Nam pla (Thai fish sauce)

Per 1 ounce:
Calories, 60; Protein, 1 g; Fat, 7 g (89% cal.); Cholesterol, 0 mg;
Carbohydrates, 1 g; Fiber, 0 g; Sodium, 190 mg.

■ Procedure

1. Heat the oil over moderate heat in a saucepan.
2. Add the curry paste and cook until it is aromatic.

3. Stir in the water or stock and bring to a simmer.
4. Add the coconut milk and nam pla. Bring to a simmer and simmer several minutes to blend the flavors.

VARIATION

Thai Green Curry Sauce
Substitute green curry paste for the red paste in the recipe.

THAI CURRIES

In Thai cuisine, curry sauces are typically made as integral sauces (see p. 183). With a variety of ready-made curry pastes on hand, it is simple to sauté the desired meat or seafood, prepare a sauce flavored with a curry paste, and stew the meat in the sauce with the desired vegetables.

In European and North American kitchens, on the other hand, curry sauces are often prepared separately and added to the plate at service time. The recipes included here can be used either way. To use the curry sauce recipe as an integral sauce, add the curry paste to the pan in which you have sautéed your meat or fish item. Finish the sauce as directed in the recipe, and return the meat to the sauce to finish cooking.

Thai curry pastes are available commercially. If none is available, use the recipes included here. Commercial pastes are usually of excellent quality and contain ingredients that are hard to obtain in Western kitchens. The curry paste recipes here are useful when commercial curry pastes and unusual Asian ingredients are not available.

Red Curry Paste

Yield: 1 lb 4 oz (560 g)

U.S.	Metric	Ingredients
2 oz	60 g	Galangal, peeled and chopped (see note)
6 oz	180 g	Shallots, chopped
2 oz	60 g	Garlic, chopped
3 oz	90 g	Cilantro roots (see note)
2 tbsp	30 mL	Lime zest, chopped
5 tbsp	75 mL	Cayenne
4	4	Lemon grass stalks, tender parts only, chopped
3 fl oz	90 mL	Vegetable oil

Per 1 ounce:
Calories, 50; Protein, 4 g; Fat, 4.5g (77% cal.); Cholesterol, 0 mg;
Carbohydrates, 3 g; Fiber, 1 g; Sodium, 0 mg.

■ Procedure

1. Combine all ingredients in a food processor. Process until the mixture forms a smooth paste.
2. Refrigerate and use as needed to make curry sauces.

Note: Galangal is a root that resembles fresh ginger in appearance but has a somewhat different taste. If it is not available, use fresh ginger.

Cilantro roots are the roots attached to ordinary cilantro that are usually discarded. Save, wash thoroughly, and use for this preparation. If not available, use cilantro stems.

Green Curry Paste

Yield: 15 oz (475 g)

U.S.	Metric	Ingredients
15	15	Serrano chiles, seeded and chopped
2 oz	60 g	Shallots, chopped
2 oz	60 g	Garlic, chopped
4	4	Lemon grass stalks, tender parts only, chopped
2 oz	60 g	Cilantro roots, chopped (see note to Red Curry Paste)
2 oz	60 g	Cilantro leaves, chopped
½ oz	15 g	Galangal, peeled and chopped (see note to Red Curry Paste)
2 tbsp	30 mL	Lime zest, chopped
1 tsp	5 mL	Nutmeg
3 fl oz	90 mL	Vegetable oil

■ P r o c e d u r e

1. Combine all ingredients in a food processor. Process until the mixture forms a smooth paste.
2. Refrigerate and use as needed to make curry sauces.

Per 1 ounce:
Calories, 60; Protein, 1 g; Fat, 6 g (77% cal.); Cholesterol, 0 mg; Carbohydrates, 3 g; Fiber, 1 g; Sodium, 195 mg.

Indonesian Peanut Sauce

Yield: 1 pt (500 mL)

U.S.	Metric	Ingredients
8 oz	250 g	Peanut butter
8 fl oz	250 mL	Hot water
4–6	4–6	Garlic cloves, crushed to a paste
2–3	2–3	Serrano chiles, seeded, chopped fine
1 tbsp	15 mL	Fresh ginger root, peeled and chopped fine
1 tbsp	15 mL	Brown sugar
1 tbsp	15 mL	Lime juice
1 fl oz	30 mL	Soy sauce

■ P r o c e d u r e

1. Combine all ingredients in a food processor. Process until the mixture forms a smooth sauce.
2. Refrigerate.

Per 1 ounce:
Calories, 90; Protein, 4 g; Fat, 7 g (66% cal.); Cholesterol, 0 mg; Carbohydrates, 4 g; Fiber, 1 g; Sodium, 190 mg.

Dashi

Yield: qt (2 L)

U.S.	Metric	Ingredients
4 ½ pt	2.25 L	Water, cold
2 oz	60 g	Kombu (giant kelp for stock)
1½ oz	50 g	Katsuobushi (dried bonito flakes)

■ P r o c e d u r e

1. Put the water in a pot and add the kombu. Bring to a boil over moderately high heat.
2. Just as the water comes to a boil, remove the kombu.
3. Remove from the heat and immediately add the bonito flakes. Let the flakes settle to the bottom. This will take 1–2 minutes.
4. Strain through a china cap lined with cheesecloth. Use the dashi within 1 day.

Per 1 ounce:
Calories, 2; Protein, 0 g; Fat, 0 g (0% cal.); Cholesterol, 0 mg; Carbohydrates, 0 g; Fiber, 0 g; Sodium, 3 mg.

V A R I A T I O N S

Vegetarian Dashi
Omit the bonito flakes and use only the kombu.

Instant dashi is also available. Its quality is good enough for simmered dishes and miso soup, but not for good clear soup. Follow label instructions.

Yakitori Sauce

Yield: 10 fl oz (300 mL)

U.S.	Metric	Ingredients
8 fl oz	240 mL	Soy sauce
3 fl oz	90 mL	Sake (Japanese rice wine)
2 fl oz	60 mL	Mirin (sweet Japanese rice wine)
3 oz	90 g	Sugar

■ P r o c e d u r e

1. Combine all the ingredients in a saucepan. Simmer until the sugar is dissolved and the liquid is reduced by about one-fourth.

Per 1 ounce:
Calories, 70; Protein, 2 g; Fat, 0 g (0% cal.); Cholesterol, 0 mg;
Carbohydrates, 13 g; Fiber, 0 g; Sodium, 1650 mg.

Ponzu Sauce

Yield: 30 fl oz (900 mL)

U.S.	Metric	Ingredients
2 fl oz	60 mL	Mirin (sweet Japanese rice wine)
12 fl oz	375 mL	Soy sauce
12 fl oz	375 mL	Lemon juice
6 fl oz	150 mL	Rice vinegar
½ oz	15 g	Katsuobushi (shaved dried bonito flakes)
1 piece about 2½ in. square	1 piece about 6 cm square	Kombu (Japanese kelp)

■ P r o c e d u r e

1. Heat the mirin in a small saucepan. Tilt the pan toward the flame to ignite (or light with a match) and burn off the alcohol.

2. Combine the mirin with the remaining ingredients. Refrigerate overnight.

3. Strain. Press on the solids to force out all liquid.

Per 1 ounce:
Calories 15; Protein, 1 g; Fat, 0 g (0% cal.); Cholesterol, 0 mg;
Carbohydrates, 3 g; Fiber, 0 g; Sodium, 650 mg.

Sesame Miso Sauce

Yield: 12 fl oz (360 mL)

U.S.	Metric	Ingredients
2 oz	60 g	Sesame seeds
8 oz	240 g	Red miso (see p. 660)
2½ oz	75 g	Sugar
2 fl oz	60 mL	Mirin (sweet Japanese rice wine)

■ P r o c e d u r e

1. Over low heat, toast the sesame seeds in a dry sauté pan until they are aromatic and have darkened slightly.

2. Grind the toasted seeds in a mortar or spice grinder.

3. Mix the ground sesame seeds with the remaining ingredients. Stir well.

Per 1 ounce:
Calories, 110; Protein, 3 g; Fat, 3 g (26% cal.); Cholesterol, 0 mg;
Carbohydrates, 15 g; Fiber, 1 g; Sodium, 680 mg.

White Wine Cream Sauce for Fish

Yield: 1½ pt (750 mL)

U.S	Metric	Ingredients
2 oz	60 g	Shallots, chopped
14 fl oz	400 mL	Dry white wine
1 pt 12 oz	800 mL	Fish stock
14 fl oz	400 mL	Heavy cream
4 oz	125 g	Butter
1½ oz	45 g	Chopped parsley
to taste	to taste	Salt
to taste	to taste	Pepper

■ P r o c e d u r e

1. Combine the shallots and white wine in a saucepan. Reduce until almost dry.
2. Add the fish stock and reduce by two-thirds.
3. Add the cream and reduce slightly.
4. Swirl in the butter (monter au beurre).
5. Add the chopped parsley. Season to taste.

Per 1 ounce:
Calories, 105; Protein, 1 g; Fat, 10 g (83% cal.); Cholesterol, 35 mg; Carbohydrates, 1 g; Fiber, 0 g; Sodium, 50 mg.

 ## Yogurt Sour Cream Sauce

Yield: 1 pt 4 oz (600 mL)

U.S	Metric	Ingredients
1 tbsp	15 g	Butter
3½ oz	100 g	Shallots, chopped fine
5 fl oz	150 mL	White wine
1½ pt	700 mL	Chicken stock
8 oz	250 g	Sour cream
8 oz	250 g	Yogurt, plain

■ P r o c e d u r e

1. Melt the butter in a pan and sweat the shallots until soft.
2. Add the wine and reduce by half, then add the chicken stock and reduce again until syrupy.
3. Strain into a clean pan.
4. Allow to cool slightly before adding the sour cream and the yogurt. Reheat gently and season.

Per 1 ounce:
Calories, 45; Protein, 1 g; Fat, 3.5 g (65% cal.); Cholesterol, 10 mg; Carbohydrates, 2 g; Fiber, 0 g; Sodium, 20 mg.

 ## Sauce Vierge

Yield: 1 pt (500 mL)

U.S	Metric	Ingredients
7 fl oz	200 mL	Olive oil
4 fl oz	110 mL	Lemon juice
2 tsp	7 g	Chopped garlic
1 tbsp	7 g	Chopped basil
5½ oz	160 g	Tomatoes, peeled, seeded, diced
2 oz	50 g	Black olives, diced
to taste	to taste	Salt
to taste	to taste	Pepper
to taste	to taste	Hot pepper sauce

■ P r o c e d u r e

1. Warm the olive oil.
2. Add the lemon juice, garlic, basil, tomatoes, and olives.
3. Season to taste with salt, pepper, and hot pepper sauce.
4. Serve warm.

Per 1 ounce:
Calories, 120; Protein, 0 g; Fat, 13 g (94% cal.); Cholesterol, 0 mg; Carbohydrates, 2 g; Fiber, 0 g; Sodium, 30 mg.

Port Wine Sauce

Yield: 1 pt (500 mL)

U.S.	Metric	Ingredients
1 qt 4 oz	1.25 L	Ruby port wine
4 fl oz	125 mL	Glace de viande
as needed	as needed	Cornstarch or arrowroot
to taste	to taste	Salt
to taste	to taste	White pepper
2 oz	60 g	Butter

Per 1 ounce:
Calories, 60; Protein, 1 g; Fat, 3 g (40% cal.); Cholesterol, 10 mg; Carbohydrates, 4 g; Fiber, 0 g; Sodium, 55 mg.

■ P r o c e d u r e

1. Using a stainless-steel saucepot, reduce the port wine over moderate heat by three-fourths.
2. Add the glace de viande.
3. If desired, thicken lightly with a slurry of cornstarch or arrowroot mixed with cold water.
4. Season to taste with salt and white pepper.
5. Just before serving, swirl in the raw butter (monter au beurre).

 ## Applesauce

Yield: about 1 qr (1 L)

U.S.	Metric	Ingredients
4 lb	2 kg	Apples (see note)
to taste	to taste	Sugar (see step 4)
to taste	to taste	Lemon juice

Per 1 ounce:
Calories, 25; Protein, 0 g; Fat, 0 g (0% cal.); Cholesterol, 0 mg; Carbohydrates, 6 g; Fiber, 1 g; Sodium, 0 mg.

Note: Use tart cooking apples such as Rome. Do not use Red Delicious.

■ P r o c e d u r e

1. Cut the apples into quarters and remove the cores. Skins may be left on because they will be strained out later. (Red peels will color the sauce pink.) Dice the apples coarsely.
2. Place the apples in a heavy saucepan with about 2 oz (60 mL) water. Cover.
3. Set the pan over low heat and cook the apples slowly until very soft. Stir occasionally.
4. Add sugar to taste. The amount needed depends on the sweetness of the apples, but the sauce should be tart, not too sweet.
5. Add a little lemon juice to taste.
6. Pass the sauce through a food mill.
7. If the sauce is too thin or watery, let simmer, uncovered, until thickened.
8. Serve warm or cold with roast pork or duck.

 ## Barbecue Sauce

Yield: ½ gal (2 L)

U.S.	Metric	Ingredients
1 qt	1 L	Tomato purée
1 pt	500 mL	Water
⅔ cup	150 mL	Worcestershire sauce
½ cup	125 mL	Cider vinegar
½ cup	125 mL	Vegetable oil
8 oz	250 g	Onion, chopped fine
4 tsp	20 mL	Finely chopped garlic
2 oz	60 g	Sugar
1 tbsp	15 mL	Dry mustard
2 tsp	10 mL	Chili powder
1 tsp	5 mL	Black pepper
to taste	to taste	Salt

■ P r o c e d u r e

1. Place all ingredients in a heavy saucepan and bring to a boil. Reduce heat and simmer about 20 minutes, until slightly reduced and flavors are well blended. Stir occasionally during cooking so the sauce does not scorch on the bottom.
2. Adjust seasoning.

Per 1 ounce
Calories, 25; Protein, 0 g; Fat, 2 g (60% cal.); Cholesterol, 0 mg; Carbohydrates, 3 g; Fiber, 0 g; Sodium, 30 mg.

Note: This sauce is not intended to be eaten as is but to be cooked with other foods. See recipe for Barbecued Spareribs (p. 299) and for Barbecued Pork Sandwich (p. 745).

Chile Barbecue Sauce

Yield: 2½ pt (1.25 L)

U.S.	Metric	Ingredients
1½ pt	750 mL	Bottled chili sauce
8 fl oz	250 mL	Soy sauce
2 oz	60 g	Dark brown sugar
1½ fl oz	45 mL	Worcestershire sauce
1 pt	500 mL	Water
6 fl oz	175 mL	Lemon juice
1 tbsp	15 mL	Hot red pepper sauce
2	2	Whole chipotle chiles
3 tbsp	45 mL	Chili powder

Per 1 ounce:
Calories, 35; Protein, 1 g; Fat, 0 g (0% cal); Cholesterol, 0 mg;
Carbohydrates, 8 g; Fiber, 1 g; Sodium, 620 mg.

■ **Procedure**

1. Combine all ingredients in a heavy saucepot. Bring to a boil.
2. Simmer 15 minutes.
3. Strain.
4. Adjust the seasoning with salt if necessary. (It is not likely that additional salt will be needed; the soy sauce is salty.)

Soy Barbecue Sauce

Yield: 1 qt (1 L)

U.S.	Metric	Ingredients
12 fl oz	375 mL	Japanese-style soy sauce
4 oz	125 mL	Brown sugar
8 fl oz	250 mL	Sake (Japanese rice wine) or dry sherry
8 fl oz	250 mL	Water
6 fl oz	175 mL	Lemon juice
2 tbsp	30 mL	Chopped fresh ginger root
1 tbsp	15 mL	Chopped garlic
8 fl oz	250 mL	Vegetable oil

Per 1 ounce:
Calories, 90; Protein, 1 g; Fat, 7 g (66% cal.); Cholesterol, 0 mg;
Carbohydrates, 5 g; Fiber, 0 g; Sodium, 610 mg.

■ **Procedure**

1. In a saucepot, combine all ingredients except the oil.
2. Bring to a simmer. Reduce by one-third.
3. Strain.

4. Add the oil. Before using, mix well to emulsfuy; this is easily done in a blender.

Fruit Salsa

Yield: 2 lb (1 kg)

U.S.	Metric	Ingredients
8 oz	250 g	Honeydew melon, seeded, rind removed
8 oz	250 g	Papaya, peeled and seeded
8 oz	250 g	Mango, peeled and pitted
4 oz	125 g	Red bell pepper, cored and seeded
1 oz	30 g	Jalapeño pepper, stemmed and seeded
3 oz	90 g	Red onion, cut brunoise
4 fl oz	125 mL	Lime juice
2 tbsp	30 mL	Chopped cilantro
to taste	to taste	Salt

Per 1 ounce:
Calories, 15; Protein, 0 g; Fat, 0 g (0% cal.); Cholesterol, 0 mg;
Carbohydrates, 3 g; Fiber, 0 g; Sodium, 0 mg.

■ **Procedure**

1. Chop the melon, papaya, mango, bell pepper, and jalapeño pepper into fine dice. Be careful to save the juices that are released.
2. Combine the chopped fruit with their juices, peppers, onion, lime juice, and cilantro in a bowl.
3. Season to taste with salt.
4. Refrigerate until served.

Shallot Oil

Yield: 1 pt (500 mL)

U.S.	Metric	Ingredients
2–3 tbsp	30 g	Shallots, chopped
1 pt	500 mL	Flavorless oil, such as canola, corn, safflower, grapeseed

Per 1 ounce:
Calories, 240; Protein, 0 g; Fat, 27 g (100% cal.);
Cholesterol, 0 g; Carbohydrates, 0 g; Fiber, 0 g; Sodium, 0 mg.

■ P r o c e d u r e

1. Combine the chopped shallots and the oil in a jar. Shake well.
2. Let stand for 30 minutes. Refrigerate.
3. The oil is ready to use as soon as it has taken on the desired flavor, which may be in 1–2 hours. After 2 days, strain the oil through a paper coffee filter. Store in the refrigerator.

V A R I A T I O N S

Ginger Oil, Horseradish Oil, or Garlic Oil
Substitute ginger root, horseradish, or garlic for the shallots in the basic recipe. For best results, chop the ginger or horseradish very fine in a food processor or grate with a fine-holed grater. For garlic oil, substitute olive oil for the flavorless oil desired.

Lemon or Orange Oil
Substitute 3–4 tbsp (30 g) grated lemon or orange zest for the shallots in the basic recipe.

Rosemary Oil, Sage Oil, Thyme Oil, or Oregano Oil
Substitute 3½ oz (100 g) chopped fresh rosemary, sage, thyme, or oregano for the shallots in the basic recipe.

Cinnamon Oil, Cumin Oil, Curry Oil, Ginger Oil, or Paprika Oil
Substitute 3 tbsp (45 mL) of one of the above ground, dried spices for the shallots in the basic recipe. In a small pan, combine the spice with just enough of the oil to make a thin paste. Heat gently just until the spice starts to give off an aroma. Be careful not to burn the spice. Paprika, especially, darkens quickly. Add the spice mixture to the remaining oil. Let stand, refrigerate, and filter as in the basic recipe.

Basil Oil, Parsley Oil, Chervil Oil, or Cilantro Oil
Select the desired quantity of one of the above fresh herbs. Drop into boiling water. Blanch for 10 seconds. Drain and refresh under cold water. Drain again and pat dry with towels. Put the herbs in a blender and add a small amount of olive oil. Blend to make a paste. Measure the volume of the paste and add 4 times that volume of olive oil. Shake and let stand. Refrigerate and strain as in the basic recipe.

 Tartar Sauce

Yield: about 1 qt (1 L)

U.S.	Metric	Ingredients
4 oz	125 g	Dill pickles or sour gherkins
2 oz	60 g	Onions
2 oz	60 g	Capers
1 qt	1 L	Mayonnaise
2 tbsp	30 mL	Chopped parsley

Per 1 ounce:
Calories, 200; Protein, 0 g; Fat, 22 g (98% cal.); Cholesterol, 15 mg;
Carbohydrates, 1 g; Fiber, 0 g; Sodium, 240 mg.

■ P r o c e d u r e

1. Chop the pickles and onions very fine. Chop the capers if they are large, or leave whole if small.
2. Press the pickles and capers in a fine sieve or squeeze out in a piece of cheesecloth so they don't make the sauce too liquid.
3. Combine all ingredients in a stainless-steel bowl and mix well.

V A R I A T I O N

Rémoulade Sauce
Add 1 tbsp (15 mL) anchovy paste or mashed anchovies to tartar sauce.

Aioli I

Yield: about 1 pt 4 oz (600 mL)

U.S.	Metric	Ingredients
10	10	Garlic cloves
⅛ tsp	0.5 mL	Salt
3	3	Egg yolks
1 pt	500 mL	Olive oil
1–2 tbsp	15–30 mL	Lemon juice

Per 1 ounce:
Calories, 200; Protein, 1 g; Fat, 22 g (99% cal.); Cholesterol, 30 mg;
Carbohydrates, 1 g; Fiber, 0 g; Sodium, 15 mg.

■ **P r o c e d u r e**

1. Crush the garlic to a fine paste with the salt.
2. Add the egg yolks and beat until thoroughly combined.
3. A few drops at a time, begin adding the olive oil, beating constantly. Do not add the oil any faster than it can be absorbed.
4. After about half the oil is added, the mixture will be very stiff. Add a few drops of the lemon juice at this point.
5. Continue adding the remaining oil gradually. From time to time, add a few more drops of the lemon juice. The finished aioli should be like a stiff mayonnaise. Adjust the seasoning with additional salt if necessary.

 Horseradish Sauce (Sauce Raifort)

Yield: about 1 pt (500 mL)

U.S.	Metric	Ingredients
1 cup	250 mL	Heavy cream
¼ cup	60 mL	Prepared horseradish, drained
to taste	to taste	Salt

Per 1 ounce:
Calories, 50; Protein, 0 g; Fat, 6 g (93% cal.); Cholesterol, 20 mg;
Carbohydrates, 1 g; Fiber, 0 g; Sodium, 10 mg.

Note: This sauce should be made just before service.

■ **P r o c e d u r e**

1. Whip the cream until stiff, but do not overwhip
2. Mix the horseradish with a little of the whipped cream, then fold into the rest of the cream.
3. Season to taste with salt.

 Cocktail Sauce

Yield: 2 qt (2L)

U.S.	Metric	Ingredients
1 qt	1 L	Ketchup
2½ cups	600 mL	Chili sauce
1 cup	250 mL	Prepared horseradish
4 fl oz	125 mL	Lemon juice
2 tbsp	30 mL	Worcestershire sauce
dash	dash	Hot red pepper sauce

Per 1 ounce:
Calories, 30; Protein, 1 g; Fat, 0 g (0% cal.); Cholesterol, 0 mg;
Carbohydrates, 7 g; Fiber, 0 g; Sodium, 330 mg.

Note: Serve as a dip with shrimp, crab, lobster, raw clams, or raw oysters.

■ **P r o c e d u r e**

1. Combine all ingredients and mix.
2. Chill.

Mignonette Sauce

Yield: 1 qt (1 L)

U.S.	Metric	Ingredients
1 qt	1 L	Wine vinegar
8 oz	250 g	Shallots, cut brunoise
1 tsp	5 mL	Salt
1 tsp	5 mL	White pepper
2 tsp	5 mL	Dried tarragon

■ P r o c e d u r e

1. Combine all ingredients.
2. Chill.
3. Serve 1 fl oz (30 mL) per portion as a cocktail sauce for oysters or clams on the half shell.

Per 1 ounce:
Calories, 5; Protein, 0 g; Fat, 0 g (0% cal.) Cholesterol, 0 mg;
Carbohydrates, 1 g; Fiber, 0 g; Sodium, 75 mg.

 Lime and Ginger Chutney

Yield: 14 oz (400 g)

U.S	Metric	Ingredients
4	4	Limes
1¾ oz	50 g	Raisins
1 fl oz	30 mL	Brandy
3½ oz	100 g	Onions, chopped fine
1	1	Garlic clove, chopped fine
1 oz	25 g	Ginger root, grated
small pinch	small pinch	Saffron
1	1	Bay leaf
2	2	Cloves
3½ fl oz	100 mL	White wine vinegar
2 fl oz	60 mL	Lemon juice
6 fl oz	175 mL	Orange juice
2½ oz	75 g	Brown sugar
1 tsp	5 mL	Tomato paste

■ P r o c e d u r e

1. Grate the zest of the limes, then peel and segment the limes. Cut each segment into 4 or 5 pieces.
2. Soak the raisins in the brandy.
3. In a stainless-steel saucepan, combine the grated lime zest, soaked raisins, onions, garlic, ginger, saffron, bay leaf, cloves, white wine vinegar, lemon juice, orange juice, brown sugar, and tomato paste. Simmer until almost dry. Cool.
4. Add the lime segments and stir in.
5. Serve at once, or keep 2–3 weeks in a sterilized jar.

Per 1 ounce:
Calories, 50; Protein, 1 g; Fat, 0 g (0% cal.); Cholesterol, 0 mg;
Carbohydrates, 13 g; Fiber, 1 g; Sodium, 5 mg.

 Fig Compote

Yield: 1 lb 4 oz (625 g)

U.S.	Metric	Ingredient
1 lb	500 g	Dried figs, preferably light rather than black figs
4 fl oz	125 mL	Lemon juice
8 fl oz	250 mL	Water
2 tbsp	30 mL	Sugar
¼ tsp	1 mL	Ground cumin
¼ tsp	1 mL	Cinnamon
⅛ tsp	0.5 mL	Ground cloves
⅛ tsp	0.5 mL	Cayenne

■ P r o c e d u r e

1. Trim the figs by cutting off the hard stem ends.
2. Cut the figs into medium dice.
3. Combine all ingredients in a saucepan.
4. Bring to a boil. Reduce heat and simmer until the liquid has evaporated.
5. Serve warm or cooled.

Per 1 ounce:
Calories, 60; Protein, 1 g; Fat, 0 g (0% cal.); Cholesterol, 0 mg;
Carbohydrates, 17 g, Fiber, 2 g; Sodium, 0 mg.

■ TERMS FOR REVIEW

stock	sauce	monter au beurre	brown butter
broth	slurry	leading sauce	compound butter
mirepoix	roux	fond lié	emulsion
sachet	white roux	small sauce	integral sauce
bouquet garni	blond roux	demi-glace	pan gravy
venting	brown roux	béchamel	jus
reduction	beurre manié	velouté	au jus
glaze	whitewash	espagnole	salsa
glace de viande	liaison	gastrique	relish
glace de volaille	au sec	coulis	chutney
glace de poisson	deglaze	clarified butter	

■ QUESTIONS FOR DISCUSSION

1. Which bones make a more gelatinous stock, beef or veal?

2. The stockpot is often considered a good way to use trimmings from meats and vegetables. Do you agree? Explain.

3. How should vegetables for mirepoix be cut?

4. Explain the importance of blanching bones before making stocks.

5. Why should stock not be boiled? Should a stockpot be covered? Why or why not?

6. Explain the procedure for cooling stock. Why is it important?

7. Why is an understanding of stocks important even if you work in an establishment that uses only bases?

8. You have just prepared a suprême sauce, but your supervisor says it's too thin. It must be served in five minutes. What can you do to correct it?

9. What are the two methods for preparing starches so they can be incorporated into hot liquids? Why are they necessary, and how do they work?

10. Why is it necessary to be able to thicken a sauce with a roux without making lumps if the sauce is going to be strained anyway?

11. You are preparing a gravy for a batch of Swiss steaks that are to be frozen for later use. What thickening agent will you use?

12. Name the five leading sauces and their major ingredients. List at least two small sauces made from each.

13. What precautions must be taken when finishing and holding allemande sauce?

14. What are the similarities between espagnole and pan gravy? The differences?

15. What precautions are necessary when making hollandaise to avoid overcooking the eggs or curdling the sauce?

CHAPTER 9

Soups

The popularity of soups today may be due to increased nutrition consciousness, to a desire for simpler or lighter meals, or to an increased appreciation of how appetizing and satisfying soups can be. Whatever the reasons, they emphasize the importance of soup-making skills.

If you have already studied the preparation of stocks and sauces in Chapter 8, you now have at your disposal the major techniques for the preparation of soups. You know how to make stocks and how to use thickening agents such as roux and liaison.

A few more techniques are necessary for you to master before you are able to prepare all the types of soups that are popular today. As in sauce-making, basic techniques are the building blocks you can use to create a wide variety of appetizing soups.

UNDERSTANDING SOUPS

Soup, according to the dictionary, is a liquid food derived from meat, poultry, fish, or vegetables. This definition is all right as far as it goes, but there's a lot it doesn't tell us. Is a stock, straight from the stockpot, a soup? Is beef stew liquid enough to be called soup?

We're interested more in production techniques than in definitions. However, a few more definitions are necessary before we can go into the kitchen, so we can talk to each other in the same language. Definitions aren't rules, so don't be alarmed if you hear other books or chefs use these terms differently. What matters is that you learn the techniques and are able to adapt them to many uses.

After reading this chapter, you should be able to

1. **Describe three basic categories of soups.**

2. **Identify standard appetizer and main course portion sizes for soups.**

3. **State the procedures for holding soups for service and for serving soups at the proper temperatures.**

4. **Prepare clarified consommé.**

5. **Prepare vegetable soups and other clear soups.**

6. **Prepare cream soups.**

7. **Prepare purée soups.**

8. **Prepare bisques, chowders, specialty soups, and national soups.**

CLASSIFICATIONS OF SOUPS

Soups can be divided into three basic categories: clear or unthickened soups, thick soups, and special soups that don't fit the first two categories.

Most of these soups, no matter what their final ingredients may be, are based on stock. Thus, the quality of the soup depends on the stock-making skills discussed in Chapter 8.

CLEAR SOUPS

Clear soups are all based on a clear, unthickened broth or stock. They may be served plain or garnished with a variety of vegetables and meats.

1. *Broth* and *bouillon* are two terms used in many ways. In general, they both refer to simple, clear soups without solid ingredients. We have already defined broth (Chapter 8) as a flavorful liquid obtained from the simmering of meats and/or vegetables. Broths are discussed in more detail on page 209.

2. Vegetable soup is a clear, seasoned stock or broth with the addition of one or more vegetables and, sometimes, meat or poultry products and starches.

3. Consommé is a rich, flavorful stock or broth that has been clarified to make it perfectly clear and transparent. The process of clarification is a technique we study in detail.

    Far from being just a plain old cup of broth, a well-made consommé is one of the greatest of all soups. Its sparkling clarity is a delight to the eye, and its rich, full flavor, strength, and body make it a perfect starter for an elegant dinner.

THICK SOUPS

Unlike clear soups, thick soups are opaque rather than transparent. They are thickened either by adding a thickening agent, such as a roux, or by puréeing one or more of their ingredients to provide a heavier consistency.

1. Cream soups are soups that are thickened with roux, beurre manié, liaison, or other added thickening agents, plus milk and/or cream. They are similar to velouté and béchamel sauces—in fact, they may be made by diluting and flavoring either of these two leading sauces.

    Cream soups are usually named after their major ingredient, such as cream of chicken or cream of asparagus.

2. Purées are soups that are naturally thickened by puréeing one or more of their ingredients. They are not as smooth and creamy as cream soups.

Purées are normally based on starchy ingredients. They may be made from dried legumes (such as split pea soup) or from fresh vegetables with a starchy ingredient such as potatoes or rice added. Purées may or may not contain milk or cream.

3. **Bisques** are thickened soups made from shellfish. They are usually prepared like cream soups and are almost always finished with cream.

   The term *bisque* is sometimes used on menus for a variety of vegetable soups. In these cases, it is really a marketing term rather than a technical term, so it is impossible to give a definition that covers all uses.

4. **Chowders** are hearty soups made from fish, shellfish, and/or vegetables. Although they are made in many ways, they usually contain milk and potatoes.

5. **Potage** is a term sometimes associated with certain thick, hearty soups, but it is actually a general term for soup. A clear soup is called a *potage clair* in French.

SPECIALTY AND NATIONAL SOUPS

This is a catch-all category that includes soups that don't fit well into the main categories and soups that are native to particular countries or regions.

Specialty soups are distinguished by unusual ingredients or methods, such as turtle soup, gumbo, peanut soup, and cold fruit soup.

Cold soups are sometimes considered specialty soups, and, in fact, some of them are. But many other popular cold soups, such as jellied consommé, cold cream of cucumber soup, and vichyssoise (vee shee swahz) are simply cold versions of basic clear and thick soups.

VEGETARIAN SOUPS AND LOW-FAT SOUPS

A great variety of vegetable-based soups are suitable for vegetarian menus. To plan vegetarian menus, review the categories of vegetarianism discussed on page 656. Vegetable soups for vegans must contain no meat or any other animal product and must be made with water or vegetable stock. To bind thick soups, use a starch slurry or a roux made with oil rather than butter. Lacto-vegetarians, on the other hand, accept soups containing butter, milk, or cream.

Because the appeal of vegetarian vegetable soups depends entirely on the freshness and the quality of the vegetables and not on the richness of meat stocks, be especially careful to use high-quality ingredients and to avoid overcooking.

Clear soups are especially suitable for people seeking low-fat foods. Consommés and clear vegetable soups are virtually fat-free, especially if the vegetables were not sweated in fat before being simmered.

Thick soups can be kept low in fat by thickening them with a slurry of starch (such as arrowroot, potato starch, or cornstarch) and cold water rather than with a roux. For cream soups, reduce or omit the cream and instead use evaporated skim milk. Purée soups are usually more adaptable than cream soups to low-fat diets because the vegetable purée adds body and richness to the soup without requiring added fat. A little yogurt or evaporated skim milk can be used to give creaminess to a purée soup. Even garnishing a serving of soup with a teaspoonful of whipped cream gives a feeling of richness while adding only a gram or two of fat.

SERVICE OF SOUPS

STANDARD PORTION SIZES

Appetizer portion: 6 to 8 oz (200 to 250 mL)

Main course portion: 10 to 12 oz (300 to 350 mL)

TEMPERATURE

Serve hot soups hot, in hot cups or bowls.

Serve cold soups cold, in chilled bowls or even nested in a larger bowl of crushed ice.

HOLDING FOR SERVICE

Strangely enough, some chefs who take the greatest care not to overcook meats or vegetables nevertheless keep a large kettle of soup on the steam table all day. You can imagine what a vegetable soup is like after four or five hours at these temperatures.

1. Small-batch cooking applies to soups as well as to other foods. Heat small batches frequently to replenish the steam table with fresh soup.

2. Consommés and some other clear soups can be kept hot for longer periods if the vegetable garnish is heated separately and added at service time.

GARNISH

Soup garnishes may be divided into three groups.

1. **Garnishes in the soup.**
    Major ingredients, such as the vegetables in clear vegetable soup, are often considered garnishes. This group of garnishes also includes meats, poultry, seafood, pasta products, and grains such as barley or rice. They are treated as part of the preparation or recipe itself, not as something added on.
    Consommés are generally named after their garnish, such as consommé brunoise, which contains vegetables cut into brunoise shape [⅛-inch (3-mm) dice].
    Vegetable cream soups are usually garnished with carefully cut pieces of the vegetable from which they are made.
    An elegant way to serve soup with a solid garnish is to arrange the garnish attractively in the bottom of a heated soup plate. This plate is set before the diner, and then the soup is ladled from a tureen by the dining room staff.

2. **Toppings.**
    Clear soups are generally served without toppings to let the attractiveness of the clear broth and the carefully cut vegetables speak for themselves. Occasional exceptions are toppings of chopped parsley or chives.
    Thick soups, especially those that are all one color, are often decorated with a topping. Toppings should be placed on the soup just before service so they won't sink or lose their fresh appearance. Their flavors must be appropriate to the soup.
    Do not overdo soup toppings. The food should be attractive in itself.
    Topping suggestions for thick soups:

    Fresh herbs (parsley, chives), chopped

    Fried herbs, such as parsley, sage, chervil, celery leaves, leek julienne

    Fine julienne of vegetables

    Sliced almonds, toasted

    Grated cheese

    Sieved egg yolks

    Chopped or riced egg whites

    Croutons

    Grated parmesan cheese

    Crumbled bacon

    Paprika

    Flavored butters

    Flavored oils

    Sour cream, crème fraîche, or whipped cream, either plain or flavored with herbs or spices

3. **Accompaniments.**

American soups are traditionally served with crackers. In addition to the usual saltines, other suggestions for crisp accompaniments are:

Melba toast

Corn chips

Breadsticks

Cheese straws

Profiteroles (tiny unsweetened cream-puff shells)

Whole-grain wafers

CLEAR SOUPS

BROTHS

The difference between a broth and a stock is that a broth, according to the most common definition, is made by simmering meat and vegetables, while a stock is made by simmering bones and vegetables. Because of this difference, a well-made stock is generally richer in gelatin content than a broth, because gelatin is derived from cartilage and connective tissue. A broth, on the other hand, usually has a more pronounced flavor of meat or poultry than a stock. A more neutral flavor is desired in a stock, which is used as the base for many sauces as well as soups. A broth, on the other hand, is an excellent choice as the base of a soup when a distinct meat flavor is desired.

Nevertheless, broths are not often specially made in food service operations. The cost of the meat makes them expensive, unless the meat can be used for another purpose, or unless the restaurant has a good supply of meat trimmings that might otherwise be wasted. Instead, broth is usually a by-product of simmering meat or poultry. The recipes for Simmered Fresh Beef Brisket (p. 325) and for "Boiled" Fowl (p. 400) produce not only the cooked meat or poultry but also flavorful broths that can be served as soups when properly seasoned and garnished.

Note that the broths resulting from both these recipes are white. To prepare a brown meat broth, follow the procedure in the recipe for Simmered Fresh Beef Brisket (p. 325), but brown the meat and mirepoix well before adding water. Flavorful cuts such as beef shank, chuck, and neck are good for making broths.

For those operations that determine that making broths especially for soups is cost-effective, a recipe for beef broth is provided below.

Broths can be served as is, with only seasoning and perhaps a light garnish added. For example, plain chicken broth is commonly served as a restorative for invalids. More often, however, broths are used in place of stocks in vegetable soups and other clear soups, as discussed in the section beginning on page 214.

Like stock, broth can be made with water. For especially rich, flavorful broths, use stock in place of water in the broth recipe.

Beef Broth

Yield: 6 qt (6 L)

U.S.	Metric	Ingredients	
10 lb	5 kg	Beef: shank, chuck, oxtail, short ribs, or mixed trimmings, or a mixture of these	
2 fl oz	60 mL	Vegetable oil	
2 gal	8 L	Water, beef stock, or remouillage (p. 157)	
		Mirepoix	
1 lb	500 g	Onion, chopped	
8 oz	250 g	Carrots, chopped	
8 oz	250 g	Celery, chopped	
1 fl oz	30 mL	Vegetable oil	
8 oz	250 g	Tomatoes, canned or fresh	
		Sachet	
1	1	Bay leaf	
¼ tsp	1 mL	Dried thyme	
¼ tsp	1 mL	Peppercorns	
6–8	6–8	Parsley stems	
2	2	Whole cloves	
to taste	to taste	Salt	
as desired	as desired	Meat, vegetables, or other garnish for soup	

■ P r o c e d u r e

1. In a stockpot, brown the beef in the vegetable oil.
2. Add the water or stock and bring to a simmer. Skim the surface to remove any froth or scum.
3. Continue to simmer for 2 hours.
4. Brown the mirepoix in the second quantity of oil.
5. Add the mirepoix and the tomatoes to the stockpot.
6. With a little water, deglaze the pan used to brown the mirepoix and add the liquid to the stockpot.
7. Continue to simmer for an additional 30 minutes.
8. Add the sachet. Simmer an additional 30–45 minutes.
9. Strain the broth. Discard the sachet, vegetables, and any unusable meat trimmings. Reserve any good cuts of meat for garnishing the broth or another use.
10. For serving as a soup, season and garnish to taste.

Per 1 serving:
Calories, 130; Protein, 8 g; Fat, 11 g (3% cal.); Cholesterol, 26 mg; Carbohydrates, 1 g; Fiber, 0 g; Sodium, 55 mg.

CONSOMMÉ

When we define consommé as a clarified stock or broth, we are forgetting the most important part of the definition. The word *consommé* means, literally, "completed" or "concentrated." In other words, a consommé is a strong, concentrated stock or broth. In classical cuisine, this was all that was necessary for a stock to be called a consommé. In fact, two kinds were recognized: ordinary (or unclarified) consommé and clarified consommé.

Rule number one for preparing consommé is that the stock or broth must be strong, rich, and full-flavored. Clarification is second in importance to strength. A good consommé, with a mellow but full aroma and plenty of body (from the natural gelatin) that you can feel in your mouth, is one of the great pleasures of fine cuisine. But clarification is an expensive and time-consuming procedure, and, quite frankly, it's not worth the trouble if the soup is thin and watery.

HOW CLARIFICATION WORKS

Coagulation of proteins was an important subject in our discussion of stock-making because one of our major concerns was how to keep coagulated proteins from making the stock cloudy. Strangely enough, this same process of coagulation enables us to clarify stocks to perfect transparency.

Remember that some proteins, especially those called *albumins*, dissolve in cold water. When the water is heated, they gradually solidify or coagulate and rise to the surface. If we control this process carefully, these proteins collect all the tiny particles that cloud a stock and carry them to the surface. The stock is then left perfectly clear.

If, on the other hand, we are not careful, these proteins break up as they coagulate and cloud the liquid even more, just as they can do when we make stock.

BASIC INGREDIENTS

The mixture of ingredients we use to clarify a stock is called the **clearmeat** or the **clarification**.

1. *Lean ground meat* is one of the major sources of protein that enables the clearmeat to do its job. It also contributes flavor to the consommé. The meat must be lean because fat is undesirable in a consommé. Beef shank, also called *shin beef*, is the most desirable meat because it is high in albumin proteins as well as in flavor and gelatin, and it is very lean.

    Beef and/or chicken meat are used to clarify chicken consommé. Meat is not used, obviously, to make fish consommé. Ground lean fish may be used, but it is normal to omit flesh altogether and use only egg whites.

2. *Egg whites* are included in the clearmeat because, being mostly albumin, they greatly strengthen its clarifying power.

3. *Mirepoix* and other seasoning and flavoring ingredients are usually included because they add flavor to the finished consommé. They do not actually help in the clarification, except possibly to give solidity to the raft. The **raft** is the coagulated clearmeat, floating in a solid mass on top of the consommé.

    The mirepoix must be cut into fine pieces so it will float with the raft.

    A large amount of a particular vegetable may be added if a special flavor is desired, as in, for example, essence of celery consommé.

4. *Acid ingredients* (tomato products for beef or chicken consommé, lemon juice or white wine for fish consommé) are often added because the acidity helps coagulate the protein. They are not absolutely necessary—the heat will coagulate the protein anyway—but many chefs like to use them.

Figure 9.1
Preparing consommé

(a) The stock is well mixed with the clarification ingredients and set on a burner to begin heating.

Procedure for Preparing Consommé

1. Start with a well-flavored, cold, strong stock or broth. If your stock is weak, reduce it until it is concentrated enough, then cool it before proceeding, or plan on simmering the consommé longer to reduce while clarifying.

2. Select a heavy stockpot or soup pot, preferably one with a spigot at the bottom. The spigot enables you to drain off the finished consommé without disturbing the raft.

3. Combine the clearmeat ingredients in the soup pot and mix them vigorously.

4. Optional step: Mix in a small amount of cold water or stock—about 4 to 8 oz per pound (250 to 500 mL per kg) of meat—and let stand 30 to 60 minutes. This allows more opportunity for the proteins that do the clarifying to dissolve out of the meat.

    Note: Chefs disagree on the importance of this step. Some let the mixture stand overnight in the refrigerator. Others skip this step altogether. Check with your instructor.

5. Gradually add the cold, degreased stock and mix well with the clearmeat.

    The stock must be **cold** so it doesn't cook the proteins on contact.

    Mixing distributes the dissolved proteins throughout the stock so they can collect all the impurities more easily.

6. Set the pot over a moderately low fire and let it come to a simmer very slowly.

7. Stir the contents occasionally so the clearmeat circulates throughout the stock and doesn't burn to the bottom.

8. When the simmering point is approaching, stop stirring. The clearmeat will rise to the surface and form a raft.

(b) The raft begins to rise to the top.

9. Move pot to lower heat so the liquid maintains a slow simmer. Do not cover. Boiling would break up the raft and cloud the consommé. The same principle operates in stock-making.

10. Let simmer 1½ hours without disturbing the raft.

11. Strain the consommé through a china cap lined with several layers of cheesecloth.

    If you are not using a stockpot with a spigot, ladle the consommé out carefully without breaking up the raft.

    Let the liquid drain through the cheesecloth by gravity. Do not force it, or fine particles will pass through and cloud the consommé.

12. Degrease.

    Remove all traces of fat from the surface. Strips of clean brown paper passed across the surface are effective in absorbing every last speck of fat without absorbing much consommé.

13. Adjust the seasonings.

    Kosher salt is preferred to regular table salt because it has no impurities or additives that could cloud the stock.

(c) The raft has almost completely formed. The consommé will continue to simmer for a total of 1½ hours.

Emergency Procedures

1. **Clarifying hot stock.**

   If you do not have time to cool the stock properly before clarifying, at least cool it as much as you can. Even 10 minutes in a cold-water bath helps. Then, mix ice cubes or crushed ice with the clearmeat. This will help keep it from coagulating when the hot stock hits it. Proceed as in the basic method.

   Finally, review your production planning so you can avoid this emergency in the future.

2. **Clarifying without meat.**

   In a pinch, you can clarify a stock with egg whites alone. Use at least 3 or 4 egg whites per gallon (4 liters) of stock, plus mirepoix if possible. Great care is necessary because the raft will be fragile and easily broken up.

   Egg whites and mirepoix alone are often used for clarifying fish stocks.

3. **Failed clarification.**

   If the clarification fails because you let it boil, or for some other reason, it can still be rescued, even if there is no time for another complete clarification.

   Strain the consommé, cool it as much as you can, then slowly add it to a mixture of ice cubes and egg whites. Carefully return to a simmer as in the basic method and proceed with the clarification.

   This should be done in emergencies only. The ice cubes dilute the consommé, and the egg white clarification is risky.

4. **Poor color.**

   Beef or veal consommé made from brown stock should have an amber color. It is not dark brown like canned consommé. Chicken consommé is a very pale amber.

   It is possible to correct a pale consommé by adding a few drops of caramel color to the finished soup. But for best results, check the color of the stock before clarification. If it is too pale, cut an onion in half and place it cut side down on a flattop range until it is black, or char it under a broiler. Add this to the clearmeat. The caramelized sugar of the onion will color the stock.

 ## Consommé

Yield: 1 gal (4 L)   Portions: 16   Portion size: 8 fl oz (250 mL)
**   20   6 fl oz (250 mL)**

U.S.	Metric	Ingredients
1 lb	500 g	Lean beef, preferably shin, ground
		Mirepoix, chopped into small pieces.
8 oz	250 g	Onion
4 oz	125 g	Celery
4 oz	125 g	Carrot
8 oz	250 g	Egg whites
8 oz	250 g	Canned tomatoes, crushed
6–8	6–8	Parsley stems, chopped
pinch	pinch	Dried thyme
1	1	Bay leaf
2	2	Whole cloves
½ tsp	2 mL	Peppercorns, crushed
5 qt	5 L	Beef or veal stock, cold
		(brown or white)

Per serving:
Calories, 30; Protein, 3 g; Fat; 1g (31% cal.); Cholesterol, 15 mg;
Carbohydrates, 2 g; Fiber, 0 g; Sodium, 75 mg.

■ **Procedure**

1. Review the information on preparing consommé, page 211.
2. Combine the beef, mirepoix, egg whites, tomatoes, herbs, and spices in a tall, heavy stockpot. Mix the ingredients vigorously with a wooden paddle or a heavy whip.

3. Add about 1 pint (500 mL) cold stock and stir well. Let stand about 30 minutes. (Optional step: see p. 211 for explanation.)
4. Gradually stir in the remaining cold stock. Be sure the stock is well mixed with the other ingredients.
5. Set the pot on moderately low heat and let it come to a simmer very slowly. Stir occasionally.
6. When the simmering point is approaching, stop stirring.
7. Move the pot to lower heat and simmer very slowly for about 1½ hours. Do not stir or disturb the raft that forms on top.
8. Very carefully strain the consommé through a china cap lined with several layers of cheesecloth.
9. Degrease thoroughly.
10. Season to taste.

VARIATIONS

Double Consommé
Use twice the quantity of beef in the basic recipe. Add 8 oz (250 g) leeks to the mirepoix.

Chicken Consommé
Use chicken stock instead of beef or veal stock. Add to the clearmeat 8 oz (250 g) chicken trimmings (such as wing tips and necks) that have been chopped and browned in a hot oven. Omit tomato and add 1 fl oz (30 mL) lemon juice.

Cold Jellied Consommé
Unflavored gelatin must often be added to consommé to make jellied consommé. The amount needed depends on the strength of the stock and on the amount of jelling desired. Classically, a chilled consommé is only half jelled, more like a thick syrup. Some people, however, prefer a gelatin content high enough to solidify the consommé. In the following guidelines, use the lower quantity of gelatin for a partially jelled soup, the higher quantity for a fully jelled soup. Also, for tomatoed consommé (madrilène), increase the gelatin slightly because the acidity of the tomatoes weakens the gelatin.

1. If the stock is thin when cold, add 1–2 oz (30–60 g) gelatin per gallon (4 L).
2. If the stock is slightly jelled and syrupy when cold, add ½–1 oz (15–30 g) gelatin per gallon (4 L).
3. If the stock is jelled when cold, no gelatin is needed. Add up to ½ oz (15 g) per gallon (4 L) if a firmer texture is desired.

Gelatin may be added to the clearmeat (in step 2 of the recipe). This is the best method because there is no danger of clouding the consommé. It may also be added to the finished consommé after softening it in cold water. See page 717 for instructions on the use of gelatin.

Consommé Madrilène
Increase the tomatoes in the basic recipe to 24 oz (750 g). Use beef, veal, or chicken stock. Serve hot or jellied.

Essence of Celery Consommé
Increase the celery in the basic recipe to 1 lb (500 g).

Consommé au Porto
Flavor the finished consommé with 6–8 fl oz (200–250 mL) port wine per gallon (4 L).

Consommé au Sherry
Flavor the finished consommé with 6–8 fl oz (200–250 mL) sherry wine per gallon (4 L).

GARNISHED CONSOMMÉS

For the following consommés, prepare and cook the garnish separately. At service time, add 1–2 tbsp (15–30 mL) of the garnish to each portion. See page 134 for description of cuts.

Consommé Brunoise
Onion or leek, carrot, celery, and turnip (optional), cut brunoise. Sweat lightly in butter and simmer in a little consommé until tender.

Consommé Julienne
Onion or leek, carrot, and celery, cut julienne. Prepare like brunoise garnish.

Consommé Printanière
Small dice of spring vegetables: carrot, turnip, celery, green beans. Prepare like brunoise garnish.

Consommé Paysanne
Thin slices of leeks, carrots, celery, turnip, and cabbage. Prepare like brunoise garnish.

Consommé with Pearl Tapioca
Cooked pearl tapioca.

Consommé Vermicelli
Cooked broken vermicelli (very thin spaghetti).

Chicken and Celery Consommé

Yield: 1 gal (4 L)   Portions: 16   Portion size: 8 fl oz (250 mL)

U.S.	Metric	Ingredients
2 lb 12 oz	1.2 kg	Chicken leg meat, minced or coarsely ground
12	12	Egg whites
1 lb 6 oz	600 g	Celery, cut as for mirepoix
½ oz	15 g	Salt
½ oz	15 g	Black peppercorns, crushed
3	3	Thyme sprigs
2	2	Bay leaves
20	20	Parsley stems
5½ qt	5.5 L	Chicken stock
10 oz	300 g	Chicken breast
as needed	as needed	Chicken stock
6 oz	180 g	Celery, cut julienne

Per serving:
Calories, 35; Protein, 4 g; Fat, 1 g (27% cal.); Cholesterol, 15 mg; Carbohydrates, 2 g; Fiber, 0 g; Sodium, 460 mg.

■ Procedure

1. Place the minced chicken, egg whites, celery, salt, pepper, and herbs in a saucepot.

2. Stir in the stock and bring to simmering point over a moderate heat. Stir occasionally, paying particular attention to possible sticking or scorching of the ingredients on the base of the pot.

3. Stop stirring as simmering point is approaching and simmer very gently without disturbing for 30 minutes.

4. Strain the consommé through a china cap lined with several layers of cheesecloth. Skim and degrease thoroughly. Transfer to a clean pot.

5. Poach the chicken breast in chicken stock for 10 minutes.

6. Cool the chicken in the stock to retain juiciness, then cut into cubes.

7. At service time, reheat the soup and ladle into warm bowls. Sprinkle each portion with cubed chicken and the julienne of celery.

VEGETABLE SOUPS

Clear vegetable soups are made from a clear stock or broth, not necessarily clarified, with the addition of one or more vegetables and, sometimes, meat or poultry and/or pasta or grains. Most vegetable soups are made from meat or poultry stock or broth. Meatless or vegetarian soups are made from vegetable broth or water.

Guidelines for Preparing Vegetable Soups

Procedures for making these soups are not complicated. Most of them are made simply by simmering vegetables in stock until done. But care and attention to details are still necessary for producing a high-quality soup.

1. **Start with a clear, flavorful stock or broth.**

   This is one reason it's important to be able to make stocks that are clear, not cloudy.

2. **Select vegetables and other ingredients whose flavors go well together.**

   Don't just throw in everything you've got. Judgment, combined with experience, must be used to create a pleasing combination. Five or six vegetables are usually enough. More than that often makes a jumble.

3. **Cut vegetables uniformly.**

   Neat, careful cutting means uniform cooking and attractive appearance. Sizes of cuts are important, too. Pieces should be large enough to be identifiable but small enough to eat conveniently with a spoon.

4. **Cooking vegetables slowly in a little butter before combining with liquid improves their flavor and gives the soup a mellower, richer taste.**

5. **Cook starches such as grains and pasta separately and add to the soup later.**

   Cooking them in the soup makes it cloudy. Potatoes are sometimes cooked directly in the soup, but they should be rinsed of excess starch after cutting if you want to keep the soup as clear as possible.

6. **Observe differences in cooking times.**

   Add long-cooking vegetables first, short-cooking vegetables near the end. Some vegetables, like tomatoes, should be added to the hot soup only after it is removed from the fire.

7. **Don't overcook.**

   Some cooks feel that soups must be simmered a long time to extract flavors into the liquid. But you should already have done this when you made the stock! Vegetables in soup should be no more overcooked than vegetable side dishes, especially as the soup will probably spend a longer time in the steam table.

Clear Vegetable Soup

Yield: 6 qt (6 L) U.S.	Portions: 24 Metric	Portion size: 8 fl oz (250 mL) Ingredients
4 oz	125 g	Butter or chicken fat
1½ lb	750 g	Onions, small dice
1 lb	500 g	Carrots, small dice
1 lb	500 g	Celery, small dice
12 oz	375 g	Turnip, small dice
6 qt	6 L	Chicken stock
1 lb	500 g	Drained canned tomatoes, coarsely chopped
to taste	to taste	Salt
to taste	to taste	White pepper
12 oz	375 g	Frozen peas, thawed

Per serving:
Calories, 80; Protein, 3 g; Fat, 4.5 g (46% cal.); Cholesterol, 15 mg; Carbohydrates, 9 g; Fiber, 2 g; Sodium, 125 mg.

Clear Vegetable Soup with Cranberry Beans

■ Procedure

1. Heat the butter in a heavy saucepot over medium-low heat.
2. Add the onions, carrots, celery, and turnip. Sweat the vegetables in the butter over low heat until they are about half cooked. Do not let them brown.
3. Add the stock. Bring to a boil and skim carefully. Simmer until vegetables are just barely tender.
4. Add the tomatoes and simmer another 5 minutes.
5. Degrease the soup and season with salt and white pepper.
6. Just before serving, add the peas.

VARIATIONS

Other vegetables may be used in addition to or in place of one or more of the vegetables in the basic recipe. Add with the vegetables sweated in butter:

Leeks	Green cabbage
Rutabagas	Parsnips

Add to the simmering soup, timing the addition so that all the vegetables are done at the same time:

Potatoes	Lima beans
Green beans	Corn

Other cuts may be used for the vegetables instead of small dice, such as batonnet, julienne, or paysanne (see p. 134).

Vegetable Rice Soup
Add 1½–2 cups (350–500 mL) cooked rice to the finished soup.

Chicken Vegetable Rice Soup
Add 12 oz (375 g) cooked, diced chicken to vegetable rice soup.

Vegetable Beef Soup
Use beef stock instead of chicken stock. Add 12 oz (375 g) cooked, diced beef when the tomatoes are added. Also, add the juice from the tomatoes.

Vegetable Beef Barley Soup
Add 1½–2 cups (350–500 mL) cooked barley to vegetable beef soup.

Piquant Vegetable Soup with Chickpeas

Yield: 6 qt (6 L)   Portions: 24   Portion size: 8 fl oz (250 mL)

U.S.	Metric	Ingredients
2 fl oz	60 mL	Vegetable oil
1¼ lb	625 g	Red onion, small dice
1 tbsp	15 mL	Garlic, chopped
1 lb	500 g	Green bell pepper, small dice
2–4 oz	60–125 g	Jalapeño or other green chile, cut brunoise
5 qt	5 L	Chicken stock or vegetable stock
1¼ lb	625 g	Tomatoes, peeled, seeded, and chopped
1¼ lb	625 g	Cooked chickpeas
8 oz	250 g	Corn kernels, frozen or fresh
8 oz	250 g	Green beans, cooked until just tender and cut into ½-in. (1-cm) pieces
to taste	to taste	Salt
to taste	to taste	White pepper
to taste	to taste	Hot red pepper sauce (optional)
		Garnish:
12 oz	375 g	Grated cheddar cheese
⅓ cup	75 mL	Chopped cilantro or whole cilantro leaves

Per serving:
Calories, 160; Protein, 8 g; Fat, 8 g (45% cal.); Cholesterol, 20 mg; Carbohydrates, 14 g; Fiber, 3 g; Sodium, 105 mg.

■ P r o c e d u r e

1. Heat the oil in a soup pot over moderate heat.
2. Add the onion, garlic, bell pepper, and green chile. Sweat the vegetables in the oil over low heat until they are about half-cooked. Do not let them brown.
3. Add the stock. Bring to a boil and skim carefully. Simmer until the vegetables are just barely tender.
4. Add the tomatoes, chickpeas, and corn. Simmer another 5 minutes.
5. Shortly before serving, add the cooked green beans. (The beans should be cooked separately and added at the end so their color won't be destroyed by the acidity of the tomatoes.)
6. Add salt and white pepper to taste. Add hot pepper sauce if desired
7. To serve, ladle a portion into soup plates and sprinkle with grated cheese and a little chopped cilantro.

V A R I A T I O N

Piquant Vegetable Soup with Roasted Garlic
Roast 1 head of garlic, as explained on page 567. Separate and peel the cloves. Add them to the soup in step 4.

Mushroom Barley Soup

Yield: 6 qt (6 L)   Portions: 24   Portion size: 8 fl oz (250 mL)

U.S.	Metric	Ingredients
8 oz	250 g	Barley
10 oz	300 g	Onion, cut brunoise
5 oz	150 g	Carrot, cut brunoise
5 oz	150 g	White turnip, cut brunoise
2 oz	60 g	Butter or chicken fat
5 qt	5 L	Chicken stock
2 lb	1 kg	Mushrooms, diced
4 oz	125 g	Butter or chicken fat
to taste	to taste	Salt
to taste	to taste	White pepper

Per serving:
Calories, 60; Protein, 3 g; Fat, 1 g (15% cal.); Cholesterol, 20 mg; Carbohydrates, 10 g; Fiber, 3 g; Sodium, 75 mg.

■ P r o c e d u r e

1. Cook the barley in boiling water until tender. Drain.
2. In a heavy saucepot or stockpot, sweat the vegetables in the fat until they are about half-cooked. Do not let them brown.
3. Add the chicken stock. Bring to a boil. Reduce heat and simmer until the vegetables are just tender.
4. While the soup is simmering, sauté the mushrooms briefly in fat without letting them brown.
5. Add the mushrooms and the drained, cooked barley to the soup. Simmer another 5 minutes.
6. Degrease the soup. Season to taste with salt and pepper.

OTHER CLEAR SOUPS

In addition to vegetable soups, many other clear or unthickened soups are known to various cuisines. They range from simple broths to elaborate concoctions of meats, vegetables, starches, and other ingredients. Although many contain vegetables, we don't classify them as vegetable soups because other ingredients are generally more prominent.

 ## Chicken Noodle Soup

Yield : 6 qt (6 L)   Portions: 24   Portions size: 8 fl oz (250 mL)

U.S.	Metric	Ingredients
10 oz	300 g	Egg noodles
10 oz	300 g	Cooked chicken meat
6 qt	6 L	Chicken stock
to taste	to taste	Salt
to taste	to taste	White pepper
as desired	as desired	Chopped parsley

■ P r o c e d u r e

1. Cook the noodles in boiling, salted water. (See Procedure for cooking pasta, p. 638.) Drain and rinse in cold water.
2. Cut the chicken into small dice.
3. Bring the stock to a simmer. Season to taste with salt and white pepper. If stock doesn't have enough flavor, add more stock and reduce to concentrate the flavor.
4. Just before service, add the chicken and noodles to the stock. Let them heat through before serving.
5. Garnish each portion with a little chopped parsley.

V A R I A T I O N S

Beef Noodle Soup
Prepare as in basic recipe, using beef and beef stock.

Chicken or Beef Noodle Soup with Vegetables
Before adding the chicken and noodles, simmer 10 oz (300 g) diced carrots and 5 oz (150 g) diced celery in the stock until tender.

Per serving:
Calories, 70; Protein, 6 g; Fat, 1.5 g (21% cal.); Cholesterol, 25 mg; Carbohydrates, 7 g; Fiber, 0 g; Sodium, 20 mg.

Note: See Chapter 13 (p. 400) for preparing "boiled" chicken and broth for use in soups. Other leftover cooked chicken may also be used.

 ## Brunswick Soup

Yield: 6 qt (6 L)   Portions: 24   Portion size: 8 fl oz (250 mL)

U.S.	Metric	Ingredients
10 oz	300 g	Onions, small dice
1 oz	30 g	Butter or oil
5 qt	5 L	Chicken stock
1¼ lb	600 g	Tomato concassé
1¼ lb	600 g	Lima beans, frozen
1¼ lb	600 g	Okra, fresh or frozen, cut in ¼-in. (½-cm) pieces
1 lb	475 g	Corn, frozen
1¼ lb	600 g	Cooked chicken meat and giblets, small dice
to taste	to taste	Salt
to taste	to taste	White pepper

■ P r o c e d u r e

1. In a heavy pot, sweat the onions in the butter until about half cooked. Do not brown.
2. Add the chicken stock and bring to a boil. Simmer about 10 minutes.
3. Add the remaining vegetables and the chicken. Simmer until the vegetables are tender, about 10–15 minutes.
4. Season to taste with salt and white pepper.

Per serving:
Calories, 120; Protein, 10 g; Fat, 3 g (23% cal.); Cholesterol, 40 mg; Carbohydrates, 13 g; Fiber, 3 g; Sodium, 45 mg.

Chicken Tomato Bouillon with Pesto

Yield: 6 qt (6 L)   Portions: 24   Portion size: 8 fl oz (250 mL)

U.S.	Metric	Ingredients
6 qt	6 L	Chicken stock
2 qt	2 L	Tomato juice
8 oz	250 g	Celery, chopped
8 oz	250 g	Onion, chopped
1½ tsp	7 mL	Dried basil
½ tsp	2 mL	Dried thyme
to taste	to taste	Salt
to taste	to taste	Pepper
pinch	pinch	Sugar
12 fl oz	375 mL	Pesto (p. 644) thinned with olive oil

Per serving:
Calories, 210; Protein, 3 g; Fat 21 g (87% cal.); Cholesterol, 10 mg; Carbohydrates, 4 g; Fiber, 1 g; Sodium, 410 mg.

Chicken Tomato Bouillon with Pesto

■ P r o c e d u r e

1. Place the stock, juice, celery, onion, basil, and thyme in a saucepot. Bring to a boil.

2. Simmer about 45 minutes, until vegetables are soft and flavors are well blended.

3. Strain and season with salt, pepper, and a pinch of sugar.

4. Garnish each portion with 1 tbsp (15 mL) pesto lightly swirled into the soup.

V A R I A T I O N S

Chicken Tomato Bouillon with Rice
Add 2 cups (500 mL) cooked rice at service time.

Cold Chicken Tomato Bouillon
Chill the soup and add a few drops of lemon juice to taste. Serve each portion with a spoonful of sour cream.

Oxtail Soup

Yield: 6 qt (6 L) *Portions: 24* *Portion size: 8 fl oz (250 mL)*

U.S.	Metric	Ingredients
6 lb	2.7 kg	Oxtails
		Mirepoix:
10 oz	300 g	Onion, medium dice
5 oz	150 g	Carrot, medium dice
5 oz	150 g	Celery, medium dice
6 qt	6 L	Brown stock (see note)
		Sachet:
1	1	Bay leaf
pinch	pinch	Dried thyme
6	6	Peppercorns
2	2	Whole cloves
1	1	Garlic clove
1¼ lb	600 g	Carrots, small dice
1¼ lb	600 g	White turnips, small dice
10 oz	300 g	Leeks, white part only, cut julienne
4 oz	125 g	Butter
10 oz	300 g	Tomatoes (canned), drained, coarsely chopped
2 fl oz	60 mL	Sherry (optional)
to taste	to taste	Salt
to taste	to taste	Pepper

Per serving:
Calories, 240; Protein, 24 g; Fat, 11 g (45% cal.); Cholesterol, 90 mg;
Carbohydrates, 6 g; Fiber, 2 g; Sodium, 220 mg.

■ P r o c e d u r e

1. Using a heavy chef's knife, cut the oxtails into sections at the joints.
2. Place the oxtails in a bake pan and brown in a 450°F (230°C) oven. When they are partially browned, add the mirepoix to the pan and brown it along with the oxtails.
3. Place the oxtails and mirepoix in a stockpot with the stock.
4. Pour off the fat from the pan in which the meat was browned. Deglaze the pan with a little of the stock and add this to the stockpot.
5. Bring to a boil. Reduce heat to a simmer and skim well. Add the sachet.
6. Simmer until the meat is tender, about 3 hours. Add a little water if necessary during cooking to keep the meat completely covered.
7. Remove the pieces of oxtail from the broth. Trim the meat off the bones and dice it. Place it in a small pan with a little of the broth. Keep warm if the soup is to be finished immediately, or chill for later use.
8. Strain the broth. Degrease carefully.
9. Sweat the carrots, turnips, and leeks in the butter until about half-cooked
10. Add the broth. Simmer until vegetables are tender.
11. Add the tomatoes and the reserved oxtail meat. Simmer another minute.
12. Add the sherry, if desired. Season to taste with salt and pepper.

V A R I A T I O N

Oxtail soup is often clarified. Chill the broth after step 7 and clarify like consommé. See page 211 for procedure.

Note: Water is sometime used instead of stock. If this is done, brown 4–5 lb (about 2 kg) beef or veal bones with the oxtails and simmer in the soup with them. Double the quantity of mirepoix.

Asian-Style Shrimp Soup with Egg Flowers

Yield: 3 qt (3 L)   **Portions: 12**   **Portion size: 8 fl oz (250 mL)**

U.S.	Metric	Ingredients
3 lb 4 oz	1.5 kg	Small shrimp
3 lb 4 oz	1.5 kg	Crab shells (see note)
2 fl oz	60 mL	Oriental sesame oil
1 lb	450 g	Onion, peeled and chopped
10 oz	300 g	Celery stalks, medium dice
1	1	Garlic head, cut in half horizontally
7 oz	190 g	Red bell pepper, seeded, medium dice
1 oz	30 g	Black peppercorns, coarsely crushed
1 oz	30 g	Sea salt
2½ oz	75 g	Fresh ginger root, peeled, fine dice
6	6	Lemon grass stalks, roughly chopped
4½ qt	4.5 L	Chicken stock
7 oz	190 g	Red bell pepper, small dice
10 oz	300 g	Lean chicken meat, minced
1	1	Lemon grass stalk, chopped
2 oz	30 g	Dill stems
1	1	Kaffir lime leaf (optional; see note)
2 pieces	2 pieces	Star anise
1 tbsp	15 mL	Tomato paste
2 tbsp	2 g	Saffron threads
3	3	Egg whites
		Garnish:
3	3	Egg whites
4 oz	125 g	Small shrimp, peeled and cooked
8 tsp	18 g	Chives, chopped
8 tsp	18 g	Dill sprigs
4 tsp	18 g	Japanese pickled ginger

■ Procedure

1. Using a pestle and mortar, crush the whole shrimp and the crab shells.

2. Heat the sesame oil in a brazier over medium heat. Add the shrimp, crab shells, onion, celery, garlic, and red pepper. Fry until golden, stirring.

3. Add the peppercorns, sea salt, ginger root, and lemon grass to the pot and mix well.

4. Pour in the chicken stock, stir, and bring to a boil. Cook at a low simmer, uncovered, for 1 hour. Cool and refrigerate overnight if you want to develop a stronger flavor.

5. Strain the stock into a clean saucepot. Heat the stock until warm, not hot.

6. In a food processor or blender, blend together the red pepper, chicken meat, lemon grass, dill stems, kaffir lime leaf, star anise, tomato paste, and saffron threads.

7. Add the egg whites and mix in well.

8. Add this mixture to the warm stock. Whisk continuously over medium heat. When just about to boil, a frothy crust will form. Stop whisking.

9. Make a small hole in the center of the crust with a spoon, taste the soup beneath, and season through the hole.

10. Cook at low simmer for 20 minutes, then strain through a china cap lined with cheesecloth.

11. At service time, reheat the soup.

12. Whisk the egg whites to break them up, but do not whip to a froth. Pour into the soup in a thin steady stream, stirring slowly with a fork to create a fine thread effect.

13. Serve the soup in warm bowls and garnish with the shrimp, chives, dill sprigs, and Japanese pickled ginger.

Per serving:
Calories, 120; Protein, 13 g; Fat, 7 g (50% cal.); Cholesterol, 120 mg; Carbohydrates, 3 g; Fiber, 0 g; Sodium, 1250 mg.

Note: If crab shells are not available, substitute half their weight of whole small shrimp or shells. Kaffir lime leaves are available in markets that sell Asian or Indian spices.

THICK SOUPS

CREAM SOUPS

Learning to cook professionally, as you have already heard, is not learning recipes but learning basic techniques that you can apply to specific needs.

The basic techniques of sauce-making were discussed in Chapter 8. If we tell you that cream soups are simply diluted velouté or béchamel sauces, flavored with the ingredient for which they are named, you should almost be able to make a cream of celery soup without further instructions.

It's not *quite* that simple. There are some complications, but they are mostly a matter of detail. You already know the basic techniques.

THE CLASSIC CREAM SOUPS

In the great kitchens of several decades ago, cream soups were exactly as we have just described: diluted, flavored sauces. In fact, what we now call cream soups were divided into two groups, veloutés and creams.

1. Velouté soups consisted of

    Velouté sauce

    Puréed flavoring ingredient

    White stock, to dilute

    Liaison, to finish

2. Cream soups consisted of

    Béchamel sauce

    Puréed flavoring ingredient

    Milk (or white stock), to dilute

    Cream, to finish

These methods were natural to large kitchens that always had quantities of velouté and béchamel sauces on hand. Making a soup was simply a matter of finishing off a sauce.

Modern cooks view these methods as complicated and have devised other methods that seem simpler. But most of the sauce steps are involved—you still have to thicken a liquid with roux (or other starch), cook and purée the ingredients, and add the milk or cream.

The classical method is still important to learn. It will give you versatility, it makes excellent soup, and besides, it really isn't any harder or longer, in the final analysis. In addition, we explain two other methods much in use today.

But first, we consider a problem frequently encountered with cream soups.

CURDLING

Because cream soups contain milk or cream or both, curdling is a common problem. The heat of cooking and the acidity of many of the other soup ingredients are the causes of this curdling.

Fortunately, we can rely on one fact to avoid curdling: *roux and other starch thickeners stabilize milk and cream.* Caution is still necessary because soups are relatively thin and do not contain enough starch to be completely curdle-proof.

Observe the following guidelines to help prevent curdling:

1. Do not combine milk and simmering soup stock without the presence of roux or other starch. Do one of the following:
   * Thicken the stock before adding milk.
   * Thicken the milk before adding it to the soup.
2. Do not add cold milk or cream to simmering soup. Do one of the following:
   * Heat the milk in a separate saucepan.
   * Temper the milk by gradually adding some of the hot soup to it. Then add it to the rest of the soup.
3. Do not boil soups after milk or cream has been added.

STANDARDS OF QUALITY FOR CREAM SOUPS

1. **Thickness.**
   About the consistency of heavy cream. Not too thick.

2. **Texture.**
   Smooth; no graininess or lumps (except garnish, of course).

3. **Taste.**
   Distinct flavor of the main ingredient (asparagus in cream of asparagus, etc.). No starchy taste from uncooked roux.

Basic Procedures for Making Cream Soups

The following methods apply to most cream soups. Individual ingredients may require variations.

Method 1

1. Prepare Velouté Sauce (p. 172) or Béchamel Sauce (p. 171), using roux.

2. Prepare the main flavoring ingredients. Cut vegetables into thin slices. Sweat them in butter about 5 minutes to develop flavor. *Do not brown.* Green leafy vegetables must be blanched before stewing in butter. Cut poultry and seafood into small pieces for simmering.

3. Add flavoring ingredients from step 2 to the velouté or béchamel and simmer until tender. Exception: Finished tomato purée is added for cream of tomato; further cooking is not necessary.

4. Skim any fat or scum carefully from the surface of the soup.

5. Purée the soup using a food mill (Figure 9.2) or an immersion blender (Figure 9.3), and then strain it through a fine china cap. Alternatively, just strain it through a fine china cap, pressing down hard on the solid ingredients to force out the liquid and some of the pulp. The soup should be very smooth.

   Poultry and seafood ingredients may be puréed or reserved for garnish.

6. Add hot white stock or milk to thin the soup to proper consistency.

7. Adjust seasonings.

8. At service time, finish with liaison (p. 165) or heavy cream.

Method 2

1. Sweat vegetable ingredients (except tomatoes) in butter; do not let them color.

2. Add flour. Stir well to make a roux. Cook the roux for a few minutes, but do not let it start to brown.

3. Add white stock, beating with a whip as you slowly pour it in.

4. Add any vegetables, other solid ingredients, or flavorings that were not sautéed in step 1.

5. Simmer until all ingredients are tender.

6. Skim any fat that has risen to the surface.

7. Purée and/or strain (as in Method 1).

8. Add hot white stock or milk to thin soup to proper consistency.

9. Adjust seasonings.

10. At service time, finish with heavy cream or liaison.

Method 3

1. Bring white stock to a boil.

2. Add vegetables and other flavoring ingredients. If desired, first slowly cook some or all of the vegetables in butter for a few minutes to develop flavors.

3. Simmer until all ingredients are tender.

4. Thicken with roux, beurre manié, or other starch.

5. Simmer until no starch taste remains.

6. Skim fat from surface.

7. Purée and/or strain (as in Method 1).

8. Add hot or tempered milk and/or cream. A light cream sauce may be used, if desired, to avoid thinning the soup or curdling the milk.

9. Adjust seasonings.

Figure 9.2
Using a food mill.
(a) Purée soft foods by turning the crank of the mill to force them through small holes.

(b) Scrape the solids from the bottom of the mill after all the food has been forced through the plate.

Figure 9.3
Using an immersion blender to purée a soup.

Cream of Celery Soup (Cream Soup Method 1)

Yield: 6 qt (6 L)   Portions: 24   Portion size: 8 fl oz (250 mL)

U.S.	Metric	Ingredients	■ P r o c e d u r e
3 lb	1.5 kg	Celery, small dice	1. Review cream soup guidelines and Method 1 (p. 222).
12 oz	375 g	Onion, small dice	2. Sweat the celery and onions in the butter in a heavy saucepot until they are almost tender. Do not let them brown.
3 oz	90 g	Butter	
4½ qt	4.5 L	Velouté sauce, made with chicken or veal stock (see note)	3. Add the velouté to the pot. Simmer until the vegetables are very tender.
			4. Skim any fat or scum from the soup.
			5. Pass the soup through a food mill to purée it.
			6. Pass the puréed soup through a fine china cap or through cheesecloth.
3 pt	1.5 L	Milk or white stock, hot	7. Add enough hot milk or stock to bring the soup to the proper consistency.
to taste	to taste	Salt	8. Heat the soup again, but do not let it boil.
to taste	to taste	White pepper	9. Season to taste.
3 cups	750 mL	Heavy cream, hot Optional garnish:	10. At service time, add the cream. Add the garnish if desired.
6 oz	175 g	Celery, cut julienne, cooked	

Per serving:
Calories, 320; Protein, 5 g; Fat, 27 g (75% cal.); Cholesterol, 90 mg; Carbohydrates, 15 g; Fiber, 1 g; Sodium, 240 mg.

Note: Béchamel may be used in place of velouté if desired. This is often done for vegetarian menus.

V A R I A T I O N S ,   M E T H O D   1

For the following cream soups, make the substitutions in the basic recipe as indicated. Frozen and canned vegetables may be used, where appropriate, in place of fresh. Also, trimmings may be used if they are clean and of good quality, such as the bottom ends of asparagus and broccoli stalks.

Cream of Asparagus
Use 3 lb (1.5 kg) asparagus stalks in place of celery. Optional garnish: cooked asparagus tips.

Cream of Broccoli
Use 3 lb (1.5 kg) broccoli in place of celery. Optional garnish: small cooked broccoli florets.

Cream of Carrot
Use 3 lb (1.5 kg) carrots in place of celery. Garnish: chopped parsley.

Cream of Cauliflower
Use 3 lb (1.5 kg) cauliflower in place of celery. Optional garnish: tiny cooked cauliflower florets.

Cream of Corn
Use 3 lb (1.5 kg) whole kernel corn (fresh, frozen, or canned) in place of celery. Do not sweat the corn with the onions. Instead, sweat the onions alone, add the velouté, then add the corn. Garnish: corn kernels.

Cream of Cucumber
Use 3 lb (1.5 kg) peeled, seeded cucumber in place of celery. Optional garnish: small, diced, cooked cucumber.

Cream of Mushroom
Use 1½ lb (750 g) mushrooms in place of celery. Optional garnish: julienne, brunoise, or sliced cooked mushrooms.

Cream of Pea
Use 3 lb (1.5 kg) frozen green peas in place of celery. Do not sweat the peas with the onions. Add them after the velouté has been added.

Cream of Spinach
Use 3 lb (1.5 kg) fresh spinach or 2 lb (900 g) frozen spinach in place of celery. Do not sweat the spinach with the onion. Blanch it, drain it well, and add it to the velouté in step 3.

Cream of Watercress
Use 1½ lb (750 g) watercress in place of celery.

Cream of Chicken.
Reduce celery to 6 oz (175 g) and add 6 oz (175 g) carrot (note that, together with the onion, this makes 1½ lb [750 g] mirepoix). Use a velouté sauce made with a strong, flavorful chicken stock. After the soup is strained, add 6 oz (175 g) cooked chicken meat, cut into julienne or fine dice.

Cold Cream Soups
Most cream soups are delicious cold as well as hot. For example, cold cream of cucumber soup is a special favorite in summer. Procedure:
1. Chill soup after step 9 in recipe.
2. Add cold cream after soup is well chilled.
3. Dilute with extra milk, cream, or stock if soup becomes too thick.
4. Season carefully. Cold foods require more seasonings.

Cream of Mushroom Soup (Cream Soup Method 2)

Yield: 6 qt (6 L)   Portions: 24   Portion size: 8 fl oz (250 mL)

U.S.	Metric	Ingredients	
12 oz	375 g	Butter	
12 oz	375 g	Onion, chopped fine	
1½ lb	750 g	Mushrooms, chopped	
9 oz	275 g	Flour	
4½ qt	4.5 L	White stock, chicken or veal, hot	
3 pt	1.5 L	Milk, hot	
to taste	to taste	Salt	
to taste	to taste	White pepper	
3 cups	750 mL	Heavy cream, hot Optional garnish:	
6 oz	175 g	Mushrooms, cut brunoise, sautéed in butter	

■ P r o c e d u r e

1. Review cream soup guidelines and Method 2 (p. 222).
2. Heat the butter in a heavy saucepot over moderate heat.
3. Add the onions and mushrooms. Sweat the vegetables without letting them brown.
4. Add the flour and stir to make a roux. Cook the roux for a few minutes, but do not let it start to brown.
5. Gradually beat in the stock. Bring to a boil, stirring with a whip as it thickens.
6. Simmer until vegetables are very tender.
7. Skim the soup carefully.
8. Pass the soup through a food mill to purée it.
9. Pass the puréed soup through a fine china cap or through cheesecloth.
10. Add enough hot milk to the soup to bring it to the proper consistency.
11. Heat the soup again, but do not let it boil.
12. Season to taste.
13. At service time, add the cream. Add the garnish, if desired.

Per serving:
Calories, 300; Protein, 5 g; Fat 25 g (75% cal.); Cholesterol, 85 mg;
Carbohydrates, 14 g; Fiber, 1 g; Sodium, 170 mg.

V A R I A T I O N S ,   M E T H O D   2

For each variation, replace the mushrooms with the vegetable and quantity indicated. See the note to the variations for Cream of Celery Soup, page 223.

Cream of Asparagus
3 lb (1.5 kg) asparagus

Cream of Broccoli
3 lb (1.5 kg) broccoli

Cream of Carrot
3 lb (1.5 kg) carrots

Cream of Cauliflower
3 lb (1.5 kg) cauliflower

Cream of Celery
3 lb (1.5 kg) celery

Cream of Corn
3 lb (1.5 kg) whole kernel corn

Cream of Cucumber
3 lb (1.5 kg) peeled, seeded cucumber

Cream of Green Pea
3 lb (1.5 kg) frozen peas. Add after step 5.

Cream of Spinach
3 lb (1.5 kg) fresh or 2 lb (900 g) frozen spinach. Blanch, drain, and add after step 5.

Cream of Watercress
1½ lb (750 g) watercress.

Cream of Chicken
6 oz (175 g) celery and 6 oz (175 g) carrot. Use strong chicken stock. Add 6 oz (175 g) cooked chicken meat, cut into julienne or fine dice, to the finished soup after straining.

Cream of Broccoli Soup (Cream Soup Method 3)

Yield: 6 qt (6 L)   Portions: 24   Portion size: 8 fl oz (250 mL)

U.S.	Metric	Ingredients	Procedure
4½ qt	4.5 L	White stock, chicken or veal	1. Bring the stock to a boil in a heavy saucepot.
3 lb	1.5 kg	Broccoli (fresh or frozen), chopped	2. Add the broccoli and onion. (*Optional:* Vegetables may be sweated in butter first to develop flavors.)
12 oz	375 g	Onion, chopped fine	3. Simmer until the vegetables are tender. Do not overcook or the broccoli will lose its fresh, green color.
9 oz	275 g	Butter, clarified	4. Combine the butter and flour in a saucepan to make a roux. Cook the roux a few minutes, but do not let it color. Cool the roux slightly. (*Note:* Beurre manié may be used instead of roux.)
9 oz	275 g	Flour	5. Beat the roux into the soup. Simmer until no starch taste remains.
			6. Pass the soup through a food mill, then through a fine china cap or cheesecloth.
3 pt	1.5 L	Milk, hot	7. Add enough hot milk to bring the soup to proper consistency.
to taste	to taste	Salt	8. Heat the soup again, but do not let it boil.
to taste	to taste	White pepper	9. Season to taste.
3 cups	750 mL	Heavy cream, hot	10. At service time, add the heavy cream. If desired, add the garnish.
		Optional garnish:	
6 oz	175 g	Small broccoli florets, cooked	

Per serving:
Calories, 280; Protein, 6 g; Fat, 22 g (69% cal.); Cholesterol, 75 mg; Carbohydrates, 16 g; Fiber, 2 g; Sodium, 150 mg.

VARIATIONS, METHOD 3

For other cream soups, replace the broccoli with 3 lb (1.5 kg) of any of the following:

Asparagus	Celery	Green peas
Carrots	Corn	Spinach
Cauliflower		

Cream of Tomato Soup

Yield: 6 qt (6 L)   Portions: 24   Portion size: 8 fl oz (250 mL)

U.S.	Metric	Ingredients
4 oz	125 g	Salt pork, diced
4 oz	125 g	Onion, medium dice
2 oz	60 g	Carrots, medium dice
2 oz	60 g	Celery, medium dice
2 oz	60 g	Flour
3 qt	3 L	White stock
2 lb	1 kg	Canned tomatoes
2 lb	1 kg	Tomato purée
		Sachet:
1	1	Bay leaf
pinch	pinch	Dried thyme
1	1	Whole clove
2	2	Peppercorns, crushed
2 qt	2 L	Cream sauce, hot
to taste	to taste	Salt
to taste	to taste	White pepper

Per serving:
Calories, 210; Protein, 5 g; Fat, 15 g (64% cal.); Cholesterol, 45 mg;
Carbohydrates, 14 g; Fiber, 1 g; Sodium, 230 mg.

■ Procedure

1. In a heavy saucepot, cook the salt pork over medium heat to render the fat.
2. Add the onion, carrots, and celery. Sweat until they are slightly softened.
3. Add the flour and stir to make a roux. Cook the roux a few minutes.
4. Slowly beat in the stock. Bring to a boil, stirring while the liquid thickens slightly.
5. Add the tomatoes, tomato purée, and sachet. Simmer about 1 hour.
6. Strain through a china cap. Press down on the solids with a ladle to force out all the juices and some of the pulp. (*Alternative method:* Pass through a food mill, then strain.)
7. If the soup is being made ahead, chill the tomato base and proceed to the next step just before service.
8. Return the tomato base to the saucepot and bring back to a simmer.
9. Stir in the hot cream sauce.
10. If the soup is too thick, thin with a little stock.
11. Season to taste with salt and pepper.

VARIATIONS

If you study this recipe, you will see that the first part (through step 6) is essentially a tomato sauce. The recipe can be broken down as follows:

1 part	Tomato sauce
1 part	Stock
1 part	Cream sauce

Using this formula, you can also make cream of tomato soup from Tomato Sauce I (p. 176) or from canned tomato sauce. You can also make it from canned tomato purée if you simmer it with extra herbs, seasonings, and mirepoix. Check all seasonings and flavors carefully when using canned, prepared products.

Wild Rice and Mushroom Soup

Yield: 4 qt (4 L) *Portions: 16* *Portion size: 8 fl oz (250 mL)*

U.S.	Metric	Ingredients	
¾ cup	180 mL	Wild rice, washed and drained	**■ P r o c e d u r e**
18 fl oz	540 mL	Water	1. Combine the wild rice and water in a heavy saucepan. Bring to a boil. Reduce heat, cover tightly, and cook until tender. Reserve.
6 oz	180 g	Butter	2. Heat the butter in a heavy saucepot over moderate heat.
6 oz	180 g	Onion, chopped fine	3. Add the onion and carrot and cook slowly for a few minutes until the vegetables start to become tender.
6 oz	180 g	Carrot, cut brunoise	
4½ oz	135 g	Flour	4. Add the flour. Stir to combine the flour with the butter to make a roux. Cook the roux for a few minutes, but do not let it start to brown.
4½ pt	2250 mL	Chicken stock, hot	5. Gradually beat in the stock, using a whip to blend the stock smoothly with the roux. Bring to a boil, stirring with the whip until the stock thickens.
			6. Simmer until the vegetables are completely tender and the soup has no taste of raw flour.
			7. Skim the soup carefully.
2 oz	60 g	Butter	8. While the soup is simmering, heat the butter in a sauté pan. Sauté the mushrooms.
12 oz	375 g	Mushrooms, sliced	9. After the soup has been skimmed, add the mushrooms.
1½ pt	750 mL	Milk, hot	10. Stir the hot milk into the soup.
to taste	to taste	Salt	11. Add the cooked wild rice from step 1. Simmer 2–3 minutes.
to taste	to taste	White pepper	12. Season to taste with salt and white pepper.
12 fl oz	375 mL	Heavy cream, hot	13. At service time, stir in the cream.
as needed	as needed	Chopped parsley	14. Garnish the top of each portion with a sprinkling of chopped parsley.

Per serving:
Calories, 380; Protein, 7 g; Fat, 29 g (68% cal.); Cholesterol, 90 mg;
Carbohydrates, 24 g; Fiber, 2 g; Sodium, 160 mg.

Wisconsin Cheddar and Broccoli Soup

Yield: 3 qt (3 L)   *Portions: 12*   *Portion size: 8 fl oz (250 mL)*

U.S.	Metric	Ingredients
8 oz	250 g	Butter
6 oz	180 g	Onion, chopped fine
4 oz	125 g	Celery, chopped fine
8 oz	250 g	Broccoli stems, coarsely chopped
4 oz	125 g	Mushrooms, chopped
4½ oz	140 g	Flour
4½ pt	2250 mL	White stock
1 pt	500 mL	Milk, hot
12 oz	375 g	Broccoli florets, cooked
1 lb	500 g	Sharp cheddar cheese, grated
8 fl oz	250 mL	Heavy cream, hot
to taste	to taste	Salt
to taste	to taste	White pepper

■ Procedure

1. Heat the butter in a heavy saucepot over moderate heat.
2. Add the onion, celery, broccoli stems, and mushrooms. Sweat the vegetables without letting them brown.
3. Add the flour and stir to make a roux. Cook the roux for a few minutes, but do not let it start to brown.
4. Gradually beat in the stock. Bring to a boil, stirring with a whip, as it thickens.
5. Simmer until the vegetables are very tender.
6. Skim the soup carefully.
7. Pass the soup through a food mill to purée it.
8. Pass the puréed soup through a chinois or fine strainer.
9. Add the hot milk to the soup.
10. Heat the soup again, but do not let it boil.
11. Separate the broccoli florets into pieces small enough to be eaten with a soup spoon. Add them to the soup.
12. If the soup is to be served at once, proceed to the next step. Otherwise, cool the soup in a cold-water bath and refrigerate until service time. Reheat the soup to a simmer when ready to finish.
13. Add the cheese to the soup and stir until all the cheese is melted.
14. Carefully reheat the soup, but do not let it boil, or else the cheese may curdle or separate.
15. Stir in the heavy cream.
16. Season to taste with salt and white pepper.

Per serving:
Calories, 460; Protein, 13 g; Fat, 38 g (75% cal.); Cholesterol, 115 mg; Carbohydrates, 15 g; Fiber, 2 g; Sodium, 410 mg.

Wisconsin Cheddar and Broccoli Soup

PURÉE SOUPS

TECHNIQUES

Purée soups are made by simmering dried or fresh vegetables, especially high-starch vegetables, in stock or water, then puréeing the soup. Thus, they are relatively easy to prepare. Purée soups are not as smooth and refined as cream soups but are heartier and coarser in texture and character.

Techniques vary greatly depending on the ingredients and the desired result.

Basic Procedure for Making Purée Soups

1. Sweat mirepoix or other fresh vegetables in fat.
2. Add liquid.
3. Add dried or starchy vegetables.
4. Simmer until vegetables are tender. Fresh vegetables should be completely cooked but not overcooked or falling apart.
5. Purée soup in a food mill or with an immersion blender.

   Variation: Some soups made from dried legumes, such as bean soup, are not puréed but are served as is or slightly mashed.
6. Purée soups are generally not bound with an added starch but rely on the starches present in the vegetables. Some fresh vegetable purées, however, settle out. These may be thickened with a little starch if desired.
7. Add cream if required.
8. Adjust seasonings.

Purée of Green Pea Soup with Mint Cream

Yield: 6 qt (6 L)	Portions: 24	Portion size: 8 fl oz (250 mL)
U.S.	**Metric**	**Ingredients**

U.S.	Metric	Ingredients	Procedure
2 oz	60 g	Butter	1. Heat the butter in a heavy saucepot over moderately low heat.
6 oz	175 g	Onions, small dice	2. Add the onions and sweat them without letting them brown.
4 qt	4 L	Chicken stock	3. Add the stock and bring to a boil.
6 lb	3 kg	Peas, fresh or frozen	4. Add the peas. Simmer until the peas are soft, about 5 minutes.
to taste	to taste	Salt	5. Pass the soup through a food mill or purée with an immersion blender.
to taste	to taste	White pepper	6. Return the stock to a simmer. Add additional stock if necessary to bring to a proper consistency.
			7. Adjust the seasoning.
8 oz	250 mL	Heavy cream	8. At service time, heat the heavy cream and stir into the soup.
		Garnish:	9. Whip the cream until it forms soft peaks. Fold in the shredded mint leaves.
12 oz	375 mL	Heavy cream	10. Immediately before serving, place 1 tbsp (15 mL) mint cream on top of each portion. (Within a few minutes, the whipped cream will melt into a mint-flecked foam.)
¼ cup	60 mL	Mint leaves, finely shredded	

Per serving:
Calories, 200; Protein, 7 g; Fat, 11 g (50% cal.); Cholesterol, 40 mg; Carbohydrates, 18 g; Fiber, 6 g; Sodium, 40 mg.

Purée of Carrot Soup (Potage Crècy)

Yield: 6 qt (6 L)   Portions: 24   Portion size: 8 fl oz (250 mL)

U.S.	Metric	Ingredients
4 oz	125 g	Butter
4 lb	2 kg	Carrots, small dice
1 lb	500 g	Onions, small dice
5 qt	5 L	Chicken stock or white veal stock
1 lb	500 g	Potatoes, small dice
to taste	to taste	Salt
to taste	to taste	White pepper
		Optional:
1½–2 cups	350–500 mL	Cream, hot

■ P r o c e d u r e

1. Heat the butter in a heavy saucepot over moderately low heat.
2. Add the carrots and onions, and sweat the vegetables until they are about half cooked. Do no let them brown.
3. Add the stock and potatoes. Bring to a boil.
4. Simmer until the vegetables are tender.
5. Purée the soup by passing it through a food mill or by using an immersion blender.
6. Bring the soup back to a simmer. If necessary, add more stock to thin the soup to the proper consistency.
7. Season to taste.
8. If desired, finish the soup with hot cream at service time.

Per serving:
Calories, 90; Protein, 2 g; Fat, 4.5 g (40% cal.); Cholesterol, 15 mg; Carbohydrates, 13 g; Fiber, 3 g; Sodium, 95 mg.

V A R I A T I O N S

Rice may be used in place of potatoes as the binding agent in the above recipe or in any of the variations below except purée of potato, purée of potato and leek, and purée of watercress. Use 8 oz (250 g) raw rice in place of 1 lb (500 g) potatoes. The soup must be simmered until the rice is very soft.

Purée of Cauliflower Soup (Purée Dubarry)
Use 4 lb (2 kg) cauliflower in place of carrots.

Purée of Celery or Celery Root Soup
Use 4 lb (2 kg) celery of celery root in place of carrots.

Purée of Jerusalem Artichoke Soup
Use 4 lb (2 kg) Jerusalem artichoke in place of carrots.

Purée of Potato Soup (Potage Parmentier)
Omit carrots from basic recipe, add 10 oz (300 g) leeks to the onions and increase the potatoes to 5 lb (2.5 kg).

Purée of Potato and Leek Soup
Use 2 lb (1 kg) leeks in place of the carrots. Increase the potatoes to 2½ lb (1.25 kg).

Purée of Turnip Soup
Use 4 lb (2 kg) white turnips in place of carrots.

Purée of Watercress Soup
Prepare like purée of potato soup, but add 5 bunches watercress, chopped, when the potatoes are almost tender.

Purée of Mixed Vegetable Soup
Decrease carrots to 1¼ lb (600 g). Add 10 oz (300 g) each celery, turnips, leeks, and cabbage.

Potage Solferino
Combine equal parts purée of potato and leek soup and cream of tomato soup.

Purée of Split Pea Soup

Yield: 6 qt (6 L) **Portions: 24** **Portion size: 8 fl oz (250 mL)**

U.S.	Metric	Ingredients
6 oz	175 g	Salt pork
		Mirepoix:
10 oz	300 g	Onion, small dice
5 oz	150 g	Celery, small dice
5 oz	150 g	Carrot, small dice
6 qt	6 L	Ham stock (see note)
1	1	Ham bone or
		ham hock (optional)
3 lb	1.5 kg	Green split peas
		Sachet:
1	1	Bay leaf
2	2	Whole cloves
6	6	Peppercorns
to taste	to taste	Salt
to taste	to taste	Pepper

■ Procedure

1. Cut the salt pork into fine dice or pass through a grinder.
2. Cook the salt pork slowly in a heavy saucepot to render the fat. Do not brown the pork.
3. Add the mirepoix and sweat in the fat until the vegetables are slightly softened.
4. Add the ham stock and ham bone. Bring to a boil.
5. Rinse the split peas under cold water. Drain in a strainer and add to the stock. Also add the sachet.
6. Cover and simmer until the peas are tender, about 1 hour.
7. Remove the ham bone and sachet.
8. Pass the soup through a food mill.
9. Bring the soup back to a simmer. If it is too thick, bring it to proper consistency with a little stock or water.
10. Season to taste.
11. If a ham hock was used, trim off the meat. Dice it and add it to the soup.

Per serving:
Calories, 230; Protein, 13 g; Fat, 7 g (26% cal.); Cholesterol, 5 mg; Carbohydrates, 32 g; Fiber, 12 g; Sodium, 590 mg.

Note: Water may be used if ham stock is not available. In this case, the optional ham bone or ham hock should be used to provide flavor. Simmer the water and bone together for 1 hour or more before making the soup to extract more flavor.

VARIATIONS

Other dried vegetables are made into soups using the same procedure. Most dried beans should be soaked in cold water overnight to reduce cooking time. (Split peas may be soaked, but they cook quickly enough without soaking.)

Purée of White Bean Soup
Use 3 lb (1.5 kg) navy beans. Soak the beans overnight. Use chicken or veal stock in place of ham stock.

Purée of Yellow Split Pea Soup
Use yellow split peas instead of green.

Purée of Lentil Soup
Use 3 lb (1.5 kg) brown lentils. Soak overnight. Use either ham stock or white stock. Garnish with diced cooked bacon or ham or sliced frankfurters.

Purée of Kidney Bean Soup
Use 3 lb (1.5 kg) red kidney beans. Soak them overnight. Use white stock and add 2½ cups (600 mL) red wine to the soup when the beans are almost tender. Garnish with croutons sautéed in butter.

Purée of Black Bean Soup
Use 3 lb (1.5 kg) black turtle beans. Soak them overnight. Use white stock and the optional ham bone. Add 8 oz (250 mL) Madeira or sherry to the finished soup. Garnish with lemon slices and chopped hard-cooked egg.

Purée Mongole
Combine 3 qt (3 L) purée of green split pea soup and 2 qt (2 L) tomato purée. Dilute to proper consistency with about 1–2 qt (1–2 L) white stock. Garnish with cooked peas and with cooked julienne of carrots and leeks.

Nonpuréed Bean Soups
Prepare any of the above soups as directed, but purée only about one-fourth of the beans. Add this purée to the soup as a thickening agent.

Butternut Squash Soup with Caramelized Apples

Yield: 6 qt (6 L)   Portions: 24   Portion size: 8 fl oz (250 mL)

U.S.	Metric	Ingredients		Procedure
8 oz	250 g	French bread	1.	Cut the bread into slices ½ in. (1 cm) thick.
2 oz	60 g	Butter	2.	Fry the bread in the butter until golden brown. (If desired, prepare additional croutons for garnish at the same time; see step 8.)
2 oz	60 g	Butter	3.	Heat the butter in a heavy saucepot over moderately low heat.
8 oz	250 g	Onions, small dice	4.	Add the onions, leeks, and carrots. Sweat them until they are about half cooked. Do not let them brown.
8 oz	250 g	Leeks, small dice		
12 oz	375 g	Carrots, small dice	5.	Add the squash, the stock, and the browned bread from step 2. Simmer until the vegetables are tender.
4 lb	2 kg	Butternut squash, medium dice		
5 qt	5 L	Chicken stock	6.	Purée the soup with a food mill or an immersion blender.
1½ tsp	7 mL	Salt	7.	Bring the soup back to a simmer. Taste and adjust the seasonings.
½ tsp	2 mL	White pepper		
½ tsp	2 mL	Ground allspice		
½ tsp	2 mL	Ground ginger		
24	24	Croutons (see procedure)	8.	Prepare croutons by browning slices of French bread in butter as in steps 1 and 2. For best appearance, use a slender loaf so croutons aren't too big.
1½ lb	750 g	Tart, firm cooking apples		
1 oz	30 g	Butter	9.	Peel and core apples. Cut into small dice.
2 oz	60 g	Brown sugar	10.	Heat the butter in a sauté pan and add the apples and sugar. Cook over moderate heat until the apples are brown and caramelized.
12 oz	375 mL	Heavy cream (optional)	11.	At service, heat the heavy cream (if using) and add to the soup.
as needed	as needed	Additional heavy cream or crème fraîche for garnish, if desired	12.	For each portion, ladle the soup into a broad soup plate. Decorate the top of the soup with a swirl of cream, if desired. Heap a generous tablespoon (15 mL) of apple onto a crouton and carefully place in the soup.

Per serving:
Calories, 150; Protein, 3 g; Fat, 6 g (34% cal.); Cholesterol, 20 mg;
Carbohydrates, 23 g; Fiber, 4 g; Sodium, 280 mg.

Purée of Spring Vegetable Soup

Yield: 6 qt (6 L)   Portions: 24   Portion size: 8 fl oz (250 mL)

U.S.	Metric	Ingredients
2 oz	60 g	Butter
2 lb	1 kg	Leeks, white part only, small dice
2 lb	1 kg	New potatoes, peeled, small dice
1 lb	500 g	Celery, small dice
1 lb	500 g	Peas, fresh or frozen
¼ cup	60 mL	Chopped parsley
1 tbsp	15 mL	Chopped fresh tarragon
6 qt	6 L	Light vegetable stock or chicken stock
8 oz	250 mL	Heavy cream
to taste	to taste	Salt
to taste	to taste	White pepper
		Garnish:
8 oz	250 mL	Heavy cream
2 tbsp	30 mL	Chopped chives

■ P r o c e d u r e

1. Heat the butter in a heavy soup pot over low heat.
2. Add the leeks, potatoes, and celery. Sweat over low heat until fairly tender, about 10–15 minutes.
3. Add the peas, parsley, and tarragon. Sweat another 5 minutes.
4. Add the stock. Simmer 10 minutes or more, until the vegetables are tender but not overcooked.
5. Purée the soup with a food mill. If you use an immersion blender, pass the soup through a food mill or sieve after puréeing it in order to remove fibers from the celery.
6. Heat the cream and stir it into the soup.
7. Adjust the seasoning with salt and white pepper.
8. Whip the cream until it forms soft peaks. Fold in the chives.
9. At service time, garnish each portion of soup with a spoonful of the chive cream. (Within a few minutes, the whipped cream will melt into a chive-flecked foam.)

Per serving:
Calories, 160; Protein, 4 g; Fat, 10 g (53% cal.); Cholesterol, 35 mg; Carbohydrates, 16 g; Fiber, 3 g; Sodium, 65 mg.

Potage Cressonière (Watercress Soup)

Yield: 4 qt (4 L)   Portions: 16   Portion size: 8 fl oz (250 mL)

U.S.	Metric	Ingredients
3 bunches	3 bunches	Watercress
1 lb	500 g	Leeks, white part only
3½ oz	100 g	Butter
3 qt	3 L	Chicken stock or water
2 lb 8 oz	1.2 kg	Potatoes, peeled and cut into large pieces
7 oz	200 g	Crème fraîche
to taste	to taste	Salt
to taste	to taste	White pepper

■ P r o c e d u r e

1. Wash the watercress and separate the leaves from the stems. Set some of the nicer leaves aside for the garnish. Coarsely chop the stems and set aside.
2. Quickly blanch the leaves in boiling salted water and refresh. Once completely cooled, drain. Squeeze out any excess water and finely chop.
3. Thinly slice the leeks and sweat in butter with the watercress stems. Gently cook until tender and all the liquid has evaporated.
4. Add the chicken stock or water and the potatoes. Bring to a boil.
5. Reduce the heat to a simmer and cook for 30 minutes or until the potatoes are tender. Add the cream, then add the blanched watercress.
6. Blend in a blender until smooth, then strain. Season to taste.
7. Serve in a shallow soup bowl and garnish with fresh watercress leaves.
8. This soup can also be served cold.

Per serving:
Calories, 170; Protein, 4 g; Fat, 10 g (51% cal.); Cholesterol, 30 mg; Carbohydrates, 18 g; Fiber, 2 g; Sodium, 90 mg.

Navy Bean Soup

Yield: 6 qt (6 L)   Portions: 24   Portion size: 8 fl oz (250 mL)

U.S.	Metric	Ingredients	■ P r o c e d u r e
2 lb	1 kg	Dried navy beans	1. Soak the beans overnight in cold water.
4 oz	125 g	Bacon, diced	2. Place the bacon in a heavy saucepot over medium heat. Render the fat from the bacon, but do not cook until crisp.
4 oz	125 g	Onions, small dice	3. Add the vegetables and cook over low heat until almost tender.
8 oz	250 g	Carrots, small dice	
8 oz	250 g	Celery, small dice	
4 oz	125 g	Leeks, sliced	
3	3	Garlic cloves, chopped	
5 qt	5 L	Stock or water	4. Add the stock or water and the ham hock. Bring to a boil.
1	1	Ham hock	5. Drain the beans and add them to the liquid. Also add the bay leaf, thyme, and pepper.
1	1	Bay leaf	
½ tsp	2 mL	Dried thyme	6. Cover and simmer until the beans are tender.
½ tsp	2 mL	Pepper	
1 qt	1 L	Canned tomatoes, with juice, crushed	7. Add the tomatoes to the soup and simmer another 15 minutes. Remove the bay leaf.
			8. Remove the ham hock from the soup. Cut off and dice the meat and add it to the soup. Discard the bones.
			9. Mash the beans lightly with a paddle or pass about one-fourth of the beans through a food mill. Add this purée back to the soup to thicken it.
			10. If the soup is too thick, thin it with a little stock.
			11. Adjust the seasoning.

Per serving:
Calories, 180; Protein, 10 g; Fat, 4 g (19% cal.); Cholesterol, 5 mg; Carbohydrates, 28 g; Fiber, 7 g; Sodium, 510 mg.

 Apple and Parsnip Soup with Floating Calvados Cream

Yield: 6 qt (6 L)   Portions: 24   Portion size: 8 fl oz (250 mL)

U.S.	Metric	Ingredients	■ P r o c e d u r e
6 oz	180 g	Butter	1. Heat the butter in a heavy saucepot over moderately low heat. Add the onions and sweat without letting them brown.
1 lb 6 oz	670 g	Onions, sliced thin, large dice	2. Add the parsnips and apples, stirring to mix.
2 lb	1 kg	Parsnips, peeled, large dice	3. Add the stock and bring to a boil. Simmer until the parsnips and apples are tender, about 30 minutes.
2 lb	1 kg	Cooking apples, peeled, cored, large dice	4. Pass the soup through a food mill or purée in a blender. Then pass through a china cap.
6 qt	6 L	Chicken stock	5. Pour into a clean saucepot and bring to a boil.
to taste	to taste	Salt	6. If the soup is too thick, thin with a little stock. Season to taste with salt and white pepper.
to taste	to taste	White pepper	
2½ pt	1.2 L	Heavy cream	7. Whip the cream until lightly thickened but not stiff. Do not overwhip. Mix the Calvados into the cream. This further mixing should thicken the cream so that it holds peaks.
12 fl oz	360 mL	Calvados	8. At service time, garnish each portion of the soup with a spoonful of the cream. Pass under the salamander or broiler very briefly to lightly brown the cream. Serve immediately.

Per serving:
Calories, 160; Protein, 1.5 g; Fat, 12 g (68% cal.); Cholesterol, 45 mg; Carbohydrates, 7 g; Fiber, 1 g; Sodium, 46 mg.

Potato and Leek Soup with Sorrel

Yield: 6 qt (6 L)	**Portions: 24**	**Portion size: 8 fl oz (250 mL)**
U.S.	**Metric**	**Ingredients**
5 oz	140 g	Butter
1 lb 4 oz	600 g	Onions, sliced thin
1 lb 4 oz	600 g	Leeks, white part only, sliced thin
5 lb	2.4 kg	Potatoes, peeled, large dice
5 qt	4.8 L	Chicken stock
to taste	to taste	Salt
to taste	to taste	White pepper
12 oz	360 g	Fresh sorrel leaves

Procedure

1. Heat the butter in a large saucepot over moderately low heat. Add the onions and leeks. Sweat them without letting them brown.
2. Add the potatoes to the saucepot and stir.
3. Add the stock, season, and bring to a boil. Simmer until the vegetables are very tender.
4. Purée the soup with a blender or food processor or use an immersion blender, then pass through a china cap if necessary.
5. Pour into a clean saucepot and bring to a boil.
6. If the soup is too thick, thin with a little stock.
7. Wash and pick over the sorrel, removing thick stalks. Coarsely shred and add to the soup to serve.

Per serving:
Calories, 150; Protein, 3 g; Fat, 5 g (30% cal.); Cholesterol, 20 mg; Carbohydrates, 23 g; Fiber, 3 g; Sodium, 70 mg.

Spicy Black Bean Soup

Yield: 6 qt (6 L)	**Portions: 24**	**Portion size: 8 fl oz (250 mL)**
U.S.	**Metric**	**Ingredients**
2 lb	1 kg	Black turtle beans
1½ fl oz	50 mL	Olive oil
8 oz	250 g	Onions, small dice
4	4	Garlic cloves, chopped
2 oz	60 g	Jalapeño or other fresh green chile, chopped
4 tbsp	60 mL	Chili powder
1½ tsp	7 mL	Ground cumin
1½ tsp	7 mL	Ground coriander
1	1	Bay leaf
5 qt	5 L	White stock, vegetable stock, or water
1 lb	500 g	Tomatoes (canned), drained and chopped
to taste	to taste	Salt
to taste	to taste	Hot pepper sauce
		Garnish:
8 oz	250 g	Avocado, medium dice
8 oz	250 g	Tomato, medium dice

Procedure

1. Soak the beans overnight in cold water.
2. Heat the olive oil in a heavy soup pot over moderate heat.
3. Add the onions, garlic, and jalapeño. Cook over low heat until almost tender.
4. Add the chili powder, cumin, coriander, and bay leaf. Stir to mix in with the oil and vegetables.
5. Add the stock or water. Drain the soaked beans and add them to the pot.
6. Cover and simmer until the beans are just tender.
7. Add the tomatoes. Continue to simmer another 15–30 minutes, until the beans are completely tender and the flavors are well blended.
8. Add salt and hot pepper sauce to taste.
9. Carefully mix together the diced avocado and tomato. Garnish each portion of the soup with a spoonful of this mixture.

Per serving:
Calories, 170; Protein, 10 g; Fat, 4.5 g (22% cal.); Cholesterol, 5 mg; Carbohydrates, 25 g; Fiber, 9 g; Sodium, 55 mg.

Spicy Black Bean Soup

Chilled Leek and Potato Soup with Shrimp and Fennel Salad

Yield: 3 qt (3 L) plus garnish   Portions: 12
`Portion size: 8 fl oz (250 mL) plus garnish*

U.S.	Metric	Ingredients
1½ lb	750 g	Leeks, white part only
1½ lb	750 g	Potatoes, peeled
2 fl oz	60 mL	Olive oil
4½ pt	2.25 L	Chicken stock
to taste	to taste	Salt
to taste	to taste	White pepper
12 oz	375 g	Tender fennel bulbs, trimmed (see note)
4 tsp	20 mL	Lemon juice
1 fl oz	30 mL	Olive oil
to taste	to taste	Salt
to taste	to taste	Pepper
36	36	Small cooked shrimp (see note)
8 fl oz	250 mL	Heavy cream
8 fl oz	250 mL	Buttermilk

Per serving:
Calories, 240; Protein, 8 g; Fat, 15 g (55% cal.); Cholesterol, 55 mg; Carbohydrates, 22 g; Fiber, 3 g; Sodium, 90 mg.

Note: The fennel must be young and tender, as it is eaten raw. If only large bulbs are available, use the interior part and save the outer layers for another purpose.

Grilled shrimp are especially good for this soup.

■ **Procedure**

1. Cut the leeks and potatoes into thin slices.
2. Sweat the leeks in olive oil without letting them brown.
3. Add the stock and potatoes and bring to a boil. Simmer until the vegetables are tender.
4. Pass the soup through a food mill.
5. If the soup is too thick, add a little stock to bring to proper consistency.
6. Chill the soup thoroughly.
7. Add salt and white pepper to taste.
8. While the soup is chilling, prepare the garnish. Cut the fennel in half lengthwise through the base, then cut lengthwise into paper-thin slices (a slicing machine may be used). Cut these slices lengthwise into rough julienne.
9. Toss the fennel with the lemon juice, then with half the olive oil. Add salt and pepper to taste.
10. Toss the shrimp with the remaining olive oil.
11. Stir the heavy cream and buttermilk into the chilled soup.
12. Arrange the fennel salad in the center of broad soup plates. Arrange 3 shrimp on top of each mound of fennel.
13. Place the soup plate in front of the diner, then ladle in a portion of soup from a tureen.

VARIATIONS

The fennel and shrimp garnish may be omitted for a simpler presentation. Water may be substituted for the stock. Leeks are flavorful enough to make a delicious soup even without stock.

Vichyssoise

Substitute butter for the olive oil. Omit the buttermilk and increase the heavy cream to 16–20 fl oz (500–600 mL). Omit the fennel and shrimp salad garnish. Garnish with chopped chives.

Chilled Leek and Potato Soup with Shrimp and Fennel Salad

BISQUES

A bisque is a cream soup made with shellfish. At one time, bisques were thickened with rice, but today they are more frequently thickened with roux. Bisques are made basically like other cream soups, but they seem more complex because of the handling of the shellfish and the variety of flavoring ingredients often used. Expensive to prepare and rich in taste, they are considered luxury soups.

The term *bisque* has come to be used for a great variety of other soups, primarily because the word sounds nice. In this book, we reserve the term for shellfish cream soups.

Shrimp Bisque

Yield: 2 qt (2 L)   **Portions: 10**   **Portion size: 6 fl oz (200 mL)**

U.S.	Metric	Ingredients
1 oz	30 g	Butter
2 oz	60 g	Onions, cut brunoise
2 oz	60 g	Carrots, cut brunoise
1 lb	500 g	Small shrimp, shells on
small piece	small piece	Bay leaf
pinch	pinch	Dried thyme
4	4	Parsley stems
1 oz	30 g	Tomato paste
2 oz	60 mL	Burnt brandy (see note)
6 oz	200 mL	White wine
1 qt	1 L	Fish velouté
1 pt	500 mL	Fish stock
1 cup	250 mL	Heavy cream, hot
to taste	to taste	Salt
to taste	to taste	White pepper

Procedure

1. Heat the butter in a saucepan over medium heat.
2. Add the onions and carrots. Sauté until they are lightly browned.
3. Add the shrimp, bay leaf, thyme, and parsley stems. Sauté until the shrimp turn red.
4. Add the tomato paste and stir well.
5. Add the brandy and wine. Simmer until reduced by half.
6. Remove the shrimp. Peel and devein them. Return the shells to the saucepan.
7. Cut the shrimp into small dice and reserve for garnish.
8. Add the fish velouté and stock to the saucepan. Simmer 10–15 minutes.
9. Strain. Return the soup to the saucepan and bring back to a simmer.
10. At service time, add the hot cream and the diced shrimp. Season to taste.

Per serving:
Calories, 220; Protein, 8 g; Fat 17 g (70% cal.); Cholesterol, 110 mg; Carbohydrates, 6 g; Fiber, 0 g; Sodium, 180 mg

Note: Burnt brandy is brandy that has been heated in a saucepan and flamed (carefully) to burn off the alcohol.

VARIATIONS

This recipe is based on Method 1 for making cream soups (p.222), because it uses velouté as a base. You can also use fish stock instead of velouté and thicken the soup in other ways:

1. Beat in a beurre manié (p. 164), a little at a time, after step 8, until properly thickened.
2. Stir in a cornstarch slurry (cornstarch in cold water), a little at a time.
3. Simmer 2 oz (60 g) rice in 1 pt (500 mL) of the stock, until the rice is completely cooked. Liquefy in a blender or force through a fine sieve to purée the rice, and add to the soup. (This is the classical method.)

To reduce food cost, you may reduce the quantity of shrimp and add extra shrimp shells for flavor. Or, instead of using all the cooked shrimp for garnish, save most of them for another use.

Paprika is often used instead of tomato paste to color and flavor bisques. Substitute 1 tbsp (15 mL) Spanish paprika for the 1 oz (30 g) tomato paste.

Lobster Bisque

In place of shrimp, use live lobster, cut as shown in Figure 14.12. (Alternatively, to reduce food costs, use crushed lobster shells or rock lobster tails.)

CHOWDERS

Chowders are chunky, hearty soups that are so full of good things that they sometimes are more like stews than soups. Many types of chowder are simply cream soups or purée soups that are not puréed but left chunky. Like other specialty regional soups, chowders resist categorization. However, most of them are based on fish or shellfish or vegetables, and most contain potatoes and milk or cream.

 Potato Chowder

Yield: 6 qt (6 L)   Portions: 24   Portion size: 8 fl oz (250 mL)

U.S.	Metric	Ingredients	■ P r o c e d u r e
8 oz	250 g	Salt pork	1. Grind the salt pork or cut into very fine dice.
12 oz	375 g	Onions, medium dice	2. Render the pork fat in a heavy saucepot.
3 oz	90 g	Celery, medium dice	3. Add the onions and celery. Cook in the fat over moderate heat until nearly tender. Do not brown.
4 oz	125 g	Flour	4. Add the flour. Stir into the fat to make a roux. Cook the roux slowly for 4–5 minutes, but do not let it brown.
3½ qt	3.5 L	Chicken stock	5. Using a wire whip, slowly stir in the stock. Bring to a boil, stirring to make sure the liquid is smooth.
3 lb	1.5 kg	Potatoes, medium dice	6. Add the potatoes. Simmer until all the vegetables are tender.
3 pt	1.5 L	Milk, hot	7. Stir in the hot milk and cream.
1 cup	250 mL	Heavy cream, hot	8. Season to taste with salt and white pepper.
to taste	to taste	Salt	
to taste	to taste	White pepper	
as needed	as needed	Chopped parsley	9. Sprinkle each portion with a little chopped parsley for garnish.

Per serving:
Calories, 210; Protein, 5 g; Fat 14 g (58% cal.); Cholesterol, 35 mg;
Carbohydrates, 18 g; Fiber, 1 g; Sodium, 180 mg.

V A R I A T I O N S

Corn Chowder

Version 1. Prepare as in basic recipe, but reduce potatoes to 2¼ lb (1.1 kg). When vegetables are tender, add 3 lb (1.5 kg) frozen or drained canned whole-kernel corn. (If using canned corn, replace part of the chicken stock with the corn liquid.)

Version 2. Prepare as in basic recipe, but reduce potatoes to 1½ lb (750 g). Add 3 lb (1.5 kg) canned cream-style corn when vegetables are tender.

Corn and Crab Chowder with Basil

| Yield: 6 qt (6 L) | Portions: 24 | Portion size: 8 fl oz (250 mL) |
U.S.	Metric	Ingredients
3 fl oz	90 mL	Vegetable oil
12 oz	375 g	Onions, medium dice
2	2	Garlic cloves, chopped
3 oz	90 g	Flour
3½ qt	3.5 L	Mild fish stock or chicken stock
8 fl oz	250 mL	Dry white wine
2 lb	1 kg	Potatoes, medium dice (see note)
2	2	Bay leaves
2 lb	1 kg	Corn kernels, fresh or frozen
½ cup	125 mL	Fresh basil leaves, shredded
2 lb	1 kg	Crabmeat
1 pt	500 mL	Milk, hot
8 fl oz	250 mL	Heavy cream, hot
to taste	to taste	Salt
to taste	to taste	White pepper

■ Procedure

1. Heat the oil in a heavy soup pot over moderate heat.
2. Add the onions and garlic.
3. Cook over moderate heat until nearly tender. Do not brown.
4. Add the flour. Stir into the fat to make a roux. Cook the roux slowly for 4–5 minutes, but do not let it brown.
5. Using a wire whip, slowly stir in the stock. Bring to a boil, stirring to make sure the liquid is smooth. Add the wine.
6. Add the potatoes and bay leaves. Simmer until the potatoes are tender.
7. Add the corn kernels and shredded basil. Return the soup to a simmer.
8. Add the crabmeat.
9. Stir in the hot milk and cream.
10. Season to taste with salt and pepper.

V A R I A T I O N

If a thicker soup is desired, increase the flour to 4 oz (125 g) and the oil to 4 fl oz (125 mL).

Per serving:
Calories, 220; Protein, 12 g; Fat, 9 g (36% cal.); Cholesterol, 45 mg; Carbohydrates, 22 g; Fiber, 2 g; Sodium, 160 mg.

Note: For attractive color, use small red-skinned potatoes and do not peel them.

Corn and Crab Chowder with Basil

New England Clam Chowder

Yield: 6 qt (6 L)   *Portions: 24*   *Portion size: 8 fl oz (250 mL)*

U.S.	Metric	Ingredients
2 qt	2 L	Canned, minced clams, with their juice, or fresh shucked clams, with their juice (see note)
1½ qt	1.5 L	Water
10 oz	300 g	Salt pork, ground or cut into fine dice
1 lb	500 g	Onions, small dice
4 oz	125 g	Flour
2 lb	1 kg	Potatoes, small dice
2½ qt	2.5 L	Milk, hot
1 cup	250 mL	Heavy cream, hot
to taste	to taste	Salt
to taste	to taste	White pepper

■ P r o c e d u r e

1. Drain the clams but reserve the juice. If you are using fresh clams, chop them, being sure to save all the juice.
2. Combine the juice and water in a saucepan. Bring to a boil.
3. Remove from the heat and keep the liquid hot for step 7.
4. In a heavy saucepot or stockpot, render the salt pork over medium heat.
5. Add the onions and cook slowly until they are soft, but do not brown.
6. Add the flour and stir to make a roux. Cook the roux slowly for 3–4 minutes, but do not let it brown.
7. Using a wire whip, slowly stir the clam liquid and water into the roux. Bring to a boil, stirring constantly to make sure the liquid is smooth.
8. Add the potatoes. Simmer until tender. (If you are using large, tough chowder clams, pass them once through a grinder and add them with the potatoes.)
9. Stir in the clams and the hot milk and cream. Heat gently, but do not boil.
10. Season to taste with salt and white pepper.

Per serving:
Calories, 300; Protein, 16 g; Fat, 17 g (52% cal.); Cholesterol, 65 mg; Carbohydrates, 19 g; Fiber, 1 g; Sodium, 350 mg.

Note: If whole clams in the shell are used, you will need about 8–10 qt (8–10 L). Scrub them well. Combine with the 1½ qt (1½ L) water in a stockpot and simmer until the shells are open. Remove the clams from the shells and chop. Strain the liquid.

V A R I A T I O N S

Manhattan Clam Chowder
Substitute 4 fl oz (125 mL) oil or 4 oz (125 g) butter for the salt pork. Add 10 oz (300 g) celery, small dice; 10 oz (300 g) carrots, small dice; and 1 tsp (5 mL) chopped garlic to the onions in step 5. Omit flour. Instead of milk, use 2½ qt (2½ L) chopped canned tomatoes and their juices. Omit cream.

New England Fish Chowder
Follow the procedure for New England clam chowder, but omit clams and water. Use 3 qt (3 L) fish stock instead of the clam juice and water mixture in step 7. Remove all skin and bones from 1¼ lb (625 g) haddock fillets. Cut into ¾-in. (2-cm) chunks. Add to the finished soup and keep hot (do not boil) until the fish is cooked, about 5 minutes.

SPECIALTY SOUPS AND NATIONAL SOUPS

 ## French Onion Soup Gratinée

Yield: 7½ qt (7.5 L)	Portions: 24	Portion size: 10 fl oz (300 mL)
U.S.	**Metric**	**Ingredients**
4 oz	125 g	Butter
5 lb	2.5 kg	Onions, sliced thin
6½ qt	6.5 L	Beef stock, or half beef and half chicken stock
to taste	to taste	Salt
to taste	to taste	Pepper
4–6 fl oz	125–175 mL	Sherry (optional)
as needed	as needed	French bread (see procedure)
1½ lb	750 g	Gruyère or Swiss cheese, or a mixture, coarsely grated

Per serving:
Calories, 320; Protein, 15 g; Fat, 15 g (42% cal.); Cholesterol, 50 mg; Carbohydrates, 31 g; Fiber, 3 g; Sodium, 410 mg.

■ Procedure

1. Heat the butter in a stockpot over moderate heat. Add the onions and cook until they are golden. Stir occasionally.
   Note: The onions must cook slowly and become evenly browned. This is a slow process and will take about 30 minutes. Do not brown too fast or use high heat.

2. Add the stock and bring to a boil. Simmer until the onions are very tender and the flavors are well blended, about 20 minutes.

3. Season to taste with salt and pepper. Add the sherry, if desired.

4. Keep the soup hot for service.

5. Cut the bread into slices about ⅜ in. (1 cm) thick. You will need 1 or 2 slices per portion, or just enough to cover the top of the soup in its serving crock.

6. Toast the slices in the oven or under the broiler.

7. For each portion fill an individual service soup crock with hot soup. Place 1 or 2 slices of the toast on top and cover with cheese. Pass under the broiler until the cheese is bubbling and lightly browned. Serve immediately.

VARIATIONS

Onion soup may be served without gratinéeing and with cheese croutons prepared separately. Toast the bread as in basic recipe. Place on a sheet pan. Brush lightly with butter and sprinkle each piece with grated cheese. (Parmesan may be mixed with the other cheese.) Brown under the broiler. Garnish each portion with 1 cheese crouton. (This method is less expensive because it uses much less cheese.)

French Onion Soup Gratinée

Roasted Garlic Soup with Black Olive Crostini

Yield: 3 qt (3 L)   Portions: 12   Portion size: 8 fl oz (250 mL)

U.S.	Metric	Ingredients
3 oz	90 g	Butter
6	6	Whole heads of garlic, separated into cloves and peeled
2 lb	900 g	Onion, peeled and chopped
2 lb	900 g	Potato, peeled and diced
1½ qt	1.5 L	Milk
1½ qt	1.5 L	Chicken stock
to taste	to taste	Salt
to taste	to taste	Pepper
7 fl oz	200 mL	Olive oil
7 oz	200 g	Pitted black olives, finely chopped
12 slices	12 slices	French bread

■ P r o c e d u r e

1. Heat the butter in a heavy saucepot over a medium heat. Cook the garlic cloves until golden brown, stirring to color evenly. If desired, start the cooking on top of the stove and finish in the oven at 375°F (190°C), stirring from time to time.

2. Add the onions and stir for 2–3 minutes. Add the potato and sweat the mixture without letting the vegetables brown, stirring to prevent the potatoes from sticking. Cook until the onion is soft.

3. Add the milk and the stock. Bring to a boil. Simmer until the potatoes are soft enough to crush, 30–40 minutes.

4. Pass the soup through a food mill or purée in a blender. Pour into a clean saucepot and season to taste with salt and pepper.

5. Add the olive oil to the finely chopped olives to bind them as a thick, spreadable paste.

6. Toast the slices of French bread on each side. Spread one side with the olive mixture.

7. At service time, bring the soup back to a simmer. If necessary, thin the soup with a little stock to achieve the correct consistency. Serve 1 crostino per person with the soup.

Per serving:
Calories, 470; Protein, 10 g, Fat, 29 g (54% cal.); Cholesterol, 35 mg; Carbohydrates, 45 g; Fiber, 4 g; Sodium, 430 mg.

Viennese-Style Vegetable Broth

Yield: 6 qt (6 L)   Portions: 24   Portion size: 8 fl oz (250 mL)

U.S.	Metric	Ingredients
3½ oz	100 g	Butter
7 oz	200 g	Onions, cut brunoise
7 oz	200 g	Turnip, cut brunoise
7 oz	200 g	Carrot, cut brunoise
4½ qt	4.5 L	Chicken stock
7 oz	200 g	Tender young green beans, cut brunoise or sliced thin
7 oz	200 g	Leeks, cut brunoise
7 oz	200 g	Zucchini, cut brunoise
1½ oz	45 g	Chopped parsley
1 tbsp	10 g	Fresh marjoram leaves, chopped fine (see note)
1½ tsp	5 g	Fresh thyme (see note)
1 pt	400 mL	Heavy cream
4	4	Egg yolks

■ P r o c e d u r e

1. Heat the butter in a saucepot over medium heat. Add the onion, turnip, and carrot brunoise to the pot and sweat without coloring.

2. Add the stock to the pot and quickly bring to a boil. Add the beans, leeks, and zucchini. Simmer for 5 minutes.

3. Add the herbs to the soup. Season to taste.

4. At service time, mix together the cream and egg yolks to make a liaison. Slowly stir a little hot soup into the liaison, then add the tempered liaison to the soup. Carefully reheat the soup, but do not let it boil. Serve immediately.

Per serving:
Calories, 130; Protein, 2 g, Fat, 12 g (79 % cal.); Cholesterol, 75 mg; Carbohydrates, 5 g; Fiber, 1 g; Sodium, 65 mg.

Note: If fresh marjoram and thyme are not available, use one-third their quantity of dried herbs.

Borscht

Yield: 6 qt (6 L) *Portions: 24* *Portion size: 8 fl oz (250 mL)*

U.S.	Metric	Ingredients
2 lb	1 kg	Beef brisket or shank (see note)
3½ qt	3½ L	Water or beef stock
4 oz	125 g	Butter
8 oz	250 g	Onion, sliced thin
8 oz	250 g	Leeks, white part and about ½ in. (1 cm) of green, cut julienne
8 oz	250 g	Cabbage, shredded
2 No. 2½ cans	2 No. 2½ cans	Beets (about 60 oz/ 1.7 kg) (see note)
4 oz	125 g	Tomato purée
4 fl oz	125 mL	Vinegar
2 tbsp	30 g	Sugar
to taste	to taste	Salt
to taste	to taste	White pepper
as needed	as needed	Sour cream

Per serving:
Calories, 150; Protein, 9 g; Fat, 9 g (53% cal); Cholesterol, 40 mg; Carbohydrates, 9 g; Fiber, 1 g; Sodium, 250 mg.

Note: Leftover cooked beef may be used. In this case, use 16–20 oz (500–625 g) cooked beef and use stock, not water. If fresh raw beets are used, shred or grate them and sweat them with the onions.

■ P r o c e d u r e

1. Simmer the beef in the water or stock until tender.
2. Remove the cooked beef from the broth and cut it into small dice.
3. Measure the broth and, if necessary, add water to bring it back up to 3 qt (3 L).
4. Return the meat to the broth.

5. Heat the butter in a heavy pot. Add the onion, leeks, and cabbage. Cook slowly in the butter for about 5 minutes.

6. Drain the beets and save the juice. Grate the beets on a coarse grater or chop them fine.
7. Add the mixture of onions, leek, and cabbage, the beets, beet juice, tomato purée, vinegar, and sugar to the meat and broth.
8. Bring to a boil and simmer until the vegetables are tender.
9. Season to taste with salt, white pepper, and more vinegar if desired.

10. Serve each portion topped with a spoonful of sour cream.

V A R I A T I O N S

Cold Borscht
Omit beef. Strain soup through a china cap, pressing down on the vegetables to force out all juices. Chill the soup and add lemon juice to taste. Serve with sour cream.

Gulyas

Yield: 3 qt (3 L) *Portions: 12* *Portion size: 8 fl oz (250 mL)*

U.S.	Metric	Ingredients
2 oz	60 g	Pork fatback or bacon
8 oz	250 g	Onions, medium dice
1 lb 8 oz	750 g	Beef chuck or shank
2	2	Garlic cloves, chopped fine
½ tsp	2 mL	Caraway seeds
2 tbsp	12 g	Hungarian paprika
1 tbsp	15 mL	Tomato paste
2½ qt	2.5 L	Water or brown stock, hot
1 lb	500 g	Potatoes, peeled, medium dice
to taste	to taste	Salt
to taste	to taste	Pepper

■ P r o c e d u r e

1. Grind the fatback or bacon or cut it into fine dice. Render the fat in a heavy pot. After the fat has rendered, remove the solids with a slotted spoon and discard or save for another use.
2. Add the onions to the fat in the pot and sweat. Do not brown.
3. Cut the beef into medium dice. Add to the onions and cook over low heat for 10 minutes.
4. Add the garlic, caraway seeds, paprika, and tomato paste. Stir them in well.
5. Add the liquid. Simmer until the beef is almost tender. This may take 1 hour or more, depending on the type and quality of the meat.

6. Add the potatoes and simmer until done.
7. Season to taste with salt and pepper.

Per serving:
Calories, 210; Protein, 12 g; Fat, 14 g (60% cal.); Cholesterol, 40 mg; Carbohydrates, 9 g; Fiber, 1 g; Sodium, 45 mg.

Seafood Gumbo

Yield: 5 qt (5 L)   Portions: 16   Portion size: 10 fl oz (300 mL) plus 1½ oz (45 g) rice

U.S.	Metric	Ingredients
3 fl. oz	90 g	Vegetable oil
6 oz	180 g	Onion, small dice
4 oz	120 g	Celery, small dice
4 oz	120 g	Green bell pepper, small dice
1 oz	30 g	Garlic, chopped fine
1½ tsp	7 mL	Dried thyme
1½ tsp	7 mL	Dried basil
1 tsp	5 mL	Dried oregano
2	2	Bay leaves
1 tsp	5 mL	Cayenne
1 tsp	5 mL	Black pepper
2 tsp	10 mL	Paprika
1 gal	4 L	Fish stock, hot
8 oz	250 g	Blond roux (p. 162)
10 oz	300 g	Canned tomatoes, chopped
1 lb	500 g	Okra, trimmed, cut into ¾-in. (2-cm) slices
1 lb	500 g	Small shrimp, peeled and deveined
1 lb	500 g	Lump crabmeat
1 tbsp	15 mL	Filé powder
to taste	to taste	Salt
1½ lb	750 g	Cooked rice

Per serving:
Calories, 290; Protein, 18 g; Fat, 14 g (44% cal.); Cholesterol, 80 mg;
Carbohydrates, 22 g; Fiber, 2 g; Sodium, 580 mg.

Seafood Gumbo

■ Procedure

1. Heat the oil in a stockpot or heavy soup pot. Add the onion, celery, green pepper, garlic, herbs, and spices. Cook over low heat until the vegetables are soft.

2. Add the stock. Bring the mixture to a boil.

3. Beat in the roux to thicken the soup.

4. Add the tomatoes. Simmer 10 minutes.

5. Add the okra. Simmer until the okra is tender, about 10 to 15 minutes more.

6. Add the shrimp and crabmeat. Simmer 10 minutes.

7. Sprinkle the filé powder over the top of the soup and stir it in. Simmer another 2 minutes.

8. Remove from heat and season to taste with salt.

9. To serve, spoon about 1½ oz (45 g) cooked rice into a soup bowl. Ladle 10 fl oz (300 mL) soup over the rice.

V A R I A T I O N S

Substitute diced white fish fillets (such as grouper, snapper, or monkfish) for part of the crabmeat. Add 12 oz (375 g) shucked oysters.

Chicken and Andouille Gumbo

Substitute chicken stock for the fish stock. Omit the shrimp and crabmeat. Instead, use 1½ lb (750 g) diced raw chicken meat and 8 oz (250 g) sliced andouille sausage. Brown the chicken in oil, and add the chicken and sausage in step 6. Simmer until the chicken is completely cooked.

Pho Bo (Vietnamese Beef and Rice Noodle Soup)

Yield: 3 qt (3 L)   Portions: 12   Portion size: 8 fl oz broth, plus garnish

U.S.	Metric	Ingredients
3 qt	3 L	Beef broth
12 slices	12 slices	Fresh ginger root
3 stalks	3 stalks	Lemon grass, coarsely chopped
6 oz	180 g	Shallots, sliced thin
1	1	Cinnamon stick
3 fl oz	90 mL	Nuoc nam (Vietnamese fish sauce) or nam pla (Thai fish sauce)
to taste	to taste	Salt
1 lb 8 oz	750 g	Beef tenderloin or other tender beef steak
1 lb 8 oz	750 g	Rice sticks (see p. 638)
		Garnishes
as desired	as desired	Shallots, sliced thin
as desired	as desired	Mung bean sprouts
as desired	as desired	Fresh mint leaves
as desired	as desired	Fresh cilantro leaves
as desired	as desired	Fresh red chiles, seeded and sliced thin
as desired	as desired	Lime wedges
as desired	as desired	Chile paste with garlic

■ P r o c e d u r e

1. Combine the broth, ginger, lemon grass, shallots, and cinnamon stick in a stockpot. Simmer 30 minutes.
2. Strain. Discard the solids.
3. Add the fish sauce.
4. Taste and add salt if necessary
5. Partially freeze the beef to make it easier to slice.
6. Slice the beef into paper-thin slices.
7. Just before service, drop the rice sticks into boiling water. Bring the water back to a boil and drain immediately.
8. For service, bring the broth back to a boil.
9. Place each garnish in a separate bowl and arrange on the dining table.
10. Place 2 oz (60 g) beef slices in the bottom of each soup bowl.
11. Ladle 8 fl oz (250 mL) broth over the beef slices. The boiling broth cooks the beef in moments.
12. Add rice noodles to the bowl.
13. Allow guests to help themselves to garnishes to flavor soup as desired.

Per serving:
Calories, 380; Protein, 23 g; Fat, 25 g (58% cal.); Cholesterol, 105 mg;
Carbohydrates, 17 g; Fiber, 1 g; Sodium, 800 mg.

Pho Bo

Chinese Hot and Sour Soup

Yield: 3 qt (3 L)

U.S.	Metric	Ingredients
8	8	Dried black mushrooms
16	16	Dried cloud ear (also called tree ear) mushrooms
as needed	as needed	Boiling water
2½ qt	2.5 L	Chicken stock
8 oz	250 g	Lean pork, cut julienne (see note)
6 oz	180 g	Bamboo shoots, cut julienne
3 fl oz	80 g	Soy sauce
2 tsp	10 mL	White pepper
8 tbsp	120 mL	Cornstarch
8 fl oz	250 mL	Cold water
3 fl oz	90 mL	Rice vinegar or wine vinegar
2 tsp	10 mL	Oriental sesame oil
2	2	Eggs, lightly beaten
1	1	Scallion, sliced thin
2 tbsp	30 mL	Cilantro, chopped

■ P r o c e d u r e

1. Place the two types of dried mushrooms in separate bowls. Add enough boiling water to each to cover the mushrooms. Let stand until the mushrooms are soft.
2. Drain the mushrooms, squeezing them lightly. Reserve the soaking liquid.
3. Cut off and discard the stems from the black mushrooms. Cut the caps into thin strips.
4. Cut off any coarse, woody stems from the cloud ear mushrooms. Cut the mushrooms into half-inch (1-cm) pieces.

5. Combine the stock and the mushroom liquid in a saucepot. Bring to a boil.
6. Add the mushrooms, pork, bamboo shoots, soy sauce, and white pepper.
7. Simmer 3 minutes.

8. Mix the cornstarch with the water until smooth.
9. Add the cornstarch mixture to the simmering soup, stirring constantly.
10. Simmer until the soup is lightly thickened.

11. Add the vinegar and sesame oil to the soup.
12. Slowly drizzle in the beaten egg, stirring slowly but constantly, so that the egg coagulates in thin shreds.

13. At service time, top each portion with a few slices of scallion and a pinch of chopped cilantro.

Per serving:
Calories, 170; Protein, 11 g; Fat, 5 g (27% cal.); Carbohydrates, 20 g; Cholesterol, 50 mg; Fiber, 5 g; Sodium, 710 mg.

Note: To cut raw pork into julienne more easily, partially freeze it first.

Chinese Hot and Sour Soup

Chilled Tomato and Basil Soup

Yield: 2½ qt (2.5 L)   *Portions: 10*   *Portion size: 8 fl oz (250 mL)*

U.S.	Metric	Ingredients	■ P r o c e d u r e
4 lb	2 kg	Tomatoes, ripe	1. Peel, seed, and chop the tomatoes (see p. 533), reserving the juice and seeds.
			2. Transfer the seeds and juice to a strainer. Reserve the juice and discard the seeds.
1 tbsp	15 mL	Olive oil	3. Heat the olive oil in a heavy saucepot over moderate heat. Add the garlic and sweat until soft, but do not let it brown.
¼ oz	7 g	Garlic, chopped	
1½ qt	1.5 L	Chicken broth	4. Add the tomatoes, tomato juice, and chicken broth. Bring to a boil, and simmer 20 minutes.
2 tsp	10 mL	Fresh green or red chiles, seeded and chopped	5. Add the chiles and lemon zest. Simmer another 5 minutes.
1 tsp	5 mL	Grated lemon zest	6. Cool completely.
1 oz	30 g	Fresh basil, cut chiffonade (p. 139)	7. In a food processor or blender, purée the soup until smooth.
			8. Transfer to a bowl, a bain-marie, or other container. Stir in the basil and lemon juice.
2 fl oz	60 mL	Lemon juice	9. Chill.
to taste	to taste	Salt	10. Add salt to taste.
		Garnish	11. At service time, top each portion with a little basil chiffonade.
as desired	as desired	Fresh basil, cut chiffonade	

V A R I A T I O N

For a vegetarian alternative, substitute vegetable stock or water for the chicken stock. If desired, garnish each portion with a spoonful of yogurt or sour cream.

Per serving:
Calories, 60; Protein, 2 g; Fat, 2 g (27% cal.); Cholesterol, 5 mg; Carbohydrates, 10 g; Fiber, 2 g; Sodium, 25 mg.

Ecuadorian Quinoa and Peanut Soup

Yield: 3 qt (3 L)   *Portions: 12*   *Portion size: 8 fl oz (250 mL)*

U.S.	Metric	Ingredients	■ P r o c e d u r e
1 oz	30 g	Butter	1. Prepare annatto butter: Melt the butter and add the annatto seeds. Heat together for 10 minutes over low heat. Strain the butter and discard the seeds.
½ oz	15 g	Annatto seeds	
1 oz	30 g	Butter	2. Heat the second quantity of butter in a heavy saucepot. Add the onion and garlic. Sweat until the vegetables are soft.
10 oz	300 g	Onion, chopped fine	
½ oz	15 g	Garlic, chopped fine	3. Stir in the annatto butter.
2 qt 8 fl oz	2.25 L	Water	4. Add the water, quinoa, and potatoes. Simmer 25–30 minutes, until the quinoa and potatoes are very tender.
8 oz	250 g	Quinoa, rinsed well and drained	
10 oz	300 g	Potatoes, medium dice	
5 oz	150 g	Peanuts, roasted, unsalted, skinless	5. Grind the peanuts to a powder in a food processor. Do not process so long that they turn to peanut butter.
1 pt	500 mL	Milk	6. Add the peanuts, milk, and cilantro to the soup. Simmer an additional 15 minutes.
3 tbsp	45 mL	Chopped fresh cilantro	
to taste	to taste	Salt	7. Add salt to taste.

V A R I A T I O N

Peanuts may be omitted if desired, and change the name of the soup to Ecuadorian Quinoa Soup.

Per serving:
Calories, 230; Protein, 8 g; Fat, 12 g (46% cal.); Cholesterol, 15 mg; Carbohydrates, 24 g; Fiber, 3 g; Sodium, 55 mg.

Tortilla Soup

Yield: 3 qt (3 L)   Portions: 12
Portion size: 8 fl oz (250 mL) broth, plus garnish

U.S.	Metric	Ingredients
12 oz	375 g	Tomatoes, whole, ripe
12 oz	375 g	Onion, chopped
1½ tbsp	22 mL	Garlic, chopped
1 fl oz	30 mL	Vegetable oil
3 qt	3 L	Chicken stock or broth
to taste	to taste	Salt
		Garnishes in the soup:
1 lb	500 g	Fresh, mild cheese, such as Mexican queso fresco or cotija, or Monterey jack, crumbled or grated
12	12	Corn tortillas, cut into strips ¼ in. (6 mm) wide and deep-fried until crisp
as desired	as desired	Garnishes served separately: Dried pasilla chiles, fried crisp and crumbled Lime wedges Avocado, diced Sour cream or Mexican crema

■ Procedure

1. Place the tomatoes on a foil-lined pan and place under a pre-heated broiler. Broil until the tomatoes are softened and the skin is blistered and blackened.
2. Peel and core the tomatoes.
3. Purée the tomatoes, onion, and garlic together in a food processor.
4. Heat the oil in a heavy saucepot over moderately high heat.
5. Add the tomato mixture. Cook, stirring frequently, until the mixture is thick and several shades darker in color.
6. Add the stock or broth, stirring to make a smooth mixture. Simmer 30 minutes.
7. Season to taste with salt.
8. Place a little crumbled or grated cheese in the bottom of each soup bowl (about 1½ oz [40 g] per portion) and top with tortilla strips.
9. Ladle the soup over the tortillas.
10. Serve immediately, with the remaining garnish on the side in small bowls.

VARIATION

For a heartier soup with more protein, add cooked, shredded chicken, using about 2 oz (60 g) per portion.

Per serving:
Calories, 250; Protein, 13 g; Fat, 10 g (37% cal.); Cholesterol, 20 mg; Carbohydrates, 26 g; Fiber, 2 g; Sodium, 440 mg.

Tortilla Soup

Summer Vegetable and Smoked Tomato Soup

Yield: 2 qt (2 L)   Portions: 8   Portion size: 8 fl oz (250 mL)

U.S.	Metric	Ingredients	Procedure
8 oz	250 g	Roma tomatoes	1. Using hot smoking equipment or a stovetop smoker (p. 71), smoke the tomatoes until they are soft. 2. Peel the tomatoes and chop them coarsely. Set aside.
1½ fl oz	45 mL	Olive oil	3. Heat the olive oil over low heat in a heavy saucepot.
4 oz	125 g	Red bell pepper, chopped fine	4. Add the peppers, zucchini, carrot, and garlic. Sweat the vegetables until they are tender.
4 oz	125 g	Yellow bell pepper, chopped fine	5. Add the chicken stock, cayenne, parsley, and basil. Bring to a simmer. Simmer 15–20 minutes.
4 oz	125 g	Orange bell pepper, chopped fine	6. Stir in the tomatoes. Simmer another 10 minutes.
4 oz	125 g	Zucchini, chopped fine	7. Add salt to taste.
3 oz	90 g	Carrot, chopped fine	
1 oz	30 g	Garlic, chopped fine	
2 qt	2 L	Chicken stock or vegetable stock	
⅛ tsp	1 mL	Cayenne	
1 tbsp	15 mL	Chopped fresh parsley	
1 tbsp	15 mL	Chopped fresh basil	
to taste	to taste	Salt	
8 oz	250 g	Cooked orzo or other pastina	8. At service time, reheat the soup and add the orzo.
as desired	as desired	Romesco (p. 762; optional)	9. Serve the soup with a small bowl of romesco on the side, to be added to the soup by the diner.

Per serving:
Calories, 120; Protein, 3 g; Fat, 6 g (44% cal.); Cholesterol, 6 mg;
Carbohydrates, 14 g; Fiber, 2 g; Sodium, 25 mg.

Red Lentil and Apricot Soup

Yield: 3 qt (3 L)   Portions: 12   Portion size: 8 fl oz (250 mL)

U.S.	Metric	Ingredients	Procedure
1 fl oz	30 mL	Vegetable oil	1. Heat the oil in a heavy saucepot over moderate heat.
6 oz	180 g	Onion, small dice	2. Add the onions and garlic. Sweat until tender.
½ oz	15 g	Garlic, chopped fine	
3 qt	3 L	Vegetable stock	3. Add the stock to the pot. Bring to a boil.
1 lb 4 oz	600 g	Red lentils, sorted, rinsed, and drained	4. Add the lentils, sachet, and cayenne. Simmer 5 minutes.
		Sachet:	5. Add the tomatoes and apricots. Continue to simmer until the lentils and apricots are completely tender.
1	1	Bay leaf	6. Remove and discard the sachet.
¼ tsp	1 mL	Dried thyme	
4	4	Peppercorns	
2	2	Whole cloves	
⅛ tsp	0.5 mL	Cayenne	
5 oz	150 g	Tomato concassé	
12 oz	375 g	Dried apricots, coarsely chopped	
1 fl oz, or to taste	30 mL, or to taste	Lemon juice	7. Season to taste with lemon juice and salt.
to taste	to taste	Salt	

Per serving:
Calories, 280; Protein, 14 g; Fat, 3.5 g (11% cal.); Cholesterol, 0 mg;
Carbohydrates, 49 g; Fiber, 13 g; Sodium, 15 mg.

Japanese Clear Soup with Shrimp

Portions: 10   Portion size: 6 fl oz (200 mL)

U.S.	Metric	Ingredients
2 qt	2 L	Dashi (p. 195)
to taste	to taste	Salt
1 tbsp	15 mL	Japanese soy sauce
		Garnish:
1–2 strips	1–2 strips	Lemon zest
15	15	Snow peas
10	10	Medium shrimp

Per serving:
Calories, 15; Protein, 2 g; Fat, 0 g (0% cal.); Cholesterol, 10 mg;
Carbohydrates, 1 g; Fiber, 0 g; Sodium, 115 mg.

■ **P r o c e d u r e**

1. Bring the dashi to a simmer. Carefully add salt to taste.
2. Add soy sauce. (The soup should be crystal clear.)

3. Cut lemon zest into very fine julienne.
4. Trim and wash the snow peas. Cut them crosswise at an angle, making diamond shapes. Blanch them 1 minute in boiling water. Drain and cool.
5. Peel and devein the shrimp. Blanch them in boiling water just until cooked, no more than 1 minute. Drain.
6. Rinse soup cups or bowls in hot water to warm them. In each bowl put 1 shrimp, a few pieces of snow peas, and a few threads of lemon zest.
7. Make sure that the soup is very hot—almost at the boiling point—and ladle 6 oz (200 mL) into each bowl. Serve at once.

V A R I A T I O N S

Garnish: Clear soup garnish can be varied considerably. Always use just a few carefully chosen items. Don't clutter the bowl. The effect should be like an elegant little still-life painting seen through the perfectly clear soup. All cutting should be done carefully and neatly. Garnish items include:

Tofu, cut in small cubes

Cooked pork loin or chicken breast, cut in small dice, batonnet, or julienne

Lobster tail, in thin slices

Cooked fish, separated into flakes (use a type that separates into large, firm flakes, such as snapper or cod)

Small clams, steamed and removed from shell (the broth can be clarified, diluted, and used for soup base instead of dashi)

Carrots, cut julienne

Fresh white mushrooms, sliced thin

Dried shiitake mushrooms, soaked, simmered, and cut into julienne

Wakame (a type of seaweed); soak until soft, cut into small pieces and discard the hard ribs, and simmer in the soup 2 minutes

Chinese cabbage, shredded

Watercress leaves

Fresh ginger root, cut into fine shreds (use only a few shreds per serving)

Bamboo shoots, sliced thin

White radish, sliced thin or shredded

Miso Soup

Miso soup is made simply by dissolving miso (fermented paste made of soybeans, barley, and/or rice) in dashi. The two main categories of miso are *white miso*, which is actually light yellowish in color and has a sweet, mild taste, and *red* or *dark miso,* which comes in varying shades of reddish brown and is stronger and saltier in taste. General proportions for soup are 4 tbsp (60 mL) red miso or 6 tbsp (90 mL) white miso, per quart (liter) of dashi. Put the miso in a small bowl and carefully stir in a ladleful of hot dashi. Stir until completely lump-free. Add enough dashi so the miso is thin and pourable. (Do not add miso directly to soup, or it will not mix in properly.) Carefully stir the dissolved miso into the remaining hot dashi. Season to taste and, if desired, add 1–2 tsp (5–10 mL) soy sauce. Add desired garnish as for clear soup, except that the garnish can be added directly to the soup kettle. Because this is a heartier soup, it is more often garnished with tofu and vegetables than is more delicate seafood. Stir before serving, as the miso settles out.

Caldo Verde

Portions: 16   Portion size: 10 fl oz (300 mL)

U.S.	Metric	Ingredients
2 fl oz	60 mL	Olive oil
12 oz	350 g	Onion, chopped fine
1 clove	1 clove	Garlic, chopped fine
4 lb	1.8 kg	Potatoes, peeled and sliced
4 qt	4 L	Water
1 lb	450 g	Hard, spicy garlic sausage (see note)
to taste	to taste	Salt
to taste	to taste	Pepper
2 lb	900 g	Kale

■ P r o c e d u r e

1. Heat oil in a soup pot. Add the onion and garlic. Cook slowly until soft, but do not brown.
2. Add the potatoes and water. Simmer until the potatoes are very tender.
3. Purée the soup or, for a coarser texture, simply mash it in the pot.
4. Cut the sausage into thin slices. Heat it slowly in a sauté pan to cook off some of the fat. Drain.
5. Add the sausage to the soup. Simmer 5 minutes. Season to taste.
6. Remove the hard center ribs from the kale. Shred the leaves as fine as possible, about as thin as threads.
7. Add to the soup. Simmer 5 minutes. Check the seasoning.
8. This soup should be accompanied by chunks of coarse peasant bread.

Per serving:
Calories, 270; Protein, 10 g; Fat, 15 g (48% cal.); Cholesterol, 25 mg; Carbohydrates, 26 g; Fiber, 3 g; Sodium, 370 mg.

Note: Because authentic Portuguese *chouriço* sausage is not widely available, you may substitute Spanish *chorizo* or Italian pepperoni.

 ## Lightly Saffroned Mussel Soup

Yield: about 3¼–3½ qt (3.25–3.51 L)   Portions: 12
Portion size: 10 fl oz (300 mL)

U.S.	Metric	Ingredients
4 qt	4 L	Mussels
2½ oz	80 g	Shallots, minced
3	3	Garlic cloves, crushed
2 oz	70 g	Celery
1	1	Bouquet garni (see p. 152)
1½ pt	800 mL	White wine
3½ oz	100 g	Carrot, cut julienne
3½ oz	100 g	Leek, cut julienne
3 oz	80 g	Celery, cut julienne
1½ oz	50 g	Butter
1 pt 3 fl oz	600 mL	Crème fraîche
4 knife tips	4 knife tips	Powdered saffron (see note)
18	18	Egg yolks
to taste	to taste	Pepper
3 tbsp	20 g	Minced chives

■ P r o c e d u r e

1. Clean the mussels thoroughly.
2. Place the mussels, shallots, garlic, celery, bouquet garni, and white wine in a covered pot. Cook until the mussels are open.
3. Remove the mussels with a slotted spoon. Remove the mussels from their shells and, if necessary, remove any remaining beards from the mussels. Discard the shells.
4. Carefully strain the cooking liquid through cheesecloth, pouring carefully so that any sand is left in the cooking pot.
5. Sweat the julienned vegetables in the butter until just tender. Reserve for garnishing the soup.
6. Measure the cooking liquid and add enough fish stock to bring the volume to 3 qt (3 L). Bring to a boil. Allow to reduce by 30–50%, depending on the saltiness of the liquid.
7. Place half of the crème fraîche in a small bowl. Stir a little of the hot broth into the cream, then stir into the broth. Add the saffron and bring back to a boil.
8. Mix the egg yolks with the remaining crème fraîche. Temper with a little of the hot soup, then add the mixture to the soup. Place on low heat and heat gently without letting it boil.
9. Taste and season with a little pepper and, if necessary, salt. (Because mussels are salty, you will probably not need to add salt. Taste carefully.)
10. To serve, place the julienned vegetables and the mussel meats in the bottoms of warmed broad soup plates, using about 1 oz (25 g) vegetables and 2½ oz (70 g) mussels per portion. Ladle the hot soup into the plates. Sprinkle with chives.

Per serving:
Calories, 510; Protein, 30 g; Fat, 32 g (58% cal); Cholesterol, 420 mg; Carbohydrates, 13 g; Fiber, 1 g; Sodium, 660 mg.

Note: To measure something as precious as saffron powder, use the tip of a clean, dry knife to measure out the amount needed. If using saffron threads instead of powder, use a generous pinch of the threads.

Velouté Agnes Sorel (Chicken and Leek Soup)

Yield: 3–3½ qt (3–3.5 L) plus garnish   *Portions: 12*
Portion size: 8 fl oz, plus 2½ oz garnish (250 mL, plus 75 g garnish)

U.S.	Metric	Ingredients
2	2	Chickens, 3 lb (1.5 kg) each
2	2	Carrots, medium
2	2	Onions, medium
2	2	Celery stalks
1	1	Leek
5 qt	5 L	Water
1	1	Bouquet garni (see p. 152)
13 oz	400 g	Leeks, white part only
1 lb	500 g	White button mushrooms
3 oz	100 g	Butter
3 oz	100 g	Rice powder (see note)
5 oz	150 g	Crème fraîche
5 oz	150 g	Crème fraîche
4	4	Egg yolks
5 oz	150 g	Cooked cured beef tongue

Per serving:
Calories, 300; Protein, 15 g; Fat, 21 g (63% cal.); Cholesterol, 145 mg;
Carbohydrates, 13 g; Fiber, 1 g; Sodium, 230 mg.

Note: If rice powder (also called cream of rice) is not available, substitute an equal weight of potato starch.

■ P r o c e d u r e

1. Trim the chickens. Trim the vegetables as necessary.
2. Place the chickens in the water with the whole vegetables and bouquet garni. Simmer for 30 minutes.
3. Remove the chickens from the broth. Strain the broth.

4. Thinly slice the leeks.
5. Wash the mushrooms. Cut the white part of the caps into julienne until you have 7 oz (200 g) julienne. Set the mushroom julienne aside for the garnish. Slice the remainder of the mushrooms.
6. Sweat the sliced mushrooms and the leeks in butter.
7. Add 3 qt (3 L) of the poaching liquid. Simmer about 30 minutes.
8. Dissolve the rice powder in a little of the hot liquid, then gradually stir into the broth. Simmer a few minutes until thickened.
9. Transfer to a blender or food processor and process until smooth.
10. Mix in the crème fraîche, then strain through a fine sieve.

11. Mix the second amount of crème fraîche and the egg yolk together in a small bowl. Add some of the hot liquid to temper, and mix well.
12. Incorporate the liaison into the soup over very low heat. Do not allow the soup to boil, or the egg yolks will curdle.

13. Remove the breast meat from the chickens. Save the legs for another use. Cut the breast meat into julienne. Similarly, cut the cured tongue into julienne.
14. Gently sauté the reserved mushroom julienne in just enough butter to coat the bottom of a sauté pan.
15. To serve, place the julienned garnish in the bottom of a serving bowl, then pour the hot soup over the garnish.

Zuppa di Ceci e Riso

Portions: 16   Portion size: 6 fl oz (175 mL)

U.S.	Metric	Ingredients
3 fl oz	90 mL	Olive oil
1	1	Garlic clove, chopped
1½ tsp	7 mL	Rosemary, chopped fine
1 lb	450 g	Canned plum tomatoes, crushed or chopped
5 pt	2.5 L	White stock (chicken, veal, or pork)
6 oz	175 g	Rice (raw)
1½ lb	700 g	Cooked chickpeas, drained
to taste	to taste	Salt
to taste	to taste	Pepper
3 tbsp	45 mL	Chopped parsley

Per serving:
Calories, 170; Protein, 6 g; Fat, 7 g (36% cal.); Cholesterol, 5 mg; Carbohydrates, 22 g; Fiber, 4 g; Sodium, 55 mg.

■ P r o c e d u r e

1. Heat the oil over moderate heat. Add the garlic and rosemary. Cook for a few seconds.
2. Add the tomatoes. Bring to a boil, then simmer until most of the juice has evaporated.
3. Add the stock and the rice. Simmer for 15 minutes.
4. Add the chickpeas and continue to simmer until the rice is tender and the flavors are well blended.
5. Season to taste with salt and pepper.
6. Sprinkle each portion with a little chopped parsley.

Minestrone

Yield: 6 qt (6 L)   *Portions: 24*   *Portion size: 8 fl oz (250 mL)*

U.S.	Metric	Ingredients
4 fl oz	125 mL	Olive oil
1 lb	500 g	Onions, sliced thin
8 oz	250 g	Celery, small dice
8 oz	250 g	Carrots, small dice
2 tsp	10 mL	Garlic, chopped
8 oz	250 g	Green cabbage, shredded (See p. 519 for technique)
8 oz	250 g	Zucchini, medium dice
1 lb	500 g	Canned tomatoes, crushed
5 qt	5 L	White stock
1 tsp	5 mL	Dried basil
6 oz	175 g	Small macaroni, such as ditalini
1½ lb	750 g	Drained, canned cannellini or other white beans (2 No.2 cans)
¼ cup	60 mL	Chopped parsley
to taste	to taste	Salt
to taste	to taste	Pepper
as needed	as needed	Parmesan cheese, grated

■ Procedure

1. Heat the oil in a heavy pot over medium heat.
2. Add the onions, celery, carrots, and garlic. Sweat them in the oil until they are almost tender. Do not brown.
3. Add the cabbage and zucchini. Stir to mix the vegetables. Continue to sweat them for another 5 minutes.
4. Add the tomatoes, stock, and basil. Bring to a boil, reduce heat, and simmer until the vegetables are almost cooked. (Do not overcook. The soup will continue to cook when the pasta is added.)
5. Add the pasta and continue to simmer the soup until the pasta is cooked.
6. Add the beans and bring the soup back to a boil.
7. Add the parsley. Season to taste with salt and pepper.
8. Just before service, stir in the parmesan cheese, or serve the cheese separately.

Per serving
Calories, 150; Protein, 7 g; Fat, 7 g (40% cal.); Cholesterol, 10 mg; Carbohydrates, 17 g; Fiber, 3 g; Sodium, 200 mg.

Scotch Broth

Yield: 6 qt (6 L)   *Portions: 24*   *Portion size: 8 fl oz (250 mL)*

U.S.	Metric	Ingredients
6 qt	6 L	White lamb stock
4 oz	125 g	Barley
1½ lb	750 g	Lean, boneless lamb shoulder or shank, cut in small dice
4 oz	125 g	Butter
12 oz	375 g	Onions, cut brunoise
8 oz	250 g	Carrots, cut brunoise
8 oz	250 g	Celery, cut brunoise
4 oz	125 g	Leeks, cut brunoise
4 oz	125 g	Turnips, cut brunoise
to taste	to taste	Salt
to taste	to taste	White pepper
as needed	as needed	Chopped parsley

■ Procedure

1. Bring 1 qt (1 L) of the stock to a boil in a saucepan.
2. Add the barley and cover the pan. Simmer until tender.
3. Bring the remaining 5 qt (5 L) of stock to a boil in another pot.
4. Add the lamb and cover the pot. Simmer until the meat is almost tender.
5. Heat the butter in a heavy pot over medium heat. Add the vegetables and sweat them in the butter until nearly tender.
6. Add the lamb and stock from step 4. Simmer until the meat and vegetables are tender.
7. Add the cooked barley and stock from step 2. Simmer about 5 minutes, until the flavors are well blended.
8. Season to taste with salt and pepper.
9. At serving time, sprinkle each portion with a little chopped parsley.

Per serving:
Calories, 120; Protein, 8 g; Fat, 7 g (51% cal.); Cholesterol, 50 mg; Carbohydrates, 7 g; Fiber, 2 g; Sodium, 80 mg.

Gazpacho

Yield: 2½ qt (2.5 L)   Portions: 12   Portion size: 6 fl oz (200 mL)

U.S.	Metric	Ingredients	Procedure
2½ lb	1.2 kg	Tomatoes, peeled and chopped fine	1. If a blender is available, combine all ingredients in the blender and process until liquefied.
1 lb	500 g	Cucumbers, peeled and chopped fine	2. If a blender is not available, combine all ingredients except the olive oil. Pass through a food mill. If a smoother soup is desired, then pass through a fine sieve. Rub the solids through the sieve to purée them. Place the mixture in a stainless-steel bowl. Using the wire whip, slowly beat in the olive oil.
8 oz	250 g	Onions, peeled and chopped fine	
4 oz	125 g	Green bell peppers, seeded and chopped fine	
½ tsp	2 mL	Crushed garlic	
2 oz	60 g	Fresh white bread crumbs	
1 pt	500 mL	Water or tomato juice, cold	
3 fl oz	90 mL	Red wine vinegar	
4 fl oz	125 L	Olive oil	
to taste	to taste	Salt	3. Add salt, pepper, and cayenne or pepper sauce to taste.
to taste	to taste	Pepper	4. If necessary, adjust the tartness by adding a little lemon juice or vinegar.
to taste	to taste	Cayenne or hot red pepper sauce	
to taste	to taste	Lemon juice or vinegar	5. Chill the soup thoroughly.
		Garnish:	6. Combine garnish ingredients in a small bowl or bain-marie.
2 oz	60 g	Onion, small dice	7. At service time, ladle 6 oz (200 mL) gazpacho into chilled soup cups. Top with 1–2 tbsp (15–30 g) diced vegetable garnish. If desired, gazpacho may be served with ice cubes.
2 oz	60 g	Cucumber, small dice	
2 oz	60 g	Green pepper, small dice	

Per serving:
Calories, 130; Protein, 2 g; Fat, 10 g (63% cal.); Cholesterol, 0 mg;
Carbohydrates, 11 g; Fiber, 2 g; Sodium, 36 mg.

Gazpacho

Chilled Melon and Mint Soup

Yield: 3 qt (3 L)   **Portions: 12**   **Portion size: 8 fl oz (250 mL)**

U.S.	Metric	Ingredients
3 lb	1.4 kg	Galia melon (see note)
3 lb 8 oz	1.6 kg	Charentais melon (see note)
4 lb	1.9 kg	Honeydew melon
1 lb 4 oz	600 g	Watermelon
to taste	to taste	Lemon juice
to taste	to taste	Sugar
2 oz	60 g	Mint leaves, finely chopped
		Garnish:
as needed	as needed	Mint sprigs

■ P r o c e d u r e

1. Quarter the melons. Scrape the seeds from the galia, Charentais, and honeydew melons. Remove as many seeds as possible from the watermelon. Cut the flesh of each type of melon into balls with a ball cutter and place in a bowl. Cover and refrigerate.

2. Scoop the remaining flesh from the melons. Place in a food processor and purée. (Do not use a blender unless you remove all the watermelon seeds first, as it will chop the seeds into fine bits.) Strain to remove watermelon seeds.

3. Taste and, if required, add lemon juice and sugar to taste.

4. Stir in the chopped mint. Pour over the melon balls and chill for at least 2 hours.

5. At service time, ladle into chilled bowls and garnish with sprigs of mint.

Per serving:
Calories, 60; Protein, 1 g; Fat, 0 g (0% cal.); Cholesterol, 0 mg; Carbohydrates, 15 g; Fiber, 1 g; Sodium, 15 mg.

Note: If galia melon is not available, use yellow-fleshed honeydew. If Charentais melon is not available, use cantaloupe.

Chilled Melon and Mint Soup

■ TERMS FOR REVIEW

clear soup	puréed soup	potage	clarification
vegetable soup	bisque	national soup	clearmeat
consommé	chowder	coagulation	raft
cream soup			

■ QUESTIONS FOR DISCUSSION

1. You have 3 gallons (12 liters) of vegetable soup in the walk-in, prepared by a cook on the morning shift. You are going to serve the soup this evening, and your dinner service lasts from 6 until 10 p.m. How should you prepare the soup for service?

2. What are the most important characteristics of a good consommé?

3. Why is it important not to boil consommé during clarification?

4. What is the function of egg whites in clearmeat? mirepoix? tomato product?

5. In what order would you add the following items to a vegetable soup during cooking?

Carrots	Shredded cabbage	Tomatoes
Barley	Diced cooked beef	

6. Using Method 1 or 2, describe how you would prepare cream of watercress soup.

10 Understanding Meats and Game

Meat is muscle tissue. It is the flesh of domestic animals (cattle, hogs, and lambs) and of wild game animals (such as deer). As a cook, chef, or food service operator, you will spend more of your time and money on meats than on any other food.

It is important, then, to understand meats thoroughly in order to cook them well and profitably. Why are some meats tender and some tough? How can you tell one cut from another when there are so many? How do you determine the best way to cook each cut?

In order to answer questions like these, it is helpful to start at the most basic level of composition and structure. We then proceed to discuss grading and inspection, basic cuts, and appropriate cooking and storage methods. In addition, we discuss the characteristics of variety meats and of popular game meats. Only then can we best approach the individual cooking methods and recipes presented in the following chapters.

COMPOSITION, STRUCTURE, AND BASIC QUALITY FACTORS

After reading this chapter, you should be able to

1. **Describe the composition and structure of meat and explain how they relate to meat selection and cooking methods.**

2. **Explain the use of the federal meat inspection and grading system in selecting and purchasing meats.**

3. **Explain the effect that aging has on meat and identify the two primary aging methods.**

4. **Identify the primal cuts of beef, lamb, veal, and pork, and list the major fabricated cuts obtained from each of them.**

5. **Select appropriate cooking methods for the most important meat cuts, based on the meat's tenderness and other characteristics.**

6. **Prepare variety meats.**

7. **Identify the characteristics of game meats and select the appropriate cooking methods for them.**

8. **Determine doneness in cooked meat.**

9. **Store fresh meat and frozen meat to gain the maximum shelf life.**

COMPOSITION

Muscle tissue consists of three major components: water, protein, and fat.

WATER

Water is about 75 percent of muscle tissue. With such a high percentage of water, you can see why *shrinkage* can be a big problem in cooking meat. Too much moisture loss means dry meat, loss of weight, and loss of profit.

PROTEIN

Protein is an important nutrient and the most abundant solid material in meat. About 20 percent of muscle tissue is protein.

As we learned in Chapter 4, protein **coagulates** when it is heated. This means it becomes firmer and loses moisture. Coagulation is related to doneness. When protein has coagulated to the desired degree, the meat is said to be "done." Doneness is discussed later in this chapter.

After protein has coagulated, applying higher heat *toughens* it.

FAT

Fat accounts for up to 5 percent of muscle tissue. Of course, more fat may surround the muscles. A beef carcass can be as much as 30 percent fat.

Because of health and dietary concerns, many meat animals are being bred and raised with a lower fat content than in past years. Nevertheless, a certain amount of fat is desirable for three reasons:

1. **Juiciness.**
    Marbling is fat that is deposited within the muscle tissue. The juiciness we enjoy in well-marbled beef is due more to fat than to moisture.

    Surface fat protects the meat—especially roasts—from drying out during cooking as well as in storage. Adding surface fats where they are lacking is called **barding**.

2. **Tenderness.**
    Marbling separates muscle fibers, making them easier to chew.

3. **Flavor.**
    Fat is perhaps the main source of flavor in meat. A well-marbled Prime (top grade) steak tastes "beefier" than the same cut of a lower grade.

CARBOHYDRATE

Meat contains a very small amount of carbohydrates. From the standpoint of nutrition, its quantity is so small that it is insignificant. It is important, however, because it plays a necessary part in the complex reaction, called the Maillard reaction (see p. 65), that takes place when meats are browned by roasting, broiling, or sautéing. Without these carbohydrates, the desirable flavor and appearance of browned meats would not be achieved.

STRUCTURE

MUSCLE FIBERS

Lean meat is composed of long, thin muscle fibers bound together in bundles. These determine the *texture* or *grain* of a piece of meat. Fine-grained meat is composed of small fibers bound in small bundles. Coarse-textured meat has large fibers.

Feel the cut surface of a tenderloin steak, and compare its smooth texture to the rough cut surface of brisket or bottom round.

CONNECTIVE TISSUE

Muscle fibers are bound together in a network of proteins called connective tissue. Also, each muscle fiber is covered in a sheath of connective tissue.

It is important for the cook to understand connective tissue for one basic reason: *Connective tissue is tough.* To cook meats successfully, you should know

- Which meats are high in connective tissue and which are low.
- What the best ways are to make tough meats tender.

1. **Meats are highest in connective tissue if**
- They come from muscles that are more exercised. Muscles in the legs, for example, have more connective tissue than muscles in the back.
- They come from older animals. Veal is more tender than meat from a young steer, which, in turn, is more tender than meat from an old bull or cow. (Young animals have connective tissue, too, but it becomes harder to break down as the animal ages.)

2. **Meats high in connective tissue can be made more tender by using proper cooking techniques.**
   There are two kinds of connective tissue: collagen, which is white in color, and elastin, which is yellow.

- Collagen.
  Long, slow cooking in the presence of moisture breaks down or dissolves collagen by turning it into gelatin and water. Of course, muscle tissue is about 75 percent water, so moisture is always present when meats are cooked. Except for very large roasts, however, long cooking by a dry-heat method has the danger of evaporating too much moisture and drying out the meat. Therefore, *moist-heat cooking methods at low temperatures are most effective for turning a meat high in connective tissue into a tender, juicy finished product.*
      Other factors also help tenderize collagen:

  Acid helps dissolve collagen. Marinating meat in an acid mixture, or adding an acid such as tomato or wine to the cooking liquid, helps tenderize it.

  Enzymes are naturally present in meats. They break down some connective tissue and other proteins as meat ages (see "Aging," pp. 261–262). These enzymes are inactive at freezing temperatures, slow-acting under refrigeration, active at room temperature, and destroyed by heat above 140°F (60°C).

  Tenderizers are enzymes such as papain (extracted from papaya) that are added to meats by the cook or injected into the animal before slaughter. Exercise care when using enzyme tenderizers. Too long an exposure at room temperature can make the meat undesirably mushy.

- Elastin.

    Older animals have a higher proportion of elastin than younger animals.

    Elastin is not broken down in cooking. Tenderizing can be accomplished only by *removing the elastin* (cutting away any tendons) and by mechanically breaking up the fibers, as in

    Pounding and cubing (cubed steaks)

    Grinding (hamburger)

    Slicing the cooked meat very thin against the grain (as in London broil)

INSPECTION AND GRADING

Cooks and food service operators in Canada are assisted in their evaluation of meats by a federal inspection and grading system.

INSPECTION

1. **Inspection** is a *guarantee of wholesomeness*, not of quality or tenderness. It means the animal was not diseased and the meat is clean and fit for human consumption.

2. That the meat passed inspection is indicated by a round stamp with a crown and the number of the processing plant (Figure 10.1).

3. Inspection is required by law. All meat must be inspected.

    The following discussion explains the above three points in more detail.

    The Canadian Food Inspection Agency (CFIA) is responsible for carrying out meat inspection. All meat that is shipped from province to province or is exported to other countries is required to be inspected. This includes about 90 percent of all meats processed in Canada. The remainder is subject to provincial inspection regulations, which are similar to the federal regulations. The CFIA also inspects all meat imported into Canada.

    Beginning 24 hours before slaughter, all livestock process at federally registered plants undergoes a two-step inspection process. First, all live animals are inspected in order to separate any animal that may be diseased or otherwise unsuitable for slaughter. Certified veterinarians examine these separated animals for wholesomeness.

    After slaughter, the internal organs and lymph nodes of each animal are inspected, and any animal found to be diseased is removed from further processing. Condemned carcasses are disposed of as required by the CFIA.

QUALITY GRADING

1. **Grading** is a *quality* designation.

2. Quality grading is indicated by a maple leaf stamp (Figure 10.2a).

3. Yield grading indicates the proportion of lean meat in a carcass. It is indicated by a triangular stamp. Figure 10.2b shows a yield grade stamp.

4. Grading is *not required by law*.

    Quality grading is based on the texture, firmness, and color of the lean meat, the age or maturity of the animal, and the marbling (the fat within the lean).

    All these factors must be considered together. For example, old, tough meat can still have marbling, but it would rate a low grade because of the other factors.

Beef Grades

The Canadian Beef Grading Agency is responsible for grading Canadian beef. This private, nonprofit organization administers the grades according to federal standards. Grading is voluntary, and producers must pay a fee for the service.

There are 13 Canadian beef grades. The best grades, beginning with the highest, are Prime, AAA, AA, and A. All prime and A grades must be from young animals. The meat

Figure 10.1
Canada inspection stamp for meat
Courtesy of the Canadian Food Inspection Agency

Figure 10.2
Canada quality grade stamp (a) and yield grade stamp (b) for meat
Courtesy of the Canadian Food Inspection Agency

(a)

(b)

must be firm, fine grained, and well developed. The muscle tissue must be bright red. The fat must be white and firm. Carcasses that meet these initial requirements are then divided into grades based on the amount of marbling, as follows:

Canada Prime—slightly abundant marbling or higher

Canada AAA—small marbling or higher

Canada AA—at least slight marbling, but less than small

Canada A—at least trace marbling, but less than slight

About 90 percent of all graded Canadian beef carcasses fall within these four grades. Prime and A grades are indicated by a red grade stamp.

Beef carcasses graded as prime or one of the A grades is also yield graded, as follows:

Canada 1—59 percent or more of lean, usable meat

Canada 2—54-58 percent lean, usable meat

Canada 3—53 percent or less of lean, usable meat

Canada B grades are, starting with the highest, B1, B2, B3, and B4. These grades are also given to young animals, but animals that do not meet the requirements for the A grades. They are indicated by a blue stamp.

The lowest grades are D1, D2, D3, D4, and E (there are no C grades). These grades are all from mature animals. The meat is used primarily for ground beef and processed products. They are indicated by a brown stamp.

Veal Grades

Veal carcasses are divided into ten grades: four A grades (A1 through A4), four B grades (B1 through B4), and two C grades (C1 and C2). Grades are based on muscling, meat color, and fat cover. The A grades are the highest, with the best muscling and some creamy white fat. Color ranges from light pink (A1) to red (A4).

Pork Grades

Pork is not graded the way other meats are. Within the industry, carcasses are yield-graded based on the ratio of fat to lean. The carcasses are not stamped, however, and the meat is trimmed at the processing plant before shipment. Thus, the grading system is of concern only to producers in that it is used to determine the price the packer pays the producer.

Lamb Grades

Most lamb produced and sold in Canada is ungraded. Nevertheless, a grading system has been established, so you may find lamb graded Canada AAA, the highest grade. Other grades are Canada C1, Canada C2, Canada D1, and Canada D4. Grades are determined based on the maturity of the carcass, the condition of the break joint in the leg (the joint in young carcasses breaks easily and shows evidence of a blood supply), the color of the muscle (young carcasses have pink to light red meat, not dark red), the color of the fat (white rather than yellow), and the overall muscling and fat cover.

AGING

GREEN MEAT

Soon after slaughter, an animal's muscles stiffen due to chemical changes in the flesh. This stiffness, called *rigor mortis*, gradually disappears. Softening takes three to four days for beef, less time for smaller carcasses like veal, lamb, and pork. This softening is caused by enzymes in the flesh.

Green meat is meat that has not had enough time to soften. It is tough and relatively flavorless. Because it takes several days for meats to reach the kitchen from the slaughterhouse, green meat is seldom a problem with commercially available meats, except when meat is frozen while still green. The problem is sometimes encountered with game killed for home consumption, if the hunter cuts and freezes the meat when it is too fresh.

AGED MEAT

Enzyme action continues in muscle tissue even after meat is no longer green. This tenderizes the flesh even more and develops more flavor. Holding meats in coolers under controlled conditions to provide time for this natural tenderizing is called **aging**.

Beef and lamb can be aged because high-quality carcasses have enough fat cover to protect them from bacteria and from drying. Veal has no fat cover, so it is not aged. Pork does not require aging.

Aging does not mean just storing meat in the refrigerator. *There is a difference between aged meat and old meat.* Conditions must be carefully controlled so the meat becomes naturally tender without spoiling. There are two primary methods used for aging.

1. **Wet aging.**
    Today, most wholesale meat carcasses are broken down into smaller cuts and enclosed in plastic vacuum packs. These packs are usually known by the trade name **Cryovac**®. The air- and moisture-proof packaging protects the meat from bacteria and mold, and it prevents weight loss due to drying. (However, Cryovac-aged meats often lose more weight in cooking than do dry-aged meats.) Vacuum-pack meats must be refrigerated.

2. **Dry aging.**
    Dry aging is the process of storing meats, usually large cuts, under carefully controlled conditions. The meat is not packaged or wrapped, and it is exposed to air on all sides. Temperature, humidity, and air circulation are precisely controlled to prevent spoilage. Ultraviolet lights are sometimes used in aging coolers to kill bacteria.
    Dry-aged meat can lose up to 20 percent of its weight through moisture loss, depending on the size of the cut and how long it is aged. Consequently, dry aging is a more expensive process than wet aging. Dry-aged meats are usually available from specialty purveyors only and at a higher price than wet-aged meats. Many customers are willing to pay a premium for fine dry-aged steaks because they are considered the best for flavor and texture.

Aging increases tenderness and flavor. An off taste is not characteristic of aged meat. *If a meat smells or tastes spoiled, it probably is.* Sometimes meats in vacuum packs have a musty aroma when first opened, but this disappears quickly.

Aging costs money. Storage costs, weight losses due to drying, and heavier trimming due to dried and discolored surfaces all add to the price of aged meat (although wet aging costs less than dry aging). As a meat purchaser, you will have to decide how much quality is worth how much cost for your particular establishment.

IMPS/CMC CLASSIFICATIONS

The IMPS/CMC system assigns a series of numbers to each major category of meat, as detailed in Table 10.1. Beef, for example, is the 100 series. This means that all large beef cuts, from whole carcass to primals and prepared roasts, are assigned a three-digit number from 100 to 199. Portion-size and smaller cuts of beef, such as steaks and stew meat, are assigned a four-digit number, also beginning with 1. For example, a whole beef rib, roast-ready, has the number 109; a beef rib steak, bone in, is 1103.

Note that variety meats and processed meat products, such as cured and smoked meats and sausages, are also categorized (see Table 10.1).

UNDERSTANDING THE BASIC CUTS

The following discussion of meat cuts focuses on the four primary meat categories in the wholesale and retail markets: beef, lamb, veal, and pork. Keep in mind, however, that game animals, discussed later in the chapter, have the same bone and muscle structure and are generally divided into the same or similar cuts as nongame animals.

Meat cuts are based on two factors:

1. The muscle and bone structure of the meat.
2. Uses and appropriate cooking methods of various parts of the animal.

Food service suppliers may follow a set of specifications called **Institution Meat Purchase Specifications** (IMPS). (The **Canadian Meat Council** [CMC] has published a manual that includes the IMPS numbers and names of cuts. The CMC manual also includes cuts that are specific to Canada.) All cuts are described in detail and listed by number. This simplifies purchasing, as you can order by number for exactly the cut you want.

AVAILABLE FORMS: CARCASSES, PARTIAL CARCASSES, PRIMALS, AND FABRICATED CUTS

Beef, lamb, veal, and pork may be purchased in some or all of these forms. Mutton and goat are also given classification numbers, as indicated in Table 10.1, but they have minimal importance in Canadian food service and are not covered here.

CARCASSES

The carcass is the whole animal, minus entrails, head, feet, and hide (except pork, from which only the entrails and head are removed). Whole carcasses are rarely purchased by food service operators because of the skill and labor required in cutting and because of the problem of total utilization.

SIDES, QUARTERS, FORESADDLES, HINDSADDLES

These represent the first step in breaking down a carcass.

Again, these larger cuts are no longer frequently used in food service. Fewer establishments cut their own meats.

1. Beef is split first through the backbone into sides. Sides are divided between the 12th and 13th ribs into forequarter and hindquarter.

2. Veal and lamb are not split into sides but are divided in half into foresaddle and hindsaddle, or the front half and the hind half. The cut is made between the 11th and 12th ribs.

3. Pork carcasses are not divided in this way. They are cut directly into primal cuts (see below).

PRIMAL OR WHOLESALE CUTS

These are the primary divisions of quarters, foresaddles, hindsaddles, and carcasses. These cuts, called primal cuts, are still used, to some extent, in food service, because they

1. Are small enough to be manageable in many food service kitchens.

2. Are still large enough to allow a variety of cuts for different uses or needs.

3. Are easier to utilize completely than quarters or halves.

Each primal may be fabricated, or cut up and trimmed, in several ways. Primal cuts are always the starting point for smaller cuts. For this reason, it will benefit you to be able to identify each one. Study the charts and photos in Figures 10.3 through 10.6. Learn the names of the primals, their location on the carcass, and the most important cuts that come from each. Then, whenever you work with a piece of meat, try to identify it exactly and match it with its primal cut.

(Text continues on p. 267)

Table 10.1 IMPS/CMC Meat Categories	
Series Number	**Series Name**
100	Fresh Beef
200	Fresh Lamb and Mutton
300	Fresh Veal and Calf
400	Fresh Pork
500	Cured, Cured and Smoked, and Cooked Pork Products
600	Cured, Dried, and Smoked Beef Products
700	Variety Meats and Edible By-Products
800	Sausage Products
11	Fresh Goat

Figure 10.3 Beef

Figure 10.3 (a) Primal (wholesale) beef meat cuts

Figure 10.3 (b) Primal (wholesale) beef cuts and their bone structure

Beef rib, roast ready

Beef chuck, boneless, separated into blade, clod, and arm

Beef rib steak

Beef short loin

Beef porterhouse steak

Beef loin

Beef T-bone steak

Beef tenderloin, trimmed

Beef boneless strip loin

Beef outside (bottom) round

Beef round steak

Beef inside (top) round

Beef knuckle, untrimmed

Beef shank, cross cuts

Beef flank steak

Figure 10.4 Veal

Neck · Shoulder · Rack · Loin (Trimmed) · Sirloin · Leg (Sirloin off) · Breast · Flank · Shank · Leg (Sirloin on)

Figure 10.4 (a) Primal (wholesale) veal meat cuts

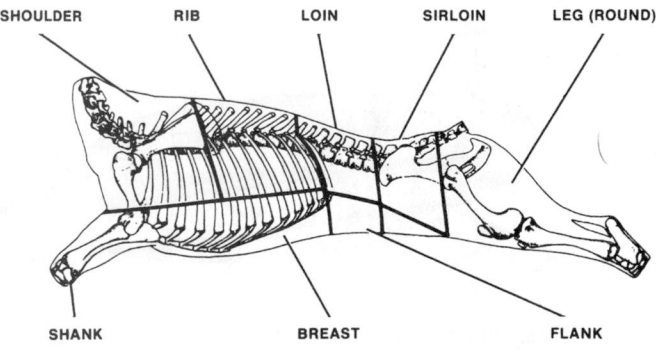

SHOULDER · RIB · LOIN · SIRLOIN · LEG (ROUND) · SHANK · BREAST · FLANK

Figure 10.4 (b) Primal (wholesale) veal cuts and their bone structure

Veal rib roast

Veal breast

Figure 10.5 Lamb

Neck

Rib or rack

Loin

Leg

Shoulder

Shank

Breast

Sirloin

Leg (Sirloin off)

Figure 10.5 (a) Primal (wholesale) lamb meat cuts

SHOULDER   NECK   RIB   LOIN   SIRLOIN   LEG

FORE SHANK   BREAST   FLANK   HIND SHANK

Figure 10.5 (b) Primal (wholesale) lamb cuts and their bone structure

Lamb loin roast   **Lamb arm chop**   **Lamb shoulder blade chop**   **Lamb rib chop**   **Lamb loin chop**

Lamb, square-cut shoulder, whole   **Lamb, whole leg**   **Lamb, boneless shoulder, rolled and tied**   **Lamb foreshank**

Figure 10.6 Pork

Shoulder butt
or Shoulder blade

Fat back

Loin

Jowl

Ham

Foot

Foot

Hock   Shoulder   Bacon side   Side ribs
         (Picnic)   (Belly)

Figure 10.6 (a) Primal (wholesale) pork meat cuts

SHOULDER BUTT   CLEAR PLATE   LOIN   LEG (FRESH OR SMOKED HAM)
                 FAT BACK

JOWL   PICNIC SHOULDER   SIDE RIBS   BACON (SIDE PORK)

Figure 10.6 (b) Primal (wholesale) pork cuts and their bone structure

Pork tenderloin   **Pork shoulder butt**

Full pork loin (includes ribs)   **Pork loin chops**   **Pork rib half and loin half roasts**

FABRICATED CUTS

Primal cuts are fabricated into smaller cuts for roasts, steaks, chops, cutlets, stewing meat, ground meat, and so forth, according to individual customer requirements and, if applicable, IMPS/CMC specifications.

The amount of trim and exact specifications can have many variations. For example, a beef primal rib can be trimmed and prepared for roasting at least nine ways.

Portion-controlled cuts are ready-to-cook meats cut according to a customer's specifications. Steaks and chops are ordered either by weight per steak or by thickness. Portion-controlled cuts require the least work for the cook of all meat cuts. They are also the most expensive per pound of all categories of cuts.

BONE STRUCTURE

Knowing the bone structure of meat animals is essential for:

1. **Identifying meat cuts.**
   The distinctive shapes of the bones are often the best clue to the identification of a cut. Note how the shapes of the bones in the photographs in Figures 10.3 through 10.6 help your recognition.

2. **Boning and cutting meats.**
   Bones are often surrounded by flesh. You will need to know where they are even if you can't see them.

3. **Carving cooked meats.**
   Same reason as number 2.

Study the chart of the beef skeleton in Figure 10.7 and learn the names of the major bones. Then compare the charts in Figures 10.3 through 10.6. You will see that the bone structures for all the animals are identical (except for pork, which has more than 13 ribs). Even the names are the same.

Figure 10.7
Beef bone structure

1. Neck bone	**4. Blade bone**	**10. Pelvis**
2. Backbone	**5. Arm bone**	**10a. Hip bone**
2a. Feather bone	**6. Foreshank bone**	**10b. Rump or aitch bone**
2b. Finger bone	**7. Breastbone**	**11. Leg or round bone**
2c. Chine bone	**8. Rib cartilage**	**12. Knee cap**
3. Tailbone	**9. Ribs**	**13. Hindshank bone**

The photographs in Figures 10.3 through 10.6 depict typical primal and fabricated cuts of beef, lamb, veal, and pork.

MEAT-CUTTING TERMINOLOGY

Although the public refers to retail meat cutters as *butchers*, the meat industry uses this term another way. To **butcher** means to kill and dress a meat animal. To **fabricate** means to cut raw meat into smaller pieces.

A third term, **carve**, also means to cut meat, but this always refers to cooked meat.

BEEF, LAMB, VEAL, AND PORK CUTS

Beef Primal Cuts and Fabricated Cuts

Primal	Major Bones	Common Fabricated Cuts	Primary Cooking Methods
Forequarter			
Chuck (square cut)	Ribs 1–5 Blade bone Backbone (including chine and feather bones) Neck bones Arm bone	Shoulder clod Triangle Boneless inside chuck Chuck tender (top blade) Chuck short ribs Cubed (delicatized) steaks Stew meat Ground chuck	Moist heat
Brisket	Rib bones Rib cartilage Breast bone	Boneless brisket and corned beef brisket Ground beef	Moist heat
Shank	Shank bone	Stew meat Ground beef	Moist heat
Note: Square-cut chuck, brisket, and shank, in one piece, are called *center-cut chuck*.			
Rib	Ribs 6–12 Backbone (chine and feather bones)	Rib roasts (prime rib) Rib steaks Short ribs	Dry heat Moist heat
Plate	Rib bones Tip of breastbone Rib cartilage	Short ribs Stew meat Ground beef	Moist heat
Hindquarter			
(Long loin)		Tenderloin (to have tenderloin in one piece, it must be stripped out of loin before loin is split into short loin and sirloin)	Dry heat
Short loin	Rib 13 Backbone [chine, feather bones, fingerbones (see note)]	Club (wing) steaks T-bone steaks Porterhouse steaks Strip loin Strip loin steaks Short tenderloin	Dry heat
Sirloin	Backbone Hip bone (part of pelvis)	Top sirloin steak, boneless Bottom sirloin steak, boneless Tenderloin butt	Dry heat
Flank	Tip of rib 13	Flank steak Ground beef	Moist heat (exception: flank steak cooked as London broil)
Hip or round	Round (leg) bone Aitch bone (part of pelvis) Shank bone Tailbone	Sirloin tip (knuckle) Inside (top) round Outside (bottom) round Eye of round (part of outside round) Rump Hind shank	Moist heat and dry heat

Note: Finger bones are the short horizontal bones attached to those chine bones that have no ribs attached. They are stems of the Ts in T-bones.

Lamb Primal Cuts and Fabricated Cuts

Primal	Major Bones	Common Fabricated Cuts	Primary Cooking Methods
Foresaddle (front half)			
Shoulder	Ribs 1–6 Arm Blade Backbone (chine and feather bones) Neck bones	Shoulder roasts Shoulder chops Stew meat Ground lamb	Moist heat and dry heat
Breast and shank	Rib bones Breast bone Shank bone	Riblets Breast Stew meat Ground lamb	Moist heat
Rib or rack (see note)	Ribs 7–11 or 7–13 Backbone	Rib roasts (rack) Crown roast Ribs chops	Dry heat
Hindsaddle (hind-half)			
Loin (with or without flank)	Backbone (chine, feather bones, finger bones)	Loin roast Loin chops	Dry heat
Leg	Backbone Tailbone Pelvis (hip bone, aitch bone) Round bone Hind shank	Leg roast Leg chops Sirloin chops Shank	Dry heat Moist heat

Note: Rack and loin attached are called *whole loin double or back*; used mostly for chops. The whole loin may be divided after the 13th rib to yield a rib or rack section containing ribs 7–13.

Veal Primal Cuts and Fabricated Cuts

Primal	Major Bones	Common Fabricated Cuts	Primary Cooking Methods
Foresaddle (front half)			
Shoulder (square cut)	Ribs 1–6 Blade bone Backbone (chine and feather bones) Neck bones Arm bone	Shoulder roasts Shoulder chops Shoulder clod steaks Cubed steaks Stew meat Ground veal	Moist heat and dry heat
Breast	Rib bones Rib cartilage Breast bone	Boneless breast Cubed steaks Ground veal	Moist heat
Shank	Shank bone	Shank cross-cuts (osso buco)	Moist heat
Rib or rack (see note)	Ribs 7–11 or 7–13 Backbone (chine and feather bones)	Rib roast (rack) Rib chops	Dry heat and moist heat

Note: Rack plus connecting portions of breast is called a *bracelet* or *rib and flank, double.*

Primal	Major Bones	Common Fabricated Cuts	Primary Cooking Methods
Hindsaddle (hind-half)			
Loin (with or without flank)	Ribs 12 and 13 or no ribs Backbone (chine, feather bones, finger bones)	Saddle (loin roast) Loin chops	Dry heat and moist heat
Leg	Backbone Tailbone Pelvis (hip bone, aitch bone) Round bone Hind shank	Leg roast Scaloppine or cutlets Shank (osso buco)	Dry heat Moist heat

Note: Rack and loin attached are called *back* or *whole loin*; used mostly for chops. The whole loin may be divided after the 13th rib to yield a rib or rack section containing ribs 7–13.

Pork Primal Cuts and Fabricated Cuts

Primal	Major Bones	Common Fabricated Cuts	Primary Cooking Methods
Foresaddle			
Shoulder picnic	Shoulder (arm) bone Shank bone	Fresh and smoked picnic shoulder Hocks Ground pork Sausage meat	Moist heat
Shoulder butt (shoulder blade)	Blade bone (rib bones, back and neck bones are removed)	Shoulder butt steaks Shoulder roasts Daisy (smoked) Ground pork Sausage meat	Dry heat and moist heat
Loin	Rib bones (see note) Backbone (chine, feather bones, finger bones) Hip bone	Loin roast Loin chops (rib end and tenderloin end) Boneless loin Country-style ribs Canadian-style bacon (smoked)	Dry heat and moist heat
Ham	Aitch bone Leg bone Hind shank bone	Ham Smoked ham Ham steaks	Dry heat and moist heat
Belly	None	Bacon	Dry heat and moist heat
Side ribs	Rib bones Breast bone	Side ribs (belly ribs)	Moist heat
Fatback (back fat)	None	Fresh and salt fatback Salt pork Lard	(Used as cooking fats)
Jowl	None	Jowl	Moist and dry heat
Feet	Foot bones		Moist heat

Note: Pork has more than 13 ribs (unlike beef, lamb, and veal) due to special breeding to develop long loins.

SELECTING MEATS FOR YOUR OPERATION

DECIDING WHICH FORMS TO PURCHASE

Whether you buy whole carcasses, fabricated cuts, or anything in between depends on four factors:

1. How much meat-cutting skill you or your staff has.
2. How much work and storage space you have.
3. Whether or not you can use all cuts and lean trim on your menu.
4. Which form gives you the best cost per portion after figuring in labor costs.

Meat purveyors can usually cut meat more economically than food service operators can because they deal in large volume. Carcasses or primal cuts cost less per pound than fabricated cuts, but they have more waste (fat and bone) and require more labor (which costs money). However, some operators still do some of their own cutting, depending on how they can answer the four questions above. They feel that cutting their own meat gives them greater control over quality.

Some compromises are available. If you want the quality of freshly cut steaks, for example, you might buy boneless strip loins and cut your own steaks to order. You need not buy primal loins.

SPECIFICATIONS

When buying meat, you must indicate the following specifications:

1. **Item name.**
    Include IMPS/CMC number, if applicable.
    Example: 173 Beef Short Loin, Regular

2. **Grade.**
    Example: Canada AAA

3. **Weight range for roasts and large cuts.**
    Portion weight or thickness (not both) for steaks and chops.

4. **State of refrigeration: chilled or frozen.**

5. **Fat limitations, or average thickness of surface fat.**
    Example: 2 cm average, 2.5 cm maximum.
    (This does not apply to veal.)

Meat purchasers may also have to make the choice of whether or not to purchase irradiated meat. **Irradiation** is the process of exposing foods to radiation in order to kill bacteria, parasites, and other potentially harmful organisms. Irradiation does not harm the meat, make it radioactive, or change its structure, flavor, or nutritional value. In Canada, the irradiation of ground beef and poultry is awaiting approval from Health Canada. Currently, only potatoes, onions, wheat flour, whole wheat flour, and whole or ground spices and dehydrated seasonings are approved for irradiation and sale. The Canadian Food Inspection Agency (CFIA) requires that prepackaged wholly irradiated foods include labeling along with a statement that the product has been irradiated and the international symbol for irradiation, the radura, shown on this page.

Some operators refuse to purchase irradiated foods because they or their customers may have concerns about their health effects. The procedure has generated much controversy for other reasons as well. For example, some see the availability of the process as an excuse to avoid normal sanitation procedures. Nevertheless, there is so far no evidence that these foods are harmful for human beings to eat.

Figure 10.8
The radura is the international symbol for irradiation.

COOKING AND HANDLING MEATS

TENDERNESS AND APPROPRIATE COOKING METHODS

The heat of cooking affects tenderness in two ways:

1. It tenderizes connective tissue if moisture is present and cooking is slow.
2. It toughens protein. Even meats low in connective tissue can be tough and dry if cooked at excessively high heats for too long.

THE PRINCIPLE OF LOW-HEAT COOKING

1. High heat toughens and shrinks protein and results in excessive moisture loss. Therefore, low-heat cooking should be the general practice for most meat cooking methods.

2. Broiling seems to be a contradiction to this rule. The reason carefully broiled meat stays tender is that it is done quickly. It takes time for the heat to be conducted to the interior of the meat, so the inside never gets very hot. Meat broiled to the point of being well done, however, is likely to be dry.

3. Roasts cooked at low temperatures have better yields than those roasted at high heat. That is, they shrink less and lose less moisture.

4. Because both liquid and steam are better conductors of heat than air, moist heat penetrates meat quickly. Therefore, to avoid overcooking, meat should be simmered, never boiled.

BREAKING DOWN CONNECTIVE TISSUE

Remember that connective tissue is highest in muscles that are frequently exercised and in mature animals.

Look again at the primary cooking methods (column 4) in the table of meat cuts (p. 268). You should detect a pattern of tender cuts, cooked primarily by dry heat; slightly less tender cuts, cooked sometimes by dry and sometimes by moist heat; and least tender cuts, cooked almost always by moist heat.

The concept of moist-heat cooking needs further explanation as it applies to breaking down connective tissue in meat. The usual explanation of the effect of moist heat on connective tissue is that heat breaks down collagen in the presence of moisture. But meat is about 75 percent water, so *moisture is always present*. Collagen breaks down because of long, slow cooking, no matter what cooking method is used.

The catch is that, for small cuts of meat, dry-heat cooking methods are usually short, quick methods. Cooking must be short, in part because too long an exposure to dry heat results in excessive moisture loss from the product. The terms *moist-heat cooking method* and *dry-heat cooking method* refer to the way in which heat is transferred from the heat source to the food, whether by dry means like hot air or radiation, or moist means like steam or simmering liquid. Because the product is surrounded by moisture when it is simmered, steamed, or braised, moist-heat cooking methods promote moisture retention, not moisture loss, so the cooking time can be as long as desired.

A tough steak on the grill or in the oven doesn't have enough time to become tender before it is dried out. On the other hand, large cuts of less tender meat can be roasted successfully because they are too large to dry out during a long roasting time. A 40-pound (18-kg) roast steamship round of beef can be tender because it takes hours to cook even to the rare stage. A grilled steak cut from the same round, however, is likely to be tough.

To summarize: Long, slow cooking tenderizes collagen. Moist-heat methods are most suitable for long, slow cooking. Dry-heat methods usually are short, quick cooking methods, suitable only for tender cuts, except when larger items are roasted for a relatively long time.

1. **Rib and loin cuts.**
    Always the most tender cuts, used mostly for roasts, steaks, and chops.

    Beef and lamb. Because these meats are often eaten rare or medium done, the rib and loin are used almost exclusively for roasting, broiling, and grilling.

    Veal and pork. Pork is generally eaten well done, and veal is most often eaten well done, although many people prefer it slightly pink in the center. Therefore, these meats are occasionally braised, not to develop tenderness but to help preserve juices. Veal chops, which are very low in fat, may be broiled if great care is taken not to overcook them and dry them out. A safer approach is to use a method with fat, such as sautéing or pan-frying, or to use moist heat.

MILK-FED, GRAIN-FED, OR GRASS-FED

The properties of meats are determined, in part, by the diet of the animals. Most of the beef on the market in North America is grain-fed, even though grass, not grain, is the natural diet of cattle. Feeding cattle grain enables producers to raise and fatten them for market more quickly than letting them browse on grass does. Grain-fed beef is tender and has more marbling than grass-fed beef, and it is preferred by most North American consumers. Grass-fed or pastured beef is usually perceived as less tender and less juicy, although it is lower in saturated fat and may have more health benefits. Its flavor is often described as "beefier" than that of grain-fed beef. Grass-fed beef is common in some other countries, such as the beef-eating and -producing nation of Argentina. In North America, producers of pastured beef are campaigning for more consumer recognition.

The effect of diet can be seen in other meat animals. Traditionally,

(continues next page)

2. **Hip, leg, or round.**

   Beef. The cuts of the round are less tender and are used mostly for braising.

   Top grades, such as Canada Prime and Canada AAA, can also be roasted. The roasts are so large that, roasted at low temperatures for a long time, the beef's own moisture helps dissolve collagen. Inside round (top round) is favored for roasts because of its size and relative tenderness.

   Beef round is very lean. It is best roasted rare. Lack of fat makes well-done round taste dry.

   Veal, lamb, and pork. These meats are from young animals and therefore are tender enough to roast.

   Legs make excellent roasts because large muscles with few seams and uniform grain allow easy slicing and attractive portions.

   Figure 10.9 shows the muscle structure of the round in cross section. A center-cut steak from a whole round of beef, lamb, veal, or pork has this same basic structure.

3. **Chuck or shoulder.**

   Beef. Beef chuck is a tougher cut that is usually braised. Although chuck is not the ideal choice for braising if uniform slices are desired, it makes braised dishes of excellent eating quality. Its connective tissue is easily broken down by moist cooking, yielding moist, tender meat with abundant gelatin content

   Veal, lamb, and pork. These are most often braised but are young enough to be roasted or cut into chops for broiling. Shoulder roasts are not the most desirable because they consist of many small muscles running in several directions. Therefore, they do not produce attractive, solid slices.

4. **Shanks, breast, brisket, and flank.**
   These are the least tender cuts, even on young animals, and are almost always cooked by moist heat.

   Shanks are desirable for braising and simmering because their high collagen content is converted into gelatin that gives body to braising liquids and good eating quality to the meat.

   Beef flank steaks can be broiled (as London broil) if they are cooked rare and cut across the grain into thin slices. This cuts the connective tissue into chewable pieces (see mechanical tenderization, p. 260).

5. **Ground meat, cubed steaks, and stew meat.**
   These can come from any primal cut. They are usually made from trimmings, although whole chucks are sometimes ground into chopped meat. Ground meat and cubed steaks can be cooked by dry or moist heat because they have been mechanically tenderized. Stew meat is, of course, cooked by moist heat.

OTHER FACTORS INFLUENCING CHOICE OF COOKING METHODS

1. **Fat content.**
   Meats high in fat, such as Prime beef or lamb, are generally cooked without added fat, such as by roasting or broiling.

   Meats low in fat, such as veal, are often cooked with added fat to prevent dryness. Sautéing, pan-frying, or braising is generally preferable to broiling for veal chops that are cooked well done.

   Fat can be added to lean meats in two ways:

   - **Barding.** Tying slices of fat, such as pork fatback, over meats with no natural fat cover to protect them while roasting.

   - **Larding.** Inserting strips of fat with a larding needle into meats low in marbling.

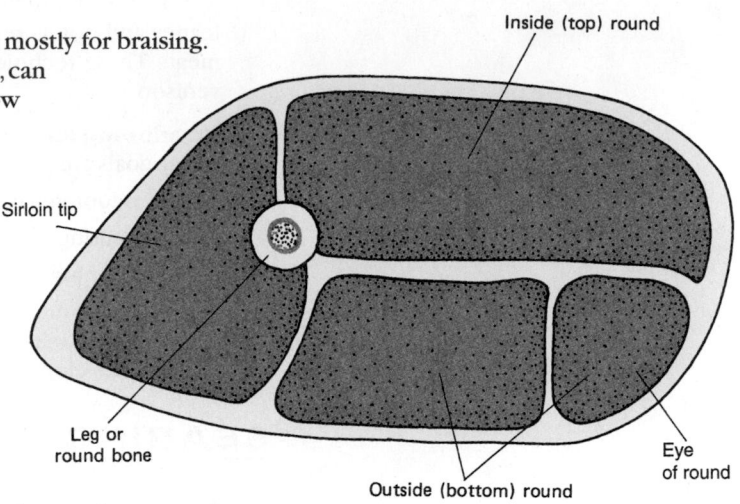

Figure 10.9
Location of the muscles in a whole center-cut round steak of beef, veal, lamb, or pork

the highest-quality veal is considered to be so-called milk-fed veal, more properly called formula-fed. The meat is light pink in color and mild and delicate in flavor. Calves that are fed solid food or that are allowed into a pasture have darker, more reddish meat with a somewhat beefier flavor. Ethical objections are raised about the raising of formula-fed veal because the animals are penned and not allowed much movement. As for the flavor of milk-fed versus pastured veal, this is a matter of personal preference.

The youngest lamb is called *spring lamb.* It is slaughtered before it begins a diet of solid food, and its meat is light in color and delicate in flavor. Older lamb is darker in color and has a more pronounced flavor. After the age of one year, it is no longer called lamb but *mutton,* and it has a still darker color and stronger flavor. Little mutton is sold in North America. (In some markets the name mutton may also be used for goat meat, although this is not traditional English usage.)

These two techniques were developed in Europe when meats were much leaner and not as tender. They are not often used with today's tender, grain-fed meats. These techniques are useful, however, when cooking lean game, such as venison.

2. **Developing tenderness is not the only goal of cooking.**
    Other goals are

    •   Developing flavor.

    •   Preventing excessive shrinkage and nutrient loss.

    •   Developing appearance.

    You must often compromise to get a balanced result. For example, preliminary browning of a roast at high heat increases shrinkage but may be desirable for some roasts to develop flavor and appearance.

SEARING AND "SEALING"

Searing

The purpose of searing meats at high heat is to create desirable flavor and color by browning the surfaces. It was long believed that searing the surface of meat "seals the pores," keeping in juices.

This does not actually happen. Meat does not have pores but rather an open network of fibers. Think of the surface of a steak as resembling the cut end of a thick rope. There are no pores to seal. It is true that heavy browning creates a kind of crust on the surface of the meat, but this crust is no more waterproof than an unbrowned surface.

You can easily demonstrate that this is true. Place a steak or chop on a hot griddle or grill and sear it well. Turn it over and continue cooking. As it cooks, you will see meat juices driven up through the seared top surface. You will continue to hear a sizzling sound, which is the sound of moisture escaping from the meat and quickly vaporizing. Remove the finished steak from the grill and let it set on a plate for a few minutes, and you will see a small pool of juices collect. Everyone who has cooked a steak has seen this demonstration that searing doesn't seal.

Roasts cooked from the start at a low temperature retain more juices than roasts that are seared at high heat first.

Steaks, chops, and cutlets cooked quickly at high heat retain more moisture at first because the intense heat instantly evaporates the juices from the surface of the meat and forces internal juices further into the meat. This permits browning, because moisture would create steam and inhibit browning. However, overcooked steaks are dry whether or not they were seared.

Blanching and "Sealing"

Dropping meat into boiling water doesn't seal the pores either. What actually happens is this: Many proteins dissolve in cold water. When heated, these proteins coagulate and become froth or scum on the surface of the water. When meat is placed into boiling water, some of the protein coagulates inside that meat and not as much is carried out of the meat with the lost moisture. Prolonged cooking shrinks meat as much if started in boiling water as if started in cold water.

COOKING FROZEN MEATS

Some sources recommend cooking some meats from the frozen state, without thawing, in order to eliminate drip loss that occurs during defrosting. However, it is usually better to thaw before cooking because of the following reasons:

1. Frozen meats lose no moisture from defrosting but lose more during cooking. The total loss is about the same as for thawed meats. Besides, the perception of juiciness depends as much or more on fat content than on moisture content.

2. Cooking frozen meats complicates the cooking process and requires adjustments in procedure. It is possible for roasts to be cooked on the outside but still be frozen in the center. Frozen steaks, too, are more difficult to cook evenly than thawed steaks. Thawed meats, on the other hand, are handled like fresh meats.

3. Cooking frozen meats requires extra energy, and energy is expensive. A hard-frozen roast may take 3 times as long to cook as a thawed roast.

DONENESS

DEFINITIONS

The meaning of the term **doneness** depends on whether the cooking method uses dry heat or moist heat.

1. **Dry heat.**
    Meat is "done" when the proteins have reached the desired degree of coagulation (see p. 65), as indicated by internal temperature.

2. **Moist heat.**
    Meat is "done" when connective tissues have broken down enough for the meat to be palatable. With a few exceptions, meat cooked by moist heat is always well done.

DRY-HEAT COOKING

The object of dry-heat cooking is to achieve the desired degree of doneness (protein coagulation) while preserving natural tenderness and juiciness.

Degree of Doneness

As meat cooks, its pigments change color. These color changes indicate degrees of doneness.

Red meat (beef and lamb) changes from red to pink to gray or gray-brown.
*   Rare: browned surface; thin layer of cooked (gray) meat; red interior
*   Medium: thicker layer of gray; pink interior
*   Well done: gray throughout
    (Of course, there are stages in between.)

White meat (veal and pork) changes from pink or gray-pink to white or off-white. It is generally cooked well done, although many cuts of veal may be considered done when still slightly pink in the center.

As explained on page 23, trichinosis is a disease caused by a parasite that lives in the muscle tissue of hogs as well as of some wild animals. In countries in which this disease is a problem, pork must be cooked long enough to eliminate this danger. This parasite is killed at 137°F (58°C), but, to be safe, pork should be cooked to at least 150° to 155°F (66° to 68°C). At this stage, pork is only medium to medium-well done. Some people are happy to eat pork that is still pink in the center, but most people prefer it to be cooked slightly more than this. On the other hand, it is not necessary to cook pork to 185°F (85°C), as older guidelines said. At this temperature, pork is overcooked and dry. For diners who avoid any trace of pink in pork, perhaps the best doneness range is 160° to 170°F (71° to 77°C).

Testing Doneness

Determining doneness is one of the most difficult and critical aspects of meat cooking. Anyone can put a steak on the grill or a roast in the oven. But it takes experience and skill to take it off the fire at the right time.

Color change cannot be used by the cook to test doneness because it would be necessary to cut the meat. Piercing the meat and examining the color of the juices is not a reliable method.

Internal Temperature

Testing the interior of meat with a meat thermometer is the most accurate method of testing doneness. Thermometers are of two types: *standard*, which are inserted before roasting and left in the roast; and *instant-read*, which are inserted at any time, read as soon as the needle stops moving, and pulled out. Whatever thermometer you use, make sure it is *clean* and *sanitary* before inserting it in the meat.

The tip of the thermometer should be inserted into the center of the thickest part of the flesh, not touching fat or bone. Table 10.2 gives internal temperatures of meats at various degrees of doneness.

Table 10.2
Interior Temperatures of Cooked Meats

Meat	Rare	Medium	Well Done
Beef	130°F (54°C)	140°–145°F (60°–63°C)	160°F (71°C)
Lamb	130°F (54°C)	145°F (63°C)	160°F (71°C)
Veal	—	145°–150°F (63°–66°C)	160°F (71°C)
Pork	—	—	165°F–170°F (74°–77°C)

In general, regional traditions of eating well-done or overcooked meats are decreasing, and more people are eating meat cooked rare. For decades, meats cooked to an internal temperature of 140°F (60°C) were called rare, but by today's standards, this is more like medium. Current preferences are reflected in the temperatures given in Table 10.2.

It should be stated that health agencies caution that meats may contain harmful bacteria and parasites. Although studies are still being done, these agencies suggest that meats should be cooked to at least 145°F (63°C) in order to be completely safe. Whether or not 145°F (63°C) is the lowest safe temperature for cooking meats, it is not really accurate to call it rare. In any case, tastes vary from region to region. You should be guided by the preferences of your customers.

You may recall from Chapter 2 that cooking foods to lower temperatures can make them safe. Note, however, that according to Table 2.3 on page 29, the lower the final internal temperature, the longer the product must be held at that temperature. Thus, for example, a roast may be brought to an internal temperature of only 130°F (54°C), but it can be considered safe only if it is held at that temperature for at least 112 minutes.

Clearly, it is not possible to keep a rare steak at its final temperature for 112 minutes before serving it. According to safety standards, then, rare steaks are not considered safe. Those who prefer their steaks rare, however, are not likely to be swayed by this argument and will continue to request meat done to their liking. Each food service operator has to decide whether to please these customers or to follow food safety guidelines.

In any case, whether or not 145°F (63°C) is the lowest safe temperature for cooking most meats, it is not really accurate to call it rare.

Carry-Over Cooking

Internal temperature continues to rise even after the meat is removed from the oven. This is because the outside of roasting meat is hotter than the inside. This heat continues to be conducted into the meat until the heat is equalized throughout the roast.

Carry-over cooking can raise internal temperatures from 5°F (3°C) for small cuts to as much as 25°F (14°C) for very large roasts, such as a steamship round. The usual range is 10°F to 15°F (6°C to 8°C) for average roasts. Exact temperature change depends on the size of the cut and on the oven temperature.

Remove roasts from the oven when internal temperature is 10° to 15°F (6° to 8°C) below the desired reading. Let the roast stand 15 to 30 minutes before slicing. For example, a beef rib roast cooked rare should be removed from the oven when the thermometer reads about 115° to 120°F (46° to 49°C). Carry-over cooking will bring the temperature to 130°F (54°C) after the roast has stood for 30 minutes.

Touch

The small size of steaks and chops makes using a thermometer impractical. The cook must depend on his or her sense of touch.

Meat gets firmer as it cooks. Pressing it lightly with the finger indicates its doneness. Press the center of the lean part, not the fat.

Rare. Feels soft, gives to pressure, though not as soft and jellylike as raw meat.

Medium. Feels moderately firm and resilient, springs back readily when pressed.

Well done. Feels firm, does not give to pressure.

Time-Weight Ratio

Many charts give roasting times per pound of meat. However, these can be approximate only and should be used in estimating and planning cooking times, not in determining doneness.

Many factors other than weight and oven temperature determine cooking time:

1. Temperature of meat before roasting.

2. Amount of fat cover (fat acts as an insulator).

3. Bones (bones conduct heat faster than flesh, so boneless roasts cook more slowly than bone-in roasts of the same weight).

4. Size, type, and contents of oven.

5. Number of times oven door is opened.

6. Shape of the cut (a flat or a long, thin cut cooks more quickly per pound than a round, compact cut).

You can see why roasting requires experience and judgment. To be really accurate and useful, a complete roasting chart that took all variables into consideration, including all meat cuts, sizes, oven temperatures, and so on, would be the size of a small book.

Point 6 above is a key point. It is the *thickness* of a cut, *not its weight*, that determines cooking time—the time needed for the heat to penetrate to the center. Half a pork loin roasts in about the same time as a whole pork loin, even though it weighs half as much. The thickness is the same.

Perhaps the most useful roasting time charts are those you make yourself. When you regularly roast the same cuts in the same way with the same equipment and find they always take the same length of time, you may use those times as indicators of doneness. Many food service operators have developed charts based on their own practices, and the correct times are indicated on their individual recipe cards.

MOIST-HEAT COOKING

Meat cooked by moist heat is cooked well done and actually beyond well done. Doneness is indicated by tenderness, not by temperature.

Piercing with a meat fork is the usual test for doneness. When the prongs of the fork go in and slide out easily, the meat is done.

Low temperatures—no higher than simmering—are essential to avoid toughening protein in moist-cooked meats. Oven temperatures of 250° to 300°F (120° to 150°C) are usually sufficient to maintain a simmer.

JUICINESS

Three main factors determine the juiciness—or, more accurately, the *perception* of juiciness—in cooked meat. Despite the myths about basting with stock and about searing meat to "seal in the juices," the following are the only factors that have any significant effect on juiciness.

1. **Internal fat.**
   Fat makes meat taste juicy. This is why well-marbled meats taste juicier than lean meats. We understand the health effects of too much fat in the diet, but there is no getting around the fact that high fat content makes meat taste juicier. When lean meats are cooked, other measures (such as using sauces and, especially, avoiding overcooking) are used to increase palatability.

2. **Gelatin.**
   This factor is most important in braised meats. Gelatin, converted from connective tissue, helps bind water molecules and hold them in the meat. Also, the texture of the gelatin improves the texture of the meat in the mouth. This is why braised beef shank tastes so much juicier than braised outside round.

3. **Protein coagulation.**
   As you know, as protein coagulates or is cooked, it breaks down and begins to lose water. The more it is cooked, the more it contracts and forces out moisture. No mat-

ter how much you try to sear to "seal in the juices," this moisture will be lost. The only way to minimize the loss is to avoid overcooking.

COOKING VARIETY MEATS

Variety meats, also known as *offal*, include various organs, glands, and other meats that don't form a part of the dressed carcass of the animal.

For cooking purposes, we can divide the most popular variety meats into two groups:

Glandular meats	*Muscle meats*
Liver	Heart
Kidneys	Tongue
Sweetbreads	Tripe
Brains	Oxtails

Glandular meats do not consist of muscle tissue like regular meats but instead are internal organs or glands. This fact is important for two reasons.

First, because they do not consist of bundles of muscle fibers, the texture of glandular meats is unlike that of regular meats. Because they are not muscle tissue, they are naturally tender and do not need long, slow cooking like muscular variety meats do. If organ meats are dry and tough, it is usually because they have been overcooked.

Second, glandular meats are much more perishable than muscle meats. While some muscle meats, especially beef, benefit from aging, organ meats must be very fresh to be of the best quality. Liver, sweetbreads, and brains must be used within a day or two after purchase. If brains or sweetbreads must be kept longer, they should be blanched as described below so they will keep another day or two.

Heart, tongue, oxtails, and tripe are made of muscle tissue, just like other meats from the carcass. They are all tough, however, and must be cooked for a long time by simmering or braising in order to be made tender.

LIVER

Calf's liver is the most prized because it is tender and delicate in flavor. It is easily recognized by its pale, pinkish color. Most calf's liver is served pan-fried, sautéed, or broiled.

Beef liver is darker in color (see accompanying photo), stronger in flavor, and tougher than calf's liver. It is also pan-fried or broiled, and it is frequently braised.

Pork liver is also available, but it is used mostly in pâtés and sausages.

Top: calf's liver slice. Bottom: beef liver slice.

Preparation

- Remove outer skin.
- Slice on the bias about ¼ inch (½ cm) thick. Slicing is easier if liver is partially frozen.
- Remove tough membranes.

Cooking

- Cook to order. Do not cook ahead.
- To broil: Brush with (or dip in) oil or melted butter. Broil according to basic procedure for meats.
- To pan-fry, griddle, or sauté: Dredge in seasoned flour. Cook in desired fat over moderately high heat.
- *Do not overcook*, unless customer requests well done. To be moist, liver must be slightly pink inside. Liver cooked well done is very dry.
- Serve with bacon, French-fried or smothered onions, or seasoned butter.

KIDNEYS

Veal and lamb kidneys are the most popular, especially in the more upscale restaurants. They are usually prepared by sautéing and broiling. Beef kidneys are tougher and more strongly flavored. They are often cooked by braising and served in specialty items, like steak and kidney pie. Pork livers not often used.

Veal kidneys weigh about 8 to 12 oz (225 to 350 g) each. Lamb kidneys are very small, about 1½ to 3 oz (40 to 85 g) each. If you purchase whole lamb or veal carcasses, you will find a pair of kidneys inside the cavity, attached to the small of the back in the region of the tenderloin and surrounded by a heavy layer of fat or suet.

Left: lamb kidney. Right: veal kidney.

Preparation

If the kidney is encased in fat, pull the fat away with your hands and use a knife to cut it away from the core area where the ducts emerge from inside the kidney.

Lamb kidneys are usually broiled and served two or three per portion, or as part of a mixed grill. Butterfly them by splitting them almost in half, starting at the curved or convex side. Spread them open and skewer them to hold them open during cooking.

Veal kidneys can be broiled like lamb kidneys, but they are most often cut up, sautéed, and served in a sauce. To prepare them for sautéing, first split them in half. Remove the white ducts from the center. Then cut into large dice or thick slices.

Cooking

There are two main pitfalls to cooking kidneys. First, they become tough and rubbery if overcooked. Properly cooked, they are pink in the middle and still tender and juicy. Cooking time is very short.

Second, they have a high moisture content, which can interfere with proper sautéing. Make sure the pan is very hot before adding the kidneys, and do not overcrowd the pan. Failure to do this results in kidneys that are boiled in their juices rather than sautéed.

To avoid overcooking when sautéing over high heat, do not try to brown the kidneys too heavily. Brown them only lightly and remove them from the pan when they are still somewhat rare. Set them aside while you deglaze the pan and prepare the sauce. During this time, some juices will be released from the kidneys. Drain this juice and add it to the sauce if desired, or discard it if you feel that the flavor is too strong. Finally, add the kidneys to the sauce and warm them gently. Do not let them simmer long. Serve at once.

SWEETBREADS

Sweetbreads are the thymus glands of calves and young beef animals. (The gland gradually disappears as the animal matures.) They are considered a delicacy and are often expensive. Sweetbreads are mild in flavor and delicate in texture. They are usually braised or breaded and sautéed in butter.

Before cooking, sweetbreads should be prepared according to the following procedure (see Figure 10.10):

1. Soak in several changes of cold water for several hours or overnight. This removes blood, which would darken the meat when cooked.

2. Blanch in simmering salted water for 10 minutes. Some chefs like to add a little lemon juice or vinegar to the water to preserve whiteness and make the meat firmer.

3. Refresh under cold water and peel off membranes and connective tissue.

4. Press between two trays, with a light weight on top, and refrigerate for several hours. If desired, wrap in cheesecloth before pressing, as shown in Figure 10.10.

5. Prepare for cooking:

   - For braising, leave whole or cut into large dice.

   - For breading and sautéing, split in half horizontally. Pass through Standard Breading Procedure or dredge in flour.

Figure 10.10 Preparing sweetbreads.

(a) Raw sweetbreads.

(b) After the sweetbread has been blanched, peel off the membrane.

(c) Wrap the sweetbreads in clean cheesecloth.

(d) Tie the ends securely.

(e) Place in a hotel pan or other flat pan and top with another pan.

(f) Place weights in the top pan and refrigerate for several hours.

BRAINS

Brains are not a popular item, but they are delicate in both flavor and texture. Calf's brains are the most frequently used.

Brains are very perishable and should be cooked as soon as possible. They are also fragile and must be handled carefully.

Brains must be pre-prepared according to the following procedure. They may then be served hot with black butter (p. 177) or cooled, then dipped in batter, deep-fried, and served with tomato sauce.

1.   Soak in fresh water, as for sweetbreads.

2.   Peel off outer membrane (this may be done before or after poaching).

3.   Poach 20 minutes in court bouillon made of 1 oz (25 mL) lemon juice or vinegar per pint (500 mL) of salted water, plus a bouquet garni.

4.   Drain and serve immediately, or cool in fresh, cold water.

HEART

Heart, usually from veal or beef, is very tough and lean. It can be braised or simmered, or it may be ground and added to chopped meat for casserole dishes and meatloaf.

Before cooking, trim coarse fibers and veins inside and at top.

TONGUE

Cooked beef *tongue* is popular as a cold, sliced meat for sandwiches. It may be fresh, cured, or smoked. Veal and lamb tongues are also available.

Tongue is almost always cooked by simmering. After simmering, remove the skin and trim the gristle at the base of the tongue before slicing.

OXTAILS

Oxtails contain flavorful meat and a rich gelatin content, making them highly desirable for soups and stews.

To disjoint oxtails, cut into sections at the joints with a French knife or butcher knife. Do not use a cleaver, or you may splinter the bones.

TRIPE

Tripe is the muscular stomach lining of meat animals. Although lamb and pork tripe are sometimes available, beef tripe is by far the most widely used. Because cattle have four stomachs, there are four kinds of beef tripe. Honeycomb tripe, from the second stomach, is the kind most widely available. Other kinds, however, can be substituted in recipes that call for honeycomb tripe. In France, another type of beef tripe, known as **gras-double**, is popular; it is smooth rather than honeycombed.

Most tripe that comes from the market has been partially cooked, but it still requires several hours of simmering to be made tender. Undercooked tripe is chewy and somewhat rubbery, but tripe that has simmered long enough is tender, with a pleasant gelatinous texture.

To prepare, first remove any lumps of fat by pulling or cutting them off. Next, blanch the tripe, if desired. Although it is already partially cooked when purchased, blanching freshens it. Place it in a pot with cold, salted water. Bring to a boil, simmer 5 to 10 minutes, drain, and rinse under cold water.

OTHER VARIETY MEATS

Intestines

The most common use for intestines is to make sausage casings. These are discussed in Chapter 26.

Chitterlings are pork intestines that are treated like tripe. They are blanched or simmered, then braised or fried. Chitterlings are generally available in 10-pound (4.5-kg) pails. Because they shrink a great deal when simmered, this quantity yields only 3 pounds (1.3 kg) or less of finished product.

Caul

Pig's **caul** is a fatty membrane covering the animal's stomach. It looks somewhat like a delicate piece of lace. Its main uses are to line terrines and to wrap forcemeats and other foods so they hold their shape during cooking and do not dry out. Sausage patties wrapped in caul are called *crêpinettes* (see p. 839). The advantage of using caul instead of fatback to line terrines is that the caul is so thin it melts away almost completely during cooking.

Feet

Feet are exceptionally rich in gelatin. For this reason, they are added to soups, stews, and stocks to add richness and body. Indeed, some stews made with feet, such as Tripes à la Mode de Caen, may be so rich in gelatin that not only do they solidify when cold but they can even be unmolded and sliced like cold cuts.

Pig's feet are readily available in most markets. Calf's feet and ox's feet are also available, but often only on the wholesale market. The feet from older animals have less gelatin. If a recipe calls for a calf's foot but none is available, in most cases you can substitute two pig's feet.

GAME AND SPECIALTY MEATS

The term **game** is used to refer to poultry and meat animals normally found in the wild. However, most of the "wild" game that has become so popular on restaurant menus is actually from farm-raised animals. Venison farms, in particular, have become numerous and productive, supplying a growing demand.

Farm-raised game birds are discussed along with other poultry in Chapter 12. This section is concerned with furred game.

Although a great variety of game, large and small, can be found on hunters' tables, the supply of game for the restaurant and retail markets is more limited. Venison, the most popular game item, is the main subject of this section. Other products, such as boar and hare, are occasionally available as well. In addition, domestic rabbit is considered here, although its meat has little in common with true game.

The French terms for game meats are often used on menus and in cooking manuals and references. To clarify these terms, a list of those most commonly used follows:

Chevreuil: often translated as "venison" but refers specifically to the roe deer, the most prized European variety

Cerf: red deer; often farm raised

Daim: fallow deer; often farm raised

Marcassin: young boar, especially boar under six months of age

Sanglier: boar

Lapin: rabbit

Lapereau: young rabbit

Lièvre: hare

Levraut: young hare

Venaison: usually translated as "venison," the term in fact refers to the meat of any game animal

VENISON

Several varieties of deer are raised on farms for use as meat, including the red deer and the smaller fallow deer. Deer meat is typically called *venison*. An important advantage of farm-raised venison, besides its year-round availability, is that the cook can be assured that it is from young, tender animals. In the wild, young animals less than two years old are likely to have tender meat, but the meat rapidly becomes tough as the animal matures and ages. The tradition of marinating game for several days in strong wine marinades originates, in large part, from efforts to tenderize hunted game enough to make it palatable.

Marination, Flavor, and Tenderness

The first thing to be said about farm-raised venison is that it is milder in flavor than venison hunted in the wild. It has little, if any, of the strong, gamy flavor usually associated with wild game. In fact, a farm-raised venison steak tastes rather like an especially flavorful lean cut of beef. Those who enjoy strong, gamy flavors may even find farmed venison a little bland. Although it does have some tenderizing effect, marination is not necessary for commercially raised venison because the meat is already tender. Nevertheless, marinating is widely used as a flavoring technique. Much of the flavor traditionally associated with venison, in fact, is due less to its gaminess than to the red wine marinades that were invariably used.

To retain more of the natural flavor of the meat, cook it without marination, or let it marinate for only a short period (30 minutes to 3 or 4 hours) with the desired seasonings and flavoring ingredients. Modern quick marinades are often simple and may contain only a few ingredients.

Fat Content

Venison, like other game, is very low in fat. This makes it especially popular with health-conscious diners. It also makes the meat likely to become dry unless the cook takes great care.

The loin and leg, being tender, are best cooked by dry-heat methods and served rare or medium done. If cooked longer, they will dry out. Roast these cuts whole, either bone-in or deboned, or cut them into steaks, cutlets, and medallions, and sauté, pan-fry, or broil them, taking care not to overcook.

Whole leg of venison, completely boned, seamed, and vacuum packed, is available. Weights range from 5 to 10 pounds (2 to 4.5 kg). Whole bone-in saddle weighs from 5 to 20 pounds (2.3 to 9 kg), while the loin muscle weighs about half that after boning and trimming.

Tougher cuts, chiefly the shoulder, neck, and breast, are braised, stewed, or made into ground meat or sausage. These cuts are also lean, but because they are higher in connective tissue and gelatin, they take more readily to stewing and braising.

To generalize, farm-raised venison can be treated like very lean beef. Take care not to cook it to the point of dryness.

BONE STRUCTURE OF GAME

The bone and muscle structure of furred game such as venison and elk is the same as that of familiar meats such as beef and lamb. The carcasses are also broken down and fabricated in the same ways. After you have become familiar with the charts and diagrams on pages 264–267, you can apply the same cuts to venison and other large game.

Unlike those larger game animals, however, rabbit is cut differently, so separate illustrations are provided in this section, beginning on page 283.

BOAR

Boar is a type of wild pig. Its meat is somewhat similar to pork, except that it is leaner and its flavor fuller and richer. Boar is now raised commercially on a few farms and is available in limited quantities.

Boar is somewhat more difficult to cook than venison and other game because, like pork, it must be cooked until well done. At the same time, it is leaner and less tender than domestic pork, so it often tends to be somewhat dry and chewy. Special care must be taken to cook it adequately without overcooking. Because boar is usually tougher than farm-raised venison, its legs or hams are better suited for braising or slow roasting, while the loins can be used for roasts or cut into medallions and sautéed.

Traditionally, boar is handled much like venison, and typical recipes call for red wine marinades. Although marinating a white meat in red wine may seem strange at first, this treatment actually works very well with boar. The red wine accentuates the more pronounced flavor of boar (as compared to pork) and makes it taste more like game.

OTHER LARGE GAME

Various other meats are sometimes found in food service kitchens. *Elk, caribou, moose,* and *antelope* are all similar to venison and are handled in much the same way. The first three of these, especially moose, are larger than deer, so it may be necessary to allow for longer cooking times when using venison recipes for them.

Buffalo, or *American bison,* is raised on ranches in the western United States and Canada and handled like beef. Flavor and cooking characteristics are similar to those of beef, but the meat is somewhat richer in flavor and has less fat and cholesterol than beef.

RABBIT

Domestic rabbit is a versatile meat that can be cooked in most of the same ways as chicken. In fact, in some countries it is classified as poultry. Some typical recipes for rabbit are included in Chapter 11, but nearly any chicken recipe can be used for domestic rabbit as well. In addition, many recipes for veal or pork are adaptable to rabbit.

Rabbit's light, delicate meat is often compared to chicken, but there are differences. It is somewhat more flavorful than chicken, with a mild but distinctive taste that is not exactly like that of other poultry or meat. Also, it is very lean (more like chicken or turkey breast than legs) and can become dry if overcooked.

**Figure 10.11
Cutting rabbit for stews and sautés.**

(a) Cut off the hind legs, separating them at the hip joint.

(b) Cut off the forelegs by cutting under the shoulder blade.

(c) Cut off the hip bone.

(d) Cut through the backbone to separate the bony rib section from the meaty loin or saddle.

(e) Carefully separate the remaining rib bones from the loin and remove them. The saddle can then be cut crosswise through the backbone into pieces if desired.

(f) This is the cut-up rabbit, with the forelegs and rib section on the left, the saddle in the center, and the hind legs and hip bone on the right.

Rabbit takes well to marination, and, of course, it can also be cooked without prior marination. Either way, it can be cooked by long, slow simmering, braising, or stewing, or it can be quickly cooked by sautéing, grilling, or roasting.

The structure of rabbit, of course, is like that of other land mammals rather than like that of poultry. Cutting methods divide the meaty hind legs, the bonier forelegs, and the choice saddle or back section (râble in French). The whole carcass, cut up, is used for stews and sautés, while the saddle alone is often roasted. It may be boned or bone-in. (See Figure 10.11.)

Small rabbits, 3 pounds (1.5 kg) or less, are the best for cooking. Mature rabbits, weighing about 4 to 5 pounds (about 2 kg), tend to be tougher and drier.

HARE

Hare is a wild cousin of the rabbit. (Please note that rabbits and hares are different animals. The American jackrabbit, for example, is actually a hare, not a rabbit.) Unlike domestic rabbit, with its light-colored, delicate meat, hare has flesh that is dark reddish-brown and gamy.

Hares seven to eight months old and weighing about 6 pounds (2.7 kg) make the best eating. Larger ones, more than 8 pounds (3.6 kg), are likely to be tough and stringy.

Because its structure is the same, hare is cut the same way as rabbit.

Roast Saddle of Hare

Like other game, hare is very lean and therefore becomes dry if overcooked. If roasted, it should be removed from the oven while rare or at least still pink. Rare roast hare has an attractive, deep red color. A typical classic preparation of saddle of hare is as follows. Note that this is also the classic treatment for roast venison.

1. Marinate the saddle of hare in a red wine marinade (such as the venison marinade on p. 304).

2. Brown it on top of the stove and roast it rare or medium done, about 15 minutes at 425°F (220°C).

3. Remove the loin muscles from the bone and cut lengthwise into thin slices. Remove the tenderloins from the underside of the saddle and leave whole or slice as desired.

4. Serve it with a poîvrade sauce (p. 175).

STORAGE OF MEATS

The quality of the finished product depends not only on proper selection and cooking of meats but also on proper storage. Fresh meat is highly perishable. The high cost of meat makes it essential to avoid spoilage.

FRESH MEATS

1. Check purchases on arrival to ensure that purchased meat is of good quality.

2. Do not wrap tightly. Bacteria and mold thrive in moist, stagnant places. Air circulation inhibits their growth. Store loosely to allow air circulation between pieces, but cover cut surfaces to prevent excessive drying.

3. Do not open vacuum-packed meats until ready to use.

4. Store at 32° to 36°F (0° to 2°C). Meat does not freeze until about 28°F (−2°C).

5. Keep meats separated in cooler (or, even better, in separate coolers) and on worktable to avoid cross-contamination.

6. Use as soon as possible. Fresh meats keep well for only two to four days. Ground meats keep even less well because so much surface area is exposed to bacteria.

Cured and smoked products may keep up to one week. Frequent deliveries are better than long storage.

7. Do not try to rescue meats that are going bad by freezing them. Freezing will not improve the quality of spoiling meat.

8. Keep coolers clean.

FROZEN MEATS

1. Wrap frozen meats well to prevent freezer burn.

2. Store at 0°F (–18°C) or colder.

3. Rotate stock—first in, first out. Frozen meats do not keep indefinitely. Recommended shelf life at 0°F (–18°C) for beef, veal, and lamb: 6 months; for pork: 4 months (pork fat turns rancid easily in the freezer).

4. Defrost carefully. Tempering in the refrigerator is best. Defrosting at room temperature encourages bacterial growth.

5. Do not refreeze thawed meats. Refreezing increases loss of quality.

6. Keep freezers clean.

■ TERMS FOR REVIEW

coagulation	aging	butcher	sweetbreads
marbling	Cryovac	fabricate	tripe
connective tissue	dry aging	carve	gras-double
collagen	Institution Meat Purchase	irradiation	caul
elastin	Specifications	barding	game
inspection	Canadian Meats Council	larding	venison
grading	primal cuts	doneness	boar
yield grade	fabricated cuts	carry-over cooking	hare
green meat	portion-controlled cuts	variety meats	

■ QUESTIONS FOR DISCUSSION

1. Many people assume that the leaner a meat is, the better it is. Do you agree? Explain.

2. What is connective tissue? Why is it important for the cook to understand connective tissue?

3. Flank steak (beef) is high in connective tissue, yet it is often broiled and served in thin slices as London broil. How is this possible?

4. You are in charge of a large hospital food service. Why might you choose Canada Grade AA or A rather than a higher grade beef for making pot roast and stew?

5. Why are portion-controlled meats so widely used in food service, even though their per-pound cost is higher?

6. Can you explain why veal loin, a tender cut, is sometimes braised, while veal shoulder, a less tender cut, is sometimes roasted?

7. Which of the following cuts are you more likely to braise? Which might you roast?

Beef chuck	Corned beef brisket
Lamb shanks	Ground pork
Veal rib	Beef strip loin
Beef rib	Lamb leg
Pork shoulder	

8. Table 10.2 indicates the internal temperature of rare roast beef as 130°F (54°C). Why, then, would you remove a roast rib from the oven when the temperature on the meat thermometer reads 115°F (46°C)?

9. Why are weight-time roasting charts inadequate for determining the doneness of roast meats?

10. Describe the fat content of game meats such as venison, boar, and elk. Explain how the fat content affects how game meats are handled and cooked.

11. How does farm-raised venison differ from wild venison?

CHAPTER 11

Cooking Meats and Game

This chapter presents basic cooking methods as they apply to beef, lamb, veal, pork, and game such as venison. It is important that you have read and understood the basic material in Chapter 10, especially the sections on matching particular cuts to appropriate cooking methods and on testing for doneness. If necessary, please review those sections as well as the discussion of basic cooking methods in Chapter 4.

The procedures given here are general. Be aware that they may be modified slightly in specific recipes. Nevertheless, the basic principles still hold. In addition, your instructors may wish to show you variations or methods that differ from those presented here.

The recipes that follow each of the procedures for roasting, sautéing, braising, and so on are intended to illustrate the basic techniques. Each time you prepare one of these recipes, you should be thinking not just about that one product but about the techniques you are using and how they can be applied to other products. It is helpful to compare the recipes in each section, to see how they are alike and how they are different. This way you will be learning to cook, not just to follow recipes.

ROASTING AND BAKING

Remember the definitions of *roast* and *bake* (Chapter 4): to cook foods by surrounding them with hot, dry air, usually in an oven. Roasting is a dry-heat method. No water is used, and the meat is not covered, so steam can escape. There is no real distinction between the terms *roast* and *bake*. Both terms are used for the same procedure, but the word *bake* is more likely to be used for small cuts of meat, as well as vegetables, fish, breads, and pastries.

In principle, roasting meats is a simple procedure. The prepared cut of meat is placed in an oven at a selected temperature, and it is removed when done. What could be easier?

However, there are many variables, and chefs often disagree about proper roasting procedures, especially when it comes to the fine points. In this section, you will learn a roasting procedure that you can apply to most meats. But first we discuss in more detail several of the points of disagreement and some of the possible variations.

SEASONING

Salt added to the surface of meat just before roasting will penetrate the meat only a fraction of an inch during cooking. The same is true of the flavors of herbs, spices, and aromatics. In the case of smaller cuts of meat, such as beef tenderloin or rack of lamb, the seasoned, browned crust that forms during roasting is an important part of the flavor of the finished dish. Although opinions vary, many chefs advocate seasoning such roasts immediately before roasting so the salt doesn't have time to draw moisture to the surface, which inhibits browning.

In the case of large roasts, such as beef ribs and steamship rounds, there is so little crust in proportion to meat that seasoning before roasting has little effect. Also, if the surface of the roast is mostly fat covering or bone, the seasoned fat and bones may not even be served, so the seasoning has little effect.

With roasts of any size, two alternatives to seasoning just before roasting are often used:

- Marinate the meat or apply seasonings in advance, to give the time for flavors to penetrate. See page 141 for a discussion of marinades and dry seasoning rubs.
- Serve the meat with a flavorful sauce, gravy, or jus. The sauce serves as a seasoning and flavoring for the meat.

Another way to add flavor to roasted meats is to smoke-roast them. Commercial smoker ovens roast meats in the same way as conventional ovens, except that they also have a smoke-generating unit that passes smoke through the oven chamber, flavoring foods as they cook. The flavor of wood smoke in cooked meats is so popular that some restaurants have even installed wood-burning hearth ovens to bake and roast meats, pizza, and other items.

Stovetop smoke roasting is an alternative to smoker ovens. The procedure is explained on page 71. Although there are no recipes for smoke-roasted meats in this chapter, examples of smoke-roasted fish and poultry can be found on pages 374 and 462.

TEMPERATURE

Low-Temperature Roasting

As we discussed on page 274, it was once thought that starting the roast at a high temperature "seals the pores" by searing the surface, thus keeping in more juices.

We now know that this is not the case. Repeated tests have shown that *continuous roasting at a low temperature* gives a superior product with

1. Less shrinkage.
2. More flavor, juiciness, and tenderness.
3. More even doneness from outside to inside.
4. Greater ease in carving.

After reading this chapter, you should be able to

1. **Cook meats by roasting and baking.**
2. **Cook meats by broiling, grilling, and pan-broiling.**
3. **Cook meats by sautéing, pan-frying, and griddling.**
4. **Cook meats by simmering.**
5. **Cook meats by braising.**
6. **Cook variety meats.**

Low roasting temperatures generally range from 250° to 325°F (120° to 160°C), depending on

1. The size of the cut. The larger the cut, the lower the temperature. This ensures that the outer portion is not overcooked before the inside is done.
2. The operation's production schedule. Lower temperatures require longer roasting times, which may or may not be convenient for a particular operation.

Searing

If a well-browned, crusted surface is desired for appearance, such as when the roast is to be carved in the dining room, a roast may be started at high temperature (400° to 450°F/200° to 230°C) until it is browned. The temperature should then be lowered to the desired roasting temperature and the meat roasted until done, as for low-temperature roasting.

High-Temperature Roasting

Very small pieces of meat that are to be roasted rare may be cooked at a high temperature, from 375° to 450°F (190° to 230°C). The effect is similar to that of broiling: a well-browned, crusted exterior and a rare interior. The meat is in the oven for so short a time that there is little shrinkage. Examples of cuts that may be roasted at a high temperature are rack of lamb and beef tenderloin.

Convection Ovens

If a convection oven is used for roasting, the temperature should be reduced about 50°F (25°C). Many chefs prefer not to use convection ovens for large roasts because the drying effect of the forced air seems to cause greater shrinkage. On the other hand, convection ovens are effective in browning and are good for high-temperature roasting.

FAT SIDE UP OR FAT SIDE DOWN

Roasting meats fat side up provides continuous basting as the fat melts and runs down the sides. This method is preferred by perhaps the majority of chefs, although there is not complete agreement.

In this book, we use the fat-side-up method. In the classroom, you should be guided by the advice of your instructor.

BASTING

Basting is unnecessary if the meat has a natural fat covering and is roasted fat side up. For lean meats, *barding* has the same effect. Barding is covering the surface of the meat with a thin layer of fat, such as sliced pork fatback or bacon.

If a roast is basted by spooning pan drippings over it, use only the fat. Fat protects the roast from drying, while moisture washes away protective fat and allows drying. Juices used in basting will not soak into the meat.

Basting with drippings or juices may be used to increase the appetite appeal of the roast because it enhances browning. Gelatin and other solids dissolved in the juices are deposited on the surface of the meat, helping form a flavorful brown crust. This does not increase juiciness, however. Some cookbooks claim that basting forms a waterproof coating that seals in juices, but this is not the case.

Basting sometimes produces more tender roasts for an unexpected reason: Frequent basting interrupts and slows down the cooking. Every time the oven door is opened, the temperature in the oven drops considerably, so the roasting time is longer and more connective tissue breaks down. Thus, it is not the basting but the lower temperature that increases tenderness.

USE OF MIREPOIX

Mirepoix is often added during the last part of the roasting time to flavor the roast and to add extra flavor to the pan juices.

Many chefs feel, however, that the mirepoix adds little flavor, if any, to the roast and that it is actually harmful because the moisture of the vegetables creates steam around the roast. Mirepoix can be more easily added when the gravy is being made. If no gravy or juice is to be served, there may be no need for mirepoix at all.

The use of mirepoix is more important for white meats—veal and pork—which, because they are usually cooked well done, lose more juices and need a good gravy or jus to give them moistness and flavor.

GRAVY AND JUS

The general procedures for making pan gravy are given in Chapter 8 (p. 183). Read or review this section if necessary. The procedure for making jus, given here in the recipe for roast prime rib of beef au jus, is the same except that no roux or other thickening agents are used. In other words, use the methods for making pan gravy (p. 184), but eliminate steps 5 and 6 from Method 1 and step 3 from Method 2.

Basic Procedure for Roasting Meats

1. Collect all equipment and food supplies. Select roasting pans that have low sides (so moisture vapor does not collect around the roast) and that are just large enough to hold the roast. If pans are too large, drippings will spread out too thin and burn.

2. Prepare or trim meat for roasting. Heavy fat coverings should be trimmed to about ½ inch (1 cm) thick.

3. If desired, season meat several hours ahead or the day before.

4. Place meat fat side up on a rack in the roasting pan. The rack holds the roast out of the drippings. Bones may be used if no rack is available. Bone-in rib roasts need no rack because the bones act as a natural rack.

5. Insert a meat thermometer (clean and sanitary) so the bulb is in the center of the meat, not touching bone or fat. (Omit this step if you are using an instant-read thermometer.)

6. Do not cover or add water to the pan. Roasting is a dry-heat cooking method.

7. Place meat in oven, which has been preheated to desired temperature.

8. Roast to desired doneness, allowing for carry-over cooking.

9. If desired, add mirepoix to the pan during the last half of the cooking period.

10. Remove roast from oven and let stand in a warm place 15 to 30 minutes. This allows the juices to be reabsorbed through the meat so less juice is lost when the meat is sliced. Also, resting the meat makes slicing easier.

11. If the meat must be held, place it in an oven or warmer set no higher than the desired internal temperature of the roast.

12. While the roast is resting, prepare jus or pan gravy from the drippings. Mirepoix may be added to the drippings now if it was not added in step 8.

13. Slice the roast as close as possible to serving time. In almost all cases, slice the meat against the grain for tenderness.

Roast Rib of Beef au Jus

Yield: 10 lb (4.5 kg) boneless, trimmed meat
Portions: 25   Portion size: 6½ oz (175 g)
*   20   8 oz (225 g)*
*   1½ oz (50 mL) jus*

U.S.	Metric	Ingredients
20 lb	9 kg	Beef rib, roast ready, bone in (one average-size rib roast)
		Mirepoix:
8 oz	250 g	Onions
4 oz	125 g	Carrots
4 oz	125 g	Celery
2 qt	2 L	Brown stock
to taste	to taste	Salt
to taste	to taste	Pepper

Per 5½ ounces:
Calories, 810; Protein, 52 g; Fat, 65 g (74% cal.); Cholesterol, 180 mg; Carbohydrates, 0 g; Fiber, 0 g; Sodium, 150 mg.

■ Procedure

1. Place the meat fat side up in a roasting pan.
2. Insert a meat thermometer so the bulb is in the center of the meat, not touching bone or fat.
3. Place meat in a preheated 300°F (150°C) oven. Roast until rare or medium done, as desired, *allowing for carryover cooking*.
    Thermometer readings:
    Rare: 120°F (49°C)
    Medium 130°F (54°C)
    (Outer slices will be cooked more than center.)
    Roasting time will be at least 3–4 hours.
4. Remove the meat from the pan and let stand in a warm place 30 minutes before carving.
5. Drain off all but about 3–4 oz (100 g) of the fat from the roasting pan. Be careful to retain any juices in the pan. Add the mirepoix to the pan (see Figure 11.1).
6. Set the pan over high heat and cook until mirepoix is brown and moisture has evaporated, leaving only fat, mirepoix, and browned drippings.
7. Pour off any excess fat.
8. Pour about 1 pt (500 mL) of stock into the roasting pan to deglaze it. Stir over heat until brown drippings are dissolved.
9. Pour the deglazing liquid and mirepoix into a saucepot with the remaining stock. Simmer until mirepoix is soft and liquid is reduced by about one-third.
10. Strain through a china cap lined with cheesecloth into a bain-marie. Skim fat carefully. Season to taste with salt and pepper.
11. For service, stand the roast on its widest end. Cut down beside the bones to free the meat, and slice the meat across the grain.
12. Serve each portion with 1½ oz (50 mL) jus.

V A R I A T I O N S

Roast Rib-Eye Roll, Top Round, Sirloin, or Strip Loin
These cuts may be roasted by the same procedure; roast them on a rack.

Roast Beef with Gravy
Roast desired cut of beef according to the basic recipe. Prepare gravy according to the following recipe.

**Figure 11.1
Preparing pan jus.**

(a) After removing the cooked meat from the roasting pan, degrease the pan. Add mirepoix to the pan and brown on the stovetop or in the oven.

(b) Deglaze with brown stock.

(c) Pour the mirepoix and deglazing liquid into a saucepan. Simmer for the desired time.

(d) Strain through a fine chinois or through a china cap lined with cheesecloth.

Roast Beef Gravy

Yield: approx. 1½ qt (1.5 L)
Portions: 25   Portion size: 2 fl oz (60 mL)

U.S.	Metric	Ingredients	Procedure
as needed	as needed	Pan drippings from roast beef (previous recipe)	1. After removing the roast, add the mirepoix to the drippings in the roasting pan.
		Mirepoix:	2. Set the pan over high heat and cook until mirepoix is brown and moisture has evaporated, leaving only fat, mirepoix, and browned drippings (see Figure 11.1).
8 oz	250 g	Onions	
4 oz	125 g	Carrots	
4 oz	125 g	Celery	3. Pour off and save the fat.
2 qt	2 L	Brown stock	4. Deglaze the pan with some of the stock. Pour the deglazing liquid and mirepoix into a saucepot with the remaining stock. Add the tomato purée. Bring to a boil and reduce heat to a simmer.
4 oz	125 g	Tomato purée	
4 oz	125 g	Flour	5. Make a brown roux with the flour and 4 oz (125 g) of the reserved fat. Cool the roux slightly and beat it into the simmering stock to thicken it.
to taste	to taste	Salt	6. Simmer 15–20 minutes, until all raw flour taste is cooked out and liquid is reduced slightly.
to taste	to taste	Pepper	
to taste	to taste	Worcestershire sauce	7. Strain through a china cap into a bain-marie.
			8. Season to taste with salt, pepper, and Worcestershire sauce.

Per serving:
Calories. 35; Protein, 1 g; Fat, 1.5 g (40% cal.); Cholesterol, 5 mg; Carbohydrates, 4 g; Fiber, 0 g; Sodium, 10 mg.

VARIATION

Jus Lié
Omit tomato paste and roux. Thicken liquid with 1½ oz (50 g) cornstarch or arrowroot blended with ½ cup (100 mL) cold water or stock.

Roast Loin of Pork with Sage and Apples

Portions: 25   Portion size: 1 chop, about 6 oz (175 g) with bone
2 fl oz (60 mL) gravy

U.S.	Metric	Ingredients
14½ lb	6.6 kg	Pork loins, center cut, bone in
1 tsp	5 mL	Salt
½ tsp	2 mL	Pepper
1 tbsp	15 mL	Dried sage
		Mirepoix:
8 oz	250 g	Onion
4 oz	125 g	Carrot
4 oz	125 g	Celery
8 oz	250 g	Apples, peeled, cored, and diced
2½ qt	2.5 L	Chicken stock, veal stock, or pork stock
5 oz	150 g	Flour
to taste	to taste	Salt
to taste	to taste	Pepper
8	8	Tart apples
2 oz	60 g	Butter
1 tbsp	15 mL	Sugar

Per serving:
Calories, 420; Protein, 40 g; Fat, 22 g (48% cal.); Cholesterol, 105 mg;
Carbohydrates, 13 g; Fiber, 2 g; Sodium, 210 mg.

■ P r o c e d u r e

1. With a meat saw, cut off the chine bones so the loins can be carved into chops after roasting.
2. Rub the pork with salt, pepper, and sage.
3. Place the chine bones in a roasting pan. Place the pork loins fat side up on top of the bones. Insert a meat thermometer into the thickest part of the muscle.
4. Place in oven at 325°F (165°C) and roast for 1 hour.
5. Place the mirepoix and the apples in the bottom of the pan and continue to roast until the thermometer reads 160°F (71°C). Total cooking time is about 2–2½ hours.
6. Remove the roast from the pan and hold in a warm place.
7. Set the roasting pan over moderate heat and cook until moisture has evaporated and mirepoix is well browned. Drain off and reserve fat.
8. Deglaze the pan with the stock and pour the contents into a saucepot. Skim well.
9. Make a browned roux with the flour and 5 oz (150 g) of the pork fat. Thicken the gravy with the roux and simmer 15 minutes, until thickened and slightly reduced.
10. While the gravy is simmering, core the apples. They may be peeled or not, as desired. Cut the apples crosswise into slices about ⅜ in. (1 cm) thick. Sauté the slices in a little butter over moderately high heat. Sprinkle them with sugar as they cook. Continue to sauté on both sides until browned and caramelized.
11. Strain the gravy and adjust the seasonings.
12. Cut the roast into chops between the rib bones. Serve each portion with 2 oz (60 mL) gravy. Garnish with caramelized apple slices.

V A R I A T I O N S

Other pork cuts may be roasted as in basic recipe: full loin, loin ends, boneless loin, fresh ham, shoulder.

Roast Loin or Rack of Veal with Sage and Apples
Substitute loin or rack of veal for pork in the basic recipe. Use brown stock instead of white stock.

Roast Stuffed Shoulder of Lamb

Portions: 10　Portion size: 5 oz (150 g) meat and stuffing
2 fl oz (60 mL) gravy

U.S.	Metric	Ingredients
		Stuffing:
4 oz	125 g	Onion, fine dice
1 tsp	5 mL	Garlic, chopped fine
2 fl oz	60 g	Olive oil, vegetable oil, *or* butter
3 oz (about 2 cups)	100 g	Soft, fresh bread crumbs
⅓ cup	80 mL	Chopped parsley
½ tsp	2 mL	Dried rosemary
¼ tsp	1 mL	Black pepper
½ tsp	2 mL	Salt
1	1	Egg, beaten
1	1	Boneless lamb shoulder, about 4 lb (1.8 kg)
as needed	as needed	Oil
as needed	as needed	Salt
as needed	as needed	Pepper
as needed	as needed	Dried rosemary
		Mirepoix:
4 oz	125 g	Onions, chopped
2 oz	60 g	Carrots, chopped
2 oz	60 g	Celery, chopped
2 oz	60 g	Flour
1 qt	1 L	Brown beef stock or lamb stock
4 oz	125 g	Tomatoes, canned
to taste	to taste	Salt
to taste	to taste	Pepper

Per serving:
Calories, 390; Protein, 31 g; Fat, 25 g (57% cal.); Cholesterol, 120 mg; Carbohydrates, 11 g; Fiber, 1 g; Sodium, 275 mg.

■ **P r o c e d u r e**

1. Sauté the onion and garlic in oil until soft. Remove from heat and cool.
2. Combine onion and garlic with the remaining stuffing ingredients and mix lightly.

3. Lay the lamb shoulder out flat, fat side down.
4. Spread the lamb with the stuffing and roll it up. Tie the roll tightly.
5. Rub the meat with oil, salt, pepper, and rosemary.
6. Place the meat on a rack in a roasting pan. Insert a meat thermometer into the thickest part of the meat (not into the stuffing).
7. Place in a 325°F (165°C) oven. Roast the meat about 1½ hours.

8. Place the mirepoix in the bottom of the roasting pan. Baste the meat with fat and continue to roast until the thermometer reads 160°F (71°C). Total cooking time is about 2½ hours.
9. Remove the roast from the pan and let stand in a warm place.

10. Set the roasting pan over high heat to clarify the fat and finish browning the mirepoix. Drain off about three-fourths of the fat.
11. Add the flour to the pan to make a roux, cooking it until it is brown.
12. Stir in the stock and tomatoes and bring to a boil. Simmer, while stirring, until the gravy is thickened and reduced to about 1½ pt (750 mL.).
13. Strain and skim excess fat.
14. Season to taste with salt and pepper.
15. Slice the roast crosswise, so that each slice contains stuffing in the center. When slicing, be careful to keep the slices from falling apart. Serve each portion with 2 oz (60 mL) gravy.

V A R I A T I O N S

Roast Boneless Shoulder of Lamb
Roast tied, boneless lamb shoulder as in basic recipe, without stuffing.

Roast Leg of Lamb
Prepare leg of lamb for roasting as shown in Figure 11.2. Rub with oil, salt, pepper, rosemary, and garlic. Roast as in basic recipe (without stuffing) to rare, medium, or well-done stage. Leg of lamb may be served with natural juices (au jus) instead of thickened gravy, if desired. Approximate yield: 8 lb (3.6 kg) AP leg of lamb yields about 3½ lb (1.6 kg) cooked meat. Yield is less if cooked well done. See Figure 11.3 for carving technique.

Roast Leg of Lamb Boulangère
1½ hours before lamb is done, transfer the meat to a rack over a pan of Boulangère Potatoes (p. 596) and finish cooking.

Figure 11.2 Preparing a leg of lamb for roasting. Fresh hams may be prepared using the same basic technique.

(a) Begin by removing the hip and tail bones.

(b) With a sharp-pointed boning knife, cut along the hip bone to separate bone from meat. Always cut against the bone.

(c) Continue until the hip bone and tailbone are completely removed. Note the round ball joint at the end of the leg bone in the center of the meat.

(d) Trim off excess external fat, leaving a thin covering.

(e) Pull off the skin or fell on the outside of the leg.

(f) Full leg of lamb, ready for roasting. The end of the shankbone and part of the shank meat have been removed.

(g) The leg may be tied into a more compact shape.

(h) The sirloin portion may be cut off and used for another purpose, such as shish kebabs.

Figure 11.3
Carving a leg of lamb. Hams and other leg roasts may be carved using the same basic technique shown here.

(a) Place the roast on a clean, sanitary cutting board. Begin by making a vertical cut through to the bone about 1 in. (2.5 cm) from the end of the shank meat. The small collar of shank meat forms a guard to protect the hand in case the knife slips.

(b) Using long, smooth strokes, cut thin slices on a slight bias as shown.

(c) When slices become too large, angle the knife. When the top of the roast has been completely sliced, turn over and repeat the procedure on the bottom of the roast.

Roast Rack of Lamb

Portions: 8   Portion size: 2 chops   1 fl oz (30 mL) jus

U.S.	Metric	Ingredients
2	2	Racks of lamb, 8 ribs each
to taste	to taste	Salt
to taste	to taste	Pepper
to taste	to taste	Dried thyme
2	2	Garlic cloves, chopped
1 pt	500 mL	White or brown veal stock

Per serving:
Calories, 280; Protein, 19 g; Fat, 22 g (72% cal.); Cholesterol, 75 mg;
Carbohydrates, 0 g; Fiber 0 g; Sodium, 70 mg.

■ P r o c e d u r e

1. Prepare lamb for roasting as shown in Figure 11.4.

2. Place any trimmed-off bones in the bottom of a roasting pan. Place the meat fat side up on top of the bones. Season with salt, pepper, and thyme.

3. Place in hot oven (450°F/230°C) and roast to desired doneness. Rack of lamb is usually roasted rare or medium. Test doneness with a meat thermometer or by the touch method, as for steaks. Total time will be about 30 minutes.

4. Remove the lamb from the roasting pan and hold in a warm place. Leave bones in pan.

5. Set the roasting pan over moderate heat to caramelize the juices and clarify the fat. Pour off the fat.

6. Add the garlic to the pan and cook 1 minute.

7. Deglaze the pan with the stock and reduce by half. Strain, degrease, and season to taste.

8. Cut the meat between the ribs into chops. Serve 2 chops per portion with 1 oz (30 mL) jus.

V A R I A T I O N S

Rack of Lamb aux Primeurs (with Spring Vegetables)

Place the racks on one or two heated serving platters. Garnish the platters with an assortment of spring vegetables, cooked separately: tournéed carrots, tournéed turnips, buttered peas, green beans, rissolé potatoes. Pour the jus into a warm gooseneck or sauceboat. Carve and serve the meat, vegetables, and jus in the dining room.

Rack of Lamb Persillé

Prepare as in basic recipe. Combine the ingredients for Persillade (pear-see-yahd), listed below. Before carving and serving, spread the top (fat side) of each rack with 1 tbsp (15 g) soft butter. Pack the persillade onto the top of the racks and brown under the salamander.

Persillade
4 cloves garlic, minced
2 oz (60 g) fresh bread crumbs (about 1 cup)
⅓ cup (80 mL) chopped parsley

**Roast Rack of Lamb; White Beans Bretonne; and
Steamed Brussels Sprout Leaves**

Figure 11.4
Preparing a rack of lamb for roasting.

(a) Begin by cutting down on both sides of the feather bones all the way to the chine bone.

(b) If a meat saw is available, turn the rack over and cut through the rib bones at the points where they attach to the chine bone.

(c) If a meat saw is not available, use a cleaver. Stand the roast up on end and cut through the rib bones at the point where they join the chine bone. This will separate one rack.

(d) Repeat the procedure on the other side of the chine.

(e) The two halves are separated from the chine.

(f) Trim excess fat from the top of the meat, leaving a thin protective covering. During this step, you should also remove the shoulder blade cartilage, which is embedded in the layers of fat.

(g) To trim the fat and meat from the ends of the bones (called frenching the bones), first cut through the fat in a straight line down to the bone, keeping the cut about 1 in. (2.5 cm) from the tip of the eye muscle.

(h) Score the membrane covering the rib bones. Pull and cut the layer of fat from the bones.

(i) The roast is trimmed and ready to cook.

Smoke-Roasted Pork Shoulder

Yield: approx 4 lb (2 kg) trimmed, boneless meat

U.S.	Metric	Ingredients
8 lb	4 kg	Pork shoulder or butt
2 oz, or as needed	60 g, or as needed	Spice Rub I (below)

Per serving:
Calories, 60; Protein, 7 g; Fat, 3 g (49% cal.); Cholesterol, 25 mg;
Carbohydrates, 0 g; Fiber, 0 g; Sodium, 140 mg.

■ P r o c e d u r e

1. Trim excess external fat from the meat.
2. Rub the meat with the spice rub so it is completely coated with a thin layer.
3. Refrigerate the meat overnight.
4. Cook the meat on racks in a smoke roaster at 250–275°F (120–135°C) until very tender, about 6 hours. When done, the meat should be tender enough to pull apart with a fork.
5. The pork may be cut from the bones and sliced or cut into chunks and served with a barbecue sauce on the side, or it may be shredded, mixed with a little barbecue sauce, and used as a sandwich filling.

V A R I A T I O N

Smoke-Roasted Shoulder of Boar
Substitute shoulder of boar for the pork shoulder.

Spice Rub I

Yield: approx. 6 oz (180 g)

U.S.	Metric	Ingredients
1½ oz	45 g	Paprika
1 oz	30 g	New Mexico chili powder
2 tbsp	30 mL	Dried oregano
2 tbsp	20 mL	Dried thyme
4 tsp	20 mL	Ground coriander
4 tsp	30 g	Ground cumin
2 oz	30 mL	Salt
2 tbsp		Black pepper

Per serving:
Calories, 60; Protein, 7 g; Fat, 3 g (49% cal.); Cholesterol, 25 mg;
Carbohydrates, 0 g; Fiber, 0 g; Sodium, 140 mg.

■ P r o c e d u r e

1. Combine all ingredients and mix well.
2. Store in a tightly sealed container in a dark place.

Barbecued Spareribs

Portions: 24   Portion size: 10 oz (300 g)

U.S.	Metric	Ingredients
18 lb	8.5 kg	Fresh pork spareribs
6 oz, or as needed	180 g, or as needed	Spice Rub I or II
2½ qt	2.5 L	Barbecue Sauce (p. 198) or Chili Barbecue Sauce (p. 199)

Per serving:
Calories, 730; Protein, 47 g; Fat, 54 g (68% cal.); Cholesterol, 190 mg; Carbohydrates, 11 g; Fiber, 2 g; Sodium, 1010 mg.

■ P r o c e d u r e

1. Weigh the spareribs and cut them into 12-oz (350-g) portions.
2. Rub the ribs with the spice rub so they are completely coated with a thin layer.
3. Refrigerate overnight.
4. Place the ribs in a roasting pan with the inside of the ribs down.
5. Place the ribs in a smoker oven or a conventional oven at 300°F (150°C). Bake for 1 hour.
6. Drain the fat from the pans.
7. Spoon about 1 pt (500 mL) barbecue sauce over the ribs to coat them with a thin layer. Turn them over and coat with more sauce.
8. Bake 45 minutes. Turn and coat the ribs with the remaining sauce.
9. Bake until tender, about 30–60 minutes more.
10. Serve the portions whole, or cut into separate ribs for easier eating.

Barbecued Spareribs

 ## Spice Rub II

Yield: approx. 7 oz (200 g)

U.S.	Metric	Ingredients
1½ oz	45 g	Paprika
1½ oz	45 g	Chili powder
2 tsp	10 mL	Dry mustard
2 tbsp	30 mL	Onion powder
1 tsp	5 mL	Celery seed
2 tsp	10 mL	Dried thyme
1 oz	30 g	Sugar
2 oz	60 g	Salt
2 tbsp	30 mL	Black pepper

Per serving:
Calories, 60; Protein, 7 g; Fat, 3 g (49% cal.); Cholesterol, 25 mg; Carbohydrates, 0 g; Fiber, 0 g; Sodium, 140 mg.

■ P r o c e d u r e

1. Combine all ingredients and mix well.
2. Store in a tightly sealed container in a dark place.

Roast Pork Tenderloin with Leeks and Whole-Grain Mustard Sauce

Portions: 12   Portion size: about 8 oz (250 mL) meat
2 fl oz (60 mL) sauce

U.S.	Metric	Ingredients
4 lb	1.8 kg	Leek, white part only, cut julienne
3½ oz	100 g	Butter
5 lb	2.4 kg	Pork tenderloins
to taste	to taste	Salt
to taste	to taste	Pepper
as needed	as needed	Oil
3½ oz	100 g	Shallots, chopped
5 fl oz	150 mL	Dry vermouth
1 pt 4 fl oz	600 mL	Créme fraîche
2½ oz	75 g	Whole-grain mustard
		Garnish:
as needed	as needed	Chervil springs

Per serving:
Calories, 640; Protein, 46 g; Fat, 37 g (53% cal.); Cholesterol, 160 mg;
Carbohydrates, 26 g; Fiber, 4 g; Sodium, 300 mg.

■ P r o c e d u r e

1. Sweat the julienned leek in the butter. Season to taste. Cover and keep warm.
2. Trim the pork fillets and season with salt and pepper.
3. Brown in a little oil. Transfer to an oven preheated to 475°F (250°C) for 10 minutes.
4. Remove the pork fillets, cover with aluminum foil, and set aside to rest. Remove most of the fat from the pan.
5. Add the shallots to the pan. Sweat the shallots, then deglaze with the dry vermouth. Reduce by two-thirds.
6. Add the cream. Bring to a boil, then strain through a fine sieve.
7. Season to taste, then add the mustard. Once the mustard has been added, do not allow the mixture to boil.
8. Slice the pork. Spoon the leeks onto the center of the dinner plates, then arrange the sliced pork around the leeks. Pour 2 oz (60 mL) sauce around the meat. Garnish with sprigs of chervil.

Roasted Loin of Pork with Ginger

Portions: 12   Portion size: 1 chop, about 6½ oz (190 g) with bone
2 fl oz (60 mL) sauce

U.S.	Metric	Ingredients
8 lb	3.6 kg	Pork loin, center cut, bone in
3½ fl oz	100 mL	Oil
3½ fl oz	100 mL	Soy sauce
2½ oz	75 g	Ginger root, fine dice
to taste	to taste	Salt
to taste	to taste	Pepper
12 oz	350 g	Onion, diced
3½ oz	100 g	Carrot, diced
12	12	Garlic cloves, peeled, left whole
1 tbsp	25 g	Tomato paste
1 qt	1 L	Chicken stock
3½ fl oz	100 mL	Honey (preferably acacia honey)
7 fl oz	200 mL	Cider vinegar
to taste	to taste	Salt
to taste	to taste	Pepper

Per serving:
Calories, 410; Protein, 45 g; Fat, 18 g (40% cal.); Cholesterol, 100 mg;
Carbohydrates, 15 g; Fiber, 1 g; Sodium, 170 mg.

■ P r o c e d u r e

1. Trim the pork racks of excess fat and sinews. With a meat saw, cut off the chine bones so that the loin can be cut into chops after cooking. French the bones if desired (see Figure 11.4). The trimmed loin should weigh about 6–6½ lb (2.8 kg). Reserve the trimmings (except for the fat).
2. Mix together the oil, soy sauce, ginger, and seasonings. Marinate the pork with its trimmings for at least 1 hour.
3. Remove the pork rack from the marinade, leaving any pieces of ginger adhering to the meat. Place in an oiled roasting pan and place in an oven preheated to 350°F (175°C).
4. After 10 minutes of roasting, add the bones and trimmings, the onion, carrot, and garlic cloves, and continue roasting until the pork is done, about 1 hour 20 minutes to 1 hour 50 minutes in all.
5. Remove the roast from the pan and hold in a warm place.
6. Place the roasting pan on the stovetop. Add the tomato paste and cook for a few minutes, then add the chicken stock. Cook for 15 minutes.
7. Strain. Reserve the garlic cloves. Skim off any fat.
8. Combine the honey with the vinegar in a saucepan and cook until lightly caramelized.
9. Add the strained cooking liquid and cook for a few minutes, then add the garlic cloves. Reduce until the sauce is thickened enough to lightly coat the back of a spoon. Strain, pressing the garlic cloves well. Season to taste.
10. Serve the pork sliced with the sauce around.

Note: A mixture of caramelized sugar and vinegar is called a *gastrique*. It is used as the base of many sweet and savory sauces, such as orange sauce for roast duck and other sauces with fruit, because it gives a good balance of sweetness and acidity.

Baked Pork Chops with Prune Stuffing

Portions: 25   Portion size: 1 chop
2 fl oz (60 mL) gravy

U.S.	Metric	Ingredients
25	25	Prunes, pitted
1½ lb	750 g	Basic Bread Dressing (p. 424)
25	25	Pork chops, cut thick (at least ¾ in./2 cm)
as needed	as needed	Oil
to taste	to taste	Salt
to taste	to taste	Pepper
8 fl oz	250 mL	Water or white wine
3½ pt	1.75 L	Brown sauce or demi-glace
2 fl oz	60 mL	Sherry (optional)

■ **P r o c e d u r e**

1. Soak the prunes in hot water 15 minutes. Drain and cool.
2. Prepare the dressing and add the prunes. Keep refrigerated until ready to use.
3. Cut a pocket in the pork chops as shown in Figure 11.5.
4. Stuff the pockets with the prune dressing, using 1 prune per chop. Fasten the openings with picks or skewers.
5. Oil a baking pan and place the chops in it. Brush them with oil and season with salt and pepper.
6. Place the chops under the broiler just until lightly browned.
7. Transfer the pan to an oven at 350°F (175°C) and bake for about ½ hour, until chops are cooked through.
8. Remove the chops from the pan and place in a hotel pan for holding. Remove picks.
9. Deglaze the baking pan with the water or wine, degrease, and strain the liquid into the hot brown sauce.
10. Bring to a boil and reduce the sauce slightly to bring to the proper consistency.
11. Add the sherry (if using) and adjust seasoning.
12. Serve 1 chop per portion with 2 oz (60 mL) gravy.

Per serving:
Calories, 500; Protein, 49 g; Fat, 26 g (47% cal.); Cholesterol, 125 mg; Carbohydrates, 16 g; Fiber, 1 g; Sodium, 290 mg.

Figure 11.5
For stuffed pork chops, cut a pocket in the chops as shown.

Glazed Ham with Cider Sauce

Portions: 25   Portion size: 5 oz (150 g) ham
2 fl oz (60 mL) sauce

U.S.	Metric	Ingredients
15 lb	7 kg	Smoked ham
3–4 tbsp	45–60 mL	Prepared mustard
6 oz	175 g	Brown sugar
¼ tsp	1 mL	Ground cloves
1½ qt	1.5 L	Apple cider
8 oz	250 g	Raisins, seedless (optional)
3 oz	100 g	Brown sugar
⅓ tsp	2 mL	Nutmeg
1 tsp	5 mL	Grated lemon rind
6 tbsp	50 g	Cornstarch
to taste	to taste	Salt

■ P r o c e d u r e

1. Place the ham(s) in a stockpot with enough water to cover. Bring to a boil and reduce heat to a simmer. Simmer for 1 hour. Drain.

2. Cut off skin and excess fat. Leave fat covering about ½ in. (1 cm) thick. Score the fat with a knife.

3. Place the ham fat side up in a roasting or baking pan. Spread with a thin layer of prepared mustard. Mix the sugar and cloves and sprinkle over the ham.

4. Bake at 350°F (175°C) about 1 hour. (*Caution:* Sugar burns easily, so check ham after 30–45 minutes.)

5. Place cider, raisins, sugar, nutmeg, and lemon rind in saucepan and simmer 5 minutes.

6. Mix cornstarch with a little cold water or cold cider and stir into the sauce. Simmer until thickened.

7. Add salt to taste.

8. Slice ham (as for leg of lamb, Figure 11.3). Serve 5-oz (150-g) portion with 2 oz (60 mL) sauce on the side.

V A R I A T I O N S

Ham with Brown Cider Sauce
When ham is baked, drain fat from pan and deglaze with 1½ pt (750 mL) cider. Add 1½ qt (1.5 L) demi-glace or espagnole and simmer until reduced and thickened. Flavor to taste with mustard and a little sugar.

Fruit-Glazed Ham
Omit mustard-sugar glaze. During last half of baking, spoon fruit preserves (apricot, pineapple, or peach) over ham to glaze.

Per serving:
Calories, 300; Protein, 32 g; Fat, 7 g (21% cal.); Cholesterol, 70 mg; Carbohydrates, 25 g; Fiber, 1 g; Sodium, 1680 mg.

Note: The amount of cooking required depends on type of ham. Aged country hams must be soaked 24 hours in cold water, scrubbed, and simmered about 20 minutes per pound (500 g). Hams labeled *tenderized* or *ready to cook* may be baked without simmering (starting with step 2) or may be just blanched before baking (place in cold water, bring to a boil, and drain).

Home-Style Meatloaf

Portions: 25   Portion size: 4 oz (125 g)

U.S.	Metric	Ingredients
1 lb	500 g	Onions, fine dice
8 oz	250 g	Celery, fine dice
2 oz	60 mL	Oil
12 oz	375 g	Soft bread crumbs
12 fl oz	375 mL	Tomato juice, stock, or milk
2½ lb	1.25 kg	Ground beef
2½ lb	1.25 kg	Ground pork
2½ lb	1.25 kg	Ground veal
5	5	Eggs, beaten slightly
1 tbsp	15 mL	Salt
½ tsp	2 mL	Black pepper
3 pt	1.5 L	Tomato sauce, Spanish sauce, Creole sauce, or sour cream sauce

Per serving:
Calories, 360; Protein, 27 g; Fat, 21 g (53% cal.); Cholesterol, 135 mg; Carbohydrates, 16 g; Fiber, 2 g; Sodium, 680 mg.

■ P r o c e d u r e

1. Sauté the onions and celery in oil until tender. Remove from pan and cool thoroughly.

2. In a large bowl, soak the bread crumbs in the juice, stock, or milk.

3. Add the sautéed vegetables, the meat, eggs, salt, and pepper. Mix gently until evenly combined. Do not overmix.

4. Form the mixture into 2 or 3 loaves in a baking pan, or fill loaf pans with the mixture.

5. Bake at 350°F (175°C) about 1–1½ hours, until done. Test with a meat thermometer for internal temperature of 165°F (74°C).

6. For service, cut the loaves into 4-oz (125-g) slices. Serve with 2 oz (60 mL) sauce per portion.

V A R I A T I O N S

Home-Style All-Beef Meatloaf
In place of the mixture of beef, pork, and veal, use 7½ lb (3.75 kg) ground beef.

Italian-Style Meatloaf
Add the following ingredients to the basic mix:

4 tsp (20 mL) chopped garlic, sautéed with the onion
1 oz (30 g) parmesan cheese
⅔ cup (150 mL) chopped parsley
1½ tsp (7 mL) basil
1 tsp (5 mL) oregano

Salisbury Steak
Divide meat mixture for all-beef meatloaf into 6-oz (175-g) portions. Form into thick, oval patties and place on sheet pan. Bake at 350°F (175°C) for about 30 minutes.

Baked Meatballs
Divide basic meat mixture or Italian-Style Meatloaf mixture into 2½-oz (75-g) portions using a No. 16 scoop. Form into balls and place on sheet pans. Bake at 350°F (175°C). May be served with tomato sauce over pasta.

Loin or Rack of Venison Grand Veneur

Portions: 8   Portion size: ¼ loin or rack (2 chops)

U.S.	Metric	Ingredients
2	2	Loins or racks of venison (2½–3 lb/ 1.1–1.4 kg each)
2 qt	2 L	Red Wine Marinade for Game (below)
12 oz	350 g	Pork fatback for barding (quantity approximate)
1 pt	500 mL	Poîvrade Sauce (p. 175)
1 oz	30 g	Red currant jelly
3 fl oz	90 mL	Heavy cream
1 lb	480 g	Chestnut purée (fresh or canned), thinned to a soft texture with a little demi-glace and cream

Per serving:
Calories, 990; Protein, 67 g; Fat, 65 g (60% cal.); Cholesterol, 345 mg; Carbohydrates, 8 g; Fiber, 1 g; Sodium, 200 mg.

■ P r o c e d u r e

1. Trim the venison, removing all silverskin. Because venison is very lean, there will be very little fat to remove.

2. Marinate the venison for 2 days, using enough marinade to cover the meat completely. (The quantity indicated is approximate.)

3. Cut the fatback into thin sheets on a slicing machine. Bard the venison by covering the meat with the sheets of fat and tying them in place.

4. Roast the meat at 450°F (230°C) until rare, about 30–45 minutes.

5. When the meat is done, set it aside in a warm place for 15 minutes. Degrease the roasting pan and deglaze it with a little of the marinade. Reduce slightly and strain it into the poîvrade sauce.

6. Heat the sauce with the jelly until the jelly is melted and dissolved.

7. Temper the cream with a little of the sauce, then add to the rest of the sauce.

8. Cut the meat into chops, or else cut the meat from the bones in one piece and slice into medallions.

9. Serve each portion with 2 oz (60 mL) sauce and garnish with 2 oz (60 g) chestnut purée.

V A R I A T I O N

Leg of Venison Grand Veneur
Leg of venison can be prepared and served in the same way. A whole leg of venison weighing 4–5 lb (about 2 kg) yields 8–10 portions. This larger cut should be marinated slightly longer, 2–3 days.

Red Wine Marinade for Game

Yield: 2 qt (2 L)

U.S.	Metric	Ingredients
4 oz	125 g	Carrots, chopped fine
4 oz	125 g	Onions, chopped fine
4	4	Garlic cloves, crushed
25	25	Parsley stems
2 tsp	10 mL	Dried thyme
4	4	Bay leaves
2 tsp	10 mL	Dried ground sage
1 tsp	5 mL	Peppercorns, crushed
4	4	Cloves
8 fl oz	250 mL	Red wine vinegar
2 qt	2 L	Red wine

Per serving:
Calories, 25; Protein, 0 g; Fat, 0 g (0% cal.); Cholesterol, 0 mg; Carbohydrates, 23 g; Fiber, 5 g; Sodium, 200 mg.

■ P r o c e d u r e

1. Combine all ingredients in a nonreactive container (e.g. stainless steel, glass, plastic; do not use aluminum).

2. Marinate meat as desired or as indicated in recipe. Marinating times may vary from a few hours to several days. After marinating, use the liquid as a cooking medium and as the base for a sauce.

Roast Loin of Rabbit with Risotto

Portions: 8   Portion size: 5–6 oz (140–160 g) rabbit, 4 oz (125 g) risotto, plus sauce and garnish

U.S.	Metric	Ingredients	**Procedure**
2½–3 lb	1.1–1.3 kg	Boneless saddles of rabbit	1. Trim the meat as necessary, leaving the meat in whole pieces.
as needed	as needed	Oil	2. Heat the oil in a sauté pan. Add the rabbit meat and brown on all sides.
			3. Transfer to an oven heated to 450°F (230°C) and roast for 5–10 minutes, until medium done (slightly pink in center). Remove the meat from the pan and keep warm.
2 oz	60 g	Shallots, chopped fine	4. Add the shallots, carrots, mushrooms, and garlic. Brown lightly.
2 oz	60 g	Carrots, chopped fine	5. Add the vermouth or wine and reduce by half.
4 oz	125 g	Mushrooms, chopped fine	6. Add the stock and reduce by half.
1	1	Garlic clove, chopped fine	7. Strain. Season to taste with salt.
4 fl oz	125 g	Dry white vermouth or white wine	
1 pt	500 mL	Rabbit stock or chicken stock, rich and concentrated	
to taste	to taste	Salt	
2 lb	1 kg	Risotto alla Parmigiana (p. 626)	8. Place a mound of risotto in the center of each plate.
as desired	as desired	Steamed, buttered spinach	9. Cut the rabbit meat into thick slices and arrange around the risotto.
as desired	as desired	Carrots, small dice, cooked, hot	10. Arrange small mounds of spinach between the slices of meat.
as desired	as desired	Zucchini, small dice, cooked, hot	11. Place a few pieces of diced carrot and zucchini on the plate.
			12. Spoon the sauce onto the plate around the meat.

Per serving:
Calories, 510; Protein, 38 g; Fat, 24 g (42% cal.); Cholesterol, 105 mg; Carbohydrates, 33 g; Fiber, 5 g; Sodium, 280 mg.

BROILING, GRILLING, AND PAN-BROILING

Broiling and grilling are dry-heat cooking methods, which use very high heat to cook meat quickly. Properly broiled meats have a well-browned, flavorful crust on the outside, and the inside is cooked to the desired doneness and still juicy.

It may be helpful to think of broiling and grilling as browning techniques rather than cooking techniques. This is because the best, juiciest broiled meats are those cooked to the rare or medium-done stage. Because of the intense heat, it is difficult to broil meats to the well-done stage and still keep them juicy. Pork and veal, which are usually eaten well done, are generally better griddled, sautéed, or braised than broiled or grilled. (Veal can be broiled successfully if the customer prefers it still a little pink inside.)

For best results, only high-quality, tender cuts with a good fat content should be broiled.

TEMPERATURE CONTROL

The object of broiling is not just to cook the meat to the desired doneness but also to form a brown, flavorful, crusty surface.

The goal of the broiler cook is to create the right amount of browning—not too much or too little—by the time the inside is cooked to the desired doneness. To do this, he or she must broil the item at the right temperature.

In general, the shorter the cooking time, the higher the temperature, or else the meat won't have time to brown. The longer the cooking time, the lower the temperature, or the meat will brown too much before the inside is done.

Cooking time depends on two factors:

1. The desired doneness.
2. The thickness of the cut.

In other words, a well-done steak should be cooked at a lower heat than a rare one. A thin steak cooked rare must be broiled at a higher temperature than a thick one cooked rare.

To control the cooking temperature of a broiler, raise or lower the rack. On a grill, set different areas for different temperatures and grill meats in the appropriate area.

SEASONING

As with roasting, chefs disagree on when to season. Some feel that meats should not be seasoned before broiling. This is because salt draws moisture to the surface and retards browning. Others feel that seasoning before broiling improves the taste of the meat because the seasonings become part of the brown crust rather than something sprinkled on afterward.

Generally, if you have a professional broiler that has been properly preheated, it is not difficult to brown meat that has been salted. Low-powered broilers such as those found in home kitchens, on the other hand, do not get as hot. In such cases, it is better to salt after broiling, not before.

One way around this problem is to serve the meat with a *seasoned butter* (p. 179). Another option is to marinate the meat in seasoned oil 30 minutes or more before broiling. Be sure to dry marinated meats well before placing them on the broiler.

Procedure for Broiling or Grilling Meats

In a broiler, the heat source is above the food. In a grill, the heat is below the food. Except for this difference, the basic procedure is the same for both. Make sure you understand how to test broiled meats for doneness (p. 275) before starting.

1. Collect and prepare all equipment and food supplies. Trim excess fat from meats to avoid flare-ups that can char the meat too much and coat it with smoky residue. If necessary, score the fatty edges of meats to prevent curling.
2. Preheat the broiler or grill.
3. If necessary, brush the grill with a wire brush to clean off any charred food particles.
4. Brush the meat with oil, or dip it in oil and let the excess drip off. Place the item on the broiler or grill. The oil helps prevent sticking and keeps the product moist. It may be unnecessary for meats high in fat. Using too much oil can cause grease fires. Alternatively, wipe the grill with an oiled towel before placing the meat on it.
5. When one side is brown and the meat is cooked halfway, turn it over with a fork (piercing only the fat, never the meat, or juices will be lost) or with tongs. Figure 11.6 illustrates the technique for grill-marking steaks and other meats.
6. Cook the second side until the meat is cooked to the desired doneness.

   If the meat is to be brushed with a glaze or sauce, such as a barbecue sauce, it is usually best to wait until the product is partially cooked on each side before applying the first coat. Many glazes or sauces burn if cooked too long. After the item has cooked on both sides and is one-half to three-fourths done, brush the top with a light coat of the sauce. Turn over and repeat as necessary.
7. Remove from broiler or grill and serve immediately.

Figure 11.6
Grill-marking steaks.

(a) Place the meat on a preheated grill at an angle as shown.

(b) When the meat is about one-fourth done, turn the meat about 60 to 90 degrees, as shown. Do not turn it over.

(c) When the steak is about half done, turn it over. The grill marks will appear as shown.

SAUCES AND ACCOMPANIMENTS FOR GRILLED AND BROILED MEATS

Many kinds of sauces and accompaniments are appropriate for grilled meats, including compound butters, butter sauces such as béarnaise; brown sauce variations such as Bercy, mushroom, and bordelaise; tomato sauce variations; and salsas and relishes. For other examples, see the recipes in this section. Note that, unlike pan sauces made by deglazing sauté pans (see p. 313), all these sauces are prepared in advance because broiling or grilling does not give you the opportunity to deglaze a pan.

Part of the appeal of broiled and grilled meats is their brown, crisp surface. For this reason, it is best not to cover the item with the sauce. Also, less sauce is usually served with grilled items than with sautéed items. Serve the sauce on the side or around the meat or, at most, in a thin ribbon across only part of the meat.

Similarly, vegetables and accompaniments for broiled and grilled meats should, in most cases, not be heavily sauced. Grilled vegetables are often good choices as accompaniments.

PAN-BROILING

Broiling very thin steaks (minute steaks) to the rare stage is difficult because the heat is not high enough to form a good brown crust without overcooking the inside.

Pan-broiling in a heavy iron skillet is an answer to this problem.

Procedure for Pan-Broiling Meats

1. Preheat an iron skillet over a high flame until it is very hot. Do not add fat. (The pan should, of course, be well seasoned.)
2. Proceed as for grilling. Pour off any fat that accumulates during cooking, if necessary.

Broiled Strip Loin Steak Maître d'Hôtel

Yield: 10 portions

U.S.	Metric	Ingredients	Procedure
10	10	Strip loin steaks, boneless, 10–12 oz (300–350 g) each	1. Trim steaks as necessary, leaving a thin layer of fat on the edge.
to taste	to taste	Salt	2. Season the steaks to taste with salt and pepper. Brush lightly with oil.
to taste	to taste	Black pepper	3. Place the steaks on a preheated grill or broiler.
as needed	as needed	Vegetable oil	4. When the steak is about one-fourth done, turn it about 60–90 degrees to grill-mark it (see Figure 11.6).
			5. When the steak is half-done, turn it over and complete the cooking to the desired doneness. If turning with a fork, pierce the fat, not the meat, or juices will be lost.
5 oz	150 g	Maître d'Hôtel Butter (p. 179)	6. Remove the steaks from the broiler and immediately place on a hot plate. Top each steak with a ½-oz (15-g) slice of seasoned butter.

Per 8 ounces:
Calories, 550; Protein, 60 g; Fat, 33 g (55% cal.); Cholesterol, 185 mg; Carbohydrates, 0 g; Fiber, 0 g; Sodium, 250 mg.

VARIATIONS

Other steaks may be cooked by the same method, including *rib steak*, *rib eye steak*, *tenderloin*, *club steak*, *porterhouse*, *T-bone*, and *sirloin*. *Chopped beef patties* may also be prepared using this recipe.

Other seasoned butters and sauces make good accompaniments to broiled steaks, including:

Garlic butter Chasseur sauce Mushroom sauce (brown) Béarnaise sauce
Anchovy butter Madeira sauce Bercy sauce (brown) Foyot sauce
Bordelaise sauce Perigueux sauce Lyonnaise sauce Choron sauce
Marchand de vin sauce

Broiled Lamb Chops
Prepare as for broiled steaks, using rib, loin, or shoulder chops.

London Broil

Portions: 24   Portion size: 5 oz (150 g)

U.S.	Metric	Ingredients
10 lb	4.75 kg	Flank steak (5 steaks)
		Marinade:
1 pt	500 mL	Vegetable oil
2 fl oz	60 mL	Lemon juice
2 tsp	10 mL	Salt
2 tsp	10 mL	Black pepper
1 tsp	5 mL	Dried thyme
1½ qt	1.5 L	Mushroom Sauce (brown) (p. 175)

■ Procedure

1. Trim all fat and connective tissue from beef.

2. Combine the marinade ingredients in a hotel pan. Place the steaks in the pan and turn them so they are coated with oil. Cover and refrigerate at least 2 hours.

3. Remove the meat from the marinade and place in a preheated broiler or grill. Broil at high heat about 3–5 minutes on each side, until well browned outside but rare inside (see note).

4. Remove from broiler and let rest 2 minutes before slicing.

5. Slice the meat very thin on a sharp angle across the grain (see Figure 11.7).

6. Weigh 5-oz (150-g) portions. Serve each portion with 2 oz (60 mL) sauce.

VARIATIONS

Thick-cut steaks from the round or chuck are sometimes used for London broil.

Teriyaki-Style London Broil
Marinate the steaks in a mixture of the following ingredients: 2½ cups (600 mL) Japanese soy sauce, 6 oz (200 mL) vegetable oil, 4 oz (125 mL) sherry, 6 oz (175 g) chopped onion, 2 tbsp (30 g) sugar, 2 tsp (10 mL) ginger, 1 crushed clove garlic. Marinate at least 4 hours or, preferably, overnight. Broil as in basic recipe.

Per serving:
Calories, 520; Protein, 41 g; Fat, 37 g (65% cal.); Cholesterol, 110 mg; Carbohydrates, 3 g; Fiber, 0 g; Sodium, 370 mg.

Note: Flank steak should be broiled rare. If cooked well done, it will be tough and dry.

Figure 11.7
Slicing London broil flank steak.

(a) Holding the knife at a sharp angle, slice the meat in very thin slices across the grain. Use a table fork or kitchen fork to hold the meat steady. Some chefs slice the meat toward the fork.

(b) Others prefer to slice away from the fork. The result is the same.

Beef Fajitas

Portions: 12   Portion size: 4 oz (150 g) plus garnish

U.S.	Metric	Ingredients
3 fl oz	90 mL	Vegetable oil
6 fl oz	180 mL	Lime juice
4 tsp	20 mL	Ground cumin
4 tsp	20 mL	Chili powder
4	4	Garlic cloves, chopped fine
4 tsp	20 mL	Salt
2 tsp	10 mL	Pepper
4 lb	1.9 kg	Beef skirt steak or flank steak, trimmed of fat
1 fl oz	30 mL	Vegetable oil
1 lb 8 oz	700 g	Bell peppers, assorted colors, cut into strips.
1 lb 8 oz	700 g	Onion, in thick slices
24, or as desired	24, or as desired	Flour tortillas, steamed to soften
as desired	as desired	Garnishes:
		Guacamole or sliced avocado
		Sour cream
		Shredded lettuce
		Diced tomato
		Salsa Cruda (p. 191)

■ P r o c e d u r e

1. To make a marinade, mix together the oil, lime juice, cumin, chili powder, garlic, salt, and pepper.
2. Place the meat in a nonreactive container with the marinade, turning the meat so it is coated on all sides. Refrigerate for 2–4 hours.
3. Remove the meat from the marinade. Grill the meat on both sides on a grill or under a broiler until it is lightly charred and rare to medium done, as desired.
4. While the beef is grilling, heat the oil in a large sauté pan over high heat.
5. Add the peppers and sauté briefly, keeping them slightly crisp.
6. Remove the peppers from the pan and sauté the onions in the same way.
7. When the beef is done, remove it from the grill and let it rest 5 minutes.
8. Slice the meat across the grain into thin slices.
9. Serve the meat strips and vegetables on a hot plate or sizzle platter. Serve the tortillas and the garnishes on the side in separate containers. Diners make their own soft tacos by rolling meat, vegetables, and choice of condiments in tortillas.

Per serving:
Calories, 740; Protein, 44 g; Fat, 22 g (27% cal.); Cholesterol, 60 mg; Carbohydrates, 88 g; Fiber, 6 g; Sodium, 830 mg.

 Broiled Smoked Pork Chop with Flageolet Beans and Wilted Arugula

Portions: 15   Portion size: 1 pork chop, 8 oz (250 g)
about 5 oz (150 g) vegetable

U.S.	Metric	Ingredients
15	15	Smoked pork loin chops, bone-in, about 8 oz (250 g) each
as needed	as needed	Vegetable oil
4 lb 12 oz	2.2 kg	Flageolet Beans with Wilted Arugula (see note)

■ P r o c e d u r e

1. Brush the chops very lightly with oil. Place on a preheated grill or broiler until grill-marked on both sides and heated through. Smoked pork chops are fully cooked, so it is necessary only to heat them through.
2. Serve each chop with 5 oz (150 g) of the beans with arugula.

Per serving:
Calories, 620; Protein, 57 g; Fat, 26 g (39% cal.); Cholesterol, 110 mg; Carbohydrates, 26 g; Fiber, 9 g; Sodium, 3110 mg.

Note: The quantity of beans and arugula required for this recipe is equal to the yield of the recipe on p. 613.

Broiled Smoked Pork Chop with Flageolet Beans and Wilted Arugula

Grilled Marinated Pork Tenderloin with Sweet Potato Purée and Warm Chipotle Salsa

Portions: 10　Portion size: 5 oz (150 g) meat

U.S.	Metric	Ingredients
4 lb	2 kg	Pork tenderloin
2 oz	60 g	Onion, chopped fine
1	1	Garlic clove, chopped fine
2 tbsp	30 mL	Powdered red New Mexico chile (see note)
1 tsp	5 mL	Salt
½ tsp	2 mL	Dried oregano
¼ tsp	1 mL	Ground cumin
⅛ tsp	0.5 mL	Cinnamon
2 fl oz	60 mL	Lime juice
1 fl oz	30 mL	Olive oil
1 clove	1 clove	Garlic, unpeeled
1 lb	500 g	Plum tomatoes or other small tomatoes
2	2	Whole chipotle chiles in adobo (canned)
½ tsp	2 mL	Salt
2–3 tsp	10–15 mL	Sauce from the canned chiles
3 lb	1.5 kg	Sweet potatoes
to taste	to taste	Salt

Per serving:
Calories, 410; Protein, 41 g; Fat, 10 g (22% cal.); Cholesterol, 110 mg; Carbohydrates, 38 g; Fiber, 5 g; Sodium, 630 mg.

Note: For a slightly different flavor, or if powdered New Mexico chile is not available, use a regular chile powder blend.

■ Procedure

1. Trim fat and membranes from the tenderloins (see Figure 11.8).

2. Mix together the onion, garlic, powdered chile, salt, oregano, cumin, cinnamon, lime juice, and oil.

3. Coat the meat with this mixture. Wrap and refrigerate several hours or overnight.

4. Roast the garlic and tomatoes in an oven preheated to 450°F (230°C) for 10 minutes.

5. Remove the skins from the tomatoes and garlic. Place them in a blender.

6. Carefully cut open the chiles. Scrape out and discard the seeds. Chop the chiles.

7. Add the chiles, salt, and the sauce from the chiles to the blender. Blend to make a coarse purée. Add more salt if needed.

8. Bake the sweet potatoes at 400°F (200°C) until soft. Cut in half and scoop out the flesh. Pass through a food mill to purée. Season lightly.

9. Scrape the onions and garlic off the meat (they will burn if left on).

10. Grill the meat until just well done. Be careful not to overcook, or the meat will be dry.

11. To serve, place 3 oz (90 g) sweet potato purée on the plate. Slice the meat across the grain into medallions. Arrange 5 oz (150 g) meat on top of the sweet potato. Drizzle with 1½ oz (45 mL) tomato chipotle salsa.

Grilled Marinated Pork Tenderloin with Warm Chipotle Salsa

Figure 11.8 Trimming a pork tenderloin.

Grilled Chopped Lamb "Steaks" with Rosemary and Pine Nuts

Portions: 25   Portion size: 5 oz (150 g)

U.S.	Metric	Ingredients
6 oz	175 g	Onions, chopped fine
2 fl oz	60 g	Salad oil
6½ lb	3.25 kg	Ground lamb
8 oz	250 g	Soft, fresh bread crumbs
8 oz	250 g	Toasted pine nuts
10 fl oz	300 mL	Milk
½ cup	30 g	Chopped parsley
2 tsp	10 mL	Rosemary
2½ tsp	12 mL	Salt
1 tsp	5 mL	White pepper
25 strips	25 strips	Bacon

Per serving:
Calories, 460; Protein, 25 g; Fat, 37 g (72% cal.); Cholesterol, 95 mg;
Carbohydrates, 7 g; Fiber, 1 g; Sodium, 520 mg.

■ P r o c e d u r e

1. Sauté the onion in oil until tender. Do not brown. Cool thoroughly.
2. Combine all ingredients except bacon in a bowl. Mix gently until evenly combined. Do not overmix.
3. Scale the meat into 5-oz (150-g) portions. Form the portions into thick patties, about ¾ inch (2 cm) thick.
4. Wrap a strip of bacon around each patty and fasten with picks.
5. Grill or broil the patties under moderate heat until done, turning once (see note).
6. Remove picks before serving.

V A R I A T I O N S

Ground beef or veal may be used instead of lamb.

Grilled Chopped Beef "Steaks" with Marjoram
Substitute ground beef for ground lamb. Substitute marjoram for the rosemary. Omit the pine nuts.

Note: Patties may be browned under the broiler, arranged on a sheet pan, and finished in the oven at 375°F (190°C).

Shish Kebab

Portions: 25   Portion size: 6 oz (175 g)

U.S.	Metric	Ingredients
10 lb	4.5 kg	Lamb leg, boneless, trimmed
		Marinade:
1 qt	1 L	Olive oil, or part olive and part vegetable oil
½ cup	125 mL	Lemon juice
5	5	Garlic cloves, crushed
4 tsp	20 mL	Salt
1½ tsp	7 mL	Pepper
1 tsp	5 mL	Dried oregano

Per serving:
Calories, 280; Protein, 37 g; Fat, 14 g (46% cal.); Cholesterol, 115 mg;
Carbohydrates, 0 g; Fiber, 0 g; Sodium, 125 mg.

■ P r o c e d u r e

1. A day before cooking, trim any remaining fat and connective tissue from the lamb. Cut into 1-in. (2½-cm) cubes. Keep all the cubes the same size for even cooking.
2. Combine the marinade ingredients and pour over the lamb in a hotel pan. Mix well. Refrigerate overnight.
3. Drain the meat and weigh out 6-oz (175-g) portions. Thread each portion onto a skewer.
4. Place skewers on a grill or broiler rack and broil at moderate heat until medium done, turning over once when they are half cooked.
5. To serve, place each portion on a bed of Rice Pilaf (p. 625). The skewers should be removed by the waiter in the dining room or by the cook in the kitchen.

Note: Shish kebabs are sometimes made with vegetables (onions, green peppers, cherry romatoes, mushrooms) on the same skewer with the meat. However, it is easier to control cooking times if vegetables are broiled on separate skewers. Also, the meat is less likely to steam in the moisture from the vegetables.

Broiled Lamb Kidneys with Bacon

Portions: 10   Portion size: 2 kidneys
2 strips bacon

U.S.	Metric	Ingredients
20	20	Bacon strips
20	20	Lamb kidneys
as needed	as needed	Melted butter or oil
to taste	to taste	Salt
to taste	to taste	Pepper

Per serving:
Calories, 410; Protein, 26 g; Fat, 33 g (73% cal.); Cholesterol, 515 mg;
Carbohydrates, 1 g; Fiber, 0 g; Sodium, 580 mg.

■ Procedure

1. Cook the bacon on a griddle or in the oven on a sheet pan until crisp. Drain fat and keep bacon warm.

2. Split the kidneys in half lengthwise and cut out the white fat and gristle in center.

3. Arrange the kidneys on skewers, 4 half-kidneys per skewer.

4. Brush the kidneys well with melted butter or oil and season with salt and pepper.

5. Broil the kidneys under high heat, turning once, until browned on the outside but still slightly rare. (Test by pressing with finger, as for testing steaks.)

6. Serve immediately with 2 slices of bacon per portion. Mustard is often served with kidneys.

Grilled Venison with Lime Butter

Portions: 8   Portion size: 3–4 oz (90–125 g)

U.S.	Metric	Ingredients
2 lb	1 kg	Boneless, trimmed venison (see step 1)
1 tsp	5 mL	Sichuan peppercorns, toasted
1 fl oz	30 mL	Lime juice
to taste	to taste	Salt
2 oz	60 g	Butter
½ tsp	2 mL	Sichuan peppercorns, toasted and crushed
2 tsp	10 mL	Grated lime zest
½ tsp	2 mL	Lime juice
to taste	to taste	Salt

Per serving:
Calories, 190; Protein, 26 g; Fat, 9 g (43% cal.); Cholesterol, 110 mg;
Carbohydrates, 1 g; Fiber, 0 g; Sodium, 115 mg.

■ Procedure

1. Select a piece or pieces of venison suitable for broiling and slicing in the manner of London broil. Make sure the venison is well trimmed of all silverskin.

2. Rub the meat with Sichuan peppercorns. Sprinkle with lime juice and salt. Let marinate for 30 minutes.

3. Soften the butter and mix in the crushed peppercorns, lime zest, lime juice, and salt. Refrigerate until needed.

4. Grill or broil the venison until rare or medium rare. Remove from the heat and let rest for a few minutes.

5. Cut on the bias, across the grain, into thin slices, like London broil.

6. Arrange the slices on plates. Top each portion with a small slice of lime butter, about 1½ tsp (8 g).

Grilled Loin of Elk

Portions: 12   Portion size: 5–6 oz (150–180 g)

U.S.	Metric	Ingredients
8 fl oz	250 mL	Red wine
2 fl oz	60 mL	Vegetable oil
2 oz	60 g	Shallots, sliced
1 tbsp	15 mL	Lemon zest, grated
¼ tsp	1 mL	Cayenne
1 tbsp	15 mL	Salt
1 tsp	5 mL	Black pepper
12	12	Steaks, 5–6 oz (150–180 g) each, cut from trimmed, boneless loin of elk

Per serving:
Calories, 180; Protein, 33 g; Fat, 45 g (75% cal.); Cholesterol, 80 mg;
Carbohydrates, 0 g; Fiber, 0 g; Sodium, 115 mg.

■ Procedure

1. Mix together the wine, oil, shallots, lemon zest, cayenne, salt, and pepper in a nonreactive container big enough to hold the elk steaks.

2. Place the steaks in the container, turning them to coat them with the marinade.

3. Refrigerate for 2 hours. The steaks should remain in the marinade only long enough to flavor them lightly.

4. Remove the steaks from the marinade and pat them dry with clean towels.

5. Broil or grill to rare or medium doneness.

SAUTÉING, PAN-FRYING, AND GRIDDLING

If you review the general definitions of sautéing, pan-frying, and griddling in Chapter 4, you will see that the differences among these methods are largely a matter of degree. Sautéing uses high heat and a small amount of fat and is usually used for small pieces of food. Pan-frying uses moderate heat, a moderate amount of fat, and is usually employed with larger items, such as chops. But at what point does moderate heat become high heat and a small amount of fat become a moderate amount of fat? It is impossible to draw an exact dividing line between sautéing and pan-frying.

Each time you cook a piece of meat, you must judge how much heat and how much fat to use to do the job best. This depends on the kind of food and the size of the pieces. Following are guidelines to help you make the right judgments.

Guidelines for Sautéing, Pan-frying, and Griddling

1. Use only tender cuts for sautéing.
2. Smaller or thinner pieces of meat require higher heat. The object is to brown or sear the meat in the time it takes to cook it to the desired doneness. Very small or thin pieces cook in just a few moments.
3. If large or thick items are browned over high heat, it may be necessary to finish them at lower heat to avoid burning them.
4. The amount of fat needed is the amount required to conduct the heat to all surfaces so the item cooks evenly. Flat items need much less fat than irregularly shaped items like chicken pieces.
   Sautéing small pieces of meat requires little fat because the items are tossed or flipped so that all sides come in contact with the hot pan.
5. When sautéing small pieces of food, do not overload the pan, and do not flip or toss the food more than necessary. This will cause the temperature to drop too much, and the meat will simmer in its own juices instead of sauté.
6. Use clarified butter or oil or a mixture of the two for sautéing. Whole butter burns easily.
7. Dredging meats in flour promotes even browning and helps prevent sticking. Flour meats immediately before cooking, not in advance, or the flour will get pasty. Also, shake off excess flour before adding meat to the pan.
8. Meats to be pan-fried are often breaded. Review page 142 for Standard Breading Procedure.
9. When pan-frying several batches, strain or skim the fat between batches. Otherwise, burned food particles from previous batches may mar the appearance of the meat.
10. Griddling and pan-frying are preferable to broiling and grilling for cooking pork and veal chops because the lower temperatures keep these meats moister when cooked well done. Hamburgers cooked well done are also moister if cooked on a griddle.

DEGLAZING THE PAN

A sauce made by deglazing the pan often accompanies sautéed meats. To **deglaze** means to swirl a liquid in a sauté or other pan to dissolve cooked particles of food remaining on the bottom. (Review discussions of deglazing in Chapter 4, p. 72, and in Chapter 8, p. 156 and p. 167). The deglazing liquid can be used to flavor a sauce in one of two ways:

1. Add the reduced deglazing liquid to a prepared sauce. The deglazing liquid adds flavor and color to the sauce.
2. Use the deglazing liquid to make a freshly prepared sauce. Add stock or other liquids and other flavoring and thickening ingredients and finish the sauce as indicated in the recipe.

STIR-FRYING

The Chinese technique of stir-frying is very much like sautéing, except that in sautéing, the food items are usually tossed by flipping the pan, while in stir-frying, the pan is left stationary while the foods are tossed with spatulas or other tools. Although true Chinese stir-frying is done in a round-bottomed pan called a wok over a special burner, you can use the same technique with a standard sauté pan.

General Procedures for Sautéing and Pan-Frying Meats

The following procedures are presented side by side so you can compare them. Keep in mind that these are the two extremes and that many recipes require a procedure that falls somewhere between the two.

The procedure for pan-frying applies to griddling as well, although only a small amount of fat can be used on a griddle.

Sautéing

1. Collect all equipment and food supplies.
2. Prepare meats as required. This may include dredging with flour.
3. Heat a small amount of fat in a sauté pan until very hot.
4. Add the meat to the pan. Do not overcrowd the pan.
5. Brown the meat on all sides, flipping or tossing it in the pan as necessary so it cooks evenly.
6. Remove meat from pan. Drain excess fat, if any.
7. Add any sauce ingredients to be sautéed, such as shallots or mushrooms, as indicated in the recipe. Sauté them as necessary.
8. Add liquid for deglazing, such as wine or stock. Simmer while swirling and scraping the pan to release food particles on the bottom so they can dissolve in the liquid. Reduce the liquid.
9. Add a prepared sauce or other sauce ingredients and finish the sauce as indicated in the recipe.
10. Serve the meat with the sauce, or return the meat to the sauce in the pan to reheat briefly and coat it with the sauce. Do not let the meat cook in the sauce. Serve.

Pan-Frying

1. Collect all equipment and food supplies.
2. Prepare meats as required. This may include breading or dredging with flour.
3. Heat a moderate amount of fat in a sauté pan or skillet until hot.
4. Add the meat to the pan.
5. Brown the meat on one side. Turn it with a spatula and brown the other side. Larger pieces may need to be finished at reduced heat after browning. If required, they may finish cooking, uncovered, in the oven.
6. Serve immediately.

Basic Procedure for Stir-Frying

1. Heat a wok or sauté pan over high heat until very hot.
2. Add a small quantity of oil and let it heat.
3. Add seasonings for flavoring the oil—one or more of the following: salt, garlic, ginger root, scallions.
4. If meat, poultry, or seafood items are part of the dish, add them at this point. As when sautéing, do not overload the pan. Leave the food pieces untouched for a few moments so they begin to brown properly. Then stir and toss them with a spatula so they sear and cook evenly.
5. If any liquid seasoning for the meat, such as soy sauce, is used, add it now, but only in small quantities, so the meat continues to fry and does not start to simmer or stew.
6. Remove the meat from the pan or leave it in, depending on the recipe. If a small quantity of quick-cooking vegetables is used, the meat can sometimes be left in the pan and the vegetables cooked with it. Otherwise, remove the meat when it is almost done and keep it on the side while cooking the vegetables.
7. Repeat steps 2 and 3 if necessary.
8. Add the vegetables to the pan and stir-fry. If more than one vegetable is used, add the longer-cooking ones first and the quicker-cooking ones last.
9. Some dishes are dry-fried, meaning prepared without liquid or sauce. In this case, simply return the meat item, if any, to the pan to reheat with the vegetables, then serve. Otherwise, proceed to the next step.
10. Add liquid ingredients, such as stock or water, and continue to cook and stir until the vegetables are almost cooked.
11. Add the meat item, which was removed in step 6, to the pan to reheat.
12. Optional but widely used step: Add a mixture of cornstarch and water to the pan and cook until lightly thickened.
13. Serve at once.

Breaded Veal Cutlets

Portions: 24   Portion size: 4 oz (125 g)

U.S.	Metric	Ingredients
6 lb	3 kg	Veal cutlets (scaloppine): 24 pieces, 4 oz (125 g) each. (See Figure 11.9 for preparation of veal.)
to taste	to taste	Salt
to taste	to taste	Pepper
		Standard Breading Procedure (see note):
4 oz	125 g	Flour
4	4	Eggs
1 cup	250 mL	Milk
1½ lb	750 g	Bread crumbs, dry or fresh
8 oz	250 mL	Oil or clarified butter, or a mixture of oil and butter
12 oz	375 g	Butter

■ P r o c e d u r e

1. Lightly flatten each piece of veal with a meat mallet. Do not pound too hard, or you may tear the meat.

2. Season the meat with salt and pepper and pass through Standard Breading Procedure (see p. 142).

3. Heat about ¼ in. (½ cm) oil or butter in a large sauté pan. Place the cutlets in the pan and pan-fry until golden brown. Turn and brown the other side. Remove from the pan and place on hot plates.

4. Heat the butter in a small saucepan or sauté pan until lightly browned. Pour ½ oz (15 g) brown butter over each portion.

V A R I A T I O N S

Veal Cutlet Sauté Gruyère
Top each cooked cutlet with 1 or 2 thin slices of tomato and a slice of Gruyère cheese. Pass under a broiler to melt cheese. Serve with tomato sauce placed under the cutlet or in a ribbon (cordon) around the cutlet.

Schnitzel à la Holstein
Top each portion with a fried egg and 4 anchovy fillets placed around the edge of the egg.

Veal Cutlet Viennese Style (Wiener Schnitzel)
Top each cutlet with 1 peeled lemon slice and 1 anchovy fillet rolled around a caper. Garnish the plate with chopped hard-cooked egg white, sieved egg yolk, and chopped parsley.

Veal Parmigiana
Top each cutlet with 2 fl oz (60 mL) tomato sauce, a slice of mozzarella cheese, and 2 tbsp (30 mL) parmesan cheese. Pass under a broiler to melt cheese.

Veal Cordon Bleu
Use 2 thin 2-oz (60-g) cutlets per portion. Sandwich 1 thin slice ham and 1 thin slice Swiss cheese between 2 cutlets. Pound edges lightly to seal. Bread and fry as in basic recipe.

Breaded Pork Cutlets
Cutlets from pork leg or loin may be breaded and pan-fried like veal. They must be cooked well done.

Per serving:
Calories, 550; Protein, 31 g; Fat, 38 g (63% cal.); Cholesterol, 165 mg; Carbohydrates, 19 g; Fiber, 1 g; Sodium, 380 mg.

Note: Quantities given for breading materials are only guidelines. You may need more or less, depending on the shapes of the meat pieces, the care used in breading, and other factors. In any case, you will need enough so that even the last piece to be breaded can be coated easily and completely.

Veal Cutlet, Viennese Style

Veal Scaloppine alla Marsala

Portions: 10   Portion size: 4 oz (125 g)

U.S.	Metric	Ingredients
2½ lb	1.25 kg	Small veal scaloppine: 20 pieces, 2 oz (60 g) each.(See Figure 11.9 for preparation of veal.)
to taste	to taste	Salt
to taste	to taste	White pepper
for dredging	for dredging	Flour
2 fl oz	60 mL	Oil
4 fl oz	125 mL	Marsala wine
8 fl oz	250 mL	Strong white stock, veal or chicken (see note)
2 oz	60 g	Butter, cut in pieces
2 tbsp	30 mL	Chopped parsley

Per serving:
Calories, 360; Protein, 27 g; Fat, 26 g (65% cal.); Cholesterol, 115 mg; Carbohydrates, 2 g; Fiber, 0 g; Sodium, 120 mg.

■ P r o c e d u r e

1. Lightly flatten each piece of veal with a meat mallet. Do not pound hard, or you may tear the meat.
2. Dry the meat, season it with salt and pepper, and dredge in flour. Shake off excess. (Do not do this step until immediately before cooking.)
3. Heat the oil in a large sauté pan until very hot. Add the veal and sauté over high heat just until lightly browned on both sides. (If necessary, sauté the meat in several batches.)
4. Remove the meat from the pan and drain the excess oil.
5. Add the Marsala to the pan and deglaze.
6. Add the stock and reduce over high heat by about half.
7. Add the pieces of butter and swirl the pan until they are melted and blended with the sauce.
8. Add the veal to the pan and bring just to the simmer. Turn the meat to coat it with the sauce.
9. Serve immediately, 2 pieces per portion, sprinkled with chopped parsley.

Note: Brown sauce may be used instead of white stock. However, the stock makes a more delicate product without masking the flavor of the veal.

V A R I A T I O N S

Veal Scaloppine with Sherry
Substitute sherry for the Marsala.

Veal Scaloppine à la Crème
Prepare as in basic recipe but omit the wine. Deglaze the pan with the stock. Add 1 cup (250 mL) heavy cream and reduce until thickened. Omit the butter. Season the sauce with a few drops of lemon juice. Taste carefully for salt.

Veal Scaloppine with Lemon
Substitute 3 fl oz (90 mL) lemon juice for the 4 fl oz (125 mL) wine. After plating, top each piece of veal with 1 lemon slice and sprinkle with chopped parsley.

Veal Scaloppine with Mushrooms and Cream
Prepare as for Veal Scaloppine à la Crème, but sauté ½ lb (250 g) sliced mushrooms in butter in the sauté pan before deglazing.

Figure 11.9 Trimming and cutting veal for scaloppine.

(a) Remove all tendons and connective tissue (silverskin) from the veal. Slip the point of a thin boning knife under the skin. Angle the edge of the blade upward against the skin and cut it away carefully without cutting through the meat.

(b) Holding the blade of the knife at an angle if necessary to get a broader slice, *cut across the grain* of the meat as shown to make thin slices.

(c) Broader slices can be cut from narrower pieces of meat by butterflying. Cut the slice almost through the meat but . . .

(d) . . . leave it attached.

(e) Then cut a second slice the same way, but cut all the way through.

(f) A butterflied scaloppine is twice as large as a single slice. Unfortunately, it has a seam in the center that often detracts from the appearance of the finished dish, unless the veal is breaded or covered with a topping.

(g) If desired, pound the cutlet to an even thickness with a cutlet mallet. This helps disguise the seam in a butterflied cutlet.

Figure 11.10 Preparing beef tenderloin.

(a) A whole, untrimmed beef tenderloin.

(b) Pull off the heavy fat from the outside of the tenderloin, freeing it with a knife as necessary.

(c) Separate the strip of gristly meat, or chain, from the side of the tenderloin. Use this piece for ground meat.

(d) Carefully remove the silverskin.

(e) The fully trimmed tenderloin before cutting.

(f) Cut into steaks of the desired size.

(g) This tenderloin has been cut into a variety of steaks as a demonstration. From left to right: four fillet steaks, two large pieces for chateaubriand, two tournedos, four filets mignons. In front: trimmings from both ends.

 ## Tournedos Vert-Pré

Portions: 1   Portion size: 5–6 oz (150–175 g)

U.S.	Metric	Ingredients
1 oz	30 g	Clarified butter
2	2	Tournedos (see note), 2½–3 oz (75–90 g) each
2 slices	2 slices	Maître d'Hôtel Butter (p. 179)
as needed	as needed	Allumette Potatoes (p. 603)
as needed	as needed	Watercress

Per serving:
Calories, 640; Protein, 27 g; Fat, 59 g (83% cal.); Cholesterol, 185 mg; Carbohydrates, 0 g; Fiber, 0 g; Sodium, 410 mg.

Note: Tournedos (TOOR-nuh-doe; singular form: one tournedos) are small tenderloin steaks cut about 1½ inches (4 cm) thick. The same recipe may be used for fillet steaks, which are larger but thinner cuts from the tenderloin. See Figure 11.10 for cutting tenderloin.

■ P r o c e d u r e

1. Heat the butter in a small sauté pan over moderately high heat.
2. Place the tournedos in the pan and cook until well browned on the bottom and about half cooked.
3. Turn the meat over and continue to cook until rare or medium done, according to customer's request.
4. Place the tournedos on a hot dinner plate and top each with a slice of maître d'hôtel butter. Garnish the plate with a portion of allumette potatoes and a generous bunch of watercress. Serve immediately, while the butter is still melting.

V A R I T I O N S

Tournedos Béarnaise
Pan-fry tournedos as in basic recipe and serve with béarnaise sauce.

Tournedos Bordelaise
Pan-fry as in basic recipe. Top each steak with 1 slice poached beef marrow and coat lightly with bordelaise sauce.

Tournedos Chasseur
Pan-fry as in basic recipe. Plate the steaks and deglaze the sauté pan (drained of cooking fat) with ½ fl oz (15 mL) white wine. Add 2 fl oz (60 mL) chasseur sauce, bring to a simmer, and pour around the tournedos.

Tournedos Rossini
Pan-fry as in basic recipe. Set the tournedos on croutons (rounds of bread cut the same size as the steaks and fried in butter until golden). Top each steak with 1 slice pâté de foie gras (goose liver pâté) and 1 slice truffle (if available). Coat lightly with Madeira sauce.

Tournedos Rossini; Berny Potatoes; Braised Lettuce

Pork Chops Charcutière

Portions: 24 **Portion size: 6 oz (175 g) chop**
2 fl oz (60 mL) sauce

U.S.	Metric	Ingredients
24	24	Pork chops, 6 oz (175 g) each
as needed	as needed	Oil
1½ qt	1.5 L	Charcutière Sauce (p. 175)

Per serving:
Calories, 260; Protein, 28 g; Fat, 13 g (46% cal.); Cholesterol, 90 mg; Carbohydrates, 4 g; Fiber, 0 g; Sodium, 180 mg.

■ Procedure

1. Trim excess fat from chops if necessary.
2. Add enough oil to a skillet or sauté pan or to a griddle to make a thin film. Heat over moderate heat.
3. Place the chops in the hot pan or on griddle and cook until browned and about half-done. Turn over and cook until well done and browned on the second side.
4. Place the chops on hot dinner plates for service (or place them in a hotel pan if they must be held).
5. Spoon a ribbon of sauce (2 oz/60 mL) around each plated chop.

V A R I A T I O N S

Pork Chops Robert
Use Robert sauce instead of charcutière sauce.

Pork Chops Piquante
Use piquante sauce.

Veal Chops
These may be cooked by the same basic procedure and served with an appropriate sauce, such as a well-seasoned demi-glace or a mixture of demi-glace and cream. Other suggestions; ivory sauce, Hungarian sauce, mushroom sauce (white), aurora sauce.

Sautéed Veal Chop; Zucchini with Tomatoes

Thai Green Curry of Pork with Vegetables

Portions: 12 **Portion size: 7 oz (200 g)**

U.S.	Metric	Ingredients
2 fl oz	60 mL	Vegetable oil
2 lb	1 kg	Boneless pork loin, cut into thin slices
1 lb	500 g	Bok choy, cut into 1-in. (2.5-cm) pieces
10 oz	300 g	Yellow summer squash, sliced
8 oz	250 g	Green bell pepper, medium dice
6 oz	180 g	Shiitake mushrooms, sliced
1 tbsp	15 mL	Garlic, chopped
12	12	Scallions, sliced
18 fl oz	550 mL	Thai Green Curry Sauce (p. 194), hot

■ Procedure

1. Heat half the oil in a large sauté pan or wok.
2. Over high heat, stir-fry the pork just until it loses its pink color. Cook it in several batches if necessary. Remove from pan.
3. Add the rest of the oil to the pan.
4. With the pan still over high heat, add the bok choy, squash, peppers, mushrooms, garlic, and scallions. Stir-fry for a few minutes, keeping the vegetables crisp.
5. Return the pork to the pan and add the sauce. Simmer until the pork is cooked through.
6. Serve immediately with steamed rice.

Per serving:
Calories, 250; Protein, 18 g; Fat, 19 g (64% cal.); Cholesterol, 40 mg; Carbohydrates, 6 g; Fiber, 2 g; Sodium, 310 mg.

Note: This method of making a curry is designed for advance preparation and quick, last-minute cooking. A more traditional method is to make the sauce as an integral sauce. Stir-fry the meat and vegetables, add curry paste (see sauce recipe, p. 173), and cook until aromatic. Add the coconut milk, other liquids, flavorings, and any other ingredients indicated in the sauce recipe, and finish cooking.

Thai Green Curry of Pork with Vegetables

Entrecôte Sauté Bordelaise (Sirloin Steak with Red Wine and Shallot Sauce)

Portions: 12   Portion size: 1 steak, 6 oz (175 g)
3 fl oz (95 mL) sauce

U.S.	Metric	Ingredients
12	12	Strip loin steaks, 6–7 oz (180–200 g) each
5 fl oz	150 mL	Oil
3 oz	90 g	Butter
1 lb 4 oz	600 g	Shallots, chopped fine
1 pt 4 fl oz	600 mL	Red wine
2½ pt	1.2 L	Brown stock
to taste	to taste	Salt
to taste	to taste	Pepper
1½ oz	50 g	Butter (optional)
5 oz	150 g	Bone marrow, poached and diced (optional)
1 oz	30 g	Chopped parsley

■ Procedure

1. Season the steaks and sear in a hot sauté pan with the oil. Cook until rare and rest the steaks in a warm place. Degrease the pan.
2. For the sauce, add the first quantity of butter to the pan and gently sauté the shallots until lightly golden. Add the wine and reduce by 90 percent. Add the stock and continue to reduce by another 50 percent.
3. Season the sauce to taste with salt and pepper and, if desired, finish with the second amount of butter to add a gloss to the sauce.
4. Rewarm the steaks and place on hot plates with the sauce around. Place the warm diced bone marrow on top of the steaks and garnish with chopped parsley.

Per serving:
Calories, 400; Protein, 29 g; Fat, 27 g (61% cal.); Cholesterol, 90 mg; Carbohydrates, 9 g; Fiber, 0 g; Sodium, 135 mg.

Côte de Veau Grandmère (Veal Chops with Bacon, Mushrooms, and Onions)

Portions: 12   Portion size: 1 chop, 5 oz (150 g) vegetable garnish

U.S.	Metric	Ingredients
1 lb 5 oz	650 g	Pearl onions
1 oz	30 g	Butter
1 tbsp	15 g	Sugar
1 lb 2 oz	550 g	Slab bacon
1 oz	30 g	Butter
1 oz	30 g	Butter
1 lb 5 oz	650 g	Button mushrooms
4 lb	1.8 kg	Potatoes
8 fl oz	250 mL	Oil
1½ oz	45 g	Butter
to taste	to taste	Salt
12	12	Veal rib chops, about 7–8 oz (200–250 g) each
as needed	as needed	Oil
as needed	as needed	Butter
1 qt	900 mL	Brown stock
to taste	to taste	Salt
to taste	to taste	Pepper
to taste	to taste	Lemon juice
3 tbsp	20 g	Chopped parsley

■ Procedure

1. Peel the pearl onions and place in a pan large enough to cook in a single layer.
2. Add the butter and sugar and add enough water to cover. Cover with a round of parchment paper and cook until all the water has evaporated and the onions are coated with a fine glaze. Continue cooking, constantly moving the onions until they are evenly colored.
3. Cut the bacon into small cubes. Blanch in water and drain.
4. Brown in melted butter.
5. Heat the butter and cook the mushrooms until the liquid has evaporated. Strain and set aside.
6. Tourné the potatoes into small olive shapes. Rinse and pat dry.
7. Cook in very hot oil, moving often. After about 5 minutes, add the butter to finish cooking. (Adding the butter too early will soften the potatoes and make them stick to the pan, causing them to break up.) Strain off excess oil and season with salt.
8. Toss the onions, bacon, mushrooms, and potatoes together.
9. Pan-fry the veal chops in a little oil and butter.
10. Remove from the pan and keep warm.
11. Degrease the pan and deglaze with the stock. Reduce until thick enough to coat the back of a spoon.
12. Season with salt, papper, and a few drops of lemon juice.
13. Serve the chop on the center of the plate and spoon the mixed vegetables and bacon around. Coat the chop with the sauce and sprinkle with chopped parsley.

Per serving:
Calories, 740; Protein, 29 g; Fat, 52 g (64% cal.); Cholesterol, 150 mg; Carbohydrates, 37 g; Fiber, 4 g; Sodium, 510 mg.

Lamb Medallions with Thyme and Garlic Cream

Portions: 8   Portion size: ½ lamb rack

U.S.	Metric	Ingredients
40	40	Garlic cloves, peeled
10 fl oz	300 mL	Milk
10 oz	300 g	Crème fraîche
to taste	to taste	Salt
to taste	to taste	White pepper
4 racks	4 racks	Lamb (2 hotel racks)
as needed	as needed	Olive oil
2 tbsp	30 mL	Fresh thyme leaves
		Optional ingredients (see step 6):
as needed	as needed	Oil
5 oz	150 g	Carrots, chopped
5 oz	150 g	Onions, chopped
2 stems	2 stems	Celery, chopped
2 cloves	2 cloves	Garlic, chopped
1 lb	500 g	Tomatoes, chopped
1	1	Bouquet garni
3½ fl oz	100 mL	White wine (optional)
as needed	as needed	Water
to taste	to taste	Salt
to taste	to taste	Pepper
3 fl oz	90 mL	Oil
2 oz	60 mL	Butter
8 portions	8 portions	Tomato and Zucchini Tian (p. 571; optional)

Per serving:
Calories, 470: Protein, 20 g; Fat, 40 g; (76% cal.), Cholesterol, 105 mg; Carbohydrates, 8 g; Fiber, 0 g; Sodium, 150 mg.

■ Procedure

1. Simmer the peeled garlic cloves in the milk for 3–4 minutes.
2. Add the crème fraîche and finish cooking at a simmer until soft (the cloves should give easily when pressed with the back of a spoon).
3. Purée in a blender until smooth. Season to taste.
4. Bone the lamb racks. Trim the meat of excess fat and connective tissue.
5. Rub the meat with a little olive oil and coat lightly with fresh thyme. Allow to marinate for several hours or overnight.
6. If you have a good-quality brown lamb stock on hand, simmer 1 qt (1 L) of it until reduced to a rich syrup and reserve. If you do not have lamb stock on hand, use the bones from the racks to make the jus, following steps. 7–11
7. Chop the bones. Heat some oil in a deep pan. Add the bones and trimmings and brown.
8. Add the vegetables and bouquet garni. Stir, coating well with the oil. Cook for a few minutes.
9. Deglaze with the white wine or water and stir to dissolve the caramelized cooking juices. Cook until almost completely reduced.
10. Reduce to a simmer and cook for 30 minutes, skimming regularly. If the jus reduces too quickly, add more water.
11. Strain and degrease further if necessary and continue to reduce until syrupy.
12. Season the lamb with salt and pepper.
13. Brown in the oil and butter in a sauté pan. Finish cooking at reduced heat on top of the stove or, for more even cooking, in the oven at 400°F (200°C) for about 6 minutes, until rare or medium rare. Allow to rest 10 minutes. Slice each piece into 6 medallions.
14. To serve, pour a little garlic cream sauce on the plate and arrange the medallions on top. Drizzle with a little of the reduced lamb jus. Serve each portion with a vegetable tian on a side dish.

Fillet of Lamb with Mint and Cilantro Jus

Portions: 12   Portion size: 6 ½ oz (185 g) meat
2 ½ fl oz (70 mL) sauce

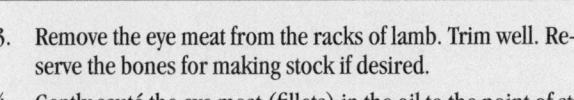

U.S.	Metric	Ingredients	Procedure
9 lb	4.5 kg	Spinach	1. Carefully pick and wash the spinach. Drain well. Set aside.
1 lb	500 g	Large tomatoes	2. Peel, seed, and chop the tomatoes. Set aside.
4	4	Hotel racks of lamb (or 8 single racks)	3. Remove the eye meat from the racks of lamb. Trim well. Reserve the bones for making stock if desired.
as needed	as needed	Oil	4. Gently sauté the eye meat (fillets) in the oil to the point of still just pink, taking care to brown them on all sides. Remove from the pan and hold in a warm place.
6	6	Shallots, large, chopped	
1½ qt	1.5 L	Brown veal stock	
to taste	to taste	Salt	5. Degrease the pan. Add the shallots and lightly sauté before adding the stock. Reduce to about 14 oz (850 mL) and season to taste. Finish with the chopped cilantro and mint.
1 oz	30 g	Fresh cilantro, chopped	
1 oz	30 g	Fresh mint, chopped	
3½ fl oz	100 mL	Hazelnut oil	6. Heat a clean sauté pan. Add the hazelnut oil and quickly cook the spinach until just wilted. Drain and season.
10 oz	300 g	Pine nuts, toasted	
			7. For each portion, place a ring mold, about 2½–3 in. (6–8 cm) in diameter, on the center of a plate. Pack the spinach into the mold and remove the ring.
			8. Slice the rested lamb fillet and arrange neatly on the bed of spinach. Surround with the herb jus and sprinkle with the chopped tomatoes and pine nuts.

Fillet of Lamb with Mint and Cilantro Jus

Per serving:
Calories, 390; Protein, 27 g; Fat, 26 g (57% cal); Cholesterol, 40 mg; Carbohydrates, 17 g; Fiber, 9 g; Sodium, 240 mg.

Calf's Liver Lyonnaise

Portions: 10   Portion size: 1 slice liver
1½ oz (50 g) onion garnish

U.S.	Metric	Ingredients	Procedure
2 lb	1 kg	Onions	1. Peel and slice the onions.
3 oz	90 g	Butter	2. Heat the butter in a sauté pan and add the onions. Sauté them over medium heat until tender and golden brown.
1 cup	250 mL	Demi-glace or strong brown stock	3. Add the demi-glace or stock and cook a few minutes, until the onions are nicely glazed. Season to taste.
to taste	to taste	Salt	
to taste	to taste	Pepper	4. Place in a bain-marie and keep warm for service.
10 slices	10 slices	Calf's liver, ¼ in. (6 mm) thick, about 4 oz (125 g) each	5. Season the liver and dredge in flour. Shake off excess flour.
as needed	as needed	Salt	6. Pan-fry the liver in butter or oil over moderate heat until browned on both sides and slightly firm to the touch. Do not overcook or use high heat.
as needed	as needed	Pepper	
as needed	as needed	Flour	7. Serve each portion with 1½ oz (50 g) onion mixture.
as needed	as needed	Clarified butter or oil	

Per serving:
Calories, 310; Protein, 24 g; Fat, 19 g (54% cal); Cholesterol, 445 mg; Carbohydrates, 13 g; Fiber, 1 g; Sodium, 250 mg.

Medallions of Venison Poîvrade with Cassis

Portions: 8   Portion size: 2 medallions, 2–3 oz (60–90 g) each

U.S.	Metric	Ingredients
16	16	Medallions of venison, cut from the loin, ¾ in. (2 cm) thick, about 2–3 oz (60–90 g) each
to taste	to taste	Salt
to taste	to taste	Pepper
as needed	as needed	Butter or oil
4 fl oz	125 mL	Chicken stock
12 fl oz	375 mL	Poîvrade Sauce (p. 175)
1 fl oz	30 mL	Crème de cassis (blackcurrant liqueur.)

Per serving:
Calories, 260; Protein, 26 g; Fat, 11 g (39% cal.); Cholesterol, 120 mg; Carbohydrates, 4 g; Fiber, 2 g; Sodium, 150 mg.

■ **P r o c e d u r e**

1. Season the meat with salt and pepper. Sauté in butter or oil, keeping the meat rare.
2. Remove the meat from the sauté pan and set it aside in a warm place.
3. Degrease the sauté pan. Deglaze it with the chicken stock and reduce the stock by half.
4. Add the sauce and the cassis to the pan and bring to a simmer. Strain the sauce.
5. Serve 2 medallions per portion. Spoon the sauce around the meat, using about 1½ oz (45 mL) per portion. Garnish the plate with appropriate seasonal vegetables.

V A R I A T I O N

Medallions of Boar Poîvrade with Cassis
Prepare as in the basic recipe, substituting loin of boar for the venison. Cook the meat until it is almost well done but still a little pink inside. Do not overcook, or the meat will be dry.

 ## Sautéed Veal Sweetbreads with Shiitake Mushrooms and Port Wine Sauce

Portions: 10   Portion size: 4 oz (125 g) sweetbreads, plus sauce and garnish

U.S.	Metric	Ingredients
2½ lb	1.25 kg	Sweetbreads, blanched, trimmed, and pressed according to the procedure on page 279
to taste	to taste	Salt
to taste	to taste	Pepper
as needed	as needed	Flour
as needed	as needed	Clarified butter
as needed	as needed	Clarified butter
1¼ lb	625 g	Shiitake mushrooms, caps only, cut into strips
to taste	to taste	Salt
to taste	to taste	Pepper
1 pt	500 mL	Port Wine Sauce (p. 175)

Per serving:
Calories, 330; Protein, 23 g; Fat, 16 g (43% cal.); Cholesterol, 340 mg; Carbohydrates, 17 g; Fiber, 1 g; Sodium, 270 mg.

■ **P r o c e d u r e**

1. Slice the sweetbreads in half horizontally.
2. Season the sweetbreads with salt and pepper. Dredge them with flour and shake off the excess.
3. Heat the butter in a sauté pan over moderately high heat. Sauté the sweetbreads until golden brown on both sides. Place on hot dinner plates.
4. Heat additional butter in the sauté pan and quickly sauté the mushrooms over high heat just until tender, about 1 minute. Add salt and pepper to taste.
5. Spoon the sauce around (not over) the sweetbreads. Distribute the mushrooms around the sweetbreads.
6. Serving suggestion: A green vegetable, such as small green beans, makes a good additional complement to the plate.

V A R I A T I O N

Instead of dredging the sweetbreads in flour, bread them using the Standard Breading Procedure (p. 143). Omit the port wine sauce and top each portion with a little beurre noisette.

Stir-Fried Beef with Green Peppers

Portions: 16   Portion size: 4 oz (125 g)

U.S.	Metric	Ingredients
2½ lb	1.2 kg	Flank steak
4 fl oz	125 mL	Soy sauce
1 fl oz	30 mL	Sherry or shaoxing wine
5 tsp	25 mL	Cornstarch
6	6	Green bell peppers
4 slices	4 slices	Ginger root
1–2	1–2	Garlic cloves, sliced
2 fl oz	60 g	Scallions, sliced
3–4 fl oz	90–125 mL	Oil
½ tsp	2 mL	Salt
2 fl oz	60 mL	Chicken stock

Per serving:
Calories, 180; Protein, 16 g; Fat, 11 g (54% cal.); Cholesterol, 35 mg;
Carbohydrates, 5 g; Fiber, 1 g; Sodium, 525 mg.

■ Procedure

1. Cut the flank steak lengthwise (with the grain) into strips 2 in. (5 cm) wide. Then cut the strips crosswise into very thin slices. (This is easier if the meat is partially frozen.)
2. Toss the meat with the soy sauce, sherry, and cornstarch. Let marinate 30 minutes or longer.
3. Core and seed the peppers. Cut them into large dice.
4. Have the ginger, garlic, and scallions ready in separate containers.
5. Stir-fry the beef in 3 or more batches, depending on the size of the pan or wok. Use a little of the oil for each batch, as needed.
6. As each batch of the beef is cooked, remove it from the pan and set it aside.
7. Heat additional oil in the pan and add the salt, ginger, garlic, and scallions. Stir-fry for a few seconds to develop flavor.
8. Add the peppers and stir-fry until lightly cooked but still crisp.
9. Add the stock and toss the vegetables a few times.
10. Return the meat to the pan. Toss the meat with the vegetables until it is hot and evenly combined with the peppers. Serve at once.

VARIATIONS

Other vegetables may be used instead of the peppers, such as celery, broccoli, snow peas, green beans, asparagus, mushrooms, bok choy. Or use 2 or 3 fresh vegetables, plus water chestnuts and/or bamboo shoots.

Chicken or pork may be used instead of beef. If chicken is used, cut it into medium dice or batonnet. Also, reduce the quantity of soy sauce to avoid discoloring the light meat of the chicken.

 ## Costolette di Vitello Ripiene alla Valdostana

Portions: 16   Portion size: 1 chop

U.S.	Metric	Ingredients
16	16	Veal rib chops
12 oz	350 g	Fontina cheese
to taste	to taste	Salt
to taste	to taste	White pepper
1½ tsp	7 mL	Rosemary
		Standard Breading Procedure:
as needed	as needed	Flour
as needed	as needed	Egg wash
as needed	as needed	Bread crumbs
as needed	as needed	Butter

Per serving:
Calories, 500; Protein, 35 g; Fat, 30 g (56% cal.); Cholesterol, 185 mg;
Carbohydrates, 19 g; Fiber, 1 g; Sodium, 530 mg.

■ Procedure

1. Remove the chine and feather bones so that only the rib bone is attached to each chop.
2. Cut a pocket in each, as shown in Figure 11.5.
3. Flatten the chops lightly with a cutlet pounder to increase the diameter of the eye. Be careful not to tear a hole in the meat.
4. Cut the cheese into thin slices.
5. Stuff the chops with the cheese, making sure all of the cheese is inside the pockets, with none hanging out. Press the edges of the pockets together and pound lightly to seal. If this is done carefully, you don't need to skewer them shut.
6. Season the chops with salt and pepper.
7. Set up a breading station. Crumble the rosemary and mix it with the bread crumbs.
8. Bread the chops.
9. Sauté the chops in butter and serve immediately.

VARIATIONS

Costolette alla Milanese
Omit the cheese stuffing and the rosemary. Do not cut pockets in the meat. Flatten the chops with a cutlet pounder until they are half their original thickness. Bread and sauté them as in the basic recipe.

SIMMERING

Meats are not often simmered. Part of the reason simmered meats are not as popular may be that they lack the kind of flavor produced by browning with dry heat.

However, simmering is used effectively for less tender cuts for which browning is not desired or not appropriate. Popular examples of simmered meats are cured products such as ham and corned beef, fresh or cured tongue, fresh beef brisket, and white stews such as veal blanquette.

The term **stewing** means cooking small pieces of meat by simmering or braising (a composite method that includes both browning and simmering). Stews cooked by braising are covered in the next section.

One difference between stews and many other simmered meats is that stews are served in a sauce or gravy made of the cooking liquid.

LIQUIDS AND FLAVORING INGREDIENTS FOR SIMMERED MEATS

The kind of meat to be cooked determines the kind and amount of cooking liquid to use as well as the kinds of flavorings and seasonings to use.

- For fresh meats, use enough liquid to cover the meat completely, but don't use too much, as flavors will be diluted. Water is the main cooking liquid, but other liquids, such as wine, can be added to flavor the meat. Use herbs, spices, and a generous amount of mirepoix to give a good flavor to the meat.

- For cured meats, especially meats that are heavily salted or smoked, use a generous amount of water to help draw excess salt or smoky flavor from the meat. In some cases, such as country hams, the water may even have to be changed during cooking to remove salt from the meat. Heavily seasoned cured meats, such as corned beef, are often simmered in pure, unseasoned water, but milder cured meats may be simmered with mirepoix and herbs. Do not add salt, however, because cured meats already contain a great deal of salt.

Basic Procedure for Simmering Meats

1. Collect all equipment and food supplies.

2. Prepare meat for cooking. This may include cutting, trimming, or tying.

3. Prepare the cooking liquid:
   - For fresh meats, start with boiling liquid, usually seasoned.
   - For cured and smoked meats, start with cold, unsalted liquid to help draw out some of the salt from the meats.
   - For both kinds of meats, use enough liquid to cover the meat completely.
   - Add mirepoix and seasonings as desired. (See the discussion of seasonings and flavorings above.)

4. Place the meat in the cooking liquid and return (or bring) to a boil.

5. Reduce heat to a simmer and skim the surface. Meat must never boil for any length of time. Simmering yields a more tender, juicier product than boiling.

6. Simmer until the meat is tender, skimming as necessary. To test for doneness, insert a kitchen fork into the meat. The meat is tender if the fork slides out easily. This is called *fork tender*.

7. If the meat is to be served cold, cool it in its cooking liquid to retain moistness. Cool rapidly in a cold-water bath, as for stocks.

Simmered Fresh Beef Brisket ("Boiled Beef")

Portions: 25   Portion size: 4 oz (125 g)

U.S.	Metric	Ingredients
10 lb	5 kg	Fresh beef brisket, well trimmed
		Mirepoix:
8 oz	250 g	Onion, coarsely chopped
4 oz	125 g	Carrot, coarsely chopped
4 oz	125 g	Celery, coarsely chopped
2 cloves	2 cloves	Garlic
1	1	Bay leaf
½ tsp	2 mL	Peppercorns
2	2	Whole cloves
6	6	Parsley stems
to taste	to taste	Salt

Per serving:
Calories, 280; Protein, 35 g; Fat, 15 g (49% cal.); Cholesterol, 110 mg; Carbohydrates, 0 g; Fiber, 0 g; Sodium, 90 mg.

■ P r o c e d u r e

1. Place beef in a stockpot with enough boiling water to cover. Return the water to a boil, reduce heat to a simmer, and skim the scum carefully.
2. Add the mirepoix and seasonings.
3. Simmer until the meat is tender when tested with a fork.
4. Transfer the meat to a steam table pan and add enough of the broth to barely cover (to keep the meat moist), or cool the meat with some of the broth in a cold-water bath and refrigerate.
5. To serve, cut the meat into thin slices across the grain. Slice at an angle to make the slices broader. Serve each portion with Horseradish Sauce (p. 173), prepared horseradish, or mustard and with boiled vegetables, such as carrots, potatoes, or turnips.
6. Strain the broth and save for soups or sauces. If desired, use some of the broth to make horseradish sauce to accompany the meat.

V A R I A T I O N S

Beef tongue (fresh, cured, or smoked), beef shank, various cuts of beef chuck, beef short ribs, fresh or smoked ham, pork shoulder, and lamb shoulder or leg may be cooked using the same method.

Simmered Pork Shoulder with Cabbage
Cook fresh or smoked pork shoulder or pork butt as in basic recipe. Cut 5 lb (2.3 kg) cabbage (for 25 portions) into wedges and simmer in some of the pork broth. Serve each portion of meat with a cabbage wedge. For 25 portions, 4 oz (125 g) each, use about 15 lb (7.5 kg) bone-in, skin-on shoulder.

Simmered Pork Shoulder; Braised Red Cabbage, Kasha Pilaf with Parsley, Roasted Onions

New England Boiled Dinner

Portions: 16   Portion size: 3 oz (90 g) meat, plus assorted vegetables

U.S.	Metric	Ingredients
5½ lb	2.75 kg	Corned beef brisket

■ P r o c e d u r e

1. Trim excess fat from corned beef if necessary.
2. Place the beef in a stockpot or steam kettle. Cover with cold water.
3. Bring to a boil and reduce heat to a simmer. Simmer until the meat feels tender when pierced with a fork. Cooking time will be about 2–3 hours.
4. To hold and serve hot, place the cooked meat in a steam table pan and add some of the cooking liquid to keep it moist.

U.S.	Metric	Ingredients
2 heads	2 heads	Green cabbage
2 lb	1 kg	Turnips
2 lb	1 kg	Carrots
30	30	Pearl onions
30	30	Baby beets
30	30	Small red-skinned potatoes
as needed	as needed	Horseradish Sauce (p. 173) or prepared horseradish

5. Prepare the vegetables: Cut each cabbage into 8 wedges; pare the turnips and carrots and cut them into serving-size pieces; peel the onions; scrub the beets and potatoes.
6. Cook the cabbage, turnips, carrots, onions, and potatoes separately in a little of the beef cooking liquid.
7. Steam the beets, then peel them.
8. To serve, cut the meat across the grain into slices, holding the knife at an angle to get broader slices. Serve with horseradish sauce or prepared horseradish.

Per serving:
Calories, 560; Protein, 31 g; Fat, 24 g (38% cal.); Cholesterol, 85 mg; Carbohydrates, 57 g; Fiber, 12 g; Sodium, 400 mg.

V A R I A T I O N

To serve the corned beef cold, cool the beef, with some of its cooking liquid to keep it moist, in a cold-water bath. When cool, remove from the liquid and refrigerate, covered. Cold corned beef may be reheated in its cooking liquid.

Blanquette of Veal

Portions: 25   Portion size: 5 oz (150 g)

U.S.	Metric	Ingredients
10 lb	5 kg	Boneless, trimmed veal breast, shoulder, or shank
1	1	Medium onion stuck with 2 cloves
1	1	Bouquet garni
4 tsp	20 mL	Salt
2½ qt (approximately)	2.5 L (approximately)	White veal stock
		Roux:
4 oz	125 g	Butter, clarified
4 oz	125 g	Flour
		Liaison:
5	5	Egg yolks
1 pt	500 mL	Heavy cream
to taste	to taste	Lemon juice
pinch	pinch	Nutmeg
pinch	pinch	White pepper

Per serving:
Calories, 350; Protein, 35 g; Fat, 21 g (55% cal.); Cholesterol, 230 mg; Carbohydrates, 4 g; Fiber, 0 g; Sodium, 550 mg.

Note: Blanching eliminates impurities that discolor the sauce. This step can be omitted, but the product will have a less attractive appearance.

■ **P r o c e d u r e**

1. Cut the veal into 1-in. (2½-cm) dice.
2. Blanch the meat: Place in a saucepot and cover with cold water. Bring to a boil, drain, and rinse the meat under cold water (see note).
3. Return the meat to the pot and add the onion stuck with cloves, bouquet garni, and salt.
4. Add enough stock to just cover the meat.
5. Bring to a boil, skim, cover, and lower heat to a slow simmer.
6. Simmer until meat is tender, about 1½ hours. Skim when necessary.
7. Strain the stock into another pan. Reserve the meat and discard the onion and bouquet garni.
8. Reduce the stock to about 2⅓ pt (1.25 L).
9. Meanwhile, prepare a white roux with the butter and flour. Beat into the stock to make a velouté sauce and simmer until thickened and no raw flour taste remains.
10. Remove the sauce from the heat. Beat the egg yolks and cream together, temper with a little of the hot sauce, and stir into the sauce.
11. Combine the sauce and meat. Heat gently but do not boil.
12. Season to taste with a few drops of lemon juice, a pinch of nutmeg and white pepper, and more salt if needed.

V A R I A T I O N S

Blanquette of Lamb
Prepare as in basic recipe, using lamb shoulder or shank. If desired, use white lamb stock.

Blanquette of Pork
Prepare as in basic recipe, using pork shoulder or butt. If desired, use white pork stock.

Irish Lamb Stew

Portions: 16   Portion size: 8 oz (250 g) meat, vegetables, and broth

U.S.	Metric	Ingredients
3½ lb	1.75 kg	Lean, boneless lamb shoulder or shanks
3 pt (approximately)	1.5 L (approximately)	Water or white lamb stock
1	1	Small onion stuck with 2 cloves
		Sachet:
1	1	Bay leaf
1 clove	1 clove	Garlic
4	4	Whole peppercorns
6	6	Parsley stems
¼ tsp	1 mL	Dried thyme
to taste	to taste	Salt
1 lb	500 g	Onions, sliced thin
8 oz	250 g	Leeks (white part), sliced
2 lb	1 kg	Potatoes, peeled and sliced thin
as needed	as needed	Chopped parsley

Per serving:
Calories, 200; Protein, 18 g; Fat, 7 g (33% cal.); Cholesterol, 60 mg; Carbohydrates, 14 g; Fiber, 2 g; Sodium, 55 mg.

■ **P r o c e d u r e**

1. Cut meat into 1-in. (2½-cm) cubes.
2. Bring the water to a boil in a large, heavy saucepot. Add the lamb. There should be just enough liquid to cover the meat; add more liquid if necessary.
3. Return to a boil, reduce heat to a simmer, and skim the scum carefully.
4. Add the onion stuck with cloves, the sachet ingredients tied in a piece of cheesecloth, and salt to taste. Simmer 1 hour.

5. Add the onions, leeks, and potatoes. Continue to simmer until the meat is tender and the vegetables are cooked. The potatoes should break down somewhat and thicken the stew.
6. Remove and discard the sachet and the onion stuck with cloves. Correct the seasoning.
7. Garnish each portion with chopped parsley.

V A R I A T I O N

Carrots and white turnips may be cooked with the stew or cooked separately and added as a garnish.

 Tripes à la Mode de Caen

Yield: approx. 5 lb (2.4 kg)   Portions: 8   Portion size: 10 oz (300 g)

U.S.	Metric	Ingredients
4 lb 8 oz	2.2 kg	Beef tripe
2	2	Calf's feet (see note)
8 oz	250 g	Onion, medium dice
6 oz	185 g	Carrots, sliced
6 oz	185 g	Leek, sliced
		Sachet:
12	12	Peppercorns, lightly crushed
2	2	Bay leaf
12	12	Parsley stems
½ tsp	2 mL	Dried thyme
4	4	Whole cloves
2 pt	1 L	Dry white wine
1 pt	500 mL	White stock
to taste	to taste	Salt
3 oz	90 mL	Calvados (apple brandy)

Per serving:
Calories, 640; Protein, 159 g; Fat, 28 g (40% cal.); Cholesterol, 345 mg; Carbohydrates, 8 g; Fiber, 1 g; Sodium, 200 mg.

■ **P r o c e d u r e**

1. Trim all fat from the tripe. Put the tripe in a pot of cold water and bring it to a boil. Simmer 5 minutes. Drain and rinse in cold water. Cut the tripe into 1½-in. (4-cm) squares.
2. Cut the feet into pieces with a meat saw as necessary so that they fit into the braising pan.
3. Combine all the ingredients, except the Calvados, in a braising pan or other heavy pot. Salt lightly. Bring to a boil, cover tightly, and put in an oven at 325°F (160°C). Cook 5 hours or longer, until the tripe is very tender.
4. Remove the feet and bone them out. Dice the skin and meat and return it to the pot. Discard the bone, fat, and connective tissue.
5. Stir in the Calvados. Adjust the seasoning. Simmer a few minutes to blend in the flavor of the Calvados.
6. Serve with boiled potatoes.

Note: If calf's feet are not available, substitute twice the number of pig's feet. Do not omit, or the tripe stew will not have enough gelatin to give it the proper texture.

This dish is from the Normandy region of France, famed for, among other things, its apples. The traditional recipe calls for hard cider, but white wine is an acceptable substitute.

Pearl Balls

Yield: about 40 pieces

U.S.	Metric	Ingredients
2 cups	500 mL	Glutinous rice
3 tbsp	45 mL	Cornstarch
1 fl oz	30 mL	Water, cold
2 lb	900 g	Ground pork
4	4	Scallions, minced
8	8	Water chestnuts, minced
2 tsp	10 mL	Minced fresh ginger root
2	2	Eggs, beaten
1 fl oz	30 mL	Soy sauce
1 fl oz	30 mL	Sherry or shaoxing wine
2 tsp	10 mL	Sugar
1½ tsp	7 mL	Salt

Per 1 piece:
Calories, 70; Protein, 5 g; Fat, 3.5 g (49% cal.); Cholesterol, 25 mg; Carbohydrates, 3 g; Fiber, 0 g; Sodium, 145 mg.

■ P r o c e d u r e

1. Wash the rice in several changes of cold water. Drain. Add enough fresh water to cover by 1 in. (2½ cm). Let soak for at least 30 minutes.
2. Mix together the cornstarch and water.
3. Combine all ingredients except the glutinous rice and mix together.
4. Form the meat mixture into small meatballs, about 1 oz (30 g) each.
5. Drain the rice. Roll the balls in the rice so that they are well coated.
6. Line a rack or perforated steamer pan with cheesecloth. Arrange the meatballs in the pan, allowing about ½ in. (1–2 cm) between them.
7. Steam for 30–45 minutes, until the rice is translucent and the pork is done.

V A R I A T I O N S

Fried Pork Balls
Omit the rice coating and cook the meatballs by deep-frying them.

Wontons
The pork mixture can be used for wonton filling. Put a small spoonful of meat in the center of a wonton skin. Moisten the edges with beaten egg, then fold the skin in half to make a triangle (or, if you are using round wonton skins, a semicircle) enclosing the filling. Moisten one of the two corners (on the folded edge) with egg, then twist the wonton to bring the two corners together. Press the corners together to seal. Makes 60 or more wontons, depending on size. Wontons can be cooked by simmering, steaming, or deep-frying. They are often served in chicken broth as wonton soup.

Shredded Pork (Carnitas)

Yield: about 3½ lb (1.6 kg)

U.S.	Metric	Ingredients
6 lb	2.8 kg	Pork butt or shoulder, boned
1	1	Onion, medium, cut in half
1	1	Garlic clove, chopped
1 tbsp	15 mL	Salt
¼ tsp	1 mL	Pepper
1 tsp	5 mL	Dried oregano
1 tsp	5 mL	Cumin seeds

Per ounces:
Calories, 390; Protein, 31 g; Fat, 28 g (67% cal.); Cholesterol, 120 mg; Carbohydrates, 0 g; Fiber, 0 g; Sodium 590 mg.

■ P r o c e d u r e

1. Remove most of the large chunks of fat from the pork, leaving a little of it on. Cut the meat into strips measuring 1 x 2 in. (2.5 x 5 cm).
2. Put the pork in a large pot with the rest of the ingredients. Add water to barely cover the meat.
3. Bring to a boil, reduce heat, and simmer slowly, uncovered, until all the liquid has evaporated. By this time, the meat should be tender. If it is not, add more water and continue to cook until it is.
4. Remove the onion and discard it.
5. Lower the heat and let the meat cook in the rendered fat, stirring from time to time, until the meat is browned and very tender. Shred the meat slightly.
6. Serve as a snack, an appetizer, or a filling for tortillas, either as it is or moistened with any of the sauces in this section or with guacamole.

V A R I A T I O N S

Picadillo
Add a little extra water to the basic recipe so that some liquid will be left when the meat is tender. Drain and degrease the liquid and use it to make Tomato Broth for Chiles Rellenos (p. 190). Heat 3 oz (90 g) oil or lard and sauté 6 oz (175 g) onion, medium dice, and 4 cloves garlic, chopped. Add the meat, plus a sachet containing 10 peppercorns, 1 small cinnamon stick, and 6 cloves, and brown slowly. Add 4 oz (125 g) raisins, 4 oz (125 g) slivered almonds, and 2 lb (900 g) peeled, seeded, chopped tomatoes. Cook slowly until almost dry. Serve as is or as a stuffing for Chiles Rellenos (p. 578).

Shortcut Picadillo
Instead of preparing Shredded Pork, use 5 lb (2.3 kg) raw ground pork. Sauté it with the onion and garlic in the picadillo recipe, then proceed as directed with the rest of the recipe.

Dillkött

Portions: 16   Portion size: 6 oz (175 g)

U.S.	Metric	Ingredients
7 lb	3.2 kg	Boneless, trimmed veal shoulder, breast, or shank
1	1	Medium onion stuck with 2 cloves
		Sachet:
1	1	Bay leaf
5–6	5–6	Parsley stems
6	6	Peppercorns
2 qt	2 L	Water
1 tbsp	15 mL	Salt
2 tbsp	30 mL	Fresh dill weed, chopped (see note)
		Roux:
2 oz	60 g	Butter
2 oz	60 g	Flour
1 fl oz	30 mL	Lemon juice or wine vinegar
1½ tsp	7 mL	Brown sugar
2 tbsp	30 mL	Fresh dill weed, chopped
2 tbsp	30 mL	Capers, drained

Per serving:
Calories, 280; Protein, 36 g; Fat, 12 g (41% cal.); Cholesterol, 165 mg; Carbohydrates, 3 g; Fiber, 0 g; Sodium, 640 mg.

Note: If fresh dill is not available, substitute one-third its quantity of dried dill.

■ P r o c e d u r e

1. Cut the veal into 1-in. (2.5-cm) dice.
2. Put the meat in a pot with the onion, sachet, water, and salt. Bring to a boil and skim well.
3. Reduce the heat and add the dill. Simmer slowly until the meat is very tender, about 1½–2 hours.
4. Strain off the broth into another pan. Discard the onion and the sachet.

5. Reduce the broth over high heat to 1 qt (1 L).
6. Make a blond roux with the flour and butter. Thicken the broth with it.
7. Add the lemon juice, brown sugar, dill, and capers. Adjust the seasonings.

V A R I A T I O N

Dillkött på Lamm
Substitute lamb shoulder or shank for the veal.

Lamb Tagine with Chickpeas

Portions: 12   Portion size: 10 oz (285 g) meat, vegetables, and sauce

U.S.	Metric	Ingredients
3 fl oz	90 mL	Vegetable oil
8 oz	240 g	Onion, chopped fine
½ oz	15 g	Garlic, crushed
1 tsp	5 mL	Ground ginger
1 tsp	5 mL	Turmeric
1 oz	30 g	Fresh cilantro, chopped
2 tsp	10 mL	Salt
1 tsp	5 mL	Pepper
5½ lb	2.5 kg	Lamb shoulder, boneless, trimmed of fat, cut into 1½-in. (4-cm) pieces
1 pt	500 mL	Water
1½ lb	675 g	Chickpeas, cooked or canned, drained
1½ lb	675 g	Carrots, cut into 1-in. (2.5-cm) pieces
6 oz	180 g	Mediterranean-type olives, such as kalamata, pitted
3 fl oz	90 mL	Lemon juice
to taste	to taste	Salt

Per serving:
Calories, 620; Protein, 43 g; Fat, 40 g (57% cal.); Cholesterol, 145 mg; Carbohydrates, 24 g; Fiber, 7 g; Sodium, 640 mg.

■ P r o c e d u r e

1. In a heavy braising pan or casserole, mix together the oil, onion, garlic, ginger, turmeric, cilantro, salt, and pepper.
2. Add the lamb to the pan and toss with the spice mixture to coat all the pieces.
3. Add the water. Bring to a boil, and then cover tightly. Simmer slowly on top of the stove or in an oven heated to 325°F (165°C) for 1½ hours.

4. Add the chickpeas and carrots to the pan. If necessary, add a little more water if the tagine is becoming dry.
5. Return to the heat and cook until the carrots and the meat are very tender.

6. Add the olives and lemon juice and stir. Simmer another 5 minutes.
7. Remove the meat and vegetables with a slotted spoon.
8. Degrease the cooking liquid.
9. Reduce the cooking liquid over moderate heat until it has the consistency of thick gravy.
10. Season the liquid with salt if necessary. Pour over the meat and vegetables.

Poached Beef Tenderloin with Beef Short Rib Ravioli in Morel Consommé

Portions: 16   Portion size: 4 oz (125 g) meat, 3 oz (90 g) ravioli,
3 mushrooms, 3 fl oz (90 mL) consommé

U.S.	Metric	Ingredients
2 lb	1 kg	Trimmed meat from Braised Short Ribs (p. 335)
½ cup	125 mL	Chopped parsley
¼ cup	60 mL	Grated parmesan cheese
2 lb	1 kg	Fresh Egg Pasta (p. 640)
48	48	Dried morel mushrooms
as needed	as needed	Hot water
3 pt	1.5 L	Consommé (p. 212)
4 lb	2 kg	Beef tenderloin, completely trimmed of fat and silverskin, in 1 or 2 pieces
to taste	to taste	Salt
to taste	to taste	Pepper
4 qt	4 L	Brown stock

Per serving:
Calories, 680; Protein, 46 g; Fat, 40 g (55% cal.); Cholesterol, 210 mg;
Carbohydrates, 29 g; Fiber, 1 g; Sodium, 180 mg.

■ P r o c e d u r e

1. Prepare the ravioli filling: Shred the meat and place it in a bowl. Add the chopped parsley and cheese. Mix well.

2. If the meat mixture is dry, moisten with a little of the short rib braising liquid or brown stock.

3. Roll out the pasta and, using the meat mixture as a filling, make ravioli following the procedure illustrated on page 641.

4. If desired, cook the ravioli in advance. Simmer in salted water until just tender. Drain. Rinse briefly with cold water to stop the cooking. Toss with a little vegetable oil to keep them from sticking. Refrigerate, covered, until needed.

5. Place the mushrooms in a bowl and add hot water to cover. Let soak until soft.

6. Drain the mushrooms, squeezing them lightly. Strain and reserve the soaking liquid.

7. Combine the soaking liquid with an equal volume of the consommé. Bring to a simmer. Cook until the mushrooms are tender.

8. Drain the mushrooms. Strain the cooking liquid again and add it to the consommé.

9. Season the beef with salt and pepper.

10. Bring the stock to a boil in a pot large enough to hold both the stock and the beef.

11. Lower the beef into the stock. Adjust the heat and cook at a slow simmer until the meat reaches the desired doneness, as determined by a meat thermometer. The temperature at the center of the meat should be 120°F (49°C) for rare, 130°F (54°C) for medium. Cooking time will be about 20–30 minutes for rare, slightly longer for medium.

12. Remove the meat from the liquid and let rest in a warm place for about 15 minutes.

13. Reserve the stock for another use, such as for making the next batch of consommé.

14. While the meat is cooking, bring the consommé to a simmer and hold.

15. If the ravioli were cooked in advance, reheat them by dropping them for a moment into boiling water. Drain. If they were not cooked ahead, cook them now in simmering salted water until just tender.

16. Slice the meat. Arrange it in heated broad soup plates with the ravioli and the morels. Ladle 3 fl oz (90 mL) consommé into each bowl.

BRAISING

Braising is a combination of dry-heat and moist-heat cooking methods. Meats are first browned or seared in fat or in a hot oven, then simmered in a flavorful liquid until tender.

The popularity of properly braised items is due to the flavor imparted by the browning and by the sauce made from the braising liquid. Clearly, the quality of a braised meat depends greatly on the quality of the stock the meat is cooked in. Other liquids used in braising include wine, marinades, tomato products, and, occasionally, water.

POPULAR TYPES OF BRAISED MEAT DISHES

1. **Large cuts.**
    Large cuts of meat braised whole, sliced, and served with a sauce or gravy are sometimes called **pot roasts**.

2. **Individual portion cuts.**
    Meats may be cut into portion sizes before braising instead of afterward. When portion cuts of beef round are braised in a brown sauce, the process is sometimes called swissing, and the product is called **Swiss steak**.

    Other braised portion cut meats include short ribs, lamb shanks, and pork chops.

3. **Stews.**
    Stews are made of meats cut into small pieces or cubes. Most stews are made by braising, but some are cooked by simmering only, without first browning or searing the meat.

    Stews are usually made with enough liquid or gravy to cover the meat completely while cooking. However, so-called dry stews are braised in their own juices or in a very little added liquid.

    Brown stews are made by browning the meat thoroughly before simmering. **Fricassées** are white stews made by cooking white meat in fat over low heat without letting it brown, then adding liquid. Compare this to **blanquettes**, which are white stews made by simmering the meat in stock without first cooking it in fat. The cooking method for blanquettes, therefore, is simmering rather than braising.

    Note: This use of the term *fricassée* is its traditional or classical usage. Today the word is often used for many kinds of stews.

    Many other dishes can be classified as braised stews, even if we don't normally think of them that way. Chili, for example, is a braised dish made of finely cut or ground beef or pork. Even meat sauce for spaghetti (p. 639) is actually a braised meat or a stew.

    Many chefs prefer to use the term *braising* only for large cuts of meat and use the term *stewing* for small cuts. However, the basic cooking method—using first dry heat, then moist heat—is the same for both large and small cuts.

Guidelines for Braising Meats

The basic principle of braising is a combination of searing or browning and then simmering. This process accomplishes two things: *it cooks the meat*, and *it produces a sauce*. (You will use some of your sauce-making techniques when you braise meats.)

Before giving basic procedures that apply to most popular braised meats, we discuss factors that affect the quality of the finished product.

1. Seasoning.

   The meat may be seasoned before browning, or it may receive its seasonings from the cooking liquid while braising. But remember that salt on the surface of meat retards browning. Also, herbs may burn in the high heat necessary for browning.

   Marinating the meat for several hours or even several days before browning is an effective way to season because the seasonings have time to penetrate. The marinade is often included as part of the braising liquid.

2. Browning.

   Dry the meat thoroughly before browning. Small pieces for stew may be dredged in flour for better browning. In general, red meats are well browned; white meats are browned less heavily, usually until they are golden.

3. Amount of braising liquid.

   The amount of liquid to be added depends on the type of preparation and on the amount of sauce required for serving. Do not use more liquid than necessary, or the flavors will be less rich and less concentrated.

   Pot roasts usually require about 2 oz (60 mL) sauce per portion, and this determines the amount of liquid needed. The size of the braising pot used should allow the liquid to cover the meat by one-third to two-thirds.

   Stews usually require enough liquid to cover the meat.

   Some items are braised with no added liquid. They are browned, then covered, and the item cooks in its own moisture, which is trapped in by the pan lid. Pork chops are frequently cooked in this way. If roasted, sautéed, or pan-fried items are covered during cooking, they become, in effect, braised items.

4. Vegetable garnish.

   Vegetables to be served with the meat may be cooked along with the meat or cooked separately and added before service.

   If the first method is used, the vegetables should be added just long enough before the end of cooking for them to be cooked through but not overcooked.

5. Adjusting the sauce.

   Braising liquids may be thickened by a roux either before cooking (Method 2) or after cooking (Method 1). In some preparations, the liquid is left unthickened or is naturally thick, such as tomato sauce.

   In any case, the sauce may require further adjustment of its consistency by

   • Reducing.

   • Thickening with roux or beurre manié or other thickening agent.

   • The addition of a prepared sauce, such as demi-glace or velouté.

Basic Procedures for Braising Meats

Method 1: Braising in Unthickened Liquid

1. Collect all equipment and food supplies.
2. Cut or trim meat as required. Dry it thoroughly. For stews, the meat may be dredged with flour.
3. Brown the meat thoroughly on all sides in a heavy pan with a small amount of fat, or in an oven.
4. Remove the meat from the pan and brown mirepoix in the fat left in the pan.
5. Return the meat to the pan and add the required amount of liquid.
6. Add a sachet or other seasonings and flavorings.
7. Bring the liquid to a simmer, cover the pot tightly, and simmer in the oven or on top of the range until the meat is tender.

   Oven braising provides more uniform heat. Temperatures of 250° to 300°F (120° to 150°C) are sufficient to maintain a simmer. Do not let boil.
8. Remove the meat from the pan and keep it warm.
9. Prepare a sauce or gravy from the braising liquid. This usually includes the following:
   - Skim fat.
   - Prepare a brown roux with this fat or with another fat if desired.
   - Thicken the braising liquid with the roux. Simmer until the roux is cooked thoroughly.
   - Strain and adjust seasonings.
10. Combine the meat (sliced or whole) with the sauce.

Method 2: Braising in Thickened Liquid

1. Collect all equipment and food supplies.
2. Prepare meat for cooking, as required.
3. Brown meat thoroughly in a heavy pan with fat or in a hot oven.
4. Remove meat from pan (if required) and brown mirepoix in remaining fat.
5. Add flour to make a roux. Brown the roux.
6. Add stock to make a thickened sauce. Add seasonings and flavorings.
7. Return meat to pan. Cover and simmer in oven or on range until meat is tender.
8. Adjust sauce as necessary (strain, season, reduce, dilute, etc.).

Method 3: Classic Fricassées

1. Follow Method 2, *except:*
   - Do not brown the meat. Cook it gently in the fat without browning.
   - Add flour to the meat in the pan and make a blond roux.
2. Finish the sauce with a liaison of egg yolks and cream.

Beef Pot Roast

Portions: 25   Portion size: 4 oz (125 g) meat
2 fl oz (60 mL) sauce

U.S.	Metric	Ingredients
10 lb	5 kg	Beef bottom round, well trimmed (see note)
4 fl oz	125 mL	Oil
		Mirepoix:
8 oz	250 g	Onions, medium dice
4 oz	125 g	Celery, medium dice
4 oz	125 g	Carrots, medium dice
6 oz	175 g	Tomato purée
		or
12 oz	375 g	Tomatoes, canned
2½ qt	2.5 L	Brown stock
		Sachet:
1	1	Bay leaf
pinch	pinch	Dried thyme
6	6	Peppercorns
1 clove	1 clove	Garlic
4 oz	125 g	Bread flour

Per serving:
Calories, 320; Protein, 38 g; Fat, 15 g (45% cal.); Cholesterol, 90 mg; Carbohydrates, 4 g; Fiber, 0 g; Sodium, 70 mg.

Note: Other cuts of beef from the round, or from the chuck or brisket, may be used instead of bottom round. Braised round makes the best slices, but it tends to be dry. Chuck and brisket are moister when braised because they have a higher fat content.

For quicker, more uniform cooking and easier handling, cut meats for braising into 5–7 lb (2–3 kg) pieces.

■ Procedure

1. Dry the meat so it will brown more easily. Heat the oil in a brazier over high heat and brown the meat well on all sides. Remove from pan. (*Alternative method:* Brown meat in a very hot oven.)

2. Add the mirepoix to the brazier and brown it.

3. Add the tomato product, the stock, and the sachet ingredients tied in cheesecloth. Bring to a boil, cover, and place in a preheated oven set at 300°F (150°C), or just hot enough to maintain a simmer.

4. Braise the meat until tender, about 2–3 hours.

5. Remove meat from pan and keep warm for service in a covered pan. Discard sachet. (See alternate method of service given below.)

6. Skim the fat from the braising liquid and reserve 4 oz (125 g) of it.

7. Make a brown roux with the flour and the reserved fat. Cool the roux slightly.

8. Bring the braising liquid to a simmer and beat in the roux. Simmer the sauce at least 15–20 minutes, until thickened and reduced slightly.

9. Strain the sauce and adjust the seasonings.

10. Slice the meat across the grain. The slices should not be too thick. Serve each 4-oz (125-g) portion with 2 fl oz (60 mL) sauce.

VARIATIONS

Alternative Method of Service: Cool beef as soon as it is cooked. For service, slice cold meat on an electric slicer and arrange in hotel pans. Add sauce, cover pans, and reheat in oven or steamer. Individual portions may also be reheated to order in the sauce.

Braised Beef Jardinière
Garnish the finished product with 1 lb (500 g) each carrots, celery, and turnips, all cut batonnet and boiled separately, and 1 lb (500 g) pearl onions, boiled and sautéed until brown.

Braised Lamb Shoulder
Prepare boned, rolled shoulder of lamb according to the basic recipe. Use either regular brown stock or brown lamb stock.

Braised Short Ribs

Portions: 25   Portion size: 10 oz (300 g) meat with bone
2 fl oz (60 mL) sauce

U.S.	Metric	Ingredients
25	25	Short rib sections, 10 oz (300 g) each
8 oz	250 mL	Oil
10 oz	300 g	Onion, cut brunoise
5 oz	150 g	Celery, cut brunoise
5 oz	150 g	Carrot, cut brunoise
5 oz	150 g	Bread flour
2½ qt	2.5 L	Brown stock
5 oz	150 mL	Tomato purée
2	2	Bay leaves
to taste	to taste	Salt
to taste	to taste	Pepper

Per serving:
Calories, 299; Protein, 29 g; Fat, 17 g (52% cal.); Cholesterol, 55 mg; Carbohydrates, 6 g; Fiber, 0 g; Sodium, 70 mg.

Figure 11.11
Tie short ribs as shown so the meat will stay on the bone during cooking.

■ Procedure

1. Tie the short ribs, as shown in Figure 11.11.
2. Dry the meat so it will brown more easily.
3. Heat the oil in a heavy skillet until very hot. Brown the steaks well on both sides. Transfer the browned steaks to a braising pan or baking pan.
4. Add the onion, celery, and carrot to the fat in the skillet and sauté until lightly browned.
5. Stir in the bread flour to make a roux. Cook until the roux is browned.
6. Stir in the stock and tomato purée and simmer until the sauce thickens. Add the bay leaves and season to taste with salt and pepper.
7. Pour the sauce over the steaks. Cover and braise in the oven at 300°F (150°C) until tender, about 2 hours.
8. Transfer the steaks to a hotel pan for service.
9. Strain the sauce (optional). Degrease. Adjust the seasoning and consistency and pour over the steaks.

V A R I A T I O N S

Short ribs and other variations may be braised in a prepared brown sauce or espagnole instead of a specially made sauce. Omit steps 4, 5, and 6.

If desired, use 1 lb (500 g) chopped canned tomatoes instead of the purée.

Swiss Steak
Instead of the short ribs, use beef round steaks, about 5 oz (150 g) per portion. Omit celery and carrot if desired.

Swiss Steaks in Tomato Sauce
Reduce flour to 2½ oz (75 g). For braising liquid, use 2½ pt (1.25 L) brown stock, 2½ lb (1.25 kg) chopped canned tomatoes with their juice, and 1¼ lb (625 g) tomato purée. Season with bay leaf, oregano, and basil. After removing cooked steaks, reduce sauce to desired consistency. Do not strain. Garnish each portion with chopped parsley.

Swiss Steaks with Sour Cream
Prepare as in first Swiss Steak recipe. When steaks are cooked, finish the sauce with 1 pt (500 mL) sour cream, 2½ fl oz (75 mL) Worcestershire sauce, and 2 tbsp (30 g) prepared mustard.

Swiss Steaks in Red Wine Sauce
Prepare as in first Swiss Steak recipe, but add 1 pt (500 mL) dry red wine to the braising liquid.

Braised Oxtails
Allow 1 lb (500 g) oxtails per portion. Cut into sections at joints.

Braised Lamb Shanks
Allow 1 lamb shank per portion. Add chopped garlic to mirepoix if desired.

Beef Stew

Portions: 25   Portion size: 8 oz (250 g)

U.S.	Metric	Ingredients
6 lb	3 kg	Beef chuck, boneless and well trimmed of fat
4 fl oz	125 mL	Oil
1 lb	500 g	Onion, fine dice
2 tsp	10 mL	Chopped garlic
4 oz	125 g	Flour
8 oz	250 g	Tomato purée
2 qt	2 L	Brown stock
		Sachet:
1	1	Bay leaf
pinch	pinch	Thyme
small sprig	small sprig	Celery leaves
1 lb	500 g	Celery, EP
1½ lb	750 g	Carrots, EP
1 lb	500 g	Small pearl onions, EP
8 oz	250 g	Tomatoes, canned, drained, and coarsely chopped
8 oz	250 g	Peas, frozen, thawed
to taste	to taste	Salt
to taste	to taste	Pepper

■ **P r o c e d u r e**

1. Cut the meat into 1-in. (2½-cm) cubes.
2. Heat the oil in a brazier until very hot. Add the meat and brown well, stirring occasionally to brown all sides. If necessary, brown the meat in several small batches to avoid overcrowding the pan.
3. Add the onion and garlic to the pan and continue to cook until onion is lightly browned.
4. Add the flour to the meat and stir to make a roux. Continue to cook over high heat until the roux is slightly browned.
5. Stir in the tomato purée and stock and bring to a boil. Stir with a kitchen spoon as the sauce thickens.
6. Add the sachet. Cover the pot and place in an oven at 325°F (165°C). Braise until the meat is tender, about 1½–2 hours.
7. Cut the celery and carrots into large dice.
8. Cook the celery, carrots, and onions separately in boiling salted water until just tender.
9. When meat is tender, remove the sachet and adjust seasoning. Degrease the sauce.
10. Add celery, carrots, onions, and tomatoes to the stew.
11. Immediately before service, add the peas. Alternatively, garnish the top of each portion with peas. Season with salt and pepper.

Per serving:
Calories, 240; Protein, 27 g; Fat, 9 g (34% cal.); Cholesterol, 60 mg; Carbohydrates, 13 g; Fiber, 2 g; Sodium, 150 mg.

Note: For more elegant service, remove the cooked meat from sauce before adding the vegetables. Strain the sauce and pour it back over the meat.

V A R I A T I O N S

Vegetables for garniture may be varied, as desired.

Beef Stew with Red Wine
Prepare as in basic recipe, but use 2½ pt (1.25 L) dry red wine and 1½ pt (750 mL) brown stock instead of 2 qt (2 L) brown stock.

Boeuf Bourguignon
Prepare Beef Stew with Red Wine, using rendered salt pork or bacon fat instead of oil. (Cut the pork into batonnet shapes, sauté until crisp, and save the cooked pork for garnish.) Increase garlic to 2 tbsp (30 mL). Omit vegetable garnish (celery, carrots, pearl onions, tomatoes, and peas) indicated in basic recipe, and substitute lardons (cooked salt pork or bacon pieces), small mushroom caps browned in butter, and boiled pearl onions browned in butter. Serve with egg noodles.

Navarin of Lamb (Brown Lamb Stew)
Prepare as in basic recipe, using lamb shoulder instead of beef chuck. Increase garlic to 2 tbsp (30 mL).

Brown Veal Stew
Prepare as in basic recipe, using veal shoulder or shank.

Brown Veal with White Wine
Prepare Brown Veal Stew, replacing 1 pt (500 mL) stock with white wine.

Beef Pot Pie
Fill individual casserole dishes with stew and vegetable garnish. Top with pie pastry (p. 980). Bake in a hot oven (400°–450°F/200°–225°C) until crust is brown.

Boeuf à la Mode

Portions: 15   Portion size: 5½ (175 g) meat
2 fl oz (60 mL) sauce

U.S.	Metric	Ingredients
1 lb 4 oz	600 g	Fatback
1½ fl oz	50 mL	Cognac or brandy
to taste	to taste	Salt
to taste	to taste	Pepper
8 lb	4 kg	Beef rump roast (in one or more pieces)
as needed	as needed	Oil
1 lb 10 oz	800 g	Carrot, diced
7 oz	200 g	Celery, diced
2 oz	70 g	Garlic, diced
1 lb	500 g	Tomatoes, cut into quarters
1 tbsp	15 mL	Tomato paste
1 fl oz	30 mL	Cognac or brandy
10 fl oz	300 mL	White wine
1 qt	1 L	Brown veal stock
1 qt	1 L	Water
1	1	Bouquet garni (see p. 152)
1	1	Calf's foot, blanched (see note)
to taste	to taste	Salt
to taste	to taste	Pepper
3 tbsp	20 g	Chopped parsley

Per serving:
Calories, 740; Protein, 56 g; Fat, 51 g (63% cal.); Cholesterol, 190 mg; Carbohydrates, 8 g; Fiber, 2 g; Sodium, 150 mg.

Note: The purpose of the calf's foot is to provide gelatin to add body and texture to the sauce. If a calf's foot is not available, use 2 pig's feet.

Figure 11.12
Larding meat using a large needle.

■ P r o c e d u r e

1. Cut the fatback into long, thin strips to fit a larding needle (Figure 11.12). Marinate in the cognac and season with salt and pepper.
2. Trim the rump roast well, removing as much fat and sinew as possible. Reserve the trimmings.
3. Lard the roast, piercing lengthwise in 3 rows. The strips of fat should be about 1–1½ inches (3–4 cm) apart. Stagger the rows so that the fat is evenly distributed.
4. Heat some oil in a braising pan and brown the rump roast along with the trimmings.
5. Once evenly browned, remove the roast and add the carrot, celery, and garlic. Sweat for a few minutes.
6. Add the tomatoes and the tomato paste. Cook for a few minutes.
7. Deglaze with the cognac and white wine. Reduce by half. Add the veal stock and water.
8. Return the meat to the pot and add the bouquet garni and blanched calf's foot. Bring to a boil, then cover and place in a 350°F (175°C) oven. Cook for about 3 hours. (If the liquid evaporates too quickly, add more water.)
9. Once cooked, remove the meat and set aside. Remove the calf's foot, debone, and cut the meat and skin into small dice.
10. Strain the braising liquid and discard the solids. Reduce the liquid until it is thick enough to lightly coat the back of a spoon. Season to taste, then add the diced calf's foot.
11. Serve sliced, coated with the sauce, sprinkled with some chopped parsley.

V A R I A T I O N

Beef Stew with Carrots
Omit the fatback and both quantities of cognac. Use beef chuck, cut for stew, instead of the beef rump. Add 2½ lb (1.2 kg) chopped onion with the celery and carrot and reduce the garlic to ½ oz (15 g). Use half the quantity of stock and omit the water. Braise as in the basic recipe. Serve with Glazed Carrots (p. 554), cut tourné rather than sliced.

(a) Cut a strip of fatback to fit inside the needle.

(b) Insert the needle through the meat. Pull out the needle, holding the strip of fat so that it stays inside the meat.

Lombatine di Maiale alla Napoletana

Portions: 16   Portion size: 1 chop, 3–4 oz (90–125 g) vegetables

U.S.	Metric	Ingredients
6	6	Italian peppers or bell peppers; red or green
1 lb 8 oz	700 g	Mushrooms
3 lb	1.4 kg	Tomatoes
6 fl oz	175 mL	Olive oil
2	2	Garlic cloves, crushed
16	16	Pork loin chops
to taste	to taste	Salt
to taste	to taste	Pepper

Per serving:
Calories, 430; Protein, 45 g; Fat, 23 g (49% cal.); Cholesterol, 125 mg; Carbohydrates, 9 g; Fiber, 2 g; Sodium, 100 mg.

Note: Charring and peeling the peppers is optional, but it improves the flavor and removes the peel, which would otherwise come off during cooking and make the vegetable mixture less attractive.

■ P r o c e d u r e

1. Char the peppers over a gas flame until the skin is black. Rub off the blackened skin under cold running water. Remove and discard the seeds and core and cut the peppers into batonnet (see note).

2. Slice the mushrooms.

3. Peel, seed, and chop the tomatoes.

4. Heat the olive oil in a large sauté pan or brazier. Add the garlic cloves. Sauté them until they are light brown, then remove and discard them.

5. Season the chops with salt and pepper. Brown them in the olive oil. When they are well browned, remove and set them aside.

6. Add the peppers and mushrooms and sauté briefly, until wilted.

7. Add the tomatoes and return the chops to the pan. Cover and cook on the range or in a low oven until the pork is done. The vegetables should give off enough moisture to braise the chops, but check the pan from time to time to make sure it is not dry.

8. When the chops are done, remove them from the pan and keep them hot. If there is a lot of liquid in the pan, reduce it over high heat until there is just enough to form a little sauce for the vegetables.

9. Adjust the seasoning. Serve the chops topped with the vegetables.

V A R I A T I O N

Pollo con Peperoni all'Abruzzese
Double the quantities of peppers. Increase the tomatoes to 4½ lb (2 kg). Omit the mushrooms and garlic. Add 1 lb (450 g) sliced onions and sauté them with the peppers. Instead of pork, use 8–10 lb (3.6–4.5 kg) chicken parts. Season with a little basil. If desired, reduce the quantity of chicken in the above recipe and add some Italian pork sausages.

Lombatine di Maiale alla Napoletana

Chile con Carne

Portions: 24   Portion size: 8 oz (250 g)

U.S.	Metric	Ingredients
2½ lb	1.25 kg	Onion, small dice
1¼ lb	625 g	Green bell pepper, small dice
1 oz	30 g	Garlic, chopped
4 fl oz	125 g	Oil
5 lb	2.5 kg	Ground beef
1 No. 10 can	1 No. 10 can	Tomatoes
10 oz	300 g	Tomato paste
2½ pt	1.25 L	Brown stock
3 oz	90 g	Chili powder
to taste	to taste	Salt
to taste	to taste	Pepper

Per serving:
Calories, 310; Protein, 20 g; Fat, 19 g (54% cal.); Cholesterol, 55 mg; Carbohydrates, 16 g; Fiber, 4 g; Sodium, 380 mg.

■ Procedure

1. Sauté the onion, pepper, and garlic in oil in a heavy saucepot until tender but not browned. Remove from the pot.
2. Add the meat to the pot and brown over high heat, breaking up the meat with a spoon as it browns. Drain off the fat.
3. Return the vegetables to the pot and add the remaining ingredients.
4. Simmer uncovered until the chili has reduced to desired thickness, about 45–60 minutes. Stir occasionally during the cooking period.

VARIATION

Chile with Beans
Add 4 lb (2 kg) (drained weight) cooked or canned and drained kidney beans or pinto beans about 15 minutes before end of cooking.

Game Chile
In place of the ground beef, use ground bison, venison, elk, caribou, or boar.

Texas Red

Yield: 6 lb 12 oz (3 kg)   Portions: 12   Portion size: 9 oz (250 g)

U.S.	Metric	Ingredients
6 lb	2.75 kg	Lean beef, preferably chuck or shank, well trimmed
2 fl oz	60 mL	Vegetable oil
1 oz	30 g	Garlic, chopped fine
5 oz	140 g	Chili powder
1½ tbsp	22 mL	Ground cumin
1½ tbsp	22 mL	Dried oregano
1–2 tsp	5–10 mL	Cayenne
2 qt	2 L	Brown stock or beef broth
2 oz	60 g	Cornmeal or masa harina
4 fl oz	120 mL	Cold water
to taste	to taste	Salt

Per serving:
Calories, 380; Protein, 46 g; Fat, 16 g (38% cal.); Cholesterol, 90 mg; Carbohydrates, 12 g; Fiber, 5 g; Sodium, 200 mg.

■ Procedure

1. Cut the beef into 1-in. (2.5-cm) cubes.
2. In a brazier, brown the beef in the vegetable oil over high heat. Brown a little at a time so as not to overcrowd the pan.
3. Add the garlic, chili powder, cumin, oregano, and cayenne to the beef over moderate heat. Stir and cook a few minutes, until the spices are aromatic.
4. Add the stock. Bring to a boil, cover, and place in an oven at 325°F (165°C) for 1½–2 hours, or until the beef is tender.
5. Degrease the cooking liquid carefully.
6. Mix the cornmeal or masa harina with the cold water to make a smooth paste.
7. Stir the cornmeal mixture into the beef mixture.
8. Simmer 30 minutes to thicken the cooking liquid.
9. Season to taste with salt.

VARIATION

Texas Short Ribs
In place of the lean beef, use 7 lb 8 oz (3.4 kg) beef short ribs. After the ribs are tender, remove them from the braising liquid and carefully degrease the liquid. Add just enough cornmeal or masa harina to lightly thicken the liquid, approximately half the amount in the basic recipe.

Texas Red

Braised Beef with Ancho Chiles

Yield: 3 lb 12 oz (1.7 kg)   Portions: 10   Portion size: 6 oz (170 g) meat, 2 fl oz (60 mL) jus

U.S.	Metric	Ingredients
6 lb	2.75 kg	Beef chuck, well trimmed, in large pieces
as needed	as needed	Vegetable oil
1 lb	900 g	Onion, sliced
4 oz	120 g	Slab bacon, in 1 piece
4	4	Whole dried ancho chiles, stems and seeds removed (see note)
1 oz	30 g	Garlic, coarsely chopped
¼ tsp	1 mL	Ground cumin
¼ tsp	1 mL	Dried thyme
¾ tsp	3 mL	Dried oregano
2 oz	60 g	Tomato paste
3 pt	1.5 L	White stock
1 tbsp	15 mL	Salt
1 tsp	5 mL	Pepper

■ P r o c e d u r e

1. In a braising pan, brown the beef well in vegetable oil. Brown just a little of the meat at a time if necessary to prevent overcrowding the pan. Remove the meat from the pan.

2. Using additional oil as needed, brown the onions over moderate heat until they are well browned but not scorched.

3. Return the beef to the pot and add the remaining ingredients.

4. Bring to a boil, cover, and place in an oven at 325°F (165°C). Braise for about 2 hours, until the meat is very tender.

5. Remove the meat from the braising liquid and keep warm. Discard the bacon.

6. Degrease the cooking liquid.

7. Remove the chiles from the liquid. Place the chiles, skin side down, on a cutting board, and carefully scrape the soft pulp from the inside surface. Discard the thin, transparent skins. Stir the pulp back into the cooking liquid.

8. Reduce the liquid over moderate heat to about 1½ pt (700 mL).

9. Taste and add additional salt and pepper if needed.

Per serving:
Calories, 410; Protein, 56 g; Fat, 16 g (36% cal.); Cholesterol, 110 mg; Carbohydrates, 9 g; Fiber, 3 g; Sodium, 920 mg.

Note: If whole chiles are not available, or if it is necessary to save the labor of scraping the pulp of the chiles after cooking (step 7), substitute 2½ tbsp (40 mL) ground ancho chiles for the whole chiles.

Duet of Beef and Corn: Braised Beef with Ancho Chiles on Grits with Cheddar, paired with sliced grilled steak on Corn with Poblanos, garnished with roasted diced squash

Braised Pork Loin with Olives

Portions: 12   Portion size: 1 chop, about 6½ oz (190 g) with bone
2 fl oz (60 mL) sauce

U.S.	Metric	Ingredients
8 lb	3.6 kg	Pork loin, center cut, bone in
as needed	as needed	Oil
to taste	to taste	Salt
to taste	to taste	Pepper
5 oz	150 g	Carrot, chopped
5 oz	150 g	Onion, chopped
1 lb	450 g	Tomatoes, chopped
2 oz	60 g	Pitted black olives, sliced
2 oz	60 g	Pitted green olives, sliced
2½ tbsp	20 g	Flour
15 fl oz	450 mL	White wine
1½ qt	1.5 L	Brown veal stock
1	1	Bouquet garni (see p. 152)
to taste	to taste	Salt
to taste	to taste	Pepper
2 oz	60 g	Pitted black olives, sliced into rings and blanched
2 oz	60 g	Pitted green olives, sliced into rings and blanched
2 tbsp	15 g	Chopped parsley

■ **P r o c e d u r e**

1. Trim the pork racks of excess fat and sinews. With a meat saw, cut off the chine bones so that the loin can be cut into chops after cooking. French the bones if desired (see Figure 11.4). The trimmed loin should weigh about 6–6½ lb (2.8 kg). Reserve the trimmings.

2. Season the racks and brown along with the trimmings. Remove the racks and trimmings and set aside.

3. Heat a little oil in a braising pan.

4. Add the carrots and onion and sweat. Add the tomatoes and the sliced olives.

5. Mix in the flour and cook for a few minutes. Deglaze with the white wine and reduce until almost dry.

6. Add the veal stock, the pork racks, trimmings, and the bouquet garni. Bring to a boil, then cover and place in a 350°F (175°C) oven to cook for around 1½–2 hours, until tender.

7. Remove the racks and set aside. Strain the braising liquid and discard the solids.

8. Reduce the liquid until it coats the back of a spoon, then season to taste.

9. Add the sliced blanched olives.

10. Cut the rack into chops. Serve coated with the sauce and sprinkled with chopped parsley.

Per serving:
Calories, 510; Protein, 51 g; Fat, 30 g (54% cal.); Cholesterol, 150 mg; Carbohydrates, 6 g; Fiber, 1 g; Sodium, 415 mg.

Daube d'Agneau Provençale (Braised Lamb Provençale)

Portions: 12   Portion size: 4 oz (125 g)
2 fl oz (60 mL) sauce

U.S.	Metric	Ingredients	
8 lb	3.8 kg	Lamb shoulder (see note)	**■ P r o c e d u r e**
to taste	to taste	Salt	1. Trim the lamb shoulder of excess fat and sinews.
to taste	to taste	Pepper	2. Season the lamb with salt and pepper. Brown in hot oil in a braising pan.
as needed	as needed	Oil	
4 oz	125 g	Carrot, large dice	3. Add the carrot, onion, shallot, and garlic. Sweat the vegetables.
3 oz	90 g	Onion, large dice	
1½ oz	45 g	Shallot, large dice	4. Add the herbs. Deglaze the pan with the red wine, cover, and place in the oven to cook at 350°F (175°C) for 2½–3 hours.
1 oz	30 g	Garlic cloves, halved	
2 tsp	5 g	Dried Marjoram	5. Remove from the pan and strain the cooking liquid.
4 tsp	10 g	Dried Basil	
4 tsp	10 g	Dried Rosemary	
1½ qt (2 bottles)	1.5 L (2 bottles)	Heavy red wine	
10 oz	300 g	Onion, chopped fine	6. Sweat the onion and garlic in olive oil. Add the diced tomato and the tomato paste. Stir well and cook for a few minutes. Add the chopped olives, season, and cook until thick.
1 oz	30 g	Garlic, chopped fine	
1½ fl oz	50 mL	Olive oil	
1 lb 10 oz	800 g	Tomatoes, peeled, seeded, and diced	7. Degrease the lamb cooking liquid. Mix in the tomato mixture. Cook for a few minutes to allow the flavors to blend.
1 tsp	5 g	Tomato paste	8. Adjust the seasoning.
4 oz	125 g	Finely chopped black olives	9. Serve the lamb sliced, with the sauce on top.
to taste	to taste	Salt	
to taste	to taste	Pepper	

Per serving:
Calories, 370; Protein, 34 g; Fat, 17 g (41% cal.); Cholesterol, 80 mg;
Carbohydrates, 11 g; Fiber, 2 g; Sodium, 190 mg.

Note: This recipe specifies bone-in lamb shoulder. The lamb is sliced from the bone after cooking. If desired, substitute 4½ lb (2 kg) trimmed, boneless lamb shoulder for ease in handling. The result will be somewhat less flavorful, however, because the bones contribute to flavor and to the texture of the sauce.

Veal Fricassée
Pork Fricassée

See Chicken Fricassée variations, page 410.

Veal Shank with Orange

Portions: 12   Portion size: 8 oz (250 g) cooked weight
2½ fl oz (70 mL) sauce

U.S.	Metric	Ingredients
3½ fl oz	100 mL	Oil
1 oz	30 g	Butter
12 pieces	12 pieces	Veal shank, cut crosswise into thick slices, about 11 oz (320–350 g) each
12 oz	350 g	Carrot, chopped
12 oz	350 g	Onion, chopped
3 oz	90 g	Garlic, chopped
8 oz	250 g	Tomatoes, cut into quarters
2½ tbsp	20 g	Flour
10 fl oz	300 mL	White wine
1 pt 4 oz	600 mL	Fond Lié (p. 174) or espagnole
1	1	Bouquet garni (see p. 152)
4 tbsp	50 g	Sugar
2 fl oz	60 mL	Wine vinegar
¾ oz	20 g	Orange zest, cut brunoise and blanched
¾ oz	20 g	Lemon zest, cut brunoise and blanched
1 oz	30 g	Carrot, cut brunoise
1 oz	30 g	Onion, cut brunoise
1 tbsp	15 mL	Chopped parsley

▪ P r o c e d u r e

1. Heat the oil and butter. Season the veal and brown. Remove and set aside.
2. Add the carrot, onion, garlic, and tomato. Sweat briefly.
3. Add the flour and cook for a few minutes. Deglaze with the white wine. Reduce until almost dry.
4. Add the fond lié and bouquet garni.
5. Return the veal to the pan. Cover and cook in a 350°F (175°C) oven for 1¼–1¾ hours, until the veal is tender.
6. Remove the veal. Strain the braising liquid and skim off the fat.
7. Combine the sugar and vinegar in a stainless-steel pan. Cook until lightly caramelized. Once colored, stop the cooking by adding the strained cooking liquid. Reduce until it coats the back of a spoon.
8. Strain and add the blanched orange and lemon zest, the carrot, and the onion. Simmer for a few minutes. Season to taste and mix in the chopped parsley before serving.

Per serving:
Calories, 470; Protein, 62 g; Fat, 15 g (29% cal.); Cholesterol, 170 mg; Carbohydrates, 17 g; Fiber, 2 g; Sodium, 310 mg.

Veal Shank with Orange

Hungarian Goulash (Veal, Beef, or Pork)

Portions: 25   Portion size: 8 oz (250 g)

U.S.	Metric	Ingredients
7½ lb	3.75 kg	Boneless, lean meat: Veal (shoulder, shank, or breast), or beef (chuck), or pork (shoulder or butt)
5 fl oz	150 mL	Oil, lard, or rendered beef suet
2½ lb	1.25 kg	Onions, fine dice
5 tbsp	75 mL	Hungarian paprika
2 tsp	10 mL	Garlic, crushed
½ tsp	2 mL	Caraway seeds
10 oz	300 g	Chopped, drained canned tomatoes or tomato purée
2½ qt	2.5 L	White stock
2½ lb	1.25 kg	Potatoes, medium dice
to taste	to taste	Salt

Per serving:
Calories, 250; Protein, 27 g; Fat, 10 g (35% cal.); Cholesterol, 35 mg;
Carbohydrates, 14 g; Fiber, 2 g; Sodium, 120 mg.

■ P r o c e d u r e

1. Cut the meat into 1-in. (2½-cm) cubes.
2. Heat the fat in a brazier and sauté the meat until lightly seared on all sides.
3. Add the onions and sweat over moderate heat. Continue to cook until most of the liquid that forms is reduced.
4. Add the paprika, garlic, and caraway seeds and stir.

5. Add the tomatoes and stock, cover, and simmer until the meat is almost tender, about 1 hour in the oven (325°F/165°C) or on the range.

6. Add the potatoes and continue to cook until the meat and potatoes are tender.
7. The potatoes will thicken the sauce slightly but, if necessary, reduce the sauce slightly. Degrease and season to taste.
8. Serve with spaetzle or noodles.

Rabbit with Mustard

Portions: 8   Portion size: approximately 8 oz (250 g), including sauce

U.S.	Metric	Ingredients
4–5 lb	2 kg	Rabbit
as needed	as needed	Oil
½ oz	15 g	Butter
1 oz	30 g	Shallots, chopped
2 oz	60 g	Prepared mustard, Dijon-style or grainy
to taste	to taste	Salt
to taste	to taste	Pepper
¼ tsp	1 mL	Dried thyme
8 fl oz	250 mL	White wine
8 fl oz	250 mL	Chicken stock
8 fl oz	250 mL	Heavy cream

Per serving:
Calories, 450; Protein, 30 g; Fat, 28 g (58% cal.); Cholesterol, 150 mg;
Carbohydrates, 2 g; Fiber, 0 g; Sodium, 260 mg.

■ P r o c e d u r e

1. Clean and cut up the rabbit for stewing.
2. Brown the rabbit in oil in a heavy pan.
3. Remove the rabbit pieces from the pan and keep them warm. Degrease the pan.

4. Add the butter to the pan. Sweat the shallots in the butter, but do not brown.
5. Add the mustard, salt, pepper, thyme, wine, and stock to the pan and return the browned rabbit to the pan. Cover and braise slowly over low heat or in a low oven until the meat is cooked.
6. Remove the rabbit from the liquid and set aside.

7. Reduce the cooking liquid by about one-third. Skim any excess fat from the top.
8. Temper the heavy cream and add it to the reduced liquid. Simmer and reduce until the sauce is lightly thickened. Adjust the seasonings. Return the rabbit pieces to the sauce.

Sauerbraten

Portions: 25   Portion size: 4 oz (125 g)
2 fl oz (60 mL) sauce

U.S.	Metric	Ingredients
10 lb	5 kg	Beef bottom round, trimmed (see note)
		Marinade:
1 qt	1 L	Red wine vinegar
1 qt	1 L	Water
1 lb	500 g	Onion, sliced
8 oz	250 g	Carrots, sliced
2	2	Garlic cloves, chopped
2 oz	60 g	Brown sugar
2	2	Bay leaves
3	3	Whole cloves
1 tsp	5 mL	Peppercorns, crushed
2 tsp	10 mL	Salt
as needed	as needed	Vegetable oil, if needed for browning meat
8 fl oz	250 mL	Red wine
4 oz	125 g	Gingersnap crumbs

Per serving:
Calories, 260; Protein, 37 g; Fat, 8 g (32% cal.); Cholesterol, 80 mg; Carbohydrates, 4 g; Fiber, 0 g; Sodium, 110 mg.

Note: If you are preparing this item in large quantities and are using whole bottom round (called gooseneck), separate the eye of round from the bottom round and cut the bottom round in half lengthwise, so that two pieces are about the size of the eye of round.

Brisket or chuck may also be used for sauerbraten. They will not make attractive slices, but the eating quality will be very good.

■ P r o c e d u r e

1. Place the trimmed beef in a nonmetallic crock or barrel.
2. Add all the marinade ingredients to the crock. If the meat is not completely covered by the liquid, add equal parts vinegar and water until it is. Cover.
3. Refrigerate for 3–4 days. Turn the meat in the marinade every day.
4. Remove the meat from the marinade. Dry the meat thoroughly with paper towels.
5. Brown the meat on all sides. This may be done on the range in an iron skillet, on a very hot griddle, under the broiler, or in a brazier in a hot oven.
6. Place the meat in a braising pan. Strain the marinade. Add the vegetables to the meat and enough of the liquid to cover the meat by half. Cover and braise in a 300°F (150°C) oven until the meat is tender, about 2–3 hours.
7. Remove the meat from the braising liquid and transfer to a hotel pan. Set aside.
8. Strain 2 qt (2 L) of the braising liquid into a saucepan and skim off fat. Bring to a boil. Reduce to about 1½ qt (1.5 L).
9. Add wine and boil another 2–3 minutes.
10. Reduce heat to a simmer and stir in the gingersnap crumbs. Simmer another 3–4 minutes. Remove from heat and let stand 5 minutes to allow the crumbs to be completely absorbed.
11. Slice the meat across the grain. Serve 4 oz (125 g) meat per portion, overlapping the slices on the plate. Ladle 2 oz (60 mL) sauce over the meat.

V A R I A T I O N

Sauerbraten with Sour Cream Gravy
Marinate and braise meat as in basic recipe. Prepare gravy through step 8. Thicken the sauce with a roux made of 4 oz (125 g) butter or beef fat, 4 oz (125 g) flour, and 2 oz (60 g) sugar. Cook the roux until well browned and thicken the sauce. Omit wine and add 8 oz (250 mL) sour cream.

Braised Sweetbreads

Portions: 10   Portion size: 3½ oz (100 g) sweetbreads (cooked weight)
2 fl oz (60 mL) sauce

U.S.	Metric	Ingredients
3 lb	1.5 kg	Sweetbreads
2 oz	60 g	Butter
		Mirepoix:
6 oz	175 g	Onion, medium dice
3 oz	90 g	Carrot, medium dice
3 oz	90 g	Celery, medium dice
3½ pt	750 mL	Demi-glace, hot

Per serving:
Calories, 500; Protein, 21 g; Fat, 42 g (75% cal.); Cholesterol, 350 mg; Carbohydrates, 10 g; Fiber, 1 g; Sodium, 340 mg.

■ **P r o c e d u r e**

1. Prepare (blanch and trim) sweetbreads according to the procedure on page 280. Leave them whole or cut into uniform serving pieces.
2. Heat the butter in a large sauté pan (straight-sided). Add the mirepoix and cook over medium heat until lightly browned.
3. Place the sweetbreads on top of the mirepoix and pour in the demi-glace.
4. Cover tightly and place in oven at 325°F (165°C), until the sweetbreads are very tender and well flavored with the sauce, about 45–60 minutes.
5. Remove the sweetbreads from the sauce and place in a hotel pan.
6. Bring the sauce to a rapid boil and reduce slightly. Strain and adjust seasoning. Pour over sweetbreads.

 Swedish Meatballs

Portions: 25   Portion size: 3 meatballs, 5 oz (150 g) cooked weight
2 fl oz sauce (60 mL)

U.S.	Metric	Ingredients
10 oz	300 g	Onion, chopped fine
2 fl oz	60 mL	Oil
10 oz	300 g	Dry bread crumbs
2 cups	500 mL	Milk
10	10	Eggs, beaten
5 lb	2.5 kg	Ground beef
1¼ lb	625 g	Ground pork
2½ tsp	12 mL	Dried dill weed
½ tsp	2 mL	Nutmeg
½ tsp	2 mL	Allspice
2 tbsp	30 g	Salt
2 qt	2 L	Brown sauce, hot
2½ cups	625 mL	Light cream, hot
1 tsp	5 mL	Dried dill weed

Per serving:
Calories, 440; Protein, 27 g; Fat, 29 g (61% cal.); Cholesterol, 180 mg; Carbohydrates, 15 g; Fiber, 1 g; Sodium, 810 mg.

■ **P r o c e d u r e**

1. Sauté the onions in oil until tender but not brown. Cool thoroughly.
2. Combine the bread crumbs with the milk and egg and let soak for 15 minutes.
3. Add the cooked onion and the crumb mixture to the meat in a mixing bowl. Add the spices and salt and mix gently until well combined.
4. Portion the meat with a No. 20 scoop into 2-oz (60-g) portions. Roll into balls and place on a sheet pan.
5. Brown in a 400°F (200°C) oven.
6. Remove meatballs from sheet pan and place in baking pans in a single layer.
7. Add the hot cream and dill to the hot brown sauce and pour over the meatballs.
8. Cover the pans and bake at 325°F (165°C) for 30 minutes, until the meatballs are cooked.
9. Skim fat from sauce.
10. Serve 3 meatballs and 2 fl oz (60 mL) sauce per portion.

Veal Curry with Mangoes and Cashews

Portions: 25   Portion size: 8 oz (250 g)

U.S.	Metric	Ingredients
9 lb	4.5 kg	Boneless, lean veal (shoulder, shank, or breast)
8 fl oz	250 mL	Oil
2½ lb	1.25 kg	Onions, medium dice
2 tbsp	30 mL	Garlic, chopped
5 tbsp	75 mL	Curry powder (see note)
1 tbsp	15 mL	Ground coriander
2½ tsp	12 mL	Paprika
1 tsp	5 mL	Ground cumin
1 tsp	5 mL	Pepper
½ tsp	2 mL	Cinnamon
2	2	Bay leaves
2 tsp	10 mL	Salt
4 oz	125 g	Flour
2 qt	2 L	White stock
10 oz	300 g	Tomato concassé
8 fl oz	250 mL	Heavy cream, hot
4–5	4–5	Mangoes
as needed	as needed	Boiled or steamed rice
8 oz	250 g	Cashews, coarsely chopped
½ cup	125 mL	Chopped parsley

■ Procedure

1. Cut the veal into 1-in. (2½ cm) cubes.
2. Heat the oil in a brazier over medium heat and add the meat. Cook the meat in the fat, stirring occasionally, until seared on all sides but only lightly browned.
3. Add the onions and garlic to the pan. Sauté until softened, but do not brown.
4. Add the spices and salt and stir. Cook 1 minute.
5. Stir in the flour to make a roux and cook another 2 minutes.
6. Add the stock and tomatoes. Bring to a boil while stirring.
7. Cover and simmer slowly in the oven (300°F/150°C) or on top of the range until the meat is tender, 1–1½ hours.
8. Degrease, discard the bay leaf, and add the cream. Adjust the seasonings.
9. Peel the mangoes with a paring knife or vegetable peeler. Cut the mango flesh from the stone in thick slices. Cut into medium dice.
10. To serve, place a bed of rice on a plate. Spoon the curry onto the center of the rice. Top with diced mango. Sprinkle with chopped cashews and chopped parsley.

V A R I A T I O N S

In place of the mango and cashews, serve meat curries with an assortment of other condiments, such as raisins, chutney, peanuts, chopped scallions or onions, diced pineapple, diced banana, diced apple, shredded coconut, and poppadums.

Lamb Curry
Substitute lean boneless lamb shoulder, breast, or leg for the veal.

Per serving:
Calories, 430; Protein, 31 g; Fat, 26 g (64% cal.); Cholesterol, 95 mg; Carbohydrates, 18 g; Fiber, 2 g; Sodium, 330 mg.

Note: If desired, increase curry powder to taste and omit other spice (except bay leaf).

Saltimbocca alla Romana

Portions: 16   Portion size: 2 pieces

U.S.	Metric	Ingredients
32	32	Veal scaloppine, about 1½–2 oz (45–60 g) each
to taste	to taste	Salt
to taste	to taste	White pepper
32	32	Thin slices of prosciutto, about the same diameter as the scaloppine
32	32	Fresh sage leaves
4 oz	125 g	Butter
12 fl oz	350 mL	White wine

■ P r o c e d u r e

1. Pound the scaloppine with a cutlet pounder. Season with salt and white pepper. Put 1 slice of prosciutto and 1 sage leaf on top of each and fasten with a toothpick.
2. Sauté briefly in butter on both sides.
3. Add the wine and continue to cook until the meat is done and the wine is partly reduced, no more than 5 minutes.
4. Remove the meat from the pan and serve, ham side up, with a spoonful of the pan juices over each.

Per serving:
Calories, 320; Protein, 28 g; Fat, 21 g (60% cal.); Cholesterol, 115 mg; Carbohydrates, 0 g; Fiber, 0 g; Sodium, 800 mg.

Carbonnade à la Flammande

Portions: 16   Portion size: 6–7 oz (175–200 g)

U.S.	Metric	Ingredients
3 lb	1.4 kg	Onions
as needed	as needed	Beef fat or vegetable oil
6 oz	175 g	Flour
2 tsp	10 mL	Salt
1 tsp	5 mL	Pepper
5 lb	2.3 kg	Beef chuck, 1-in. (2.5-cm) dice
2½ pt	1.25 L	Dark beer
2½ pt	1.25 L	Brown stock
		Sachet:
2	2	Bay leaves
1 tsp	5 mL	Dried thyme
8	8	Parsley stems
8	8	Peppercorns
1 tbsp	15 mL	Sugar

■ P r o c e d u r e

1. Peel the onions. Cut them into small dice.
2. Cook over moderate heat in a little fat until golden. Remove from the heat and set aside.
3. Season the flour with salt and pepper. Dredge the meat in the flour. Shake off the excess flour.
4. Brown the meat well in a sauté pan. Do a little at a time to avoid overcrowding the pan. As each batch is browned, add it to the pot with the onions.
5. Deglaze the sauté pan with the beer and add it to the pot. Add the stock, sachet, and sugar.
6. Bring to a boil, cover, and transfer to the oven, Cook at 325°F (160°C) until very tender, about 2–3 hours.
7. Degrease. Adjust the consistency of the sauce. If it is too thin, reduce over moderately high heat. If it is too thick, dilute with brown stock.
8. Taste and adjust the seasonings. Serve with plain boiled potatoes.

Per serving:
Calories, 450; Protein, 30 g; Fat, 29 g (52% cal.); Cholesterol, 100 mg; Carbohydrates, 19 g; Fiber, 1 g; Sodium, 290 mg.

■ TERMS FOR REVIEW

deglaze   pot roast   fricassée
stewing   Swiss steak   blanquette

■ QUESTIONS FOR DISCUSSION

1. List four advantages of roasting at a low temperature.

2. When might you use high temperatures for roasting?

3. What is the purpose of basting?

4. In the recipe for Home-Style Meatloaf (p. 303), why are the sautéed vegetables cooled after cooking in step 1?

5. Which steaks require the highest broiler heat, thick ones or thin ones? steaks to be cooked rare or steaks to be cooked well done?

6. Why is it important not to overload the pan when sautéing meats?

7. Why is the menu term *boiled beef* inaccurate?

CHAPTER 12

Understanding Poultry and Game Birds

The versatility, the popularity, and the relatively low cost of poultry items make them ideal for all kinds of food service operations, from elegant restaurants to cafeterias and fast-food restaurants. Also, chicken and turkey are popular among diet-conscious people because they are lower in fat and cholesterol than other meats.

Game birds, such as pheasant, are also increasing in popularity and availability because they are now raised domestically by many producers. Farm-raised game birds are similar, in many ways, to chicken, so learning techniques for cooking and handling chicken teaches you a great deal about handling these other birds as well.

Learning about poultry is, in some ways, easier than learning about meats like beef and lamb. Because chickens, turkeys, and other poultry are much smaller, they are not cut up in such detail.

However, poultry has its own cooking problems, so it is important to observe both the similarities and the differences between meat and poultry.

After reading this chapter, you should be able to

1. Explain the differences between light meat and dark meat, and describe how these differences affect cooking.

2. Describe four techniques that help keep chicken or turkey breast moist while roasting.

3. Define the following terms used to classify poultry: *kind, class,* and *style.*

4. Identify popular types of farm-raised game birds and the cooking methods appropriate to their preparation.

5. Store poultry items.

6. Determine doneness in cooked poultry, both large roasted birds and smaller birds.

7. Truss poultry for cooking.

8. Cut up chicken into parts.

COMPOSITION AND STRUCTURE

The flesh of poultry and game birds is muscle tissue, as is the flesh of beef, lamb, veal, pork, and game. Its composition and structure are essentially the same as those of meat. Review the section on meat composition and structure (Chapter 10, pp. 258–260). Remember that muscle tissue is composed of

Water (about 75 percent)

Protein (about 20 percent)

Fat (up to 5 percent)

Other elements, including carbohydrate, in small quantities

Remember that muscles consist of *muscle fibers* held together in bundles by *connective tissue.*

MATURITY AND TENDERNESS

We learned in Chapter 10 that the tenderness of a piece of meat—or poultry—is related to *connective tissue* and that connective tissue increases with

• Use or exercise of the muscle.

• Maturity or age of the animal or bird.

1. Use or exercise is of less concern in poultry. Most poultry is so young that it is relatively tender throughout. However, there are some differences, discussed in the next section, between light meat and dark meat.

2. Maturity is a major consideration when selecting poultry. Young, tender birds are cooked by dry-heat methods, such as broiling, frying, and roasting, as well as by moist-heat methods. Older, tougher birds need slow, moist heat to be made palatable.

Maturity is the major factor in categorizing each kind of poultry (see p. 354).
Skin color is determined by diet and is not related to the flavor or tenderness of the poultry.

FREE-RANGE CHICKENS

Most chickens on the market are produced by large operations that house their poultry indoors in carefully controlled environments and feed them scientifically monitored diets. This process enables the industry to raise healthy chickens quickly and in large numbers to meet the great demand. Many people feel that these chickens lack flavor because they are not allowed to move around outdoors. Some farmers, in response, offer free-range chickens, which are allowed to move around freely and eat outdoors in a more natural environment.

It is important to note that there is no legal definition of *free-range*, and that free-range chickens are considerably more expensive than ordinary chickens. Many people, however, feel that free-range chickens are more flavorful and are worth the extra cost. Because quality varies from producer to producer, it is necessary to do careful taste-testing to determine whether you want to purchase free-range poultry for your operation.

A term related to *free-range* is **organic**, which refers to food produced without using most conventional pesticides, fertilizers made with synthetic ingredients or sewage sludge, bioengineering, or ionizing radiation. The National Standard of Canada for Organic Agriculture sets detailed requirements for organic foods. In addition, individual provinces may set further requirements.

LIGHT MEAT AND DARK MEAT

Poultry is not divided into as many small cuts as are meats. Chicken and turkey, however, are usually thought of as consisting of two kinds of parts, depending on the color of the meat. These color differences reflect other differences:

"Light meat"—breast and wings

> Less fat
>
> Less connective tissue
>
> Cooks faster

"Dark meat"—legs (drumsticks and thighs)

> More fat
>
> More connective tissue
>
> Takes longer to cook

Duck, goose, and squab have all dark meat, but the same differences in connective tissue hold true.

The dark color of dark meat is due to a protein called *myoglobin*. This protein stores oxygen for muscles to use during periods of great activity. The breast muscles of birds are used for flying, and because chickens and turkeys rarely, if ever, fly, these muscles don't need a great deal of myoglobin. In flying birds, such as ducks, the breast muscles have more myoglobin and thus are darker. Active muscles, in addition to being darker, also have more connective tissue.

The cook must observe these differences when preparing poultry.

1. **Cooking whole birds.**
   Everyone has tasted chicken or turkey breast so dry it was difficult to swallow. In fact, light meat is overcooked more often than not because it cooks faster than the legs and is done first. In addition, the breast has less fat than the legs, so it tastes much drier when cooked (or overcooked).

   A major problem in roasting poultry is cooking the legs to doneness without overcooking the breast. Chefs have devised many techniques to help solve this problem. Here are some of them.

   - Roasting breast down for part of the roasting period. Gravity draws moisture and fat to the breast rather than away from it.

   - Basting with fat only, not with water or stock. Fat protects against drying, but moisture washes away protective fat.

   - Barding, or covering the breast with a thin layer of pork fat. This is usually done with lean game birds.

   - Separating breast from leg sections and roasting each for a different time. This is often done with large turkeys.

2. **Cooking poultry parts.**
   Many recipes have been devised especially for certain poultry parts, such as wings, drumsticks, and boneless chicken breasts. These recipes take into account the different cooking characteristics of each part. For example, flattened boneless chicken breasts can be quickly sautéed and remain juicy and tender. Turkey wings, when braised, release enough gelatin to help make a rich sauce.

   Many of these items have especially high customer appeal, especially boneless chicken breast, and are served in the most elegant restaurants.

   Several of the chicken and turkey recipes in Chapter 13 are for specific parts. Those that use cut-up whole chickens can easily be adapted for specific parts. For example, you may want to buy whole chickens, braise the leg sections, and reserve the breasts for other preparations.

Figures 12.1
Inspection stamps for poultry
Courtesy of the Canadian Food Inspection Agency

1

2

3

Figures 12.1
Inspection stamps for poultry
Courtesy of the Canadian Food Inspection Agency

Figures 12.2
Grade stamp for poultry
Courtesy of the Canadian Food Inspection Agency

INSPECTION AND GRADING

Like meat, poultry is subject to federal inspection and grading, which is controlled by the Canadian Food Inspection Agency (CFIA). (*Note:* Unlike for meats, poultry inspection and grading stamps are not stamped on the birds but are printed on tags and packing cases.)

INSPECTION

1. A guarantee of wholesomeness (fit for human consumption).
2. Indicated by a round or oval stamp (Figure 12.1).
3. Required by Canadian law.

GRADING

1. Based on quality.
2. Indicated by a maple leaf stamp and letter grade (Figure 12.2).
3. Not required by law but widely practiced in Canada and the United States.

Canadian poultry grades are Canada Grade A, Canada Utitlity, and Canada Grade C (A being the best). The grade stamps are colored red for Grade A, blue for Utility, and brown for Grade C. (In limited circumstances, the stamps may be colored black. For example, when non-prepackaged items are shipped in a carton, it is permissible to print the carton in black rather than in color.) These grades are based on

Shape of carcass (lack of defects)	Pinfeathers (present or absent)
Amount of flesh	Skin tears, cuts, broken bones
Amount of fat	Blemishes and bruises

Most poultry used in food service is Grade A. Some utility-grade poultry is also used, although most utility- and nearly all C-grade poultry is used by canners and processors.

CLASSIFICATION AND MARKET FORMS

The following terms are used to classify poultry:

Kind—the species, such as chicken, turkey, or duck.

Class—the subdivision of kind, depending on age and sex.

Style—the amount of cleaning and processing.

Live: almost never purchased in food service.

Dressed: killed, bled, and plucked. Also rarely seen in food service.

Ready to cook: dressed and eviscerated, with head and feet removed.

- Whole.
- Cut up, or parts.

State of refrigeration—chilled or frozen.

Table 12.1 describes the kinds and classes of domestic poultry. *Chicken* is the most common kind of poultry in the kitchen. As indicated in the table, age or maturity determines the differences among the various classes of chicken. *Rock Cornish game* hens (usually called Cornish hens), *broilers,* and *fryers* are young, tender chickens suitable for sautéing, broiling, or frying, while *roasters* and *capons* are larger chickens that are usually roasted. Older *hens* and (rarely marketed) *roosters* must be simmered or braised to make them tender.

Table 12.1
Domestic Poultry Classes and Characteristics

Kind /Class	Description	Age	Weight range
Chicken			
Rock Cornish game hen	Special breed of young chicken, very tender and delicate.	5 weeks or less	¾-2 lb (0.34-0.9 kg)
Broiler or fryer	Young chicken of either sex. Tender flesh and flexible cartilage. Smooth skin.	6-12 weeks	Broiler: 1½-2½ lb (0.7-1.1 kg) Fryer: 2½-3½ lb (1.1-1.6 kg)
Roaster	Young chicken of either sex. Tender flesh and smooth skin, but less flexible cartilage.	3-5 months	3½-5 lb (1.6-2.3 kg)
Capon	Castrated male chicken. Flesh very tender and well flavored. Large breast. Expensive.	Under 8 months	5-8 lb (2.3-3.6 kg)
Hen or fowl	Mature female. Tough flesh and coarse skin. Hardened breastbone cartilage.	Over 10 months	3½-6 lb (1.6-2.7 kg)
Cock or rooster	Mature male. Coarse skin. Tough, dark meat.	Over 10 months	4-6 lb (1.8-2.7 kg)
Turkey			
Fryer-roaster	Young bird of either sex. Tender flesh, smooth skin, and flexible cartilage.	Under 16 weeks	4-9 lb (1.8-4 kg)
Young turkey (hen or tom)	Young turkeys with tender flesh but firmer cartilage.	5-7 months	8-22 lb (3.6-10 kg)
Yearling turkey	Fully matured turkey that is still reasonably tender.	Under 15 months	10-30 lb (4.5-14 kg)
Mature turkey or old turkey (hen or tom)	Old turkey with tough flesh and coarse skin.	Over 15 months	10-30 lb (4.5-14 kg)
Duck			
Broiler or fryer duckling	Young tender duck with soft bill and windpipe.	Under 8 weeks	2-4 lb (0.9-1.8 kg)
Roaster duckling	Young tender duck with bill and windpipe that are just starting to harden.	Under 16 weeks	4-6 lb (1.8-2.7 kg)
Mature duck	Old duck with tough flesh and hard bill and windpipe.	Over 6 months	4-6 lb (1.8-2.7 kg)
Goose			
Young goose	Young bird with tender flesh.	Under 6 months	6-10 lb (2.7-4.5 kg)
Mature goose	Tough old bird	Over 6 months	10-16 lb (4.5-7.3 kg)
Guinea			
Young guinea	Domestic relatives of the pheasant. Tender.	3-6 months	¾-1½ lb (0.34-0.7 kg)
Mature guinea	Tough.	Up to 12 months	1-2 lb (0.45-0.9 kg)
Pigeon			
Squab	Very young pigeons with light, tender meat.	3-4 weeks	Under 1 lb (0.45 kg)
Pigeon	Older pigeons with tough, dark meat.	Over 4 weeks	1-2 lb (0.45-0.9 kg)

In addition to the common classes of chicken listed in the table, you may also find **poussin** (poo-san) on the market in certain localities. Similar to Rock Cornish game hen but often smaller, a poussin is a young chicken weighing 1 pound (450 g) or less. It commands a fairly high price because of the special techniques required for raising it.

Turkeys are larger birds that are usually roasted, although the cooking of turkey parts is increasingly common. For example, legs may be stewed or braised for special dishes (see, for example, Mole Poblano, p. 409), while breasts are cut into cutlets or scaloppine and sautéed like veal cutlets.

Ducks and *geese* also are usually roasted, although duck parts are sometimes cooked separately. Boneless breast of duck is sautéed or broiled and served rare, sliced into small medallions, and the legs may be braised. Ducks and geese have a thick layer of fat under the skin. Compared with chicken and turkey, they have a low yield. For example, a 2-kg duck yields about 500 g raw lean meat, and a 2-kg chicken yields about 1 kg raw lean meat.

Most ducks marketed in North America are a breed called **White Pekin**; this includes the well-known Long Island duck. A specialty item available in some markets is **magret** (mah-gray). This is the boneless breast of a breed of duck called **moulard**. It is thicker and meatier than the breast of a regular Pekin.

Guineas are a domestically raised descendant of the pheasant. They taste like a flavorful chicken and are usually cooked and handled like young chickens.

Squabs are young, domestically raised pigeons, usually weighing less than 1 pound (450 g). Their rich, dark meat, which is usually cooked slightly rare to avoid dryness, has a slightly gamy flavor that combines well with flavorful brown sauces.

Clockwise from left: duckling, free-range chicken, poussin, guinea fowl, squab, quail

GAME BIRDS AND SPECIALTY PRODUCTS

In recent years, the availability of such birds as quail and squab has increased dramatically, and they are seen regularly on restaurant menus. The poultry items discussed in this section are classified as game birds, but they are all, in fact, raised domestically. While farm-raised pheasants and partridge lack the full gamy flavor of their wild cousins, they do have a richer, somewhat gamelike taste when compared to chicken. With bland, factory-raised chickens dominating the market, cooks and eaters are turning more and more to exotic poultry and are willing to pay the higher price.

Traditionally, true wild game is hung and allowed to age, usually before plucking and dressing. The purpose is essentially the same as for aging beef, namely to allow the natural enzymes in the meat to tenderize it and to develop flavor. Often, game is hung until it becomes high, to the point where spoiled meat is mistaken for aged meat. With today's farm-raised game birds, this procedure is not appropriate. Anyway, most customers prefer a fresh taste to a strong, gamy one.

Quail are small, weighing about 4 to 5 ounces (110 to 140 g) each. A normal portion is two birds. They have meaty breasts for their size, but not much meat on the legs. Quail are richly flavored without being gamy. The French name is *caille*.

Partridges are about the size of Rock Cornish game hens, weighing about 1 pound (450 g) each. It is important to look for young, tender birds because mature partridge is likely to be tough. They have excellent flavor, but not as delicate as squab or pheasant. The French names are *perdreau* (young partridge) and *perdrix* (mature partridge).

Pheasant is a popular game bird, and farm-raised pheasant is widely available. Most pheasant sold weighs from 2 to 2½ pounds (900 to 1125 g), but young pheasant weighing 1 pound (450 g) or less is also available. This bird has delicate, light-colored meat with subtle flavor similar to that of chicken. Most recipes for chicken are also suitable for pheasant, but the simplest preparations are usually the best, because the flavor stands well on its own and is easily covered by too many spices. Pheasant can be dry if overcooked. The French name is *faisan*.

Many varieties of *wild duck* are eaten, but mallard is the most common. Farm-raised mallards weigh from 1½ to 3 pounds (700 to 1350 g). Unlike domestic duck, wild duck is very lean. It has dark, flavorful flesh.

Handling game birds is easy if you remember that their structure is basically the same as the structure of chickens. All the cutting and trussing techniques you learn for chicken can be applied to these other birds.

Because farm-raised game birds are usually young and tender, they can be roasted, sautéed, grilled, and barbecued. The most important thing to remember about them is that they are usually very lean. Therefore, they are best served slightly rare. If cooked to well done, they become dry. This is especially true of wild duck, which is almost inedible if overcooked. Wild duck is usually left rarer than the other birds discussed here. Its meat is then red and juicy.

Pheasant is also very dry if well done. Its light-colored meat is best if still slightly pink at the bone. Quail doesn't become as dry, but it too has the best flavor if still slightly pink at the bone.

Another category of farm-raised birds increasing in popularity is the category technically known as **ratites. Ostrich** and **emu** are the most familiar members of this category. Meat from both birds is widely available. It is lean and red and resembles venison or very lean beef in appearance, although it is slightly lighter in color than venison.

Because ostrich and emu are so lean, they are best cooked to the medium rare or, at most, medium stage to avoid dryness. Recommended internal temperature is 155° to 160°F (68° to 71°C). Grilling, sautéing, and pan-frying are the best cooking methods for small, tender cuts, while larger tender cuts can be roasted. Moist-heat methods, especially braising, are sometimes recommended for less tender cuts, but this often results in excessively dry meat because it is so lean. Take care to avoid overcooking if you braise ostrich or emu. Another option is to grind the less tender cuts. Mixed with seasonings and added moisture, ground emu and ostrich can make excellent burgers, meatballs, and meatloaf.

Ostrich and emu are best cooked like other lean red meats and game. Recipes for venison, in particular, are often excellent when applied to these meats, as are recipes for grilled or sautéed beef. Ostrich producers often recommend cooking their product like veal. This may be slightly misleading because veal is often cooked medium well or well done. Nevertheless, grilled, sautéed, and roast veal recipes can often be used for ostrich and emu as well, as long as the meat is not overcooked. Two recipes developed specifically for ostrich or emu are included in Chapter 13 as a sample. For other cooking ideas, look for appropriate recipes in Chapter 11 based on the guidelines just described.

HANDLING AND STORAGE

FRESH POULTRY

1. Fresh poultry is extremely perishable. It should arrive packed in ice and be kept in ice until used.
2. Ideally, use poultry within 24 hours of receiving. Never hold it for more than 4 days.
3. Poultry often carries salmonella bacteria. Wash all equipment and cutting surfaces after handling poultry to avoid contamination of other foods.

FROZEN POULTRY

1. Store frozen poultry at 0°F (–18°C) or lower until ready to thaw.
2. Thaw in original wrapper in refrigerator, allowing 1 to 2 days for chickens, 2 to 4 days for larger birds. If pressed for time, thaw in cold, running water in original wrapper.
3. Do not refreeze thawed poultry.

DONENESS

Domestic poultry is almost always cooked well done (except squab and sautéed or grilled duck breast). Many cooks, however, cannot tell the difference between well done and overcooked. Chicken and turkey are low in fat, so they quickly become dry and unpalatable when overcooked. Even duck and goose, which are very fatty, taste dry and stringy if cooked too long.

Skilled chefs with years of experience can often tell the doneness of a roast chicken or turkey just by looking at it. Until you have gained that much experience, you should rely on other methods.

FOR LARGE ROASTED BIRDS

An *internal temperature* of 180°F (82°C), tested with a thermometer, is the most accurate guide. The thermometer should be inserted into the thickest muscle of the inner part of the thigh, away from the bone. (*Note:* This temperature has been determined by the Canadian Food Inspection Agency to be a safe temperature for cooked poultry. While the poultry will be safe when it reaches this temperature, it will also be unavoidably somewhat dry.)

The thigh is tested rather than the breast because the thigh is the last part of the bird to become fully cooked.

FOR SMALLER BIRDS, COOKED BY ANY METHOD

Doneness of smaller birds is determined in the following ways.

1. Looseness of joints. The leg moves freely in its socket.
2. Clear juices. Juices inside the cavity of a roasted bird are clear yellow rather than cloudy and red or pink.
3. Flesh separating from bone. Muscles begin to pull away from bones, especially breastbone and leg bones. Excessively shrunken flesh means it's overcooked and dry.
4. Firmness to touch. Test with finger pressure as you would a steak (see p. 276). This method is especially useful for sautéed boneless chicken breasts.

Not recommended: Do not test by piercing deeply with a fork and twisting the flesh. Too many valuable juices will be lost.

TRUSSING METHODS

Trussing means tying the legs and wings against the body to make a compact, solid unit. It has two main purposes:

1. Even cooking. Extended legs and wings cook too quickly.
2. More attractive appearance, especially when presented or served whole or carved in the dining room.

One of many trussing methods is illustrated in Figure 12.3. Your instructor may wish to show you other methods.

Figure 12.3
Trussing chicken.

(a) Place the chicken breast up with the neck end toward you. Tuck the first joint of the wings behind the back.

(b) Press the legs forward and down against the body.

(c) Pass the center of a length of twine under the hip bone just ahead of the tail.

(d) Bring the twine up and across the ends of the legs.

(e) Pass the twine under the ends of the legs as shown and pull tight.

(f) Bring the ends of the twine toward the neck end of the bird. Pull firmly on the twine while pressing on the breast portion with the thumbs as shown.

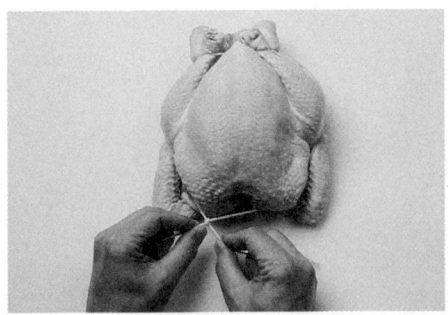

(g) Tie the twine tightly.

(h) The stub of the neck holds the twine in place, preventing it from slipping behind the back.

(i) The trussed chicken.

CUTTING UP CHICKEN

There are many ways to cut up chickens. Every chef has his or her own preferred methods. Some of these methods are illustrated, step by step, in Figures 12.4, 12.5, and 12.6. They show how to split a chicken for broiling and how to cut whole chickens into quarters and eighths, for both bone-in parts and semi-boneless pieces.

As for meats, it is important to know the bone structure of chicken in order to cut it up. The best way to learn this is to practice cutting chickens.

**Figure 12.4
Splitting chicken for broiling.**

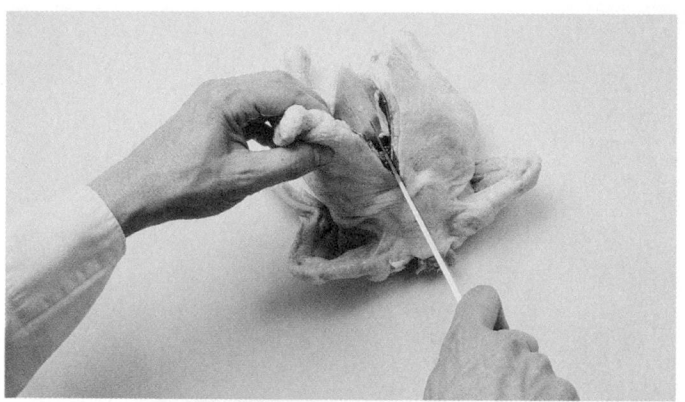

(a) Hold the chicken up by the tail. Cut through the bones to one side of the backbone, all the way to the neck.

(b) Split the chicken open.

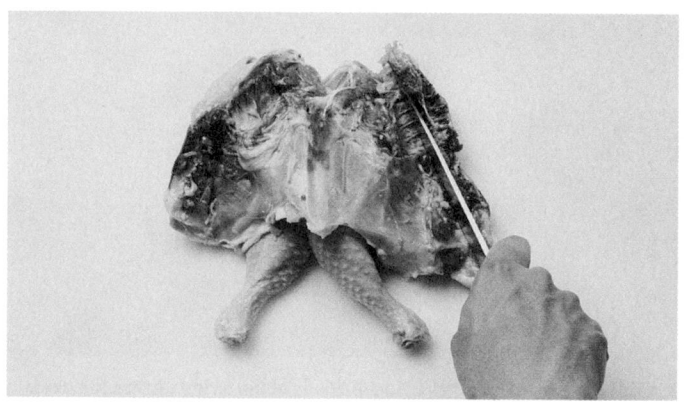

(c) Cut off the backbone as shown.

(d) Pull out the breastbone or keel bone. This helps the chicken lie flat and cook evenly.

(e) For a portion size of one-half chicken, cut the chicken in half down the center of the breast. Make a split in the skin below the leg and slip the end of the leg through it as shown to hold the chicken in shape.

(f) Portion-size Cornish game hens are left whole.

Figure 12.5
Cutting chicken into quarters and eighths, bone in.

(a) Place the chicken on the cutting board breast up. Split the chicken down the center of the breast with a heavy knife as shown.

(b) Spread the chicken open and cut through the bones on one side of the backbone.

(c) Cut off the backbone completely. Save for stocks.

(d) Cut through the skin between the leg and the breast.

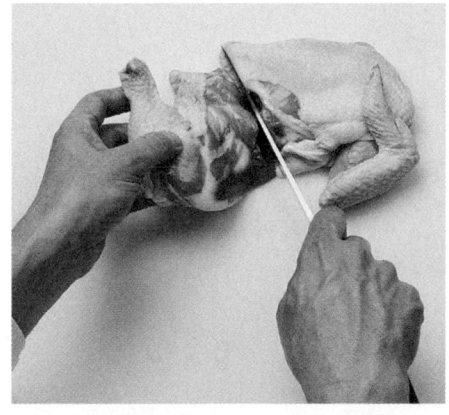

(e) Pull the leg back and cut off the entire leg section. Repeat with the other half. The chicken is now in quarters.

(f) To cut into eighths, cut the drumstick and thigh apart at the joint.

(g) Cut the breast and wing quarter into two equal pieces. (Another method is simply to cut off the wing.)

(h) The chicken cut into eighths. Note that the first joint of each wing has been cut off.

Figure 12.6
Cutting up chickens, semiboneless.

(a) Cut off the wings at the second joint. Save for stocks.

(b) Cut through skin between the leg and body.

(c) Turn the chicken on its side and pull the leg back. Carefully start to cut the flesh from the bone, being sure to get the "oyster," the little nugget of tender meat in the hollow of the hip bone. Cut through the ligaments at the hip joint.

(d) Holding the chicken steady with the knife, pull off the leg. Repeat with the other leg.

(e) Turn the breast portion upright. Cut down along one side of the ridge of the breastbone to separate the breast meat from the bone.

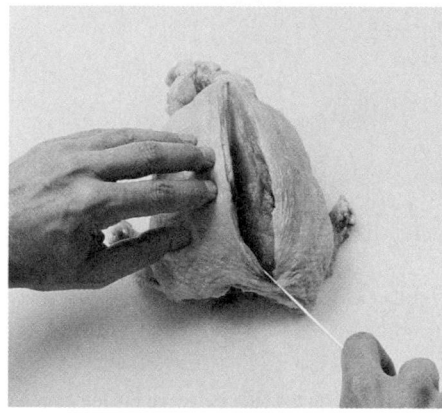

(f) Continue the cut along the wishbone to the wing joint.

(g) Holding the chicken by the wing, cut through the wing joint.

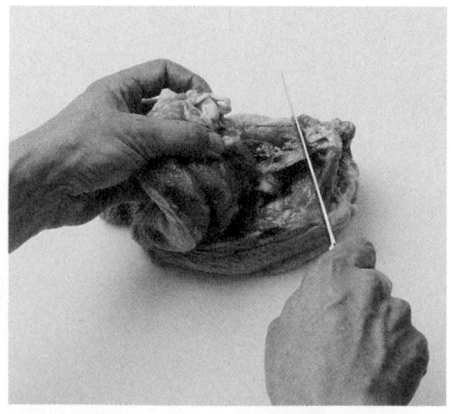

(h) Holding the carcass steady with the knife, pull back on the wing and breast meat.

(i) Pull the breast meat completely off the bone. Be sure to hold on to the small "tenderloin" muscle inside the breast so it doesn't separate from the rest of the meat. Repeat with the other side.

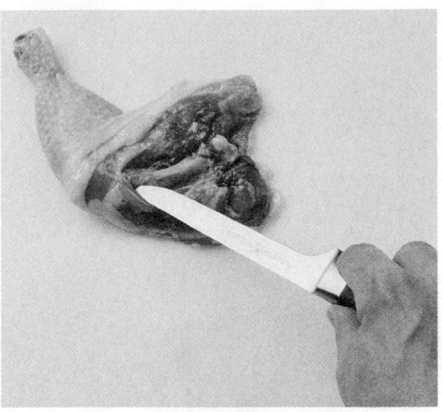

(j) If desired, remove the thigh bone. Cut down along both sides of the bone to separate it from the meat.

(k) Lift out the bone and cut it off at the joint.

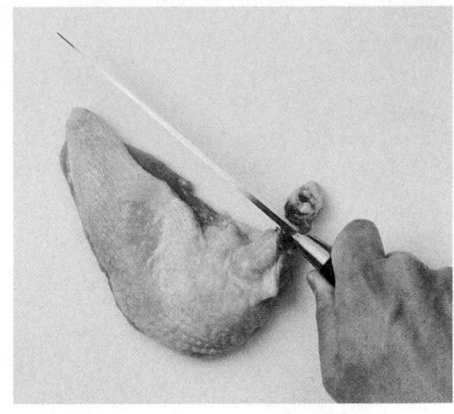

(l) For a neater appearance, chop off the end of the wing bone with the heel of the knife.

(m) The cut-up chicken. From left: breast portions without and with wing bone; leg portions without and with thigh bone; wing sections and carcass for stockpot. The drumstick and thigh (bone-in) may be cut apart at the joint, as in Figure 12.5.

■ TERMS FOR REVIEW

maturity	kind	fowl	partridge
light meat	class	White Pekin	pheasant
dark meat	style	magret	ratite
free-range	broiler/fryer	moulard	ostrich
organic	roaster	guinea	emu
inspection	capon	squab	trussing
grading	hen	quail	

■ QUESTIONS FOR DISCUSSION

1. Why are hens or fowl not roasted in commercial kitchens?

2. Why is the breast section so often dry when whole chickens and turkeys are roasted? Can you suggest ways to remedy this problem?

3. Give a brief description of each of the following classes of poultry. Be sure to mention relative tenderness and approximate size.

Capon	Young tom turkey
Roaster duckling	Rock Cornish hen
Broiler/fryer	Yearling turkey
Roaster	Hen or fowl

4. How should fresh and frozen poultry be stored?

5. Describe five methods for determining doneness in poultry items.

6. What is the purpose of trussing poultry?

7. Why are most game birds better if not cooked until well done?

13

Cooking Poultry and Game Birds

The muscle tissue of domestic poultry and game birds, as we have said, has basically the same structure as the muscle tissue of meat animals. In particular, the breast meat of chicken and turkey is so similar to veal that they are interchangeable in many recipes.

Imaginative cooks realize that even when two meats are quite different—chicken and beef, for example—interesting new dishes can be made with substitutions that might seem unusual. For example, it is possible to make a delicious chili from chicken or turkey meat, a preparation that has the added advantage of having a lower food cost than beef chili.

Because the basic cooking methods for poultry are the same as for meat, they are not repeated here. But you may want to review them before proceeding with any of the recipes in this chapter. Also, please review the discussion of light and dark meat (p. 353) in the previous chapter, as well as the methods for testing doneness (p. 358).

After reading this chapter, you should be able to

1. Cook poultry by roasting and baking.

2. Cook poultry by broiling and grilling.

3. Cook poultry by sautéing, pan-frying, and deep-frying.

4. Cook poultry by simmering and poaching.

5. Cook poultry by braising.

6. Identify the safety, quality, and practicality concerns associated with preparing dressings and stuffings.

7. List basic ingredients for dressings and stuffings.

8. Prepare dressings and stuffings.

ROASTING AND BAKING

The general procedures for roasting and baking meats also apply to poultry, as illustrated by the following recipes. However, there are some differences in the ways poultry items are handled. The guidelines below should be observed.

Remember that poultry items are almost always cooked well done (except for squab and game birds).

SEASONING AND BASTING

1. Seasonings and, if desired, a little mirepoix or a bouquet garni should be placed inside the cavity. You need to season the skin only if it is to be served and eaten, as the seasonings will not penetrate the skin.

2. Oil the skin before roasting to help in browning and to protect against drying. The skin may be basted with *fat only* during roasting, but this is unnecessary if the bird is roasted breast down (and turned breast up just at the end of the roasting period to brown).

   Basting is beneficial for large turkeys, which must be subjected to dry heat for several hours. If you baste large poultry during roasting, do it every 20 to 30 minutes. More frequent basting results in the loss of a great deal of heat from the oven because the door is opened so frequently.

3. Basting is unnecessary for duck and goose, which have a great deal of fat under the skin. These birds are usually roasted breast up for that reason.

TEMPERATURE

Selection of roasting temperature depends on the product being roasted.

1. *Low-temperature roasting* is best for large items such as turkeys and capons. It results in a tender, juicy product. Review pages 272 and 288 for a discussion of low-temperature roasting.

   Large turkeys may be roasted at 250° to 325°F (120° to 165°C). For most operations, however, cooking times at the lower end of this range are too long. In addition, if a turkey is stuffed (see pp. 423–424), it is not advisable to roast it at a very low temperature because the interior temperature will take too long to rise, providing a good breeding ground for bacteria.

   Some recipes call for starting large turkeys at a high temperature for 15 to 30 minutes in order to brown them. This is usually not necessary because they will likely brown anyway during the long cooking time.

   Smaller items, such as roasting chickens, are usually roasted at 325° to 375°F (165° to 190°C). Small items roasted at low temperatures may not brown well by the time they are done. In such cases, the heat can be turned up for a few minutes when they are almost done in order to brown them.

2. The *searing* method may be used for chickens under 4 to 5 pounds (2 kg) and for baked chicken parts. That is, start roasting in the oven at 450°F (230°C) for 15 minutes, then reduce the oven temperature to 250° to 325°F (120° to 160°C). These small items cook so quickly that continuous roasting at a low temperature produces very little browning.

   Ducks and geese also may be started at a high temperature in order to melt off some of the heavy fat layer under the skin and to make the skin brown and crisp.

3. *High-temperature roasting* is used for small items such as squab and game birds, which are often served rare. Cornish hens and other small poultry under 3 pounds (1.35 kg) may also be flash-roasted. Great care is necessary when roasting at high temperatures, however, because the poultry will quickly become overcooked if left in the oven only a few minutes too long. For example, a 2½-pound (1.2 kg) chicken or guinea hen roasted at 450°F (230°C) may be perfectly cooked and nicely browned after 45 minutes but overcooked and dry if left another 10 minutes.

   Ducks may also be roasted at a continuously high temperature (400° to 425°F/200° to 220°C) because their fat content protects them from drying. Great care should be used to prevent overcooking, however, because this can happen very quickly at these temperatures. (Goose should not be roasted at a continuously high temperature because of its larger size and the length of time it takes to cook.)

BAKED POULTRY

Roasting and baking are the same process. Cutting up the chicken doesn't change the cooking method. Baked chicken or turkey parts are treated like roasted poultry.

Chicken parts are sometimes coated with seasoned crumbs or flour and rolled in fat before baking. Such products are sometimes misleadingly called *oven-fried* because of their resemblance to breaded fried chicken.

 ### Baked Chicken

Portions: 24   Portion size: ¼ chicken

U.S.	Metric	Ingredients
8 oz	250 g	Flour
5 tsp	25 mL	Salt
½ tsp	2 mL	White pepper
2 tsp	10 mL	Paprika
½ tsp	2 mL	Dried thyme
15 lb	7 kg	Fryer chicken parts or quarters (see note)
1 lb	500 g	Melted butter, oil, or a mixture of butter and oil

Per serving:
Calories, 450; Protein, 38 g; Fat, 30 g (61% cal.); Cholesterol, 150 mg; Carbohydrates, 6 g; Fiber, 0 g; Sodium, 590 mg.

Note: If you are starting with whole chickens, cut them into quarters or eighths, as shown in Figure 12.5. Any chicken parts may be used for this recipe. For example, you might bake just the legs and use the breasts and wings for other preparations.

■ P r o c e d u r e

1. Combine the flour and seasonings in a pan.
2. Dry the chicken pieces with paper towels if they are wet. Dredge in the seasoned flour.
3. Dip the chicken in the fat so that all sides are coated. Let excess drip off.
4. Arrange the chicken pieces on a sheet pan or in baking pans, skin side up. If using both dark and light meat parts, place them on separate pans.
5. Bake the chicken at 350°F (175°C) until done, about 1 hour.

V A R I A T I O N S

Baked Herbed Chicken
Add 1 tbsp (15 mL) dried tarragon, 1 tsp (5 mL) dried marjoram, 2 tbsp (30 mL) fresh chives, and 2 tbsp (30 mL) dried parsley to the flour mixture. Omit paprika.

Baked Rosemary Chicken
Prepare as in basic recipe. After placing chicken parts in baking pans, sprinkle with dried rosemary, about 4 tsp (20 mL) for 24 portions. Fifteen minutes before chicken is done, sprinkle with 3–4 fl oz (90–125 mL) lemon juice.

Baked Chicken Parmesan
Instead of flour for dredging, use 1 cup (100 g) parmesan cheese mixed with 1½ cups (150 g) fine dry bread crumbs. Season as in basic recipe.

Roast Chicken with Natural Gravy

Portions: 24   Portion size: ¼ chicken
2 fl oz (60 mL) jus

U.S.	Metric	Ingredients
6	6	Chickens, 3–3½ lb (1.4–1.6 kg) each
to taste	to taste	Salt
to taste	to taste	Pepper
as needed	as needed	Oil or butter
		Mirepoix:
6 oz	175 g	Onion, medium dice
3 oz	90 g	Carrots, medium dice
3 oz	90 g	Celery, medium dice
3 qt	3 L	Strong chicken stock
2 oz	60 g	Cornstarch or arrowroot
2 fl oz	60 mL	Water or stock, cold
to taste	to taste	Salt
to taste	to taste	Pepper

Per serving:
Calories, 350; Protein, 45 g; Fat, 17 g (45% cal.); Cholesterol, 105 mg; Carbohydrates, 2 g; Fiber, 0 g; Sodium, 140 mg.

■ Procedure

1. Remove giblets from chickens. Check inside cavities to make sure they have been well cleaned. Reserve giblets for other use.
2. Season the insides of the chickens with salt and pepper.
3. Truss the chickens (see Figure 12.3).
4. Rub the outside of the chickens with oil or butter (butter promotes faster browning). Season the skin with salt and pepper, as it will be served with the meat.
5. Place the mirepoix in a roasting pan. Place a rack over the mirepoix, and place the chickens breast down on the rack.
6. Place the chickens in an oven preheated to 450°F (230°C). After 15 minutes (not longer), turn the heat down to 325°F (165°C).
7. When the chickens have been in the oven for 45–60 minutes, turn them breast side up. Baste with the fat in the roasting pan and finish roasting. Total cooking time is about 1½ hours.
8. Remove the chickens from the roasting pan and hold them in a warm place for service.
9. Set the roasting pan on the range over high heat and brown the mirepoix well, but do not let it burn. Pour off the fat.
10. Add the stock to deglaze the pan. Boil until the gravy is reduced by about one-third. Degrease carefully. See Figure 13.1.
11. Stir the starch with the cold water or stock. Stir it into the gravy. Bring to a boil and simmer until thickened.
12. Strain into a bain-marie, using a china cap lined with cheesecloth. Season carefully with salt and pepper.
13. Quarter the chickens, or carve them as shown in Figure 13.2. Serve a quarter chicken with 2 oz (60 mL) gravy.

VARIATIONS

Roast Herbed Chicken
Place 3–4 parsley stems and a pinch each of tarragon and marjoram in the cavity of each bird.
After turning the chicken breast up in the roasting pan, rub the skin with chopped parsley, tarragon, and marjoram.

Roast Chicken with Gravy
Save 4 oz (125 g) of the fat skimmed from the juices and make a blond roux with the fat and 4 oz (125 g) bread flour. Beat the roux into the juices and simmer until thickened.

Roast Chicken with Cream Gravy
Prepare as in basic recipe, but use only 1½ qt (1.5 L) chicken stock. Boil until reduced to 1 qt (1 L) and strain (step 9). Add 1 qt (1 L) hot milk and thicken with 8 oz (250 g) blond roux. Finish with 4 fl oz (125 mL) heavy cream.

Roast Chicken with Natural Gravy; Whipped Potatoes, Glazed Root Vegetables, Roasted Garlic, Peas

Figure 13.1
Preparing pan gravy.

(a) Remove the rack of cooked poultry from the roasting pan.

(b) If the mirepoix is not already browned, set it over a burner to brown it. Degrease the pan.

(c) Deglaze the pan with stock.

(d) Bring to a simmer and cook until reduced by about one-third. Stir in a starch slurry or a roux to thicken. Simmer until the desired texture is reached.

(e) Strain the gravy.

Figure 13.2
Carving roast chicken.

(a) Place the chicken on a clean, sanitary cutting board. Cut through the skin between the leg and the breast sections.

(b) Pull the leg away from the body of the chicken with the fork. Using the knife, cut between the thigh bone and the hip to separate the leg completely.

(c) Hold the chicken steady by bracing the backbone with the fork. Cut through the breast between the two halves, just to one side of the keel bone.

(d) Pull the breast section away from the bone. With the knife, cut through the joint where the wing bone is attached to the body. Separate the breast and wing section completely from the carcass. Repeat steps (a) through (d) on the other side of the chicken.

(e) Cut the wings from the breast portions and cut the drumsticks apart from the thighs.

Roast Turkey with Giblet Gravy

Yield: about 7 lb (3.5 kg) sliceable meat   Portions: 22   Portion size: 5 oz (150 g)
28   4 oz (125 g)
36   3 oz (100 g)

U.S.	Metric	Ingredients
1	1	Turkey, dressed, 20 lb (10 kg)
to taste	to taste	Salt
to taste	to taste	Pepper
as needed	as needed	Oil
		Mirepoix:
8 oz	250 g	Onions, chopped medium
4 oz	125 g	Carrots, chopped medium
4 oz	125 g	Celery, chopped medium
3 qt	3 L	Chicken stock, hot
6 oz	175 g	Bread flour
to taste	to taste	Salt
to taste	to taste	Pepper

■ P r o c e d u r e

1. Remove the giblets from the cavity of the turkey. Check inside the turkey to make sure it has been well cleaned. Lock the wings in place by twisting the wing tips behind the back of the turkey.

2. Season the inside of the turkey with salt and pepper. Rub the skin thoroughly with oil.

3. Place the turkey on one side in a roasting pan, on a rack if possible (see note).

4. Place in an oven preheated to 325°F (165°C). (Lower temperatures are preferable if production schedule permits. See p. 366 for explanation.)

5. Roast for 1½ hours. Turn the turkey on the other side. Roast another 1½ hours. Baste turkey with drippings (fat only) every 30 minutes.

6. While turkey is roasting, place turkey heart, gizzard, and neck in a saucepan. (Reserve the liver for another use, or add it to bread dressing.) Cover the giblets with water and simmer until very tender, about 2–3 hours. Reserve the broth and the giblets for gravy.

7. Turn the turkey breast up. Place the mirepoix in the pan.

8. Return the turkey to the oven and continue to roast. Baste occasionally by spooning the fat in the pan over the turkey.

9. The turkey is done when a thermometer inserted into the thickest part of the inside of the thigh reads 180°F (82°C). Total roasting time is about 5 hours. (See Chapter 12 for a discussion of how to determine doneness.)

10. Remove the turkey from the roasting pan and let stand in a warm place at least 15 minutes before carving.

11. Drain off and save the fat from the roasting pan.

12. Set the roasting pan with the mirepoix and drippings on the range to reduce the moisture and brown the mirepoix. Brown lightly if a light gravy is desired. Brown heavily if a dark gravy is desired.

13. Deglaze the pan with about 1 qt (1 L) of the chicken stock. Pour into a saucepan with the rest of the stock and the giblet broth (from step 6). Bring to a simmer. Degrease well.

14. Make a blond roux with the flour and 6 oz (175 g) of the fat from the roasting pan. Beat the roux into the gravy to thicken it.

15. Simmer at least 15 minutes, until the gravy is smooth and no raw flour taste remains. Strain and season.

16. Chop or dice the giblets very fine and add to the gravy.

17. Slice the turkey and serve desired portion with 2 fl oz (60 mL) gravy. See Figure 13.3 for slicing techniques. For quantity service, see procedures demonstrated in Figure 13.4.

Per 5 ounces:
Calories, 460; Protein, 68 g; Fat, 16 g (33% cal.); Cholesterol, 135 mg; Carbohydrates, 6 g; Fiber, 0 g; Sodium, 170 mg.

Note: Because of the difficulty of handling large turkeys, many chefs do not use a rack. Also, large turkeys are easier to turn if they are placed first on one side, then on the other, rather than breast down.

For more even cooking, separate leg and thigh sections from breast section. Roast dark and light meat on separate pans, if many turkeys are being prepared. Remove each part from oven when done.

V A R I A T I O N S

Roast Capons and Large Chickens
Prepare like roast turkey. Reduce roasting time, depending on size of bird. A 6-lb (2.7- kg) bird requires about 3 hours at 325°F (165°C).

Roast Turkey, Chicken, or Capon with Cream Gravy
Prepare as in basic recipe, but use half stock and half milk for the gravy instead of all stock. When gravy is finished, add 8 oz (250 mL) heavy cream.

Figure 13.3 Carving roast turkey.

(a) Place the turkey on a clean, sanitary cutting board. Cut through the skin between the leg and the body. Pull the leg outward with a fork. The leg should pull off easily, but use the knife as necessary to separate the thigh from the hip.

(b) Cut the drumstick and thigh apart at the joint. Repeat with the other leg.

(c) Cut the meat from the drumstick and thigh in thin slices.

(d) Make a horizontal cut just above the wing, cutting all the way through to the bones of the body cavity. This cut helps the breast slices separate evenly.

(e) With long, smooth strokes, cut the breast into thin slices.

(f) When the slices become too large, change the angle of the knife slightly as shown. Continue until both sides of the breast are completely sliced.

(g) An alternative method is to cut off an entire half breast in one piece. This piece can then be sliced as shown. Cut across the grain, holding the knife at an angle to get broader slices.

(f)

(g)

Figure 13.4
Quantity service of roast turkey and dressing.

(a) Using a scoop, place measured portions of baked dressing in hotel pans as shown or on sheet pans.

(b) Place measured portions of dark meat slices on top of the mounds of dressing.

(c) Place light meat slices on last, using the best-looking slices for the tops. Cover the pans. Refrigerate if they are to be held for later service. To serve, ladle a small amount of stock over the portions to keep them moist, and reheat, covered, in a moderate oven. Ladle 2 fl oz (60 mL) gravy over the portions when served.

Roast Duckling with Caramelized Apples

Portions: 12   Portion size: ¼ duckling
                        2 fl oz (60 mL) sauce

U.S.	Metric	Ingredients	
			■ **P r o c e d u r e**
3	3	Ducklings, about 4½ lb (2 kg) each	1. Clean the ducklings well. Season them inside and out with salt and pepper. Place the orange zest inside the cavities.
to taste	to taste	Salt	2. Truss the ducks.
to taste	to taste	Pepper	3. Heat some oil in a roasting pan. Brown the ducks well. Place in an oven preheated to 425°F (220°C). Roast for 45 minutes or until done.
1 oz	30 g	Orange zest	
as needed	as needed	Oil	
2½ oz	75 g	Sugar	4. Place the sugar and vinegar in a casserole and bring to a boil. Cook until light caramel in color.
5 fl oz	150 mL	Red wine vinegar	5. Deglaze with the orange and lemon juices. Reduce until syrupy. Add two-thirds of the brown stock. Reduce by one-third.
9 fl oz	275 mL	Orange juice	
2½ fl oz	75 mL	Lemon juice	
1 qt	1 L	Brown stock	6. Once the ducks are cooked, remove and discard the excess fat in the pan. Place pan on the stovetop and deglaze the pan using the remaining brown stock. Add the deglazing liquid to the other sauce.
4 tsp	10 g	Potato starch	
1 fl oz	30 mL	Orange liqueur (optional)	
1½ oz	45 g	Orange zest, cut julienne, blanched	7. Dilute the potato starch with a little water and, if desired, the orange liqueur.
¾ oz	25 g	Lemon zest, cut julienne, blanched	8. Bring the sauce to a boil and add a little to the diluted potato starch. Then mix the starch into the rest of the sauce and simmer until thickened.
			9. Season and strain. Add the julienned zest.
2½ lb	1.2 kg	Apples	10. Peel, core, and slice the apples into thin wedges.
3 oz	90 g	Clarified butter	11. Heat the clarified butter in a sauté pan. Add the apples and toss until well coated. Sprinkle with the sugar and cook until lightly caramelized.
2 oz	60 g	Sugar	12. Remove the string from the duck and carve. Serve the sliced duck with the apples neatly arranged on the plate. Spoon the sauce around.

Per serving:
Calories, 740; Protein, 40 g; Fat, 52 g (63% cal.); Cholesterol, 145 mg;
Carbohydrates, 28 g; Fiber, 2 g; Sodium, 200 mg.

Duckling in Paprika

Portions: 12   Portion size: ¼ duck
2 fl oz (60 mL) sauce

U.S.	Metric	Ingredients
3	3	Ducklings, about 4½ lb (2 kg) each
4 tsp	10 g	Paprika
to taste	to taste	Salt
to taste	to taste	Pepper
3 fl oz	90 mL	Oil
4 oz	125 g	Onions, diced
4 oz	125 g	Carrots, diced
2½ oz	75 g	Celery, diced
1 tsp	3 g	Paprika
10 fl oz	300 mL	White wine (see note)
2½ pt	1.2 L	Brown stock
to taste	to taste	Salt
to taste	to taste	Pepper

Per serving:
Calories, 630; Protein, 40 g; Fat, 49 g (71% cal.); Cholesterol, 130 mg; Carbohydrates, 1 g; Fiber, 0 g; Sodium, 135 mg.

■ Procedure

1. Clean the ducklings well. Rub them with the paprika and season them inside and out with salt and pepper. Reserve any trimmings, including neck, heart, and gizzard.
2. Heat the oil in a roasting pan. Brown the ducks well. Place in an oven preheated to 425°F (220°C). Roast for 45 minutes or until done, basting often.
3. Remove the ducks from the pan and set aside. Drain off most of the fat.
4. Place the roasting pan on the stovetop and add the onions, carrots, celery, and duck trimmings. Brown the vegetables, then drain off the excess fat thoroughly.
5. Add the paprika. Mix well and cook for a few minutes.
6. Deglaze with the white wine and reduce a few minutes before adding the brown stock. Reduce until thick enough to coat the back of a spoon. Skim off any fat from the surface. Strain and season.
7. Carve the duckling and serve the sauce around.

Note: If you do not wish to use wine in this recipe, substitute water or stock for deglazing. Adjust the flavor balance of the finished sauce with a little fresh lemon juice.

Herb-Roasted Squab

Portions: 8   Portion size: 1 squab
1 fl oz (30 mL) jus

U.S.	Metric	Ingredients
2 tbsp	15 g	Chopped fresh parsley
2 tbsp	15 g	Chopped fresh tarragon
2 tbsp	15 g	Chopped fresh chervil
4 oz	125 g	Soft butter
to taste	to taste	Salt
to taste	to taste	Pepper
8	8	Squab
2 fl oz	60 mL	Oil
2½ oz	75 g	Carrots, chopped
2½ oz	75 g	Onions, chopped
2 oz	60 g	Celery, chopped
2–3	2–3	Garlic cloves, chopped
4 fl oz	125 mL	White wine
1½ pt	750 mL	Water
1	1	Bouquet garni (see p. 152)
to taste	to taste	Salt
to taste	to taste	Pepper

■ Procedure

1. Mix the chopped herbs into the soft butter and season with salt and pepper.
2. Trim the squab by removing the wing tips and setting aside. Loosen the skin of the squab, being careful not to break it. Using a piping bag, pipe a small amount of the herb butter underneath the skin. Using your fingertips, spread the butter evenly under the skin. Truss for roasting.
3. Heat the oil in a braising pan or roasting pan. Brown the squab and finish cooking in the oven at 425°F (220°C). Start on the side and roast for about 5 minutes, then turn over onto the other leg and roast another 5 minutes. Finally, turn the squab on their backs and finish cooking for 10–20 minutes. Total cooking time for squab is about 20–30 minutes, depending on size. The breast should still be pink inside, or it will be dry. Remove the squab and set aside in a warm place.
4. Degrease the pan and add the trimmings, carrots, onions, celery, and garlic. Cook until lightly browned.
5. Deglaze with white wine, then add the water and bouquet garni. Reduce by two-thirds. Strain and skim. Season to taste.
6. The squab may be served halved or whole but, in any case, remove the backbone first, using a pair of shears.

Per serving:
Calories, 1120; Protein, 64 g; Fat, 94 g (76% cal.); Cholesterol, 335 mg; Carbohydrates, 1 g; Fiber, 0 g; Sodium, 310 mg.

Smoke-Roasted Spiced Chicken Breasts with Fruit Salsa

Portions: 12   Portion size: 1 chicken breast
3 oz (90 g) vegetable garnish
2 oz (60 g) salsa

U.S.	Metric	Ingredients
2 tbsp	30 mL	Paprika
1½ tsp	7 mL	Ground cumin
¾ tsp	4 mL	Dried thyme
1½ tsp	7 mL	Ground coriander
1½ tsp	7 mL	Salt
¾ tsp	4 mL	Pepper
12	12	Chicken breasts, boneless and skinless, about 5 oz (150 g) each
as needed	as needed	Vegetable oil
2 lb 4 oz	1.1 kg	Wheatberries with Pecans and Poblanos (p. 630)
24 oz	725 g	Fruit Salsa (p. 199)
as needed	as needed	Cilantro sprigs for garnish

■ Procedure

1. Combine the paprika, cumin, thyme, coriander, salt, and pepper.
2. Coat the chicken breasts with the spice mixture.
3. Brush lightly with oil. Allow to marinate, refrigerated, for 3 to 4 hours.
4. Set up a smoke-roasting system as shown in Figure 4.1. Heat the pan of wood chips or sawdust on top of the stove until smoke starts to appear. Lay the chicken breasts on the rack, cover, and turn the heat to medium-low. Smoke-roast for 10 minutes.
5. Transfer the pan to an oven preheated to 400°F (200°C) and continue roasting for another 10 minutes.
6. For each portion, place a 3-oz (90-g) portion of wheatberries on the center of a plate. Slice a chicken breast on the diagonal and arrange the slices, overlapping, on top of the wheatberries. Spoon 2 oz (60 g) salsa around the chicken and wheatberries. Garnish with cilantro.

Per serving:
Calories, 200; Protein, 29 g; Fat, 6 g (27% cal.); Cholesterol, 80 mg; Carbohydrates, 7 g; Fiber, 1 g; Sodium, 360 mg.

Quail Baked with Prosciutto and Herbs

Portions: 8   Portion size: 2 quail

U.S.	Metric	Ingredients
2 oz	60 g	Butter
4 tsp	20 mL	Sage, crumbled
1 tsp	5 mL	Dried rosemary, crumbled
2 tbsp	30 mL	Chopped parsley
to taste	to taste	Salt
to taste	to taste	Pepper
16	16	Quail, whole
16 slices	16 slices	Prosciutto, sliced paper-thin
2 fl oz	60 mL	Balsamic vinegar or red wine vinegar
4 fl oz	125 mL	Chicken stock

■ P r o c e d u r e

1. Melt the butter. Add the herbs and seasonings.

2. Brush the quail heavily with the herb butter. Wrap a slice of prosciutto around the breast of each quail.

3. Place the quail in a casserole just large enough to hold them. Cover and bake at 400°F (200°C) until done, about 30 minutes.

4. When they are done, remove the quail from the casserole and keep them warm. Without degreasing it, deglaze the pan with the vinegar and reduce au sec. Add the chicken stock and bring to a boil.

5. Place 1 tbsp (15 mL) sauce on each plate and place 2 quail on top. Garnish with your choice of vegetable accompaniment.

V A R I A T I O N S

Chicken, squab, and guinea hens can be cooked using this recipe. Cut them into pieces, brush each piece with the herb butter, and wrap with a slice of prosciutto. If desired, the skin can be removed before the pieces are brushed with the herb butter.

Per serving:
Calories, 500; Protein, 47 g; Fat, 34 g (61% cal.); Cholesterol, 185 mg;
Carbohydrates, 1 g; Fiber, 0 g; Sodium, 900 mg.

BROILING AND GRILLING

Tender, young poultry items may be cooked on the grill or broiler using the same procedure as for steaks and chops.

Use lower temperatures than for meats. The outside can be burned easily before the inside is cooked through. Poultry skin, in particular, browns and then burns very easily. For quantity production, broiled chicken is sometimes finished in the oven on sheet pans, preferably on racks.

Start poultry pieces skin side down. This helps keep flavorful juices from dripping out. Brush generously with melted butter or other fat before and during broiling.

Because the skin of broiled chicken is often eaten, it may be seasoned before cooking.

- Large or thick poultry items are not well suited to broiling and grilling because it takes so long for the heat to penetrate to the center and cook them through. For example, turkey thighs could be broiled if you kept the heat low enough, but, in practice, this is rarely done. On the other hand, if you boned them out and flattened them lightly with a cutlet mallet, you would make them more suitable for broiling and grilling.

- Grilled meat and poultry items are fairly simple, straightforward dishes, without the variety of ingredients and components you find in, for example, stews. However, there are several ways you can give variety to grilled poultry:

1. **Marinate the poultry or rub it with seasonings before cooking.**
   Keep in mind that marinade ingredients such as sugar and tomato burn easily, so use these with care. Also, herbs on the surface of the poultry burn easily. Charred rosemary can give a pleasant aroma to the food, but herbs such as parsley, if used in large quantity and allowed to burn, may taste like burned leaves.

2. **Baste with seasoned butter, marinade, or other flavorings during broiling.**
   Again, be careful with ingredients that burn easily. Use them only toward the end of cooking.

3. **Serve with an appropriate sauce or seasoned butter.**
   Flavored butters can be placed on top of the grilled poultry, but sauces should be underneath or on the side so they don't detract from the crisp, browned skin.

4. **Select vegetable garnishes for variety and interest.**
   Well-chosen and carefully plated garnishes should be thought of as part of the whole presentation, not just something served on the side.

Broiled Chicken

Portions: 10   Portion size: ½ chicken

U.S.	Metric	Ingredients
5	5	Broiler chickens, about 2 lb (900 g) each
4 fl oz	125 mL	Melted butter (or oil)
to taste	to taste	Salt
to taste	to taste	Pepper

Per serving:
Calories, 600; Protein, 59 g; Fat, 39 g (60% cal.); Cholesterol, 215 mg;
Carbohydrates, 0 g; Fiber, 0 g; Sodium, 270 mg.

■ **P r o c e d u r e**

1. Split the chickens in half and prepare for broiling, as shown in Figure 12.4.
2. Brush the chickens on both sides with melted butter. Season with salt and pepper.
3. Place the chickens skin side down on broiler rack (or on grill). Broil at moderately low heat until the chicken is half cooked and well browned on one side.
4. Turn the chickens over. (Use tongs or fork, but do not pierce the flesh with the fork.) Continue to broil until the chicken is done (no pink near thigh bone) and well browned on second side. (See first variation below for oven method.)
5. Remove from broiler. To serve, place half a chicken on dinner plate, skin side up.

V A R I A T I O N S

Broiled Chicken, Quantity Method
For large quantities, or for bigger chickens (quartered instead of halved), use slightly higher heat (set the broiler rack higher), and broil until browned on both sides, as in basic recipe. Remove from broiler and place in baking pans or on sheet pans. Finish cooking in the oven at 325°–350°F (165°–175°C).

Broiled Rock Cornish Game Hen
Remove backbones from hens and prepare for broiling (see Figure 12.4). Broil as in the basic recipe for any of the variations. Serve 1 hen per portion.

Broiled Tarragon Chicken
Before brushing with melted butter, rub each chicken half with ¼ tsp (1 mL) dried tarragon and 1–2 tsp (5–10 mL) chopped fresh parsley. Broil as in basic recipe.

 Chicken Paillard with Grilled Vegetables

Portions: 12   Portion size: 1 chicken breast, about 6 oz (175 g)

U.S.	Metric	Ingredients
12	12	Boneless, skinless chicken breasts, about 6 oz (175 g) each
3	3	Garlic cloves, chopped
1 tbsp	15 mL	Fresh rosemary, chopped
1½ tsp	7 mL	Salt
½ tsp	2 mL	Pepper
3 fl oz	90 mL	Lemon juice
3 fl oz	90 mL	Olive oil
as desired	as desired	Grilled Vegetable Medley (p. 574)
12	12	Fresh rosemary sprigs

Per serving:
Calories, 250; Protein, 34 g; Fat, 11 g (41% cal.); Cholesterol, 95 mg;
Carbohydrates, 1 g; Fiber, 0 g; Sodium, 370 mg.

■ **P r o c e d u r e**

1. Place each chicken breast between sheets of plastic film. With a meat mallet, carefully pound to a uniform thickness of about ¼ in. (6 mm).
2. Combine the garlic, rosemary, salt, and pepper. Lightly rub the flattened chicken breasts on both sides with the mixture. Sprinkle both sides with the lemon juice, then with the olive oil. Let marinate for 2–4 hours in the refrigerator.
3. Preheat a grill or broiler to very hot. Place the chicken breasts on the grill, skin side (that is, the side that had the skin on) down, and grill until about one-fourth done. Rotate on the grill, as in Figure 11.6, to mark. Continue to cook until about half done. Turn over and continue to grill until just cooked through.
4. Plate and serve at once with an assortment of grilled vegetables. Garnish each portion with a sprig of rosemary.

Broiled Poussin or Cornish Hens with Mustard Crust

Portions: 10   Portion size: 1 hen
1½ fl oz (40 mL) sauce

U.S.	Metric	Ingredients
10	10	Poussins or Cornish hens, about 1 lb (450 g) each
8 oz	250 g	Melted butter
to taste	to taste	Salt
to taste	to taste	Pepper
7 oz	225 g	Dijon mustard
4 oz	125 g	Fresh white bread crumbs
10	10	Broiled tomato halves
10 oz	300 g	Broiled mushrooms

Per serving:
Calories, 920; Protein, 81 g; Fat, 60 g (59% cal.); Cholesterol, 300 mg; Carbohydrates, 12 g; Fiber, 2 g; Sodium, 1630 mg.

■ Procedure

1. Lift the neck skin of each chicken and remove the wishbone by scraping the meat from the bone with a small sharp knife. Remove the backbone and split open, as shown in Figure 12.4. Tuck each wing tip behind the breast as shown. Push a skewer through a middle wing joint, through the breast, and through the second middle wing joint. Push another skewer through from one thigh to the other. Place skin side up on an oiled tray.

2. Brush with butter (reserve remaining butter for step 4) and season with salt and pepper.

3. Broil at a low heat to lightly color the skin. Transfer to the oven, set at 375°F (180°C), and cook for 30 minutes.

4. When the Cornish hens have been in the oven for 30 minutes, spread the mustard evenly over the skin. Sprinkle with the bread crumbs and drizzle with the remaining butter. Broil (grill) at high heat to golden brown and crisp.

5. Remove the chicken from the broiler, remove the skewers, and place a whole chicken on a dinner plate, skin side up. Garnish with 1 broiled tomato half and 1 oz (30 g) broiled mushrooms.

Grilled Spiced Squab with Couscous and Fig Compote

Portions: 12   Portion size: 1 squab, plus garnish

U.S.	Metric	Ingredients
12	12	Whole squab
1 tbsp	15 mL	Salt
1 tbsp	15 mL	Quatre épices (p. 839)
¾ tsp	3 mL	Dried thyme
¾ tsp	3 mL	Black pepper
as needed	as needed	Olive oil
3 pt	750 mL	Water
1½ tsp	7 mL	Salt
12 oz	375 g	Instant couscous (uncooked)
1 lb	500 g	Tender, young salad greens, such as mesclun
6 fl oz	175 mL	Basic vinaigrette (p. 723) made with red wine vinegar and olive oil
36	36	Cherry tomatoes, cut in half
12 oz	360 g	Fig Compote (p. 202)

Per serving:
Calories, 1300; Protein, 69 g; Fat, 94 g (68% cal.); Cholesterol, 325 mg; Carbohydrates, 42 g; Fiber, 5 g; Sodium, 1180 mg.

■ P r o c e d u r e

1. Split the squab for broiling, as shown in Figure 12.4, leaving the birds in one piece.
2. Combine the salt, spices, thyme, and pepper. Rub the squab with the spice mixture. Refrigerate for several hours.
3. Brush the squab lightly with olive oil. Place on the grill or broiler, starting skin side down. Grill or broil, turning as necessary, until the breast portion is medium rare.
4. Combine the water and salt in a saucepan and bring to a boil. Stir in the couscous. Cover and let stand for 5 minutes. Remove the cover and fluff with a kitchen fork.
5. Wash and drain the salad greens. Toss with the vinaigrette. Place a small mound of the greens at the top of each dinner plate. Top with the halved cherry tomatoes.
6. At the bottom center of each plate, place a small mound of couscous. In the center of the plate, above the couscous, place 1 oz (30 g) fig compote.
7. Split the squab in half. Place 1 half squab on each side of the couscous.

V A R I A T I O N

Grilled Spiced Cornish Hen
Prepare and grill Cornish hens using the same procedure as in the basic recipe, but make sure the chicken is more thoroughly cooked.

Grilled Chicken with Garlic and Ginger

Portions: 8   Portion size: approximately 12 oz (375 g), bone in

U.S.	Metric	Ingredients
6–8 lb	2.8–3.6 kg	Chicken parts or halves, or whole Cornish hens
6 fl oz	180 mL	Lemon or lime juice
2 fl oz	60 mL	Vegetable oil
1 oz	30 g	Fresh ginger root, grated
2 tsp	10 mL	Garlic, chopped fine
to taste	to taste	Salt
to taste	to taste	Pepper
as needed	as needed	Melted butter
to taste	to taste	Ginger oil (p. 200), optional

Per serving:
Calories, 430; Protein, 42 g; Fat, 27 g (59% cal.); Cholesterol, 140 mg; Carbohydrates, 1 g; Fiber, 0 g; Sodium, 150 mg.

■ Procedure

1. Cut the chickens into parts or halves for broiling. If using Cornish hens, split down the back and flatten, or cut into halves.
2. Combine the lemon or lime juice, oil, ginger, garlic, salt, and pepper to make a marinade.
3. Marinate the chicken for 3–4 hours.
4. Remove the chicken from the marinade. Broil or grill the chicken until done. Baste with the marinade several times during cooking.
5. Shortly before the chicken is done, brush the pieces once or twice with melted butter.
6. If desired, drizzle a few drops of ginger oil around the chicken after plating.

VARIATIONS

Substitute any of the following for the chicken parts in the above recipe or in any of the following variations:

Chicken or turkey brochettes (cubes of boneless meat on skewers)
Boneless chicken breast
Turkey cutlets (thick slices of turkey breast)
Turkey paillards (broad slices of turkey breast pounded thin)
Chicken or turkey thighs, boned out and lightly pounded

Southwestern Grilled Chicken
Substitute the following ingredients for the marinade in the basic recipe:

4 oz	120 g	Tomato, puréed
4 tsp	20 mL	Very finely chopped jalapeño
4 tbsp	60 mL	Chopped cilantro
3 fl oz	90 mL	Red wine vinegar

Spicy Barbecue-Style Grilled Chicken
Substitute the following ingredients for the marinade in the basic recipe. Toss the chicken pieces by hand so they are well coated.

2 fl oz	60 mL	Worcestershire sauce
1 fl oz	30 mL	Red wine vinegar
4 tsp	20 mL	Paprika
2 tsp	10 mL	Chili powder
1 tsp	5 mL	Dry mustard
1 tsp	5 mL	Crushed garlic
½ tsp	2 mL	Black pepper
1 tsp	5 mL	Salt

Grilled Chicken Oriental Style
Substitute the following ingredients for the marinade in the basic recipe. Brush the chicken with the marinade frequently during grilling.

8 fl oz	250 mL	Soy sauce
2 fl oz	60 mL	Rice wine or sherry
2 fl oz	60 mL	Chicken stock or water
1 fl oz	30 mL	Lemon juice
2 tsp	10 mL	Sugar
4 tsp	20 mL	Ginger root, grated

Grilled Chicken Marinated in Yogurt and Spices
Substitute the following ingredients for the marinade in the basic recipe. Marinate the chicken overnight.

8 oz	250 g	Unflavored yogurt
2 oz	60 g	Onion, grated
½ tsp	2 mL	Crushed garlic
½ tsp	2 mL	Grated ginger root
1 tsp	5 mL	Ground cumin
½ tsp	2 mL	Ground cardamom
pinch	pinch	Mace
½ tsp	2 mL	Cayenne
½ tsp	2 mL	Black pepper
1 tsp	5 mL	Salt

TANDOORI CHICKEN

The *tandoor* is a clay oven widely used in northern India. With wood or coal as a fuel, it cooks foods quickly at a high temperature. Tandoori chicken is especially popular in Indian restaurants in North America and Europe. In the original version, whole chickens are marinated in yogurt and spices, usually strongly colored with a red food coloring, then impaled on skewers and lowered into the tandoor. Western kitchens approximate this dish by cooking the chicken on a grill or in a very hot oven.

The marinade for Grilled Chicken Marinated in Yogurt and Spices (p. 380) is similar to typical marinades for tandoori chicken, but without the red coloring.

 ## Grilled Quail Marinated in Soy Barbecue Sauce

Portions: 12   Portion size: 2 quail

U.S.	Metric	Ingredients
24	24	Quail
1 qt	1 L	Soy Barbecue Sauce (p. 199)

Per serving:
Calories, 790; Protein, 58 g; Fat, 53 g (81% cal.); Cholesterol, 215 mg; Carbohydrates, 14 g; Fiber, 0 g; Sodium, 1780 mg.

■ **P r o c e d u r e**

1. Remove the backbones and split open the quails, as shown in Figure 12.4. Keep each quail in one piece.
2. Marinate the quail in the barbecue sauce for 2 hours. Drain.
3. Place the quail on a preheated broiler or grill. Cook, turning as necessary, until they are browned and the breast meat is medium done. Do not overcook, or the breast meat will be dry.

 ## Grilled Ostrich or Emu with Adobo Spices

Portions: 8   Portion size: 4 oz (125 g)

U.S.	Metric	Ingredients
		Spice rub:
1 tbsp	15 mL	Powdered ancho or pasilla chiles
½ tsp	2 mL	Salt
¼ tsp	1 mL	Dried oregano
¼ tsp	1 mL	Ground cumin
¼ tsp	1 mL	Black pepper
8	8	Ostrich or emu steaks or fillets, 4 oz (125 g) each

Per serving:
Calories, 130; Protein, 25 g; Fat, 3 g (21% cal.); Cholesterol, 85 mg; Carbohydrates, 0 g; Fiber, 0 g; Sodium, 230 mg.

■ **P r o c e d u r e**

1. Combine the ingredients for the spice rub. (*Note:* The quantities given are enough to mildly spice the meat. For a spicier product, double the quantities.)
2. Rub the spices over both sides of the steaks to lightly but evenly coat them.
3. Refrigerate for 1 hour or longer.
4. Grill or broil until medium done. Minimum safe internal temperature is 155°F or 68°C (see p. 29).
5. Cut into thin slices across the grain.

Grilled Spiced Turkey Burger

Portions: 10   Portion size: 5 oz (150 g)

U.S.	Metric	Ingredients	Procedure
6 oz	180 g	Onion, chopped fine	1. Sweat the onions in the oil until soft. Cool completely.
1 tbsp	15 mL	Vegetable oil	
3 lb	1.5 kg	Ground turkey	2. Combine the onions, turkey, salt, spices, and water in a bowl. Toss gently until uniformly mixed.
1 tbsp	15 mL	Salt	
1 tbsp	15 mL	Curry powder	3. Divide the mixture into 5-oz (150-g) portions (or as desired). Form each portion into a thick patty.
1½ tsp	7 mL	Grated lemon zest	
½ tsp	2 mL	Pepper	4. Grill or broil until just well done, but avoid overcooking, which makes the burger dry.
¼ tsp	1 mL	Cinnamon	
½ tsp	2 mL	Ground coriander	
¼ tsp	1 mL	Ground cumin	
¼ tsp	1 mL	Ground cardamom	
4 fl oz	125 mL	Water	
as desired	as desired	Tomato Raisin Chutney (p. 192), or other chutney as desired	5. Plate the burgers. Top each with a spoonful of chutney and a small mound of greens. (Alternatively, serve the burger and garnish as a sandwich on whole-grain bread.)
as desired	as desired	Microgreens or cilantro leaves	

Per serving:
Calories, 250; Protein, 27 g; Fat, 14 g (52% cal.); Cholesterol, 100 mg;
Cholesterol, 2 g; Fiber, 1 g; Sodium, 800 mg.

Grilled Spiced Turkey Burger; Tomato Raisin Chutney; Curry Oil

SAUTÉING, PAN-FRYING, AND DEEP-FRYING

Because chicken and turkey are lean, tender meats, cooking in fat is an appropriate and popular way to prepare them. The procedures for sautéing and pan-frying meats apply to chicken as well. Also, please note the following guidelines that apply particularly to poultry and game bird items.

Tender game birds and specialty poultry items may also be cooked by sautéing or pan-frying. For most game birds, only the breasts are usually cooked by these methods. The legs are small and have more connective tissue, so they require longer cooking. They are often braised or roasted until tender and served as garnish for the breast, either bone-in or as boneless meat.

For lean items, such as squab, partridge, and quail, the breasts are best if not cooked well done but kept somewhat pink inside, or even rare, to preserve moisture. Breast of pheasant and guinea may also be served with a little pink in the interior, although because this meat is so similar to the white meat of chicken, many customers may prefer it well done.

Dark red poultry, such as ostrich and emu steaks and breast of duck, are also lean and most often served medium to medium rare. Remember, however, that the minimum safe temperature for ostrich and emu is 155°F (68°C). Refer to page 29. Duck breasts present a special case for pan-frying because of the heavy layer of fat between the skin and the meat. Pan-fried duck breasts are started skin side down and cooked until much of the fat has rendered and the skin is crisp. This will take several minutes, or most of the cooking time. To finish, they are turned over and cooked skin side up for just a few moments, until they reach the desired doneness.

SAUTÉING

1. Boneless chicken breasts, thin slices of turkey breast, and other quick-cooking items are ideal for sautéing.

2. Larger items, such as bone-in chicken cut into eighths, are harder to cook to doneness by sautéing because they need longer cooking times. Such items are often browned by sautéing and then finished by another method, such as baking or braising. Breasts of game birds, on the other hand, may be cooked rare or medium and can thus be easily cooked from start to finish on the stovetop.

3. In classical cuisine, there are preparations for chicken called *sautés*, many of which are actually made by braising. The basic procedure for sautéing meats is used, except that the chicken is only partially cooked by sautéing. It is then finished by simmering briefly in the sauce made by deglazing the pan. Recipes for this kind of preparation are included under "Braising," page 410.

PAN-FRYING

1. Pan-fried chicken is usually breaded or floured before cooking for even browning and crispness.

2. About ¼ inch (½ cm) or more of fat is needed in the pan to pan-fry chicken.

3. The side that is to be face up on the plate should be browned first for best appearance. This is called the *presentation side*. For chicken pieces, this is usually the skin side.

4. After browning on all sides over moderately high heat, lower the heat so the chicken will cook to doneness without overbrowning. Pan-fried chicken takes about 30 to 45 minutes to cook.

DEEP-FRYING

1. The procedure for deep-frying is like that for pan-frying, except that the item doesn't have to be turned because it is submerged in the hot fat. Review page 73 for deep-frying instructions.

2. Pieces from small chickens (under 2½ lb/1 kg) are best for deep-frying. Larger pieces require such a long cooking time that the surface may brown too much. If necessary, fried items may be finished in the oven.

3. Fry chicken at 325° to 350°F (160° to 175°C) for even cooking.

 Pan-Fried Chicken

| Portions: 24 | Portion size: ½ chicken | |
| 48 | ¼ chicken | |
U.S.	Metric	Ingredients
12	12	Chickens, 2½ lb (1.1 kg) each
1 lb	450 g	Flour
5 tsp	25 mL	Salt
1 tsp	5 mL	White pepper
as needed	as needed	Oil

Per ½ chicken:
Calories, 820; Protein, 75 g; Fat, 51 g (57% cal.); Cholesterol, 235 mg; Carbohydrates, 11 g; Fiber, 0 g; Sodium, 580 mg.

■ Procedure

1. Cut chickens into 8 pieces, as shown in Figure 12.5.
2. Place the flour in a small hotel pan and season with salt and pepper.
3. Pour about ¼ in. (0.5 cm) oil into enough heavy iron skillets to hold all the chicken pieces in a single layer. Heat over moderately high heat.
4. Dredge the chicken pieces in the seasoned flour and shake off excess.
5. Place the pieces skin side down in the hot oil. Let the pieces fall away from you to avoid splashing hot oil on yourself.
6. Fry the chicken until golden brown on the bottom. Turn the pieces with tongs and brown the other side.
7. Lower the heat slightly to avoid overbrowning. Continue to cook the chickens, turning once or twice more, until cooked through. Breast meat cooks faster than leg meat— remove it when it is done. Total cooking time will be 20–40 minutes, depending on the size of the chickens and the temperature of the fat.
8. Remove the chicken from the pan and drain well. Place on hot dinner plates or hold for service in counter pans. Do not cover pans or hold too long, or chicken will lose its crispness.

V A R I A T I O N S

For slightly crustier, browner chicken, dip in milk before dredging in flour.

Alternative Method, Quantity Service: Brown chickens in hot oil as in basic recipe. Place on sheet pans or in baking pans skin side up, and finish cooking in a 350°F (175°C) oven.

Country-Style Fried Chicken
Fry chickens as in basic recipe. For 24 portions: Pour all but 4 oz (125 g) fat from the pans. Add 4 oz (125 g) flour and make a blond roux. Stir in 2½ qt (2.5 L) milk and bring to a boil. Stir constantly as the gravy thickens. Simmer a few minutes to eliminate all raw starch taste, and season with salt and white pepper. Adjust the consistency with stock, water, or additional milk, if necessary. Strain. Serve the chicken with gravy and mashed potatoes.

Sautéed Boneless Breast of Chicken with Mushroom Sauce

Portions: 10   Portion size: 1 chicken breast, about 4 oz (125 g)
                    2 fl oz (60 mL) sauce

U.S.	Metric	Ingredients
2 oz	60 g	Clarified butter
10	10	Boneless, skinless chicken breasts from 5 chickens, 3½ lb (1.6 kg) each
to taste	to taste	Salt
to taste	to taste	White pepper
2 oz	60 g	Flour for dredging
10 oz	300 g	Mushrooms (white), sliced
1 fl oz	30 mL	Lemon juice
2½ cups	600 mL	Suprême sauce, hot

■ **P r o c e d u r e**

1. Add enough clarified butter to a sauté pan to just cover the bottom with a thin film. Place on the range over moderate heat.
2. While the pan is heating, season the chicken breasts and dredge in flour. Shake off excess flour.
3. Place the breasts in the hot pan, presentation side (that is, the side that had the skin) down.
4. Sauté over moderate heat until lightly browned and about half cooked. The heat must be regulated so the chicken doesn't brown too fast.
5. Turn the chicken over and complete the cooking.
6. Remove the chicken from the pan and place on hot dinner plates for service. Keep warm.
7. Add the mushrooms to the pan and sauté briefly. After a few seconds, before the mushrooms start to darken, add the lemon juice. Toss the mushrooms in the pan as they sauté.
8. Add the suprême sauce to the pan and simmer for a few minutes, until reduced to the proper consistency. (The juices from the mushrooms will dilute the sauce.)
9. Ladle 2 fl oz (60 mL) sauce over each portion and serve immediately.

V A R I A T I O N S

Alternative (Quick) Method: Sauté the chicken as in basic recipe. Plate and ladle 2 fl oz (60 mL) prepared Mushroom Sauce (p. 173, made with suprême sauce as a base) over each portion.

Other sauces based on chicken stock may be used in place of mushroom sauce to serve with sautéed chicken breasts, including suprême, aurora, Hungarian, and ivory.

Per serving:
Calories, 360; Protein, 36 g; Fat, 20 g (51% cal.); Cholesterol, 145 mg; Carbohydrates, 8 g; Fiber, 1 g; Sodium, 200 mg.

Sautéed Chicken Breast with Ivory Sauce, Broccoli, Parisienne Potatoes

Deep-Fried Chicken

Portions: 24   Portion size: ½ chicken

U.S.	Metric	Ingredients
12	12	Chickens, about 2 lb (900 g) each
		Standard Breading Procedure (see note):
8 oz	250 g	Flour
2 tsp	10 mL	Salt
1 tsp	5 mL	White pepper
2	2	Eggs
2½ cups	600 mL	Milk
1½ lb	750 g	Dry bread crumbs

Per serving:
Calories, 880; Protein, 63 g; Fat, 58 g (61% cal.); Cholesterol, 205 mg; Carbohydrates, 22 g; Fiber, 1 g; Sodium, 520 mg.

Note: Quantities given for breading materials are only guidelines. You may need more or less, depending on the shapes of the chicken pieces, the care used in breading, and other factors. In any case, you will need enough so that even the last piece to be breaded can be coated easily and completely.

■ P r o c e d u r e

1. Cut chickens into 8 pieces, as shown in Figure 12.5.
2. Set up breading station: seasoned flour, egg wash, and crumbs (see p. 143).
3. Pass the chicken through the Standard Breading Procedure.
4. Heat the fat in a deep fryer to 325°–350°F (165°–175°C).
5. Fry the chicken until golden brown and cooked through. Fry light meat and dark meat pieces in separate baskets, as the light meat cooks faster.
6. Remove from the fat, drain well, and serve immediately.

V A R I A T I O N

Alternative Method: For larger chickens or for quantity service, brown the chicken in the deep fryer. Drain, place on sheet pans, and finish in the oven at 350°F (175°C).

Fried Chicken Maryland
Fry the chicken as in basic recipe. Serve each portion with the following sauce and garnish:

    2 fl oz (60 mL) cream sauce, suprême sauce, or horseradish sauce made with béchamel, placed on the plate under the chicken
    2 strips crisp bacon (p. 804), placed in a cross on top of the chicken
    2 corn fritters (p. 577)
    2 banana quarters, breaded and fried

Fried Chicken Breast Strips
Cut boneless, skinless chicken breasts into strips about ¾ inch (2 cm) wide. Bread and fry as in basic recipe. Serve with desired dipping sauce, such as barbecue sauce or blue cheese dressing.

Turkey Scaloppine with Shiitake Mushrooms and Roasted Shallots

Portions: 10   Portion size: 4 oz (125 g) plus garnish

U.S.	Metric	Ingredients
2½ lb	1.25 kg	Boneless, skinless turkey breast
15 oz	450 g	Shiitake mushrooms, caps only
to taste	to taste	Salt
to taste	to taste	White pepper
for dredging	for dredging	Flour
2 fl oz	60 mL	Oil
½ oz	15 g	Butter
30	30	Roasted shallots (prepared using the recipe for Roasted Winter Vegetables, p. 567)

Per serving:
Calories, 280; Protein, 31 g; Fat, 11 g (36% cal.); Cholesterol, 85 mg;
Carbohydrates, 13 g; Fiber,1 g; Sodium, 140 mg.

■ **Procedure**

1. Cut the turkey breast across the grain into 20 scaloppine, about 2 oz (60 g) each, using the procedure for cutting veal (Figure 11.9).
2. Lightly flatten each piece of turkey with a meat mallet.
3. Refrigerate until ready to cook.
4. Slice the mushroom caps into strips about ¼ in. (5 mm) wide.
5. Dry the meat, season it with salt and pepper, and dredge in flour. Shake off excess. (Do not do this step until immediately before cooking.)
6. Heat the oil in a large sauté pan until very hot. Add the turkey in a single layer and sauté over high heat just until lightly browned on both sides. (If necessary, sauté the meat in several batches.)
7. Remove the meat from the pan and keep warm. Drain any excess oil from the pan.
8. Add the butter to the pan. When it is hot, add the mushrooms and sauté for about 1 minute, just until the mushrooms are cooked. Adjust the seasoning.
9. Place the meat on hot dinner plates and top with the mushrooms. Arrange 3 roasted shallots on each plate.

Turkey Scaloppine with Shiitake Mushrooms and Roasted Shallots

Quail with Balsamic Glaze

Portions: 12 (see note)   Portion size: 1 quail plus garnish

U.S.	Metric	Ingredients
1 pt	500 mL	Balsamic vinegar
½ tsp	2 mL	Rosemary, dried
1 lb	500 g	Dried black-eyed peas
3 fl oz	90 mL	Olive oil
1½ fl oz	45 mL	Lemon juice
to taste	to taste	Salt
to taste	to taste	Pepper
1 fl oz	30 mL	Olive oil
4	4	Garlic cloves, chopped
1½ lb	750 g	Swiss chard, greens only (reserve the thick stalks for another use)
to taste	to taste	Cayenne
to taste	to taste	Salt
to taste	to taste	Pepper
12	12	Quail
to taste	to taste	Salt
to taste	to taste	Pepper
3 fl oz	90 mL	Oil
4 fl oz	125 mL	Balsamic vinegar
12 fl oz	375 mL	Red Bell Pepper Coulis (p. 189)

■ P r o c e d u r e

1. Combine the balsamic vinegar and rosemary in a stainless-steel pan. Reduce to about 2 oz (60 mL), until syrupy. Strain.

2. Soak and simmer the black-eyed peas until cooked. See page 610 for information on cooking dried beans. The black-eyed peas may be cooked ahead of time and cooled.

3. Heat the olive oil in a saucepan. Add the peas and cook until heated through. Add the lemon juice. Season to taste with salt and pepper.

4. In another saucepan or sauté pan, heat the olive oil and add the garlic. Cook briefly.

5. Add the chard leaves. Stir while cooking over high heat to wilt the greens and evaporate excessive moisture. Cook just until tender.

6. Season to taste with cayenne, salt, and pepper.

7. Cut each quail into four semiboneless parts, as shown in Figure 12.6. Leave the third wing joint in the breast sections. Season lightly with salt and pepper.

8. Heat the oil in sauté pan or pans. Add the legs and pan-fry until well browned and slightly crisp on the outside.

9. When the legs are almost cooked, add the breast sections, skin side down, and pan-fry until medium rare, turning as necessary to brown both sides.

10. Remove the quail from the pan and degrease. Return to the pan and add the balsamic vinegar (not the reduced vinegar from step 1). Cook over moderate heat, turning the pieces until they are lightly glazed.

11. For each portion, make a bed of Swiss chard on the center of the plate. Top with black-eyed peas. Arrange 2 leg portions and 2 breast portions on top of the peas.

12. Drizzle 1 fl oz (30 mL) coulis around the arrangement. Then drizzle 1 tsp (5 mL) reduced balsamic glaze around the arrangement.

Per serving:
Calories, 600; Protein, 37 g; Fat, 36 g (54% cal.); Cholesterol, 110 mg; Carbohydrates, 33 g; Fiber, 5 g; Sodium, 200 mg.

Note: One quail per portion is suitable for a first-course portion. For main courses, use 2 quail per portion.

Quail with Creole Spices

Portions: 12 as first course *Portion size: 1 quail, 2 oz (60 g) vegetables, 1½ oz (45 g) rice*
6 as main course *2 quail, 4 oz (125 g) vegetables, 3 oz (90 g) rice*

U.S.	Metric	Ingredients
12	12	Quail
1½ tsp	7 mL	Paprika
¼ tsp	1 mL	Cayenne
¼ tsp	1 mL	Dried oregano
¼ tsp	1 mL	Dried thyme
¼ tsp	1 mL	Pepper
½ tsp	2 mL	Salt
2 fl oz	20 mL	Vegetable oil
6 oz	180 g	Onion, chopped fine
1	1	Garlic clove, chopped fine
4 oz	125 g	Celery, small dice
4 oz	125 g	Green bell pepper, small dice
1 lb	500 g	Tomatoes, canned, chopped, with their juice
1 oz	30 g	Tomato purée
1 tsp	5 mL	Dried thyme
2 tbsp	30 mL	Chopped parsley
to taste	to taste	Salt
to taste	to taste	Pepper
18 oz	550 g	Steamed white rice

■ P r o c e d u r e

1. Remove the backbones from the quail, spread the birds open, and flatten them as illustrated in Figure 12.4f.
2. Mix together the paprika, cayenne, oregano, thyme, pepper, and salt.
3. Lay out the quail skin side up and sprinkle them generously with the spice mixture.
4. Heat the oil in one or more sauté pans over moderate heat. Pan-fry the quail on both sides until well browned and cooked through.
5. Remove the quail from the pan and keep warm.
6. Pour off all but about 1 fl oz (30 mL) fat from the pan.
7. Add the onion, garlic, celery, and green pepper to the pan. Sauté over medium heat until the onion just starts to brown.
8. Add the tomatoes, tomato purée, and thyme. Simmer 10 minutes, until the juices are somewhat reduced and thickened.
9. Stir in the parsley.
10. Add salt and pepper to taste.
11. To serve, place a scoop of hot rice on a dinner plate. Spoon the vegetables around the rice. Lean the quail against the mound of rice.

Per serving:
Calories, 300; Protein, 23 g; Fat, 16 g (48% cal.); Cholesterol, 85 mg;
Carbohydrates, 16 g; Fiber, 2 g; Sodium, 221 mg.

Quail with Creole Spices

Sautéed Chicken with Tomatoes and Mushrooms

Portions: 12   Portion size: ¼ chicken

U.S.	Metric	Ingredient
3	3	Chickens, about 2¾ lb (1.3 kg) each
to taste	to taste	Salt
to taste	to taste	Pepper
as needed	as needed	Vegetable oil
2 oz	60 g	Butter
4 oz	120 g	Shallots, chopped fine
4	4	Garlic cloves, chopped fine
1½ lb	700 g	Mushrooms, sliced or quartered (see note)
10 fl oz	280 mL	White wine
1½ lb	700 g	Tomato concassé
12 fl oz	360 mL	Demi-glace
2 tbsp	30 mL	Chopped parsley
to taste	to taste	Salt

■ P r o c e d u r e

1. Cut each chicken into 8 pieces, as shown in Figure 12.5.
2. Season the chicken lightly with salt and pepper.
3. Pour about ⅛ in. (3 mm) oil into one or more sauté pans over moderate heat.
4. Sauté the chicken pieces until they are cooked through. Regulate the heat so the chicken browns well but does not scorch by the time it is done.
5. Remove the chicken from the sauté pans and keep it hot. (Alternative method: Brown the chicken well in the sauté pans, transfer the chicken pieces to a sheet pan or hotel pans, without crowding them, and finish cooking in a 375°F [190°C] oven.)

6. Drain the oil from the sauté pans and discard. Add the butter to the pans over moderately high heat.
7. Add the shallots, garlic, and mushrooms. Sauté until tender and lightly browned.
8. Add the wine. Reduce by half.
9. Stir in the tomatoes and demi-glace. Return the mixture to a boil.
10. Stir in the chopped parsley. Season to taste with salt.
11. Spoon the tomato mixture onto plates and top with the chicken. (If the chicken has cooled, it can be reheated in the tomato mixture, but do not let it cook further.)

Per serving:
Calories, 470; Protein, 72 g; Fat, 28 g (53% cal.); Cholesterol, 140 mg; Carbohydrates, 9 g; Fiber, 2 g; Sodium, 370 mg.

Note: Use white button mushrooms or a mixture of mushrooms, such as shiitake, portobello, and cremini.

Sautéed Chicken with Tomatoes and Mushrooms

Tangerine-Marinated Breast of Duck

Portions: 12   Portion size: 6 oz (180 g)

U.S.	Metric	Ingredients
12	12	Boneless duck breast halves, skin on, about 6 oz (180 g) each
1½ oz	45 mL	Shallots, chopped fine
1 fl oz	30 mL	Soy sauce
4 fl oz	120 mL	Tangerine juice
½ tsp	2 mL	Grated tangerine zest
¼ tsp	1 mL	Cinnamon
¼ tsp	1 mL	Crushed star anise
1 lb 8 oz	720 g	Wheatberries with Pecans (p. 630, prepared without poblanos)
as needed	as needed	Microgreens
12 fl oz	360 mL	Oriental Vinaigrette (p. 725), optional

■ P r o c e d u r e

1. With a sharp knife, score the duck skin in a diamond pattern. Cut through the skin and into the layer of fat but not into the meat.
2. In a nonreactive container, combine the shallots, soy sauce, tangerine juice and zest, cinnamon, and star anise and mix together.
3. Add the duck breasts, turning them to coat on both sides. Refrigerate 2–4 hours.
4. Remove from the marinade. Pat dry the breasts with clean towels. Discard the marinade and any pieces of star anise clinging to the meat.
5. Pan-fry the breasts skin side down in a sauté pan over moderately high heat for about 6 minutes, until the skin is well browned and crisp and much of the fat has rendered. Turn over and pan-fry another 4 minutes. The breasts should still be rare.
6. Remove from the pans and let rest 5 minutes in a warm place.
7. Place 2 oz (60 g) wheatberries on each plate.
8. Cut each duck breast diagonally into thin slices. Fan the slices out, leaning them against the mound of wheat berries.
9. Top the wheatberries with a small mound of microgreens.
10. If desired, drizzle a little vinaigrette onto the plate around the duck breast.

Per serving:
Calories, 320; Protein, 31 g; Fat, 15 g (43% cal.); Cholesterol, 165 mg;
Carbohydrates 13 g; Fiber, 2 g; Sodium, 280 mg.

Sautéed Chicken Breasts with Lemon Grass and Three Peppers

Portion: 12   Portion size: 1 chicken breast,
4 oz (125 g) vegetable garnish
2½ fl oz (75 mL) sauce

U.S.	Metric	Ingredients
2 stalks	2 stalks	Lemon grass
2 fl oz	50 mL	Olive oil
12 oz	350 g	Yellow bell pepper, cut brunoise
12 oz	350 g	Green bell pepper, cut brunoise
12 oz	350 g	Red bell pepper, cut brunoise
1 oz	30 g	Garlic, chopped fine
7 oz	200 g	Onion, chopped fine
1½ oz	40 g	Fresh ginger root, chopped fine
2 oz	50 g	Cilantro, chopped fine
4 tsp	10 g	Dry mustard
1 pt 4 fl oz	600 mL	Chicken stock
12	12	Boneless chicken breasts, about 7 oz (200 g) each
to taste	to taste	Salt
to taste	to taste	Pepper
3 oz	90 g	Clarified butter
5 oz	150 g	Peanut butter
5 fl oz	150 mL	Peanut oil or sesame oil
to taste	to taste	Salt
to taste	to taste	Pepper

Per serving:
Calories, 610; Protein, 48 g; Fat, 41 g (61% cal.); Cholesterol, 140 mg;
Carbohydrates, 12 g; Fiber, 2 g; Sodium, 230 mg.

Note: Most lemon grass is too fibrous to be eaten, so it must be removed after it
has been used as seasoning. If you have access to tender, edible lemon grass,
simply chop it fine and add it with the other chopped herbs.

■ P r o c e d u r e

1. Cut the bulbous bases (the bottom 2½–3 in./5–7 cm) from the lemon grass; discard the tops. Crush the lemon grass bases and chop fine. Tie in a square of cheesecloth (see note).

2. Heat the olive oil in a saucepan over moderate heat. Add the brunoise of peppers. Sauté briefly.

3. Add the garlic, onion, ginger, cilantro, and the sachet of lemon grass. Sauté briefly.

4. Mix in the dry mustard and add the chicken stock. Simmer for 20 minutes.

5. Strain the vegetables, reserving both the vegetables and the cooking liquid. Discard the lemon grass.

6. Season the chicken breasts with salt and pepper.

7. Over moderate heat, pan-fry the chicken breasts in clarified butter until well browned and cooked through. (Alternatively, brown them on top of the stove, then finish cooking them in a hot oven.)

8. Place the reserved cooking liquid from step 5 in a blender. Add the peanut butter and blend to mix well.

9. Add the oil and blend until emulsified. Add salt and pepper to taste.

10. To serve, make 3 quenelles, about 1 oz (40 g) each, of the vegetable garnish (see Figure 13.5) and place at the top of a dinner plate. Slice the chicken breast and fan out with a little sauce just below.

Sautéed Chicken Breasts with Lemon Grass and Three Peppers

Figure 13.5
Shaping quenelles with two spoons.

(a) Pick up a portion with one spoon. Position a second spoon as shown.

(b) Scoop the mixture with the second spoon. If the mixture is stiff, press the spoons together lightly while scooping to help shape the quenelle.

(c) Again scoop the mixture with the first spoon to complete the shape.

Chicken Pojarski Princesse

Portion: 12   Portion size: 2 pieces, 2 oz (55 g) each

U.S.	Metric	Ingredients
2 lb 4 oz	1 kg	Chicken breast, boneless and skinless
15 fl oz	450 mL	Heavy cream
to taste	to taste	Salt
to taste	to taste	Pepper
7 oz	200 g	Fresh white bread crumbs
as needed	as needed	Oil or clarified butter
12 oz	350 g	Asparagus tips, cooked

Procedure

1. Ensure the chicken is thoroughly trimmed of all tendons. Chop finely, either by hand or in a grinder fitted with a large plate. Do not use a food processor, as it will not create the proper texture.

2. Mix the cream into the chicken, adding a little at a time, only as fast as it is absorbed. Season well with salt and pepper. The mixture will be very soft. Keep it as cold as possible. (Test the seasoning by pan-frying a small bit and tasting.)

3. Divide the mixture into 24 equal amounts and drop each into the bread crumbs, rolling to cover completely. Mold, while still in the bread crumbs, into cutlet shapes.

4. Fry the cutlets gently in the clarified butter or oil until golden brown.

5. Allow 2 pieces per person and serve garnished with the asparagus tips.

Per serving:
Calories, 190; Protein, 4 g; Fat, 16 g (75% cal.); Cholesterol, 50 mg; Carbohydrates, 8 g; Fiber, 1 g; Sodium, 80 mg.

Goujons of Chicken in Salad with Sesame Seeds

Portions: 12   Portion size: 4 oz (125 g) meat
2½–3 oz (80 g) salad/garnish

U.S.	Metric	Ingredients		Procedure
3½ lb	1.6 kg	Chicken breast, skinless and boneless		1. Prepare the chicken by cutting into strips (goujons).
9 fl oz	275 mL	Sesame oil		2. Mix the sesame oil, vinegar, soy sauce, ginger, and garlic together in a bowl. Add the strips of chicken and stir well to coat. Cover and marinate while preparing the remaining ingredients.
1½ fl oz	40 mL	Cider vinegar		
4 tsp	20 mL	Soy sauce		
3½ oz	100 g	Ginger root, peeled, chopped fine		
12	12	Garlic cloves, crushed		
		Sauce:		3. Process all the sauce ingredients in a blender or food processor until smooth.
3	3	Garlic cloves		
2 oz	60 g	Ginger root, peeled, chopped fine		
10 fl oz	300 mL	Light soy sauce		
6 fl oz	175 mL	Sesame oil		
pinch	pinch	Sugar		
1 lb	500 g	Carrots, cut batonnet		4. For the garnish, put the carrots into a pan and just cover with water. Add the honey and simmer until the water has evaporated and the carrots are tender and lightly caramelized. Allow to cool.
2 fl oz	20 mL	Honey		
10 oz	300 g	Flour, seasoned with salt and pepper		5. Remove the strips of chicken from the marinade and dry on paper towels.
3	3	Eggs, beaten		6. Toss in seasoned flour, beaten eggs, and then the sesame seeds.
10 oz	300 g	Sesame seeds		7. Deep-fry in hot oil.
2 heads	2 heads	Boston lettuce		8. Separate the lettuce leaves and wash. Dress the lettuce with a little sauce and place in the center of individual plates. Top with the remaining sauce and the cooked goujons and carrots. Garnish with cilantro leaves.
as needed	as needed	Cilantro for garnish		

Per serving:
Calories, 600; Protein, 33 g; Fat, 41 g (61% cal);
Cholesterol, 80 mg; Carbohydrates, 27 g; Fiber, 4 g; Sodium, 1280 mg.

Goujons of Chicken in Salad with Sesame Seeds

Chicken Stir-Fry with Walnuts

Portions: 12   Portion size: 6 oz (175 g)

U.S.	Metric	Ingredients
2½ lb	1.2 kg	Boneless, skinless chicken meat
1 lb	450 g	Green or red bell peppers
1 lb	450 g	Scallions
3 tbsp	45 mL	Cornstarch
4 fl oz	125 mL	Soy sauce
4 oz	125 g	Walnut pieces (or unsalted peanuts)
¼ tsp	1 mL	Ground ginger
⅛ tsp	0.5 mL	Cayenne
1½ cups	350 mL	Chicken broth or water
2 fl oz	60 mL	Oil

■ P r o c e d u r e

1. Remove all fat from the chicken. Cut into ½-in. (1-cm) dice.
2. Cut the peppers in half and remove the core and seeds. Cut into strips ¼ in. (½ cm) wide.
3. Cut off the roots and withered parts of the green tops of the scallions. Split the scallions in half lengthwise and cut into 1-in. (2½-cm) pieces. Combine with the peppers.
4. Stir the cornstarch with the soy sauce until smooth.
5. Have the remaining ingredients ready in separate containers. Everything must be ready before starting to cook because cooking takes only a few minutes.

6. Heat half the oil in a large sauté pan or skillet until very hot, almost smoking.
7. Add the peppers and scallions and sauté rapidly for about 2 minutes, until the vegetables are only slightly cooked. Remove from the pan.
8. Add the remaining oil to the pan and again get it very hot.
9. Add the chicken and sauté rapidly until no longer pink. If the chicken sticks to the pan, use a spatula to stir.
10. Add the nuts, ginger, and cayenne and sauté another minute.
11. Quickly stir the cornstarch mixture (the starch settles out) and add it and the stock or water to the pan. Stir to deglaze the pan and bring to a simmer.
12. Add the sautéed vegetables and simmer just until heated through. Correct the seasonings.
13. Serve immediately with boiled or steamed rice.

Per serving:
Calories, 270; Protein, 22 g; Fat, 16 g (53% cal.); Cholesterol, 60 mg; Carbohydrates, 10 g; Fiber, 2 g; Sodium, 610 mg.

Chicken Teriyaki

Portions: 16   Portion size: 1 chicken breast or thigh

U.S.	Metric	Ingredients
		Teriyaki sauce;
3 fl oz	75 mL	Sake
7 fl oz	175 mL	Soy sauce
6 fl oz	150 mL	Mirin (sweet rice wine)
2 tbsp	25 mL	Sugar
as needed	as needed	Vegetable oil
16	16	Boneless chicken breasts or thighs, skin on or off as desired

Per serving:
Calories, 280; Protein, 31 g; Fat,11 g (38% cal.); Cholesterol, 85 mg; Carbohydrates, 6 g; Fiber, 0 g; Sodium, 780 mg.

■ P r o c e d u r e

1. Combine the sake, soy sauce, mirin, and sugar. Heat to a simmer to dissolve the sugar. Cool.

2. Heat a thin film of oil in a skillet. Put in the chicken pieces, skin side down. Cook until browned and half done. Turn and cook the other side.

3. Remove the chicken and degrease the pan.

4. Deglaze the pan with the teriyaki sauce and bring the sauce to a boil.

5. Return the chicken to the pan. Turn it in the pan until it is lightly glazed.

6. Remove the chicken from the pan and reserve the sauce. Cut each piece of chicken crosswise, on the diagonal, into strips ½ in. (1 cm) wide.

7. Plate the chicken, keeping each piece assembled in its original form. Spoon a little of the sauce on top.

V A R I A T I O N S

Other items, such as small beefsteaks, fish fillets, and scallops, can be cooked this way. In the case of fish fillets, keep the skin on, if possible, and use the skin side as the presentation side.

TERIYAKI

The Japanese word *yaki* is often translated as "grilled," although it is less specific in Japanese and is also used to mean pan-broiled or griddled. **Teriyaki** can be translated as "glaze-grilled." In the West, the term usually refers to a meat or fish that is marinated in a soy-sauce mixture before being cooked, and sometimes the meat is even simmered in the sauce. In Japan, however, the item is usually not marinated, and the teriyaki sauce is applied only at the end of cooking to give the food an attractive and flavorful glaze.

Japanese food is, in general, delicately seasoned. Western palates, however, usually demand more seasoning. For example, few Japanese would douse a bowl of plain rice with soy sauce, as Westerners tend to do in Asian restaurants.

For a more Western-style teriyaki, you may marinate the chicken in the accompanying recipe in the teriyaki sauce for several hours or overnight before pan-frying it. The result, however, will not be as authentic.

Chicken Breasts Parmesan

Portions: 10   Portion size: 1 chicken breast, about 4 oz (125 g)

U.S.	Metric	Ingredients
3 oz	90 g	Flour
1 tsp	5 mL	Salt
½ tsp	2 mL	White pepper
4	4	Eggs
3 oz	90 g	Parmesan cheese
1 fl oz	30 mL	Milk
10	10	Boneless, skinless chicken breasts from 5 chickens, 3½ lb (1.6 kg) each
4 oz	125 mL	Clarified butter
20	20	Lemon slices

Per serving:
Calories, 350; Protein, 40 g; Fat, 18 g (47% cal.); Cholesterol, 190 mg; Carbohydrates, 5 g; Fiber, 0 g; Sodium, 510 mg.

■ **P r o c e d u r e**

1. Place the flour in a small counter pan and season with salt and white pepper.
2. Beat the eggs in a bowl and mix in the parmesan cheese and milk. Place the bowl next to the seasoned flour when ready for service.
3. Flatten the chicken breasts lightly with a meat mallet.
4. If cooking to order, select a sauté pan just large enough to hold in a single layer the number of portions being cooked. If cooking all the chicken breasts at once, use a very large skillet or enough sauté pans to hold all the breasts in a single layer.
5. Place the pan (or pans) over moderate heat and add enough clarified butter to just cover the bottom.
6. Dip the chicken breasts in the flour and shake off excess. Dip in the cheese batter, turning the pieces to coat both sides.
7. Cook over moderate heat until the bottom is golden. Turn the pieces over. Reduce the heat to low and continue to cook until the chicken is cooked through. It should feel somewhat firm when done.
8. Place each portion on a hot plate and top with 2 lemon slices. Serve immediately.

V A R I A T I O N

Alternative Method: As soon as the first side is browned, turn the pieces over, cover the pans, and place in an oven at 350°F (175°C) for 8–10 minutes. This procedure requires less attention from the cook, an advantage in busy kitchens.

Vietnamese Stir-Fried Chicken with Chile

Portions: 10   Portion size: 6 oz (180 g) chicken and vegetables, 6 oz (180 g) rice noodles

U.S.	Metric	Ingredients
3 lb	1.4 kg	Chicken breast, boneless and skinless
6 fl oz	180 mL	Nuoc nam (Vietnamese fish sauce) or nam pla (Thai fish sauce)
3	3	Garlic cloves, chopped fine
½ tsp	2 mL	Black pepper
1 lb	450 g	Rice sticks (p. 638)
4 fl oz	120 mL	Nuoc Cham (p. 193)
3 fl oz	90 mL	Vegetable oil
6	6	Thai green chiles or serrano chiles, seeded and sliced thin
12	12	Scallions, sliced
8 oz	240 g	Snow peas, trimmed and blanched
6 oz	180 g	Tomato concassé
2 tbsp	30 mL	Sesame seeds, toasted
1 pt	500 mL	Nuoc Cham

■ P r o c e d u r e

1. Cut the chicken breasts into 1-in. (2.5-cm) pieces.
2. In a bowl, toss the chicken with the fish sauce, garlic, and pepper. Marinate 15–20 minutes.
3. Soak the rice sticks in warm water for 20 minutes. Drain.
4. Drop the rice sticks into boiling water. As soon as the water returns to a boil, drain.
5. Toss the rice sticks with the nuoc cham. Keep warm while cooking the chicken.
6. Heat the oil in a sauté pan or wok over high heat.
7. Drain the chicken, reserving the marinade. Add the chicken to the pan. Stir-fry until the chicken is about half cooked.
8. Add the chiles, scallions, and reserved marinade. Continue to stir-fry until the chicken is nearly done.
9. Add the snow peas and stir-fry 1 minute, until the snow peas are just cooked and still crisp.
10. Add the tomato. Stir-fry just until the tomato is hot.
11. Place the rice noodles in the center of dinner plates.
12. Top with the chicken mixture.
13. Sprinkle with sesame seeds.
14. Serve with additional nuoc cham in small ramekins on the side.

Per serving:
Calories, 410; Protein, 38 g; Fat, 16 g (35% cal.); Cholesterol, 110 mg; Carbohydrates, 28 g; Fiber, 2 g; Sodium, 3320 mg.

Vietnamese Stir-Fried Chicken with Chile

SIMMERING AND POACHING

Simmering and poaching are both methods of cooking in a liquid. The major difference is the temperature. In simmering, the liquid is a little below the boiling point and bubbling very gently. In poaching, the temperature is even lower, and the liquid is not really bubbling. Also, less liquid is usually used for poaching.

SIMMERING

1. The simmering method is used to cook fowl and other tough items, which require long cooking in moist heat to be made tender. Cooking time is about 2½ hours.

2. The cooking liquid is usually water seasoned with salt and, most often, with mirepoix and herbs.

3. Simmered fowl yields a rich, flavorful broth. The meat can be used for soups, creamed dishes, casseroles, salads, and similar preparations.

4. Start the fowl in *cold water* if a flavorful soup is your main objective. Start with *hot water* to retain more flavor in the meat.

POACHING

1. The poaching method is used to gently cook tender poultry in order to retain moisture and to develop a light, subtle flavor. Cooking time is usually short because the product is naturally tender.

2. The cooking liquid is usually stock, sometimes with the addition of wine and other flavorings and seasonings. Cold liquid is added to the poultry product in the pan to cover partway, and the pan must be covered to retain steam. Covering also helps prevent drying and discoloration.

3. After cooking, the liquid may be used to make a sauce, such as suprême sauce, to serve with the cooked product.

4. It is important to drain the poultry well after cooking, since any remaining liquid may spoil the appearance of the sauce on the plate.

5. Poaching may be done on the rangetop or in the oven. Oven poaching provides more even heat.

"Boiled" Fowl

This preparation and the variation that follows are usually not served as is. Instead, they are the basis for several other recipes in this section that call for simmered or cooked chicken or turkey and for chicken or turkey stock or velouté. The cooked meat can also be used for chicken or turkey salads.

Yield: about 4½–5 lb (2–2.3 kg) cooked meat

U.S.	Metric	Ingredients
3	3	Fowls, about 5 lb (2.3 kg) each
		Mirepoix:
8 oz	250 g	Onion, coarsely chopped
4 oz	125 g	Celery, coarsely chopped
4 oz	125 g	Carrots, coarsely chopped
		Sachet:
1	1	Bay leaf
6	6	Parsley stems
¼ tsp	1 mL	Peppercorns
2	2	Whole cloves
1 tsp	5 mL	Salt

Per 1 ounce:
Calories, 70; Protein, 10 g; Fat, 2.5 g (36% cal.); Cholesterol, 30 mg; Carbohydrates, 0 g; Fiber, 0 g; Sodium, 65 mg.

■ Procedure

1. Truss the fowls. This step is optional but recommended because it keeps the chicken from falling apart, especially if you are cooking more than one in the pot.

2. Place the fowls in a stockpot.

3. Add boiling water to cover and return to a boil. Skim the scum carefully.

4. Add the mirepoix and sachet.

5. Simmer until the fowls feel tender when pressed on the thigh, about 2½ hours.

6. If the meat and broth are to be used immediately for another preparation, remove the fowl from the liquid. Place in another pan and keep covered until needed. Strain the broth.

7. If the meat and broth are not needed right away, leave the fowls in the broth and cool quickly in a cold water bath, as for cooling stocks (pp. 154). When completely cool, remove the fowls and refrigerate, covered. Strain the broth and refrigerate.

8. To use, disjoint the fowls, remove all bones and skin, and dice or cut as required.

V A R I A T I O N

Simmered Chicken or Turkey

Simmer young chickens or turkey as in basic recipe. They may be whole or disjointed. A 3-lb (1.4-kg) chicken will take about 45–60 minutes. Turkey will take about 1½–3 hours depending on size. Do not overcook young poultry, and do not let the liquid boil.

Poached Chicken Breast Princesse

Portions: 24   Portion size: ½ chicken breast,
2 fl oz (60 mL) sauce, plus garnish

U.S.	Metric	Ingredients
24	24	Boneless, skinless half chicken breasts from 12 chickens, 3 lb (1.2 kg) each
as needed	as needed	Butter
as needed	as needed	Salt
as needed	as needed	White pepper
¼ cup	60 mL	Lemon juice
1½ qt (approximately)	1.5 L (approximately)	Chicken stock, cold
		Beurre manié:
3 oz	90 g	Butter, softened
3 oz	90 g	Flour
2½ cups	600 mL	Heavy cream, hot
to taste	to taste	Salt
72	72	Asparagus tips, cooked, hot

Per serving:
Calories, 330; Protein, 37 g; Fat, 17 g (47% cal.); Cholesterol, 140 mg; Carbohydrates, 6 g; Fiber,1 g; Sodium, 140 mg.

■ Procedure

1. Select a baking pan just large enough to hold the chicken breasts in a single layer. Butter the inside of the pan.
2. Season the chicken breasts with salt and pepper. Place them in the pan, presentation side (that is, the side that had the skin on) up.
3. Sprinkle with the lemon juice and add enough chicken stock to barely cover the chicken.
4. Cover the chicken with a buttered piece of parchment or waxed paper.
5. Bring to a simmer on top of the stove. Finish poaching in a 325°F (165°C) oven or over low heat on the stove. Cooking time will be 5–10 minutes.
6. Remove the chicken breasts from the liquid. Place them in a hotel pan, cover, and keep them warm.
7. Reduce the poaching liquid over high heat to about 2½ pt (1.1 L).
8. Knead the butter and flour together to make a beurre manié (p. 164).
9. With a wire whip, beat the beurre manié into the simmering stock to thicken it. Simmer a minute to cook out any starchy taste.
10. Add the hot cream to the sauce. Season to taste.
11. Place each chicken breast, well drained, on a plate and coat with 2 fl oz (60 mL) sauce. Garnish with 3 asparagus tips. Serve immediately.

VARIATIONS

Alternative Method: Poach the chicken as in basic recipe. Plate immediately and coat with prepared suprême sauce. Save poaching liquid for next day's sauce.

Other sauces may be used to coat poached chicken breasts, including:
Allemande
Aurora
Hungarian
Ivory
Mushroom

Poached Chicken Breast Florentine
Poach the chicken as in basic recipe. Place each portion on a bed of buttered spinach (well drained). Coat with Mornay sauce. Optional: Sprinkle with parmesan cheese and brown under the broiler.

Chicken or Turkey Pot Pie

Portions: 25   Portion size: 3 oz (90 g) meat
2 oz (60 g) vegetables
4 fl oz (125 mL) sauce

U.S.	Metric	Ingredients
5 lb	2.3 kg	Cooked chicken or turkey meat (light and dark meat)
12 oz	350 g	Potatoes, medium dice
12 oz	350 g	Carrots, medium dice
12 oz	350 g	Tiny white onions, peeled
12 oz	350 g	Peas
3 qt	3 L	Chicken velouté
to taste	to taste	Salt
to taste	to taste	Pepper
2 tsp	10 mL	Dried tarragon
25	25	Flaky pie pastry covers (p. 980)

Per serving:
Calories, 520; Protein, 25 g; Fat, 32 g (55% cal.); Cholesterol, 80 mg;
Carbohydrates, 34 g; Fiber, 5 g; Sodium, 430 mg.

■ P r o c e d u r e

1. Cut the chicken or turkey into ¾ in. (1-cm) dice.
2. Cook the vegetables separately in boiling salted water. Drain and cool.
3. Season the velouté to taste with salt and pepper. Add the tarragon.
4. Prepare the pastry and cut out circles to cover the tops of casserole serving dishes. You will need about 2 oz (60 g) pastry per portion.
5. Divide the light and dark meat evenly among individual serving casseroles (3 oz/ 90 g per portion).
6. Divide the vegetables evenly among the casseroles (about ½ oz/15 g per portion of each vegetable).
7. Ladle about 4 fl oz (125 mL) velouté into each casserole.
8. Top the dishes with the pastry. Cut holes in the centers to allow steam to escape.
9. Place the dishes on a sheet pan. Bake at 400°F (200°C) until the crust is well browned.

V A R I A T I O N S

Vegetable ingredients may be varied as desired. Other vegetables that may be used include celery, mushroom caps, and lima beans.

Chicken or Turkey Stew

Prepare the meat, vegetables, and velouté as in basic recipe. Omit pastry. Combine the ingredients in a saucepot and bring to a simmer. Hold for service.

Chicken Blanquette I

Portions: 25   Portion size: 5 oz (150 g)

U.S.	Metric	Ingredients
5 lb	2.5 kg	Cooked chicken meat, 1-in. (2½-cm) dice
2½ pt	1.1 L	Chicken velouté
		Liaison:
5	5	Egg yolks
1 pt	500 mL	Heavy cream
to taste	to taste	Lemon juice
pinch	pinch	Nutmeg
pinch	pinch	White pepper
pinch	pinch	Salt

Per serving:
Calories, 240; Protein, 21 g; Fat, 16 g (60% cal); Cholesterol, 135 mg; Carbohydrates, 3 g; Fiber, 0 g; Sodium, 160 mg.

■ P r o c e d u r e

1. Combine the chicken with the sauce and bring to a simmer.
2. Remove from the heat. Beat the egg yolks and cream together. Temper with a little of the hot sauce, and stir into the sauce.
3. Return the pot to the heat and bring to just below the simmer. Do not boil.
4. Season to taste with a few drops of lemon juice and a pinch each of nutmeg, white pepper, and salt.

V A R I A T I O N S

Chicken Blanquette II
Follow the recipe for Veal Blanquette, page 326. Use 12 lb (6 kg) disjointed chicken (raw) in place of the 10 lb (5 kg) veal. Use chicken stock instead of veal stock.

Chicken Blanquette à l'Ancienne (Ancient Style)
Garnish each portion with 2 cooked pearl onions and 1 cooked mushroom cap, fluted if possible (see p. 525).

Chicken Blanquette Brunoise
Add to the sauce 4 oz (125 g) each of carrot, celery, and leeks or onions, all cut brunoise and sautéed lightly in butter.

Chicken Blanquette Argenteuil
Garnish each portion with 3 cooked asparagus tips.

Stuffed Chicken Breasts Doria

Portions: 12   Portion size: 1 stuffed chicken breast
1½–2 fl oz (50 mL) sauce

U.S.	Metric	Ingredients		Procedure
3½ oz	100 g	Shallots, chopped fine	1.	To make the stuffing, sweat the shallots in the butter until soft. Allow to cool.
2 oz	60 g	Butter		
1 lb	500 g	Chicken leg meat	2.	Process the chicken leg meat in a food processor for a few seconds.
2	2	Egg whites		
7 fl oz	200 mL	Crème fraîche	3.	Add the cooled shallots, egg whites, crème fraîche, herbs, and bread crumbs. Process briefly to combine. Season and chill.
3 tbsp	25 g	Finely chopped mixed fresh herbs		
1 oz	50 g	Fresh white bread crumbs		
12	12	Chicken breasts, boneless, about 6 oz (175 g) each	4.	Flatten the chicken breasts and the smaller fillets that come with them. Cut a pocket in each breast and stuff with the filling. This can be done easily by piping the stuffing in with a pastry bag.
			5.	Place the smaller fillet over the top and wrap each breast in foil or nonstick paper, securing the ends with string.
			6.	Cover with the stock and poach gently for 20–25 minutes. Leave in the hot stock.
2	2	Cucumbers	7.	Cut the cucumbers into 1½-in. (4-cm) lengths and into quarters, removing the seeds. Turn (tourné) into barrel shapes (see Figure 7.18).
			8.	Blanch in boiling water for 1–2 minutes, then drain and refresh under cold water. Drain and set aside.
1 tbsp	15 g	Butter	9.	Sauté the cucumber in the butter until tender, but do not let it brown.
1–1½ pt	600 mL	Yogurt Sour Cream Sauce (p. 197)		
as needed	as needed	Chives, chopped, for garnish	10.	Unwrap the chicken and cut into slices. Arrange on plates and spoon the sauce around the chicken. Garnish with the cucumber and chives.

Per serving:
Calories, 410; Protein, 45 g; Fat, 21 g (47% cal.); Cholesterol, 165 mg;
Carbohydrates, 7 g; Fiber,1 g; Sodium, 220 mg.

Stuffed Chicken Breasts Doria

Chicken Stew with Sorrel

Portions: 12   Portion size: ¼ chicken
2½ fl oz (75 mL) sauce
vegetable garnish

U.S.	Metric	Ingredients
36	36	Baby carrots
36	36	Baby turnips
36	36	Baby leeks
36	36	Pearl onions
36	36	Snow pea pods
as needed	as needed	Chicken stock
36	36	Cherry tomatoes
7 oz	200 g	Sorrel
1 oz	30 g	Butter
3	3	Chickens, about 3¼ lb (1.5 kg) each
2 qt	2 L	Chicken stock
5 fl oz	150 mL	Heavy cream, hot
		Liaison:
5 oz	150 mL	Heavy cream
5	5	Egg yolks
to taste	to taste	Salt
to taste	to taste	Pepper

Per serving:
Calories, 620; Protein, 50 g; Fat, 37 g (53% cal.); Cholesterol, 270 mg;
Carbohydrates, 24 g; Fiber, 5 g; Sodium, 320 mg.

■ **P r o c e d u r e**

1. Trim and peel the baby vegetables. Poach with onions and snow peas in chicken stock. Cool. Reserve the vegetables and the stock.
2. Peel the cherry tomatoes (optional).
3. Shred the sorrel. Cook in butter until wilted.

4. Cut the chickens into 8 pieces each (see Figure 12.5).
5. Simmer in the chicken stock until cooked.
6. Remove the chicken from the stock and keep warm.
7. Strain the stock and measure out 1½ pt (750 mL), reserving the remainder for another purpose.
8. Add the hot cream to the hot stock and bring to a simmer.
9. Mix the egg yolks and the cream to make a liaison. Temper with a little of the hot stock, then add the mixture back to the stock. Also add the sorrel. Cook over low heat until lightly thickened, but do not allow to boil. Season to taste.
10. Reheat the tomatoes and the baby vegetables in their stock, then drain.
11. Plate the chicken and coat lightly with the sauce. Arrange the vegetables around the chicken.

Oyako Donburi

Portions: 16   Portion size: see procedure

U.S.	Metric	Ingredients
2 qt	2 L	Dashi
5 fl oz	150 mL	Soy sauce
5 oz	150 g	Sugar
2 fl oz	60 mL	Sake (optional)
3 qt	3 L	Raw Japanese short-grain rice
1½ lb	725 g	Boneless, skinless chicken meat
16	16	Scallions
16	16	Eggs

Per serving:
Calories, 570; Protein, 23 g; Fat, 8 g (13% cal.); Cholesterol, 240 mg; Carbohydrates, 98 g; Fiber, 4 g; Sodium, 600 mg.

Note: The name of this dish, oyako, means "parent and child," referring to the chicken and eggs. A donburi is a type of serving bowl, and the word also refers to foods served in this type of bowl, generally rice with toppings and sauce.

■ **P r o c e d u r e**

1. Combine the dashi, soy sauce, sugar, and sake in a saucepan. Bring to a simmer to dissolve the sugar. Remove from heat and reserve.

2. Cook the rice by following steps 1–4 in the recipe for sushi rice, page 500. Keep it hot.

3. Cut the chicken into strips 1 in. (2½ cm) wide, then slice diagonally ¼ in. (6 mm) thick.

4. Trim the roots and the coarser greens from the scallions, leaving the tender green parts intact. Cut diagonally into ½-in. (1-cm) pieces.

5. For each portion, put 1½ oz (45 g) chicken, 1 sliced scallion, and 4½ fl oz (125 mL) dashi mixture in a small sauté pan. Simmer until the chicken is nearly done.

6. Break 1 egg into a bowl. Mix lightly but do not beat.

7. Pour the egg in a stream around the chicken in the skillet. Continue to simmer until the egg is half set.

8. Put 1½ cups (375 mL) hot rice in a large, deep soup bowl.

9. When the egg is nearly set, give the egg and chicken mixture a light stir and pour the contents of the skillet over the rice.

V A R I A T I O N

Tendon

Omit the chicken, scallions, and egg in the recipe above. Reduce the dashi to 1 qt (1 L) and double the amount of sake. Top each bowl of rice with 1 piece of shrimp tempura (p. 481) and 2 pieces of vegetable tempura. Pour about 2½ fl oz (75 mL) hot dashi mixture over the rice and serve. (The name of this dish comes from the first syllables of "tempura" and "donburi.")

Red-Cooked Chicken

Portions: 16   Portion size: ⅛ chicken

U.S.	Metric	Ingredients
2	2	Chickens, about 4 lb (1.8 kg) each
2 cloves	2 cloves	Star anise
3 slices	3 slices	Ginger root
1 tbsp	15 mL	Sichuan peppercorns
½ pt	250 mL	Soy sauce
2 pt	1 L	Water or chicken stock
1 oz	30 g	Sugar
2	2	Scallions
2 fl oz	60 mL	Sherry or shaoxing wine

■ P r o c e d u r e

1. Cut each chicken into eighths.
2. Tie the star anise, ginger root, and Sichuan peppercorns in a cheesecloth bag.
3. Combine the soy sauce and water or stock in a pot and add the spice bag, sugar, scallions, and sherry. Bring to a boil.
4. Add the chicken. Simmer until tender.
5. Serve the chicken hot or cold. If it is to be served cold, cool it and store it in the cooking liquid. The liquid may be reused for another batch.

V A R I A T I O N S

The star anise and Sichuan peppercorns may be omitted for a simpler version of this dish.

Other meats (using cuts appropriate for simmering) may be cooked this way, including pork, beef, tripe, and duck.

Per serving:
Calories, 260; Protein, 29 g; Fat, 14 g (49% cal.); Cholesterol, 90 mg; Carbohydrates, 3 g; Fiber, 0 g; Sodium, 990 mg.

COOKING STYLES IN CHINESE DISHES

A popular misconception in the Western world about Chinese cooking is that nearly all dishes are stir-fried. An important advantage of stir-frying if cooking fuel is scarce is that, although preparation times are long, due to all the required cutting and slicing, cooking times are short. Once the mise en place is done, stir-fried dishes can be sent to the table in a matter of minutes.

Although stir-frying is an important technique in China, many other cooking techniques are also used, especially simmering and steaming. Two of the recipes in this section, Tea-Smoked Duck and Red-Cooked Chicken, are typical examples of steaming and simmering.

Although both these recipes begin with whole poultry, the birds are cut into small pieces before they are served. In a typical Chinese meal, meats, fish, and vegetables are not so much main dishes as they are accompaniments to rice or, sometimes, noodles. Portion sizes of protein items are small, and the dishes are served family-style in the center of the table. Each diner takes a small quantity of the desired dishes to eat between bites of rice.

Because China is so large and has such an array of climates, there is no single cooking style. The styles of Beijing in the north, Guangdong (Canton) in the southeast, and Sichuan (Szechuan) in the interior, are perhaps as different as the styles of Germany, France, and Italy.

Tea-Smoked Duck

Yield: 1 duck

U.S.	Metric	Ingredients
3 tbsp	45 mL	Coarse salt
1 tbsp	15 mL	Sichuan peppercorns
1	1	Duck, about 5 lb (2.3 kg)
6	6	Scallions, trimmed
4 slices	4 slices	Ginger root
3 oz	90 g	Raw rice
½ cup	125 mL	Brown or black tea leaves
2 oz	60 g	Sugar

Per ⅙ recipe:
Calories, 520; Protein, 30 g; Fat, 43 g (75% cal.); Cholesterol, 130 mg; Carbohydrates, 2 g; Fiber, 1 g; Sodium, 2969 mg.

■ Procedure

1. Toast the salt and Sichuan peppercorns in a dry skillet over moderate heat, until peppercorns are fragrant.
2. Cool the mixture, then crush with a rolling pin.

3. Clean the duck well, removing excess fat. Flatten the duck slightly by pressing down on the breastbone to break it.
4. Rub the duck inside and out with the salt and peppercorn mixture.
5. Put the duck in a hotel pan, weight it down, and refrigerate it for 1–2 days.

6. Rinse the duck.
7. Put the scallions and ginger slices in the cavity.
8. Steam the duck for 1–1½ hours, until tender.

9. Line a large wok or other heavy pan with aluminum foil.
10. Mix together the rice, tea leaves, and sugar. Put the mixture in the bottom of the wok.
11. Put the duck on a rack over the tea mixture and cover the pan tightly.
12. Set the pan over high heat for 5 minutes, then over moderate heat for 20 minutes. Turn the heat off and let stand another 20 minutes without uncovering.
13. Cool the duck. Chop it into pieces measuring 1–2 in. (3–5 cm), bones and all. Alternatively, bone it out and cut the meat into strips 1 in. (2.5 cm) wide. This dish is normally served at room temperature.

VARIATIONS

For spicier duck, add 1 tsp (5 mL) five-spice powder to the dry marinade after toasting.

Crispy Duck

This variation may be made with smoked duck or with steamed but unsmoked duck (step 8). When the duck is cool, cut it into quarters. You may bone it if desired, but try to keep it in its original shape. Deep-fry until the skin is crisp. Drain, cut up, and serve at once. (Optional step: Rub cornstarch into the skin before deep-frying.)

Mole Poblano de Pollo *or* de Guajolote

Portions: 16   Portion size: 3 fl oz (90 mL) sauce
chicken or turkey quantity variable

U.S.	Metric	Ingredients
15	15	Mulato chiles (see note)
1½ oz	45 g	Sesame seeds
4 oz	125 g	Almonds
3	3	Tortillas
6 oz	175 g	Lard, or rendered chicken fat, turkey fat, or pork fat
¼ tsp	1 mL	Ground cloves
½ tsp	2 mL	Cinnamon
½ tsp	2 mL	Black pepper
¼ tsp	1 mL	Ground coriander
8 oz	225 g	Tomatoes, canned or fresh
4	4	Garlic cloves, chopped
1 oz	30 g	Bitter (unsweetened) chocolate, grated or broken into pieces
10–14 lb	4.5–6.5 kg	Chicken (pollo) or turkey (guajolote), disjointed
6 oz	175 g	Onion, chopped
2 oz	60 g	Carrot, chopped
1	1	Garlic clove
8	8	Peppercorns
4 tsp	20 mL	Salt
as needed	as needed	Water
as needed	as needed	Lard
to taste	to taste	Salt

■ P r o c e d u r e

1. Remove and discard the seeds and stem ends of the chiles. Grind the chiles to a powder.

2. Grind the sesame seeds in a spice grinder or with a mortar and pestle. Set them aside and grind the almonds in the same way.

3. Fry the tortillas in the fat for about 30 seconds. Drain and reserve the fat for step 6. Break the tortillas into pieces.

4. Put the ground sesame, ground almonds, tortillas, cloves, cinnamon, pepper, and coriander into the container of a blender.

5. Peel the tomatoes if they are fresh. Add the tomatoes and the garlic to the blender. Blend to a smooth purée. If the mixture is too thick to blend, add a little chicken or turkey broth or water.

6. Heat the reserved fat from step 3 in a saucepot over moderate heat. Add the powdered chiles and cook for about 30 seconds. Be careful not to let it burn.

7. Add the purée from the blender. Cook 5 minutes, stirring constantly. The mixture will be very thick.

8. Add the chocolate. Stir constantly until the chocolate is completely blended in. The sauce may be prepared to this point 1–2 days ahead of time and held in the refrigerator.

9. Put the poultry, onion, carrot, garlic, peppercorns, and salt in a large pot. Add enough water to cover.

10. Simmer until the poultry is tender.

11. Remove the poultry from the broth and set aside to keep warm.

12. Strain the broth. Measure 3 pt (1.5 L) broth and stir it into the chile sauce base. Simmer slowly for 30–45 minutes, until the flavors have blended and the mixture has the consistency of a light sauce. (Reserve the remaining broth for another use.)

13. Heat the lard in a sauté pan and brown the cooked poultry pieces lightly. (This step is optional.)

14. Add the poultry to the sauce and simmer a few minutes until quite hot.

15. Adjust the seasoning with salt, if necessary, and serve.

Per serving:
Calories, 510; Protein, 38 g; Fat, 36 g (63% cal.); Cholesterol, 120 mg; Carbohydrates, 9 g; Fiber, 4 g; Sodium, 420 mg.

Note: Instead of mulato chile peppers, you may use ancho or pasilla chiles or a mixture of different kinds. If none of these is available, you may substitute about 1 cup (125 g) chili powder.

MOLE POBLANO

Internationally, the most common examples of Mexican cooking—enchiladas, burritos, tacos, and tamales—represent only a small part of the varied cooking styles of Mexico. Beyond these few dishes, mole poblano is one of the few dishes widely known outside its home.

The Spanish word *salsa* means, literally, "sauce," and includes a wide variety of cooked and uncooked sauces and condiments. In Mexican cuisine, a *mole* (mo-lay) is a more specific kind of sauce, one that is cooked, contains chiles in addition to spices, and is usually thickened with corn, ground seeds, or nuts. It is a more complex preparation than most salsas. The best-known mole, mole poblano, meaning mole from the town of Puebla, contains bitter chocolate in addition to its other seasonings.

Mole does not mean chocolate sauce, and simply putting chocolate in a sauce does not make it a mole. In addition, many moles contain no chocolate.

BRAISING

A moist-heat cooking method, braising may be used to tenderize tough poultry products. Also, as for veal and pork, it can be used to provide moistness and flavor to tender poultry items. Coq au vin, the well-known braised chicken in red wine, was originally made with a tough old rooster (coq), but today the same recipe is applied to tender young chicken.

Poultry products are braised using the same procedures as for meats, except that mirepoix is frequently omitted. Other flavoring ingredients may be used instead, depending on the recipe. Methods 1 and 2 (p. 333) are used when the chicken is to be browned.

 ## Chicken Fricassée

Portions: 24   Portion size: ¼ chicken
3 fl oz (90 mL) sauce

U.S.	Metric	Ingredients
6	6	Chickens, 2½–3 lb (1.1–1.4 kg) each
to taste	to taste	Salt
to taste	to taste	White pepper
6 oz	175 g	Butter
12 oz	350 g	Onion, cut brunoise
6 oz	175 g	Flour
3 qt (approximately)	3 L (approximately)	Chicken stock
		Sachet:
1	1	Bay leaf
1	1	Small piece of celery
4	4	Parsley stems
¼ tsp	1 mL	Thyme
		Liaison:
5	5	Egg yolks, beaten
1 pt	500 mL	Heavy cream
2 tbsp	30 mL	Lemon juice
to taste	to taste	Salt
to taste	to taste	White pepper
to taste	to taste	Nutmeg

Per serving:
Calories, 440; Protein, 39 g; Fat, 27 g (56% cal.); Cholesterol, 175 mg; Carbohydrates, 8 g; Fiber, 0 g; Sodium, 180 mg.

■ Procedure

1. Cut the chickens into 8 pieces each. Season with salt and white pepper.
2. Melt the butter in a brazier over moderate heat.
3. Add chicken and onion. Sauté very lightly so that the chicken is seared on all sides, but do not brown.
4. Add the flour and stir so that it combines with the fat to make a roux. Cook another 2 minutes, without browning.
5. Gradually stir in enough stock to cover the chicken. Bring to a simmer, stirring, until the sauce thickens.
6. Add the herbs, tied in cheesecloth (sachet).
7. Cover and place in a slow oven (300°F/150°C) or over very low heat on the range. Cook until tender, about 30–45 minutes.
8. Remove the chicken from the sauce and keep it warm in a covered pan.
9. Degrease the sauce. Reduce it over high heat to proper thickness. You should have about 2 qt (2 L) sauce. Strain through cheesecloth.
10. Combine the egg yolks and cream. Temper with a little hot sauce, and add the liaison to the sauce. Bring to just below the simmer. Do not boil.
11. Season to taste with lemon juice, salt, white pepper, and nutmeg. Pour the sauce over the chicken.

VARIATIONS

Chicken Fricassée with Tarragon
Add 1 tbsp (15 mL) dried tarragon to the sachet.

Chicken Fricassée à l'Indienne
Add 4 tbsp (60 mL) curry powder when making the roux.

Fricassée of Turkey Wings
Prepare as in basic recipe, using 1 or 2 turkey wings per portion, depending on size. Cut large turkey wings into 2 pieces.

Veal Fricassée
Prepare as in basic recipe, using 10 lb (4.5 kg) boneless veal shoulder, cut into large dice. Use white veal stock.

Pork Fricassée
Use 10 lb (4.5 kg) boneless, diced pork and pork, veal, or chicken stock.

Fricassée à l'Ancienne
Fricassée Brunoise
Fricassée Argenteuil
Use same garnishes as Chicken Blanquette variations (p. 403).

Method 3 (p. 333) is used for fricassées, white stews in which the chicken is sautéed without browning.

BRAISED "SAUTÉS"

If you review the procedure for sautéing meats (p. 314), you will see that if the product is not completely cooked when browned in step 5 and then finished by simmering it in the sauce in step 10, the result is a braised item. This procedure may be used for classical "sautés," which are often braised items. (An alternative method is to finish cooking the chicken or meat in a covered pan in the oven while you are making the sauce. This is also braising because the cover holds in moisture.)

Chicken Chasseur

Portions: 10 **Portion size: ½ chicken**
3 fl oz (90 mL) sauce

U.S.	Metric	Ingredients
5	5	Chickens, 2–2¼ lb (0.9–1 kg) each (see note)
to taste	to taste	Salt
to taste	to taste	Pepper
2 fl oz	60 mL	Oil
2 oz	60 g	Shallots or onions, cut brunoise
8 oz	250 g	Mushrooms, sliced
8 fl oz	250 mL	White wine
1½ pt	750 mL	Demi-glace
8 oz	250 g	Tomato concassé, fresh
		or
4 oz	125 g	Drained, chopped canned tomatoes
to taste	to taste	Salt
to taste	to taste	Pepper
2 tbsp	30 mL	Chopped parsley

■ P r o c e d u r e

1. Cut the chickens into 8 pieces. Season the chicken with salt and pepper.

2. Heat the oil in a brazier or large sauté pan. Brown the chicken well on all sides.

3. Remove the chickens from the pan. Cover and keep them hot.

4. Add the shallots and mushrooms to the pan and sauté lightly without browning.

5. Add the white wine and reduce by three-fourths over high heat.

6. Add the demi-glace and tomatoes and bring to a boil. Reduce slightly. Season with salt and pepper.

7. Place the chickens in the sauce. Cover and simmer slowly on the stove or in the oven at 325°F (165°C), about 20–30 minutes, until done.

8. When the chicken is done, remove it from the pan and reduce the sauce slightly over high heat. Add the chopped parsley and check the seasonings.

9. Serve ½ chicken (2 pieces dark meat and 2 pieces light meat) per portion. Cover with 3 fl oz (90 mL) sauce.

Per serving:
Calories, 780; Protein, 76 g; Fat, 47 g (55% cal.); Cholesterol, 250 mg; Carbohydrates, 72 g; Fiber, 1 g; Sodium, 290 mg.

Note: Large chickens may be used, if desired. For 3½-lb (1.6-kg) chickens, use ¼ chicken per portion (1 piece dark meat and 1 piece light meat).

V A R I A T I O N S

Alternative Method: Brown chickens as in basic recipe. Drain excess fat. Ad 1 qt (1 L) prepared chasseur sauce and finish cooking the chickens as in basic method.

Chicken Bercy
Method 1: Prepare as in basic recipe, but omit the mushrooms and tomato.

Method 2: Brown chickens as in basic recipe. Add 1 qt (1 L) prepared Bercy sauce and simmer the chickens until done.

Chicken Portugaise
Method 1: Prepare as in basic recipe, but omit the mushrooms and wine. Use 4 oz (125 g) onions, cut brunoise, and add 1 tsp (5 mL) chopped garlic. Substitute tomato sauce for the demi-glace.

Method 2: Brown chicken as in basic recipe. Add 1 qt (1 L) portugaise sauce and simmer the chicken until done.

Chicken Hongroise
Prepare as in basic recipe, but sauté chicken only lightly. Do not brown. Omit mushrooms and wine. Use Hungarian (hongroise) sauce instead of demi-glace. When the chicken is cooked, add 4–6 fl oz (125–175 mL) heavy cream (tempered or heated) to the sauce. Omit parsley garnish. Serve with rice pilaf.

Braised Duckling with Sauerkraut

Portions: 12　Portion size: ¼ duckling
4 oz (125 g) kraut

U.S.	Metric	Ingredients
3	3	Ducklings, 5 lb (2.2 kg) each
2 oz	60 mL	Oil
		Sachet:
1	1	Bay leaf
½ tsp	2 mL	Dried thyme
6–8	6–8	Parsley stems
½ recipe (about 3 lb)	½ recipe (about 1.5 kg)	Braised Sauerkraut (p. 561)

Per serving:
Calories, 680; Protein, 45 g; Fat, 53 g (71% cal.); Cholesterol, 145 mg; Carbohydrates, 4 g; Fiber, 2 g; Sodium, 600 mg.

■ **P r o c e d u r e**

1. Cut the ducklings into 8 pieces, the same way you would disjoint a chicken. (See Figure 12.5.) Trim off all excess fat.

2. Heat the oil in a sauté pan or brazier. Place the duck pieces in the pan skin side down, and cook over moderately high heat until the skin is well browned. A great deal of fat will render out.

3. Turn the pieces over and continue to brown on all sides.

4. Drain all the fat from the pan. Turn the duck pieces skin side up.

5. Tie the herbs in a cheesecloth bag and place in the pan with the duck.

6. Cover the pan and place in a 325°F (165 °C) oven for about 30 minutes. Do not add any liquid. The duck will cook in its own juices.

7. While the duck is cooking, prepare the sauerkraut, but cook it only 30 minutes.

8. Remove the duck from its pan and bury it in the partially cooked sauerkraut. Carefully degrease the duck pan without losing any of the juices. Pour the juices over the duck and sauerkraut.

9. Cover and continue braising the duck and sauerkraut for another hour.

10. When done, remove the duck and place in a hotel pan or on a serving platter. Remove the sauerkraut with a slotted spoon and place in another hotel pan, or around the duck on the platter.

11. Degrease the juices. Pour some of the juices over the duck and some over the sauerkraut.

V A R I A T I O N

Braised Duckling with Cabbage
Prepare as in basic recipe, but substitute ½ recipe Braised Green or White Cabbage (p. 560) for the ½ recipe Sauerkraut.

Paprika Chicken

Portions: 24   Portion size: ¼ chicken
3 fl oz (90 mL) sauce

U.S.	Metric	Ingredients
4 fl oz	125 mL	Oil
6	6	Chickens, disjointed, 3–3½ lb (1.4–1.6 kg) each
1½ lb	700 g	Onions, chopped fine
1 lb	450 g	Green bell pepper, small dice
2 oz	60 g	Flour
6 tbsp	90 mL	Hungarian paprika
1 pt	500 mL	Chicken stock
1 lb	450 g	Canned tomatoes, crushed
2 tsp	10 mL	Salt
1 pt	500 mL	Sour cream

■ P r o c e d u r e

1. Heat the oil in a skillet and brown the chicken lightly on all sides.
2. Remove the chicken from the pan and place in a brazier.
3. Add the onion and green pepper to the fat in the pan. Sauté until soft but not browned.
4. Add the flour and stir to make a roux. Cook the flour slowly for a few minutes.
5. Add the paprika and stir to blend in.
6. Stir in the chicken stock, tomatoes, and salt. Bring to a boil. The sauce will be very thick at this point.
7. Pour the sauce over the chicken. Cover and simmer over very low heat or in a 325°F (165 °C) oven until the chicken is tender, about 30–40 minutes.

8. When the chicken is tender, remove it from the sauce and place in a hotel pan.
9. Degrease the sauce. Stir in the sour cream. Simmer a minute, but do not boil. Adjust the seasonings.
10. Pour the sauce over the chicken in the hotel pan.
11. Serve with egg noodles, spaetzle (p. 651), or rice.

Per serving:
Calories, 440; Protein, 46 g; Fat, 24 g (50% cal.); Cholesterol, 120 mg;
Carbohydrates, 8 g; Fiber, 1 g; Sodium, 370 mg.

Poulet Sauté Basquaise (Basque-Style Chicken)

Portions: 12   Portion size: ¼ chicken or 2 pieces (about 8 oz or 250 g)

U.S.	Metric	Ingredients
3	3	Chicken, about 2¾–3 lb (1.3 kg) each
to taste	to taste	Salt
to taste	to taste	Pepper
as needed	as needed	Oil
5 fl oz or as needed	150 mL or as needed	Olive oil
1 lb 4 oz	600 g	Onion
1 lb 12 oz	800 g	Green bell peppers
1 lb 12 oz	800 g	Red bell peppers
9	9	Garlic cloves, chopped
1½ lb	750 g	Tomatoes, peeled, seeded, and quartered
10 fl oz	300 mL	White wine
8 oz	250 g	Prosciutto, cut batonnet
as needed	as needed	Butter

■ P r o c e d u r e

1. Cut each chicken into 8 pieces (see Figure 12.5) and season with salt and pepper.
2. Heat the oil in a large pan and sauté, skin side down first, in batches until lightly browned.
3. Remove the chicken from the pan and drain on kitchen paper. Discard the excess fat in the pan.
4. Place the pan back over low heat and add oil. Gently sauté the onion, peppers, garlic, and tomatoes. Cook for 10 minutes, uncovered.
5. Add the wine and cook for a further 30 minutes.
6. Return the browned chicken pieces to the pan and simmer until done. Check that the juices on the chicken are running clear. Check the seasoning.
7. Pan-fry the prosciutto lightly in butter.
8. Serve the chicken coated with the sauce and topped with the ham and the buttery juices in the pan.

Per serving:
Calories, 570; Protein, 48 g; Fat, 33 g (52% cal.); Cholesterol, 125 mg; Carbohydrates,16 g; Fiber, 3 g; Sodium, 610 mg.

Poulet Sauté au Vinaigre (Lyonnaise-Style Chicken with Tomatoes and Vinegar)

Portions: 12   Portion size: ¼ chicken

U.S.	Metric	Ingredients
3	3	Chickens, about 2½ lb (1.2 kg) each
to taste	to taste	Salt
to taste	to taste	Pepper
3½ fl oz	100 mL	Oil
1 pt 4 oz	600 mL	Tarragon vinegar
3 oz	90 g	Beurre manié
3 lb 12 oz	1.7 kg	Tomatoes, peeled, seeded, and chopped
as needed	as needed	Tarragon sprigs for garnish

■ P r o c e d u r e

1. Cut each chicken into 8 pieces. Season with salt and pepper.
2. Heat the oil in a large pan and sauté the chicken pieces until golden brown, skin side first. You may have to do this in batches. Remove excess oil from the pan.
3. Add half the vinegar to the pan with the chicken and simmer, covered, for 10 minutes. Turn the pieces over and cook for a further 10 minutes. Check that the chicken is cooked by ensuring the juices run clear when pricked with a fork.
4. While the chicken is cooking, heat the rest of the vinegar in a second pan and boil for 4 minutes.
5. Whisk the beurre manié into the reduced vinegar. Add this to the pan containing the chicken pieces, together with the tomatoes. Simmer for 10 minutes. Check the seasoning.
6. Serve the chicken on hot plates and pour the sauce over the meat. Garnish with the tarragon. This dish should be served with rice.

Per serving:
Calories, 450; Protein, 38 g; Fat, 28 g (56% cal.); Cholesterol, 125 mg; Carbohydrates, 12 g; Fiber, 2 g; Sodium, 150 mg.

Pheasant en Cocotte

Portions: 4   Portion size: ½ pheasant (see note)

U.S.	Metric	Ingredients
4 oz	110 g	Tiny white onions
8 oz	220 g	Small new potatoes
½ oz	15 g	Butter
2	2	Pheasants, 2 lb (900 g) each (see note)
to taste	to taste	Salt
to taste	to taste	Pepper
1 oz	25 g	Butter
1 fl oz	25 g	Brandy (optional)
4 fl oz	110 g	Brown stock or demi-glace

■ P r o c e d u r e

1. Peel the onion and potatoes.
2. Brown the onions and potatoes in the butter, then cover them and let them steam over low heat until they are about half-cooked. They will finish cooking with the pheasant.
3. Season the pheasants with salt and pepper. Truss them.
4. In a casserole just large enough to hold the birds, brown the pheasants well in butter over moderate heat, making sure that all sides are well browned.
5. If the butter has burned during the browning, wipe out the casserole or transfer the birds to a clean casserole and add a little fresh butter.
6. Add brandy, if it is being used. Also add the onion and potatoes. Cover tightly and place in a 375°F (190°C) oven. Cook until done, about 30–45 minutes, or 15–30 minutes if you have substituted baby pheasants. Halfway through the cooking time, remove the cover and baste with butter. Replace the cover.
7. When the pheasant is done, remove it from the casserole and keep it warm. Deglaze the casserole with the stock and reduce lightly.
8. The pheasant, with its vegetable garnish and sauce, may be sent to the dining room in its own casserole, to be carved and plated by the dining room staff. Alternatively, it can be carved like chicken (see p. 369) and plated in the kitchen. Plate the pheasant with the vegetable garnish and moisten with a spoonful of the sauce.

V A R I A T I O N S

Other birds, such as partridges, guinea fowl, small chickens, and Cornish hens, may be prepared using this recipe.

Other garnishes may be used in place of the onions and potatoes, such as:

　Mushrooms
　Cabbage, blanched and sautéed with a little pork fat
　Whole chestnuts, cooked separately
　Peas
　Sliced artichoke bottoms

Per serving:
Calories, 850; Protein, 92 g; Fat, 46 g (49% cal.); Cholesterol, 305 mg; Carbohydrates,14 g; Fiber, 1 g; Sodium, 250 mg.

Note: Very small pheasants of 1 lb (each) may be substituted, using 1 pheasant per portion.

Fricassée de Volaille Vallée d'Auge
(Fricassée of Chicken with Apples and Cider)

Portions: 12   Portion size: ¼ chicken
4 oz (125 g) sauce and mushrooms

U.S.	Metric	Ingredients	Procedure
3	3	Chickens, about 2¾ lb (1.3 kg) each	1. Cut each chicken into 8 pieces and season with salt and pepper.
to taste	to taste	Salt	2. Heat the oil in a large pan, add the butter, and sauté the chicken skin side down in batches until lightly browned. Discard the excess fat.
to taste	to taste	Pepper	
2½ fl oz	75 mL	Oil	3. Add the Calvados to the chicken in the pan and ignite to burn off the alcohol.
2½ oz	75 g	Butter	
7 fl oz	200 mL	Calvados	4. Add the shallots and cook gently until they have softened, then pour in the cider. Cover and barely simmer for 20–25 minutes. Turn the chicken pieces after 15 minutes.
5 oz	150 g	Shallots	
1½ qt	1.5 L	Fermented cider (see note)	
1 lb	500 g	Mushrooms	5. Sauté the mushrooms in the butter in another pan, covered, for 5 minutes.
1½ oz	50 g	Butter	6. Five minutes before the end of the cooking time for the chicken, add the mushrooms and their juices to the chicken.
1½ pt	750 mL	Heavy cream	
			7. Add the cream.
			8. When cooked, remove the chicken from the pan and keep warm. Reduce the sauce until it coats the back of a spoon. Adjust the seasoning, then return the chicken pieces to the pan and simmer until they are thoroughly heated through.
1 lb 4 oz	600 g	Apples, Golden Delicious	9. To prepare the apples, core but do not peel. Cut across into slices about ¼ in. (¼–½ cm) thick and fry in the clarified butter until golden on both sides. Serve with the chicken and garnish with parsley.
5 oz	150 g	Clarified butter	
1½ oz	40 g	Chopped parsley	

Per serving:
Calories, 890; Protein, 43 g; Fat, 63 g (63% cal.); Cholesterol, 260 mg;
Carbohydrates, 22 g; Fiber, 2 g; Sodium, 330 mg.

Note: If fermented cider is not available, substitute 1 qt (1 L) apple juice (unsweetened) plus 1 pt (500 mL) dry white wine.

Chicken en Cocotte with Côte du Rhône

Portions: 12   Portion size: ¼ chicken
2½ fl oz (75 mL) sauce

U.S.	Metric	Ingredients	Procedure
3	3	Chickens, about 4½ lb (2 kg) each	1. Cut each chicken into 8 pieces. Season the chicken with salt and pepper.
to taste	to taste	Salt	2. Brown the chicken in the clarified butter. Remove the chicken from the pan.
to taste	to taste	Pepper	
1½ oz	50 g	Clarified butter	3. Add the shallots to the pan. Sweat, then sprinkle with the flour and mix well to make a roux. Cook for a few minutes.
2½ oz	75 g	Shallots	
⅔ oz	20 g	Flour	4. Deglaze with the red wine. Reduce by two-thirds, then add the chicken stock.
1 pt 5 oz	650 mL	Red wine, preferably Côte du Rhône	5. Return the chicken pieces to the pan, cover, and cook in the oven at 400°F (200°C) until the chicken is cooked.
1 qt	1 L	Chicken stock	
4 fl oz	125 mL	Cream, hot	6. Remove the chicken from the cooking liquid and strain. Skim off any fat from the surface, then reduce until it coats the back of a spoon.
3 tbsp	50 g	Black olive purée	
2 tbsp	6 g	Chopped fresh basil	7. Add the cream and reduce again.
3 tbsp	50 g	Butter	8. Mix in the olive purée and half of the chopped basil.
to taste	to taste	Salt	9. Swirl in the butter (monter au beurre) and check the seasoning.
to taste	to taste	Pepper	
as needed	as needed	Basil leaves for garnish	10. Just before serving, mix in the remaining chopped basil.
			11. Decorate with a few leaves of basil.

Per serving:
Calories, 630; Protein, 67 g; Fat, 33 g (48% cal.); Cholesterol, 190 mg;
Carbohydrates, 4 g; Fiber, 0 g; Sodium, 290 mg.

Ballotine de Poulet Grandmère
(Stuffed Boneless Chicken Legs with Mushrooms, Onion, and Bacon)

Portions: 12   Portion size: 1 chicken leg
6–7 oz (195 g) sauce and vegetables

U.S.	Metric	Ingredients
12	12	Chicken legs, about 10 oz (300 g) each, skin on
3 oz	90 g	Shallot, chopped fine
1½ oz	45 g	Carrot, cut brunoise
1½ oz	45 g	Celery, cut brunoise
2 oz	60 g	Butter
6 oz	175 g	Fresh white bread crumbs
3 (approximately)	3 (approximately)	Eggs, beaten
to taste	to taste	Salt
to taste	to taste	Pepper
12 pieces	12 pieces	Pork caul, approximately 13 oz (375 g) total (see note)
2 fl oz	60 mL	Oil
12 oz	350 g	Mirepoix, small dice
5 fl oz	150 mL	White wine (see note)
1½ oz	45 g	Tomato paste
1½ qt	1.5 L	Brown stock
5 oz	150 g	Beurre manié
to taste	to taste	Salt
to taste	to taste	Pepper
12 oz	350 g	Slab bacon
10 oz	300 g	Pearl onions
1 lb	500 g	Button mushrooms
as needed	as needed	Parsley sprigs for garnish

■ P r o c e d u r e

1. Carefully remove the bones from both thigh and drumstick of the chicken legs, following the procedure shown in Figure 13.6. Be sure to remove all cartilage. Chop and reserve the bones.

2. Sweat the shallot, carrot, and celery in butter until soft. Cool. Bind with bread crumbs and just enough egg to make a soft but not too wet consistency. Season.

3. Fill the bone cavity of the chicken legs with this stuffing, then roll up the legs to enclose the filling. If caul is available, roll neatly in pork caul and tie to secure. Alternatively, simply tie the rolls securely without the caul.

4. Heat the oil in large, shallow pan and brown the legs. Remove from the pan.

5. Add the chopped chicken bones and the mirepoix to the pan. Cook until golden.

6. Deglaze with the wine and reduce by 90 percent. Stir in the tomato paste and the stock. Bring to the boil and thicken lightly with beurre manié.

7. Place the chicken legs in the pan, ensuring that the liquid comes only halfway up them. Bring to a boil, then continue cooking, uncovered, in the oven at 350°F (180°C) for about 30 minutes. During this time, baste with the braising liquid to give the legs a glaze.

8. Remove the chicken legs from the liquid and keep warm. Strain the liquid into a clean pan, degrease, and season with salt and pepper, adjusting consistency if necessary.

9. Prepare the garnish: Cut the bacon into lardons (batonnet). Blanch the lardons by placing them in cold water and bringing to a boil, cooking for 5 minutes in total, then frying them in a sauté pan until golden brown. Sauté the onions and mushrooms in the bacon fat until glazed and golden. Combine all three.

10. Remove the strings from the chicken legs, slice neatly, and serve on hot plates with the sauce around. Sprinkle the mixed garnish over the chicken and finish with parsley sprigs.

Per serving:
Calories, 680; Protein, 46 g; Fat, 46 g (61% cal.); Cholesterol, 205 mg; Carbohydrates,19 g; Fiber, 2 g; Sodium, 610 mg.

Note: Caul is a thin, lacy membrane of fat surrounding the abdominal cavity of pigs and other animals. Wrapping in caul helps maintain the shape of the roll and prevent the stuffing from escaping, and it melts away almost entirely during cooking. If it is not available, simply omit.

If you do not wish to use wine in this recipe, substitute water or stock for deglazing. Adjust the flavor balance of the finished sauce with a little fresh lemon juice.

Ballotine de Poulet Grandmère

Figure 13.6 Boning and stuffing a chicken leg.

(a) Make a shallow cut along the thigh bone.

(b) Continue to cut along the bone to free it from the meat.

(c) Continue the cut along the entire length of the leg bone to expose all the bone.

(d) Remove the bone completely from the meat.

(e) Place a portion of the stuffing along the length of the meat and roll the leg into a cylinder to enclose the stuffing.

(f) Tie securely.

Salmis of Partridge

Portions: 4   Portion size: 1 partridge

U.S.	Metric	Ingredients
4	4	Partridges, about 1 lb (450 g) each (see variations)
as needed	as needed	Salt
as needed	as needed	Pepper
as needed	as needed	Butter, melted
1 oz	30 g	Shallots
½ oz	15 g	Butter
3–4	3–4	Peppercorns, crushed
10 fl oz	300 ml	Red wine
6 fl oz	180 ml	Demi-glace
to taste	to taste	Salt
2 oz	60 g	Butter

Per serving:
Calories, 920; Protein, 118 g; fat, 21 g (26% cal.); Cholesterol 435 mg; Carbohydrates, 5 g; Fiber, 0 g; Sodium, 390 mg.

Note: A salmis (sahl mee) is a dish, usually of game or poultry, prepared by roasting the item partway and finishing it in a sauce. The sauce is usually made with red or white wine and flavored by adding the juices from the carcass or by simmering the carcass in the sauce. The meat may then be simply reheated with the sauce or simmered in it for a longer time.

■ Procedure

1. Season the birds with salt and pepper and brush them with melted butter.
2. Roast them in hot oven (475°F/250°C), keeping them rare.
3. Cut off the legs. Put them under the broiler for a few minutes with the insides toward the heat and broil until well done.
4. Carefully cut each side of the breast from the carcass in one piece. Set aside and keep warm.
5. Chop the carcasses.
6. Sauté the chopped carcasses and the shallots in butter for a few minutes.
7. Add the peppercorns and red wine. Reduce by two-thirds.
8. Add the demi-glace and bring to a boil. Strain through a fine sieve, pressing down on the solids to squeeze out as much liquid as possible.
9. Combine the breasts and the sauce in a saucepan and heat gently until the meat is hot and cooked to the desired degree. It should remain pink on the inside.
10. Strain the sauce again. Season with salt. Finish the sauce by setting over low heat and swirling in the butter.
11. Serve the breasts with the sauce, and garnish with the broiled legs.

VARIATIONS

This recipe can be prepared with any of the following in place of the partridge. The number of birds to use will depend on their size.

Pheasant   Squab   Wild duck   Guinea hen

Coq au Vin

Portions: 12   Portion size: ¼ chicken
2½ fl oz (75 mL) sauce

U.S.	Metric	Ingredients	Procedure
12 oz	350 g	Salt pork or slab bacon	1. Cut the salt pork or bacon into batonnet shapes, 1 × ¼ × ¼ in. (2 × ½ × ½ cm).
1 fl oz	30 mL	Oil	2. Place the bacon pieces in a saucepan. Cover with cold water. Bring to a boil and drain.
			3. Add the oil to a large sauté pan and place over moderate heat. When hot, add the blanched bacon. Sauté until lightly browned. Remove with a slotted spoon and set aside.
3	3	Chickens, 3½ lb (1.6 kg) each, cut into 8 pieces	4. Increase the heat to high. Add the chickens to the fat remaining in the pan and brown well on all sides. Remove the chicken from the pan.
24	24	Tiny white onions, peeled and parboiled	5. Add the onions and mushrooms to the pan and sauté until browned. Remove with a slotted spoon and set aside with the bacon pieces. Pour off the fat from the pan.
1½ lb	700 g	Small mushroom caps	
1 qt	1 L	Dry red wine	6. Add the wine and stock to the pan and bring to a boil.
1 pt	500 mL	Chicken stock	7. Add the thyme, bay leaf, and garlic, tied in a piece of cheesecloth.
		Sachet:	8. Return the chicken to the pan. Bring the liquid back to a boil. Cover and cook in a 300°F (150°C) oven or over very low heat on top of the stove until chicken is done, about 30–40 minutes.
½ tsp	2 mL	Dried thyme	
1	1	Bay leaf	
4	4	Large garlic cloves, crushed	
		Beurre manié:	9. Remove the chicken from the cooking liquid and place in a heated pan or on a serving platter. Garnish with the mushrooms, onions, and bacon pieces.
2 oz	60 g	Butter, softened	10. Degrease the cooking liquid carefully.
2 oz	60 g	Flour	11. Place over high heat and boil until the liquid is reduced to about 1 qt (1 L).
to taste	to taste	Salt	12. Mix the butter and flour to make beurre manié. Beat in the beurre manié a little at time, just enough to thicken the sauce lightly.
as needed	as needed	Chopped parsley	13. Add salt to taste.
			14. Strain the sauce over the chicken and garnish.
			15. At service time, sprinkle each portion with a little chopped parsley.

Per serving:
Calories, 690; Protein, 50 g; Fat, 41 g (54% cal.); Cholesterol, 165 mg; Carbohydrates, 10 g; Fiber, 2 g; Sodium, 480 mg.

Coq au Vin

Arroz con Pollo (Spanish Rice with Chicken)

Portions: 24   Portion size: ¼ chicken
5 oz (150 g) rice

U.S.	Metric	Ingredients
6	6	Chickens, 3 lb (1.4 kg) each
3 fl oz	90 mL	Olive oil
1 lb	500 g	Onion, small dice
1 lb	500 g	Green bell peppers, medium dice
4 tsp	20 mL	Garlic, chopped fine
2 tsp	10 mL	Paprika
1 qt	1 L	Long-grain rice, raw
3 pt	1.5 L	Chicken stock
2 lb	900 g	Fresh tomatoes, 1-in. (2½-cm) dice *or*
1½ lb	700 g	Canned tomatoes, diced
to taste	to taste	Salt
to taste	to taste	Pepper
1¼ lb	600 g	Frozen peas, thawed
4 oz	125 g	Pimientos, cut into thin strips

■ P r o c e d u r e

1. Cut the chickens into 8 pieces each.
2. Heat the olive oil in a large sauté pan. Brown the chickens on all sides. Transfer the pieces to a brazier as they are browned. Drain off and discard about one-third of the fat in the pan.
3. Place the onion, green pepper, and garlic in the sauté pan in which the chicken was browned. Sauté over medium heat until the vegetables are almost tender.
4. Add the paprika and rice and stir until the grains are coated with fat.
5. Add the stock and tomatoes. Bring to a boil. Season the liquid to taste with salt and pepper.
6. Pour the contents of the pan over the chicken in the brazier. Cover and place in a 325°F (165°C) oven until the rice and chicken are cooked, about 20–30 minutes.
7. At service time, stir in the peas and garnish the top with pimiento strips.

Per serving:
Calories, 580; Protein, 49 g; Fat, 26 g (41% cal.); Cholesterol, 145 mg;
Carbohydrates, 35 g; Fiber, 3 g; Sodium, 160 mg.

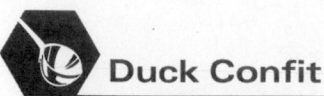
Duck Confit

Portions: 8 (see note)

U.S.	Metric	Ingredients
8 lb	3.6 kg	Duck parts, preferably legs
1 oz	30 g	Salt
1 tsp	5 mL	White pepper
½ tsp	2 mL	Nutmeg
½ tsp	2 mL	Powdered bay leaf
pinch	pinch	Ground cloves
as needed	as needed	Extra duck fat

Per serving:
Calories, 620; Protein, 35 g; Fat, 52 g (77% cal.); Cholesterol, 155 mg; Carbohydrates, 0 g; Fiber, 0 g; Sodium, 1480 mg.

Note: The exact weight of the finished confit can vary considerably.

■ P r o c e d u r e

1. Trim off excess fat from the duck and reserve.
2. If you are using duck legs (the ideal part for this preparation), leave the thigh attached to the drumstick.
3. Rub the duck pieces with the salt and spices. Refrigerate overnight.
4. Render the trimmed fat plus as much extra fat as needed. You will need enough rendered fat to completely cover the duck pieces.
5. Put the duck and the rendered fat in a brazier, large saucepan, or casserole. Simmer gently in the fat over low heat or in a 300°F (150°C) oven until very tender, about 1½–2 hours.
6. Remove the cooked duck from the fat and pack into a clean crock or other container. Pour the melted fat over the meat so that it is completely covered, but be careful not to pour in any of the juices. (The degreased juices may be used for another purpose, such as cooking beans.)
7. Remove duck pieces and use as needed. For best storage, remaining pieces must be kept covered by the fat. For serving, the confit is usually browned in a little of the fat until it is heated through and the skin is crisp. Serve with such accompaniments as braised cabbage, cooked white beans, or sautéed potatoes with garlic, or on a bed of salad greens.

CONFIT OF DUCK AND GOOSE

Confit means "preserved." Confit of duck and goose originated as a byproduct of the production of foie gras, as a way to make use of and preserve the meat of birds that are raised and fed for their enlarged, fattened livers. After the parts are cooked by the procedure in the recipe on this page, they are packed in crocks and enough fat is poured over them to seal them from the air, thus preserving them for a time.

Today, of course, refrigeration makes this method of preserving unnecessary. But confit is more popular than ever because of the tenderness and flavor this cooking method yields. In the case of ducks, the legs are usually made into confit, while the boneless breasts are reserved for pan-frying and serving rare. A special breed of duck called *moulard*, with a large, meaty breast, is used for foie gras production. It is this duck whose legs are traditionally made into confit. However, the legs of any domestic duck can be used in this recipe.

DRESSINGS AND STUFFINGS

Stuffing chickens and turkeys is usually not practical in production kitchens. Baking the stuffing separately gives better results, for these reasons:

1. **Safety.**
   Stuffing inside a bird is an ideal breeding ground for bacteria that cause food poisoning.

2. **Quality.**
   Additional roasting time is needed to heat the stuffing through. The result is often overcooked poultry.

3. **Efficiency**
   Filling poultry with stuffing and removing it after roasting is impractical, time consuming, and messy.

Stuffing that is baked separately is usually called *dressing*.
   Is poultry ever stuffed? Yes. Small birds served whole as one or two portions can be stuffed and often are. Stuffed Cornish hens or small game birds such as quail are popular items.

BASIC INGREDIENTS OF DRESSINGS

1. Starch base, such as bread or rice.
2. Aromatic vegetables, generally onions and celery.
3. Fat, such as butter or chicken fat, for sautéing the vegetables and for providing richness.
   Dressings for chicken and turkey, which are lean, may require more fat than dressings for duck and goose, which are fatty.
4. Liquid, usually stock, to provide moisture.
5. Seasonings, herbs, and spices.
6. Eggs, sometimes added as a binder but not always necessary.
7. Other ingredients for flavor, character, and bulk, such as:

Sausage	Chestnuts
Oysters	Fruits
Giblets	Nuts

Guidelines for Making Dressings

1. All ingredients that require cooking must be completely cooked before combining with other dressing ingredients. They will cook very little more during baking or roasting.
2. Cool all ingredients before combining to avoid growth of dangerous bacteria.
3. Never let baked or unbaked dressing stay in the Food Danger Zone (41° to 135°F/5° to 57°C) longer than 1 hour.
   - Refrigerate unbaked dressing if it is not to be baked immediately.
   - Hold baked dressing above 135°F (57°C) for service or chill as rapidly as possible.
   - Reheat baked dressing rapidly in oven or steamer to an internal temperature of 180°F (82°C).
4. Bake dressing in shallow pans (2 in/5 cm deep) for rapid cooking, to get it above the Danger Zone quickly.
5. Do not overmix bread dressings, or they will become pasty. Toss ingredients together lightly.
6. For light texture, do not pack dressings into baking pans; instead, spoon loosely.
7. If you stuff poultry instead of baking the dressing separately, fill the birds loosely. Do not pack. Stuffings expand during cooking.

Basic Bread Dressing

Yield: about 4 lb (2 Kg)

U.S.	Metric	Ingredients
1 lb	500 g	Onion, small dice
½ lb	250 g	Celery, small dice
½ lb	250 g	Fat such as butter, chicken fat, or bacon fat
2 lb	1 kg	White bread, 2 days old
1 oz	30 g	Chopped fresh parsley
1 tsp	5 mL	Sage
½ tsp	2 mL	Dried thyme
½ tsp	2 mL	Dried marjoram
½ tsp	2 mL	White pepper
2 tsp	10 mL	Salt
1–2 pt	0.5–1 L	Chicken stock, cold

Per 1 ounce:
Calories, 70; Protein, 1 g; Fat, 3.5 g (47% cal.); Cholesterol, 10 mg;
Carbohydrates, 8 g; Fiber, 0 g; Sodium, 175 mg.

■ P r o c e d u r e

1. Sauté the onion and celery lightly in the fat until tender but not browned. Cool thoroughly.

2. Cut the bread into small cubes. If desired, crusts may be trimmed first.

3. Combine the bread and cooked vegetables in a large stainless-steel bowl. Add the herbs and seasonings and toss gently until all ingredients are well mixed.

4. Add the stock a little at a time, and mix the dressing lightly after each addition. Add just enough to make the dressing slightly moist, neither dry nor soggy. Adjust the seasonings.

5. Place in a greased baking pan and bake at 375°F (190°C), until hot at the center, about 1 hour.

V A R I A T I O N S

Sausage Dressing
Cook 1 lb (500 g) crumbled pork sausage meat, drain, and cool. Use some of the drained fat to cook the vegetables for the dressing. Add the cooked sausage to the dressing before adding the stock.

Chestnut Dressing
Reduce the bread to 1½ lb (750 g). Add 1 lb (500 g) cooked, coarsely chopped chestnuts to the dressing before adding the stock.

Mushroom Dressing
Cook 2 lb (1 kg) sliced mushrooms with the onion and celery. Proceed as in basic recipe.

Giblet Dressing
Add ½ lb (250 g) cooked, chopped chicken or turkey gizzards and hearts to the dressing before adding the stock.

Cornbread Dressing
Substitute cornbread for all or part of the white bread in Basic Bread Dressing or Sausage Dressing.

■ QUESTIONS FOR DISCUSSION

1. Describe the three roasting methods discussed in this chapter: low-temperature roasting, searing, and high-temperature roasting. When is each used?

2. True or false: Chicken should be broiled at a lower temperature than steaks. Explain your answer.

3. What is meant by the term *presentation side*?

4. Why is it difficult to cook large chicken pieces by deep-frying? How can this problem be solved?

5. What are the differences between simmering and poaching as applied to poultry?

6. Give three reasons for baking dressing in a separate pan rather than stuffing it into roast poultry.

14

Understanding Fish and Shellfish

A t one time, fresh fish was enjoyed only in limited areas—along the seacoast and, to a lesser extent, around lakes and rivers. Today, thanks to modern refrigeration and freezing technology, fish products are enjoyed much more widely.

For the cook, the difficulties of understanding fish and shellfish are, in some ways, the reverse of those for meat. With meat, we are presented with only a few animals, but a bewildering array of cuts from each. With fish, we see only a few cuts but hundreds of species, each with its own characteristics and cooking requirements.

For this reason, it is especially important that students learn the basic principles of structure, handling, and cooking so they can utilize the many varieties of seafood in a systematic way.

Fish products are divided into two categories: fin fish, or fish with fins and internal skeletons, and shellfish, or fish with external shells but no internal bone structure. Because they have many differences, it is helpful to look at them separately, as we do in this chapter.

After reading this chapter, you should be able to

1. Explain how the cooking qualities of fish are affected by its lack of connective tissue.

2. Determine doneness in cooked fish.

3. Demonstrate the appropriate cooking methods for fat and lean fish.

4. List seven basic market forms of fish.

5. Dress and fillet round fish and flatfish.

6. List and describe common varieties of saltwater and freshwater fin fish used in North American food service.

7. Identify the characteristics of fresh fish, and contrast them with characteristics not-so-fresh fish.

8. Store fish and fish products.

9. Understand the popular varieties of shellfish, and discuss their characteristics.

10. Outline the special safe handling and cooking procedures for shellfish.

11. Open clams and oysters, split lobster, and peel and devein shrimp.

FIN FISH

COMPOSITION AND STRUCTURE

The edible flesh of fish, like that of meat and poultry, consists of water, proteins, fats, and small amounts of minerals, vitamins, and other substances. The differences, however, are perhaps more important than the similarities.

Fish has very little connective tissue. This is one of the most important differences between fish and meat. It means that

1. *Fish cooks very quickly*, even at low heat (just enough heat to coagulate the proteins).

2. *Fish is naturally tender.* Toughness is the result not of connective tissue but of the toughening of the protein by high heat.

3. *Moist-heat cooking methods* are used not to create tenderness but to preserve moistness and provide variety.

4. *Cooked fish must be handled very carefully* or it will fall apart.

SPECIAL PROBLEMS IN COOKING FISH

DONENESS AND FLAKING

When fish is cooked, the flesh breaks apart into its natural separations. This is called **flaking**. Most books, somewhat misleadingly, say that fish is done when it flakes *easily*. Unfortunately, some cooks interpret this as "nearly falling apart." Because fish continues to cook in its retained heat even when removed from the fire, it is often dreadfully overcooked by the time it reaches the customer. *Fish is very delicate and is easily overcooked.*

Observe these tests for doneness:

1. The fish *just separates* into flakes—that is, it is beginning to flake but does not yet fall apart easily.

2. If bone is present, the flesh separates from the bone, and the bone is no longer pink.

3. The flesh has turned from translucent to opaque (usually white, depending on the kind of fish).

Remember, the major flaw in fish preparation is *overcooking*.

COOKING FAT FISH AND LEAN FISH

The fat content of fish ranges from 0.5 percent to 20 percent.

Lean fish are those that are low in fat. Examples: Flounder, sole, cod, red snapper, bass, perch, halibut, pike.

Fat fish are those that are high in fat. Examples: Salmon, tuna, trout, butterfish, mackerel.

Cooking Lean Fish

Because lean fish has almost no fat, it can easily become dry, especially if overcooked. It is often served with sauces to enhance moistness and give richness.

Moist-heat methods. Lean fish is especially well suited to poaching. This method preserves moistness.

Dry-heat methods. Lean fish, if it is broiled or baked, should be basted with butter or oil. Take special care not to overcook it, or the fish will be dry.

Dry-heat methods with fat. Lean fish may be fried or sautéed. The fish gains palatability from the added fat.

Cooking Fat Fish

The fat in these fish enables them to tolerate more heat without becoming dry.

Moist-heat methods. Fat fish, like lean fish, can be cooked by moist heat. Poached salmon and trout are very popular.

Dry-heat methods. Fat fish are well suited to broiling and baking. The dry heat helps eliminate excessive oiliness.

Dry-heat methods with fat. Large fat fish, like salmon, and stronger-flavored fish, like bluefish and mackerel, may be cooked in fat, but care should be taken to avoid excessive greasiness. Smaller ones, like trout, are often pan-fried. Drain the fish well before serving.

CUTTING FISH

MARKET FORMS

Fish are available in several forms, as illustrated in Figure 14.1. Or they may be cut by the cook into these forms, depending on how they are to be cooked.

BUYING PROCESSED FISH VERSUS CUTTING THEM YOURSELF

Most food service establishments purchase fish in the forms in which they intend to cook them. They find it less expensive to pay the purveyor to do the cutting than to hire and train the personnel and to allocate the storage and workspace to do it in-house.

Some restaurants still buy whole fish. Here are a few reasons why they do:

1. Their clientele demands it. Some high-priced luxury restaurants stake their reputations on using only the freshest, most unprocessed ingredients. They are able to charge enough to cover their high labor costs.

2. They are in the heart of a fresh fish market, where fresh whole fish, delivered daily, are economical. They can best take advantage of seasonal bargains.

3. They are high-volume specialty restaurants and find it more economical to clean the fish themselves and watch the market for the best prices every day.

4. They make fish stocks and use the bones.

5. They serve the whole fish. Examples: sautéed or poached trout presented whole; whole cold poached fish as a buffet display.

Your purchasing decisions will depend on what you plan to do with the fish and what forms are most economical for those purposes.

Figure 14.1
Market forms of fish.

(a) Whole or round: completely intact, as caught

(b) Drawn: viscera removed

(c) Dressed: viscera, scales, head, tail, and fins removed

(d) Steaks: cross-section slices, each containing a section of backbone

(e) Fillets: boneless sides of fish, with skin on or off

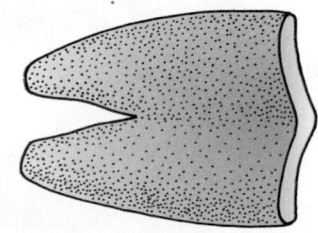

(f) Butterflied fillets: both sides of a fish still joined, but with bones removed

(g) Sticks or tranches: cross-section slices of fillets

Figure 14.2
Dressing a fish.

(a) Scale the fish. Lay the fish flat on work surface. Rub a scaling tool or the back of a knife against the scales from tail to head. Repeat until all scales are removed. Rinse. (Exceptions: Trout, with very tiny scales, and scaleless fish, like catfish, are not scaled.)

DRESSING AND FILLETING

Although most of you will work with ready-to-cook fish products, you should know how to clean and fillet whole fish.

1. **Dressing.**
   Figure 14.2 illustrates how to dress a whole fish.

2. **Filleting.**
   There are two basic shapes of fish: flatfish (like flounder and sole) and round fish (like cod and trout). They are filleted differently. Flatfish have four fillets; round fish have two. Figures 14.3 and 14.4 show the two methods for filleting these fish.

(b) Eviscerate. Slit the belly and pull out viscera. Rinse cavity.

(c) Cut off tail and fins. Scissors are easiest to use.

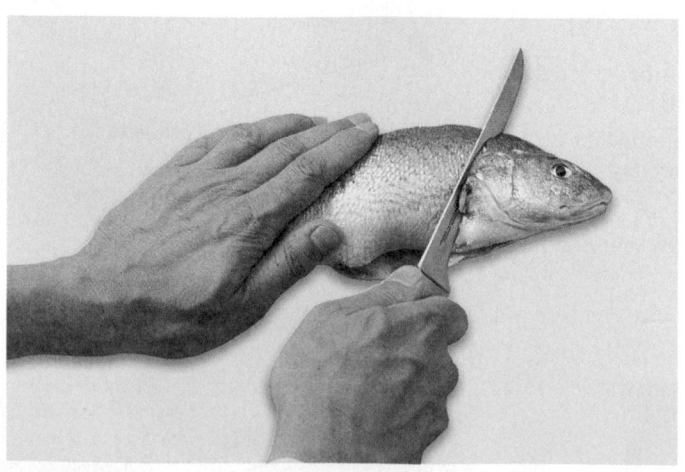

(d) Remove head. Cut through flesh just behind gills. Cut or break backbone at the cut and pull off head.

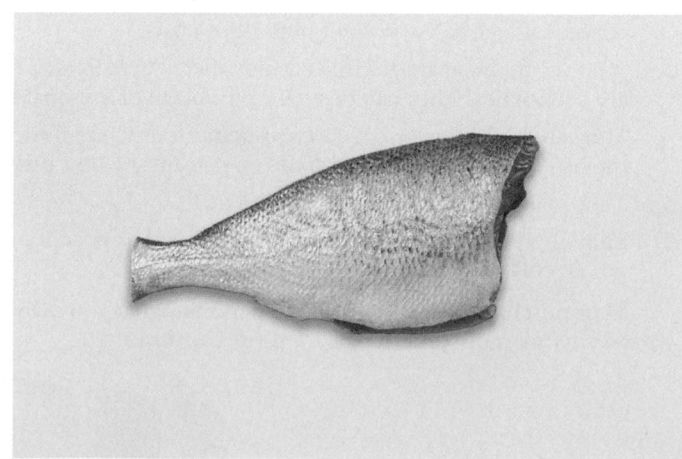

(e) The fish is dressed.

Figure 14.3 Filleting flatfish.

(a) Use a thin-bladed, flexible knife. Cut off the head, just behind the gills. (This step is optional.)

(b) Make a cut from head to tail just to one side of the center line, down to the backbone.

(c) Turn the knife so that it is almost parallel to the table. Making long, smooth cuts, cut horizontally against the backbone toward the outer edge of the fish. Gently separate the fillet from the bone.

(d) Remove the fillet completely. Repeat to remove the three remaining fillets.

(e) To skin, place the fillet skin side down on the work surface with the tail pointing toward you. Holding the skin at the tail end, slide the knife between the skin and flesh, scraping against the skin to avoid cutting into the fillet. *Note:* Dover or English sole is skinned before filleting. Cut through the skin at the tail. Holding the tail with one hand, peel off the skin toward the head. *Caution:* Do not do this with flounder. You will tear the flesh.

Figure 14.4 Filleting round fish.

(a) Cut into the top of the fish along one side of the backbone from head to tail. Cut against the bone with smooth strokes of the knife to separate the flesh from the bone.

(b) Cut under the flesh toward the tail; detach it.

(c) Cut along the curved rib bones and finish detaching the fillet at the head end. Turn the fish over and repeat to remove the second fillet. Lightly run your finger along the flesh side of the fillets to see if any bones remain in them. Pull out any you find. Skin the fillets as for flatfish.

VARIETIES AND CHARACTERISTICS

Hundreds of varieties of fish are eaten around the world. However, relatively few species account for the majority of the fish used in food service in the United States and Canada. Below are the most common varieties that are used fresh. Some are illustrated in the following photographs.

There is a significant difference in flavor between freshwater fish and saltwater fish, because saltwater fish, as might be expected, have more salt in their flesh. The following survey of fish varieties divides them into these two basic categories. However, some fish may spend part of their lives in the ocean and part in fresh water. Salmon, for example, lives in the ocean but migrates up rivers to lay eggs or *spawn*. Fish that live in salt water but spawn in fresh water are called **anadromous**. Shad and arctic char are two other examples of anadromous fish. On the other hand, fish that live in fresh water but swim downstream to spawn in the ocean are called **catadromous**. Eel is a catadromous fish.

In the following listing, fish are categorized by where they spend most of their adult lives. Thus, anadromous fish such as salmon are listed with saltwater fish, while the catadromous fish such as eel are listed with freshwater fish.

SALTWATER FISH—FLATFISH

These are all popular in commercial kitchens. Flatfish have lean, white flesh and a mild, delicate flavor. They are all very flat, oval in shape, with both eyes on one side of the head.

You should note that, in North American waters, there are no true sole. All such fish marketed as sole, such as lemon sole, gray sole, and Pacific Dover sole, are actually flounder. True Dover sole, from Atlantic waters off Europe, is the only actual sole in this list. Also, be aware that both true Dover sole and the flounder called Pacific Dover sole are both sometimes called English sole.

Flounder

Flounder

Type: Lean.

Varieties: Winter flounder, lemon sole, gray sole, Pacific Dover sole, sand dab.

Characteristics: White flesh; fine flakes; mild, sweet flavor.

Weight: ½ to 5 lb (0.2 to 2.3 kg).

Sole (Dover sole or English sole)

Type: Lean.

Characteristics: Narrower, more elongated than flounder. Flesh similar to flounder, but firmer in texture. One of the most prized of all fish. Expensive.

Weight: 1 to 2 lb (0.5 to 1 kg).

Halibut

Type: Lean.

Characteristics: Looks like a giant flounder, with thicker flesh, delicate flavor. Cut into steaks and fillets.

Weight: 4 to 100 lb or more (2 to 45 kg).

Turbot

Type: Lean.

Characteristics: Large, broad flatfish. White, firm, delicate flesh.

Weight: 1 to 25 lb (0.5 to 11 kg).

Dover sole

SALTWATER FISH—ROUND FISH

Arctic Char

Type: Fat. Anadromous.

Characteristics: Similar to both salmon and trout, to which it is related. Flesh is similar to salmon but with less fat, although with more fat than trout.

Weight: Usually around 4 lb (1.8 kg), but can be as large as 25 lb (11 kg).

Black Sea Bass

Type: Lean.

Characteristics: Small, black-skinned fish with firm, delicate, sweet white flesh.

Weight: Up to 3 lb (1.5 kg).

Black sea bass

Bluefish

Type: Fat.

Characteristics: Flavorful, oily flesh that is bluish when raw, grayish when cooked. Abundant and inexpensive.

Weight: 1 to 10 lb (0.5 to 4.5 kg).

Chilean Sea Bass

Type: Fat.

Varieties: This fish is not a bass; the name is a marketing term for the Patagonian toothfish. Because it has become seriously overfished, due to its popularity, numbers have declined dramatically. Fishing is highly regulated, and imports to North America must be labeled as legally caught, although there is much illegal fish on the market. Many chefs have agreed to stop serving this fish in order to slow or halt the illegal fishing that threatens its survival.

Characteristics: White, oily flesh with large flakes, firm texture, and mild flavor.

Weight: Usually around 20 lb (9 kg), although it can be much larger.

Bluefish

Cod

Type: Lean.

Varieties: Small, young cod is called scrod.

Characteristics: Lean, white, delicately flavored flesh with large flakes. One of the most widely used food fish in North America. Most fish sticks and similar items are made from cod.

Weights: Scrod: 1 to 2½ lb (0.5 to 1 kg). Cod: 2½ to 25 lb and up (1 to 11 kg).

Cod

Escolar

Type: Fat.

Characteristics: A firm, white oily fish containing a fat that is not metabolized by the human body. Because of this fat, some people can become ill when eating this fish. The fat seems to act like a laxative. In the United States, the Food and Drug Administration banned escolar in 1990, but its sale is once again legal. It is legal in Canada, although the government has issued a safety advisory. Food service operators who serve escolar should advise customers of its potential dangers.

Weight: 65 to 110 lb (30 to 35 kg).

Grouper

Type: Lean.

Characteristics: Many varieties with varying shape and skin color. Firm white fish, similar in texture and flavor to red snapper. Tough skin.

Weight: Up to 700 lb (300 kg), but most groupers on the market weigh 5 to 15 lb (2.3 to 7 kg).

Grouper

Haddock

Type: Lean.

Varieties: Finnan haddie is smoked haddock, not a separate kind of fish.

Characteristics: Similar to cod, but generally smaller.

Weight: 1 to 5 lb (0.5 to 2.3 kg).

Herring

Type: Fat.

Characteristics: Small, full-flavored, oily fish. Most herring sold to food service and retail establishments is pickled or smoked rather than fresh, but fresh herring is sometimes available. Smoked herring are sometimes called kippers. Fresh herring are excellent butterflied or left whole and grilled. Because of their high fat content, they do not keep well, so they should be checked carefully for freshness when purchased.

Weight: Up to 8 oz (240 g).

Jack

Type: Fat.

Varieties: Members of the jack family include kingfish, blue runner, yellowtail, amberjack, and golden thread. The best-known jack is the pompano, listed separately.

Blue runner, a type of Jack

Jack

Characteristics: Smooth, shiny skin; firm, oily flesh; strong flavor. Some varieties are much stronger in flavor than others.

Weight: Varies greatly depending on variety.

John Dory

Also known as St. Peter's fish, St. Pierre.

Type: Lean.

Characteristics: Identified by the characteristic black spot ("St. Peter's thumbprint") on each side of the body behind the head. Firm, sweet, white flesh with fine flakes; broad, thin fillets.

Weight: About 2 lb (900 g) average.

Boston mackerel

Mackerel

Type: Fat.

Varieties: Spanish and Boston mackerel are the most common small varieties. King mackerel is larger, usually cut into steaks.

Characteristics: Fat, firm flesh with rich flavor and slightly dark color.

Weight: ½ to 5 lb (0.2 to 2.3 kg).

Spanish mackerel

Mahi-Mahi

Also known as dorado and dolphinfish (not related to the mammal called dolphin).

Type: Lean.

Characteristics: Firm, fine-textured, pinkish flesh with rich, sweet taste. Becomes very dry when overcooked, so best cooked with moist heat or with fat or served with a sauce.

Weight: 5 to 40 lb (2.3 to 18 kg).

Mahi-mahi

Monkfish

Also known as lotte, anglerfish, bellyfish.

Type: Lean.

Characteristics: Large, ugly fish, but only tail is used. White, very firm flesh with fine texture, somewhat like lobster. Rich flavor. Holds up well in soups and stews, but dries out easily if cooked dry without fat.

Weight: 5 to 50 lb (2.3 to 23 kg).

Monkfish

Ocean Perch

Type: Lean.

Varieties: Many. Red-skinned varieties (redfish) are especially popular and more expensive.

Characteristics: Mild, somewhat bony.

Weight: Depends on variety, but typically about 1 lb (0.5 kg).

Orange Roughy

Type: Lean.

Characteristics: A South Pacific fish increasingly available in some markets. Texture and flavor similar to red snapper.

Weight: ¾ to 2 lb (0.3 to 1 kg).

Pompano

Pompano

Type: Fat.

Characteristics: Small fish with rich, sweet-flavored flesh. Expensive. A variety of jack (see entry above).

Weight: ¾ to 2 lb (0.3 to 1 kg).

Porgy

Type: Lean.

Characteristics: Small, oval fish. Sweet and mild, but quite bony.

Weight: Up to 2 lb (1 kg).

Porgy

Red Mullet

Also known as rouget barbet (roo-zhay bar-bay), rouget.

Type: Lean.

Varieties: A member of the goatfish family. In addition to the Mediterranean variety discussed here, similar varieties are found in North American waters.

Characteristics: Mediterranean fish resembling a small red snapper. Rich flavor with a slight taste of shrimp or lobster. Always cooked with skin on, because much of the desired flavor comes from the skin.

Weight: Usually 12 oz or less (350 g or less).

Red mullet

Red Snapper

Type: Lean.

Characteristics: Firm, delicate, sweet white flesh with large flakes. Large, coarse bones. Skin is red. Highly prized; popular in restaurants.

Weight: 1 to 15 lb (0.5 to 7 kg).

Red snapper

Salmon

Salmon

Type: Fat. Anadromous.

Varieties: Atlantic, chinook, sockeye, coho, chum, humpback.

Characteristics: Rich pink to red flesh, with somewhat meaty texture and flavor. One of the most prized of all fish. Much is canned or smoked.

Weight: 4 to 25 lb (2 to 11 kg).

Sardine

See Herring. True sardines are closely related to herring, but are scarce. Most fish sold as sardines are actually small herring. Usually sold canned.

Shad

Type: Fat. Anadromous.

Characteristics: Oily, rich flavor and many bones in several rows in each fillet. Its roe (egg sacs) are especially prized. Fresh shad is highly seasonal (February to June).

Weight: 1½ to 5 lb (0.7 to 2.3 kg).

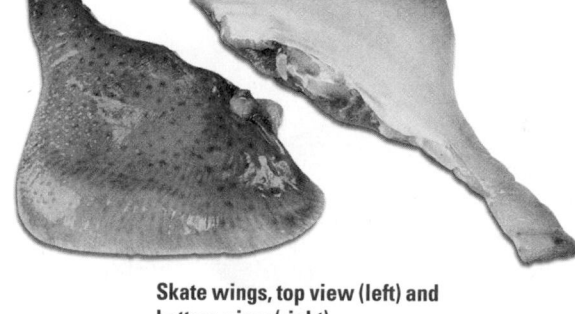

Shark

Type: Fat.

Varieties: Mako shark is the variety usually used.

Characteristics: Firm texture, similar to swordfish, but softer and a little moister and with finer grain; less expensive. Has cartilage skeleton, no bones. Usually cut into steaks.

Weight: 25 to 40 lb (11 to 18 kg).

Skate

Also known as ray.

Type: Lean.

Characteristics: May be sold whole, but often only the triangular wings are marketed. Skeleton is cartilage, not bone; tough skin, gray on top, white on bottom. Flesh consists of sweet, white, gelatinous strips of meat extending the width of the wings; two fillets per wing, one above and one below the cartilage.

Weight: Some varieties weigh up to a ton, but most sold for food weigh 1 to 4 lb (0.5 to 2 kg) per wing.

Skate wings, top view (left) and bottom view (right)

Striped Bass

Type: Lean.

Varieties: Wild striped bass is highly prized but available in only small numbers in recent years. Farmed striped bass, developed in response to demand, is a cross between white bass and wild striped bass.

Characteristics: Firm, white, delicately flavored fish with large flakes.

Weight: 1 to 10 lb (0.5 to 4.5 kg).

Striped bass

Swordfish

Type: Fat.

Characteristics: Very large, fat fish with dense, meaty, not flaky, texture. High yield. Sold mostly as steaks. Expensive.

Weight: Up to 1,000 lb (450 kg).

Tilefish

Type: Lean.

Characteristics: Firm, sweet, mild white flesh, pinkish when raw. Used mostly for steaks, but smaller ones can be filleted or poached whole.

Weight: 4 to 8 lb (1.8 to 3.6 kg).

Tilefish

Triggerfish

Type: Lean.

Characteristics: Tough-skinned fish with firm, meaty, white to gray-white flesh. Low yield because of large head.

Weight: About 2 lb (900 g) average.

Triggerfish

Tuna

Type: Fat.

Varieties: Yellowfin and bluefin have red flesh, gray when cooked. Albacore (more often canned than used fresh) has pink flesh, off-white when cooked. Some other varieties are also available.

Characteristics: Meaty texture and appearance. Belly cuts much fattier than back ("loin"). Red-fleshed varieties often served raw as sashimi or sushi. When cooked, usually cut into steaks and grilled. Should not be cooked well done, or will be very dry.

Weight: Depends on variety. May be several hundred pounds (100 kg and up).

Wahoo or Ono

Type: Fat.

Characteristics: Firm flesh similar in texture to mackerel and tuna, to which it is related. Pale pink flesh turns white when cooked. The biology of this fish is not well known, and there are concerns about overfishing. It is a popular sport fish.

Weight: 11 to 80 lb (5 to 35 kg), but can be much larger.

Weakfish

Also called sea trout, but unrelated to trout.

Type: Lean.

Characteristics: Mild, light-gray flesh with soft texture.

Weight: Up to 10 lb (4.5 kg).

Weakfish

Whiting

Type: Lean.

Characteristics: Fragile, white flesh with mild flavor. Fillets must be handled carefully or they will break up.

Weight: ¼ to 3 lb (0.1 to 1.4 kg).

Whiting

FRESHWATER FISH

Catfish

Type: Fat to somewhat lean, depending on origin.

Varieties: Bullhead is similar but is not the same species.

Characteristics: Firm flesh with abundant flavor. Layer of fat directly under skin. Catfish has no scales and is usually skinned before frying or pan-frying. Farmed catfish is milder and usually leaner than wild catfish.

Weight: 1 to 8 lb (0.5 to 3.6 kg).

Catfish

Eel

Type: Fat.

Characteristics: A long, slender, snakelike fish with a slippery skin. Flesh is firm, mild, and oily. Must be alive until shortly before cooking or flesh will be mushy. Skin before cooking and fillet or cut into 1½-inch (4 cm) lengths. Popular in Japanese restaurants (where it is called unagi), served filleted and grilled, basted with a soy-based glaze.

Weight: Typically 2 to 4 lb (900 g to 1.8 kg) but can be much smaller or larger.

Perch

Type: Lean.

Varieties: Yellow perch is the most common. Walleyed pike is actually a perch, not a pike. Zander (French: *sandre*) is a popular European perch sometimes mislabeled in North America as European walleye, although it is different from, and usually less expensive than, true walleye.

Characteristics: Mild-flavored, flaky white flesh with firm texture and fine grain.

Weight: ½ to 5 lb (0.2 to 2.3 kg).

Pike

Type: Lean.

Varieties: Northern pike is most common in the North America. Walleyed pike or walleye is not a pike but a perch.

Characteristics: Firm white flesh similar to perch but not as thick, and with many small bones.

Weight: 2 to 12 lb (1 to 5.4 kg).

Tilapia

Type: Lean.

Characteristics: Nearly always from aquafarms, because wild tilapia often taste muddy. Firm, mild white flesh.

Tilapia

Weight: Up to 3 lb (1.4 kg); usually about 1½ lb (700 g).

Trout

Trout

Type: Fat.

Varieties: Lake trout, river trout, brook trout, rainbow trout, steelhead trout, many local varieties.

Characteristics: Soft, fine-textured flesh with rich, delicate flavor. Color of flesh may be white, pink, or reddish.

Weight: Lake trout: 4 to 10 lb (2 to 4.5 kg). Others: ½ to 3 lb (0.2 to 1.4 kg).

Whitefish

Type: Fat.

Characteristics: Flaky, white flesh with somewhat sweet flavor.

Weight: 1½ to 6 lb (0.7 to 2.7 kg).

Zander (see Perch)

Whitefish

HANDLING AND STORAGE

Fish and shellfish are some of the most perishable foods you will handle. It is especially important to store them carefully and use them quickly. The fishy taste that turns many people away from fish is actually a sign of decomposition. Fresh fish should taste and smell sweet and fresh.

Guidelines for checking fish quality are summarized in Table 14.1.

STORING FRESH FISH

Objectives

1. To maintain temperature of 30° to 34°F (-1° to 1°C).

2. To keep the fish moist.

3. To prevent fish odors and flavors from being transferred to other foods.

4. To protect the delicate flesh from being bruised or crushed.

Table 14.1 Checklist for Fish Freshness		
Characteristics	**Fresh Fish**	**Not-So-Fresh Fish**
Odor	Fresh and mild, no off odors	Strong fishy odor
Eyes	Clear, shiny, bulging	Cloudy, sunken
Gills	Red or pink	Gray or brown
Texture of flesh	Firm, elastic	Soft, dents easily
Scales	Shiny, tight on skin	Loose, not shiny

Note: Because most fish is not purchased whole or dressed but as fillets, steaks, or other portions, odor must be your primary check for freshness.

Methods

1. On crushed ice—the preferred method. Use drip pans to allow for drainage of melted ice. Change ice daily. Cover container or store in separate box away from other foods.

   Whole fish should be **drawn** (that is, viscera removed; see Figure 14.1) as soon as possible because the entrails deteriorate quickly. Whole or drawn fish are not wrapped. Cut fish (fillets, steaks, portions) should be wrapped or left in original moisture-proof wrap.

2. In refrigerated box at 30° to 34°F (-1° to 1°C)—if crushed ice storage is not available or practical. Wrap all fish or leave in original moisture-proof wrap.

Storage Time

Fresh fish may be stored for 1 or 2 days. If it must be kept longer, you may (1) wrap and freeze it immediately, or (2) cook and then refrigerate it for later use in recipes calling for cooked fish.

Check stored fish for freshness just before you use it. Even if it was fresh when received, it may not be fresh after a few days in storage.

FROZEN, CANNED, AND OTHER PROCESSED FISH

Federal Inspection

The Canadian Food Inspection Agency (CFIA) conducts a program of fish and fish product inspection to promote the safety of fish and shellfish products produced in Canada and imported into Canada. The agency sets the guidelines for product quality and establishes standards for fish and seafood processing plants, for fishing boats, and for equipment used to handle and store fish. These standards cover all aspects of the harvesting and processing of fish products. In order to be approved by the CFIA, a processing facility must use procedures that follow the principles of HACCP (see p. 33). For domestic fish products, the "Canada Inspected" logo is indicated by a round stamp with a maple leaf (Figure 14.5).

Standards cover all aspects of the harvesting and processing of fish products. The program is required for fish that is imported, exported, or shipped between provinces.

Figure 14.5
Canadian Inspected logo
Courtesy of the Canadian Food Inspection Agency

Frozen Fish

Frozen seafood products account for more of the fish served today than does fresh. If it were not for the wide availability of frozen seafood products, commercial kitchens would serve much less fish than they do.

Checking Quality

1. Frozen products should be frozen, not thawed, when received.
2. Look for fresh, sweet odor or none at all. Strong, fishy odor means poor handling.
3. Items should be well wrapped, with no freezer burn.
4. Some frozen fish is *glazed* with a thin layer of ice to prevent drying. Check for shiny surface to make sure glaze has not melted off or evaporated.

Storage

1. Store at 0°F (–18°C) or colder.
2. Keep well wrapped to prevent freezer burn.
3. Maximum storage time:

   Fat fish: 2 months.

   Lean fish: 6 months.
4. Rotate stock—first in, first out.

Thawing and Handling

1. *Frozen raw fish.*
   - Thaw in refrigerator, never at room temperature. Allow 18 to 36 hours, depending on size. Alternative method, if pressed for time: Keep in original moisture-proof wrapper and thaw under cold running water.
   - Small pieces (fillets, steaks, portions) up to 8 oz (250 g) can be cooked from frozen state to make handling easier and to prevent excessive drip loss. Large fish should be thawed for more even cooking from surface to interior.
   - Fillets or other portions that are to be breaded or prepared in some other way before cooking may be partially thawed (for example, for a few seconds in a microwave), then prepped and cooked. They will be easier to handle than if fully thawed.
   - Handle thawed fish as you would fresh fish.
   - Do not refreeze.

2. *Breaded and battered fish, fully prepared entrées, and other frozen, prepared fish items.*
   - Read and follow package directions.
   - Most of these items are cooked from the frozen state, usually in the deep fryer, oven, microwave, or steamer.

Canned Fish

1. Check cans for signs of damage. Discard swollen cans (or return to the supplier).
2. Store, like other canned goods, in a cool, dry place.
3. Opened canned fish should be placed in covered containers, labeled with the contents and date, and refrigerated. It will keep for 2 or 3 days.

SHELLFISH

Shellfish are distinguished from fin fish by their hard outer shells and their lack of backbones or internal skeletons.

There are two classifications of shellfish:

1. **Mollusks** are soft sea animals that fall into three main categories:
   - **Bivalves**, which have a pair of hinged shells (such as clams and oysters).
   - **Univalves**, which have a single shell (such as abalone and conch).
   - **Cephalopods** (such as octopus, squid, and cuttlefish).

   From the scientist's point of view, there are other mollusks as well, but they do not concern us here.

2. **Crustaceans** are animals with segmented shells and jointed legs.

MOLLUSKS

The most important mollusks in commercial kitchens are oysters, clams, mussels, scallops, squid, and octopus.

OYSTERS

Characteristics

St. James River oysters

1. Oysters have rough, irregular shells. The bottom shell is slightly bowl-shaped. The top shell is flat.
2. The flesh of the oyster is extremely soft and delicate and contains a high percentage of water.
3. Oysters are available all year, even in months without an R in their names, but they are at their best in the fall, winter, and spring.
4. There are four main varieties in the United States and Canada, depending on their origin. Note in particular that the dozens of varieties of Eastern oysters are all the same species; they all have different flavors, however, depending on the environment in which they grew.

   Eastern: Known by many local names, depending on their place of origin, such as Bluepoint (Long Island), Box Oyster (Long Island), Chesapeake Bay, Chincoteague (Virginia), Cotuit (Nantucket), Kent Island (Maryland), Malpeque (Prince Edward Island, Canada), Patuxent (Maryland), Apalachicola (Florida), Breton Sound (Louisiana), Wellfleet (Massachusetts).

   Olympia: Very small, from the Pacific coast.

   Belon: European oyster now grown in North America. Shells are flatter than those of Eastern oysters. More properly called *European flat oysters*, reserving the term *Belon* for those flat oysters grown near the mouth of the Loire River in France. Prized for their intense, briny flavor.

   Japanese or Pacific: Usually large oysters from the Pacific coast. The much smaller kumamoto oyster is of the same species.

Pine Island oysters

Figure 14.6
Opening oysters.

(a) Examine the shell to see that it is tightly closed, indicating a live oyster. Rinse the shell under cold, running water. Hold oyster in left hand, as shown. (Left-handers will hold oyster in right hand.) Hold the oyster knife near the tip as shown. Insert the knife between the shells near the hinge.

(b) Twist the knife to break the hinge.

(c) Slide the knife under the top shell and cut through the *adductor* muscle (which closes the shells) near the top shell. Try not to cut the flesh of the oyster, or it will lose plumpness. Remove the top shell.

(d) Carefully cut the lower end of the muscle from the bottom shell to loosen oyster. Remove any particles of shell from the oyster before serving.

Market Forms

1. Live, in the shell.
2. Shucked—fresh or frozen. Shucked oysters are graded by size as follows.

Grade	Number per Gallon (3.8 liters)
Extra Large or Counts	160 or fewer
Large or Extra Selects	161 to 210
Medium or Selects	211 to 300
Small or Standards	301 to 500
Very Small	Over 500

3. Canned—rarely used in food service.

Checking Freshness

1. Oysters in the shell must be alive to be good to eat. Tightly closed shells, or shells that close when jostled, indicate live oysters. Discard dead ones.
2. Live or shucked oysters should have a very mild, sweet smell. Strong odors indicate spoilage.

Opening Oysters

1. Scrub shells thoroughly before opening.
2. Oysters to be served raw must be opened in a way that leaves the bottom shell intact and the tender oyster undamaged. The technique illustrated in Figure 14.6 is one common way of opening oysters. Your instructor may wish to show you another method.
3. Oysters to be cooked may be opened by spreading them on a sheet pan and placing them in a hot oven just until the shells open. Remove from shells and cook immediately. Discard any that do not open.

Storage

1. Keep live oysters in a cold, wet place in the cartons or sacks in which they arrived. They should keep at least 1 week.
2. Store fresh shucked oysters in the original container in refrigerator at 30° to 34°F (–1° to 1°C). They will keep up to 1 week.
3. Keep frozen oysters in freezer, at 0°F (–18°C) or colder, until ready for use. Thaw in refrigerator for 24 hours or more, depending on size of container.

Cooking Oysters

1. Cook just enough to heat through to keep oysters juicy and plump. Overcooking makes them shrunken and dry.
2. Cooking methods: Poaching, deep-frying, baking on the half-shell with toppings, in soups and stews.

CLAMS

Characteristics

There are two major kinds of clams from the east coast of North America: hard shell and soft shell. The West Coast also has some local varieties.

1. Hard-shell clams or quahogs. These go by different names, depending on size.

   Littlenecks are the smallest. They are the most tender for eating raw or for steaming.

   Cherrystones are medium-sized, and perhaps the most common. They can be eaten raw and are good for steaming, though tougher than littlenecks.

   Chowders, the largest, are also called *quahogs* in the Northeast. Rather tough, they are chopped for cooking in chowders or cut into strips for frying.

2. **Soft-shell clams.** These are sometimes called *longnecks* because of the long tube that protrudes from between the shells. They have very thin shells that do not close completely.

They are also called *steamers* because the usual way to serve them is to steam them and serve them with their own broth and with melted butter for dipping.

3. **Cockles.** These are not actually clams but are in a different family, even though they look like tiny clams, usually no more than an inch (2.5 cm) across. They can be cooked like clams and are almost always served in the shell.

Market Forms (Hard-Shell Clams)

1. Live, in the shell.
2. Shucked, fresh or frozen.
3. Canned, whole or chopped.

Clams, clockwise from top left: steamers, littlenecks, cherrystones, chowder clams.

Checking Freshness

Same as for oysters. Clams in the shell must be alive. Live and shucked clams should smell fresh.

Opening Clams

1. Scrub shells thoroughly before opening.
2. Hard-shell clams are sometimes sandy inside, and soft-shell clams nearly always are. They can be flushed as follows:
   - Make a salt brine, using ⅓ cup salt per gallon of water (20 mL salt per liter).
   - Soak the clams in the brine for 20 minutes.
   - Drain and repeat until the clams are free of sand.

Cockles

Figure 14.7
Opening clams.

(a) Examine the shell to see that it is tightly closed, indicating a live clam. Rinse the shell under cold, running water. Avoid jostling the clam too much, or it will "clam up" tighter. Hold clam in left hand as shown (or in right hand if you are left-handed). Place the sharp edge of the clam knife against the crack between the shells.

(b) Squeeze with the fingers of the left hand, forcing the knife between the shells.

(c) Change the angle of the blade as shown in the illustration and slide the knife against the top shell to cut the adductor muscles (clams have two; oysters have only one). Be careful not to cut or pierce the soft clam.

d) Open the clam and finish detaching the meat from the upper shell.

(e) Cut the muscles against the lower shell to loosen the clam completely. Discard the top shell. Remove any particles of shell from the clam before serving.

- Some chefs put cornmeal in the water and refrigerate the clams in it for a day. The clams eat the cornmeal and expel the sand.
- Rinse in fresh water before using.

3. Opening hard-shell clams is different from opening oysters. This technique is illustrated in Figure 14.7.

4. Like oysters, clams to be cooked may be opened by spreading on sheet pans and placing in a hot oven *just* until the shells open. Discard any that do not open, because they were likely dead before cooking.

Storage

Same as for oysters.

Cooking Clams

1. Clams become tough and rubbery if overcooked. Cook just enough to heat through.

2. When steaming clams in the shell, steam just until shells open.

3. Cooking methods: Steaming, poaching, deep-frying, baking on the half-shell with toppings, simmering in soups and chowders.

Mussels, left to right: green, blue (wild), blue (farm-raised).

MUSSELS

Characteristics

The most common mussels resemble small black or dark-blue clams. Their shells are not as heavy as clamshells. Their flesh is yellow to orange in color and firm but tender when cooked. Mussels are harvested worldwide and are also extensively farmed.

Green mussels, from New Zealand and Southeast Asia, are larger and have a lighter-colored gray or tan shell with a green edge. Green mussels often command premium prices.

Market Forms

Most mussels are sold live in the shell. Many are also sold shucked and packed in brine.

Checking Freshness

1. Like oysters and clams, mussels must be alive to be good to eat. Check for tightly closed shells or shells that just close when jostled.

2. Discard any mussels that are very light in weight or seem to be hollow. Also, discard any that are much too heavy—they are probably full of sand.

New Zealand green lips

Cleaning

1. Clean shells thoroughly:
   - Scrub well under cold running water.
   - Scrape off barnacles, if any, with a clam knife.
   - Remove the beard, a fibrous appendage protruding from between the shells (see Figure 14.8). Do not do this until just before cooking, because it may kill the shellfish.

Figure 14.8
When cleaning mussels, pull off the fibrous beard that extends from between the shells.

2. Mussels may be sandy inside if not commercially grown. They may be soaked in brine and flour or cornmeal like clams (see previous section) to rid them of sand.

Storage

Keep refrigerated (32° to 35°F/0° to 2°C) and protect from light. Store in original sack and keep sack damp.

Cooking

Unlike oysters and clams, mussels are almost never served raw. They are usually steamed and served in their cooking broth, in soups, or chilled and served with mayonnaise-type sauces. Cook only until shells open and mussels are heated through. Do not overcook. Discard any that are not open after cooking.

SCALLOPS

Characteristics

1. Scallops are almost always sold shucked. The only part we usually eat is the *adductor muscle*, which closes the shell. If live scallops in the shell are available, leave the orange, crescent-shaped coral attached to the adductor muscle when shucking.

2. There are two main kinds of scallops:

   Bay scallops: Small, with delicate flavor and texture; expensive; 32 to 40 per pound (70 to 88 per kilogram) on average.

   Sea scallops: Larger, not as delicate as bay scallops, but still tender unless overcooked; 10 to 15 per pound (22 to 33 per kilogram) on average.

3. Scallops are creamy white in color and have a sweet flavor.

4. They are available all year.

Market Forms

1. Fresh, shucked. Sold by volume or weight.
2. Frozen.
   - IQF (individually quick frozen).
   - In 5-lb (2.3-kg) blocks.

Scallops with roe or coral

Checking Freshness

A sweet, clean smell is a sign of freshness. Strong fishy odor or a brownish color is a sign of age or spoilage.

Handling

1. Shucked scallops can be cooked without further preparation. They are improved, however, if you pull off the small, tough tendon or sinew on the side of each.
2. Large sea scallops are sometimes cut into smaller pieces before cooking.

Storage

Keep scallops covered and refrigerated (30° to 34°F/−1° to 1°C). Do not let them rest directly on ice, or they will lose flavor and become watery.

Cooking Scallops

Scallops are cooked in almost every way that fish are cooked. The most popular methods are sautéing, deep-frying, broiling, and poaching.

CEPHALOPODS

The term **cephalopod** means "head-foot," referring to the fact that these animals have tentacles, or "legs," attached to the head, surrounding the mouth. The most important cephalopods in the North American kitchen are squid and octopus. A third type, cuttlefish, is similar to squid but is usually seen only in limited markets.

SQUID

Squid, usually referred to on menus by their Italian name, **calamari**, are classified as mollusks, even though they have no external shell. They are soft-bodied animals somewhat resembling octopus, but they have 10 tentacles, 2 of them longer than the others.

Squid must be skinned and eviscerated. The head, beak, and the internal plastic-like quill are discarded. The hollow body and tentacles are eaten. Figure 14.9 illustrates how to clean squid.

Somewhat chewy, squid are cut up and either fried quickly or simmered for about 45 minutes in a seasoned liquid or sauce.

Note: The similar **cuttlefish** has a shorter, thicker body than does squid. Instead of a thin, transparent interior quill, it has a hard, chalky cuttlebone.

OCTOPUS

Octopus (the name means "eight feet") range in size from less than an ounce to many pounds. All sizes are firm-textured, even chewy, but the larger sizes are usually considered too tough to eat. Because of its texture, octopus requires either mechanical tenderization (such as pounding with a mallet) or long, slow cooking in a court bouillon.

Like squid, octopus is cleaned by cutting off the tentacles, discarding the head and beak, and eviscerating the body cavity. Pull the skin off the body pouch and tentacles; it may be necessary to parboil the octopus for a few minutes to loosen the skin. The skin is reddish gray, turning purple-red when cooked.

**Figure 14.9
Cleaning squid.**

(a) Pull off the head. The interior organs will come out with it.

(b) Pull off the skin.

(c) Pull out the plasticlike quill from the body sac. Rinse out the sac to clean it well.

(d) Cut off the tentacles just above the eyes. Discard the head and organs.

(e) Be sure to remove the hard beak, which is found at the center of the tentacle cluster, as shown by the tip of the knife in this picture.

(f) The body sac may be left whole for stuffing or cut into rings for frying, sautéing, or stewing.

CRUSTACEANS

The most important crustaceans in commercial kitchens are lobsters, rock lobsters or langoustes, shrimp, and crabs.

LOBSTERS

Characteristics

1. The northern lobster is perhaps the most prized of all shellfish. It has a large, flexible tail, four pairs of legs, and two large claws. Its shell is dark green or bluish green but turns red when cooked.

2. Meat from the tail, claws, and legs is eaten. It is white and sweet, with a distinctive taste. Claw meat is considered especially good. The coral (roe or eggs), which is dark green when raw and red when cooked, and the green tomalley (liver) in the thorax or body portion are also eaten.

3. Lobsters are classified by weight.

Chicken   1 lb (450 g)
Quarters   1¼ lb (575 g)
Selects   1½ to 2¼ lb (675 to 1025 g)
Jumbos   over 2½ lb (1130 g)

4. Lobsters weighing over 20 lb (9 kg) have been caught, but they are rare.

Figure 14.10
Splitting a lobster for broiling.

(a) Place the lobster on its back on a cutting board. With a firm thrust of a French knife, pierce the head.

(b) Bring the knife down firmly through the center of the lobster to split it in half.

(c) With the hands, crack the back of the shell by spreading the lobster open.

(d) Pull out and discard stomach, a sac just behind the eyes.

(e) If desired, remove the tomalley for use in the crumb stuffing.

(f) With a sharp blow of the back of the knife, crack the claws.

(g) The lobster is ready for broiling. If it is broiled as shown, the end of the tail should be weighted down to keep it from curling.

(h) You may also split the tail all the way through and curl up the two sides as shown. In this position, weighting the tail is not necessary. Note that the claws have been broken off and placed beside the lobster.

Figure 14.11
Cutting a lobster for sautés and stews.

(a) Place the lobster on the cutting board. Pierce the head with a firm thrust of the knife point to kill the lobster quickly.

(b) Cut off the legs and claws.

(c) Remove the tail section from the thorax, either by breaking it off or by inserting the knife behind the thorax as shown and cutting through the flesh.

5. Yield: A 1-lb lobster yields about ¼ lb cooked meat, or a 500-g lobster yields about 125 g cooked meat.

6. Sometimes customers request female lobsters in order to get the coral, so you should be able to tell females from males. Look at the pairs of tiny legs (called *swimmerets*) under the tail. If the pair closest to the front is soft and flexible, the lobster is female. If it is hard, the lobster is male.

Market Forms

1. Live.

2. Cooked meat, fresh or frozen.

Checking Freshness

1. Live lobster must be alive when cooked. This is indicated by movement of the legs and claws and by a tightly curled tail.

2. If the lobster is dead when cooked, the meat will fall apart. If it is alive, the meat will be firm and the tail will spring back when straightened.

(d) Cut the thorax in half lengthwise.

(e) Remove and discard the stomach, a sac just behind the eyes.

(f) Remove the tomalley and coral for use in the sauce to accompany the lobster.

(g) Cut the tail into pieces where the segments join. This is a small lobster. Large tails should be cut into more pieces (at least four or five) so that each piece is not too large.

(h) The cut-up lobster, ready to cook.

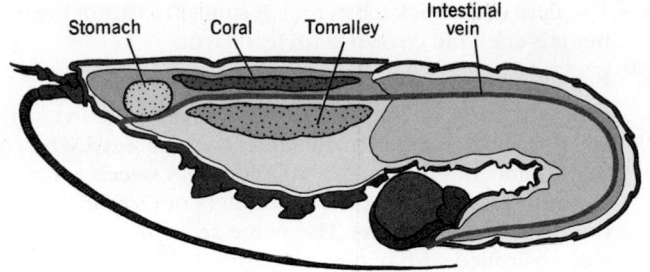

Figure 14.12
Cross section of a female lobster showing the location of the stomach, tomalley, coral, and vein.

3. Sleepers (dying lobsters) should be cooked immediately so the meat will still be usable.

4. Cooked lobster meat (fresh or thawed) should smell fresh and sweet.

Handling

1. Live lobsters are either cooked live or cut up before cooking (as for broiling or sautéing). Live lobsters are plunged head-first into boiling water to kill them instantly. They are then simmered for 5 to 6 minutes per pound (500 g). If served hot, they are drained well and split in half, and the claws are cracked.

2. Splitting and cutting up live lobsters is necessary for certain preparations. Figure 14.10 shows splitting a lobster for broiling. Figure 14.11 shows cutting up a lobster for sautés and stews. Note that the methods are somewhat different.

3. The thorax section contains three parts you should recognize. Figure 14.12 shows their location.

   • The stomach, or sac, located just behind the eyes, is often sandy and should be discarded.

   • The tomalley, or liver, is pale green. It is eaten plain or removed, mashed, and added to sauces that accompany the lobster.

   • The coral, or roe, is red when cooked and dark green when raw. It is present only in females. Like the tomalley, it is considered a delicacy.

   • The intestinal vein may be removed from the split lobster if it contains dark material, but is often left in if its clear.

Storage

1. Live lobsters can be kept in two ways:

   • Packed in moist seaweed or in moist, heavy paper, kept in a cool place.

   • In saltwater. Special lobster tanks are used in restaurants for display and for allowing customers to select their own lobster. Air must be bubbled through the water to keep the lobsters alive.

2. Cooked lobster meat must be covered and refrigerated at 30° to 34°F (–1° to 1°C). It is very perishable and should be used in 1 or 2 days.

Cooking Lobsters

1. Lobster meat becomes tough if cooked at too high a temperature or for too long. Boiling too long will also make the meat dry. Whole lobster is usually cooked by dropping into boiling water and then simmering for 5 to 6 minutes per pound (500 g). For jumbo lobsters, reduce the cooking time slightly.

2. Whole or cut-up lobster can be cooked by simmering in water or court bouillon, simmering in sauce or soup, sautéing, baking, or broiling.

ROCK LOBSTERS

Characteristics

1. Rock lobsters are also known as *spiny lobsters* or *langoustes*. They are warm-water relatives of northern lobsters but have no claws. Only the tails are marketed, sold as *lobster tails*.

Figure 14.13
Peeling and deveining shrimp.

(a) Pull off the legs with your forefinger.

(b) Peel back the shell as shown and remove.

(c) For deep-fried and broiled shrimp, leave on the tail section of the shell for appearance. This also gives you something to hold when dipping the shrimp in batter.

2. The flesh of the rock lobster tail is similar to that of the northern or Maine lobster, but it is drier and coarser, with less flavor.

3. Rock lobster tails weigh from 2 to 12 oz (60 to 340 g).

4. **Langoustines**, or *langostinos*, are smaller relatives of the rock lobster. These small shellfish are often marketed as **rock shrimp**. When out of the shell, they look like shrimp, but their flavor is milder and sweeter than that of shrimp. The term **scampi** (plural form of *scampo*) refers not to shrimp but to a variety of langoustine from Italian waters. The name *scampi* is often used, incorrectly, for large shrimp broiled with butter and garlic.

Market Forms

Nearly all rock lobster tails are sold IQF (individually quick frozen).

Handling and Cooking

1. Rock lobsters are handled and cooked much like northern lobsters. The most common cooking methods are steaming, simmering, and broiling.

2. Tails to be broiled will be moister if poached for 5 minutes before splitting and broiling.

3. Tails steamed or simmered whole should have the shells split before serving as a convenience to the customer.

SHRIMP

Characteristics

1. Shrimp are small crustaceans that look somewhat like tiny, clawless lobsters. Only the tail is marketed and eaten, as a rule.

2. Shrimp come in many varieties, depending on where they are caught, but the particular variety is usually of little importance to the cook.

3. Shrimp are classified by count per pound—the higher the count, the smaller the shrimp. (For example, 16/20 means 16 to 20 per pound.) Classification systems differ by market. That is, in different markets a given size shrimp may have different names.

4. Large shrimp are more expensive per pound, but they require less work to peel and devein.

5. Yield: 1 lb raw shrimp (tails) in the shell yield about ½ lb peeled, cooked shrimp (500 g raw yields 250 g peeled, cooked).

6. The term **prawn** is sometimes used for large shrimp, sometimes for langoustines (see above). Use of the term varies from region to region.

(d) For most other preparations, remove the tail section of the shell.

(e) With a paring knife, make a shallow cut down the back of the shrimp and pull out the intestinal vein, which is just below the surface.

(f) To butterfly shrimp, make the cut in step (e) deeper so the shrimp can be spread open as shown.

Market Forms

1. *Green shrimp* are raw shrimp in the shell.
    Fresh: Not widely available, except near source of supply.
    Frozen: In 5-lb (2.3-kg) blocks.
2. P/D (peeled, deveined): Usually IQF (individually quick frozen).
3. PDC (peeled, deveined, and cooked): Usually IQF.
    Note: IQF shrimp are usually glazed (see p. 440).

Checking Freshness

1. Frozen shrimp should be solidly frozen when received.
2. Glazed shrimp should be shiny, with no freezer burn.
3. All shrimp should smell fresh and sweet. A strong fishy or iodine smell indicates age or spoilage.

Storing

1. Like other frozen fish, shrimp should be kept frozen at 0°F (–18°C) or lower until ready for use.
2. Thaw in refrigerator, allowing sufficient slack time.
3. Fresh or thawed shrimp in the shell are stored on crushed ice, like whole fish.
4. Peeled shrimp lose soluble nutrients and flavor when stored unwrapped on ice. They should be wrapped before placing on ice or covered and simply refrigerated.

Handling

1. Shrimp served hot must normally be peeled and deveined before cooking. Figure 14.13 shows how.
2. Shrimp to be served cold may be peeled after cooking to preserve flavor.
3. Large shrimp are sometimes butterflied, as shown in Figure 14.13f. This is done for appearance (makes shrimp seem larger, with more surface area for breading) and to speed cooking by reducing thickness.

Cooking Shrimp

Like most shellfish, shrimp become tough and rubbery when cooked at too high a heat. Shrimp can be cooked by simmering, deep-frying, sautéing, broiling, and baking.

CRABS

Six kinds of crabs are important in commercial kitchens.

1. **Alaskan king crab.**
    Largest of the crabs, weighing from 6 to 20 lb (2.7 to 9 kg). The meat can be removed in large chunks, making it especially attractive to serve in restaurants. It is expensive.

2. **Alaskan snow crab.**
    Smaller than the king crab. Often used as a less expensive substitute.

3. **Dungeness crab.**
    Another West Coast crab, weighing 1½ to 4 lb (0.7 to 1.8 kg). The meat is very sweet.

4. **Blue crab.**
    Small crab from the East Coast, weighing about 5 oz (150 g). Most frozen crabmeat is from blue crabs.

5. **Soft-shell crab.**
    Actually a molting blue crab, harvested before the new shell has hardened. It is sautéed or fried and eaten shell and all; only the gills and head are removed.

Blue crab

Dungeness crab

Alaskan king crab legs

Alaskan snow crab legs

Soft-shell crabs must be cleaned before being cooked. The procedure is shown in Figure 14.14.

6. **Stone crab.**
   Popular in the Southeast. Only the claws are eaten.

Market Forms

1. Live. Crabs taste best when fresh, but very few (except soft-shell crabs) are purchased live because of the labor required to pick the meat. An average blue crab yields less than 1 ounce (30 g) meat.

2. Cooked, frozen, in the shell.

   King crab legs, whole and split.

   Snow and stone crab claws.

   Soft-shell crabs, whole.

3. Cooked, frozen meat. All varieties.

Freshness and Storage

1. Live crabs should be kept alive until cooked. They are packed in damp seaweed and kept cool.

2. Frozen crabmeat should be treated like any other frozen fish. It is very perishable when thawed.

Handling and Cooking

1. Hard-shell crabs are picked of their meat after cooking.

- Simmer 10 to 15 minutes in salted water (½ cup salt per gallon or 30 mL per liter). Cool rapidly in ice water.
- Break off the pointed shell on the underside (called the *apron*) and remove the top shell.
- Remove and discard the spongy gills and the stomach, which is just behind the eyes.
- Pick out the body meat.
- Crack the legs and claws with a mallet or the back of a heavy knife and pick out the meat.

2. Soft-shell crabs.
- With a knife or shears, cut off the head section, just behind the eyes.
- Lift the pointed, outside corners of the top shell and pull out the spongy gills.
- Cut off the apron, the small flap on the underside.
- Dredge the crab in flour for sautéing, or bread or batter it for deep-frying.

Figure 14.14 Cleaning soft-shell crabs.

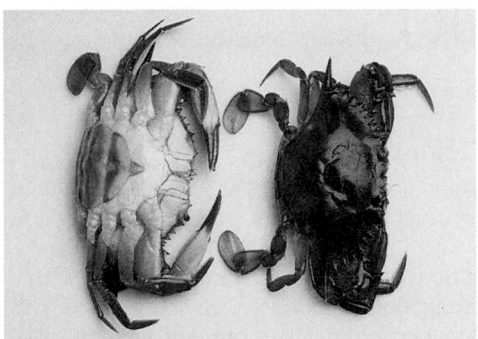

(a) Soft-shell crabs, seen from the bottom and top.

(b) Cut off the head just behind the eyes.

(c) Pull out the stomach sac.

(d) Pull back one side of the soft top shell to reveal the feathery gills.

(e) Pull off the gills. Repeat on the other side.

(f) Cut off the apron on the underside. The wide apron indicates that this is a female crab. Males have a much narrower apron.

3. Frozen crabmeat.

- Crabmeat is usually watery. You may need to squeeze out excess moisture before cooking. Whenever possible, save the liquid for use in sauces and soups.

- Frozen crabmeat is already cooked. It needs only to be heated through to be prepared for serving.

CRAYFISH

Crayfish or *crawfish* (the preferred term in the southern United States) are freshwater relatives of the lobster. Not long ago, they were used almost exclusively in Southern regional cuisine and in French restaurants. With the spreading popularity of Southern cuisines, including Creole and Cajun, they have become more widely available.

Crayfish are marketed live and frozen (peeled tail meat or whole).

MISCELLANEOUS SEAFOOD

Several other seafood items play a role in food service kitchens. They are classified with fish, even though some of them spend part or all of their lives on land, like frogs and snails.

Snails or *escargots* are popular hors d'oeuvres when baked in their shells with a highly seasoned butter. Fresh snails require long, slow cooking before being baked with escargot butter, but canned snails are fully cooked and ready to prepare. Canned snails can be improved, however, by first simmering them in white wine and seasonings.

Frogs' legs are often compared to chicken in taste and texture (but then, so are a lot of things). Only the hind legs are used, and they are sold in pairs. They may be sautéed, deep-fried, or poached and served with a sauce.

Surimi is a processed seafood product made by grinding lean, inexpensive, white fish, combining it with flavorings, and forming it into various shapes. The most popular shapes are shredded crab and crab leg segments, but other items, such as lobster claws, are also available. Coloring is added for a realistic appearance. Originally from Japan, surimi has found growing acceptance in North America because of the reasonably good quality of the product and the high cost of crab and lobster.

■ TERMS FOR REVIEW

fin fish	anadromous	cockle	rock shrimp
shellfish	catadromous	adductor muscle	scampi
flaking	drawn	squid	prawn
lean and fat fish	mollusks	calamari	soft-shell crab
dressed	bivalve	cuttlefish	crayfish
fillet	univalve	coral	surimi
flatfish	crustacean	tomalley	
round fish	cephalopod	langoustine	

■ QUESTIONS FOR DISCUSSION

1. Fish has very little connective tissue. How does this affect the ways in which you handle it and cook it?

2. Based on what you learned about fat and lean fish and about individual species of fish, can you suggest at least one cooking method for each of the following?

Mackerel	Salmon
Cod	Perch
Flounder	Swordfish
Trout	Whitefish
Red snapper	Halibut

3. List and describe the major market forms of fresh fish.

4. What are the differences between filleting flatfish and round fish? Describe or demonstrate.

5. You have just received delivery of fresh whole red snapper and fresh cod fillets. What should you check before ac-cepting the shipment? After accepting the fish, what do you do with them?

6. You are making a casserole of shrimp with a prepared Newburg sauce and frozen, glazed cooked shrimp. When you add the frozen shrimp to the sauce, it thins out so much it is no longer usable. Why did this happen, and how could you have prevented it?

7. What is the most important indication of freshness in fresh oysters, clams, lobsters, and crabs? Describe how you would preserve this freshness.

8. How does opening oysters differ from opening clams, and how is it similar?

9. What happens to most kinds of shellfish when they are overcooked?

15

Cooking Fish and Shellfish

Because most fish and shellfish have little connective tissue, the procedures for cooking them are somewhat different from those for cooking meats and poultry. When we cook meats, we are often concerned with tenderizing the product. Fish is naturally tender, however, and cooking—especially overcooking—is more likely to toughen the product and dry it out.

In this chapter, we apply basic cooking principles to the preparation of fish dishes. Our goals are to cook the product just to doneness, to preserve moisture and texture, and to preserve and enhance natural flavors.

Of course, your study of these procedures depends on your understanding of the basic information on fish in the previous chapter. In particular, you may want to review the sections on testing for doneness and on fat and lean fish and their appropriate cooking methods.

BAKING

Whole fish and fish portions may be cooked by baking in an oven. Although large whole fish may be baked, this is usually not practical in volume food service. The method is more often used with steaks and fillets and with small fish. Baking is also a popular method for preparing shellfish such as stuffed clams or oysters.

Baking is often combined with other cooking methods. For example, partially broiled fish can be finished by baking. Baked fish casseroles are usually made with cooked fish.

Whole fish or portions of fish baked in the oven may also be referred to as roasted, as is currently the fashion. The term *roasting* may be applied both to basic baking and to moist baking, discussed below.

After reading this chapter, you should be able to

1. **Cook fish and shellfish by baking.**

2. **Cook fish and shellfish by broiling.**

3. **Cook fish and shellfish by sautéing and pan-frying.**

4. **Cook fish and shellfish by deep-frying.**

5. **Cook fish and shellfish by poaching in court bouillon.**

6. **Cook fish and shellfish by poaching in fumet and wine.**

7. **Cook fish and shellfish by mixed cooking techniques.**

8. **Prepare dishes made of raw seafood.**

Guidelines for Baking Fish

1. Fat fish are better for baking because they are less likely to dry out.

2. Lean fish may be baked successfully if great care is taken not to overcook them. Basting with butter or oil helps prevent drying.

3. In most cases, baking temperatures are from 350° to 400°F (175° to 200°C). Large fish are best baked at the lower end of this range so they bake more evenly.

   It is also possible to bake thin fillets or slices of fillets (cut like scaloppine) at very high temperatures. Great care must be used in this case because the fish may cook in a minute or less, and a few seconds too long might ruin it. The effect of the high heat is almost like broiling, and the normal guidelines for broiling thin fish fillets should be followed, as explained in the next section.

4. It is not possible to give specific baking times because fish vary so much in shape and composition. Different ingredients and types of baking pans also affect the baking time. The following guideline is helpful, however: Measure the thickness of the fish at the thickest point. At 400°F (200°C), baking time is about 10 minutes per inch (2.5 cm) of thickness.

5. Serving baked fish with a sauce or seasoned butter enhances its moistness and improves palatability. Serving with lemon also enhances the fish.

6. If fish is baked with a moist topping or sauce, strictly speaking, it is no longer being cooked by a dry-heat method. However, because the basic procedure is the same, the fish is treated as if it were.

Procedure for Baking Fish

1. Collect all equipment and food supplies.

2. Prepare and season fish (whole, steaks, fillets) as directed in the recipe.

3. Place the fish on oiled or buttered baking sheets. Brush tops with oil or butter.

   Alternative method: Dip fish in oil or melted butter to coat both sides. Place on baking sheets.

4. Apply toppings, if desired. Examples: seasoned bread crumbs, lemon slices, mushrooms or other vegetable garnish, and sauces.

5. Bake at 350° to 400°F (175° to 200°C) until done. If the fish is lean and has no moist topping, baste with oil or butter during baking.

MOIST BAKING OR BRAISING

As we noted above, if fish is baked with moist ingredients or with liquids, strictly speaking, the method is no longer a dry-heat method, although such preparations are included in this section. In French cooking, baking fish—usually whole fish or large pieces—with vegetables and liquid is called *braising*. To avoid confusion with the braising method as applied to meats, however, we avoid that term and refer to such dishes as *baked*.

This procedure is the same as the basic procedure for baking fish described above, with the following special features:

1. The baking pan should be just large enough to hold the fish, so you will not need too much liquid.

2. The bottom of the pan is buttered or oiled, then covered with a layer of sliced or chopped vegetables, such as carrots, onions, shallots, and mushrooms. The vegetables may be raw or first sautéed gently in butter or oil. The fish is then placed on top of the vegetables.

3. Frequently, a small amount of liquid, such as equal parts wine and fish stock, is added. Just enough liquid is used to cover the fish about halfway or less. During baking, the fish is basted with this liquid.

4. The fish may be baked uncovered or covered only lightly. It should not be covered tightly, however, because the liquid must be able to reduce somewhat so it will become more concentrated and more flavorful. Remember also that more liquid will be released from the fish, diluting the cooking liquid.

5. For service, the fish is removed from the dish. The liquid is strained, degreased, reduced, and finished in various ways, such as by adding butter, cream, or velouté sauce.

You can see that this is a sort of combination technique. Because it often uses wine and other liquids, the method is, in some ways, similar to poaching in wine, as explained on page 483.

 ## Baked Cod Fillets Portugaise

Portions: 24   Portion size: 5 oz (150 g) fish   2 fl oz (60 mL) sauce

U.S.	Metric	Ingredients
24	24	Cod fillets, 5-oz (150-g) portions
⅓ cup	75 mL	Lemon juice
8 fl oz	250 mL	Melted butter or oil
to taste	to taste	Salt
to taste	to taste	White pepper
1½ qt	1.5 L	Portuguaise Sauce (p. 176)

■ Procedure

1. Place cod fillets on a well-oiled baking sheet or baking pan, flesh side up (that is, skin side down).

2. Brush the fish lightly with lemon juice. Then brush generously with the butter or oil and season lightly with salt and pepper.

3. Place the pan in a preheated 350°F (175°C) oven until done, about 10–15 minutes.

4. Halfway through the cooking time, check the fish and, if the tops appear to be drying out, brush with more butter or oil.

5. Serve each portion with 2 fl oz (60 mL) sauce. Nap the sauce across the center of the portion. Do not cover the entire fillet.

Per serving:
Calories, 170; Protein, 16g; Fat, 10 g (53% cal.); Cholesterol, 60 mg; Carbohydrates, 4 g; Fiber, 1 g; Sodium, 250 mg.

VARIATIONS

Many other fish may be baked according to the basic recipe, such as

Haddock (fillets or steaks)	Pike (fillets)	Halibut (steaks or fillets)	Salmon (fillets or steaks)
Snapper (fillets)	Perch (fillets)	Bluefish (fillets)	Swordfish (steaks)
Bass (fillets)	Flounder (fillets)	Mackerel (fillets)	Whitefish (fillets)

Other appropriate sauces may be used, such as

Melted butter	Tomato and tomato-based sauces such as Creole (not for salmon or for very delicate fish like flounder)
Beurre noisette	Mustard (for strong-flavored fish only, such as mackerel or bluefish)
Maitre d'hôtel butter	Curry (not for salmon or other fat fish)

Baked Fish with Tomatoes and Mushrooms

Portions: 10   Portion size: 1 fish

U.S.	Metric	Ingredients
10	10	Small whole fish, about 12 oz (375 g) each (see note)
to taste	to taste	Salt
to taste	to taste	Pepper
pinch	pinch	Dried thyme
10	10	Parsley sprigs
as needed	as needed	Olive oil
8 oz	250 g	Onion, small dice
1 oz	30 g	Shallots, minced
8 oz	250 g	Mushrooms, chopped
1 lb	500 g	Tomato concassé
8 fl oz	250 mL	Dry white wine

Per serving:
Calories, 350; Protein, 55 g; Fat, 9 g (24% cal.); Cholesterol, 120 mg; Carbohydrates, 6 g; Fiber, 1 g; Sodium, 210 mg.

Note: Many types of fish can be used, including sea bass, red snapper, porgy, perch, and trout. As an alternative use thick steaks or thick pieces of fillet from larger fish such as cod or tilefish.

■ Procedure

1. Scale and clean the fish but leave the heads on. Season the fish inside and out with salt and pepper, and put a small pinch of thyme and a sprig of parsley in the cavity of each.

2. Select as many baking pans as necessary to just hold the fish in a single layer. Oil the pans with a little olive oil.

3. Sauté the onions and shallots in a little olive oil for about 1 minute. Add the mushrooms and sauté lightly.

4. Put the sautéed vegetables and the tomatoes in the bottoms of the baking pans.

5. Put the fish in the pans. Oil the tops lightly. Pour in the wine.

6. Bake at 400°F (200°C) until the fish is done. The time will vary but will average 15–20 minutes. Baste often with the liquid in the pan.

7. Remove the fish and keep them warm until they are to be plated.

8. Remove the vegetables from the pans with a slotted spoon and check for seasonings. Serve a spoonful of the vegetables with the fish, placing it under or alongside each fish.

9. Strain, degrease, and reduce the cooking liquid slightly. Just before serving, moisten each portion with 1–2 tbsp (15–30) mL of the liquid.

VARIATIONS

Baked Fish à la Menagère
Use butter instead of olive oil. Substitute sliced leeks for part or all of the onion. Omit the tomatoes. Add 4 oz (125 g) sliced carrot and cook it with the leek. Slice the mushrooms instead of chopping them, and add them to the pan raw. Add 1 cup (250 mL) fish stock along with the wine. After straining and reducing the cooking liquid in step 9, thicken it very lightly with a little beurre manié. Enrich the sauce with a little raw butter or cream.

Baked Stuffed Mackerel

Portion: 10   Portion size: 1 fish, with stuffing

U.S.	Metric	Ingredients	Procedure
10	10	Mackerel, about 8–12 oz (250–375 g) each, or other small fish	1. Fillet the fish (see p. 431, Figure 14.4), but leave the skin on.
8 oz	250 g	Fresh bread crumbs	2. Combine the crumbs, butter, and herbs in a bowl. Toss lightly until mixed.
3 fl oz	90 mL	Melted butter	
1 tbsp	15 mL	Chopped parsley	3. Mix the beaten egg, lemon zest, and lemon juice. Add to the crumbs and mix gently. Season to taste.
½ tsp	2 mL	Dried thyme	
1	1	Egg, beaten	
¼ tsp	1 mL	Grated lemon zest	
2 fl oz	60 mL	Lemon juice	
to taste	to taste	Salt	
as needed	as needed	Oil or melted butter	4. Place 10 fillets (that is, half of each fish) on a well-oiled baking sheet, skin side down.
			5. Top each fillet with 1½ oz (50 g) stuffing. (Portion with a No. 24 scoop.) Shape the stuffing to fit the length of the fish.
			6. Place the second fillet on top and press down lightly.
			7. Brush fish with oil or melted butter.
			8. Bake at 350°F (175°C) until done, about 15–20 minutes.

Per serving:
Calories, 600; Protein, 43 g; Fat, 41 g (63% cal.); Cholesterol, 165 mg; Carbohydrates, 12 g; Fiber, 1 g; Sodium, 330 mg.

 Baked Clams Oreganata

Portions: 10   Portion size: 3 clams (appetizer portion)

U.S.	Metric	Ingredients	Procedure
30	30	Cherrystone clams	1. Open the clams (see Figure 14.8 for technique). Catch the juice in a bowl.
			2. Remove the clams from the shell. Place them in a strainer over the bowl of juice. Let them drain 15 minutes in the refrigerator. Save the 30 best half-shells.
			3. Chop the clams into small pieces.
2 fl oz	60 mL	Olive oil	4. Heat the oil in a sauté pan. Add the onion and garlic. Sauté about 1 minute but do not brown.
1 oz	30 g	Onions, shallots, or scallions, chopped fine	5. Add *half* the clam juice and reduce by three-fourths over high heat.
1 tsp	5 mL	Finely chopped garlic	6. Remove from the heat and add the lemon juice, crumbs, parsley, oregano, and white pepper. Mix gently to avoid making the crumbs pasty.
1 fl oz	30 mL	Lemon juice	
10 oz	300 g	Fresh bread crumbs	
1 tbsp	15 mL	Chopped parsley	7. Taste and adjust seasonings if necessary. (Clams are usually very salty.)
¾ tsp	3 mL	Dried oregano	
⅛ tsp	0.5 mL	White pepper	8. Cool the mixture. Mix in the chopped clams.
⅓ cup	25 g	Parmesan cheese	9. Fill the 30 clam shells with the mixture. Sprinkle with parmesan cheese and (very lightly!) with paprika.
as needed	as needed	Paprika	
			10. Place on a sheet pan and refrigerate until needed.
10	10	Lemon wedges	11. For each order, bake 3 clams in hot oven (450°F/230°C) until they are hot and the top is brown.
			12. Garnish with lemon wedge.

Per serving:
Calories, 180; Protein, 10 g; Fat, 8 g (41% cal.); Cholesterol, 20 mg; Carbohydrates, 16 g; Fiber, 1 g; Sodium, 230 mg.

Note: Clams and oysters are often baked on a bed of rock salt to hold them steady. The rock salt also holds heat well.

Smoke-Roasted Salmon Fillet with Pepper Salad

Portions: 12   Portion size: 4 oz (125 g) fish
4 oz (125 g) garnish.

U.S.	Metric	Ingredients
3 lb	1.5 kg	Salmon fillets
1 fl oz	30 mL	Vegetable oil
¾ tsp	3 mL	Ground coriander
¾ tsp	3 mL	Ground cumin
¼ tsp	1 mL	Ground cloves
½ tsp	2 mL	Ground fennel
½ tsp	2 mL	Black pepper
1 tsp	5 mL	Salt
3 lb	1.5 kg	Basque-Style Pepper Salad (p. 692)

■ P r o c e d u r e

1. Cut the salmon fillets into 4-oz (125-g) portions.

2. Brush the salmon lightly with oil.

3. Combine the spices and salt. Sprinkle over the fish to coat them in a light, even layer.

4. Set up a smoke-roasting system as shown in Figure 5.1. Heat the pan of wood chips or sawdust on top of the stove until smoke starts to appear. Lay the salmon fillets on the rack, cover, and turn the heat to medium-low. Smoke-roast for 2 minutes.

5. Transfer the pan to an oven preheated to 400°F (200°C) and continue roasting for another 8–10 minutes, until the fish is just cooked through.

6. Arrange the salmon fillets and the pepper salad on plates. Serve immediately.

Per serving:
Calories, 370; Protein, 22 g; Fat, 29 g (70% cal.); Cholesterol, 70 mg; Carbohydrates, 6 g; Fiber, 2 g; Sodium, 250 mg.

Smoke-Roasted Salmon Fillet with Pepper Salad

Roasted Monkfish Wrapped in Prosciutto

Portion: 12   Portion size: 6 oz (175 g) fish
2⅓ oz (70 g) relish

U.S.	Metric	Ingredients
6 oz	175 g	Sugar
10 fl oz	300 mL	Water
1½	1½	Lemons, zest only
3	3	Rosemary sprigs
4 lb 8 oz	2.2 kg	Monkfish fillets
1 lb	500 g	Prosciutto, sliced
as needed	as needed	Olive oil
5 oz	150 g	Black olives, pitted, coarsely chopped
12 oz	375 g	Tomatoes, peeled, seeded, and chopped
4 oz	125 g	Capers
½ oz	15 g	Chives, chopped
7 fl oz	200 mL	Olive oil
as needed	as needed	Whole chives for garnish

■ P r o c e d u r e

1. To prepare a syrup, dissolve the sugar in the water over low heat, bring to the boil, then remove from the heat. Add the lemon zest and rosemary sprigs and let stand to cool.

2. Brush the monkfish with the syrup and lay on the prosciutto. Roll the prosciutto around the fish and tie securely with string.

3. Brush with olive oil and sear under a broiler or salamander. Finish cooking in a moderately hot oven (375°F/190°C). Remove from the oven and allow to rest a few minutes.

4. Prepare a relish by mixing together the olives, tomato, capers, chives, and olive oil.

5. Slice the rested monkfish into thick slices resembling tournedos, allowing 3 per person. Arrange on plates. Spoon the relish around the fish. Garnish with whole chives laid across the plate.

Per serving:
Calories, 460; Protein, 36 g; Fat, 29 g (55% cal.); Cholesterol, 70 mg; Carbohydrates, 17 g; Fiber, 1 g; Sodium, 1260 mg.

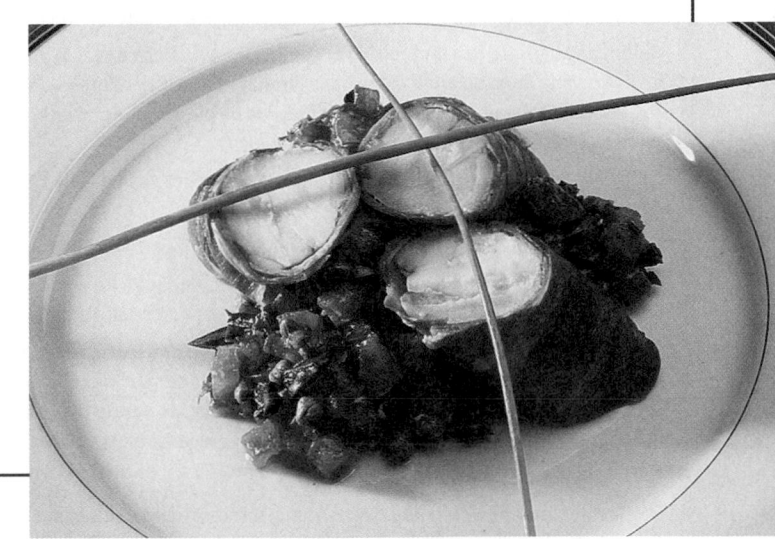

Roasted Monkfish Wrapped in Prosciutto

Baked Oysters with Balsamic Vinegar, Arugula, and Pine Nuts

Portions: 12   Portion size: 3 oysters (appetizer portion)

U.S.	Metric	Ingredients
36	36	Oysters
½ oz	15 mL	Balsamic vinegar
1 oz	30 g	Arugula, chopped
1 oz	30 g	Pine nuts, toasted
1½ fl oz	45 mL	Olive oil

■ P r o c e d u r e

1. Open the oysters as shown in Figure 14.7. Arrange the oysters on a sheet pan.

2. Top each oyster with a few drops of balsamic vinegar, then with a little chopped arugula, a few pine nuts, and, finally, about ¼ tsp (1.2 mL) olive oil. If the oysters are not salty, you may wish to add a little salt.

3. Bake at 450°F (230°C) for a few minutes, just until the oysters are hot. Serve immediately.

Per serving:
Calories, 70; Protein, 3 g; Fat, 6 g (77% cal.); Cholesterol, 15 mg; Carbohydrates, 2 g; Fiber, 0 g; Sodium, 75 mg.

BROILING AND GRILLING

Broiled and grilled seafood items, like grilled meats, are increasingly popular. Customers perceive them as simpler and more healthful and, because they are prepared quickly, as fitting the faster pace of modern life.

Grilled dishes are, in their purest form, simple and straightforward, but they lend themselves to many variations in presentation. By varying sauces, vegetable accompaniments, and garnishes, you can offer a great assortment of grilled fish on the menu. And, because the sauces and accompaniments are generally prepared ahead of time, these dishes are still quick to prepare, even if the presentation is elaborate.

A slightly crisped, browned, or grill-marked surface is important to the appeal of grilled or broiled fish. Do not cover the item with sauce, and do not serve too much sauce. A small piece of seasoned butter or a drizzle of a flavorful condiment or sauce can be used to decorate the top of the item. In most other cases, it is better to place sauces on the side. Appropriate healthful sauces include vegetable coulis and salsas. For richer dishes, beurre blanc is a good accompaniment, especially for lean fish like halibut.

Another popular approach is to serve the fish without a sauce, except perhaps for a small dab of a condiment such as a relish or chutney, and to complement the fish with an attractive variety of vegetables.

Guidelines for Broiling or Grilling Fish

1. Because of the intense heat of the broiler, great care is needed to avoid overcooking the fish.

2. Select appropriate fish for broiling or grilling. Small slices and thin fillets are usually too delicate to be placed directly on the grid of a broiler or grill. Arrange them on oiled sheet pans, broiler platters, or other baking dishes or pans, and cook under a broiler. Whole fish or thick slices of firm fish such as salmon, shark, and swordfish can be placed directly on the grill if care is taken to avoid breaking them up. Be sure the grid is clean and oiled to prevent sticking.

3. Fat fish is best for broiling because it doesn't get as dry as lean fish. However, all fish, fat or lean, should be coated with a fat before broiling to reduce drying.

4. Lean fish may be dredged in flour before dipping in oil or melted butter. The flour helps form a flavorful browned crust.

5. Instead of being dredged with flour, fish may be coated with fat and then with bread crumbs or cornmeal. Use caution, however, as bread crumbs burn very easily. Use this technique only with items that cook quickly.

6. If the fish has an attractive skin (such as red snapper and black sea bass), the skin may be left on and used as the presentation side. This enhances appearance and also helps hold the delicate flesh together. Make sure the fish is thoroughly scaled. To prevent splitting during cooking, score the skin with a sharp knife, making a series of parallel cuts across the fish or cutting in a diamond pattern for larger fish. For small fillets, scoring may not be necessary.

7. Broil fish to order and serve immediately.

8. Broiled fish may be garnished *lightly* with paprika if more color is desired. But don't overdo it. A common fault in broiling or baking fish is coating them with a heavy layer of paprika, which ruins their delicate flavor.

9. Thick cuts should be turned once during broiling in order to cook evenly. Thin pieces may be arranged on an oiled pan and broiled on one side only. Lobster is also broiled without turning.

Procedure for Broiling or Grilling Fish

1. Collect all equipment and food supplies.

2. Prepare the fish as required: Season and coat with oil or butter, with flour and then fat, or with fat and then bread crumbs or cornmeal.

3. Preheat the broiler or grill.

4. With a wire brush, remove burned or charred particles of food from the broiler grate or grill. Brush the grate with an oiled cloth to coat it lightly with oil.

5. Broil thick cuts on both sides, turning once. Broil thin pieces on one side only.

6. Serve immediately, with appropriate sauce and garnish.

Broiled Fish Steaks Maître d'Hôtel

Portions: as needed   Portion size: 5–6 oz (150–175 g)

U.S.	Metric	Ingredients
as needed	as needed	Fish steaks, 5–6 oz (150–175 g) each (see note)
to taste	to taste	Salt
to taste	to taste	White pepper
as needed	as needed	Oil or melted butter
as needed	as needed	Maître d'hôtel butter
as needed	as needed	Lemon wedges

Per serving:
Calories, 320; Protein, 27 g; Fat, 22 g (63% cal.); Cholesterol, 105 mg; Carbohydrates, 2 g; Fiber, 1 g; Sodium, 2460 mg.

Note: Salmon, tuna, and swordfish steaks are ideal for broiling, but they are also expensive. Other fish steaks that may be broiled include cod, haddock, halibut, king mackerel, and large bluefish.

Fillets may also be broiled using this recipe if they are thick or firm enough to avoid breaking up on the grill.

■ P r o c e d u r e

1. Season the steaks with salt and pepper.
2. Place the oil or melted butter in a small pan. Dip both sides of the steaks in it to coat completely.
3. Place on the rack of a preheated broiler. Broil under medium heat until half cooked. Turn over with a spatula. At this point, it may be necessary to brush the tops of the steaks with more oil or butter if they are becoming dry.
4. Complete the cooking on the second side.
5. Plate the fish. Place a slice of seasoned butter on top of each steak. Garnish the plate with a lemon wedge. Serve immediately.

V A R I A T I O N

For lean white fish (halibut, cod, etc.), dredge in flour and shake off excess before dipping in the melted butter or oil. Broil as in basic recipe.

Other compound butters may be used in place of maître d'hôtel butter.

For fat fish, omit the butter and serve the fish with a small quantity of flavorful vinaigrette.

 ## Grilled Tuna with Sauce Vierge and Spinach

Portions: 12   Portion size: 5 oz (150 g) tuna
4 oz (125 g) spinach
1⅓ fl oz (40 mL) sauce

U.S.	Metric	Ingredients
7 fl oz	200 mL	Olive oil
⅔ oz	20 g	Garlic, chopped
1½ tsp	10 g	Basil, chopped
1	1	Small chile, such as cayenne, coarsely chopped
to taste	to taste	Salt
to taste	to taste	Pepper
12	12	Tuna steaks, 5 oz (150 g) each
3 lb	1.5 g	Cooked spinach, buttered
1 pt	500 mL	Sauce Vierge (p. 197)

■ P r o c e d u r e

1. Combine the olive oil, garlic, basil, chile, salt, and pepper to make a marinade.
2. Marinate the tuna for 1 hour.
3. Grill the tuna steaks, keeping them medium rare.
4. For each portion, place 4 oz (125 g) hot spinach on a plate. Place the tuna steak on top. Drizzle the sauce around.

Per serving:
Calories, 500; Protein, 35 g; Fat, 39 g (68% cal.); Cholesterol, 75 mg; Carbohydrates, 6 g; Fiber, 3 g; Sodium, 210 mg.

Grilled Tuna with Sauce Vierge and Spinach

Grilled Mahi-Mahi with Fruit Salsa

Portions: 12   Portion size: 6 oz (180 g)

U.S.	Metric	Ingredients
3 fl oz	90 mL	Lemon juice
1 tsp	5 mL	Salt
¼ tsp	1 mL	White pepper
⅛ tsp	0.5 mL	Cayenne
12	12	Mahi-mahi fillets, 6 oz (180 g) each
4 fl oz, or as needed	125 mL, or as needed	Vegetable oil
1 lb 2 oz	600 g	Fruit Salsa (p. 199)

Per serving:
Calories, 210; Protein, 32 g; Fat, 6 g (27% cal.); Cholesterol, 125 mg;
Carbohydrates, 5 g; Fiber, 1 g; Sodium, 170 mg.

■ P r o c e d u r e

1. In a nonreactive container, mix together the lemon juice, salt, white pepper, and cayenne.

2. Place the fish fillets in the mixture, turning them to coat all sides. Let stand 15 minutes.

3. Remove the fish from the marinade. Dip the fillets in the oil and remove, letting the excess oil drip off.

4. Grill the fillets on a preheated, seasoned grill or broiler. Grill until just done. Do not overcook, or the fish will be dry.

5. Plate the fillets. Next to each fillet, place 1½ oz (50 g) fruit salsa.

 ## Broiled Mako Shark Steaks with Browned Garlic Vinaigrette

Portions: 10   Portion size: 6 oz (175 g)

U.S.	Metric	Ingredients
15–20	15–20	Garlic cloves
8 fl oz	250 mL	Olive oil
10	10	Mako shark steaks, about 6 oz (175 g) each
to taste	to taste	Salt
to taste	to taste	Pepper
4 fl oz	125 mL	Olive oil
2 fl oz	60 mL	Red wine vinegar
to taste	to taste	Salt
to taste	to taste	Pepper
2 tbsp	30 mL	Chopped parsley

Per serving:
Calories, 530; Protein, 36 g; Fat, 42 g (71 % cal.); Cholesterol, 85 mg;
Carbohydrates, 2 g; Fiber, 0 g; Sodium, 135 mg.

■ P r o c e d u r e

1. Cut the garlic cloves crosswise into thick slices.

2. Heat the oil in a small sauté pan over moderate heat. Add the garlic and sauté gently until light golden brown. Do not allow the garlic to become too dark, or it will be bitter.

3. Remove the browned garlic with a slotted spoon. Reserve the garlic and the oil separately.

4. Brush the shark steaks with about half the garlic-flavored oil from step 3. Season to taste with salt and pepper.

5. Place the steaks on a heated broiler or grill and broil until just done. Do not overcook or the steaks will be dry.

6. Beat the remaining oil from step 3 with the additional oil and the vinegar to make a basic vinaigrette. Season to taste with salt and pepper.

7. Plate the shark steaks and top with the browned garlic from step 3. Drizzle about 1 fl oz (30 mL) vinaigrette around the fish. Sprinkle with chopped parsley.

V A R I A T I O N

Substitute other firm fish steaks, such as swordfish or tuna, for the shark.

Broiled Salmon in Escabeche

Portions: 12   Portion size: 5–6 oz (150–180 g)

U.S.	Metric	Ingredients
4 fl oz	120 mL	Lime juice
1 tsp	5 mL	Salt
½ tsp	2 mL	Pepper
½ tsp	2 mL	Ground cumin
½ tsp	2 mL	Ground allspice
12	12	Salmon steaks, 5–6 oz (150–180 g) each
2 fl oz	60 mL	Vegetable oil
12 oz	360 g	Onion, sliced ⅛ in. (3 mm) thick
6	6	Garlic cloves, peeled and halved
4	4	Pickled jalapeños, sliced
		Sachet:
6	6	Whole cloves
½ tsp	2 mL	Whole allspice
1 tsp	5 mL	Peppercorns
½ tsp	2 mL	Cumin seed
3	3	Bay leaves, broken
1 tsp	5 mL	Dried oregano
1-in. piece	2–3 cm piece	Cinnamon stick
6 fl oz	180 mL	Cider vinegar
1 pt	500 mL	Water
as needed	as needed	Vegetable oil
as needed	as needed	Cilantro leaves

Per serving:
Calories, 260; Protein, 31 g; Fat, 12 g (43% cal.); Cholesterol, 80 mg; Carbohydrates, 5 g; Fiber, 0 g; Sodium, 150 mg.

ESCABECHE

The word *escabeche* (ess ka bey chay) is Spanish for "brine," and *en escabeche* means "pickled." Many foods *en escabeche* are popular in the cuisines of Mexico, especially seafood and vegetables. The method originated as a way to preserve foods by pickling them in vinegar and spices. Today, with refrigeration available, they are enjoyed for their flavors more than their keeping qualities.

In a true escabeche, the food is left in the vinegar mixture for a time at room temperature or refrigerated long enough for it to develop a pickled taste. It is later served at room temperature or rewarmed. In addition, fish prepared this way is often pan-fried in oil before being pickled. The accompanying recipe is modified from the traditional methods for a lighter flavor. The fish is grilled rather than pan-fried, and the spice and vinegar mixture is served with it as a sauce rather than being used to pickle it.

■ Procedure

1. In a nonreactive container, mix together the lime juice, salt, pepper, ground cumin, and ground allspice.
2. Place the salmon steaks in the mixture, turning them to coat both sides.
3. Refrigerate 30–60 minutes.
4. Heat the oil in a sauté pan over moderate heat.
5. Add the onion. Sauté until lightly browned.
6. Add the garlic and jalapeños. Sauté 2–3 minutes.
7. Add the sachet, vinegar, and water. Simmer over low heat until reduced by half.
8. Remove the salmon from the marinade and pat dry with clean towels.
9. Dip the salmon in oil and remove, letting the excess oil drip off.
10. Grill the steaks on a preheated, seasoned grill or broiler. Grill until just done. Do not overcook, or the fish will be dry.
11. Serve each steak with about 1½ fl oz (45 mL) onion, spice, and vinegar mixture. Top with a few cilantro leaves.

V A R I A T I O N

For a more traditional escabeche, add the fish to the hot vinegar mixture and cool. After 1 hour, refrigerate the fish in the liquid. To serve, rewarm to room temperature or slightly warmer.

Broiled Lobster

Portions: 1   Portion size: 1 lobster

U.S.	Metric	Ingredients
1	1	Live lobster, 1–1½ lb (450–700 g)
1 tsp	5 mL	Finely chopped shallot
1 tbsp	15 g	Butter
1 oz	30 g	Dry bread crumbs
3 tbsp	45 mL	Chopped parsley
to taste	to taste	Salt
to taste	to taste	Pepper
as needed	as needed	Melted butter
2 fl oz	60 mL	Melted butter
as needed	as needed	Lemon wedges

Per serving:
Calories, 760; Protein, 12 g; Fat, 71 g (82% cal.); Cholesterol, 210 mg; Carbohydrates, 22 g; Fiber, 1 g; Sodium, 1090 mg.

■ P r o c e d u r e

1. Split the lobster as shown in Figure 14.11. Remove and discard the stomach (just behind the eyes) and the vein that runs through the tail. The liver and coral may be left in or removed and added to the stuffing (step 3), as desired.

2. Sauté the shallot in the butter just until it starts to become tender.

3. Optional step: Chop the lobster coral and liver (tomalley) and add to the pan. Sauté just until firm, about 10–20 seconds.

4. Add the bread crumbs and brown them lightly in the butter. Remove from the heat.

5. Add the parsley. Season the crumbs with salt and pepper.

6. Place the lobster shell side down on a small sheet pan or in a shallow baking pan. Fill the body cavity with the crumb mixture. Do not put the crumbs over the tail meat.

7. Brush the tail well with melted butter.

8. Place a few of the legs on top of the stuffing. If the lobster was split by the first method, shown in Figure 14.11g, weight the end of the tail down to keep it from curling.

9. Place the lobster under the broiler at least 6 in. (15 cm) from the heat. Broil until the crumbs are well browned.

10. At this point, the lobster will probably not be completely cooked, unless it is very small and the broiler heat very low. Place the pan with the lobster in a hot oven to finish cooking.

11. Remove the lobster from the heat and serve immediately with a small cup of melted butter and with lemon garnish.

V A R I A T I O N

Broiled Rock Lobster Tail
Rock lobster is usually dry if broiled like lobster. A better method is to poach it in salted water (see pp. 482) until just cooked. Then split the tails, brush with butter, and run under the broiler for 1–2 minutes.

Broiled Shrimp, Scampi Style

Portions: 10   Portion size: 4½ oz (125 g)

U.S.	Metric	Ingredients
50	50	Shrimp, size 16/20
6 oz	175 g	Butter
½ cup	125 mL	Oil, preferably olive oil (see note)
1 tbsp	15 mL	Garlic, very finely chopped
1 fl oz	30 mL	Lemon juice
2 tbsp	30 mL	Chopped parsley
to taste	to taste	Salt
to taste	to taste	Pepper

■ P r o c e d u r e

1. Peel, devein, and butterfly the shrimp, as shown in Figure 14.14. Leave tails on.
2. Place shrimp in individual service casserole dishes or in a shallow baking pan, tails up and cut side down. (Shrimp will curl more when cooked, so tails stand up as shrimp are broiled.)
3. Keep refrigerated until needed.

4. Heat butter and oil in a saucepan until the butter is melted.
5. Add the garlic, lemon juice, parsley, salt, and pepper.
6. Pour the butter sauce over the shrimp.
7. Place under the broiler at medium heat. Broil until the tops are lightly browned. (Don't worry if the tips of the tails burn a little; this is normal.)
8. Transfer the shrimp to the oven above the broiler for a few minutes to finish cooking.

Per serving:
Calories, 250; Protein, 7 g; Fat, 25 g (88% cal.); Cholesterol, 95 mg; Carbohydrates, 1 g; Fiber, 0 g; Sodium, 210 mg.

Note: All butter may be used, instead of a mixture of butter and oil. Or, if you are using a good-quality olive oil, use more oil and less butter or all olive oil.
    Serve this dish with rice or with plenty of bread to soak up the flavorful butter.

V A R I A T I O N S

The shrimp can be marinated for 1–2 hours in the oil, chopped garlic, lemon juice, and seasonings. Add the butter at cooking time. Or omit the butter when cooking, and serve small cups of garlic butter on the side.

Shrimp Brochettes
Marinate the shrimp as indicated above. Put the shrimp on skewers and broil, basting several times with the marinade and melted butter.

Broiled Scallops
Place the scallops in individual service casseroles (5–6 oz/150–175 g per portion). Top each portion with 1 tbsp (15 mL) dry bread crumbs. Pour the butter sauce over the scallops and broil as in basic recipe.

Broiled Fish Fillets or Steaks with Garlic Butter
Use fillets or steaks of any lean, white fish. Place fish on sheet pans and prepare according to procedure for Broiled Scallops, using the bread crumbs.

Oysters Casino

Portions: 12   Portion: 3 oysters (appetizer portion)

U.S.	Metric	Ingredients
36	36	Oysters
½ lb	225 g	Butter
2 oz	60 g	Green bell pepper, chopped fine
1 oz	30 g	Pimiento, chopped fine
1 oz	30 g	Shallots, chopped fine
¼ cup	60 mL	Chopped parsley
1 fl oz	30 mL	Lemon juice
to taste	to taste	Salt
to taste	to taste	White pepper
9 strips	9 strips	Bacon

Per serving:
Calories, 610; Protein, 26 g; Fat, 51 g (75% cal.); Cholesterol, 230 mg; Carbohydrates, 12 g; Fiber, 0 g; Sodium, 860 mg.

Note: Broiled or baked oysters and clams are often placed on beds of rock salt to hold them steady.

■ Procedure

1. Open oysters as shown in Figure 14.7. Discard top shell.
2. Place oysters on a sheet pan or in a shallow baking pan (see note).
3. Place the butter in the bowl of a mixer and beat with the paddle attachment until soft and smooth.
4. Add the green pepper, pimiento, shallots, parsley, and lemon juice. Mix until evenly combined. Season to taste with salt and pepper. (Casino butter can be rolled in parchment, refrigerated or frozen, and sliced to order.)
5. Cook the bacon in the oven or on the griddle until about half cooked. Drain.
6. Cut each strip into 4 pieces.
7. Place about 2 tsp (10 mL) butter mixture on top of each oyster.
8. Top each oyster with a piece of bacon.
9. Run the oysters under the broiler until the bacon is brown and the oysters are hot. Do not overcook.

VARIATIONS

Clams Casino
Prepare as in basic recipe, using cherrystone or littleneck clams.

SAUTÉING AND PAN-FRYING

As in meat cookery, the exact distinction between sautéing and pan-frying fish is impossible to draw. For many purposes, the two terms are used interchangeably.

A classic method for sautéing fish is called à la meunière (mun yair). In this preparation, the product is dredged in flour and sautéed in clarified butter or oil. It is then plated and sprinkled with lemon juice and chopped parsley, and freshly prepared hot brown butter (beurre noisette) is poured over it. When the hot butter hits the lemon juice, it creates a froth. The fish should then be served at once.

Other sautéed fish preparations may call for Standard Breading Procedure (p. 143) or for dredging the fish with a product other than flour, such as cornmeal. Also, a variety of garnishes may be used.

The procedures and variations just described apply to most popular sautéed and pan-fried fish recipes. In general, because most types of fin fish are so delicate, especially if filleted, they do not lend themselves to a great many sautéing variations. Rather, variety is created with accompaniments, sauces, and garnishes. On the other hand, firm shellfish, like shrimp and scallops, are easy to sauté, and there is a greater variety of recipes for them.

Guidelines for Sautéing and Pan-Frying Fish and Shellfish

1. Lean fish are especially well suited to sautéing because the cooking method supplies fat the fish lack.

   Fat fish may also be sautéed, as long as you take care not to get it too greasy.

2. Sautéed fish is usually given a coating of flour, breading, or other starchy product before sautéing. This forms a crust that browns attractively, enhances the flavor, and helps hold the fish together and prevent sticking.

3. Fish may be soaked in milk briefly before dredging in flour. This helps the flour form a good crust.

4. Clarified butter and oil are the preferred fats for sautéing and pan-frying. Whole butter is likely to burn, unless the fish items are very small.

5. Use a minimum of fat. About ⅛ inch (3 mm), or enough to cover the bottom of the pan, is enough.

6. Observe the guidelines for the basic sautéing procedure (p. 314). In particular, be sure the pan is hot before adding the fish to it. After the item has begun to cook, adjust the heat as necessary. Small items, such as shrimp and scallops, are sautéed over high heat. Larger items, such as whole fish or thick steaks, require lower heat to cook evenly.

7. Very large fish may be browned in fat and then finished in the oven, uncovered.

8. Brown the most attractive side—the presentation side—first. For fillets, this is usually the flesh side or the side against the bone, not the skin side.

9. Handle fish carefully during and after cooking to avoid breaking the fish or the crisp crust.

10. Sauté or fry to order and serve immediately.

Procedure for Cooking Fish à la Meunière

1. Collect all equipment and food supplies.
2. Heat a small amount of clarified butter in a sauté pan.
3. Season the fish and dredge in flour. Shake off excess.
4. Place the fish in the pan, presentation side down.
5. Sauté the fish, turning once with a spatula, until both sides are brown and the fish is just cooked through.
6. Remove the fish from the pan with a spatula and place on serving plate, presentation side up.
7. Sprinkle fish with lemon juice and chopped parsley.
8. Heat some raw butter in the sauté pan until it turns light brown. Pour it over the fish immediately.
9. Serve at once.

Fillets of Sole Meunière

Portions: 10　Portion size: 4 oz (125 g)

U.S.	Metric	Ingredients
20	20	Sole fillets, 2 oz (60 g) each
to taste	to taste	Salt
to taste	to taste	White pepper
3 oz	90 g	Flour
6 oz	175 g	Clarified butter or oil, or a mixture of butter and oil
1 fl oz	30 mL	Lemon juice
¼ cup	60 mL	Chopped parsley
5 oz	150 g	Butter
20	20	Slices of peeled lemon

Per serving:
Calories, 370; Protein, 20 g; Fat, 29 g (71% cal.); Cholesterol, 130 mg; Carbohydrates, 7 g; Fiber, 0 g; Sodium, 370 mg.

■ P r o c e d u r e

1. Have all ingredients ready, but do not season and flour the fish until immediately before cooking.

2. Unless you are cooking to order, use as many sauté pans as necessary to hold all the fillets, or cook them in several batches. Place the sauté pans over medium heat so that they will be ready as soon as the fish is floured.

3. Season the fillets with salt and pepper. Place the clarified butter in the hot pans to heat. Dredge the fish in flour and shake off excess. Place the fish in the pans flesh side (presentation side) down.

4. Sauté until lightly browned. Turn over with a spatula and brown the other side. Be careful not to break the fillets when turning.

5. Remove the fillets from the pan with a spatula, being careful not to break them. Plate the fish on hot dinner plates.

6. Sprinkle the fish with lemon juice and chopped parsley.

7. Heat the butter in small saucepan or sauté pan until it turns light brown (beurre noisette).

8. Pour the hot butter over the fish.

9. Quickly place a lemon slice on top of each fillet and serve immediately.

V A R I A T I O N S

Other white fish fillets, as well as shellfish such as scallops and shrimp, may be cooked by the same procedure.

Placing fish in milk before dredging in flour helps form an attractive, well-browned crust. However, the fish must be drained well before flouring, or the flour coating may be heavy and pasty.

Fillets of Fish Doré
Sauté the fish as in the basic recipe, but serve without the lemon juice, chopped parsley, and beurre noisette. Garnish the plate with lemon and parsley sprig. (Doré means "golden.")

Trout Meunlère
Prepare whole, drawn trout as in basic recipe. Dip fish in milk before dredging in flour to form a better crust.

Fish Sauté Amandine
Prepare as in basic recipe. Brown sliced almonds in the butter used for garnishing. Omit garnish of lemon slices, and garnish plate with lemon wedges.

Fish Sauté Grenobloise
Prepare as in basic recipe. Garnish the fish with capers and diced, peeled lemon sections in addition to the chopped parsley before pouring on the brown butter.

Sautéed Soft-Shell Crabs
Prepare as in basic recipe. Serve 2 per portion. Chopped parsley and lemon slices may be omitted.

Scallops Meunière

Sautéed Scallops with Tomato, Garlic, and Parsley

Portions: 10   Portion size: 4 oz (125 g)

U.S.	Metric	Ingredients
2½ lb	1.25 kg	Bay or sea scallops
2 fl oz	60 mL	Olive oil
2 fl oz	60 mL	Clarified butter
2 tsp	10 mL	Finely chopped garlic
4 oz	125 g	Drained, chopped canned or fresh tomato
¼ cup	60 mL	Chopped parsley
to taste	to taste	Salt

Per serving:
Calories, 160; Protein, 9 g; Fat, 13 g (73% cal.); Cholesterol, 35 mg; Carbohydrates, 2 g; Fiber, 0 g; Sodium, 310 mg.

■ Procedure

1. If you are using sea scallops and they are very large, cut them in halves or quarters. Dry the scallops with paper towels.
2. Heat the oil and butter in a large sauté pan until it is very hot.
3. Place the scallops in the sauté pan and sauté quickly. Shake the pan often to keep the scallops from sticking.
4. When the scallops are about half cooked, add the garlic. Continue to sauté until the scallops are lightly browned.
5. Add the tomato and parsley and sauté a few seconds, just enough to heat the tomato.
6. Add salt to taste and serve immediately.

VARIATIONS

Omitting the tomato makes a slightly different but equally good dish.

Sautéed Shrimp
Use peeled, deveined shrimp. Sauté as in basic recipe.

Escalope of Salmon with Sorrel

Portions: 12   Portion size: 3½–4 oz (115–120 g) salmon
2 fl oz (60 mL) sauce

U.S.	Metric	Ingredients
2 lb	1 kg	Sorrel
½ oz	15 g	Butter
1 pt	500 mL	Heavy cream
1 pt	500 mL	Fish stock
to taste	to taste	Salt
to taste	to taste	Pepper
3 lb	1.5 kg	Salmon fillets, boneless and skinless
as needed	as needed	Oil

Per serving:
Calories, 380; Protein, 23 g; Fat, 28 g (66% cal.); Cholesterol, 130 mg; Carbohydrates, 10 g; Fiber, 1 g; Sodium, 95 mg.

■ Procedure

1. Wash and stem the sorrel. Cut into chiffonade.
2. Over low heat, cook the sorrel with the butter until very soft, about 2–5 minutes.
3. Add the cream and simmer for 1 minute. Set aside.
4. Reduce the fish stock by four-fifths. Add the sorrel and cream mixture.
5. Place in a blender and blend until smooth. Strain into a saucepan and reheat. Season to taste and keep warm.
6. Slice the salmon fillets into thin escalopes weighing 4 oz (125 g) each (see Figure 15.1).
7. Heat a little oil over high heat in a sauté pan. Sauté the salmon slices about 1–2 minutes on each side. Remove and drain briefly on paper towels to absorb excess oil.
8. To serve, cover the bottom of a warm plate with sauce and place a salmon escalope on top.

Figure 15.1
Cutting escalopes of salmon.

(a) Holding the knife at a sharp angle, cut a thin slice of the fillet, slicing toward the tail or thin end.

(b) The cut slice. Weigh the slice to check for accuracy of cutting, then continue making slices.

Salmon with an Almond Crust

Portions: 12   Portion size: 5½ oz (165 g)

U.S.	Metric	Ingredients
3½ oz	100 g	Ground almonds
3½ oz	100 g	Fresh bread crumbs
1 oz	30 g	Chopped parsley
2	2	Eggs, beaten
4 oz	125 g	Butter, softened
to taste	to taste	Salt
to taste	to taste	White pepper
4 lb	1.8 kg	Salmon fillets
3 oz	90 g	Clarified butter
1 pt 4 oz	600 mL	Red Wine Butter Sauce for Fish (p. 180)

Per serving:
Calories, 770; Protein, 33 g; Fat, 62 g (72% cal.); Cholesterol, 250 mg; Carbohydrates, 9 g; Fiber, 1 g; Sodium, 590 mg.

■ P r o c e d u r e

1. Mix together the almonds, bread crumbs, and chopped parsley. Add the egg and mix gently.
2. Add the soft butter and mix until incorporated.
3. Season to taste with salt and white pepper.
4. Cut the salmon fillets into 5-oz (150-g) portions.
5. Pan-fry the salmon in butter, starting with the flesh side down. Brown lightly. Turn over and continue cooking skin side down. Do not cook the fish completely, as it will continue cooking with the almond crust. It should still be somewhat rare inside.
6. Spread a layer of the almond crust mixture over the salmon.
7. Place under a salamander or broiler to brown the crust and finish cooking the salmon. Adjust the height of the broiler rack so the crust is not too browned before the salmon is cooked.
8. Plate the salmon. Ladle the sauce around it, not over it.

V A R I A T I O N S

This recipe works well with other firm-fleshed fish.

Crab Cakes with Roasted Pepper Rémoulade

Portions: 16   Portion size: 4 oz (125 g)

U.S.	Metric	Ingredients
3 lb	1.4 kg	Crabmeat
4 oz	125 g	Fresh bread crumbs
6 oz	175 g	Mayonnaise
4	4	Eggs, beaten
2 tsp	10 mL	Prepared mustard
2 tsp	10 mL	Worcestershire sauce
2 tsp	10 mL	Salt
½ tsp	2 mL	White pepper
3 tbsp	45 mL	Chopped parsley
8	8	Scallions, chopped fine
as needed	as needed	Clarified butter, for cooking
3 oz	90 g	Roasted red bell peppers, peeled, cored, and seeded (see Figure 16.13)
1 pt	500 mL	Rémoulade Sauce (p. 200)
16	16	Lemon wedges

Per serving:
Calories, 440; Protein, 21 g; Fat, 36 g (72% cal.); Cholesterol, 145 mg; Carbohydrates, 7 g; Fiber, 0 g; Sodium, 1070 mg.

■ P r o c e d u r e

1. Pick over the crabmeat to remove any bits of shell.
2. Mix together the bread crumbs, mayonnaise, eggs, mustard, Worcestershire sauce, salt, pepper, parsley, and scallions. Fold in the crabmeat.
3. Form by hand into round cakes. For each portion, allow 1 large cake, about 4 oz (125 g), or 2 small cakes, about 2 oz (60 g) each (see note).
4. Pan-fry the cakes in butter until browned on both sides and cooked through.
5. Cut the roasted peppers into brunoise. Mix into the rémoulade.
6. Serve each crab cake with 1 fl oz (30 mL) sauce and 1 lemon wedge.

Note: This mixture has very little bread filler, so it may be somewhat difficult to handle. If desired, add more bread crumbs to make a firmer mixture that will pack more easily into cakes. The texture of the crabmeat may also affect the texture of the cakes and the quantity of bread crumbs needed.

Cornmeal-Crusted Soft-Shell Crabs with Cornmeal Pancakes and Roasted Tomatoes

Portions: 10   Portion size: 1 crab, 1 pancake, 2 tomato halves

U.S.	Metric	Ingredients
10	10	Plum tomatoes
10	10	Pancakes (p. 801), made without sugar and with half white flour and half cornmeal
10	10	Soft-shell crabs
8 oz	250 mL	Milk
5 oz	150 g	Cornmeal
4 fl oz	125 mL	Oil
6 oz	175 g	Butter
to taste	to taste	Salt
5 fl oz	150 mL	Rémoulade Sauce (p. 200)

Per serving:
Calories, 420; Protein, 16 g; Fat, 27 g (57% cal.); Cholesterol, 120 mg; Carbohydrates, 30 g; Fiber, 2 g; Sodium, 500 mg.

■ Procedure

1. Cut the tomatoes in half lengthwise. Carefully squeeze the tomatoes to remove most of the seeds. Place the tomatoes cut side down on an oiled sheet pan. Bake at 250°F (120°C) for 1½ hours or until they are soft and shriveled but not browned.

2. Prepare the pancakes. Keep both the pancakes and the tomatoes warm.

3. Clean the crabs, as shown in Figure 14.15.

4. Dip the crabs in milk. Drain, then dredge in cornmeal. Discard leftover milk.

5. Heat the oil and butter in enough sauté pans to hold the crabs in a single layer (or pan-fry in separate batches). Place the crabs in the pan upside down and cook over moderate heat until lightly browned. Salt lightly to taste while the crabs are cooking. Turn over and brown the other side. Remove from the pan and drain for a few seconds on paper towels to remove excess fat.

6. For each portion, place 1 pancake in the center of a plate. Top with 2 tomato halves, cut side up. Top with crab. Place 1 tbsp (15 mL) rémoulade sauce on the plate beside the crab.

Peppered Haddock with Garlic Mashed Potatoes and Parsley Sauce

Portions: 12   Portion size: 5 oz (150 g) plus garnish

U.S.	Metric	Ingredients
10 fl oz	300 mL	Olive oil
1 fl oz	30 mL	Lemon juice
½ cup	125 mL	Chopped parsley
½ tsp	2 mL	Salt
3 lb 12 oz	1.8 kg	Haddock fillets, cut into 5-oz (150-g) portions
2 tbsp	30 mL	Crushed black peppercorns
1 tsp	5 mL	Salt
2 fl oz	60 mL	Olive oil
2 lb 4 oz	1.1 kg	Garlic Mashed Potatoes (p. 589)

Per serving:
Calories, 480; Protein, 28 g; Fat, 33 g (62% cal.); Cholesterol, 95 mg; Carbohydrates, 17 g; Fiber, 2 g; Sodium, 420 mg.

■ Procedure

1. Prepare the sauce: Combine the oil, lemon juice, chopped parsley, and salt in a blender. Process until the parsley is puréed.

2. Coat the fish fillets evenly with a light sprinkling of crushed peppercorns. Season with salt.

3. Heat the olive oil in as many sauté pans as necessary to hold the fish in a single layer.

4. Place the fish in the pans, presentation side down, and sauté over moderate heat until lightly browned and about half cooked. Turn over and finish the cooking.

5. Place a 3-oz (90-g) portion of potatoes in the center of each plate. Top with the fish fillet. Drizzle about 1 fl oz (30 mL) sauce in a circle around the fish.

VARIATIONS

Other firm-fleshed white fish, such as cod, sea bass, striped bass, red snapper, or grouper, may be substituted.

Peppered Haddock with Purée of Flageolet Beans
Substitute Purée of Flageolet Beans with Garlic (p. 613) for the potatoes.

Peppered Haddock with Garlic Whipped Potatoes and Parsley Sauce

Spicy Shrimp or Scallop Sauté

Portions: 10   Portion size: 4 oz (125 g)

U.S.	Metric	Ingredients
1 tsp	5 mL	Paprika
¼ tsp	1 mL	Cayenne
¼ tsp	1 mL	Black pepper
½ tsp	2 mL	White pepper
¼ tsp	1 mL	Dried thyme
¼ tsp	1 mL	Dried basil
¼ tsp	1 mL	Dried oregano
½ tsp	2 mL	Salt
2½ lb	1.25 kg	Peeled, deveined shrimp or scallops
6 oz	175 g	Onion, sliced
1	1	Garlic clove, chopped
as needed	as needed	Clarified butter

Per serving:
Calories, 160; Protein, 18 g; Fat, 9 g (50% cal.); Cholesterol, 185 mg;
Carbohydrates, 2 g; Fiber, 0 g; Sodium, 390 mg.

■ P r o c e d u r e

1. Mix together the spices, herbs, and salt.
2. If the shrimp or scallops are wet, dry them with paper towels. If you are using sea scallops and they are large, cut them into halves or quarters.
3. Toss the shrimp or scallops with the dry seasonings.
4. Sauté the onion and garlic in a little clarified butter until they are tender and only lightly browned. Remove them from the pan and set them aside.
5. Add a little more butter to the pan and sauté the seafood just until it is cooked.
6. Return the onion and garlic to the pan and toss to combine. Serve immediately, accompanied by white rice.

V A R I A T I O N

For spicy fish fillets, season them well with the dry seasoning mix in the basic recipe. Then dredge them in flour and sauté as for meunière.

Spicy Shrimp Sauté; Steamed Rice; Sautéed Grated Zucchini

Shrimp and Cucumber in Thai Red Curry

Portions: 12   *Portion size: 6 oz (180 g)*

U.S.	Metric	Ingredients
2 fl oz	60 mL	Vegetable oil
2½ lb	1.2 kg	Shrimp, medium to large, peeled and deveined
12 oz	375 g	Cucumber, peeled, seeded, medium dice
18 fl oz	550 mL	Thai Red Curry Sauce (p. 194)

Per serving:
Calories, 200; Protein, 17 g; Fat, 16 g (65% cal.); Cholesterol, 140 mg; Carbohydrates, 2 g; Fiber, 2 g; Sodium, 450 mg.

Note: This method of making a curry is designed for advance preparation and quick, last-minute cooking. A more traditional method is to make the sauce as an integral sauce. Stir-fry the shrimp, add curry paste (see sauce recipe, p. 194), and cook until aromatic. Add the coconut milk, other liquids, flavorings, and any other ingredients indicated in the sauce recipe, and finish cooking.

■ **P r o c e d u r e**

1. Heat the oil in a sauté pan or wok over high heat.
2. Add the shrimp and stir-fry until well seared.
3. Add the cucumber and stir-fry 1 minute.
4. Add the curry sauce. Cook a few minutes longer, until the shrimp are completely cooked.
5. Serve with rice.

Shrimp and Cucumber in Thai Red Curry

 ## Skate with Caper Butter

Portions: 12   *Portion size: 4 oz (125 g)*

U.S.	Metric	Ingredients
12	12	Skate fillets, 4 oz (125 g) each
to taste	to taste	Salt
to taste	to taste	White pepper
3 fl oz	90 mL	Vegetable oil
3 fl oz	90 mL	Clarified butter
as needed	as needed	Flour
1 oz	30 g	Shallots, chopped fine
6 fl oz	180 mL	White wine
1 fl oz	30 mL	Lemon juice
12 tbsp	180 mL	Capers, drained
12 oz	360 g	Butter, cut into small pieces
to taste	to taste	Salt

Per serving:
Calories, 450; Protein, 2 g; Fat, 37 g (90% cal.); Cholesterol, 115 mg; Carbohydrates, 5 g; Fiber, 0 g; Sodium, 510 mg.

■ **P r o c e d u r e**

1. Season the fillets with salt and white pepper.
2. Heat the oil and clarified butter in a sauté pan over moderate heat.
3. Dredge the fillets in flour and shake off excess.
4. Sauté the fish, browning it lightly on both sides, until done.
5. Place the fillets on hot dinner plates.

6. Drain the butter and oil from the sauté pan, leaving a thin film on the bottom.
7. Add the shallots and sauté just until they are soft.
8. Add the wine. Reduce until about 1 fl oz (30 mL) remains.
9. Add the lemon juice and capers.
10. Whip in the raw butter as for making beurre blanc (p. 179).
11. Season the caper butter to taste with salt.
12. Pour the butter over the fish fillets.

V A R I A T I O N

For a different kind of caper butter, plate the sautéed skate and top each portion with 1 tbsp (15 mL) capers. Pour hot beurre noisette over the fish, using 1–2 tbsp (15–30 mL) butter per portion.

Pan-Fried Catfish with Shrimp Etouffée

Portions: 12   Portion size: 4 oz (125 g) catfish, 3½ oz (100 g) etouffée

U.S.	Metric	Ingredients		Procedure
3 oz	90 g	Butter	1.	Heat the butter in a sauté pan over moderate heat.
1½ lb	750 g	Shrimp, small, peeled, and deveined	2.	Add the shrimp. Sauté just until they turn pink.
6 oz	180 g	Onion, chopped	3.	Remove the shrimp from the pan with a slotted spoon, leaving the butter in the pan.
3 oz	90 g	Green bell pepper, chopped	4.	Add the onion, green pepper, celery, scallions, and garlic to the pan. Sauté until soft.
3 oz	90 g	Celery, chopped	5.	Stir in the flour to make a roux. Continue to cook until the roux is brown.
2 oz	60 g	Scallion, sliced thin		
2	2	Garlic cloves, chopped	6.	Stir in the water or stock. Bring to a simmer, stirring constantly, and simmer until thickened and no longer tasting of raw flour.
3 tbsp	45 mL	Flour		
12 fl oz	375 fl oz	Water or fish stock		
¼ tsp	1 mL	Dried thyme	7.	Add the shrimp, thyme, paprika, cayenne, pepper, and Worcestershire sauce. Simmer 3–4 minutes, until the shrimp are cooked.
½ tsp	2 mL	Paprika		
¼ tsp	1 mL	Cayenne		
¼ tsp	1 mL	Black pepper	8.	Stir in the parsley.
1 tbsp	15 mL	Worcestershire sauce	9.	Add salt to taste.
4 tbsp	60 mL	Chopped parsley		
to taste	to taste	Salt		
1½ tsp	7 mL	Salt	10.	Mix together the salt and spices.
1½ tsp	7 mL	Paprika	11.	Cut the catfish fillets into 4-oz. (125-g) portions.
¼ tsp	1 mL	Cayenne	12.	Sprinkle the fillets with the spice mixture to coat both sides lightly.
½ tsp	2 mL	Dried thyme		
¼ tsp	1 mL	Black pepper	13.	Sauté the catfish in clarified butter until lightly browned on both sides and cooked through.
¼ tsp	1 mL	White pepper		
3 lb	1.4 kg	Catfish fillets	14.	To serve, portion the shrimp etouffée on hot dinner plates. Top with the catfish fillets.
as needed	as needed	Clarified butter		
			15.	Serve with rice.

Per serving:
Calories, 270; Protein, 32 g; Fat, 13 g (44% cal.); Cholesterol, 165 mg;
Carbohydrates, 5 g; Fiber, 1 g; Sodium, 560 mg.

DEEP-FRYING

Deep-frying is perhaps the most popular method of preparing fish in North America. While fried fish may not be the most subtle or refined preparation, it can be of very high quality if the fish is fresh and not overcooked, the frying fat is of good quality, and the item is served without delay after cooking.

Lean fish—either small whole fish or small portions such as fillets or sticks—and shellfish such as shrimp, clams, oysters, and scallops are best for deep-frying.

Fish to be fried is breaded or battered to protect it from the frying fat and to protect the frying fat from it. Also, the breading or batter provides a crisp, flavorful, and attractive coating.

Frozen breaded fish portions are widely used. They should be fried without thawing.

Fried fish is usually served with lemon and/or a cold sauce such as tartar, rémoulade, or cocktail sauce on the side.

Frying and breading procedures are discussed in detail in Chapter 7. There is no need to repeat them here, but you should review those sections if necessary. Also, the batter recipes on page 576 are suitable for fish as well as for vegetables.

 ## Fried Breaded Fish Fillets

Portions: 25   Portion size: 4 oz (125 g)

U.S.	Metric	Ingredients
		Standard Breading Procedure (see note):
4 oz	125 g	Flour
4	4	Whole eggs, beaten
1 cup	250 mL	Milk
1¼ lb	625 g	Dry bread crumbs
25	25	4-oz (125-g) fillets of lean, white fish, such as haddock, perch, pike, bass, sole, or flounder
to taste	to taste	Salt
to taste	to taste	White pepper
25	25	Parsley sprigs
25	25	Lemon wedges
25 fl oz	750 mL	Tartar sauce

Per serving:
Calories, 490; Protein, 25 g; Fat 36 g (66% cal.); Cholesterol, 115 mg; Carbohydrates, 16 g; Fiber, 1 g; Sodium, 430 mg.

Note: Quantities given for breading materials are only guidelines. You may need more or less, depending on the shapes of the fish pieces, the care used in breading, and other factors. In any case, you will need enough so that even the last piece to be breaded can be coated easily and completely.

■ P r o c e d u r e

1. Set up a breading station (see p. 143): Place the flour in one pan, the eggs beaten with milk in a shallow bowl, and the bread crumbs in another pan.

2. Season the fish lightly with salt and white pepper.
3. Bread the fish fillets by passing them through the flour, egg wash, and crumbs. Press the crumbs on firmly. (See p. 143 for detailed breading instructions.)
4. Fry the fillets in deep fat heated to 350°F (175°C) until golden brown.

5. Drain and serve immediately. Garnish each portion with a parsley sprig and lemon wedge. Serve with 1 fl oz (25 mL) tartar sauce.

V A R I A T I O N S

Breaded fish fillets may also be pan-fried in butter or oil (see previous section).

Fried Breaded Scallops
Prepare as in basic recipe. Use wire baskets in the breading station to simplify the procedure, as explained on page 143.

Fried Breaded Shrimp
Peel, devein, and butterfly shrimp, as shown in Figure 14.14. Leave tails on. Bread and fry as in basic recipe.

Fried Oysters or Clams
Prepare like scallops.

Cod Cakes

Portions: 25   Portion size: 2 cakes, 2½ oz (75 g) each

U.S.	Metric	Ingredients
4 lb	1.8 kg	Cooked cod
4 lb	1.8 kg	Potato purée (p. 588)
3	3	Whole eggs
2	2	Egg yolks
to taste	to taste	Salt
to taste	to taste	White pepper
pinch	pinch	Ground ginger
		Standard Breading Procedure:
as needed	as needed	Flour
as needed	as needed	Egg wash
as needed	as needed	Bread crumbs
as desired	as desired	Tomato sauce *or* tartar sauce

Per serving:
Calories, 280; Protein, 23 g; Fat, 6 g (19% cal.); Cholesterol, 110 mg; Carbohydrates, 33 g; Fiber, 2 g; Sodium, 360 mg.

■ P r o c e d u r e

1. Flake the fish until it is well shredded.
2. Combine with the potato, egg, and egg yolk. Mix well.
3. Season to taste with salt, pepper, and a little ground ginger.
4. Scale the mixture into 2½-oz (75-g) portions. Shape into round, slightly flattened cakes.
5. Pass the cakes through Standard Breading Procedure.
6. Deep-fry at 350°F (175°C) until golden brown.

7. Serve 2 cakes per portion. Accompany with tomato sauce or tartar sauce.

V A R I A T I O N

Salmon or Tuna Cakes
Prepare as in basic recipe, using well drained canned salmon or tuna.

If you have duchesse potato mixture on hand, simply combine equal parts fish and duchesse mixture. No additional eggs are needed, as the potatoes already contain eggs.

 Deep-Fried Calamari with Spicy Tomato Sauce and Aioli

Portions: 12   Portions size: 6 oz (175 g) squid
2 fl oz (60 mL) each sauce

U.S.	Metric	Ingredients
4½ lb	2.25 kg	Small cleaned squid (see Figure 14.10)
4 fl oz	125 mL	Lemon juice
1 lb	500 g	Flour
3 tbsp	45 mL	Salt
1½ pt	750 mL	Tomato Sauce for Pasta (p. 639)
to taste	to taste	Hot red pepper sauce
1½ pt	750 mL	Aioli I (p. 201) or Aioli II (p. 728)

Per serving:
Calories, 700; Protein, 30 g; Fat, 50 g (64% cal.); Cholesterol, 395 mg; Carbohydrates, 33 g; Fiber, 2 g; Sodium, 1710 mg.

■ P r o c e d u r e

1. Slice the body sacs of the squid crosswise into rings. Leave the tentacle sections whole, or cut them in half if they are large.
2. Combine the squid with the lemon juice and marinate, refrigerated, for 2–3 hours.
3. Mix the flour and salt.
4. Drain the squid and dry on clean towels. Immediately before cooking, toss the squid with the flour, then shake in a large strainer to remove excess flour.
5. Deep-fry at 350°F (175°C) just until lightly golden. Remove from the fryer and drain.

6. Heat the tomato sauce and season to taste with the hot pepper sauce.
7. Heap the fried squid in the center of the serving plates, accompanied by 2 fl oz (60 mL) of each of the sauces in small cups.

V A R I A T I O N

For other versions of deep-fried calamari, bread the squid (see Standard Breading Procedure) or dip in batter, using one of the batter recipes for Onion Rings (p. 576); the recipe for Beer Batter is recommended. Follow steps 6–8 in the Onion Ring recipe for battering and frying.

Shrimp and Vegetable Tempura

Portions: 16 **Portion size: 3 shrimp, plus vegetables**

U.S.	Metric	Ingredients	Procedure
48	48	Large shrimp	1. Peel the shrimp, leaving the tails attached. Devein and butterfly them.
4	4	Green bell peppers	2. Core and seed the peppers. Cut each one lengthwise in 8 wedges or strips.
1 lb 4 oz	600 g	Sweet potatoes	3. Peel the sweet potatoes. Cut into slices about ⅛ in. (4 mm) thick.
32	32	Small mushrooms (or halves or quarters of large mushrooms)	4. Clean the mushrooms and trim the bottoms of the stems.
1½ lb	750 g	Cake flour or other low-gluten flour	5. Sift the flour into a mixing bowl.
1½ pt	750 mL	Water, ice-cold	6. Mix together the water and egg yolks.
6	6	Egg yolks	7. Mix the liquid into the flour until just combined. Do not worry about a few lumps. The batter should be somewhat thinner than pancake batter.
1½ pt	750 mL	Dashi (p. 195)	8. Make a dipping sauce by combining the dashi, soy sauce, and mirin.
5 fl oz	150 mL	Soy sauce	
3 fl oz	100 mL	Mirin (sweet rice wine)	
as needed	as needed	Flour for dredging	9. Divide the shrimp and vegetables equally among the 16 portions. Fry the vegetables first, then the shrimp, by dredging with flour, shaking off the excess, then dipping in the batter and dropping into clean frying fat at 350°F (175°C). Fry just until lightly golden.
8 oz	250 g	Grated daikon (large white Japanese radish)	
3 tbsp	45 mL	Grated fresh ginger root	10. Drain and serve at once. Tempura is traditionally served on a bamboo tray covered with a clean piece of absorbent paper. Accompany with about 2 fl oz (60 mL) dipping sauce in a shallow bowl. Put a small mound each of grated daikon and grated ginger on each serving tray. The diner mixes these to taste into the dipping sauce.

Per serving:
Calories, 380; Protein, 11 g; Fat 12 g (28% cal.); Cholesterol, 115 mg; Carbohydrates, 56 g; Fiber, 3 g; Sodium, 560 mg.

TEMPURA

Tempura (TEM-poo-rah) is not a native Japanese dish but rather originated with the deep-fried dishes that Portuguese traders and missionaries introduced to Japan in the sixteenth century. Japanese cooks transformed the dish by perfecting a particularly light, lacy batter and by serving the tempura with a dipping broth based on dashi (p. 195) and soy sauce and flavored with grated ginger and daikon radish.

POACHING AND SIMMERING

Poaching is cooking in a liquid at very low heat. Fillets and other small portions are sometimes cooked in a small amount of liquid, usually fish fumet and/or wine, and served with a sauce made of the poaching liquid. This procedure is called **shallow poaching**, because the item is only partially submerged in the liquid. Whole fish and thick steaks may be cooked completely submerged in a seasoned liquid called *court bouillon*. The liquid is not used to make a sauce, and the fish may be served hot or cold. This procedure is called the **submersion method**. Because these are two distinct procedures, we discuss them separately.

The two methods are illustrated in their most basic form in the recipes on pages 485 and 486. In addition, this section contains recipes using a variety of techniques for preparing fish dishes by cooking in flavorful liquids.

THE SUBMERSION METHOD: POACHING AND SIMMERING IN COURT BOUILLON

Court bouillon may be defined as water containing seasonings, herbs, and usually an acid, used for cooking fish. The name means "short broth" in French, so called because it is made quickly, unlike stocks.

In quantity food service, this method is perhaps used most often for cooking large whole fish that are to be decorated and served cold on a buffet. Slightly higher simmering temperatures are used for cooking crustaceans, such as lobster, crab, and shrimp.

The famous preparation called **truit au bleu** (blue trout) is made by poaching trout that are alive until cooking time. The fish must be alive and must not be washed in order for the fish to turn blue. Live fish have a protective slippery coating on the skin, and the blue color results from the vinegar in the court bouillon reacting with this coating.

Guidelines for Poaching Fish in Court Bouillon

1. Both fat and lean fish may be cooked by this method.

2. Seasoned liquid for cooking fish may be as simple as salted water. More often, however, it contains flavoring ingredients such as spices, herbs, and mirepoix, and acid ingredients such as lemon juice, vinegar, and white wine.

3. Cook flavoring ingredients in court bouillon to extract the flavors before cooking the fish.

4. Cooking temperature is 160° to 180°F (70° to 80°C), well below boiling. A temperature of 160°F (70°C) is sufficient to cook fish, and it reduces the likelihood of overcooking. Higher temperatures are harmful to the delicate texture and flavor of fish.

   Lobsters, crabs, and shrimp may be cooked at a *simmer* because their textures are less fragile. The terms *boiled lobster* and *boiled fish* are often used but inaccurate. Lobster and fish should never be boiled.

5. Start shellfish, small fish, and portion cuts in hot liquid to preserve flavors. Start large fish in cold liquid to cook more evenly and to avoid sudden contractions that would split the skin and spoil the appearance.

6. Special fish poachers with racks are best for poaching. They allow the fish to be removed from the liquid without damage. If these utensils are not available, wrap the fish in cheesecloth so it can be lifted out easily, or tie the fish loosely to a board.

7. Serve poached fish with an appropriate sauce, such as hollandaise for hot fish and a mayonnaise-based sauce for cold fish. Mild vinaigrettes go well with both hot and cold poached fish.

Procedure for Poaching Fish in Court Bouillon

1. Collect all equipment and food supplies.
2. Prepare court bouillon.
3. Place the fish in a suitable pan with liquid to cover.

    Start small fish and portions in simmering liquid.

    Start shellfish in boiling liquid.

    Start large fish in cold liquid.
4. Cook fish at below the simmer, 160° to 180°F (70° to 80°C). Lobsters, crabs, and shrimp may be cooked at a gentle simmer.
5. If fish is to be served hot, remove from liquid and serve immediately.
6. If fish is to be served cold, stop the cooking by adding ice to the liquid, and cool the fish in the court bouillon to retain moisture.

SHALLOW POACHING

The procedure of shallow-poaching fish is based on one of the great dishes of classical cuisine: sole or other white fish poached in fumet and white wine. If well prepared, it can be one of the most exquisite dishes on the menu.

This method of preparation is best for lean, delicate white fish, such as sole, halibut, turbot, haddock, cod, pike, and perch. It is also used for salmon and trout. The fish is always served with a sauce made from the **cuisson**—that is, the poaching liquid.

The procedure and recipe given here are for fillets of sole au vin blanc (in white wine). This is the basic preparation, and most other classical poached fish recipes are variations on it. Many of the variations involve only different garnishes.

Because of the delicacy of flavors, this preparation requires good-quality fish and well-made stock, and the wine should have a good flavor. A cheap, bad-tasting wine will spoil the dish.

The basic classical procedure is detailed in this section. Using this procedure as a pattern, the technique of shallow poaching can also be used for other fish preparations, substituting other cooking liquids for the fumet, wine, velouté, and cream.

CUISSON

The basic meaning of the French word *cuisson* is "cooking." If you order a steak in a restaurant in Paris and are asked how you would like the cuisson, you are being asked whether you would like the meat cooked rare, medium, or well done.

In the context of poaching or simmering foods, *cuisson* refers to the cooking liquid, which may be used as the base of a sauce. This term is commonly used in restaurant kitchens on both sides of the Atlantic.

Procedure for Poaching Fish in Fumet and Wine

1. Collect all equipment and food supplies. Select a pan just large enough to hold the fish portions in a single layer. This will enable you to use a minimum amount of poaching liquid. Also, use a pan with low, sloping sides. This makes it easier to remove the fragile cooked fish from the pan.
2. Butter the bottom of the pan and sprinkle with chopped shallots.
3. Arrange the fish portions in the pan in a single layer. Season them lightly.
4. Add enough fish fumet and white wine to almost cover the fish. Use no more liquid than necessary so the flavor will be more concentrated and less reduction will be required later.
5. Cover the fish with a piece of buttered parchment or other paper and cover the pan with a lid. The paper holds in the steam to cook the top of the fish. It is sometimes omitted if the pan has a tight lid, but it does help the fish cook more evenly.
6. Bring the liquid just to a simmer and finish poaching in the oven at moderate heat. Thin fillets will cook in just a few minutes. Fish may be poached on top of the range, but the oven provides more even, gentle heat from both top and bottom.
7. Drain the liquid into a wide pan and keep the fish warm. After a few minutes of standing, more liquid will drain from the fish. Add this to the rest.
8. Reduce the cuisson over high heat to about one-fourth its volume.
9. Add fish velouté and heavy cream and bring to a boil. Adjust seasoning with salt, white pepper, and lemon juice.
10. Strain the sauce.
11. Arrange the fish on plates for service, coat with the sauce, and serve immediately.

Variations in Sauce Production

Using a prepared velouté, as in the standard method just given, makes the sauce production very quick, and the procedure can easily be used for cooking to order.

An alternative method may be used if no velouté is available or if a large quantity of fish is being poached for banquet service:

1. Use a larger quantity of fumet and wine for cooking the fish and reduce it by only about half, depending on the amount of sauce needed.

2. Thicken the liquid with roux or beurre manié and simmer until no raw starch taste remains.

3. Finish the preparation as in the basic method.

Another popular method uses no starch thickener. Instead, the reduced poaching liquid is lightly bound with heavy cream or raw butter.

- To bind the sauce with cream, add about 2 ounces (60 mL) heavy cream per portion to the reduced cooking liquid and continue to reduce until the sauce is lightly thickened.

- To bind with butter, whip raw butter into the reduced cooking liquid as for *monter au beurre* (p. 167). Use about ½ ounce (15 g) butter or more per portion.

A further variation is known as à la nage, which means "swimming." To serve poached seafood à la nage, reduce the cooking liquid only slightly, season, and strain it carefully. If desired, enrich the liquid with a very small quantity of butter. Serve the seafood with the liquid in a soup plate or other plate deep enough to hold the juices.

In one recipe in this section, the fish is steamed above the wine rather than poached in it. But the dish is finished by making a sauce from the wine and fumet in a fairly traditional manner (even though the wine is red rather than white!).

The procedure of shallow poaching in wine and fumet can also be adapted to other preparations. In place of the fumet and wine in step 4, substitute other liquids as directed in the recipe. To finish the sauce, reduce the cuisson and, instead of finishing the sauce with velouté and cream, finish the sauce as directed in the individual recipe.

GLAZING

Poached fish is sometimes glazed before serving. This is done as follows:

1. According to the particular recipe, combine the finished sauce with egg yolk, hollandaise sauce, and/or lightly whipped cream. Alternatively, combine the reduction of the cooking liquid with Mornay sauce instead of fish velouté.

2. Coat the fish with the sauce and run the plate or platter under the salamander or broiler for a few seconds, until the sauce is golden brown.

   Note: It's a good idea to test a little of the sauce under the salamander before coating the fish to make sure it will brown.

Court Bouillon for Fish

Yield: 1 gal (4 L)

U.S.	Metric	Ingredients
1 gal	4 L	Water
8 fl oz	250 mL	White vinegar, wine vinegar, *or* lemon juice
8 oz	250 g	Onions, sliced
4 oz	125 g	Celery, sliced
4 oz	125 g	Carrots, sliced
2 oz	60 g	Salt
¼ tsp	2 mL	Peppercorns, crushed
1	1	Bay leaf
½ tsp	1 mL	Dried thyme
10–12	10–12	Parsley stems

■ P r o c e d u r e

1. Combine all ingredients in a stockpot or saucepot and bring to boil.

2. Reduce heat and simmer 30 minutes.

3. Strain and cool.

Per 1 ounce:
Calories, 0; Protein, 0 g; Fat, 0 g (0% cal.); Cholesterol, 0 mg;
Carbohydrates, 0 g; Fiber, 0 g; Sodium, 170 mg.

Poached Whole Fish

Portions: 10   Portion size: 4 oz (125 g)

U.S.	Metric	Ingredients
5 lb	2.5 kg	Drawn fish
		or
4 lb	2 kg	Dressed fish (1 large or 2 or more smaller fish; see note)
3 qt or as needed	3 L or as needed	Court bouillon, cold
		Suggested sauces:
		Hollandaise
		Mousseline
		Beurre noisette
		Herb vinaigrette

Per serving:
Calories, 220; Protein, 47 g; Fat, 2 g (9% cal.); Cholesterol, 140 mg; Carbohydrates, 0 g; Fiber, 0 g; Sodium, 320 mg.

Note: For attractive presentations, such as for buffet work, fish is often poached with the head on. Suggested fish for poaching whole:

Haddock	Red snapper	Striped bass
Cod	Salmon	Trout

■ Procedure

1. Place the clean dressed or drawn fish on the lightly oiled rack of a fish poacher. If a rack is unavailable, wrap the fish in cheesecloth or tie it loosely on a board so that it can be lifted out when cooked.

2. Place the fish in the poaching pan and pour in enough cold court bouillon to cover the fish completely.

3. Set the pan over moderately low heat and slowly bring barely to a simmer.

4. Reduce heat to very low and cook the fish at below the simmering point until done. The fish will feel firm, not mushy, at its thickest part, and the backbone, as seen inside the cavity, will no longer be pink. Total cooking time will vary from 5 to 20 minutes, depending on the size of the fish and exact cooking temperature. In general, plan on about 8–10 minutes for every inch of thickness at the thickest point.

5. For serving hot: Remove fish from liquid, drain well, and serve immediately with choice of sauce.

   For serving cold: Add ice to the court bouillon to stop the cooking. Cool the fish rapidly in the liquid and refrigerate. Drain when chilled.

VARIATION

Poached Fish Steaks
Prepare as in basic recipe, except start with boiling court bouillon. Drain the cooked fish, remove skin and center bone, and serve immediately with selected sauce. Suggested fish steaks: cod, haddock, halibut, turbot, salmon.

"Boiled" Shellfish (Lobster, Crab, Shrimp)
Prepare as for fish steaks using *salted water, court bouillon*, or *acidulated water* (4 oz lemon juice and ½ oz salt per quart of water/125 mL lemon juice and 15 g salt per liter). Water may simmer when cooking shellfish.

Sole Vin Blanc (Poached Fillets of Sole in White Wine Sauce)

Portions: 25   **Portion size: 4 oz (125 g) fish**
                    2 fl oz (60 mL) sauce

U.S.	Metric	Ingredients
6¼ lb	3 kg	Sole fillets: 50 fillets, 2 oz (60 g) each
3 oz	90 g	Butter
3 oz	90 g	Shallots, fine dice
10 fl oz	300 mL	White wine
2½ cups or as needed	600 mL or as needed	Fish stock
3½ pt	1.75 L	Fish velouté
3	3	Egg yolks
8 fl oz	250 mL	Heavy cream
2 oz	60 g	Butter
to taste	to taste	Salt
to taste	to tastes	White pepper
as needed	as needed	Lemon juice

■ P r o c e d u r e

1. Fold the fillets in half or roll them up, starting with the large end (see Figure 15.2). Be sure the skin side of the fillet is on the inside of the fold or the roll (called paupiette).

2. Butter the inside of shallow hotel pans or baking pans. Sprinkle with the shallots. Lay the fillets on top of the shallots in a single layer.

3. Pour the wine into the pan and add enough stock to almost cover the fish.

4. Butter a piece of parchment or waxed paper cut the same size as the pan. Cover the fish closely with it, buttered side down. Cover the pan.

5. Set the pan on the range and bring just barely to a simmer. Do not boil.

6. Place the pan in a hot oven (400°F/200°C) and cook the fish until it is just barely done, about 5 minutes.

7. Drain the poaching liquid into a broad sauté pan. Keep the fish covered in a warm, not hot, place. If more liquid collects under the fish as it stands, add this to the rest.

8. Reduce the poaching liquid over high heat to about one-fourth its volume.

9. Add the velouté and bring to a simmer. Reduce to about 1 qt (1 L).

10. Beat the egg yolks, then mix in the cream to make a liaison.

11. Whip in a little of the hot velouté to temper the liaison. Stir the tempered liaison into the sauce.

12. Swirl in the raw butter (monter au beurre). Season to taste with salt, pepper, and a few drops of lemon juice if necessary.

13. To serve, place 2 fillets on a dinner plate and coat with 2 fl oz (60 mL) sauce.

Per serving:
Calories, 260; Protein, 25 g, Fat, 14 g (51% cal.); Cholesterol, 125 mg;
Carbohydrates, 4 g; Fiber 0 g; Sodium, 190 mg.

**Paupiettes of Sole Dugléré; Buttered Spinach;
Steamed Potatoes**

VARIATIONS

Any lean white fish may be poached using this recipe or any of the variations below, including:

Halibut	Cod	Perch
Turbot	Pike	Scallops
Haddock		

For a sauce that is lower in fat, omit the liaison and the final monter au beurre. Finish the sauce with the desired amount of heavy cream, 6–12 fl oz (175–350 mL).

À la Carte Serice, Fast Method: Poach fish as in basic recipe. Plate the fish as soon as it is cooked. Coat it with a *pre-prepared white wine sauce*. The poaching liquid may be reused throughout the service period, then used to make velouté for the next day's sauce. Other sauces based on fish velouté or béchamel may be used instead of white sauce:

Bercy	Normandy	Nantua
Herb	Mushroom	Mornay

Glazed Poached Fish

Prepare as in basic recipe. Immediately before serving, fold 1 pt (500 mL) hollandaise and 8 fl oz (250 mL) heavy cream, whipped, into the sauce. Coat the fish and brown it quickly under the salamander.

Poached Fish Bonne Femme

Add 1½ lb (700 g) sliced mushrooms to the shallots in the poaching pan. Poach as in basic recipe. Omit egg yolks. Do not strain the sauce.

Poached Fish Dugléré

Add 1½ lb (400 g) tomato concassé (p. 533) and 4 tbsp (60 mL) chopped parsley to the pan when poaching the fish. Poach as in basic recipe. Omit liaison, but stir 5 oz (150 g) raw butter into the sauce before serving. Do not strain.

Poached Fish Mornay

Strain the reduced poaching liquid (after step 8) and add a little of it to a thick Mornay Sauce for Glazing (p. 171), just enough to thin it to the desired consistency. Coat the fish with the sauce and brown under the salamander or broiler.

Note: Scallops are often prepared à la Mornay and served in scallop shells with a duchesse potato border. The dish is called Coquille St. Jacques Mornay. (St. Jacques is the French term for scallop, and coquille means "shell.")

Poached Fish Florentine

Prepare like Poached Fish Mornay, but place the cooked fish on beds of cooked, buttered spinach before coating with sauce.

Seafood à la Nage

Double the quantity of fish stock. Omit the velouté, liaison, and final butter. After poaching, reduce the cooking liquid only slightly. Season carefully and strain. Serve the seafood with the broth.

Figure 15.2
Rolling and folding sole fillets.

(a) To make paupiettes, or rolled fillets of sole, lay the fillets on the work surface, skin side up. Starting at the large end, roll tightly. As the fish cooks, the connective tissues on the skin side shrink and keep the roll tight. If you roll the fillet skin side out, it unrolls as it cooks.

(b) If the fillets are to be poached flat or folded, first make a series of very shallow cuts in the skin side as shown. This helps keep the tissues from shrinking and deforming the fillet. Fold so the flesh side is out (skin side on the inside).

Poached Fingers of Salmon and Turbot with Saffron and Julienne of Vegetables

Portions: 10   Portion size: 5 oz (150 g) fish
2 fl oz (60 mL) broth

U.S.	Metric	Ingredients
8 oz	250 g	Leeks
8 oz	250 g	Carrots
8 oz	250 g	Celery or celery root
8 oz	250 g	Onion, sliced thin
2½ qt	2.5 L	Water, cold
to taste	to taste	Salt
to taste	to taste	Pepper
2 lb 4 oz	1 kg	Turbot fillets
2 lb 4 oz	1 kg	Salmon fillets
large pinch	large pinch	Saffron threads
to taste	to taste	Salt
to taste	to taste	Pepper
1 oz	30 g	Chopped chives

Per serving:
Calories, 280; Protein, 36 g; Fat, 11 g (37% cal.); Cholesterol, 110 mg:
Carbohydrates, 7 g; Fiber, 2 g; Sodium, 240 mg.

■ P r o c e d u r e

1. Cut the leeks, carrots, and celery or celery root into julienne and keep the trimmings.

2. Place the trimmings into a deep pan with the onion and cover with the water. Bring slowly to a boil and skim to remove any impurities.

3. Simmer for 30 minutes, then strain into a shallow poaching pan and keep barely simmering to reduce to 1½ qt (1.5 L). Season.

4. Skin the fillets. Cut the fish into pieces, 1 x 4 in. (2 x 6 cm), and add to the cooking liquid with the vegetable strips and saffron.

5. Simmer for 5 minutes. Check the seasoning. Serve in broad soup plates with the cooking liquid. Sprinkle with chopped chives.

Poached Fingers of Salmon and Turbot with Saffron and Julienne of Vegetables

Poached Salmon with Lentils in Cream

Portions: 12   Portion size: 4 oz (125 g) salmon
5 oz (150 g) lentils
2 fl oz (60 mL) sauce

U.S.	Metric	Ingredients
3 lb	1.5 kg	Salmon fillets
as needed	as needed	Court bouillon
3 lb 12 oz	1.8 kg	Lentils in Cream (p. 613)
1½ pt	750 mL	White Wine Cream Sauce for Fish (p. 197)

Per serving:
Calories, 640; Protein, 31 g; Fat, 46 g (34% cal.); Cholesterol, 175 mg;
Carbohydrates, 20 g; Fiber, 8 g; Sodium, 420 mg.

■ P r o c e d u r e

1. Cut the salmon fillets into 4-oz (125-g) portions.

2. Poach in the court bouillon until just cooked, about 10 minutes.

3. For each portion, cover the center of a plate with 5 oz (150 g) lentils. Place the salmon on top.

4. Dot with the sauce and serve.

Pesce con Salsa Verde

Portions: 16 Portion size: 1 piece of fish, plus 1½ oz (45 mL) sauce

U.S.	Metric	Ingredients	Procedure
		Court bouillon:	1. Combine the court bouillon ingredients in a pot. Simmer for 15 minutes.
4 oz	125 g	Onion, sliced	
1 oz	30 g	Celery, chopped	
6–8	6–8	Parsley stems	
1	1	Bay leaf	
¼ tsp	1 mL	Fennel seeds	
1½ tsp	7 mL	Salt	
1 pt	500 mL	White wine	
3 qt	3 L	Water	
		Salsa verde:	2. Soak the bread in the vinegar for 15 minutes, then squeeze it out.
3 slices	3 slices	White bread, crusts removed	3. Combine the parsley, garlic, capers, and anchovies on a cutting board and chop them very well.
4 oz	125 g	Wine vinegar	
1½ oz	50 g	Parsley, leaves only	4. Mash the egg yolks and the bread pulp together in a bowl, then add the chopped parsley mixture and mix together until well combined.
1 clove	1 clove	Garlic	
3 tbsp	45 mL	Capers, drained	
4	4	Anchovy fillets	5. Very slowly beat in the olive oil as though you were making mayonnaise. When all the oil has been added, the sauce should have a creamy texture, not as thick as mayonnaise.
3	3	Hard-cooked egg yolks	
1 pt	500 mL	Olive oil	
to taste	to taste	Salt	6. Season to taste with salt and pepper.
to taste	to taste	Pepper	
16	16	Fish steaks, fillets, or small whole fish	7. Poach the fish in the court bouillon.
			8. Drain well. Top each portion with 1½ oz (45 mL) sauce and serve immediately.

Per serving:
Calories, 510; Protein, 20 g; Fat, 45 g (81% cal.); Cholesterol, 100 mg; Carbohydrates, 4 g; Fiber, 0 g; Sodium, 340 mg.

Note: Some of the fish that can be used for this recipe are halibut, sea bass, striped bass, red snapper, bluefish, and porgy.

Sole Fillets Steamed in Beaujolais

Portions: 12 Portion size: 4 oz (125 g) fish
1½–2 fl oz (50 mL) sauce

U.S.	Metric	Ingredients	Procedure
3 lb	1.5 kg	Sole fillets: 24 fillets, 2 oz (60 g) each	1. Fold the fillets in half. Be sure that the skin side of the fillet is on the inside of the fold.
1½ pt	750 mL	Beaujolais wine	2. Place the wine on to boil in a wide pan. Place a round rack above the wine. Arrange the fish on the rack in a single layer, cover, and cook in the steam of the boiling wine (the side of the fish exposed to the steam will take on a light color).
1½ pt	750 mL	Fish stock	
10 oz	300 g	Butter	
to taste	to taste	Salt	
to taste	to taste	Pepper	3. Set the fish aside and keep warm. Reduce the wine to a glaze.
as needed	as needed	Chervil sprigs for garnish	4. Add the fish stock. Reduce until the sauce is thick enough to lightly coat the back of a spoon. Swirl in the butter (monter au beurre). Strain. Season to taste.
			5. To serve, ladle some sauce onto the plate and arrange the sole in the center. Garnish with a sprig of chervil.

Per serving
Calories, 300; Protein, 24 g; Fat, 21 g (64% cal.); Cholesterol, 110 mg; Carbohydrates, 0 g; Fiber, 0 g; Sodium, 290 mg.

Bourride of Monkfish

Portions: 12   Portion size: about 5 oz (150 g) fish
2 oz (60 g) vegetables
2½ fl oz (70 mL) sauce

U.S.	Metric	Ingredients
2	2	Baking potatoes, large
5	5	Garlic cloves
to taste	to taste	Salt
to taste	to taste	Pepper
7 fl oz	200 mL	Olive oil
7 fl oz	200 mL	Peanut oil
4 oz	125 g	Onion, cut julienne
8 oz	250 g	Carrot, cut julienne
4 oz	125 g	Leek, cut julienne
1 fl oz	30 mL	Olive oil
12 oz	375 g	Peas
1½ pt	750 mL	White wine
1 pt 6 oz	700 mL	Fish stock
5 lb	2.5 kg	Monkfish fillets, boneless and skinless
as needed	as needed	Butter
to taste	to taste	Salt
to taste	to taste	Pepper

Per serving:
Calories, 750; Protein, 31 g; Fat, 64 g (77% cal.); Cholesterol, 135 mg;
Carbohydrates, 10 g; Fiber, 2 g; Sodium, 110 mg.

■ P r o c e d u r e

1. Bake the potatoes. While they are still hot, peel them and pass through a food mill to purée.
2. Peel and chop the garlic. Crush to a fine paste with a little salt and pepper.
3. Mix the garlic into the potato puree.
4. A little at a time, whip the olive oil and peanut oil into the potato as though making mayonnaise. It is important to add just a few drops at a time at first to get a smooth mixture.
5. Sweat the onion, carrot, and leek in the olive oil over low heat, covered, until tender. Set aside
6. Cook the peas in boiling salted water until tender. Drain, cool under cold water, drain again, and set aside.
7. Reduce the white wine by half, then add the fish stock. Simmer for 5 minutes.
8. Cut the monkfish into 48 equal pieces.
9. Butter the inside of a braising pan large enough to hold the monkfish in a single layer. Season the monkfish and place in the braising pan.
10. Pour the hot fish stock over the fish and simmer for 5–8 minutes or until done.
11. Remove the fish. Add it to the julienned vegetables and set aside.
12. Bring the cooking liquid to a boil and reduce by half (about 20 oz/600 mL), skimming regularly.
13. If the fish has cooled, reheat it and the vegetables briefly in the reduced cooking liquid. Strain again.
14. Whip the cooking liquid into the potato garlic mixture from step 4. Adjust the seasoning as necessary. Strain through a fine sieve.
15. Arrange the fish, julienned vegetables, and peas on plates (allowing 4 pieces of fish per portion) or on a serving platter. Pour the strained sauce over the fish.

Zuppa di Vongole

Portions: 16

U.S.	Metric	Ingredients
15 lb ·	7 kg	Small clams, such as littlenecks
1 pt	500 mL	Water
6 fl oz	175 mL	Olive oil
5 oz	150 g	Onion, small dice
3–5	3–5	Garlic cloves, chopped
6 tbsp	90 mL	Chopped parsley
12 fl oz	350 mL	White wine
1½ lb	700 g	Canned plum tomatoes, with juice, coarsely chopped

Per serving:
Calories, 680; Protein, 93 g; Fat,18 g (25% cal.); Cholesterol, 240 mg; Carbohydrates, 22 g; Fiber, 1 g; Sodium, 470 mg.

■ P r o c e d u r e

1. Scrub the clams under cold water to remove sand and grit from the shells.
2. Put the clams and water in a heavy covered pot and heat gently, just until the clams open. Set the clams aside. Strain and reserve the liquid.
3. Depending on how you wish to serve them, you can leave the clams in the shell or shell all but 4–6 of them per portion to use as garnish.

4. Heat the olive oil in a large pot. Sauté the onion until soft but not brown.
5. Add the garlic and cook another minute.
6. Add the parsley and the wine and boil for 1 minute.
7. Add the tomatoes and the reserved clam juice. Simmer 5 minutes.
8. Taste for seasoning and adjust if necessary.
9. Add the clams and reheat them gently. Do not overcook, or the clams will be tough.
10. Serve with plenty of crusty bread for dipping in the broth.

V A R I A T I O N S

Zuppa di Cozze
Substitute mussels for the clams.

Zuppa di Frutti di Mare
Use a mixture of clams, mussels, squid (cut up), and shrimp (shelled). Keep all the items separate. Cook the clams and mussels as in the basic recipe. Add the squid at the same time as the tomatoes and broth. Simmer slowly, covered, until tender. Add the shrimp and cook just 1 minute before adding the clams and mussels.

Zuppa di Pesce
Use a mixture of shellfish and fin fish, as desired. Add each type of fish just long enough before the end of cooking so that it cooks through without overcooking.

STEAMING AND MIXED COOKING TECHNIQUES

The recipes in this section are included here because they are difficult to classify as one of the basic cooking methods, although they are all based on moist-heat methods. Most of the recipes have two characteristics in common:

1. The item cooks in its own juices and, usually, a small amount of added liquid.

2. The item is served with its flavorful cooking liquid.

In some cases, enough liquid is added to barely cover, and the item simmers. In other cases, little liquid is added and the item cooks in the steam trapped by the pot lid.

The French term **étuver** (ay too vay) is used for this kind of procedure, in which the item cooks slowly in very little liquid. The word is usually translated as "stew," but this may be misleading. More precisely, it means "to cook or steam in its own juices" or "to sweat."

Note that all the procedure variations in this section are moist-heat cooking methods, but that the items are not submerged in liquid but rather steamed in an enclosed container. For this reason, simple steaming procedures are also discussed in this section.

In addition, this section includes two traditional recipes for dishes made with cooked seafood.

COOKING EN PAPILLOTE

An unusual version of the third variation at the left is called **cooking en papillote** (on poppy-yote), or in paper. The fish item, plus flavoring ingredients and sauce, is tightly enclosed in a piece of parchment so that steam cannot escape. When the paper package is heated, the item steams in its own moisture. All the juices, flavors, and aromas are held inside the paper, which is not opened until it is placed before the customer.

Sometimes a starch-thickened sauce is used in cooking fish en papillote. In this case, the fish is usually precooked (poached) so it will not exude juices that would dilute and spoil the sauce. The problem with this method is that the fish is often overcooked by the time it reaches the customer.

STOVETOP STEAMING

The simplest method of steaming is to place the item on a rack above simmering liquid, cover the pan, and steam until done. Because it does not come in contact with seasoned liquid or fat during cooking, steamed seafood is usually delicate in flavor, even more so than submersion-poached seafood. For this reason, this method is usually used when the cook wants to emphasize the pure, natural taste of the best-quality seafood.

Three methods are available to season and flavor steamed seafood:

1. Apply salt and other seasonings directly to the item.

2. Season the steaming liquid with aromatic herbs and other ingredients. The steam rising from the liquid carries a little of the aroma to the fish. This method gives only the subtlest and most delicate flavors to fish and is most effectively used with mild-tasting seafood.

3. Serve the seafood with an appropriate sauce. Accompaniments as simple as melted butter and lemon wedges are classic accompaniments to steamed seafood.

COMPARTMENT STEAMING

Several precautions should be observed if you cook fish and shellfish in a compartment steamer.

1. Watch the cooking time carefully. Fish cooks quickly, especially in the high heat of a steamer, and is easily overcooked.

Variations

Note the following three variations represented by the recipes in this section.

1. The product is cooked for a few minutes in fat over low heat, along with mirepoix or onion, to begin extracting juices. A little liquid is then added, the pot is covered, and the item is cooked. Example: Fisherman's Stew.

2. The product is sautéed over high heat. Then other ingredients and liquids are added and the item is cooked, covered, over low heat. Examples: Lobster à l'Americaine and Fricassée of Lobster.

3. The product is simply placed in a pot with liquids and flavoring ingredients. The pot is covered, and the item is steamed or simmered. Example: Moules Marinière.

2. Avoid pressure-steaming fish and shellfish, if possible. The high temperatures toughen fish protein very quickly. Such items as lobster tails can become rubbery.

3. Use solid pans to retain juices, and use the juices for sauces and soups.

Procedure for Steaming Seafood

1. Collect all equipment and food supplies. Select a pan large enough to hold the seafood and a rack that will hold the seafood above the simmering liquid.
2. Prepare the fish or seafood items for cooking. Trim and portion as necessary. Season as desired.
3. Pour water or other cooking liquid into the pan. There should be enough to last the entire cooking period without going dry, but not so much that it comes in contact with the seafood. Add aromatics and seasonings as desired. Bring to a boil.
4. Place the seafood on the rack and set above the liquid. Cover the pan and steam until done.
5. Remove the seafood from the rack. Serve with desired sauce and/or accompaniments.

 ## Lobster à l'Americaine

Portions: 2   Portion size: ½ lobster

U.S.	Metric	Ingredients
1	1	Live lobster, about 1½ (700 g)
1 oz	30 g	Butter, softened
2 fl oz	60 mL	Oil
1 tbsp	15 mL	Finally chopped shallot
½ tsp	2 mL	Finally chopped garlic
2 fl oz	60 mL	Brandy
6 fl oz	200 mL	White wine
4 fl oz	125 mL	Fish stock
4 oz	125 g	Tomato concassé
		or
2 oz	60 g	Tomato purée
1 tbsp	15 mL	Chopped parsley
¼ tsp	1 mL	Dried tarragon
pinch	pinch	Cayenne

Per serving:
Calories, 340; Protein, 7 g; Fat, 26 g (67% cal); Cholesterol, 50 mg;
Carbohydrates, 5 g; Fiber, 1 g; Sodium, 230 mg.

Procedure

1. Cut up the lobster, as shown in Figure 14.12.
2. Remove the tomalley (liver) and coral (if any). Mash them in a small bowl with the soft butter.
3. Heat the oil in a sauté pan and add the lobster pieces. Sauté over high heat until the shells turn red.
4. Drain off the oil by tilting the pan and holding the lobster in with the pan lid.
5. Add the shallot and garlic to the pan. Sauté for a few seconds.
6. Remove from the heat (to avoid burning yourself if the brandy flares up) and add the brandy. Return to the heat and add the wine, fish stock, tomato, chopped parsley, tarragon, and cayenne.
7. Cover the pan and simmer until the lobster is cooked, about 10–15 minutes.
8. Remove the lobster from the cooking liquid and place it on a serving platter or in broad soup plates for service. The meat may be left in the shell or removed from the shell, as desired.
9. Reduce the cooking liquid over high heat to about 6 oz (175 mL).
10. Remove from the heat and stir in the mixture of butter, tomalley, and coral from step 2. Heat the sauce gently for a minute, but do not boil or it will curdle. Adjust the seasoning.
11. Strain the sauce and pour it over the lobster. Serve immediately.

VARIATIONS

Lobster Newburg
(Note: See p. 496 for Seafood Newburg using cooked shellfish.) Prepare through step 4. Omit remaining ingredients. Instead, add 1 tbsp (15 mL) brandy, 3 tbsp (45 mL) sherry or Marsala or Madeira wine, and 3 fl oz (100 mL) fish stock. Cover and simmer as in basic recipe. Remove lobster meat from shells and discard shells. Reduce cooking liquid by half and add 1 cup (250 mL) heavy cream or light cream sauce. Reduce the sauce slightly and finish by adding the mixture of butter, tomalley and coral (step 10 of basic recipe). If desired, flavor with more sherry. Pour sauce over the lobster meat.

Shrimp à l'Americaine or Shrimp Newburg
Shrimp may be cooked using the main recipe or the variation. They should be shelled before combining with the finished sauce.

Moules Marinière (Steamed Mussels)

Portions: 10

U.S.	Metric	Ingredients
7 lb	3.2 kg	Mussels, in shells
3 oz	90 g	Shallots or onions, chopped fine
6	6	Parsley stems
¼ tsp	1 mL	Pepper
1 cup	250 mL	White wine
¼ cup	60 mL	Chopped parsley
3 oz	90 g	Butter
to taste	to taste	Salt
to taste	to taste	Lemon juice

Per serving:
Calories, 220; Protein, 20 g; Fat, 11 g (44% cal.); Cholesterol, 65 mg; Carbohydrates, 8 g; Fiber, 0 g; Sodium, 540 mg.

■ P r o c e d u r e

1. Scrub the mussels well with a stiff brush and remove the beards. Clean them well by soaking them according to the procedure given in Chapter 14.

2. Place the mussels in a stockpot or large saucepot. Add the shallots or onions, parsley stems, pepper, and wine.

3. Cover the pot and set it over moderately high heat. Cook until the mussels open, about 5 minutes.

4. Drain the mussels and strain the liquid through cheesecloth into a broad saucepan. Bring to a boil.

5. Add the parsley and butter. Swirl the liquid in the pan until the butter is melted. Season to taste with salt and a few drops of lemon juice.

6. For service, remove the top shells of the mussels (or leave them on, if desired). Place the mussels in broad soup plates and pour the sauce over them.

V A R I A T I O N

Steamed Mussels (without wine)
Substitute water for the wine and add 2 fl oz (60 mL) lemon juice. Increase the onion or shallot to 6 oz (175 g) and add 3 oz (90 g) sliced celery.

Mussels in Cream
Prepare the basic recipe. Reduce the cooking liquid by half and add 1 cup (250 mL) heavy cream or a liaison of 2 egg yolks and 1 cup (250 mL) heavy cream.

Moules Marinière

Mackerel en Papillote

Portions: 1   Portion size: 4 oz (125 g)

U.S.	Metric	Ingredients
1	1	Mackerel fillet, 4 oz (125 g) (see note)
2 tsp	10 mL	Melted butter
to taste	to taste	Salt
to taste	to taste	White pepper
2 tsp	10 mL	Chopped parsley
pinch	pinch	Dried marjoram
1 tsp	5 mL	Very finely chopped shallots,
2	2	Thin lemon slices

Per serving:
Calories, 290; Protein, 20 g; Fat, 23 g (71% cal.); Cholesterol, 85 mg; Carbohydrates, 1 g; Fiber, 0 g; Sodium, 150 mg.

Note: Pompano or bluefish may be used.

VARIATION

Instead of the parsley, shallots, and lemon slices, top fillets with a thin layer of Duxelles (p. 558).

■ Procedure

1. Cut out a piece of parchment in a heart shape, as shown in Figure 15.3. (Foil may be used instead of parchment.) The piece must be big enough to hold the fish and still have room for crimping the edges. Oil the parchment and place on the workbench oiled side down. (If using foil, place it oiled side up.)

2. Place the fillet on one side of the heart. Brush with melted butter and sprinkle with salt, pepper, parsley, marjoram, and chopped shallot, Lay the lemon slices on top.

3. Fold and crimp the parchment, as shown in the illustration, to enclose the fish tightly.

4. Place the folded package in a sauté pan or, if several orders are being done at once, on a sheet pan. Set on the range to start the cooking.

5. As soon as the paper begins to puff, place the pan in a hot oven (450°F/230°C). Bake until the parchment is puffed and browned, about 5–8 minutes. (If the paper doesn't brown, you may run it under the broiler for a second.)

6. Serve immediately. The parchment should be cut open in front of the customer.

Figure 15.3 Preparing foods en papillote.

(a) Cut out a heart-shaped piece of parchment by folding a parchment sheet in half and cutting half a heart from the folded side. Oil or butter the parchment and place on the work surface, oiled side down.

(b) Place the fish fillet or other item plus any sauce, topping, or seasoning, on one side of the heart.

(c) Fold over the other half of the heart. Starting at the top of the fold, make a small crimp in the edges as shown.

(d) Continue crimping around the edge. Each crimp holds the previous one in place.

(e) When you reach the bottom of the heart, fold the point under to hold it in place. The papillote is now ready for cooking.

Steamed Sea Bass with Garlic and Ginger

Portions: 10   Portion size: 5–6 oz (150–180 g)

U.S.	Metric	Ingredients
10	10	Sea bass fillets, skin on, 5–6 oz (150–180 g) each
10	10	Scallions, trimmed, halved lengthwise
10 thin slices	10 thin slices	Ginger root, peeled
4–5	4–5	Garlic cloves
5	5	Scallions, sliced thin
5 fl oz	150 mL	Soy sauce
5 fl oz	150 mL	Peanut oil

Per serving:
Calories, 280; Protein, 29 g; Fat, 17 g (54% cal.); Cholesterol, 60 mg; Carbohydrates, 4 g; Fiber, 1 g; Sodium, 1130 mg.

■ **P r o c e d u r e**

1. With the point of a sharp knife, lightly score the skin of the sea bass, making 3 or 4 diagonal cuts across the fillets.
2. Arrange the scallions on the rack of a steamer.
3. Place the fillets, skin side up, on top of the scallions.
4. Cut the ginger slices into thin shreds.
5. Cut the garlic cloves into paper-thin slices.
6. Scatter the ginger and garlic on top of the fillets.
7. Pour water into the bottom of a steamer and bring to a boil.
8. Place the steamer rack holding the fish in the steamer, cover, and steam just until the fish is done, about 4 to 8 minutes, depending on the thickness of the fish.
9. Remove the fish and the scallions from the steamer. Discard the scallions.
10. Place the fillets on hot plates.
11. Sprinkle the tops of the fillets with scallion slices.
12. Pour 1 tbsp (15 mL) soy sauce over each portion.
13. Heat the peanut oil until it is very hot, almost smoking.
14. Pour 1 tbsp (15 mL) oil over each portion.
15. Serve immediately.

V A R I A T I O N

Instead of finishing with soy sauce and hot oil, serve with Ponzu Sauce (p. 196) or Oriental Vinaigrette (p. 725).

 ## Seafood Newburg

Portions: 25   Portion size: 7 oz (200 g)

U.S.	Metric	Ingredients
2½ lb	1.2 kg	Cooked sea scallops
2½ lb	1.2 kg	Cooked crabmeat
1¼ lb	600 g	Cooked, peeled shrimp
4 oz	125 g	Butter
2½ tsp	12 mL	Paprika
8 fl oz	250 mL	Sherry
2½ qt	2.5 mL	Cream sauce, hot
to taste	to taste	Salt
to taste	to taste	White pepper

Per serving:
Calories, 330; Protein, 26 g; Fat, 19 g (53% cal.); Cholesterol, 145 mg; Carbohydrates, 11 g; Fiber, 0 g; Sodium, 550 mg.

■ **P r o c e d u r e**

1. If the sea scallops are large, cut them in halves or quarters.
2. Pick over the crabmeat to make sure there are no pieces of shell. If there are large pieces of meat, cut them into ½-in. (1-cm) dice.
3. Cut the shrimp in half lengthwise.
4. Heat the butter in a large saucepan or sauté pan. Add the paprika and the seafood. Sauté over moderate heat until heated through and coated lightly with butter.
5. Add sherry and simmer for a minute.
6. Add the cream sauce and bring to a simmer. Season to taste with salt and white pepper.
7. Serve with rice or in patty shells.

V A R I A T I O N

Different proportions of seafood may be used. Lobster meat may also be included.

Seafood Curry
Omit paprika and sherry. Substitute curry sauce (made with fish velouté) for the cream sauce. Garnish with toasted, sliced almonds, if desired.

Fisherman's Stew

Portions: 10   Portion size: see step 9

U.S.	Metric	Ingredients	
2 lb	900 g	Fish steaks or fillets (see note for suggested fish)	
10	10	Clams, in shell	
20	20	Mussels, in shell (or 10 more clams)	
5	5	Lobster tails, small (or use 10 large shrimp)	
4 fl oz	125 mL	Olive oil	
8 oz	250 g	Onions, sliced	
8 oz	250 g	Leeks, cut julienne	
2 tsp	10 mL	Chopped garlic	
¼ tsp	1 mL	Fennel seed	
12 oz	350 g	Tomato concassé or drained, chopped canned tomato	
2 qt	2 L	Fish stock	
4 fl oz	100 mL	White wine (optional but recommended)	
2	2	Bay leaves	
2 tbsp	30 mL	Chopped parsley	
¼ tsp	1 mL	Dried thyme	
2 tsp	10 mL	Salt	
¼ tsp	1 mL	Pepper	
20–30	20–30	French bread slices, dry or toasted	

■ P r o c e d u r e

1. Cut the fish into 3-oz (90 g) serving pieces.
2. Scrub the clams and mussels well.
3. Cut the lobster tails in half lengthwise with a heavy chef's knife. Remove the intestinal vein.
4. Heat the oil in a heavy saucepot or large straight-sided sauté pan.
5. Add the onions, leeks, garlic, and fennel seed. Sweat them in the oil for a few minutes.
6. Add the pieces of fish and the lobster tails (or shrimp). Cover and cook over low heat for a few minutes to begin extracting juice from the fish.
7. Remove the cover and add the clams and mussels.
8. Add the tomato, fish stock, wine, bay leaves, parsley, thyme, salt, and pepper. Cover and bring to a boil. Reduce heat and simmer about 15 minutes, until the clams and mussels are open.
9. To serve, place 2 or 3 thin slices of French bread in the bottoms of soup plates. For each portion, place 1 piece of fish, 1 clam, 2 mussels, and half of 1 lobster tail in each plate. Ladle 8 fl oz (250 mL) broth over the fish.

Per serving:
Calories, 470; Protein, 32 g; Fat, 26 g (51% cal.); Cholesterol, 90 mg;
Carbohydrates, 25 g; Fiber, 2 g; Sodium, 910 mg.

Note: Any firm fish may be used, such as halibut, cod, haddock, sea bass or striped bass, red snapper, or mackerel. Avoid delicate fish like flounder or sole, which break up easily during cooking.
   If desired, reduce or eliminate shellfish from the recipe and increase the quantity of fish.

Seafood Casserole au Gratin

Portions: 25   Portion size 6 oz (175 g)

U.S.	Metric	Ingredients
3¾ lb	1.7 kg	Cooked, flaked cod or other firm, white fish
2½ lb	1.1 kg	Cooked crabmeat, shrimp, scallops, or lobster meat, or a mixture of any of these
4 oz	125 g	Butter
2 qt	2 L	Mornay sauce, hot
4 oz	125 g	Parmesan cheese

Per serving:
Calories, 330; Protein, 33 g; Fat, 18 g (51% cal); Cholesterol, 120 mg; Carbohydrates, 6 g; Fiber, 0 g; Sodium, 520 mg.

■ P r o c e d u r e

1. Pick over the fish and shellfish to make sure it contains no bones or pieces of shell.

2. Heat the butter in a wide saucepan or straight-sided sauté pan. Add the fish and shellfish. Sauté lightly over moderate heat until the fish is heated through and coated with butter.

3. Add the mornay sauce and bring just to a simmer. Taste and adjust seasonings.

4. Ladle 6-oz (175-g) portions into individual service casseroles. Sprinkle with parmesan cheese.

5. Heat under the broiler at low heat until the tops are lightly browned.

V A R I A T I O N S

Other combinations of seafood may be used. If desired, use all fish or all shellfish.

Other sauces may by used instead of Mornay, including

Cream sauce	White wine sauce
Cheddar cheese sauce	Mushroom sauce (made from
Nantua sauce	fish velouté)

Salmon or Tuna Casserole

Use drained, canned salmon or tuna, and use cream sauce, cheddar cheese sauce, or mushroom sauce (made with fish velouté) instead of Mornay sauce. Combine the parmesan cheese with an equal quantity of buttered bread crumbs before topping. If desired, prepare in a baking pan instead of individual casseroles.

SEAFOOD SERVED RAW

Raw oysters and clams have long been enjoyed in North American restaurants as well as in homes. Smoked salmon, too, has always been a popular raw seafood item, although many people don't think of it as raw fish because it has been processed.

More recently, with the popularity of Japanese sushi and sashimi, many more people enjoy eating items made with raw fish, and chefs are experimenting with new ways to serve raw seafood items. Because of the danger of contamination from polluted fishing waters, however, many health officials advise against serving raw seafood. Nevertheless, these items remain popular. If you choose to serve raw seafood, observe the following guidelines:

1. Use only the freshest fish.

2. Buy the fish from a reliable purveyor.

3. Use only saltwater seafood from clean waters. Do not use freshwater fish, which is more likely than saltwater fish to contain parasites. To destroy possible parasites in saltwater fish, freeze it, and then thaw it before use.

4. Observe the strictest sanitation procedures.

5. Keep the fish cold. Handle it as little as possible.

Four kinds of raw fish recipes are included in this chapter. **Fish tartare** is a mixture of chopped raw fish mixed with various condiments and seasonings. **Fish carpaccio** is a dish consisting of very thin slices of firm, meaty fish such as tuna, served with various garnishes and usually with a piquant sauce such as a vinaigrette. *Carpaccio* (karpachio) is the Italian word for a dish of thin slices of raw beef, served the same way. **Seviche** or *ceviche* (seh vee chay, or, in Spanish, seh bee chay) is a preparation, native to Latin America, of raw seafood marinated in an acid mixture. The acid coagulates the protein so the texture of the raw fish resembles that of cooked fish. It is common to say that the acid "cooks" the fish. However, because the food is not subjected to heat, it is important to still think of the item as raw, for sanitation reasons. Sushi is seasoned Japanese short-grain rice that is usually, but not always, garnished with raw fish.

Sushi has become especially popular in Western countries, but there is much confusion about it. Sushi is often equated with raw fish, but in fact the term refers to cooked rice lightly flavored with seasoned vinegar. The rice is served with various garnishes, which include not only raw fish (the most popular garnish) but also cooked seafood and many kinds of vegetables and pickles.

Tartare of Sea Bass and Salmon

Yield: 3 lb (1.5 kg)	Portions: 12	Portion size: 4 oz (125 g)
U.S.	Metric	Ingredients
1 lb 4 oz	600 g	Salmon fillet, skinless and boneless
12 oz	375 g	Sea bass fillet, skinless and boneless
3 fl oz	90 mL	Lemon juice
2½ oz	75 g	Dijon mustard
3½ oz	100 g	Shallots, chopped
6 fl oz	175 mL	Olive oil
to taste	to taste	Salt
to taste	to taste	Pepper
7 tbsp	40 g	Chopped fresh parsley
4 tbsp	25 g	Chopped fresh chervil
3 tbsp	17 g	Chopped fresh chives
12 oz	375 g	Tomato, peeled and seeded
as needed	as needed	Chervil sprigs

Per serving:
Calories, 250; Protein, 16 g; Fat, 19 g (68% cal.); Cholesterol, 40 mg; Carbohydrates, 4 g; Fiber, 1 g; Sodium, 190 mg.

■ Procedure

1. Chop the fish with a knife. Refrigerate until ready to mix and serve.
2. Whip together the lemon juice, mustard, and shallots. Gradually whip in the oil until well emulsified. Season to taste, then mix in the chopped herbs.
3. Mix into the chopped fish.
4. Cut a small brunoise of tomato.
5. The tartare can be presented either in quenelles (see Figure 13.5.) or molded in a ring mold (see Figure 15.4). Sprinkle the plate with the tomato and decorate with springs of chervil.

Tartare of Sea Bass and Salmon

Figure 15.4
Shaping food with a ring mold.

(a) Position a ring mold on the plate. Fill with the food and level the top with a palette knife or spatula.

(b) Carefully lift off the mold.

Sushi Rice

Yield: about 2½ lb (1.1 kg)

U.S.	Metric	Ingredients
3 cups	750 mL	Japanese short-grain rice (see note)
3½ cups	900 mL	Water, cold
3–4 fl oz	100–125 mL	Sushi vinegar (see note)

Per 1 ounce:
Calories, 40; Protein, 1 g; Fat, 0g (0% cal.); Cholesterol, 0 mg; Carbohydrates, 9 g; Fiber, 0 g; Sodium, 105 mg.

Note: Do not confuse Japanese short-grain rice with glutinous rice, which is an entirely different product. Sushi vinegar is commercially available, but it can also be made in the kitchen. Combine 1 pint (500 mL) Japanese rice vinegar, 8 oz (250 g) sugar, and 4 oz (125 g) salt. Heat and stir until the sugar and salt are dissolved, then cool.

■ **P r o c e d u r e**

1. Wash the rice in several changes of cold water. Drain well.

2. Put the drained rice in a heavy saucepan and add the measured water. Cover tightly and let stand at least 30 minutes.

3. With the cover in place, set the pan over high heat and bring to a boil. When it boils, reduce the heat to medium and let cook until all the water is absorbed. Do not remove the cover to check, but listen to the sounds. The bubbling will stop, and there will be a faint hissing sound.

4. Reduce the heat to very low and cook another 5 minutes. Then remove from heat and let stand at least 15 minutes before removing the cover. You now have the basic white rice that is eaten with Japanese meals.

5. In Japan, mixing in the vinegar is done in special wooden tub that is used only for this purpose (to avoid off flavors). The advantage of wood is that it absorbs excess moisture. If you use a nonabsorbent mixing bowl, transfer the rice to a clean bowl whenever the mixing bowl becomes coated with moisture. Using a wooden paddle or plastic spatula, break up the hot rice to get rid of all lumps. At the same time, fan the rice to cool it.

6. When the rice is slightly warm to the touch, begin adding the sushi vinegar. Add a little at a time while mixing gently. The rice is ready when it has a glossy apperance and a very mild taste of the vinegar. The vinegared rice is best if used within 2–3 hours, and it must not be refrigerated.

V A R I A T I O N S

Nigirizushi (Finger Sushi)

1. Prepare *wasabi* (green horseradish) by mixing wasabi powder with a little water to form a thick paste. Let stand, covered, a few minutes to allow flavor to develop.

2. Prepare sushi toppings by cutting very fresh fish fillets (use saltwater fish or smoked salmon) into slices about 1½ x 2½ in. (4 x 6 cm). Tuna, the most popular fish for sushi, is tender and is usually cut about ¼ in. (6 mm) thick. Other fish are cut thinner.

3. Wet your hands with cold water to keep the rice from sticking to them, then pick up about 2 tbsp (30 mL) sushi rice. Shape it into firm oval about 1½ in. (4 cm) long (see Figure 15.5). Pick up a slice of fish in one hand. Dip a finger of the other hand in the wasabi and spread a very small amount on the underside of the fish slice. Drape the fish over the rice, with the wasabi underneath next to the rice, and press it gently but firmly in place. Serve with soy sauce for dipping.

Kappa-maki (Cucumber Roll)

To make rolled sushi, you will need a special bamboo mat called a *sudare* (see Figure 15.5). You could also use a sheet of parchment, but the roll will be harder to make.

1. Peel a cucumber. Cut it in half and scrape out the seeds. Cut lengthwise into julienne.

2. Cut a sheet of *nori* (a type of seaweed for rolled sushi) in half crosswise. Toast it by passing it briefly above a burner flame, being careful not to burn it.

3. Put the bamboo mat on the table in front of you with the bamboo strips horizontal. Put the half-sheet of nori on the mat, smooth side down.

4. Cover the two-thirds of the nori closest to you with a layer of sushi rice about ¼ in. (6 mm) thick.

5. Spread a light streak of wasabi from right to left across the middle of the rice.

6. Lay strips of cucumber evenly on top of the strip of wasabi.

7. Lift the edge of the mat closest to you and roll up firmly. This is best done by lifting the mat with the thumbs while holding the cucumber in place with the fingers. Press the roll in the mat gently but firmly to make it tight.

8. Wipe the blade of a very sharp knife, then cut the roll in half crosswise. Do not saw the roll but cut it cleanly with a single stroke. Wiping the blade on a damp cloth after every cut, cut each half roll into 3 or 4 pieces.

Tekka-maki (Tuna Roll)

Make Kappa-maki, but instead of cucumber, use raw tuna cut into batonnet strips.

Chirashizushi (Scatter Sushi)

Fill a serving bowl half full of sushi rice. Carefully and attractively arrange an assortment of raw fish, cooked shrimp, crabmeat, and neatly cut vegetables such as snow peas, cucumbers, carrots, mushrooms, and pickled ginger on top of the rice.

Figure 15.5 Making sushi.

(a) For nigirizushi, wet your hands with cold water to keep the rice from sticking to them. Form a bit of rice into a small oval in one hand.

(b) In the other hand, pick up a slice of fish and smear a dab of wasabi on the bottom of it.

(c) Top the rice with the fish, wasabi side against the rice, and press in place in the palm of one hand with two fingers of the other.

(d) Turn it over and press the same way. Then press the sides with the thumb and forefinger to finish shaping it.

(e) For rolled sushi, put a half piece of nori on the sudare (bamboo mat). Wetting your hands with cold water to keep the rice from sticking to them, spread a layer of sushi rice over the bottom two-thirds of the nori.

(f) Lay strips of the filling across the middle of the rice.

(g) Holding the filling in place with the fingers, lift the corner of the mat with the thumbs and roll up.

(h) Press the mat firmly and evenly to make a tight roll.

(i) Cut the roll in half with a single forward stroke, using a dampened knife.

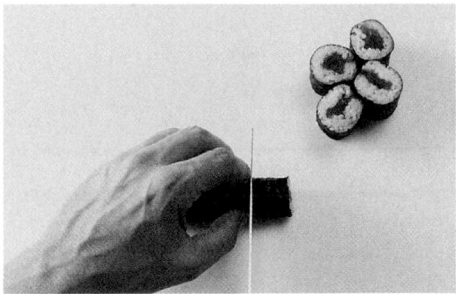

(j) Wipe the blade between cuts, and cut each half-roll into three or four pieces.

SUSHI: A JAPANESE CLASSIC

Fish and rice dominate the cuisine of the island nation of Japan, and these two staples are combined in sushi, a classic Japanese preparation that is especially popular in the West. Sushi originated many years ago as a way of preserving fish by salting it and packing it with vinegared rice. When the fish was eaten, the rice was discarded.

In Japan, it takes many years of apprenticeship to become a sushi master, or *itamae* (ee-tah-mah-eh). A master is skilled in preparing rice properly, making rice fingers of just the right size and compactness for *nigirizushi,* and especially in selecting, judging, and cutting the many varieties of fresh seafood used as toppings.

When one is eating nigirizushi, it is considered improper to dip the rice ball into soy sauce. The large amount of soy sauce absorbed by the rice masks the fresh flavor of the toppings and makes the rice ball break up. Instead, turn the sushi over and dip the seafood topping lightly in the sauce.

Incidentally, in Japanese, an initial s sound, as in the word *sushi*, may change to a z sound when it is in the middle of a compound word, as in *nigirizushi.*

Scallop Seviche

Portions: 12   Portion size: 4 oz (125 g)

U.S.	Metric	Ingredients	■ P r o c e d u r e
2 lb	1 kg	Sea scallops (see note)	1. Cut the scallops into quarters vertically, then slice crosswise ¼ in. (6 mm) thick.
8 fl oz	250 mL	Lime juice	2. In a nonreactive container, mix together the scallops, lime juice, and onion.
4 oz	125 g	Red onion, chopped fine	3. Refrigerate about 12 hours, until the scallops have the texture of cooked scallops.
1	1	Jalapeño, seeded and chopped fine	4. Drain the scallops and onions, discarding the lime juice.
6 tbsp	90 mL	Chopped cilantro	5. Gently toss the scallops with the jalapeño, cilantro, avocado, and tomato.
2	2	Avocados, medium dice	
8 oz	250 g	Tomato, peeled and seeded, small dice	6. Add salt to taste.
to taste	to taste	Salt	7. Mix in the olive oil
4 fl oz	125 mL	Olive oil	
as needed	as needed	Lettuce leaves	8. To serve, line small bowls or cups with lettuce leaves and spoon in the seviche.

Per serving:
Calories, 220; Protein, 14 g; Fat, 15 g (61% cal.); Cholesterol, 25 mg; Carbohydrates, 8 g; Fiber, 2 g; Sodium, 130 mg.

Note: As an alternative to sea scallops, use bay scallops and leave them whole.

Scallop Seviche

Tuna Carpaccio with Sheep's–Milk Cheese

Portions: 12   Portion size: 5 oz (150 g) tuna
2½ oz (70 g) garnish
1½ fl oz (45 mL) sauce

U.S.	Metric	Ingredients
7 fl oz	200 mL	Lime juice
3 oz	80 g	Shallots, chopped
12 fl oz	375 mL	Olive oil
to taste	to taste	Salt
to taste	to taste	Pepper
4½ lb	2 kg	Fresh tuna
1 lb	500 g	Sheep's milk cheese (see note)
3½ oz	100 g	Red pepper
3½ oz	100 g	Green bell pepper
7 oz	200 g	Scallions
⅔ oz (3 tbsp)	20 g	Fresh basil

■ P r o c e d u r e

1. Combine the lime juice, shallots, and olive oil to make a marinade, seasoning it with salt and pepper.
2. Slice the tuna into paper-thin slices, using a slicing machine. Marinate, refrigerated, for 2 hours.
3. Cut the cheese into very thin slices.
4. Cut the peppers into a small brunoise. Blanch and refresh. Drain well on paper towel.
5. Thinly slice the scallions.
6. Chop the basil.
7. Drain the tuna, reserving the marinade. Cut out rounds using a round cutter. Do the same with the cheese. Arrange in a single layer on a plate, alternating cheese and tuna, with the rounds slightly overlapping.
8. Sprinkle with the chopped scallions, peppers, and chopped basil.
9. Whisk the marinade until emulsified and drizzle over. Decorate with whole basil leaves.

Per serving:
Calories, 620; Protein, 50 g; Fat, 44 g (64% cal.); Cholesterol, 120 mg; Carbohydrates, 6 g; Fibers, 1 g; Sodium, 200 mg.

Note: The cheese used for this recipe is a hard cheese, with a smooth texture, golden color, and nutty flavor. It is similar in flavor to Edam. Substitute a similar cheese as necessary.

■ TERMS FOR REVIEW

meunière	au bleu	étuver	fish carpaccio
shallow poaching	cuisson	en papillote	sushi
submersion method	à la nage	fish tartare	seviche
court bouillon			

■ QUESTIONS FOR DISCUSSION

1. What major precaution must be taken when baking or broiling lean fish?
2. Describe the procedure for cooking fish à la meunière.
3. Which side of a fish fillet is the presentation side?
4. What techniques can you use for lifting whole poached fish out of court bouillon without breaking it or damaging its appearance?
5. What temperatures are best for poaching fish?
6. What is one advantage of using the oven to poach fish fillets?
7. Describe two methods for making a finished sauce out of the cooking liquid (fumet and wine) used for poaching fish fillets.
8. Discuss the precautions a cook should take to ensure that raw fish is safe to eat.

16
Understanding Vegetables

Vegetables were, at one time, abused and neglected, relegated to the minor role of unimportant side dishes, to be taken or left, or not even noticed on the table.

Today, however, lowly vegetables are much more appreciated, not only for their nutritional importance but for the variety, flavor, eye appeal, and even elegance and sophistication they bring to the menu. Modern cooks owe it to themselves and their customers to treat vegetables with understanding, respect, and imagination.

Because they are so perishable, vegetables require extra care from receiving to service. *Freshness* is their most appealing and attractive quality, and one must be especially careful to preserve it. The goals of proper vegetable cookery are to preserve and enhance fresh flavor, texture, and color, to prepare and serve vegetables that are not just accepted but sought after.

After reading this chapter, you should be able to

1. **Describe the factors that influence texture, flavor, color, and nutritional changes when cooking vegetables.**

2. **Cook vegetables to their proper doneness.**

3. **Judge quality in cooked vegetables based on color, appearance, texture, flavor, seasonings, and appropriateness of combination with sauces or other vegetables.**

4. **Perform pre-preparation tasks for fresh vegetables.**

5. **Calculate yields based on trimming losses.**

6. **Determine the quality of frozen, canned, and dried vegetables.**

7. **Prepare vegetables using the batch cooking method and the blanch and chill method.**

8. **Store fresh and processed vegetables.**

CONTROLLING QUALITY CHANGES DURING COOKING

As a cook, you have a choice of many kinds of vegetables and many cooking methods. Not surprisingly, then, you are also faced with the necessity of learning many rules for cooking vegetables.

Many guides to vegetable cookery simply present a long list of rules to memorize. You will be able to understand the principles more easily, however, if you first learn how vegetables change as they are cooked and how to control those changes. In other words, it is suggested you not just memorize what to do but understand why you do it.

Cooking affects vegetables in four ways. It changes the following:

1. Texture.
2. Flavor.
3. Color.
4. Nutrients.

How much these four characteristics change determines whether your final product is attractive and delicious to the customer or whether it ends up in the garbage. You can control these changes if you understand how they happen.

Unfortunately, there is still legitimate controversy among chefs about proper vegetable cooking techniques. Modern technology has not yet solved all the problems that experienced chefs tackle successfully every day in the kitchen.

CONTROLLING TEXTURE CHANGES

Changing the texture is one of the main purposes of cooking vegetables.

FIBER

The fiber structures of vegetables (including cellulose and pectins) give them shape and firmness. Cooking softens some of these components.

The *amount of fiber* varies

1. In different vegetables. Spinach and tomatoes have less than carrots and turnips, for example.

2. In different examples of the same vegetables. Old, tough carrots have more fiber than young, fresh carrots.

3. In the same vegetable. The tender tips of asparagus and broccoli have less fiber than their tougher stalks.

Fiber is made *firmer* by

1. **Acids.**
Lemon juice, vinegar, and tomato products, when added to cooking vegetables, extend the cooking time.

2. **Sugars.**
Sugar strengthens cell structure. You will use this principle primarily in fruit cookery. For firm poached apples or pears, for example, cook in a heavy syrup. For applesauce, cook apples until soft before sweetening.

Fiber is *softened* by

1. **Heat.**
   In general, longer cooking means softer vegetables.

2. **Alkalis.**
   Do not add baking soda to green vegetables. Not only does it destroy vitamins but it also makes the vegetables unpleasantly mushy.

STARCH

Starch is another vegetable component that affects texture.

1. *Dry starchy foods* like dried legumes (beans, peas, lentils), rice, and macaroni products must be cooked in enough water for the starch granules to absorb moisture and soften. Dried beans are usually soaked before cooking to replace lost moisture.

2. *Moist starchy vegetables* like potatoes and sweet potatoes have enough moisture of their own, but they must still be cooked until the starch granules soften.

DONENESS

A vegetable is said to be done when it has reached the desired degree of tenderness. This stage varies from vegetable to vegetable. Some, such as winter squash, eggplant, and braised celery, are considered properly cooked when they are quite soft. Most vegetables, however, are best cooked very briefly, until they are crisp-tender or **al dente** (firm to the bite). At this stage of tenderness, they not only have the most pleasing texture but also retain maximum flavor, color, and nutrients.

Guidelines for Achieving Proper Doneness in Vegetables

1. Don't overcook.
2. Cook as close to service as possible. Holding vegetables in a steam table continues to cook them.
3. If vegetables must be cooked in advance, slightly undercook them, cool rapidly in cold water, drain, and refrigerate, then reheat to order.
4. For uniform doneness, cut vegetables into pieces of uniform size before cooking.
5. Vegetables with both tough and tender parts need special treatment so the tender parts are not overcooked by the time the tougher parts are done. For example,

   Peel the woody stalks of asparagus.

   Peel or split broccoli stalks.

   Pierce the base of brussels sprouts with a sharp knife.

   Remove the heavy center stalks of lettuce leaves before braising.

6. Don't mix batches of cooked vegetables. They are likely to be cooked to slightly different levels of doneness.

CONTROLLING FLAVOR CHANGES

COOKING PRODUCES FLAVOR LOSS

Many flavors are lost during cooking by dissolving into the cooking liquid and by evaporation. The longer a vegetable is cooked, the more flavor it loses.

Flavor loss can be controlled in several ways:

1. Cook for as short a time as possible.

2. Use boiling salted water. Starting vegetables in boiling water shortens cooking time. The addition of salt helps reduce flavor loss.

3. Use just enough water to cover to minimize leaching. Note that this rule contradicts rule 1 in that adding vegetables to a small quantity of water lowers the temperature more, so cooking time is extended. Save your questions on this until you have finished reading the sections on color and nutritional changes.

4. Steam vegetables whenever appropriate. Steam cooking reduces leaching out of flavor and shortens cooking time.

Strong-Flavored Vegetables

With certain strong-flavored vegetables, it is desirable to lose some of the flavor to make them more appealing to the taste. These include the onion family (onions, garlic, leeks, shallots), the cabbage family (cabbage, brussels sprouts, cauliflower, broccoli), and some root vegetables (turnips, rutabagas).

When cooking strong-flavored vegetables, leave uncovered to allow these flavors to escape, and use larger amounts of water.

COOKING PRODUCES FLAVOR CHANGES

Cooked vegetables do not taste like raw vegetables because cooking produces certain chemical changes. As long as the vegetables are not overcooked, this change is desirable. It produces the flavors one looks for in vegetable dishes.

Overcooking produces undesirable changes in members of the cabbage family. They develop a strong, unpleasant flavor. Cabbage and its relatives should be cooked quickly, uncovered.

COOKING AND SWEETNESS

Young, freshly harvested vegetables have a relatively high sugar content that makes them taste sweet. As they mature, or as they sit in storage, the sugar gradually changes to starch. This is especially noticeable in corn, peas, carrots, turnips, and beets.

To serve sweet-tasting vegetables:

1. Try to serve young, fresh vegetables that have been stored for as short a time as possible.

2. For older vegetables, especially those just listed, add a small amount of sugar to the cooking water to replace lost sweetness.

CONTROLLING COLOR CHANGES

It is important to preserve as much natural color as possible when cooking vegetables. Because customers may reject or accept a vegetable on the basis of its appearance, it can be said that its visual quality is as important as its flavor or nutritional value.

Pigments are compounds that give vegetables their color. Different pigments react in different ways to heat and to acids and other elements that may be present during cooking, so it is necessary to discuss them one at a time. Table 16.1 summarizes this information.

WHITE VEGETABLES

White pigments, called flavones, are the primary coloring compounds in potatoes, onions, cauliflower, and white cabbage and in the white parts of such vegetables as celery, cucumbers, and zucchini.

White pigments stay white in acid and turn yellow in alkaline water. To keep vegetables such as cauliflower white, add a little lemon juice or cream of tartar to the cook-

Table 16.1
Vegetable Color Changes During Cooking

Color	Examples of Vegetables	Cooked with Acid	Cooked with Alkali	Overcooked
White	Potatoes, turnips, cauliflower, onions, white cabbage	White	White	Yellowish, gray
Red	Beets, red cabbage (not tomatoes, whose pigment is like that in yellow vegetables)	Red	Blue or blue-green	Greenish blue, faded
Green	Asparagus, green beans, lima beans, broccoli, brussels sprouts, peas, spinach, green peppers, artichokes, okra	Olive green	Bright green	Olive green
Yellow (and orange)	Carrots, tomatoes, rutabagas, sweet potatoes, squash, corn	Little change	Little change	Slightly faded

ing water. (Don't add too much, though, as this may toughen the vegetable.) Covering the pot also helps keep acids in.

Cooking for a short time, especially in a steamer, helps maintain color (and flavor and nutrients as well). Overcooking or holding too long in a steam table turns white vegetables dull yellow or gray.

RED VEGETABLES

Red pigments, called anthocyanins, are found in only a few vegetables, mainly red cabbage and beets. Blueberries also are colored by these red pigments. (The red color of tomatoes and red peppers is due to the same pigments that color carrots yellow or orange.)

Red pigments react very strongly to acids and alkalis.

Acids turn them a brighter red.

Alkalis turn them blue or blue-green (not a very appetizing color for red cabbage).

Red beets and red cabbage, therefore, have their best color when cooked with a small amount of acid. Red cabbage is often cooked with tart apples for this reason.

When a strongly acid vegetable is desired, such as Harvard Beets or Braised Red Cabbage, add just a small amount of acid at first. Acids toughen vegetables and prolong cooking time. Add the rest when the vegetables are tender.

Red pigments dissolve easily in water. This means

1. Use a short cooking time. Overcooked red vegetables lose a lot of color.
2. Use only as much water as is necessary.
3. Cook beets whole and unpeeled, with root and an inch of stem attached, to protect color. Skins easily slip off cooked beets.
4. When steaming, use solid pans instead of perforated pans to retain the red juices.
5. Whenever possible, serve the cooking liquid as a sauce with the vegetable.

GREEN VEGETABLES

Green coloring, or chlorophyll, is present in all green plants. Green vegetables are common in the kitchen, so it is important to understand the special handling required by this pigment.

Acids are enemies of green vegetables. Both *acid* and *long cooking* turn green vegetables to a drab olive green.

Protect the color of green vegetables by

1. Cooking uncovered to allow plant acids to escape.
2. Cooking for the shortest possible time. Properly cooked green vegetables are tender-crisp, not mushy.

3. Cooking in small batches rather than holding for long periods in a steam table.

Steaming is rapidly becoming the preferred method for cooking green vegetables. Steam cooks food rapidly, lessens the dissolving out of nutrients and flavor, and does not break up delicate vegetables. Overcooking, however, can occur rapidly in steamers.

Do not use baking soda to maintain green color. Soda destroys vitamins and makes texture unpleasantly mushy and slippery.

How much water should be used when boiling? A large quantity of water helps dissolve plant acids, helps preserve colors, and speeds cooking. But some cooks feel that an excessive amount of nutrients are lost. See the next section for further discussion.

YELLOW AND ORANGE VEGETABLES

Yellow and *orange* pigments, called **carotenoids**, are found in carrots, corn, winter squash, rutabaga, sweet potatoes, tomatoes, and red peppers. These pigments are very stable. They are little affected by acids or alkalis. Long cooking can dull the color, however. Short cooking not only prevents dulling of the color but also preserves vitamins and flavors.

CONTROLLING NUTRIENT LOSSES

Vegetables are an important part of our diets because they supply a wide variety of essential nutrients. They are our major sources of vitamins A and C and are rich in many other vitamins and minerals. Unfortunately, many of these nutrients are easily lost.

Six factors are responsible for most nutrient loss:

1. High temperature.
2. Long cooking.
3. Leaching (dissolving out).
4. Alkalis (baking soda, hard water).
5. Plant enzymes (which are active at warm temperatures but destroyed by high heat).
6. Oxygen.

Some nutrient loss is inevitable because it is rarely possible to avoid all of these conditions at the same time. For example,

- Pressure steaming shortens cooking time, but the high temperature destroys some vitamins.
- Braising uses low heat, but the cooking time is longer.
- Baking eliminates the leaching out of vitamins and minerals, but the long cooking and high temperature cause nutrient loss.
- Boiling is faster than simmering, but the higher temperature can be harmful and the rapid activity can break up delicate vegetables and increase loss through leaching.
- Cutting vegetables into small pieces decreases cooking time, but it increases leaching by creating more exposed surfaces.
- Even steaming allows some leaching out of nutrients into the moisture that condenses on the vegetables and then drips off.

COOKING IN A LITTLE
LIQUID VERSUS A LOT OF LIQUID

This is an area of controversy with good arguments on both sides.

1. Using a lot of liquid increases vitamin loss by leaching. Use just enough liquid to cover. Save the cooking liquid for reheating the vegetables or for stocks or soups.

2. Using a little liquid increases cooking time. When the vegetables are combined with the small quantity of boiling water, the temperature is lowered greatly and the vegetables must sit in warm water while it again heats up. Also, plant enzymes may destroy some vitamins before the water again becomes hot enough to destroy them.

Tests have shown that, for these reasons, no more nutrients are lost when vegetables are cooked in a lot of water than when vegetables are cooked in just enough water to cover.

When cooking green vegetables, there is an added advantage to using a lot of water. Plant acids are more quickly diluted and driven off, better preserving the color.

The best cooking methods, nutritionally, are usually those that produce the most attractive, flavorful products.

*   They are more likely to be eaten. Discarded vegetables benefit no one, no matter how nutritious they are.

*   Factors that destroy nutrients are often those that also destroy color, flavor, and texture.

GENERAL RULES OF
VEGETABLE COOKERY

Now that you understand how vegetables change as they cook, let's summarize that information in some general rules. You should now be able to explain the reasons for each of these rules.

*   Don't overcook.

*   Cook as close to service time as possible and in small quantities. Avoid holding for long periods on a steam table.

*   If the vegetable must be cooked ahead, undercook slightly and chill rapidly. Reheat at service time.

*   Never use baking soda with green vegetables.

*   Cut vegetables uniformly for even cooking.

*   Start with boiling, salted water when boiling green vegetables and other vegetables that grow above the ground. Roots and tubers are started in cold, salted water for more even cooking.

*   Cook green vegetables and strong-flavored vegetables uncovered.

*   To preserve color, cook red and white vegetables in a slightly acid (not strongly acid) liquid. Cook green vegetables in a neutral liquid.

*   Do not mix a batch of freshly cooked vegetables with a batch of the same vegetable that has been cooked earlier and kept hot in a steam table.

STANDARDS OF QUALITY IN COOKED VEGETABLES

1. **Color.**
   Bright, natural colors.
   Green vegetables, in particular, should be a fresh, bright green, not olive green.

2. **Appearance on plate.**
   Cut neatly and uniformly. Not broken up.
   Attractively arranged or mounded on plate or dish.
   Not swimming in cooking water.
   Imaginative and appropriate combinations and garnishes are always well received.

3. **Texture.**
   Cooked to the right degree of doneness.
   Most vegetables should be crisp-tender, not overcooked and mushy, but not tough or woody either.
   Vegetables intended to be soft (potatoes, squash, sweet potatoes, tomatoes, vegetable purées) should be cooked through, with a pleasant, smooth texture.

4. **Flavor.**
   Full, natural flavor and sweetness, sometimes called *garden-fresh* flavor. Strong-flavored vegetables should be pleasantly mild, with no off flavors or bitterness.

5. **Seasonings.**
   Lightly and appropriately seasoned. Seasonings should not be too strong and not mask the natural garden flavors.

6. **Sauces.**
   Butter and seasoned butters should be fresh and not used heavily; vegetables should not be greasy.
   Cream sauces and other sauces should not be too thick or too heavily seasoned. As with seasonings, sauces should enhance, not cover up.

7. **Vegetable combinations.**
   Interesting combinations attract customers.
   Flavors, colors, and shapes should be pleasing in combination.
   Vegetables should be cooked separately and then combined to allow for different cooking times.
   Acid vegetables (like tomatoes) added to green vegetables will discolor them. Combine just before service.

HANDLING VEGETABLES

FRESH VEGETABLES

WASHING

1. Wash all vegetables thoroughly.
2. Root vegetables that are not peeled, such as potatoes for baking, should be scrubbed very well with a stiff vegetable brush.

3. Wash green, leafy vegetables in several changes of cold water. Lift the greens from the water so the sand can sink to the bottom. Pouring off into a colander dumps the sand back onto the leaves.

4. After washing, drain well and refrigerate lightly covered. The purpose of covering is to prevent drying, but covering too tightly cuts off air circulation. This can be a problem if the product is stored more than a day because mold is more likely to grow in a damp, closed space. Use a drain insert in the storage container to allow drainage.

SOAKING

1. With a few exceptions, do not soak vegetables for long periods. Flavor and nutrients leach out.

2. Cabbage, broccoli, brussels sprouts, and cauliflower may be soaked for 30 minutes in cold salted water to eliminate insects, if necessary.

3. Limp vegetables can be soaked briefly in cold water to restore crispness.

4. Dried legumes are soaked for several hours before cooking to replace moisture lost in drying. Dried beans absorb their weight in water.

PEELING AND CUTTING

1. Peel most vegetables as thinly as possible. Many nutrients lie just under the skin.

2. Cut vegetables into uniform pieces for even cooking.

3. Peel and cut vegetables as close to cooking time as possible to prevent drying and loss of vitamins through oxidation.

4. For machine paring, sort vegetables for evenness of size to minimize waste.

5. Treat vegetables that brown easily (potatoes, eggplant, artichokes, sweet potatoes) with an acid, such as lemon juice, or an antioxidant solution, or hold under water until ready to use (some vitamins and minerals will be lost).

6. Save edible trim for soups, stocks, and vegetable purées.

TRIMMING LOSS: CALCULATING YIELDS AND AMOUNTS NEEDED

The percentage yield of a vegetable indicates, on the average, how much of the **AP weight** (as purchased weight) is left after pre-prep to produce the ready-to-cook item, or **EP weight** (edible portion weight). You can use this figure to do two basic calculations.

1. **Calculating yield.**
   Example: You have 10 lb AP brussels sprouts. Yield after trimming is 80 percent. What will your EP weight be?

   First, change the percentage to a decimal number by moving the decimal point two places to the left.

   80% = 0.80

   Multiply the decimal by your AP weight to get EP yield.

   10 lb x 0.80 = 8 lb

2. **Calculating amount needed.**
   Example: You need 10 lb EP brussels sprouts. What amount of untrimmed vegetable do you need?

   Change the percentage to a decimal number.

   80% = 0.80

   Divide the EP weight needed by this number to get the AP weight.

   $$\frac{10\ lb}{0.80} = 12\frac{1}{2}\ lb$$

CLASSIFYING VEGETABLES

Many people are bothered by the fact that tomatoes are referred to as vegetables when they are, in fact, fruits. Yes, tomatoes are fruits, and carrots are roots, and spinach is a leaf, and they are all vegetables.

To a botanist, the term *fruit* refers to a specific part of a plant, just as do the terms stem, root, and leaf. A fruit is defined as the ripened ovary or ovaries of a seed-bearing plant, and it contains the seeds. In other words, if it has seeds, it's a fruit. We shouldn't be misled by the fact that a few fruits are sweet. Many, if not most, fruits in nature are not sweet at all. Some examples of fruits used in the vegetable kitchen are tomatoes, eggplant, peppers, green beans, okra, cucumbers, squash, pea pods, walnuts, and avocados.

There are many ways of classifying vegetables. Some are more helpful to the cook than others. Putting vegetables into groups based on their botanical origin is not always helpful. For example, okra and eggplant are both fruits, but they are handled and cooked so differently that this information doesn't really help us.

The following vegetable categories are based, in part, on how the vegetables are used in the kitchen. For example, the vegetables listed under roots and tubers come from several unrelated families, but they all have fairly solid, uniform textures and are handled in similar ways. This is not a scientific classification, and it is not the only way to group vegetables.

Note that the first three categories are all fruits or, in a few cases, seeds from fruits.

- The gourd family: cucumber, winter and summer squashes, pumpkin, chayote
- Seeds and pods: beans, peas, corn, okra
- Other tender-fruited vegetables: avocado, eggplant, sweet and hot peppers, tomato
- Roots and tubers: beet, carrot, celery root, parsnip, radish, turnip, rutabaga, Jerusalem artichoke, potato, sweet potato, jícama
- The cabbage family: cabbage, broccoli, cauliflower, brussels sprouts, kohlrabi, bok choy
- The onion family: onion, scallion, leek, garlic, shallot
- Leafy greens: spinach, beet greens, lettuces, endive and chicory, Swiss chard, sorrel, watercress, collards, kale, turnip greens (the last three are also members of the cabbage family)
- Stalks, stems, and shoots: globe artichoke, asparagus, celery, fennel, fiddlehead ferns, bamboo shoots
- Mushrooms

FRESH VEGETABLES: EVALUATING AND PREPARING

This section lists the fresh vegetables commonly used in North American kitchens, including many products that have become familiar from Asian and Latin cuisines. Tips for evaluation and trimming the products, as well as the average trimming yield, are indicated. Vegetables are listed alphabetically, rather than by family classification, to make them easier to find.

Artichokes, Globe

Identification: Artichokes are the unopened or immature flowers of a type of thistle. They vary in size and coloration but are usually round to somewhat elongated, colored light to medium green, sometimes with purple tints.

Related Varieties: Baby artichokes are not actually babies but come from a different place on the plant and are at their full size. Especially young baby artichokes may be tender enough to eat whole, with little trimming except for removing the top points of the leaves.

Evaluation: Look for compact, tight leaves; heavy for size; few or no brown blemishes.

Preparation: Wash. Cut 1 inch (2–3 cm) off tops. Cut off stem and lower leaves. Scrape out choke (fuzzy center) with melon ball cutter. (Remove choke before or

Figure 16.1
Trimming artichoke bottoms.

(a) Cut or break off the stem flush with the bottom of the artichoke, as shown.

(b) Break off the outer leaves.

(c) Alternatively, trim the outer leaves with a knife as shown, being careful not to cut into the base of the artichoke.

(d) Cut off the remaining leaves above the base.

(e) With a paring knife, trim off the green outer peel to give the base a smooth, neat appearance.

(f) With a ball cutter or tablespoon, scrape out the fuzzy choke.

(g) A trimmed artichoke bottom on the left; a trimmed whole artichoke on the right. Note that the points of the leaves have been cut off and the center choke removed.

Figure 16.2
To keep the cut stem end of an artichoke from darkening during steaming or boiling, tie a slice of lemon over the cut surface.

after cooking.) Dip in lemon juice immediately. To prepare bottoms, see Figures 16.1 and 16.2.

Percentage Yield: 80% (whole, trimmed), 30% (bottoms only)

Artichokes, Jerusalem (see Sunchoke)

Asparagus

Identification: Spear-shaped new shoot or stem that emerges from the plant's roots in the spring. The pointed spear tip sprouts branches when the shoot is left to grow.

Related Varieties: *White asparagus* is the same plant as green, but soil is mounded over the shoots, protecting from the sun so they do not turn green. In Europe, white asparagus is more common than green. The flavor is milder than that of green, although North American white asparagus is usually more bitter than European. *Purple asparagus* turns dark green when cooked. It is tender and sweet.

Evaluation: Look for tightly closed tips; firm, not withered, stalks. For white asparagus, buy only product that has been kept chilled for its entire storage time; unchilled white asparagus becomes fibrous.

Figure 16.3
Trimming asparagus.

(a) With a vegetable peeler, pare the stalk from about 2 in. (5 cm) below the tip down to the base.

(b) Cut or break off the hard, woody bottoms of the stems.

Preparation: Break off woody lower ends. Remove lower scales, which may harbor sand, or peel lower part of stalk. Figure 16.3 shows an alternative method. Cut tips to uniform lengths and/or tie them in bundles for cooking. White asparagus should be peeled the entire length of the stalk. Purple asparagus needs no peeling; just trim the bottoms.

Percentage Yield: 55% (green, peeled)

(c) Another method used by many chefs is to break off the stems first . . .

(d) . . . and then peel the stem.

Avocados

Identification: The egg-shaped fruit of a small tree, with a leathery skin, tender, pale-green flesh, and a single large seed or pit in the center.

Related Varieties: There are several varieties that fall into two main categories: (1) The Mexican or Californian avocados, mostly the Hass variety, that have rough dark green skins that turn black when ripe. These have a rich, buttery flesh with a high oil content. (2) The West Indian or Florida type, with smoother skins that remain green. These are juicier and have a lower oil content.

Evaluation: Look for fresh appearance; fruit heavy for size; no blemishes or bruises.

Preparation: Ripen at room temperature, 2–5 days. Cut in half lengthwise and remove pit (see Figure 16.4). Peel (skin pulls away easily from ripe fruit). Dip or rub with lemon juice immediately to prevent browning.

Percentage Yield: 75%

Figure 16.4
Preparing avocados.

(a) To remove the pit or seed from the cut avocado, strike it sharply (but carefully) with the heel of a chef's knife.

(b) Twist the knife slightly and pull out the pit.

Bamboo Shoots

Identification: The young shoots of various species of bamboo plants, harvested as they just begin to emerge from the ground. They are roughly cone-shaped, with tough, brown skins and a creamy, crisp, tender interior.

Evaluation: Look for solid, heavy shoots with no soft spots or cracks; no trace of sour smell.

Preparation: Peel down to the creamy white or pale yellowish cone-shaped core. Slice and boil in salted water until tender, then cut as desired for use in recipes.

Percentage Yield: Varies greatly, depending on size of shoots, which range from a few ounces to a pound (less than 100 grams to 500 grams) or more.

Beans, Dried (see Chapter 19)

Beans, Fava

Identification: Also called *broad bean*. Unlike most of our common beans, which originated in the Western Hemisphere, favas are Old World beans. The large pods hold four to six beans in a soft, white lining. The flat beans slightly resemble limas, but they are not as starchy. Flavor is subtle and nutlike.

Evaluation: Select small to medium pods that are fresh green in color, not overly large. Yellowing pods may be too mature. Some spots on pods are normal.

Preparation: Preparation is labor-intensive. Shell the beans, parboil, then peel off skins or husks (Figure 16.5).

Percentage Yield: 15–20%

Figure 16.5
Preparing fava beans.

(a) Split open the pods and remove the beans.

(b) Blanch the beans for a few minutes. This cooks the beans and loosens the skins. Peel off the outer skins. Unpeeled beans are on the left, peeled beans on the right.

Beans, Fresh Shell

Identification: These are the fresh, moist versions of the many types of dried beans.

Related Varieties: Although many types of beans are grown to be shelled, most of these are dried, and, with the exception of *cranberry* or *borlotti beans, southern-peas* or *cowpeas*, and *black-eyed peas*, few are available fresh. Soybeans and lima beans have their own entries below.

Evaluation: Look for firm, fresh, moderately filled-out pods containing firm but not hard seeds. Avoid yellow or brownish pods, which are likely to be too mature.

Preparation: Shell and rinse. Cook before serving; raw beans can be harmful.

Percentage Yield: 40%

Beans, Lima

Identification: Flat, pale-green beans in flat, slightly fuzzy pods, with three or four beans per pod. Larger ones tend to be starchier than small or baby limas.

Related Varieties: Many varieties are grown, but they are not usually distinguished from one another in the market.

Evaluation: Beans should be plump, with tender skins.

Preparation: Shell, wash, and drain.

Percentage Yield: 40%

Beans, Snap

Identification: Fresh green beans and other varieties are in the same family as shell beans, except they are grown to be picked immature for their tender, edible pods.

Related Varieties: Green beans are the most common. Some green varieties, picked

Green Beans

when very small and tender, are known as *haricots verts* (ah ree coh vehr, French for "green beans"). Other varieties include yellow or wax beans, purple beans, and flat, Italian-style green beans.

Evaluation: Look for firm and straight beans, with few shriveled ends; even color, without blemishes. Should be tender and crisp enough to break when bent to a 45-degree angle. Enclosed seeds should be small, not large and bulging.

Preparation: Wash. Cut or snap off ends. Remove any spots. Leave whole or cut into desired lengths.

Percentage Yield: 88%

Beans, Soy—see Soybeans

Beets

Identification: A tender, bulbous, somewhat sweet root, usually but not always dark red. The tops can also be cooked like other greens; handle and treat beet tops like Swiss chard (see below), which is in the beet family.

Related Varieties: Beets come in several shapes and colors in addition to the common red, including yellow, pink, orange or brick red, and white. Chioggia (kee oh ja) are striped red and white. Shapes include round, elongated oval, and cylindrical.

Evaluation: Look for firm, round, uniform size; smooth skin. Tops, if any, should be fresh or just wilted, but not yellow or deteriorated. Large, rough beets are often woody.

Preparation: Cut off tops, leaving 1 inch (2–3 cm) of stem attached to beets. Leave roots on to avoid loss of color and juice during cooking. Scrub well. Steam, boil, or bake before peeling.

Percentage Yield: 40–45% (75% if purchased without tops)

Bok Choy

Bok Choy

Identification: An Asian member of the cabbage family, related to Chinese cabbage, except the stalk is thicker and fleshier and the green portion is smoother and darker in color. Leaves and stalks are tender, crisp, and juicy.

Related Varieties: Several varieties all form compact, elongated bunches. The most common variety forms large heads or bunches with white stems. *Shanghai bok choi* is smaller, with pale green stems. *Choy sum* is allowed to become more mature, so the central stem or core is longer, and there may be small yellow flowers among the leaves.

Evaluation: Fresh, green appearance for all varieties, with no wilting or discoloration.

Preparation: Cut in half lengthwise and wash under running water to remove soil from the crooks of the stalks. Trim bottom by cutting off a thin slice, or cut out core. Cut as desired. Small varieties may be cooked whole.

Percentage Yield: 80%

Broccoli

Figure 16.6
Prepare tough bottoms of broccoli stalks by pulling off the fibrous peel, as shown.

Identification: A green vegetable in the cabbage family, consisting of tight clusters of tiny green flower buds on fleshy stalks.

Related Varieties: Pale green *broccoflower* is closer in character to cauliflower than to broccoli and should be handled like cauliflower. *Broccolini* is a relatively new broccoli hybrid with slender stems and small, loose florets (flower bud heads). *Broccoli rabe* (also called *broccoli raab*, *broccoletti di rape*, *rapini*, and *cima de rapa*), like broccolini, has slenderer stems and loose florets, but it also has tender leaves attached to the stems, and the stems are slightly ribbed rather than smooth. Broccoli has a stronger, more mustardy flavor. Several varieties of *Chinese broccoli* are similar to broccoli rabe, in both shape and flavor, except the stems are smoother and fleshier.

Evaluation: Look for dark green, tightly closed buds in regular broccoli and broccoflower. Broccoli rabe and Asian types should be dark green with crisp, not wilted, leaves.

Preparation: Wash well. Soak in salted water 30 minutes if necessary to remove insects. Split large stalks into smaller sizes for portioning. Split thick stalks partway for faster cooking, or cut tops from stalks. Tougher stalks may be peeled (Figure 16.6).

Percentage Yield: 65–75%

Brussels Sprouts

Identification: This cabbage relative resembles a tiny cabbage head. The clusters of leaves grow in rows along a thick stalk. Flavor is somewhat stronger than that of green cabbage.

Related Varieties: Red or purple (the color of red cabbage) brussels sprouts exist but are not often seen, probably because their flavor and texture is less appealing to most people.

Evaluation: Look for bright green, tight heads; uniform size.

Preparation: Trim bottom ends and remove yellowed outer leaves (but don't cut off too much of the bottom or you will lose too many leaves). For more even cooking, pierce base with sharp knife point. Rinse well. Rinse in cold salted water 30 minutes if necessary to remove insects.

Percentage Yield: 80%

Brussel sprouts

Cabbage: Green, Red, and Savoy

Identification: Cabbages are large leaf clusters in dense, round heads (heads may also be flat or elongated, depending on the variety). Cabbage and mustard are in the same family, a relationship that can be detected in the faintly peppery taste.

Evaluation: For both green and red cabbage, look for a firm head, heavy for size. Good color. Crisp leaves, finely ribbed. Savoy cabbage is not as heavy, with darker green, ruffled leaves.

Preparation: Remove coarse or discolored outer leaves. Remove core and rinse whole, or cut into quarters and then remove core. For wedges, core is left in, but with bottom trimmed, to hold sections together. (See Figure 16.7)

Percentage Yield: 80%

Green cabbage

Figure 16.7
Cutting and shredding cabbage.

(a) Cut the cabbage head into quarters. Then cut out the core as shown.

Red cabbage

(b) With a French knife, cut into thin shreds.

Savoy cabbage

Cabbage, Chinese

Identification: Heads of tender, crinkly, pale green leaves with broad, flat center stalks. The flavor is mild and slightly spicy.

Related Varieties: There are two main varieties, with different head shapes, although the flavor and texture are virtually the same for both. The head of *napa cabbage* is stout and barrel-shaped. A more elongated, slender head cabbage is often called *celery cabbage* for its shape. See also Bok Choy, a closely related cabbage.

Evaluation: Look for firm, tightly packed heads with no dry or browned tips, crisp and not limp or wilted.

Preparation: Wash. Cut as desired, discarding the center core.

Percentage Yield: 85%

Cactus Pads or Nopales

Identification: Nopales are tender pads of the prickly pear cactus. When cooked, their texture is slippery, like that of okra, and their flavor slightly resembles cooked green pepper or possibly green beans with a slight sourness.

Evaluation: Try to purchase pads with the spines removed. Look for full, firm, crisp pads, not wilted or soft ones.

Preparation: If spines are present, wear rubber gloves and brush them vigorously under running water, then with a vegetable peeler remove the eyes that held the spines. Trim the base if necessary. Cut as desired. Can be sautéed, boiled, steamed, or grilled.

Percentage Yield: 90%

Carrots

Identification: Long, pointed, orange roots. Among the most widely used vegetables.

Evaluation: Look for bright orange color; crisp, straight, and well shaped; smooth surface. Large carrots are sometimes woody.

Preparation: Trim top and bottom ends. Pare with hand peeler.

Percentage Yield: 75–80%

Cauliflower

Cauliflower

Identification: White or off-white, tight cluster of tiny flowers (florets) branching off a central stalk. Member of the cabbage family.

Related Varieties: *Broccoflower* is a light green relative that looks like a cross between broccoli and cauliflower. Handle like regular cauliflower.

Evaluation: Look for white color, not yellow or brownish; fine-grained, tightly closed buds; fresh green, well-trimmed leaves.

Preparation: Remove leaves and trim tough part of stalk. Cut away discolored parts. Wash. Soak in salted water 30 minutes if necessary to remove insects. Separate into florets, leaving portion of center stalk attached to each one to minimize trim loss. If cooking whole, cut out center of stalk for more even cooking.

Percentage Yield: 55%

Celery

Identification: Pale green stems that form bunches or clusters attached at root end. One of the most common vegetables.

Evaluation: Look for bunches that are straight, compact, well trimmed; fresh green color.

Preparation: Cut off root end. Separate stems and scrub well. Reserve leaves and tough outer stems for stocks, soups, mirepoix. Ribbed outer side of stems may be peeled to remove strings.

Percentage Yield: 75%

Celery Root or Celeriac

Identification: A variety of celery grown for its round, fleshy white root.

Evaluation: Select firm and heavy roots. Large ones are often soft and spongy in the center.

Preparation: Wash well, peel, and cut as desired.

Percentage Yield: 75%

Celery root

Chayote

Identification: A member of the gourd or squash family, this vegetable has a crisp texture and a mild flavor that is somewhere between zucchini and cucumber. It is roughly pear-shaped, although more rounded, with a thin yellow-green skin and creamy white flesh. It is also known as *mirliton* and *vegetable pear*.

Evaluation: Look for firm, solid chayotes without blemishes.

Preparation: Skin can be left on if served raw, but peel chayotes to be cooked, because the skin toughens. The soft seed in the middle can also be eaten.

Percentage Yield: 100% if unpeeled; 85–90% if peeled

Chayote

Chestnut

Identification: Chestnuts are the seed or nut of a variety of trees grown primarily in Europe. They have a thin, hard, dark brown outer shell and a bitter inner skin surrounding a soft, starchy meat.

Evaluation: Look for plump, firm nuts with no blemishes on the shells.

Preparation: The shell and skin must be removed before use. With the point of a paring knife, cut an X in the shell on the flat side of each nut. Roast at 350°F (180°C) for 15 minutes or blanch in boiling water. Peel while still hot.

Percentage Yield: 75%

Corn

Identification: Corn is a grain that is used as a vegetable if immature. It grows in rows on the outside of a central woody cob and is covered with a leafy husk. Varieties grown for vegetable use are sweeter than grain varieties.

Evaluation: Look for fresh, moist husks, not dry; no worm damage; kernels well filled, tender, and milky when punctured.

Preparation: Strip off husks, remove silk, and cut off bottom stump. Cut into two or three sections as desired, if serving on cob, or cut from cob. Keep refrigerated and use as soon as possible.

Percentage Yield: 28% after husking and cutting from cob

Cucumber

Identification: A member of the gourd family, like squash, the cucumber has a thin green skin and a crisp, mild, juicy off-white flesh.

Related Varieties: Cucumbers are of two types, slicing and pickling. The common green slicing cucumber, with dark green skin, is most often used in food service. The long, slender hothouse cucumber, also called *seedless* and *burpless*, is another common slicing cucumber. Pickling cucumbers, also called *Kirbys*, range in size from tiny gherkins to the large ones used to make dill pickles. They are somewhat drier and a little more flavorful than the slicing types. Their green skin is a little lighter in color than that of slicing cucumbers, and the surface is bumpy.

Evaluation: Look for vegetables that are firm, crisp, dark green, well shaped. Yellow color means the cucumber is overmature.

Preparation: Wash. Trim ends. Peel if skin is tough or has been waxed. Skin may be scored to make decorative slices (see Figure 16.8).

Percentage Yield: 75–95%, depending on peeling

Figure 16.8
Cucumber garnishes can be made more decorative by scoring the cucumber before slicing or cutting.

(a) Scoring with a fork.

(b) Scoring with a channel knife.

Eggplant

Identification: Eggplants are members of the same family as tomatoes, peppers, and potatoes. They have purple, white, or pale green skin and a firm but spongy off-white flesh containing tiny edible seeds.

Related Varieties: Worldwide, there are dozens of varieties. In the West, the most common is the large, oblong, purple-skinned variety. Smaller, elongated varieties are sometimes called *Italian eggplant*. White-skinned varieties are round, egg-shaped (the origin of the name *eggplant*), or long and slender. Japanese eggplants are small, long and slender, with a purple instead of green stem. Asian types include small round, green-skinned fruits, including a Thai eggplant no larger than a pea. The flesh of these varieties is similar in flavor, varying in texture or density from soft to almost hard.

Evaluation: Eggplants should be firm, not soft. Common purple types should be shiny, dark purple color; heavy and plump; without blemishes or soft spots.

Preparation: Wash. Trim off stem end. Peel if skin is tough. Cut just before use. Dip in lemon juice or antioxidant solution to prevent discoloration if not to be cooked within a few minutes after peeling and cutting.

Percentage Yield: 90% (75% if peeled)

Italian eggplant   **White eggplant**

Fennel

Identification: The clustered or bunched stems form a bulbous base. The fleshy bulb is white with a pale hint of green, while the stems are darker green. The aroma and flavor have a faint suggestion of licorice.

Related Varieties: The vegetable fennel is more properly known as *Florence fennel*, to distinguish it from the varieties grown as a spice (seed) and herb. The vegetable is sometimes incorrectly called *anise*, which is a different plant.

Evaluation: Look for bright, pale green color with few or no brown spots. Fresh green tops, not wilted or spoiled. Compact, heavy for size.

Preparation: Trim stems and feathery leaves. Split in half through the base. If the fennel is large, cut out the core as for cabbage if it is fibrous or tough.

Percentage Yield: 80%

Fennel

Fiddlehead Fern

Identification: This spring vegetable is the early shoot of a fern, usually ostrich fern, harvested just as it emerges from the ground. It consists of a tightly curled stem lined with the tiniest beginnings of leaves. It is usually handled and cooked like tender asparagus.

Evaluation: Look for jade-green, firm and resilient, not wilted, fiddleheads with fresh-looking, not spoiled, cut ends and leaf tips.

Preparation: Trim the cut ends. Rinse well.

Percentage Yield: 85%

Figure 16.9
Peeling and crushing garlic.

(a) Place the garlic on the worktable. Hold a broad knife blade over it as shown and strike it firmly with the palm of the hand.

(b) You can now peel the garlic easily.

(c) Chop or mince the garlic.

(d) To make a paste of the garlic, sprinkle it with salt and mash it firmly with the back of the knife blade.

Garlic

Identification: A pungent member of the onion family, garlic forms bunches of cloves attached at the root end and covered with a papery skin.

Related Varieties: There are many varieties, with white or purplish skins. Some are more pungent than others. Elephant garlic is the size of an apple, with relatively few large cloves; it is milder than other garlics.

Evaluation: Skin may be white or pink. No brown spots, soft spots, or spoilage; dry skin; no green shoots.

Preparation: Separate cloves as needed, or strike whole bulb with heel of hand to separate. To peel cloves, crush slightly with side of heavy knife. Peel and trim root end (see Figure 16.9).

Percentage Yield: 88%

Greens, Cabbage Family (Collards, Turnip Greens, Kale)

Identification: These sturdy, flavorful greens are nearly always cooked because they are too tough to eat raw, unless very young. The kale varieties have curly or ruffled dark green leaves (except the ornamental varieties, which may have touches of red or other colors). Turnip greens resemble large, lobed mustard or arugula leaves. Collards are similar, generally with heavier stems and more rounded leaves.

Evaluation: Avoid browned, yellowed, or dried leaves. Look for smaller leaves that are dark green and have a moist feel.

Preparation: Strip the leaves off the stems if they are tough. Cut off any discolored parts. Wash well in several changes of water.

Percentage Yield: 80%

Collard greens

Turnip greens

Kale

Jícama

Jícama

Identification: Jícama (HEE kama) is a large, round tuber with a thin brown skin and crisp, mild, juicy, creamy white flesh similar to water chestnuts.

Evaluation: Look for smooth, almost shiny skin with no blemishes.

Preparation: Peel. Cut as desired.

Percentage Yield: 85%

Kohlrabi

Kohlrabi

Identification: Kohlrabi, when trimmed, resembles a root vegetable, but it is actually a swollen stem. A member of the cabbage family, its pale white, crisp flesh resembles, in texture and flavor, the interior of a broccoli stem. The skin is tough and must be removed.

Related Varieties: Purple-skinned kohlrabi, except for the skin color, are similar to the more common green.

Evaluation: Look for uniform light green color; 2–3 inches (5–8 cm) in diameter. Crisp and firm. No woodiness.

Preparation: Peel like turnips, being sure to remove the full thickness of skin.

Percentage Yield: 55%

Leeks

Identification: A long, slender member of the onion family with distinctive flavor, milder than onions.

Related Varieties: *Ramps* are wild leeks with broad, flat leaves and bulbs that resemble those of scallions. They have a pungent, garlicky flavor.

Evaluation: Look for fresh green leaves; 2–3 inches (5–8 cm) of white. White part should be crisp and tender, not fibrous.

Preparation: Cut off roots and green tops. Cut deeply through white part, separate the layers slightly, and wash carefully to remove all embedded soil (see Figure 16.10).

Percentage Yield: 50%

**Figure 16.10
Cleaning leeks.**

(a) Trim off the root end and as much of the green as desired.

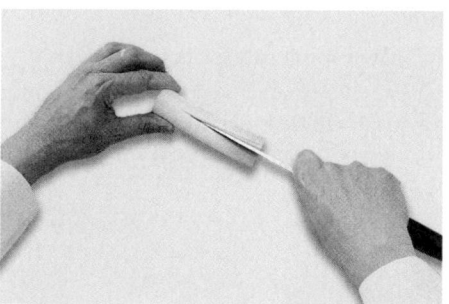

(b) Make one or two deep cuts to within 1 in. (2.5 cm) of the root end.

(c) Spread apart the layers, as shown. Carefully wash out all embedded dirt under running water.

Lettuce

Identification: See Chapter 21 for full description of salad greens.

Percentage Yield: 75%

Mushrooms, White

Identification: Mushrooms are the fruiting body of a fungus—that is, the part of the fungus that produces spores for reproduction.

Evaluation: Select firm, white caps, closed at the stem. Stems should be relatively short. No dark spots, bruises, or mold.

Preparation: Trim bottoms of stems. Just before cooking, wash quickly in cold water; drain well. If you desire to keep the mushrooms white, add a small amount of acid (lemon juice, vinegar, ascorbic acid) to the rinse water. To flute mushrooms, see Figure 16.11.

Percentage Yield: 90%

White mushrooms

Figure 16.11
Basic methods for fluting mushrooms.

(a) Grasping the blade of a paring knife, hold the edge against the center of the mushroom cap at a sharp angle.

(b) The first cut is completed.

(c) Continue making cuts all around the mushroom.

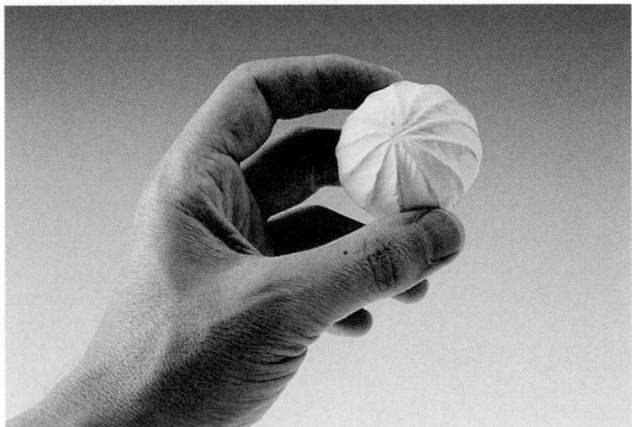

(d) The fluted mushroom cap.

Mushrooms, Exotic and Wild Varieties

Identification: See pages 534–536.

Figure 16.12
To prepare okra, cut off the stem ends.

Okra

Identification: Okra is the pod or fruit of a member of the mallow family. It is long and tapered, with ridges running its length. Inside the pod are tender seeds and a thick, sticky juice. The flavor is very mild.

Related Varieties: Common okra varieties are green. Red-skinned varieties, which turn green when cooked, are uncommon but available.

Evaluation: Look for tender, full pods, not dry or shriveled. Ridges should be soft. Seeds should be soft and white. Uniform color.

Preparation: Wash. Trim ends (see Figure 16.12). Slice or leave whole.

Percentage Yield: 82%

Onions, Dry

Identification: A pungent, many-layered bulbous root that is the kitchen's most common vegetable.

Related Varieties: Onions come in almost limitless varieties, from tiny white, yellow, and red pearl onions and cipolline (chip oh lee neh, Italian pearl onions) to medium and large yellow onions, the workhorse of the kitchen, to large red and white onions. Mild varieties include Vidalia, Walla-Walla, and Maui. These are often said to be sweeter, but they do not contain more sugar than regular varieties. Rather, they have less of the chemical compounds that make onions strong.

Evaluation: Select onions that are clean, hard, well shaped; no mold or black fungus; no green shoots. Skins should be very dry.

Preparation: Cut off root and stem ends. Peel. Wash. Cut or slice as needed (see Figure 7.10).

Percentage Yield: 90%

Yellow onions

White onion

Red onions

Pearl onions

Onions, Green (Scallions)

Identification: These are very young, immature bulb onions, sold with their stems. Scallions are almost always white varieties of onions, although red varieties can sometimes be found.

Evaluation: Scallions should have fresh, crisp green tops; little or no bulb formation at white part.

Preparation: Cut off roots and wilted ends of green tops. Amount of green left on varies with recipe or use.

Percentage Yield: 60–70%

Parsley

Identification: Parsley is the most common fresh herb used in kitchens. It is used in such quantities that it is included here with vegetables.

Related Varieties: The two main varieties are curly parsley and flat or Italian parsley.

Evaluation: Select bright green, unwilted leaves with no rot.

Preparation: Wash well and drain. Remove yellow leaves and large stems (save stems for stocks). Separate into sprigs for garnish, or chop leaves.

Percentage Yield: 85%

Parsnips

Identification: The parsnip is a long, conical root vegetable that looks like a carrot, only more tapered and with a wider top. Its skin is tan and its interior is yellow-beige, with a distinctive, sweet flavor.

Evaluation: Look for firm, smooth, well-shaped parsnips, with light, uniform color. Large ones are often woody.

Preparation: Refrigerating for two weeks develops sweetness. Trim ends and peel. Rinse.

Percentage Yield: 70–75%

Parsnip

Pea Greens or Pea Shoots

Identification: These are the tender tips, with leaves, of pea vines, usually snow peas.

Evaluation: Look for fresh, medium-green leaves and tender, not woody, stems.

Preparation: Wash well; trim ends of stems, especially if they are tough. Cook like spinach.

Percentage Yield: 90–95%

Pea shoots

Peas, Green

Identification: The tender, immature seed of a legume (see Chapter 19).

Evaluation: Look for firm, fresh, moderately filled-out pods. Peas lose sweetness quickly after harvest, so locally grown, just-harvested peas are best. Frozen peas are likely to be sweeter than fresh peas that have been stored for some time.

Preparation: Shell and rinse. (Peas are not often purchased in the pod by food service operations because of the labor required for shelling.)

Percentage Yield: 40%

Peas, Edible Pod

Identification: Unlike shell peas, above, whose pods are too fibrous to be eaten, these peas have tender, edible pods and so are always served in the pod.

Related Varieties: The two main varieties are the flat-podded *snow pea*, with tiny undeveloped seeds, and the rounder *sugar pea* or *sugar snap pea*, with larger seeds.

Evaluation: Look for fresh green color, crisp pods, no blemishes.

Preparation: Remove stem end. Pull off strings at side veins. Wash.

Percentage Yield: 90%

Sugar snap peas   **Snow peas**

Peppers, Sweet

Identification: Peppers are the fruit of a plant related to tomatoes, eggplant, and potatoes. Both sweet and hot peppers are members of the *Capsicum* family. They have fleshy walls and a hollow interior, with a seedy core just below the stem. Also called *bell peppers*.

Related Varieties: Green, red, yellow, orange, and purple peppers are widely available.

Evaluation: Shiny color; well shaped; no soft spots or shriveling.

Preparation: Wash. Cut in half lengthwise and remove core, seeds, and white membranes. Peppers to be julienned or diced may have the interior ribs trimmed. Or leave whole (as for stuffed peppers) and cut out core from the end. Peppers are often roasted and peeled as preparation for use in recipes (see Figure 16.13).

Percentage Yield: 82%

Red pepper   **Green pepper**

Yellow pepper   **Orange pepper**

**Figure 16.13
Roasting peppers.**

(a) Roast the peppers over an open flame until the skins blacken. For large quantities, you may do this under a broiler or in a hot oven. In this case, the skins will not darken as much but can still be peeled off.

(b) Wrap the peppers in plastic film while they are still hot. This helps loosen the skins.

(c) Peel off the loosened skin. You may do this under running water to help rinse off charred skin, but some nutrients and flavor may be lost.

Peppers, Hot, or Chiles

Identification: Relatives of sweet peppers, but containing a compound called capsaicin, which makes them spicy hot. (*Chile* is the original Spanish spelling; also spelled *chili* and *chilli*.)

Related Varieties: Many varieties are available worldwide. The heat of any particular pepper is determined by how much capsaicin it contains and is measured in Scoville units. A mildly hot jalapeño averages about 2,500–3,000 units, while the intensely hot habanero averages around 200,000 units. Commonly used fresh chiles include the jalapeño, serrano, poblano, California, New Mexico, Thai green, and cayenne.

Evaluation: See Peppers, Sweet.

Preparation: Larger fresh chile peppers, such as ancho, mulato, New Mexico, and Anaheim, are usually roasted and prepared like sweet peppers (see above). Small peppers, such as cayenne, jalapeño, and serrano, are usually chopped or sliced and used as seasoning. Remove core, veins, and seeds carefully; wear rubber gloves if you are sensitive to the hot oils, and avoid touching the eyes or any sensitive part of the skin after working with chiles.

Percentage Yield: 80–90%

Green cayenne chiles

Italian hot peppers

Jalapeños and cherry peppers

Potatoes, White

Identification: See Chapter 18.

Percentage Yield: 80%

Potatoes, Sweet

Identification: Sweet potatoes are any of several types of tubers, usually bulbous, with tapered or pointed ends. They are unrelated to potatoes and to yams. (True yams are an entirely different vegetable, with starchy white flesh. They are not often seen in North America, except in Hispanic and some other specialty markets.)

Related Varieties: There are two basic groups of sweet potatoes, those with a creamy white or pale yellow flesh and those with orange flesh. The variety that has a moister, deeper orange flesh is sometimes referred to, incorrectly, as the yam. These varieties are interchangeable for most purposes. Skin colors range from beige to orange to red, depending on the variety.

Evaluation: Look for clean, dry surface. Firm, not shriveled or blemished. Fat, regular shapes are preferable because of less waste in trimming and portioning.

Preparation: Scrub, boil, or steam, then peel. May be peeled before cooking but must be dipped in antioxidant to prevent discoloring. Machine paring is wasteful with irregular shapes.

Percentage Yield: 80%

Sweet potato

Radishes

Identification: Crisp, juicy root vegetables in the mustard family, with a peppery taste.

Related Varieties: In North America and Western Europe, the word *radish* usually indicates the small, round or tapered, red-skinned and white-fleshed variety, or sometimes the white icicle radish. Other important radishes are the turnip-size *black radish*, eaten raw or cooked, and the very large, long Asian *daikon* (the name is Japanese for "big root"), with white skin and flesh, also served raw or cooked. Cooked radishes are somewhat like turnips both in flavor and texture.

Evaluation: Select firm, tender, crisp radishes, with good shape and color.

Preparation: Cut off root and stem ends. Wash. Decorative cuts are shown in Figure 16.14.

Percentage Yield: 90%

Radishes

Rutabagas

Identification: See Turnip.

Salsify

Identification: The name *salsify* (sal si fee) refers to either of two distantly related long, slender root vegetables with off-white flesh and a flavor, when cooked, that is sometimes said to resemble artichoke.

Related Varieties: True salsify, or white salsify, has brownish-white roots, often forked and branched, with many root hairs attached. Scorzonera (score tso nerra), or black salsify, is straight, long, and slender, with dark brown skin. Both have off-white flesh.

Evaluation: Select medium-size roots, as larger ones may be fibrous. They should be as smooth as possible.

Preparation: Scrub with a brush. Peel with a swivel peeler and immediately drop into water containing an acid, such as lemon juice or vinegar, to prevent discoloration. Wear gloves to prevent staining the hands.

Percentage Yield: 65–70%

Figure 16.14
Radishes can be cut into many decorative forms, including those shown here.

Shallots

Identification: Shallots are small, dry-skinned onions that grow in clusters attached at the root end. They have a brown, papery skin and white and purple flesh. Their flavor is milder than that of onions.

Evaluation: Same as for dry onions.

Preparation: Same as for dry onions.

Percentage Yield: Same as for dry onions.

Shallots

Sorrel

Identification: A tender leafy green with a tart, astringent taste, used in small quantities, usually to flavor sauces. The leaf resembles spinach but is longer and not as dark green.

Evaluation: Same as for spinach.

Preparation: Pull off coarse stems. Wash in several changes of water if sandy. For most purposes, sorrel is cut into chiffonade (p. 139).

Percentage Yield: 90%

Soybeans

Identification: Most soybeans are allowed to mature and dry and are harvested and processed as a grain. The use of tender, unripe soybeans, known as *edamame* (edd ah mah meh), is a popular adoption from Japanese cuisine. The small, fuzzy pods usually hold three light green, roundish beans.

Evaluation: Same as shell beans.

Preparation: Rinse, boil in the pod until the beans are tender, and shell.

Percentage Yield: 50%

Green Soybeans

Spinach

Identification: A tender, dark green leaf, probably the most popular of leafy vegetables after lettuce.

Related Varieties: Two main types are curly-leafed and flat-leafed.

Evaluation: Look for fresh, crisp, dark green leaves. No rot or slime or badly bruised leaves.

Preparation: Remove stems and damaged leaves (Figure 16.15). Wash in several changes of water. Use a large quantity of water and lift spinach up and down to float off sand and dirt. Lift from water and drain well.

Percentage Yield: 50–70%

Figure 16.15
When trimming spinach leaves, remove the heavy center rib along with the stem.

Squash, Summer

Identification: Several types of tender-skinned members of the gourd family are called *summer squash*. They all have tender seeds in a firmly filled seed cavity, unlike the hard seeds encased in a fibrous mesh in the hollow interior of winter squash.

Related Varieties: Green-skinned *zucchini* is well known and the most popular. *Yellow straight* and *crookneck* squashes are similar in flavor and use. *Pattypan* squash has a squat, round shape, slightly resembling the popular idea of a flying saucer. They can be yellow, dark green, or pale green. Many other types are available, but they are less common.

Evaluation: Look for firm, heavy, and crisp squash, with tender skins, no blemishes.

Preparation: Wash or scrub well. Trim ends.

Percentage Yield: 90%

Zucchini

Yellow summer squash

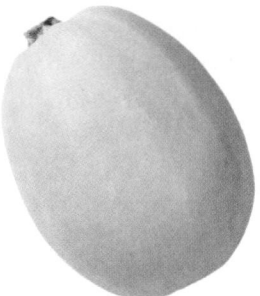

Spaghetti squash

Squash, Winter, including Pumpkin

Identification: Winter squash are mature members of the gourd family, with thick skins and hard seeds in a hollow cavity. They are starchier and less moist than summer squash and, unlike summer squash, are not generally eaten raw.

Related Varieties: Many types, of all sizes and shapes, are available, including Hubbard, acorn, butternut, buttercup, kabocha, turban, delicata, sweet dumpling, and pumpkin. Spaghetti squash has a fibrous flesh that, when cooked and scraped out of the shell, resembles a tangled pile of spaghetti.

Evaluation: Heavy and firm. Hard rind. No blemishes.

Preparation: Wash. Cut in half. Scrape out seeds and fibers. Cut into portion sizes. For puréed or mashed squash either steam or bake, then remove peel; or peel, dice, then steam.

Percentage Yield: 65–85%

Butternut squash

Squash Blossoms

Identification: Young, yellow blossoms of any summer squash.

Related Varieties: Female flowers are attached to the ends of new squashes. They fall off after the squash is a day or two old so must be harvested, attached to the tiny fruit, in a timely manner. Male blossoms contain the pollen and grow on a separate part of the same plant. Both types are used, often for stuffing, or simply sliced and sautéed.

Evaluation: Squash blossoms should be fresh and bright yellow, not wilted. They are best if used within a day or two of harvest.

Preparation: Open the flower petals gently and carefully rinse in water.

Percentage Yield: 100%

Acorn squash

Sunchokes or Jerusalem Artichokes

Identification: *Sunchoke* is a relatively new marketing term for a Jerusalem artichoke, created because the vegetable is not an artichoke and has nothing to do with Jerusalem. Sunchokes are knobby brown tubers with crisp, creamy white flesh.

Evaluation: Look for firm sunchokes with clean brown skin, no soft or green spots, and no sprouts.

Preparation: Wash and peel off brown skin.

Percentage Yield: 80%

Swiss Chard

Identification: A leafy green related to the beet. Chard leaves resemble beet greens, both in flavor and appearance, except the center stalks of chard are broader.

Related Varieties: Red-stemmed, white-stemmed, and yellow-stemmed chard are available.

Evaluation: Fresh, dark green color, not wilted. Crisp, not wilted or rubbery stalks.

Preparation: Wash thoroughly. Trim ends of stalks. Remove leafy greens from stalks by cutting along the margins of the stalk down the center of the leaf. Center stalks may be cooked separately like asparagus.

Percentage Yield: 85%

Red-stemmed Swiss chard

Tomatoes

Identification: One of the most widely used vegetables, the fruit of a plant in the nightshade family, related to eggplant, potatoes, and peppers.

Related Varieties: In addition to the common red slicing tomato and the small cherry tomato, dozens of varieties of heirloom tomatoes are grown and marketed. These come in all shades of red, pink, yellow, and green, all with somewhat different flavors.

Evaluation: Firm but not hard, with little or no green core. Smooth, without bruises, blemishes, cracks, or discoloration. If underripe, let stand two to three days at room temperature. Do not refrigerate.

Preparation: For use with skin on: Wash, remove core. To peel: Plunge into boiling water for 10–20 seconds (riper tomatoes take less time). Cool immediately in ice water. Slip skins off and remove core. (Note: Many chefs core the tomatoes and cut a shallow x in the skin at the bottom before blanching in boiling water. Other chefs, wishing to avoid even the slightest loss of flavor and nutrients from the exposed flesh into the water, first blanch the tomatoes and then core them and pull off the skins, which slip off just as easily.) See Figure 16.16 for further techniques.

Percentage Yield: 90% (peeled)

White-stemmed Swiss chard

Figure 16.16
Preparing tomato concassé.

(a) Blanch and peel the tomato and cut it in half crosswise. Gently squeeze out the seeds, as shown.

(b) Dice the seeded tomato or chop it coarsely.

Tomatillo

Tomatillos

Identification: A small green fruit vegetable resembling a green cherry tomato encased in a papery husk. It is not a tomato, although it is in the same family as tomatoes, eggplant, peppers, and potatoes. Widely used in Mexican cuisine.

Evaluation: Look for hard, dry tomatillos with tight husks.

Preparation: Remove the husks and rinse.

Percentage Yield: 95%

Turnips and Rutabagas

Identification: Root vegetables in the mustard family, related to cabbages.

Related Varieties: Turnips are white with purple skin around the stem end. The flesh is white. Rutabagas, also called *swedes*, are much larger and have yellow-orange flesh.

Evaluation: Look for roots that are firm and heavy, with good color and no blemishes. White turnips over 2½ inches (6–7 cm) in diameter may be woody or spongy.

Preparation: Peel heavily by hand or in machine to remove thick skin (see Figure 16.17). Rinse.

Percentage Yield: 75–80%

Figure 16.17
Peel rutabagas and turnips deeply enough to remove the full thickness of skin, as pointed out in this photograph.

Water Chestnuts

Identification: Water chestnuts are corms, or swollen underground stem bases, of plants that grow in moist, warm environments. They are small and roundish, with dark brown skin and crisp white flesh.

Evaluation: Look for solid water chestnuts with no sign of softness, bruising, rot, or shriveling. They spoil easily.

Preparation: Scrub well with a brush, as they are often muddy. Peel with a paring knife.

Percentage Yield: 75%

Watercress

Watercress

Identification: See discussion of salad greens in Chapter 21.

Evaluation: Bright green, crisp, unbruised leaves.

Preparation: Wash well. Remove heavy stems and discolored leaves.

Percentage Yield: 90%

MUSHROOMS: A SPECIAL TOPIC

Because of the great interest today in exotic mushrooms, and because eating some poisonous species of wild mushrooms can be fatal, it is important for the cook to be familiar with at least the most popular varieties of exotic mushrooms, both cultivated and wild.

Although hundreds of mushroom varieties are edible, until recently only the common cultivated button mushroom was used with any frequency in most commercial kitchens. Now, however, many varieties are available. Some of these mushrooms, especially the wild ones, are expensive, but the demand always seems to exceed the supply.

Strictly speaking, the term *wild* should be used only for those mushrooms that are not cultivated but that are hunted and gathered in the wild. In the kitchen and on menus, however, exotic cultivated varieties, such as shiitakes, are often referred to as *wild mushrooms* because they are seen as rare and unusual, like true wild mushrooms, and they are generally more flavorful than the button mushroom.

One important advantage of cultivated exotic mushrooms is that they are available all year, while certain wild mushrooms may be in season for only a few weeks annually.

Cultivated Exotic Mushrooms

1. **Shiitake.**
   Sometimes known as *Black Forest mushroom* or *golden oak mushroom*, the shiitake is also available in dried form as *Chinese black mushroom*. The fresh mushroom is golden brown to dark brown. It has a firm, fleshy texture and a broad, dome-shaped cap with creamy white gills. The stem is rather tough, so it is trimmed off and chopped fine or used in stocks.

Shiitake mushrooms

2. **Oyster mushroom.**
   Also called pleurotte, it is a light tan or cream-colored fan-shaped mushroom with a short stem at the side. Tender, with delicate flavor, it is best prepared simply so its mild flavor is not overwhelmed by stronger-tasting ingredients. (*Note:* The name *oyster* refers to the shape of the mushroom, not its taste.)

3. **Enoki mushroom.**
   Also called *enokitake* or *enokidake*, this mushroom has a tiny white cap on a long, slender stem, and grows in clusters or bunches that are attached at the base. The base is trimmed off before use. The enoki mushroom has a crisp texture and a fruity, slightly acidic but sweet flavor. It is often used raw (for example, in salads or as garnish) or in clear soups. When used in cooked dishes, it should be added in the last few minutes so as not to be overcooked.

Oyster mushrooms

4. **Cremini mushroom.**
   The cremini is a variety of the common cultivated button mushroom, but it has a brown or tan skin. It may have a slightly more robust flavor than white cultivated mushrooms.

5. **Portobello mushroom.**
   This is a mature cremini whose cap has opened and spread into a broad, flat disk. It may be 6 inches (15 cm) or more across. Portobello (note the correct spelling) are often grilled, brushed with olive oil, and served plain as a first course.

Wild Mushrooms

Of the many varieties of edible wild mushrooms, those described here are among the most prized as well as the most likely to be found on menus. As a rule, they are expensive and of limited availability.

Cremini mushrooms

Wild mushrooms should be carefully examined for spoilage and insect infestation. Cut away any damaged parts.

The four varieties described here are also available dried (see p. 538). Dried mushrooms have a high price per pound but are more economical to use than fresh wild mushrooms because they are equivalent to about 7 or 8 times their weight of fresh mushrooms. In addition, they have a more intense, concentrated flavor, so a little goes a long way.

Caution: Never eat any wild mushroom that has not been identified by an expert. Many mushrooms are poisonous, and some are deadly. Many species are difficult to identify, and some poisonous varieties resemble edible ones.

1. **Morel.**
   Several varieties exist, including black, golden, and nearly white. The morel is shaped somewhat like a conical sponge, with a pitted surface, on a smooth stem. It is completely hollow. The most prized of spring mushrooms, it is usually sautéed in butter or cooked in a sauce and is especially good with cream.

2. **Bolete.**
   Other names for this mushroom include *cep*, *cèpe* (sepp; the French term), *porcino* (por chee no; the Italian term; the plural is *porcini* [por chee nee]), and *steinpilz*

(shtine pilts; the German term). It is a brown-capped mushroom with a light-colored, bulbous stem. The interior flesh is creamy white. The underside of the cap has no gills but many tiny pores. With a meaty but smooth texture and rich, earthy flavor, it is often sautéed or braised with garlic and olive oil or butter. It is available late summer to fall.

3. **Chanterelle.**
   Also called *girolle*, the chanterelle is yellow to orange in color and shaped like an umbrella that has turned inside out. The underside of the cone-shaped cap has ridges instead of gills. It has a rich, woodsy aroma and flavor and is best cooked simply, such as sautéed in butter, perhaps with garlic. It is available summer and fall.

4. **Black trumpet.**
   This mushroom is closely related to the chanterelle but is black in color and has much thinner flesh. It is also called *black chanterelle*, *horn of plenty*, and *trompette de la mort* (French name, meaning "trumpet of death," so called because of its black color). In spite of this French name, it is edible and delicious.

PROCESSED VEGETABLES

It is generally agreed that the quality of frozen and canned vegetables can never equal that of the best-quality fresh product at its peak of maturity, prepared properly, and cooked while still fresh. However, because of the high perishability of fresh produce, seasonal variations in availability and price, and the amount of labor required to handle fresh produce in commercial kitchens, food service relies, to a great extent, on processed vegetables. Therefore, it is important to know how to handle processed foods properly. Your goal should be to make them as close as possible in quality to the best fresh produce.

The quality of processed vegetables varies greatly. For example, frozen cauliflower always lacks the slightly crunchy texture of properly cooked fresh cauliflower. In fact, most frozen vegetables are a bit mushier than fresh because cell walls rupture during freezing. On the other hand, frozen peas are almost universally accepted, not just for their convenience but for their dependably high quality in comparison with the highly perishable fresh product.

In the section of Chapter 7 called "Handling Convenience Foods," we learned that convenience foods are products that have been partially or completely prepared or processed by the manufacturer. This means you should treat frozen and canned vegetables as though they are partially or fully cooked fresh vegetables, which deserve the same care in handling, heating, seasoning, and presentation.

HANDLING FROZEN VEGETABLES

Checking Quality

Examine all frozen products when received to make sure they have experienced no loss of quality. Check in particular for the following:

1. **Temperature.**
   Check the temperature inside the case with a thermometer. Is it still 0°F (–18°C) or below, or have the vegetables begun to thaw during shipment?

2. **Large ice crystals.**
   A little frost is normal, but lots of ice means poor handling.

3. **Signs of leaking on the carton.**
   This is another obvious sign of thawing.

4. **Freezer burn.**
   Open a package and check the vegetables themselves. Is the color bright and natural, or is there yellowing or drying on the surface?

Cooking

Frozen vegetables have been partially cooked, so final cooking time is shorter than for fresh products.

Cook from the frozen state. Most vegetables need no thawing. They can go directly into steamer pans or boiling salted water.

Exceptions: Corn on the cob and vegetables that freeze into a solid block, such as spinach and squash, should be thawed in the cooler first for more even cooking.

Seasoning: Most frozen vegetables are slightly salted during processing, so add less salt than you would to fresh products.

HANDLING CANNED VEGETABLES

Checking Quality

1. **Reject damaged cans on receipt.**
   Puffed or swollen cans indicate spoilage. Small dents may be harmless, but large dents may mean the can's protective lining has been damaged. Avoid rusted or leaking cans.

2. **Know the drained weight.**
   This varies with different grades of different vegetables and should be specified when ordering. Typical drained weights are 60 to 65 percent of total contents. You must know this drained weight in order to calculate the number of servings the can contains.

   Some canned products, such as tomato sauce and cream-style corn, have no drained weight because the entire contents are served.

3. **Check the grade.**
   Grades are determined by the packers or by federal inspectors. They are based on factors like color, absence of defects, and sieve size (size of individual pieces). Check to make sure you receive the grade you ordered (and paid for).

   In the United States, the federal grades are

   U.S. Grade A or Fancy

   U.S. Grade B or Extra Standard (for vegetables) or Choice (for fruits)

   U.S. Grade C or Standard

Cooking

1. Wipe the top of the can clean before opening. Use a clean can opener.

2. Drain the vegetable and place half the liquid in a cooking pot. Bring it to a boil. This shortens the heating time of the vegetable.

3. Add the vegetable and heat to serving temperature. *Do not boil for a long time.* Canned vegetables are fully cooked—in fact, usually overcooked. They need reheating only.

   Note: Health officials recommend holding vegetables at 190°F/88°C for 10 minutes or more—20 to 30 minutes for nonacid vegetables like beets, green beans, or spinach—to eliminate the danger of botulism. See Chapter 2.

4. Heat as close to serving time as possible. Do not hold in steam table for long periods.

5. Season and flavor with imagination. Canned vegetables require more creativity in preparation than fresh because they can be pretty dreary when served plain.

6. Season the liquid while it is coming to a boil, before you add the vegetable. This will give the flavors of the herbs and spices time to blend.

7. Butter enhances the flavor of most vegetables, and it carries the flavors of the other seasonings you choose to add.

8. Dress up the vegetables with added flavors and garnishes, such as beets or sauerkraut with caraway, limas or green beans with crisp crumbled bacon, corn with sautéed minced onion and green or red pepper, carrots with butter and tarragon or orange juice and brown sugar.

The combinations suggested in the table in Chapter 17 apply to canned vegetables as well as to fresh and frozen.

HANDLING DRIED VEGETABLES

There are two basic kinds of dried vegetables.

Dried Legumes

Dried beans and peas have been used as food for thousands of years, and they continue to be important foods even today. In fact, with today's increased interest in healthful eating and in vegetables of all sorts, many more interesting varieties of beans are widely available now than only a few years ago.

Although legumes are dried forms of seed vegetables, they are hard and starchy and handled much like grains (which are also dried seeds). Grains and legumes are discussed in more detail in Chapter 19.

Freeze-Dried and Other Dehydrated Vegetables

Drying has always been an important method for preserving vegetables, especially before modern canning and freezing techniques were developed. Modern technology has developed new methods for drying foods, so a great variety of dried products is on the market, including dried potatoes, onions, carrots, celery, beans, peppers, tomatoes, and mushrooms.

Follow manufacturers' directions for reconstituting these products. Many need to be soaked in cold or warm water for specific lengths of time. They continue to absorb water as they are simmered.

Instant dried products, especially potatoes, require only the addition of a boiling liquid and seasonings to be ready to serve. Again, manufacturers' directions vary with their brands.

An important category of dried vegetables is dried mushrooms. Many flavorful wild mushrooms are in season for only a short time and are in limited supply at high prices. They are available year round in dried form, however. The most popular types—morels, chanterelles, and porcini—are illustrated, along with dried shiitake, a cultivated mushroom that originated in Japan and China.

Dried mushrooms, clockwise from top left: morels, porcini, shiitake, chanterelles.

Dried mushrooms should be soaked in hot water until soft, then drained and lightly squeezed before being cooked. The flavorful soaking liquid is strained and used as a flavoring for cooking liquids and sauces.

PRODUCTION AND HOLDING PROBLEMS IN QUANTITY COOKING

We have emphasized throughout this chapter that vegetables should be cooked as close as possible to serving time. They lose quality rapidly when held in a steam table.

In quantity cooking, however, it is rarely possible to cook individual vegetable portions to order. After 20 to 30 minutes at steam table temperatures, even carefully prepared vegetables are usually overcooked.

Two systems have been devised to help solve this problem. Batch cooking is especially well suited to set meal service, and the blanch and chill method is most helpful in extended meal service. Needs vary from institution to institution, and you will probably find both techniques useful in one kitchen.

BATCH COOKING

Rather than cooking all your vegetables in one batch large enough for the entire meal service, this method (described in Chapter 7, p. 131) involves dividing the food into smaller batches and cooking them one at a time, as needed.

BLANCH AND CHILL METHOD

It is usually impractical to cook vegetables completely to order. Too much time is required. But if the vegetables have been partially cooked, the time needed to finish them to order is short.

Partially cooking, chilling, and finish-cooking is not as good, nutritionally, as cooking completely to order, but it is almost as good. It's certainly better than holding vegetables for hours at serving temperature, and it gives the cook complete control over the degree of doneness when served.

Procedure for Batch Cooking

1. Steamers and small tilting trunnion kettles behind the service line are the most useful kinds of equipment for vegetable batch cooking.

2. Divide each vegetable into batches small enough to be served within 20 to 30 minutes. Arrange in steamer pans ready to be placed in steamers or in containers ready for pouring into the kettles.

3. Keep the prepped vegetables in the cooler until needed.

4. Cook batches as needed. In planning, allow time for loading and unloading the equipment, for cooking, for finishing the product with the desired seasoning, sauce, or garnish, and for carrying to the serving line.

5. Undercook slightly if the vegetable must be held before serving.

6. Have all your seasonings, sauces, and garnishes ready for finishing the dish.

7. Do not mix batches. They will be cooked to different degrees, and colors and textures usually will not match.

Procedure for Blanching and Chilling

1. Steam or simmer the vegetable until partially cooked to desired degree. (In the case of French fries, blanch by deep-frying.)

   The amount of cooking required depends on the vegetable and on the method by which it will be reheated or finished. Frozen vegetables need less cooking than fresh. Often, they need only be thawed.

2. Chill immediately in ice water. (Needless to say, French fries are an exception.)

3. Drain and keep chilled until needed.

4. Finish to order by desired cooking method.

   For example, one or more portions can be placed in a strainer and lowered briefly into a ready pot of boiling water.

   Sautéing in butter is a popular method for finishing such items as peas, green beans, and carrots.

   Potato croquettes are an example of a more complicated application of this same method. The potatoes are boiled or steamed, puréed, seasoned, formed, and breaded in advance. They are then deep-fried to order.

STORAGE

FRESH VEGETABLES

1. Potatoes, onions, and winter squash are stored at cool temperatures (50–65°F/10–18°C) in a dry, dark place.
2. Other vegetables must be refrigerated. To prevent drying, they should be kept covered or wrapped, or the humidity in the cooler must be high. Allow for some air circulation to help prevent mold.
3. Peeled and cut vegetables need extra protection from drying and oxidation. Cover or wrap, and use quickly to prevent spoilage. Potatoes, eggplants, and other vegetables that brown when cut should be treated with an acid or antioxidant. As an alternative, they can be blanched to destroy the enzymes that cause browning. Raw, cut potatoes are sometimes held in cold water for a short time.
4. Store all fresh vegetables for as short a time as possible. They lose quality rapidly. Peas and corn lose sweetness even after a few hours in storage.
5. Keep refrigerators and storage areas clean.

FROZEN VEGETABLES

1. Store at 0°F (–18°C) or colder, in original containers, until ready for use.
2. Do not refreeze thawed vegetables. Quality will be greatly reduced.

DRIED VEGETABLES

1. Store in a cool (less than 75°F/24°C), dry, well-ventilated place.
2. Keep well sealed and off the floor.

CANNED VEGETABLES

1. Keep in a cool, dry place, away from sunlight and off the floor.
2. Discard cans that show signs of damage or spoilage (swollen, badly dented, or rusted cans). When in doubt, throw it out.

LEFTOVERS

1. The best way to store leftovers is not to create them in the first place. Careful planning and small-batch cooking reduce leftovers.
2. Don't mix batches.
3. Store leftover creamed vegetables for one day only. Then either use or discard. Before storing, cool rapidly by placing the container on ice.

TERMS FOR REVIEW

al dente	anthocyanins	trimming loss	sieve size
pigment	carotenoids	AP weight	batch cooking
flavones	chlorophyll	EP weight	blanch and chill

QUESTIONS FOR DISCUSSION

1. Give two reasons for not adding baking soda to the cooking water for green vegetables.

2. Besides appearance, why is proper, uniform cutting of vegetables important?

3. What are some advantages of steam-cooking vegetables over boiling or simmering?

4. You are trying a recipe for blueberry muffins. When you break open a finished muffin, you see that the baked dough around each berry is green. What caused this? How can you correct it? (*Hint:* The batter is made with buttermilk and leavened with baking soda. Even though berries aren't discussed in this chapter, the information about color changes will enable you to answer this question.)

5. Discuss the reasons for cooking green vegetables in a large quantity of water and in just enough water to cover.

6. You are to prepare buttered, steamed asparagus and must produce 50 portions of 3 ounces (90 g) each. How much untrimmed fresh asparagus will you need?

17

Cooking

Vegetables

Now that you have studied the whys and wherefores of vegetable cooking, you should be able to proceed to actual preparation with a clear understanding of what you are doing.

This chapter outlines briefly the basic methods of vegetable preparation. Successful performance of these methods relies on your knowledge of the principles we have discussed.

The recipes given here reinforce your understanding through actual practice. The emphasis is on the method rather than on the particular vegetable used because each method applies to many vegetables. For this reason, variations are listed after basic recipes rather than presented as separate complete recipes. As in other chapters, recipes for sauces that appear in Chapter 8 and are used as components of subsequent preparations are not repeated here.

Most of the recipes are applicable to fresh, frozen, or canned vegetables, even though variations are not listed for each. You have learned how to handle these products in order to make proper substitutions. Review pages 436–438 if necessary.

Potatoes and other starchy foods, such as rice and pasta, are covered in the next chapter. However, the basic cooking methods here apply to potatoes as well as to other vegetables.

BOILING AND STEAMING

Nearly all vegetables may be cooked by boiling or by steaming. These are the two most frequently used methods because they are easy, economical, and adaptable to a great variety of preparations.

Boiling and steaming are basic cooking methods. In most cases, additional steps are required after the basic cooking is completed in order to make the product ready for serving. These steps include adding butter, seasonings, flavorings, and sauces.

Unless they are to be served immediately, boiled or simmered vegetables are drained as soon as they are cooked and then cooled quickly under cold water. This is called *shocking* or *refreshing*, and it prevents the vegetables from being overcooked in their retained heat. Normally, they are then reheated quickly by sautéing in butter or other fat. Seasonings and sauces can be added at this stage. We classify this cooking method as boiling even though the vegetables are finished by sautéing to reheat them. This section includes recipes for boiled vegetables finished with a variety of sauces, flavorings, and seasonings.

In other cases, the product is only partially cooked by boiling or steaming and is finished by another cooking method, such as sautéing or baking. Recipes of this sort are usually included under the final cooking method.

We speak of the cooking method as *boiling* even though, in many cases, *simmering* is a more appropriate term. Green vegetables are generally boiled so they cook quickly, preserving color and nutrients. In many cases, however, the agitation and high temperature of boiling break up delicate vegetables, and simmering is more appropriate.

Steaming as a method for cooking vegetables is becoming more and more widely used, especially as more varieties of advanced equipment become available. It may be the ideal method for cooking certain vegetables, such as broccoli, that easily break or turn watery or mushy when simmered.

After reading this chapter, you should be able to

1. Identify vegetables that are well suited to the different vegetable cooking methods.

2. Cook vegetables by boiling and steaming.

3. Cook vegetables by sautéing and pan-frying.

4. Cook vegetables by braising.

5. Cook vegetables by baking.

6. Cook vegetables by broiling and grilling.

7. Cook vegetables by deep-frying.

Procedure for Boiling Vegetables

1. Collect all equipment and food products.

2. Trim, peel, and cut vegetables as required. See pages 514–534 for prep requirements.

3. Add the required amount of water to the pot (saucepot, steam-jacketed kettle, tilting skillet, or whatever equipment you are using).

   Most vegetables are cooked in just enough water to cover, but many green vegetables and strong-flavored vegetables may be cooked in a large quantity of water (2 or 3 times their volume). See page 511 for discussion.

4. Add salt (approximately 1½–2 tablespoons per gallon of water/6–8 grams per liter) and bring to a boil.

5. Place the vegetables in the pot and return the water to a boil.

6. Reduce heat to a simmer and cook the vegetables, covered or uncovered, as indicated, to required doneness.

   • Green vegetables and strong-flavored vegetables are cooked uncovered.

   • Other vegetables are cooked covered.

7. Drain the vegetables quickly to avoid overcooking.

8. If the vegetables are to be served at once, complete the recipe and serve.

9. If the vegetables are not to be served at once, cool them (except potatoes and starchy vegetables) in cold water, drain as soon as cool, and refrigerate until needed.

Procedure for Steaming Vegetables

This method is used both for pressurized and nonpressurized compartment steam cookers and for simple range-top steamers that consist of a perforated basket over a pot of boiling water.

1. **Know your equipment. Read all operating instructions supplied with your equipment. Each model is a little different.**
2. **Collect all equipment and food products.**
3. **Trim and cut vegetables as required.**
4. **Preheat the steamer.**
5. **Arrange vegetables in pans or baskets for cooking. Make shallow, even layers for uniform cooking.**
   - **Use perforated pans for best steam circulation.**
   - **Use solid pans if cooking liquid must be retained.**
6. **Insert pans or baskets in steamer and close door or lid.**
7. **Steam for required time. Consult timing charts supplied with your model of steamer.**
8. **Remove vegetables from steamer. If it is a pressure steamer, *pressure must return to zero before door is opened.***
9. **Finish vegetables according to recipe and serve at once, or cool quickly for later use.**

   Vegetables that form compact layers do not steam well. They do not allow the steam to circulate, so they cook unevenly. Examples: spinach and other greens, peas, whole-kernel corn, frozen puréed squash.

PURÉEING VEGETABLES

Vegetable purées are served as side dishes or garnishes, and they are also used as ingredients in other preparations. For example, spinach purée is an ingredient in the Spinach Timbale custard on page 568.

Purées were introduced in the discussion of soups in Chapter 9. The vegetable purées we are discussing here are similar, although they are of course much thicker than soups. Procedures for puréeing vary depending on what vegetable is puréed and how the purée is to be used, but some general guidelines can be stated:

Guidelines for Puréeing Vegetables

1. **Vegetables to be puréed should be cooked until tender. Undercooked vegetables make a grainy purée. Be careful not to overcook green vegetables, which discolor when cooked too long.**

   Exception: **A few vegetables, such as avocados and tomatoes, are tender enough to be puréed raw. Whether or not they are cooked depends on the individual vegetable and the desired use for the purée.**
2. **Vegetables for puréeing can be cooked by any method, but the most commonly used methods are boiling, steaming, and baking. Baking is used most often for starchy vegetables such as sweet potatoes and white potatoes.**
3. **Vegetables cooked by boiling or simmering should be drained well when done. If a stiff purée is desired, it may be necessary to dry the cooked vegetable before puréeing. Place the colander of drained vegetables on a sheet pan and set in a moderate oven for a few minutes to dry.**
4. **Always purée cooked vegetables while they are still hot. Cold vegetables are harder to purée to a smooth texture.**
5. **Select appropriate equipment. Ricers, food processors, vertical cutter/mixers (VCMs), food mills, and sieves can be used for puréeing. Food mills, ricers, and sieves make lump-free purées, but they may leave a grainy texture, depending on the vegetable. Food processors and VCMs can create a smooth texture, especially with starchy vegetables, but they do not eliminate vegetable fibers and may leave a few lumps. First using a processor and then passing the purée through a food mill yields the smoothest result.**
6. **Season and finish the purée as desired. Butter or cream is often used to finish vegetable purées. Alternatively, use the purée as an ingredient in another recipe as directed.**

Peas, Carrots and Pearl Onions with Tarragon Butter

Portions: 15   Portion size: 3 oz (100 g)

U.S.	Metric	Ingredients
12 oz	375 g	Pearl onions
1 lb	500 g	Carrots
1 lb 8 oz	750 g	Peas, frozen
2 oz	60 g	Butter
1½ tsp	7 mL	Dried tarragon
1 tbsp	15 mL	Chopped parsley
to taste	to taste	Salt
to taste	to taste	White pepper

Per serving:
Calories, 90; Protein, 3 g; Fat, 3.5 g (34% cal.); Cholesterol, 10 mg;
Carbohydrates, 12 g; Fiber, 3 g; Sodium, 90 mg.

Peas, Carrots, and Pearl Onions with Tarragon Butter

■ P r o c e d u r e

1. Blanch the onions for 20 seconds in boiling water. (Blanching makes them easier to peel.) Drain, refresh under cold water, and drain again. Peel the onions.

2. Bring salted water to a boil in a saucepan. Add the onions, return to a boil, reduce heat to a simmer, and simmer until tender. Drain, refresh under cold water, and drain again.

3. Peel the carrots and cut into batonnet.

4. Bring salted water to a boil in a saucepan. Add the carrots, return to a boil, reduce heat to a simmer, and simmer until tender. Drain, refresh briefly, and drain again.

5. Bring a third pan of salted water to a boil. Add the frozen peas. Return to a boil, reduce heat, and simmer until tender. This only takes a few seconds. Frozen peas have already been blanched and need very little cooking. Drain, refresh, and drain again.

6. Mix together the three vegetables.

7. Heat the butter in as many sauté pans as necessary to hold the vegetables without overcrowding.

8. Add the vegetables and the tarragon. Toss over heat until the vegetables are hot and coated with the butter. Add the parsley and toss to mix.

9. Season to taste with salt and white pepper.

Quantity preparation: Cook and drain the vegetables and combine in a steam table pan. Heat the butter with the herbs and ladle over the vegetables. Season and serve.

V A R I A T I O N S

Herbs may be omitted for a simpler preparation, if desired.

Buttered Vegetables
The following vegetables may be cooked by simply boiling or steaming method and dressed with butter for service, as in basic recipe:

Asparagus	Cabbage	Parsnips
Beans, green or yellow	Carrots	Peas
Beans, lima	Cauliflower (see note)	Rutabagas
Beets	Celery	Spinach
Broccoli (see note)	Corn (on cob or whole kernel)	Turnips
Brussels sprouts	Kohlrabi	

Note: Dress each portion of broccoli spears with butter just when served. Butter runs off broccoli quickly. Do not sauté for á la carte service. Reheat in boiling water, then add butter. Other large vegetables, such as cauliflower, may also be prepared like broccoli.

Herbed Vegetables
Season buttered vegetables with fresh chopped parsley or other appropriate fresh or dried herbs (see table on p. 579). Dried herbs should be heated a few minutes with the vegetable to release flavor.

Amandine
Especially for green beans, broccoli, celery, cauliflower. For each 2 lb (900 g) EP of vegetable, sauté 2 oz (60 g) slivered or sliced almonds in 2–3 oz (60–90 g) butter until lightly browned. (Caution: Almonds darken quickly.) Combine with cooked vegetable.

Hollandaise
Especially for broccoli, asparagus, cauliflower, brussels sprouts, leeks, and artichoke hearts or bottoms. At service time, nap each portion of vegetable with 2 fl oz (60 mL) hollandaise sauce.

Polonaise
Especially for cauliflower, broccoli, brussels sprouts, and, sometimes, asparagus and green beans. For each 5 lb (2.3 kg) EP of vegetable, sauté 1½ pt (750 mL) fresh bread crumbs in about 6 oz (175 g) butter until golden. Chop the whites and yolks of 2–4 hard-cooked eggs separately. Combine the crumbs, chopped egg, and 4 tbsp (60 mL) chopped parsley. Sprinkle this mixture over the cooked vegetable immediately before serving.

Puréed Butternut Squash

Portions: 25   Portion size: 3 oz (90g)

U.S.	Metric	Ingredients
7½ lb	3.5 kg	Butternut squash
6 oz	175 g	Butter
3 oz	90 g	Brown sugar
2 tsp	10 mL	Salt
to taste	to taste	White pepper
to taste	to taste	Nutmeg or ground ginger

Per serving:
Calories, 90; Protein, 1 g; Fat, 6 g (51% cal.); Cholesterol, 15 mg; Carbohydrates, 12 g; Fiber, 2 g; Sodium, 250 mg.

Note: If squash is too wet, cook out some of the moisture in a shallow pan over medium heat.

■ P r o c e d u r e

1. Peel the squash, cut in half, and scrape out seeds. Cut into large dice.
2. Place in perforated steamer pan. Steam until tender. (Alternative method: Place in heavy pot. Add 1 in. [3 cm] water, cover, and cook slowly until tender. Drain well.)
3. Purée the squash with a food mill. Add the butter, sugar, and seasonings. Whip until light, but do not overwhip or squash will become watery.

V A R I A T I O N S

Add 3–4 fl oz (90–125 mL) heavy cream, heated. Sugar may be reduced or omitted if the squash has a good flavor.

Mashed Rutabagas or Yellow Turnips
Prepare as in basic recipe. If desired, add a small amount of whipped potato.

Creamed Spinach

Yield: about 1 lb (500 g)
Portions: 25   Portion size: 3½ oz (100 g)

U.S.	Metric	Ingredients
10 lb AP	4.5 kg AP	Spinach, fresh
2½ pt	1.2 L	Cream sauce, hot
to taste	to taste	Nutmeg
to taste	to taste	Salt
to taste	to taste	White pepper

Per serving:
Calories, 120; Protein, 6 g; Fat, 7 g (50% cal.); Cholesterol, 20 mg; Carbohydrates, 10 g; Fiber, 3 g; Sodium, 150 mg.

Note: For frozen chopped spinach, partially thaw 2½ packages (2½ lb/1.1 kg each). Cover with boiling salted water and break spinach apart. Cook only until hot and drain. Squeeze out excess liquid and combine with cream sauce.

■ P r o c e d u r e

1. Trim spinach and wash carefully in several changes of water. Drain. (See note.)
2. Place 2 in. (5 cm) water in a heavy pot, cover, and bring to a boil. Add the spinach. Stir several times, so it cooks evenly.
3. As soon as the spinach is thoroughly wilted, drain in a colander, pressing with the back of a kitchen spoon to squeeze out excess liquid.
4. Chop the spinach coarsely.
5. Combine with the cream sauce in a hotel pan. Season to taste with nutmeg, salt, and pepper. (The spinach must not taste strongly of nutmeg.)

V A R I A T I O N S

Creamed Vegetables
The following vegetables, cut into small pieces if necessary, may be cooked by boiling or steaming and combined with cream sauce, as in basic recipe. For 25 portions, use 5–6 lb (about 2½ kg) EP vegetables and 2½–3½ pt (1.2–1.7 L) cream sauce.

Asparagus	Cabbage	Okra
Beans, green or yellow	Carrots	Onions, small white
Beans, lima	Cauliflower	Peas
Broccoli	Celery	
Brussels sprouts	Kohlrabi	

Broccoli Mornay

Portions: 24   Portion size: 3½ oz (100 g) broccoli
2 fl oz (60 mL) sauce

U.S.	Metric	Ingredients
7½ lb	3.4 kg	Broccoli
1½ qt	1.5 L	Mornay sauce, hot

Per serving:
Calories, 160; Protein, 9 g; Fat, 10 g (53% cal.); Cholesterol, 30 mg; Carbohydrates, 11 g; Fiber, 4 g; Sodium, 180 mg.

Note: This method of cooking in a shallow pan is used to prevent damaging the blossom ends, which are easily broken. Other delicate vegetables, such as asparagus, are also sometimes cooked in shallow water in hotel pans or sauté pans.

Broccoli may be cooked in a steamer, following basic steaming method.

■ P r o c e d u r e

1. Trim and wash broccoli. Separate large pieces into smaller serving pieces. Split or peel stems for even cooking.

2. Arrange broccoli in hotel pan with flowers to the outside, stems in center.

3. Pour in boiling salted water to partially cover. Cover with clean, wet towels and set on rangetop.

4. Simmer until blossom parts are nearly tender. Fold back towels from edges to uncover blossoms. This releases steam and helps avoid overcooking. Leave stems covered and continue to simmer until stems feel tender but al dente when pierced with a knife, Drain well.

5. Nap each portion with 2 fl oz (60 mL) Mornay sauce at service time. Ladle the sauce across the stems without covering the blossoms.

V A R I A T I O N S

Other vegetables may be served with cheese sauce, such as cauliflower and brussels sprouts.

Broccoli with Cheddar Cheese Sauce
Prepare as in basic recipe, but substitute cheddar cheese sauce for the Mornay sauce.

Vegetable Tagliatelle

Portions: 16   Portion size: about 4 oz (125 g)

U.S	Metric	Ingredients
1lb 8 oz	800 g	Zucchini, trimmed
1 lb 8 oz	800 g	Carrots, peeled and trimmed
1 lb 8 oz	800 g	Celery root, peeled
2 oz	60 g	Butter

Per serving:
Calories, 70; Protein, 1 g; Fat, 3 g (40% cal.); Cholesterol, 10 mg; Carbohydrates, 9 g; Fiber, 3 g; Sodium, 100 mg.

■ P r o c e d u r e

1. Cut vegetables lengthwise into thin slices, about ⅛ in. (3 mm) thick, then cut into long, thin strips so the vegetables resemble flat noodles (tagliatelle).

2. Blanch each vegetable separately in boiling salted water. Vegetables should be tender but still firm. Refresh under cold water and drain.

3. Just before serving, heat the butter in a saucepan over moderate heat. Add the vegetables and toss in the butter until hot.

Cauliflower au Gratin

Portions: 25   Portion size: 3 oz (90 g) cauliflower
1½ oz (45 g) sauce and topping

U.S.	Metric	Ingredients
5 lb EP	2.3 kg EP	Cauliflower
1 tbsp	15 mL	Lemon juice (see note)
1 qt 6 fl oz	1.2 L	Béchamel or Mornay sauce, hot
1½ oz	45 g	Dry bread crumbs
1½ oz	45 g	Parmesan cheese, grated
2½ oz	75 g	Butter, melted

Per serving:
Calories, 60; Protein, 3 g; Fat, 3.5 g (50% cal.); Cholesterol, 10 mg;
Carbohydrates, 5 g; Fiber, 2 g; Sodium, 80 mg.

Note: Adding lemon juice to cooking water helps to keep white vegetables
white. It may be omitted if desired.

■ P r o c e d u r e

1. Separate the cauliflower into florets.
2. Place the cauliflower and lemon juice in boiling, salted water. Return to boil, lower heat, and cover. Simmer until just tender. Do not overcook, as it will cook further in the sauce. Drain.
3. Butter the bottom of a baking pan or hotel pan and place the cauliflower in it about 2 in. (5 cm) deep. (Individual ovenproof serving dishes may be used instead.)
4. Cover with the hot sauce.
5. Mix together the bread crumbs and cheese and sprinkle evenly over the top. Drizzle melted butter over the top.
6. Bake at 350°F (175°C) for about 20 minutes to heat through. Brown the top under the broiler or salamander.

V A R I A T I O N S

Substitute cheddar cheese sauce for the béchamel or Mornay, and use grated cheddar cheese instead of parmesan for topping.

Other vegetables may be prepared au gratin, such as asparagus, Belgian endive, broccoli, brussels sprouts, celery, celery root, leeks, and turnips.

Cauliflower au Gratin

Green Beans Basquaise

Portions: 12   Portion size: 4 oz (110 g)

U.S.	Metric	Ingredients
1 lb 12 oz	800 g	Green beans, trimmed
4 fl oz	125 mL	Olive oil
6 oz	175 g	Green bell pepper, cut brunoise
6 oz	175 g	Red bell pepper, cut brunoise
6 oz	175 g	Yellow bell pepper, cut brunoise
to taste	to taste	Salt
to taste	to taste	Pepper

■ P r o c e d u r e

1. Boil the green beans in salted water until tender but firm. Drain and cool under cold water. Drain.
2. Heat the olive oil over medium heat. Add the peppers and sweat.
3. Add the green beans and toss in the hot oil until the beans are hot.
4. Season to taste.

Per serving:
Calories, 120; Protein, 2 g; Fat, 10 g (69% cal.); Cholesterol, 0 mg;
Carbohydrates, 8 g; Fiber, 2 g; Sodium, 0 mg.

Mixed Vegetables with Herbs

Portions: 16   Portion size: 4 oz (125 g)

U.S.	Metric	Ingredients
2 lb	1 kg	Asparagus
1 lb 6 oz	600 g	Zucchini
14 oz	400 g	Celery root
14 oz	400 g	Turnips
4 oz	125 g	Butter
6	6	Shallots, chopped
1½ fl oz	45 mL	Lemon juice
1 fl oz	30 mL	Water
to taste	to taste	Salt
2 tbsp	30 mL	Chopped parsley
2 tbsp	30 mL	Chopped chives

■ **P r o c e d u r e**

1. Trim and peel the asparagus (see Figure 16.3). Cook in boiling salted water until tender but firm. Refresh under cold water and set aside.
2. Trim the zucchini, celery root, and turnips as necessary. Cut into batonnet.
3. Cook each vegetable separately in boiling salted water. Refresh under cold water and drain.
4. Melt the butter in a large sauté pan. Add the shallots, lemon juice, water, and salt. Cook until the shallots are tender.
5. Add the vegetables. When hot, mix in the herbs

Per serving:
Calories, 80; Protein, 2 g; Fat, 6 g (67% cal.); Cholesterol, 15 mg; Carbohydrates, 7 g; Fiber, 3 g; Sodium, 105 mg.

Green Beans with Sesame Dressing

Portions: 16   Portion size: 2 oz (60 g)

U.S.	Metric	Ingredients
1 cup	250 mL	White sesame seeds
1½ fl oz	50 mL	Soy sauce
2 tbsp	30 g	Sugar
2 fl oz	60 mL	Dashi or water
2 lb	1 kg	Green beans

■ **P r o c e d u r e**

1. Toast the sesame seeds in a dry skillet, stirring and tossing regularly, until light golden.
2. Using a spice grinder or mortar and pestle, grind the sesame seeds to a paste.
3. Mix in the soy sauce and sugar. Thin with dashi or water. Set aside.
4. Wash the green beans and trim the ends. Cut into 1-in. (2½-cm) lengths.
5. Cook the beans in boiling, salted water until crisp-tender. Drain, cool under cold running water, and drain again.
6. Mix the beans with the dressing.

Per serving:
Calories, 80; Protein, 3 g; Fat, 4.5 g (48% cal.); Cholesterol, 0 mg; Carbohydrates, 8 g; Fiber, 3 g; Sodium, 150 mg.

V A R I A T I O N S

Other mild green vegetables, such as spinach and asparagus, can be served the same way.

Sesame Miso Dressing
Reduce the sesame seeds to ½ cup (125 mL). Omit the soy sauce and sugar, and add 4 oz (125 g) white or red miso. Use mirin (sweet rice wine) instead of dashi or water to thin the dressing. Use as a dressing for vegetables, in the same manner as sesame dressing.

Green Beans with Sesame Dressing

Green Beans with Roasted Peppers and Bacon

Portions: 16   Portion size: 3½ oz (100 g)

U.S.	Metric	Ingredients
3 lb	1.35 kg	Green beans
1 lb	450 g	Red bell peppers
8 oz	225 g	Slab bacon
to taste	to taste	Salt

Per serving:
Calories, 90; Protein, 4 g; Fat, 6 g (53% cal.); Cholesterol, 10 mg; Carbohydrates, 8 g; Fiber, 3 g; Sodium, 115 mg.

■ **P r o c e d u r e**

1. Trim the stem ends from the green beans.
2. Wash and drain the beans.
3. Boil the beans in a large pot of salted water until just tender. Drain.
4. Rinse under cold water to cool the beans and stop the cooking, or drop them into ice water. Drain again. Refrigerate until needed.
5. Roast and peel the peppers (see p. 529). Trim and discard the stem, seed core, and inner membranes.
6. Cut into batonnet.
7. Cut the bacon into batonnet about 1 in. (2.5 cm) long.
8. In a heavy sauté pan, cook the bacon over moderate heat until crisp.
9. Remove the bacon from the pan with a slotted spoon and reserve. Reserve about 2 oz (60 g) of the fat in the pan, discarding the rest.
10. Add the beans and the red peppers to the pan with the bacon fat and toss over heat until hot.
11. Taste and add salt if necessary. The salt from the bacon may be enough.
12. Add the crisp bacon and toss to mix.
13. Serve immediately.

V A R I A T I O N S

Green Beans with Pecans and Browned Shallots
Omit the bacon and peppers. Brown 12 oz (360 g) thinly sliced shallots in butter. Add 12 oz (360 g) broken pecans and continue to cook until the pecans are hot. Reheat the beans in butter instead of bacon fat, and toss with the shallots and pecans.

Compote of Carrots and Onions

Portions: 12   Portion size: 3½–4 oz (110–120 g)

U.S.	Metric	Ingredients
3 lb 8 oz	1.6 kg	Carrots
14 oz	400 g	Onions, chopped
1 tbsp	15 mL	Olive oil
12 fl oz	350 mL	Water
to taste	to taste	Salt and pepper
to taste	to taste	Ground ginger

Per serving:
Calories, 80; Protein, 2 g; Fat, 1.5 g (16% cal.); Cholesterol, 0 mg; Carbohydrates, 16 g; Fiber, 4 g; Sodium, 80 mg.

■ **P r o c e d u r e**

1. Trim and peel the carrots. Cut them in half lengthwise, then cut them into slices.
2. In a large pan, cook the onions over low heat in the olive oil for about 5 minutes.
3. Add the carrots and water. Season to taste with salt, pepper, and ground ginger. Cover and cook over medium heat for about 20 minutes. Check from time to time to make sure that the liquid hasn't evaporated and that the vegetables aren't scorching. This could happen if the cover is loose or if the heat is too high.
4. Remove the cover and cook another 5–10 minutes to allow the moisture to evaporate, stirring occasionally, until the desired consistency is reached. Adjust the seasoning if necessary and serve.

Collards with Ham

Portions: 16   Portion size: 4 oz (125 g)

U.S.	Metric	Ingredients
2 lb	1 kg	Smoked ham hocks
6 lb	3 kg	Collard greens
to taste	to taste	Black pepper
2 tsp, or to taste	20 mL, or to taste	Hot pepper sauce
as needed	as needed	Cider vinegar

■ **P r o c e d u r e**

1. Simmer the ham hocks in enough water to cover until the meat is tender, about 1½ to 2 hours.
2. Remove the hocks from the liquid, and reserve the liquid in the pot.
3. Remove the meat from the bone and cut into small dice.
4. Trim the stems from the greens. Wash the greens in several changes of cold water.
5. Add the greens to the ham stock. Simmer until very tender, about 45 to 60 minutes.
6. Drain the greens, reserving the liquid.
7. Chop the greens coarsely.
8. Combine the greens with the ham.
9. Add enough of the reserved cooking liquid to moisten the greens well. Reheat as necessary.
10. Add pepper and hot pepper sauce to taste.
11. Serve with vinegar on the side, for diners to add to taste.

V A R I A T I O N S

Turnip greens, mustard greens, or kale may be substituted for the collards.

Per serving:
Calories, 240; Protein, 20 g; Fat, 14 g (51% cal.); Cholesterol, 60 mg; Carbohydrates, 10 g; Fiber, 6 g; Sodium, 95 mg.

Note: This is a traditional Southern preparation that disregards all the rules of cooking green vegetables and preserving vegetable color.

Brussels Sprouts Paysanne

Portions: 24   Portion size: 6 oz (175 g)

U.S.	Metric	Ingredients
4 lb 8 oz	2 kg	Brussels sprouts
1 lb 4 oz	600 g	Carrot
1 lb 4 oz	600 g	Celery
1 lb 4 oz	600 g	Leek
1 lb 4 oz	600 g	Onion
7 oz	200 g	Prosciutto
5 oz	150 g	Butter
3 tbsp	20 g	Chopped parsley
to taste	to taste	Salt

■ **P r o c e d u r e**

1. Clean the brussels sprouts and cook in boiling salted water until tender.
2. Cut the vegetables into paysanne as follows: Cut the carrot and celery into ¹⁄₁₆-in. (2–mm) slice. Cut each slice into strips, ¼ in. (6 mm) wide. Cut the strips into triangles. Cut the leek and onion into triangles approximately the same size.
3. Cut the prosciutto into julienne.
4. Sweat the paysanne vegetables in the butter. Once cooked, add the ham and the brussels sprouts. Cook for around 10 minutes, then mix in the chopped parsley. Adjust the seasoning if necessary.

V A R I A T I O N

Substitute bacon for the prosciutto. Render the bacon, then use the bacon fat instead of the butter for sweating the vegetables.

Per serving:
Calories, 130; Protein, 6 g; Fat, 7 g (41% cal.); Cholesterol, 20 mg; Carbohydrates, 17 g; Fiber, 5 g; Sodium, 310 mg.

Artichokes Gribiche

Portions: 10   Portion size: 1 artichoke
2½ fl oz (80 mL) sauce

U.S.	Metric	Ingredients
10	10	Artichokes
3	3	Lemons
1½ pt	800 mL	Sauce Gribiche (p. 724)

Per serving:
Calories, 480; Protein, 6 g; Fat, 45 g (82% cal.); Cholesterol, 65 mg;
Carbohydrates, 16 g; Fiber, 7 g; Sodium, 310 mg.

■ P r o c e d u r e

1. Trim the artichokes for cooking whole, as shown in Figure 16.1.
2. Cut the lemons into ¼-in. (5-mm) slices. Tie a slice of lemon to the base of each artichoke to prevent discoloration (see Figure 16.2).
3. Cook in gently simmering water until tender, about 30–40 minutes.
4. Serve warm or cooled, with the sauce on the side, for dipping.

 ## Artichokes Clamart

Portions: 10   Portion size: 1 artichoke heart
1 oz (30 g) peas

U.S.	Metric	Ingredients
10	10	Artichokes, large
1	1	Lemon, cut in half
1 oz	30 g	Flour
3 pt	1.5 L	Water, cold
1½ fl oz	50 mL	Lemon juice
1 tbsp	15 mL	Salt
10 oz	300 g	Peas, frozen
3 oz	90 g	Butter
to taste	to taste	Salt
to taste	to taste	White pepper
pinch	pinch	Dried basil

Per serving:
Calories, 150; Protein, 6 g; Fat, 7 g (38% cal.); Cholesterol, 20 mg;
Carbohydrates, 20 g; Fiber, 9 g; Sodium, 580 mg.

■ P r o c e d u r e

1. Prepare artichoke bottoms by trimming, as shown in Figure 16.1. Rub the cut surfaces with the lemon as you work to keep them from darkening.
2. Mix the flour with a little water, then add it to the remaining water in a saucepan. Add the lemon juice and salt. Bring to a boil. This mixture is called a blanc. It helps keep the artichokes white as they cook.
3. Add the artichokes to the blanc and simmer until just tender, about 30 minutes. Drain.
4. Place the peas in a saucepan with boiling salted water and simmer until just heated through. Drain.
5. Heat 1 oz (30 g) of the butter in a sauté pan and sauté the peas briefly. Season with salt, pepper, and basil, tossing over heat briefly so that the basil can release its flavor.
6. At the same time, heat the remaining 2 oz (60 g) butter in another sauté pan. Place the cooked artichoke bottoms in the pan and sauté over medium heat until the artichokes are well coated with butter and are hot. Season with salt and pepper.
7. Arrange artichokes in a hotel pan and fill with the peas. (Do not do this in advance because the lemon juice in the artichokes will discolor the peas.)

V A R I A T I O N S

Artichoke bottoms can be filled with other vegetables, such as asparagus tips, tiny tournéed carrots, tournéed turnips, or mushrooms. They may also be used as containers for a sauce served with grilled meat items. Either way, they are used mostly as garnish for meats.

Glazed Root Vegetables

Portions: 12   Portion size: 3½–4 oz (110–120 g)
Portions: 25   Portion size: 3 oz (90 g)

U.S.	Metric	Ingredients
3 lb	1.4 kg	Carrots
1½ lb	600 g	Parsnips
2½ lb	1 kg	Turnips
3 oz	90 g	Butter
2 oz	60 g	Sugar
to taste	to taste	Salt

Per serving:
Calories, 90; Protein, 1 g; Fat, 3 g (30% cal.); Cholesterol, 5 mg; Carbohydrates, 15 g; Fiber, 4 g; Sodium, 85 mg.

■ P r o c e d u r e

1. Trim and peel the carrots, parsnips, and turnips. Tournéed root vegetables (see Figure 7.18) are often prepared by this method.

2. Place the vegetables in a saucepan with boiling salted water to cover. Simmer until tender. Drain.

3. Heat the butter in a sauté pan. Add the vegetables and sprinkle with the sugar. Season to taste with salt. Sauté until the vegetables are well glazed.

V A R I A T I O N S

Single vegetables as well as other combinations of vegetables may be glazed by this method, including celery root, pearl onions, rutabagas, and chestnuts, in addition to carrots, parsnips, and turnips.

Glazed Carrots

Glazed Carrots (Carrots Vichy)

Portions: 25   Portion size: 3 oz (90 g)

U.S.	Metric	Ingredients
6½ lb	3 kg	Carrots
as needed	as needed	Water (see note)
5 oz	150 g	Butter
2 tbsp	30 g	Sugar
2 tsp	10 mL	Salt
to taste	to taste	White pepper
as needed	as needed	Chopped parsley

Per serving:
Calories, 100; Protein, 2 g; Fat, 5 g (43% cal.); Cholesterol, 10 mg; Carbohydrates, 13 g; Fiber, 2 g; Sodium, 240 mg.

Note: Sometimes Vichy water or other bottled mineral water is used, but it is not necessary.

■ P r o c e d u r e

1. Trim, peel, and slice the carrots.

2. Place them in a saucepan or straight-sided sauté pan. Add water to barely cover the carrots. Add the butter, sugar, and salt.

3. Bring to a boil. Lower heat and simmer until the carrots are tender and the water is nearly evaporated. If done properly, these should happen at the same time. Toss the carrots so that they are well coated with the glaze that is left in the pan.

4. Season with pepper. Garnish with chopped parsley.

Spinaci alla Romana

Portions: 16   Portion size: 3 oz (90 g)

U.S.	Metric	Ingredients
6 lb	2.7 kg	Spinach
1½ fl oz	45 mL	Olive oil
1½ oz	45 g	Fat from prosciutto or pork, small dice
1½ oz	45 g	Pine nuts
1½ oz	45 g	Raisins
to taste	to taste	Salt
to taste	to taste	Pepper

Per serving:
Calories, 100; Protein, 5 g; Fat, 7 g (57% cal.); Cholesterol, 5 mg; Carbohydrates, 7 g; Fiber, 3 g; Sodium, 90 mg.

■ P r o c e d u r e

1. Trim and wash the spinach. Cook in a small quantity of boiling water until wilted. Drain, cool under running water, and drain again. Press excess water out of the spinach, but do not squeeze too dry.
2. Heat the oil in a pan. Add the fat and render it. Remove and discard the cracklings (solid pieces remaining from the fat).
3. Add the spinach, pine nuts, and raisins. Sauté until hot.
4. Season with salt and pepper.

V A R I A T I O N S

Chopped garlic may be sautéed in the fat before the spinach is added.

Lean prosciutto, sliced thin, then diced, may be added.

Spinaci alla Piemontese
Omit the oil, fat, nuts, and raisins. Heat 8 chopped anchovy fillets and 2 chopped garlic cloves in 4 oz (125 g) butter, then add the boiled, drained spinach and sauté.

 ## Cipolline in Agrodolce

Portions: 16   Portion size: 3½ oz (100 g)

U.S.	Metric	Ingredients
4½ lb	2 kg	Pearl onions
1 pt	500 mL	Water
2 oz	60 g	Butter
3 fl oz	90 mL	Wine vinegar
1½ oz	45 g	Sugar
1½ tsp	7 mL	Salt

Per serving:
Calories, 120; Protein, 2 g; Fat, 3 g (23% cal.); Cholesterol, 10 mg; Carbohydrates, 21 g; Fiber, 1 g; Sodium, 270 mg.

■ P r o c e d u r e

1. Blanch the onions for 1 minute. Drain and peel.
2. Put the onions in a sauté pan in a single layer. Add the water and butter and cook slowly, uncovered, for about 20 minutes, until fairly tender. Add a little water if necessary during cooking so that the pan does not become dry. Stir gently from time to time.
3. Add the vinegar, sugar, and salt. Cover lightly. Cook over low heat until the onions are very tender and the liquid is syrupy, about 30 minutes. If necessary, remove the cover toward the end of the cooking time to let the liquid reduce. The onions should be lightly browned by the time they are done.

SAUTÉING AND PAN-FRYING

Remember that the main differences between sautéing and pan-frying are in the amount of fat used and in the cooking time. *Sautéing* means cooking quickly in a small amount of fat. The product is often tossed or flipped in the pan over high heat. *Pan-frying* means cooking in a larger amount of fat, usually for a longer time at lower heat, and the product is not tossed or flipped. In practice, the two methods are often similar, and the distinction between them is hard to draw.

Both methods may be used for finish-cooking precooked or blanched vegetables as well as for completely cooking vegetables from the raw state. Sautéing in butter is especially popular for finishing precooked and chilled vegetables for service.

Stir-frying is a quick-cooking technique used in Asian cookery. In effect, it is similar to sautéing, except the pan is left stationary and the items being cooked are stirred and flipped in hot fat with spatulas or other tools. For the basic stir-frying procedure, see page 314. This is the general procedure for stir-frying all foods, including meats. To use the procedure for vegetables only, omit steps 4, 5, and 6.

Procedure for Sautéing Vegetables

This method is used for precooked or blanched vegetables and for tender, small-cut vegetables that cook quickly.

1. Collect all equipment and food products.
2. Prepare vegetables as required.
3. Place sauté pan on high heat.
4. When the pan is hot, add a small amount of clarified butter, oil, or other fat, enough to coat the bottom of the pan. (Clarified butter is used because the milk solids in whole butter burn quickly at the high heat necessary for sautéing.)
5. As soon as the fat is hot, add the vegetable. Do not overload the pan, or the temperature will be lowered too much and the vegetables will simmer instead of sauté.
6. After the heat has recovered, flip the pan a few times to turn and toss the vegetables (see Figure 17.1). Let the pan set again over the heat.
7. Continue to flip the vegetables as often as necessary for them to cook or heat evenly and become coated with the cooking fat. (Don't flip more than necessary, however. It may be fun and a good way to show off, but it's a waste of time and accomplishes nothing except breaking fragile vegetables. Also, the heat must have time to recover between flips.)
8. As soon as the vegetables are cooked, or heated through if precooked, remove from the pan and serve. Browning may or may not be desirable, depending on the vegetable and the particular preparation.

Flipping action of wrist

Figure 17.1 To flip foods in a sauté pan, give the handle a sharp twist upward with the wrist. Be sure to move the pan back far enough to catch the foods as they come down.

Procedure for Pan-Frying Vegetables

Note: A griddle is often used for this procedure if only a small amount of fat is required.

1. Collect all equipment and food products.
2. Prepare vegetables as required.
3. Place a sauté pan or cast-iron skillet on moderately high heat. Add required amount of fat to the pan and let it heat.
4. Place prepared vegetables in the pan. Adjust the heat so the product cooks through with the desired amount of browning but without burning the outside.
5. Turn vegetables with a spatula and continue to cook until done.
6. Remove from pan. If necessary, drain on absorbent paper to eliminate excess fat.

Pan-Fried Eggplant with Tomato Sauce

Portions: 24   Portion size: 3½ oz (100 g) eggplant
2 fl oz (60 mL) sauce

U.S.	Metric	Ingredients
6½ lb	3 kg	Eggplant
		Breading:
6 oz	175 g	Flour
1½ tsp	7 mL	Salt
½ tsp	2 mL	White pepper
1 pt	500 mL	Egg wash
1¼ lb	600 g	Bread crumbs
as needed	as needed	Oil for frying
1½ qt	1.5 L	Tomato sauce

■ P r o c e d u r e

1. Wash and trim eggplants. Pare if skins are tough. Cut crosswise into ¼-in. (0.5-cm) slices.
2. Hold in strongly salted cold water up to 30 minutes. (This step may be omitted, but it helps prevent darkening and eliminates some bitter flavors.)
3. Set up breading station, seasoning the flour with the salt and pepper.
4. Drain the eggplants and dry them well. Pass through Standard Breading Procedure (see p. 143).
5. Heat ¼ in. (0.5 cm) oil in a heavy iron skillet or sauté pan. Pan fry the breaded eggplant on both sides until browned. Remove from pan with slotted spatula and drain on absorbent paper.
6. Serve 2–3 slices per portion, depending on size. Nap each portion with 2 fl oz (60 mL) tomato sauce. Ladle the sauce in a band across the eggplant; do not cover completely.

Per serving:
Calories, 260; Protein, 7 g; Fat, 13 g (44% cal.); Cholesterol, 70 mg; Carbohydrates, 30 g; Fiber, 4 g; Sodium, 490 mg.

V A R I A T I O N S

Instead of Standard Breading Procedure, simply dredge slices in seasoned flour and pan-fry.

Pan-Fried Eggplant Creole
Use Creole sauce instead of tomato sauce.

Eggplant Parmigiana
Pan-fry as in basic recipe. Top each fried slice with a thin slice of mozzarella cheese. Arrange in layers in a baking pan, covering each layer with tomato sauce and sprinkling with parmesan cheese. Bake 30 minutes at 350°F (175°C).

Zucchini Sauté Provençale

Portions: 25   Portion size: 3½ oz (100 g)

U.S.	Metric	Ingredients
6 lb	2.7 kg	Zucchini
6 fl oz	175 mL	Olive oil
6 oz	175 g	Shallots or onions, minced
4–6	4–6	Garlic cloves, chopped
to taste	to taste	Chopped parsley
to taste	to taste	Salt
to taste	to taste	White pepper

■ P r o c e d u r e

1. Wash and trim the zucchini. Cut crosswise into thin slices.
2. Heat the oil in two or three sauté pans (or sauté in several batches—do not overload the pans). Add the shallot or onion and the garlic. Sauté until soft but not browned.
3. Add the zucchini and sauté until slightly browned but still somewhat crisp.
4. Add the parsley and toss to mix. Season to taste.

Per serving:
Calories, 80; Protein, 1 g; Fat, 7 g (72% cal.); Cholesterol, 0 mg; Carbohydrates, 5 g; Fiber, 1 g; Sodium, 5 mg.

V A R I A T I O N S

Cut the zucchini into other shapes, but keep them small enough to cook quickly. Examples: batonnet, julienne, dice, and shredded on a coarse grater.

Shredded Zucchini with Shallots
Shred the zucchini on a coarse grater. Sauté with shallots as in basic recipe, but without browning. Omit the garlic and parsley.

Zucchini with Tomatoes
Sauté as in basic recipe. When half-cooked, add 2½ pt (1.2 L) drained, chopped, canned tomatoes or fresh tomatoes concassé (p. 533). Finish cooking. Season with oregano and basil.

Zucchini with Cream
Shred zucchini on grater. Salt lightly and let stand in a colander for 30 minutes. Press out excess liquid. Sauté as in basic recipe, but without browning. Add 2½ cups (600 mL) heavy cream and simmer 2 minutes.

Sautéed Mushrooms

Portions: 25   **Portion size: 3½ oz (100 g)**

U.S.	Metric	Ingredients
6½ lb	3 kg	Mushrooms, fresh
10 oz	300 g	Clarified butter, or half oil, half butter
to taste	to taste	Salt
to taste	to taste	Pepper

Per serving:
Calories, 120; Protein, 2 g; Fat, 11 g (80% cal.); Cholesterol, 30 mg; Carbohydrates, 4 g; Fiber, 2 g; Sodium, 115 mg.

Note: If mushrooms must be kept light in color, add lemon juice to the pan when the mushrooms are added. Use about 1 fl oz (30 mL) lemon juice per pound (500 g) of mushrooms.

■ P r o c e d u r e

1. Rinse the mushrooms quickly and dry them with towels. Trim off the bottoms of the stems and slice the mushrooms.

2. Heat two or three sauté pans over high heat (or sauté in several batches—do not overload pans). Add the fat to the pans. Place the mushrooms in the pan and sauté over high heat until browned. Do not overcook, or the mushrooms will shrivel and lose a great deal of moisture.

3. Season with salt and pepper.

V A R I A T I O N S

Garnish with chopped parsley.

Instead of slicing, leave small mushroom caps whole, or cut in halves or quarters.

Creamed Mushrooms
Prepare as in basic recipe, using lemon juice to keep light color. Combine with 2½ pt (1.2 L) hot cream sauce. Season with a little nutmeg.

Duxelles
Chop mushrooms very fine. Squeeze out moisture in a towel. Sauté in butter with 3 oz (90 g) minced shallot or onion until dry. Season with salt, pepper, nutmeg. Used in vegetable and meat stuffings. May be moistened with heavy cream or stretched with bread crumbs.

 ## Corn with Poblanos

Portions: 12   **Portion size: 3 oz (90 g)**

U.S.	Metric	Ingredients
12 oz	360 g	Poblano chiles
2 lb	900 g	Corn, fresh or frozen
1½ fl oz	45 mL	Olive oil
8 oz	240 g	Onion, chopped fine
1 tsp	5 mL	Dried oregano
to taste	to taste	Salt
to taste	to taste	Pepper

Per serving:
Calories, 180; Protein, 6 g; Fat, 7 g (30% cal.); Cholesterol, 0 mg; Carbohydrates, 30 g; Fiber, 9 g; Sodium, 25 mg.

■ P r o c e d u r e

1. Roast and peel the chiles as illustrated on page 529. Remove and discard the stem, seeds, and inner membranes.

2. Cut the chiles into batonnet.

3. If the corn is frozen, drop into boiling water until thawed, then drain.

4. Heat the olive oil in a sauté pan over moderately high heat.

5. Add the onion and sauté until it is soft and beginning to brown.

6. Add the poblanos, corn, and oregano. Sauté until hot and well blended.

7. Add salt and pepper to taste

V A R I A T I O N S

Gratin of Corn and Poblanos
Prepare as in the main recipe. Transfer to a gratin dish and cover with a generous layer of Monterey jack or similar mild cheese. Place under a salamander or broiler until the cheese is melted and lightly browned.

Corn and Poblanos in Cream
Prepare as in the main recipe, but in step 6 add 12 fl oz (360 mL) heavy cream. Simmer until the cream is thickened and reduced by about one-third.

Stir-Fried Mixed Vegetables

Portions: 16   Portion size: 4 oz (125 g)

U.S.	Metric	Ingredients
1½ lb	750 g	Chinese cabbage
16	16	Dried black mushrooms
6 oz	175 g	Bamboo shoots, drained
4 oz	125 g	Celery
4 oz	125 g	Carrots
15 oz can	425 g can	Baby corn
4	4	Scallions
2–3 fl oz	60–90 mL	Oil
1	1	Garlic cloves, crushed (optional)
5 slices	5 slices	Ginger root
1 tsp	5 mL	Salt
12 fl oz	350 mL	Water or chicken stock
1 fl oz	30 mL	Soy sauce (optional)
¼ cup	25 g (60 mL)	Cornstarch
3 fl oz	100 mL	Water, cold
1 tsp	5 mL	Sesame oil (optional)

Per serving:
Calories, 90; Protein, 2 g; Fat, 4 g, (36% cal.); Cholesterol, 0 mg;
Carbohydrates, 14 g; Fiber, 3 g; Sodium, 165 mg.

■ Procedure

1. Cut off the root end of the cabbage and separate the leaves. Cut out the thick center ribs, then cut them crosswise into 2-in. (5-cm) chunks. Cut the thin, leafy parts into shreds.
2. Soak the mushrooms in boiling water to cover. When soft, drain and squeeze dry, reserving the liquid. Discard the stems and cut the caps into julienne.
3. Cut the bamboo shoots into thin slices.
4. Cut the celery on the diagonal into thin slices.
5. Cut the carrots into julienne.
6. Drain the baby corn.
7. Slice the scallions at a sharp angle into shreds.

8. Heat the oil in a wok or large sauté pan.
9. Add the garlic and cook about 15 seconds to flavor the oil, then remove and discard the garlic.
10. Add the ginger and salt and let cook about 15 seconds.
11. Add the cabbage ribs and stir-fry 1–2 minutes.
12. Add the remaining vegetables, except for the shredded cabbage leaves. Continue to stir-fry for another 1–2 minutes. Add the shredded cabbage.
13. Add the stock and soy sauce and continue to stir and cook until the vegetables are cooked but still crisp.
14. Mix the cornstarch with the cold water, then stir it, a little at a time, into the vegetables to thicken the sauce. Do not add it all at once because you may not need it all. The sauce should not be too thick, about the consistency of a light velouté sauce.
15. Stir in the sesame oil and serve at once.

V A R I A T I O N S

This is a basic procedure for stir-fried vegetables. One or two vegetables, or any harmonious assortment, can be cooked using the same recipe, merely substituting different vegetable ingredients.

BRAISING

Braising, as you know, is a slow, moist-heat cooking method using a small amount of liquid. When meats are braised, they are seared or browned in fat before liquid is added. Braised vegetables are not always cooked in fat before liquid is added, although some kind of fat is used in the preparation.

Braised vegetable preparations tend to be more complex than boiled or steamed vegetables, and the cooking times are longer. Unfortunately, there are so many variations of braised vegetables that it is not possible to prescribe a single basic procedure. Instead, we discuss the procedures in general terms and use the recipes to illustrate them.

Characteristics of Vegetable Braising Procedures

1. Fat is added to a braising or baking pan or a saucepan and heated. Finely diced mirepoix or other flavoring ingredients may be cooked briefly in the fat. The fat contributes to flavor and eating quality.

2. The vegetable (blanched or raw) is placed in the pan. It may or may not be cooked in the fat before the liquid is added, depending on the recipe.

3. Liquid is added—stock, water, wine, or a combination of liquids. The liquid generally covers the vegetable only partway.

4. The pot or saucepan is covered and the vegetable is cooked slowly in the oven or on the rangetop.

5. The flavorful cooking liquid is served with the vegetable. It is sometimes drained off and reduced over high heat before serving in order to concentrate flavor.

Braised Red Cabbage

Portions: 25   Portion size: 5 oz (150 g)

U.S.	Metric	Ingredients
6 lb	3 kg	Red cabbage
12 oz	375 g	Bacon, diced
1 lb	500 g	Onions, sliced
1 oz	30 g	Sugar
1½ pt	750 mL	White stock (chicken, pork, veal) or water
1 lb	500 g	Apples (unpeeled), cored and diced
4	4	Cloves
6	6	Whole allspice
1	1	Cinnamon stick
4 fl oz or more	125 mL	Cider vinegar or red wine vinegar
1 cup	250 mL	Red wine (or more vinegar)
to taste	to taste	Salt
to taste	to taste	Pepper

Per serving:
Calories, 130; Protein, 3 g; Fat, 8 g (54% cal.); Cholesterol, 10 mg; Carbohydrates, 11 g; Fiber, 3 g; Sodium, 110 mg.

■ Procedure

1. Remove the outer leaves of the cabbage and cut it into quarters. Remove the core and shred the cabbage with a knife (Figure 16.7) or a power shredder attachment. Do not chop; cabbage should be in long, fine shreds.

2. Render the bacon in a large, heavy pot. Add the onions and sugar and cook until the onion is soft.

3. Add the cabbage and stir over heat until it is coated with fat.

4. Add the stock, apples, and the spices, tied in a cheesecloth bag. Cover and simmer until cabbage is nearly tender, about 30 minutes.

5. Add the vinegar and red wine and simmer another 10 minutes. Remove spice bag.

6. Taste and correct seasoning. If not tart enough or color is not red enough, add more vinegar.

VARIATIONS

Substitute lard, salt pork, or chicken fat for the bacon. Vegetable oil may be used, but it does not contribute to flavor.

Eliminate cinnamon, cloves, and allspice. Add 1 tbsp (15 mL) caraway seeds to onions when sautéing them.

Braised Green or White Cabbage
Prepare as in the basic recipe, but season with 1 bay leaf, 6–8 parsley stems, 6 peppercorns, and a pinch of thyme instead of the cinnamon, cloves, and allspice. Omit sugar, apples, wine, and vinegar. Butter may be used as cooking fat if desired.

Braised Red Cabbage

Sauerkraut

Portions: 25   Portion size: 4½ oz (125 g)

U.S.	Metric	Ingredients
1 No. 10 can	1 No. 10 can	Sauerkraut
2 oz	60 g	Lard or bacon fat
1 lb	500 g	Onions, sliced
1 pt	500 mL	Dry white wine (optional)
1½ qt (approximately)	1.5 L (approximately)	Chicken stock
5	5	Juniper berries
2	2	Bay leaves
2	2	Cloves
1 tsp	5 mL	Caraway or cumin seed
2	2	Garlic cloves
to taste	to taste	Salt

Per serving:
Calories, 50; Protein, 2 g; Fat, 2.5 g (38% cal.); Cholesterol, 5 mg; Carbohydrates, 7 g; Fiber, 3 g; Sodium, 790 mg.

■ Procedure

1. Rinse the sauerkraut in cold water. Drain and press out water. Taste and rinse again if still too briny. (See Appendix 2, p. 1026, for can sizes and substitutions.)

2. Heat the lard in a heavy pot and sauté the onions until soft. Add the sauerkraut, wine (if used), and enough stock so that the sauerkraut is covered by about three-fourths. Tie the spices and garlic in cheesecloth and add to the pot.

3. Cover and simmer for 1½ hours on the rangetop or in a slow oven (300°F/150°C).

4. Remove the spice bag. Taste the sauerkraut and adjust seasoning.

VARIATION

Choucroute Garni
Double quantities per portion. Cook a variety of fresh and smoked pork products and sausages in the sauerkraut. Add each item at the proper time so that it is in the sauerkraut for its correct cooking time. Suggestions: fresh or smoked pork chops, slab bacon, bratwurst, frankfurters, smoked pork shoulder. Serve as a main course. Accompany with boiled potatoes.

Fresh Sauerkraut

U.S.	Metric	Ingredients
as desired (see step 1)	as desired (see step 1)	Green cabbage
as needed (see step 5)	as needed (see step 5)	Kosher salt

Per 1 ounce:
Calories, 5; Protein, 0 g; Fat, 0 g (0% cal.); Cholesterol, 0 mg; Carbohydrates, 2 g; Fiber, 1 g; Sodium, 280 mg.

■ Procedure

1. Sauerkraut can be made in as large a quantity as desired, depending on the containers available. For practicality, it is best to start with at least 5 lb (2.3 kg).

2. Trim and discard the outer leaves and any damaged areas from the cabbage.

3. Quarter the heads. Remove and discard the cores.

4. Slice the cabbage into fine shreds, preferably on a slicing machine.

5. Weigh the cabbage. Divide the weight by 40 to get the weight of salt needed.

6. Measure the salt and toss it with the shredded cabbage to mix evenly.

7. Pack the salted cabbage tightly into one or more nonreactive containers. Cover the top of the cabbage with a layer of plastic film and place a weight on top. If the cabbage is well packed, the juices drawn out by the salt should just cover the cabbage. (Note: The salt begins drawing out juices within minutes after being mixed with the cabbage.)

8. Place the cabbage in a cool place to ferment, preferably about 60°F (15°F). After a day or two the cabbage and liquid will begin to bubble slowly. Keep covered and let stand until the bubbling stops and the cabbage smells like sauerkraut. The fermentation may take from several days to about 2 weeks, depending on the temperature.

9. Discard any discolored cabbage from the top layer.

10. Refrigerate to stop the fermentation. The sauerkraut is ready for use.

Peas á la Française

Portions: 16   Portion size: 3 oz (90 g)

U.S.	Metric	Ingredients
3 oz	90 g	Butter
2 oz	60 g	Onion, chopped, or whole tiny pearl onions, peeled
2½ lb	1.1 kg	Peas, frozen
8 oz	225 g	Lettuce, shredded
2 tbsp	30 mL	Chopped parsley
1 tsp	5 mL	Salt
2 tsp	10 mL	Sugar
4 fl oz	125 mL	Chicken stock or water, hot
1 tbsp	15 mL	Beurre manié

■ P r o c e d u r e

1. Heat the butter in a saucepan. Add the onions and sauté lightly.

2. Add the peas, lettuce, parsley, salt, and sugar. Cook over moderate heat, stirring a few times, until the vegetables begin to steam.

3. Add the stock or water. Bring to a boil, cover, and simmer over low heat or in oven until peas are tender.

4. Stir in a little beurre manié to thicken the cooking liquid and simmer another 2–3 minutes. Adjust seasoning. (For larger quantities, drain off liquid and thicken separately.)

Per serving:
Calories, 100; Protein, 4 g; Fat, 5 g (43% cal.); Cholesterol, 15 mg;
Carbohydrates, 11 g; Fiber, 4 g; Sodium, 250 mg.

Braised Celery

Portions: 25   Portion size: 3 oz (90 g)

U.S.	Metric	Ingredients
6 lb	3 kg	Celery
4 oz	125 g	Butter
3 pt (approximately)	1.5 L (approximately)	Brown stock or chicken stock
to taste	to taste	Salt
to taste	to taste	Pepper
as needed	as needed	Beurre manié (optional)

■ P r o c e d u r e

1. Trim and wash the celery. If it is very stringy, peel the outside of the ribs, or use the tender inner stems and save the outside ones for mirepoix. Cut into 1½-in. (4-cm) lengths. Split broad pieces lengthwise so all pieces are about the same size.

2. Heat the butter in a braising pot and add the celery. Cook over moderate heat until the celery is just beginning to soften.

3. Add enough stock to cover the celery by about two-thirds. Season with salt and pepper to taste. Cover and cook slowly in the oven or on the rangetop until tender, about 20–30 minutes.

4. Drain the celery and keep it warm in a steam table pan. Reduce the stock over high heat to about 2½ pt (1.25 L). If desired, thicken slightly with beurre manié. Adjust the seasonings and pour the sauce over the celery.

Per serving:
Calories, 50; Protein, 1 g; Fat, 4 g (64% cal.); Cholesterol, 10 mg;
Carbohydrates, 4 g; Fiber, 2 g; Sodium, 130 mg.

V A R I A T I O N S

Bacon fat may be used instead of butter. For extra flavor, add finely diced mirepoix to the fat in the pan before adding celery.

Braised Celery Hearts
Prepare as in basic recipe, but use celery hearts (the tender inner stalks, connected at the root), cut into wedges.

Braised Celery with Brown Sauce
Add 2½ pt (1.25 L) brown sauce or demi-glace to the reduced cooking liquid and reduce again to reach desired consistency. Add to celery.

Braised Celery Root
Prepare as in basic recipe, using sliced, blanched knob celery (celeriac).

Braised Lettuce
Blanch romaine lettuce to wilt leaves. Fold leaves into neat, portion-size bundles. Arrange on finely cut sautéed mirepoix and braise as in basic recipe, without sautéing the lettuce.

Carrots with Orange and Cumin

Portions: 12   Portion size: 3½ oz (100 g)

U.S.	Metric	Ingredients
3 lb 4 oz	1.5 kg	Carrots
3½ oz	100 g	Butter
⅛ tsp	1 g	Cumin seed
¼ tsp	2 g	Ground cumin
to taste	to taste	Salt
to taste	to taste	White pepper
10 fl oz	300 mL	Orange juice

Per serving:
Calories, 120; Protein, 2 g; Fat, 7 g (51% cal.); Cholesterol, 20 mg; Carbohydrates, 13 g; Fiber, 2 g; Sodium, 70 mg.

■ P r o c e d u r e

1. Trim and peel the carrots. Cut into thin slices.

2. Sweat the carrots in the butter for a few minutes, then add the cumin and salt and pepper to taste.

3. Add the orange juice. Cook, loosely covered, over low heat until tender. Remove the cover and continue to cook until most of the liquid has evaporated.

V A R I A T I O N

Carrot Purée with Orange and Cumin
Transfer the cooked carrots to the bowl of a food processor or a food mill. Purée until smooth. Place back on the heat to remove any excess moisture. Mix in 3–4 oz (100 g) butter (monter au beurre). Adjust the seasoning.

Ratatouille

The method for this preparation is unlike that for the other braised vegetables in this section because no liquid is added. It is classified as a braised item because the vegetables are first sautéed in fat, then simmered in their own juices.

Portions: 20   Portion size: 4 oz (125 g)

U.S.	Metric	Ingredients
1 lb	500 g	Zucchini
1 lb	500 g	Eggplant
1 lb	500 g	Onions
4	4	Green bell peppers
4	4	Garlic cloves
2 lb	1 kg	Tomatoes (canned may be used if necessary)
6 oz, or more as needed	200 mL, or more as needed	Olive oil
½ cup	125 mL	Chopped parsley
1	1	Bay leaf
¼ tsp	1 mL	Dried thyme
to taste	to taste	Salt
to taste	to taste	Pepper

Per serving:
Calories, 110; Protein, 1 g; Fat, 9 g (67% cal.); Cholesterol, 0 mg; Carbohydrates, 9 g; Fiber, 2 g; Sodium, 5 mg.

■ P r o c e d u r e

1. Prepare the vegetables: Cut the zucchini into ½-in. (1-cm) slices. Peel the eggplant and cut into large dice. Slice the onions. Remove the cores and seeds of the peppers and cut into 1-in. (2½-cm) dice. Chop the garlic. Peel and seed the tomatoes and cut into large dice (leave canned tomatoes whole; they will break up during cooking).

2. Sauté the zucchini in a little of the olive oil until it is about half cooked. Remove from pan.

3. Sauté the eggplant in olive oil until half cooked. Remove from pan.

4. Sauté the onions and peppers until half cooked. Add the garlic and sauté another minute.

5. Combine all vegetables and seasonings in brazier or heavy saucepan. Cover and cook in a slow oven (325°F/160°C) for about 30 minutes, until vegetables are tender and flavors are well blended. If the vegetables are too juicy, cook uncovered on a rangetop for a few minutes to reduce. Be careful not to scorch the vegetables on the bottom.

6. Adjust seasonings. Serve hot or cold.

Eggplant, Sichuan Style

Portions: 16   Portion size: 2–2½ oz (60–75 g)

U.S.	Metric	Ingredients
2 oz	60 mL	Chili paste with garlic (Sichuan paste)
1 fl oz	30 mL	Soy sauce
2 fl oz	60 mL	Sherry or shaoxing wine
1 fl oz	30 mL	Red wine vinegar
1 tsp	5 mL	Sugar
2 fl oz	60 mL	Chicken stock or water
2½ lb	1.1 kg	Eggplant
4	4	Garlic cloves
1 tsp	5 mL	Ginger root
6	6	Scallions
2–3 fl oz	60–90 mL	Oil
1 tbsp	15 mL	Sesame oil

Per serving:
Calories, 70; Protein, 1 g; Fat, 4.5 g (57% cal.); Cholesterol, 0 mg; Carbohydrates, 8 g; Fiber, 2 g; Sodium, 250 mg.

■ P r o c e d u r e

1. Mix together the chili paste, soy sauce, wine, vinegar, sugar, and stock or water.

2. Peel the eggplant if the skin is tough. Otherwise, leave it on. Cut the eggplant into 1-in. (2½-cm) dice.

3. Mince the garlic, ginger, and scallions.

4. Heat the plain oil in a sauté pan and sauté the eggplant until lightly browned.

5. Add the garlic, ginger, and scallions and sauté another minute.

6. Add the chili paste mixture and stir in. Cover and cook over low heat until the eggplant is tender, about 15–20 minutes.

7. Uncover. The sauce should be quite thick so, if necessary, cook uncovered for a few minutes to reduce the liquid.

8. Add the sesame oil and serve.

 Lecsó

Portions: 16   Portion size: 4 oz (125 g)

U.S.	Metric	Ingredients
1 lb 8 oz	750 g	Onions
3 lb	1.5 kg	Green peppers or Hungarian or Italian frying peppers
3 oz	100 g	Tomatoes, as ripe as possible
3 tbsp	20 g	Lard
to taste	to taste	Hungarian paprika
pinch	pinch	Salt

Per serving:
Calories, 110; Protein, 2 g; Fat, 6 g (46% cal.); Cholesterol, 5 mg; Carbohydrates, 14 g; Fiber, 3 g; Sodium, 10 mg.

■ P r o c e d u r e

1. Peel the onion and cut into fine dice.

2. Core and seed the peppers. Cut into thin slices.

3. Peel, seed, and chop the tomatoes.

4. Heat the lard over low heat. Add the onion and cook slowly for 5–10 minutes, until it is quite soft.

5. Add the peppers and cook for another 5–10 minutes.

6. Add the tomatoes and paprika. Cover and simmer for 15–20 minutes, until vegetables are tender.

7. Season to taste with salt. Add 1–2 pinches of sugar if desired.

V A R I A T I O N S

This dish may be used as a vegetable or an appetizer or served with rice or boiled noodles. Smoked sausages are often added to it as a luncheon dish, or it may be served with eggs prepared in a variety of ways. The portion size indicated is rather large because this dish is often served as part of a main course. For a side dish portion, you may want to reduce the portion size to 2½–3 oz (75–100 g).

Gratin of Fennel

Portions: 12   Portion size: 3½ oz (100 g)

U.S.	Metric	Ingredients
4½ lb	2 kg	Fennel bulbs
12 oz	360 g	Onion (optional)
3 oz	90 g	Butter
1 tsp, or to taste	5 mL, or to taste	Salt
¼ tsp, or to taste	1 mL, or to taste	White pepper
8 fl oz	250 mL	Water, chicken stock, or vegetable stock
4 oz	125 g	Parmesan cheese, grated

Per serving:
Calories, 140; Protein, 6 g; Fat, 9 g (53% cal.); Cholesterol, 20 mg; Carbohydrates, 12 g; Fiber, 5 g; Sodium, 490 mg.

■ Procedure

1. Trim the stems and the root ends of the fennel bulbs.
2. Cut lengthwise—that is, from stem end to root end—into quarters. If the bulbs are large, cut each quarter into 2 wedges.
3. Cut the onion into thin slices.
4. Heat the butter in a sauté pan over moderate heat.
5. Add the fennel and onion. Sauté for 2–3 minutes, turning the fennel to coat it with the butter.
6. Sprinkle with the salt and white pepper. Add the liquid.
7. Cover tightly. Cook over very low heat or in an oven heated to 325°F (165°C) until the fennel is tender, about 20 minutes. Check once or twice during cooking to make sure the liquid hasn't all evaporated. Add a little more liquid if necessary to keep the vegetables moist.
8. When the fennel is tender, the liquid should be nearly all evaporated. If it is not, set the pan over moderate heat, uncovered, to cook off the liquid.
9. Transfer the fennel to individual-portion gratin dishes or to one or more larger gratin dishes.
10. Distribute the grated cheese over the top of the fennel.
11. Place under a broiler or salamander or in a hot oven until the top is browned.

BAKING

You could, if you wished, cook carrots by placing them in a pot of boiling water, placing the pot in a hot oven, and cooking until tender. This is not a different cooking technique, however. It's plain old simmering. You'd just be using the heat of the oven rather than the rangetop to simmer the water.

When we talk about baking vegetables, we usually mean one of two things:

1. Cooking starchy vegetables, such as potatoes, winter squash, and sweet potatoes, and other moist, dense-textured vegetables such as tomatoes, beets, eggplant, onions, and turnips, from the raw to the finished state. Starch vegetables are baked because the dry heat produces a desirable texture. Baked potatoes, for example, do not have the same texture as boiled or steamed potatoes.

    In some areas, it is fashionable to refer to such baked vegetables as roasted.

    In theory, any vegetable with enough moisture can be baked like potatoes, but the drying effects of the oven and the long cooking time make it undesirable for most small vegetables, such as peas and green beans.

2. Finishing certain vegetable combinations, sometimes known as casseroles. The vegetables in these items are usually parcooked by simmering or steaming before they are baked.

    Vegetable casseroles are baked for either of two reasons:

    - The slow, all-around heat allows the product to cook undisturbed. The agitation and stirring of range-top cooking is not always desirable. Baked beans could be finished on top of the range, but they would be mushier and more broken. Custard-based timbales would be pourable, not firmly set.

    - The dry heat produces desirable effects, such as browning and caramelizing of sugars. For example, you could put a pan of candied sweet potatoes in a steamer, but the moist heat would not allow a glaze to form.

Procedure for Baking Vegetables

1. Collect all equipment and food products.
2. Prepare vegetables as required.
3. Place in appropriate pan and set in preheated oven.
4. Bake to desired doneness.

Baked Acorn Squash

Portions: 24   Portion size: ½ squash

U.S.	Metric	Ingredients
12	12	Acorn squash, small
as needed	as needed	Butter, melted
5 oz	150 g	Brown sugar
2½ tsp	12 mL	Salt
2 fl oz	60 mL	Sherry (optional)

Per serving:
Calories, 130; Protein, 2 g; Fat, 2 g (13% cal.); Cholesterol, 5 mg; Carbohydrates, 28 g; Fiber, 3 g; Sodium, 270 mg.

■ **P r o c e d u r e**

1. Wash and cut squash in half lengthwise. Scrape out seeds. (If using large squash, cut into portion sizes.)

2. Brush cut surfaces and cavity with melted butter. Place close together cut side down on baking sheet. (This helps squash cook faster without drying by retaining steam.)

3. Bake at 350°F (175°C) until almost tender, about 30–40 minutes.

4. Turn the squash cut side up and brush again with butter. Sprinkle the cavities with sugar and salt. Add a few drops of sherry to each if desired.

5. Bake 10–15 minutes more, until surface is glazed.

V A R I A T I O N S

Hubbard, buttercup, and other winter squash varieties may be cut into portion sizes and baked as in basic recipe.

Gingered Squash
Mix 1½ tsp (7 mL) ground ginger with the sugar in basic recipe.

Puréed Squash
Bake cut Hubbard squash until tender. Remove from shell and purée in food mill. Add butter, salt, and pepper to taste.

Baked Acorn Squash

Roasted Winter Vegetables

Portions: 16   Portions size: 4 oz (125 g)

U.S.	Metric	Ingredients
12 oz	375 g	Carrots, peeled
12 oz	375 g	Celery root, peeled
8 oz	250 g	Turnips, peeled
8 oz	250 g	Parsnips, peeled
12 oz	375 g	Waxy potatoes, peeled
8 oz	250 g	Butternut squash, peeled and seeded
12	12	Shallots, peeled
12	12	Garlic cloves, peeled
4 fl oz	125 mL	Olive oil
1½ tsp	7 mL	Dried thyme
1½ tsp	7 mL	Coarse salt
1 tsp	5 mL	Coarsely ground black pepper

Per serving:
Calories, 120; Protein, 1 g; Fat, 7 g (51% cal.); Cholesterol, 0 mg; Carbohydrates, 14 g; Fiber, 3 g; Sodium, 230 mg.

■ Procedure

1. Cut the carrots, celery root, turnips, parsnips, potatoes, and squash into 1-in. (2.5 cm) dice.

2. Place these cut vegetables, plus the shallots and garlic cloves, in a baking pan.

3. Pour the olive oil over the vegetables and sprinkle with the thyme, salt, and pepper. Toss or mix until the vegetables are well coated with oil. Add more oil if necessary.

4. Bake at 375°F (190°C) for about 45 minutes, until the vegetables are tender and lightly browned. Turn or stir the vegetables several times during baking so that they cook evenly. Do not allow them to become too browned, or they may be bitter.

V A R I A T I O N S

Vegetable proportions may be varied as desired. Other vegetables, such as sweet potatoes, stalk celery, onions, and rutabagas may be added.

Roasted Onions

Substitute 4 lb (2kg) onions, sliced ¼ in. (5 mm) thick, for all the vegetables in the basic recipe. Bake as in the basic recipe, cooking until the onions are browned and caramelized. Onions lose a lot of moisture during baking, so total yield is only about 2¼ lb (1.1 kg).

Roasted Summer Vegetables

Omit the parsnips, turnips, celeriac, and butternut squash. Substitute an assortment of summer vegetables in desired proportions, such as eggplant, summer squash, fennel, bell peppers, cherry tomatoes, and baby turnips. Season with fresh chopped basil and parsley. For another version of Roasted Summer Vegetables, see Provençale Vegetables Confit, p. 569.

Roasted Garlic

Yield: approximately 6 oz (175 g) garlic pulp

U.S.	Metric	Ingredients
6	6	Garlic heads, whole
1 fl oz	30 mL	Olive oil

Per 1 ounce:
Calories, 90; Protein, 2 g; Fat, 5 g (48% cal.); Cholesterol, 0 mg; Carbohydrates, 10 g; Fiber, 1 g; Sodium, 5 mg.

■ Procedure

1. Preheat an oven to 400°F (200°C).

2. Rub the heads of garlic with olive oil.

3. Place on a sheet pan in the oven. Roast for about 30 minutes, until soft.

4. Remove from the oven and cool slightly.

5. For roasted garlic pulp, cut the heads in half crosswise and squeeze out the pulp.

6. For roasted garlic cloves to use as garnish, separate the cloves. Serve peeled or unpeeled.

V A R I A T I O N

For whole roasted heads of garlic to use as garnish, cut off the tops (the pointed end) of the heads before rubbing with oil.

Roasted Garlic

Glazed Sweet Potatoes

Portions: 25   Portion size: 5 oz (150 g)

U.S.	Metric	Ingredients
8 lb	3.6 kg	Sweet potatoes
6 fl oz	175 mL	Water
1½ cups	350 mL	Light corn syrup or maple syrup
6 oz	175 g	Brown sugar
8 fl oz	250 mL	Orange juice
2 fl oz	60 mL	Lemon juice
2 oz	60 g	Butter
1 tsp	5 mL	Cinnamon
¼ tsp	1 mL	Ground cloves
½ tsp	2 mL	Salt

■ **P r o c e d u r e**

1. Scrub the sweet potatoes and boil or steam until nearly tender. Do not overcook.
2. Spread the potatoes on a sheet pan to cool.
3. Peel the potatoes when they are cool enough to handle. Remove dark spots. Cut into neat, uniform pieces for easy portioning. Arrange in a buttered baking pan.
4. Place the water, syrup, and sugar in a saucepan. Stir over heat until sugar is dissolved. Add the remaining ingredients and boil until the mixture is reduced to about 1½ pt (700–800 mL) and forms a heavy syrup.
5. Pour the syrup over the potatoes.
6. Bake at 350°F(175°C) until potatoes are thoroughly cooked and glazed, about 45–60 minutes. Baste with the syrup several times during baking.

Per serving:
Calories, 190; Protein, 2 g; Fat, 2 g (9% cal.); Cholesterol, 5 mg; Carbohydrates, 44 g; Fiber, 2 g; Sodium, 100 mg.

Spinach Timbales

Portions: 15   Portion size: 3 oz (90 g)

U.S.	Metric	Ingredients
2 lb	1 kg	Cooked spinach
to taste	to taste	Salt
to taste	to taste	White pepper
to taste	to taste	Nutmeg
6	6	Eggs
4 fl oz	125 mL	Heavy cream
as needed	as needed	Butter

■ **P r o c e d u r e**

1. Purée the spinach in a food processor. Season to taste with salt, white pepper, and nutmeg.
2. Add the eggs and process another few seconds to mix well.
3. Add the cream and mix in.
4. Pass the mixture through the fine disk of a food mill.
5. Butter the insides of 4-oz (125-mL) timbale molds. Place 3 oz (90 g) spinach mixture in each mold. Rap each one sharply on the worktable to remove air bubbles.
6. Set the molds in a hot water bath and bake at 375°F (190°C) until set, about 25–40 minutes.
7. When set, remove them from the oven. Let stand 10 minutes to allow them to settle.
8. The timbales can be kept warm for a short time in the water bath. At service time, unmold and serve at once.

Per serving:
Calories, 80; Protein, 4 g; Fat, 6 g (66% cal.); Cholesterol, 100 mg; Carbohydrates, 3 g; Fiber, 1 g; Sodium, 85 mg.

Southwestern Corn and Pinto Bean Gratin

Portions: 10   Portion size: 4 oz (125 g)

U.S.	Metric	Ingredients
4 oz	125 g	Onion, small dice
2 fl oz	60 mL	Oil
1–2 tbsp	15–30 mL	Chili powder
4 oz	125 g	Red bell peppers, small dice
4 oz	125 g	Green bell peppers, small dice
1 lb	500 g	Whole-kernel corn (see note)
1 lb	500 g	Cooked pinto beans (see note)
to taste	to taste	Salt
to taste	to taste	Pepper
as needed	as needed	Water or chicken stock
4 oz	125 g	Fresh white bread crumbs

Per serving:
Calories, 190; Protein, 6 g; Fat, 7 g (0% cal.); Cholesterol, 0 mg;
Carbohydrates, 29 g; Fiber, 6 g; Sodium, 70 mg.

Note: Use either frozen corn (thawed) or fresh corn cut from the cob. If you use canned beans, first rinse them under cold water and drain well.

■ P r o c e d u r e

1. Over low heat, sweat the onion in the oil until soft but not browned.
2. Stir in the chili powder and cook another minute.
3. Add the peppers and continue to sweat just until they begin to soften.
4. Add the corn and beans and mix. Adjust the seasoning with salt and pepper. If the mixture seems dry (the beans may absorb a lot of moisture), moisten with a little water or stock.
5. Transfer the vegetables to a shallow baking pan or gratin dish. Top with a thin layer of bread crumbs.
6. Bake at 375°F (190°C) until the mixture is very hot and the top is lightly browned. If necessary, brown the top lightly under a salamander or broiler.

V A R I A T I O N

Substitute roasted fresh chiles, such as poblanos or New Mexico peppers, for all or part of the bell peppers.

Provençale Vegetables Confit

Portions: 24   Portion size: about 4 oz (125 g)

U.S.	Metric	Ingredients
1 lb	450 g	Eggplant
1 lb 6 oz	625 g	Zucchini
1 lb	450 g	Red bell peppers, seeded
7 oz	200 g	Green bell peppers, seeded
1 lb 2 oz	525 g	Fennel bulbs
1 lb	450 g	Cherry tomatoes
1 lb 8 oz	725 g	Pearl onions, peeled
3 oz	90 g	Garlic, finely chopped
3½ oz	100 g	Shallots, chopped
1½ oz	45 g	Fresh basil, finely chopped
2 tbsp	30 mL	Fresh thyme, finely chopped
10 fl oz	300 mL	Olive oil

Per serving:
Calories, 160; Protein, 2 g; Fat, 12 g (66% cal.); Cholesterol, 0 mg;
Carbohydrates, 12 g; Fiber, 3 g; Sodium, 80 mg.

■ P r o c e d u r e

1. Cut the eggplant, zucchini, peppers, and fennel into batonnet. (Peel the eggplant if desired.)
2. Halve the cherry tomatoes and set them aside.
3. Mix the vegetables, except the tomatoes, together with the onions, garlic, shallots, chopped basil, and thyme. Spread out on the bottom of a roasting pan and drizzle with the olive oil. Mix well until the vegetables are well coated.
4. Cook gently at 300°F (150°C) for 1 hour.
5. Add the tomatoes, then cook another 10 minutes.
6. Season to taste and serve.

Eggplants Bayaldi

Portions: 24 as a first course   *Portion size: ½ eggplant, about 8 oz (250 g)*
          12 as vegetarian main course   *Portion size: 1 eggplant*

U.S.	Metric	Ingredients	Procedure
12	12	Small eggplants, about 8 oz (250 g) each	1. Cut the eggplants in half lengthwise. Using a knife, carefully dig out the flesh without puncturing the skin. Set aside the flesh until you have around 2½ lb (1.2 kg).
to taste	to taste	Salt	2. Place the eggplant skins on a baking sheet. Season and lightly drizzle with oil. Cook for about 5–10 minutes in the oven at 400°F (200°C). They should hold their shape but be somewhat tender.
to taste	to taste	Cayenne	
to taste	to taste	Olive oil	
3½ oz	100 g	Garlic, chopped	3. Sweat the garlic in the olive oil. Add the eggplant flesh and cook until soft. Add 3 tbsp (20 g) chopped basil. Season to taste.
1½ fl oz	50 mL	Olive oil	
1½–2 oz	50 g	Fresh basil, chopped	
to taste	to taste	Salt	
to taste	to taste	Pepper	
4 oz	125 g	Shallots	4. Sweat the shallots in the olive oil and add the tomato. Cook until thick, then mix in the remaining basil (from step 3). Season to taste with salt and cayenne.
1½ fl oz	50 mL	Olive oil	
4 lb 6 oz	2 kg	Tomatoes, peeled, seeded, and chopped	
to taste	to taste	Salt	
to taste	to taste	Cayenne	
12	12	Small tomatoes about 1 oz (30 g) each	5. Thinly slice the tomatoes.
14 oz	400 g	Grated Swiss cheese	6. Spread some of the tomato sauce in the bottom of the cooked eggplant skins. Top with the cooked eggplant flesh. Top with overlapping slices of tomato, and sprinkle with the grated cheese.
			7. Place in a hot oven until the cheese is melted and golden brown.

Per serving:
Calories, 200; Protein, 7 g; Fat, 14 g (60% cal.); Cholesterol, 15 mg;
Carbohydrates, 14 g; Fiber, 4 g; Sodium, 55 mg.

Tomato and Zucchini Tian

Portions: 12   Portion size: 3½ oz (100 g)

U.S.	Metric	Ingredients
1 lb 4 oz	600 g	Zucchini, large
1 lb 8 oz	700 g	Tomatoes, small (about the same diameter as the zucchini)
to taste	to taste	Salt
to taste	to taste	White pepper
2–3 fl oz	60–90 mL	Olive oil
1½ oz	40 g	Fresh bread crumbs

Per serving:
Calories, 70; Protein, 1 g; Fat, 5 g (62% cal.); Cholesterol, 0 mg; Carbohydrates, 6 g; Fiber, 1 g; Sodium, 25 mg.

■ **P r o c e d u r e**

1. Trim the ends off the zucchini and cut into very thin rounds. Quickly blanch in boiling salted water.

2. Core the tomatoes but do not peel. Cut the tomatoes in rounds the same thickness as the zucchini.

3. Place 12 ring molds, 4 in. (10 cm) in diameter, on an oiled baking sheet (see note). Inside the ring molds, alternately place the zucchini and tomato in overlapping circles. Season and drizzle with olive oil. Sprinkle with the bread crumbs. Lift off the rings and bake the vegetables in the oven for 10 minutes at 350°F (180°C).

Note: If you have only one ring mold, fill if as directed, lift off, and repeat for the remaining tians.

 Elote con Queso

Portions: 16   Portions size: 3½ oz (100 g)

U.S.	Metric	Ingredients
6	6	Anaheim chiles (see note)
4 oz	125 g	Onion
2 oz	60 g	Butter
2½ lb	1.2 kg	Whole-kernel corn (frozen or fresh)
to taste	to taste	Salt
10 oz	300 g	Mild cheddar cheese, grated

Per serving:
Calories, 160; Protein, 7 g; Fat, 9 g (48% cal.); Cholesterol, 25 mg; Carbohydrates, 15 g; Fiber, 2 g; Sodium, 150 mg.

Note: Canned, diced chiles (10–12 oz/300–350 g, drained) may be used in place of the fresh Anaheims. Omit steps 1 and 2 in the procedure.

■ **P r o c e d u r e**

1. Char the chiles over an open flame or under a broiler until the skin is black. Rub off the blackened skin under running water.

2. Remove and discard the seeds and stem ends from the chiles. Cut the chiles into medium dice.

3. Cut the onion into small dice. Cook it slowly in the butter until it is soft. Do not brown.

4. Add the diced chile and cook 5 minutes.

5. Add the corn and cook over moderate heat until it is thawed (if using frozen corn) or no longer raw (if using fresh corn).

6. Add salt to taste.

7. Put the corn in a shallow baking pan or in individual gratin dishes and bake at 350°F (175°C), covered, for 10 minutes.

8. Uncover and top with the grated cheese. Bake until very hot and the cheese is melted and bubbling.

V A R I A T I O N S

If you wish, this may be cooked entirely on top of the range. Simply mix in the grated cheese before serving.

Fresh zucchini, cut into small dice, may be substituted for one-third to one-half of the corn. Add to the onion at same time as the chiles.

Moussaka

Portions: 16   Portion size: 9 oz (250 g)

U.S.	Metric	Ingredients
1 lb	450 g	Onions, small dice
3	3	Garlic cloves, chopped
2 fl oz	60 mL	Olive oil
3½ lb	1.6 kg	Ground lamb or beef
2 lb 4 oz	1 kg	Tomatoes, canned or fresh, peeled and chopped, with juice
4 fl oz	100 mL	Red wine
2 tbsp	30 mL	Chopped parsley
1½ tsp	7 mL	Dried oregano
¼ tsp	1 mL	Cinnamon
to taste	to taste	Salt
to taste	to taste	Pepper
4 lb	1.8 kg	Eggplant
as needed	as needed	Olive oil
to taste	to taste	Salt
1 qt	1 L	Béchamel, cold
to taste	to taste	Salt
to taste	to taste	White pepper
to taste	to taste	Nutmeg
4	4	Eggs
as needed	as needed	Olive oil
as needed	as needed	Dry bread crumbs
2 oz	60 g	Romano or parmesan cheese, grated

Per serving:
Calories, 470; Protein, 24 g; Fat, 33 g (62% cal.); Cholesterol, 140 mg; Carbohydrates, 20 g; Fiber, 4 g; Sodium, 580 mg.

■ P r o c e d u r e

1. Sauté the onion and garlic in the olive oil until soft. Remove with a slotted spoon.
2. Add the meat to the pan and brown lightly.
3. Return the onion and garlic to the pot and add the tomato, wine, parsley, oregano, and cinnamon. Simmer, uncovered, until the liquid has reduced and the mixture is thick.
4. Season to taste with salt and pepper.

5. Peel the eggplant if the skin is tough. Cut into ½-in. (1-cm) slices.
6. Fry the eggplant slices in olive oil until tender. Set aside and season with salt.

7. Season the béchamel (which should be quite thick when cold) with a little salt, white pepper, and nutmeg.
8. Beat the eggs and mix into the béchamel.

9. Oil the bottom of a hotel pan or other pan measuring 12 × 20 in. (30 × 50 cm) with olive oil. Sprinkle lightly with bread crumbs.
10. Arrange the eggplant slices in the pan so that they completely cover the bottom. Push them together as necessary.
11. Put the meat mixture on the eggplant in a smooth layer.
12. Pour the béchamel over the top and sprinkle with the grated cheese.
13. Bake at 350°F (175°C) until hot and the top is golden, about 45–60 minutes.
14. Cut into squares to serve.

BROILING AND GRILLING

Grilled quick-cooking vegetables such as peppers, zucchini, large mushroom caps, and eggplant are pleasant accompaniments to grilled and roasted meats and poultry. Cut the vegetables into broad slices, brush with oil, and grill until lightly cooked and lightly browned. Heavy browning may produce an unpleasant burned taste. Grilled vegetables are often dressed with vinaigrette.

Broiling is also used to finish cooked or partially cooked vegetables by browning or glazing them on top. Bread crumbs are sometimes used to give a pleasing brown color and to prevent drying. Casseroles or gratin dishes that do not brown sufficiently in the oven may be browned for a few seconds under the broiler or salamander.

Procedure for Broiling or Grilling Vegetables

1. Collect equipment and food supplies.
2. Prepare the vegetables as necessary, including cutting them into required shapes and seasoning or marinating them.
3. Preheat the broiler or grill.
4. If necessary, brush the grill with a wire brush to clean it of any charred food particles.
5. Place the vegetables directly on the grill or broiler grate. Alternatively, place tender vegetables on broiler platters or sheet pans and set under the broiler. Cook the vegetables to the desired doneness and color, turning them as necessary.
6. Remove from broiler or grill and serve immediately.

 ## Broiled Tomato Slices

Portion: 10   Portion size: about 2 slices
3–4 oz (100 g)

U.S.	Metric	Ingredients
2½ lb	1.1 kg	Tomatoes
2 fl oz	60 g	Melted butter (or olive oil)
to taste	to taste	Salt
to taste	to taste	White pepper
		Topping (optional)
1 cup	100 g	Dry bread crumbs
4 fl oz	100 g	Melted butter or olive oil
1 oz	30 g	Onion, minced very fine

Per serving:
Calories, 60; Protein, 1 g; Fat, 5 g (65% cal.); Cholesterol, 10 mg; Carbohydrates, 5 g; Fiber, 1 g; Sodium, 55 mg.

■ Procedure

1. Wash the tomatoes, cut out the core ends, and slice crosswise into ½-in. (1-cm) slices.
2. Place the slices in a single layer on an oiled baking sheet.
3. Drizzle melted butter or oil over the tomatoes and sprinkle with salt and pepper.
4. Place in a broiler, 4 in. (10 cm) from the heat, and broil just until bubbling and hot but still firm enough to hold shape.
5. Serve 2 slices per portion, depending on size.

6. To use optional ingredients, cook tomatoes halfway. Combine topping ingredients and sprinkle over tomatoes. Brown under broiler.

VARIATIONS

Herbed Broiled Tomatoes
Top tomatoes with ¼ cup (60 mL) chopped parsley and ½ tsp (2 mL) dried basil or oregano before broiling, or mix herbs with crumb topping.

Parmesan Broiled Tomatoes
Add ½ cup (125 mL) grated parmesan cheese to crumb topping.

Grilled Vegetable Medley

Yield: about 3 lb (1.5 kg)   Portions: 9   Portion: 5 oz (150 g)

U.S.	Metric	Ingredients
3–3½ lb	1.5–1.75 kg	Assorted vegetables;
		Small eggplants
		Zucchini
		Yellow summer squash
		Bell peppers
		Radicchio
		Large onions
as needed	as needed	Olive oil
to taste	to taste	Salt
as needed	as needed	Balsamic vinegar

Per serving:
Calories, 180; Protein, 1 g; Fat, 16 g (78% cal.); Cholesterol, 0 mg; Carbohydrates, 9 g; Fiber, 2 g; Sodium, 10 mg.

■ Procedure

1. Prepare the vegetables: Trim off the stem ends of the eggplants and cut them lengthwise into thick slices. If they are very small, just cut them in half lengthwise. Trim the stem ends of the zucchini and yellow squash. Cut lengthwise into thick slices. Core and seed the peppers and cut into quarters lengthwise. Remove any bruised outer leaves of the radicchio and cut in halves or quarters through the base, leaving the core in to hold the leaves together. Cut the onion into thick slices, holding the rings of each slice together with a bamboo skewer.

2. Brush the vegetables with olive oil and sprinkle them with salt.

3. Grill the vegetables over medium heat, turning as necessary, until they are tender and lightly grill-marked. Cooking time will vary for different vegetables. Regulate the heat or distance from the flame so that the vegetables cook without browning too much.

4. Remove from the grill and brush with a little balsamic vinegar, and, if desired, a little more olive oil. Serve warm.

V A R I A T I O N S

Other vegetables and vegetable assortments may be grilled in the same manner. Suggestions include large mushroom caps, Belgian endive, blanched potatoes, fennel, asparagus, leeks, and scallions.

Grilled vegetables may be served with various sauces, such as aioli, sauce Vierge, salsa cruda, and vinaigrette variations.

Grilled Vegetable Kebabs

Portions: 12   Portion size: 3 oz (90 g)

U.S.	Metric	Ingredients
6 oz	180 g	Zucchini, trimmed
6 oz	180 g	Yellow summer squash, trimmed
6 oz	180 g	Red or orange bell peppers, cut into 1½-in. (2.5 cm) squares
12 oz	360 g	Red onion, large dice
12	12	Mushroom caps, medium
12 fl oz	360 mL	Olive oil
½ oz	15 g	Garlic, crushed
1½ tsp	7 mL	Dried rosemary
½ tsp	2 mL	Dried thyme
2 tsp	10 mL	Salt
½ tsp	2 mL	Black pepper

Per serving:
Calories, 50; Protein, 1 g; Fat, 3 g (53% cal.); Cholesterol, 0 mg; Carbohydrates, 5 g; Fiber, 1 g; Sodium, 40 mg.

Note: Soaking bamboo skewers in water ahead of time helps delay their charring.

■ Procedure

1. Cut the zucchini and yellow squash into 12 equal slices each.

2. Arrange the vegetables on 12 bamboo skewers (see note). Give each skewer an equal arrangement of vegetable pieces.

3. Place the skewers in a single layer in a hotel pan.

4. Mix together the oil, garlic, herbs, salt, and pepper to make a marinade.

5. Pour the marinade over the vegetables, turning them to coat them completely.

6. Marinate 1 hour. Turn the skewers once or twice during marination to ensure that the vegetables are coated.

7. Remove the skewers from the marinade and let the excess oil drip off.

8. Broil the skewers until the vegetables are lightly charred on the surface but still somewhat crisp in the center.

9. Serve immediately.

V A R I A T I O N S

Other assortments of vegetables may be used, and the skewers may be made larger if desired. Any vegetables that you want to be completely cooked when served, such as cauliflower florets, should be blanched and cooled before being skewered, as they will not cook completely on the skewer.

DEEP-FRYING

The principles of deep-frying that you have already learned are applied to vegetables as well as to other foods.

- Review "Deep-Frying," Chapter 4, page 73.
- Review "Breadings" and "Batters," Chapter 7, pages 142–144.
- Review "Shrimp and Vegetable Tempura," Chapter 15, page 481. This batter and basic procedure can be used for many vegetables.

Potatoes (covered in the next chapter) and onion rings are the most popular fried vegetables, but many others may be fried, too.

Deep-fried vegetables may be divided into five categories:

1. Vegetables dipped in batter and fried.
2. Vegetables breaded and fried.
3. Vegetables fried without a coating.

    Potatoes are the obvious example. Other starchy vegetables, such as sweet potatoes, may be fried without breading or batter if they are cut thin to reduce cooking time. The sugar in them burns easily if they are cooked too long.

    Thin slices and shavings of vegetables, deep-fried until light and crisp, make an attractive and interesting garnish for many dishes. Root vegetables, such as beets, celery root, and parsnips, can be sliced thin and fried like potato chips (slice long roots like parsnips lengthwise). Other vegetables, such as leeks and celery, can be cut into thin shreds or julienne and fried. These may be dusted in flour before frying.

4. Small vegetables or cuts mixed with a batter and dropped with a scoop into hot fat. The term *fritter* is used for this preparation, as well as for that in category 1.

5. *Croquettes:* thick vegetable purées or mixtures of small pieces of vegetable and a heavy béchamel or other binder, formed into shapes, breaded, and fried.

Procedure for Deep-Frying Vegetables

1. Collect all equipment and food products.
2. Preheat fryer to proper temperature.

    Most vegetables are fried at 325°–350°F (160°–175°C).
3. Prepare food items as required. Apply breading or batter if necessary.
4. Place proper amount of food in fryer. Do not overload.
5. Fry to desired doneness.
6. Remove food from fryer and let fat drain from it.
7. Serve at once, or, if necessary, hold uncovered in a warm place for the shortest possible time.

VEGETABLES FOR DEEP-FRYING

Most vegetables large enough to coat with breading or batter may be fried. Tender, quick-cooking vegetables can be fried raw. Others may be precooked by simmering or steaming briefly to reduce the cooking time they need in the frying fat.

Raw vegetables for frying in breading or batter:

Eggplant	Onion rings	Tomatoes
Mushrooms	Peppers	Zucchini

Blanched or precooked vegetables for frying in breading or batter:

Artichoke hearts	Carrots	Fennel
Asparagus	Cauliflower	Okra
Beans, green and yellow	Celery	Parsnips
Broccoli	Celery root	Turnips
Brussels sprouts	Cucumbers	

Onion Rings

Portions: 20   Portion size: 3 oz (90 g), 8–10 pieces

U.S.	Metric	Ingredients
2	2	Eggs, beaten
1 pt	500 mL	Milk
10 oz	300 g	Cake flour
2 tsp	10 mL	Baking powder
½ tsp	2 mL	Salt
½ tsp	2 mL	Paprika (optional: for color)
3 lb	1.4 kg	Onions, large
as needed	as needed	Flour

Per serving:
Calories, 130; Protein, 3 g; Fat, 6 g (40% cal.); Cholesterol, 20 mg; Carbohydrates, 17 g; Fiber, 1 g; Sodium, 95 mg.

■ P r o c e d u r e

1. Combine the eggs and milk in a bowl.
2. Mix the flour, baking powder, salt and paprika together and add to the milk. Mix well. The batter should have the consistency of a thin pancake batter.
3. Peel the onions and cut crosswise into ¼-in. (½-cm) slices. Separate into rings (save unusable pieces for another purpose).
4. Place the onions in cold water, if they are not used immediately, to maintain crispness.
5. Drain and dry the onions thoroughly.
6. Dredge with flour and shake off excess. (This step isn't always necessary, but it helps the batter adhere.)
7. Dip a few pieces at a time in the batter and fry in deep fat (350°F/175°C) until golden brown.
8. Drain and serve immediately.

V A R I A T I O N S

Beer Batter
Substitute light beer for the milk. Omit baking powder because the carbonation of the beer acts as a leavener.

Buttermilk Batter
Substitute buttermilk for the milk and use 1 tsp (5 mL) baking soda instead of the 2 tsp (10 mL) baking powder.

Other Fried Vegetables
Any of the vegetables on the list at the beginning of this section may be fried in these batters.

Onion Rings

 Celery Leaf Fritters

Portions: 12   Portion size: about 4 oz (125 g)

U.S.	Metric	Ingredients
8 oz	250 g	Flour
1 tsp	5 g	Salt
2¾ oz	80 mL	Butter, melted
12–13 fl oz	400 mL	Water, cold
4	4	Egg whites, beaten to stiff peaks
96 pieces (8 per portion)	96 pieces (8 per portion)	Leafy celery tops

Per serving:
Calories, 130; Protein, 3 g; Fat, 8 g (55% cal.); Cholesterol, 10 mg; Carbohydrates, 12 g; Fiber, 1 g; Sodium, 220 mg.

■ P r o c e d u r e

1. Mix together the flour, salt, and melted butter.
2. Gradually mix in the cold water until a thin batter forms. It should be about the consistency of a crêpe batter.
3. Fold in the beaten egg whites.
4. Dip the celery leaves into the batter, then drop into a deep fryer heated to 350°F (180°C).
5. Drain and serve immediately.

Pea Fritters with Sesame

Yield; about 2 lb (1 kg)   Portions: 10   Portion size: 4 fritters, about ¾ oz (25 g) each

U.S.	Metric	Ingredients
3 lb	1.5 kg	Peas, fresh or frozen
4 tsp	20 g	Butter, softened
3	3	Egg yolks
3 tbsp	20 g	Fresh mint leaves, chopped fine
to taste	to taste	Salt
to taste	to taste	Pepper
6 oz	175 g	Flour
to taste	to taste	Salt
to taste	to taste	White pepper
3	3	Whole eggs, beaten
4 oz	125 g	Sesame seeds
4 oz	125 g	Dry bread crumbs
as needed	as needed	Mint leaves for garnish

Per serving:
Calories, 360; Protein, 13 g; Fat, 18 g (45% cal.); Cholesterol, 115 mg;
Carbohydrates, 37 g; Fiber, 9 g; Sodium, 110 mg.

■ P r o c e d u r e

1. Bring a large pan of water to a boil and simmer the peas for 8 minutes or until tender. Drain thoroughly and process in a food processor or blender to a very thick paste. Push through a five sieve to remove the skins.

2. Beat the softened butter and egg yolks into the pea mixture and add the chopped mint. Season well to taste and chill until firm.

3. Shape the pea mixture into slightly flattened patties, approximately 2 in. (5 cm) in diameter.

4. Prepare a Standard Breading Procedure, seasoning the flour with salt and white pepper and mixing the sesame seeds with the bread crumbs.

5. Pass the pea patties through the breading procedure. Chill for 30 minutes.

6. Deep-fry the fritters in batches at 350°F (180°C) until golden. Drain and serve warm, garnished with mint leaves.

Vegetable Fritters

Portions: 20   Portion size: 3 oz (90 g)
2 pieces

U.S.	Metric	Ingredients
		Batter:
6	6	Eggs, beaten
1 pt	500 mL	Milk
1 lb	500 g	Flour
2 tbsp	30 mL	Baking powder
1 tsp	5 mL	Salt
1 oz	30 g	Sugar
1½ lb EP	700 g EP	Vegetables: Choice of corn, cooked diced carrots, baby lima beans, diced asparagus, diced celery or celery root, turnip, eggplant, cauliflower, zucchini, parsnips

Per serving:
Calories, 140; Protein, 4 g; Fat, 6 g (37% cal.); Cholesterol, 45 mg;
Carbohydrates, 19 g; Fiber, 1 g; Sodium, 230 mg.

■ P r o c e d u r e

1. Combine the eggs and milk.

2. Mix together the flour, baking powder, salt, and sugar. Add to the milk and eggs and mix until smooth.

3. Let the batter stand for several hours in a refrigerator.

4. Stir the cold, cooked vegetables into the batter.

5. Drop with a No. 24 scoop into deep fat at 350°F (175°C). Hold the scoop just above the hot fat when dropping. Fry until golden brown.

6. Drain well and serve.

V A R I A T I O N S

For lighter fritters, beat egg whites separately and fold into batter.

Fruit Fritters
Increase sugar to 2 oz (60 g). Use fresh, frozen, or canned fruits such as blueberries, diced pineapple, or apple. Fruit must be well drained. Dust each portion with powdered sugar at service time. (Batter may be seasoned with cinnamon, vanilla, brandy, or other appropriate flavoring.)

Chiles Rellenos

Portions: 16　Portion size: 1 pepper

U.S.	Metric	Ingredients
16	16	Chiles poblanos (see note)
3 lb (approximately)	1.4 kg (approximately)	Picadillo (p. 328) (see note)
12	12	Egg yolks
1 fl oz	30 mL	Water
1 oz	30 g	Flour, sifted
½ tsp	2 mL	Salt
12	12	Egg whites
as needed	as needed	Flour for dredging
3–4 pt	1.5–2 L	Tomato Broth for Chiles Rellenos (p. 190)

Per serving:
Calories, 430; Protein, 24 g; Fat, 30 g (62% cal.); Cholesterol, 210 mg; Carbohydrates, 17 g; Fiber, 2 g; Sodium, 460 mg.

Note: Anaheim peppers or frying peppers may be used if poblanos are not available, but the results will not be as flavorful. The exact amount of filling needed depends on the size of the peppers.

■ P r o c e d u r e

1. Char the chiles over a gas flame until the skin is blackened. Rub off the blackened skin under running water.
2. Slit one side of each pepper and remove the seeds, but be careful to keep the peppers intact.
3. Stuff the peppers with the picadillo.
4. Beat the egg yolks and water slightly, then mix in the flour and salt.
5. Whip the whites until they form soft peaks. Fold them into the yolk mixture.
6. Carefully dust the filled peppers with flour, then dip in the egg batter. Deep-fry at 350°F (175°C) until lightly browned. (*Hint:* Carefully lower each pepper into the fat with the slit side up. If the slit tends to open, spoon a little of the batter over the slit. This helps keep the opening sealed and the filling in the pepper.)
7. For each portion, ladle 3–4 fl oz (90–125 mL) broth into a broad serving bowl or soup plate. Place 1 chile in the center of the bowl and serve at once.

V A R I A T I O N S

For cheese-filled chiles, use chunks of American munster or Monterey jack cheese instead of the picadillo.

For baked chiles rellenos, omit the egg batter and simply bake the stuffed chiles in a casserole until they are heated through. Serve with the tomato broth as in the basic recipe.

Chile Relleno

Suggested Vegetable Seasonings, Flavorings, and Combinations

Asparagus	Lemon juice, brown butter, mustard sauce, parmesan cheese; hard-cooked egg, peas, artichokes, mushrooms
Beans, green	Dill, basil, tarragon, oregano, garlic, brown butter, soy sauce; almonds, sesame seed, onion, tomato, celery, mushrooms, bacon
Beans, lima	Oregano, sage, thyme, sour cream, cheddar cheese; corn, peas, onions, mushrooms, pimiento, bacon
Beets	Lemon, allspice, caraway, cloves, dill, ginger, horseradish, bay leaf, orange, sour cream, onion
Broccoli	Lemon, mustard sauce, almonds, buttered toasted bread crumbs, hard-cooked egg
Brussels sprouts	Caraway, dill, parmesan cheese, cheddar cheese, chestnuts
Cabbage	Caraway, celery seed, dill, mustard, nutmeg, garlic; bacon, ham, carrots, onion
Carrots	Parsley, dill, fennel, tarragon, ginger, nutmeg, bay leaves, caraway, mint, orange; celery, peas, zucchini
Cauliflower	Dill, nutmeg, mustard, curry, cheese, tomato sauce; hard-cooked egg, peas, almonds
Celery	Parsley, tarragon, onion, green or red pepper, potatoes
Corn	Chili powder, mild cheddar or jack cheese, tomato, bacon, lima beans
Cucumber	Dill, garlic, mint, tarragon; peas
Eggplant	Garlic, marjoram, oregano, parsley, parmesan cheese; tomato, chopped walnuts
Mushrooms	Nutmeg, parsley, lemon, paprika, dill, sherry, parmesan cheese, cayenne, heavy cream; peas, spinach, artichokes, green beans
Okra	Garlic, coriander, sage; tomatoes, corn
Onions	Nutmeg, sage, thyme, cheese sauce, sour cream; peas
Peas	Mint, basil, dill, sage; mushrooms, pearl onions, turnips, potatoes, carrots, water chestnuts, Jerusalem artichokes
Spinach	Nutmeg, garlic, heavy cream; mushrooms, hard-cooked egg, cheese
Squash, summer (including zucchini)	Cumin, basil, oregano, mustard seed, rosemary, garlic, parmesan cheese, parsley; tomato, carrots (with zucchini), onion, almonds, walnuts
Squash, winter	Cinnamon, nutmeg, allspice, cloves, ginger; apples, bacon, pecans
Sweet potatoes	Allspice, cinnamon, cloves, nutmeg, ginger, brandy, orange; almonds, apples, bananas
Tomatoes	Basil, bay leaf, garlic, celery seed, oregano, thyme, rosemary, chili powder; peppers, black olives
Turnips	Parsley, chives, nutmeg; mushrooms, potatoes, peas

■ QUESTIONS FOR DISCUSSION

1. Which of the following vegetables would you simmer uncovered?

   Asparagus, Green beans, Beets, Brussels sprouts, Carrots, Cauliflower, Peas, Sweet potatoes, Rutabagas, Turnips

2. Why are greens such as spinach not well suited to cooking in a compartment steamer?

3. In the recipe for Peas, Carrots, and Pearl Onions (p. 546), why could you not save a step and cook the three vegetables together in one pot?

4. Why is it important to drain vegetables well before combining with a cream sauce?

5. Which of the two methods for making glazed root vegetables (see Glazed Root Vegetables, p. 554, and Glazed Carrots, p. 554) might be more appropriate for á la carte service, or cooking to order? Why?

6. We have learned that green vegetables are supposed to be cooked in a neutral liquid because acids destroy green pigments. But the recipe for artichokes says to cook them with lemon juice. What's going on here?

7. Describe briefly how you would make breaded, fried onion rings rather than onion rings with batter.

18
Potatoes

The eating habits of most nations place a great deal of importance on a category of foods we call *starches*. In fact, for a large portion of the world's peoples, starch is the mainstay of the diet and supplies most of the day's calories. In North America and Europe, the most important starches are potatoes, rice, pasta, and bread. It is true that we do not depend on these high-carbohydrate foods as much as many of the world's people do who eat far less meat than we do. Nevertheless, even as diet fashions and fads come and go, starches appear at nearly all our meals.

Because we eat them often and have devised a great many ways of preparing them, starchy foods require extra study beyond that which we have given to other vegetables. In this chapter, we turn our attention primarily to the preparation of our most important vegetable, the potato. Grains and other starches are discussed in Chapter 19.

UNDERSTANDING POTATOES

In classical cuisine, the potato is one of the most important of all foods. To many of us today, potatoes are considered an ordinary and humble food. Escoffier, however, treated the potato with great respect. His *Guide Culinaire* lists more than 50 potato preparations, far more than for any other vegetable or starch.

Considering how important the potato is in the cuisines of Europe and North America, it is surprising to think that this vegetable wasn't widely used until the last half of the eighteenth century. Although the potato had been brought to Europe from the New World a few hundred years earlier, it wasn't until then that an army pharmacist named Antoine-Auguste Parmentier began promoting its use. To this day, many classical recipes featuring the potato are called *Parmentier* (par mawn tyay).

Botanically, the potato is a tuber, which is an enlarged underground stem with buds (or eyes) that become new shoots. Traditional main courses in western cooking feature a protein item, one or more vegetables, and a starch. The potato is, of course, a vegetable, but because of its high starch content it usually serves the same function on the menu as grains and other starchy foods.

Potatoes are traditionally classified as either starchy, low-moisture varieties or as waxy, high-moisture varieties. The following section summarizes the main characteristics of these two categories as well as traditional uses for each. Today, many potato varieties are available that were largely unknown not long ago. As always, chefs love to experiment with new foods and to find new uses for them. For example, they don't feel limited to russets for baking. So, after reading about the two main categories of potatoes below, continue to the next section for an introduction to some of the many varieties available today.

After reading this chapter, you should be able to

1. Classify potatoes into two types, describe the general properties of each type, and identify the most suitable cooking method for each type.

2. Identify characteristics of high-quality potatoes and describe how to store them.

3. Cook potatoes by boiling and steaming.

4. Prepare potato purée.

5. Cook potatoes by baking, sautéing, pan-frying, and deep-frying.

TYPES

Potatoes are classified according to their starch content. The amount of starch determines the use for which they are usually considered most suitable. Keep in mind that these categories are only general. Within each group is a range of starch and moisture content. For example, different varieties of **waxy potatoes** have different moisture content, depending not only on the variety of potato but also on the growing and storage conditions.

1. **Waxy potatoes.**
   High moisture content, high sugar content, low starch content.

   Usually small and round in shape, but some varieties can be large, and some may be elongated. Flesh is white, yellow, or even blue or purple. Skin is white, red, yellow, or blue.

   Hold shape well when cooked. Firm, moist texture.

   Use for boiling whole, for salads, soups, hashed browns, and any preparation where the potato must hold its shape.

   Do not use for deep-frying. High sugar content will cause dark streaks and poor texture.

Waxy potatoes, clockwise from top left: small and large red-skinned potatoes, white potatoes, large and small yellow potatoes.

2. **Mature or starchy potatoes.**
   High starch content, low moisture and sugar.
   Light, dry, and mealy when cooked.

   - **Russets** or Idahos.
        Long, regularly shaped potatoes with slightly rough skin.
        Ideal choice for the traditional baked potato. Best potato for French fries because the high starch content produces an even, golden color and good texture. Also, the regular shape means little trimming loss.
        May be mashed, but is generally too expensive for that purpose.
        Sizes are indicated by count per 50-pound carton. For example, 100s average 8 ounces each.

   - **All-purpose** (sometimes called *chef potatoes*).
        Not as dry and starchy as russets.
        Irregularly shaped. Less expensive than russets.
        Suitable for most purposes, but not usually used for baking because of irregular shape. Especially useful for puréeing or mashing, or any preparation in which the shape of the whole potato is not important.
        Note: Very knobby potatoes are wasteful when pared in a mechanical peeler.

Starchy potatoes, left to right: russet potatoes, all-purpose or chef potatoes.

VARIETIES

For most of us, selecting the right potato for a particular preparation means selecting from among russets, all-purpose potatoes, and red- or white-skinned boiling potatoes, as these are often the only types found in the kitchen. For basic potato cookery, then, the information in the preceding section tells us what we need to know. Today's chefs, however, can use more information in order to take advantage of the many varieties of potatoes available today, as growers discover new varieties and rediscover heirloom potato varieties. The following are some of the many potatoes available.

First, the term **new potato** needs explanation. Not all small potatoes are new potatoes, and not all new potatoes are small. Normally, potatoes are not harvested until the green, bushy tops turn brown and die back. At this point, the potatoes are mature. Their skin has thickened, and their starch content has developed. Any variety of potato that is harvested before it is mature, while leaves and stems are still green, are new potatoes. Because they have not matured, they have a lower starch content and tender, thin skin. Although most new potatoes are small, usually less than 1½ inches (4 cm) in diameter, this is not always the case.

New potatoes are shipped and sold as soon as they are harvested. By contrast, potatoes that are harvested mature are held at a controlled temperature and humidity for about two weeks in order to toughen their skins further and heal cuts and other damage. This curing process gives the potatoes greater keeping quality.

Russets, often called *Idaho potatoes* because so many russets are grown in that state, are high-starch potatoes with a regular, elongated shape, brown or reddish-brown, rough skin, and white flesh. These are the standard choice for baking and deep-frying.

All-purpose potatoes are also white-fleshed potatoes. They have a moderate starch content and moderate moisture, making them suitable for many kinds of preparations, indicated in the previous section. White-fleshed potatoes may also be harvested young, when they have more moisture, less starch, and a thin skin. Young white potatoes are used mostly for boiling.

Yellow-fleshed potatoes include many varieties. *Yukon Gold* is a round, medium-size potato that ranges from waxy to somewhat starchy, depending on age and growing conditions. They are used for many purposes, including baking. *Yellow Finn* is also used for baking, and it has a smooth, creamy texture when baked, unlike the grainy, starchy texture of baked russets. Other yellow potatoes include *Bintje* (waxy), *Butte* (fairly starchy), *Concord* (waxy), *Charlotte* (waxy), and *Island Sunshine* (medium starch).

Blue potatoes (All-Blue)

Fingerling potatoes

Red-skinned varieties may have white, pink, or yellow flesh. Most of them are of the waxy type. *Red Bliss* has long been one of the most popular waxy potatoes. Other red-skinned potatoes include *All-Red* (pink flesh), *Early Ohio* (white flesh), *Early Rose* (white flesh), and *Rose Gold* (yellow flesh).

Blue-skinned, white-fleshed varieties are similar to red-skinned varieties, except that their skins range in color from dark reddish blue to purple. When cooked, the skins may keep their color or turn brown, grayish, or another color, depending on the variety. Several varieties are grown, including *Blue Pride*, *Caribe*, and *Kerry Blue*.

Blue- or purple-fleshed varieties are the novelty item among potatoes. They may be waxy or somewhat starchy, depending on the variety. The two most common purple-fleshed potatoes are *Peruvian Blue*, also called *Purple Peruvian*, with dark violet flesh that lightens somewhat when cooked, and *All-Blue*, with purple or reddish purple flesh that becomes lavender when cooked.

Fingerling potatoes are small potatoes, usually firm and waxy, with a long, narrow shape. Most popular fingerlings are yellow-skinned and yellow-fleshed, but red-skinned, yellow-fleshed fingerlings, red-skinned, pink-fleshed fingerlings, and purple fingerlings are also grown. Among the available varieties are *Austrian Crescent* (yellow), *French Fingerling* (red skin, yellow flesh), *Russian Banana* (yellow), *La Ratte* (yellow), *Ruby Crescent* (pinkish yellow skin, yellow flesh), and *Red Thumb* (red skin, pink flesh).

Each of these many potato varieties has a slightly different flavor, texture, and cooking characteristics. Experiment with any variety you find available and adapt it to the most appropriate preparations.

CHECKING FOR QUALITY

Look for these signs of high-quality potatoes:

1. Firm and smooth, not soft or shriveled.

2. Dry skin.

3. Shallow eyes.

4. No sprouts. Sprouting potatoes are high in sugar.

5. No green color. Green areas develop on potatoes stored in light. These areas contain a substance called **solanine**, which has a bitter taste and is poisonous in large quantities. All green parts should be cut off before cooking.

6. Absence of cracks, blemishes, and rotten spots.

STORING AND HANDLING

Keep in a cool, dry, dark place, ideally at 55°–60°F (13°–16°C). If they will be used quickly, you may keep them at room temperature.

Do not refrigerate. Temperatures below 45°F (7°C) convert potato starch to sugar. Refrigerated potatoes must be stored at 50°F (10°C) for two weeks to change the sugar back to starch.

New potatoes do not keep well. Purchase only one week's supply at a time.

Potatoes begin to turn brown as soon as they are peeled. To prevent browning, place potatoes in cold water as soon as they are peeled. Potatoes may be peeled in advance and stored a short time under water, although some nutrients will be lost.

Remove all green parts when peeling potatoes (see "Checking for Quality" above).

MARKET FORMS

The demands of time and labor have made processed potato products widely used, and many forms are available. Many of these products are very good, and there is no doubt that they save time. However, for best quality, there is no substitute for fresh potatoes, *if they are well prepared.*

1. **Fresh, unprocessed.**

2. **Peeled. Treated to prevent browning.**
   Keep refrigerated (below 40°F/4°C) for five to seven days.

3. **Canned whole, cooked.**

4. **French fries. Blanched in deep fat and frozen.**
   Available in a wide variety of sizes and cuts. Cook from the frozen state.
   Refrigerated French fries are also available.

5. **Other frozen, prepared products.**
   Available as hashed browns, puffs, stuffed baked, and croquettes; in casseroles with
   a variety of sauces.

6. **Dehydrated.**
   Granules or flakes for mashed potatoes to be reconstituted with hot water or milk
   and butter or other desired flavorings.
   Other products: many varieties and preparations. May need soaking in water
   before cooking.

COOKING POTATOES

Some potato recipes are simple, but many are complex and use a combination of cooking methods. For example, to make potato croquettes, you must first boil or steam the
potatoes, purée them and combine the purée with other ingredients, shape them, bread
them, and, finally, deep-fry them.

Cooking methods are essentially the same as the methods for vegetables discussed
in the previous chapter. If necessary, review these methods before proceeding with the
following recipes.

BOILING AND STEAMING POTATOES

These methods for cooking potatoes are given in the first recipe in this section. Boiled
or steamed potatoes are served as is and are also the basis for many other preparations.

Potatoes are peeled or left unpeeled for boiling and steaming. For most purposes,
they are peeled. Peel thoroughly with a swivel peeler and remove all eyes. Place peeled
potatoes immediately in a container of cold water to prevent browning.

If potatoes are cooked with the skins on and peeled after cooking, it is best to peel
while they are still hot, because the skins pull off more easily. New potatoes are usually
cooked and served with the skins on. Fingerling potatoes are peeled after cooking if
the skins are tough, or they may be served with the skins on if tender.

Two additional points should be noted:

1. Boiled potatoes are generally started in cold water rather than hot. This allows for
   more even cooking and heat penetration from outside to inside during the relatively long cooking time required.

2. Potatoes are never cooled in cold water, unlike most vegetables. This would make
   them soggy.

Boiled Potatoes (Pommes Natures)

Portions: 25   Portion size: 5 oz (150 g)

U.S.	Metric	Ingredients
10 lb	4.5 kg	Potatoes

Per serving:
Calories, 140; Protein, 3 g; Fat, 0 g (0% cal.); Cholesterol, 0 mg; Carbohydrates, 32 g; Fiber, 3 g; Sodium, 10 mg.

Note: Potatoes may be cut, shaped, or trimmed as desired. They may be left in neat but irregular shapes, trimmed or tournéed into large, medium, or small sizes (see Figure 7.18), or cut with a ball scoop (see Figure 7.17) for parisienne boiled potatoes. Allow for greater trimming loss if preparing tournéed or parisienne potatoes.

■ P r o c e d u r e

1. Peel and eye potatoes. Be sure that all traces of dark peel are removed.

2. Cut potatoes into 25 uniform portions, 1 or 2 pieces per portion. Trim pieces to shape (see note). Save the trimmings for other use.

3. Place in a pot and cover with salted water. Bring to boil, lower heat, and simmer until tender.

4. Drain and let the potatoes steam dry in the colander for a minute.

5. Serve immediately or place in a hotel pan, cover with a clean, damp towel, and hold for service.

V A R I A T I O N S

Steamed Potatoes (Pommes Vapeurs)
Prepare as in basic recipe, but steam in perforated pan instead of boiling.

Parsley Potatoes
Prepare as in basic recipe. Brush or pour 4 oz (125 mL) melted butter onto the potatoes and sprinkle with chopped parsley.

New Potatoes
Prepare as in basic recipe, using small new potatoes. Scrub well but do not peel. Serve 1–3 per portion, depending on size.

   Optional: Peel a narrow band around potato before cooking to prevent skin from splitting.

Creamed Potatoes
Prepare new potatoes or all-purpose potatoes as in basic recipe. Cut or slice to desired size, or leave small new potatoes whole. Combine with 2 qt (2 L) hot cream sauce. Heat over low heat, but do not boil, and hold for service.

Hungarian Potatoes

Portions: 25 Portion size: 4 oz (125 g)

U.S.	Metric	Ingredients
4 oz	125 g	Butter
8 oz	250 g	Onion, chopped
2 tsp	10 mL	Paprika
1 lb	500 g	Tomatoes, peeled, seeded, diced
5 lb	2.5 kg	Potatoes, peeled and cut into thick slices
1 qt (approximately)	1 L (approximately)	Chicken or beef stock, hot
to taste	to taste	Salt
to taste	to taste	Pepper
½ cup	125 mL	Chopped parsley

▪ P r o c e d u r e

1. Heat the butter a large saucepan and add the onion and paprika. Cook until onion is soft.

2. Add the tomatoes and potatoes. Pour in enough stock just to cover the potatoes. Add a small amount of salt (about 2 tsp/10 mL), but undersalt because liquid will reduce.

3. Simmer until potatoes are cooked and liquid is mostly evaporated or absorbed. Stir gently from time to time.

4. Season to taste.

5. Garnish with chopped parsley at service time.

V A R I A T I O N

Bouillon Potatoes
Prepare as in basic recipe but omit paprika and tomatoes. Slice onion instead of chopping it, and sauté 6 oz (175 g) carrot, cut julienne, with the onion. Trim the potatoes into portion–size pieces instead of slicing them.

Per serving:
Calories, 110; Protein, 2 g; Fat, 4 g (31% cal.); Cholesterol, 10 mg; Carbohydrates, 18 g; Fiber, 2 g; Sodium, 45 mg.

Colcannon

Portions: 16 Portion size: 5 oz (150 g)

U.S.	Metric	Ingredients
4 lb	1.8 kg	Potatoes
2 lb	900 g	Cabbage
6 oz	175 g	Leeks or scallions
4 oz	125 g	Butter
6 oz	175 mL	Milk or cream, hot
2 tbsp	30 mL	Chopped parsley (optional)
to taste	to taste	Salt
to taste	to taste	White pepper
as needed	as needed	Additional hot milk or cream

▪ P r o c e d u r e

1. Peel and eye the potatoes. Cut them into uniform sizes. Simmer in salted water until tender.

2. While the potatoes are cooking, trim the cabbage and cut it into wedges. Steam until tender.

3. Cook the leeks or scallions very slowly in a little of the butter until tender.

4. Mash the potatoes and add the leeks or scallions and the rest of the butter. Mix in the milk or cream and the parsley.

5. Chop the cabbage fine and stir it into the potatoes until well mixed. Season with salt and white pepper.

6. If the mixture seems dry, mix in additional milk or cream to bring to a smooth, moist consistency.

Per serving:
Calories, 160; Protein, 3 g; Fat, 6 g (33% cal.); Cholesterol, 15 mg; Carbohydrates, 24 g; Fiber, 3 g; Sodium, 75 mg.

Potato and Eggplant Stew with Cilantro

Portions: 12   Portion size: 6 oz (180 g)

U.S.	Metric	Ingredients
2 fl oz	60 mL	Vegetable oil
2 tsp	10 mL	Cumin seeds
12 oz	337 mL	Onion, chopped fine
2 tbsp	30 mL	Finely chopped garlic
2 tbsp	30 mL	Grated fresh ginger root
½ tsp	2 mL	Turmeric
1½ lb	750 g	Eggplant, peeled, medium dice
2 lb	1 kg	Potatoes, medium dice
1 lb	500 g	Tomatoes, canned, chopped, with their juice
6 fl oz	180 mL	Water
4 tbsp	60 mL	Chopped fresh cilantro
to taste	to taste	Salt

■ Procedure

1. Heat the oil in a large saucepot over moderate heat.
2. Add the cumin. Cook until the seeds are aromatic and start to darken, about 15 to 20 seconds.
3. Add the onion, garlic, ginger, and turmeric. Sauté until the onions are soft and lightly browned.
4. Add the eggplant and stir together with the onion. Sauté 2 minutes.
5. Add the potatoes, tomatoes, and water. Cover and simmer until the potatoes are tender. Stir occasionally, and add a little more water if the potatoes become dry.
6. Stir in the cilantro.
7. Season with salt.

Per serving:
Calories, 140; Protein, 3 g; Fat, 5 g (31% cal.); Cholesterol, 0 mg;
Carbohydrates, 22 g; Fiber, 4 g; Sodium, 55 mg.

POTATO PURÉE

Potato purée is an important product in most kitchens, even though it is not served as is. It is the basis of many popular preparations, including mashed or whipped potatoes, **duchesse potatoes**, and potato croquettes. (Please note that this usage of the term is different from classic European usage, where *purée de pommes de terre* means mashed or whipped potatoes.)

Starchy potatoes are usually used for purées. The flesh of starchy potatoes breaks apart easily and can absorb large quantities of butter, milk, and other enriching ingredients. Moderately waxy potatoes can also be puréed. The flesh doesn't break apart as easily, however, so they are harder to purée. Also, they don't absorb as much fat or liquid.

Avoid excessive mixing of potato purée. Too much whipping or mixing damages cell walls, releasing excess starch that makes the purée gluey in texture.

Following is the basic procedure for making potato purées.

Procedure for Making Potato Purée

1. Select starchy or moderately waxy potatoes.
2. Wash, peel, and eye carefully.
3. Cut into uniform sizes for even cooking.
4. Simmer or steam until tender. Potatoes for purée must be thoroughly cooked, or the purée will be grainy. But they must not be overcooked, or they will be watery.
5. Drain in a colander (if simmered). Set the colander on a sheet pan and place in an oven for several minutes to dry out the potatoes. If potatoes are too moist, they will be too loose or slack when liquid is added later.
6. While the potatoes are still hot, pass them through a food mill or ricer to purée. A mixer with the paddle attachment may be used to break up the potatoes for whipped potatoes, but there is no guarantee that it will remove all lumps.

    Equipment used for puréeing should not be cold, or it will cool the potatoes too much. Heat equipment under hot water before use.
7. Add ingredients to the purée as indicated in the individual recipe. Avoid excessive mixing in order to prevent glueyness.

Mashed or Whipped Potatoes

Portions: 25   Portion size: 5 oz (150 g)

U.S.	Metric	Ingredients
9 lb	4 kg	Potatoes
6 oz	175 g	Butter
1 cup	250 mL	Light cream, hot
as needed	as needed	Milk, hot
to taste	to taste	Salt
to taste	to taste	White pepper

Per serving:
Calories, 190; Protein, 3 g; Fat, 8 g (36% cal.); Cholesterol, 20 mg; Carbohydrates, 29 g; Fiber, 3g; Sodium, 65 mg.

■ Procedure

1. Peel and eye the potatoes and cut them into uniform sizes. Simmer in salted water to cover until tender.

2. Drain well and let the potatoes steam dry for a few minutes.

3. Pass the potatoes through a food mill or ricer into the bowl of a mixer. Alternative method: Place potatoes in mixer with paddle attachment. Mix until well broken up. Replace paddle with whip and beat until well puréed. Do not overwhip, or potatoes will become pasty.

4. Beat in butter, then cream.

5. Add enough hot milk to bring potatoes to proper consistency. They should be soft and moist, but firm enough to hold their shape, not runny.

6. Add salt and white pepper to taste.

7. If desired, whip *briefly* at high speed until potatoes are light and fluffy. Do not overwhip.

VARIATIONS

Garlic Mashed Potatoes
Method 1: Simmer 6–8 whole, peeled cloves of garlic with the potatoes. Purée the garlic and the potatoes together.

Method 2: Purée 1 or 2 heads roasted garlic (p. 567) and mix into the potatoes before adding cream.

Ancho Mashed Potatoes
Add Ancho Sauce (p. 191) to taste to whipped potatoes before adding milk. Reduce the quantity of milk as necessary to achieve the proper consistency.

Duchesse Potatoes

Portions: 25   Portion size: 4 oz (100 g)

U.S.	Metric	Ingredients
7 lb	3 kg	Potatoes, peeled and quartered
4 oz	100 g	Butter, melted
to taste	to taste	Salt
to taste	to taste	White pepper
to taste	to taste	Nutmeg
10	10	Egg yolks
as needed	as needed	Egg wash (optional)

Per serving:
Calories, 150; Protein, 3 g; Fat, 6 g (34% cal.); Cholesterol, 95 mg; Carbohydrates, 23 g; Fiber, 2 g; Sodium, 45 mg.

■ Procedure

1. Steam the potatoes or simmer them in salted water until tender. Drain in a colander and let dry in an oven for several minutes.
2. Pass the potatoes through a food mill or ricer.
3. Add butter and mix to a smooth paste. Season to taste with salt, pepper, and just a little nutmeg (the potatoes should not taste strongly of nutmeg).
4. If the potatoes are very moist, stir over a low flame to stiffen. They must be much stiffer than mashed potatoes.
5. Add the egg yolks (off the fire) and beat until smooth.
6. Put the mixture in a pastry bag with a star tube and bag out into desired shapes on sheet pans or as platter borders (see Figure 18.1). Cone-shaped spiral mounds are most popular for individual portion service.
7. If desired, brush lightly with egg wash for greater browning.
8. At service time, place potatoes in hot oven (400°–425°F/200°–230°C) until lightly browned. Platter borders may be browned under the salamander.

VARIATION

Duchesse potato mixture is also used as base for Potato Croquettes (p. 604) and is considered one of the basic hot kitchen preparations.

Figure 18.1
Using the pastry bag: duchesse potatoes.

(a) Turn down the top of the pastry bag as shown. Slip your hand under this collar and hold the top open with your thumb and forefinger while you fill it with duchesse potato mixture.

(b) Turn the top of the bag up again and gather the loose top together as shown. Hold the bag shut with your thumb and forefinger. To force out the potatoes, squeeze the top of the bag in the palm of your hand. Use your free hand to guide the tip or hold the item being filled or decorated. You can make potato croquettes quickly by forcing out the potato mixture in long strips, using a large plain tube. Cut the strips into 2-in. (5-cm) lengths with a knife.

(c) Duchesse potatoes are often used to decorate platters, as in this illustration. This technique is also used in decorating cakes and desserts with icing, whipped cream, or meringue.

(d) Single portions of duchesse potatoes are usually piped out into a tall spiral shape. They are then browned in the oven.

(e) Dauphine and Lorette Potatoes may be bagged out into many shapes, such as these small stars. Some cookies are also shaped this way.

BAKING

Preparing baked potatoes is a simple procedure that is widely misunderstood and needlessly complicated. Properly baked potatoes are white, fluffy, mealy, and steamy. Poorly baked potatoes, unfortunately common, are gray and soggy.

Russet potatoes are most often used for baked potatoes. However, many varieties are now available on the market, some of which are excellent for baking and yield different flavors and textures. Don't be afraid to experiment with some of the varieties listed on pages 583–584.

Procedure for Baking Potatoes

1. For standard baked potatoes, select russets or other regularly shaped starchy potatoes.

2. Scrub well and pierce the ends with a fork or skewer so steam can escape.

3. For crisp skins, rub lightly with oil. For more tender skins, leave dry.

4. Place on sheet pans or on sheet pan racks in a preheated 400°F (200°C) oven and bake until done, about 1 hour. To test doneness, squeeze gently. Done potatoes yield to gentle pressure.

   Note: Using sheet pan racks eliminates the hard spot that forms where the potato is in contact with the sheet pan.

5. Remove from oven.

6. To hold for service, keep warm and uncovered so the potatoes will not be made soggy by trapped steam. Hold no more than 1 hour, if possible, though they will keep longer with some loss of quality.

   Note that nothing was said about wrapping potatoes in foil. Foil-wrapped potatoes do not bake but rather steam in their own moisture. The texture of a steamed potato is entirely different from that of a baked potato. Save yourself the trouble and expense of wrapping in foil and serve a better product.

 Baked Potatoes

Portion size: 1 potato

U.S.	Metric	Ingredients
as needed	as needed	Idaho or baking potatoes
as needed	as needed	Vegetable oil (optional)

■ Procedure

1. Scrub the potatoes well and pierce the ends with a skewer or fork to allow steam to escape.

2. Leave potatoes dry or oil them lightly if a crisp skin is desired.

3. Place on sheet pan in 400°F (200°C) oven. Bake until done, about 1 hour. Test for doneness by squeezing a potato gently.

Per serving:
Calories, 130; Protein, 3 g; Fat, 0 g (0% cal.); Cholesterol, 0 mg; Carbohydrates, 31 g; Fiber, 3 g; Sodium, 10 mg.

Stuffed Baked Potatoes

Portions: 10   Portion size: 1 potato

U.S.	Metric	Ingredients
10	10	Baking potatoes, about 7–8 oz (200–225 g) each
2 oz	60 g	Butter, melted
4 oz	100 mL	Light cream or milk, hot
to taste	to taste	Salt
to taste	to taste	White pepper
3 tbsp	45 mL	Dry bread crumbs
3 tbsp	45 mL	Parmesan cheese, grated
1 oz	30 g	Butter, melted

Per serving:
Calories, 270; Protein, 5 g; Fat, 10 g (32% cal.); Cholesterol, 30 mg; Carbohydrates, 42 g; Fiber, 4 g; Sodium, 140 mg.

■ P r o c e d u r e

1. Bake the potatoes according to the basic method.

2. Remove from the oven. Cut a slice off the top of each potato and scoop out the pulp, leaving a shell about ¼ in. (½ cm) thick.

3. Pass the pulp through a food mill or ricer. Beat in the butter and enough cream or milk to make a smooth purée. Season to taste. (Note that this preparation is basically the same as whipped potatoes.)

4. Fill the potato shells with the purée, using a pastry bag or kitchen spoon. (A pastry bag is faster and neater.) Place them on a baking sheet.

5. Mix the bread crumbs and parmesan cheese and top the potatoes with this mixture. Sprinkle with melted butter.

6. Place in hot oven (400°F/200°C) until potatoes are heated through and tops are browned, about 15 minutes.

V A R I A T I O N S

For each variation listed, add the indicated ingredients to the potato purée mixture. Proportions are for about 2½–3 lb (1.1–1.4 kg) purée.

1. 2 oz (60 g) grated parmesan cheese
2. 8 oz (225 g) minced onion, sautéed in butter
3. 4 oz (100 g) cooked ham, small dice
   4 oz (100 g) mushrooms, chopped and sautéed in butter
4. 8 oz (225 g) bacon, diced and cooked crisp
   1 green pepper, chopped and sautéed in butter or bacon fat

Macaire Potatoes

Scoop out the pulp completely and discard the skins. Mash the pulp with a kitchen fork or break it up with the paddle of a mixer. Omit the melted butter and cream or milk. Instead, mix in 7 oz (200 g) soft butter. Season. Form into small cakes and pan-fry in clarified butter until golden brown on both sides.

Oven Roast Potatoes

Portions: 25   Portion size: 4 oz (125 g)

U.S.	Metric	Ingredients
10 lb AP	4.5 kg	Potatoes
as needed	as needed	Vegetable oil or olive oil
to taste	to taste	Salt
to taste	to taste	White pepper

Per serving:
Calories, 160; Protein, 3 g; Fat, 2.5 g (14% cal.); Cholesterol, 0 mg; Carbohydrates, 32 g; Fiber, 3 g; Sodium, 10 mg.

■ P r o c e d u r e

1. Peel and eye potatoes. Cut into 25 uniform portions and trim pieces to shape. Save the trimmings for other use.

2. Dry the potatoes well and rub with oil. Place in oiled baking pan and season with salt and pepper.

3. Place in 400°F (200°C) oven and bake until browned and cooked through, about 1 hour. Halfway through baking time, turn potatoes and brush with additional oil.

Roasted New Potatoes with Herbs and Garlic

Portions: 10   Portion size: 4 oz (125 g)

U.S.	Metric	Ingredients
3 lb	1.5 kg	New potatoes, fingerling potatoes, or other small potatoes
3 fl oz	90 mL	Olive oil
2 tbsp	30 mL	Fresh rosemary, coarsely chopped
1 tbsp	15 mL	Fresh thyme
2 tbsp	30 mL	Finely chopped garlic
2 tsp	10 mL	Salt

■ P r o c e d u r e

1. Wash the potatoes, drain, and let dry.
2. Cut round potatoes in half, or, if using small fingerlings, leave them whole.
3. Place the potatoes in a roasting pan.
4. Pour the oil over the potatoes and sprinkle with the herbs, garlic, and salt. Toss or mix so all the potatoes are coated.
5. Bake at 400°F (200°C) until the potatoes are tender, about 45 minutes.

Per serving:
Calories, 270; Protein, 5 g; Fat, 8 g (26% cal.); Cholesterol, 0 mg; Carbohydrates, 45 g; Fiber, 4 g; Sodium, 480 mg.

BAKED "EN CASSEROLE"

A number of preparations call for potatoes baked in a baking pan or casserole, with or without liquid added. The best-known is scalloped potatoes. A characteristic of most of these preparations is that they are baked uncovered at least part of the time so that a brown crust forms on top. (Note that two versions of Gratin Dauphinoise are included here. The first is a modern version, while the second is a more traditional version.)

 ## Gratin Dauphinoise I

Portions: 24   Portion size: 4 oz (125 g)

U.S.	Metric	Ingredients
5 lb	2.5 kg	Firm-fleshed potatoes
2 tsp	10 mL	Salt
¼ oz	7 g	Garlic, chopped
1 qt	1 L	Cream
1 pt	500 mL	Milk
to taste	to taste	White pepper

■ P r o c e d u r e

1. Peel the potatoes and cut into thin slices (as for potato chips). Do not place the sliced potatoes in water.
2. Toss the potatoes in the salt and chopped garlic and arrange in an even layer in a buttered full-size hotel pan or a roasting pan of equivalent size.
3. Mix together the cream and milk and lightly season with pepper. Bring to a boil.
4. Pour over the potatoes, then place the pan in the oven at 400°F (200°C) for about 30 minutes or until the potatoes are tender and the sauce is thick.

Per serving:
Calories, 300; Protein, 4 g; Fat, 23 g (67 % cal.); Cholesterol, 85 mg; Carbohydrates, 21 g; Fiber, 2 g; Sodium, 490 mg.

Gratin Dauphinoise

Gratin Dauphinoise II

Portions: 15   Portion size: 5 oz (150 g)

U.S.	Metric	Ingredients
3 lb	1.4 kg	Potatoes
to taste	to taste	Salt
to taste	to taste	White pepper
to taste	to taste	Nutmeg
½ lb	225 g	Gruyère cheese, grated
1 pt	500 mL	Milk
1 cup	250 mL	Heavy cream
3	3	Egg yolks

Per serving:
Calories, 220; Protein, 8 g; Fat, 13 g (53% cal.); Cholesterol, 85 mg;
Carbohydrates, 18 g; Fiber, 1g; Sodium, 80 mg.

■ P r o c e d u r e

1. Peel and eye the potatoes. Cut into very thin slices.
2. Place some of the potatoes in a layer in a buttered baking pan. Season with salt, pepper, and a very small amount of nutmeg. Sprinkle with a little of the cheese. Repeat until all the potatoes and about three-fourths of the cheese are used up.
3. Combine the milk and half the cream and heat to a simmer. Beat the egg yolks with the remaining cream. Slowly stir in the hot milk mixture.
4. Pour the milk mixture over the potatoes. Top with remaining cheese.
5. Bake uncovered at 350°F (175°C) until done, about 45–60 minutes.

V A R I A T I O N

Savoyarde Potatoes
Prepare as above, but use chicken stock instead of milk.

Scalloped Potatoes

Portions: 25   Portion size: 5 oz (150 g)

U.S.	Metric	Ingredients
2½ qt	2.5 L	Milk
3 oz	90 g	Butter
3 oz	90 g	Flour
2 tsp	10 mL	Salt
to taste	to taste	White pepper
7½ lb	3.5 kg	Potatoes

Per serving:
Calories, 200; Protein, 6 g; Fat, 6 g (27% cal.); Cholesterol, 20 mg;
Carbohydrates, 31 g; Fiber, 2 g; Sodium, 80 mg.

Note: Unthickened milk may be used instead of a thin white sauce, but the milk is more likely to curdle. The roux helps prevent curdling.

■ P r o c e d u r e

1. Make a thin white sauce (béchamel) using the ingredients listed (see p. 171). Keep hot while preparing the potatoes.
2. Peel and eye the potatoes. Cut into slices ⅛ in. thick (3 mm).
3. Place the potatoes in a buttered baking pan, making several layers.
4. Pour in the white sauce. Lift the potatoes slightly so that the sauce can run between the layers.
5. Cover with foil or greased paper and place in oven at 350°F (175°C) for 30 minutes.
6. Uncover and continue to bake until top is lightly browned and potatoes are tender.

V A R I A T I O N S

Scalloped Potatoes with Onions
Add 1¼ lb (600 g) sliced onions to baking pan with the potatoes.

Scalloped Potatoes with Cheese
Add 1 lb (500 g) shredded cheddar cheese to baking pan with potatoes. Top with additional cheese before browning.

Scalloped Potatoes with Ham
Add 2½ lb (1.4 kg) diced ham.

Boulangère Potatoes

Portions: 25   Portion size: 5 oz (150 g)

U.S.	Metric	Ingredients
2½ lb	1.1 kg	Onions, sliced
5 oz	150 g	Butter or fat drippings from roast (see note)
7½ lb	3.5 kg	Potatoes, peeled and cut into thick slices
1 qt	1 L	Stock, chicken or lamb (if available), hot
to taste	to taste	Salt
to taste	to taste	Pepper

Procedure

1. Sauté the onions in butter or fat until they are translucent and just beginning to brown.

2. Add the potatoes and toss until coated with fat.

3. Place in a baking pan or in a roasting pan under a partially cooked roast. Pour in the hot stock. Season.

4. Bake 1–1½ hours at 350°F (175°C) or at the roasting temperature of lamb, until potatoes are done. Add more stock during cooking if necessary to keep potatoes from drying out.

Per serving:
Calories, 160; Protein, 3 g; Fat, 5 g (27% cal.); Cholesterol, 15 mg; Carbohydrates, 28 g; Fiber, 3 g; Sodium, 55 mg.

Note: Boulangère potatoes may be cooked separately, but they are usually cooked with a roast, especially leg of lamb (see p. 294).

If the potatoes are cooked with a roast, they must be added to the pan at the right time so they will be done at the same time as the meat.

Potatoes au Gratin

Portions: 25   Portion size: 6 oz (175 g)

U.S.	Metric	Ingredients
7½ lb	3.5 kg	Potatoes
2 qt	2 L	Cheddar Cheese Sauce (p. 171), hot
⅔ cup	150 mL	Dry bread crumbs
2 tsp	10 mL	Paprika
2 oz	60 g	Butter, melted (optional)

Procedure

1. Scrub the potatoes and simmer or steam them until tender but still firm.

2. Drain and spread on sheet pan to cool.

3. When the potatoes are cool enough to handle, peel and cut them into uniform ⅜-in. (1-cm) dice.

4. Combine with the hot cheese sauce in a baking pan.

5. Mix the bread crumbs and paprika and sprinkle over the potatoes. Drizzle the butter evenly over the top.

6. Bake at 350°F (175°C) about 30 minutes, until hot and browned.

Per serving:
Calories, 190; Protein, 7 g; Fat, 6 g (29% cal.); Cholesterol, 20 mg; Carbohydrates, 26 g; Fiber, 2 g; Sodium, 150 mg.

Note: Cream sauce may be used instead of cheese sauce. Grated cheese (cheddar or parmesan) may be sprinkled over the potatoes before topping them with bread crumbs.

Anna Potatoes

Portions: 10   Portion size: 5 oz (150 g)

U.S.	Metric	Ingredients
4 lb AP	1.8 kg	Boiling potatoes
12 oz	350 g	Butter
to taste	to taste	Salt
to taste	to taste	White pepper

■ P r o c e d u r e

1. Select round, uniformly sized potatoes. The appearance of this dish is important, so the slices should be neat and even.

2. Peel and eye the potatoes and cut into thin slices. Hold in cold water until ready to use.

3. Clarify the butter (see p. 178).

4. Heat about ¼ in. (½ cm) butter in a heavy 9-in. (23-cm) cast iron skillet. The skillet must be well seasoned so the potatoes will not stick. Remove from heat.

5. Drain the potatoes and dry them well. Select the most uniform slices for the bottom layer. Arrange the slices in circles in the bottom of the pan. Shingle the slices and reverse the direction of each circle. See Figure 18.2 for illustration of this technique. Season this layer with salt and pepper and ladle some clarified butter over it.

6. Continue making layers, seasoning and buttering each layer, until the ingredients are used up. The potatoes will be mounded over the top of the pan, but they will compress as they cook. There will be a great deal of butter in the pan, but it will be drained after cooking and can be reused.

7. Place the pan over a moderate fire and heat until the pan is sizzling. Shake the pan lightly to make sure the potatoes are not sticking.

8. Cover with foil and bake in a hot oven (450°F/230°C) for about 40 minutes, until potatoes are tender. Test for doneness by piercing center with paring knife. Remove the foil and bake 10 minutes more.

9. Drain off excess butter (remember that it's hot!) and carefully invert the potato cake onto a baking sheet. The potatoes should have stayed intact in a round cake, but if any slices fall off, put them back in place. Set the potatoes back in the oven if necessary for even browning.

10. Cut into wedges for service.

V A R I A T I O N

Voisin Potatoes

Prepare as in basic recipe, but sprinkle each layer of potatoes with grated Swiss cheese.

Per serving:
Calories, 260; Protein, 3 g; Fat, 14 g (47 % cal.); Cholesterol, 35 mg; Carbohydrates, 32 g; Fiber, 3 g; Sodium, 150 mg.

Note: Small molds may be used instead of the large pan for individual service.

**Figure 18.2
Anna Potatoes.**

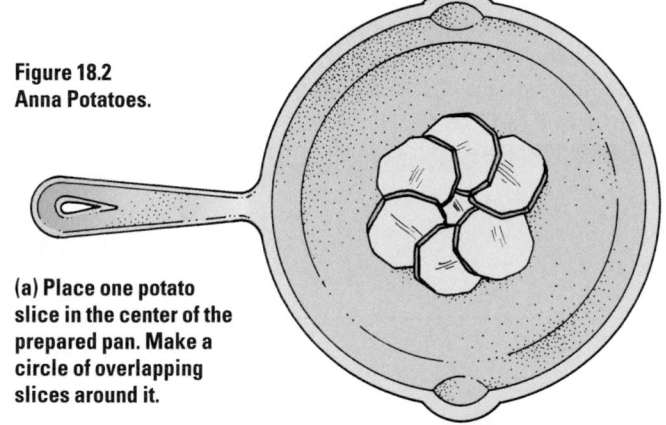

(a) Place one potato slice in the center of the prepared pan. Make a circle of overlapping slices around it.

(b) Make another circle of overlapping slices around this, but reverse the direction, as shown. Continue building up layers of potatoes, butter, and seasonings as directed in the recipe.

SAUTÉING AND PAN-FRYING

The procedures for sautéing and pan-frying potatoes are basically the same as for other vegetables (p. 556).

There are many sautéed and pan-fried potato preparations. Some are made with raw potatoes, others with precooked or blanched potatoes. Many of these recipes are especially useful because they are excellent ways to utilize leftover boiled potatoes.

This group of recipes may be divided into two categories based on production technique.

1. **Potatoes mixed or tossed while cooking.**

    The procedure for sautéing vegetables, page 556, is used for these preparations. The potatoes are cut into pieces or into small shapes and cooked in a small amount of fat. They are turned or tossed in the pan so that they brown on all sides. This category includes rissolé, parisienne, noisette, château, and American fried or home-fried potatoes.

2. **Potatoes cooked and served in compact cakes.**

    The procedure for pan-frying vegetables (see p. 556) is the basic method used for these preparations. The potatoes are not mixed while cooking but are made into cakes, which are browned on both sides. This category includes hashed browns and variations, as well as potato pancakes and macaire potatoes (see p. 593).

 ## Hashed Brown Potatoes

Portions: 25   Portion size: 4½ oz (125 g)

U.S.	Metric	Ingredients
7½ lb	3.4 kg	Boiled potatoes, cooled and peeled
10 oz	275 g	Oil, clarified butter, or a mixture of oil and clarified butter
to taste	to taste	Salt
to taste	to taste	Pepper

Per serving:
Calories, 180; Protein, 2 g; Fat, 7 g (35% cal.); Cholesterol, 0 mg; Carbohydrates, 27 g; Fiber, 2 g; Sodium, 5 mg.

■ P r o c e d u r e

1. Chop the potatoes into small pieces.

2. Ladle a thin layer of oil or butter into a well-seasoned 6-in. (15-cm) sauté pan and set it over high heat. A griddle may also be used for this preparation.

3. When the fat is hot, add 1 portion of potatoes and flatten them into a round cake. Shake the pan back and forth to keep the potatoes from sticking.

4. When the potatoes are well browned on the bottom, flip them over or turn them with an offset spatula. Try to keep the potato cake unbroken. Season with salt and pepper.

5. When the second side is done, tilt the pan to drain off any excess fat for reuse, holding the potatoes in the pan with the spatula. Slide the potatoes out of the sauté pan onto a plate.

6. Repeat with remaining portions.

V A R I A T I O N S

Any of the following can be added to the potatoes to vary the flavor: chopped parsley, chives, bacon, hard-cooked egg, grated cheese, and garlic.

Roesti Potatoes

Shred boiled potatoes on the large holes of a hand grater, or use a machine. Prepare as in basic recipe. Potatoes should be very crisp. (These are sometimes called "hashed brown potatoes" but, strictly speaking, hashed browns are made with chopped potatoes, as hash means "to chop.")

Lyonnaise Hashed Browns

Combine 1¼ lb (600 g) onion, chopped and sautéed in butter, with the chopped or shredded potatoes before pan-frying.

Rissolé or Cocotte Potatoes

Portions: 25   Portions size: 4 oz (125 g)

U.S.	Metric	Ingredients
14 lb	7 kg	Potatoes (see note)
10 oz	300 g	Clarified butter
to taste	to taste	Salt
to taste	to taste	White pepper

Per serving:
Calories, 290; Protein, 4 g; Fat, 11g (34% cal.); Cholesterol, 30 mg; Carbohydrates, 45 g; Fiber, 4 g; Sodium, 125 mg.

Note: The quantity of potatoes needed varies, depending on how heavily they are trimmed. Save trimmings for purées or other uses.

■ P r o c e d u r e

1. Peel and eye the potatoes and trim or tourné them into small oval shapes about 1½ in. (4 cm) long. (See Figure 7.18 for technique.)

2. Place the potatoes in a saucepan, cover with salted water, and bring to a boil. Reduce heat and simmer 7–8 minutes or until about three-fourths cooked.

3. Drain and turn out onto a sheet pan to steam dry.

4. Heat the clarified butter in a large sauté pan. Add the potatoes and sauté over moderate heat until golden brown and fully cooked. (Potatoes may also be browned in deep fat if speed of service is critical.)

5. Season with salt and pepper.

V A R I A T I O N S

Alternative Method: Potatoes may be sautéed without prior blanching. Sauté over low heat and keep covered during the first half or three-fourths of the cooking period so that the potatoes will cook fully without becoming overbrowned. Potatoes cooked this way absorb more butter than those that are blanched first. Thus they are tastier, but they also are higher in calories.

Parisienne and Noisette Potatoes
Prepare as in basic recipe, but cut potatoes with melon ball cutter. Parisienne potatoes are cut with a scoop slightly larger than 1 in. (about 3 cm). Noisette potatoes are smaller than 1 in. (about 2½ cm). Blanch for 3–5 minutes or cook from raw state.

Château Potatoes
Prepare as in basic recipe, but tourné the potatoes into larger ovals, about 2 in. (5 cm) long.

 ## Lyonnaise Potatoes

Portions: 25   Portion size: 4½ oz (125 g)

U.S.	Metric	Ingredients
6½ lb	3 kg	Boiled potatoes, cooled and peeled
1½ lb	700 g	Onions
8 oz	225 g	Clarified butter, vegetable oil, or mixture of oil and butter
to taste	to taste	Salt
to taste	to taste	White pepper

Per serving:
Calories, 190; Protein, 2 g; Fat, 9 g (42% cal.); Cholesterol, 25 mg; Carbohydrates, 26 g; Fiber, 2 g; Sodium, 95 mg.

Note: This preparation may be made on a griddle instead of in a sauté pan.

■ P r o c e d u r e

1. Cut the potatoes into slices about ¼ in. (½ cm) thick.

2. Peel the onions, cut in half lengthwise, and slice into julienne.

3. Heat half the fat in a sauté pan and sauté the onions until they are golden. Remove from the pan with a slotted spoon and set aside.

4. Put the rest of the fat into the pan. Set the pan on high heat and add the potatoes.

5. Sauté the potatoes, tossing them in the pan until well browned on all sides.

6. Add the onions and continue to sauté for another minute, until onions and potatoes well mixed and the flavors are blended.

7. Season to taste.

V A R I A T I O N S

Home Fries or American Fries
Prepare as in basic recipe, but omit onions.

Potatoes O'Brien
Cook 10 oz (300 g) diced bacon until crisp. Remove bacon from pan. Sauté 10 oz onion (300 g), cut in fine dice, and 10 oz (300 g) green bell pepper, cut in fine dice, in bacon fat. Sauté 6½ lb (3 kg) diced potatoes as in basic recipe and add vegetables.

Add the crisp bacon and 4 oz (125 g) diced pimiento to finish, and season to taste.

Potato Pancakes

Portions: 20   Portion size: 2 pancakes, about 2 oz (60 g) each

U.S.	Metric	Ingredients
6 lb	2.7 kg	Potatoes
1 lb	450 g	Onions
2	2	Lemons
6	6	Eggs
¼ cup	60 mL	Chopped parsley (optional)
2 tsp	10 mL	Salt
½ tsp	2 mL	White pepper
2 oz or more	60 g or more	Flour (see note)
as needed	as needed	Oil for pan-frying

Per serving:
Calories, 220; Protein, 5 g; Fat, 10 g (40% cal.); Cholesterol, 65 mg; Carbohydrates, 29 g; Fiber, 3 g; Sodium, 260 mg.

Note: Matzoh meal or dried potato starch may be used instead of flour for binding the batter.

■ P r o c e d u r e

1. Peel the potatoes and onions. Grate them together into a stainless-steel bowl. Juice the lemons, add the juice to the potatoes to prevent discoloration, and toss to mix.

2. Place the potatoes in a china cap and squeeze out the excess liquid. Hold the liquid and let the starch settle out. Drain off the liquid from the starch.

3. Return the potatoes to a stainless-steel bowl and add the potato starch.

4. Beat in the eggs, parsley, salt, and pepper.

5. Stir in enough flour to bind the potato mixture. (If the batter is too thin, the pancakes will fall apart in the pan. Test-fry a little first, and add more flour if necessary.)

6. Pour about ¼ in. (½ cm) oil into a heavy iron skillet. Heat the oil over moderately high heat. The oil should reach about 325°F/160°C.

7. Measuring with a solid kitchen spoon, place portions of the batter in the pan to make individual pancakes.

8. Pan-fry, turning once, until golden brown on both sides.

9. Remove from the pan with a slotted spoon or spatula and drain briefly on absorbent paper.

10. Alternative method: Lightly brown in oil and place in one layer on a sheet pan. Finish in the oven (375°F/190°C) until brown and crisp.

Potatoes with Chickpeas and Chiles

Portions: 12   Portion size: 4½ oz (125 g)

U.S.	Metric	Ingredients
2½ lb	1.1 kg	Boiled potatoes, cooled and peeled
4 fl oz	120 mL	Vegetable oil
8 oz	225 g	Onion, small dice
1 oz	10 g	Garlic, chopped fine
1 tsp	5 mL	Ground coriander
¼ tsp	1 mL	Cinnamon
¼ tsp	1 mL	Black pepper
4	4	Jalapeño chiles, seeded and sliced
1 lb	450 g	Chickpeas, cooked or canned, drained
1 fl oz	15 mL	Lemon juice
to taste	to taste	Salt

■ P r o c e d u r e

1. Cut the potatoes into large dice.
2. Heat the oil in a sauté pan.
3. Add the onion, garlic, coriander, cinnamon, and pepper. Sauté until the onion is lightly browned.
4. Add the chiles and sauté another 2 minutes.
5. Add the potatoes and chickpeas. Sauté until the potatoes and chickpeas are hot and the potatoes are lightly browned.
6. Sprinkle the lemon juice over the potatoes and stir in.
7. Add salt to taste.

Potatoes with Chickpeas and Chiles

Per serving:
Calories, 240; Protein, 5 g; Fat, 10 g (38% cal.); Cholesterol, 0 mg; Carbohydrates, 32 g; Fiber, 5 g; Sodium, 10 mg.

DEEP-FRYING

All the rules of deep-frying that you learned in Chapter 4 apply to potatoes. Review page 73 to refresh your memory.

There are two kinds of deep-fried potato preparations:

1. **Potatoes fried raw.**

   These are potatoes that are simply cut into various shapes and deep-fried until golden and crisp. They include all the varieties of French fries as well as potato chips.

   Russet or Idaho potatoes are most suitable for frying because of their high starch content and their regular shape, which permits less trimming loss.

2. **Preparations made from cooked, puréed potatoes.**

   Most of these products are made from duchesse potato mixture. They include potato croquette variations, Dauphine potatoes, and Lorette potatoes.

   Starchy potatoes are used for these recipes, as they are for duchesse potatoes, because they make a good dry, mealy purée.

FRENCH FRIES

Because French fries, or deep-fried potatoes, are one of the most popular items in North American food service, you must know how to prepare them well. Most French fries served are made from blanched, frozen products, but it is also important to know how to make them from fresh potatoes.

The recipe on page 603 gives the complete procedure for preparing French fries. Note that they are fried in two stages. It is possible to cook them in one step, but this is impractical in a volume operation because of the long cooking time. The more common practice is to blanch them in frying fat. This is done at a lower temperature so they will cook through without becoming brown. They are then drained and refrigerated until service time. Portions can then be finished to order in a few minutes.

Frozen products have been prepared through step 5 in the recipe and then frozen. To use them, simply begin with step 6.

French Fries

Portions: as needed (2¼ lb AP/1 kg AP potatoes will yield about 1 lb/450 g cooked potatoes)

U.S.	Metric	Ingredients
as needed	as needed	Idaho potatoes

Per 3.2 ounces:
Calories, 290; Protein, 4 g; Fat, 15 g (46% cal.); Cholesterol, 0 mg; Carbohydrates, 36 g; Fiber, 3 g; Sodium, 200 mg.

■ P r o c e d u r e

1. Peel and eye the potatoes.
2. Cut the potatoes into strips ⅜ in. (1 cm) square and about 3 in. (7½ cm) long. (See Figure 7.10 for cutting procedure.) Hold the cut potatoes in cold water until needed, to prevent discoloration.
3. Line sheet pans with several layers of brown paper and have them ready by the deep fryer.
4. Drain and dry the potatoes well. Deep-fry in fat heated to 325°F (160°C) until they are just beginning to turn a pale golden color. At this point, they should be cooked through and soft.
5. Remove the potatoes from the fryer and turn them out onto the sheet pans in a single layer to drain. Refrigerate.
6. At service time, fry the potatoes in small quantities in fat heated to 350°–375°F (175°–190°C) until brown and crisp.
7. Drain well. Salt them lightly away from the fryer or let customers salt their own. Serve immediately.

V A R I A T I O N S

Pont-Neuf Potatoes
Prepare as in basic recipe, but cut the potatoes in thicker strips, about ½ in. (1¼ cm) square or slightly larger. Blanching time will be slightly longer.

**Allumette Potatoes
(Shoestring or Matchstick Potatoes)**
Cut the potatoes into thin strips, slightly less than ¼ in. thick (about ½ cm). Because they are so thin, they are usually fried in one step (without blanching) until very crisp.

Straw Potatoes
Cut into very thin strips, about ⅛ in. (3 mm) thick. Fry in one step in hot fat (375°F/190°C).

Steakhouse Fries
Scrub but do not peel potatoes. Cut in half lengthwise, then cut each half lengthwise into 4–6 wedges, depending on size. Prepare as in basic recipe.

Potato Chips
Cut potatoes into very thin slices, less than ⅛ in. (3 mm) thick. Fry in one step in hot fat (375°F/190°C).

Waffle or Gaufrette Potatoes
Set the fluted blade of a mandoline (a special slicer) so that it cuts very thin slices. Cut potatoes into round slices, turning the potato about 90 degrees between slices so that you cut waffle shapes (see Figure 18.3). Fry like potato chips.

**Figure 18.3
Gaufrette Potatoes**

(a) Set the fluted blade of the mandoline so that it cuts very thin slices.

(b) Slice the potatoes, turning the potato about 90 degrees between slices so that the ridges on the two sides of each slice cross each other.

(c) You may need to adjust the thickness of the cut after the first slice or two. The slices should be thin enough to have holes.

Potato Croquettes

Note: These are made from duchesse potato mixture. The procedure for duchesse potatoes is repeated here for the sake of convenience.

Portions: 20   Portion size: 3 pieces, 1½ oz (40 g) each

U.S.	Metric	Ingredients
7 lb	3 kg	Potatoes, peeled and quartered
4 oz	100 g	Butter
to taste	to taste	Salt
to taste	to taste	White pepper
to taste	to taste	Nutmeg
10	10	Egg yolks
		Standard Breading Procedure:
as needed	as needed	Flour
as needed	as needed	Egg wash
as needed	as needed	Bread crumbs

■ **P r o c e d u r e**

1. Steam the potatoes or simmer in salted water until tender. (Steaming is preferable because it results in a drier product.) Drain in a colander (if simmered) and let dry in an oven for a few minutes.

2. Pass the potatoes through a food mill or ricer.

3. Add the butter and mix to a smooth paste. Season to taste with salt, pepper, and nutmeg.

4. Set over moderate fire and stir the mixture to dry it out well. If it is not dry enough, the croquettes will not hold their shape. Alternative method: Add enough cornstarch or dry potato starch to absorb excess moisture and stiffen the mixture.

5. Remove from the fire, add the egg yolks, and beat in thoroughly.

6. To shape croquettes, two methods are available: (a) Spread the mixture out to cool in a pan, cover with plastic or buttered paper to keep a crust from forming, and refrigerate. Dust hands with flour and shape potatoes by hand into cylinders the shape of corks, about 2 in. (5 cm) long. They should be about 1½ oz (40 g) each. (b) Dust sheet pans with flour. Place the warm potato mixture in a pastry bag fitted with a large, plain tip. Bag out the potatoes into long strips on the pans (see Figure 18.1). With a knife, cut the strips into 2-in. (5 cm) lengths.

7. Set up the breading station and pass the potatoes through Standard Breading Procedure (p. 143).

8. At service time, fry croquettes in deep fat at 350°F (175°C) until golden brown. Drain well.

9. Serve immediately, 3 pieces per portion.

Per serving:
Calories, 443; Protein, 9 g; Fat, 20 g (42% cal.); Cholesterol, 155 mg; Carbohydrates, 54 g; Fiber, 3 g; Sodium, 315 mg.

V A R I A T I O N S

Other shapes may be used as desired.

Add 8 oz (225 g) of any one of the following to the potato mixture:

Grated cheese   Minced, sautéed onion   Chopped, sautéed mushrooms   Chopped ham   Finely chopped nuts

Berny Potatoes
Shape into small balls. Bread with finely slivered almonds instead of bread crumbs. (In classical cuisine, minced truffles are added to the potato mixture.)

Lorette Potatoes
Prepare like Dauphine Potatoes and add 1 oz grated parmesan cheese per pound of mixture (60 g per kg). Shape as desired (the classic shape is a small crescent) and fry without breading.

Dauphine Potatoes
Method 1: For each pound of duchesse or croquette potato mixture, add ⅓ lb Pâte à Choux or cream puff paste (p. 998), made without sugar and with half the amount of butter. To fry, bag out into desired shapes on greased brown paper. Slide into hot fat. Remove paper when potatoes float loose. **Method 2:** Hold pastry bag over deep fryer. Force out potato mixture and cut off short lengths with the back of a knife, letting them drop into the hot fat.

Potato Croquettes with Peppers

Yield: 36 pieces

U.S.	Metric	Ingredients
3	3	Small red bell peppers
3	3	Small green bell peppers
1 lb 7 oz	700 g	Potatoes, peeled
1 oz	25 g	Butter, softened
1	1	Egg yolk
		Standard Breading Procedure

Per serving:
Calories, 270; Protein, 6 g; Fat, 12 g (40% cal.); Cholesterol, 55 mg; Carbohydrates, 34 g; Fiber, 2 g; Sodium, 240 mg.

■ P r o c e d u r e

1. Halve the red and green peppers and place under a hot grill until the skin is black and blistered. Cool.

2. Remove the skin and seeds, and cut peppers into ¼-in. (½-cm) dice.

3. Boil the potatoes and prepare a basic potato purée as explained on page 588.

4. Mix the peppers gently with the mashed potato, butter, and egg yolk. Season well.

5. With flour-dusted hands, shape the potato mixture into 36 balls. Set up Standard Breading Procedure (p. 143) and bread the croquettes.

6. Just before service, deep-fry the croquettes at 350°F (175° C). Drain well.

■ TERMS FOR REVIEW

waxy potato	all-purpose	blue-skinned, white-fleshed	solanine
russet	yellow-fleshed	blue- or purple-fleshed	duchesse potatoes
new potato	red-skinned	fingerling	hashed

■ QUESTIONS FOR DISCUSSION

1. True or false: French fries made from fresh potatoes are always better than French fries made from frozen, blanched potato strips. Explain.

2. If mature, starchy potatoes are best for puréeing (mashed, duchesse, etc.), then why doesn't everyone use russets or Idahos, which are the starchiest?

3. Why is it not a good idea to put parisienne potatoes on your menu unless you are also serving a puréed potato product?

4. Many of the potato recipes in this chapter do not indicate what type of potato to use. For each of those recipes, indicate whether you would select all-purpose, russet, or waxy potatoes.

CHAPTER 19

Legumes, Grains, Pasta, and Other Starches

This chapter continues the discussion of starchy foods. The previous chapter focuses on a fresh vegetable, the potato, one of the most important starches on European and North American menus. This chapter, by contrast, discusses preparations based on dried foods: legumes and grains.

For most of human history—and prehistory—grains have been the most important source of nutrients and calories to sustain life, and this remains true today in many parts of the world. For example, in parts of Asia, rice is eaten at nearly every meal. In Japan, the standard words for breakfast, lunch, and dinner can be translated as "morning rice," "noon rice," and "evening rice."

In many regions, dried beans, eaten together with rice, are a more common source of protein than meat or fish. Dried legumes are actually matured, dried versions of some of the fresh vegetables discussed in earlier chapters and are not immediately thought of as starches. However, they do have a high starch content and, because of their dried nature, are handled much like grains.

Pastas and noodles are important starchy foods made from grains, usually wheat, but also rice and other grains. In this chapter we look primarily at the noodle products inherited from Italian cuisine, but we also learn about noodles from other cuisines.

DRIED LEGUMES

A **legume** is a plant that bears seed pods that split along two opposite sides when ripe. Legumes include beans, peas, lentils, and a number of other plants. In culinary usage, we use the word to refer to the seeds from these pods, especially when they are mature and dried. (Do not confuse the English meaning of *legume* with that of the French word *legume*, which means "vegetable.")

Dried beans and peas have been used as food for thousands of years, and they continue to be important foods today. In fact, with today's increased interest in healthful eating and in vegetables of all sorts, as well as a greater knowledge of cuisines from around the world, many more interesting varieties of beans are widely available now than only a few years ago.

Legumes are high in protein and, thus, are important in vegetarian diets. They are rich in B vitamins and minerals. Some legumes, like the soybean, are also rich in fat.

TYPES AND VARIETIES

The three most important types of dried legumes in Western kitchens are kidney beans, peas, and lentils. In addition, several other unrelated legumes, including chickpeas, fava beans, soybeans, and lima beans, play smaller roles on the menu. The following descriptions include most of the commonly available beans.

Kidney Beans

Most of the many-colored beans in the illustrations are types of kidney beans. These are all varieties of one species of plant—the same plant that gives us the common green bean. Their flavors and textures vary slightly, but their cooking and handling characteristics are similar, although some may require longer cooking times than others.

A subgroup of this family is sometimes called **haricot beans** (*haricot* is the French word for "bean"). These are all varieties of green beans (*haricots verts*), which are allowed to ripen until the seeds are mature and dry. The members of this group are white beans of various sizes. The term *kidney bean* is then used for the remaining beans in this family, which have colors other than white.

The most common kinds of kidney beans and haricot beans are summarized in Table 19.1.

Peas

Dried *green* and *yellow* peas are the same peas we eat as a fresh vegetable, but they are left on the vine until mature and dry. They are usually split, with the hull removed, in order to speed cooking time, although whole peas are also available.

Split peas cook quickly without preliminary soaking,

Black-eyed peas and *pigeon peas* are popular in the southern United States as well as in parts of Africa and the Caribbean. They are not related to green or yellow peas nor to kidney beans but, like regular peas, are often sold fresh in the pod as well as dried. Black-eyed peas are small white, kidney-shaped beans with a black spot where the bean attaches to the pod. Pigeon peas are small and round or oval, with beige skin flecked with brown.

Lentils

Lentils are small, lens-shaped legumes. They have a shorter cooking time than kidney beans, even when whole, and do not need soaking. If desired, however, they may be soaked, resulting in an even shorter cooking time.

The most prized lentils are the tiny *green lentils* commonly known as *Le Puy* lentils, because the best ones are grown in Le Puy, France. (*Note:* Only lentils actually grown in Le Puy should be given this name. If grown elsewhere, they are simply called green lentils.) They have a dark green or gray-green hull and, unlike other lentils, keep their shape fairly well when cooked.

The larger *brown lentils* are the most common lentils in Western kitchens. They range in color from medium brown to greenish-brown.

After reading this chapter, you should be able to

1. Distinguish the major types of dried legumes.

2. Cook dried legumes.

3. Distinguish the major types of rice.

4. Distinguish the major types of other grains used in food service.

5. Prepare grains by simmering and by the pilaf and risotto methods.

6. Distinguish major kinds and shapes of commercial pasta and determine their quality.

7. Prepare fresh and commercial pasta products, and list the steps involved in the alternate steam-table method of its preparation.

Table 19.1
The Kidney Bean/Haricot Bean Family

Name	Description
Haricot beans	
Navy bean	small, oval white bean
Pea bean	similar to but smaller than navy bean
Rice bean	tiny white bean slightly larger than a grain of cooked rice
Great Northern bean	medium-small white bean
White kidney bean, cannellini	large, white kidney-shaped bean
Soissons (swah sohn)	medium white bean
Flageolet	small, pale green bean, harvested while immature and then dried
Kidney beans	
Red kidney bean	dark red-brown medium bean with tough skin
Pink kidney bean	pink-red bean similar to red kidney
Pinto bean	medium kidney bean with tan skin splotched with pink-brown
Black bean or turtle bean	small, black, oval kidney bean
Cranberry bean or borlotti bean	medium kidney bean, pale pink skin spotted with red
Brown or Swedish bean	small, oval, brown-skinned bean
Calypso bean	medium oval bean, white with black patches
Appaloosa bean	Medium kidney-shaped bean with black and white skin

Top row: navy beans, garbanzo beans or chickpeas, great northern beans. Bottom row: baby lima beans, cannelini beans or white kidney beans, rice beans

Top row: black turtle beans, dried fava beans. Bottom row: Swedish brown beans, calypso beans, flageolet beans.

Top row: red kidney beans, pink beans, appaloosa beans. Bottom row: cranberry beans or borlotti, Christmas lima beans, pinto beans.

Top row: yellow split peas, green lentils, green split peas. Bottom row: brown lentils, red lentils, black-eyed peas.

Red lentils have long been a mainstay in India and have become popular in the West only recently. They are tiny, salmon-pink lentils that have been split, with the dark hull removed. Red lentils turn yellow when cooked and break apart to form a purée.

Yellow lentils are small split lentils similar to red lentils but less often seen.

Other Legumes

A number of other legumes are also important.

Lima beans, also called *butter beans*, are flat, broad beans ranging from creamy white to pale pastel green in color, in a range of sizes from large to small. They have a starchy texture and a distinctive flavor unlike that of any of the kidney beans. Like peas, they are often harvested when they are immature and moist and eaten as a fresh vegetable.

Chickpeas, also called *garbanzos* or, in Italian, *ceci* (chay chee), are round, hard, yellow-brown beans about twice the size of peas and best known as the main ingredient in hummus (p. 762). They stay firm and whole when cooked and have a nutty flavor. Dried chickpeas are also ground into flour.

Fava beans are broad, flat beans, the matured dried form of the vegetable discussed on page 517. The brilliant green of the immature vegetable turns a creamy brown color when the bean is dried. The skin of the dried fava is tough and the texture is starchy.

Soybeans are one of the world's most important bean crops because of their high protein content as well as their rich oil content. Fresh soybeans are used as a vegetable (p. 531). Dried soybeans are very hard and require a long cooking time, but they are not often cooked and eaten directly. Rather, they are used to make a variety of other foods, such as soy sauce, soybean paste or *miso*, and tofu or bean curd. These products are discussed in Chapter 20.

Mung beans are small, round beans with a dark green skin and white interior. They are often sprouted to make the bean sprouts widely used in Chinese cooking. As dried legumes, they are available whole or hulled and split. The split form has a much shorter cooking time. Split mung beans break apart when cooked to make a purée. Mung beans belong to the same family as pigeon peas and black-eyed peas.

Adzuki beans are small, oval beans with a thick red skin. They are used primarily in Asian cooking in sweet as well as savory dishes.

Dal, or *dhal*, is the generic term in India for dried legume. Legumes used in Indian cuisine include *moong dal* (mung bean), *masoor dal* (red lentil), *urad dal* (a tiny, white split lentil), and *chana* (chickpea).

COOKING LEGUMES

Because dried beans, peas, and lentils are dry and hard, they must be rehydrated—that is, they must absorb water—in order to be made edible. Thus, the primary cooking method used to prepare dried legumes is simmering. Once the beans are cooked and tender, they can be finished in a variety of ways. The recipes in this section give a sample of ways to prepare legumes. Additional recipes are included in Chapter 9 ("Soups") and Chapter 21 ("Salads and Salad Dressings").

Procedure for Preparing Dried Legumes

1. Pick over to remove any foreign particles and rinse well.
2. Soak overnight in 3 times their volume of water. (Split peas and some lentils do not require soaking. Check package directions.)
3. Drain the beans. Place them in a pot and add fresh cold water to cover by 1–2 inches (2½–5 cm).
4. Bring to a boil. Reduce heat and simmer, covered, until tender. Do not boil, or the vegetables may toughen. Some beans require up to 3 hours of simmering.
5. Check texture for doneness. A properly cooked bean is soft and creamy in texture, not hard or grainy. Unless a purée or soup is desired, kidney beans should remain intact, not cooked so long that they are falling apart. Other peas and beans will form a purée or remain whole, depending on the type.
6. If you forget to soak beans overnight, an alternative method can be used. Put the beans in a cooking pot with 3 times their volume of cold water. Bring to a boil. When water just starts to boil, cover tightly and remove from the heat. Let stand 1 hour. Then proceed with step 3 above.

Baked Beans, New England Style

Portion: 20   Portion size: 4½ oz (125 g)

U.S.	Metric	Ingredients
2 lb	900 g	Dried beans, navy or Great Northern
		Bouquet garni:
1	1	Bay leaf
6–8	6–8	Parsley stems
¼ tsp	1 mL	Dried thyme
		A few celery tops
1 cup	250 mL	Molasses
2 oz	60 g	Brown sugar
1 tbsp	15 mL	Dry mustard
1 tbsp	15 mL	Salt
8 oz	225 g	Salt pork, medium dice

Per serving:
Calories, 290; Protein, 10 g; Fat, 10 g (31% cal.); Cholesterol, 10 mg; Carbohydrates, 41 g; Fiber, 7 g; Sodium, 520 mg.

■ Procedure

1. Soak the beans overnight in enough water to cover by 2 in. (5 cm.).
2. Place the beans and liquid in a pot and add the bouquet garni. Bring to a boil and skim foam. Reduce heat to a simmer. Cover and simmer 45 minutes–1 hour or until beans are just tender but not soft. Add more water if necessary during cooking.
3. Drain the beans, reserving the cooking liquid. Discard the bouquet garni.
4. Mix together the molasses, brown sugar, dry mustard, salt, and 1 qt (1 L) of the bean cooking liquid. If there is not enough bean liquid, add water to make up the difference.
5. Mix the beans, molasses mixture, and salt pork in a 4-qt (4-L) pot or deep baking pan.
6. Bake, covered, at 300°F (150°C) for 2–2½ hours. Add more liquid if necessary during baking.

VARIATIONS

Michigan Baked Beans
Reduce molasses to ¼ cup (60 mL) and add 2 cups (500 mL) tomato sauce or tomato purée.

Frijoles de la Olla (Mexican Pinto Beans)

Portions: 16–20   Portion size: 4 oz (125 g)

U.S.	Metric	Ingredients
1½ lb	750 g	Dried pinto beans or pink beans
3 qt	3 L	Water, cold (see note)
6 oz	175 g	Onion, sliced thin
1–2	1–2	Garlic cloves, chopped
1	1	Jalapeño or other green chile, chopped (optional)
2 oz	60 g	Lard or rendered pork fat
2 tsp	10 ml	Salt

Per serving:
Calories, 170; Protein, 8 g; Fat, 4 g (20% cal.); Cholesterol, 5 mg; Carbohydrates, 27 g; Fiber, 9 g; Sodium, 290 mg.

Note: The beans may be soaked overnight, if desired (although many Mexican cooking authorities feel that the results are not as good). If they are soaked, reduce the water for cooking to 1½ pt (750 mL).

■ Procedure

1. Combine the beans, water, onion, garlic, and chile in a pot. Bring to a boil, reduce heat, and simmer, covered, for 1½ hours. Check the pot from time to time and add more water, if needed, to keep the beans covered.
2. Add the lard and salt. Continue to simmer until the beans are tender. Do not let the beans go dry. There should always be some broth. Add hot water if necessary.
3. The beans will hold refrigerated for several days.

VARIATIONS

Frijoles Refritos
For the quantity of beans in the basic recipe, make in at least 3 batches. Mash the beans coarsely. Heat 2 oz (60 g) lard in a large sauté pan. Add 2 oz (60 g) chopped onion and fry until soft, but do not brown. Add one-third of the cooked, mashed beans (about 1½ lb or 750 g, including broth) to the pan. Stir and mash the beans over heat until the beans start to dry out and pull away from the sides of the pan. Roll the mass out of the pan like an omelet. Sprinkle with grated cheese (mild cheddar or Monterey jack) and serve with tortilla chips.

Vegetarian Pinto Beans
Omit the lard or pork fat from the basic recipe.

White Beans, Bretonne Style

Yield: about 6 lb (3 kg)   Portions: 20   Portion size: 5 oz (150 g)

U.S.	Metric	Ingredients
2 lb	1 kg	Dried white beans
1	1	Carrot, small
1 stem	1 stem	Celery
1	1	Onion, small, peeled
		Sachet (tied in cheesecloth):
1	1	Bay leaf
6–8	6–8	Parsley stems
3–4	3–4	Peppercorns
1	1	Clove
pinch	pinch	Thyme
4 oz	125 g	Butter
8 oz	250 g	Onion, diced
2	2	Garlic cloves, chopped
1 lb	500 g	Canned tomatoes, with juice, coarsely chopped
as needed	as needed	Pan juices from roast lamb (optional; see note)
to taste	to taste	Salt
to taste	to taste	Pepper

■ P r o c e d u r e

1. Soak the beans overnight in cold water.
2. Drain the beans and place in a pot with enough water to cover by 1 in. (2.5 cm). Add the carrot, celery, onion, and sachet. Simmer until the beans are tender but not soft or broken (1–3 hours, depending on the beans). Drain but save the liquid. Discard the vegetables and sachet.
3. Heat the butter in a large saucepot or brazier. Sauté the onion and garlic until soft. Add the tomatoes and cook a few minutes to reduce liquid.
4. Add the beans to this mixture and stir carefully. Simmer until heated through and flavors are blended. If too dry, add some of the bean cooking liquid. Add pan drippings, if you are using them. Season to taste.

Note: This preparation is often served with roast leg of lamb or other lamb roast. If so, the pan drippings may be used to flavor the beans.

Per serving:
Calories, 200; Protein, 11 g; Fat, 5 g (22% cal.); Cholesterol, 10 mg; Carbohydrates, 29 g; Fiber, 7 g; Sodium, 90 mg.

Black Bean Cakes with Salsa

Yield: 20 cakes, 2 oz (60 g) each   Portions: 10   Portion size: 2 cakes, 1½ fl oz (45 mL) salsa

U.S.	Metric	Ingredients
1 fl oz	30 mL	Olive oil
1 lb	500 g	Onion, cut brunoise
2–4	2–4	Garlic cloves, chopped
1–2	1–2	Jalapeño peppers, seeded and cut brunoise
2 tsp	10 mL	Ground cumin
2 lb	1 kg	Cooked black beans (see note)
1 tsp	5 mL	Dried oregano
to taste	to taste	Salt
to taste	to taste	Pepper
3 fl oz	100 mL	Olive oil
1 pt	450 mL	Salsa Cruda (p. 191)

■ P r o c e d u r e

1. Heat the olive oil in a sauté pan over moderately low heat.
2. Add the onions and garlic and sweat until very soft. Do not brown.
3. Add the jalapeño and ground cumin. Cook slowly another few minutes.
4. Add the beans and oregano. Cook until heated through.
5. Transfer the mixture to a food processor and process to form a coarse purée. The mixture should be thick enough to hold its shape but not too dry. If necessary, moisten with a little water.
6. Taste and adjust the seasoning with salt and pepper.
7. Divide the mixture into 2-oz (60-g) portions. Form into small, flat cakes.
8. Brown the cakes lightly on both sides in hot olive oil in a sauté pan. They will be very soft; handle carefully.
9. Serve 2 cakes per portion with 1½ fl oz (45 mL) salsa.

Per serving:
Calories, 260; Protein, 9 g; Fat, 12 g (41% cal.); Cholesterol, 0 mg; Carbohydrates, 30 g; Fiber, 9 g; Sodium, 180 mg.

Note: Canned black beans may be used, but they should be drained and rinsed.

Lentils in Cream

Yield: 3 lb 12 oz (1.8 kg)   Portions: 12   Portion size: 5 oz (150 g)

U.S.	Metric	Ingredients		Procedure
1 lb 4 oz	600 g	Small green lentils	1.	Blanch the lentils and drain.
7 oz	200 g	Carrots, cut in large chunks	2.	Return to the pan and cover with enough cold water to cover by at least 2 in. (5 cm).
7 oz	200 g	Onion, cut in large chunks	3.	Add the carrot, onion, celery, bacon, garlic, and bouquet garni.
7 oz	200 g	Celery, cut in large chunks		
7 oz	200 g	Bacon	4.	Simmer until tender but still firm. Drain, reserving the liquid. Discard the vegetables, bacon, and bouquet garni.
6	6	Garlic cloves		
1	1	Bouquet garni		
2 oz	60 g	Onion, cut brunoise	5.	Sweat the onion, carrot, and celery in the clarified butter.
2 oz	60 g	Carrot, cut brunoise	6.	Add the lentils along with 10 fl oz (300 mL) of the cooking liquid. Bring to a boil and cook for a few minutes.
1 oz	30 g	Celery, cut brunoise		
1 oz	30 g	Clarified butter	7.	Add the cream, return to a simmer, and stir in the butter, then the mustard and chopped parsley. Season to taste.
4 fl oz	125 mL	Heavy cream, hot		
2 fl oz	60 g	Butter		
2 tbsp	30 mL	Dijon mustard		
1 oz	30 g	Chopped parsley		
to taste	to taste	Salt		
to taste	to taste	Pepper		

Per serving:
Calories, 320; Protein, 12 g; Fat 20 g (54% cal.); Cholesterol, 40 mg; Carbohydrates, 26 g; Fiber, 12 g; Sodium, 200 mg.

Purée of Flageolet Beans with Garlic

Yield: 4 lb (2 kg)   Portions: 16   Portion size: 4 oz (125 g)

U.S.	Metric	Ingredients		Procedure
1½ lb	750 g	Dried flageolet beans	1.	Rinse and drain the beans. Soak overnight in enough cold water to cover by several inches (5 cm or more).
1	1	Sachet (p. 152)		
3 pt	1.5 L	Water or light vegetable stock	2.	Drain. Add the sachet and the water or stock. Simmer until the beans are tender, about 45 minutes. Discard the sachet.
6–8	6–8	Garlic cloves, peeled and chopped	3.	Mash the chopped garlic with the salt.
			4.	Drain the beans. Place the beans in a food processor with the garlic and olive oil. Blend to a purée.
2 tsp	10 mL	Salt		
12 fl oz	375 mL	Olive oil	5.	With the motor running, pour in the lemon juice. The purée should have the consistency of soft mashed potatoes.
3 fl oz	90 mL	Lemon juice		
to taste	to taste	Additional salt	6.	Adjust seasoning to taste with salt and pepper if necessary.
to taste	to taste	Pepper	7.	Serve warm as a vegetable accompaniment (reheat as necessary) or cold as a dip.

VARIATIONS

Other beans, such as white kidney beans and pinto beans, may be substituted.

Flageolet Beans with Wilted Arugula
Cook the beans as in the basic recipe but do not purée. Use 3 cloves garlic and 4 fl oz (125 mL) olive oil. Chop the garlic and sauté in the olive oil. Add 1 lb (500 g) coarsely chopped arugula and sauté just until wilted. Add this mixture to the drained, hot beans. Season to taste.

Per serving:
Calories, 320; Protein, 9 g; Fat, 22 g (60% cal.); Cholesterol, 0 mg; Carbohydrates, 24 g; Fiber, 8 g; Sodium, 290 mg.

Pasta e Fagioli

Portions: 12   Portion size: 8 fl oz (240 mL)

U.S	Metric	Ingredients
12 oz	360 g	Dried cranberry beans
4 fl oz	120 mL	Olive oil
6 oz	180 g	Pancetta (unsmoked Italian-style bacon), ground or chopped fine
6 oz	180 g	Onion, chopped fine
3 oz	90 g	Carrot, chopped fine
3 oz	90 g	Celery, chopped fine
4	4	Fresh sage leaves, chopped
1 tbsp	15 mL	Fresh rosemary, chopped
3 tbsp	45 mL	Chopped fresh parsley
2½ qt	2.5 L	Water
1 oz	30 g	Tomato paste
to taste	to taste	Salt
1 lb	450 g	Dried fettuccine, broken
12 tsp	60 mL	Grated parmesan cheese
3 fl oz	90 mL	Olive oil

Per serving:
Calories, 440; Protein, 15 g; Fat, 22 g (44% cal.); Cholesterol, 10 mg; Carbohydrates, 48 g; Fiber, 9 g; Sodium, 350 mg.

Note: If cranberry beans are not available, use white kidney beans.

■ P r o c e d u r e

1. Clean and rinse the beans. Soak in cold water overnight.

2. Heat the olive oil in a heavy saucepot over moderate heat. Add the pancetta and cook, stirring from time to time, until crisp. Remove with a slotted spoon, leaving the fat in the pot.

3. Add the onion, carrot, celery, sage, rosemary, and parsley to the pot. Sweat in the reserved fat just until the vegetables start to become tender.

4. Drain the beans and add them to the pot. At the same time, add the water. Bring to a boil, reduce heat, and simmer until the beans are almost tender, about 45 minutes.

5. Add the tomato paste. Continue to simmer until the beans are very tender.

6. Remove about half of the soup and pass it through a food mill to purée it. Return it to the pot with the rest of the soup.

7. Season to taste with salt.

8. At this point the soup should be thick but still liquid enough to cook the pasta when it is added. If necessary, add a little more water.

9. Add the pasta and simmer until it is tender.

10. Stir in the reserved pancetta.

11. Serve each portion topped with 1 teaspoon (5 mL) cheese and a drizzle of olive oil.

Pasta e Fagioli

Hoppin' John

Portions: 12   Portion size: 6 oz (180 g)

U.S.	Metric	Ingredients
1 lb	450 g	Dried black-eyed peas
8 oz	225 g	Bacon, chopped
8 oz	225 g	Onion, chopped fine
½ tsp	2 mL	Red pepper flakes
as needed	as needed	Water or chicken stock
1 lb	450 g	Long-grain rice
to taste	to taste	Salt

Per serving:
Calories, 210; Protein, 9 g; Fat, 2 g (9% cal.); Cholesterol, 5 mg; Carbohydrates, 37 g; Fiber, 5 g; Sodium, 100 mg.

■ P r o c e d u r e

1. Clean, soak, and cook the peas according to the procedure for cooking dried legumes (p. 610). Drain. Reserve the cooking liquid.

2. Render the bacon in a heavy saucepot, cooking until crisp.

3. Remove the bacon with a slotted spoon and set aside.

4. Add the onion and the red pepper to the pot. Cook until the onion is soft.

5. Measure the reserved cooking liquid from step 1. Add enough water or chicken stock to measure 2 qt (2 L).

6. Add the liquid, the cooked beans, and the rice to the pot. Bring to a boil, reduce heat, and cover. Cook at a low simmer until the rice is tender, about 15 minutes or a little longer.

7. Remove from the heat and let stand, covered, for 5 minutes.

8. Fluff the rice with a fork while stirring in the reserved bacon, and salt to taste.

Masoor Dal (Red Lentils with Spices)

Portions: 12   Portion size: 8 fl oz (240 mL)

U.S.	Metric	Ingredients
1 lb 4 oz	575 g	Red lentils
2½ qt	2.5 L	Water
4	4	Garlic cloves, chopped
4 thin slices	4 thin slices	Fresh ginger root
2 tbsp	30 mL	Chopped fresh cilantro
2 tsp	10 mL	Turmeric
½ tsp	2 mL	Cayenne
1½ fl oz	45 mL	Lemon juice
to taste	to taste	Salt
2 fl oz	6 mL	Vegetable oil
2 tsp	10 mL	Cumin seed

Per serving:
Calories, 200; Protein, 12 g; Fat, 5 g (21% cal.); Cholesterol, 0 mg; Carbohydrates, 30 g; Fiber, 8 g; Sodium, 20 mg.

■ P r o c e d u r e

1. Sort, rinse, and drain the lentils.

2. Put the lentils and water in a saucepot. Bring to a boil. Skim off any froth that rises to the top.

3. Add the garlic, ginger, cilantro, turmeric, and cayenne. Simmer until the lentils are very tender and falling apart, about 1½ hours.

4. Add the lemon juice and salt to taste.

5. To finish the dal, heat the oil in a small sauté pan. When it is very hot, add the cumin seed and cook a few seconds, until the cumin is aromatic.

6. Pour the oil and seeds into the dal and stir in.

Cranberry Beans with Asparagus

Portions: 12   Portion size: 5 oz (150 g)

U.S.	Metric	Ingredients	■ **P r o c e d u r e**
1½ lb	700 g	Asparagus	1. Peel and trim the bottom of the asparagus stalks (see p. 516). 2. Cook the asparagus in boiling, salted water until just tender. Drain, cool in cold water, and drain again. 3. Cut the asparagus into pieces about 1½ inches (4 cm) long.
2 fl oz	60 mL	Olive oil	4. Heat the olive oil in a sauté pan over moderate heat.
4 oz	125 g	Shallots, chopped fine	5. Add the shallots and garlic. Cook until tender and lightly browned.
¼ oz	7 g	Garlic, chopped fine	
3 lb	1.4 kg	Cranberry beans, cooked or canned, drained	6. Add the beans to the pan. Toss over heat until the beans are hot. 7. Add the asparagus and herbs. Heat another minute or two, until the asparagus is hot.
2 tbsp	30 mL	Chopped fresh parsley	8. Add salt to taste.
1 tbsp	15 mL	Chopped fresh basil	
1 fl oz	30 mL	Red wine vinegar	9. Just before serving, stir in the vinegar and the cheese.
⅓ cup	80 mL	Grated parmesan cheese	

Per serving:
Calories, 180; Protein, 10 g; Fat, 5 g (24% cal.); Cholesterol, 0 mg;
Carbohydrates, 25 g; Fiber, 10 g; Sodium, 50 mg.

Cranberry Beans with Asparagus

Chickpeas in Spicy Tomato Sauce

Portions: 10   Portion size: 5 oz (150 g)

U.S.	Metric	Ingredients	Procedure
8 oz	250 g	Onion, chopped	1. Put the onion, garlic, ginger, cardamom, cloves, cinnamon, pepper, and cayenne in a blender. Blend to a smooth purée. If necessary, add a little water to help the blending.
1 oz	30 g	Garlic, chopped	
1 oz	30 g	Fresh ginger root, peeled and chopped	2. Heat the oil in a sauté pan over moderate heat.
½ tsp	2 mL	Ground cardamom	3. Add the onion and spice purée to the hot oil. (*Caution:* Hold your face away from the pan as you do this to avoid the onion fumes.)
½ tsp	2 mL	Ground cloves	
1 tsp	5 mL	Cinnamon	
1 tsp	5 mL	Black pepper	4. Cook over moderate heat, stirring, until the mixture is reduced to a thick, golden-brown paste.
½ tsp	2 mL	Cayenne	
2 fl oz	60 mL	Vegetable oil	
1½ lb	750 g	Tomatoes, canned, with their juice	5. Purée the tomatoes and their juice in a blender or food processor.
3 lb	1.5 kg	Chickpeas, cooked or canned, drained	6. Stir the tomatoes into the onion paste.
to taste	to taste	Salt	7. Simmer, stirring regularly, until reduced by half to form a thick tomato paste.
			8. Add the chickpeas. Stir over heat until the chickpeas are hot.
			9. Add salt to taste.

Per serving::
Calories, 300; Protein, 13 g; Fat, 9 g (26% cal.); Cholesterol, 0 mg;
Carbohydrates, 44 g; Fiber, 12 g; Sodium, 100 mg.

GRAINS

Wheat and rice are without doubt the world's two most important grains. Unlike rice, wheat is rarely cooked and eaten as a whole grain. Rather, its primary use is to be ground into flour for making breads and other baked goods. The use of grain flours in baked goods is the subject matter of the last seven chapters of this book. In this section, we look at other uses of grains in food service kitchens.

TYPES OF GRAINS

Grains are the edible seeds of various members of the grass family. Each seed consists of four parts:

- The husk—an inedible fibrous outer layer that is removed during processing
- The endosperm—the starchy mass that forms most of the kernel
- The bran—a tough but edible layer covering the endosperm
- The germ—the tiny embryo that forms the new plant when the seed sprouts

A product labeled *whole grain* consists of the endosperm, bran, and germ. The grain may be polished or milled to remove the bran and germ. White rice and other polished grains are only the endosperm.

Although rice appears on menus more often than other grain starches, several other grains can also be served as side dishes to add variety to your menu. The most popular of these grains are described following the section on rice.

Top row: basmati rice, glutinous rice, plain long-grain rice. Bottom row: Japanese short-grain rice, jasmine rice, arborio rice.

Top row: true wild rice, wehani rice, cultivated wild rice. Bottom row: parboiled or converted rice, brown long-grain rice.

Rice

Regular milled white rice has been milled to remove the outer bran coating. This process removes some vitamins and minerals, but it produces a white, lighter-textured product that most people prefer. White rice appears in several forms:

> **Enriched rice** has received a coating of vitamins to compensate for some of the nutrients lost in milling.
>
> **Short-grain** and **medium-grain** rice have small, round kernels that become sticky when cooked. They are used for such preparations as rice pudding and rice molds. In addition, the regular boiled rice used in Japanese cuisine for everyday eating and for making sushi is short-grain rice.
>
> **Long-grain** rice has long, slender grains that stay separate and fluffy when properly cooked. It is used for side dishes, entrées, casseroles, and so on.

Parboiled or **converted** rice is a specially processed long-grain rice. It has been partially cooked under steam pressure, redried, and then milled or polished. This process results in a higher vitamin and mineral content.

Parboiled rice is the most widely used in food service. The grains stay firm, separate, and light, and the product holds well in the steam table without becoming mushy or sticky. However, the flavor and texture are not like those of regular long-grain rice, so it is not always preferred by all customers.

Converted rice takes slightly more liquid and time to cook.

Instant rice has been precooked and dried so it can be prepared quickly. It does not hold well after cooking, and the grains quickly lose their shape and become mushy.

Brown rice has had the bran layer left on, giving it a light brown color, a slightly coarse, crunchy texture, and nutty flavor. Brown rice is available as short, medium, or long grain. Brown rice takes about twice as long to cook as white rice.

Arborio rice is one of several Italian varieties of a type of short-grain rice that is essential for making the highest-quality risotto (see p. 623). It is the variety most often found here and the one specified in recipes. Two other varieties used for risotto but less widely available are *carnaroli* and *vialone nano*.

Basmati rice is an extra-long-grain rice widely used in India and surrounding countries. It has a distinctive nutty flavor. Brown basmati rice is also available.

Jasmine rice is a long-grain white rice from Thailand and other parts of Southeast Asia. It is very fragrant, a little like basmati rice but more delicate or floral.

Wehani rice is another aromatic rice, red in color, with a rich, earthy flavor.

Wild pecan rice is a cultivated, not wild, long-grain rice from Louisiana. It is aromatic, with a nutty flavor, from which it gets the name *pecan*.

Glutinous rice, also called **sticky rice**, is a sweet-tasting short-grain rice that becomes quite sticky and chewy when cooked. It is used for a number of special dishes, including desserts, in Chinese and Japanese cuisines. It is often cooked by soaking and steaming rather than boiling (see the recipe on page 668). Contrary to what you may read elsewhere, however, it is not the rice used for sushi, which is made with regular Japanese short-grain rice.

Wild rice is not a type of rice but an unrelated grain, so it is discussed with specialty grains below.

Corn

Unlike other grains, which have a husk covering each seed, **corn** has a set of husks covering the entire seed head, or ear. Also unlike other grains, corn is eaten as a fresh vegetable, although different varieties are grown as grain and as a vegetable.

Corn as a grain is not often cooked whole. More often, it is ground into **cornmeal** and cooked into a porridge or used in baked goods. *Meal* can be defined as a coarsely ground grain, as distinguished from *flour*, which is finely ground grain. Common cornmeal is yellow or white, depending on the variety of corn it is made from.

Polenta is Italian-style cornmeal. Polenta has become popular in North America in recent years. Its preparation and uses are explained and illustrated on pages 632–633.

Hominy is corn that has been treated with lye. When it is cracked into a coarse meal, it becomes **grits**, popular in the southern United States and wherever the foods of the South are appreciated. Hominy in whole-grain form is known in Mexican cuisine as **pozole** (poh soh leh). It requires several hours of simmering.

Blue corn, usually available as blue cornmeal, is derived from early varieties of corn grown by Native Americans.

Wheat

The most common use for wheat is to be made into flour. The milling process for white flour separates the bran and germ. **Wheat germ** and **wheat bran** can be purchased separately. They are usually used as additions to baked goods and some other dishes to enrich their nutritional content and to add flavor interest.

Whole wheat grains that have been cut into smaller pieces are called **cracked wheat**. This product is often added to breads and also can be cooked like pilaf (see p. 623).

Whole wheatberries are the whole grain minus the hulls. They are generally cooked by boiling or simmering, but cooking time can be several hours. Soaking overnight reduces the cooking time to about 1 hour.

Bulgur is a type of cracked wheat that has been partially cooked or parched. It is usually available in coarse, medium, and fine granulations. Its cooking time is shorter than regular cracked wheat and, in fact, the fine granulations can be prepared simply by pouring boiling water over them and letting them stand for ½ hour. This type of bulgur is often served cold, mixed with lemon juice, olive oil, chopped scallions, and fresh herbs.

Green wheat is wheat that is harvested while it is immature and dried. It can be cooked like cracked wheat.

Couscous (koose koose) is not actually a grain, although it resembles one. It is made from semolina wheat, a variety of high-protein wheat, and is sort of a granular pasta. It is cooked by soaking and then steaming, using a fairly time-consuming process. **Instant couscous** is prepared simply by adding the dry product to hot or boiling water and letting it stand 5 minutes.

Top row: Egyptian green wheat, hulled whole wheatberries. Bottom row: couscous, kasha, farro.

Other Grains

Wild rice is not actually rice but is the seed of a grass native to the northern United States and Canada. The grains are long, slender, hard, and dark brown or nearly black in color. Because of its unique nutty flavor, scarcity, and high price, wild rice is considered a luxury food.

Wild rice is now widely cultivated, but the cultivated type is slightly different from that which is harvested in the wild. Grains of cultivated wild rice are generally larger and firmer, but the texture of the cooked rice is coarser and the flavor less complex. Cultivation has helped reduce the price of wild rice, however.

Farro (far oh) is a wheat-like grain that may be an ancestor of modern wheat. It has been used in the Mediterranean region for thousands of years and is still widely known in Tuscany and other parts of Italy. Farro has a flavor similar to that of wheat. It is higher in protein than wheat and can often be eaten by people who have wheat allergies. In North America, farro is known as spelt, although the Italian name is catching on. (Some sources argue that spelt and farro are different grains, but according to the International Plant Genetic Resources Institute, "the only registered varieties of farro belong to *T. spelta* or spelt."

Kamut (kah moot), like farro, is an ancient relative of wheat. It is similar to spelt in composition and flavor.

Buckwheat is technically not a grain because it is the seed not of a grass but of a plant with branched stems and broad, arrow-shaped leaves. Whole buckwheat is often ground into flour. When the grains are crushed into coarse pieces, they are called buckwheat groats and can be cooked like rice. Toasted buckwheat is called kasha. The toasting gives it a nutty flavor. Kasha is popular in Eastern European and Jewish cooking. Kasha is also cooked like pilaf (p. 623).

Barley is usually purchased as pearled barley, which has been milled to remove the outer bran layers. It is commonly used in soups, but it can also be cooked by the pilaf method and served like rice, although it has a longer cooking time.

Top row: quinoa, triticale, pearl barley. Bottom row: blue cornmeal, pozole, bulgur wheat.

Oats are most familiar in North America as a breakfast food. **Steel-cut oats** are whole grains that have been cut into small pieces, somewhat resembling cracked wheat. They are usually cooked as a porridge. **Rolled oats** are whole grains that have been steamed until soft and then flattened between rollers. This processing reduces their cooking time considerably. If they are cooked and not just softened during the steaming process, they become instant oats. These need no additional cooking, only reconstituting with boiling water.

Millet is a small, round yellow grain that is an important food source in much of Africa and Asia. It has a high protein content and a mild flavor. Millet is often used as bird seed in North America. It can be cooked like rice.

Quinoa (keen wah) is a grain native to the South American Andes that has only recently become an occasional feature of North American menus. Quinoa is very high in good-quality protein and lower in carbohydrates than other grains. It is a tiny, round grain with an ivory color and a mild, delicate flavor. When cooked, the germ of the grain unwinds, making it look as though each grain has a tail. Before cooking, quinoa must be washed and rinsed well to remove a bitter coating that occurs naturally on the grain.

Triticale is a high-protein hybrid of wheat and rye. It is often ground into flour, but it can also be cooked whole like rice. Triticale has a nutty, sweet flavor.

Amaranth is a tiny, yellow-brown seed with a somewhat spicy, nutty flavor when cooked. It contains high-quality protein and thus is useful in vegetarian diets.

STORING AND HANDLING GRAINS

Store raw grains at room temperature in a dark, dry place and in a tightly sealed container to keep out moisture and insects. Milled grains such as white rice that have had the germ removed will keep for many months. Whole grains are somewhat more perishable because the fat content of the germ can become rancid.

Depending on the source, whole grains may need to be picked over like dried beans (see p. 610) to remove foreign matter such as tiny stones or bits of soil. In addition, whole grains should usually be washed and drained before cooking.

Rice, our most commonly cooked grain, should be rinsed in cold water before boiling or steaming. This removes the excess starch that makes rice sticky. The rice industry recommends *not* washing rice because it removes some of the vitamin coating of enriched rice. But that's probably a small price to pay for a more attractive product. This is a decision you will have to make in your own operation.

Do not buy low-grade rice, which tends to be dirty, or rice that has been coated with talc.

Rice cooked by the pilaf method (p. 623) does not need to be washed (unless it is dirty) because the fat coating each kernel helps keep the grains separate and reduces stickiness.

Converted rice and instant rice do not need to be washed.

COOKING GRAINS

Most grains are cooked by one of three cooking methods: the simmering method, the pilaf method, and the risotto method.

Simmering Methods

The most common method for cooking rice and other whole grains is to place the washed grain in a heavy pot with the right amount of water or other liquid to hydrate it, bring it to a simmer, cover, and cook slowly until all the water is absorbed. The exact amount of liquid needed varies considerably, depending on these factors:

1. The type of grain, its age, and its moisture content.
2. Tightness or looseness of the cover (degree of moisture loss during cooking).
3. Desired moistness of the finished product.

Because of all these factors, it is difficult to be precise when determining how much liquid to use. It is better to add too much liquid than too little. With too little moisture, the grain will not cook to tenderness. If a little too much is added, remove the pan from the heat, keeping it tightly covered, and let it stand for a few minutes. Liquid remaining in the bottom of the pan is likely to be absorbed. If there is much excess liquid, drain it off.

A second method, called the *pasta method*, can be used. This method is called the pasta method because the item is cooked in a large quantity of water and drained. This method is good for producing separate, unsticky grains. However, some nutrients are lost in the cooking water, so chefs disagree about the value of this method.

Procedure for Simmering Rice and Other Grains

1. For whole grains, wash the grain in cold water as necessary. Drain.
2. Combine the grain with the proper amount of water or other liquid in a heavy saucepot. Bring to a boil. Stir.
3. Cover and cook over very low heat for the proper cooking time, depending on the grain.
4. Test for doneness. Cook a few additional minutes if necessary.
5. Remove from the heat. Drain excess liquid if necessary. Let stand, covered, to allow moisture to be absorbed uniformly by the grain.
6. For rice and any grains that stick together, fluff with a fork and turn out into a hotel pan to let steam escape and stop the cooking.

Variation: Pasta Method

1. Drop the washed, drained grain into a large pot of boiling, salted water.
2. When just tender, pour into a strainer and drain well.
3. Place in a hotel pan. Cover and steam dry in oven for 5 to 10 minutes, or leave uncovered and place in a steamer to steam dry.

Simmering Meals and Cereals

Procedures for cooking meals and cereals such as polenta and oatmeal differ somewhat from procedures for cooking whole grains. Cracked or flaked cereals such as rolled oats consist of large particles. They are usually stirred into boiling water. Because of the size of the particles, there is little danger of lumping.

Boiled and Steamed Rice

Yield: about 3 lb (1.4 kg)   *Portions:* 10   *Portion size:* 4½–5 oz (140 g)
                                         12   4 oz (115 g)
                                         16   3 oz (90 g)

Proportions	U.S.	Metric
Regular long-grain white rice		
Rice	1 lb	475 g
Water	1 qt	1 L
Salt	1 tsp	5 mL
Butter	1 oz	30 g
Parboiled long-grain rice		
Rice	1 lb	475 g
Water	4½ cups	1.1 L
Salt	1 tsp	5 mL
Butter	1 oz	30 g
Medium-grain white rice		
Rice	18 oz	525 g
Water	1 qt	1 L
Salt	1 tsp	5 mL
Butter	1 oz	30 g
Brown rice		
Rice	12 oz	350 g
Water	1 qt	1 L
Salt	1 tsp	5 mL
Butter	1 oz	30 g

Per 4¹/2–5 oz (140 g) serving:
Calories 200; Protein, 4 g; Fat, 2.5 g (12% cal.); Cholesterol, 5 mg;
Carbohydrates, 39 g; Fiber 1 g; Sodium, 260 mg.

■ P r o c e d u r e s

Rangetop

1. Wash rice in cold water until water is clear (optional step; see pp. 620–621 for note on washing rice).
2. Combine all ingredients in a heavy pot. Bring to boil. Stir. Cover and cook over very low heat.

   Cooking times:
   Long- and medium-grain: 15–20 minutes
   Parboiled: 20–25 minutes
   Brown: 40–45 minutes

3. Test rice for doneness. Cook 2–4 minutes more if necessary.
4. Turn rice out into a hotel pan. Fluff with fork or slotted spoon to let steam escape.

Oven

1. Wash rice in cold water until water is clear (optional step; see pp. 620–621 for note on washing rice).
2. Bring salted water to boil. Combine all ingredients in a shallow steamer pan. Cover with foil or tight lid. Place in 375°F (175°C) oven.

   Cooking times:
   Long- and medium-grain: 25 minutes
   Parboiled: 30–40 minutes
   Brown: 1 hour

3. Test rice for doneness. Bake 2–4 minutes more if necessary.
4. Fluff rice with fork or slotted spoon to let steam escape.

Steamer

1. Wash rice in cold water until water is clear (optional step; see pp. 620–621 for note on washing rice).
2. Bring salted water to boil. Combine all ingredients in a shallow steamer pan. Place uncovered pan in steamer for cooking time recommended by equipment manufacturer.

   Cooking times:
   Depend on type of steamer.

3. Test rice for doneness. Steam 2–4 minutes more if necessary.
4. Fluff rice with fork or slotted spoon to let steam escape.

Granular meals such as cornmeal can be stirred into boiling water if care is taken to add the grain slowly and stir constantly and vigorously while doing so, in order to avoid lumps. See the recipe for polenta (p. 632). Alternatively, combine the meal with cold liquid, stir, and bring to a simmer while continuing to stir. Mixing the meal with cold liquid separates the granules to prevent lumping.

Procedure for Simmering Meals and Cereals

1. Measure the correct amount of liquid into a pot and bring to a boil.
2. Measure the correct amount of meal or cereal.
3. Add the cereal slowly to the boiling liquid, stirring constantly.
4. Stir until some thickening takes place. Depending on the grain, continue to stir constantly, or stir only occasionally. Some cereals, such as oatmeal, become gummy with excessive stirring.
5. Reduce heat to a slow simmer and cook to desired doneness and consistency.
6. To prevent drying, keep the cooked grain covered until serving.

Variation: Simmering Meals and Granular Cereals

The procedure is the same as above, except the cereal is mixed with cold liquid. This separates the grains to prevent lumping. Place the mixture in a pot, bring to a simmer, and cook as in the basic procedure.

The Pilaf Method

The pilaf method is equivalent to braising. The grain is first sautéed in fat, then cooked in liquid—preferably in the oven for uniform heating—until the liquid is absorbed (see Figure 19.1). The fat helps keep the grains separate and adds flavor.

It is normal to measure rice by volume when making pilaf, as the proportions are based on volume measure. One pint of raw rice weighs about 14 ounces, or 1 pound measures about 2¼ cups (1 liter weighs about 875 grams, or 1 kilogram measures 1.15 liters). Regarding exact measurements, see the note following the pilaf recipe.

Procedure for Cooking Grain by the Pilaf Method

1. Heat the desired fat (such as butter or olive oil) in a heavy pan. Add chopped onion or other aromatic vegetable, if desired, and sauté until soft but not browned.
2. Add the grain. Stir to coat the grains with fat.
3. Cook the grain in the fat, stirring, to toast the grain lightly.
4. Add the proper amount of hot liquid.
5. Bring to a simmer, stirring occasionally.
6. Cover tightly. Cook on the stovetop or, preferably, in an oven, for the correct length of time, depending on the grain.
7. Remove from the heat and let stand, covered, to allow the moisture to be absorbed uniformly by the grain.

The Risotto Method

Risotto is a classic Italian preparation made by a special procedure that is like neither the boiling method nor the pilaf method. After sautéing the rice, add a small amount of stock or other liquid and stir until the liquid is absorbed. Repeat this procedure until the rice is cooked but still firm. Risotto should be served quickly, as it does not hold well. The finished product has a creamy consistency due to the starch that is cooked out of the rice. The grains are not fluffy and separate.

The word *risotto* comes from the Italian word *riso*, meaning "rice." Other grains can be cooked using the same method, although strictly speaking they should not be called *risotto*. In Italy, farro cooked by the risotto method is called *farotto*, and orzo pasta cooked this way is called *orzotto*. In the English-speaking world, however, the word *risotto* is more likely to be understood and is often used on menus, but with the grain specified if any type other than rice is used.

Procedure for Cooking Grain by the Risotto Method

1. Heat the desired fat (such as butter or olive oil) in a heavy pan. Add chopped onion or other aromatic vegetable, if desired, and sauté until soft but not browned.

2. Add the grain. Stir to coat the grains with fat.

3. Cook the grain in the fat, stirring, to toast the grain lightly.

4. Add a small amount of boiling liquid. Cook slowly, stirring, until the liquid is absorbed by the grain.

5. Add a second small quantity of liquid and repeat the procedure.

6. Continue adding a small quantity of liquid at a time, stirring constantly, and waiting until the liquid is absorbed before adding more.

7. Stop adding liquid when the grain is tender but still firm. It should be moist and creamy but not runny.

Figure 19.1 Making rice pilaf.

(a) Sweat the onion or shallot.

(b) Add the rice and sauté briefly.

(c) Pour in the hot stock or other liquid.

(d) Bring to a boil and cover. Cook at low heat on top of the stove or in the oven for the required time.

(e) The finished pilaf.

Rice Pilaf

U.S.	Metric	Ingredients
	Yield: about 3 lb (1.4 kg)	Portion: 10	Portions size: 5 oz (150 g)
		12	4 oz (125 g)
		16	3 oz (90 g)
2 oz	60 g	Butter
3 oz	90 g	Onions, fine dice
1 pt (see note)	500 mL (see note)	Long-grain rice
1½–2 pt (see note)	750 mL–1 L (see note)	Chicken stock or water, boiling
to taste	to taste	Salt

Per 5 oz (150 g) serving:
Calories, 190; Protein, 4 g; Fat, 5 g (23% cal.); Cholesterol, 15 mg; Carbohydrates, 33 g; Fiber, 1 g; Sodium, 50 mg.

Note: Rice for pilaf is measured by volume rather than by weight. Use 1½–2 times its volume in stock or water (1¾ times is the normal proportion for long-grain rice). For example, use 2 pints liquid per pint of rice if you desire a moister product or if you are using parboiled rice. Use 1½ pints liquid if you desire a drier product and if your cover is tight enough to retain most of the steam.

■ P r o c e d u r e

1. Heat the butter in a heavy saucepan. Add the onion and sauté until it begins to soften. Do not brown.

2. Add the rice, without washing. Stir over heat until the rice is completely coated with butter.

3. Pour in the boiling liquid. Return the liquid to a boil with the rice. Taste and adjust seasonings; cover tightly.

4. Place in a 350°F (175°C) oven and bake for 18–20 minutes, until liquid is absorbed and rice is dry and fluffy. Taste the rice and, if it is not done, replace in oven 3–5 minutes.

5. Turn out into a hotel pan and fluff the rice with a fork. This releases steam and prevents further cooking. Keep hot for service.

6. If desired, additional raw butter may be stirred into finished rice.

V A R I A T I O N S

Tomato Pilaf
Prepare as in basic recipe, using 12–16 oz (375–500 mL) chicken stock and 1½ lb (700 g) chopped tomatoes with juice.

Spanish Rice
Prepare like Tomato Pilaf, but use bacon fat and sauté 6 oz (175 g) diced green bell pepper, 1 crushed clove garlic, and 1 tbsp (15 mL) paprika with the onion.

Turkish Pilaf
Sauté ¼ tsp (1 mL) turmeric with the rice. To finished rice, add 4 oz (125 g) tomato concassé or drained, chopped canned tomatoes, 4 oz (125 g) cooked peas, and 4 oz (125 g) raisins (soaked and drained). Let stand 10–15 minutes before serving.

Cracked Wheat Pilaf
Prepare as in basic recipe, using cracked wheat instead of rice.

Orzo Pilaf
Prepare as in basic recipe, using orzo (rice-shaped pasta) instead of rice.

Barley Pilaf
Prepare as in basic recipe, using pearled barley instead of rice. Use 2½ pints (1.25 L) stock and bake 45 minutes.
Mushrooms are often added to barley pilaf.

Additions to Rice Pilaf

Pimiento	Peas	Ham, diced or cut julienne
Chopped nuts	Green bell pepper, diced	Raisins or currants
Celery, diced	Spinach, chopped	Water chestnuts
Carrot, diced or grated	Mushrooms	Bacon
Scallions	Olives, chopped or sliced	

Risotto alla Parmigiana

Portions: 10   Portion size: 5 oz (150 g)

U.S.	Metric	Ingredients
1 oz	30 g	Butter
1 fl oz	30 mL	Vegetable oil
1 oz	30 g	Onion, chopped fine
1 lb	450 g	Italian Arborio rice
1½ qt (approximately)	1.4 L (approximately)	Chicken stock, hot
1 oz	30 g	Butter
3 oz	90 g	Parmesan cheese, grated
to taste	to taste	Salt

Per serving:
Calories, 260; Protein, 7 g; Fat, 11 g (38% cal.); Cholesterol, 25 mg;
Carbohydrates, 34 g; Fiber, 3g; Sodium, 210 mg.

■ Procedure

1. Heat the butter and oil in a large, straight-sided sauté pan. Add the onion and sauté until soft. Do not brown.

2. Add the rice and sauté until well coated with the fat.

3. Using a 6-oz (150-mL) ladle, add one ladle of stock to the rice. Stir the rice over medium heat until the stock is absorbed and the rice is almost dry.

4. Add another ladle of stock and repeat procedure. Do not add more than one ladleful of stock at a time.

5. Stop adding stock when the rice is tender but still firm. It should be very moist and creamy, but not runny. The cooking should take about 30 minutes.

6. Remove from the heat and stir in the raw butter and parmesan cheese. Salt to taste.

VARIATIONS

Restaurant Method: Prepare basic pilaf (p. 624) using 1 lb Italian Arborio rice to 1 qt chicken stock (500 g rice to 1 L stock). To finish for service, place desired number of portions in a sauté pan and moisten with additional stock. Simmer until slightly moist and creamy, as in basic recipe. Finish with raw butter and parmesan cheese.

Risotto Milanese
Prepare as in basic recipe, but add ¼–½ tsp (1–2 mL) saffron soaked in 1 cup (200 mL) stock near the end of cooking.

Risotto with Mushrooms
Add 4–8 oz (100–200 g) mushrooms, chopped and sautéed in butter, near the end of cooking time.

Risi Bisi
Add 1 lb (450 g) cooked peas and ¼ cup (60 mL) chopped parsley to basic risotto. (This is not authentic Risi Bisi, which is considered a thick soup in Italy. However, it is similar.)

Risotto Milanese

Figure 19.2 Making risotto.

(a) Sauté the onion or shallot until soft.

(b) Add the rice. Sauté until coated with the fat.

(c) Add a ladleful of stock to the rice. Stir until it is absorbed.

(d) Continue adding stock and stirring until the rice is cooked.

(e) For Risotto Milanese, add saffron steeped in hot stock near the end of the cooking period.

(f) Finish by stirring in parmesan cheese and butter.

Basic Fried Rice

Portions: 16   Portion size: 6 oz (175 g)

U.S.	Metric	Ingredients
4 lb	1.8 kg	Cooked rice, cold
4–6 fl oz	125–175 mL	Oil
1 lb	450 g	Cooked meat (cut into shreds) or seafood (flaked or sliced)
3 oz	90 g	Scallions, sliced thin
1 lb	450 g	Vegetables (see variations), shredded or small dice
4–6 fl oz	125–175 mL	Soy sauce (optional)
to taste	to taste	Salt
4–8	4–8	Eggs, beaten

Per serving:
Calories, 280; Protein, 11 g; Fat, 10 g (33% cal); Cholesterol, 70 mg; Carbohydrates, 35 g; Fiber, 2 g; Sodium, 35 mg.

■ Procedure

1. Break up the rice to remove all lumps.

2. Divide the rice and other ingredients into two or more batches, depending on the size of the pan or wok. Do no more than 1–2 lb (0.5–1 kg) rice at one time. If you fry too much at once, it will not fry properly.

3. Heat a small amount of oil in the wok. Add the meat and stir-fry 1–2 minutes.

4. Add the scallions and stir-fry for 1 minute.

5. Add any raw vegetables and stir-fry until almost done.

6. Add the rice and stir-fry until it is hot and lightly coated with oil.

7. Add any cooked vegetables and mix in.

8. Add soy sauce, if used, and salt.

9. Add beaten egg and mix in. Stir-fry lightly to cook the egg, then serve.

V A R I A T I O N S

The quantities given in the basic recipe are only guidelines, but rice should be the predominant ingredient. You can omit the meat or fish items. For plain rice, you can omit the vegetables too.

Eggs can be omitted, or they can be added to fried rice in several other ways:

1. Remove the meat and vegetables from the pan when they are cooked. Add the egg to the pan and scramble. Add the rice, return the meat and vegetables to the pan, and continue with the recipe.

2. In step 9, push the rice to the sides of the pan. Add the egg to the well in the middle. When it starts to set, gradually mix in the rice.

3. Scramble the eggs separately and add to the rice at the end.

4. Mix the raw beaten egg with the cold cooked rice before cooking.

Suggested Ingredients

Meats: cooked pork, beef, chicken, duck, ham, bacon, Chinese sausage

Seafood: shrimp (diced or whole), crab, lobster

Vegetables: bamboo shoots, bean sprouts, celery, peas, mushrooms, onions, peppers, water chestnuts

Bulgur Pilaf with Lemon

Portions: 12   Portion size: 2½ oz (75 g)

U.S.	Metric	Ingredients
1 oz	30 g	Butter or vegetable oil
4 oz	125 g	Onion, chopped fine
8 oz	250 g	Bulgur, coarse
4 tsp	20 mL	Grated lemon zest
1½ pt	750 mL	Chicken stock or vegetable stock, hot
to taste	to taste	Salt
to taste	to taste	Pepper
4 tbsp	60 mL	Chopped chives

Per serving:
Calories, 90; Protein, 3 g; Fat, 2 g (20% cal.); Cholesterol, 25 mg; Carbohydrates, 15 g; Fiber, 4 g; Sodium, 25 g.

■ Procedure

1. Heat the butter in a saucepan. Add the chopped onion and sauté gently without browning until the onion is soft.

2. Add the bulgur. Stir to coat with butter. Stir over heat for 1 minute to lightly toast the grain.

3. Add the grated lemon zest and stir to mix.

4. Stir in the hot stock. Add salt and pepper to taste. Bring to a simmer.

5. Cover the pot and cook over low heat or in an oven heated to 350°F (175°C) until the bulgur is tender, about 20 minutes.

6. Uncover and fluff the grain with a kitchen fork. Add the chives and toss to mix in.

Arroz à la Mexicana

Portions: 16   Portion size: 4½ oz (125 g)

U.S.	Metric	Ingredients
1½ lb	700 g	Long-grain rice
3 fl oz	90 mL	Oil
12 oz	350 g	Tomato purée
3 oz	90 g	Onion, chopped fine
2	2	Garlic cloves, mashed to a paste
3½ pt	1.75 L	Chicken stock
1 tbsp	15 mL	Salt

Per serving:
Calories, 230; Protein, 4 g; Fat, 6 g (24% cal.); Cholesterol, 5 mg; Carbohydrates, 39 g; Fiber, 1 g; Sodium, 440 mg.

■ Procedure

1. Rinse the rice well to remove excess starch. Soak in cold water for at least 30 minutes. Drain well.
2. Heat the oil in a pot and add the rice. Stir over moderate heat until it begins to brown lightly.
3. Add the tomato purée, onion, and garlic. Cook until the mixture is dry. Be careful not to let it burn.
4. Add the chicken stock and salt. Stir. Simmer, uncovered, over medium heat until most of the liquid has been absorbed.
5. Cover, turn the heat to very low, and cook for 5–10 minutes, until the rice is tender.
6. Remove from the heat and let it stand, without removing the cover, for 15–30 minutes before serving.

VARIATION

Arroz Verde

Omit the tomato purée. Purée in a blender the onion and garlic along with the following: 6 fl oz (175 mL) water, 3 tbsp (45 mL) chopped fresh cilantro leaves, ¾ cup (45 g or 200 mL) chopped parsley, and 3 oz (90 g) green chiles (or part green chiles and part green bell peppers). Use this purée in place of the tomato purée. Reduce the quantity of stock to 3 pt (1.5 mL). You may use water instead of stock.

Arroz à la Mexicana

 ## Barley with Wild Mushrooms and Ham

Portions: 10   Portion size: 3½ oz (110 g)

U.S.	Metric	Ingredients
1 oz	30 g	Dried porcini mushrooms
4 fl oz	125 mL	Water, hot
1 fl oz	30 mL	Oil
4 oz	125 g	Onions, small dice
4 oz	125 g	Celery, small dice
10 oz	300 g	Barley
1 pt 4 fl oz	600 mL	Brown stock, chicken stock, or vegetable broth
4 oz	125 g	Cooked ham, small dice
to taste	to taste	Salt

Per serving:
Calories, 170; Protein, 7 g; Fat, 6 g (30% cal.); Cholesterol, 10 mg; Carbohydrates, 24 g; Fiber, 6 g; Sodium, 125 mg.

■ Procedure

1. Soak the dried porcini in hot water until they are soft. Drain the mushrooms and squeeze them out, reserving all the soaking liquid. Strain or decant the liquid to remove any sand or grit. Chop the mushrooms.
2. Heat the oil in a heavy pot. Add the onion and celery. Sauté briefly.
3. Add the barley and sauté briefly, as for making rice pilaf.
4. Add the stock and mushroom liquid. Bring to a boil. Stir in the chopped mushrooms and the ham. Add salt to taste.
5. Cover tightly. Cook on top of the stove over low heat or in the oven at 325°F (160°C) until the barley is tender and the liquid is absorbed, about 30–45 minutes.

VARIATIONS

Add other vegetables to the barley, such as diced carrots, turnips, fennel, or parsnips. Add them at the same time as the onion and celery, or cook them separately and add them at the end of cooking.

Wheatberries with Pecans and Poblanos

Portions: 12   Portion size: 4 oz (125 g)

U.S.	Metric	Ingredients
1 lb 8 oz	750 g	Whole wheatberries, rinsed and soaked overnight in cold water (see note)
2 qt	2 L	Water, cold
2 fl oz	60 mL	Olive oil
3 oz	90 g	Chopped pecans
3 oz	90 g	Roasted poblano pepper, diced
to taste	to taste	Salt

Per serving:
Calories, 280; Protein, 8 g; Fat, 10 g (31% cal.); Cholesterol, 0 mg; Carbohydrates, 42 g; Fiber, 7 g; Sodium, 0 mg.

Note: This recipe was developed using soft wheatberries with the bran left on. Other types of wheatberries may be used, but the yields and cooking times will vary. For example, the white wheatberries shown in the illustration on page 619 cook in less than 30 minutes and yield 3 times their dry weight (about 4½ lb/2.25 kg for this recipe). When using a new type of product, test cooking time and yield with a small quantity before adapting it to production.

■ Procedure

1. Drain the soaking water from the wheatberries. Add the wheatberries to the cold water in a pot. Bring to a boil. Reduce heat to a simmer, cover, and simmer until the wheatberries are tender but still slightly crunchy. This will take about 1 hour. Remove from heat and allow to stand, covered, for 10 minutes. Drain.

2. Heat the olive oil in a sauté pan. Add the pecans and diced poblano peppers. Sauté about 1 minute.

3. Add the cooked wheatberries. Toss over heat until the mixture is hot. Season to taste.

VARIATIONS

Substitute any green chile or any sweet bell pepper for the poblanos.

Brown Rice, Barley, Farro, or Cracked Wheat with Pecans and Poblanos
Substitute cooked brown rice, cooked barley, cooked farro, or cracked wheat pilaf for the cooked wheatberries.

Wheatberries with Pecans and Poblanos

Paella (Spain)

Portions: 16   **Portion size: see procedure**

U.S.	Metric	Ingredients
2	2	Chickens, 2½–3 lb (1.1–1.4 kg) each
as needed	as needed	Olive oil
8 oz	225 g	Chorizo sausage (see note)
2 lb	900 g	Lean pork, cut into large dice
16	16	Large shrimp, peeled and deveined
2 lb	900 g	Squid, cleaned (p. 446), cut into rings
2	2	Red bell peppers, large dice
2	2	Green bell peppers, large dice
16	16	Small clams
16	16	Mussels
8 fl oz	250 mL	Water
as needed	as needed	Chicken stock
1 tsp	5 mL	Saffron
12 oz	350 g	Onion, small dice
6	6	Garlic cloves, minced
2 lb	900 g	Tomatoes, chopped
2 tsp	10 mL	Dried rosemary
2 lb	900 g	Short-grain rice, such as Italian arborio
2 tsp	10 mL	Salt
to taste	to taste	Pepper
4 oz	125 g	Cooked green peas
16	16	Lemon wedges

Per serving:
Calories, 630; Protein, 52 g; Fat, 22 g (32% cal.); Cholesterol, 260 mg; Carbohydrates, 52 g; Fiber, 5 g; Sodium, 630 mg.

■ P r o c e d u r e

1. Cut each chicken into 8 pieces.
2. In a large sauté pan, brown the chicken in olive oil. Remove and set aside.
3. Using additional oil as needed, briefly sauté the sausage, pork, shrimp, squid, and peppers. Do each ingredient separately, then remove to separate containers.
4. Combine the clams and mussels with the water in covered pot. Steam them just until they open.
5. Remove the shellfish and set them aside. Strain the liquid, then add enough chicken stock to measure 2 qt (2 L).
6. Add the saffron to the stock mixture.
7. In the skillet used for browning the meats, sauté the onion and garlic until soft. Use additional olive oil if necessary.
8. Add the tomatoes and rosemary. Cook until most of the liquid has evaporated and the tomatoes form a rather dry paste.
9. Add the rice and stir. Add the chicken, sausage, pork, squid, and peppers.
10. Bring the stock mixture to a boil in a separate pot, then add to the rice and stir. Add salt and pepper to taste.
11. Bring to a simmer, cover, and put in an oven heated to 350°F (175°C) for 20 minutes. (This dish is traditionally made uncovered on top of the stove, but making it in the oven is more practical for restaurants because it requires less attention.)
12. Remove the pan from the oven. Check the moisture level and add more stock, if necessary. It should be quite moist but not soupy.
13. Sprinkle the peas over the rice. Then arrange the shrimp, clams, and mussels on top. Cover loosely and let stand 10 minutes to heat the shellfish.
14. For each portion, allow 8 oz (225 g) rice and vegetables, 1 shrimp, 1 clam, 1 mussel, 1 piece of chicken, and at least 1 piece each of pork, sausage, and squid. Garnish each portion with 1 lemon wedge.

Note: If chorizo sausage is not available, use pepperoni sausage or other hard, spicy sausage. You may cut the sausage into ½-ounce (15-g) chunks before sautéing or cut them up just before serving.

Paella

Polenta

Yield: about 5 lb (2.5 kg)

U.S.	Metric	Ingredients
5 pt	2.5 L	Water
1 tbsp	15 mL	Salt
1 lb	500 g	Polenta (Italian coarse-grained yellow cornmeal)

Per 1 ounce:
Calories, 20; Protein, 0 g; Fat, 0 g (0% cal.); Cholesterol, 0 mg; Carbohydrates, 4 g; Fiber, 0 g; Sodium, 90 mg.

■ P r o c e d u r e

1. Bring the water and salt to a boil in a saucepot.
2. Very slowly sprinkle the cornmeal into the boiling water, stirring constantly. This must be done slowly and carefully to avoid lumps (see Figure 19.3).
3. Cook over low heat, stirring almost constantly. The polenta will become thicker as it cooks and will eventually start to pull away from the sides of the pot. This will take about 20–30 minutes.
4. Lightly moisten a large flat surface, such as a wooden board or a platter.
5. Pour the polenta onto this board or platter. Serve immediately, hot, or let cool and use in any of a number of ways, including the variations below.

V A R I A T I O N S

Freshly made hot polenta is good with many kinds of stews and other braised dishes that provide plenty of flavorful juices for the polenta to soak up. It is also served with grilled dishes.

Polenta con Sugo di Pomodoro
Serve hot polenta with tomato sauce or Meat Sauce (p. 639).

Polenta con Salsicce
Serve hot polenta with pork sausages cooked with tomatoes or tomato sauce.

Polento al Burro e Formaggio
Stir 6 oz (175 g) fresh butter and 2–3 oz (60–90 g) grated parmesan cheese into hot polenta as soon as it is cooked.

Polenta Fritta or Grigliata
Let polenta cool and cut it into slices ½ inch (1 cm) thick. Pan-fry in oil until a thin crust forms. Alternatively, heat slices on a grill or broiler until hot and lightly grill-marked.

Polenta Grassa
This can be prepared in two ways.

1. Pour a layer of hot polenta into a buttered baking dish. Cover with sliced fontina cheese and dot with butter. Cover with another layer of polenta, then another layer of cheese and butter. Bake until very hot.
2. Prepare as in the first method, but instead of the hot, freshly made polenta, use cold polenta cut into thin slices.

Polenta Pasticciata
Prepare Meat Sauce (p. 639), using pork sausage in addition to the beef. Also, add sautéed sliced mushrooms to the sauce. Cut cold polenta into thin slices. Fill a baking pan with alternating layers of polenta slices, meat sauce, and parmesan cheese. Bake until hot.

Polenta Pasticciata

Figure 19.3 Making polenta.

(a) Slowly sprinkle the polenta into the simmering water, stirring constantly to avoid lumps.

(b) Simmer while stirring until the polenta reaches the desired texture. Serve at once or proceed to the next step.

(c) Pour the polenta into a sheet pan and cool.

(d) Cut into desired shapes.

 ## Grits with Cheddar Cheese

Portions: 12   Portion size: 6 oz

U.S.	Metric	Ingredients
2 cups	500 mL	Hominy grits
2 qt	2 L	Water
1 tsp	5 mL	Salt
8 oz	250 g	Cheddar cheese, grated

Per serving:
Calories, 170; Protein, 7 g; Fat, 7 g (35% cal.); Cholesterol, 20 mg; Carbohydrates, 22 g; Fiber, 1 g; Sodium, 310 mg.

Grits

■ P r o c e d u r e

1. Stir the grits into the water in a saucepan.

2. If you are using stone-ground grits, let them settle, then skim off any hulls that float to the surface.

3. Bring the mixture to a boil while stirring.

4. Simmer the grits, stirring every 5–10 minutes. If you are using quick-cooking grits, they will be done in about 7-10 minutes but can be cooked longer if a thicker product is desired. If you are using regular grits, cooking time is about 45 minutes, and you may have to add water as they thicken. In any case, continue to cook until creamy, adding water as necessary.

5. Stir in salt to taste.

6. Add the cheese and stir until it is melted.

V A R I A T I O N S

For regular grits, omit the cheese. Serve topped with a pat of butter. If desired, substitute milk for one-third of the water.

Farrotto with Pecorino Cheese

Portions: 10   Portion size: 4 oz (1150 g)

U.S.	Metric	Ingredients
1 lb	450 g	Farro
2 fl oz	60 mL	Olive oil
1 oz	30 g	Onion, chopped fine
1½ qt (approximately)	1.5 L (approximately)	Vegetable stock, hot
1 oz	30 g	Butter
4 oz	120 g	Pecorino cheese, grated

■ Procedure

1. Soak the farro in cold water for 45 minutes. Drain.
2. Boil the farro in boiling salted water for 20 minutes. Drain. At this point, the farro should be about half-cooked.

3. Heat the olive oil in a sauté pan over moderate heat.
4. Sweat the onion in the oil until soft.
5. Add the farro. Stir and cook over moderate heat for 2 minutes.
6. Ladle in 4 fl oz (125 mL) stock. Stir over moderate heat until the stock is absorbed and the farro is almost dry.
7. Add another ladleful of stock and repeat the procedure.
8. Stop adding stock when the farro is tender.

9. Stir in the butter and cheese. Serve immediately.

Farrotto with Pecorino Cheese

Per serving:
Calories, 260; Protein, 8 g; Fat, 12 g (39% cal.); Cholesterol, 15 mg; Carbohydrates, 34 g; Fiber, 0 g; Sodium, 102.7 mg.

Kasha Pilaf with Egg

Portions: 10   Portion size: 4 oz (125 g)

U.S.	Metric	Ingredients
2 cups	250 mL	Buckwheat groats (kasha)
2	2	Eggs, lightly beaten
2 oz	60 g	Chicken fat or butter
1 qt	1 L	Water or chicken stock
2 tsp	10 mL	Salt
½ tsp	2 mL	Pepper

■ Procedure

1. Put the buckwheat in a sauté pan over moderate heat.
2. Add the eggs and stir vigorously so all the grains are coated with egg.
3. Continue to cook, stirring, until the grains are dry.
4. Add the fat and stir.
5. Add the water or stock, salt, and pepper. Bring to a boil, cover, and set over low heat to simmer for 10 minutes, until the liquid is absorbed.

Per serving:
Calories, 180; Protein, 5 g; Fat, 7 g (35% cal.); Cholesterol, 50 mg; Carbohydrates, 24 g; Fiber, 2 g; Sodium, 480 mg.

PASTA, NOODLES, AND DUMPLINGS

Macaroni products, or pastas, are popular alternatives to other starch foods. The word **pasta** is Italian for "paste," so called because pasta is made from a mixture of wheat flour and water and, sometimes, eggs.

Not so many years ago, many of us knew only spaghetti with tomato sauce and elbow macaroni with cheese, among all pasta products. Today, thanks to the influence of Italian cooks, we have a choice of a great variety of pasta dishes.

In addition, noodle products play an important role in other cuisines, notably those of Asia. These include not only wheat noodles but also noodles made of rice and other starches. Although most of our attention here is devoted to Italian-style pastas, we take a look at these other products as well.

ITALIAN-STYLE PASTAS

Italian pastas have spread beyond their original borders to become one of the most popular foods in North America and Europe. Please note that when we use the term *Italian-style pasta* we are referring only to the noodle products themselves, not to the dishes prepared from them. Appearing on menus are many dishes that are made with Italian-style pastas but that are not recognizably Italian in any way, as they use ingredients from other cuisines, including those of Asia and Latin America. Adopted by chefs from many cultures, Italian pastas have become citizens of the world.

Kinds, Characteristics, and Quality Factors

Commercial dried pasta is made from dough that has been shaped and dried. To refer to this category of food, we sometimes use the term **macaroni**, meaning any dried pasta made from flour and water. These include spaghetti, lasagne, elbow macaroni, and many other shapes.

The best dried macaroni pastas are made from **semolina**, a high-protein flour from the inner part of durum wheat kernels. Lower-quality products are made from farina, a softer flour.

Specialty pastas include ingredients in addition to semolina and water. Whole wheat pasta may be made with all whole wheat flour or a mixture of semolina and whole wheat. Other grain flours, including buckwheat and farro (spelt), are used in other specialty items.

Spinach pasta is perhaps the most popular of the pastas that contain vegetable purées. Others include red peppers, hot chile, seaweed, beet, tomato, and pumpkin.

Pasta containing *squid ink* is black in color and goes well with seafood sauces.

When purchasing macaroni products (unflavored), look for a good yellow color, not gray-white. The product should be very hard, brittle, and springy, and it should snap with a clean, sharp-edged break. When cooked, it should be firm and hold its shape well. Poor-quality pastas are soft and pasty when cooked.

In addition to pastas made of flour and water, dried **egg pastas** are also available. They contain at least 5½ percent egg solids in addition to the flour and water. They are usually sold as flat noodles of various widths.

Fresh egg pasta is made from flour and eggs and, sometimes, a small quantity of water and/or oil. Use a regular all-purpose or bread flour. Hard semolina flour, used for factory-made spaghetti and macaroni, is not appropriate for fresh egg pasta. Softer flour makes a more tender pasta. Soft egg noodle products are also available fresh and frozen from manufacturers. They take less time to cook than dried macaroni products.

Other flours, such as whole wheat flour, can be used to make fresh noodles. When you are making them yourself, you can experiment with ingredients. Keep in mind that flours other than wheat flour don't form much gluten (see p. 895), so they should be mixed with some wheat flour. Buckwheat flour added to white flour makes especially tasty noodles that are featured in a northern Italian classic called Pizzoccheri (peet so kerry; p. 648).

Vegetable purées and other flavoring ingredients are often added to fresh egg pasta. Spinach, tomato, beet, mushrooms, fresh herbs, dried hot pepper, grated lemon zest, saffron, and squid ink are among the many possibilities.

Shapes and Their Uses

Pasta is made in hundreds of shapes and sizes. Each shape is appropriate for different preparations because of the way different kinds of sauce cling to them or the way their textures complement the texture of the topping. The illustration shows some of the most popular kinds. Table 19.2 describes the most common shapes and gives suggestions for use.

Remember that fresh egg pasta and factory-made spaghetti and macaroni are different products. It makes no sense to say that one type is better than the other. Italian cooks use fresh and dried pasta in different ways, with different recipes for each type. Factory pasta has a chewy, robust texture, good with robust sauces, while fresh egg pasta is tender and more delicate. Fresh egg pasta absorbs sauces more deeply than factory macaroni products. In general, factory-made pasta is ideal for olive oil–based sauces, and fresh homemade pasta is better with butter or cream-based sauces.

Top row: elbow macaroni, pepe bucato, radiatore, ziti, conchiglie.

Middle row: fettuccine; spaghettini; fusilli; (three small piles, from top to bottom) orzo, stelline, and ditalini; lasagne; spaghetti; (two small piles, from top to bottom) gemelli and rigatoni.

Bottom row: bow ties (farfalle), penne, manicotti.

OTHER NOODLE PRODUCTS

Asian countries have a wide variety of noodle products. We can divide these into two categories: wheat noodles and noodles made of other starches.

Noodles Made of Wheat

Most of the Asian wheat noodles we know in the West are from China and Japan.

Chinese noodles are made from either flour and water or flour, water, and egg. If they contain egg, they are usually labeled as *egg noodles*. Flat noodles come in a variety of widths, from very thin to nearly an inch (2.5 cm) wide. Round noodles come in a variety of thicknesses, from thin vermicelli to thicker, spaghetti-like noodles.

Table 19.2
Commercial Pasta Shapes and Uses

Name	Description	Suggested Uses
Spaghetti	Long, round	With great variety of sauces, especially tomato sauces
Spaghettini	Thin, long, round	Like spaghetti, especially with olive oil and seafood sauces
Vermicelli	Very thin	With light, delicate sauces and, broken, in soups
Linguine	Looks like slightly flattened spaghetti	Like spaghetti; popular with clam sauces
Perciatelli	Looks like thick, hollow spaghetti	Like spaghetti, but can handle heavy, chunky sauces
Fusilli	Long, shaped like a corkscrew	Thick, creamy sauces
Macaroni	Long, hollow tubes	Especially good with hearty meat sauces
Elbow macaroni	Short, bent macaroni	Cold, in salads; baked, in casseroles
Penne or mostaccioli	Hollow tubes, cut diagonally; may be smooth or ridged	Baked, with meat sauce or with tomato sauce and cheese; freshly cooked, with tomato sauce
Ziti	Short, hollow tubes, cut straight	
Rigatoni	Larger tubes, with ridges	
Manicotti (sometimes called *cannelloni*, which are actually rolled from fresh egg noodle dough)	Large hollow tubes, sometimes with ridges	Stuff with cheese or meat filling
Orecchiette	Little ears	Chunky vegetable sauces
Rotelle, ruote	Wheels	Chunky tomato, meat, or vegetable sauces; in soups
Radiatore	Radiators; curled, ruffled shapes	Cold, in salads; hot, with chunky sauces
Fettuccine	Flat egg noodles	Rich cream sauces or meat sauces
Tagliagelle	Wide, flat egg noodles	
Lasagne	Broad, flat noodles, often with rippled edges	Bake with meat, cheese, or vegetable fillings
Conchiglie	Shells	With seafood or meat sauces; small sizes can be used in salads
Bow ties or farfalle		With sauces containing chunks of meat, sausage, or vegetables
Pastina (little pasta)		In soups; cold, in salads; buttered, as a side dish
Ditalini	Very short, hollow tubes	
Orzo	Rice-shaped	
Stelline	Tiny stars	
Acini di pepe	"Peppercorns"	
Pepe bucato	Peppercorns with holes	
Rotelline	Little wheels	
Semi di melone	Melon seeds	

Cantonese noodles are a special type of Chinese wheat noodles made by stretching a single large piece of dough in one length until it is as thin as spaghetti. Some restaurants feature a skilled noodle maker performing this amazing feat in the dining room. Cantonese noodles are available fresh or dried.

Japanese wheat noodles come in several varieties. **Udon** are thick, white noodles made from wheat flour. They are available fresh in vacuum packs or dried. **Somen** are thin, white wheat noodles usually packaged in small bundles. Tamago somen are made with egg in addition to wheat flour and water (*tamago* means "egg").

Soba are thin noodles made with buckwheat in addition to wheat flour. A special variety of buckwheat noodle is **chasoba**, made with powdered green tea in addition to the buckwheat.

In spite of the *soba* in the name, **chukasoba** contain no buckwheat. They are wheat noodles made with flour and water, with an alkali such as sodium carbonate added to the water. The noodles are yellow in color, leading some people to think they are egg noodles, but they contain no egg. These noodles are used in the popular ramen dishes familiar in the West from the single-portion packages of noodles and soup stock, found in nearly every supermarket.

Noodles Made of Other Starches

With the increased popularity of Southeast Asian and Chinese cuisines in the West, rice noodles have become familiar. Rice noodles are available as very fine, almost hairlike noodles called rice vermicelli, and as flat noodles of various widths. Rice noodles are sometimes known as rice sticks.

Rice vermicelli is usually cooked by deep-frying the dry noodle, without using any water. The noodles puff up and become crisp and tender. This type of noodle is too fine to reconstitute with water because it easily becomes a sticky mass. Rice vermicelli can also be broken apart and stir-fried.

Flat rice noodles are usually not cooked in water because boiling or simmering makes them too soft and sticky. Rather, they are covered with hot water and soaked until tender. This takes from a few minutes to about 20 minutes, depending on the thickness of the noodle and the temperature of the water. The noodles are drained and added to stir-fried dishes and soups at the last minute of cooking.

Bean thread noodles, also called cellophane noodles, are made with mung bean starch. They are very thin noodles that resemble rice vermicelli. Like rice noodles, they are either deep-fried or soaked in hot water until tender and then added to soups and braised dishes.

COOKING PASTA

Doneness

Pasta should be cooked al dente, or "to the tooth." This means that cooking should be stopped when the pasta still feels firm to the bite, not soft and mushy. Much of the pleasure of eating pasta is its texture (that's why there are so many shapes), and this is lost if it is overcooked.

Testing Doneness and Serving

Many suggestions have been made for testing doneness, but none is more reliable than breaking off a very small piece and tasting it. As soon as the pasta is al dente, the cooking must be stopped at once. Half a minute extra is enough to overcook it.

Cooking times differ for every shape and size of pasta. Timing also depends on the kind of flour used and the moisture content. Times indicated on the package are often too long.

Fresh egg pasta, if it has not been allowed to dry, takes only 1 to 1½ minutes to cook after the water has returned to a boil.

Italian practice is to toss the pasta with the sauce the minute it is drained. The sauce immediately coats all surfaces of the pasta, and cheese, if there is any, melts in the heat of the boiling hot noodles. If you are attempting to serve an authentic Italian pasta dish, follow this practice rather than simply topping the pasta with the sauce.

Pasta is best if cooked and served immediately. Whenever possible, you should try to cook pasta to order. Fresh pasta, in particular, cooks so quickly that there is little reason to cook it in advance. In volume operations, however, commercial pasta may have to be cooked ahead of time. The following procedures can be used for quantity cookery.

Yields

One pound (450 g) uncooked dried pasta yields about 3 pounds (1.4 kg) cooked pasta. This is enough for four to six main-course portions or eight to ten side-dish or first-course portions.

One pound (450 g) uncooked fresh pasta yields about 2 to 2½ pounds (900 to 1,100 g) cooked pasta.

Procedure for Cooking Pasta in Large Quantities

1. Use at least 4 quarts boiling, salted water per pound of pasta (4 L per 500 g). Use about 1½ tablespoons (25 g) salt per 4 quarts (4 L) water.
2. Have the water boiling rapidly and drop in the pasta. As it softens, stir gently to keep it from sticking together and to the bottom.
3. Continue to boil, stirring a few times.
4. As soon as it is al dente, drain immediately in a colander and rinse with cold running water until the pasta is completely cooled. Otherwise, it would continue to cook and become too soft. (If you are cooking just a few portions to serve immediately, just drain well and do not rinse. Sauce and serve without a moment's delay.)
   If the pasta is to be used cold in a salad, it is ready to be incorporated into the recipe as soon as it has cooled.
5. If the pasta is to be held, toss gently with a small amount of oil to keep it from sticking.
6. Measure portions into mounds on trays. Cover with plastic film and refrigerate until service time. (Do not store pasta in cold water. The pasta will absorb water and become soft, as though it had been overcooked.)
7. To serve, place the desired number of portions in a china cap and immerse in simmering water to reheat. Drain, plate, and add sauce.

Alternative Method: Steam Table Service

Pasta gradually becomes soft and mushy when kept hot for service, but it will hold reasonably well for 30 minutes. It will not be as good as if freshly cooked, however. This method should not be used unless cooking pasta to order is not possible in a particular food service operation.

1. Follow steps 1 to 3 above.
2. Drain the pasta while still slightly undercooked. Rinse briefly in cool water, enough to stop the cooking and rinse off starch but not enough to cool the pasta. Pasta should still be quite warm.
3. Transfer to steam table pan and toss with oil to prevent sticking.
4. Hold for up to 30 minutes.

Tomato Sauce for Pasta

Yield: 3 qt (3 L)   Portions: 32   Portion size: 3 fl oz (mL)

U.S.	Metric	Ingredients
1 pt	500 mL	Olive oil (see note)
½ lb	225 g	Onion, chopped fine
½ lb	225 g	Carrot, chopped fine
½ lb	225 g	Celery, chopped fine
1 No. 10 can	1 No. 10 can	Whole tomatoes
2	2	Garlic cloves, minced
1 oz	30 g	Salt
1 tbsp	15 mL	Sugar

Procedure

1. Heat the olive oil in a large saucepot. Add the onions, carrots, and celery and sauté lightly for a few minutes. Do not let them brown.
2. Add remaining ingredients. (See Appendix 2 for can sizes and substitutions.) Simmer, uncovered, about 45 minutes, until reduced and thickened.
3. Pass through a food mill. Taste and adjust seasonings.

Per serving::
Calories, 190; Protein, 1 g; Fat, 18 g (82% cal.); Cholesterol, 0 mg; Carbohydrates, 8 g; Fiber, 2 g; Sodium, 660 mg.

Note: The quantity of olive oil may seem high, but it is only 1 tbsp for a 3-oz portion (15 mL per 90 g). These are typical proportions for basic tomato sauce in Italy, where sauces are not used in such large quantities as in North America. If a lower-fat sauce is desired, oil may be cut in half. Except for meat sauce, most Italian sauces are cooked less than American-style tomato sauce and have fewer ingredients. As a result, they have a more pronounced fresh tomato taste.

VARIATIONS

Omit onion, carrot, and celery. Reduce oil to 8 fl oz (250 mL). Add fresh chopped parsley and basil to taste.

Meat Sauce
Brown 2 lb (1 kg) ground beef, ground pork, or a mixture of beef and pork, in oil or rendered pork fat. Add 8 fl oz (250 mL) red wine, 2 qt (2 L) tomato sauce, 1 qt (1 L) beef or pork stock, and parsley, basil, and oregano to taste. Simmer 1 hour, uncovered.

Tomato Cream Sauce
Use butter instead of olive oil in basic recipe. At service time, add 1 cup heavy cream per quart of tomato sauce (250 mL per liter). Bring to simmer and serve.

Tomato Sauce with Sausage
Slice 3 lb (1.4 kg) fresh Italian sausage and brown in oil. Drain and add to basic tomato sauce. Simmer 20 minutes.

Tomato Sauce with Sausage and Eggplant
Prepare like Tomato Sauce with Sausage, but use 1½ lb (700 g) each sausage and peeled, diced eggplant.

Tomato Sauce with Ham and Rosemary
Cook 1 lb (450 g) ham, cut into fine dice, and 2 tbsp (30 mL) dried rosemary leaves in a little olive oil for a few minutes. Add to basic tomato sauce (after it has been passed through the food mill) and simmer 5 minutes.

Fresh Egg Pasta

Yield: 1½ lb (700 g)

U.S.	Metric	Ingredients
1 lb	450 g	Bread flour
5	5	Eggs
½ fl oz	15 mL	Olive oil
pinch	pinch	Salt

Per 1 ounce:
Calories, 90; Protein, 4 g; Fat, 2 g (20% cal.);
Cholesterol, 45 mg; Carbohydrates, 14 g; Fiber, 0 g;
Sodium, 20 mg.

■ P r o c e d u r e

1. Put the flour in a mound on a work surface. Make a well in the center and add the eggs, oil, and salt.

2. Working from the center outward, gradually mix the flour into the eggs to make a dough.

3. When it is firm enough to knead, begin kneading the dough, incorporating more flour. If the dough is still sticky when all the flour has been incorporated, add more flour, a little at a time. Knead well for at least 15 minutes.

4. Cover the dough and let it rest for at least 30 minutes.

5. Cut the dough into 3 to 5 pieces. Set the rollers of a pasta machine at the widest opening. Pass the pieces of dough through the machine, folding them in thirds after each pass and dusting them lightly with flour to keep them from getting sticky. Continue passing each piece through the machine until it is smooth. See Figure 19.4.

6. Working with one piece of dough at a time, decrease the width between the rollers one notch and pass the dough through them again. After each pass, turn the rollers one notch narrower, dust the dough with flour, and pass it through again. Continue until the dough is as thin as desired. The pasta is now ready to cut into desired shapes and to cook. See below for cutting instructions.

V A R I A T I O N S

Cutting Instructions

Fettuccine or Tagliatelle: Roll dough thin and cut with wide cutting rollers.

Taglierini: Roll dough thin and cut with narrow cutting rollers.

Papardelle: Cut by hand, using a fluted cutting wheel, into long noodles about ¾ inch (18 mm) wide.

Tonnarelli: Roll dough to the same thickness as the width of the narrow cutting roller. Cut with the narrow cutting rollers. The result is like square spaghetti.

Bow ties: Cut into rectangles about 1½ x 3 in. (4 x 8 cm). Pinch in the middle to make a bow.

Lasagne: Cut by hand into broad strips about 8–12 in. (20–30 cm) long.

Spinach Pasta

Clean 1 lb (450 g) AP spinach, discarding stems. Simmer 5 minutes in salted water. Drain, rinse in cold water, and squeeze dry. Chop as fine as possible. Incorporate in basic pasta recipe, adding it to the flour at the same time as the eggs. Reduce the quantity of eggs to 4.

Other Colored Pastas

Other colored vegetables, in small quantities, cooked until tender and puréed or chopped fine, can be substituted for spinach to color pasta. For example, try experimenting with beets, red bell peppers, and carrots.

Whole Wheat Pasta

Substitute whole wheat flour for half of the white flour.

Buckwheat Pasta

In place of the 1 lb (450 g) white flour, use 10 oz (280 g) buckwheat flour and 6 oz (180 g) white flour. Omit the olive oil.

Figure 19.4 Working with fresh egg pasta.

(a) Set the rollers of the machine at their widest setting. Pass the piece of dough through the rollers, fold in thirds, and repeat until the dough is smooth.

(b) Decrease the opening between the rollers one notch at a time and pass the dough through them to roll to desired thickness.

(c) Pass the rolled-out dough through the appropriate cutters to make pasta of desired size and shape.

(d) To make ravioli, lay a thin sheet of pasta on the workbench. Deposit portions of filling on the dough using a spoon, small scoop, or pastry bag.

(e) Cover with another sheet of pasta.

(f) Press down between the mounds of filling to seal the layers of pasta together. Try to remove air bubbles from between the layers.

(g) Cut out the ravioli with cutters, or cut them apart with a pastry wheel.

 ## Ravioli with Cheese Filling

Portions: 25   Portion: 5 oz (150 g) uncooked or approximately 7 oz (200 g) cooked

U.S.	Metric	Ingredients
3 lb	1.4 kg	Ricotta cheese
8 oz	250 g	Parmesan cheese, grated
5	5	Egg yolks
¾ cup	50 g	Chopped parsley
½ tsp	2 mL	Nutmeg
to taste	to taste	Salt
to taste	to taste	White pepper
4½ lb	2 kg	Fresh pasta

Per serving:
Calories, 410; Protein, 21 g; Fat, 17g (38% cal.); Cholesterol, 205 mg; Carbohydrates, 42 Fiber, 1 g; Sodium, 270 mg.

■ **P r o c e d u r e**

1. Mix together the ricotta, parmesan, egg yolks, parsley, and seasonings.

2. Roll the pasta into thin sheets.

3. Over half the pasta, make small mounds of the cheese filling about 1 tsp (5 mL) each, arranging them in a checkerboard pattern about 1½–2 in. (4–5 cm) apart.

4. Lay the remaining pasta over the top and press down between the mounds of cheese to seal well (see Figure 19.4). While doing this, try to avoid sealing large air bubbles inside the ravioli. *Note:* If the pasta is fresh and moist, the layers will seal together if pressed firmly. If it is dry, moisten the bottom layer lightly between the mounds of cheese, using a brush dipped in water. Do not get the pasta too wet.

5. Cut the ravioli apart with a pastry wheel. Check each piece to be sure it is completely sealed.

6. The cheese filling does not keep well, so the ravioli should be cooked the same day they are made. They can be held briefly on sheet pans covered with dry, clean towels; turn them over from time to time so they do not stick. Alternatively, cook them immediately in boiling salted water, keeping them slightly underdone. Drain and rinse under cold water, drain, and toss with oil or melted butter. Spread in a single layer on a sheet pan and refrigerate. They can then be reheated to order by sautéing them briefly in butter or oil or by dipping them in boiling water.

7. Serve with your choice of sauce, such as tomato sauce, meat sauce, tomato cream sauce, or just melted butter and parmesan cheese.

Fettuccine Alfredo

Portions: 10   Portion size: 6–7 oz (175–200 g)

U.S.	Metric	Ingredients
1 cup	250 mL	Heavy cream
2 oz	60 g	Butter
1½ lb	700 g	Fresh fettuccine
1 cup	250 mL	Heavy cream
6 oz	175 g	Freshly grated parmesan cheese
to taste	to taste	Salt
to taste	to taste	Pepper

Per serving:
Calories, 500; Protein, 17 g; Fat, 32 g (56% cal.); Cholesterol, 195 mg; Carbohydrates, 35 g; Fiber, 1 g; Sodium, 430 mg.

■ Procedure

1. Combine the cream and butter in a sauté pan. Bring to a simmer, reduce by one-fourth, and remove from heat.

2. Drop the noodles into boiling salted water, return to a full boil, and drain. The noodles must be slightly undercooked because they will cook further in the cream.

3. Put the drained noodles in the pan with hot cream and butter. Over low heat, toss the noodles with two forks until they are well coated with the cream.

4. Add the remainder of the cream and the cheese and toss to mix well. (If the noodles seem dry at this point, add a little more cream.)

5. Add salt and pepper to taste.

6. Plate and serve immediately. Offer additional grated cheese at the table.

VARIATIONS

Fettuccine with Vegetables I (Fettuccine Primavera)

Fresh, lightly cooked vegetables can be added to fettuccine to make a great variety of dishes. In the basic recipe, use about half the quantity of cream. Select 4–6 fresh vegetables, cook them al dente, cut into appropriately small sizes and shapes, and add them to the pasta when it is being tossed in the cream. The following are examples of appropriate vegetables:

Mushrooms	Tiny green beans
Peas	Asparagus
Broccoli	Artichoke hearts
Red or green bell pepper	Zucchini

Small quantities of finely diced ham, prosciutto, or bacon can also be added as a flavor accent.

Fettuccine with Vegetables II

Prepare like Fettuccine with Vegetables I, but omit all butter and cream. Instead, toss the freshly cooked fettuccine and cooked vegetables with olive oil. Add parmesan cheese as desired.

Fettuccine with Seafood

Use half the quantity of cream and cheese in the basic recipe. Prepare like Fettuccine with Vegetables I, adding only 1 to 3 types of vegetables. At the same time, add desired quantity of cooked seafood, such as shrimp, scallops, crab, or lobster. For a fuller flavor, reduce a small amount of fish stock and white wine with the cream in the first step.

Fettuccine with Gorgonzola

Prepare as in basic recipe, except use light cream instead of heavy cream in the first step. Omit the second quantity of heavy cream, and instead add 6 oz (175 g) gorgonzola cheese (Italian blue cheese). Reduce the quantity of parmesan cheese to 2 oz (60 g).

Fettuccini with Vegetables II

Spaghettini Puttanesca

Portions: 10   Portion size: approximately 12 oz (350 g)

U.S.	Metric	Ingredients
3½ lb	1.6 kg	Tomatoes, preferably fresh
2 fl oz	60 mL	Olive oil
5	5	Garlic cloves, chopped
15	15	Anchovy fillets, chopped
3 tbsp	30 g	Capers, drained
5 oz	150 g	Black olives, pitted and sliced
½ tsp	2 mL	Dried oregano
3 tbsp	45 mL	Chopped parsley
1 fl oz	30 mL	Olive oil
to taste	to taste	Salt
to taste	to taste	Pepper
2 lb	900 g	Spaghettini

■ P r o c e d u r e

1. Peel, seed, and dice the tomatoes, and let them stand in a colander. If using canned tomatoes, drain them and chop them coarsely.
2. Heat the olive oil in a sauté pan over moderate heat. Add the garlic and sauté for a minute.
3. Add the anchovy fillets and sauté for a few seconds.
4. Add the tomatoes, capers, and olives. Bring to a boil. Cook 2–3 minutes.
5. Remove from heat. Add the oregano, the parsley, and the second quantity of olive oil. Season to taste with salt and pepper.
6. Boil the spaghettini, drain, toss with the sauce, and serve immediately. Grated cheese is usually not served with this dish.

Per serving:
Calories, 500; Protein, 16 g; Fat 13 g (23% cal.); Cholesterol, 5 mg; Carbohydrates, 80 g; Fiber, 9 g; Sodium, 460 mg.

Linguine with White Clam Sauce

Portions: 10   Portion size: approximately 12 oz (350 g)

U.S.	Metric	Ingredients
4 dozen	4 dozen	Cherrystone clams
1 cup	250 mL	Olive oil
4–6	4–6	Garlic cloves, sliced thin
½ tsp	2 mL	Red pepper flakes
½ cup	125 mL	Dry white wine (optional)
2 tsp	10 mL	Dried oregano
2 lb	900 g	Linguine
4 tbsp	60 mL	Chopped parsley
to taste	to taste	Black pepper

■ P r o c e d u r e

1. Open the clams. Strain and reserve 1 pt (500 mL) of their juice. Chop the clams coarsely.
2. Heat the olive oil in a large sauté pan. Add the garlic and brown it very lightly. Do not let it get too brown, or it will be bitter.
3. Add the red pepper and then, very carefully, add the wine. (If the pan is very hot, you may want to cool it a little first to prevent dangerous spattering when the liquid is added.) Reduce the wine by half.
4. Add the reserved clam juice and reduce by half.
5. Add the oregano.
6. Drop the linguine into boiling, salted water and boil al dente. Drain and plate.
7. While the linguine is boiling, add the chopped clams and the parsley to the olive oil mixture. Heat gently, just until the clams are hot. Do not overcook them, or they will be tough.
8. Add pepper to taste. (Because clams are salty, the sauce will probably not need any salt, but taste to make sure.)
9. Spoon the sauce over the hot linguine and serve at once.
10. Many people prefer this dish without parmesan cheese, but provide it on the side for those who want it.

Per serving:
Calories, 600; Protein, 21 g; Fat, 24 g (36% cal.); Cholesterol, 25 mg; Carbohydrates, 74 g; Fiber, 7 g; Sodium, 40 mg.

Baked Lasagne

Portions: 24   Portion size: 8 oz (225 g)

U.S.	Metric	Ingredients
1½ lb	700 g	Ricotta cheese
2 oz	60 g	Parmesan cheese, grated
2	2	Eggs
to taste	to taste	Salt
to taste	to taste	Pepper
2 lb	900 g	Fresh pasta or spinach pasta
3 qt	3 L	Meat Sauce (p. 639)
1½ lb	700 g	Mozzarella cheese, shredded
4 oz	125 g	Parmesan cheese, grated

Per serving:
Calories, 450; Protein, 26 g; Fat, 25 g (50% cal.); Cholesterol, 150 mg; Carbohydrates, 29 g; Fiber, 2 g; Sodium, 590 mg.

■ P r o c e d u r e

1. Mix together the ricotta, parmesan, and eggs. Season to taste with salt and pepper.

2. Cut the fresh pasta into lasagne noodles. Cook them in boiling salted water, drain, and rinse in cold water. Lay them out in a single layer on oiled sheet pans.

3. Ladle a little meat sauce into a standard hotel pan, 12 x 20 inches (20 x 50 cm). Spread it across the bottom.

4. Arrange a layer of noodles in the pan. Then add a layer of the ricotta mixture, a layer of noodles, a layer of sauce, and a layer of mozzarella.

5. Continue making layers of noodles, ricotta, sauce, and mozzarella until all ingredients are used. Top with parmesan cheese.

6. Bake at 375°F (190°C) for about 45 minutes. Cover lightly with foil at first to keep it from drying out, but remove the foil for the last 15 minutes of baking time.

V A R I A T I O N S

Other ingredients can be added to lasagne, such as sliced cooked meatballs, sausages, zucchini, eggplant, and so forth. It is best to add only one or two ingredients so the lasagne doesn't seem like a catchall for leftovers.

If meat items are added to the lasagne, you may use plain tomato sauce instead of meat sauce. The ricotta mixture may also be omitted, especially if other protein items are added or if the quantity of mozzarella is increased.

 Pesto (Fresh Basil Sauce)

Yield: about 3 cups (750 mL)   Portions: 12   Portion size: 2 oz (60 mL)

U.S.	Metric	Ingredients
2 qt	2 L	Fresh basil leaves
1½ cups	375 mL	Olive oil
2 oz	60 g	Walnuts or pine nuts (pignoli)
6	6	Garlic cloves
1½ tsp	7 mL	Salt
5 oz	150 g	Parmesan cheese, grated
1½ oz	50 g	Romano cheese, grated

Per 1 ounce:
Calories, 350; Protein, 8 g; Fat, 35 g (88% cal.); Cholesterol, 15 mg; Carbohydrates, 3 g; Fiber, 1 g; Sodium, 550 mg.

■ P r o c e d u r e

1. Wash the basil leaves and drain well.

2. Put the basil, oil, nuts, garlic, and salt in a blender or food processor. Blend to a paste, but not so long that it is smooth. It should have a slightly coarse texture.

3. Transfer the mixture to a bowl and stir in the cheese.

4. To serve, cook pasta to order according to the basic procedure. Just before the pasta is done, stir a little of the hot cooking water into the pesto to thin it, if desired. Toss the drained pasta with the pesto and serve immediately. Pass additional grated cheese.

Vegetable Ravioli in Lemon Grass Broth

Portions: 12   Portion size: 4 oz (125g) (uncooked weight)
2 fl oz (60mL) broth

U.S.	Metric	Ingredients
1 lb	500 g	Chinese cabbage
6	6	Scallions
6 oz	175 g	Snow peas
4 oz	125 g	Carrots
4 oz	125 g	Mushrooms, trimmed
2 fl oz	60 mL	Vegetable oil
1 fl oz	30 mL	Soy sauce
1 tsp	5 mL	Sesame oil
2 tbsp	30 mL	Chopped cilantro
to taste	to taste	Salt
1 lb 8 oz	750 g	Fresh pasta dough
as needed	as needed	Water or egg wash
4 stalks	4 stalks	Lemon grass
1 oz	30 g	Ginger root, sliced
4	4	Scallions, sliced
1 qt	1 L	Water
to taste	to taste	Salt
as needed	as needed	Cilantro leaves for garnish

Per serving:
Calories, 250; Protein, 9 g; Fat, 9 g (33% cal.); Cholesterol, 90 mg;
Carbohydrates, 32 g; Fiber, 3 g; Sodium, 190 mg.

■ P r o c e d u r e

1. Cut the Chinese cabbage into fine shreds.
2. Trim and slice the scallions.
3. Trim the snow peas and cut diagonally into thin julienne.
4. Trim, peel, and grate the carrots.
5. Chop the mushrooms coarsely.
6. Heat the oil in a large sauté pan. Add the vegetables and sauté until wilted.
7. Add the soy souce. Lower the heat to moderate and continue to cook until the vegetables are tender and there is no liquid in the pan.
8. Remove from the heat and cool. Add the sesame oil and the cilantro. Adjust the seasoning with salt.
9. Roll the pasta dough into thin sheets. Lay half the sheets on the worktable.
10. Place mounds of the vegetable mixture about 3–4 in. (8–10cm) apart on the pasta, using about ½ oz (15 g) for each mound. This quantity makes about 60 ravioli, or 5 per portion.
11. Brush the exposed pasta with water or egg wash. Top with the remaining sheets of pasta. Press the layers of pasta together to seal them, at the same time pressing around the vegetable mounds to eliminate air bubbles. Cut into round or square ravioli
12. Trim off and discard the tops of the lemon grass stalks. Crush the bases, then chop coarsely.
13. Combine the lemongrass, ginger, scallions, and water in a saucepan. Simmer 10–15 minutes, until the water is lightly flavored. Strain and season to taste with salt.
14. Drop the ravioli into boiling salted water. Reduce the heat and simmer about 3 minutes, until the pasta is cooked.
15. Remove the ravioli with a skimmer and drain well.
16. Arrange the ravioli in broad soup plates and pour the lemon grass broth over them. Garnish with a few leaves of cilantro.

Rigatoni or Penne with Sausage and Clams

Portions: 8   Portion size: approximately 10 oz (300 g) pasta and sauce, plus 3 clams

U.S.	Metric	Ingredients
1 fl oz	30 mL	Olive oil
8 fl oz	250 g	Italian sausage, cut into ½-in. (1- cm) slices
4 oz	125 g	Onion, chopped
4 oz	125 g	Green bell pepper, diced
4 oz	125 g	Red bell pepper, diced
6 oz	180 g	Tomatoes, peeled, seeded, chopped
pinch	pinch	Saffron
to taste	to taste	Hot red pepper flakes
1 lb	500 g	Rigatoni or penne
24	24	Littleneck clams, well scrubbed
to taste	to taste	Salt
to taste	to taste	Pepper
8 tsp	40 mL	Chopped parsley

Per serving:
Calories, 340; Protein, 18 g; Fat, 9 g (24% cal); Cholesterol, 30 mg; Carbohydrates, 47 g; Fiber, 6 g; Sodium, 170 mg.

■ P r o c e d u r e

1. Heat the oil in a sauté pan. Add the sausage and sauté until just cooked. Remove with a slotted spoon.
2. Add the onion and diced peppers to the fat in the pan. Sauté briefly until just starting to get tender.
3. Add the tomatoes, saffron, and hot pepper. Simmer about 5 minutes.
4. Meanwhile, add the penne or rigatoni to boiling salted water and boil al dente.
5. Shortly before the pasta is cooked, return the sausage to the pan with the vegetable mixture. Set over moderately high heat. Add the clams and cover. Cook just until the clams open. Do not overcook, or they will be tough. Season with salt and pepper.
6. Drain the pasta and immediately transfer to pasta bowls for serving.
7. Top with the contents of the pan, dividing the clams, sausage, and vegetables evenly among the servings.
8. Sprinkle with chopped parsley. Serve immediately.

V A R I A T I O N S

Mussels may be substituted for clams. Adjust the quantity as desired. If neither clams nor mussels are available, the dish can be made with shrimp, although its flavor and character will be quite different.

Rigatoni or Penne with Sausage, Peppers, and Tomatoes

Omit the seafood from the recipe and double the quantity of sausage.

Macaroni and Cheese

Portions: 15   Portion size: 6 oz (175 g)

U.S.	Metric	Ingredients
1 lb	450 g	Elbow macaroni
1 qt	1 L	Medium Béchamel, hot (p. 171)
1 tsp	5 mL	Dry mustard
dash	dash	Tabasco
1 lb	450 g	Cheddar cheese, grated
		Garnish:
as needed	as needed	Bread crumbs
as needed	as needed	Paprika

■ P r o c e d u r e

1. Cook macaroni according to basic method for boiling pasta. Drain and rinse in cold water.

2. Flavor the white sauce with the dry mustard and Tabasco.
3. Mix the macaroni with the cheese. Combine with the béchamel.
4. Pour into a buttered half-size hotel pan. Sprinkle with bread crumbs and paprika.
5. Bake at 350°F (175°C) until hot and bubbling, about 30 minutes.

Per serving:
Calories, 330; Protein, 14 g; Fat, 17 g (46% cal.); Cholesterol, 50 mg; Carbohydrates, 31 g; Fiber, 1 g; Sodium, 290 mg.

Note: Cheese sauce may be used instead of béchamel. If you do so, reduce grated cheese to 4 oz (100 g) or omit.

Fettuccine with Chiles and Grilled Chicken

Portions: 8   Portion size: approximately 12 oz (360 g)

U.S.	Metric	Ingredients
1 lb	450 g	Chicken breasts, boneless and skinless
to taste	to taste	Chili powder
to taste	to taste	Salt
as needed	as needed	Olive oil or corn oil
4 fl oz	120 mL	Sour cream
1 fl oz	30 mL	Lime juice
12 oz	360 g	Tomatoes, peeled, seeded, and chopped
1 tsp	5 mL	Garlic, minced
2 fl oz	60 mL	Olive oil or corn oil
4 oz	120 mL	Mild green chiles (see note), roasted, peeled (p. 529), and cut into small strips
to taste	to taste	Salt
10–12 oz	300–360 g	Fresh fettuccine (see note)
8 oz	240 g	Monterey jack cheese, grated
6 oz	180 g	Avocado, sliced

Per serving:
Calories, 440; Protein, 24 g; Fat, 27 g (55% cal.); Cholesterol, 65 mg; Carbohydrates, 25 g; Fiber, 3 g; Sodium, 260 mg.

Note: Green bell peppers may be substituted for the chiles if desired.
To add to the character of the dish, prepare fresh egg pasta according to the recipe on page 640, adding 5 tbsp (75 mL) chili powder for each pound (450 g) of flour.

■ **P r o c e d u r e**

1. Season the chicken breasts lightly with chili powder and salt. Coat with oil. Marinate in the refrigerator until ready to cook.

2. Mix together the sour cream and lime juice. Refrigerate until needed.

3. Warm the tomatoes and garlic gently in the oil. Add the chile pepper strips. Season to taste with salt.

4. Grill the chicken.

5. Cook the pasta in boiling water. Drain and immediately toss together with the tomato mixture.

6. Add the cheese and toss lightly. Check for seasonings and add more salt if necessary. Put into pasta bowls or serving plates.

7. Slice the grilled chicken. Arrange the sliced chicken and sliced avocado on top of the pasta.

8. Drizzle with the sour cream mixture. Serve at once.

V A R I A T I O N

To serve as a main course, increase the quantity of chicken as desired.

Pizzoccheri

Portions: 12   Portion size: 8 oz (240 g)

U.S.	Metric	Ingredients
1½ lb	700 g	Buckwheat pasta dough (p. 640)
4 oz	120 g	Butter
2 oz	60 g	Garlic, crushed
1 lb	450 g	Small, waxy potatoes, cut into ¼-in. (6-mm) slices
2 lb	900 g	Swiss chard, stalks only, cut into 2-in. (5-cm) pieces
8 oz	240 g	Taleggio cheese, sliced into small pieces
4 oz	120 g	Parmesan cheese, grated

Per serving:
Calories, 380; Protein, 18 g; Fat, 18 g (42% cal.); Cholesterol, 135 mg; Carbohydrates, 38 g; Fiber, 4 g; Sodium, 610 mg.

■ **P r o c e d u r e**

1. Prepare the pasta: Roll the buckwheat pasta dough into sheets slightly thicker than for fettuccine. Cut the sheets into strips 1 in. (2.5 cm) wide, then cut the strips diagonally into pieces about 3 in. (8 cm) long.

2. Prepare the garlic butter: Heat the butter in a small saucepan and add the garlic. Cook until the garlic is golden brown, then strain the butter and discard the garlic.

3. Drop the potatoes and chard into a large pot of boiling salted water. Cook at a slow boil just until the potatoes are tender.

4. When the potatoes are cooked, drop the buckwheat noodles into the water with the potatoes. Boil until the pasta is just cooked but al dente. Drain immediately in a colander.

5. Transfer the mixture to a large, buttered gratin dish or to several small gratin dishes.

6. Pour the garlic butter over the mixture and toss gently to coat the noodles, potatoes, and chard with the butter.

7. Add the Taleggio and parmesan cheeses and mix in gently.

8. Bake at 400°F (200°C) until the mixture is hot and bubbling and the top is lightly browned, about 10 minutes.

Pizzoccheri

Whole Wheat Maltagliate with Porcini and Peas

Portions: 8   Portion size: 8 oz (240 g)

U.S.	Metric	Ingredients
1½ lb	700 g	Whole wheat pasta dough (p. 640)
2 oz	60 g	Dried porcini mushrooms
6 fl oz	180 mL	Olive oil
1 tbsp	15 mL	Finely chopped garlic
4 tbsp	60 mL	Chopped fresh parsley
1 lb	450 g	Peas, fresh or frozen
2 oz	60 g	Butter
to taste	to taste	Black pepper
4 oz	120 g	Parmesan cheese, grated

■ P r o c e d u r e

1. Prepare the pasta: Roll out the dough into sheets as for making fettuccine. By hand, cut the pasta into triangles about 3 in. (8 cm) across.

2. Put the dried mushrooms in a bowl and cover them with hot water. Let stand 30 minutes.

3. Lift the mushrooms out of the water, squeezing them dry and letting the water run back into the bowl.

4. Cut the mushrooms into ½-in. (1-cm) pieces.

5. Strain the soaking liquid through a paper filter to remove sand or soil.

6. Heat the olive oil in a sauté pan. Add the garlic. Cook until the garlic is soft.

7. Add the mushrooms. Stir to coat with oil.

8. Add the soaking liquid, parsley, and peas. Simmer until almost all the liquid has evaporated.

9. In a separate pot, boil the pasta in salted water until al dente.

10. Drain and immediately add to the peas.

11. Add the butter and pepper. Toss to coat the noodles with oil and butter.

12. Add the grated cheese and toss to mix.

13. Serve immediately.

Per serving:
Calories, 600; Protein, 23 g; Fat, 36 g (53% cal.); Cholesterol, 160 mg; Carbohydrates, 50 g; Fiber, 7 g; Sodium, 360 mg.

Whole Wheat Maltagliate with Porcini and Peas

Rice Sticks, Singapore Style

Yield: 2 qt (2 L)
Portions: 10   Portion size: 8 oz (225 g)

U.S.	Metric	Ingredients
1 oz	30 g	Dried Chinese black mushrooms
1 tbsp	15 mL	Soy sauce
4 fl oz	120 mL	Water or chicken stock
5 tbsp	75 mL	Madras curry powder
1 lb	450 g	Thin rice noodles (rice sticks)
1 tbsp	15 mL	Vegetable oil
3	3	Eggs, beaten
2 fl oz	60 mL	Vegetable oil
4	4	Scallions, cut diagonally into thin shreds
1 tbsp	15 mL	Finely chopped garlic
1 tbsp	15 mL	Finely chopped fresh ginger root
1 tsp	5 mL	Salt
8 oz	225 g	Small shrimp, peeled and deveined
8 oz	225 g	Mung bean sprouts
4 oz	110 g	Red bell peppers, cut julienne
4 oz	110 g	Cooked pork or chicken, cut julienne

Per serving:
Calories, 320; Protein, 13 g; Fat, 10 g (28% cal.); Cholesterol, 115 mg;
Carbohydrates, 45 g; Fiber, 3 g; Sodium, 500 mg.

■ Procedure

1. Soak the dried mushrooms in warm water until soft.
2. Remove the mushrooms from the water and squeeze them dry. Cut off and discard the stems.
3. Cut the mushroom caps into julienne.
4. Mix together the soy sauce, water or stock, and curry powder.
5. Soak the noodles in warm, not hot, water until softened, about 20 minutes. Drain.
6. Heat the oil in a wok or large sauté pan. Add the egg and swirl it to cover the bottom of the pan in a thin layer.
7. As soon as the egg is set, remove it to a cutting board. Cut into thin shreds.
8. Heat the rest of the oil in the same wok or pan until very hot.
9. Add the scallions, garlic, ginger, and salt. Stir-fry for 1 minute.
10. Add the shrimp and stir-fry until the shrimp is about half cooked.
11. Add the bean sprouts, peppers, mushrooms, and meat. Continue to stir-fry until the sprouts and peppers are cooked but still somewhat crisp.
12. Add the noodles and continue to stir-fry until the items are well mixed and hot.
13. Add the curry mixture. Quickly stir and toss the mixture to distribute it evenly. Continue to stir-fry until the liquid is absorbed.
14. Return the shredded omelet to the pan and toss to mix in.
15. Serve immediately.

SINGAPORE NOODLES

The city-nation of Singapore sits at the tip of the Malay Peninsula, which juts into the Indian Ocean. Situated as it is between India and China, Singapore has been an important stop on trade routes between East and West. Thus, it is not surprising that its cooking should show the influences of many regions, such as curry from India and rice noodles from south China.

That's a good story, but there isn't much evidence that the dish called Rice Stick Singapore Style, or Singapore Noodles, was invented in Singapore. Rather, it was probably invented in Chinese restaurants in Europe in the 1970s and quickly became popular around the world. Today, it is one of the most popular dishes in Chinese restaurants from Hong Kong to London.

Use a good brand of Madras curry powder to create the true flavor of this dish.

Rice Sticks, Singapore Style

DUMPLINGS

Dumplings are starch products made from soft doughs or batters and cooked by simmering or steaming. They are served as side dishes and in soups and stews. Many national cuisines have their own kinds of dumplings. (For Chinese filled dumplings or wontons, see p. 328.)

Potato Dumplings

Portions: 10   Portion size: 5 oz (150 g)

U.S.	Metric	Ingredients
2½ lb	1.1 kg	Boiled potatoes, peeled, cold
12 oz	350 g	Flour
2 tsp	10 mL	Salt
2	2	Eggs
4 oz	125 g	Butter
4 oz	125 g	Dry bread crumbs

■ Procedure

1. Grate the potatoes into a mixing bowl.
2. Add the flour and salt and mix lightly until just combined.
3. Add the eggs and mix well to form a stiff dough. Work in more flour if necessary.
4. Divide the dough into 20 equal portions. Roll each piece into a ball. Refrigerate 1 hour. Dumplings may be made ahead up to this point.
5. Heat the butter in a sauté pan and add the bread crumbs. Sauté for a few minutes, until the crumbs are toasted and brown. Set aside.
6. Place the dumplings into a pot of boiling salted water. Stir so that they rise to the top and don't stick to the bottom of the pan. Simmer 10 minutes.
7. Remove with a slotted spoon and place in a single layer in a hotel pan (or onto serving plates).
8. Top with the toasted buttered bread crumbs. Serve 2 pieces per order. (Dumplings may also be served with melted butter or with pan gravy.)

VARIATIONS

One or more of the following may be added to the dough: ¼ cup (60 mL) chopped parsley; 4 oz (125 g) diced bacon, cooked crisp; 2 oz (60 g) onion, chopped fine and sautéed in butter or bacon fat.

Per serving:
Calories, 360; Protein, 8 g; Fat, 11 g (28% cal); Cholesterol, 65 mg; Carbohydrates, 57 g; Fiber, 3 g; Sodium, 680 mg.

Spaetzle

Portions: 15   Portion size: 4 oz (125 g)

U.S.	Metric	Ingredients
6	6	Eggs
1½ cups	375 mL	Milk or water
1 tsp	5 mL	Salt
⅛ tsp	0.5 mL	Nutmeg
⅛ tsp	0.5 mL	White pepper
1 lb or more	450 g or more	Flour
as needed	as needed	Butter, for service

■ Procedure

1. Beat the eggs in a bowl and add the milk or water, salt, nutmeg, and pepper.
2. Add the flour and beat until smooth. You should have a thick batter. If it is too thin, beat in a little more flour.
3. Let the batter stand 1 hour before cooking to relax the gluten.
4. Set a colander (or a spaetzle machine, if available) over a large pot of boiling salted water. The colander should be high enough so that the steam doesn't cook the batter in the colander.
5. Place the batter in the colander and force it through the holes with a spoon.
6. After the spaetzle float to the top of the water, let them simmer 1–2 minutes, then remove them with a skimmer. Cool quickly in cold water and drain well.
7. Cover and refrigerate until service.
8. Sauté portions to order in butter until hot. Serve immediately.

Per serving:
Calories, 260; Protein, 7 g; Fat, 15 g (52% cal.); Cholesterol, 120 mg; Carbohydrates, 24 g; Fiber, 1 g; Sodium, 310 mg.

Potato Gnocchi with Tomato Sauce

Portions: 16   Portion size: 4½ oz (140g)

U.S.	Metric	Ingredients
4 lb	2 kg	All-purpose potatoes
1 lb	500 g	Flour
3 pt	1.5 L	Tomato Sauce for Pasta (p. 639)
1½ cup	350 mL	Grated parmesan cheese

Per serving:
Calories, 380; Protein, 10 g; Fat, 17 g (40% cal.); Cholesterol, 5 mg;
Carbohydrates, 47 g; Fiber, 4 g; Sodium, 680 mg.

■ **P r o c e d u r e**

1. Wash the potatoes but do not peel. Boil until tender.

2. Peel the potatoes while they are still hot, and force them though a food mill.

3. Add about three-fourths of the flour to the potatoes and knead to make a soft, sticky mixture. Continue to work in more flour to form a soft, smooth dough. It should still be somewhat sticky. You may not need all the flour.

4. Divide the dough into smaller pieces. Roll each piece into a sausage shape about ½ in. (1.56 cm) thick. Cut into pieces about ¾ in. (2 cm) long.

5. To shape the gnocchi, pick up one piece of the dough and press it with the fingertip against the times of a fork. Then flip the piece with the finger and allow it to drop on the worktable. This will give the piece grooves on one side and an indentation on the other side.

6. Drop the gnocchi into a large quantity of boiling salted water. When they float to the surface, let them boil 10–15 seconds, then remove with a skimmer or slotted spoon.

7. Plate the gnocchi. Top each portion with 2 fl oz (60 mL) tomato sauce and 1 tbsp (15 mL) grated parmesan cheese.

V A R I A T I O N S

Gnocchi may be served with other pasta sauces, such as pesto, or simply with melted butter and grated cheese.

■ TERMS FOR REVIEW

legume	wehani rice	wild rice	commercial dried pasta
haricot bean	wild pecan rice	farro	macaroni
lentil	glutinous or sticky rice	spelt	semolina
dal	corn	kamut	egg pasta
endosperm	cornmeal	buckwheat	Chinese noodle
bran	polenta	kasha or buckwheat groats	Cantonese noodle
germ	hominy	barley	udon
regular milled white rice	grits	oats	somen
enriched rice	pozole	pearled barley	soba
short-grain rice	blue corn	oats	chasoba
medium-grain rice	wheat germ	steel-cut oats	chukasoba
long-grain rice	wheat bran	rolled oats	rice noodle
parboiled or converted rice	cracked wheat	instant oats	rice vermicelli
instant rice	whole wheatberry	millet	rice stick
brown rice	bulgur	quinoa	bean thread
arborio rice	green wheat	triticale	cellophane noodle
basmati rice	couscous	amaranth	al dente
jasmine rice	instant couscous	pasta	dumpling

■ QUESTIONS FOR DISCUSSION

1. Describe how to prepare dried beans, lentils, and peas for cooking.

2. What is the main difference between cooking dried kidney beans and dried lentils?

3. Describe the three basic methods for cooking grains.

4. Should rice be washed before cooking? Always, sometimes, or never? Discuss.

5. Can wild rice and long-grain rice be cooked together to decrease the portion cost of wild rice? Explain.

6. What factors determine how much water is needed to cook rice?

7. Describe two ways in which rice noodles are cooked or prepared.

8. Describe the procedure for making cheese ravioli, starting with a freshly made piece of pasta dough.

20

Cooking for Vegetarian Diets

Vegetarian diners are an important and growing segment of the dining public. In the United States, for example, it is estimated that about 15 million people consider themselves vegetarians. Young people in particular embrace many forms of vegetarianism. In college dining rooms, the proportion of clients choosing vegetarian options may be as high as 40 percent. Clearly, food service cannot afford to ignore this segment.

It is important that cooks and chefs who want to please their customers know something about the needs of vegetarian diners. Beyond the financial benefits of serving foods that appeal to the widest range of customers, chefs find that there are other benefits as well. Vegetarians are often more knowledgeable and enthusiastic about their dining choices because they have thought more about them. Accomplished cooks often say that meeting the challenge of cooking for knowledgeable diners is one of the most satisfying aspects of their jobs and that vegetarian menus give them new opportunities for creativity.

In addition to people who have a strong commitment to vegetarianism, many others eat meat on other occasions but choose vegetarian items simply because the choices are so appealing in a particular dining facility. Chefs who create satisfying, innovative choices for vegetarians often find that creating a good vegetarian menu selection is one of their best professional decisions.

UNDERSTANDING VEGETARIAN DIETS

Preparing food for anyone who follows a restricted diet requires understanding the nature and limitations of that diet. Vegetarian diets present challenges because there are several types of vegetarianism.

TYPES OF VEGETARIAN DIETS

A vegetarian diet is one consisting entirely or mostly of foods derived from plants. Most committed vegetarians fall into one of the categories listed below.

The vegan diet is the most restrictive form of vegetarianism. Vegans eat plant products only. All animal products, including dairy products and eggs, are off limits. Even foods that might sound safe are off limits to the strictest vegans. Examples of such foods include honey, because it comes from bees, and cane sugar, which may be refined with the use of animal products (more on this subject on p. 661). When preparing a vegetarian menu, the chef should keep in mind that a menu appropriate to a vegan diet has the broadest appeal because it can be eaten by all categories of vegetarians.

Lacto-vegetarians eat dairy products in addition to plant products but will not eat other animal products.

Ovo-vegetarians eat eggs in addition to plant products.

Lacto-ovo-vegetarians eat dairy and egg products as well as plant products.

Pesco-vegetarians eat fish and plant products but not meat or poultry. They may or may not eat dairy and egg products.

Vegetarianism may be based on strong ethical or moral beliefs or on health concerns. Naturally, the chef who cares for his or her customers is eager to respect these beliefs and concerns. Vegetarians may have chosen their diet based on deeply held ethical or religious beliefs and may be strongly dedicated to following their diet rigorously.

In addition, many people choose vegetarianism for health reasons. Vegetarian diets are usually low in fat and cholesterol and in addition are free of the hormones and drugs often used in the raising of meat animals. Environmental concerns also lead some people to vegetarianism. Producing plant foods requires fewer natural resources than raising meat animals. Economic factors are yet another consideration in that vegetables and grains are, on average, much less expensive than meat, poultry, and seafood. Finally, some people are occasional vegetarians simply because they enjoy the foods.

NUTRITIONAL CONSIDERATIONS

Because vegetarians eliminate major categories of foods from their diets, any nutrients obtained from animal products are lost and must be obtained from other foods. Refer to the Food Guide Pyramid on page 123. Note that although dairy products, meats, fish, and eggs do not form the largest portions of the pyramid, they form an important part. When those foods are eliminated, the pyramid must be rebuilt, as in Figure 20.1, in order to ensure adequate nutrition.

Protein

The subject of complete proteins and complementary proteins was introduced in Chapter 6 (see p. 121). Because this subject is so important for vegetarian diets, the subject is discussed in greater detail here.

The major nutritional concern of a vegetarian diet is getting enough protein. Dairy products, eggs, and fish supply adequate amounts of good-quality protein, but vegans must plan their diets carefully in order to get adequate protein. Some plant products, such as grains, nuts, and dried beans, contain proteins. Note that in the standard Food

After reading this chapter, you should be able to

1. **Describe the main types of vegetarian diets.**

2. **Describe complementary proteins and describe how to include them in the diet.**

3. **List three nutrients other than proteins that non-vegetarians get mostly from animal products, and describe how vegetarians can include these nutrients in their diets.**

4. **Name and describe five food types derived from soybeans.**

5. **Explain why refined sugar may not be permitted in a vegan diet.**

6. **List seven guidelines for building a vegetarian menu.**

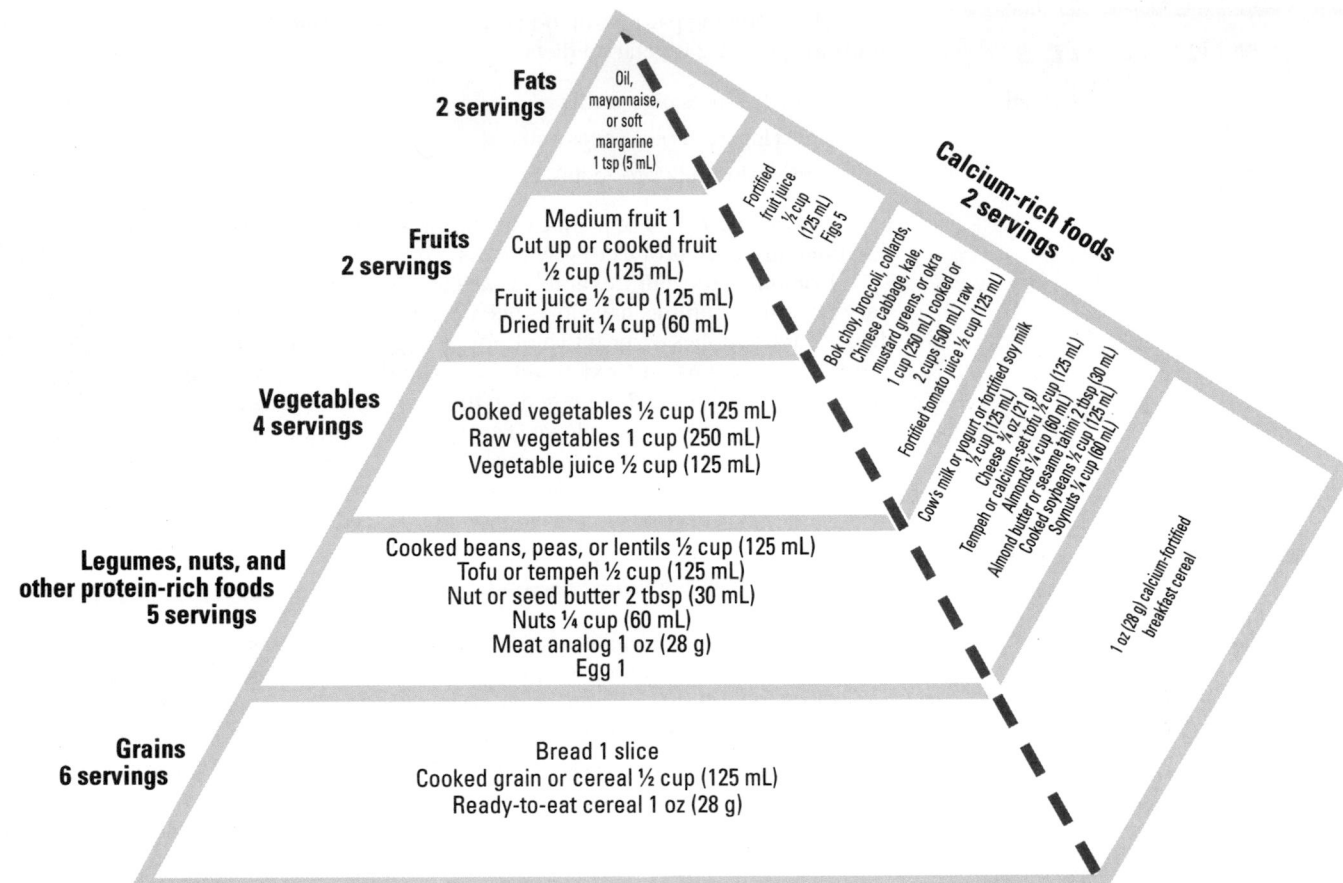

Figure 20.1
Vegetarian food guide pyramid.
Reprinted from *Journal of the American Dietetic Program,* Volume 103, Messina, Virginia, Melina, Vesanto, and Mangels, Ann Reed, "A new food guide for North American vegetarians," pages 771-775, Copyright 2003, with permission from American Dietetic Association.

Guide Pyramid on page 123, dried beans and nuts are included in the meat group. However, with the important exception of soybeans and soy products such as tofu, most of these protein foods, *when eaten alone*, are not adequate for human nutrition.

Proteins are long chains of smaller compounds called amino acids. There are, in all, 20 amino acids that, when joined in various combinations, make up over 100,000 proteins in the human body. Eleven of these amino acids can be made in the body, so it is not necessary to include them in the diet. All remaining nine amino acids must be included in the diet in order for the body to make all the proteins it needs. These are called essential amino acids.

Any food protein that contains all nine essential amino acids is called a complete protein. Proteins found in meat, poultry, seafood, milk and milk products, and eggs are complete proteins.

Some plant foods, especially dried legumes, grains, nuts, and seeds, contain incomplete proteins. This means that one or more of the essential amino acids is either missing or is not present in high enough concentration. Soybeans, quinoa, and amaranth are unusual among grains and legumes, because they contain complete proteins.

The key to getting enough protein in a plants-only diet is to eat, in the course of each day, a balance of these foods, so that amino acids missing from one of these foods is supplied by another one of them. Such proteins are called complementary proteins. For example, kidney beans are high in the amino acids isoleucine and lysine, but low in some of the others. Millet is low in lysine but high in the amino acids that kidney beans are missing. So if both kidney beans and millet are eaten during the day, all the essential amino acids are included in the diet.

Including Complementary Proteins in the Diet

Contrary to what you might think after reading the preceding discussion, you do not have to be a biochemist to prepare vegetarian menus. A basic understanding of what foods go together to supply complete proteins is the best place to start and will carry you a long way.

The following pairings of food categories are the most useful complementary proteins for planning vegetarian diets:

Dried legumes plus grains

Dried legumes plus seeds and nuts

Grains plus milk products

The first two of these pairings are important in vegan diets. The third pairing can be included in the diets of lacto-vegetarians.

Examining the cultures and cuisines of other lands, we see that these complementary protein groupings have long been a part of the staple diet of peoples who have had limited supplies of meats. Think, for example, of the beans and corn tortillas (dried legumes plus grains) of Mexico and the rice and dal (also grains plus dried legumes) of India. People who have long relied on these foods have found tasty and varied ways to prepare them. Studying traditional vegetarian cuisines is a useful way to learn how to include these items in your own menus.

Other Nutrients

In addition to protein, other nutrients normally found in animal products must be supplied in other ways in vegetarian diets.

Vitamin B$_{12}$. This vitamin is found only in animal foods, including milk and eggs. Vegans must obtain it from grain foods, such as breakfast cereals, that have been fortified with this vitamin, or else take vitamin supplements. Vegetarians who eat sufficient dairy products and eggs usually can get enough vitamin B$_{12}$.

Vitamin D. This vitamin is found in vitamin D–fortified milk, and it is created in the skin on exposure to sunlight. A vegan or other vegetarian who doesn't get enough exposure to sunlight can get this nutrient from vitamin-fortified cereals or some soy beverages.

Calcium. Dairy products are rich in calcium, but vegans and other vegetarians who don't consume dairy products must get calcium from other sources, including green leafy vegetables and dried legumes. Calcium supplements or calcium-fortified beverages may be necessary in vegan diets.

MENUS FOR VEGETARIAN DIETS

To a meat eater, the idea of a vegetarian diet might seem monotonous or boring, but the reality can be the opposite. A typical meat-based diet often features the same few meats—beef, pork, chicken, and occasionally fish—over and over, accompanied by the same few simple vegetable side dishes and potatoes. By contrast, a diet in which vegetables are the focus and not a routine side dish can feature dozens of fresh vegetables, a great variety of grains and legumes, and, for at least some vegetarians, dairy products and possibly eggs to round out the selection.

The appeal of vegetarian menus can be seen in many fine restaurants that feature tasting menus (see p. 90). At such restaurants, the dinner menu each evening may offer a multi-course vegetarian menu in addition to the meat and seafood options. It is common for a pair of diners, even non-vegetarians, to order one vegetarian menu and one non-vegetarian menu so they can sample all the chef's creations.

INGREDIENTS

Because animal protein is omitted from vegetarian diets, some important ingredients get more attention than they do in meat diets. Several categories of plant foods take on the role of main courses.

Dried Legumes

Dried beans, peas, and lentils are some of the most important sources of proteins for vegans and other vegetarians. These are listed and discussed in detail in Chapter 19. Refer to that information as necessary in your menu planning.

One legume not mentioned earlier is the peanut, which is not a nut but a legume with an unusual growing habit. As the plants grow, the branches bearing the pods bend to the ground so the pods develop underground. Although peanuts are used in the kitchen like other nuts, nutritionally they are similar to other legumes. Keep this in mind when planning complementary proteins.

Dried soybeans are high in protein, but they are rarely cooked and served like other dried beans. They are very hard and take hours of cooking if whole, and when cooked they do not appeal to most tastes. Furthermore, their protein is not as usable as the protein in products derived from soybeans, such as soy milk and tofu. These are so important that they are discussed separately below.

Grains

Like legumes, grains are discussed in detail in Chapter 19. They are sources of complementary proteins when eaten with legumes or dairy products. Of the grains described, rice is no doubt the most important worldwide. Many vegans and other vegetarians use brown rice instead of white rice to take advantage of its vitamin and fiber content. Wheat and corn are also important protein foods. In the form of bread, noodles, and tortillas, these grains are especially versatile.

Don't overlook the other grains. Products such as farro, barley, millet, and triticale add variety to the menu. Quinoa and amaranth are especially valuable for vegan diets because they contain complete protein.

Nuts and Seeds

Nuts and seeds are rich in protein, so almonds, cashews, hazelnuts, pecans, walnuts, pistachios, pumpkin seeds, sesame seeds, and sunflower seeds are useful in vegetarian diets. They are high in fat, however, so they can't be relied on as heavily as other vegetable proteins.

Nut butters, such as cashew butter and almond butter, are simply nuts or seeds that have been roasted and ground to a paste. They are a flavorful and attractive way to include these foods in a diet. Sesame butter, or tahini, is especially prominent in Mediterranean diets and is used in many recipes. See, for example, the recipe for hummus on page 762, which uses legumes (chickpeas) and seeds (tahini) to supply complementary proteins.

Soy Products

Borrowed from Asian cuisines, soy derivatives such as tofu have long been familiar in the West and have been important sources of protein for many people.

Soy milk is made by soaking dried soybeans, draining them, grinding them, combining them with water, boiling, and then straining the resulting milky liquid.

Plain soy milk can be used in cooking and as a beverage. Many brands of flavored and sometimes sweetened soy beverages are also available, and these can also be used in coffee beverages and in desserts.

Tofu, or **bean curd**, is made by curdling soy milk, just as cheese is made by curdling dairy milk. The result is a soft, white cake with a mild, faintly beany flavor that is adaptable to many sauces and accompaniments.

Tofu is available in several varieties, described here. Most types are available packed in water in sealed plastic packages. It keeps well as long as it is unopened, but it should be used within a day or two of opening.

Japanese silken tofu is the softest type. Unlike other tofu varieties, the curd of silken tofu is not pressed to remove moisture. Silken tofu has the most delicate texture and also the mildest flavor. In Japan it is regularly eaten cold with a light dipping sauce, or it is diced and added as a garnish to miso soup (p. 250).

Japanese cotton tofu is firmer than the silken variety and can stand up to more vigorous handling. It is often deep-fried or added to stir-fried dishes.

Chinese firm tofu is the firmest of these three tofu types and is the coarsest in texture. It can be fried, stir-fried, grilled, baked in casseroles, simmered in stews, and put on skewers.

Silken tofu

Firm tofu

When tofu is to be marinated, fried, or stewed, removing excess moisture first helps the tofu absorb the added flavors more readily. Place the cakes of tofu on several layers of paper towels or on a perforated sheet pan, cover with several more layers of paper towels, place a weighted tray or sheet pan on top, and let stand for about 15 minutes.

To make tofu even firmer and less likely to break apart when cooked, press it as above and then deep-fry until it has a light golden color. Or drop it into simmering water and simmer for 5 minutes. Precooking coagulates the proteins, making them firmer.

Tempeh is a fermented soybean product that originated in Indonesia. In addition to the original versions made with only soybeans, it is also made from soy plus grains, including barley, millet, and rice. Tempeh is sold in cakes and has a dense, meaty texture. It can be sliced or diced and braised, sautéed, stir-fried, baked, and added to casseroles.

Miso, also called **bean paste**, is a paste made of fermented soybeans, sometimes with the addition of wheat, rice, or barley, depending on the variety. There are several types of miso ranging from light, sweet, and mild to dark, salty, and robust. The lightest, called *white miso* (*shiromiso* in Japanese), is yellow, with a sweet flavor and soft, moist texture. It is often used in soups (p. 250) and in dressings or sauces for vegetables (p. 550). Other light miso types may be darker yellow and saltier. *Red miso* (*akamiso*) is brown or reddish brown, salty, and fuller in flavor. It may be smooth or chunky. Red miso is used in soups and in cooked dishes rather than in uncooked dressings. The thickest, darkest, strongest-tasting miso is *hatcho miso*. It is dark brown and thick enough to cut, almost like fudge. It is used in soups and cooked dishes.

Textured vegetable protein (TVP) is made from defatted soy flour, processed and dried to give it a spongelike texture. It is available unflavored or flavored to resemble various meats. To prepare TVP, mix with water, let stand until softened, and then add to recipes as you would meat. Because it doesn't taste exactly like real meat, it is best used in highly flavored or seasoned dishes such as chili. TVP is high in protein and fiber and free of cholesterol. It is useful on some menus for its nutritional value, but some vegetarians avoid it because they are not interested in highly processed foods that pretend to be meat.

Dairy and Eggs

For lacto-ovo vegetarians, milk products and eggs are valuable sources of protein, vitamin D, calcium, and other nutrients. Cheeses and eggs, however, are high in fat and cholesterol, so it is a good idea not to rely on them for one's sole source of protein.

Dairy products and eggs are discussed in later chapters.

MODIFYING RECIPES

You have probably noticed by now that many of the recipes in this book are labeled with a small icon indicating that they are vegetarian. These include recipes for lacto-ovo vegetarians as well as vegans. The presence of any egg or dairy product indicates that the recipe cannot be used on a vegan menu, although it is suitable for other vegetarians. Before using any of these recipes on vegetarian menus, please note the discussion of sugar below.

Other recipes, in this book and elsewhere, can be modified for vegetarian diets. Always read the list of ingredients to make sure they are all permitted. If any of the ingredients is a packaged or manufactured food, read the list of ingredients on the package as well. Remember:

- No animal product of any kind may be used as an ingredient in a recipe intended for vegans.

- Dairy products (such as milk, cream, butter, and cheese) and eggs may be included as ingredients in recipes for lacto-ovo vegetarians, and thus they may be labeled as vegetarian. However, they will not be eaten by vegans.

- Service staff must be adequately trained to accurately answer patrons' questions about the menu.

Sometimes a soup, salad, or side dish recipe consists primarily of plant products but contains one or more animal products, such as a stock. The following methods can be used to modify existing recipes to adapt them for vegetarian menus:

1. Remove meat, poultry, and fish stocks from recipes and substitute an equal quantity of water or vegetable stock.

2. Omit sauces based on meat, poultry, or fish stocks and, for vegans, omit sauces using dairy products or eggs. Substitute another suitable sauce. Vinaigrettes, salsas, vegetable coulis, and flavored oils are often good sauces for vegetarian dishes.

3. For vegans, substitute oil for butter. Substitute soy milk or other soy products for dairy products.

Sugar in Vegetarian Recipes

Refined white sugar and most brown sugar are processed either from sugar cane or sugar beets. Refineries that process sugar from cane often use charcoal made from animal bones as a filter. Sugar made from beets, however, is not made with bone char. Vegans and many other vegetarians often avoid all refined sugar because of the difficulty of determining the sugar's origin. For home use, they may use unbleached sugar or beet sugar, but away from home it is easier just to avoid sugar altogether.

Some of the recipes in this book labeled as vegetarian may have sugar as an ingredient. *If you use any of these recipes on a vegetarian menu, make sure to use sugar from a purely vegetarian source, such as beet sugar or unbleached sugar.*

Other recipes in this book may appear to be vegetarian but are not labeled as such. For example, the recipe for Cocktail Sauce (p. 201) contains only plant products, and sugar is not listed as an ingredient. However, two of the ingredients, ketchup and chili sauce, contain sugar. Because there is no way to tell the source of the sugar, the recipe can't easily be adapted to a vegetarian menu. In this book, no recipe is labeled as vegetarian if one of the ingredients is a manufactured product that may contain sugar or other impermissible ingredient.

CENTER OF THE PLATE

In the world of food service, the expression *center of the plate* is often used to describe the meat, poultry, fish or other principal item that is the focus of the main course. For vegetarian menus, we need to rethink the concept of center of the plate somewhat.

One of the problems in developing vegetarian menu choices is constructing a plate that is satisfying as a main course. Appetizers or first courses are less of a problem. Vegetarians and non-vegetarians alike enjoy soups, salads, and vegetable dishes as first courses. Similarly, a succession of four to six small courses in a tasting menu can be pleasing and satisfying. A main course, on the other hand, must usually feel like a complete meal in its own right, and a selection of steamed vegetables on a plate will usually not satisfy.

Begin by thinking about the categories of foods we rely on for complementary proteins: legumes, grains, seeds and nuts, and dairy products, and, if appropriate, soy products like tofu. Dishes made with these ingredients tend to be more substantial than simple vegetables and thus are often suitable for main courses, especially when combined with vegetables and perhaps a sauce or condiment.

Complex dishes—dishes that have had something done to them beyond simple boiling or steaming—are appealing vegetarian main courses. For example, a baked squash stuffed with a well-seasoned grain and vegetable mixture holds its own in the center of the plate. Regional cuisines give us other examples, such as a bean-filled enchilada served with rice and a spicy tomato sauce.

Some kinds of preparations work as main courses whether or not they are made with meat. Examples are listed below. These types of dishes can be prepared many ways using only plant products, with or without the use of dairy products or eggs.

Stews

Curries

Chili

Stir-fries served with rice or noodles

Risotto

Pasta

Pizza

Pot pies, or foods served inside dough or pastry

Casseroles

Gratins

The ingredient information and prep and cooking procedures in other chapters in this book, especially in the chapters on vegetables; potatoes; legumes, grains, pastas, and other starches; and salads, give you the tools you can use to build creative and satisfying vegetarian menus. Many of the recipes in those chapters can be used by vegetarians without modification. In addition, examples of other vegetarian items are in this chapter.

Guidelines for Building a Vegetarian Menu

1. Offer dishes containing no ingredients of animal origin, to appeal to vegans, and offer dishes containing dairy products and eggs for vegetarians who eat those foods.

2. Select a variety of legumes, grains, and seeds, and use them in combinations that provide complementary proteins.

3. Complementary proteins don't need to be on the same plate. For example, you could offer a grain salad as a first course and a vegetable stew with beans as a main course.

4. Use a wide variety of vegetables.

5. Offer dishes made with tofu and other soybean derivatives.

6. To limit fat and cholesterol, consider using low-fat milk products and use eggs sparingly.

7. Offer foods containing nutrients, such as vitamin B_{12}, that are of special concern to vegetarians (see p. 658).

8. Read the ingredient labels of all packaged food products to make sure they contain no ingredients of animal origin.

Yellow Split Pea and Vegetable Curry with Spiced Rice and Cucumber Raita

Portions: 12   Portion size: 3½ oz (100 g) rice,
6 oz (180 g) vegetable curry,
2 oz (60 mL) raita

U.S.	Metric	Ingredients
		Spiced rice:
1 lb	500 g	Long-grain brown rice, preferably basmati
2 fl oz	60 mL	Vegetable oil
4 oz	125 g	Onion, chopped
1 tsp	5 mL	Finely chopped garlic
1 tsp	5 mL	Finely chopped fresh ginger root
¼ tsp	1 mL	Ground cardamom
¼ tsp	1 mL	Cinnamon
⅛ tsp	1 mL	Ground cumin
⅛ tsp	0.5 mL	Ground cloves
⅛ tsp	0.5 mL	Nutmeg
⅛ tsp	0.5 mL	Cayenne
1 qt	1 L	Water or vegetable stock, hot
2 tsp	10 mL	Salt
8 oz	250 g	Yellow split peas
1 qt	1 L	Water
2 fl oz	60 mL	Vegetable oil
8 oz	250 g	Onion, medium dice
2 tsp	10 mL	Finely chopped garlic
2 tbsp	30 mL	Curry powder
2 tsp	10 mL	Salt
8 oz	250 g	Carrots, thickly sliced
6 oz	180 g	Parsnips, large dice
6 oz	180 g	Eggplant, peeled, cut large dice
8 oz	250 g	Cauliflower, broken into small florets
8 oz	250 g	Broccoli, broken into small florets
8 fl oz	250 mL	Plain yogurt
2 fl oz	60 mL	Lemon juice or lime juice
1½ pt	750 mL	Cucumber Raita (p. 193)
as needed	as needed	Cilantro leaves
as needed	as needed	Paprika

■ Procedure

1. Wash the rice in several changes of cold water. Drain. Add cold water to cover by 1–2 inches (3–5 cm) and soak 1 hour or longer.
2. Heat the oil in a heavy saucepan.
3. Add the onion, garlic, and ginger. Sauté until the onion is lightly browned.
4. Add the spices.
5. Drain the rice and add it to the pan. Stir to coat the grains with oil.
6. Add the water or stock and the salt. Bring to a boil.
7. Cover and simmer over low heat about 40 minutes, until the rice is tender. Check after about 30 minutes to make sure the liquid hasn't all been absorbed before the rice is done. If it has, add a little more hot water.

8. Pick over the peas to remove stones and other foreign matter. Rinse and drain them.
9. Simmer the peas in the water until they are very tender and falling apart. Do not drain.

10. Heat the oil in a heavy saucepot.
11. Add the onion and garlic. Sauté until lightly browned.
12. Stir in the curry powder and salt.
13. Add the carrots, parsnips, and eggplant. Sauté for 2–3 minutes over medium heat.
14. Add the cauliflower. Sauté another minute.
15. Add the cooked peas. Simmer 15–20 minutes, until the vegetables are nearly tender.
16. Add more water if the mixture becomes too thick. The peas should have the consistency of a sauce.
17. Add the broccoli and continue to simmer until all the vegetables are tender. Taste and add more salt if necessary.
18. Stir in the yogurt and lemon or lime juice.

19. For each portion, spoon a portion of the rice to cover about two-thirds of a plate, leaving space at one side. Make a well in the center. Spoon a portion of the vegetable curry into the center of the rice.
20. To the side of the rice, spoon a portion of the raita.
21. Top the curry with a few cilantro leaves.
22. Sprinkle a dash of paprika onto the center of the raita.

V A R I A T I O N

Vegan Vegetable and Split Pea Curry
Omit the yogurt. Increase the lemon juice or lime juice to taste.

Per serving (excluding Raita):
Calories, 370; Protein, 12 g; Fat, 13 g (30% cal.); Cholesterol, 5 mg; Carbohydrates, 55 g; Fiber, 6 g; Sodium, 1030 mg.
Per serving (Raita only):
Calories, 15; Protein, 1 g; Fat, 1 g (53% cal.); Cholesterol, 0 mg; Carbohydrates, 1 g; Fiber, 0 g; Sodium, 105 mg.

Noodle Bowl with Stir-Fried Vegetables, Tofu, and Peanuts

Portions: 12   Portion size: 4 oz (125 g) noodles, 6 oz (180 g) vegetables

U.S.	Metric	Ingredients
2 fl oz	60 mL	Vegetable oil
4	4	Scallions, chopped
2	2	Garlic cloves, chopped
1 tsp	5 mL	Finely chopped ginger root
6 oz	180 g	Carrots, cut julienne
6 oz	180 g	Red bell peppers, cut batonnet
8 oz	250 g	Shiitake mushroom caps, cut batonnet
1 lb	500 g	Bok choy, cut into 1-in. (2.5-cm) pieces
4 oz	125 g	Mung bean sprouts
8 oz	250 g	Snow peas, trimmed
1 lb 4 oz	625 g	Firm tofu, pressed (p. 660), cut in ½-in. (1-cm) dice
6 oz	180 g	Roasted peanuts, shelled, skinless
3 fl oz	90 mL	Soy sauce
2 fl oz	60 mL	Hoisin sauce
4 fl oz	125 mL	Vegetable stock or water
1 tbsp	15 mL	Sesame oil or chili oil
3 lb	1.5 kg	Cooked Chinese wheat noodles or egg noodles, hot

■ P r o c e d u r e

1. Heat the oil in a large sauté pan or wok over high heat.
2. Add the scallions, garlic, and ginger. Stir-fry 1 minute.
3. Add the carrots, peppers, and mushrooms. Continue to stir-fry another minute.
4. Add the bok choy and bean sprouts. Stir-fry until the vegetables are wilted but still crisp.
5. Add the snow peas and continue to cook about 30 seconds.
6. Add the tofu and peanuts. Toss the mixture to blend, and cook until the tofu is hot.

7. Pour in the soy sauce, hoisin sauce, stock or water, and oil. Toss to mix.

8. Put the noodles into individual serving bowls and top with the vegetable mixture with its liquid.

Per serving:
Calories, 400; Protein, 19 g; Fat, 18 g (39% cal.); Cholesterol, 0 mg;
Carbohydrates, 45 g; Fiber, 6 g; Sodium, 830 mg.

Noodle Bowl with Stir-Fried Vegetables, Tofu, and Peanuts

Zucchini and Eggplant Lasagne

Portions: 12   Portion size: 8 oz (250 g)

U.S.	Metric	Ingredients
1½ lb	750 g	Eggplant
1½ lb	750 g	Zucchini
as needed	as needed	Salt
as needed	as needed	Olive oil
12 oz	375 g	Ricotta cheese
1 oz	30 g	Parmesan cheese, grated
1	1	Egg, beaten
2 tbsp	30 mL	Chopped parsley
to taste	to taste	Salt
to taste	to taste	Pepper
1½ qt	1.5 L	Tomato Sauce for Pasta (p. 639), made without sugar
1 lb	500 g	Mozzarella cheese, sliced
2 tbsp	30 mL	Fresh basil, cut chiffonade
2 oz	60 g	Parmesan cheese, grated

Per serving:
Calories, 410; Protein, 15 g; Fat, 34 g (73% cal.); Cholesterol, 65 mg; Carbohydrates, 14 g; Fiber, 4 g; Sodium, 1030 mg.

■ P r o c e d u r e

1. Trim and peel the eggplant.
2. Trim the stem ends of the zucchini.
3. Cut the eggplant and the zucchini lengthwise into slices about ⅓ inch (8 mm) thick.
4. Salt the slices lightly on both sides and let stand 15 minutes.
5. Pat dry. Brush both sides of each slice lightly with oil.
6. Arrange the eggplant and zucchini on separate sheet pans.
7. Bake the eggplant in an oven at 425°F (210°C) until the bottoms are brown. Turn over and bake another 15 minutes.
8. At the same time, bake the zucchini until softened but still somewhat crisp, 5–10 minutes.
9. Remove the vegetables from the oven and let cool. These slices will serve as noodles for the lasagna.
10. Mix together the ricotta, parmesan, egg, parsley, salt, and pepper.
11. Ladle a little tomato sauce into a half-size hotel pan, 10 × 12 inches (25 × 30 cm). Spread it across the bottom.
12. Lay the eggplant slices in a single layer over the sauce.
13. Add the ricotta mixture, carefully spreading it in an even layer over the eggplant.
14. Add the zucchini in a single layer.
15. Cover with half the remaining sauce.
16. Arrange the mozzarella slices over the top. Sprinkle the mozzarella with a little of the basil.
17. Cover with the remaining sauce.
18. Sprinkle with the second quantity of parmesan cheese.
19. Bake at 375°F (190°C) until hot and bubbling.

Pinto Bean Enchiladas

Portions: 12   Portion size: 2 enchiladas

U.S.	Metric	Ingredients
as needed	as needed	Vegetable oil
24	24	Corn tortillas
2 qt	2 L	Ancho Sauce (made with water) or the variation with tomato (p. 191) or Salsa Roja (p. 190)
2 lb 4 oz	1.1 kg	Vegetarian Pinto Beans (p. 613), warmed
2 lb	1 kg	Monterey jack cheese, grated
3 lb	1.5 kg	Arroz Verde or Arroz à la Mexicana (p. 629), made with water instead of stock
as desired	as desired	Guacamole (p. 763)
as desired	as desired	Salsa Cruda (p. 191)
as desired	as desired	Sour cream

■ P r o c e d u r e

1. Heat a thin layer of oil in a sauté pan over moderate heat.
2. One at a time, dip the tortillas in the hot oil and fry them for a few seconds, first on one side, then the other, just until they are soft. The purpose is to soften them, so do not fry until crisp. Drain and lay them on a work surface or in a pan.
3. Pour 1–2 cups (250–500 mL) sauce in a shallow pan.
4. One at a time, dip the tortillas in the sauce to coat both sides and let the excess drip off. Lay the sauced tortilla on the work surface. Place 1½ oz (45 g) beans and ½ oz (15 g) grated cheese in the center of the tortilla and roll up.
5. Add more sauce to the pan as it gets used up. You need about 1 qt (1 L) of the sauce for dipping.
6. Arrange the rolled tortillas against each other in a baking pan, putting the loose ends on the bottom. Alternatively, place them in individual gratin dishes, allowing 2 per portion.
7. Pour the remaining sauce over the tortillas, making sure to cover the ends so they don't dry out.
8. Top with the remaining cheese.
9. Bake at 375°F (190°C) until heated through, about 20 minutes.
10. Serve 2 enchiladas per portion with 4 oz (125 g) rice.
11. Serve with guacamole, salsa, and sour cream as desired.

Per serving:
Calories, 830; Protein, 35 g; Fat, 41 g (43% cal.); Cholesterol, 70 mg; Carbohydrates, 89 g; Fiber, 17 g; Sodium, 1040 mg.

Pinto Bean Enchiladas

ENCHILADAS

The Spanish word *enchilar* means to put chile on something. The word *enchilada* is short for *tortilla enchilada*, meaning a tortilla covered with chile sauce. In the non–Spanish-speaking world, an enchilada is a corn tortilla rolled around a filling. Strictly speaking, however, the tortilla must first be coated with chile sauce before being rolled. A plain, dry tortilla with a filling is more accurately called a *soft taco*.

There are two basic methods for making enchiladas. In both methods, part of the procedure is to soften the tortilla enough so it can be rolled without breaking.

Fry the tortilla just enough to soften it, then dip in sauce, fill, and roll up.

Coat the tortilla in chile sauce, then fry briefly, fill, and roll up.

Once the tortilla is filled, it can be served immediately. For North American tastes, however, it is usually baked with additional sauce and sometimes cheese toppings.

Three-Bean Chili with Tostaditas

Yield: 6 lb   Portions: 12   Portion size: 8 oz (250 g)

U.S.	Metric	Ingredients
8 oz	250 g	Black turtle beans
8 oz	250 g	White kidney beans
1	1	Bay leaf
8 oz	250 g	Red kidney beans or pinto beans
1	1	Bay leaf
2 fl oz	60 mL	Vegetable oil
2 tbsp	30 mL	Cumin seed
6 oz	180 g	Onion, medium dice
1 oz	30 g	Garlic, chopped fine
¼ cup	60 mL	Chili powder
1½ tsp	7 mL	Chipotle chili powder
1 tbsp	15 mL	Paprika
2 tbsp	30 mL	Dried oregano
2 lb	1 kg	Tomatoes, canned, chopped, with their juice
1 tsp	5 mL	Salt
24	24	Tortillas
6 fl oz	180 mL	Salsa Cruda (p. 191)

■ Procedure

1. Sort, wash, and drain the beans. Soak them overnight in cold water.
2. Drain the beans. Place them in a heavy saucepot and add enough water to cover them by 1 in. (2.5 cm).
3. Bring to a boil, reduce heat to a simmer, and simmer until the beans are just tender.
4. Keep an eye on the beans and add a little more water whenever necessary to keep the beans covered with water.
5. Repeat steps 1–4 for the white beans. It is necessary to cook the beans separately because they may have different cooking times.
6. Repeat steps 1–4 for the red or pinto beans.
7. Heat the vegetable oil in a sauté pan over moderate heat.
8. Add the cumin and cook in the oil until the cumin is aromatic.
9. Add the onion, garlic, and spices. Sauté until the onion is lightly browned.
10. Add the tomatoes and salt. Simmer 15 minutes.
11. Combine all three pots of beans in one large pot and add the spice and tomato mixture. Simmer until the beans are very tender. As before, add water if the stew becomes too dry.
12. Taste for seasonings and add more salt if necessary.
13. To make the tostaditas, cut the tortillas into quarters, and then cut each quarter into two wedges.
14. Deep-fry the tortillas until they are crisp. Drain well.
15. To serve, ladle the chili into bowls.
16. Set the bowls on large dinner plates as underliners. Arrange the tostaditas around the bowls on the plates.
17. Place 1 tbsp (15 mL) salsa on top of each portion of chili.

Three-Bean Chili with Tostaditas

Per serving:
Calories, 400; Protein, 17 g; Fat, 10 g (22% cal.); Cholesterol, 0 mg; Carbohydrates, 65 g; Fiber, 16 g; Sodium, 580 mg.

Red Rice, Spinach with Tofu Dressing, and Eggplant Dengaku

Portions: 10   Portion size: approximately 5 oz (150 g) rice, 3 oz (90 g) spinach, 3 oz (90 g) eggplant

U.S.	Metric	Ingredients
¾ cup	180 mL	Azuki beans
4½ cups	1.1 L	Water
4 cups	1 L	Glutinous rice (see p. 618)

■ P r o c e d u r e

1. Wash and drain the beans.
2. Place the beans and the water in a saucepan and bring to a boil. Simmer 10 minutes, until the beans are just soft enough to be crushed between the fingers but not completely cooked.
3. Drain. Cool both the beans and the water to room temperature. Refrigerate the beans.
4. Wash the rice in several changes of cold water. Drain.
5. Add the red bean cooking water to the rice and soak overnight.
6. The next day, drain the rice and mix it with the beans.
7. Cover the rack of a steamer with several layers of cheesecloth.
8. Place the rice and bean mixture on top of the cheesecloth in a layer no more than 1½ in. (4 cm) thick.
9. Steam until the rice and beans are tender, about 40 minutes.

U.S.	Metric	Ingredients
10 oz	280 g	Firm Japanese-style tofu
2 tbsp	30 mL	Sesame seeds
2 tsp	10 mL	Soy sauce
1 tsp	5 mL	Mirin (Japanese sweet rice wine)
1 tbsp	15 mL	Sugar
1 lb 12 oz	850 g	Spinach, fresh, cooked and lightly squeezed (see p. 547)
to taste	to taste	Salt

10. Simmer the tofu in water for 2 minutes. Drain.
11. Wrap the tofu in cheesecloth or in a clean towel and weight with a dinner plate for 30–60 minutes to remove excess moisture.
12. Lightly toast the sesame seeds in a dry skillet, and then grind them coarsely in a mortar or spice mill.
13. Rub the tofu through a fine sieve.
14. Mix the puréed tofu with the sesame seeds, soy sauce, mirin, and sugar.
15. Chop the pressed spinach into large pieces, and then mix with the tofu dressing.
16. Add salt to taste.

U.S.	Metric	Ingredients
6 oz	180 g	White miso
1	1	Egg yolk
1 tbsp	15 mL	Sake (Japanese rice wine)
1 tbsp	15 mL	Mirin (sweet Japanese rice wine)
1 tbsp	15 mL	Sugar
2 fl oz	60 mL	Vegetarian dashi (p. 195)
2 lb	900 g	Eggplant

17. In a stainless-steel bowl, combine the miso and egg yolk and stir until smooth.
18. Stir in the sake, mirin, sugar, and dashi.
19. Set the bowl in a pan of simmering water and stir until thick.
20. Cool.
21. Trim the ends off the eggplant. Cut crosswise into rounds 1 in. (2.5 cm) thick.
22. Brush the cut sides of the eggplant slices with oil.
23. Grill, broil, or pan-fry the eggplant until tender.
24. Spread a layer of the miso mixture on top of each of the rounds.
25. Pass under the broiler or salamander just until the miso topping is lightly colored.

U.S.	Metric	Ingredients
as needed	as needed	Goma-shio (see note)

26. Serve each of the three items in separate bowls, one of each per diner. Sprinkle the top of the red rice with a little goma-shio as garnish.

Per serving:
Calories, 430; Protein, 16 g; Fat, 4.5 g (9% cal.); Cholesterol, 20 mg; Carbohydrates, 81 g; Fiber, 10 g; Sodium, 770 mg.

Note: Goma-shio, or sesame salt, is a mixture of toasted black sesame seeds and coarse salt. If it is not available, toast sesame seeds and mix with a little kosher salt.

Red Rice, Spinach with Tofu Dressing, and Eggplant Dengaku

Vietnamese Vegetable Pancakes

Portions: 6   Portion size: 1 pancake

U.S.	Metric	Ingredients
		Dipping sauce:
4 fl oz	125 mL	Soy sauce
1 tsp	5 mL	Finely chopped garlic
2 tsp	10 mL	Sugar
½ tsp	2 mL	Black pepper
1 tbsp	15 mL	Chopped fresh red chile
2 tbsp	30 mL	Chopped peanuts
1 tbsp	15 mL	Lime juice
½ cup	120 mL	Rice flour
3	3	Eggs, beaten
9 fl oz	270 mL	Water
⅛ tsp	0.5 mL	Salt
4 oz	125 g	Shiitake mushroom caps, cut batonnet
1 tbsp	15 mL	Vegetable oil
2 fl oz	60 mL	Vegetable oil
6 oz	180 g	Snow peas, trimmed
6 oz	180 g	Bean sprouts
2 oz	60 g	Scallions, sliced thin

Per serving:
Calories, 400; Protein, 17 g; Fat, 10 g (22% cal.); Cholesterol, 0 mg; Carbohydrates, 65 g; Fiber, 16 g; Sodium, 580 mg.

■ Procedure

1. Combine the dipping sauce ingredients and stir until the sugar is dissolved.
2. Set aside.

3. Whip together the rice flour, eggs, water, and salt to make a thin batter. Let stand 10 minutes
4. Strain to remove any lumps.

5. Sauté the mushrooms in hot oil until tender. Cool.

6. In a well-seasoned 10-in. (25-cm) sauté pan or, preferably, a nonstick pan, heat 2 tsp (10 mL) oil until very hot.
7. Add about 2½ fl oz (75 mL) of the batter and swirl it around to cover the bottom of the pan.
8. Add one-sixth of the mushrooms and snow peas. Cover and cook 1 minute.
9. Remove the lid and add one-sixth of the bean sprouts and scallions.
10. Cook uncovered until the pancake is crisp.
11. Slide the pancake onto a dinner plate.
12. Repeat with the remaining batter and vegetables.
13. Serve with dipping sauce.

V A R I A T I O N S

For a non-vegetarian version, serve the pancake with Nuoc Cham (p. 193) instead of the soy dipping sauce.

Vietnamese Vegetable Pancake

Winter Vegetable Gratin with Feta Cheese and Bulgur Pilaf

Portions: 10   Portion size: 6½ oz (185 g) vegetables
3 oz (90 g) pilaf

U.S.	Metric	Ingredients
10 oz	300 g	Turnips, peeled
10 oz	300 g	Parsnips, peeled
10 oz	300 g	Carrots, peeled
10 oz	300 g	Cauliflower, trimmed
6 oz	180 g	Brussels sprouts, trimmed
4 oz	125 g	Pearl onions, peeled
3 oz	90 g	Olive oil or melted butter
1 tsp	5 mL	Salt
½ tsp	2 mL	Pepper
1 tsp	5 mL	Dried thyme
1 tsp	5 mL	Dried oregano
12 oz	375 g	Feta cheese, crumbled
4 oz	125 g	Olive oil or melted butter
8 oz	250 g	Fresh bread crumbs
30 oz (1 recipe)	900 g (1 recipe)	Bulgur Pilaf with Lemon (p. 628), made with vegetable stock

Per serving:
Calories, 490; Protein, 12 g; Fat, 31 g (55% cal.); Cholesterol, 35 mg;
Carbohydrates, 44 g; Fiber, 9 g; Sodium, 830 mg.

■ P r o c e d u r e

1. Cut the turnips, parsnips, and carrots into 1½-in. (4-cm) pieces.
2. Break or cut the cauliflower into small florets.
3. Cut the brussels sprouts in half lengthwise.
4. In a large bowl, toss the vegetables, including the onions, with the oil, salt, pepper, and herbs to coat them.
5. Transfer to a half-size hotel pan, 10 × 12 in. (25 × 30 cm), or a gratin dish of the same capacity. (Alternatively, bake in single-serving gratin dishes.)
6. Bake at 400°F (200°C) until the vegetables are lightly browned and tender. Stir them occasionally during cooking so they brown evenly.
7. Remove the pan from the oven and sprinkle the feta cheese over the vegetables.
8. Mix the oil or butter with the crumbs until they are evenly mixed.
9. Sprinkle the crumbs over the vegetables in an even layer.
10. Return to the oven and bake until the top is browned. If necessary, place under a broiler or salamander to finish browning.
11. Serve with bulgur pilaf.

Winter Vegetable Gratin with Feta Cheese and Bulgur Pilaf

Falafel

Yield: about 2 lb 4 oz (1.1 kg)

U.S.	Metric	Ingredients
2 lb	1 kg	Chickpeas, cooked or canned, drained
1 oz	30 g	Garlic, chopped fine
4 oz	125 g	Scallion, chopped fine
3 tbsp	45 mL	Chopped parsley
2 tsp	10 mL	Ground cumin
2 tsp	10 mL	Ground coriander
¼ tsp	1 mL	Cayenne
2 tsp	10 mL	Salt
1 tsp	5 mL	Black pepper
1 oz	30 g	Tahini (sesame paste)
2	2	Eggs, beaten
2 oz	60 g	Soft bread crumbs

■ P r o c e d u r e

1. Process the chickpeas in a food processor until well chopped but not completely puréed.
2. Add the remaining ingredients and mix well.
3. To make large falafel, use a No. 20 scoop to portion the mix. Roll each portion into a ball and then flatten into a thick patty. Handle the portions quickly and lightly. If they are handled too much, a loose crust may form during frying which will flake off after draining.
4. To make small, appetizer-size falafel, use a No. 40 or 50 scoop to portion the mix, and roll into balls.
5. Deep-fry at 375°F (190°C) until browned and crisp.

Per serving:
Calories, 70; Protein, 3 g; Fat, 3 g (36% cal.); Cholesterol, 10 mg; Carbohydrates, 9 g; Fiber, 2 g; Sodium, 150 mg.

■ TERMS FOR REVIEW

vegetarian	pesco-vegetarian	complementary proteins	tempeh
vegan	amino acid	limiting amino acid	miso
lacto-vegetarian	essential amino acid	soy milk	bean paste
ovo-vegetarian	complete protein	tofu	textured vegetable protein
lacto-ovo-vegetarian	incomplete proteins	bean curd	(TVP)

■ QUESTIONS FOR DISCUSSION

1. Explain how complementary proteins enable vegans to get enough protein in their diet without eating animal products.

2. What vitamin is most difficult for vegans to get in their diet? Why is it difficult? What are alternative sources for this vitamin?

3. Considering them as sources of protein, what makes soybeans, amaranth, and quinoa unique among foods from plants?

4. Name and describe the three main types of tofu.

5. What is TVP? Describe how to prepare it for use in recipes.

6. Explain why some refined sugars are not suitable for use in vegetarian recipes. Which sugars are unsuitable, and which sugars can be used?

21

Salads and Salad Dressings

In the days before modern refrigeration, the pantry was the storeroom where food products were kept before being brought into the kitchen. Because this room was cooler than the kitchen, it was especially suited as a work area for the production of cold food, especially aspics, chaud-froids, and other elaborate buffet preparations. In kitchens around the world, this department is often referred to by its French name, *garde manger* (gard mawn zhay).

Today, the pantry is the department responsible for cold foods and related items. This does not mean that no cooking is done in the pantry. On the contrary, garde manger chefs must be masters of a wide range of cooking techniques. In addition, they must have artistic judgment as well as the patience and dexterity to perform a great many hand operations quickly and efficiently.

This chapter deals with two groups of items prepared in the pantry: salads and salad dressings.

SALADS

Because the number and variety of salad combinations is nearly endless, it is helpful to divide salads into categories in order to understand how they are produced. For the pantry chef, the most useful way to classify salads is by ingredients: green salads, vegetable salads, fruit salads, and so on. This is because production techniques are slightly different for each kind. We use this classification when we discuss specific recipes later in this chapter.

Before the pantry chef can produce the salads, first he or she has to decide exactly what salads should be made. Therefore, you should know what kinds of salads are best for which purposes. For this reason, salads are also classified according to their function in the meal. Keep in mind that there are no exact dividing lines between the types of salads discussed below. For example, a salad that is suitable as the first course of a dinner may also be an excellent main course on a luncheon menu.

After reading this chapter, you should be able to

1. **Identify and describe five different salad types, and select appropriate recipes for use as appetizer, accompaniment, main course, separate course, or dessert salad.**

2. **Identify a dozen popular salad greens; list six categories of other salad ingredients; and recognize several examples from each category.**

3. **Judge the quality of fruits and complete the pre-preparation procedures for fruit.**

4. **Identify the four basic parts of a salad.**

5. **Prepare and arrange salads that achieve maximum eye appeal.**

6. **Set up an efficient system for producing salads in quantity.**

7. **Prepare the following types of salads: green, vegetable, bound, fruit, combination, and gelatin.**

8. **Set up a successful salad bar and buffet service.**

9. **Identify the major salad dressing ingredients.**

10. **Prepare the following: oil and vinegar dressings, mayonnaise and mayonnaise-based dressings, cooked dressings, and specialty dressings.**

TYPES OF SALADS

Today, the variety of salads on offer seems to be greater than ever in memory. Restaurants that once listed no more than two or three salads on their menu now devote an entire page to the category. New kinds of salads fill bin after bin in the prepared-food sections of supermarkets and delicatessens.

At the same time, more traditional salads have not lost their importance. In schools, hospitals, nursing homes, neighborhood diners, and mom-and-pop restaurants, cooks who may never have heard of mesclun still have to know how to clean a head of iceberg lettuce and how to prepare flavored gelatins.

The following classification of salad types describes the roles salads fill in modern menus. These categories apply to both traditional and modern recipes. Examples of both are included later in this chapter.

APPETIZER SALADS

Many establishments serve salads as a first course, often as a substitute for a more elaborate first course. Not only does this ease the pressure on the kitchen during service but it also gives the customers a satisfying food to eat while their dinners are being prepared.

In addition, more elaborate composed salads are popular as appetizers (and also as main courses at lunch) in many elegant restaurants. These often consist of a poultry, meat, or fish item, plus a variety of vegetables and garnishes, attractively arranged on a bed of greens.

Appetizer salads should stimulate the appetite. This means they must have fresh, crisp ingredients; a tangy, flavorful dressing; and an attractive, appetizing appearance.

Preportioned salads should not be so large as to be filling, but they should be substantial enough to serve as a complete course in themselves. (Self-service salad bars, of course, avoid this problem.) Tossed green salads are especially popular for this reason, as they are bulky without being filling.

The combination of ingredients should be interesting, not dull or trite. Flavorful foods like cheese, ham, salami, shrimp, and crabmeat, even in small quantities, add appeal. So do crisp raw or lightly cooked vegetables. A bowl of poorly drained iceberg lettuce with a bland dressing is hardly the most exciting way to start a meal.

Attractive arrangement and garnish are important because visual appeal stimulates the appetite. A satisfying, interesting starter puts the customer in a good frame of mind for the rest of the meal.

ACCOMPANIMENT SALADS

Salads can also be served with the main course. They serve the same function as other side dishes (vegetables and starches).

Accompaniment salads must balance and harmonize with the rest of the meal, like any other side dish. For example, don't serve potato salad at the same meal at which you are serving French fries or another starch. Sweet fruit salads are rarely appropriate as accompaniments, except with such items as ham or pork.

Side-dish salads should be light and flavorful, not too rich. Vegetable salads are often good choices. Heavier salads, such as macaroni or high-protein salads containing meat, seafood, cheese, and so on, are less appropriate, unless the main course is light. Combination salads with a variety of elements are appropriate accompaniments to sandwiches.

MAIN-COURSE SALADS

Cold salad plates have become popular on luncheon menus, especially among nutrition- and diet-conscious diners. The appeal of these salads is in variety and freshness of ingredients.

Main-course salads should be large enough to serve as a full meal and should contain a substantial portion of protein. Meat, poultry, and seafood salads, as well as egg salad and cheese, are popular choices.

Main-course salads should offer enough variety on the plate to form a balanced meal, both nutritionally and in flavors and textures. In addition to the protein, a salad platter should offer a variety of vegetables, greens, and/or fruits. Examples are chef's salad (mixed greens, raw vegetables, and strips of meat and cheese), shrimp or crab-meat salad with tomato wedges and slices of avocado on a bed of greens, and cottage cheese with an assortment of fresh fruits.

The portion size and variety of ingredients give the chef an excellent opportunity to use imagination and creativity to produce attractive, appetizing salad plates. Attractive arrangements and good color balance are important.

SEPARATE-COURSE SALADS

Many fine restaurants serve a refreshing, light salad after the main course. The purpose is to cleanse the palate after a rich dinner and to refresh the appetite and provide a pleasant break before dessert.

Salads served after the main course were the rule rather than the exception many years ago, and the practice deserves to be more widespread. A diner who may be satiated after a heavy meal is often refreshed and ready for dessert after a light, piquant salad.

Separate-course salads must be very light and in no way filling. Rich, heavy dressings, such as those made with sour cream and mayonnaise, should be avoided. Perhaps the ideal choice is a few delicate greens, such as Bibb lettuce or Belgian endive, lightly dressed with vinaigrette. Fruit salads are also popular choices.

DESSERT SALADS

Dessert salads are usually sweet and may contain items such as fruits, sweetened gelatin, nuts, and cream. They are often too sweet to be served as appetizers or accompaniments and are best served as dessert or as part of a buffet or party menu.

INGREDIENTS

Freshness and variety of ingredients are essential for high-quality salads. Lettuce, of course, is the first choice for most people, but many other foods can make up a salad.

The following tables list, by category, most of the ingredients used in popular salads. You will be able to think of others. Add them to the lists as they occur to you or as they are suggested by your instructor. The lists will be useful when you are creating your own salad ideas.

Following these lists are detailed descriptions of two groups of foods that have not been covered in previous chapters and belong especially in the pantry: salad greens and fresh fruits.

SALAD GREENS

Iceberg lettuce	Dandelion greens
Romaine lettuce	Watercress
Boston lettuce	Arugula
Bibb or limestone lettuce	Radicchio
Loose-leaf lettuce	Mesclun
Escarole	Tatsoi
Chicory or curly endive	Mâche
Frisée	Microgreens
Belgian endive	Sprouts
Chinese cabbage or celery cabbage	Edible flowers
Spinach	

VEGETABLES, RAW

Avocado	Cucumbers
Bean sprouts	Jerusalem artichokes
Broccoli	Kohlrabi
Cabbage, white, green, and red	Mushrooms
Carrots	Onions and scallions
Cauliflower	Peppers, red, green, and yellow
Celery	Radishes
Celeriac (celery root)	Tomatoes

VEGETABLES, COOKED, PICKLED, AND CANNED

Artichoke hearts	Hearts of palm
Asparagus	Leeks
Beans (all kinds)	Olives
Beets	Peas
Carrots	Peppers, roasted and pickled
Cauliflower	Pimientos
Corn	Potatoes
Cucumber pickles (dill, sweet, etc.)	Water chestnuts

STARCHES

Dried beans (cooked or canned)	Grains
Potatoes	Bread (croutons)
Macaroni products	

FRUITS, FRESH, COOKED, CANNED, OR FROZEN

Apples	Melons
Apricots	Nectarines
Bananas	Oranges
Berries	Papayas
Cherries	Peaches
Coconut	Pears
Dates	Persimmons
Figs	Pineapple
Grapefruit	Plums
Grapes	Pomegranates
Kiwi fruit	Prickly pear
Kumquats	Prunes
Mandarin oranges and tangerines	Raisins
Mangoes	

PROTEIN FOODS

Meats (beef, ham)	Bacon
Poultry (chicken, turkey)	Eggs, hard-cooked
Fish and shellfish (tuna, crab, shrimp, lobster, salmon, sardines, anchovies, herring, any fresh cooked fish)	Cheese, cottage
	Cheese, aged or cured types
Salami, prosciutto, luncheon meats, etc.	

MISCELLANEOUS

Gelatin (plain or flavored)

Nuts

LETTUCE AND OTHER SALAD GREENS

Iceberg lettuce

Iceberg Lettuce

The most popular salad ingredient. Firm, compact head with crisp, mild-tasting pale green leaves. Valuable for its texture because it stays crisp longer than other lettuces. Can be used alone but is best mixed with more flavorful greens such as romaine because it lacks flavor itself. Keeps well.

Romaine or cos lettuce

Romaine or Cos Lettuce

Elongated, loosely packed head with dark green, coarse leaves. Crisp texture, with full, sweet flavor. Keeps well and is easy to handle. Essential for Caesar salad. For elegant service, the center rib is often removed.

Boston lettuce

Boston Lettuce

Small, round heads with soft, fragile leaves. Deep green outside shading to nearly white inside. The leaves have a rich, mild flavor and delicate, buttery texture. Bruises easily and does not keep well. Cup-shaped leaves excellent for salad bases.

Bibb or limestone lettuce

Loose-leaf lettuce

Escarole or broad-leaf endive

Chicory or curly endive

Frisée

Belgian endive or witloof chicory

Chinese cabbage

Spinach

Arugula or rocket

Bibb or Limestone Lettuce

Similar to Boston lettuce, but smaller and more delicate. A whole head may be only a few inches (less than 10 cm) across. Color ranges from dark green outside to creamy yellow at the core. Its tenderness, delicate flavor, and high price make it a luxury in some markets. The small, whole leaves are often served by themselves, with a light vinaigrette dressing, as an after-dinner salad.

Loose-leaf Lettuce

Forms bunches rather than heads. Soft, fragile leaves with curly edges. May be all green or with shades of red. Wilts easily and does not keep well, but is inexpensive and gives flavor, variety, and interest to mixed green salads.

Escarole or Broad-leaf Endive

Broad, thick leaves in bunches rather than heads. Texture is coarse and slightly tough, and flavor is somewhat bitter. Mix with sweeter greens to vary flavor and texture, but do not use alone because of the bitterness. Escarole is frequently braised with olive oil and garlic and served as a vegetable in Italian cuisine.

Chicory or Curly Endive

Narrow, curly, twisted leaves with firm texture and bitter flavor. Outside leaves are dark green; core is yellow or white. Attractive when mixed with other greens or used as a base or garnish, but may be too bitter to be used alone.

Frisée

Frisée is the same plant as curly endive or chicory, but it is grown in a way that makes it more tender and less bitter. Except for the outer layer, the leaves are pale yellow, slender, and feathery, with a distinct but mild taste.

Belgian Endive or Witloof Chicory

Narrow, lightly packed, pointed heads resembling spearheads, 4–6 inches (10–15 cm) long. Pale yellow-green to white in color. Leaves are crisp, with a waxy texture and pleasantly bitter flavor. Usually expensive. Often served alone, split in half or into wedges, or separated into leaves, accompanied by a mustard vinaigrette dressing.

Chinese Cabbage

Elongated, light green heads with broad, white center ribs. Available in two forms: narrow, elongated head, often called *celery cabbage*, and thicker, blunt head, called napa cabbage. Tender but crisp, with a mild cabbage flavor. Adds excellent flavor to mixed green salads. Also used extensively in Chinese cooking.

Spinach

Small, tender spinach leaves are excellent salad greens, either alone or mixed with other greens. A popular salad is spinach leaves garnished with sliced raw mushrooms and crisp, crumbled bacon. Spinach must be washed thoroughly, and the coarse stems must be removed.

Watercress

Most commonly used as a garnish, watercress is also excellent in salads. Small, dark green, oval leaves with a pungent, peppery flavor. Remove thick stems before adding to salads.

Watercress

Arugula

Also known as *rugula* or *rocket*, these pungent, distinctively flavored greens are related to mustard and watercress. They are tender and perishable, and they often are sandy, so they must be washed carefully. Arugula was once found almost exclusively in Italian restaurants, but it has since become more widely available and is increasingly popular.

Mesclun

Mesclun is a mixture of tender baby lettuces. It is available as a mixture, but some chefs prefer to buy individual baby lettuces and make their own mixture.

Mesclun

Baby Lettuces

The small, tender leaves that make up a mesclun mix are also available separately. These include baby Bibb (both red and green), baby romaine, baby red oak leaf, and lola rossa (a red lettuce with ruffled leaves).

Sprouts

Sprouts are young plants that have just emerged from their seeds, before the true leaves develop. Sprouts from mung beans are commonly used in Chinese cooking. Alfalfa, daikon radish, and mustard sprouts are often used in delicate salads. Alfalfa sprouts have a mild flavor, while radish and mustard sprouts have a peppery flavor.

Microgreens

These are the first true leaves that develop after a seed sprouts. Tiny herb leaves and tiny leaves from lettuce and other salad greens, younger and smaller than baby lettuces, are used mostly as garnish for other dishes, both hot and cold.

Microgreens

Tatsoi

Tatsoi is a small, dark green round leaf. Its flavor has a pleasant bite similar to that of arugula, watercress, and other members of the mustard family. It is sometimes included in mesclun mixtures, although it is not actually a lettuce.

Tatsoi

Mizuna

Mizuna, also known as Japanese mustard greens, is a dark green leaf with jagged edges resembling dandelion leaves. It has a mild, mustardy taste.

Mizuna

Mâche

Also called *corn salad*, *lamb's lettuce*, *lamb's tongue*, and *field salad*, mâche is a small, very tender green with spoon-shaped leaves. It has a delicate, nutty flavor.

Mâche

Radicchio

Radicchio (ra dik ee oh), a red-leafed Italian variety of chicory, has creamy white ribs or veins and generally comes in small, round heads. It has a crunchy texture and a slightly bitter flavor. Radicchio is expensive, but only a leaf or two are needed to add color and flavor to a salad.

Radicchio

Treviso

Treviso is a red-leafed plant like radicchio, but with elongated leaves somewhat like Belgian endive. Like radicchio and endive, it belongs to the chicory family and has a slightly bitter flavor.

Treviso

Dandelion Greens

The familiar lawn ornament is also cultivated for use in the kitchen. Only young, tender leaves may be used. Older leaves are coarse and bitter, though cultivated varieties are milder than wild dandelion. Best in spring.

Precleaned, Precut Salad Greens

Precut greens are sold in large, sealed plastic bags. They save labor costs in large operations but are more perishable than unprocessed greens. Keep refrigerated, and do not open until ready to use. Unopened bags will keep for two or three days. Taste before serving to make sure the greens do not have too much antioxidant on them, making them bitter.

Granny Smith apple

Golden Delicious apple

Rome apple

Round Gala apple

Macintosh apple

Red Delicious apple

Bananas

FRESH FRUITS: EVALUATING AND PREPARING

The following is a summary of the most commonly available fresh fruits. Emphasis is on the qualities to look for when purchasing them and on how to trim and prepare the fruit for use. In addition, identification information is included for certain exotic items. Nearly everyone knows what apples, bananas, and strawberries are, but not everyone can identify a persimmon or a passion fruit. Trimming yields are also given. How to use these percentages is explained on page 513.

Apples. Mature apples have a fruity aroma, brown seeds, and a slightly softer texture than unripe fruit. Overripe or old apples are soft and sometimes shriveled. Avoid apples with bruises, blemishes, decay, or mealy texture. Summer varieties (sold until fall) do not keep well. Fall and winter varieties keep well and are available for a longer period. Apples with a good acid content are usually better for cooking than bland eating varieties like Red Delicious. Granny Smith and Golden Delicious are widely used for cooking. To prepare, wash; pare if desired. Quarter and remove core, or leave whole and core with a special coring tool. Use a stainless-steel knife for cutting. After paring, dip in solution of lemon juice (or other tart fruit juice) or ascorbic acid to prevent browning.
Percentage yield: 75%

Apricots. Only tree-ripened apricots have sufficient flavor, and they keep for a week or less under refrigeration. They should be golden yellow, firm, and plump, not mushy. Avoid fruit that is too soft, blemished, or decayed.
Wash, split in half, and remove pit. Peeling is not necessary for most purposes.
Percentage yield: 94%

Bananas. Look for plump, smooth bananas without bruises or spoilage. All bananas are picked green, so you don't need to avoid unripe fruit. Avoid overripe fruit, however.
Ripen at room temperature for three to five days; fully ripe fruit is all yellow with small brown flecks and no green. Do not refrigerate, or fruit will discolor. Peel and dip in fruit juice to prevent browning.
Percentage yield: 70%

Berries. This category includes blackberries, blueberries, cranberries, blackcurrants (cassis), red currants, white currants, lingonberries, raspberries, and strawberries. Berries should be full, plump, and clean, with bright, fully ripe color. Watch for moldy or spoiled fruits. Wet spots on carton indicate damaged fruit.
Refrigerate in original container until ready to use in order to reduce handling. Except for cranberries, berries do not keep well. Sort out spoiled berries and foreign materials. Wash with gentle spray and drain well. Remove stems from strawberries. Red currants for garnishing are often left on the stem. Handle berries carefully to avoid bruising.
Percentage yield: 92–95%

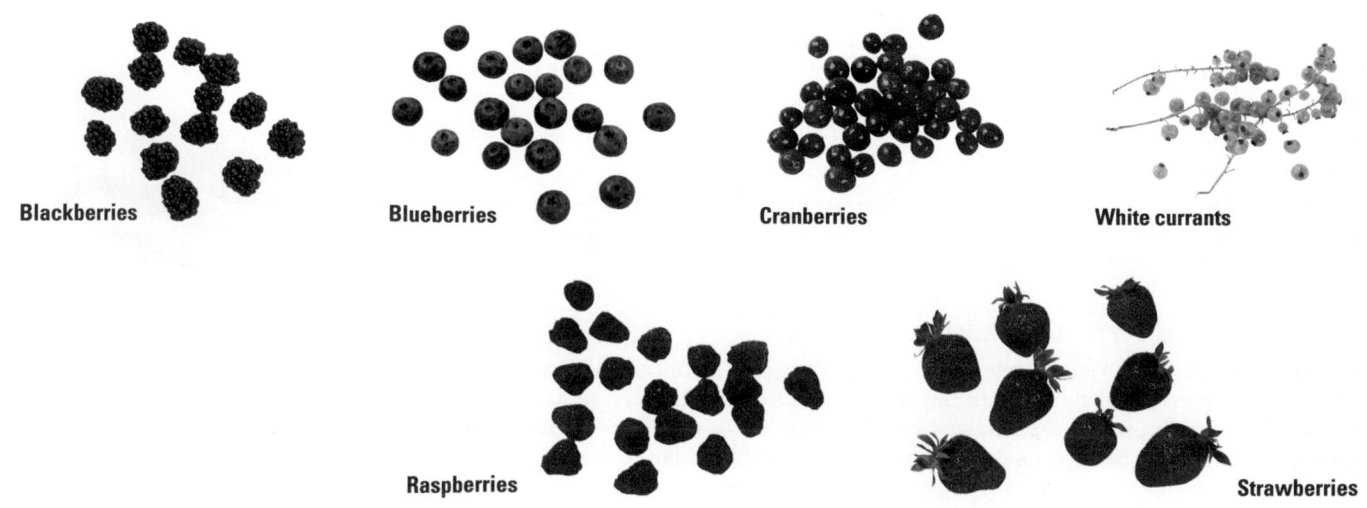

Blackberries   **Blueberries**   **Cranberries**   **White currants**

Raspberries   **Strawberries**

Cherries. Look for plump, firm, sweet, juicy cherries. Bing or black cherries should be uniformly dark to almost black.

Refrigerate in original container until ready to use. Just before use, remove stems and sort out damaged fruit. Rinse and drain well. Pit with a special pitting tool.

Percentage yield: 82% (pitted)

Coconuts. Shake to hear liquid inside; fruits with no liquid are dried out. Avoid cracked fruits and fruits with wet eyes.

Pierce eye with ice pick or nail and drain liquid. Crack with hammer and remove meat from shell (easier if placed in 350°F/175°C oven for 10–15 minutes first). Peel brown skin with paring knife or vegetable peeler.

Percentage yield: 50%

Figs. Calimyrna figs, also called *Smyrna figs*, are light green; Black Mission figs and Black Spanish figs (also called *Brown Turkey*) are purple. All figs are sweet when ripe and soft and delicate in texture. They should be plump and soft, without spoilage or sour odor.

Keep refrigerated (although firm, unripe figs can be left at room temperature, spread in one layer, for a few days to ripen slightly). Rinse and drain, handling carefully. Trim off hard stem ends.

Percentage yield: 95% (80–85% if peeled)

Grapefruit. Select fruit that is heavy for its size and has a firm, smooth skin. Avoid puffy, soft fruits or those with pointed ends, which have low yield and a lot of rind. Cut and taste for sweetness.

For sections and slices, peel with a chef's knife, removing all white pith (see p. 139). Free sections from membrane with a small knife.

Percentage yield: 45–50% (flesh without membrane); 40–45% (juiced)

Grapes. Look for firm, ripe, good-colored fruits in full bunches. Grapes should be firmly attached to stems and not fall off when shaken. Watch for rotting or shriveling at stem ends.

Refrigerate in original container. Wash and drain. Except for seedless varieties, cut in half and remove seeds with the point of a paring knife.

Percentage yield: 90%

Kiwi fruit. Kiwis are firm when unripe; they become slightly softer when ripe but do not change color significantly. Common kiwis have green flesh; golden kiwis are also available. Allow them to ripen at room temperature. Avoid fruits with bruises or soft spots.

Pare thin outer skin. Cut crosswise into slices.

Percentage yield: 80%

Kumquats. These look like tiny, elongated oranges, about the size of a medium olive. The skin and even the seeds can be eaten. In fact, the skin is sweet, while the flesh and juice are tart. Avoid soft or shriveled fruit. Kumquats keep well and are usually in good condition in the market.

Wash, drain well, and cut as desired.

Percentage yield: 95–100%

Lemons and limes. Look for firm, smooth skins. Colors may vary: Limes may be yellow, and lemons may have green on skin.

Cut in wedges, slices, or other shapes for garnish, or cut in half crosswise for juicing. Wash first if using the zest.

Percentage yield: 40–45% (juiced)

Litchis (or lychees). This Chinese fruit is about the size of a walnut or Ping-Pong ball. Its rough, leathery outer skin, which ranges from reddish to brown, is easily peeled away to reveal aromatic, juicy white flesh that surrounds an inedible pit. Look for heavy, plump fruit with good color.

Peel, cut in half, and remove the seed.

Percentage yield: 50%

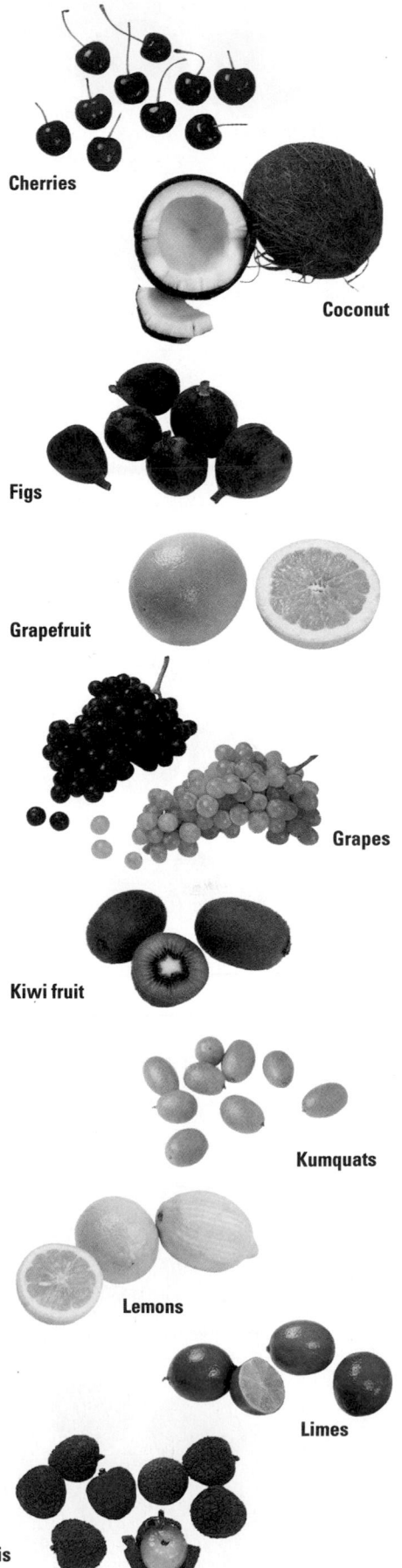

Cherries

Coconut

Figs

Grapefruit

Grapes

Kiwi fruit

Kumquats

Lemons

Limes

Litchis

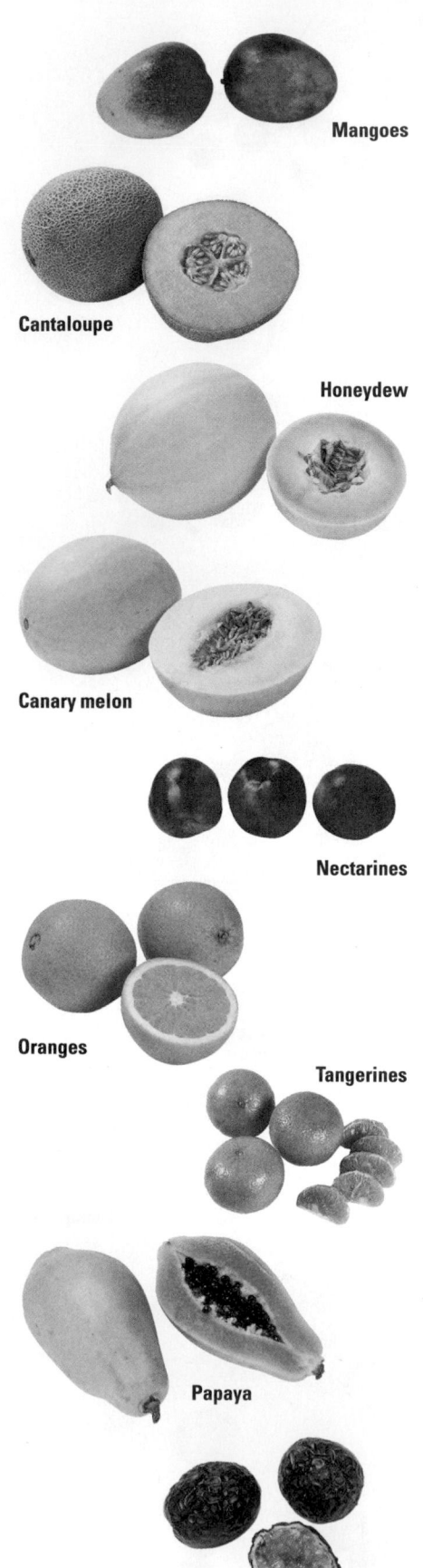

Mangoes

Cantaloupe

Honeydew

Canary melon

Nectarines

Oranges

Tangerines

Papaya

Passion fruit

Mangoes. This tropical fruit comes in two main types: oval, with a skin that ranges from green to orange to red, and kidney-shaped, with skin that is more uniform yellow when ripe. Mangoes have a thin but tough skin and yellow to yellow-orange flesh that is juicy and aromatic. Fruit should be plump and firm, with clear color and no blemishes. Avoid rock-hard fruit, which may not ripen properly.

Let ripen at room temperature until slightly soft. Peel and cut flesh away from center stone, or cut in half before peeling, working a thin-bladed knife around both sides of the flat stone.

Percentage yield: 75%

Melons. Look for the following characteristics when selecting melons. *Cantaloupes:* Smooth scar on stem end, with no trace of stem (called **full slip**, meaning the melon was picked ripe). Yellow rind, with little or no green. Heavy, with good aroma. *Honeydew:* Good aroma, slightly soft, heavy, creamy white to yellowish rind, not too green. Large sizes have best quality. *Crenshaw, Casaba, Persian, Canary, Santa Claus:* Heavy, with a rich aroma and slightly soft blossom end. *Watermelon:* Yellow underside, not white. Firm and symmetrical. Large sizes have best yield. Velvety surface, not too shiny. When cut, look for hard dark brown seeds and no white heart (hard white streak running through center).

To prepare hollow melons, wash, cut in half, and remove seeds and fibers. Cut into wedges and cut flesh from rind, or cut balls with ball cutter. For watermelon, wash, cut in half or into pieces, and cut balls with ball cutter, or cut flesh from rind and remove seeds.

Percentage yield: Watermelons: 45%; others: 50–55%

Nectarines. See peaches and nectarines.

Oranges and mandarins (including tangerines). To buy high-quality oranges, use the same guidelines as for grapefruit. Mandarins may feel puffy, but they should be heavy for their size. Unusual varieties include blood oranges, with dark red flesh and juice and intense flavor, and Seville oranges, with tart rather than sweet flesh. Seville oranges are prized for making marmalade.

Peel mandarins by hand and separate the sections. For juicing, cut oranges in half crosswise. For sections, see grapefruit.

Percentage yield: 60–65% (sections with no membranes); 50% (juiced)

Papayas. Papayas are pear-shaped tropical fruits with a mild, sweet flavor and slightly floral aroma. The flesh is yellow or pinkish, depending on the variety, and the center cavity holds a mass of round, black seeds. Papayas may weigh from less than 1 pound to several pounds (less than 500 g to more than 1 kg) each. Their skin is green when unripe, becoming yellow as they ripen. For best quality, select fruits that are firm and symmetrical, without bruises or rotten spots. Avoid dark green papayas, which may not ripen properly.

Let ripen at room temperature until slightly soft and nearly all yellow, with only a little green. Wash. Cut in half lengthwise and scrape out the seeds. Peel, if desired, or serve like cantaloupe.

Percentage yield: 65%

Passion fruit. These are tropical fruits about the size of eggs, with a brownish purple skin that becomes wrinkled when ripe. (There is also a yellow-skinned variety.) They are mostly hollow when ripe, with juice, seeds, and a little flesh inside. The tart juice has an intense, exotic flavor and aroma that is greatly prized by pastry chefs. Select fruits that are large and heavy for their size. If they are smooth, let ripen at room temperature until the skin is wrinkled.

To use, cut in half, taking care not to lose any juice. Scrape out the seeds, juice, and pulp. Seeds can be eaten, so do not discard. If you need only the juice, it is much more economical to buy the frozen juice, as fresh fruits are expensive.

Percentage yield: 40–45%

Peaches and nectarines. Peaches should be plump and firm, without bruises or blemishes. Avoid dark green fruits, which are immature and will not ripen well. Avoid fruits that have been refrigerated before ripening, as they may be mealy. Select freestone varieties of peaches. Clingstone varieties require too much labor (they are used primarily for canning).

Let ripen at room temperature, then refrigerate. Peel peaches by blanching in boiling water about 10 to 20 seconds, until skin slips off easily, and cool in ice water. (Nectarines do not need to be peeled.) Cut in half, remove pits, and drop into fruit juice, sugar syrup, or ascorbic acid solution to prevent darkening.

Percentage yield: 75%

Peaches

Bartlett pears

Bosc pears

Pears. Pears should be clean, firm, and bright, with no blemishes or bruises.

Pears for eating raw should be fully ripe and aromatic. For cooking, they are better if slightly under-ripe, as fully ripe pears are very soft when cooked. Wash, pare, cut in halves or quarters, and remove core. To prevent browning, dip in fruit juice.

Percentage yield: 75% (peeled and cored)

Persimmons. Persimmons are orange-red fruits available in two varieties. The most common is Hachiya, which is shaped somewhat like a large acorn (about 8 oz/250 g each). It is extremely tannic when unripe, making it nearly inedible until it ripens to a soft, jellylike mass. Ripe persimmons are sweet, juicy, and mild but rich in flavor. The other variety, Fuyu, is smaller and more squat in shape. It lacks the tannin content of Hachiya persimmons and can be eaten even when not fully ripe. Select plump persimmons with good red color and stem cap attached.

Ripen at room temperature until very soft, then refrigerate. Remove stem cap, cut as desired, and remove seeds, if there are any.

Percentage yield: 80%

Hachiya persimmons

Pineapple

Pineapples. Pineapples should be plump and fresh-looking, with an orange-yellow color and abundant fragrance. Avoid soft spots, bruises, and dark, watery spots.

Store at room temperature for a day or two to allow some tartness to disappear, then refrigerate. Pineapples may be cut in many ways. For slices, chunks, and dice, cut off top and bottom and pare the rough skin from the sides, using a stainless-steel knife. Remove all eyes. Cut into quarters lengthwise and cut out the hard center core. Slice or cut as desired.

Percentage yield: 50%

Prune Plums

Plums. Plums should be plump and firm but not hard, with good color and no blemishes.

Wash, cut in half, and remove pits, or serve whole.

Percentage yield: 95% (pitted only)

Red Plums

Pomegranates. The pomegranate is a subtropical fruit about the size of a large apple. It has a dry red skin or shell enclosing a mass of seeds. Each seed is surrounded by a small sphere of juicy, bright red pulp. Pomegranates are used mostly for their red, tart-sweet juice. The seeds with their surrounding pulp can also be used as an attractive garnish for desserts and even meat dishes. Look for heavy fruits without bruises. When squeezed, they should yield to gentle pressure; if they are too hard, they may be dried out.

To prepare, lightly score the skin without cutting into the seeds and carefully break the fruit into sections. Separate the seeds from the membranes. Juicing is difficult. Some methods crush the seeds and make the juice bitter. This method makes a better juice: Roll the whole pomegranate on the countertop under the palm of the hand to break the juice sacs. Then pierce a hole in the side and squeeze out the juice.

Percentage yield: 55%

Pomegranate

Prickly pears or cactus pears. This is a barrel-shaped fruit about the size of a large egg. Its skin color ranges from magenta to greenish red and it has a bright pinkish red, spongy interior with black seeds. The pulp is sweet and aromatic, but with a mild flavor. Good-quality fruits are tender but not mushy, with a good skin color, not faded. Avoid fruits with rotten spots.

If the fruit is firm, allow to ripen at room temperature, then refrigerate. As it is the fruit of a cactus, thorns grow on the skin. These are removed before shipping, but small, hard-to-see thorns may remain. To avoid getting stung, hold the fruit with a fork while you slice off the top and bottom. Still holding it with a fork, pare the sides with a knife and discard the peels without touching them. Cut or slice the pulp as desired, or force it through a sieve to purée it and remove the seeds.

Percentage yield: 70%

Prickly pears

Quinces

Rhubarb

Star fruit

Quince. Quinces grow in temperate climates and were once very popular in Europe and North America. Many old, neglected quince trees remain in New England and elsewhere. The fruit resembles a large, yellow, lumpy pear with a smooth or slightly downy skin. The raw fruit is never eaten, as it is dry and hard. When cooked (usually stewed or poached in a sugar syrup), it becomes aromatic, flavorful, and sweet, and the color of the flesh turns slightly pink. The fruit keeps well. Select fruit with good color and free of bruises or blemishes.

Cut, pare, and core like apples or pears, then cook.

Percentage yield: 75%

Rhubarb. Rhubarb is a stem, not a fruit, but it is used like a fruit. Buy firm, crisp, tender rhubarb with thick stalks, not thin and shriveled.

Cut off all traces of leaf, which is poisonous. Trim root end, if necessary. Peel with a vegetable peeler if desired, or omit this step if the skin is tender. Cut into desired lengths.

Percentage yield: 85–90% (if purchased without leaves)

Star fruit or carambola. The star fruit is a shiny, yellow, oblong fruit with five ridges running the length of the fruit, so that it forms stars when sliced crosswise. It is fragrant, ranging from tart to sweet, with a crisp texture. Look for full, firm fruits. Avoid fruits with ribs that have browned and shrunk.

Wash and slice crosswise.

Percentage yield: 99%

ARRANGEMENT AND PRESENTATION

THE STRUCTURE OF A SALAD

A plated salad may have as many as four parts: base, body, dressing, and garnish. All salads have body, and most have dressing, but base and garnish are parts of only some salads, as you will see in the following discussion.

Of course this discussion refers only to individual plated salads. When we use the term salad to refer to a bulk mixture, as in "two pounds of potato salad," references to the four parts of a salad do not apply.

Base or Underliner

A scoop of potato salad looks bare when served by itself on a salad plate as a side dish. Placing it on a bed of lettuce leaves makes it more appealing and also emphasizes its identity as a salad. Although most tossed green salads and many composed salads are presented without an underliner, bound salads and some other vegetable salads may be more attractive and appetizing when served on a bed of leafy greens.

Cup-shaped leaves of iceberg or Boston lettuce make attractive bases. They give height to salads and help confine loose pieces of food.

A layer of loose, flat leaves (such as romaine, loose-leaf, or chicory) or of shredded lettuce may be used as a base. This kind of base involves less labor and food cost, as it is not necessary to separate whole cup-shaped leaves from a head.

Body

This is the main part of the salad and, as such, receives most of our attention in this chapter.

Garnish

A garnish is an edible decorative item that is added to a salad to give eye appeal, though it often adds to the flavor as well. It should not be elaborate or dominate the salad. Remember this basic rule of garnishing: Keep it simple.

Garnish should harmonize with the rest of the salad ingredients and, of course, be edible. It may be mixed with the other salad ingredients (for example, shreds of red cabbage mixed into a tossed green salad), or it may be added at the end.

Often, the main ingredients of a salad form an attractive pattern in themselves, and no garnish is necessary. In the case of certain combination salads and other salads with many ingredients or components, there may be no clear distinction between a garnish and an attractive ingredient that is part of the body. In general, if a salad is attractive and balanced without an added garnish, don't add one.

Nearly any of the vegetables, fruits, and protein foods listed on pages 676–677, cut into simple, appropriate shapes, may be used as garnish.

Dressing

Dressing is a seasoned liquid or semiliquid that is added to the body of the salad to give it added flavor, tartness, spiciness, and moistness.

The dressing should harmonize with the salad ingredients. In general, use tart dressings for green salads and vegetable salads and use slightly sweetened dressings for fruit salads. Soft, delicate greens like Boston or Bibb lettuce require a light dressing. A thick, heavy dressing will turn them to mush.

Dressings may be added at service time (as for green salads), served separately for the customer to add, or mixed with the ingredients ahead of time (as in potato salad, tuna salad, egg salad, and so on). A salad mixed with a heavy dressing, like mayonnaise, to hold it together is called a **bound salad**.

Remember: Dressing is a *seasoning* for the main ingredients. It should accent their flavor, not overpower or drown them. Review the rules of seasoning in Chapter 4.

ARRANGING THE SALAD

Perhaps even more than with most other foods, the appearance and arrangement of a salad are essential to its quality. The colorful variety of salad ingredients gives the chef an opportunity to create miniature works of art on the salad plate.

Unfortunately, it is nearly as difficult to give rules for arranging salads as it is for painting pictures because the principles of composition, balance, and symmetry are the same for both arts. It is something you have to develop an eye for, by experience and by studying good examples.

Guidelines for Arranging Salads

1. Keep the salad off the rim of the plate.

   Think of the rim as a picture frame and arrange the salad within this frame. Select the right plate for the portion size, not too large or too small.

2. Strive for a good balance of colors.

   Plain iceberg lettuce looks pale and sickly all by itself, but it can be enlivened by mixing in darker greens and perhaps a few shreds of carrot, red cabbage, or other colored vegetable. On the other hand, don't go overboard. Sometimes just a few shades of green will create a beautiful effect. Too many colors may look messy.

3. Height helps make a salad attractive.

   Ingredients mounded on the plate are more interesting than if they are spread flat. Lettuce cups as bases add height. Often just a little height is enough. Arrange ingredients like fruit wedges or tomato slices so they overlap or lean against each other rather than lie flat on the plate.

4. Cut ingredients neatly.

   Ragged or sloppy cutting makes the whole salad look sloppy and haphazard.

5. Make every ingredient identifiable.

   Cut every ingredient into large enough pieces that the customer can recognize each immediately. Don't pulverize everything in the buffalo chopper or VCM. Bite-size pieces are the general rule, unless the ingredient can be cut easily with a fork, such as tomato slices. Seasoning ingredients, like onion, may be chopped fine.

6. Keep it simple.

   A simple, natural arrangement is pleasing. An elaborate design, a gimmicky or contrived arrangement, or a cluttered plate is not pleasing. Besides, elaborate designs take too long to make.

RECIPES AND TECHNIQUES

Thorough mise en place is extremely important in salad-making. Little cooking is involved, but a great deal of time-consuming handwork is. Salads can be made quickly and efficiently only if the station is set up properly.

Procedure for Quantity Salad Production

When salads are made in quantity, an assembly-line production system is most efficient. Figure 21.1 illustrates this technique.

Remember the rules of safe food handling. Most salad ingredients are eaten without further cooking, so it is essential to avoid cross-contamination. Use sanitary tools and work surfaces. Wash hands properly before beginning work. In some places, local health laws require the use of gloves whenever you are handling ready-to-eat foods.

Figure 21.1
Efficient production of salads in quantity.

(a) Prepare all ingredients ahead. Arrange cold salad plates on trays for easy refrigeration.

(b) Place lettuce bases on all plates.

(c) Place body of salad (in this case, potato salad) on all plates.

(d) Garnish all salads. Refrigerate until service.

1. Prepare all ingredients. Wash and cut greens. Prepare cooked vegetables. Cut all fruits, vegetables, and garnish. Mix bound and marinated salads (egg salad, potato salad, three-bean salad, etc.). Have all ingredients chilled.

2. Arrange salad plates on worktables. Line them up on trays for easy transfer to refrigerator.

3. Place bases or underliners on all plates.

4. Arrange body of salad on all plates.

5. Garnish all salads.

6. Refrigerate until service. Do not hold more than a few hours, or the salads will wilt. Holding boxes should have high humidity.

7. Do not add dressing to green salads until service, or they will wilt.

GREEN SALADS

Principles

Salad greens must be fresh, clean, crisp, cold, and well drained, or the salad will be of poor quality. Good greens depend on proper preparation.

Moisture and air are necessary to keep greens crisp.

1. Leaves wilt because they lose moisture. Crispness can be restored by washing and refrigeration. The moisture that clings to the leaves after thorough draining is usually enough. Too much water drowns them and dissolves out flavor and nutrients.

2. Air circulation is essential for the greens to breathe. Do not seal washed greens too tightly or pack too firmly. Refrigerate in colanders covered with clean, damp towels, or in specially designed perforated plastic bins. These protect from drying while allowing air circulation.

Browning or rusting occurs when cut greens are held too long. This can be partially avoided by rinsing them in a mild antioxidant and by using stainless-steel knives. Better yet, plan purchasing and production so you don't need to hold them too long.

Basic Procedure for Green Salads

1. **Wash greens thoroughly.**

   Remove core from head lettuce by striking the core gently against a flat surface, such as a cutting board or the side of a vegetable sink, and twisting it out. Do not smash it, or you'll bruise the entire head. Cut through the core of other greens or separate the leaves so all traces of grit can be removed. Wash in several changes of cold water, until completely clean. For iceberg lettuce, run cold water into the core end (after removing core), then turn over to drain.

2. **Drain greens well.**

   Lift greens from the water and drain in a colander. Tools and machines are available that quickly spin-dry greens. Poor draining results in a watered-down dressing and a soupy, soggy salad.

3. **Crisp the greens.**

   Refrigerate greens in a colander covered with damp towels or in a perforated storage bin to allow air circulation and complete drainage.

4. **Cut or tear into bite-size pieces.**

   Many people insist on tearing leaves instead of cutting, but this is a slow method if you have a large quantity to do. Also, you are more likely to crush or bruise the leaves.

   Use sharp stainless-steel knives for cutting. Bite-size pieces are important as a convenience to the customer. It is difficult to eat or cut large leaves with a salad fork.

5. **Mix the greens.**

   Toss gently until uniformly mixed. Nonjuicy raw vegetable garnish such as green pepper strips or carrot shreds may be mixed in at this time. Just make sure the vegetables are not cut into compact little chunks that will settle to the bottom of the bowl. Broad, thin slices or shreds stay better mixed.

   For tossed salads to be served immediately, add the dressing to the greens in the bowl. Toss to coat the greens with the dressing. Plate (step 6) and serve immediately. For pre-plated salads, proceed with steps 6 through 9.

6. **Plate the salads (including underliners, if used).**

   Cold plates, please. Don't use plates right out of the dishwasher.

   Avoid plating salads more than an hour or two before service, or they are likely to wilt or dry.

7. **Garnish.**

   Exceptions: (a) Garnish that is tossed with the greens in step 5. (b) Garnish that will not hold well (croutons will get soggy, avocado will discolor, etc.). Add these at service time.

8. **Refrigerate.**

9. **Add dressing immediately before service, or serve it on the side.**

   Dressed greens wilt rapidly.

Mixed Green Salad

Portions: 25   Portion size: 2½–3 oz (70–90 g)

U.S.	Metric	Ingredients
4½ lb	2 kg	Assorted salad greens
1–1½ pt	500–750 mL	Basic Vinaigrette or variation (p. 723)

■ Procedure

1. Review guidelines and procedure for preparing green salads (p. 687).
2. Wash and drain the greens thoroughly. Chill in refrigerator.
3. Cut or tear the greens into bite-size pieces.
4. Place the salad greens in a large mixing bowl and toss gently until uniformly mixed.
5. Immediately before service, add the dressing and toss to coat all the leaves with the dressing.
6. Place on cold salad plates and serve immediately.

Per serving:
Calories, 130; Protein, 1 g; Fat, 13 g (91% cal.); Cholesterol, 0 mg; Carbohydrates, 2 g; Fiber, 2 g; Sodium, 160 mg.

VARIATIONS

Any combination of salad greens may be used. When using head lettuces, make allowances for variations in trimming yields. Plan on an EP weight of 2½–3 oz (70–90 g) per portion.

Vegetable ingredients, if they are not juicy, may be tossed with the greens. See page 676 for a listing. Shredded carrot and red cabbage are useful because a small amount gives an attractive color accent.

Garnishes may be added after the salads are plated, such as

Tomato wedges	Cucumber slices	Pepper rings	Croutons
Cherry tomatoes	Radishes	Red onion rings	Hard-cooked egg wedges or slices

Service variation: Instead of tossing the salads with the dressing, plate the greens and hold for service. Ladle dressing over salads just before service, or serve dressing in a separate container.

 Spinach Salad

Portions: 25   Portion size: 3 oz (90 g)

U.S.	Metric	Ingredients
3 lb	1.4 kg	Spinach leaves, trimmed (no stems)
12 oz	350 g	Bacon
1 lb	450 g	Fresh white mushrooms
6	6	Hard-cooked eggs

■ Procedure

1. Wash the spinach in several changes of cold water until there is no trace of sand on them. Drain well. Chill in the refrigerator.
2. Cook the bacon on a griddle or in the oven on a sheet pan until crisp. Drain and let cool.
3. Crumble the bacon.
4. Wash the mushrooms and dry them well. Trim the bottoms of stems. Cut the mushrooms into thin slices.
5. Chop the eggs coarsely.
6. Place the spinach in a large bowl. Tear large leaves into smaller pieces. Smaller leaves may be left whole.
7. Add the mushrooms. Toss to mix thoroughly.
8. Portion the salad onto cold salad plates.
9. Sprinkle the salad with the chopped eggs.
10. Hold for service in refrigerator.
11. At serving time, sprinkle with the crumbled bacon.
12. Serve with a vinaigrette variation or with emulsified French dressing.

Per serving:
Calories, 60; Protein, 5 g; Fat, 3.5 g (50% cal.); Cholesterol, 55 mg; Carbohydrates, 3 g; Fiber, 2 g; Sodium, 130 mg.

Note: Bacon may be added to salads when they are assembled (step 9). However, it will be less appetizing because the fat congeals in the refrigerator. For best quality, cook the bacon as close to serving time as possible.

Caesar Salad (Method 1: Tableside Preparation)

Portions: 8   Portion size: 4 oz (125 g) plus dressing

U.S.	Metric	Ingredients
2 lb	1 kg	Romaine leaves
4 oz	125 g	White bread
1–1½ fl oz	30–45 mL	Olive oil
1–2	1–2	Garlic cloves
4–8	4–8	Anchovy fillets
8 fl oz	250 mL	Olive oil
2	2	Eggs, pasteurized
2½ fl oz	75 mL	Lemon juice
1 oz	30 g	Parmesan cheese, grated
to taste	to taste	Salt

■ P r o c e d u r e

1. Wash and drain the greens thoroughly. Chill in the refrigerator
2. Trim the crusts from the bread. Cut the bread into small cubes measuring about ⅜ in. (1 cm).
3. Heat a thin layer of olive oil in a sauté pan over moderately high heat. Add the bread cubes and sauté in the oil until golden and crisp. Add more oil as needed.
4. Remove the croutons from the pan and hold for service. Do not refrigerate.
5. Have all ingredients prepared ahead of time and arranged on a cart in the dining room.
6. Ask the customers how much garlic they would like. Depending on their answer, either rub the bowl with a cut clove of garlic and remove it, or leave it in the bowl and crush it with the anchovies.
7. Ask the customers how many anchovies, if any, they would like.
8. Mash the garlic and anchovies to a paste in the salad bowl.
9. Beat in about half the olive oil.
10. Add the greens and toss to coat with the oil mixture.
11. Break the egg over the bowl and drop it in. Toss the lettuce well.
12. Add the lemon juice, the rest of the oil, the parmesan cheese, and a little salt. Toss again until well mixed.
13. Add the croutons and toss a final time.
14. Plate and serve.

Per serving:
Calories, 370; Protein, 6 g; Fat, 33 g (80% cal.); Cholesterol, 55 mg; Carbohydrates, 12 g; Fiber, 2 g; Sodium, 270 mg.

Caesar Salad

V A R I A T I O N S

Caesar Salad (Method 2: Pantry Preparation)
Prepare the croutons and salad greens as in the basic recipe. Toss the greens with Caesar Dressing (p. 729). Plate and garnish with croutons.

Grilled Chicken Caesar
Top Caesar salads with sliced, grilled chicken breast.

Garden Salad

Portions: 25   Portion size: 3 oz (90 g) plus garnish

U.S.	Metric	Ingredients
3½ lb	1.6 kg	Mixed salad greens
8 oz	250 g	Cucumbers
4 oz	125 g	Celery
4 oz	125 g	Radishes
4 oz	125 g	Scallions
4 oz	125 g	Carrots
1½ lb	700 g	Tomatoes

Per serving:
Calories, 25; Protein, 2 g; Fat, 0.5 g (14% cal.); Cholesterol, 0 mg;
Carbohydrates; 5 g; Fiber, 2 g; Sodium, 25 mg.

■ **P r o c e d u r e**

1. Include some firm-textured, crisp lettuce in the mixed greens, such as romaine or iceberg.
2. Wash and drain the greens thoroughly. Chill in the refrigerator.
3. Score the cucumbers lengthwise with a fork (see p. 521). Peel them if they have been waxed. Cut into thin slices.
4. Cut the celery into thin slices on the bias.
5. Trim the radishes and cut into thin slices.
6. Trim the roots and wilted tops of the scallions. Cut in half crosswise. Then slice lengthwise into thin shreds.
7. Trim and peel the carrots. Shred on a medium grater.
8. Remove the core end of the tomatoes. Cut into wedges, 8–10 per tomato, depending on size.
9. Cut or tear the lettuce and other greens into bite-size pieces.
10. Place all ingredients except tomatoes in a large mixing bowl. Toss until evenly mixed.
11. Plate the salads on cold plates or bowls.
12. Garnish with tomato wedges.
13. Hold for service in refrigerator.
14. Serve with an appropriate dressing.

VEGETABLE, GRAIN, LEGUME, AND PASTA SALADS

Principles

Vegetable salads are salads whose main ingredients are vegetables other than lettuce or other leafy greens. Some vegetables are used raw, such as celery, cucumbers, radishes, tomatoes, and green peppers. Some are cooked and chilled before including in the salad, such as artichokes, green beans, beets, and asparagus. See page 676 for lists of vegetables that can be used.

Starchy items such as grains, pastas, and dried legumes can also form the body of a salad. These ingredients usually have a bland, flat taste, so they are enhanced by a well-seasoned, tart dressing. Raw or cooked vegetables are usually added to the starch item to enhance the color, flavor, and nutritional balance of the salad. Depending on the proportion of vegetables and starch item, it is not always possible to classify the salad as a vegetable or starch salad. However, the guidelines below apply to the preparation of all these salads.

In addition, protein items such as poultry, meat, seafood, and cheese may be added to vegetable and starch salads.

Some bound salads, discussed on page 702, could be considered as a subcategory of vegetable and starch salads. However, many bound salads have a protein item as a main ingredient, so we discuss them as a separate category. There is no exact dividing line between these types. Coleslaw with mayonnaise dressing, for example, may be considered to be in either category.

Guidelines for Making Vegetable, Legume, Grain, and Pasta Salads

1. Neat, accurate cutting of ingredients is important because the shapes of the vegetables add to eye appeal. The design or arrangement of a vegetable salad is often based on different shapes, such as long, slender asparagus and green beans, wedges of tomato, slices of cucumber, strips or rings of green pepper, and radish flowers.

2. Cut vegetables as close as possible to serving time, or they may dry or shrivel at the edges.

3. Cooked vegetables should have a firm, crisp texture and good color. Mushy, overcooked vegetables are unattractive in a salad. See Chapter 16 for vegetable cooking principles.

4. After cooking, vegetables must be thoroughly drained and chilled before being included in the salad.

5. Starches, pastas, and legumes should be cooked until completely tender but not overcooked. Starches absorb liquid from the dressing, so they may become mushy if they were overcooked. Undercooked grains and dried beans may be unpleasantly firm when cooled.

6. Vegetables are sometimes marinated, or soaked in a seasoned liquid, before being made into salads, as for Mixed Bean Salad and Mushrooms à la Grecque. The marinade is usually some form of oil and vinegar dressing that also serves as the dressing for the salad. Do not plate marinated salads too far ahead of time, or the lettuce base will wilt. Use crisp, sturdy greens (such as iceberg, romaine, or chicory) as bases, as they do not wilt as quickly.

7. Grains and pastas may also be marinated for a short time, but avoid marinating for more than a few hours, as they are likely to absorb too much liquid and become very soft. This is especially true of cooked pasta. Legumes should not be marinated long either, but for the opposite reason. The acid in the marinade may toughen the proteins in the beans or lentils.

Coleslaw

Portions: 25   Portion size: 3 oz (100 g)

U.S	Metric	Ingredients
1½ pt	750 mL	Mayonnaise
2 fl oz	60 mL	Vinegar
1 oz	30 g	Sugar (optional)
2 tsp	10 ml	Salt
½ tsp	2 ml	White pepper
4 lb EP	2 kg EP	Cabbage, shredded
25	25	Lettuce cups

Per serving:
Calories, 230; Protein, 2 g; Fat, 24 g (89% cal.); Cholesterol, 25 mg; Carbohydrates, 5 g; Fiber, 2 g; Sodium, 270 mg.

Procedure

1. Combine the mayonnaise, vinegar, sugar, salt, and pepper in a stainless-steel bowl. Mix until smooth.

2. Add the cabbage and mix well.

3. Taste and, if necessary, add more salt and/or vinegar.

4. Arrange the lettuce leaves as underliners on cold salad plates.

5. Using a No. 12 scoop, place a mound of coleslaw in the center of each plate.

6. Hold for service in refrigerator.

VARIATIONS

1. Use Cooked Salad Dressing (p. 730) instead of mayonnaise. Reduce or omit vinegar.

2. Substitute sour cream for half of the mayonnaise.

3. Substitute heavy cream for 1 cup (250 mL) mayonnaise.

4. Substitute lemon juice for the vinegar.

5. Use 1 pt (500 mL) basic vinaigrette and omit mayonnaise and vinegar. Flavor with 2 tsp (10 mL) celery seed and 1 tsp (5 mL) dry mustard.

6. Add 2 tsp (10 mL) celery seed to the basic mayonnaise dressing.

Mixed Cabbage Slaw
Use half red cabbage and half green cabbage.

Carrot Coleslaw
Add 1 lb (500 g) shredded carrots to the basic recipe. Reduce cabbage to 3½ lb (1.7 kg).

Garden Slaw
Add the following ingredients to the basic recipe: 8 oz (250 g) carrots, shredded; 4 oz (125 g) celery, chopped or cut julienne; 4 oz (125 g) green bell pepper, chopped or cut julienne; 2 oz (60 g) scallions, chopped. Reduce cabbage to 3½ lb (1.7 kg).

Coleslaw with Fruit
Add the following ingredients to the basic recipe: 4 oz (125 g) raisins, soaked in hot water and drained; 8 oz (250 g) unpeeled apple, cut in small dice; 8 oz (250 g) pineapple, cut in small dice. Use sour cream dressing (dressing variation 2 above) and use lemon juice instead of vinegar.

Salad of Mixed Cabbage and Apples

Yield: 7½ lb (3.5 kg)   Portions: 24   Portion size: 5 oz (150 g)

U.S.	Metric	Ingredients	Procedure
2 lb	900 g	Red cabbage	**■ P r o c e d u r e**
2 lb	900 g	Green cabbage	1. Finely shred the two cabbages, using a mandoline, a slicing machine, or the shredding blade of a food processor.
1 lb 12 oz	800 g	Granny Smith apples	2. Peel and core the apples, then cut them into a fine julienne.
1½ fl oz	45 mL	Lemon juice	Toss in the lemon juice.
1 pt 4 fl oz	600 mL	Cider vinegar	3. To make vinaigrette, whisk together the vinegar and cream, then whisk in the oil. Season to taste.
4 fl oz	125 mL	Cream	
8 fl oz	250 mL	Salad oil	
to taste	to taste	Salt	
to taste	to taste	White pepper	
1½–2 oz	50 g	Chives, chopped	4. Toss the cabbage and apples together and season with the vinaigrette. Leave to marinate 2–3 hours before serving.
			5. Just before serving, mix in the chopped chives.

Per serving:
Calories, 140; Protein, 1 g; Fat, 12 g (69% cal.); Cholesterol, 5 mg;
Carbohydrates, 11 g; Fiber, 3 g; Sodium, 15 mg.

Basque-Style Pepper Salad

Portions: 16   Portion size: 6 oz (175 g)

U.S.	Metric	Ingredients	Procedure
2 lb 6 oz	1.2 kg	Red bell peppers (about 5 medium peppers)	**■ P r o c e d u r e**
			1. Roast and peel the peppers as shown in Figure 16.13. Remove the core, seeds and veins.
2 lb 6 oz	1.2 kg	Green or yellow bell peppers	2. Cut the peppers into strips ½ in. (1 cm) wide and the length of the pepper.
1 pt	500 mL	Olive oil	3. Combine the oil, vinegar, salt, and pepper to make a dressing. Pour over the peppers in a bowl and marinate for at least 2–3 hours.
4 fl oz	125 mL	White wine vinegar	
to taste	to taste	Salt	
to taste	to taste	Pepper	4. Just before serving, finely shred most of the basil leaves and mix with the peppers, reserving a few whole leaves for garnish.
2½ oz	75 mg	Fresh basil leaves	
			5. If desired, serve with bread for dipping in the dressing.

Per serving:
Calories, 280; Protein, 1 g; Fat, 27 g (86% cal.); Cholesterol, 0 mg;
Carbohydrates, 9 g; Fiber, 3 g; Sodium, 5 mg.

Cucumber Salad with Dill and Yogurt

Portions: 10   Portion size: 3½ oz (100 g)

U.S.	Metric	Ingredients
1½ lb	750 g	Cucumbers
½ oz	15 g	Salt
1 lb	500 g	Plain yogurt
1½–2 oz	50 g	Fresh dill, chopped
to taste	to taste	Freshly ground pepper

Per serving:
Calories, 40; Protein, 2 g; Fat, 1.5g (36% cal.); Cholesterol, 5 mg;
Carbohydrates, 4 g; Fiber, 1 g; Sodium, 570 mg

■ P r o c e d u r e

1. Cut the cucumbers in half lengthwise. Scoop out the seeds and discard. Slice across into half-moon shape, ¼ in. (½ cm) thick.
2. Place the cucumber slices in colander, sprinkle with the salt, and set aside for 30 minutes.
3. Rinse off the salt under cool running water, drain, and pat dry.
4. Mix with the yogurt and dill, then season to taste with pepper.

White Bean Salad

Portions: 12   Portion size: about 6 oz (175 g)

U.S.	Metric	Ingredients
1 lb	500 g	White beans
1	1	Carrot
1	1	Onion
2	2	Whole cloves
1	1	Bouquet garni (see p. 152)
to taste	to taste	Salt
5 tbsp plus 1 tsp	80 mL	Vinegar
to taste	to taste	Salt
to taste	to taste	Pepper
6	6	Shallots, finely chopped
2 oz	60 g	Chopped mixed fresh herbs (chives, parsley, chervil)
11 fl oz	325 mL	Oil
24 oz	750 g	Tomatoes
4 oz	125 g	Carrots
2 heads	2 heads	Radicchio

Per serving:
Calories, 380; Protein, 10 g; Fat, 27 g (62% cal.); Cholesterol, 0 mg;
Carbohydrates, 28 g; Fiber, 7 g; Sodium, 20 mg.

■ P r o c e d u r e

1. Soak the beans overnight in cold water.
2. Rinse the beans and place in a large pot with 6 qt (6 L) fresh water. Add the carrot, the onion stuck with the whole cloves, and the bouquet garni. Bring to the boil and simmer 1–2 hours or until tender. After cooking for 45 minutes, add some salt. Strain and allow to cool for 10 minutes. Discard the carrot, onion with cloves, and bouquet garni.
3. Whisk together the vinegar, salt and pepper to taste, shallots, and chopped herbs.
4. Gradually whisk in the oil.
5. Peel, seed, and dice the tomatoes. Mix into the vinaigrette.
6. Once the beans have cooled to lukewarm, mix in the vinaigrette and place in the refrigerator to cool completely.
7. Grate the carrots and squeeze out the juices. Discard the juice or save for another use. Mix the carrots into the beans.
8. Shred the radicchio. Line plates with the shredded radicchio. Portion the bean salad onto the plates.

Mushrooms à la Grecque

Portions: 25   Portion size: 2½ oz (75 g)

U.S.	Metric	Ingredients
4½ lb	2 kg	Small whole mushrooms
1 qt	1 L	Water
1 pt	500 mL	Olive oil
6 fl oz	175 mL	Lemon juice
1	1	Celery rib
2 tsp	10 mL	Salt
		Sachet:
2	2	Garlic cloves, crushed
1½ tsp	7 mL	Peppercorns, lightly crushed
2 tsp	10 mL	Coriander seeds
1	1	Bay leaf
1 tsp	5 mL	Dried thyme
25	25	Lettuce cups
¼ cup	60 mL	Chopped parsley

Per serving:
Calories, 180; Protein, 3 g; Fat, 19 g (88% cal.); Cholesterol, 0 mg;
Carbohydrates, 3 g; Fiber, 1 g; Sodium, 190 mg.

■ P r o c e d u r e

1. Wash and dry mushrooms. Trim the bottoms of the stems. Leave the mushrooms whole. (If only large ones are available, cut them into quarters.)

2. Place the water, olive oil, lemon juice, celery, and salt in a stainless-steel saucepan. Tie the sachet ingredients in cheese-cloth and add to the pan.

3. Bring to a boil. Simmer 15 minutes to extract flavors from the spices.

4. Add the mushrooms. Simmer 5 minutes.

5. Remove from heat. Cool the mushrooms in the liquid.

6. Remove the celery and the sachet. Marinate the mushrooms overnight in the refrigerator. (The mushrooms will keep several days in the marinade.)

7. Arrange the lettuce leaves as underliners on cold salad plates.

8. Just before service, place a 2½-oz (75-g) portion of mushrooms in each lettuce cup, using a slotted spoon.

9. Sprinkle with chopped parsley.

V A R I A T I O N S

Other vegetables may be prepared à la Grecque using this recipe. Increase cooking time as necessary, but keep the vegetables crisp.

Artichoke hearts   Leeks
Carrots, sliced or diced Pearl onions
Cauliflower florets

Carrot Salad

Portions: 25   Portion size: 3 oz (100 g)

U.S.	Metric	Ingredients
5 lb	2.5 kg	Carrots
1½ cups	375 mL	Mayonnaise
1 cup	250 mL	Vinaigrette
to taste	to taste	Salt
25	25	Lettuce cups
13	13	Pitted black olives

■ **P r o c e d u r e**

1. Peel the carrots. Shred them on a coarse grater.
2. Combine the mayonnaise and vinaigrette. Mix until smooth.
3. Add the carrots and mix. Season to taste with salt.

4. Arrange the lettuce cups as underliners on cold salad plates.
5. Using a No. 12 scoop, place a mound of carrot salad in each lettuce cup.
6. Cut the olives in half lengthwise. Garnish the top of each salad with an olive half.

V A R I A T I O N S

Carrot Raisin Salad
Simmer 8 oz (250 g) raisins in water for 2 minutes. Cool, then drain. Mix raisins with the carrots.

Carrot Pineapple Salad
Mix 12 oz (375 g) drained pineapple tidbits with the carrots.

Carrot Celery Salad
Reduce the carrots to 3½ lb (1.7 kg). Mix 1½ lb (750 g) celery (cut julienne) or celery root (shredded) with the carrots.

Celery Salad
Use celery or celery root instead of carrots in basic recipe. Cut stalk celery into thin slices instead of shredding it. Add 2 tbsp (30 mL) French or Dijon-type mustard to the dressing.

Carrot Raisin Salad

Per serving:
Calories, 200; Protein, 1 g; Fat, 18 g (79% cal.); Cholesterol, 10 mg; Carbohydrates, 10 g; Fiber, 3 g; Sodium, 20 mg.

Pacific Rim Salad with Beef

Portions: 25   Portion size: 5 oz (150 g)

U.S.	Metric	Ingredients
2 lb	900 g	Bean sprouts
1 lb	450 g	Snow peas, trimmed and blanched
8 oz	225 g	Carrots, cut julienne
12 oz	350 g	Water chestnuts, sliced
4 oz	125 g	Scallions, chopped
4 oz	125 g	Slivered almonds, toasted
1½ lb	700 g	Cold roast beef
1¾ pt	800 mL	Oriental Vinaigrette (p. 725)
1½ lb	700 g	Chinese cabbage, shredded
50	50	Orange wedges

Per serving:
Calories, 330; Protein, 11 g; Fat, 27 g (72% cal.); Cholesterol, 25 mg;
Carbohydrates, 13 g; Fiber, 4 g; Sodium, 200 mg.

■ P r o c e d u r e

1. Mix together the bean sprouts, snow peas, carrots, water chestnuts, scallions, and almonds. Hold in the refrigerator.

2. Slice the beef about ¼ in. (6 mm) thick, then cut into thin strips.

3. About 2 hours before serving, marinate the beef in the vinaigrette for 30–60 minutes.

4. Add the mixed vegetables to the beef and vinaigrette mixture. Toss to mix well.

5. Place a bed of shredded Chinese cabbage on salad plates.

6. Portion the salad mixture onto the plates.

7. Garnish each salad with 2 orange wedges.

V A R I A T I O N S

Substitute chicken, turkey, ham, or duck meat for the beef.

Pacific Rim Salad with Beef

Mixed Vegetable Salad with Pasta

Portions: 25   Portion size: 4 oz (125 g)

U.S.	Metric	Ingredients
1½ lb	700 g	Cooked ditalini pasta, cold
1 lb	450 g	Cooked chickpeas or other dried beans, cold
12 oz	350 g	Zucchini, medium dice, raw or blanched
12 oz	350 g	Green beans, cooked, cut into ½-in. (1-cm) lengths
8 oz	250 g	Red onions, diced
6 oz	175 g	Small pitted black olives
6 oz	175 g	Celery, diced
4 oz	125 g	Green bell pepper, diced
4 oz	125 g	Red bell pepper, diced
¼ cup	60 mL	Capers, drained
4 oz	125 g	Parmesan cheese, grated
1½ pt	700 mL	Italian dressing
25	25	Lettuce leaves for underliners
25	25	Tomato wedges or cherry tomatoes

Per serving:
Calories, 290; Protein, 6 g; Fat, 22 g (67% cal.); Cholesterol, 5 mg; Carbohydrates, 18 g; Fiber, 4 g; Sodium, 420 mg.

■ P r o c e d u r e

1. Combine the pasta, beans, vegetables, and cheese in a large bowl. Toss to mix.
2. No more than 1–2 hours before service, add the dressing and toss.
3. Arrange the lettuce leaves on cold salad plates.
4. Just before service, place a 4-oz (125-g) portion of the salad on each lettuce leaf.
5. Garnish each salad with a tomato wedge.

V A R I A T I O N S

Add 1 lb (450 g) diced or sliced salami, pepperoni, or mozzarella cheese to the salad mixture.

 ## Heirloom Tomato Salad

Portions: 12   Portion size: about 4 oz (125 g)

U.S.	Metric	Ingredients
3 lb	1.5 kg	Assorted ripe heirloom tomatoes, 3–4 varieties (see procedure)
12 small bunches	12 small bunches	Mixed baby greens
6 fl oz	180 mL	Extra-virgin olive oil
3 fl oz	90 mL	Balsamic vinegar
to taste	to taste	Coarse salt
to taste	to taste	Black pepper

Per serving:
Calories, 150; Protein, 1 g; Fat, 14 g (82% cal.); Cholesterol, 0 mg; Carbohydrates, 6 g; Fiber, 1 g; Sodium, 100 mg.

■ P r o c e d u r e

1. Select the tomatoes: Use 3–4 varieties of ripe, flavorful tomatoes of varied colors (yellow, green, orange, different shades of red), depending on availability. Include at least one type of small tomato such as cherry tomato.
2. Prepare the tomatoes: Peel large tomatoes by blanching them for 10 seconds in boiling water, cutting out the core end, and pulling off the skins. Small tomatoes with tender skins can be left unpeeled. Cut large tomatoes into slices. Cut small tomatoes into quarters or halves or leave whole, depending on size.
3. Arrange the tomatoes attractively on large salad plates.
4. Place a small bunch of greens on each plate.
5. Drizzle the tomatoes with a little olive oil and then a little vinegar.
6. Sprinkle lightly with coarse salt and black pepper.

V A R I A T I O N S

Instead of the oil and vinegar, drizzle the salad with Balsamic Vinaigrette (p. 723) or Mustard Vinaigrette (p. 723).

Insalata Caprese
Use only one variety of large, red tomato. Peel and slice. Alternate overlapping slices of tomato and fresh mozzarella on a plate or platter. Sprinkle with fresh basil, cut chiffonade, coarse salt, and pepper. Drizzle with olive oil.

Vegetable Chopped Salad with Kidney Beans and Provolone

Portions: 12   Portion size: 6 oz (175 g)

U.S.	Metric	Ingredients
12 oz	360 g	Plum tomatoes, cored and seeded
12 oz	360 g	Iceberg lettuce
8 oz	240 g	Provolone cheese
8 oz	240 g	Avocado, pitted and peeled
2 oz	60 g	Scallion, trimmed
6 oz	175 g	Green olives, chopped
8 oz	240 g	Corn kernels, cooked
12 oz	360 g	Red kidney beans, cooked or canned, drained
8 fl oz	240 mL	Italian Dressing (p. 723)
12	12	Lettuce leaves

Per serving:
Calories, 290; Protein, 9 g; Fat, 23 g (68% cal.); Cholesterol, 15 mg; Carbohydrates, 15 g; Fiber, 5 g; Sodium, 660 mg.

■ P r o c e d u r e

1. Chop the tomato. The pieces should be no larger than about ¼ in. (6 mm) across.
2. Chop the lettuce into small pieces.
3. Cut the cheese into small dice.
4. Cut the avocado roughly into small dice.
5. Cut the scallions into fine slices.
6. Mix together the tomatoes, lettuce, cheese, avocado, scallions, olives, corn, and beans.
7. Add the dressing and toss to mix.
8. Arrange the lettuce leaves on cold salad plates.
9. Mound the salad on the lettuce leaves.

V A R I A T I O N S

Nearly any combination of ingredients, including cooked meats, poultry, and seafood, can be made into a chopped salad. For example, the recipe above can be made into a more substantial main-course salad by adding chopped, cooked chicken, turkey, or ham, allowing about 2 oz (60 g) per portion.

For a vegan version of the above recipe, omit the cheese. If a salad with protein is desired, add firm tofu, blanched, pressed (see p. 660), and chopped.

Mixed Bean Salad with Olives and Tomatoes

Portions: 12   Portion size: 4 oz (125 g)

U.S.	Metric	Ingredients
8 oz	250 g	Chickpeas, cooked or canned, drained
8 oz	250 g	Red kidney beans, cooked or canned, drained
8 oz	250 g	Navy or white kidney beans, cooked or canned, drained
10 oz	300 g	Tomatoes, peeled, seeded, small dice
2 oz	60 g	Green olives, pitted, sliced
2 oz	60 g	Black olives, pitted, sliced
2 oz	60 g	Red onion, chopped fine
8 fl oz	250 mL	Mustard Vinaigrette (p. 723)
2 tbsp	30 mL	Chopped parsley
12	12	Lettuce leaves

■ P r o c e d u r e

1. Combine the chickpeas and beans in a bowl. Add the tomatoes, olives, and onion. Toss gently.
2. Add the vinaigrette. Mix.
3. Cover and refrigerate 2–4 hours.
4. Before serving, mix in the chopped parsley.

5. Arrange the lettuce leaves on cold salad plates.
6. Mound the salad mixture on the lettuce leaves.

Per serving:
Calories, 220; Protein, 5 g; Fat, 16 g (62% cal.); Cholesterol, 0 mg; Carbohydrates, 17 g; Fiber, 6 g; Sodium, 320 mg.

Mixed Bean Salad with Olives and Tomatoes

Quinoa Salad with Bell Peppers

Portions: 12   Portion size: 4½ oz (135 g)

U.S.	Metric	Ingredients
9 oz	275 g	Quinoa
1½ pt	750 mL	Water
¼ tsp	1 mL	Salt
4 oz	125 g	Red bell pepper, small dice
4 oz	125 g	Green bell pepper, small dice
2 oz	60 g	Scallion, chopped fine
6 oz	180 g	Cucumber, peeled and seeded, small dice
3 oz	90 g	Dried apricots, chopped fine
8 fl oz	250 mL	Italian Dressing (p. 723)
to taste	to taste	Salt
12	12	Lettuce or radicchio leaves

■ Procedure

1. Rinse the quinoa thoroughly in cold water. Drain.
2. Combine with the water and salt. Bring to a boil. Lower heat, cover, and simmer slowly until the grain is cooked, about 15 minutes.
3. Spread the cooked grain in a shallow pan to cool.
4. Combine the cooled quinoa, bell peppers, scallions, cucumber, and apricots in a bowl.
5. Add the dressing and toss to mix.
6. Add salt to taste.
7. Arrange the lettuce leaves on cold salad plates.
8. Mound the salad mixture on the lettuce leaves.

V A R I A T I O N S

This salad can also be made with brown rice, farro, or couscous.

Per serving:
Calories, 220; Protein, 4 g; Fat, 14 g (56% cal.); Cholesterol, 0 mg; Carbohydrates, 21 g; Fiber, 2 g; Sodium, 200 mg.

Quinoa Salad with Bell Peppers

Panzanella

Portions: 10   Portion size: 4 oz (125 g)

U.S.	Metric	Ingredients
12 oz	375 g	Firm, white Italian bread
1½ lb	750 g	Ripe tomatoes, peeled
1½ oz	45 g	Red onion, chopped fine
½ oz	15 g	Fresh basil, torn into small pieces
4 fl oz	125 mL	Olive oil
2 fl oz	60 mL	Red wine vinegar
⅛ tsp	0.5 mL	Red pepper flakes
to taste	to taste	Salt
to taste	to taste	Pepper

■ Procedure

1. Use a hearty, firm bread for this recipe. If necessary, let it sit out to dry for a few hours, or dry it slightly in an oven.
2. Tear the bread into bite-size pieces. Place in a large bowl.
3. Chop the tomatoes coarsely into ½-in. (1-cm) pieces. Add to the bowl.
4. Add the remaining ingredients. Toss to mix.
5. Let stand about 1 hour, until the bread has absorbed the juices and softened.

V A R I A T I O N S

Add either or both of the following ingredients to the mixture: 8 oz (250 g) peeled, seeded cucumber, chopped; 4 oz (125 g) hearts of celery.

Per serving:
Calories, 200; Protein, 4 g; Fat, 12 g (53% cal.); Cholesterol, 0 mg; Carbohydrates, 20 g; Fiber, 2 g; Sodium, 200 mg.

Lentil Salad

Portions: 10   Portion size: 4 oz (125 g)

U.S.	Metric	Ingredients
12 oz	375 g	Green lentils
1 qt	1 L	Water
4 oz	125 g	Celery, cut brunoise
4 oz	125 g	Carrot, cut brunoise
1½ oz	45 g	Red onion, cut brunoise
1 oz	30 g	Parsley, chopped
4 fl oz	145 mL	Olive oil
2 fl oz	60 mL	Lemon juice
to taste	to taste	Salt
to taste	to taste	Pepper
12	12	Lettuce leaves

■ P r o c e d u r e

1. Pick over, rinse, and drain the lentils.
2. Place them in a saucepan with the water. Bring to a boil, reduce heat, and simmer until the lentils are just tender and not falling apart, about 25 minutes.
3. Drain the lentils and place them in a bowl.
4. While the lentils are still warm, add the celery, carrot, onion, parsley, olive oil, and lemon juice. Toss to mix.
5. Season to taste with salt and pepper.
6. Arrange the lettuce leaves on salad plates.
7. Serve the lentil salads warm or cold. Mound the salad on the lettuce leaves.

Per serving:
Calories, 200; Protein, 9 g; Fat, 11 g (44% cal.); Cholesterol, 0 mg; Carbohydrates, 23 g; Fiber, 6 g; Sodium, 35 mg.

Broccoli, Prosciutto, and Sunflower Salad

Portions: 12   Portion size: 4½ oz (140 g)

U.S.	Metric	Ingredients
4 oz	125 g	Raisins
2 lb	1 kg	Broccoli florets
4 oz	125 g	Prosciutto, sliced thin, chopped
3 oz	90 g	Sunflower seeds, toasted (shelled)
3 oz	90 g	Shallot or red onion, chopped fine
6 fl oz	180 mL	Emulsified French Dressing (p. 729)
4 fl oz	125 mL	Heavy cream

■ P r o c e d u r e

1. Place the raisins in a bowl and add warm water to cover. Let stand 1 hour.
2. Drain.
3. Combine the raisins, broccoli, prosciutto, sunflower seeds, and shallot or onion in a bowl. Toss to mix evenly.
4. Combine the dressing and cream. Add to the broccoli and toss to mix.

Per serving:
Calories, 240; Protein, 7 g; Fat, 19 g (67% cal.); Cholesterol, 15 mg; Carbohydrates, 14 g; Fiber, 3 g; Sodium, 280 mg.

Broccoli, Prosciutto, and Sunflower Salad

Tabouli

Portions: 12   Portion size: 4 oz (125 g)

U.S.	Metric	Ingredients
12 oz	375 g	Bulgur wheat, fine or medium texture
1 lb	500 g	Cucumber
1½ tsp	7 mL	Coarse salt
1½ oz	45 g	Parsley, chopped
1½ oz	45 g	Scallions, sliced thin
6 oz	180 g	Tomato, peeled, seeded, and chopped
3 fl oz	90 mL	Lemon juice
3 fl oz	90 mL	Olive oil
to taste	to taste	Salt
to taste	to taste	Pepper
12	12	Lettuce leaves

■ P r o c e d u r e

1. Place the bulgur wheat in a bowl. Pour over it about twice its volume of boiling water.
2. Cover and let stand until completely cool. The bulgur should have absorbed most or all of the water and should be tender enough to eat. If any liquid remains, drain it and squeeze out the grain gently. Fluff with a fork.
3. Peel the cucumbers and quarter them lengthwise. Scoop out and discard the seeds. Slice the cucumbers ¼ in. (6 mm) thick.
4. Toss with the coarse salt in a bowl and let stand 30 minutes.
5. Rinse, drain, and pat dry.
6. Mix together the bulgur, cucumbers, parsley, scallions, tomato, lemon juice, and olive oil.
7. Add salt and pepper to taste.
8. Arrange the lettuce leaves on cold salad plates.
9. Mound the tabouli on the lettuce leaves.

Per serving:
Calories, 170; Protein, 4 g; Fat, 7 g (36% cal.); Cholesterol, 0 mg; Carbohydrates, 24 g; Fiber, 6 g; Sodium, 240 mg.

 Wheatberry Salad with Mint

Portions: 16   Portion size: 3 oz (90 g) wheatberry mixture plus ½ oz (15 g) arugula

U.S.	Metric	Ingredients
8 oz	225 g	Wheatberries
1½ pt	700 mL	Water
1 lb	450 g	Tomatoes, peeled, seeded, chopped
2 oz	60 g	Scallions, sliced thin
1 oz	30 g	Parsley, chopped
1½ oz	45 g	Mint, chopped
4 oz	115 g	Black olives, coarsely chopped
6 fl oz	175 mL	Lemon Vinaigrette (p. 723)
to taste	to taste	Salt
12 oz	350 g	Arugula, washed and trimmed

■ P r o c e d u r e

1. Rinse and drain the wheatberries.
2. Place them in a saucepan with the water. Bring to a boil, reduce heat to a simmer, cover loosely, and simmer until tender, about 1 hour. Check from time to time that they are not boiling dry. Add more water if necessary.
3. When the wheatberries are tender, drain and transfer to a shallow pan to cool.
4. Combine the wheatberries, tomatoes, scallions, parsley, mint, and olives. Toss to mix.
5. Add the vinaigrette. Mix
6. Taste and add salt if necessary.
7. Refrigerate for 1 hour or until ready to serve.
8. Arrange the arugula on cold salad plates.
9. Top with a mound of the wheatberry salad.

Per serving:
Calories, 140; Protein, 2 g; Fat, 9 g (39% cal.); Cholesterol, 0 mg; Carbohydrates, 14 g; Fiber, 3 g; Sodium, 150 mg.

BOUND SALADS

Principles

Bound salads are mixtures of foods that are held together, or bound, with a dressing, usually a thick dressing such as mayonnaise. The term *bound* is used most often for traditional mixtures of cooked protein, starch, and vegetable items with mayonnaise, such as chicken salad, tuna salad, egg salad, and potato salad.

As noted in the discussion of vegetable and starch salads on page 690, there is no exact dividing line between that category and bound salads, so you should keep in mind the guidelines for preparing both kinds of salads when preparing bound salads.

Some of these salads, mainly those made with protein items, are also used as sandwich fillings. Sandwich filling ingredients must usually be chopped fine or cut into small dice to be practical for this use. Plated salads, by contrast, may contain larger cuts if desired.

Popular choices for cooked salads are the following:

Chicken	Lobster
Turkey	Eggs
Ham	Potatoes
Tuna	Pastas
Salmon	Rice
Crab	Mixed vegetables
Shrimp	

Guidelines for Making Bound Salads

1. Cooked ingredients must be thoroughly cooled before being mixed with mayonnaise, and the completed salad mixture must be kept chilled at all times. Mayonnaise-type salads are ideal breeding grounds for bacteria that cause food poisoning.

2. Bound salads are good ways to use leftovers such as chicken, meat, or fish, but the ingredient must have been handled according to the rules of good sanitation and food handling. The product will not be cooked again to destroy any bacteria that might grow in the salad and cause illness.

3. Potatoes for salads should be cooked whole, then peeled and cut, in order to preserve nutrients.

4. Except in the case of sandwich fillings, don't cut ingredients too small, or the final product will be like mush or paste, with no textural interest.

5. Crisp vegetables are usually added for texture. Celery is the most popular, but other choices are green peppers, carrots, chopped pickles, onions, water chestnuts, and apples. Be sure the flavors go together, however.

6. Bland main ingredients, such as potatoes and some seafoods, may be marinated in a seasoned liquid such as vinaigrette before being mixed with the mayonnaise and other ingredients. Any marinade not absorbed should be drained first to avoid thinning the mayonnaise.

7. Fold in thick dressings gently to avoid crushing or breaking the main ingredients.

8. Bound salads are usually portioned with a scoop. This has two advantages: (a) It provides portion control. (b) It gives height and shape to the salad.

9. For plated salads, serve on a base of greens, and choose attractive, colorful garnishes when appropriate. A scoop of potato or chicken salad looks pale and uninteresting when plated without a base or garnish.

Macedoine of Vegetables Mayonnaise

Portions: 25   Portion size: 4 oz (125 g)

U.S.	Metric	Ingredients
2 lb	1 kg	Cooked carrots, ¼ in. (½-cm) dice
2 lb	1 kg	Cooked white turnips, ¼-in. (½-cm) dice
1 lb	500 g	Cooked green beans, sliced in ¼-in. (½-cm) pieces
1 lb	500 g	Cooked green peas
1 pt or as needed	500 mL or as needed	Mayonnaise
to taste	to taste	Salt
to taste	to taste	White pepper
25	25	Lettuce cups
25	25	Tomato wedges

■ **P r o c e d u r e**

1. Chill all ingredients before combining.
2. Place vegetables and mayonnaise in a bowl and mix until evenly combined. Use just enough mayonnaise to bind. Season to taste with salt and white pepper.

3. Place lettuce bases as underliners on cold salad plates.
4. Using a No. 10 scoop, place a mound of salad on each plate. Garnish with 1 tomato wedge.

Per serving:
Calories, 180; Protein, 3 g; Fat, 14 g (68% cal.); Cholesterol, 10 mg; Carbohydrates, 12 g; Fiber, 4 g; Sodium, 150 mg.

Chicken or Turkey Salad

Portions: 25   Portion size: 3½ oz (100 g)

U.S.	Metric	Ingredients
3 lb	1.4 kg	Cooked chicken or turkey, ½-in. (1-cm) dice
1½ lb	700 g	Celery, ¼-in. (½-cm) dice
1 pt	500 mL	Mayonnaise
2 fl oz	60 mL	Lemon juice
to taste	to taste	Salt
to taste	to taste	White pepper
25	25	Lettuce cups
as needed	as needed	Parsley or watercress sprigs

■ **P r o c e d u r e**

1. Combine all ingredients in a mixing bowl. Toss gently until thoroughly mixed.

2. Arrange lettuce as underliners on cold salad plates.
3. Using a No. 10 scoop, place a mound of chicken salad on each plate. Garnish with parsley or watercress.
4. Hold for service in refrigerator.

Per serving:
Calories, 200; Protein, 15 g; Fat, 22 g (74% cal.); Cholesterol, 60 mg; Carbohydrates, 2 g; Fiber, 1 g; Sodium, 170 mg.

V A R I A T I O N S

Additions to Chicken Salad: Add any of the following ingredients to the basic recipe:

6 oz (175 g) broken walnuts or pecans
6 hard-cooked eggs, chopped
8 oz (225 g) seedless grapes, cut in half, and 3 oz (90 g) chopped or sliced almonds
8 oz (225 g) drained, diced pineapple
8 oz (225 g) diced avocado
1 lb (450 g) peeled, seeded, diced cucumber, *substituted for* 1 lb of the celery
8 oz (225 g) sliced water chestnuts

Egg Salad
Substitute 28 diced hard-cooked eggs for the chicken in the basic recipe.

Tuna or Salmon Salad
Substitute 3 lb (1.4 kg) drained, flaked canned tuna or salmon for the chicken in the basic recipe. Add 2 oz (60 g) chopped onion. Optional ingredient: 4 oz (100 g) chopped pickles or drained capers.

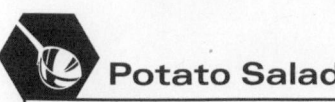 **Potato Salad**

Portions: 25   Portion size: 4 oz (125 g)

U.S.	Metric	Ingredients
5 lb AP	2.5 kg AP	Waxy potatoes (see note)
1½ cups	375 mL	Basic Vinaigrette (p. 723)
1½ tsp	7 mL	Salt
¼ tsp	1 mL	White pepper
12 oz	375 g	Celery, small dice
4 oz	125 g	Onion, chopped fine
		(Optional ingredients— see variations below)
1 pt	500 mL	Mayonnaise
25	25	Lettuce cups
50	50	Pimiento strips

Per serving:
Calories, 290; Protein, 2 g; Fat, 24 g (74% cal.); Cholesterol, 10 mg; Carbohydrates, 17 g; Fiber, 2 g; Sodium, 360 mg.

Note: See pages 582–584 for explanation of potato types. Do not use starchy, mealy potatoes for salad because they will not hold their shape.

■ **P r o c e d u r e**

1. Scrub the potatoes. Steam or boil until tender, but do not overcook.
2. Drain the potatoes. Leave in the colander or spread out on a sheet pan until cool enough to handle.
3. Peel the warm potatoes. Cut into ½-in. (1-cm) dice.
4. Combine the dressing, salt, and pepper. Add the potatoes and mix carefully to avoid breaking or crushing them.
5. Marinate until cold. For the purpose of food safety, chill the potatoes in the refrigerator before proceeding with the next step.
6. If any vinaigrette has not been absorbed by the potatoes, drain it off.
7. Add the celery, onion, and, if desired, any of the optional ingredients listed below. Mix gently.
8. Add the mayonnaise. Mix carefully until evenly blended.
9. Keep refrigerated until ready to use.
10. Arrange the lettuce as underliners on cold salad plates.
11. Using a No. 11 scoop, place a 4-oz (125-g) mound of potato salad on each plate.
12. Garnish each salad with 2 strips pimiento placed crosswise on top.
13. Hold for service in refrigerator.

V A R I A T I O N S

Optional ingredients, to be added in step 7:

   4–6 hard-cooked eggs, diced
   2 oz (60 g) green bell peppers, small dice
   2 oz (60 g) pimientos, small dice
   4 oz (125 g) chopped pickles or capers or sliced olives
   ¼ cup (60 mL) chopped parsley

Vinaigrette marination (steps 4–5) may be omitted if necessary. In this case, chill the potatoes before mixing with the dressing. Add 2 fl oz (60 mL) vinegar to the mayonnaise and check carefully for seasonings. Refrigerate for 2 hours or more before serving.

French Potato Salad

Portion: 25   Portion size: 4 oz (125 g)

U.S.	Metric	Ingredients
7 lb	3.5 kg	Waxy potatoes
8 fl oz	250 mL	Salad oil
6 fl oz	200 mL	Wine vinegar (white or red)
4 oz	125 g	Onions or shallots, chopped fine
¼ tsp	1 mL	Garlic, chopped fine
¼ cup	60 mL	Chopped parsley
1 tbsp	15 mL	Dried tarragon
to taste	to taste	Salt
to taste	to taste	Pepper

Per serving:
Calories, 180; Protein, 2 g; Fat, 9 g (46% cal.); Cholesterol, 0 mg; Carbohydrates, 22 g; Fiber, 2 g; Sodium, 5 mg.

■ **Procedure**

1. Scrub the potatoes. Steam or boil until tender, but do not overcook.
2. Drain the potatoes. Leave in the colander or spread out on a sheet pan until cool enough to handle.
3. Peel the potatoes while still hot. Cut into slices ¼-in. (½-cm) thick or into ½-in. (1-cm) dice.
4. Mix the potatoes with the remaining ingredients. Allow to stand at least 15 minutes while the potatoes absorb the dressing.
5. Serve warm or cold. This salad is a popular accompaniment to hot cooked sausages.

V A R I A T I O N

Hot German Potato Salad
Omit oil and tarragon from basic recipe. Cook 8 oz (250 g) diced bacon until crisp. Add the bacon, the bacon fat, and 1 cup (250 mL) hot chicken stock to the dressing ingredients. (More stock may be needed if the potatoes absorb a great deal.) Place the mixed salad in a hotel pan, cover, and heat in a 300°F (150°C) oven for about 30 minutes. Serve hot.

 Dilled Shrimp Salad

Portion: 25   Portion size: 3½ oz (100 g)

U.S.	Metric	Ingredients
3 lb	1.4 kg	Cooked, peeled, deveined shrimp
1½ lb	700 g	Celery, small dice
1 pt	500 mL	Mayonnaise
2 tbsp	30 mL	Lemon juice
2 tsp	10 mL	Dried dill weed (or 2 tbsp/ 30 mL chopped fresh dill)
½ tsp	2 mL	Salt
25	25	Lettuce cups
50	50	Tomato wedges

Per serving:
Calories, 200; Protein, 12 g; Fat, 15 g (67% cal.); Cholesterol, 115 mg; Carbohydrates, 5 g; Fiber, 1 g; Sodium, 300 mg.

■ **Procedure**

1. Cut the shrimp into ¼-in. (1-cm) pieces. (If the shrimp are very small, leave them whole.)
2. Combine the celery and shrimp in a bowl.
3. Mix together the mayonnaise, lemon juice, dill, and salt.
4. Add the dressing to the shrimp mixture. Mix in thoroughly.
5. Arrange the lettuce leaves as underliners on cold salad plates.
6. Using a No. 10 scoop, place a mound of shrimp salad on each plate.
7. Garnish with tomato wedges, using 2 per salad.

V A R I A T I O N S

Crab or Lobster Salad
Prepare as in basic recipe, using crab or lobster meat instead of shrimp.

Crab, Shrimp, or Lobster Louis
Use Louis Dressing (p. 728) instead of the mixture of mayonnaise, lemon juice, and dill. Serve on shredded lettuce. If food cost permits, omit celery and increase shellfish to 4½ lb/2 kg.

Rice and Shrimp Salad
Reduce shrimp in basic recipe to 1 lb (450 g) and add 2 lb (900 g) cooked rice.

Curried Rice Salad with Shrimp
Prepare Rice and Shrimp Salad but omit the dill. Instead, flavor the dressing with 1 tsp (5 mL) curry powder heated lightly in 1 teaspoon (5 mL) oil and cooled. Optional: Substitute diced green bell pepper for half the celery.

FRUIT SALADS

Principles

As their name indicates, **fruit salads** have fruits as their main ingredients. They are popular as appetizer salads, as dessert salads, and as part of combination luncheon plates, often with a scoop of cottage cheese or other mild-tasting protein food.

Guidelines for Making Fruit Salads

1. Fruit salads are often arranged rather than mixed or tossed because most fruits are delicate and easily broken. An exception is the Waldorf salad, made of firm apples mixed with nuts, celery, and a mayonnaise-based dressing.

2. Broken or less attractive pieces of fruit should be placed on the bottom of the salad, with the more attractive pieces arranged on top.

3. Some fruits discolor when cut and should be dipped into an acid such as tart fruit juice. See pages 680–684 for pre-preparation guidelines for individual fruits.

4. Fruits do not hold as well as vegetables after being cut. If both vegetable and fruit salads are being prepared for a particular meal service, the vegetable salads should usually be prepared first.

5. Drain canned fruits well before including them in the salad, or the salad will be watery and sloppy. The liquid from the canned fruit may be reserved for use in fruit salad dressing or other preparations.

6. Dressings for fruit salads are often slightly sweet, but a little tartness is usually desirable as well. Fruit juices are often used in dressings for fruit salad.

Waldorf Salad

Portions: 25   Portion size: 3 oz (90 g)

U.S.	Metric	Ingredients
1½ cups	350 mL	Chantilly Dressing (p. 728)
4 lb AP	1.8 kg AP	Crisp, red eating apples
1 lb	450 g	Celery, small dice
4 oz	100 g	Walnuts, coarsely chopped
25	25	Lettuce cups
		Optional garnish:
2 oz	60 g	Chopped walnuts

Per serving:
Calories, 150; Protein, 1 g; Fat, 12 g (69% cal.); Cholesterol, 10 mg; Carbohydrates, 11 g; Fiber, 2 g; Sodium, 40 mg.

Note: Plain mayonnaise may be used instead of Chantilly dressing.

■ Procedure

1. Prepare the dressing. Place it in a large stainless-steel bowl and have it ready in the refrigerator. (See note.)

2. Core the apples and dice them to ½ in. (1 cm) without peeling them.

3. As soon as the apples are cut, add them to the dressing and mix in to prevent darkening.

4. Add the celery and walnuts. Fold in until evenly mixed.

5. Arrange the lettuce bases as underliners on cold salad plates.

6. Using a No. 12 scoop, place a mound of salad on each plate.

7. If garnish is desired, sprinkle each salad with about 1 tsp (5 mL) chopped nuts.

8. Hold for service in refrigerator.

VARIATIONS

Any of the following ingredients may be added to the basic Waldorf mixture. If any of these changes is made, the item should no longer be called simply Waldorf Salad. Change the menu name to indicate that the product contains other ingredients. For example: Pineapple Waldorf Salad or Apple Date Salad.

8 oz (225 g) diced pineapple
4 oz (100 g) chopped dates, *substituted for* the walnuts
4 oz (100 g) raisins, plumped in hot water and drained
1 lb (450 g) shredded cabbage or Chinese cabbage, *substituted for* the celery

Arugula, Citrus, and Fennel Salad

Portions: 12   Portion size: 4 oz (125 g)

U.S.	Metric	Ingredients
1 fl oz	30 mL	Lime juice
2 fl oz	60 mL	Orange juice
½ oz	15 g	Shallots, chopped fine
1 tsp	5 mL	Grated ginger root
2 tsp	10 mL	Grated lime zest
3 fl oz	90 mL	Olive oil
to taste	to taste	Salt
2 lb	1 kg	Grapefruit
1 lb	500 g	Fennel, trimmed
6 oz	180 g	Arugula

■ Procedure

1. Mix together the lime juice, orange juice, shallots, ginger, and zest.
2. Whip in the olive oil to make a vinaigrette.
3. Add salt to taste.
4. Peel and section the grapefruit according to the procedure illustrated on page 139. You should have about 1 lb (500 g) grapefruit sections.
5. Cut the fennel bulb in half vertically. Lay the halves on the cutting board, cut side down, and cut vertically into thin slices.
6. Trim the stems from the arugula. Tear into pieces.
7. Just before serving, toss together the grapefruit, fennel, and arugula.
8. Mound on cold salad plates.
9. Drizzle 1 tbsp (15 mL) vinaigrette over each portion.

Per serving:
Calories, 90; Protein, 1 g; Fat, 7 g (66% cal.); Cholesterol, 0 mg; Carbohydrates, 7 g; Fiber, 2 g; Sodium, 25 mg.

Arugula, Citrus, and Fennel Salad

Thai Papaya and Mango Salad

Portions: 12   Portion size: 4 oz (125 g)

U.S.	Metric	Ingredients
6 fl oz	180 mL	Lime juice
1 fl oz	30 mL	Nam pla (Thai fish sauce) or nuoc nam (Vietnamese fish sauce)
2	2	Serrano chiles, seeded, chopped fine
2	2	Scallions, chopped fine
1 oz	30 g	Brown sugar or raw sugar
1½ lb	750 g	Mango, medium dice
1½ lb	750 g	Papaya, medium dice
12 oz	360 g	Napa cabbage, shredded
4 tbsp	60 mL	Chopped peanuts

■ Procedure

1. Mix together the lime juice, fish sauce, chiles, scallions, and sugar. Stir until the sugar is dissolved.
2. Mix together the mango and papaya.
3. Arrange 1 oz (30 g) cabbage on each salad plate.
4. Top with a mound of the fruit mixture.
5. Drizzle each portion with 4 tsp (20 mL) dressing.
6. Sprinkle each portion with 1 tsp (5 mL) chopped peanuts.

Per serving:
Calories, 100; Protein, 2 g; Fat, 1.5 g (13% cal.); Cholesterol, 0 mg; Carbohydrates, 21 g; Fiber, 3 g; Sodium, 240 mg.

Thai Papaya and Mango Salad

COMPOSED SALADS

Principles

Composed salads are salads made by arranging two or more elements attractively on a plate. They are called *composed* because the components are arranged on the plate rather than being mixed together. One or more of the elements may be mixed or tossed salads, but the individual mixed salads are arranged on the plate with other components for the final presentation.

Because they are more elaborate and can be substantial in size, composed salads are usually served as main courses or first courses rather than as accompaniments or side dishes.

There are so many kinds of composed salads that guidelines for preparing this category of salad are very general.

Guidelines for Preparing Composed Salads

1. Observe the guidelines for preparing each of the salad components. For example, if one of the components is a mixed green salad, observe the guidelines for preparing green salads.

2. Prepare and season each component separately and evaluate for flavor and quality. If one or more of the components is a salad, dressing may be added to each salad component separately, or in some cases dressing may be add to the entire salad just before serving.

3. Arrangements may be plated ahead of time only if the components will hold well. Add delicate items just before serving.

4. If any of the components is to be served hot or warm, prepare and add that item just before serving.

5. Flavors and textures of all components should harmonize or provide pleasing contrast. See the discussion of flavor building in Chapter 4.

6. Observe the general concepts of plating and presentation discussed in Chapter 28.

Chef's Salad

Portions: 25

U.S.	Metric	Ingredients
6 lb	3 kg	Mixed salad greens, washed, trimmed, and crisped
1½ lb	700 g	Turkey breast, cut into thin strips
1½ lb	700 g	Pullman ham, cut into thin strips
1½ lb	700 g	Swiss cheese, cut into thin strips
50	50	Tomato wedges or cherry tomatoes
50	50	Hard-cooked egg quarters
25	25	Radishes
8 oz	225 g	Carrots, cut batonnet
25	25	Green bell pepper rings

■ Procedure

1. Place the greens in cold salad bowls, approximately 4 oz (125 g) per portion.

2. Arrange the turkey, ham, and cheese strips neatly on top of the greens. Keep the items separate—do not mix them all together.

3. Arrange the remaining items attractively on the salad.

4. Hold for service. If salads must be held for over 1 hour, they should be covered so the meats and cheese don't dry out.

5. Serve with any appropriate salad dressing, served on the side in a separate container.

V A R I A T I O N S

Other vegetable garnish may be used in addition to or in place of the items in the basic recipe. See lists on pages 676–677.

Per serving:
Calories, 400; Protein, 37 g; Fat, 25 g (54% cal.); Cholesterol, 485 mg; Carbohydrates, 10 g; Fiber, 3 g; Sodium, 570 mg.

Rohkostsalatteller (German Vegetable Salad)

Portions: 16   Portion size: see Procedure

U.S.	Metric	Ingredients	Procedure
6 fl oz	175 mL	White wine vinegar	1. Make a dressing by mixing together the vinegar, sour cream, salt, sugar, and chives. Set aside.
1 pt	500 mL	Sour cream	
2 tsp	10 mL	Salt	
½ tsp	2 mL	Sugar	
2 tbsp	30 mL	Chopped chives	
1 lb	450 g	Carrots	2. Peel the carrots. Shred them on a coarse grater.
2 tbsp	30 mL	Horseradish, well drained	3. Mix the carrots with the horseradish, then with 6 fl oz (175 mL) sour cream dressing, or just enough to bind. Season to taste with salt.
to taste	to taste	Salt	
1 lb 6 oz	625 g	Cucumbers	4. Peel the cucumbers. Cut them into thin slices. Toss with the coarse salt and let stand for 1–2 hours.
1 tbsp	15 mL	Coarse salt	
2 fl oz	60 mL	White wine vinegar	5. Press the juices out of the cucumbers. Rinse off excess salt and drain.
3 fl oz	90 mL	Water	
1 tbsp	15 mL	Sugar	6. Mix together the vinegar, water, sugar, dill, and white pepper.
2 tsp	10 mL	Fresh dill weed, chopped	7. Mix this dressing with the cucumbers. If necessary, add salt to taste.
pinch	pinch	White pepper	
1 lb 4 oz	575 g	Celery root	8. Peel the celery root. Grate it on a coarse grater. Immediately mix with the lemon juice.
1½ fl oz	50 mL	Lemon juice	
5 fl oz	150 mL	Heavy cream	9. Mix in the cream. Season with salt and white pepper.
to taste	to taste	Salt	
to taste	to taste	White pepper	
2 lb	900 g	Bibb or Boston lettuce greens	10. If necessary, thin the remaining sour cream dressing with a little water until it is the consistency of heavy cream.
16	16	Tomato wedges	11. Toss the greens with the dressing. Plate in the center of large salad plates.
			12. Around the outside edge of each plate, arrange 1 tomato wedge and about 1 oz (30 g) each of the carrot, cucumber, and celery salads.

Per serving:
Calories, 140; Protein, 3 g; Fat, 10 g (58% cal.); Cholesterol, 25 mg;
Carbohydrates, 13 g; Fiber, 3 g; Sodium, 730 mg.

Roasted Beet Salad with Gorgonzola

Portions: 12   Portion size: 5 oz (150 g)

U.S.	Metric	Ingredients
1 lb 8 oz	750 g	Red beets, medium to large
1 lb 8 oz	750 g	Yellow beets, small
12 oz	375 g	Mesclun
12 fl oz	375 mL	Mustard Vinaigrette (p. 723)
6 oz	180 g	Gorgonzola cheese, crumbled

■ P r o c e d u r e

1. Wrap the red beets in foil. Wrap the yellow beets in a separate foil package.
2. Bake at 400°F (200 °C) until the beets are tender, about 1 hour.
3. Cool the beets slightly. Trim the root and stem ends, and pull off the peels.
4. Cut the red beets crosswise into thin slices.
5. Cut the yellow beets vertically into quarters.
6. Arrange the sliced beets in circles on cold salad plates.
7. Toss the mesclun with half the vinaigrette.
8. Drizzle the remaining vinaigrette over the sliced beets.
9. Place a small mound of greens in the center of each plate.
10. Arrange the quartered yellow beets around the greens.
11. Sprinkle the tops of the salads with the crumbled gorgonzola.

Per serving:
Calories, 290; Protein, 6 g; Fat, 26 g (76% cal.); Cholesterol, 15 mg; Carbohydrates, 12 g; Fiber, 3 g; Sodium, 590 mg.

Roasted Beet Salad with Gorgonzola

 ## Salade Niçoise

Portions: 25

U.S.	Metric	Ingredients
3 lb	1.4 kg	Waxy potatoes, scrubbed
3 lb	1.4 kg	Green beans, washed and trimmed
2 lbs	900 g	Mixed salad greens, washed, trimmed, and crisped
1 60-oz can	1 1700-g can	Tuna, solid pack or chunk
25	25	Anchovy fillets
50	50	Olives, black or green
50	50	Hard-cooked egg quarters
100	100	Tomato wedges
½ cup	60 mL	Chopped parsley
		Vinaigrette:
1 qt	1 L	Olive oil
1 cup	250 mL	Wine vinegar
1 tsp	5 mL	Garlic, chopped fine
1 tbsp	15 mL	Salt
½ tsp	2 mL	Pepper

■ P r o c e d u r e

1. Cook the potatoes in boiling salted water until just tender. Drain and let cool. Peel. Cut into thin slices. Hold in refrigerator, covered.

2. Cook the beans in boiling salted water. Drain and cool under cold running water. Cut into 2-in. (5-cm) pieces. Hold in refrigerator.

3. Line cold salad bowls or plates with the lettuce leaves (see note).

4. Combine the potatoes and green beans. Divide the mixture among the salad bowls, about 3 oz (90 g) per portion.

5. Drain the tuna and break it into chunks. Place a 1½-oz (50-g) portion in the center of each salad.

6. Arrange the anchovy fillets, olives, egg quarters, and tomato wedges attractively on the salads.

7. Sprinkle the salads with chopped parsley.

8. Hold for service in refrigerator.

9. Combine the dressing ingredients and mix well. Just before service, mix again and dress each salad with 1½ fl oz (50 mL) dressing.

Salade Niçoise

Per serving:
Calories, 710; Protein, 37 g; Fat, 53 g (67% cal.); Cholesterol, 440 mg; Carbohydrates, 22 g; Fiber, 5 g; Sodium, 890 mg.

Note: Salade Niçoise (nee-swahz) may be plated on large platters or in bowls to serve 2–6 portions each.

Chicken Breast Salad with Walnuts and Blue Cheese

Portions: 10

U.S.	Metric	Ingredients
10	10	Boneless, skinless chicken breasts, about 4 oz (125 g) each
as needed	as needed	Chicken stock
1 lb	450 g	Fresh white mushrooms
1 pt	500 mL	Mustard vinaigrette, made with olive oil
2 tbsp	30 mL	Chopped parsley
1 lb 4 oz	575 g	Mixed salad greens
2–3 heads	2–3 heads	Belgian endive
3 oz	90 g	Walnuts, coarsely chopped
3 oz	90 g	Blue cheese, crumbled

Per serving:
Calories, 530; Protein, 31 g; Fat, 43 g (72% cal.); Cholesterol, 75 mg; Carbohydrates, 7 g; Fiber, 3 g; Sodium, 570 mg.

■ P r o c e d u r e

1. Poach the chicken breasts in a flavorful, seasoned chicken stock, using just enough to cover them. (See Chapter 13 for information on poaching chicken.) When they are just done but still juicy, remove from the heat and cool in the poaching liquid.

2. Shortly before serving, slice the mushrooms. Toss them with about 4 oz (125 mL) vinaigrette and with the parsley so that they are lightly coated with the dressing.

3. Arrange the greens on large salad plates or dinner plates.

4. Cutting across the grain, slice each chicken breast on the slant into slices about ¼ in. (6 mm) thick. On one side of each salad plate, arrange a sliced breast single-fashion, fanning out the slices.

5. Separate the endive into leaves. Arrange some of the leaves on the other half of each plate.

6. Place a small mound of the mushroom slices on the endive.

7. Sprinkle the salads with the nuts and the blue cheese.

8. Just before serving, spoon about 1 fl oz (30 mL) dressing over each salad.

V A R I A T I O N

When plating the salads to order, toss the mixed salad greens with some of the salad dressing before plating.

Chicken Breast Salad with Walnuts and Blue Cheese

Salad of Seared Sea Scallops with Oriental Vinaigrette

Portions: 10   Portion size: 3 oz (90 g) scallops
                1½ oz (45 g) greens
                1½ fl oz (45 mL) vinaigrette

U.S.	Metric	Ingredients
1 lb	500 g	Mesclun or other delicate mixed greens
1 pt	500 mL	Oriental Vinaigrette (p. 725)
2 lb	1 kg	Sea scallops
as needed	as needed	Butter
30	30	Orange segments (free of membranes)

Per serving:
Calories, 360; Protein, 9 g; Fat, 33 g (80% cal.); Cholesterol, 20 mg;
Carbohydrates, 9 g; Fiber, 2 g; Sodium, 460 mg.

■ P r o c e d u r e

1. Wash and drain the salad greens.
2. Prepare the vinaigrette.
3. Trim the scallops by removing the small, tough side muscle. If any scallops are very large, cut them in half crosswise. Dry them well.
4. Heat a little butter in a nonstick sauté pan. Sear a few scallops at a time until they are browned on top and bottom.
5. Toss the mesclun with half the vinaigrette.
6. Mound the mesclun in the center of the plates.
7. Arrange the orange segments so that they are leaning against the mound of salad greens. Use 3 per portion.
8. Arrange the scallops around the salads.
9. Drizzle the remaining vinaigrette around the scallops.

Salad of Seared Sea Scallops with Oriental Vinaigrette

Chicory and Smoked Chicken Salad with Mustard Vinaigrette

Portions: 10   Portion size: 8 oz (250 g)

U.S.	Metric	Ingredients
10 heads	10 heads	Belgian endive
2 small heads	2 small heads	Frisée or curly endive, washed
2 fl oz	60 mL	White wine vinegar
10 fl oz	300 mL	Salad oil
2 fl oz	60 mL	Whole-grain mustard
to taste	to taste	Salt
to taste	to taste	Pepper
2 lb	1 kg	Smoked chicken, boneless, with or without skin as desired

Per serving:
Calories, 410; Protein, 15 g; Fat, 34 g (75% cal.); Cholesterol, 40 mg;
Carbohydrates, 10 g; Fiber, 9 g; Sodium, 180 mg.

■ P r o c e d u r e

1. Remove the outer leaves from the Belgian endive. For plated service, cut the base of each leaf to a point so that they fit together neatly and arrange radially on plates. For buffet presentation, omit cuts in stem and use leaves to line a bowl. Cut the remainder of the Belgian endive into julienne.
2. Break the curly endive into bite-size pieces and mix gently with the julienne of Belgian endive.
3. Briskly combine the white wine vinegar, salad oil, and whole-grain mustard with salt and pepper to taste.
4. Toss the mixed curly endive and Belgian endive julienne with the vinaigrette and pile onto the arranged plates.
5. Dice the smoked chicken and sprinkle over the endives.

Salad of Belgian Endive, Scallops, and Walnuts

Portions: 8   Portion size: 3–4 scallops (3 oz/90 g)
                              5 oz (150 g) salad

U.S.	Metric	Ingredients	
14 oz	400 g	Belgian endive	■ P r o c e d u r e
10 oz	300 g	Radicchio	1. Remove any damaged outer leaves of the Belgian endive. Then remove some undamaged leaves and set aside for the presentation (step 8).
7 oz	200 g	Carrots	2. Thinly slice the remaining endive. Thinly slice the radicchio. Peel and trim the carrots and cut into a fine julienne.
1 oz	30 g	Chives	3. Set aside some of whole chives, then mince the remaining chives.
3½ oz	100 g	Walnuts	4. Chop the walnuts.
3½ fl oz	100 mL	Balsamic vinegar	5. Make the vinaigrette. Whisk the vinegar with salt and white pepper to taste. Whisk in the two oils until the sauce is thick and well emulsified.
to taste	to taste	Salt	
to taste	to taste	White pepper	6. Toss the endive, radicchio, carrot, chives, and walnuts together with a little of the vinaigrette.
5 fl oz	150 mL	Peanut oil	
5 fl oz	150 mL	Walnut oil	
1 lb 10 oz	725 g	Sea scallops	7. Season the scallops and sear them in hot olive oil.
to taste	to taste	Salt	8. Make a dome of salad in the center of plate. Arrange 3–4 scallops around the salad. Between the scallops, place a leaf of endive, cut in half lengthwise, and place a length of chive on top. Top each scallop with a little vinaigrette and serve.
to taste	to taste	White pepper	
3½ fl oz	100 mL	Olive oil	

Per serving:
Calories, 590; Protein, 11 g; Fat, 57 g (85% cal.); Cholesterol, 15 mg;
Carbohydrates, 11 g; Fiber, 4 g; Sodium, 220 mg.

Warm Goat Cheese Salad

Portions: 12

U.S.	Metric	Ingredients	
12 slices	12 slices	Sandwich bread	■ P r o c e d u r e
12	12	Small goat cheeses, about 2½ oz (75 g) each (see note)	1. Cut the sandwich bread into ¼-in. (½-cm) slices. Toast, then cut each slice into 4 triangles.
8 oz	250 g	Frisée	2. Cut the goat cheese in half horizontally. Place under a broiler or salamander until just beginning to melt and lightly colored.
8 oz	250 g	Radicchio	3. Wash and drain the frisée, radicchio, and mâche. Tear the frisée and mâche into bite-size pieces.
4 oz	125 g	Mâche	
14 fl oz	400 mL	Walnut Herb Vinaigrette (p. 724)	4. Toss the salad greens with the vinaigrette and the chopped walnuts.
1½ oz	45 g	Chopped walnuts	5. Place a small mound of the salad greens in the center of the plate and arrange 4 pieces of toast on top, close together. Place 2 pieces of the toasted cheese on top of the toast. Decorate with whole walnut halves and sprigs of chervil.
as desired	as desired	Walnut halves	
as desired	as desired	Chervil sprigs	

Per serving:
Calories, 800; Protein, 20 g; Fat, 50 g (73% cal.); Cholesterol, 55 mg;
Carbohydrates, 22 g; Fiber, 2 g; Sodium, 540 mg.

Note: The cheese used in testing this recipe is Crottin de Chavignol, a small,
slightly aged goat cheese. If this or a similar small goat cheese is not available,
substitute a log-shaped goat cheese cut into portion sizes.

Stuffed Tomatoes Chinoise

Portions: 12   Portion size: 1 tomato with 3½ oz (100 g) filling

U.S.	Metric	Ingredients	Procedure
12	12	Tomatoes, about 7–8 oz (200–250 g) each	1. Remove the stems from the tomatoes. Slice the top third of the tomatoes, keeping the tops. Remove the seeds and ribs of the tomatoes. Season the interior with salt and overturn on paper towels. Set aside in the refrigerator for at least 30 minutes.
to taste	to taste	Salt	
1⅓ oz	4 g	Ginger root, grated	2. Place the grated ginger, rice vinegar, sesame oil, soy oil, soy sauce, and sugar in a blender. Blend until well mixed.
2 fl oz	60 mL	Rice vinegar	3. Strain the vinaigrette into a small bowl. Set aside.
2 fl oz	60 mL	Sesame oil	
1 fl oz	30 mL	Soybean oil or vegetable oil	
1 fl oz	30 mL	Soy sauce	
to taste	to taste	Sugar	
7 oz	200 g	Carrot	4. Cut the carrot, celery, and onion into a fine julienne.
3½ oz	100 g	Celery	5. Blanch the vegetables in boiling salted water for 30 seconds, then refresh in ice water. Strain and squeeze out any excess water. Spread on paper towels and keep chilled until ready to use.
3½ oz	100 g	Onion	
1 lb	500 g	Bean sprouts	6. Repeat the procedure for the bean sprouts.
1 lb	500 g	Shelled, cooked small shrimp	7. Combine the vegetables, shrimp, and chopped cilantro in a bowl. Add the vinaigrette and toss to mix.
3 tbsp	45 mL	Chopped cilantro	
2	2	Cucumbers	8. Channel the cucumbers (see Figure 16.8), then cut into thin slices.
			9. Arrange the cucumber slices into circles on plates.
			10. Fill the tomatoes with the vegetable and shrimp mixture. Place in the center of the cucumber circles and place the tops on the tomatoes.

Per serving:
Calories, 170; Protein, 12 g; Fat, 8 g (39% cal.); Cholesterol, 75 mg; Carbohydrates, 16 g; Fiber, 4 g; Sodium, 250 mg.

Stuffed Tomatoes Chinoise

Taco Salad

Portions: 12   Portion size: approximately 10 oz (300 g)

U.S.	Metric	Ingredients
12	12	Flour tortillas
2 tbsp	30 mL	Chili powder
2 tsp	10 mL	Ground cumin
2 tsp	10 mL	Dried oregano
1 tbsp	15 mL	Cornstarch
½ tsp	2 mL	Cinnamon
½ tsp	2 mL	Black pepper
12 fl oz	360 mL	Water, cold
1 fl oz	30 mL	Vegetable oil
3 oz	90 g	Onion, small dice
2 tsp	10 mL	Finely chopped garlic
2 lb 4 oz	1 kg	Ground beef
12 fl oz	360 mL	Tomato purée
to taste	to taste	Salt
1 pt	500 mL	Ranch Dressing (p. 728)
1 cup	250 mL	Salsa Cruda (p. 191)
1 lb 8 oz	750 g	Lettuce, such as romaine or iceberg, shredded
1 lb 8 oz	750 g	Pinto beans or black beans, cooked or canned, drained
12 oz	375 g	Monterey jack or mild cheddar cheese, grated
1 lb 2 oz	550 g	Tomatoes, medium dice
6 oz	180 g	Green or black olives, pitted, sliced
3 oz	90 g	Scallions, sliced thin
6 oz	180 g	Avocado, medium dice

Per serving:
Calories, 1120; Protein, 40 g; Fat, 66 g (53% cal.); Cholesterol, 115 mg; Carbohydrates, 94 g; Fiber, 13 g; Sodium, 1390 mg.

■ Procedure

1. Fit the tortillas into a taco salad shell fry basket and deep-fry until crisp. Drain and cool upside down.

2. Mix together the chili powder, cumin, oregano, cornstarch, cinnamon, and pepper.

3. Add the cold water and mix well.

4. Heat the oil in a sauté pan over moderate heat.

5. Add the onion and garlic and sauté until lightly browned.

6. Add the ground beef. Break up and fry until there are no large lumps and the beef has lost its red color.

7. Drain excess fat from the pan.

8. Add the spice mixture to the beef and bring to a boil.

9. Add the tomato purée. Return to a boil.

10. Simmer until the meat mixture is no longer liquid.

11. Season to taste with salt.

12. Keep the meat mixture warm, or refrigerate and reheat for service. Depending on the amount of fat drained in step 7, you should have about 1½ oz (45 g) meat per portion.

13. Mix together the salad dressing and salsa. Refrigerate until service. (See second variation below.)

14. Line the bottoms of the tortilla shells with lettuce.

15. Place a layer of beans and then a layer of meat on top of the lettuce.

16. Top with layers of cheese, tomatoes, olives, scallions, and, finally, a few pieces of avocado.

17. Ladle the dressing mixture over the salads. Serve immediately.

VARIATIONS

In place of the tortilla bowls, line the bottom of salad bowls with lightly crushed tortilla chips.

In place of the dressing mixture, serve the salads with separate bowls of sour cream and salsa on the side.

GELATIN SALADS

Principles

Gelatin salads have a distinguished history. Their ancestors are aspics, the highly ornamented appetizers and elaborate buffet pieces made with meat and fish stocks rich in natural gelatin extracted from bones and connective tissue. Aspics are part of the glory of classical cuisine and still an important part of modern buffet work.

It's no longer necessary to extract gelatin from bones in your kitchen. Purified, granular gelatin and gelatin sheets have long been available for use in the pantry. Many excellent gelatin-based salads can be made with little labor using these products. However, most gelatin products today are made with sweetened prepared mixes whose high sugar content and heavy reliance on artificial color and flavor make their appropriateness as salads somewhat questionable. (Often, in a cafeteria line, you will see in the salad section little squares of gelatin with a lettuce leaf underneath and a dab of mayonnaise on top, and in the dessert section the identical product, without the lettuce leaf and with a dab of whipped cream in place of the mayo.)

Nevertheless, as a professional cook, you need to know how to prepare these products because many customers expect them. You should also know how to prepare salads using unflavored gelatin, relying on fruit juices and other ingredients for flavor. Unflavored gelatin is especially valuable for preparing molded vegetable salads because shredded cabbage and other vegetables make a poor combination with highly sweetened dessert gelatin.

Guidelines for Making Gelatin Salads

1. It is important to use the right amount of gelatin for the volume of liquid in the recipe. Too much gelatin makes a stiff, rubbery product. Too little makes a soft product that will not hold its shape.

   Basic proportions for unflavored gelatin are 2½ ounces dry gelatin per gallon (19 g per liter) of liquid, *but* you will almost always need more than this because of acids and other ingredients in the recipe. Basic proportions for sweetened, flavored gelatin are 24 ounces per gallon (180 g per liter) of liquid.

   Acids, such as fruit juices and vinegar, weaken the gelatin set, so a higher proportion of gelatin to liquid is needed, sometimes as much as 4 ounces or more per gallon (30 g per liter). The setting power is also weakened by whipping the product into a foam and by adding a large quantity of chopped foods. It is impossible to give a formula for how much gelatin to use, as it varies with each recipe. Test each recipe before using it.

2. Gelatin dissolves at about 100°F (38°C), but higher temperatures will dissolve it faster.

   To dissolve unflavored gelatin, stir it into cold liquid to avoid lumping and let it stand for 5 minutes to absorb water. Then heat it until dissolved, or add hot liquid and stir until dissolved.

   To dissolve sweetened, flavored gelatin, stir it into boiling water. It will not lump because the gelatin granules are held apart by sugar granules, much the way starch granules in flour are held separate by the fat in a roux.

3. To speed setting, dissolve the gelatin in up to half of the liquid and add the remainder cold to lower the temperature. For even faster setting, add crushed ice in place of an equal weight of cold water. Stir until the ice is melted.

4. Do not add raw pineapple or papaya to gelatin salads. These fruits contain enzymes that dissolve the gelatin. If cooked or canned, however, these fruits may be included.

5. Add solid ingredients when the gelatin is partially set—that is, when thick and syrupy. This will help keep them evenly mixed rather than floating or settling.

6. Canned fruits and other juicy items must be well drained before being added or they will dilute the gelatin and weaken it.

7. For service, pour into pans and cut into equal portions when set, or pour into individual molds.

8. To unmold gelatin:
   - Run a thin knife blade around the top edges of the mold to loosen.
   - Dip the mold into hot water for 1 or 2 seconds.
   - Quickly wipe the bottom of the mold and turn it over onto the salad plate (or invert the salad plate over the mold and flip the plate and mold over together). Do not hold in the hot water for more than a few seconds, or the gelatin will begin to melt.
   - If it doesn't unmold after a gentle shake, repeat the procedure. You may also wrap a hot towel (dipped in hot water and wrung out) around the mold until it releases, but this is more time-consuming.

9. Refrigerate gelatin salads until service to keep them firm.

Jellied Fruit Salad

Portions: 25   Portion size: 4 oz (125 g)

U.S.	Metric	Ingredients
1 No. 2 can	1 No. 2 can	Pineapple cubes
8 oz	250 g	Grapefruit sections
12 oz	375 g	Orange sections
8 oz	250 g	Grapes
2 oz	60 g	Unflavored gelatin
1 cup	250 mL	Water, cold
as needed	as needed	Fruit juice: grapefruit, orange, or pineapple
6 oz	175 g	Sugar
¼ tsp	1 g	Salt
3 fl oz	90 mL	Lemon juice
25	25	Lettuce leaves for underliners
1⅔ cups	400 mL	Chantilly Dressing (p. 728)

■ P r o c e d u r e

1. Drain the pineapple and reserve the juice. You should have about 12 oz (350 g) drained fruit.
2. Cut the grapefruit and orange sections into ½-in. (1-cm) dice. (See p. 139 for cutting citrus sections.)
3. Cut the grapes in half. Remove seeds, if any.
4. Place the fruit in a colander or strainer over a bowl and hold in the refrigerator.

5. Stir the gelatin into the cold water and let stand at least 5 minutes.
6. Add enough fruit juice (or part juice and part water) to the liquid from the pineapple to measure 3½ pt (1.75 L).
7. Bring the fruit juice to a boil in a stainless-steel pan. Remove from heat.
8. Add the sugar, salt, and softened gelatin. Stir until gelatin and sugar are dissolved.
9. Cool the mixture. Add the lemon juice.
10. Chill until thick and syrupy but not set.
11. Fold the drained fruits into the gelatin mixture.
12. Pour into individual molds or into a half-size hotel pan. Chill until firm.

13. Line cold salad plates with lettuce leaves.
14. Unmold the salads or, if a hotel pan was used, cut 5 x 5 into rectangles.
15. Place a gelatin salad on each plate. Hold for service in the refrigerator.
16. At service time, top each salad with 1 tbsp. (15 mL) dressing.

Per serving:
Calories, 170; Protein, 3 g; Fat, 10 g (49% cal.); Cholesterol, 15 mg; Carbohydrates, 20 g; Fiber, 1 g; Sodium, 55 mg.

Basic Flavored Gelatin with Fruit

Portions: 25   Portion size: 4 oz (125 g)

U.S.	Metric	Ingredients
12 oz	375 g	Flavored gelatin mix
1 qt	1 L	Water, boiling
1 qt	1 L	Water or fruit juice, cold
2 lb	1 kg	Fruit, well drained

Per serving:
Calories, 70; Protein, 1 g; Fat, 0 g (0% cal.); Cholesterol, 0 mg; Carbohydrates, 18 g; Fiber, 0 g; Sodium, 40 mg.

■ **P r o c e d u r e**

1. Place the gelatin in bowl.
2. Pour in the boiling water. Stir until dissolved.
3. Stir in the cold water or juice.
4. Chill until thick and syrupy but not set.

5. Fold the fruit into the gelatin mixture.
6. Pour into molds or into a half-size hotel pan.
7. Chill until firm.
8. Unmold. If using a hotel pan, cut 5 x 5 into portions.

V A R I A T I O N S

The number of combinations of fruits and flavored gelatin is nearly limitless. The following suggestions are only a few possibilities. *Note:* When using canned fruits, use the syrup from the fruits as part of the liquid in step 3.

Black cherry-flavored gelatin; Bing cherries.
Raspberry-flavored gelatin; peach slices or halves.
Strawberry, raspberry, or cherry-flavored gelatin;
    canned fruit cocktail.
Orange-flavored gelatin; equal parts sliced peaches and pears.
Cherry-flavored gelatin; equal parts crushed pineapple
    and Bing cherries.
Lime-flavored gelatin; grapefruit sections or pear halves or slices.

SALAD BARS AND BUFFET SERVICE

Salad bars are frequent fixtures in restaurants and are popular with both customer and restaurateur. The customer enjoys being able to custom make a salad with selections from a large bowl of greens, smaller containers of assorted condiments, and a variety of dressings. The restaurateur likes them because they take some of the pressure off the dining room staff during service. Many restaurants have designed unique salad bars that have become almost a trademark. Others may not have salad bars as part of their regular meal service but rely on them for efficiency at certain times, such as weekend brunch.

For successful salad bar service, it is important to keep several points in mind:

1. Keep the salad bar attractive and well stocked from the beginning until the end of service. Refill containers before they begin to look depleted, wipe the edges of dressing containers, and clean up debris scattered by customers.

2. Keep the components simple but attractive. Elaborately arranged salad bowls lose their effect as soon as two or three customers have dug into them.

3. Select a variety of condiments to appeal to a variety of tastes. Try both familiar and unusual items to make your salad bar stand out. There is no reason to restrict the choices to the same old stuff everyone else is serving.

    There are two basic kinds of salad bar condiments:

    • **Simple ingredients.** Nearly any item in the salad ingredient list on pages 676–677 might be selected. Your choice will depend on balance of flavors and colors, customer preference, and cost.

    • **Prepared salads.** Marinated vegetable salads, such as three-bean salad, and cooked salads, like macaroni salad, are especially suitable. The choice is large.

Figure 21.2
Suggested arrangement of a salad bar. Key:
(1) plates; (2) large bowl of salad greens;
(3) condiments; (4) dressings; (5) crackers,
breads, etc.

4. Arrange the salad bar in the following order (see Figure 21.2):
   - Plates.
   - Mixed greens.
   - Condiments (put the expensive ones at the end).
   - Dressings.
   - Crackers, breads, etc., if desired.
5. Make sure your setup conforms to your state health department regulations.
6. Some portion control can be achieved by selecting the right size plates, condiment servers, and dressing ladles.

SALAD DRESSINGS

Salad dressings are liquids or semiliquids used to flavor salads. They are sometimes considered cold sauces, and they serve the same functions as sauces—that is, they flavor, moisten, and enrich.

Most of the basic salad dressings used today can be divided into three categories:

1. Oil and vinegar dressings (most unthickened dressings).
2. Mayonnaise-based dressings (most thickened dressings).
3. Cooked dressings (similar in appearance to mayonnaise dressings, but more tart, and with little or no oil content).

A number of dressings have as their main ingredient such products as sour cream, yogurt, and fruit juices. Many of these are designed specifically for fruit salads or for low-calorie diets.

INGREDIENTS

Because the flavors of most salad dressings are not modified by cooking, their quality depends directly on the quality of the ingredients.

Most salad dressings are made primarily of an oil and an acid, with other ingredients added to modify the flavor or texture.

OILS

Kinds

Corn oil is widely used in dressings. It has a light golden color and is nearly tasteless, except for a very mild cornmeal-type flavor.

Cottonseed oil, soybean oil, canola oil, and *safflower oil* are bland, nearly tasteless oils. *Vegetable oil* or *salad oil* is a blend of oils and is popular because of its neutral flavor and relatively low cost.

Peanut oil has a mild but distinctive flavor and may be used in appropriate dressings. It is somewhat more expensive.

Olive oil has a distinctive, fruity flavor and aroma and a greenish color. The best olive oils are called *virgin* or *extra-virgin*, which means they are made from the first pressing of the olives. Because of its flavor, olive oil is not an all-purpose oil but may be used in specialty salads such as Caesar salad.

Walnut oil has a distinctive flavor and a high price. It is occasionally used in fine restaurants featuring specialty salads. Other nut and seed oils, such as *hazelnut oil* and *grapeseed oil*, are sometimes used.

Quality Factors

All-purpose oils for dressings should have a mild, sweet flavor. Strongly flavored oils can make excellent salad dressings but are not appropriate with every food.

Winterized oil should be used with dressings that are to be refrigerated. These oils have been treated so they remain a clear liquid when chilled.

Rancidity is a serious problem with oils because even a hint of a rancid flavor can ruin an entire batch of dressing. A thin film of oil, such as might be left on containers through careless washing, becomes rancid very quickly. Clean all dressing containers thoroughly, and never pour a fresh batch into a jar containing older dressing.

VINEGAR

Kinds

Cider vinegar is made from apples. It is brown in color and has a slightly sweet apple taste.

White or *distilled vinegar* is distilled and purified so that it has a neutral flavor.

Wine vinegar may be white or red, and it has, naturally, a winy flavor.

Flavored vinegars have had another product added to them, such as tarragon, garlic, or raspberries.

Sherry vinegar is made from sherry wine and, consequently, has the distinctive flavor of that wine.

Balsamic vinegar is a special wine vinegar that has been aged in wooden barrels. It is dark brown in color and has a noticeably sweet taste.

Other specialty vinegars include malt vinegar, rice vinegar, and vinegars flavored with fruits, such as raspberry.

Quality Factors

Vinegars should have a good, clean, sharp flavor for their type.

Strength of acidity determines the tartness of the vinegar—and of the dressing made from it. Most salad vinegars are about 5 percent acidity, but some range as high as 7 or 8 percent. Read the label for this information. Vinegar that is too strong should be diluted with a little water before it is measured for a recipe.

White vinegar is used when a completely neutral flavor is desired for a dressing. Other vinegars are used for their characteristic flavors. Wine vinegars are usually preferred for the best-quality oil-and-vinegar dressings.

LEMON JUICE

Fresh lemon juice may be used in place of or in addition to vinegar in some preparations, when its flavor is desired.

EGG YOLK

Egg yolk is an essential ingredient in mayonnaise and other emulsified dressings. For safety, pasteurized eggs should be used (see pp. 788 and 1030), and the finished product should be refrigerated to guard against spoilage.

SEASONINGS AND FLAVORINGS

Nearly any herb or spice can be used in salad dressings. Fresh herbs are preferable to dried herbs as flavorings, especially when the dressings are used for simple, light mixed

---

BALSAMICO TRADIZIONALE (TRADITIONAL BALSAMIC VINEGAR)

True balsamic vinegar is made by small artisan producers, as distinguished from the industrial product found in most kitchens and supermarkets. It is made not from wine or wine vinegar but from grape juice, usually from white Trebbiano grapes, although four other grapes are permitted by Italian law. Balsamico tradizionale is aged in a series of small wooden barrels for at least 10 but as long as 50 years. The result is an intensely flavorful, thick, almost syrupy, dark brown liquid.

Because of the small production and the long aging, true balsamic vinegar is very expensive, the oldest bottlings being among the most expensive foods anywhere.

The familiar inexpensive balsamico vinegars most of us are familiar with are made in large quantities from wine vinegar and caramelized sugar, sometimes with the addition of a quantity of aged balsamico. The quality of inexpensive balsamic vinegars ranges from terrible to good. The better ones can be excellent salad ingredients. True balsamico tradizionale is too costly to be mixed with salad dressings. It is generally used by itself as a condiment, measured out in mere drops.

green salads. Remember that dried herbs and spices need extra time to release their flavors if they are not heated in the product. This is why most dressings are best made at
least two or three hours before serving. Review Chapter 4 to refresh your memory on
the use of herbs and spices.

Other ingredients added for flavoring include mustard, ketchup, Worcestershire
sauce, and various kinds of cheeses.

A note on blue cheese and **Roquefort cheese**: Many restaurants sell what they call
Roquefort dressing when it is actually blue cheese dressing. Roquefort is a brand name
for a special kind of blue cheese made in Roquefort, France. It is made of sheep's milk,
has a distinctive taste, and is expensive. Do not use the term *Roquefort* for blue cheese
dressings unless you are actually using this brand of cheese.

EMULSIONS IN SALAD DRESSINGS

As you know, oil and water do not normally stay mixed but separate into layers. Salad
dressings, however, must be evenly mixed for proper service, even though they are
made primarily of oil and vinegar. A uniform mixture of two unmixable liquids is called
an **emulsion**. One liquid is said to be in *suspension* in the other.

TEMPORARY EMULSIONS

A simple oil and vinegar dressing is called a **temporary emulsion** because the two
liquids always separate after being shaken.

The harder the mixture is beaten or shaken, the longer it takes for it to separate.
This is because the oil and water are broken into smaller droplets, so the droplets take
longer to recombine with each other so the oil and water can separate. When a mixture
of oil and vinegar is mixed in a blender, the resulting mixture stays in emulsion considerably longer.

Some ingredients act as weak emulsifiers. For example, when mustard is added to
the mixture, the vinaigrette stays emulsified longer. Other ingredients that work this
way include vegetable purées and stocks with a good gelatin content. Even these mixtures, however, will separate when they stand long enough. They should be mixed again
before use.

PERMANENT EMULSIONS

Mayonnaise is also a mixture of oil and vinegar, but the two liquids do not separate. This
is because the formula also contains egg yolk, which is a strong emulsifier. The egg yolk
forms a layer around each of the tiny droplets and holds them in suspension.

The harder the mayonnaise is beaten to break up the droplets, the more stable the
emulsion becomes. All emulsions, whether permanent or temporary, form more easily
at room temperature, because chilled oil is harder to break up into small droplets.

Other stabilizers are used in some preparations. Cooked dressing uses starch in addition to eggs. Commercially made dressings may use such emulsifiers as gums,
starches, and gelatin.

OIL AND VINEGAR DRESSINGS

Basic **vinaigrette**, the first recipe in this section, is a simple mixture of oil, vinegar, and seasonings. It can be used as is, but it is usually the base for other dressings, such as the variations that follow.

The ratio of oil to vinegar in a basic vinaigrette is 3 parts oil to 1 part vinegar. This is not a divine law, however, and the proportions may be changed to taste. Some chefs prefer a 2:1 ratio, while others prefer a 4:1 or even 5:1 ratio. Less oil makes the dressing more tart, while more oil makes it taste milder and oilier.

A very strong vinegar, more than 5 percent acid, may have to be diluted with water before being measured and added to the recipe.

For guidelines in the preparation of vinaigrettes, review the discussion of temporary emulsions above.

 ## Basic Vinaigrette

Yield: 1 qt (1 L)

U.S.	Metric	Ingredients
1 cup	250 mL	Wine vinegar
1 tbsp	15 mL	Salt
1 tsp	5 mL	White pepper
3 cups	750 mL	Salad oil, olive oil, or part salad oil and part olive oil

■ Procedure

1. Mix together the vinegar, salt, and white pepper until the salt is dissolved.
2. Using a wire whip, a mixing machine, or a blender, mix in the oil. (See discussion of temporary emulsions, p. 722.)
3. Mix or stir again before using.

Per 1 ounce:
Calories, 180; Protein, 0 g; Fat, 21 g (100% cal.); Cholesterol, 0 mg; Carbohydrates, 0 g; Fiber, 0 g; Sodium, 220 mg.

VARIATIONS

Mustard Vinaigrette
Add 1–2 oz (30–60 g) prepared mustard (French or Dijon type) to the basic recipe. Mix with the vinegar in step 1.

Herbed Vinaigrette
Add to the basic recipe or to the Mustard Vinaigrette variation ½ cup or 1 oz (30 g) chopped parsley, 1 tsp (5 mL) chopped fresh basil, 1 tsp (5 mL) chopped fresh marjoram or oregano, and 2 tsp (10 mL) chopped chives. If fresh herbs are not available, use half their volume of dried herbs.

Lemon Vinaigrette
In place of the wine vinegar in the basic recipe or the Mustard Vinaigrette variation, use 2½ fl oz (75 mL) wine vinegar and 5½ fl oz (175 mL) fresh lemon juice.

Balsamic Vinaigrette
Use balsamic vinegar in place of half to three-quarters of the wine vinegar in the basic recipe.

Italian Dressing
Use all or part olive oil. Add to the basic recipe 1½ tsp (7 mL) minced garlic, 1 tbsp (15 mL) dried oregano, ¼ cup (60 mL) chopped parsley.

Piquante Dressing
Add to the basic recipe 2 tsp (10 mL) dry mustard, 2 tbsp (30 mL) finely chopped onion, 2 tsp (10 mL) paprika.

Chiffonade Dressing
Add to the basic recipe the following ingredients, all chopped fine: 2 hard-cooked eggs, 4 oz (125 g) cooked or canned red beets (drained), 2 tbsp (30 mL) chopped parsley, 1 oz (30 g) onion or scallions.

Avocado Dressing
Add 1 lb (500 g) puréed avocado to the basic recipe or to Herbed Vinaigrette. Beat until smooth. Increase salt to taste.

Blue Cheese or Roquefort Vinaigrette
Mix 4 oz (125 g) crumbled blue cheese or Roquefort cheese and 4 fl oz (125 mL) heavy cream in a mixer with a paddle attachment or by hand in a stainless-steel bowl. Gradually beat in 1½ pt (750 mL) Basic Vinaigrette.

Walnut Herb Vinaigrette

Yield: 14 fl oz (400 mL)

U.S.	Metric	Ingredients
3½ fl oz	100 mL	Cider vinegar
to taste	to taste	Salt
to taste	to taste	Pepper
5 fl oz	150 mL	Walnut oil
5 fl oz	150 mL	Peanut oil
1½ tbsp	12 g	Chopped chives
1½ tbsp	12 g	Chopped chervil
1½ tbsp	12 g	Chopped parsley

■ P r o c e d u r e

1. Season the vinegar with salt and pepper.
2. Whip in the oils, little at a time.
3. Mix in the herbs. Check the seasoning and adjust as necessary.

Per 1 ounce:
Calories, 180; Protein, 0 g; Fat, 20 g (98% cal.); Cholesterol, 0 mg;
Carbohydrates, 1 g; Fiber, 0 g; Sodium, 0 mg.

 ## Sauce Gribiche

Yield: 1½ pt (750 mL)

U.S.	Metric	Ingredients
6	6	Hard-cooked egg yolks
1½ tbsp	45 mL	Prepared mustard, French or Dijon-style
to taste	to taste	Salt
to taste	to taste	Pepper
1 pt	475 mL	Olive oil
as needed	as needed	Wine vinegar or water
2 tbsp	30 mL	Chopped parsley
2 tbsp	30 mL	Chopped fresh chervil
2 tbsp	30 mL	Chopped fresh tarragon
2 tbsp	30 mL	Capers
2 tbsp	30 mL	Cornichons or sour gherkin pickles, chopped
6	6	Hard-cooked egg whites, cut julienne

■ P r o c e d u r e

1. Mash the yolks or force them through a sieve into a bowl.
2. Add the mustard, salt, and pepper, and mix well.
3. As when making mayonnaise (see p. 727), very gradually beat in the olive oil a few drops at a time at first, then in a thin stream.
4. Because the cooked yolks do not enable a stable emulsion like raw yolks do, the mixture curdles easily. When it does, beat in a little hot water. Continue adding oil alternately with hot water.
5. The mixture should have the consistency of a thin mayonnaise.
6. Add just enough vinegar to give it a slightly tart taste.

7. Stir in the herbs, capers, cornichons, and egg whites.
8. Taste and add more salt if necessary.

Per 1 ounce:
Calories, 180; Protein, 2 g; Fat, 19 g (96% cal.); Cholesterol, 50 mg;
Carbohydrates, 0 g; Fiber, 0 g; Sodium, 70 mg.

American French or Tomato French Dressing

Yield: 2 qt (2 L)

U.S.	Metric	Ingredients
4 oz	125 g	Onion
1 qt	1 L	Salad oil
12 oz	375 mL	Cider vinegar
2½ cups	625 mL	Ketchup
4 oz	125 g	Sugar
1 tsp	5 mL	Mashed garlic
1 tbsp	15 mL	Worcestershire sauce
1 tsp	5 mL	Paprika
¼ tsp	1 mL	Hot pepper sauce (such as Tabasco)
½ tsp	2 mL	White pepper

■ P r o c e d u r e

1. Grate the onion on a hand grater or grind in food chopper.
2. Combine all ingredients in a stainless-steel bowl.
3. Mix with a wire whip until well combined and sugar is dissolved. Chill.
4. Beat or stir again before serving.

Per 1 ounce:
Calories, 140; Protein, 0 g; Fat, 14 g (86% cal.); Cholesterol, 0 mg;
Carbohydrates, 5 g; Fiber, 0 g; Sodium, 115 mg.

Oriental Vinaigrette

Yield: 1½ pt (750 mL)

U.S.	Metric	Ingredients
¾ cup	200 mL	Rice vinegar or white vinegar
¼ cup	60 mL	Soy sauce
1¾ cups	425 mL	Salad oil
¼ cup	60 mL	Sesame oil
1 tbsp	15 mL	Grated fresh ginger root
2 tsp	10 mL	Pepper
¼ tsp	1 mL	Crushed garlic
½ tsp	2 mL	Hot pepper sauce
as needed	as needed	Salt

■ P r o c e d u r e

1. Combine all ingredients except salt in a bowl and mix well.
2. Taste the dressing and add salt if necessary (the soy sauce may contain enough salt).
3. Mix or stir again before using.

Per 1 ounce:
Calories, 160; Protein, 0 g; Fat, 18 g (100% cal.); Cholesterol, 0 mg;
Carbohydrates, 0 g; Fiber, 0 g; Sodium, 150 mg.

Reduced-Fat Vinaigrette

Yield: 1 qt (1 L)

U.S.	Metric	Ingredients
1 cup	250 mL	Wine vinegar
1 pt	500 mL	Jus Lié (p. 174) made with white stock, vegetable stock, or vegetable juice
1 tbsp	15 mL	Salt
1 tsp	5 mL	White pepper
1 cup	250 mL	Salad oil, olive oil, or part salad oil and part olive oil

■ P r o c e d u r e

1. Mix together the vinegar, jus lié, salt, and white pepper until the salt is dissolved.
2. Using a wire whip or a mixing machine, mix in the oil.
3. Mix or stir again before using.

Per 1 ounce:
Calories, 60; Protein, 0 g; Fat, 7 g (100% cal.); Cholesterol, 0 mg;
Carbohydrates, 0 g; Fiber, 0 g; Sodium, 220 mg.

Fat-Free Vinaigrette

Yield: 10 fl oz (300 mL)

U.S.	Metric	Ingredients
8 oz	250 g	Onions, whole, with peel
2 tbsp	30 mL	Prepared mustard, French or Dijon style
2 fl oz	60 mL	Wine vinegar
4 fl oz	125 mL	Vegetable stock or juice
2 tbsp	30 mL	Chopped parsley
to taste	to taste	Salt
to taste	to taste	Black pepper

■ P r o c e d u r e

1. Roast the onions at 350°F (175°C) until they are completely soft, about 45 to 60 minutes.
2. Cool until they are cool enough to handle. Peel.
3. Purée the onions in a blender or food processor.
4. Add the mustard, vinegar, and stock. Blend to mix well.
5. Stir in the chopped parsley.
6. Season to taste with salt and pepper.

V A R I A T I O N S

Substitute chicken stock for the vegetable stock.

Fat-Free Roasted Garlic Vinaigrette
Substitute roasted garlic for the roasted onions in the basic recipe.

See the variations following Basic Vinaigrette for other flavoring ideas.

Per 1 ounce:
Calories, 15; Protein, 0 g; Fat, 0 g (0% cal.); Cholesterol, 0 mg;
Carbohydrates, 3 g; Fiber, 0 g; Sodium, 80 mg.

EMULSIFIED DRESSINGS

Mayonnaise is the most important emulsified dressing. It is sometimes used by itself as a salad dressing, but more often it serves as the base for a wide variety of other dressings. Mayonnaise-based dressings are generally thick and creamy. In fact, many of them are made with the addition of sour cream.

Emulsified French dressing is similar to basic French dressing, except that egg yolk has been added to keep the oil and vinegar from separating. Its preparation is similar to that of mayonnaise. Emulsified French dressing is given a red-orange color and a subtle flavoring through the addition of Spanish paprika.

PREPARATION OF MAYONNAISE

Good-quality prepared mayonnaise is readily available on the market, and few establishments make their own. But it is such a basic preparation and, like the mother sauces you studied in Chapter 8, the foundation of many others. Therefore, it is important to know how to make it.

Homemade mayonnaise is not as stable as the commercial product, which is prepared with special equipment that creates a finer emulsion and which may have added stabilizers to increase its shelf life. Also, the commercial product is usually less expensive. Nevertheless, making mayonnaise in your operation takes only minutes with a power mixer, and by carefully selecting your ingredients you can make a superior-tasting product.

To make mayonnaise, you must observe several conditions in order to get an emulsion. Study these guidelines before proceeding with the recipe:

Guidelines for Making Mayonnaise

1. Use fairly bland ingredients if the mayonnaise is to be used as a base for other dressings.

   The mayonnaise will be more versatile as a base if it has no strong flavors. Olive oil and other ingredients with distinctive flavors may be used for special preparations.

2. Use the freshest eggs possible for the best emulsification. For safety, use pasteurized eggs.

3. Have all ingredients at room temperature.

   Cold oil is not easily broken into small droplets, so it is harder to make an emulsion.

4. Beat the egg yolks well in a bowl.

   Thorough beating of the yolks is important for a good emulsion.

5. Beat in the seasonings.

   It is helpful to add a little of the vinegar at this time as well. The emulsion will form more easily because the acidity of the vinegar helps prevent curdling of the egg yolk proteins. Also, the vinegar helps disperse the spices and dissolve the salt.

6. Begin to add the oil very slowly, beating constantly.

   It is critical to add the oil slowly at first, or the emulsion will break. When the emulsion has begun to form, the oil may be added more quickly. But never add more oil at once than the amount of mayonnaise that has already formed in the bowl, or the emulsion may break.

7. Gradually beat in the remaining oil alternately with the vinegar.

   The more oil you add, the thicker the mayonnaise gets. Vinegar thins it. Add a little vinegar whenever the mayonnaise gets too thick to beat.

   Beating with a power mixer using the wire whip attachment makes a more stable emulsion than beating by hand.

8. Add no more than 8 ounces (240 mL) oil per large egg yolk, or no more than 1 quart (950 mL) per 4 yolks.

   The emulsion may break if more oil is added than the egg yolks can handle.

9. Taste and correct the seasonings.

   Finished mayonnaise should have a smooth, rich, but neutral flavor, with a pleasant tartness. Its texture should be smooth and glossy, and it should be thick enough to hold its shape.

10. If the mayonnaise breaks, it can be rescued.

    Beat an egg yolk or two or some good prepared mayonnaise in a bowl, and very slowly begin to beat in the broken mayonnaise, as in step 6. Continue until all the mayonnaise has been added and re-formed.

Figure 21.3
Making mayonnaise by hand.

(a) Whip the egg yolks until light. Whip the first quantity of vinegar and seasonings.

(b) Slowly pour in the oil in a thin stream, while whipping constantly.

(c) The finished mayonnaise should be thick enough to hold its shape.

Mayonnaise

Yield: 2 qt (2 L)

U.S.	Metric	Ingredients
8	8	Egg yolks, preferably pasteurized
2 tbsp	30 mL	Vinegar
2 tsp	10 mL	Salt
2 tsp	10 mL	Dry mustard
pinch	pinch	Cayenne
3¼ pt	1.7 L	Salad oil
4 tbsp	60 mL	Vinegar
3–4 tbsp	50–60 mL	Lemon juice

Per 1 ounce:
Calories, 220; Protein, 0 g; Fat, 25 g (100% cal.); Cholesterol, 25 mg; Carbohydrates, 0 g; Fiber, 0 g; Sodium, 75 mg.

■ P r o c e d u r e

1. Review guidelines for making mayonnaise on page 727.
2. Place the egg yolks in the bowl of a mixer and beat with the whip attachment until well beaten.
3. Add 2 tbsp (30 mL) vinegar and beat well.
4. Mix together the dry ingredients and add to the bowl. Beat until well mixed.
5. Turn the mixer to high speed. Very slowly, almost drop by drop, begin adding the oil. When the emulsion forms, you can add the oil slightly faster.
6. When the mayonnaise becomes thick, thin with a little of the vinegar.
7. Gradually beat in the remaining oil alternately with the vinegar.
8. Adjust the tartness and the consistency by beating in a little lemon juice.

Mayonnaise-Based Dressings

For each of the following dressings, add the listed ingredients to *2 qt (2 L) mayonnaise* as indicated.

Thousand Island Dressing
1 pt (500 mL) chili sauce, 2 oz (60 g) minced onion, 4 oz (125 g) finely chopped green bell pepper, 4 oz (125 g) chopped drained pimiento, and (optional ingredient) 3 chopped hard-cooked eggs.

Louis Dressing
Prepare Thousand Island Dressing without the chopped eggs. Add 1 pt (500 mL) heavy cream.

Russian Dressing
1 pt (500 mL) chili sauce or ketchup, ½ cup (125 mL) drained horse-radish, 2 oz (60 g) minced onion, and (optional ingredient) 1 cup (500 mL) lumpfish or whitefish caviar.

Chantilly Dressing
1 pt (500 mL) heavy cream, whipped. Fold the whipped cream into the mayonnaise carefully to retain volume. Do this as close as possible to service time.

Blue Cheese Dressing
½ cup (125 mL) white vinegar, 2 tsp (10 mL) Worcestershire sauce, a few drops of hot red pepper sauce, and 1 lb (500 g) crumbled blue cheese. Thin to desired consistency with 1–2 cups (250–500 mL) heavy cream or half-and-half. *Variation:* Substitute sour cream for up to half of the mayonnaise.

Ranch Dressing
1½ qt (1.5 L) sour cream, 2½ pt (1.25 L) buttermilk, 8 oz (250 mL) wine vinegar, 6 oz (175 mL) lemon juice, 6 oz (175 mL) Worcestershire sauce, 6 tbsp (90 mL) chopped parsley, 4 tbsp (60 mL) chopped chives, 6 crushed garlic cloves, 4 chopped scallions, 2 oz (60 mL) prepared mustard, 1 tbsp (15 mL) celery seed.

Aioli II
Mash 2–4 oz (60–125 g) garlic with the salt in the basic recipe. Add this to the egg yolks. Use olive oil or one-half olive oil and one-half salad oil. For another version of Aioli, see page 201.

Caesar Dressing

Yield: 1 qt (1 L)

U.S.	Metric	Ingredients	
			■ P r o c e d u r e
25	25	Anchovy fillets (see note)	1. Mash the anchovies and garlic together to make a paste.
2 tsp	10 mL	Crushed garlic	
4	4	Eggs, pasteurized	2. Place the eggs in the bowl of a mixer and whip with the whip attachment until well beaten.
3 fl oz	90 mL	Lemon juice	3. Add the anchovy and garlic paste and the first quantity of lemon juice. Whip until well mixed.
2½ cups	600 mL	Olive oil	4. With the mixer on high speed, slowly begin adding the oil, as when making mayonnaise.
3 fl oz	90 mL	Lemon juice	5. When the dressing becomes thick, add a little of the remaining lemon juice.
2 oz	60 g	Parmesan cheese, grated	6. Gradually beat in the rest of the oil alternating with the rest of the lemon juice.
to taste	to taste	Salt	7. Mix in the parmesan cheese and salt.

Per 1 ounce:
Calories, 170; Protein, 2 g; Fat, 18 g (93% cal.); Cholesterol, 30 mg; Carbohydrates, 1 g; Fiber, 0 g; Sodium, 160 mg.

Note: Anchovies are a main ingredient in traditional Caesar salads but may be omitted according to taste.

Emulsified French Dressing

Yield: 2 qt (2 L)

U.S.	Metric	Ingredients	
			■ P r o c e d u r e
2	2	Eggs, preferably pasteurized	1. Place the eggs in the bowl of a mixer and beat with the whip attachment until well beaten.
1 tbsp	15 mL	Salt	2. Mix together the dry ingredients and add to the bowl. Beat until well mixed.
1 tbsp	15 mL	Paprika	
1 tbsp	15 mL	Dry mustard	3. Turn the mixer to high speed. Very slowly begin adding the oil, as when making mayonnaise.
½ tsp	2 mL	White pepper	
3 pt	1.4 L	Salad oil	4. When the dressing becomes thick, thin with a little of the vinegar.
8 fl oz	250 mL	Cider vinegar	5. Gradually beat in the remaining oil alternately with the vinegar.
4 fl oz	125 mL	Lemon juice	6. Beat in the lemon juice.
as needed	as needed	Vinegar, lemon juice, or water	7. The dressing should be pourable, not thick like mayonnaise. If it is too thick, taste for seasonings first. If the dressing is not tart enough, thin with a little vinegar or lemon juice. If it is tart enough, thin with water.

Per 1 ounce:
Calories, 190; Protein, 0 g; Fat, 21 g (100% cal.); Cholesterol, 5 mg; Carbohydrates, 0 g; Fiber, 0 g; Sodium, 110 mg.

OTHER DRESSINGS

Cooked salad dressing is similar in appearance to mayonnaise, but it has a more tart flavor, while mayonnaise is richer and milder. Cooked dressing is made with little or no oil and with a starch thickener. It may be made in the kitchen or purchased already prepared. Formerly, it was little used in commercial kitchens because of its strong flavor and tartness, but now it is preferred to mayonnaise in some regions.

You will find in many cookbooks a great variety of dressings based on neither mayonnaise nor oil and vinegar. They include dressings based on sour cream and on fruit juice and yogurt (for fruit salads), and low-calorie dressings that appeal to the dieter. The important thing to remember is that these dressings should have well-balanced flavors with a pleasant tartness, and they should harmonize with and complement the salad with which they are served.

Sour Cream Fruit Salad Dressing

Yield: About 2½ pt (1.25 L)

U.S.	Metric	Ingredients
4 oz	125 g	Currant jelly
4 fl oz	125 mL	Lemon juice
2 pt	1 L	Sour cream

Per 1 ounce:
Calories, 60; Protein, 1 g; Fat, 5 g (74% cal.); Cholesterol, 10 mg;
Carbohydrates, 3 g; Fiber, 0 g; Sodium, 15 mg.

■ P r o c e d u r e

1. Place the jelly and lemon juice in a stainless-steel bowl. Set over hot water or low heat and stir until melted.

2. Remove from heat and beat in the sour cream a little at a time. Chill the dressing.

V A R I A T I O N

Yogurt Fruit Salad Dressing
Prepare as in basic recipe, using 1 cup (250 mL) sour cream and 3 cups (750 mL) plain yogurt.

Cooked Salad Dressing

Yield: 2 qt (2 L)

U.S.	Metric	Ingredients
4 oz	125 g	Sugar
4 oz	125 g	Flour
2 tbsp	30 mL	Salt
2 tbsp	30 mL	Dry mustard
¼ tsp	1 mL	Cayenne
4	4	Eggs
4	4	Egg yolks
3 pt	1.5 L	Milk
4 oz	125 g	Butter
12 fl oz	375 mL	Cider vinegar

Per 1 ounce:
Calories, 50; Protein, 2 g; Fat, 3 g (49% cal.); Cholesterol, 35 mg;
Carbohydrates, 5 g; Fiber, 0 g; Sodium, 250 mg.

■ P r o c e d u r e

1. Mix the sugar, flour, salt, mustard, and cayenne in a stainless-steel bowl.

2. Add the eggs and yolks and beat until smooth.

3. Place the milk in a saucepan and bring to a simmer. Be careful not to scorch it.

4. Gradually beat about half the milk into the egg mixture. Then return the mixture to the saucepan.

5. Cook over low heat, stirring constantly, until very thick and no raw flour taste remains.

6. Remove from heat and stir in the butter.

7. When the butter is melted and mixed in, stir in the vinegar.

8. Immediately transfer the dressing to a stainless-steel container. Cover and cool.

Honey Lemon Dressing

Yield: 1 pt (500 mL)

U.S.	Metric	Ingredients
1 cup	250 mL	Honey
1 cup	250 mL	Lemon juice

Per 1 ounce:
Calories, 70; Protein, 0 g; Fat, 0 g (0% cal.); Cholesterol, 0 mg;
Carbohydrates, 19 g; Fiber, 0 g; Sodium, 0 mg.

■ **P r o c e d u r e**

1. Mix honey and lemon juice together until thoroughly mixed.
2. Serve with fruit salads.

V A R I A T I O N S

Honey Cream Dressing
Mix 1 cup (250 mL) heavy cream with the honey before adding the lemon juice.

Honey Lime Dressing
Use lime juice instead of lemon juice.

Fruit Salad Dressing

Yield: 1 qt (1 L)

U.S.	Metric	Ingredients
6 oz	175 g	Sugar
1 oz	30 g	Cornstarch
4	4	Eggs
1 cup	250 mL	Pineapple juice
1 cup	250 mL	Orange juice
½ cup	125 mL	Lemon juice
1 cup	250 mL	Sour cream

Per 1 ounce:
Calories, 60; Protein, 1 g; Fat, 2 g (31% cal.); Cholesterol, 30 mg;
Carbohydrates, 9 g; Fiber, 0 g; Sodium, 10 mg.

■ **P r o c e d u r e**

1. Mix the sugar and cornstarch in a stainless-steel bowl.
2. Add the eggs and beat until the mixture is smooth.
3. Heat the fruit juices in a saucepan and bring to a boil.
4. Gradually beat the hot juices into the egg mixture.
5. Return the mixture to the saucepan and bring to a boil, stirring constantly.
6. When the mixture has thickened, immediately pour it out into a stainless-steel bowl or bain-marie and chill.
7. Beat the sour cream into the chilled fruit mixture.

Low-Fat Buttermilk Yogurt Dressing

Yield: 1 pt 12 fl oz (850 mL)

U.S.	Metric	Ingredients
1 pt	500 mL	Fat-free or low-fat yogurt, unflavored
8 fl oz	250 mL	Buttermilk
1 tbsp	15 mL	Prepared mustard, French or Dijon style
1 fl oz	30 mL	Wine vinegar
1 fl oz	30 mL	Lemon juice
1 fl oz	30 mL	Worcestershire sauce
1½ tbsp	22 mL	Chopped parsley
1 tsp	5 mL	Finely chopped garlic
½ oz	15 g	Shallots, chopped fine
½ tsp	2 mL	Celery seed
4 tsp	20 mL	Sugar
to taste	to taste	Salt
to taste	to taste	Pepper

Per 1 ounce:
Calories, 15; Protein, 1 g; Fat, 0 g (0% cal.); Cholesterol, 0 mg;
Carbohydrates, 3 g; Fiber, 0 g; Sodium, 45 mg.

■ **P r o c e d u r e**

1. Mix all ingredients together until uniformly blended.

■ TERMS FOR REVIEW

appetizer salad	full slip	composed salad	emulsion
accompaniment salad	four parts of a salad	gelatin salad	temporary emulsion
main-course salad	bound salad	winterized oil	vinaigrette
separate-course salad	vegetable salad	strength of acidity	
dessert salad	fruit salad	Roquefort	

■ QUESTIONS FOR DISCUSSION

1. List three or four salads that may be served as appetizers, as accompaniments, as main dishes, as separate-course salads, and as desserts. Give reasons for your choices.

2. What is the effect of salad dressings on the crispness of salad greens, and what are some ways to solve this problem?

3. You are asked to prepare 250 Waldorf salads for a banquet. Explain the procedure you will use for the preparation. List each step, from raw ingredients to plated salads. (You may refer to the recipe on p. 706.)

4. How can you ensure that salad greens will be crisp?

5. You are making mixed green salads and have the following ingredients to choose from. Which would you toss together, and which would you add after plating or at service time? Why?

Iceberg lettuce	Chicory
Shredded red cabbage	Avocado slices
Carrot strips or shreds	Tomato wedges
Watercress	Romaine lettuce
Sliced celery	

6. You are preparing tossed green salads, potato salads, and avocado and grapefruit salads for luncheon service. How will you plan your preparation (what will you do first, second, and so on)?

7. You are trying a new recipe for a molded vegetable salad using unflavored gelatin. After evaluating the flavor, you decide it isn't tart enough and more vinegar should be added. Should you make any other adjustments?

8. When you are making mayonnaise, you should take a number of precautions to make sure a good emulsion is formed. Name as many as you can. If you forget one of these and your mayonnaise breaks, what can you do?

CHAPTER 22

Sandwiches

The sandwich is a favorite and convenient lunchtime food. It is quickly made and served and adaptable to so many variations that it satisfies nearly every taste and nutrition requirement.

Sandwiches have long been the domain of the pantry department, along with salads and other cold preparations. However, when you consider that the most popular sandwich today is the hamburger, you realize that sandwich preparation is as much the responsibility of the short-order cook as it is of the pantry cook.

Preparing hot and cold sandwiches to order is one of the fundamental skills required in modern food service. In this chapter, we start by looking at the fundamentals of sandwich-making, the basic ingredients and basic sandwich types. We then look at the setup of the sandwich station and methods for efficient production.

BREADS

One of the functions of the bread in a sandwich is to provide an edible casing for the food inside. Ideally, though, the bread should do more than this. Good-quality breads provide variety, texture, flavor, and eye appeal to sandwiches, as well as bulk and nutrients.

TYPES

Pullman or sandwich loaves of white bread are most frequently used for simple sandwiches. These are long, rectangular loaves that provide square slices of specified thickness, from ⅜ inch to ⅝ inch (10 mm to 16 mm) thick.

Commercial sandwich bread should be of fine rather than coarse texture and firm enough to accommodate spreads well. Supermarket white bread is unsuitable because it is too soft for spreading and for holding most fillings, and it becomes pasty in the mouth.

Because of its neutral flavor, white bread is suitable for the largest variety of fillings.

Other kinds of breads add variety and interest, provided that they harmonize with the filling. The following are some possibilities:

Rolls, including hard and soft rolls, hamburger and hot dog rolls, long rolls for submarine sandwiches	Cracked wheat
	Rye and pumpernickel
	Pita bread
French or Italian bread and rolls, including sourdough and ciabatta, split horizontally	Raisin bread
	Cinnamon bread
	Fruit and nut breads
Whole wheat	Focaccia

STORAGE

Fresh bread is essential for top-quality sandwiches. Stale or dry bread is undesirable. The following measures can be taken to ensure freshness.

1. Daily delivery, or as frequent as possible, depending on your location. Bread stales rapidly, and day-old bread has lost much of its freshness.

2. Keep bread tightly wrapped in moistureproof wrapping until it is used. This prevents drying and guards against absorption of odors.

3. French bread and other hard-crusted breads should not be wrapped, or the crusts will soften. These breads stale rapidly and should be used the day they are baked.

4. Store at room temperature, away from ovens or hot equipment. Do not refrigerate, because refrigerated bread becomes stale faster.

5. If bread must be kept more than one day, it may be frozen. Thaw frozen bread without unwrapping.

6. Day-old bread may be used for toasting without loss of quality.

SPREADS

PURPOSES OF SPREADS

1. To protect the bread from soaking up moisture from the filling.
2. To add flavor.
3. To add moisture or mouth feel.

After reading this chapter, you should be able to

1. Select, store, and serve fresh, good-quality breads for sandwiches.

2. Use sandwich spreads correctly.

3. Identify the most popular types of sandwich fillings.

4. Set up an efficient sandwich station.

5. Prepare the major types of sandwiches to order.

6. Prepare sandwiches in quantity.

BUTTER

Butter should be soft enough to spread easily without tearing the bread. It may be softened by whipping in a mixer or by simply letting it stand at room temperature for half an hour.

Whipping gives the butter greater volume, and this cuts food cost. However, whipped butter does not keep as well because the incorporated air speeds the development of rancidity.

Some operators whip a small amount of water or milk into the butter. This increases both spreadability and volume. However, it adds nothing to the quality of the sandwich and increases the likelihood of soaking the bread.

Margarine is sometimes used instead of butter, if food costs require it or if customers request it.

Flavored butters, such as those listed on page 179, may be used with appropriate fillings.

MAYONNAISE

Mayonnaise is often preferred to butter as a spread because it contributes more flavor. However, it does not protect the bread from moisture as well as butter does.

Because of the danger of food-borne disease, sandwiches made with mayonnaise should be served immediately or refrigerated at once and kept refrigerated until served.

OTHER SPREADS

Although butter and mayonnaise are the most widely used spreads, almost any food of a spreadable consistency can be used to add flavor interest to sandwiches, including such items as pesto (p. 644), tapenade (p. 774), liver pâté (p. 778), hummus (p. 762), babaganouj (p. 762), guacamole (p. 763), and romesco (p. 762). Be aware, however, that most of these do not protect the bread from soaking up moisture from the filling. Moist spreads are best if applied just before serving.

FILLINGS

The filling is the heart of the sandwich. As we have already said, nearly any kind of food may be served between two slices of bread. The following are some possible fillings that may be used separately or in combination.

MEATS AND POULTRY

Most meats for sandwiches are precooked, though some are cooked to order. Sliced meats dry out and lose flavor, so avoid slicing farther ahead than necessary, and keep sliced meats covered or wrapped.

Leftovers may be used, but only if they are of good quality and have been properly handled and stored to avoid contamination.

Thin slices are more tender, and sandwiches made with them are easier to eat. Also, many thin slices make a thicker sandwich than one or two thick slices of the same total weight.

1. Beef	2. Pork products	3. Poultry	4. Sausage products
Sliced roast beef, hot or cold	Roast pork	Turkey breast	Salami
Hamburger patties	Barbecued pork	Chicken breast	Frankfurters
Small steaks	Ham, all kinds		Bologna
Corned beef	Bacon		Liverwurst
Pastrami	Canadian bacon		Luncheon meats
Tongue, fresh or smoked			Grilled sausages

CHEESE

Like meats, cheese dries out rapidly when unwrapped and sliced. When slicing is done ahead, the slices should remain covered until service time. See Chapter 25 for a summary of cheese varieties.

The most popular sandwich cheeses are

Cheddar types	Cream cheese, mascarpone
Swiss types	Process cheese
Provolone	Cheese spreads

FISH AND SHELLFISH

Most seafood fillings for sandwiches are highly perishable and should be kept well chilled at all times.

Some popular seafood fillings are

Tuna	Anchovies
Sardines	Fried fish portions
Smoked salmon and lox	Grilled or pan-fried fish fillets
Shrimp	

BOUND SALADS

Refer to page 702 for preparation of bound salads. The most popular salads for sandwich fillings are tuna salad, egg salad, chicken or turkey salad, and ham salad.

VEGETABLE ITEMS

Lettuce, tomato, and onion are indispensable in sandwich production. In addition, nearly any vegetable used in salads may also be included in sandwiches. See page 702 for a listing. Grilled vegetables are popular not only in vegetarian sandwiches but also as part of the filling in meat sandwiches.

MISCELLANEOUS

Peanut butter	Fruits, fresh or dried
Jelly	Nuts (such as sliced almonds)
Egg	

TYPES OF SANDWICHES

COLD SANDWICHES

1. **Simple cold sandwiches** are those made with two slices of bread or two halves of a roll, a spread, and a filling. They are called *simple* because they are made with just two slices of bread, not because they are necessarily simple in construction. Simple cold sandwiches range from a single slice of cheese or meat between two slices of buttered bread to complex constructions like the submarine sandwich (also called a *hero sandwich* or *grinder*), a long Italian roll filled with salami, ham, capocollo, mortadella or bologna, provolone cheese, peppers, onions, olives, tomatoes, and more.

Most popular sandwiches fall into this category.

2. **Multidecker sandwiches** are made with more than two slices of bread (or rolls split into more than two pieces) and with several ingredients in the filling.

    The **club sandwich** is a popular multidecker sandwich, made of three slices of toast and filled with sliced chicken or turkey breast, mayonnaise, lettuce, tomato, and bacon. It is cut into four triangles, as shown in Figure 22.1.

Figure 22.1
Cutting a club or multidecker sandwich.

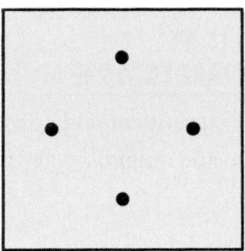

(a) Place four picks in the sandwich in the locations shown by the dots in the illustration.

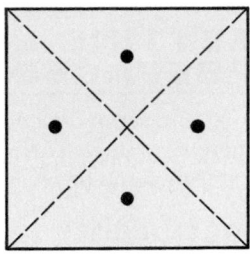

(b) Cut the sandwiches into quarters from corner to corner. Plate the sandwich with the points up.

3. **Open-faced sandwiches** are made with a single slice of bread, like large canapés, which is what they are. Like those in canapés, the filling or topping should be attractively arranged and garnished. Canapé ingredients and method are discussed in Chapter 23.

4. **Tea sandwiches** are small, fancy sandwiches generally made from light, delicate ingredients and bread that has been trimmed of crusts. They are often cut into fancy shapes. Fillings and spreads can be the same as those for canapés.

5. **Wraps** are sandwiches in which the fillings are wrapped, like a Mexican burrito, in a large flour tortilla or similar flatbread. They may be served whole or cut in half if large.

HOT SANDWICHES

1. **Simple hot sandwiches** consist of hot fillings, usually meats but sometimes fish, grilled vegetables, or other hot items, between two slices of bread or two halves of a roll. They may also contain items that are not hot, such as a slice of tomato or raw onion on a hamburger.

    Hamburgers and hot dogs and all their variations are the most popular hot sandwiches.

2. **Open-faced hot sandwiches** are made by placing buttered or unbuttered bread on a serving plate, covering it with hot meat or other filling, and topping with a sauce, gravy, cheese, or other topping. Some versions are browned under the broiler before serving. This type of sandwich is eaten with a knife and fork.

3. **Grilled sandwiches**, also called *toasted sandwiches*, are simple sandwiches that are buttered on the outside and browned on the griddle, in a hot oven, or in a panini grill (see sidebar). Sandwiches containing cheese are popular for grilling.

4. **Deep-fried sandwiches** are made by dipping sandwiches in beaten egg and, sometimes, in bread crumbs, and then deep-frying. This type of sandwich is often cooked on a griddle or in a hot oven instead, as deep-frying makes it greasy.

5. If wraps are classified as cold sandwiches, then hot burritos, quesadillas, and filled enchiladas could be considered hot sandwiches. **Pizzas** could be considered open-faced hot sandwiches, and we can define them as thin sheets of lean bread dough baked with a topping. In fact, one could classify any food made with a dough product filled or topped with another food product as a sandwich. Dough products, whether breads, puff pastry, tortillas, or egg roll skins, make useful and versatile bases or cases for foods, whether or not the result resembles something we might think of as a sandwich. Several of these items (enchiladas, quesadillas, and egg rolls) are considered in other chapters of this book. Pizzas are included in this chapter for convenience. The recipe on page 752 gives the basic procedure for baking pizzas. For other flavors, vary the toppings as desired, using the same technique for baking.

Panini grill

<table>
<tr><td>

PANINI

The basic meaning of the Italian word *panino* (plural: *panini*) is "roll," as in bread roll or dinner roll—literally, "little bread." By extension, **panini** are sandwiches made of small rolls plus fillings. The filling for a typical panino is a slice or two of cured meat, such as salami, mortadella (Italian bologna), or prosciutto. Cheese may also be used, as well as a variety of other items, such as sliced tomato and canned tuna. In summary, Italian panini are most often small, simple, cold sandwiches.

Outside of Italy, *panino* has come to mean something quite different. It is usually a hot grilled sandwich, often with a fairly substantial filling. What distinguishes panini from other grilled sandwiches is that they are made on a special griddle called a *panini grill* or *panini press*, which grills the sandwich on both sides at once while compressing or squeezing the bread and filling together. The griddle surfaces may be smooth or grooved. Grooved griddles toast grill marks onto the bread for the typical panini look.

Grilled panini often contain cheese as one of the filling ingredients. The melted cheese as well as the crisp toasted crusts are part of the attraction of this type of sandwich.

If a sandwich press is not available, you can create a similar kind of sandwich by toasting it on a standard flat griddle or grooved griddle, putting a grill brick on the sandwich to compress it and turning it over when heated halfway through to toast both sides.

For pressed sandwiches, avoid making the fillings too thick. Unlike for grilled sandwiches, it is not always necessary to butter or oil the outside surfaces of the bread. The moisture and fat in the filling may be enough to moisten the bread as it grills. Adding more sometimes makes the sandwich too greasy.

</td></tr>
</table>

MAKING SANDWICHES

The preparation of sandwiches requires a great deal of handwork. Many individual motions may be required, especially if the sandwiches are multideckers or have several ingredients. Whether you are making sandwiches in quantity or to order, your goal must be to reduce your motions to make the production as efficient and quick as possible.

SETTING UP THE STATION FOR PREPARED-TO-ORDER SANDWICHES

A station setup depends on the menu and on the available equipment and space, so there is no single correct way to set up.

Any setup involves two elements: ingredients and equipment.

Ingredients

This phase of the setup has two parts:

1. **Prepare ingredients.**
    Mix fillings, prepare spreads, slice sandwich meats and cheeses, separate lettuce leaves, slice tomatoes, prepare garnishes, and so on. In other words, have everything ready ahead of time, so nothing is left to do but assemble the ingredients.

2. **Arrange or store ingredients for maximum efficiency.**
    To reduce your movements to a minimum, the ideal setup has everything you need within easy reach of both hands. Depending on the kitchen layout, this may not be possible, especially if the sandwich menu is large. But try to get as close to it as possible.

    Arrange ingredients so you can use both hands. For example, while the left hand reaches for the bread, the right hand reaches for the butter spreader. Then, while the right hand puts the spreader back, the left reaches for the sliced ham. The right hand, on its way back from the butter, picks up a slice of cheese and so on. On a busy sandwich station, every second counts.

Two other considerations are important while we're talking about ingredients:

1. **Sanitation.**
    Because cold sandwiches are subjected to a lot of handling and are not cooked, it is especially important that ingredients be properly refrigerated and protected at all times. A refrigerated table—sort of a cold version of a steam table—is usually used. Refrigerated drawers or under-the-counter reach-ins are used for less frequently needed items.

    Wash hands carefully and thoroughly before beginning work. In addition, be aware of local sanitation requirements. In some places, laws require that workers wear gloves when handling ready-to-eat foods (see p. 26).

2. **Portion control.**
    Sliced items are portioned by the count and by weight. If portioning is by the count, you must take care, during pre-prep, to slice to the proper thickness. If done by weight, each portion can be placed on squares of waxed paper and stacked in a container.

Equipment

The equipment needed for a sandwich station depends, of course, on the menu and the size of the operation.

1. *Storage equipment* for ingredients includes refrigeration equipment for cold ingredients and a steam table for hot ingredients, such as roasted meats.

2. *Hand tools* are basic requirements for sandwich making and are often the only tools necessary. These include spreaders, spatulas, and knives, including a serrated knife and a sharp chef's knife for cutting the finished sandwich. A cutting board, of course, is also required. A power slicer may be necessary for any slicing not done ahead.

3. *Portion control equipment* includes scoops for fillings and a portion scale for other ingredients.

4. *Cooking equipment* is necessary for most hot sandwiches. Griddles, grills, broilers, and deep fryers are all used for cooking sandwich ingredients to order. Microwave ovens are sometimes used to heat ingredients or finished sandwiches.

SETTING UP AND PREPARING SANDWICHES IN QUANTITY

Once the ingredients are prepared and the hand tools assembled, all that's needed for a complete sandwich station is a large table.

Assembly-line production is the most efficient method because it simplifies movements. This is the same method applied to producing salads in quantity in Chapter 21.

Procedure for Making Simple Cold Sandwiches in Quantity

1. Prepare and assemble all ingredients.

2. Assemble necessary equipment, including wrapping materials.

3. Arrange bread slices in rows on the tabletop.

4. Spread each slice with butter or whatever spread is required.

5. Place fillings evenly and neatly on alternate slices, leaving the other slices plain. Fillings should not hang over the edges of the bread. If the filling is spreadable, spread it evenly to the edges. See Figure 22.2 for spreading technique.

6. Top the filled slices with the plain buttered slices.

7. Stack two or three sandwiches and cut with a sharp knife.

8. To hold, do one of the following:
   - Wrap separately in plastic, waxed paper, or sandwich bags.
   - Place in storage pans, cover tightly with plastic wrap, and cover with clean, damp towels. The towels must not touch the sandwiches; their purpose is to provide a moisture barrier to help prevent drying.

9. Refrigerate immediately and hold until served.

Figure 22.2
Spread sandwiches efficiently with three quick strokes as shown.

SERVICE

With a few exceptions, such as hamburgers and hot dogs, sandwiches are cut before serving. Cutting serves two purposes: It makes the sandwich easier to handle and eat, and it makes possible a more attractive presentation.

The first purpose is usually accomplished by simply cutting the sandwich in half or, if it is very large or thick, into thirds or quarters.

The second purpose can be served by displaying the cut edges rather than the crust edges to the outside. If the sandwich was neatly made, of good ingredients, and tastefully garnished, it will be appetizing and attractive. Little purpose is served by cutting and arranging the sandwich in complicated ways.

Hamburgers and other uncut sandwiches may be presented open-face to display the attractive ingredients. For example, a hamburger version often called a *California burger* is presented with the meat on the bottom half of the bun and, alongside, a lettuce leaf and a slice of tomato on the top half of the bun.

Hot sandwiches prepared to order offer the same challenges for creative and attractive presentation as other hot foods, as discussed in Chapter 28. The most important factors in the presentation are using good, fresh ingredients and preparing them with care, using proper techniques for cooking meats, poultry, fish, vegetables, and any other components of the sandwich.

COLD SANDWICH COMBINATIONS

The following suggestions are only a few of the many sandwiches that can be made from the ingredients listed in the first part of this chapter.

1. Roast beef on rye bread spread with a mixture of softened cream cheese and horseradish.
2. Beef tongue, lettuce, and tomato on onion roll; mayonnaise.
3. Bologna, provolone cheese, tomatoes, and chopped pimiento on hard roll; mayonnaise.
4. Liverwurst, onion slices, and sour pickles on pumpernickel; mayonnaise or butter.
5. Corned beef or ham, Swiss cheese, mustard, and dill pickle slices on rye; mayonnaise or butter.
6. Corned beef, coleslaw (well drained), and Swiss cheese on rye; mayonnaise or butter.
7. Ham, salami, tomato slice, Russian dressing, and lettuce on rye toast.
8. Chicken or turkey, ham, Swiss cheese, and lettuce on white or whole wheat toast; mayonnaise.
9. Chicken and cucumber slices on whole wheat; mayonnaise.
10. Turkey, bacon, Swiss cheese, and lettuce on white or whole wheat toast; mayonnaise.
11. Deviled ham, pineapple slice, and lettuce on white toast.
12. Tuna salad, lettuce, tomato, and shredded cheddar cheese on white toast.
13. Sardines and onion slices on dark rye spread with cream cheese; served open-face.

 ## California Burger

Yield: 1 sandwich

U.S.	Metric	Ingredients
1	1	Hamburger patty, 4 oz (125 g)
1	1	Hamburger roll
as needed	as needed	Butter
2 tsp	10 mL	Mayonnaise
1	1	Lettuce leaf
1	1	Thin slice of onion (optional)
1	1	Tomato slice

Per serving:
Calories, 480; Protein, 24 g; Fat, 32 g (61% cal.); Cholesterol, 85 mg; Carbohydrates, 23 g; Fiber, 2 g; Sodium, 370 mg.

■ Procedure

1. Cook the hamburger patty on a griddle or grill to desired doneness.
2. While the meat is cooking, prepare the roll. Butter the bottom half very lightly. Spread the top half with mayonnaise.
3. Place the halves of the roll side by side on a serving plate.
4. On the top half, place the lettuce leaf, the onion slice (if used), and the tomato slice.
5. When the hamburger patty is cooked, place it on the bottom half of the roll. Serve immediately, open faced.

VARIATIONS

California Cheeseburger
Prepare as in basic recipe, except place a slice of cheddar or American cheese on the hamburger patty 1 minute before it is done. Cook until the cheese melts.

Cheeseburger (plain)
Omit mayonnaise, lettuce, onion, and tomato, but add the slice of cheese as in California Cheeseburger.

Cheeseburger with Bacon
Prepare like a Cheeseburger, but place 2 half-strips of bacon on the cheese.

California Cheeseburger Deluxe
Prepare like a California Cheeseburger, but place 2 half-strips of bacon on the cheese.

California Burger

Submarine Sandwich

Yield: 1 sandwich

U.S.	Metric	Ingredients
1	1	Submarine roll
2 tbsp	30 mL	Mayonnaise
1 oz	30 g	Salami, cut in thin slices
1 oz	30 g	Ham, cut in thin slices
1 oz	30 g	Bologna, cut in thin slices
1 oz	30 g	Provolone cheese, cut in thin slices
2	2	Tomato slices
2	2	Onion slices, very thin
3	3	Green bell pepper rings

■ P r o c e d u r e

1. Split the roll horizontally, but leave it hinged on one side.
2. Spread the roll with mayonnaise.
3. Arrange the meats and cheese in the sandwich in layers. If the slices of meat are too wide to fit, fold them in half.
4. Arrange the tomato, onion, and pepper slices on top of the meats and cheese.
5. Close the sandwich. Leave it whole or cut it in half for service.
6. Serve the sandwich with mustard and olives or pickles on the side.

Per serving:
Calories, 770; Protein, 28 g; Fat, 51 g (60% cal.); Cholesterol, 85 mg; Carbohydrates, 50 g; Fiber, 5 g; Sodium, 1650 mg.

 ## Club Sandwich

Yield: 1 sandwich

U.S.	Metric	Ingredients
3 slices	3 slices	White bread, toasted
as needed	as needed	Mayonnaise
2 leaves	2 leaves	Lettuce
2 slices	2 slices	Tomato, about ¼ in. (½ cm) thick
3 strips	3 strips	Bacon, cooked crisp
2 oz	60 g	Sliced turkey or chicken breast

Per serving:
Calories, 580; Protein, 32 g; Fat, 25 g (40% cal.); Cholesterol, 75 mg; Carbohydrates, 53 g; Fiber, 3 g; Sodium, 910 mg.

■ P r o c e d u r e

1. Place the 3 slices of toast on a clean work surface. Spread the tops with mayonnaise.
2. On the first slice, place 1 lettuce leaf, then 2 slices of tomato, then 3 strips of bacon.
3. Place the second slice of toast on top, spread side down.
4. Spread the top with mayonnaise.
5. On top of this, place the turkey or chicken, then the other lettuce leaf.
6. Top with the third slice of toast, spread side down.
7. Place frilled picks on all 4 sides of the sandwich, as shown in Figure 22.1.
8. Cut the sandwich from corner to corner into 4 triangles. Each triangle will have a pick through the center to hold it together.
9. Place on a plate with the points up. The center of the plate may be filled with potato chips, French fries, or other garnish or accompaniment.

V A R I A T I O N

Bacon, Lettuce, and Tomato Sandwich (BLT)
Using only 2 slices of toast, prepare basic recipe through step 3. Omit remaining ingredients. Cut sandwich in half diagonally for service.

Club Sandwich

Grilled Cheese Sandwich

Yield: 1 sandwich

U.S.	Metric	Ingredients
1 oz	30 g	Cheddar or American cheese: 1 slice cut to the size of the bread
2 slices	2 slices	White bread
as needed	as needed	Butter

Per serving:
Calories, 360; Protein, 13 g; Fat, 20 g (49% cal.); Cholesterol, 55 mg; Carbohydrates, 34 g; Fiber, 1 g; Sodium, 580 mg.

■ P r o c e d u r e

1. Place the slice of cheese between the slices of bread.
2. Butter the outsides of the sandwich and place on a griddle preheated to 350°–375°F (175°–190°C).
3. Cook until golden brown on one side. Turn over and cook until the second side is golden brown and the cheese starts to melt.
4. Remove the sandwich from the griddle. Cut in half diagonally and serve immediately.

V A R I A T I O N S

Grilled Ham and Swiss Sandwich
Make the sandwich with a ½ -oz (15-g) slice of Swiss cheese and a 1-oz (30-g) slice of ham. Griddle as in basic recipe.

Grilled Cheese and Bacon Sandwich
Make the sandwich with 1 oz (30 g) cheddar or American cheese and 2 strips of crisp cooked bacon. Griddle as in basic recipe.

 Reuben Sandwich

Yield: 1 sandwich

U.S.	Metric	Ingredients
2 slices	2 slices	Dark rye bread
4 tsp	20 mL	Russian or Thousand Island dressing
2 oz	60 g	Corned beef, sliced very thin
1 oz	30 g	Sauerkraut, well drained
1 oz	30 g	Swiss cheese (1 or 2 slices)
as needed	as needed	Butter

Per serving:
Calories, 590; Protein, 25 g; Fat, 39 g (59% cal.); Cholesterol, 105 mg; Carbohydrates, 35 g; Fiber, 4 g; Sodium, 1580 mg.

■ P r o c e d u r e

1. Place the slices of bread on a clean work surface.
2. Spread each slice with about 2 tsp (10 mL) dressing.
3. On one of the slices, place the corned beef, then the sauerkraut, then the cheese.
4. Place the second slice of bread on top, spread side down.
5. Butter the top of the sandwich and place buttered side down on a preheated griddle. Immediately butter the other side of the sandwich, which is now on top. (This method is less messy than buttering both sides before placing it on the griddle.)
6. Griddle the sandwich, turning once, until browned on both sides and hot through.
7. Cut the sandwich into halves and serve immediately.

Monte Cristo Sandwich

Yield: 1 sandwich

U.S.	Metric	Ingredients
2 slices	2 slices	White bread
as needed	as needed	Butter
1 oz	30 g	Sliced turkey or chicken breast
1 oz	30 g	Sliced ham
1 oz	30 g	Sliced Swiss cheese
1	1	Egg, beaten
2 tbsp	30 mL	Milk

Per serving:
Calories, 570; Protein, 35 g; Fat, 30 g (48% cal.); Cholesterol, 285 mg; Carbohydrates, 37 g; Fiber, 1 g; Sodium, 650 mg.

■ **P r o c e d u r e**

1. Place the bread on a clean work surface. Spread the tops with butter.
2. Place the turkey, ham, and cheese slices on one of the pieces of bread. Top with the remaining slice of bread, buttered side down.
3. Secure the sandwich with 2 picks placed in opposite corners.
4. Beat the egg and milk together.
5. Dip the sandwich in the batter until it is completely coated and the liquid has partially soaked into the bread.
6. Fry the sandwich in deep fat at 375°F (190°C) until golden brown.
7. Cut in half and serve immediately.

Alternative Method: Omit the picks and cook on a griddle until browned on both sides.

Monte Cristo Sandwich

Barbecued Pork or Beef Sandwich

Portions: 20   Portion size: 1 sandwich with 4 oz (115 g) filling

U.S.	Metric	Ingredients
3 lb	1.3 kg	Cooked pork or beef
2¼ pt	1 L	Barbecue Sauce (p. 198)
20	20	Hamburger rolls
as needed	as needed	Butter

Per serving:
Calories, 400; Protein, 20 g; Fat, 24 g (54% cal.); Cholesterol, 65 mg; Carbohydrates, 26 g; Fiber, 2 g; Sodium, 300 mg.

■ **P r o c e d u r e**

1. Using a slicing machine or chef's knife, cut the meat into very thin slices.
2. Combine the meat and sauce in a saucepan. Simmer uncovered over low heat for 10–15 minutes, until the meat has absorbed some of the flavor of the sauce and the liquid has reduced and thickened slightly.
3. Keep the meat hot for service.
4. For each order, butter a hamburger roll. Place a 4-oz (115-g) portion of the meat mixture on the bottom half of the roll. Close the sandwich and serve immediately.

Turkey BLT Wrap

Yield: 1 sandwich

U.S.	Metric	Ingredients
1	1	Flour tortilla, 10 in. (25 cm) in diameter
½ oz	15 g	Mayonnaise
½–1 oz	15–30 g	Lettuce leaves
3	3	Tomato slices, thin
1 oz	30 g	Cooked bacon, crumbled
2 oz	60 g	Turkey breast, in thin slices

Per serving:
Calories, 810; Protein, 32 g; Fat, 35 g (52% cal.); Cholesterol, 75 mg; Carbohydrates, 42 g; Fiber, 3 g; Sodium, 920 g.

Figure 22.3
Making a wrap sandwich.

■ P r o c e d u r e

1. Spread the tortilla with the mayonnaise, leaving a ½-in. (15-mm) border around the outside unspread. (For a richer, moister sandwich, double the quantity of mayonnaise.)

2. Arrange the lettuce leaves in the center of the tortilla, leaving a border of about 2 in. (5 cm) uncovered.

3. Arrange the tomato, bacon, and turkey on top of the lettuce.

4. To roll the wrap, first fold the uncovered rim of the tortilla on opposite edges of the circle toward the center. This closes the ends of the roll to hold in the filling. Then roll the tortilla tightly. The mayonnaise on the edge of the tortilla helps seal it closed.

5. Serve whole or cut in half on the diagonal.

(a) Spread the tortilla with the desired spread. Arrange the fillings toward one edge.

(b) Fold over the sides of the tortilla so that the ends of the wrap will be closed.

(c) Roll up.

(d) The finished, cut Turkey BLT Wrap.

Vegetarian Wrap with White Beans

Yield: 1 sandwich

U.S.	Metric	Ingredients
1	1	Flour tortilla, 10 in. (25 cm) in diameter
as needed	as needed	Olive oil
½–1 oz	15–30 g	Lettuce leaves
3 oz	90 g	White Bean Salad (p. 693)
1½ oz	45 g	Cooked rice, white or brown, cold
½ oz	15 g	Green bell pepper, diced

Per serving:
Calories, 510; Protein, 13 g; Fat, 21 g (38% cal.); Cholesterol, 0 mg; Carbohydrates, 65 g; Fiber, 6 g; Sodium, 360 mg.

■ P r o c e d u r e

1. Lay the tortilla flat on the workbench. Brush it very lightly with olive oil.

2. Arrange the lettuce leaves in the center of the tortilla, leaving a border of about 2 in. (5 cm) uncovered.

3. Place the bean salad in a sieve to drain excess vinaigrette, reserving the vinaigrette. Mix together the bean salad and the rice. If the mixture is dry, add enough of the dressing back to the mixture so that it is just sufficiently moistened.

4. Mix in the diced pepper.

5. Place the bean mixture on the tortilla in an oblong mound. Roll and wrap the tortilla tightly around the filling as in the recipe for Turkey BLT Wrap above.

Falafel and Roasted Vegetables in Pita

Yield: 1 sandwich

U.S.	Metric	Ingredients
1	1	Pita
1 fl oz	30 mL	Tahini Yogurt Dressing (below)
2 oz	60 g	Falafel (p. 671), 1-oz (30-g) balls, hot
2 oz	60 g	Roasted Summer Vegetables (p. 567), hot

Per serving:
Calories, 350; Protein, 12 g; Fat, 11 g (28% cal.); Cholesterol, 20 mg;
Carbohydrates, 53 g; Fiber, 5 g; Sodium, 660 mg.

■ **P r o c e d u r e**

1. The sandwich may be made by splitting open the pita to make a pocket or by wrapping the whole pita around the filling. If you are splitting open the pita, spread the inside with 1 tbsp (15 mL) dressing.
2. Fill with the falafel and vegetables.
3. Drizzle the remaining dressing over the filling.
4. Serve immediately.

V A R I A T I O N

Traditional Falafel in Pita
Omit the roasted vegetables. Use two 2-oz (60-g) falafel patties or four 1-oz (30-g) balls. Fill the pita with the falafel, ½ oz (15 g) shredded lettuce, ½–1 oz (15–30 g) diced tomato, and the tahini yogurt dressing.

Traditional Falafel in Pita

Tahini Yogurt Dressing

Yield: 10 fl oz (300 mL)

U.S.	Metric	Ingredients
8 oz	240 g	Plain yogurt
1 oz	30 g	Tahini (sesame paste)
1 fl oz	30 mL	Lemon juice

Per 1 ounce:
Calories, 30; Protein, 1 g; Fat, 2 g (60% cal.); Cholesterol, 5 mg;
Carbohydrates, 2 g; Fiber, 0 g; Sodium, 10 mg.

■ **P r o c e d u r e**

1. Mix all ingredients together.
2. Refrigerate until needed.

Southwestern Grilled Salmon Sandwich

Yield: 1 sandwich

U.S.	Metric	Ingredients
1	1	Salmon fillet, about 4 oz (120 g)
1 tbsp	15 mL	Chili Marinade (below)
1	1	Ciabatta roll or 5-in. (13-cm) length of French baguette
2	2	Tomato slices
1½ oz	45 g	Avocado, sliced
1–2	1–2	Leaf lettuce leaves

■ P r o c e d u r e

1. Rub the salmon fillet on both sides with the marinade. Let stand 10 minutes.
2. Grill or broil the salmon until just cooked through.
3. Split the roll or baguette in half horizontally.
4. Place the salmon on the bottom half.
5. Top with the tomato slices and the avocado slices.
6. Place a lettuce leaf and the top half of the bread on top.
7. To serve, leave the sandwich whole or cut it in half.

Per serving:
Calories, 650; Protein, 39 g; Fat, 21 g (29% cal.); Cholesterol, 80 mg; Carbohydrates, 75 g; Fiber, 8 g; Sodium, 1210 mg.

Southwestern Grilled Salmon Sandwich

Chili Marinade

Yield: about 6 oz (180 g)

U.S.	Metric	Ingredients
2 oz	60 g	Chili powder
1 tbsp	15 mL	Dried oregano
½ tsp	2 mL	Ground cloves
1 oz	30 g	Garlic, crushed
2 tsp	10 mL	Salt
1 oz	30 g	Brown sugar
4 fl oz	120 mL	Red wine vinegar

■ P r o c e d u r e

1. Combine all ingredients except the vinegar and grind together to make a uniform mixture.
2. Add the vinegar and mix well.
3. Refrigerate until needed.

Per 1 ounce:
Calories, 60; Protein, 2 g; Fat, 1.5 g (19% cal.); Cholesterol, 0 mg; Carbohydrates, 12 g; Fiber, 4 g; Sodium, 870 mg.

Smoked Ham and Taleggio Panino

Yield: 1 sandwich

U.S.	Metric	Ingredients
2 tbsp	30 mL	Mayonnaise
1 tsp	5 mL	Lemon juice
¼ tsp	1 mL	Grated lemon zest
2 slices	2 slices	Firm country bread
2 thin slices	2 thin slices	Smoked ham
2 thin slices	2 thin slices	Tomato
2 slices	2 slices	Taleggio cheese
3–4 leaves	3–4 leaves	Arugula

Per serving:
Calories, 770; Protein, 30 g; Fat, 42 g (50% cal.); Cholesterol, 65 mg;
Carbohydrates, 66 g; Fiber, 3 g; Sodium, 2030 mg.

■ **P r o c e d u r e**

1. Mix together the mayonnaise, lemon juice, and zest.

2. Lay the bread on the work surface.
3. Spread the two slices of bread with the mayonnaise.
4. Top one of the slices with the ham.
5. Place the tomato slices on top of the ham.
6. Top the ham with the slices of cheese.
7. Top the cheese with the arugula leaves.
8. Place the second slice of bread on the sandwich, mayonnaise side down. Press the sandwich together firmly.
9. Cook in a panino press or on a griddle until the cheese is melted. If using a griddle, place a grill brick on the sandwich and turn it over when half done.
10. Cut in half to serve.

Smoked Ham and Taleggio Panino

Eggplant, Roasted Pepper, and Fontina Panino

Yield: 1 sandwich

U.S.	Metric	Ingredients
2 slices	2 slices	Eggplant, about ⅜ in. (1 cm) thick, peeled
as needed	as needed	Olive oil
½	½	Red bell pepper, roasted and peeled (p. 529)
1	1	Ciabatta roll or other large, flat dinner roll or bun
as needed	as needed	Olive oil
2 slices	2 slices	Fontina cheese

■ P r o c e d u r e

1. Brush both sides of the eggplant slices with oil.
2. Cook on a grill or griddle or in a sauté pan until just tender.
3. Remove the seeds, stem, and inner membranes from the pepper. Cut it in into two pieces and lay the pieces out flat.

4. Cut the roll in half horizontally.
5. Brush both halves with olive oil.
6. Lay the eggplant slices on the bottom half.
7. Top with the pepper and then the fontina cheese.
8. Place the top half of the roll in place and press together.
9. Cook in a panino press or on a griddle until the cheese is melted. If using a griddle, place a grill brick on the sandwich and turn it over when half done.
10. Cut in half to serve.

Per serving:
Calories, 640; Protein, 27 g; Fat, 26 g (36% cal.); Cholesterol, 65 mg; Carbohydrates, 75 g; Fiber, 8 g; Sodium, 1210 mg.

Grilled Vegetable Sandwich with Goat Cheese and Sun-Dried Tomatoes

Yield: 8 sandwiches

U.S.	Metric	Ingredients
8 oz	250 g	Zucchini, trimmed
8 oz	250 g	Eggplant, trimmed
8 oz	250 g	Bell peppers, any color
8 oz	250 g	Onion, large
as needed	as needed	Olive oil
as needed	as needed	Salt
as needed	as needed	Balsamic vinegar
(see step 8)	(see step 8)	Focaccia
4–6 oz	125–180 g	Sun-dried tomatoes, packed in oil, drained, cut julienne
8 oz	250 g	Fresh, soft goat cheese, sliced

■ P r o c e d u r e

1. Cut the zucchini lengthwise into slices about ¼ in. (6 mm) thick.
2. If the eggplant is large, with a thick skin, peel it. Cut large eggplant crosswise into slices ¼ in. (6 mm) thick. Cut small eggplants lengthwise to make larger slices.
3. Core and seed the peppers. Cut into quarters lengthwise.
4. Cut the onion crosswise into slices about ⅓ in. (8 mm) thick. Hold the rings of each slice together with a bamboo skewer.
5. Brush the vegetables with oil and sprinkle them with salt.
6. Grill the vegetables over medium heat, turning as necessary, until they are tender and lightly grill-marked. Cooking times will vary for different vegetables. Regulate the heat or the distance from the flame so the vegetables cook without browning too much.
7. Remove from the grill and brush with a little balsamic vinegar.

8. Cut the focaccia into 3½ x 5 in. (9 x 13 cm) rectangles. If the focaccia is thick, split the rectangles in half horizontally. If it is thin, use 2 rectangles per portion.
9. Arrange the grilled vegetables on half of the rectangles.
10. Arrange the tomatoes on top of the vegetables.
11. Top with the goat cheese and the rest of the bread rectangles.
12. For service, serve whole or cut in half at an angle.

Per serving:
Calories, 180; Protein, 8 g; Fat, 10 g (47% cal.); Cholesterol, 15 mg; Carbohydrates, 17 g; Fiber, 3 g; Sodium, 640 mg.

Grilled Portobello and Boursin Sandwich

Yield: 1 sandwich

U.S.	Metric	Ingredients
1 tbsp	15 mL	Olive oil
1½ tsp	7 mL	Balsamic vinegar
¼ tsp	1 mL	Prepared mustard, French or Dijon style
pinch	pinch	Salt
1	1	Portobello mushroom cap, large
1 oz	30 g	Boursin or other soft, creamy cheese
1	1	Whole-grain roll or bun, split in half
6–8	6–8	Arugula leaves, torn

Per serving:
Calories, 390; Protein, 7 g; Fat, 28 g (64% cal.); Cholesterol, 35 mg; Carbohydrates, 28 g; Fiber, 4 g; Sodium, 560 mg.

■ P r o c e d u r e

1. With a wire whip, mix together the oil, vinegar, mustard, and salt to make a vinaigrette.
2. Brush the mushroom cap with about two-thirds of the vinaigrette. Reserve the rest of the vinaigrette for step 6.
3. Place the mushroom cap on a grill or broiler grid, stem side down. Grill until about half cooked.
4. Turn the mushroom over so the bottom of the cap faces up. Top with the cheese.
5. Grill until the mushroom is tender and the cheese is partly melted.
6. Toss the arugula with the rest of the vinaigrette.
7. Place the mushroom cap, cheese side up, on the bottom half of the roll.
8. Top with the arugula and the top of the bun.

V A R I A T I O N

Grilled Portobello and Tomato Sandwich
Omit the cheese. Spread the bread with mayonnaise and top with the grilled mushroom, 2 tomato slices, and the arugula.

Grilled Chicken Aioli Sandwich with Tomato and Avocado

Yield: 1 sandwich

U.S.	Metric	Ingredients
1	1	Boneless skinless chicken breast, about 5 oz (150 g)
¼ tsp	1 mL	Finely chopped garlic
pinch	pinch	Salt
pinch	pinch	Pepper
1½ tsp	7 mL	Lemon juice
1½ tsp	7 mL	Olive oil
2 slices	2 slices	Hearty country-style whole-grain bread, sliced ½ in. (1 cm) thick
1 tbsp	15 mL	Aioli (p. 201 or p. 728)
2	2	Tomato slices
1 oz	30 g	Avocado, sliced
1–2	1–2	Leaf lettuce leaves

Per serving:
Calories, 690; Protein, 38 g; Fat, 31 g (41% cal.); Cholesterol, 100 mg; Carbohydrates, 64 g; Fiber, 5 g; Sodium, 810 mg.

■ P r o c e d u r e

1. Place the chicken breast between two sheets of plastic film. With a meat mallet, gently pound to a uniform thickness of about ½ in. (6 mm).
2. Combine the garlic, salt, pepper, lemon juice, and olive oil.
3. Lightly coat the chicken with this mixture. Let marinate about 2 hours in the refrigerator.
4. Preheat a grill or broiler to very hot.
5. Grill the chicken until cooked through.

6. Spread the bread slices with aioli.
7. Top one of the slices with the chicken, then the tomatoes, the avocado, and the lettuce. Top with the remaining slice of bread.
8. For service, cut in half.

Grilled Chicken Aioli Sandwich with Tomato and Avocado

Pizza Margherita

Yield: one 12-inch (30-cm) pizza

U.S.	Metric	Ingredients
12 oz	360 g	Fresh, ripe plum tomatoes or canned Italian-style plum tomatoes
1 tbsp	15 mL	Olive oil
to taste	to taste	Salt
12 oz	360 g	French Bread dough (p. 917), fermented
6	6	Fresh basil leaves, torn in half
4 oz	120 g	Fresh mozzarella cheese, preferably Italian buffalo-milk mozzarella, sliced
1 tbsp	15 mL	Parmesan cheese (optional)
1½ tbsp	22 mL	Olive oil

Per pizza:
Calories, 1450; Protein, 49 g; Fat, 63 g (39% cal.); Cholesterol, 90 mg; Carbohydrates, 170 g; Fiber, 9 g; Sodium, 1880 mg.

■ P r o c e d u r e

1. If using fresh tomatoes, peel, seed, and chop them. If using canned, chop and drain them.
2. Combine the tomatoes and oil in a saucepan. Cook uncovered over moderate heat until the tomatoes are no longer watery.
3. Add salt to taste.
4. Cool.
5. Flatten the dough and roll it out into a circle. Drape the dough over the backs of the hands and carefully stretch the circle to a diameter of 12 in. (30 cm). Leave the dough thicker around the rim than in the center.
6. Flour a peel so the dough does not stick. Lay the circle of dough on it.
7. Spread the tomatoes over the dough, leaving the rim uncovered.
8. Distribute the basil and the mozzarella cheese over the pizza.
9. If using the parmesan, sprinkle it over the pizza.
10. Drizzle with olive oil.
11. Slide directly onto the hearth of a deck oven preheated to 500°F (260°C). Bake until the dough is browned and the cheese is melted.
12. Using the peel, remove from the oven and serve immediately.

V A R I A T I O N

Pizza Marinara
Omit the mozzarella cheese and the basil. Increase the tomatoes to 2 lb (900 g). Increase the first quantity of olive oil to 1½ tbsp. In step 2, cook the tomatoes with 3 cloves garlic, sliced thin, and ½ tsp (2 mL) fresh chopped oregano or ¼ tsp dried oregano.

Pizza Margherita before baking

Pizza Margherita after baking

ASSOCIAZIONE VERACE PIZZA NAPOLETANA

Naples, Italy, takes pride in being the birthplace of pizza. Today the Associazione Verace Pizza Napoletana sets down the rules by which its members must abide if they wish to claim they serve authentic Neapolitan pizza. The rules state that the dough must contain only flour, water, salt, and natural yeast and that it must be made by hand or in an approved mixer. The pizza must be shaped by hand and baked on the hearth of a wood-burning oven. Toppings are limited to a list of approved ingredients.

Two pizzas—Margherita, topped with tomatoes, basil, and buffalo mozzarella, and Marinara, topped with tomatoes, garlic, oregano, and olive oil—are considered the original and true Neapolitan pizzas.

Pizza has grown beyond its origins to become an international favorite. In North America, most of the pizzas served make no claim to being authentically Italian and instead sport toppings such as barbecued chicken, beef with peppers and taco seasonings, and smoked salmon with artichokes, in addition to old favorites like sausage and pepperoni.

■ TERMS FOR REVIEW

pullman loaf	multidecker sandwich	tea sandwich	wrap
simple sandwich	club sandwich	grilled sandwich	panino
(hot or cold)	open-faced sandwich	deep-fried sandwich	pizza
	(hot or cold)		

■ QUESTIONS FOR DISCUSSION

1. If you cannot get daily bread delivery, what are some measures you can take to ensure that the bread in the sandwiches you serve is always fresh?

2. What precautions must you take when using mayonnaise as a sandwich spread?

3. Briefly describe the setup of a short-order sandwich station.

4. How does a setup for preparing sandwiches in quantity differ from a short-order sandwich setup?

5. Why are most sandwiches cut before serving?

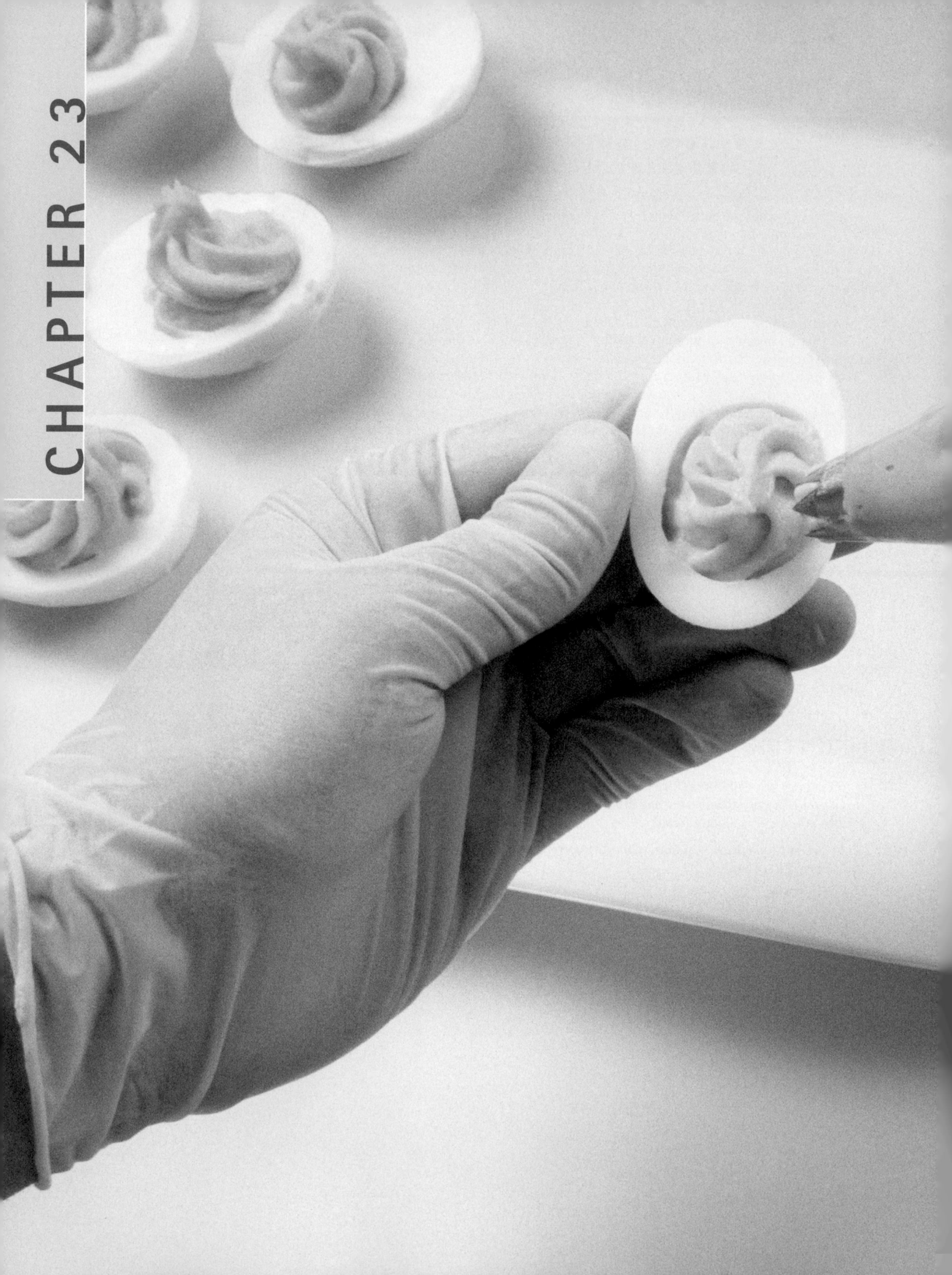

CHAPTER 23

Hors d'Oeuvres

I n addition to salads and salad dressings, the pantry or garde manger department is generally responsible for the small food items known as *appetizers* or *hors d'oeuvres*. The function of these foods is to enliven the appetite before dinner, often to the accompaniment of drinks, so they are generally small in size and spicy or piquant in flavor.

There is some confusion as to the distinction, if any, between the terms *appetizer* and *hors d'oeuvre*. In general, the first course of a multicourse meal is called an appetizer, and the finger foods served at receptions and with cocktails are called hors d'oeuvres. In some regions, however, the terms are used interchangeably.

This chapter deals not with first courses but primarily with special kinds of foods that are usually encountered away from the dinner table—foods that are the special domain of the pantry chef. They include finger foods such as canapés and relishes, indispensable accompaniments to receptions and parties.

SERVING HORS D'OEUVRES

This chapter focuses on foods that are not served as part of a normal lunch or dinner menu. These foods are usually small items that may be served at a formal reception preceding a meal, as part of a separate event not connected with a meal, or simply as accompaniments to beverages at an informal gathering.

The two most common ways of serving hors d'oeuvres are butler-style and buffet-style.

In **butler-style service**, the hors d'oeuvre selections are offered to guests by service staff carrying small trays as they pass among the assembled group. Several points should be kept in mind when planning this style of service:

- Each item should be small enough to be eaten in one or two bites.

- Each item should be easily handled by the guest. Canapés or other foods that can be picked up without soiling the fingers are ideal. For foods with a moist or oily surface, offer picks that guests can use to handle the food without touching it. Cocktail napkins should always be offered. Foods requiring a plate are better served on a cocktail buffet.

- Strive for simple, attractive arrangements on the tray. The foods should look appetizing even when only a few items are left. Trays that no longer look appealing should be brought back to the kitchen or pantry area to be refreshed and refilled.

- Ideally, each tray should hold only one food selection. For simple items, two or three selections can be presented on a single tray, but avoid making the tray too complex or overloaded.

- Avoid presenting hot and cold items on the same tray. Cold items are easiest to serve. Hot items should be brought back to the kitchen or pantry area as soon as they are no longer warm.

- For items to be offered with dips, a small bowl of the dip can be presented on the same tray as the individual hors d'oeuvres.

In **buffet-style service**, hors d'oeuvres are arranged attractively on one or more tables, and guests help themselves. Small plates can be offered on buffet tables, so it is not necessary to confine the food selections to finger foods. Cold hors d'oeuvres are usually presented arranged on trays, which can be easily replaced when they become depleted. Canapés and similar items are best arranged in neat rows, circles, or other arrangements. Raw vegetables may be piled in neat stacks, with bowls of dips placed among them. Hot items should be offered in chafing dishes, which keep them hot.

Buffet presentation is discussed in more detail in Chapter 28.

Finally, hors d'oeuvres are also served informally as accompaniments to beverages. This category is often known as *bar food* and may be served one item at a time, as ordered by the customer, or presented on a buffet. The classic bar food is the popular Spanish-style tapas, discussed on page 764.

After reading this chapter, you should be able to

1. **Name and describe the two principal methods of serving hors d'oeuvres at a reception.**

2. **Prepare canapés.**

3. **Prepare hors d'oeuvre cocktails and relishes.**

4. **Prepare dips.**

5. **Prepare a variety of other hors d'oeuvres, including antipasti, bruschette, and tapas.**

6. **Name and describe the three types of sturgeon caviar, and name and describe three other kinds of caviar.**

CANAPÉS

Canapés may be defined as bite-size open-faced sandwiches.

Canapés are perhaps the most traditional and also the most modern of hors d'oeuvres. This is no doubt because they are so varied and so versatile. Because they consist of tiny portions of food presented on bases of bread, toast, or pastry, they are perfect finger food, easily handled and easily eaten. Nearly any food that can be served in a small portion can be served as a canapé topping. The variety of possible combinations is nearly unlimited.

Most canapés consist of three parts: base, spread, and garnish.

BASE

Canapé bases may be made from several items. The following are suggestions:

Bread cutouts

Toast cutouts

Crackers

Melba toasts

Tiny unsweetened pastry shells
(short dough, filo dough, or other pastry)

Profiteroles (miniature unsweetened
cream puff shells, p. 996)

Toasted pita wedges

Tortilla chips or cups

Tiny biscuits, split in half if necessary

Polenta cutouts

Miniature pancakes

Many of these items, such as crackers and melba toasts, can be purchased ready-made, but bread and toast cutouts are the most widely used and offer the lowest food cost, though they require more labor.

Untoasted bread for canapés should be firm enough to allow the finished product to be handled easily. It may be cut thick and flattened slightly with a rolling pin to make firmer. Toast is, of course, firmer, and it gives a pleasing texture and crispness to the canapés.

Procedure for Preparing Canapés from Toast

Method 1

1. You may use ready-sliced bread (after trimming the crusts), but it is usually most efficient to use long, unsliced pullman loaves. Cut the crusts from all sides (save for bread crumbs). Cut the bread horizontally into slices ¼ inch (6 mm) thick, as shown in Figure 23.1.

2. Toast the slices in the oven or in a large toaster.

3. Let the toasts cool.

4. Cover with a thin, even layer of the chosen spread and cut into desired shapes with a knife (see Figure 23.2). Make the cuts neat and uniform.

   Alternatively, cut the toasts into desired shapes with small cutters and reserve the trim for bread crumbs. Spread each cutout with desired topping. (This method is more time-consuming, but it may be used with round or odd-shaped cutters if you desire to save food cost by not losing spread on unused trimmings.)

5. Garnish the cutouts as desired.

Method 2

1. Cut bread slices as in step 1 above.

2. Cut into desired shapes. Brush both sides of each cutout with melted butter and arrange on sheet pans. Place in a hot oven (450°F/230°C) until golden brown and very crisp, about 6 to 8 minutes.

3. Let the bases cool.

4. Assemble the canapés.

   This method is more costly but gives a crisper base that holds up better with a moist spread.

Figure 23.1
For canapés, trim the crusts from a pullman loaf. With a serrated knife, cut the loaf horizontally into thin slices.

Figure 23.2
Bread slices for canapés can be cut into several basic shapes with no waste.

SPREAD

Canapé spreads may be as simple as butter or softened cream cheese, but it is better to use a more highly flavored spread because sharp or spicy flavors are better for stimulating the appetite.

The spread should be thick enough to cling well to the base and so the garnish sticks to it without falling off.

Spreads may be divided into three basic categories, as follows.

Flavored Butters

Basic procedures for making flavored or compound butters are explained in Chapter 8 (see recipes on p. 179). Most flavored butters are made simply by blending the flavoring ingredients with the softened butter until completely mixed. Solid ingredients should be puréed or chopped very fine so the butter can be spread smoothly.

Proportions of flavoring ingredients to butter can be varied widely, according to taste. For example, to make anchovy butter, you could double the quantity of anchovies indicated in the recipe on page 179 to get a stronger flavor, or you could decrease it to get a milder flavor. Because of this variability, and because the basic procedure is so simple, you should be able to make many kinds of flavored butters without individual recipes. Use the recipes in Chapter 8 and the following list as guides. Popular and versatile flavors for butter spreads include

Lemon	Caviar	Shrimp
Parsley	Mustard	Olive
Tarragon	Horseradish	Shallot or scallion
Chive	Pimiento	Curry
Anchovy	Blue cheese	Caper

Flavored Cream Cheese

Flavored cream cheese spreads are made like flavored butters, except cream cheese is substituted for the butter. Alternatively, use a mixture of cream cheese and butter, blended together well. Flavor variations are the same as those listed above for butter.

In addition, cream cheese is often blended with sharper, more flavorful cheeses that have been mashed or grated. Adding cream cheese to firmer cheese helps make the latter more spreadable. A liquid such as milk, cream, or port wine may be added to make the mixture softer. Such cheese spreads are often flavored with spices and herbs such as paprika, caraway seeds, dry mustard, parsley, or tarragon.

Meat or Fish Salad Spreads

You can use many cold meat or fish mixtures, such as cooked salads, to make canapé spreads. Popular examples include tuna salad, salmon salad, shrimp salad, chicken salad, deviled ham, and liver pâté.

To convert a salad recipe (see pp. 703 and 705) to a spread recipe, you may need to make one or more of the following modifications:

1.   Chop the solid ingredients very fine, or grind or purée them, so the mixture is spreadable and not chunky.

2.   Do not add the liquid ingredients and mayonnaise all at once. Add them a little at a time, just until the mixture reaches a thick, spreadable consistency.

3.   Check the seasonings carefully. You may want to increase the seasonings to make the spread more stimulating to the appetite.

GARNISH

The garnish of a canapé is any food item or combination of items placed on top of the spread. It may be a major part of the canapé, such as a slice of ham or cheese, or it may be a small tidbit that is selected for color, design, texture, or flavor accent, such as a pimiento cutout, a slice of radish, a caper, or a dab of caviar. Even the spread can be used as a garnish. For example, you may make a canapé with a mustard butter spread and a

Guidelines for Assembling Canapés

1. **Good mise en place is essential.**

   Preparing thousands of canapés for large functions can be tedious work, so it is essential that all bases, spreads, and garnishes be prepared ahead of time in order that final assembly may go quickly and smoothly.

2. **Assemble as close as possible to serving time.**

   Bases quickly become soggy, and spreads and garnishes dry out easily. As trays are completed, they may be covered lightly with plastic and held for a short time under refrigeration. Be sure to observe all rules for safe food handling and storage, as you learned in Chapter 2.

3. **Select harmonious flavor combinations in spreads and garnish.**

   For example, caviar and chutney or anchovy and ham are not appealing combinations, but these combinations are:

   Mustard butter and ham

   Lemon butter and caviar

   Pimiento cream cheese and sardine

   Horseradish butter and smoked salmon or smoked tongue

   Tuna salad and capers

   Anchovy butter, hard-cooked egg slice, and olive

4. **Be sure that at least one of the ingredients is spicy or pronounced in flavor.**

   A bland canapé has little value as an appetizer.

5. **Use high-quality ingredients.**

   Canapés can be a good way to utilize leftovers, but only if the leftovers have been carefully handled and stored to retain freshness.

6. **Keep it simple.**

   Simple, neat arrangements are more attractive than elaborate, overworked designs. Besides, you don't have time to get too fancy. Be sure the canapés hold together and do not fall apart in the customers' hands.

7. **Arrange the canapés carefully and attractively on trays.**

   Much of the attraction of canapés is eye appeal, and the customer never sees just one at a time, but a whole trayful. Each tray should carry an assortment of flavors and textures, so there is something for every taste.

   Figure 23.3 shows a tray of simple, attractive canapés.

Figure 23.3
Assorted canapés, from left: gravlax with mustard cream cheese; chicken liver pâté with mustard butter and black olive; caviar, red onion, and sour cream in red potato; herbed Boursin cheese with almonds; beef tenderloin with horseradish cream cheese and capers.

slice of ham, then decorate the ham with a border or design of mustard butter piped on with a paper cone.

Here are some of the many food items that may be used alone or in combination to decorate canapés:

Vegetables, Pickles, and Relishes

Radish slices	Pickled onions	Cherry tomato slices or halves
Olives	Chutney	Watercress leaves
Pickles	Asparagus tips	Marinated mushrooms
Capers	Cucumber slices	Parsley
Pimiento		

Fish

Smoked oysters and clams	Caviar
Smoked salmon	Salmon or tuna flakes
Smoked trout	Crab meat
Herring	Lobster chunks or slices
Shrimp	Sardines
Rolled anchovy fillets	

Meats

Ham   Smoked tongue
Salami   Roast beef
Chicken or turkey breast

Other

Cheese
Hard-cooked egg slices

COCKTAILS

The term **cocktail** is used not only for alcoholic beverages and vegetable and fruit juices but also for a group of appetizers made of seafood or fruit, usually with a tart or tangy sauce. Such cocktails are always served well chilled, often on a bed of crushed ice.

Oysters and clams on the half shell are popular seafood cocktails, as are shrimp, crabmeat, lobster, and firm, flaked white fish with an appropriate sauce. Recipes for a standard tomato-based cocktail sauce and for a lighter sauce called *mignonette* are included in Chapter 8.

Fresh oysters and clams on the half shell should be opened just before they are served (see pp. 442–443) and arranged on flat plates, preferably on a bed of ice. Provide cocktail sauce in a small cup in the center or at the side of the plate. Lemon wedges should also be provided.

Cocktails of shrimp and other cooked seafood are generally served in a stemmed glass or in a small, cup-shaped bowl, which may be nestled in a bed of ice. The cocktail sauce may be put in the glass first and the seafood then arranged on top, partially immersed. Or the cocktail sauce may be added to the seafood as a topping. A third alternative is to serve the sauce separately in a small cup, as for raw oysters. Garnish the dish attractively with lettuce or other salad greens and with lemon wedges.

Fruit cups served as cocktails should be pleasantly tart and not too sweet. Many fruit salads (see Chapter 21) may be served as cocktails. Adding fresh lemon or lime juice to fruit mixtures or serving with a garnish of lemon or lime wedges provides the necessary tartness. A simple wedge of melon with lime is a refreshing cocktail.

A few drops of a flavored liqueur can also be used to perk up the flavor of a fruit cocktail.

RELISHES

The term **relish** covers two categories of foods: raw vegetables and pickled items.

RAW VEGETABLES

These are also known as **crudités** (croo dee tays; *cru* in French means "raw").

Any vegetable that can be eaten raw may be cut into sticks or other attractive, bite-size shapes and served as relishes. Most popular are celery, carrots, and radishes. Other good choices are green and red peppers, zucchini, cucumbers, scallions, cauliflower and broccoli florets, peeled broccoli stems, peeled kohlrabi, cherry tomatoes, and Belgian endive leaves. Crudités are often served with an appropriate dip (see the next section).

Raw vegetables must be served crisp and well chilled, just as in salads. Use the freshest, most attractive vegetables possible. If they are a little wilted, they can be recrisped by holding them for a short time in ice water. Serving vegetables embedded in crushed ice will maintain their crispness.

An imaginative pantry chef can make an attractive, colorful bouquet of raw vegetables.

PICKLED ITEMS

A wide variety of items such as dilled cucumber pickles, gherkins, olives, watermelon pickles, pickled peppers, spiced beets, and other preserved vegetables and fruits are served as relishes. These items are rarely made in-house but are purchased already prepared. Like raw vegetables, they should be served chilled.

DIPS

Savory **dips** are popular accompaniments to potato chips, crackers, and raw vegetables.

Proper consistency is important for any dip you prepare. It must not be so thick that it cannot be scooped up without breaking the chip or cracker, but it must be thick enough to stick to the items used as dippers. Proper consistency means thickness *at serving temperature*. Most dips become thicker when held in the refrigerator.

Many mixtures used as spreads (see section on "Canapés") can also be used as dips. Thin or soften them by adding a little mayonnaise, cream, or other appropriate liquid.

The recipes here are examples of typical dips. Many other sauces and salad dressings can be used as dips. Salsas (pp. 191 and 199) and aioli (pp. 201 and 728) are two popular examples.

 ## Blue Cheese Dip

Yield: 1 qt (1 L)

U.S.	Metric	Ingredients
12 oz	375 g	Cream cheese
5 fl oz	150 mL	Milk
6 oz	175 g	Mayonnaise
1 fl oz	30 mL	Lemon juice
1 oz	30 g	Onion, minced
½ tsp	2 mL	Hot red pepper sauce
½ tsp	2 mL	Worcestershire sauce
10 oz	300 g	Blue cheese, crumbled

Per 1 ounce:
Calories, 110; Protein, 3 g; Fat, 11 g (86% cal.); Cholesterol, 20 mg; Carbohydrates, 1 g; Fiber, 0 g; Sodium, 190 mg.

■ P r o c e d u r e

1. In a mixer with the paddle attachment, beat the cream cheese at low speed until soft and smooth.
2. With the machine running, slowly beat in the milk.
3. Add the rest of the ingredients and blend in well.
4. Taste and adjust seasonings. Chill.

V A R I A T I O N

Cheddar Cheese Dip
Substitute grated sharp cheddar cheese for the blue cheese. If desired, add chopped chives.

Garlic Cheese Dip
Add mashed garlic to taste to Cheddar Cheese Dip.

Bacon Cheese Dip
Add crumbled crisp bacon to Cheddar Cheese Dip.

Cheese and Chile Dip
Flavor Cheddar Cheese Dip with canned green chiles, chopped.

Romesco

Yield: 1 pt (500 mL)

U.S.	Metric	Ingredients
1 oz	30 g	White bread
½ fl oz	15 mL	Olive oil
3 oz	90 g	Blanched almonds
2 tsp	10 mL	Garlic, chopped
10 oz	300 g	Tomatoes, peeled
2 tsp	10 mL	Spanish paprika
⅛ tsp	0.5 mL	Cayenne
1½ fl oz	45 mL	Red wine vinegar
3–4 fl oz	90–120 mL	Olive oil
to taste	to taste	Salt
to taste	to taste	Pepper

■ P r o c e d u r e

1. Sauté the bread in olive oil until golden.
2. Toast the almonds in an oven at 350°F (175°C) for about 15 minutes or in a skillet over moderately low heat until light golden, not dark brown. Remove from the pan as soon as they are golden so they do not brown further.
3. Combine the bread, almonds, and garlic in a food processor. Grind until fine.
4. Add the tomatoes, paprika, and cayenne. Process to a paste.
5. With the machine running, gradually add the vinegar and then the oil in a slow stream.
6. Adjust the seasonings with salt and pepper. Add more vinegar if required. The sauce should not be too acidic but should have a definite sharpness.

Per 1 ounce:
Calories, 100; Protein, 2 g; Fat, 9 g (80% cal.); Cholesterol, 0 mg;
Carbohydrates, 3 g; Fiber, 1 g; Sodium, 15 mg.

Hummus (Chickpea Dip)

Yield: 1 qt (1 L)

U.S.	Metric	Ingredients
1 lb	500 g	Cooked or canned chickpeas, drained
8 oz	250 g	Tahini (sesame paste)
¼ oz	8 g	Garlic, crushed
4 fl oz	125 mL	Lemon juice
1 fl oz	30 mL	Olive oil
to taste	to taste	Salt
pinch	pinch	Cayenne
1–2 fl oz	30–50 mL	Olive oil

■ P r o c e d u r e

1. Purée the chickpeas with the tahini, garlic, lemon juice, and olive oil.
2. If necessary, thin the purée with a little water or additional lemon juice, depending on the taste.
3. Season with salt to taste and with cayenne.
4. Chill for at least 1 hour to allow the flavors time to blend.
5. Spoon the hummus into serving bowls. Drizzle additional olive oil over each bowl before serving.

Per 1 ounce:
Calories, 80; Protein, 3 g; Fat, 6 g (63% cal.); Cholesterol, 0 mg;
Carbohydrates, 5 g; Fiber, 2 g; Sodium, 0 mg.

V A R I A T I O N

Babaganouj

Substitute eggplant purée for the chickpeas. Make the eggplant purée as follows: Toast whole eggplants under a broiler, over a gas burner, or directly on a flattop range until the skin is charred and the eggplant is soft. Peel off the charred skin under running water and cut off the tops. Remove large clumps of seeds if desired. Let stand in a china cap or sieve to let excess moisture drain, then purée the pulp. Reduce the lemon juice to 2–3 fl oz (60–90 mL) and the tahini to 4 oz (125 g). Double the olive oil.

Hummus

Guacamole

Yield: approximately 1 qt (1 L)

U.S.	Metric	Ingredients
4	4	Ripe avocados, medium size
2 oz	60 g	Onion, grated
1	1	Small, hot green chile such as jalapeño, minced
1 fl oz	30 mL	Lime or lemon juice
1 fl oz	30 mL	Olive oil
to taste	to taste	Salt
12 oz	375 gl	Fresh tomato (optional)

Per serving
Calories, 45; Protein, 1 g; Fat, 4 g (75% cal.); Cholesterol, 0 mg; Carbohydrates, 2 g; Fiber, 2 g; Sodium, 0 mg.

■ P r o c e d u r e

1. Pit and peel the avocados. Mash the pulp coarsely. ... should be slightly lumpy rather than smooth.

2. Mix in the onion, minced chile, lime or lemon juice, olive oil, and salt to taste.

3. If desired, peel, seed, and dice the tomato and mix it into the avocado.

4. Cover tightly with plastic wrap placed on the surface of the guacamole. This is to protect it from air, which will darken it. For the same reason, guacamole should not be made too long before serving time. Chill the guacamole until ready to serve.

V A R I A T I O N

Sour Cream Avocado Dip
Use 1 oz (30 g) onion. Omit the olive oil and tomato. Mash the avocado to a smooth purée. Add ½–¾ pt (250–375 mL) sour cream.

Note: If fresh chiles are not available, use canned chiles or a few dashes of hot red pepper sauce.

Guacamole

MISCELLANEOUS HORS D'OEUVRES

A great variety of other foods, both hot and cold, can be served as hors d'oeuvres. If they are to be served away from the dinner table, it is best if they can be eaten with the fingers or speared with a pick. At a reception at which many hors d'oeuvres are served, it is all right if a few of them must be eaten with forks from small plates, but finger food is much easier for the guests, who are likely to be standing and holding a wineglass or cocktail glass while eating.

Of course, there are many thousands of hors d'oeuvre recipes, including many that have been adapted from the cuisines of other lands. Those included here are a sampling of some popular types.

Many of the recipes given elsewhere in this book can be adapted as hors d'oeuvre recipes. In most cases, unit size or portion size should be decreased. For example, meatballs should be made small enough to be eaten in one or two bites. Among the items most readily adapted are the following (check the Index or Recipe Table of Contents for page numbers):

Barbecued Spareribs

Shish Kebab

Deep-Fried Chicken (using wing sections)

Baked Clams Oreganata

Broiled Shrimp, Scampi Style

Broiled Scallops

Fried Breaded Scallops, Shrimp, Oysters, or Clams

Steamed Mussels (served on the half shell, with a sauce)

Cod Cakes or other fish cakes

Fish tartars

Seviche

Vegetable Fritters

Many salads

Quiche

Cheese Wafers and Straws

Sushi

Gravlax

Smoked Salmon

Smoked Trout

Smoked Duck

Pâtés, Terrines, and Galantines

Ham Mousse

Foie Gras Mousse and Terrine

In addition to the categories of hors d'oeuvres introduced so far, the following additional terms merit brief explanation.

ANTIPASTO

Italian cuisine is particularly rich in hors d'oeuvres, or *antipasti*, as they are called (singular form: antipasto). Many books give a recipe for a mixed salad called *antipasto*. This is misleading, however, because the Italian term does not refer to a specific recipe but to any typically Italian hors d'oeuvre, hot or cold.

Many menus of Italian-style restaurants offer a cold antipasto plate or platter comprising an assortment of flavorful tidbits. Typical components include the following:

Cured meats, such as salami, prosciutto, bologna, and boiled ham.

Seafood items, especially canned or preserved items such as sardines, anchovies, and tuna.

Cheeses, such as provolone and mozzarella.

Hard-cooked eggs and stuffed eggs.

Relishes, such as raw carrots, celery, fennel, radishes, cauliflower, and tomatoes, and cooked or pickled items, such as olives, artichoke hearts, small hot peppers, and onions.

Mushrooms and other vegetables prepared à la grecque (p. 694).

Cooked dried beans and other firm vegetables in a piquant vinaigrette.

BRUSCHETTA

In recent years, one of the most popular hors d'oeuvres is the Roman garlic bread called bruschetta (broo sket ta; plural: *bruschette*, pronounced broo sket teh). Bruschetta, in its most basic form, is a slice of Italian bread that is toasted, rubbed with crushed garlic, and drizzled with olive oil. When made with good bread and extra-virgin olive oil, this simple hors d'oeuvre is good on its own. But it is no doubt the variety of toppings that can be served on this garlic-bread base that accounts for its popularity.

Perhaps the best-known topping is a seasoned mixture of diced fresh tomatoes and olive oil, but this is far from the only possibility. Meats, cheeses, cooked dried beans, and raw and cooked vegetables are all appropriate. In fact, the bruschetta is a type of antipasto, and many of the items listed in the preceding section may also be served as bruschetta topping. Several variations are included among the recipes in this chapter.

Bruschette are similar to canapés in that they are toast with topping. However, they are larger and heartier than typical canapés and can be served as the appetizer course of a dinner.

TAPAS

Another type of hors d'oeuvre that has become increasingly popular is the Spanish tapa. The variety of tapas is so great that it is difficult to give a definition, except to say that a tapa is a small food item intended to be eaten with wine or other drinks, usually in taverns and bars. The Spanish term literally means "lid," and the original tapa is thought to be a small bit of food, perhaps a slice of cured ham, placed on top of a glass of sherry.

As varied as they are, tapas have a few points in common. They are served in small portions and are intended to be eaten immediately and quickly. In most cases, they are served on small plates. Many can be eaten by hand, but many others, especially those served in a sauce, are eaten with a fork. Often they are the same kinds of foods that can be served as first courses of a dinner, but presented in smaller portions.

CAVIAR

Caviar is the salted roe, or eggs, of the sturgeon. In the United States and Canada, any product labeled simply *caviar* must come from sturgeon. Roe from any other fish must be labeled as such (for example, *whitefish* caviar).

The most important caviar-producing countries have traditionally been Russia and Iran, both of which border on the Caspian Sea, where the sturgeon are harvested. Sturgeon live in other waters as well, including North American waters. Production of North American caviar has been growing in recent years, in part because of difficulties obtaining caviar from the Caspian.

To categorize it further, caviar is given the name of the species of sturgeon it is taken from. The beluga is the largest and scarcest sturgeon, and it yields the largest and most expensive eggs. Next in size are osetra and sevruga.

Although the larger eggs are generally more expensive, size or price alone does not necessarily indicate quality. All three types of caviar vary considerably in quality. The only sure way to determine the quality of a particular tin or jar of caviar is to taste it.

Good-quality caviar should be made up of shiny, whole eggs, with few, if any, broken eggs. It should not have a strong, fishy smell, and it should not look watery or oily.

Caviar that is made with a relatively low proportion of salt is labeled malassol, which means "little salt." Malassol caviar is considered to be of better quality than the more highly salted varieties. However, for those who must restrict their salt intake, there is no such thing as low-sodium caviar. Even malassol is salty.

Caviar is either fresh or pasteurized. Fresh caviar in an unopened tin will keep for a few weeks, as long as it is kept cold. Once opened, it begins to deteriorate quickly and should be eaten the same day, if possible. Pasteurized caviar is of lesser quality because it has been heat-treated. Unopened, it will keep much longer than fresh caviar, but once opened, it too should be eaten as quickly as possible, or within a few days.

Other Caviars

Roe from other fish, including trout, salmon, whitefish, and lumpfish, is also salted to make caviar. Once again, quality varies considerably, ranging from good to nearly inedible. Those of better quality are useful alternatives to expensive sturgeon caviar. Three popular types are *salmon caviar*, large red eggs, often paired with smoked salmon or other salmon products in appetizer dishes; *bleak roe*, tiny, mild-tasting, orange eggs from a fish native to the Baltic; and *tobiko*, tiny orange eggs from Japanese flying fish, introduced to the West in Japanese sushi restaurants.

Serving Caviar

The best caviar should be served ice-cold and as simply as possible. The traditional caviar accompaniments of chopped onion, lemon, chopped egg, and sour cream may be all right for inexpensive roes, but they overwhelm the delicate flavor of top-quality beluga, osetra, and sevruga. Spoons for eating caviar should be made of bone, porcelain, mother of pearl, or even plastic, but not metal, which reacts with the caviar to give it an unpleasant taste.

For more elaborate presentations, caviars a notch or two below the best quality are more economical choices. Other foods served with caviar should be fairly mild or delicate. Such items as mild smoked salmon, oysters, and potatoes are often used.

AMUSE BOUCHE

An **amuse bouche** (ah mews boosh) is a tiny appetizer or hors d'oeuvre offered, compliments of the chef and usually in more expensive restaurants, to guests seated at their tables, either before or after they have ordered from the menu. It is an opportunity to showcase an aspect of the chef's cooking style and talent and to welcome the guests.

Nearly anything that can be served in a tiny portion can be served as an amuse bouche, including salads, soups (in espresso cups), canapés, and little portions of meat, fish, or vegetable with a few drops of sauce and a garnish. Usually chefs don't use a separate category of recipe for these items but borrow something from one of their regular menus, preferably not a dish on the menu that evening, and give it a different presentation, garnish, or sauce.

 Spinach Boreks

Yield: 50 pieces

U.S.	Metric	Ingredients
2 lb	900 g	Spinach
4 oz	100 g	Butter
4 oz	100 g	Onions, chopped fine
1 oz	30 g	Scallions, chopped fine
1 oz	30 g	Fresh dill weed, chopped
1 lb	450 g	Feta cheese, crumbled
to taste	to taste	Salt
to taste	to taste	Pepper
25 sheets	25 sheets	Phyllo dough (about 1 lb/450 g)
8 oz approximately	225 g approximately	Melted butter

Per 1 piece:
Calories, 110; Protein, 2 g; Fat, 8 g (69% cal.); Cholesterol, 25 mg; Carbohydrates, 6 g; Fiber, 1 g; Sodium, 210 mg.

■ **P r o c e d u r e**

1. Trim, wash, and steam or boil the spinach just until it is thoroughly wilted.
2. Drain, cool under cold running water, and squeeze dry. Chop fine.
3. Heat the butter in a sauté pan. Sauté the onions and scallions over low heat until soft.
4. Remove from the heat and add the spinach and dill. Mix to coat the spinach lightly with butter.
5. Mix in the cheese.
6. Season to taste with salt and pepper.
7. Thaw the phyllo if it is frozen. Unwrap and unfold the stack of sheets and cut them in half lengthwise. Keep them covered to prevent drying.
8. Taking one sheet at a time, brush each lightly with melted butter. Fold the sheet in half lengthwise and butter it again.
9. Put a small mound (about ½–⅔ oz/15–20 g) of the spinach mixture toward the bottom of the strip and a little to one side, as shown in Figure 23.4.
10. Fold into triangular packets as indicated in the illustration.
11. Arrange the triangles on baking sheets with the loose ends of the phyllo on the bottom. Brush the tops with melted butter.
12. Bake at 375°F (190°C) until golden brown and crisp, about 20–25 minutes.
13. Serve warm.

V A R I A T I O N

Many other fillings can be baked wrapped in phyllo, as long as they are not too juicy. The following are some suggestions:

Diced ham, cheddar cheese, and prepared mustard

Gruyère cheese, blue cheese, walnuts

Feta and cream cheese (2 parts feta to 1 part cream cheese) mixed together, plus 1 egg yolk per 12 oz (350 g) cheese

Sautéed mushrooms and onions, crumbled bacon, parsley, parmesan cheese

Diced cooked chicken, mozzarella cheese, sun-dried tomatoes, basil

Crab meat, sautéed shellfish, cream cheese, hot pepper sauce

Ratatouille (p. 563)

Figure 23.4 Folding phyllo dough triangles.

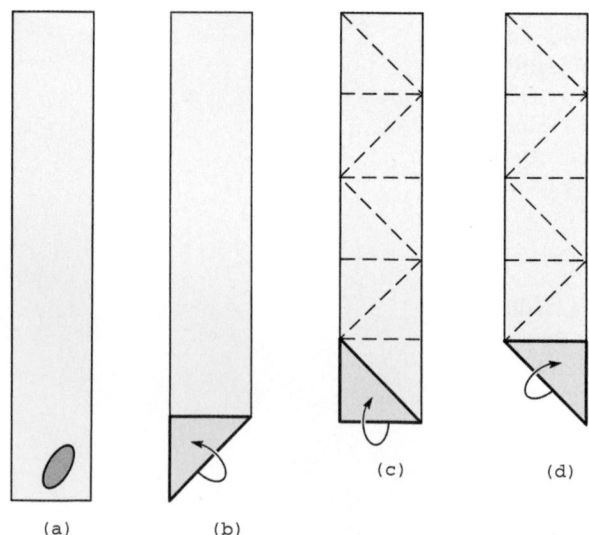

(a) **Place the filling at the bottom of the strip of buttered phyllo dough and a little to one side.**
(b) **Fold the bottom corner over at a 45-degree angle to form a triangle.**
(c, d) **Continue folding the triangle as shown in the diagram.**

Stuffed Mushrooms with Cheese

Yield: 36 pieces

U.S.	Metric	Ingredients
15 oz	425 g	Onion
2 oz	60 g	Shallot
⅔ oz	20 g	Garlic
⅓ oz	10 g	Italian parsley (flat-leaf)
1½ oz	45 g	Chives
5 fl oz	150 mL	Olive oil
3 oz	90 g	Fresh bread crumbs
36	36	Large mushrooms
3 fl oz	90 mL	Lemon juice
1 oz	30 mL	Butter
as needed	as needed	Kosher or sea salt
5 oz	150 g	Swiss cheese, grated

Per 1 piece:
Calories, 70; Protein, 2 g; Fat, 6 g (69% cal.); Cholesterol, 5 mg;
Carbohydrates, 4 g; Fiber, 1 g; Sodium, 25 mg.

■ **P r o c e d u r e**

1. Finely chop the onion, shallot, garlic, parsley, and chives.
2. Sweat the onion, shallot, and garlic in the olive oil. Once cooked, add the herbs and bread crumbs. Season to taste.
3. Remove the stems from the mushrooms and reserve for another use, such as stock or duxelles (alternatively, chop and sauté them with the ingredients in step 2). Place the mushrooms in a pot of water and add the lemon juice, butter, and salt. Bring to a boil and allow to boil for a few minutes. Remove the pan from the heat and leave the mushroom caps in the hot liquid to finish cooking.
4. Once cool enough to handle, remove the mushroom caps and drain. Arrange hollow side up on a sheet pan. Fill with the onion mixture, then sprinkle with the grated cheese. Brown under a salamander or broiler until hot and the cheese has melted.

Smoked Salmon Rolls

Yield: about 4 lb (2 kg)

U.S.	Metric	Ingredients
4 oz	125 g	Carrot, cut brunoise
8 oz	250 g	Celery, cut brunoise
5 oz	150 g	Cooked shrimp
3 oz	90 g	Crabmeat
1 lb 6 oz	700 g	Bean sprouts
½ oz	15 g	Chives
2 tsp	10 mL	Lemon zest
6 oz	175 g	Mayonnaise
2½ tsp	12 mL	Worcestershire sauce
to taste	to taste	Salt
to taste	to taste	Pepper
1 lb 4 oz	600 g	Smoked salmon (about 14 slices, 1½ oz or 40–50 g each)
as needed	as needed	Oriental Vinaigrette (p. 725)

Per 1 ounce:
Calories, 120; Protein, 3 g; Fat, 12 g (87% cal.); Cholesterol, 10 mg;
Carbohydrates, 11 g; Fiber, 0 g; Sodium, 290 mg.

■ **P r o c e d u r e**

1. Quickly blanch the carrot and celery in boiling salted water.
2. Finely chop the cooked shrimp and crab.
3. Blanch the bean sprouts.
4. Spread the blanched vegetables on paper towels to remove as much excess moisture as possible.
5. Mix together the vegetables, the crab, shrimp, chives, lemon zest, and mayonnaise. Mix in the Worcestershire sauce. Season to taste.
6. Place 2 slices of smoked salmon slightly overlapping each other on plastic film. Place some of the filling on top, roll, and twist the ends tightly so that the filling holds. When ready to serve, cut to desired length and remove the plastic.
7. To serve as hors d'oeuvres, pass with picks and with Oriental Vinaigrette as dipping sauce.

Fried Chicken Wings

Yield: 72 pieces

U.S.	Metric	Ingredients
36	36	Chicken wings
2 fl oz	60 mL	Oil
3 fl oz	90 mL	Soy sauce
1 oz	30 g	Ginger root, grated
½ oz	15 g	Garlic, chopped
as needed	as needed	Standard Breading Procedure
as needed	as needed	Tomato Sauce (p. 176)

■ **P r o c e d u r e**

1. Prepare the chicken wings. Cut off the wing tip and discard or save for stock. Cut at the joint. Loosen the skin at the narrow end of the wing drumstick (the thicker piece) and scrape and pull the skin and flesh toward the opposite joint. The result should look like half of a barbell. Cut the other half of the wing at one end, cutting off the joint. Scrape and pull the skin and flesh as for the drumstick. Disengage the smaller of the two bones and discard or save for stock.
2. Whisk together the oil, soy sauce, ginger, and chopped garlic.
3. Toss the wings in the marinade and allow to marinate overnight, stirring occasionally.
4. Bread the chicken wings. Deep-fry at 325°F (160°C).
5. Serve with Tomato Sauce for dipping.

Per 1 piece:
Calories, 90; Protein, 5 g; Fat, 6 g (63% cal.); Cholesterol, 20 mg;
Carbohydrates, 3 g; Fiber, 0 g; Sodium, 40 mg.

 Eggplant Caviar

Yield: about 2½ lb (1.2 kg)

U.S.	Metric	Ingredients
3 lb 12 oz	1.7 kg	Eggplants
to taste	to taste	Salt
10 fl oz	300 mL	Olive oil
3½ oz	100 g	Pitted black olives, chopped
2	2	Garlic cloves, crushed
1 oz	30 g	Chives, chopped fine
2 tsp	5 g	Paprika
as needed	as needed	Additional chopped olives and chives for garnish

■ **P r o c e d u r e**

1. Cut the eggplants in half lengthwise and season. Brush with oil (reserving the remaining oil for step 4) and bake for 25 minutes at 400°F (200°C) or until soft.
2. Drain the eggplants briefly to get rid of excess liquid and scrape out the flesh. Mash with a fork.
3. Add the olives, garlic, and chives.
4. Mix in the olive oil slowly, along with the paprika. Season to taste. Refrigerate for 1 hour before serving.
5. To serve, place the caviar into a chilled bowl. Decorate with additional olives and chives. Serve with melba toasts for dipping.

Per 1 ounce:
Calories, 80; Protein, 0 g; Fat, 7 g (84% cal.); Cholesterol, 0 mg;
Carbohydrates, 3 g; Fiber, 1 g; Sodium, 25 mg.

Prosciutto and Melon Balls

Yield: as desired

U.S.	Metric	Ingredients
as needed	as needed	Melon (cantaloupe, honeydew, crenshaw, etc.)
to taste	to taste	Lime juice
as needed	as needed	Prosciutto ham

Per serving:
Calories 20; Protein, 2 g; Fat, 1 g (43% cal.); Cholesterol, 5 mg;
Carbohydrates, 1 g; Fiber, 0 g; Sodium, 175 mg.

One serving equals 0.5 ounce of melon with 0.25 ounce of prosciutto.

■ P r o c e d u r e

1. Using a ball cutter, cut the melon into small balls.
2. Sprinkle the melon balls with lime juice and let stand 10 minutes.
3. Using a slicing machine, cut the ham into paper-thin slices. Cut large slices in half crosswise.
4. Shortly before serving, wrap each melon ball in a slice of ham and fasten with a pick.

V A R I A T I O N

Other fruits may be substituted for the melon, such as pineapple sticks or chunks, fresh figs (whole, halved, or quartered), and fresh pear or peach slices. Pears and peaches must be coated with lime or lemon juice to prevent darkening.

Apple Slices with Curried Chicken and Mango

Yield: 36–40 pieces, about 1½–2 oz (50–60 g) each

U.S.	Metric	Ingredients
1 lb	500 g	Apples
1½ fl oz	45 mL	Lemon juice
8 oz	250 g	Mango, flesh only
1 lb 8 oz	750 g	Cooked chicken breast meat, cooled
2 tbsp	15 g	Chopped cilantro
1 pt	500 mL	Mayonnaise
2 tsp	10 mL	Curry powder
3–4	3–4	Apples
as needed	as needed	Lemon juice
as needed	as needed	Paprika
as needed	as needed	Cilantro leaves

Per 1 piece:
Calories, 60; Protein, 6 g; Fat, 2 g (29% cal.); Cholesterol, 15 mg;
Carbohydrates, 5 g; Fiber, 1 g; Sodium, 15 mg.

■ P r o c e d u r e

1. Peel and core the apples. Cut into brunoise. Toss with the lemon juice.
2. Cut the mango into brunoise. Mix with the apples.
3. Cut the chicken breast into fine dice. Mix with the mango and apples. Mix in the chopped cilantro.
4. Season the mayonnaise with curry powder.
5. Mix enough mayonnaise into the chicken mixture so that it holds together well. (You may have some mayonnaise left over.) Keep refrigerated until ready to use.
6. Wash the apples and core them. Channel the apples (see Figure 16.8) from top to bottom at ½-in. (1-cm) intervals. Cut the apples in half vertically, then cut crosswise into slices about ¼ in. (½ cm) thick. Rub with lemon juice.
7. Form quenelles (see Figure 13.5) of the chicken mixture and place on top of each slice of apple. Decorate with paprika and cilantro.

V A R I A T I O N

The chicken mixture can also be used to fill savory tart shells and vegetables such as leaves of Belgian endive and cucumber shells.

Smoked Chicken Purses with Sun-Dried Tomatoes

Yield: 36 pieces, about ¾ oz (22 g) each

U.S.	Metric	Ingredients
3½ fl oz	100 mL	Olive oil or oil from sun-dried tomatoes
1 oz	25 g	Sun-dried tomatoes packed in oil, drained
1	1	Egg yolk
pinch	pinch	Salt
pinch	pinch	Pepper
1 tbsp	15 mL	Dijon mustard
7 oz	200 g	Smoked chicken breast
2 oz	60 g	Sun-dried tomatoes packed in oil, drained
1 oz	30 g	Chopped basil
36	36	Crêpes (recipe follows)
1–2 bunches	1–2 bunches	Chives

■ P r o c e d u r e

1. Place the oil and sun-dried tomatoes in a blender. Blend until smooth. Strain through a fine strainer.
2. In a stainless-steel bowl, whip together the egg yolk, salt, pepper, and mustard. Gradually add the flavored oil in a steady stream, whipping constantly to make a stiff mayonnaise.
3. Coarsely chop the smoked chicken. Coarsely chop the sun-dried tomatoes.
4. Mix together the chicken, tomatoes, chopped basil, and the mayonnaise from step 2. Taste and adjust seasoning if necessary.
5. Using a 4-in. (10-cm) round cutter, cut out a circle from the center of each crêpe.
6. Place about 2 tsp (10–12 g) chicken mixture in the center each circle. Gather the edges to form small purses and tie with a length of chive.

Per 1 piece:
Calories, 110; Protein, 5 g; Fat, 7 g (57% cal.); Cholesterol, 50 mg; Carbohydrates, 7 g; Fiber, 0 g; Sodium, 125 mg.

Note: Analysis is based on smoked turkey as nutrient information for smoked chicken was unavailable.

Crêpes

Yield: about 36 crêpes

U.S.	Metric	Ingredients
8 oz	250 g	Flour
1 tsp	5 g	Salt
6	6	Eggs
1 pt	500 mL	Milk
1½ oz	50 g	Browned butter
as needed	as needed	Oil

■ P r o c e d u r e

1. Whisk together the flour, salt, and eggs. Gradually mix in the milk to make a smooth batter, about the consistency of heavy cream.
2. Strain the batter through a fine sieve and whisk in the browned butter.
3. Cover with plastic wrap and set aside to rest at least 30 minutes at room temperature.
4. Heat a 5½-in. (14-cm) crêpe pan over moderate heat. Lightly oil the pan. Add about 2–3 tbsp (30–45 mL) batter and swirl to coat the bottom of the pan with a thin layer; pour any excess batter back into the bowl. Cook until the edges are brown and the bottom is golden. Flip over and cook another minute.
5. Place the crêpe on a wire rack to cool. Repeat the procedure to make additional crêpes, overlapping but not stacking them on the rack.

Per 1 crêpe:
Calories, 70; Protein, 2 g; Fat, 4 g (53% cal.); Cholesterol, 40 mg; Carbohydrates, 6 g; Fiber, 0 g; Sodium, 90 mg.

Chicken Satay

Yield: 36 pieces, about ¼–1 oz (25 g) each

U.S.	Metric	Ingredients
2	2	Garlic cloves, crushed
2 oz	60 g	Ginger root, grated
2 oz	60 g	Brown sugar
3 fl oz	90 mL	Sesame oil
1 fl oz	30 mL	Soy sauce
1 lb	900 g	Boneless, skinless chicken breasts
4 fl oz	125 mL	Water
3	3	Garlic cloves, finely chopped
8 oz	250 g	Peanut butter
4 fl oz	125 mL	Coconut milk
2 tbsp plus 2 tsp	40 mL	Honey
2 tbsp plus 2 tsp	40 mL	Lemon juice
2 tbsp plus 2 tsp	40 mL	Soy sauce
to taste	to taste	Hot pepper sauce

Per 1 piece:
Calories, 80; Protein, 4 g; Fat, 5 g (58% cal.); Cholesterol, 5 mg;
Carbohydrates, 4 g; Fiber, 0 g; Sodium, 125 mg.

■ P r o c e d u r e

1. Soak 36 bamboo skewers, 6 in. (15 cm) long, in cold water overnight (to prevent burning when grilling).
2. Place the garlic, ginger, brown sugar, sesame oil, and soy sauce in a blender and blend until smooth.
3. Cut the chicken into thin strips lengthwise. Place them in a bowl. Pour the marinade mixture (from step 2) over the chicken and stir to coat well. Cover and refrigerate for 2 hours or more.
4. Prepare a dipping sauce: Bring the water to a boil and add the chopped garlic. Simmer for 1 minute.
5. Add the peanut butter and coconut milk. Cook over medium heat for 2–3 minutes until smooth and thick.
6. Stir in the honey. lemon juice, soy sauce, and hot pepper sauce. Remove from the heat. Cool.
7. Thread the marinated chicken onto the soaked skewers.
8. Grill under a salamander or over a charbroiler for approximately 2 minutes on each side, brushing with the leftover marinade.
9. Serve with the dipping sauce.

Beef Teriyaki Skewers

Yield: 36 pieces, ⅓–½ oz (12–13 g) each

U.S.	Metric	Ingredients
1½ fl oz	45 mL	Vegetable oil
1½ fl oz	45 mL	Soy sauce
1 oz	30 g	Ginger root, grated
2	2	Garlic cloves, chopped
1 lb	500 g	Beef tenderloin

Per 1 piece:
Calories, 30; Protein, 3 g; Fat, 2 g (60% cal.); Cholesterol, 10 mg;
Carbohydrates, 0 g; Fiber, 0 g; Sodium, 75 mg.

■ P r o c e d u r e

1. Mix together the oil, soy sauce, ginger, and garlic.
2. Cut the beef into small cubes, about ¾ in. (2 cm) on a side. Marinate in the soy sauce mixture 2–3 hours, refrigerated.
3. Thread each meat cube on a wooden cocktail skewer. Cook quickly under a salamander or broiler. Serve hot.

Smoked Salmon and Trout Logs on Pumpernickel

Yield: 36 pieces, about ⅓ oz (8–10 g) each

U.S.	Metric	Ingredients
3 oz	90 g	Smoked trout
3 oz	90 g	Cream cheese
to taste	to taste	Salt
to taste	to taste	Pepper
⅔ oz	20 g	Chives, chopped
9 slices	9 slices	Pumpernickel bread
8 oz	200–250 g	Smoked salmon, sliced
as needed	as needed	Chervil or parsley for garnish

■ P r o c e d u r e

1. Remove the skin and any bones from the smoked trout.
2. Place the trout and the cream cheese in the bowl of a food processor. Process until smooth. Season with salt and pepper if necessary. Mix in the chives.
3. Transfer to a bowl and refrigerate until needed.
4. Beat the trout mixture to soften. Spread the bread with a thin layer of the trout mixture.
5. On a sheet of plastic wrap, arrange the smoked salmon slices in a row, overlapping them slightly.
6. Beat the trout mixture and spread onto the smoked salmon. Roll to form a log, twist the ends of the plastic wrap, and knot or secure with kitchen string. Place in the freezer for 10–15 minutes or until firm. Cut into slices ½ in. (1 cm) thick.
7. Trim the crusts of the bread and cut each slice into 4 triangles.
8. Place 1 slice of the trout log cut side up on each triangle. Garnish each piece with a tiny sprig of chervil or a parsley leaf.

Per 1 piece:
Calories, 35; Protein, 2 g; Fat, 1.5 g (40% cal.); Cholesterol, 5 mg; Carbohydrates, 3 g; Fiber, 0 g; Sodium, 100 mg..

 ## Prosciutto, Blue Cheese, and Walnut Parcels

Yield: 36 pieces, about ⅓ oz (18–20 g) each

U.S.	Metric	Ingredients
7 oz	200 g	Blue cheese
2 oz	60 g	Butter
2 oz	60 g	Walnuts, chopped fine
9 slices	9 slices	Whole-grain bread, toasted
12 thin slices	12 thin slices	Prosciutto
as needed.	as needed	Chervil or parsley for garnish

■ P r o c e d u r e

1. Mix the blue cheese and butter in a food processor until smooth. Transfer to a bowl and mix in the walnuts.
2. Remove the crust from the bread and spread a little of the cheese mixture on each slice. Cut each slice into 4 squares.
3. Cut each slice of the prosciutto into 3 squares, 3 in. (7–8 cm) per side.
4. Using a piping bag, pipe about ½ tbsp (8 g) filling in the center of each square. Fold the edges over the center to make a square parcel.
5. Place on the prepared squares of bread and decorate each with a tiny sprig of chervil or a parsley leaf.

Per 1 piece:
Calories, 70; Protein, 3 g; Fat, 5 g (65% cal.); Cholesterol, 10 mg; Carbohydrates, 3 g; Fiber, 0 g; Sodium, 240 mg.

Cucumber Roundels with Smoked Trout Pâté

Yield: 36 pieces, about 1 oz (30 g) each

U.S.	Metric	Ingredients
2 (approximately)	2 (approximately)	Cucumbers
6 oz	175 g	Smoked trout fillet
6 oz	175 g	Cream cheese
to taste	to taste	Salt
to taste	to taste	Pepper
to taste	to taste	Lemon juice
12–15	12–15	Pitted black olives, sliced into rings
as needed	as needed	Chervil or parsley for garnish

Per 1 piece:
Calories, 30; Protein, 1 g; Fat, 2 g (69% cal.); Cholesterol, 10 mg; Carbohydrates, 1 g; Fiber, 0 g; Sodium, 50 mg.

■ P r o c e d u r e

1. Channel the cucumbers (see Figure 16.8). Trim the ends and cut into slices ½ in. (1 cm) thick. You will need enough cucumbers to make 36 slices.
2. Using a melon baller, scoop out the seed area to create a shallow depression, being careful not to remove the seeds completely.
3. In the bowl of a food processor, process the trout and cream cheese until smooth. Season to taste with salt, pepper, and lemon juice.
4. Transfer to a piping bag fitted with a medium star tip. Lightly salt the cucumber and fill the cavity of the cucumber slices with the trout pâté (about 2 tsp/10 mL per piece).
5. Garnish each with an olive slice and a tiny spring of chervil or a parsley leaf.

 ## Feuilleté Chorizo

Yield: 72 pieces, about ⅓ oz (9–10 g) each

U.S.	Metric	Ingredients
1 lb 4 oz	600 g	Puff pastry
8 oz	250 g	Chorizo (or other spicy sausage)
1	1	Egg
pinch	pinch	Salt

Per 1 piece:
Calories, 60; Protein, 1 g; Fat, 4.5 g (67% cal.); Cholesterol, 5 mg; Carbohydrates, 4 g; Fiber, 0 g; Sodium, 60 mg.

■ P r o c e d u r e

1. Roll out the puff pastry to about ⅟₁₂ in. (2 mm) thick. Cut into 72 squares, 2 in. (5 cm) per side. Refrigerate.
2. Remove the skin from the chorizo. Grind the chorizo in a meat grinder fitted with a medium blade.
3. Beat the egg with a pinch of salt.
4. Brush each square with the egg wash and place a small mound (about ½ tsp/3 g) of the ground chorizo in the center. Fold over to form a triangle. Press the edges to seal.
5. Place on a baking sheet and brush with the egg wash. Set aside for 15 minutes, then brush with a second coating of egg wash.
6. Bake at 350°F (180°C) or until lightly browned, about 8–10 minutes.

Crab Beignets with Lime and Ginger Chutney

Yield: 36 pieces, about ¾ oz (20–22 g) each

U.S.	Metric	Ingredients
3 oz	90 g	Flour
2½ oz	70 g	Potato starch
1 tsp	6 g	Baking powder
pinch	pinch	Salt
2 tsp	10 mL	Oil
5 fl oz	150 mL	Water
1¾ oz	50 g	Onion, chopped fine
1 tbsp	15 mL	Olive oil
1¾ oz	50 g	Red bell pepper, cut brunoise
1	1	Egg
3 tbsp plus 1 tsp	50 mL	Heavy cream
½ oz	15 g	Chives, chopped fine
6 oz	175 g	Crabmeat
6 oz	175 g	Fresh bread crumbs
8 oz	250 g	Lime and Ginger Chutney (p. 202)

Per 1 piece:
Calories, 60; Protein, 2 g; Fat, 2 g (33% cal.); Cholesterol, 10 mg;
Carbohydrates, 7 g; Fiber, 0 g; Sodium, 65 mg.

■ P r o c e d u r e

1. Sift the flour, potato starch, baking powder, and salt into a bowl. Whisk in the oil and then the water.
2. Strain through a sieve. Set aside to rest for at least 30 minutes.
3. Sweat the onion in the olive oil.
4. Add the brunoise of red pepper and sweat with the onion until soft.
5. Set aside in a large bowl to cool.
6. Beat the egg with the cream and add to the cooled onion and pepper mixture. Add the chives and mix well.
7. Stir in the crab, then add the fresh bread crumbs. Mix well and season to taste.
8. Make the mixture into tightly packed balls of about ½ oz (18 g) each.
9. Dip in the batter and deep-fry at 400°F (200°C) until golden brown, about 2–3 minutes. Remove and place on paper towels to drain.
10. Serve with the Lime and Ginger Chutney on the side.

Mushrooms Stuffed with Tapenade

Yield: 50 pieces

U.S.	Metric	Ingredients
8 oz	250 g	Pitted Mediterranean or Greek black olives
1 oz	30 g	Capers, drained
1 oz	30 g	Anchovies, drained
1 oz	30 g	Tuna, drained
1 tsp	5 mL	Dijon-style mustard
2½ fl oz	75 mL	Olive oil
1 tsp	5 mL	Lemon juice
2 tbsp	30 mL	Chopped parsley
pinch	pinch	Dried thyme
to taste	to taste	Salt
to taste	to taste	Pepper
50	50	Small to medium fresh white mushrooms
as needed	as needed	Pimiento

Per 1 piece:
Calories, 30; Protein, 1 g; Fat, 25 g (74% cal.); Cholesterol, 0 mg;
Carbohydrates, 1 g; Fiber, 0 g; Sodium, 110 mg.

■ P r o c e d u r e

1. In a blender or food processor, purée the olives, capers, anchovies, tuna, mustard, oil, lemon juice, and herbs. Season to taste.
2. Chill the mixture several hours to let the flavors blend.
3. Remove the stems from the mushrooms and clean the caps.
4. Fill each cap with a small spoonful of the tapenade.
5. Garnish the top of each with a dot of pimiento.

Deviled Eggs

Yield: 50 pieces

U.S.	Metric	Ingredients
25	25	Hard-cooked eggs
½ pt	250 mL	Mayonnaise
1 fl oz	30 mL	Lemon juice or vinegar
1 tsp	5 mL	Dry mustard
1 tsp	5 mL	Worcestershire sauce
to taste	to taste	Salt
to taste	to taste	White pepper
to taste	to taste	Cayenne
as needed	as needed	Assorted garnish, such as:
		Chopped parsley
		Tiny dill sprigs
		Capers
		Diced pimiento
		Sliced stuffed olives
		Paprika
		Red or black caviar

■ Procedure

1. Halve the eggs lengthwise and remove the yolks.
2. Mash the yolks or force them through a sieve.
3. Add the remaining ingredients (except the garnish) and mix to a smooth paste.
4. Using a pastry bag with a star tip, fill the egg white halves.
5. Using a variety of garnishes, decorate the top of each egg.

VARIATION

Vary the flavor of stuffed eggs by adding any of the following ingredients to the egg yolk mixture in the basic recipe.

Anchovy: 2–3 oz (60–90 g) anchovy paste.

Curry: 2 tbsp (30 mL) curry powder, heated very gently with a little oil and cooled.

Blue cheese: 6 oz (175 g) mashed blue cheese.

Parmesan: 3 oz (90 g) grated parmesan cheese.

Tarragon: Use tarragon vinegar in the filling and add 2 tsp (10 mL) dried tarragon.

Tuna: 6 oz (175 g) well-mashed, drained tuna.

Per 1 piece:
Calories, 70; Protein, 3 g; Fat, 7 g (84% cal.); Cholesterol, 110 mg; Carbohydrates, 0 g; Fiber, 0 g; Sodium, 45 mg.

Filling deviled eggs with a pastry bag.

Miniature Gougère Puffs

Yield: about 160 pieces

U.S.	Metric	Ingredients
2½ lb	1.1 kg	Éclair paste (p. 996)
8 oz	225 g	Gruyère cheese, grated
as needed	as needed	Egg wash

■ Procedure

1. Mix together the éclair paste and the cheese.
2. Using a pastry bag with a small, plain tip, pipe small mounds of about 1 tbsp (15 mL) each onto sheet pans lined with parchment. See page 996 for guidelines on making tiny cream puff shells or profiteroles, which is essentially what these are.
3. Bake at 400°F (200°C) until puffed and brown, about 20–30 minutes.
4. Make a little slit in the side of each to allow steam to escape. Put the puffs in a warm oven until they are dry.
5. Serve warm or at room temperature.

Per 1 piece:
Calories, 25; Protein, 1 g; Fat, 1.5 g (63% cal.); Cholesterol, 15 mg; Carbohydrates, 1 g; Fiber, 0 g; Sodium, 25 mg.

Egg Rolls or Spring Rolls

Yield: 16 pieces

U.S.	Metric	Ingredients
1 oz	30 mL	Oil
6 oz	175 g	Cooked meat or poultry, cut fine julienne
6 oz	175 g	Chinese cabbage, shredded
3	3	Scallions, shredded
6 oz	175 g	Bean sprouts
5	5	Dried black mushrooms (stems discarded), soaked in boiling water, cut julienne
2 oz	60 g	Bamboo shoots, cut julienne
1½ oz	45 g	Raw shrimp, chopped
2 tsp	10 mL	Soy sauce
1 tsp	5 mL	Sherry or shaoxing wine
3 fl oz	100 mL	Chicken stock
1½ tsp	7 mL	Cornstarch
1 tbsp	15 mL	Water, cold
16	16	Egg roll skins or spring roll skins
as needed	as needed	Egg, beaten

Per 1 roll:
Calories, 180; Protein, 8 g; Fat, 8 g (38% cal.); Cholesterol, 25 mg; Carbohydrates, 21 g; Fiber, 1 g; Sodium, 240 mg.

■ **P r o c e d u r e**

1. Heat the oil in a wok or sauté pan. Stir-fry the meat, cabbage, scallions, bean sprouts, black mushrooms, bamboo shoots, and shrimp.

2. Add the soy sauce, sherry, and stock. Continue to stir and cook for another 1–2 minutes.

3. Mix the cornstarch with the cold water. Stir into the vegetable mixture and cook until reduced and thickened.

4. Remove from the heat and adjust the seasonings. Cool thoroughly.

5. Lay an egg roll skin on the worktable with one of the corners toward you. Spoon about 1½ oz (45 g) filling onto the lower half of the skin in a sort of sausage shape. (See Figure 23.5.)

6. Fold the lower corner of the skin (the corner pointing at you) over the filling so that it is covered. Then start to roll it up like a cylinder, giving it just a half turn.

7. Brush the left and right corners with a little beaten egg. Fold one corner over the filling, then the other, pressing down to seal. At this point, it should look like an open envelope.

8. Brush the top corner with beaten egg. Roll into a firm, compact cylinder. Seal the top corner well.

9. Repeat with the remaining skins and filling.

10. Deep-fry the egg rolls until the skins are crisp and brown. (*Note:* Egg roll skins are heavier than spring roll skins. They must be thoroughly fried or they will be doughy.) Drain and serve at once, with a little hot mustard or bottled duck sauce for dipping.

Figure 23.5 Rolling egg rolls.

(a) Lay an egg roll skin on the bench with one corner toward you. Place the filling as shown.

(b) Fold the lower corner of the skin over the filling and roll it up about one-third of the way.

(c) Brush the left and right corners of the skin with beaten egg.

(d) Fold the corners over the filling so that the skin resembles an open envelope.

(e) Brush the top edge with egg and roll up tightly.

(f) When completely rolled, egg rolls are ready to be cooked.

Chicken Liver Pâté

Yield: 2½ lb (1.2 kg)

U.S.	Metric	Ingredients
2 lb	1 kg	Chicken livers
to taste	to taste	Salt
as needed	as needed	Milk
4 oz	125 g	Onion, chopped
3 oz	90 g	Butter
½ tsp	2 mL	Dried oregano
¼ tsp	1 mL	White pepper
pinch	pinch	Nutmeg
pinch	pinch	Ground ginger
pinch	pinch	Ground cloves
1 tsp	5 mL	Salt
12 oz	375 g	Cream cheese
1–2 fl oz	30–60 mL	Brandy, Madeira, or port (optional)
to taste	to taste	Salt

Per 1 ounce:
Calories, 60; Protein, 3 g; Fat, 5 g (74% cal.); Cholesterol, 75 mg; Carbohydrates, 1 g; Fiber, 0 g; Sodium, 105 mg.

■ P r o c e d u r e

1. Trim fat and sinews from the livers.
2. Sprinkle the livers lightly with salt. Add milk to cover and let stand overnight, refrigerated. This step is optional, but it results in a slightly milder flavor and lighter color.
3. Sauté the onion lightly in the butter until tender but not brown.
4. Add the livers (drained and rinsed), herbs, and spices. Brown the livers lightly and cook them until they are still slightly pink in the center. Remove from the heat and cool.
5. Grind the livers and onions in a grinder or buffalo chopper.
6. Add cream cheese and continue to process to obtain a uniformly mixed paste.
7. Add brandy or wine to taste. Add additional salt if necessary.
8. Pack the mixture into containers and chill overnight.

Black Bean Quesadillas

Yield: 48 pieces

U.S.	Metric	Ingredients
12 oz	360 g	Black turtle beans, cooked or canned, drained
1–2 fl oz	30–60 mL	Water or bean cooking broth
to taste	to taste	Salt
to taste	to taste	Cayenne or ground chipotle pepper
12	12	Flour or corn tortillas
6 tbsp	90 mL	Salsa Cruda (p. 191)
1 tbsp	15 mL	Jalapeño or serrano chiles, seeded and chopped fine
2 tbsp	30 mL	Chopped cilantro
4 oz	120 g	Monterey jack or mild cheddar cheese, grated

Per 1 piece:
Calories, 110; Protein, 4 g; Fat, 4 g (30% cal.); Cholesterol, 0 mg; Carbohydrates, 17 g; Fiber, 2.4 g; Sodium, 210 mg.

■ P r o c e d u r e

1. Mash the beans coarsely.
2. Add just enough water or bean broth to moisten the beans slightly. They should not be dry.
3. Add salt and cayenne or chipotle to taste.
4. Top 1 tortilla with about 2 oz (60 g) bean mixture and spread it to cover the tortilla. Repeat this process until 6 tortillas are topped with the bean mixture.
5. For each of the 6 tortillas, sprinkle 1 tbsp (15 mL) salsa over the beans, then ½ tsp (2.5 mL) chopped chile and 1 tsp (5 mL) cilantro.
6. Lightly oil a hot griddle or sauté pan and place the tortilla on it.
7. Sprinkle about ⅔ oz (20 g) cheese over the filling in each tortilla and top with a second tortilla.
8. When the cheese is soft, flip the tortilla sandwich and heat the other side.
9. Remove from the heat and cut into 8 wedges.

Brandade de Morue

Yield: about 2½ lb (1.25 kg)

U.S.	Metric	Ingredients
2 lb	1 kg	Salt cod
1–2	1–2	Garlic cloves, crushed to a paste
8 fl oz	250 mL	Olive oil
8 fl oz	250 mL	Milk, cream, or half-and-half
to taste	to taste	White pepper
to taste	to taste	Salt
as needed	as needed	Toast points fried in olive oil

Per 1 ounce:
Calories, 80; Protein, 6 g; Fat, 6 g (69% cal.); Cholesterol, 20 mg; Carbohydrates, 0 g; Fiber, 0 g; Sodium, 175 mg.

■ **P r o c e d u r e**

1. Soak the salt cod in cold water for 24 hours, changing the water several times.
2. Put the cod in a pot with enough water to cover. Bring to a boil, reduce heat, and simmer 5–10 minutes, just until the cod is cooked and flakes. Do not overcook, or it will not absorb liquid well in the next steps. Remove the fish from the water, flake it, and remove the skin and bones.
3. Work the fish, while it is still hot, and the garlic into a smooth, lump-free paste. This can be done by hand with a bowl and wooden spoon or with a mixer with the paddle attachment. (A food processor may also be used, but be careful not to process the fish until it is totally puréed.)
4. Warm the oil and milk or cream in separate pans.
5. Gradually beat the oil into the cod paste alternately with the milk, adding just a little at a time, until the mixture is the consistency of mashed potatoes.
6. Add white pepper to taste. Salt may not be necessary because the dried cod is salty.
7. Serve warm as a dip, with toast points for dipping.

V A R I A T I O N S

Brandade can be reheated slowly over low heat, stirring frequently.

Brandade can be mixed with mashed potatoes in varying proportions.

If you add too much oil or cream in step 5, or if you add it too quickly, the brandade can break or curdle. It can usually be rescued by beating it vigorously. If this doesn't work, add a little mashed potatoes.

Bruschetta (Basic)

Yield: 24 pieces

U.S.	Metric	Ingredients
24 slices	24 slices	Italian or French bread, about 3–4 in. (8–10 cm) wide and ½ in. (6 mm) thick
4–6	4–6	Garlic cloves, cut in half
8–12 fl oz	240–360 mL	Extra-virgin olive oil
to taste	to taste	Salt
to taste	to taste	Pepper

Per serving:
Calories, 140; Protein, 2 g; Fat, 10 g (65% cal.); Cholesterol, 0 mg; Carbohydrates, 10 g; Fiber, 1 g; Sodium, 115 mg.

■ P r o c e d u r e

1. Toast the bread on a grill or under a broiler until golden brown.
2. While the bread is still hot, rub one side of each slice with a cut clove of garlic.
3. Brush or drizzle olive oil generously over each slice. The toast should be partly soaked with the oil.
4. Add salt and pepper to taste.
5. Serve warm.

V A R I A T I O N S

Bruschetta with Tomato and Basil
Toast the bread and rub with garlic as in the basic recipe. Cut 2 lb (1 kg) ripe plum tomatoes in half and remove the seeds. Cut into medium dice. Tear 16 fresh basil leaves into small pieces and mix with the tomatoes. Top the toasts with the tomatoes. Drizzle with olive oil and add salt and pepper to taste.

Bruschetta with Parmesan Cheese
Toast the bread and rub with garlic as in the basic recipe. Using a vegetable peeler, cut cheese, preferably a good-quality Parmigiano-Reggiano, into thin shavings. While the toast is still hot, top each piece with about ¼ oz (7 g) cheese and drizzle with olive oil. Sprinkle with black pepper.

Bruschetta with White Beans and Prosciutto
Toast the bread and rub with garlic as in the basic recipe. Mix 1 lb 4 oz (600 g) cooked or canned and drained white kidney beans, 2 oz (60 g) red onion cut in small dice, 6 oz (180 g) prosciutto, sliced thin and chopped, and 4 fl oz (120 mL) olive oil. Add salt and pepper to taste. Top toasts with this mixture.

Bruschette, clockwise from left: Bruschetta with White Beans and Prosciutto, Bruschetta with Parmesan Cheese, Bruschetta with Tomato and Basil

Spicy Meat Empanadas

Yield: 24 pieces

U.S.	Metric	Ingredients
8 oz	240 g	Bread flour
4 oz	120 g	Cake flour
1½ oz	45 g	Lard or vegetable shortening
¾ tsp	3 mL	Salt
6 fl oz	180 mL	Warm water
18 oz	480 g	Picadillo (p. 328)

Per 1 piece:
Calories, 130; Protein, 6 g; Fat, 6 g (43% cal.); Cholesterol, 15 mg; Carbohydrates, 12 g; Fiber, 1 g; Sodium, 140 mg.

■ Procedure

1. Sift the two flours together into a mixing bowl.
2. Add the lard or shortening and blend it thoroughly with the flour.
3. Dissolve the salt in the water and add it to the flour mixture. Mix to make a moderately stiff dough. Knead the dough for a few minutes, until smooth.
4. Let the dough rest 30 minutes.
5. Divide the dough into 24 equal parts by rolling it into a long cylinder and cutting it into equal segments.
6. Roll each piece into a ball. Cover and let rest 15–30 minutes.
7. For each empanada, flatten a ball of dough and roll out into a circle 4 in. (10 cm) in diameter.
8. Brush the rim of the circle lightly with water.
9. Place about ¾ oz. (20 g) picadillo on one side of the circle. Fold the other side over it to make a turnover. Press the dough around the filling to force out air. Seal the edge well by crimping with the tines of a fork.
10. Deep-fry at 375°F (190°C) until golden brown.
11. Serve immediately. If desired, accompany with Guacamole (p. 763) or Salsa Cruda (p. 191).

VARIATION

Empanadas with Roasted Poblanos and Cheese
Roast and peel poblano peppers as shown on page 529. Dice the poblanos. In place of the picadillo, fill the empanadas with poblanos and grated Monterey jack or mild cheddar cheese.

Cauliflower Pakoras

Yield: 30–40 pieces

U.S.	Metric	Ingredients
8 oz	240 g	Chickpea flour
¼ tsp	1 mL	Black pepper
¼ tsp	1 mL	Cayenne
½ tsp	2 mL	Ground cumin
¼ tsp	1 mL	Turmeric
½ tsp	2 mL	Baking powder
½ tsp	2 mL	Salt
12 fl oz	360 mL	Water
1½ lb	720 g	Cauliflower, trimmed

Per serving:
Calories, 50; Protein, 2 g; Fat, 3 g (49% cal.); Cholesterol, 0 mg;
Carbohydrates, 5 g; Fiber, 1 g; Sodium, 45 mg.

■ P r o c e d u r e

1. Sift together into a bowl the chickpea flour, pepper, cayenne, cumin, turmeric, baking powder, and salt.

2. Gradually stir in the water until the mixture has formed a thick batter about the consistency of ketchup. You may not need all the water.

3. Divide the cauliflower into florets no bigger than 1 in. (2.5 cm) across.

4. Dip the florets into the batter and deep-fry at 360°F (180°F) until lightly browned and tender.

V A R I A T I O N S

Other vegetables, such as peppers, onion rings, potatoes (thin slices), broccoli, eggplant, and okra, may be substituted for the cauliflower.

Cauliflower Pakoras

■ TERMS FOR REVIEW

hors d'oeuvre	cocktail	dip	tapa
appetizer	relish	antipasto	caviar
butler-style service	crudité	bruschetta	amuse bouche
canapé			

■ QUESTIONS FOR DISCUSSION

1. What is butler-style service? Describe at least five guidelines to keep in mind when planning butler-style service of hors d'oeuvres.

2. How can you avoid soggy canapé bases?

3. In order to use a ham salad recipe to make a ham spread, you may need to change the recipe slightly. What are three modifications you may need to make?

4. What is the difference between a fruit salad and a fruit cocktail?

5. What is the proper consistency or thickness for a dip?

6. List six or more items that might appear on a cold antipasto platter.

7. Describe how to prepare the simplest type of bruschetta.

8. Describe the best way to serve the best-quality caviar.

CHAPTER 24

Breakfast Preparation

When we speak of breakfast cookery, we are not just talking about a particular meal. We are referring to a particular small group of foods that appears on perhaps every breakfast menu. These items not only appear on breakfast menus but also are popular for brunches, snacks, and late suppers. Many establishments offer a breakfast menu all day long.

Eggs, of course, are the most popular breakfast food, and they are the primary subject of this chapter. In addition, this chapter examines the preparation of other breakfast staples: pancakes, waffles, French toast, and breakfast meats.

EGGS

Contrary to popular opinion, there is no law that says one must have eggs or cereal or pancakes or pastries for breakfast and must not have shrimp curry or chili or spaghetti and meatballs. Although most of us would think these last suggestions rather strange for the morning meal, there is probably no food that someone, somewhere, does not enjoy for breakfast. No doubt many Japanese, who have soybean soup, sour pickles, and rice for their first meal of the day, think Western breakfast habits are strange.

However, the egg remains a favorite breakfast food, even as we become more adventurous and explore ethnic cuisines. For such apparently simple items, eggs are used in many ways in the kitchen and require special study. We examine not only the usual breakfast preparation but other egg dishes as well, such as soufflés and custards.

After reading this chapter, you should be able to

1. Describe the composition of eggs and the major differences among grades.

2. Store eggs properly.

3. Prepare the following egg items: hard-, medium-, and soft-cooked eggs; poached eggs; fried eggs; shirred eggs; scrambled eggs; omelets; entrée soufflés; and savory custards.

4. List the key differences between waffle batter and pancake batter, and prepare each.

5. Prepare French toast, and identify the common variations possible by changing the basic ingredients.

6. Prepare each of the two general types of breakfast cereals.

7. Identify the three most common breakfast meats and prepare them.

UNDERSTANDING EGGS

COMPOSITION

A whole egg consists primarily of a yolk, a white, and a shell. In addition, it contains a membrane that lines the shell and forms an air cell at the large end, and two white strands called *chalazae* that hold the yolk centered. Figure 24.1 is a cross-sectional diagram that shows the location of these features.

1. The **yolk** is high in both fat and protein, and it contains iron and several vitamins. Its color ranges from light to dark yellow, depending on the diet of the chicken.

2. The **white** is primarily albumin protein, which is clear and soluble when raw but white and firm when coagulated. The white also contains sulfur.

    The white has two parts: a thick portion that surrounds the yolk, and a thinner, more liquid portion outside of this.

3. The **shell** is not the perfect package, in spite of what you may have heard. Not only is it fragile but it is also porous, allowing odors and flavors to be absorbed by the egg and allowing the egg to lose moisture even if unbroken.

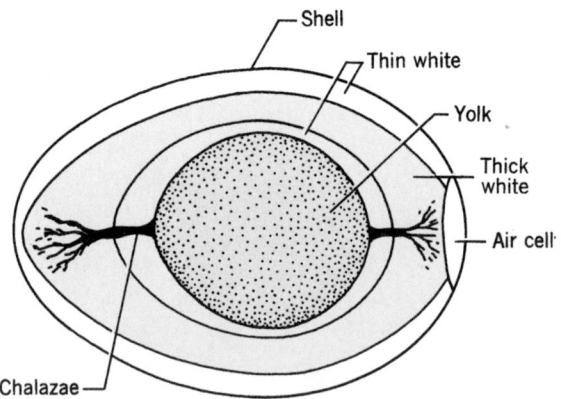

Figure 24.1
The parts of an egg. The diagram shows, in simplified form, the location of the parts of an unbroken egg, as described in the text.

GRADES AND QUALITY

Grades

In Canada, eggs are graded for quality at grading stations registered with the Canadian Food Inspection Agency (CFIA). The four grades are A, B, C, and Canada Nest Run.

The best grade (A) has a firm yolk and white that stand up high when broken onto a flat surface and do not spread over a large area. In the shell, the yolk is well centered, and the air sac is small.

As eggs age, they lose density. The thin part of the white becomes larger, and the egg spreads over a larger area when broken. Also, the air sac becomes larger as the egg loses moisture through the shell. Figure 24.3 shows the differences among grades A, B, and C.

In Canada, only grade A eggs are sold for retail use. Canada B eggs are sold for commercial baking, with their grade clearly marked. Canada C and Canada Nest Run are used for commercial processing. Grading is indicated by a maple leaf stamp (Figure 24.2).

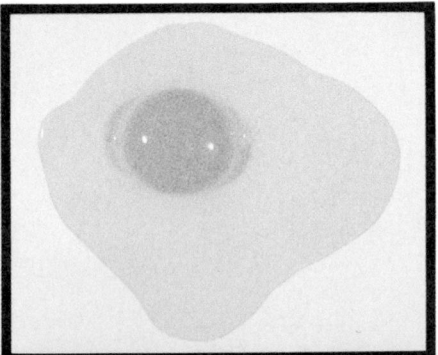

Figure 24.2
Canada grade stamp for eggs
Courtesy of the Canadian Food Inspection Agency

Figure 24.3
Egg grades. Courtesy of the USDA

(a) Grade A,

(b) Grade B, and

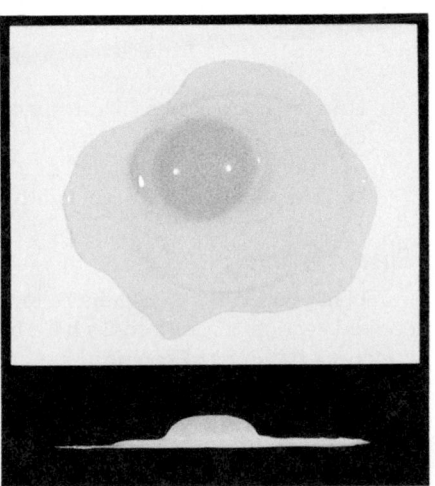

(c) Grade C eggs, as seen from the top and side. Note how the white and yolk lose thickness and spread more in the lower grades.

Maintaining Quality

Proper storage is essential for maintaining quality. Eggs keep for weeks if held at 36°F (2°C) but lose quality quickly if held at room temperature. In fact, they can lose a full grade in one day at warm kitchen temperatures. There's no point in paying for Grade A eggs if they are Grade B by the time you use them.

Store eggs away from foods that might pass on undesirable flavors or odors.

Grades and Use

One glance at Figure 24.3 will show you why Grade A is the best to use for fried or poached eggs. Lower grades spread out too much to produce a high-quality product.

For hard-cooked eggs, use Grade A eggs that have been held a few days in the refrigerator. Very fresh eggs are difficult to peel when cooked in the shell.

Grade B eggs are suitable for use in baking. If you are certain they have developed no strong flavors, they may be used for scrambled eggs, where the firmness of the whole egg is less important.

SIZE

Eggs are also graded by size. Table 24.1 gives the minimum weight per egg, including shell.

Most food service operations use large eggs, and recipes in most books are based on this size.

Table 24.1 Egg Size Classifications		
	Minimum Weight per Egg	
Size	**Canada**	**U.S.**
Jumbo	70 g or more	2½ oz or more
Extra-large	64 g	2½ oz
Large	56 g	2 oz
Medium	49 g	1½ oz
Small	42 g	1¼ oz
Peewee	less than 42 g	less than 1¼ oz

MARKET FORMS

1. **Fresh eggs or shell eggs.**
   These are most often used for breakfast cookery and are the main subject of this section.

2. **Frozen eggs.**
   - Whole eggs
   - Whites
   - Yolks
   - Whole eggs with extra yolks

   Frozen eggs are usually made from high-quality fresh eggs and are excellent for use in scrambled eggs, omelets, French toast, and in baking. They are pasteurized and are usually purchased in 30-pound (13.6-kg) cans. These take at least two days to thaw at refrigerator temperatures.

3. **Dried eggs.**
   - Whole eggs
   - Yolks
   - Whites

   Dried eggs are used primarily for baking. They are not suggested for use in breakfast cookery.
   Unlike most dehydrated products, dried eggs are not shelf-stable and must be kept refrigerated or frozen, tightly sealed.

Sanitation

In recent years, cases of salmonella food poisoning have been caused by raw or under-cooked eggs. As a result, cooks have been made more aware of egg-related sanitation concerns. Pasteurized egg products are used in more operations. For a more detailed discussion of eggs and food safety, see Appendix 5, page 1030.

EGG SUBSTITUTES

Egg yolks, in addition to being high in fat, are also high in cholesterol. Efforts to reduce cholesterol in the diet have led to the development of commercial egg substitutes. These are of two types:

1. Egg substitutes that can be used to make such dishes as scrambled eggs, omelets, and custards are made of pasteurized egg whites with the addition of a blend of ingredients to substitute for the yolks, such as vegetable oil, milk solids, vegetable gums, salt, emulsifiers, and vitamin additives. They are sold in bulk liquid form, usually frozen, and can be substituted, ounce for ounce, for whole liquid eggs in most egg preparations.

2. Eggless egg substitutes contain no egg product. They are made of flours or other starches, plus vegetable gums and stabilizers, and, sometimes, soy protein. They are intended for use in baked goods only and are not suitable for use in breakfast egg preparations or custards. If they contain no milk products (read ingredient lists on individual products), they may be used in vegan diets.

GENERAL COOKING PRINCIPLES

The most important rule of egg cookery is simple: *Avoid high temperatures and long cooking times.* In other words, do not overcook. This should be a familiar rule by now.
   Overcooking produces tough eggs, causes discoloration, and affects flavor.

Coagulation

Eggs are largely protein, so the principle of coagulation (p. 65) is important to consider.

Eggs coagulate at the following temperatures:

Whole eggs, beaten	about 156°F (69°C)
Whites	140° to 149°F (60° to 65°C)
Yolks	144° to 158°F (62° to 70°C)
Custard (whole eggs plus liquid)	175° to 185°F (79° to 85°C)

Note that whites coagulate or cook before yolks do. This is why it is possible to cook eggs with firm whites but soft yolks.

Note also that when eggs are mixed with a liquid, they become firm at a higher temperature. However, 185°F (85°C) is still much lower than the temperature of a sauté pan or skillet over high heat. As the temperature of coagulation is reached, the eggs change from semiliquid to solid, and they become opaque. If their temperature continues to rise, they become even firmer. *An overcooked egg is tough and rubbery.* Low temperatures produce the best-cooked eggs.

If egg-liquid mixtures such as custards and scrambled eggs are overcooked, the egg solids separate from the liquids, or **curdle**. This is often seen as tough, watery scrambled eggs.

Sulfur

The familiar green ring you often see in hard-cooked eggs is caused by cooking at high temperatures or cooking too long. The same green color appears in scrambled eggs that are overcooked or held too long in the steam table.

This ring results when the sulfur in the egg whites reacts with the iron in the yolk to form iron sulfide, a compound that has a green color and a strong odor and flavor. The best way to avoid green eggs is to use *low temperatures and short cooking and holding times.*

Foams

Beaten egg whites are used to give lightness and rising power to soufflés, puffy omelets, cakes, some pancakes and waffles, and other products. The following guidelines will help you handle beaten egg whites properly (see Figure 24.4).

1. **Fat inhibits foaming.**
   When separating eggs, be careful not to get any yolk in the whites. Yolks contain fats. Use very clean equipment when beating whites.

2. **Mild acids help foaming.**
   A small amount of lemon juice or cream of tartar gives more volume and stability to beaten egg whites. Use about 2 teaspoons cream of tartar per pound of egg whites (20 mL per kg).

3. **Egg whites foam better at room temperature.**
   Remove them from the cooler 1 hour before beating.

4. **Do not overbeat.**
   Beaten egg whites should look moist and shiny. Overbeaten eggs look dry and curdled and have lost much of their ability to raise soufflés and cakes.

5. **Sugar makes foams more stable.**
   When making sweet puffed omelets and dessert soufflés, add some of the sugar to the partially beaten whites and continue to beat to proper stiffness. (This will take longer than when no sugar is added.) The soufflé will be more stable before and after baking.

Figure 24.4
Whipping egg whites.

(a) The whites are just beginning to whip into a foam.

(b) The whites have reached the soft-peak stage.

(c) The whites have reached the firm-peak stage. Note the smooth texture. Whipping beyond this stage will cause the foam to break.

COOKING EGGS

SIMMERING IN THE SHELL

The term *hard-boiled egg* is not a good one to use because eggs should be simmered instead of boiled.

Eggs may be simmered in water to the soft-, medium-, or hard-cooked stage according to the following methods.

Procedures for Simmering Eggs in the Shell

Method 1

1. Collect equipment and food items.
2. Bring eggs to room temperature by (a) removing them from cooler 1 hour before cooking, or (b) placing them in warm water for 5 minutes and draining. Cold eggs are more likely to crack when placed in boiling water.
3. Place eggs in boiling water and return the water to a simmer.
4. Simmer, do not boil, for the required time:

   Soft-cooked   3 to 4 minutes

   Medium-cooked   5 to 7 minutes

   Hard-cooked   12 to 15 minutes

   Exact cooking time depends on temperature of eggs, size of eggs, and amount of water used.
5. Drain immediately and cool under cold running water to stop the cooking. Cool just a few seconds if eggs are to be served hot. Cool further if they are to be held for later use.
6. To peel, crack the shell and pull it away, starting at the large end (where the air sac is located). For easier peeling, peel while still warm, and hold under running water to help loosen shell. Very fresh eggs are hard to peel. Eggs for cooking in the shell should be several days old.

Method 2

1. Collect equipment and food items.
2. Place eggs in saucepan and cover with cold water.
3. Bring water to a boil.
4. Reduce heat and simmer for the required time:

   Soft-cooked   1 minute

   Medium-cooked   3 to 5 minutes

   Hard-cooked   9 to 10 minutes

Method 3; for Hard-Cooked Eggs Only

Proceed as in Method 2, but remove pan from heat and cover as soon as it comes to a boil. Let stand off heat for 20 minutes.

POACHING

The principles of cooking eggs in the shell are applicable to poached eggs. The only difference between the two items is the shell.

This difference, of course, complicates the cooking process, as emphasized in the following procedure. The object is to keep the eggs egg-shaped—that is, in a round, compact mass rather than spread all over the pan.

Standards of Quality for Poached Eggs

1. Bright, shiny appearance.
2. Compact, round shape, not spread or flattened.
3. Firm but tender whites; warm, liquid yolks.

Procedure for Poaching Eggs

1. Collect equipment and food items.
2. Use the freshest Grade A eggs whenever possible for best results. These maintain their shape best because the yolks and whites are firm.
3. If eggs are not very fresh, add 1 teaspoon salt and 2 teaspoons distilled vinegar per quart of water (5 mL salt and 10 mL vinegar per liter). The vinegar helps coagulate the egg white faster so it keeps a better shape.

   Vinegar is not necessary if very fresh eggs are used. Omit in this case because whites will be tougher and not as shiny if cooked with vinegar.
4. Bring water to a simmer.

   If water is boiling, eggs will toughen and may be broken up by the agitation.

   If water is not hot enough, eggs will not cook quickly enough and will spread.
5. Break eggs, one at a time, into a dish or a small plate and slide into the simmering water. Eggs will hold their shape better if they slide in against the edge of the pan.
6. Simmer 3 to 5 minutes, until whites are coagulated but yolks are still soft.
7. Remove eggs from pan with slotted spoon or skimmer.
8. To serve immediately, drain very well. For better appearance, trim off ragged edges.
9. To hold for later service, plunge immediately into cold water to stop the cooking. At service time, reheat briefly in hot water.

Eggs Benedict

Yield: 1 portion (see note)

U.S.	Metric	Ingredients
½	½	English muffin
as needed	as needed	Butter
1	1	Egg, fresh Grade A
1 slice	1 slice	Canadian bacon or ham, cooked (about 2 oz/60 g)
1½ fl oz	50 mL	Hollandaise Sauce (p. 182)

Per serving:
Calories, 660; Protein, 19 g; Fat, 58 g (79% cal.); Cholesterol, 480 mg; Carbohydrates, 15 g; Fiber, 1 g; Sodium, 1260 mg.

Note: To prepare Eggs Benedict in quantity, the eggs may be poached ahead of time, cooled in cold water, and refrigerated. At service time, reheat the eggs in simmering water for 30–60 seconds. Drain, plate, and serve.

■ Procedure

1. Toast the muffin half. Spread it with butter and place on a serving plate.
2. Poach the egg according to the basic procedure given in this section.
3. While the egg is poaching, heat the Canadian bacon or ham for 1 minute on a hot griddle or in a sauté pan. Place the meat on the toasted muffin.
4. Drain the poached egg well and place it on the Canadian bacon.
5. Ladle Hollandaise Sauce over the top. Serve immediately.

VARIATIONS

Eggs Florentine
Instead of the muffin and bacon, place the egg on a bed of hot, buttered cooked spinach (about 2 oz/60 g). Cover with Mornay sauce instead of hollandaise. Optional: Sprinkle with parmesan cheese and brown under the salamander or broiler.

Eggs Bombay
Instead of the muffin and bacon, place the egg on a bed of hot rice pilaf (about 2 oz/60 g). Cover with curry sauce instead of hollandaise.

FRYING

Fried eggs are an especially popular breakfast preparation. They should always be cooked to order and served immediately. For best quality, observe each step in the following procedure.

The choice of cooking fat is a matter of taste and budget. Butter has the best flavor, but margarine or oil may be used. Use bacon fat only if that flavor is desired by customer.

Procedure for Frying Eggs to Order

1. **Collect all equipment and food items.**

   Eggs may be fried in small, individual sauté pans (omelet pans) or on the griddle. Griddled eggs are not as attractive because they tend to spread more. See page 795 for the procedure for conditioning sauté pans to avoid sticking.

2. **Select very fresh Grade A eggs for best results.**

3. **Add about ⅛ inch (2 mm) fat to the sauté pan and set it over moderate heat, or preheat the griddle to 325°F (165°C) and ladle on a small quantity of fat.** Too much fat will make the eggs greasy. Not enough will cause them to stick, unless a pan with a nonstick coating is used.

4. **Break the eggs into a dish. This lessens the chance of breaking the yolks.**

5. **When the fat is hot enough so a drop of water sizzles when dropped into it, slide the eggs into the pan (or onto the griddle).**

   If the fat is not hot enough, the eggs will spread too much and may stick. If it is too hot, the eggs will become tough or even crisp.

6. **Reduce heat to low (if using sauté pan) and cook the eggs to order as indicated below. See Figures 24.5 and 24.6 for flipping and turning techniques.**

Figure 24.5
Flipping eggs in a pan.

(a) Lift the handle of the pan and slide the eggs to the far edge with a quick jerk.

(b) With a quick flip of the wrist, as shown by the arrow, turn the eggs over. Do not flip the eggs too hard, or the yolks may break when they land.

Figure 24.6

When frying eggs on a griddle, turn them with one smooth motion of the spatula, as shown. The left corner of the egg never actually leaves the surface of the griddle.

- **Sunny side up.** Cook slowly without flipping until white is completely set but yolk is still soft and yellow. Heat must be low, or bottom will toughen or burn before top is completely set.

- **Basted.** Do not flip. Add a few drops of water to pan and cover so steam cooks the top. A thin film of coagulated white will cover the yolk, which should remain liquid. *Note:* This preparation is sometimes called *country style*. The term *basted* is used because the same effect may be achieved by spooning hot fat over the egg as it fries. This method may make the eggs excessively greasy, however.

- **Over easy.** Fry and flip over. Cook just until the white is just set but the yolk is still liquid.

- **Over medium.** Fry and flip over. Cook until the yolk is partially set.

- **Over hard.** Fry and flip over. Cook until the yolk is completely set.

Standards of Quality for Fried Eggs

1. White should be shiny, uniformly set, and tender, not browned, blistered, or crisp at edges.

2. Yolk should be set properly according to desired doneness. Sunny-side-up yolks should be yellow and well rounded. In other styles, the yolk is covered with a thin layer of coagulated white.

3. Relatively compact, standing high. Not spread out and thin.

Huevos Rancheros

Yield: 1 portion

U.S.	Metric	Ingredients
as needed	as needed	Vegetable oil
1	1	Corn tortilla
2	2	Eggs
4 fl oz	125 mL	Salsa Roja (p. 190)
1 oz	30 g	Monterey jack or fresh Mexican white cheese, grated or crumbled

■ **P r o c e d u r e**

1. Heat a thin layer of oil in a sauté pan.
2. Fry the tortilla briefly in the oil, turning it once, until softened.
3. Remove from the pan and drain on paper towels.
4. Fry the eggs sunny side up or basted, following the procedure on page 792.
5. Place the tortilla on a warm dinner plate.
6. Top with the eggs.
7. Ladle the sauce over the whites of the eggs, leaving the yolks uncovered.
8. Top with the grated cheese.
9. If desired, add a portion of Frijoles Refritos (p. 611) to the plate.

Per serving:
Calories, 400; Protein, 22 g; Fat, 27 g (60% cal.); Cholesterol, 450 mg; Carbohydrates, 19 g; Fiber, 3 g; Sodium, 340 mg.

Huevos Rancheros

SHIRRED EGGS

Shirred eggs resemble fried eggs, except that they are baked in individual serving dishes rather than fried.

They may also be baked with or garnished with a variety of meats and sauces, as indicated in the variations that follow.

SHIRRED EGG VARIATIONS

Any of the following may be placed in the buttered shirred egg dish *before* adding the egg:

Ham or Canadian bacon, thin slice, lightly browned on griddle or in sauté pan

Bacon, cooked crisp, 3 or 4 half-strips

Corned beef hash, beef hash, or ham hash

Cheese, such as cheddar, Swiss, or Gruyère, grated

Diced chicken in cream sauce

Tomato concassé, sautéed in butter

Any of the following may be added to shirred eggs *after baking*. Place solid garnish to one side. Spoon sauces around the outside. Do not cover the yolk.

Heavy cream, hot

Brown sauces such as bordelaise, Madeira, or demiglaze

Procedure for Making Shirred Eggs

1. Collect equipment and food items.
2. Butter individual-portion casseroles or baking dishes.
3. Break eggs into dish.
4. Set over moderate heat until the eggs begin to coagulate on the bottom.
5. Place in oven at 350°F (175°C) and cook to desired doneness.
6. Serve in the same dish or casserole.

Tomato sauce

Soubise sauce

Sautéed chicken livers and brown sauce

Small grilled sausages

Mushrooms sautéed in butter or cream sauce

Asparagus tips

SCRAMBLED EGGS

Like other egg preparations, scrambled eggs are best if cooked to order. However, they may be made in larger quantities. They should be undercooked if they are to be held for volume service, as they will cook more in the steam table.

If scrambled eggs must be held over 30 minutes, they will be more stable if the eggs are mixed with a medium white sauce (béchamel) before cooking. Use about 8 ounces sauce per quart of eggs (250 mL per liter).

Do not overcook scrambled eggs or hold them too long. Overcooked eggs are tough and watery, and they eventually turn green in the steam table.

Scrambled eggs should be soft and moist, unless the customer requests "scrambled hard."

Procedure for Scrambling Eggs

1. Collect equipment and food items.
2. Break eggs into a stainless-steel bowl and beat until well blended. Season with salt and white pepper. Do not use aluminum, which may discolor the eggs.
3. If desired, add a small amount of milk or cream, about 1 to 1½ tablespoons (15 to 20 mL) for 2 eggs, or 8 to 12 ounces per quart of eggs (250 to 375 mL per liter).

   Too much liquid may make cooked eggs watery and dilutes the flavor. Heavy cream adds richness but also adds cost.
4. Heat butter in a small sauté pan (for cooking to order) or in a large skillet, as for fried eggs.

   Note: Steam kettles or tilting skillets may be used for scrambling large quantities of eggs.
5. When fat is just hot enough to make a drop of water sizzle, pour in eggs.
6. Cook over low heat, stirring gently from time to time as the eggs coagulate. Lift portions of coagulated egg so uncooked egg can run underneath.

   Too much stirring breaks up eggs into very small particles.

   Do not let the eggs brown. Keep heat low.
7. When eggs are set but still soft and moist, remove from heat. Turn out onto plate or into steam table pan.

Additions to Scrambled Eggs

Flavor variations may be created by adding any of the following ingredients to scrambled eggs before serving:

Chopped parsley and/or other herbs

Grated cheese (cheddar, Swiss, parmesan)

Diced ham

Crumbled bacon

Sautéed diced onion and green bell pepper

Diced smoked salmon

Sliced cooked breakfast sausage

OMELETS

Making omelets is like riding a bicycle. When you are learning, it seems difficult, and you can't imagine how anyone can do it. But once you have mastered the technique, it seems easy, and you don't understand how anyone could have trouble doing it.

We are talking about the plain or French omelet. There are several kinds, as described below, but the French omelet remains the most popular. Making it is a technique worth mastering.

French Omelet

Omelets may be described as sophisticated scrambled eggs. The first part of the technique is similar to that for making scrambled eggs. But the similarities end there, and the omelet emerges from the pan not as a shapeless pile of curds but an attractive oval with a light, delicate texture.

Two elements are necessary for making omelets:

1. High heat. This seems like a contradiction to our basic principle of low-temperature egg cookery. But the omelet cooks so fast that its internal temperature never has time to get too high.

2. A conditioned omelet pan. First, the pan must have sloping sides and be the right size so the omelet can be shaped properly. Second, it must be well seasoned or conditioned to avoid sticking.

Procedure for Conditioning an Omelet Pan

The following method is only one of many. Your instructor may show you another. The object is to seal the surface of the metal with a layer of baked-on oil.

1. Rub the clean pan with a thin film of vegetable oil.
2. Set the pan over moderately high heat until it is very hot.
3. Remove from heat and let cool.
4. Do not scour the pan or wash with a detergent after use. Rub with salt, which will scour the pan without harming the primed surface. Rinse only after pan has cooled, or wipe with a clean towel.
5. Reseason as often as necessary, or after each day's use.

Procedure for Making a French Omelet

See Figure 24.7 for illustration of technique.

1. Collect all equipment and ingredients.
2. Beat 2 or 3 eggs in a small bowl just until well mixed. Do not whip until frothy. Season with salt and pepper. If desired, 1 tablespoon (15 mL) water may be added to make the omelet lighter.

   For extended service, beat a large quantity of eggs. Measure each portion with a ladle.
3. Place an omelet pan over high heat.
4. When the pan is hot, add about 1 tablespoon (15 mL) clarified butter and swirl it around to coat the inside of the pan. Give it a second to get hot.

   Raw butter may be used, but great care is necessary to keep it from burning.
5. Add the eggs to the pan. They should begin to coagulate around the edges and on the bottom in a few seconds.
6. With one hand (the left, if you are right-handed), vigorously shake the pan back and forth. At the same time, stir the eggs with a circular motion with the bottom side of a fork, but do not let the fork scrape the pan.

   This is the difficult part. The most common errors are not shaking and stirring vigorously enough and using heat that is too low. The purpose of this action is to keep the eggs in motion so they coagulate uniformly.
7. Stop shaking and stirring when the eggs are almost set but still very moist. If you continue stirring, you will have scrambled eggs instead of an omelet.
8. Tilt the handle up and shake the pan so the omelet slides to the opposite side of the pan and begins to climb up the opposite slope.
9. For a filled omelet, spoon the filling across the center of the egg, perpendicular to the handle.
10. With the fork, fold the sides of the omelet over the center. The omelet should now be resting in the corner of the pan and have an approximately oval shape.
11. Grasp the handle of the pan with your palm underneath and tilt the omelet out onto a plate so it inverts and keeps an oval shape.

    The whole procedure should take less than 1 minute.

    The finished omelet should be moist on the inside, tender on the outside, and yellow or only slightly browned.

Figure 24.7
Making a French omelet. Read the accompanying text for a full description of the steps shown here.

(a) As soon as the eggs are added to the hot pan, shake the pan back and forth with one hand and stir the eggs in a circular motion with a fork.

(b) When the eggs are almost set, tilt the pan and shake the eggs down to the opposite side of the pan. Rapping the handle sharply helps move the eggs.

(c) Spoon the filling, if used, across the center.

(d) Fold over the side of the omelet to make an oval shape.

(e) Grasp the handle of the pan with your palm underneath and tilt the omelet onto a plate.

(f) The finished omelet should have a neat, oval shape. Some chefs prefer omelets that are lightly browned. Others feel that they should not be browned at all.

Suggested Omelet Fillings

Cheese

Sautéed or creamed mushrooms

Creamed or curried chicken

Creamed or buttered spinach

Sautéed onions, with or without bacon

Sautéed onions and diced potatoes

Seafood Newburg or in a cream sauce

Red caviar

Thick Spanish Sauce (p. 176)

Ratatouille (p. 563)

American-Style or Folded Omelet

This style of omelet is often called a *French omelet*, but it is not a French omelet. It was probably devised by cooks who hesitated to tackle the French method.

It is made somewhat like a French omelet, except that low heat is used and the eggs are not stirred or agitated. Instead, the edges of the cooked portion are lifted with a fork or spatula, allowing the uncooked portion to flow underneath. The finished omelet may be folded in half or like a French omelet.

The advantage of this method is that it is easier to learn.

The disadvantages are that the omelet is not as light or delicate in texture, and that the method is much slower.

Fluffy Omelet or Soufflé Omelet

These omelets are made by beating the egg whites separately and folding them into the beaten yolks, which may have some milk added. The mixture is poured into a hot, buttered omelet pan, and the omelet is finished in the oven. It is folded in half for service.

Fluffy omelets are not often made in food service because of the time they take to make.

Frittatas and Other Flat Omelets

A frittata is a flat omelet that originated in Italy. The same basic techniques are used for many popular American preparations. Flat omelets are made by mixing beaten eggs with a variety of ingredients, such as vegetables, meats, or cheese, and cooking the mixture over low heat without stirring. To finish, it is either flipped over or run under the broiler or into the oven until the top is set.

A popular American frittata (actually derived from the Chinese egg foo yung) is the Western omelet, containing diced sautéed onion, green bell pepper, and ham.

SOUFFLÉS

Soufflés are not normally featured on breakfast menus. However, they are important basic egg preparations with which you should be familiar.

Soufflés are often considered by amateur cooks to be difficult to make. Actually, they are relatively easy preparations. Many restaurants have no difficulty turning out large numbers of soufflés to order. The only hard part is making sure the waiter picks up the order when it is ready.

A standard entrée soufflé consists of three elements:

1. Base—usually a heavy béchamel sauce.
2. Flavor ingredient—cheese, vegetables, seafood, etc.
3. Egg whites, beaten

General Procedure for Preparing Entrée Soufflés

1. Prepare a heavy béchamel sauce.
2. Combine the sauce with egg yolks.
3. Prepare the flavor ingredient—grate cheese, cook and chop vegetables, and so on.
4. Combine the base and the flavor ingredient.
5. Beat egg whites and fold in.
6. Bake in a soufflé dish that has been buttered and dusted with parmesan cheese.
7. Serve immediately.

À la Carte Service

Prepare through step 4 and hold in refrigerator.

If several flavors are offered, prepare a single large batch of base and keep the flavor ingredients separate.

For each order, beat egg whites and combine with measured amount of base.

Summer Squash, Spinach, and Leek Frittata

Yield: 4 portions

U.S.	Metric	Ingredients	Procedure
4 oz	125 g	Leeks, white part and a little of the green, trimmed and cleaned	1. Split the leeks lengthwise in half, and then slice crosswise into thin slices.
10 oz	300 g	Yellow summer squash or zucchini	2. Trim and slice the squash.
1 oz	30 g	Butter	3. Heat the butter in a sauté pan over moderate heat.
8 oz	250 g	Spinach leaves (no stems)	4. Add the leeks and sauté until wilted.
			5. Add the squash and sauté until just tender.
			6. Remove from the pan and cool.
			7. Blanch the spinach in boiling water until wilted.
			8. Drain and cool the spinach in cold water. Drain again and squeeze dry.
			9. Chop the spinach coarsely and mix it with the squash.
6	6	Eggs	10. Beat the eggs and add them to the vegetables.
to taste	to taste	Salt	11. Add salt and pepper to taste
to taste	to taste	Pepper	12. Heat the butter over moderate heat in a well-seasoned or, preferably, a nonstick 10-in. (25-cm) sauté pan (see note).
½ oz	15 g	Butter	13. Add the egg mixture. Immediately lower the heat to as low as possible. Cover loosely.
			14. Cook slowly until the eggs are mostly set but creamy in the middle.
			15. Place the pan under the broiler until the eggs are set.
			16. Slide the frittata onto a plate.
			17. Cut into 4 wedges. Serve immediately.

Per serving:
Calories, 230; Protein, 12 g; Fat, 17 g (65% cal.); Cholesterol, 340 mg; Carbohydrates, 9 g; Fiber, 3 g; Sodium, 220 mg.

Note: To make individual portions to order, cook one-fourth of the egg mixture in a 6-in. (15-cm) sauté pan.

Summer Squash, Spinach, and Leek Frittata

Cheese Soufflé

Portions: 12 Portion size: 4 oz (125 g)

U.S.	Metric	Ingredients	
as needed	as needed	Butter	
as needed	as needed	Parmesan cheese or dry bread crumbs	
		Roux:	
2½ oz	75 g	Butter	
2½ oz	75 g	Flour	
1½ pt	750 mL	Milk, hot	
1½ tsp	7 mL	Salt	
1 tsp	5 mL	White pepper	
pinch	pinch	Cayenne	
pinch	pinch	Nutmeg	
12	12	Egg yolks	
10 oz	300 g	Gruyère cheese, coarsely grated (see note)	
12–15	12–15	Egg whites	
¼ tsp	1 mL	Salt	

▪ P r o c e d u r e

1. Select three 1½-qt (1½-L) soufflé dishes (4 portions each) or two 2-qt (2-L) dishes (6 portions each). Butter the insides of the dishes well. Sprinkle with cheese or crumbs so that the bottom and sides are completely coated.

2. Make a white roux with the butter and flour. Cook the roux a few minutes.

3. Beat in the hot milk. Bring to a boil, while stirring. Cool and stir until very thick and smooth.

4. Remove from the heat. Stir in the salt, pepper, cayenne, and nutmeg.

5. Add the egg yolks to the hot sauce and quickly mix in with a wire whip.

6. Stir in the cheese.

7. Beat the egg whites with the salt until they form stiff peaks. (The larger number of egg whites will make a lighter soufflé.)

8. Fold the egg whites into the cheese mixutre.

9. Pour the mixture into the prepared soufflé dishes.

10. Place the dishes in a preheated 375°F (190°C) oven. Bake for 40 minutes without opening the oven door. After this time, check for doneness by *very gently* shaking the dishes. If the centers are firm and do not jiggle, the soufflés are done. If necessary, bake another 5–10 minutes.

11. Remove from oven and serve *immediately*.

Per serving:
Calories, 290; Protein, 17 g; Fat, 21 g (65% cal.); Cholesterol, 265 mg; Carbohydrates, 8 g; Fiber, 0 g; Sodium, 600 mg.

Note: Other cheeses may be used: sharp cheddar, Swiss, a mixture of Swiss and Gruyère, or a mixture of Swiss or Gruyère and parmesan.

V A R I A T I O N S

À la Carte Service: Prepare basic recipe through step 6. Chill mixture quickly and hold in refrigerator. For each order, scale off 3½ oz (100 g) of the mixture. Beat 1 egg white and fold in. Bake in an individual soufflé dish about 20–30 minutes.

Spinach Soufflé
Reduce cheese to 5 oz (150 g). Add 5 oz (150 g) well-drained, chopped cooked spinach.

Spinach and Ham Soufflé
Add 2 oz (60 g) ground or finely chopped ham to Spinach Soufflé.

Mushroom Soufflé
Reduce cheese to 5 oz (150 g). Add 4 oz (125 g) cooked chopped mushrooms.

Other Vegetable Soufflés
Follow the procedure for Spinach Soufflé, using chopped cooked vegetables such as broccoli, asparagus, or carrots.

Salmon Soufflé
Make the sauce base with milk plus liquid from canned salmon. Add 1½ oz (45 g) tomato paste to the base. Reduce cheese to 4 oz (125 g) and add 8 oz (250 g) flaked canned salmon.

CUSTARDS

A **custard** is a liquid that is thickened or set by the coagulation of egg protein.
There are two basic kinds of custards:

1. *Stirred custard*, which is stirred as it cooks and remains pourable when done.
2. *Baked custard*, which is not stirred and which sets firm.

One basic rule governs the preparation of both custards: *Do not heat custards higher than an internal temperature of 185°F (85°C).*

This temperature, as you know, is the point at which egg-liquid mixtures coagulate. If they are heated more than this, they tend to curdle. An overbaked custard becomes watery because the moisture separates from the toughened protein.

Most custards are sweet. These preparations are covered in the baking and dessert section of this book. You may have already encountered a savory custard in the recipe for Spinach Timbales (p. 568).

The **quiche** (keesh), which is a custard baked in a pastry shell, is probably the most popular form of savory custard. The following recipe illustrates the technique for preparing savory custards.

Quiche au Fromage (Cheese Tart)

Yield: four 8-inch (20 cm) tarts | **Portion: 24 / 16** | **Portion size: ⅙ of tart / ¼ of tart**

U.S.	Metric	Ingredients	Procedure
2 lb	900 g	Mealy Pie Dough (p. 980)	1. Scale the dough into 4 pieces, 8 oz (225 g) each. 2. Roll the dough into 4 circles, ⅛ in. (3 mm) thick. 3. Fit the dough into four 8-in. (20-cm) pie pans or tart pans. 4. Hold the pie shells in the refrigerator until needed (see note).
1 lb	450 g	Swiss or Gruyère cheese, grated	5. Sprinkle 4 oz (110 g) cheese into the bottom of each tart shell.
12	12	Eggs, beaten	6. Beat together the eggs, cream, milk, and seasonings. Pour into the tart shells.
1 pt	500 mL	Heavy cream	
2 pt	950 mL	Milk	7. Place the tarts in a 375°F (190°C) oven on the bottom shelf or, if using a deck oven, directly on the deck.
2 tsp	10 mL	Salt	8. Bake until the filling is set, about 20–30 minutes.
¼ tsp	1 mL	White pepper	9. Serve hot or cold. Cut into wedges of desired size.
⅛ tsp	0.5 mL	Nutmeg	

Per serving:
Calories, 370; Protein, 12 g; Fat, 30 g (69% cal.); Cholesterol, 155 mg; Carbohydrates, 18 g; Fiber, 3 g; Sodium, 450 mg.

Note: Pastry shells may be partially baked before filling if uncooked bottoms tend to be a problem. This is sometimes the case if you are using shiny aluminum pie pans or if the bottom heat of the oven isn't strong enough. See page 982 for procedure.

VARIATIONS

Quiche Lorraine
Dice 1 lb (450 g) bacon strips and cook until crisp. Drain and add to pie shell in step 5. Omit cheese or leave it in, as desired. (Quiche Lorraine was originally made without cheese.)

Onion Quiche
Sauté 2 lb (900 g) sliced onions very slowly in 2 oz (60 g) butter until golden and tender. Cool and add to empty pie shells. Reduce cheese to 8 oz (225 g).

Spinach Quiche
Sauté 3 oz (90 g) chopped onion in 3 oz (90 g) butter until soft. Add 1½ lb (700 g) cooked, drained chopped spinach. Sauté until most of the liquid has evaporated. Cool and add to empty pie shell. Omit cheese.

Mushroom Quiche
Sauté 2 lb (900 g) sliced mushrooms and 3 oz (90 g) chopped onion in 3 oz (90 g) butter. Add 1 tbsp (15 mL) lemon juice to keep the mushrooms white. Cook until juices have evaporated. Cool and add to the empty pie shell. Omit cheese.

Seafood Quiche
Substitute 8 oz (225 g) cooked diced shrimp and 8 oz (225 g) cooked diced crabmeat for the cheese. Add 3 fl oz (90 mL) sherry and 2 oz (60 g) tomato paste to the egg mixture.

BREAKFAST BREADS, CEREALS, AND MEATS

Bread items probably play a more important role at breakfast than even eggs. Hardly an order of eggs is sold without an order of toast on the side. And for the diner who prefers a continental breakfast, coffee and a bread item such as a roll or pastry constitute the entire breakfast.

Except for toast, few breakfast breads are prepared to order. Most operations purchase such items ready-made. These products include muffins, doughnuts, Danish pastries, sweet rolls, and regional favorites such as bagels and corn bread.

In this section, we consider three items that are made to order: pancakes, waffles, and French toast. You may not think of pancakes and waffles as breads, but they are actually a form of quick bread, a category of foods we consider in more detail in the baking section of this book.

PANCAKES AND WAFFLES

Waffles and pancakes, also called *griddle cakes* and *hot cakes*, are made from pourable batters. Pancakes are made on a griddle, while waffles are made on a special tool called a *waffle iron*.

Both items should be cooked to order and served hot. Waffles lose their crispness very quickly, and pancakes toughen as they are held. However, batters may be prepared ahead and are often mixed the night before.

Serve with butter and with maple syrup or syrup blends (pure maple syrup is expensive). Other condiments that may accompany these items are fruit syrups, jams and preserves, applesauce, and fruits such as strawberries or blueberries.

INGREDIENTS AND PROCEDURES

Compare the basic pancake and waffle recipes and note how much alike the batters are, with important exceptions:

1. Waffle batter contains more fat.
2. Waffle batter contains less liquid, so it is slightly thicker.
3. Waffles are given extra lightness when the egg whites are beaten separately and folded into the batter. (Some recipes omit this step.)

A standard-size pancake requires ¼ cup (60 mL) batter. The amount of batter needed for waffles depends on the size of the waffle iron.

PRE-PREPARATION FOR VOLUME SERVICE

Pancake and waffle batters leavened by *baking powder only* may be mixed the night before and stored in the cooler. Some rising power may be lost, so baking powder may have to be increased.

Batters leavened by baking soda should not be made too far ahead because the soda will lose its power. Mix dry ingredients and liquid ingredients ahead and combine just before service.

Batters using beaten egg whites and baking powder may be partially made ahead, but *incorporate the egg whites just before service.*

Buttermilk Pancakes

Yield: 3½ pt (1.75 L) batter, enough for 25–30 large or 50 medium pancakes

U.S.	Metric	Ingredients	
1 lb	500 g	Pastry flour or all-purpose flour	**■ P r o c e d u r e**
2 oz	60 g	Sugar	1. Sift together the flour, sugar, salt, baking powder, and baking soda.
1 tsp	5 mL	Salt	
1 tbsp	15 mL	Baking powder	
1½ tsp	7 mL	Baking soda	
4	4	Eggs, beaten	2. Mix together the beaten eggs, buttermilk, and butter or oil.
1 qt	1 L	Buttermilk	3. Add the liquid ingredients to the dry ingredients. Mix just until the dry ingredients are thoroughly moistened. Do not overmix. (Note: Buttermilk makes a thick batter. Thin with a little skim milk or water if the batter seems too thick.)
4 fl oz	125 mL	Melted butter or oil	

4. Depending on the size pancake desired, measure 1–2 fl oz (30–60 mL) portions of the batter onto a greased, preheated griddle (375°F/190°C), allowing space for spreading.

5. Griddle the pancakes until the tops are full of bubbles and begin to look dry and the bottoms are golden brown. Turn and brown the other side.

6. Remove from the griddle and serve.

Per one 2-ounce pancake:
Calories, 120; Protein, 4 g; Fat, 5 g (36% cal.); Cholesterol, 40 mg; Carbohydrates, 16 g; Fiber, 0 g; Sodium, 250 mg.

 ## Waffles

Yield: 3½ pt (1.75 L) batter

U.S.	Metric	Ingredients	
1 lb 4 oz	625g	Pastry flour or all-purpose flour	**■ P r o c e d u r e**
1 tsp	5 mL	Salt	1. Sift together the flour, salt, and baking powder.
2 tbsp	30 mL	Baking powder	
6	6	Egg yolks, beaten	2. Mix together the egg yolks, milk, and butter or oil.
1½ pt	750 mL	Milk	3. Add the liquid ingredients to the dry ingredients. Mix just until the dry ingredients are thoroughly moistened. Do not overmix.
8 fl oz	250 mL	Melted butter or oil	
6	6	Egg whites	4. Whip the egg whites until they form soft peaks. Add the sugar and whip until stiff peaks form.
2 oz	60 g	Sugar	

5. Fold the egg whites into the batter.

6. Pour enough batter onto a lightly greased, preheated waffle iron to almost cover the surface with a thin layer. Close the iron.

7. Cook waffles until signal light indicates they are done or until steam is no longer emitted.

8. Remove from the iron and serve.

Per 1 ounce of batter:
Calories, 80; Protein, 2 g; Fat, 4 g (45% cal.); Cholesterol, 30 mg; Carbohydrates, 9 g; Fiber, 0 g; Sodium, 100 mg.

Buckwheat Pancakes

Yield: 2 qt (2 L) batter, enough for about 30 large or 50 medium pancakes

U.S.	Metric	Ingredients
6 oz	180 g	Buckwheat flour
8 oz	240 g	Pastry flour or all-purpose flour
4 tsp	20 mL	Baking powder
1 tsp	5 mL	Salt
4	4	Egg yolks, beaten
2 pt	1 L	Milk
4 oz	120 g	Melted butter
5 fl oz	150 mL	Honey
4	4	Egg whites

■ P r o c e d u r e

1. Sift together the flours, baking powder, and salt.

2. Mix together the egg yolks, milk, melted butter, and honey.

3. Add the liquid ingredients to the dry ingredients. Mix just until the dry ingredients are thoroughly moistened. Do not overmix.

4. Whip the egg whites until they form soft peaks.

5. Fold the egg whites into the batter.

6. Depending on the size pancake desired, measure 1–2 oz (30–60 g) portions of the batter onto a greased, preheated griddle (375°F/190°C), allowing space for spreading.

7. Griddle the pancakes until the tops are full of bubbles and begin to look dry and the bottoms are golden brown. Turn and brown the other side.

8. Remove from the griddle and serve.

Per one 2-ounce pancake:
Calories, 120; Protein, 3 g; Fat, 4.5 g (35% cal.); Cholesterol, 35 mg; Carbohydrates, 16 g; Fiber, 1 g; Sodium, 140 mg.

FRENCH TOAST

French toast in different versions is popular in many regions, and it has the added advantage of being an excellent way to utilize day-old bread.

Basic French toast consists of slices of bread dipped in a batter of eggs, milk, a little sugar, and flavorings. French toast is cooked on a griddle like pancakes.

Variations may be created by changing the basic ingredients:

Bread. White pullman bread is standard. Specialty versions can be made with French bread, rich egg bread, or whole-grain breads.

Batter. Milk is the usual liquid, mixed with egg in various proportions. Deluxe versions may include cream or sour cream.

Flavorings. Vanilla, cinnamon, and nutmeg are popular choices. Other possibilities are grated lemon and orange rind, ground anise, rum, and brandy.

The most common fault in making French toast is not soaking the bread long enough to allow the batter to penetrate. If the bread is just dipped in the batter, the final product is just dry bread with a little egg on the outside.

French toast is dusted with powdered sugar and served, like pancakes, with accompanying butter, syrups, preserves, or fruits.

Cinnamon Raisin French Toast

Portions: 6   Portion size: 2 slices

U.S.	Metric	Ingredients
6	6	Eggs
12 fl oz	375 mL	Milk
4 fl oz	125 mL	Heavy cream
4 oz	125 g	Sugar
1 tbsp	15 mL	Vanilla extract
1 tsp	5 mL	Cinnamon
⅛ tsp	0.5 mL	Nutmeg
⅛ tsp	0.5 mL	Salt
12 slices	12 slices	Cinnamon raisin bread, ¾ in. (2 cm) thick
1½ oz	45 g	Butter
as needed	as needed	Confectioners' sugar

Per serving:
Calories, 470; Protein, 15 g; Fat, 23 g (43% cal.); Cholesterol, 260 mg;
Carbohydrates, 51 g; Fiber, 2 g; Sodium, 400 mg.

■ P r o c e d u r e

1. Beat together the eggs, milk, cream, sugar, vanilla, cinnamon, nutmeg, and salt until the sugar is dissolved.

2. Soak the bread in the egg mixture until the bread is soaked through, but do not leave so long that it falls apart.

3. For each portion, heat 1½ tsp (7 mL) butter in a sauté pan large enough to hold two slices of bread.

4. Put 2 slices of bread in the pan and brown the bottoms.

5. Turn the bread over and cook for 30 seconds.

6. Transfer the sauté pan to an oven preheated to 375°F (190°C). Bake 10 minutes. The bread should be cooked through and slightly puffed up.

7. Plate, dust with confectioners' sugar, and serve immediately.

V A R I A T I O N

The amount of batter in the recipe is enough to soak about 24 thin slices of presliced bread. Regular slices of bread are thin enough to be cooked from start to finish on a griddle or in a sauté pan.

Cinnamon Raisin French Toast

CEREALS

HOT, COOKED CEREALS

Cooked cereals are of two types:

1.   Whole, cracked, or flaked cereals, such as oatmeal (rolled oats), Scotch oatmeal (cracked oats), and cracked wheat. The particles are large and can be added to boiling water without lumping.

2.   Granular cereals, such as farina and cornmeal. The particles are small and tend to lump when added to boiling water.
     For more information on cooking grains, see Chapter 19.

Procedure for Cooking Whole, Cracked, or Flaked Cereals

1.   Collect equipment and ingredients.
2.   Measure the correct amount of water and salt into a pot and bring to a boil. Read package directions for quantities.
     Using milk or part milk makes a richer cereal, but a more expensive one. Be careful not to scorch the milk if you use it.
3.   Measure the correct amount of cereal.
4.   Add the cereal slowly, stirring constantly.
5.   Stir until some thickening takes place, then stop stirring. Too much stirring makes cereal gummy.
6.   Reduce heat to a slow simmer, cover, and cook until desired doneness and consistency are reached. Cooking times vary greatly.
7.   Keep covered until service to prevent drying.

Procedure for Cooking Granular Cereals

The procedure is the same as above, except the cereal is mixed with a little cold water before being added to boiling water. This separates the grains and prevents lumping. The cold water must be calculated as part of the total amount of liquid.

COLD CEREALS

Cold, dry cereals are purchased ready prepared and need no preparation by the kitchen. Like hot cereals, they are served with accompanying milk or cream, sugar, and, sometimes, fruit such as berries or sliced bananas.

BREAKFAST MEATS

Meats and meat cooking methods are covered in previous chapters, but we mention them again because three meats in particular—bacon, sausage, and ham—appear on most breakfast menus.

BACON

Bacon is a cured, smoked pork product. It is available in whole slabs but is almost always purchased sliced. Thickness of slices is specified by number of slices per pound, usually 18 to 22 (40 to 48 per kilogram).

Low-temperature cooking applies to bacon as well as to other meats. Bacon is about 70 percent fat and shrinks a great deal. However, cooking at low temperatures minimizes shrinkage. The oven is most often used for cooking bacon in quantity, though a griddle or sauté pan may also be used.

To cook in the oven, lay out the bacon strips on sheet pans in a single layer, or, even better, on racks over sheet pans. (Bacon may be purchased already laid out on parchment.) Bake at 300° to 350°F (150° to 175°C) until about three-fourths done. Remove from the oven, being careful not to spill the hot fat. Finish individual portions to order on the griddle or in the oven, cooking them until crisp.

HAM

Ham for breakfast service is almost always precooked. Slices in 3- to 4-ounce (90- to 115-g) portions need only be heated and browned slightly on a griddle or under the broiler.

Canadian bacon is boneless pork loin that is cured and smoked like ham. It is handled like ham in the kitchen.

SAUSAGE

Breakfast sausage is simply fresh pork that has been ground and seasoned. It is available in three forms: patties, links, and bulk.

Because it is fresh pork, sausage must be cooked well done. This does not mean, however, that it should be cooked until it is just hard, dry, shrunken little nuggets, as it often is.

Most kitchens cook sausages by the same methods as bacon. For volume service, sausage is partially cooked in the oven and then finished to order. Link sausages hold better than patties because the links are protected from drying by their casings.

■ TERMS FOR REVIEW

yolk	shirred	over medium	custard
white	sunny side up	over hard	quiche
shell	basted	frittata	breakfast sausage
curdle	over easy	soufflé	

■ QUESTIONS FOR DISCUSSION

1. Which grade of eggs would you choose to prepare poached eggs? hard-cooked eggs? fried eggs? scrambled eggs? Why?

2. Is it possible to prepare hard-cooked eggs in a pressure steamer? Give reasons for your answer.

3. When separating eggs, many chefs advise breaking them one by one over a small bowl, then transferring each white to the larger bowl as it is separated. Can you give a reason for this advice?

4. Give two reasons for being careful not to add too much vinegar to egg poaching water.

5. In the recipe for waffles, what is the purpose of beating the sugar into the egg whites rather than combining it with the other dry ingredients?

6. What special precautions might you take if you were making French toast from thick slices of French bread?

25

Dairy and Beverages

Milk is one our most versatile foods, not only as a beverage but even more importantly as a cooking and baking ingredient and as a raw material for the production of a wide array of other foods, including cream, butter, and hundreds of kinds of cheese.

This chapter identifies and describes the many dairy products used regularly in the kitchen and gives guidelines for handling, storing and cooking with them. The longest section of the chapter describes the many types of cheeses produced in North America and Europe and gives examples of each type.

The chapter concludes with a discussion of coffee and tea beverages, including guidelines for their production.

DAIRY PRODUCTS

MILK AND CREAM

CATEGORIES AND DEFINITIONS

When we talk about milk and cream used in food service, we are nearly always talking about milk from cows. Milk from other animals, including goats, sheep, and water buffaloes, is used to make some cheeses, but most of the liquid milk we see, except for a small amount of goat milk, is milk from dairy cattle.

Milk is used as a beverage and also in cooking. Similarly, other milk products, including cream, butter, and cheese, are eaten as purchased and also used in cooking.

Pasteurization

Liquid milk, directly as it comes from the cow and before it has had anything done to it, is called *raw milk*. Because raw milk may contain disease-causing bacteria or other organisms, it is almost always **pasteurized** before being sold or before being processed into other products. Pasteurized milk has been heated to 161°F (72°C) and held at this temperature for 15 seconds to kill disease-causing organisms, and then quickly chilled. By law, all Grade A liquid milk and cream must be pasteurized. (Grades B and C are used in food processing and industrial uses and are rarely seen in food service or in the retail market.)

Even after pasteurizing, milk and cream are highly perishable products. Some cream products are **ultra-pasteurized** to extend their shelf life. By heating the product to a much higher temperature (275°F/135°C) for 4 seconds, this process kills not only disease-causing bacteria but nearly all organisms that cause spoilage. Ultra-pasteurized products must still be refrigerated both before and after opening.

Ultra-High-Temperature (UHT) pasteurization involves even higher temperatures. The resulting product is packed into sterile cartons. If the cartons are unopened, the milk will keep at room temperature for up to 10 months. Once opened, the milk must be refrigerated like regular pasteurized milk. UHT milk has a somewhat cooked taste and is better suited to cooking than for drinking as a beverage.

Fresh Milk Products

Whole milk is fresh milk as it comes from the cow, with nothing removed and nothing (except vitamin D) added. It contains about 3½ percent fat (known as **milk fat** or **butterfat**), 8½ percent nonfat milk solids, and 88 percent water.

Skim or **nonfat milk** has had most or all of the fat removed. Its fat content is 0.5 percent or less.

2 percent milk has a fat content of between 1.9 percent and 2.1 percent, while **partially skimmed milk** has a fat content of between 0.9 percent and 1.1 percent. Both these products must contain at least 8.5 percent milk solids (other than milk fat), the same as for whole milk. Both these products are usually fortified with Vitamin A and Vitamin D.

Fortified nonfat or *low-fat milk* has had substances added to increase its nutritional value, usually vitamins A and D and extra nonfat milk solids.

Flavored milks, such as *chocolate milk*, have had flavoring ingredients added. A label such as *chocolate milk drink* or *chocolate-flavored drink* indicates that the product does not meet the standards for regular milk. Read ingredient labels.

Except of course for nonfat milk, natural liquid milk contains fat, which, because it is lighter than water, will gradually separate and float to the top in the form of cream. **Homogenized milk** has been processed so the cream doesn't separate out. This is done by forcing the milk through very tiny holes, which breaks the fat into particles so small they stay distributed in the milk. Nearly all liquid milk on the market has been homogenized.

After reading this chapter, you should be able to

1. Describe the major milk, cream, and butter products.

2. Explain why milk curdles and why it scorches, and identify the steps to take to prevent curdling and scorching.

3. Whip cream.

4. Describe the most important kinds of cheese used in the kitchen.

5. Store and serve cheese properly.

6. Cook with cheese.

7. Prepare coffee and tea.

Fresh Cream Products

Whipping cream has a fat content of 32 to 40 percent. Whipping cream labeled *ultra-pasteurized* keeps longer than regular pasteurized cream. Pure ultra-pasteurized cream does not whip as well as regular pasteurized cream, so additives such as vegetable gums are added to it to make it more whippable.

Double cream is richer than regular whipping cream. It contains 40 percent or more milk fat.

Table cream, also called **coffee cream**, contains between 16 and 32 percent fat, usually about 18 percent.

Half-and-half has a fat content of 10 to 12 percent.

Fermented Milk and Cream Products

Sour cream has been cultured or fermented by added lactic acid bacteria, which makes it thick and slightly tangy in flavor. It has about 18 percent fat.

Crème fraîche (kremm fresh) is a slightly aged, cultured heavy cream. It is widely used for sauce-making in Europe because of its pleasant, slightly tangy flavor and its ability to blend easily into sauces. Unlike regular heavy cream, it usually doesn't require tempering and can be added directly to hot sauces. It is available commercially but is expensive. A close approximation can be made by warming 1 quart (1 L) heavy cream to about 100°F (38°C), adding 1½ ounces (50 mL) buttermilk, and letting the mixture stand in a warm place until slightly thickened, about 6 to 24 hours.

Buttermilk is fresh, liquid milk, usually skim milk, which has been cultured or soured by bacteria. It is usually called *cultured buttermilk* to distinguish it from the original buttermilk, which was the liquid left after butter-making. Buttermilk is used in recipes calling for sour milk.

Yogurt is milk (whole or low-fat) cultured by special bacteria. It has a custardlike consistency. Most yogurt has additional milk solids added, and some of it is flavored and sweetened.

Milk Products with Water Removed

Evaporated milk is milk, either whole or skim, with at least 50 percent of the water removed. It is then sterilized and canned. Evaporated milk has a somewhat cooked flavor. Evaporated milk made from skim or low-fat milk is labelled as such.

Condensed milk is whole milk that has had about 60 percent of the water removed and is heavily sweetened with sugar. It is available canned and in bulk.

Dried whole milk is whole milk that has been dried to a powder. **Nonfat dry milk** is skim milk that has been dried in the same way. Both are available in regular form and in instant form, which dissolves in water more easily.

ARTIFICIAL DAIRY PRODUCTS

A wide variety of imitation cream and dessert topping products are made from various fats and chemicals, which are listed on the label. They are used in some institutions because they keep longer and are generally less expensive than dairy products. Some people feel they are acceptable, but many find their flavors objectionable.

PROBLEMS IN COOKING MILK AND CREAM PRODUCTS

Curdling

Curdling is a process by which milk proteins solidify and separate from the whey. Curdling is usually caused by acids, tannins, salt, and heat. The mild acids in many vegetables and the tannins in potatoes are often enough to curdle milk.

Starches partially stabilize milk and cream. This is why it is possible to make soups and sauces with both milk or cream and acid ingredients. Avoid combining milk or cream with strong acids unless a starch is present.

Reducing temperatures and cooking times also helps. Curdling is more likely at high heat or with prolonged cooking.

Salt lightly, unless the milk has been stabilized by starch.

When adding milk or cream to a hot liquid, heat it first in a separate pot, or temper it by stirring a little of the hot liquid into it first.

Reconstituted dry milk is more likely to curdle than fresh milk.

**Figure 25.1
Whipping cream.**

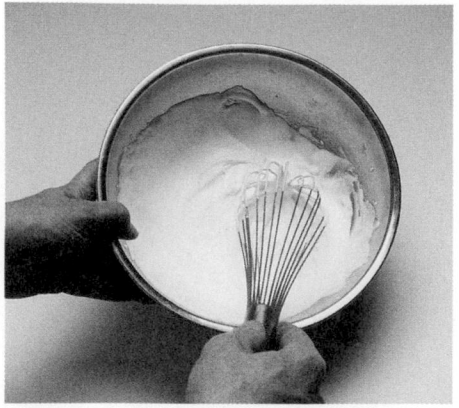

(a) The cream has begun to thicken.

**(b) The cream has reached the soft-peak stage.
Stop at this stage if the cream is to be folded into
a batter or other mixture.**

**(c) The cream has reached the firm-peak stage.
Whipping beyond this stage causes the cream to
break or separate.**

Scorching

Scorching occurs when milk that is being heated coagulates on the bottom of the pan due to high heat. This deposit is likely to burn if cooking continues.

To avoid scorching, heat milk in a double boiler, steamer, or steam-jacketed kettle rather than over direct heat.

Skin Formation

Formation of scum or skin on top of heated milk or milk sauces is caused by coagulation of proteins in contact with air. Prevent it by covering the utensil or by coating the surface with a layer of melted fat.

WHIPPING CREAM

Cream with a fat content of 32 percent or more can be whipped into a foam (see Figure 25.1). One quart or liter of cream produces up to 2 quarts or liters of whipped cream.

For the best results, observe the following guidelines:

1. Have cream and all equipment well chilled.
2. Do not sweeten until the cream is whipped. Sugar decreases stability and makes the cream harder to whip. Use powdered sugar instead of granulated sugar for best stability.
3. Do not overwhip. Stop beating when the cream forms stiff peaks. If it is whipped longer, it first becomes granular and then turns into butter and whey.
4. Cream to be folded into other ingredients should be underbeaten because the action of folding it in whips it more and may overwhip it.

BUTTER

BUTTER CHARACTERISTICS AND GRADES

Fresh **butter** in the United States and Canada consists of about 80 percent milk fat. The remainder is milk solids and water.

In Europe, butter often has a higher fat content, usually around 82 percent. Some manufacturers in North America have begun processing and selling European-style butters with this higher fat content. They are intended to replicate the qualities of European butters in cooking and baking.

In Canada, butter is graded for flavor, body, color, and salt content. Grading is mandatory. Grades are Canada 1, Canada 2, and Canada 3. Most food service operations use Canada 1.

Most butter on the market is lightly *salted*. A maximum of 2.5 percent salt is permitted. **Sweet**, or **unsalted**, butter is more perishable but has a fresher, sweeter taste.

Because of its flavor, butter is the preferred cooking fat for most purposes. It has no equal in sauce-making and is used as a sauce itself, as discussed in Chapter 8.

Clarified butter (see p. 178 for production procedure) is used as a cooking fat more often than whole butter because the milk solids in whole butter burn easily.

The smoke point of butterfat is only 350°F (177°C), so another product, such as vegetable oil, should be used when high cooking temperatures are required.

STORING

Have you ever been served butter that tasted like onions? Butter absorbs odors and flavors easily, so it should be kept well wrapped and away from other foods that might transfer odors to it in the refrigerator.

Best storage temperature is 35°F (2°C).

MARGARINE

Margarine is a manufactured product that is intended to resemble butter in taste, texture, and appearance. It is made from vegetable and animal fats, plus flavoring ingredients, emulsifiers, coloring agents, preservatives, and added vitamins. Like butter, it is about 80 percent fat. Diet and low-fat margarines have less fat and a much higher water content, so they can't be used in cooking like butter or regular margarine.

Flavors of different brands should be evaluated carefully because they vary considerably. Margarine should have a reasonably clean, fresh flavor, although you should not expect even the best to taste like high-grade butter.

Margarines that include an emulsifier called *lecithin* foam and brown like butter when heated. Those without lecithin do not. In all other respects, margarine is handled and stored like butter.

CHEESE

COMPOSITION

Cheese is a food produced by separating milk solids from whey by curdling or coagulation. This curdling is brought about by introducing selected bacteria or an enzyme called *rennet* into the milk. The resulting curds are drained, processed, and cured or aged in a variety of ways.

Processing techniques are so numerous that from a single basic ingredient (milk from cows, sheep, or goats) it is possible to produce hundreds of kinds of cheese, from cottage cheese to parmesan, from cheddar to Swiss, from blue to Limburger. Variables that produce these differences include the type of milk used, the method of curdling and the temperatures during curdling, the method of cutting and draining the curd, the way the curds are heated, pressed, or handled, and all the conditions of ripening or curing.

Ripening is the process that converts freshly made curds into distinctive, flavorful cheeses. Ripening is brought about by certain bacteria or molds that are introduced during manufacture. Much of a cheese's final character is determined by the kind of ripening agent and the way it acts on the cheese.

Cheeses can be classified by the way in which they are ripened.

Bacteria ripened from inside, such as cheddar, Swiss, Gouda, and parmesan. This category includes most hard-ripened and hard grating cheeses. These ripen uniformly throughout the interior.

Washed-rind cheeses, such as Limburger and Liederkranz. These are called washed-rind cheeses because the surface of each cheese is periodically washed with a salt brine solution during the first stages of aging and ripening. Washed-rind cheeses usually have an orange or reddish rind that is thinner than the mold rind of mold-ripened cheeses. They usually become softer as they ripen. Many washed-rind cheeses have a pungent aroma when ripe.

Blue-veined cheeses, such as Roquefort and Stilton. These contain mold cultures that spread through the interior of the cheese.

Mold-rind cheeses, such as Brie, Camembert, and St. André. These have a mold crust or rind that is white and velvety when the cheese is young but that may darken or become mottled with orange or brown as the cheese ages.

Unripened cheeses, such as cottage, cream, and baker's cheese.

The three major components of cheese are water, fat, and protein. The water content of cheese ranges from about 80 percent for a fresh, soft cheese like cottage cheese to about 30 percent for a very hard, aged cheese like parmesan.

The fat content of cheese, when it is listed on a label, generally refers to the percentage of solids. In other words, if a cheddar cheese has a 50 percent fat content, this means that the cheese would be 50 percent fat if all the moisture were removed. In fact, the cheese may have a moisture content of about 40 percent, and its actual fat content may be about 30 percent of the total.

Buffalo mozzarella

Feta

Port Salut

Brie

Double-crème (at least 60 percent fat) and **triple-crème** (at least 75 percent fat, dry weight) are very rich cheeses. Most of these styles of cheese originated in France, but they have become popular and are now made in many countries. Most of them fall into the unripened, soft-ripened, or blue-veined categories, discussed below.

VARIETIES

Hundreds, possibly even thousands, of cheeses are produced in North America and Europe. The following is a representative sampling of most of the types of cheeses commonly available. See also the accompanying photographs.

Unripened Cheeses

These are soft, white, freshly made cheeses.

Cottage cheese is a moist, loose-curd cheese that may or may not have cream added. *Baker's cheese* or *pot cheese* is similar but drier. Baker's cheese is used in cheesecakes and pastry.

Ricotta cheese is sometimes called *Italian cottage cheese*, but it is smoother, moister, and sweeter than cottage cheese.

Cream cheese is a smooth, mild cheese with a high fat content. It is extensively used in making sandwiches, canapés, and hors d'oeuvres and in baking.

Neufchâtel is similar to cream cheese but has less fat. An Italian cream cheese called *mascarpone* is very soft and rich, and it looks almost like whipped cream. It has a slightly tangy taste that goes well with fruits as a dessert.

Mozzarella is a soft, mild cheese made from whole milk or part skim milk. It has a stringy texture that comes from being pulled and stretched during production. It is widely used in pizzas and Italian-style dishes. The freshly made mozzarella one finds in Italian neighborhoods is moister and more tender than the packaged varieties.

Mozzarella di bufala, made from the milk of water buffaloes, is imported from Italy and is available in some areas at a somewhat high price. It is much softer and more delicate in texture than regular mozzarella, and it has a slightly acidic flavor that is refreshing.

Feta is a crumbly, curdy cheese that originated in Greece and other Balkan countries. Instead of being aged or cured, it is pickled in brine. This, plus the fact that it is generally made from goat's or sheep's milk, gives it a distinctive and salty flavor.

Semisoft Cheeses

Bel Paese and *fontina* from Italy, *Port Salut* from France, and American *muenster* and *brick* cheeses are the best known of a large group of cheeses that range from bland and buttery when young to more earthy and full-flavored when older. They are often used as dessert cheeses and as hors d'oeuvres.

France produces many washed-rind soft cheeses with orange rinds and with flavors that range from mild to pungent. Among the better-known ones are *Pont l'Evêque* and *Livarot* from Normandy and *Muenster* from Alsace. (These cheeses might also be categorized as soft-ripened cheeses, below, although they may not become as soft and runny as the washed-rind cheeses discussed in the next section.)

Soft-Ripened Cheeses

These cheeses ripen from the outside toward the center. When very young, they are firm and cakey and have little flavor. As they mature, they gradually become softer and, when fully ripe, may be actually runny. The ripening starts just inside the rind and spreads to the center.

Soft-ripened cheeses include two categories: mold-ripened and washed-rind or bacteria-ripened.

Brie and *Camembert* from France are ripened by mold. They are made in flat, round shapes and are covered with a crust that varies in color from white to straw. When ripe, these cheeses are creamy and flavorful, but they develop a sharp odor of ammonia when overripe.

Many rich double- and triple-crème cheeses fall into this category, including *Explorateur*, *Brillat-Savarin*, *St. André*, *Boursault*, and *Boursin* (which may be flavored with pepper or with garlic and herbs). *Chaource* is similar in texture and appearance to a double-crème cheese but is actually closer in composition to Brie, having a fat content of 45 to 50 percent.

Liederkranz, made in the United States, and its Belgian cousin, *Limburger*, are ripened by bacteria rather than mold, but they also become softer as they age. They are widely misunderstood because of their aroma. Actually, when not overripe, these cheeses are not nearly as strong as most people expect, and they have a pleasant, smooth texture.

Epoisse from Burgundy, France, is one of the great soft-ripened washed-rind cheeses. Small cheeses are packed individually in round wooden boxes. They are so soft when ripe that they are left in their boxes and served with a spoon.

Cheddar

Hard Cheeses

These are cured cheeses with a firm texture and varying degrees of mildness or sharpness, depending on their age.

Cheddar is an English invention, but American versions are so popular in the United States that it is often thought of as a distinctly American cheese. It ranges in flavor from mild to sharp and in color from light yellow to orange. Cheddar is eaten as is and is also widely used in cooking. *Colby* and *Monterey jack* are similar to very mild cheddars. Monterey jack is usually sold when quite young. In this case, it is more like American muenster and belongs in the semisoft category.

Swiss-type cheeses are also popular. Swiss-type cheeses are produced in many countries, but the original Swiss cheese from Switzerland, *Emmenthaler*, is perhaps the most flavorful. These are very firm, slightly rubbery cheeses with a nutty taste. Their large holes are caused by gases formed during ripening. *Gruyère* is another Swiss-type cheese from either Switzerland or France. It has smaller holes and a sharper, earthier flavor. Gruyère is important in cooking and it, plus Emmenthaler, are widely used for sauces, soufflés, fondue, and gratinéed items. Other cheeses related to Swiss are *Comté* from France, *Appenzeller* and *Raclette* from Switzerland, and *Jarlsberg* from Norway.

Edam and *Gouda* are the familiar round Dutch cheeses with the yellow and red wax rinds. Hard in texture, with a mellow, nutlike flavor, they are often seen on buffet platters and among dessert cheeses.

Provolone is an Italian cheese that resembles mozzarella when very young, but it becomes sharper as it ages. It is also available smoked.

Clockwise from top: Emmenthaler, Gorgonzola, Provolone, Gruyère, Gouda, Locatelli Romano, Pont l'Evêque, Baby Gouda. Lower center: Livarot.

Blue-Veined Cheeses

These cheeses owe their flavor and appearance to the blue or green mold that mottles their interiors. The most famous of the blue cheeses is *Roquefort*, made in France from sheep's milk and cured in limestone caves near the town of Roquefort. *Stilton*, from England, is a mellower, firmer blue cheese that the English call "Roquefort with a college education." Italy's *gorgonzola* is a soft, creamy cheese with an unmistakable pungency. Spanish *Cabrales* is a mellow but intensely flavorful blue cheese. Blue cheeses made in Denmark, the United States, and Canada are also widely used.

Less widely known but worth seeking out are a number of special blues, including *Bleu de Bresse, Fourme d'Ambert,* and *Pipo Crem'* from France, *Saga* from Denmark, and *Bavarian Blue* and *Blue Castello* from Germany. The last four of these are double- or triple-crèmes.

Jarlsberg

Edam

Blue Stilton

Gorgonzola

Chèvre

Goat Cheeses

Cheeses made from goat's milk are produced in dozens of varieties in France, where this type of cheese, called **chèvre** (shev r', or shev), is very popular. It has also become well known in the United States, which now has several producers. With a few exceptions, most goat cheeses are small, ranging in size from tiny buttons to logs, cakes, cones, and pyramids weighing up to 5 or 6 ounces (140 to 170 g).

Fresh, unaged chèvres are the most popular and the mildest in flavor. Their paste is very white, with a soft but interestingly dry texture. They have a distinctive peppery, slightly acidic taste. The most widely available fresh French chèvre is probably the cylindrical *Montrachet*, either plain or with a coating of ash. Other fresh goat cheeses, both domestic and imported, may be available in different localities, and many have no name other than *chèvre*.

As goat cheese ages, it becomes firmer, and the peppery, acidic flavor becomes stronger. Cheeses two or three months old can be quite powerful, while the youngest might taste almost like the unaged ones. Some names of chèvres are *Boucheron, Banon* (wrapped in chestnut leaves), *Pyramide, Crottin de Chavignol, Chabis,* and *Rocamadour. Saint-Marcellin* is made of part goat's milk and part cow's milk. Shaped into small disks, it softens rather than hardens as it ripens.

Hard Grating Cheeses

The hard grating cheeses, typified by Italian *parmesan*, are called *grana* cheeses, referring to their grainy textures. The best of all granas is called *Parmigiano-Reggiano*. It is the true parmesan, aged at least two years, and is very expensive. It is imitated widely around the world, and the imitations vary from bad to very good. Another Italian grana is *romano*. Italian romanos are made with sheep's milk, but American versions are usually made with cow's milk. Romano is stronger and saltier than parmesan.

These cheeses are often sold already grated. This is a convenience for commercial kitchens, of course, but, unfortunately, pregrated cheese has much less flavor than freshly grated cheese. A merchant was once arrested for selling what he claimed was grated parmesan cheese but was actually grated umbrella handles. A large share of pregrated cheese sold today resembles grated umbrella handles in flavor.

Process Cheeses

Up to now, we have been talking about so-called natural cheeses, made by curdling milk and ripening the curds. **Process cheese,** by contrast, is manufactured by grinding one or more natural cheeses, heating and blending them with emulsifiers and other ingredients, and pouring the mixture into molds to solidify. Process cheese is a uniform product that does not age or ripen like natural cheese. Thus, it keeps very well. It is usually mild in flavor and gummy in texture.

Because of its melting quality and low price, it is often used in cooking. However, it is not as good a value as its price implies. Because it is relatively flavorless, you have to use much more of it to get the same flavor as from a smaller quantity of sharp cheddar.

In addition to its price and keeping qualities, its chief advantages are that it melts easily and that its blandness appeals to many people who don't like more flavorful cheese.

In North America, most process cheeses are made from cheddar, while European process cheeses more often contain Swiss-type cheeses. Among them is a process cheese called *Gruyère,* which bears little resemblance to true *Gruyère*.

Process cheese food and *process cheese spread* contain a lower percentage of cheese and more moisture than a product labeled simply *process cheese. Cold pack* or *club cheese,* on the other hand, is not heated and pasteurized like process cheese but is simply ground and mixed with flavorings and seasonings to a spreadable consistency. Some brands are fairly flavorful.

North American Artisan Cheeses

Many of the fine cheeses from France, Italy, and other European countries, including many of those listed above, are handmade in small batches. By contrast, until recently, nearly all the cheese produced in North America has been made by large industrial concerns.

In recent years, the production of small-batch artisan cheeses in North America has skyrocketed. This development has been stimulated, no doubt, by the adoption of the European practice of offering a cheese course after dinner in fine dining establishments. Increased interest in specialty cheeses has created a new market for these products. North American chefs have made their cheese menus into showcases for fine local cheeses.

The American Cheese Society offers the following definitions of limited-production cheeses:

Specialty cheese is cheese of limited production, with particular attention to natural flavor and texture profiles. Specialty cheeses may be made from all types of milk and may include flavorings.

Artisan or **artisanal cheese** is cheese that is produced primarily by hand, in small batches, with particular attention to the tradition of the cheese-maker's art and using as little mechanization as possible.

Farmstead cheese is cheese that is made with milk from a farmer's own herd or flock on the farm where the animals are raised. No milk from an outside source may be used.

European cheeses are the product of hundreds of years of tradition and include nearly every type of cheese imaginable, so it is natural that North American producers looked to European cheeses as models. At the same time, the best producers have also tried to develop distinctive products that set new standards of quality. Today, cheese producers all across Canada and the United States produce cheeses that compare in quality with the best from Europe.

It is impossible in a short space to list all the fine artisan and farmstead cheeses in North America. The following are just small random samples of the hundreds of varieties from many regions.

Fresh unripened cheeses

Mozzarella Company Mascarpone, Texas

Shepherd's Way Ricotta (sheep's milk), Minnesota

Silani Sweet Cheese Ricotta, Ontario

Soft washed-rind cheeses

Harvest Moon, Colorado

Cowgirl Creamery Red Hawk, California

Le Douanier, Quebec

Colo Rouge, Colorado

Mold-rind soft-ripened

Blythedale Farm Brie and Camembert, Vermont

Groupe Fromage Cote Triple Crème, Quebec

Bittersweet Plantation Fleur-de-Teche Triple Crème, Louisiana

Sweet Grass Dairy, Georgia

Hard cheeses

Roth Kase Gruyère, Wisconsin

Gort's Gouda, British Columbia

Sylvan Star Gouda, Alberta

Belle Gioioso Romano, Wisconsin

Carr Valley Canaria, Wisconsin

Mona (sheep and cow's milk blend), Wisconsin

McCadam Cheddar, New York

Blue cheeses

Rogue River Blue, Oregon

Point Reyes Blue, California

Dragon's Breath, Nova Scotia

Firefly Farms Mountain Top Blue, Maryland

Hubbardston Blue, Massachusetts

Goat cheeses, fresh and aged

Vermont Butter and Cheese Company, Vermont

Humboldt Fog, California

Fromagerie Bergeron Patte Blanche, Quebec

Capriole Pipers Pyramid, Indiana

STORAGE AND SERVICE

Storing

Keeping qualities of cheese vary considerably. In general, *the firmer and more aged the cheese, the longer it will keep.* Cottage cheese must be used within a week, while a whole, uncut parmesan may keep a year or more.

Soft-ripened cheeses like Brie, Camembert, and Liederkranz deteriorate rapidly once they reach maturity. They are difficult cheeses to purchase because in their whole lifespan there may be only one week when they are neither underripe nor overripe.

Other ripened cheeses are not as fussy, as long as you store them under refrigeration and well wrapped to prevent drying. Cut cheeses dry especially quickly, so they must be wrapped in plastic at all times.

Serving

Serve cheese at room temperature. This is the single most important rule of cheese service. Only at room temperature will the full flavors develop. (This does not apply to unripened cheese like cottage cheese.)

Cut cheese just before service to prevent drying. Better yet, set out whole cheeses and large pieces when possible so portions can be cut to order by the customer or the service personnel.

COOKING WITH CHEESE

Three varieties of cheese account for the majority of cheese used in cooking. *Cheddar* is the most frequently used in North American dishes, especially in sauces, as casserole ingredients, and as a melted or gratinéed topping. *Swiss-type* cheeses are used more often in European-style dishes. Emmenthaler and Gruyère are essential ingredients for fondue, Mornay sauce, gratinéed dishes, soufflés, and quiches. *Parmesan-type* cheeses are used in grated form for toppings and for seasoning and flavoring purposes.

Many other varieties are called for in specialized recipes, such as mozzarella and ricotta in Italian-style dishes.

Guidelines for Cooking with Cheese

1. Use low temperatures. Cheese contains a high proportion of protein, which toughens and becomes stringy when heated too much. Sauces containing cheese should not be boiled.

2. Use short cooking times, for the same reasons. Cheese should be added to a sauce at the end of cooking. Stirring it into the hot sauce *off the heat* is usually enough to melt it.

3. Grate cheese for faster and more uniform melting.

4. Aged cheeses melt and blend into foods more easily than young cheeses.

5. Aged cheese adds more flavor to foods than young, mild cheeses, so you need less of it.

Welsh Rabbit

Portions: 25   Portion size: 4 oz (125 g)

U.S.	Metric	Ingredients
3 tbsp	45 mL	Worcestershire sauce
2 tsp	10 mL	Dry mustard
pinch	pinch	Cayenne
2½ cups	625 mL	Beer or ale
5 lb	2.5 kg	Sharp cheddar cheese, grated
25 slices	25 slices	White bread

■ P r o c e d u r e

1. Mix the Worcestershire sauce and spices in a heavy saucepan.
2. Add the beer or ale. Heat almost to a simmer.
3. Set the pan over very low heat. Add the grated cheese, a little at a time. Stir constantly. Continue to stir over low heat until the mixture is smooth and thick.
4. Remove from heat. The mixture may be kept warm in a steam table or bain-marie, but it is better if served immediately.
5. Toast the bread.
6. For each portion, place a slice of hot toast on a plate. Ladle 4 fl oz (125 mL) cheese mixture over the toast. Serve.

Per serving:
Calories, 470; Protein, 26 g; Fat, 31 g (60% cal.); Cholesterol, 95 mg; Carbohydrates, 19 g; Fiber, 1 g; Sodium, 750 mg.

Note: This dish is sometimes called Welsh Rarebit, although Rabbit is the original name.

 Sirniki (Russian Fried Cheese Cakes)

Portions: 25   Portion size: 3½ oz (100 g)

U.S.	Metric	Ingredients
5 lb	2.3 kg	Pot cheese
6 oz	175 g	Bread flour
8	8	Egg yolks
½ tsp	2 mL	Salt
2 oz	60 g	Sugar
as needed	as needed	Butter for frying
as needed	as needed	Confectioners' sugar
2½ pt	1.2 L	Sour cream

■ P r o c e d u r e

1. Place the pot cheese in a strainer lined with cheesecloth. Fold the overhanging cloth over the top of the cheese so that it is covered. Set the strainer over a bowl and refrigerate for 24 hours to drain the cheese.
2. Force the cheese through a sieve or food mill into the bowl of a mixer.
3. Add the flour, egg yolks, salt, and sugar.
4. With the paddle attachment, mix until smooth.
5. Divide the dough into 3 parts. Roll each part into a cylinder about 3 in. (7½ cm) thick. Wrap in plastic film. Refrigerate 2 hours or more.
6. At service time, cut the cheese rolls into cakes about ¾ in. (2 cm) thick.
7. Heat about ⅛ in. (3 mm) butter in a heavy sauté pan. Pan-fry the cakes over low heat until golden brown on both sides. Turn very carefully with a spatula.
8. Plate the cakes and sprinkle lightly with confectioners' sugar. Place about 1½ tbsp (20 mL) sour cream on the plate next to the cake. Serve immediately.

Per serving:
Calories, 350; Protein, 18 g; Fat, 23 g (63% cal.); Cholesterol, 130 mg; Carbohydrates, 12 g; Fiber, 0 g; Sodium, 480 mg.

Note: This dish is often served as the main course for brunch or lunch. In this case, portion sizes may be increased. Sirniki may also be served with strawberry or other preserves.

Swiss Fondue

Portions: 4   Portion size: 8 oz (250 g)

U.S.	Metric	Ingredients
1	1	Garlic clove
1 pt	500 mL	Dry white wine
1 lb	500 g	Swiss Emmenthaler cheese, or half Emmenthaler and half Gruyère, grated
1 tsp	5 mL	Cornstarch
3 tbsp	45 mL	Kirsch (see note)
to taste	to taste	Salt
to taste	to taste	White pepper
to taste	to taste	Nutmeg
2	2	Small loaves French bread, cut into bite- size pieces

■ P r o c e d u r e

1. Cut the garlic clove in half. Rub the inside of a 1½-qt (1½-L) fondue pot or casserole with the garlic.

2. Add the wine to the pot and set over moderate heat. Heat the wine until it is hot but not simmering. Do not boil.

3. Add the cheese to the wine, about one-fourth at a time. Stir well between each addition.

4. Dissolve the cornstarch in the kirsch. Stir into the cheese mixture. Stir over very low heat until smooth and slightly thickened.

5. Season to taste with salt, white pepper, and just a trace of nutmeg.

6. Set the casserole over a chafing dish heating element for service. Serve the bread cubes in baskets. To eat fondue, the diner spears a cube of bread on a special fondue fork and swirls it in the cheese mixture, which is kept hot over the heating element.

Per serving:
Calories, 870; Protein, 43 g; Fat, 35 g (36% cal.); Cholesterol, 105 mg; Carbohydrates, 70 g; Fiber, 3 g; Sodium, 1000 mg.

Note: Kirsch is a white (that is, clear) alcoholic beverage distilled from cherries. While it is traditional in Swiss fondue, it may be omitted if unavailable. In this case, dissolve the cornstarch in cold water or mix it with the grated cheese.

 Cheese Wafers

Yield: about 150 wafers

U.S.	Metric	Ingredients
1 lb	500 g	Sharp cheddar cheese, grated
8 oz	250 g	Butter, softened
12 oz	375 g	Bread flour
½ tsp	2 mL	Salt
¼ tsp	1 mL	White pepper

■ P r o c e d u r e

1. Combine all ingredients in the bowl of a mixer. Mix at low speed with the paddle attachment until the mixture forms a dough.

2. Remove from the mixer and knead lightly on a floured board until the dough holds together well.

3. Divide the dough into 4 or 5 pieces. Roll each piece into a cylinder 1 in. (2½ cm) in diameter. Wrap in waxed paper or plastic film and chill.

4. Slice the dough into thin rounds a little less than ¼ in. (½ cm) thick. Place on greased baking sheets.

5. Bake at 450°F (230°C) about 10 minutes, until crisp and lightly browned.

6. Serve hot or cold as an hors d'oeuvre or as a soup accompaniment.

V A R I A T I O N S

Cheese Straws
Roll out the dough like pie dough, slightly less than ¼ in. (½ cm) thick. Cut into strips, ¼ x 3 in. (½ x 7½ cm). Bake as in basic recipe.

Per 1 wafer:
Calories, 30; Protein, 1 g; Fat, 2.5 g (65% cal.); Cholesterol, 5 mg; Carbohydrates, 2 g; Fiber, 0 g; Sodium, 40 mg.

COFFEE AND TEA

COFFEE

Many people judge a restaurant by its coffee. Regardless of the quality of the food, one of the things they are most likely to remember about an establishment is whether the coffee is good or bad.

Whether or not that seems fair to you, it is at least a clear signal that you ought to learn to make coffee properly. Coffee-making is basically a simple procedure. All you do is pass hot water through ground coffee. The care with which you perform this operation, with attention to all the details, makes the difference between a rich, aromatic, satisfying beverage and a bitter, unpleasant liquid.

VARIETIES, ROASTS, AND BLENDS

Coffee beans are harvested as berries from a tropical shrub. Two species of coffee account for nearly all the beans grown worldwide: *Arabica* coffees are delicate plants, difficult to grow. Nevertheless, they supply about 65 to 75 percent of the world's coffee. Most of the finest coffees are from arabica beans. *Robusta* coffee plants are hardier and easier to grow. Most ordinary supermarket coffee is made from robusta beans, but robusta can also yield beans of very high quality.

Each coffee berry contains two seeds. The harvested berries are fermented and hulled, yielding green or gray-green coffee beans. The green beans are roasted to develop their flavor. The degree of roasting—light, medium, dark—affects the flavor. Most Americans drink medium roast, sometimes called *city roast*, while darker roasts, sometimes called *Viennese roast* (medium dark) and *French roast* (very dark), are popular in Europe and increasingly popular in North America. The darkest roast, *espresso roast*, is nearly black and is brewed using a special process discussed below.

Coffee is grown in many tropical countries, and each producing area is known for certain quality and flavor characteristics. Excellent coffees are grown in Colombia, Brazil, Venezuela, Mexico, Jamaica, Hawaii, Indonesia, and nations in Africa and the Middle East.

Most ground coffees are blends of several varieties. Blending enables the processor to combine desirable quantities from a number of beans to produce a well-balanced beverage.

Coffee may be purchased in whole bean or ground form. Whole beans stay fresh longer, but unopened vacuum packs of ground coffee keep well for a week or two and, for many establishments, are the easiest and most economical way to buy coffee. Ground coffee, once opened, should be kept in airtight containers and used within a few days. Better yet, buy ground coffee in premeasured packs suitable for your brewing equipment. Whole beans keep several weeks once opened and months in the freezer. The best practice, though, is to have frequent small deliveries so you always have the freshest coffee on hand.

Brewing procedures for fresh coffee are discussed in the procedures below.

In addition to the standard cup of regular hot coffee, the following coffee drinks are sometimes served.

1. **Instant coffee** is a powdered, soluble extract from coffee beans. To simplify somewhat, instant coffee is made by brewing regular coffee and drying it. In the process, the coffee loses a portion of its flavor and aroma. Most coffee lovers agree that it does not taste as good as freshly brewed coffee. Instant coffee is rarely used in food service.

2. **Decaffeinated coffee.** Caffeine is a chemical stimulant that occurs naturally in coffee, tea, and chocolate. Decaffeinated coffee is coffee from which the caffeine has been removed by solvents. It is often specially requested by some customers. In

the past, most restaurants offered decaffeinated coffee only in the instant form. Now, however, nearly all restaurants serve freshly brewed decaffeinated coffee.

3. **Espresso** or **expresso** is a strong, dark coffee made from beans roasted until they are almost black and ground to a powder. Espresso is served in small cups as an after-dinner beverage. In addition, several popular coffee drinks are made with brewed espresso, as discussed in the next section.

4. **Iced coffee** is made from double-strength brewed coffee to compensate for dilution by melting ice.

Espresso Drinks

Espresso and espresso drinks have grown in popularity in recent years, and specialty coffee shops have sprung up seemingly on almost every street corner.

Espresso is a concentrated coffee beverage brewed in special machines (see illustration) from dark-roast, finely ground beans. For each drink, the ground coffee is packed into a small metal filter, which is then firmly attached to the machine. Water is forced through the grounds under high steam pressure, making a small cup of strong beverage topped with a layer of rich foam called the *crema*. A shot of espresso is about 2 fluid ounces (55 mL), and it is usually served in a tiny cup or as a double shot in a standard coffee cup.

In addition, the following drinks are made with brewed espresso:

Cappuccino (cap oo chee no): equal parts espresso and steamed milk, topped with a generous layer of milk froth or foam.

Latte (lah tay): short for *caffe latte,* or "coffee milk." One part espresso to two (or more) parts steamed milk, without the layer of foam found on cappuccino. The French **café au lait** (cah fay oh lay; meaning "coffee with milk") is basically the same as a latte, but it may be made with strong regular dark roast coffee rather than espresso.

Macchiato (mah kee ah toe): espresso topped with a little frothed milk.

Americano: espresso diluted with hot water.

Breve (bray vay): espresso with steamed half-and-half.

Mocha (moh kah): espresso mixed with hot chocolate or cocoa, topped with whipped cream.

Specialty coffee shops also sell a great variety of flavored espresso coffee drinks, hot and cold, using flavored syrups such as caramel, vanilla, and mint.

An espresso maker
Courtesy of Cecilware

Basic Principles of Coffee Making

Coffee is made by extracting flavors from ground coffee beans by dissolving them in hot water. The essence of making good coffee is to extract enough of these solids to make a flavorful beverage, but not to brew so long as to extract those solids that make the coffee bitter.

With this principle in mind, study the following guidelines for making good coffee. The list is long, and every item is important.

1. Use fresh coffee.

    Once it is ground, coffee loses flavor and aroma rapidly. To maintain freshness, store coffee, tightly sealed, in a cool, dry place. Even with the best storage, however, you should not use coffee more than a week old. Vacuum-packed coffee keeps longer, but it too deteriorates as soon as it is opened. If you can't grind your own coffee daily (some restaurants do), at least you can arrange for frequent delivery.

2. Use the right grind and the right brewing time.

    A coarse grind requires more time for extraction than a fine grind. You must use the grind that is suited to your equipment.

Grind	Extraction Time
Fine or vacuum	2 to 4 minutes
Drip or urn	4 to 6 minutes
Regular (percolator)	6 to 8 minutes

3. Use the right proportions.

    Always measure. Recommended proportions are 1 pound of coffee and 1¾ to 2½ gallons of water, or 500 grams of coffee and 7.5 to 10.5 liters of water, depending on the strength desired.

To make weaker coffee, add more hot water after removing the used grounds. Using more water while actually making the coffee extends the brewing time, resulting in overextraction and bitterness. In fact, many experts feel that passing no more than 2 gallons of water through 1 pound of ground coffee (8 liters to 500 grams) and then diluting to taste is the surest way to avoid bitterness.

Coffee strength is a matter of customer preference and varies from region to region. For example, people in New York generally prefer stronger coffee than people in Chicago. In some areas, the preferred ratio is 1 pound (500 g) coffee to 3 gallons (12 liters) water.

4. Use fresh water.

Fresh, cold water brought to a boil contains dissolved air. Water that has been kept hot for a long time does not, so it tastes flat, and it makes flat-tasting coffee.

Tap water is usually best to use. Special filtration systems are available for tap water that has off flavors or is heavily chlorinated. Do not use chemically softened water.

5. Use water at the right brewing temperature: 195° to 200°F (90° to 93°C).

Water that is too hot extracts bitter solids. Water that is too cold does not extract enough flavor and yields coffee that is too cool for serving.

6. Use a good brewing procedure.

Most operations use either urns, for large volume, or automatic drip makers, which make one pot at a time, as shown in the photograph. These machines can make excellent coffee because water passes through the grounds only once.

Percolator-type coffee makers should not be used. They boil the coffee as it is being brewed and pass it through the grounds repeatedly.

7. Use clean equipment.

Urns and coffee makers must be cleaned every day. Coffee leaves oily deposits that quickly turn rancid or bitter and that can ruin the next batch of coffee.

8. Use good filters.

Good filters are the only way to ensure sparkling, clear coffee. Most operations use paper filters, which are discarded after use. If cloth filters are used, they must be perfectly clean and free from odors.

9. Use proper holding procedures.

Proper holding temperature is 185° to 190°F (85° to 88°C). Higher temperatures decompose the coffee quickly. Lower temperatures mean the customer gets cold coffee.

Coffee made in carafe-type coffee makers is usually kept warm over electric burners. Do not hold brewed coffee over heat longer than 30 minutes. After this time, loss of quality is considerable. If it must be held longer, transfer it as soon as it is brewed to preheated thermos containers. Plan production so that coffee is always fresh. Discard old coffee.

Decanter-type automatic drip coffee maker
Courtesy of Cecilware

Procedure for Making Coffee in an Urn

1. Be familiar with your equipment. Models differ in details.
2. Check to make sure the urn holds sufficient fresh water at the proper temperatures for brewing.
3. Fit the filter securely in place.
4. Spread a measured amount of coffee evenly in the filter. An even bed is necessary for uniform extraction.
5. Pass the correct amount of water through the ground coffee. If the urn is manual, pour the water slowly in a circular motion. If it is automatic, all you need to do is make sure the nozzle is in place.
6. Keep the top covered during brewing to retain heat.
7. Remove the filter with the used grounds as soon as brewing has been completed. Leaving the grounds in the urn results in overextraction and bitterness.
8. Mix the coffee. Because the coffee at the bottom is stronger, you must draw out some of it—about 1 gallon (4 liters) per pound (500 grams) of coffee—and pour it back into the top of the urn.
9. Hold at 185° to 190°F (85° to 88°C) for up to 1 hour, or, even better, transfer to thermos containers if the coffee must be held for more than 30 minutes, as indicated above.
10. Clean the urn thoroughly after use.

Twin urn
Courtesy of Cecilware

Using special urn brushes, clean the inside of the urn as well as inside spigots and glass gauges. Rinse and fill with several gallons of fresh water if the urn is to stand for a time. Empty and rinse with hot water before next use.

Twice a week, clean thoroughly with urn cleaning compound, following manufacturer's instructions.

TEA

Tea is one of the world's most popular beverages and is widely drunk even in coffee-drinking countries. In many regions, tea is a much more popular beverage in the home than in the restaurant. Part of the difference may be due to mishandling in the restaurant and indifference on the part of restaurateurs.

Food service professionals would do well to pay more attention to tea. First of all, it is much less expensive than coffee to serve. One pound (500 g) of tea yields 200 servings, as compared with 40 servings from 1 pound (500 g) of coffee. Moreover, tea is one of the simplest of beverages to serve and does not require the equipment or the labor of coffee service.

VARIETIES

All the world's varieties of tea are produced from one species of evergreen shrub. Most of the differences among varieties are the results of growing conditions and modifications in processing techniques.

As in the case of coffee, different regions produce teas of different quality and flavor characteristics. Most of the tea consumed in North America is imported from India and Sri Lanka (Ceylon).

Variations in processing produce three categories of tea. *Black tea* is fermented by allowing the freshly harvested leaves to oxidize in a damp place. *Green tea* is dried without fermenting. *Oolong tea* is partially fermented to a greenish-brown color. Specialty teas and flavored teas are also available.

Black teas are graded by leaf size according to a rather complicated system. This is important to remember because most people think of orange pekoe as a variety of tea, whereas it is actually a specific leaf size of any black variety.

After grading, teas are blended to ensure consistency and uniformity. A blend may contain as many as 30 individual teas.

Many excellent blends are available from many purveyors. A smart food service operator would do well to shop around rather than serve the same mediocre blend the competition serves.

Herbal Teas and Specialty Tea Drinks

Herbal teas are beverages that are brewed like tea but that are made with herbs, spices, dried fruits, and other plant ingredients in place of tea leaves, or sometimes in addition to tea leaves. In other words, most herbal tea contains no actual tea. Hundreds of flavors and blends are available, far too many to list, and most purveyors have their own proprietary blends. Mint and chamomile are among the most popular herb teas.

Chai (rhymes with pie) is a spiced milk and tea blend that originated in India and that has become popular in the West. *Chai* is the word for *tea* in several languages. The mixed beverage called *chai* is made of black tea, milk, spices such as cardamom, cinnamon, ginger, and black peppercorns, and sugar or another sweetener. In the West, chai is generally made from commercial mixes.

PACKAGING AND MARKET FORMS

Tea is packaged in bulk as loose tea and in tea bags of various sizes. Standard cup-size bags are packaged 200 to the pound (500 g), while the pot-sized bag (that is, individual service pot) is packaged at 150 to 175 per pound (500 g). This is important for you to know if you are purchasing tea because the larger bags would not be as economical if the service in your establishment is by the cup.

Larger tea bags that contain 1 or 2 oz (30 to 60 g) of tea are available for brewing larger quantities, especially for iced tea.

Instant tea is a soluble extraction made by brewing a very strong tea, using lesser grades, and drying the liquid to obtain a powder. This product is used primarily for iced tea because the processing results in the loss of much of the flavor and aroma essential to a good hot tea.

PREPARING TEA

In most restaurants, it seems, when one orders tea, one receives a cold cup, a tea bag in a little package, and a pot of warm water that has been standing in an urn for hours. This is absolutely the worst possible way to serve tea, with the possible exception of brewing a large quantity and keeping it warm all day. No wonder most people don't order tea.

Here is the right way:

Procedure for Making Hot Tea

1. Use proper proportions of tea and water. One teaspoon (5 mL) loose tea or one single-service tea bag makes a 6-oz (175-mL) cup.
2. Rinse the teapot with hot water to warm it. Use china, glass, or stainless steel. Other metals may give an off flavor.
3. Bring fresh, cold water to a boil. Water that has been kept warm for a time makes flat-tasting tea.
4. Place the loose tea or tea bag in the pot and pour the water directly over it.
5. Let the tea steep 3 to 5 minutes. Then remove the tea bag or strain off the tea from the loose leaves.

   Establishments specializing in tea service present the customer with the pot of tea and a pot of hot water so they can dilute the tea to taste.
6. Serve immediately. Tea does not hold well.

Procedure for Making Iced Tea

The following method makes 1 gallon (4 L). The tea is brewed stronger to allow for melting ice.

1. Place 2 ounces (60 g) tea in a pot.
2. Bring 1 quart (1 L) water to a boil and pour over the tea.
3. Steep 5 minutes. Remove tea bags, or strain out loose leaves.
4. Add 3 quarts (3 L) cold tap water.
5. Hold at room temperature up to 4 hours. Refrigeration may make the tea cloudy.
6. Serve over ice.

■ TERMS FOR REVIEW

pasteurized	whipping cream	curdling	farmstead cheese
ultra-pasteurized	double cream	scorching	instant coffee
ultra-high-temperature	table cream	butter	espresso
pasteurization	half-and-half	clarified butter	cappuccino
whole milk	sour cream	margarine	latte
milk fat	crème fraîche	ripened cheese	café au lait
butterfat	buttermilk	double-crème cheese	macchiato
skim milk	yogurt	triple-crème cheese	Americano
2 percent milk	evaporated milk	chèvre	breve
partially skimmed milk	condensed milk	process cheese	mocha
flavored milk	dried whole milk	specialty cheese	herbal tea
homogenized	nonfat dry milk	artisan cheese	chai

■ QUESTIONS FOR DISCUSSION

1. What is curdling, and how can you prevent it when cooking with milk?

2. What is washed-rind cheese? Describe the typical appearance of washed-rind cheese and compare it to mold-rind cheese.

3. Why does cheese combine more smoothly with a sauce at low heat than at high heat?

4. Why is using the proper grind important in making coffee?

5. Describe the procedure for making coffee in an urn.

6. Describe the proper method for making tea.

CHAPTER 26

Sausages and Cured Foods

Sausages have been popular since ancient times. They were first made to utilize and preserve trimmings and less desirable cuts from a meat carcass. Most people have heard the expression about using "every part of the hog except the squeal." The preparation of sausages is an important part of this process.

The French term charcutier (shar koo tyay; the feminine form is *charcutière* [shar koo tyair]) means one who prepares and sells pork products. The art of the charcutier is called charcuterie (shar koo tree). We use this term more generally to refer to the production of sausages, pâtés, and smoked ham and other cured and smoked products.

The main part of this chapter is devoted to the production of fresh sausages, which are easily prepared in any kitchen with relatively simple equipment. We also introduce the subject of cured and smoked sausages with an overview of curing and smoking. Preparing smoked hams and cured, air-dried meat products is an advanced subject that is beyond the scope of this book. However, reading the first section of this chapter will enable you to understand how these items are produced. A small sampling of recipes gives you some experience with curing and smoking before you proceed to the main section on sausages.

CURING AND SMOKING

Curing and smoking have been important methods for preserving foods, especially protein foods, since prehistoric times. Before the days of modern preservation techniques such as canning, freezing, and refrigeration, curing and smoking, as well as drying, enabled people to store food in times of abundance for use in times of scarcity. Today we use these techniques for their contribution to flavor perhaps even more than for their preservative qualities. We smoke foods because we like the taste, not because we must in order to preserve them.

Nevertheless, it is important to understand how curing works to preserve foods so we can avoid spoilage and food-borne disease that can result from improper curing or improper handling of cured foods.

INGREDIENTS FOR CURING FOODS

Ingredients used in cures fill two main functions: preserving the food, and changing its flavor and texture. The following discussion of cure ingredients and processes is somewhat simplified, but it introduces the most important principles.

Salt

Salt has been one of the most important food preservatives throughout most of human history. When a food comes in direct contact with salt, a two-way process takes place in an effort to make the salt concentrations inside and outside the food more nearly equal. Moisture from inside the cell walls of the food is drawn out and dilutes the salt used for the cure. At the same time, dissolved salt is absorbed into the cells to increase the salt concentration there. The result is foods that have less moisture and are saltier. Both the moisture reduction and the increased salt content make

Clockwise from top: table salt, curing salt, kosher salt

the food less hospitable to bacteria that cause spoilage and disease.

Of course, the reduced moisture and the increased salt content also change the flavor and texture of the food.

Nitrites and Nitrates

Some foods, especially meats, are susceptible to contamination by the bacteria that cause botulism (see p. 20). Nitrites and nitrates are added to the cures for these foods to make them safe from botulism infection. **Sodium nitrite** ($NaNO_2$) is the most important of these chemicals. Even in the very small quantities in which it is used, sodium nitrite has strong preservative powers. In addition, it keeps meats red or pink, which is why products like cured ham, corned beef, and certain sausages have their characteristic color.

Nitrites gradually break down inside the cured foods, but by the time they lose their effectiveness, the curing and, in some cases, smoking procedures are finished, the food is cooked or refrigerated, and the food remains safe. On the other hand, when the food is raw and air-dried, as in the case of prosciutto and various salamis, a stronger chemical, **sodium nitrate** ($NaNO_3$) is used. Nitrates break down more slowly than nitrites and therefore are effective for a longer time. (Potassium nitrate, or saltpeter, is sometimes used in cures, but it is not as safe and is strongly regulated. It should be avoided.)

Nitrates and nitrites are the subject of controversy regarding their safety. Substances called **nitrosamines** form when foods containing nitrates or nitrites are sub-

(see p. 20)

After reading this chapter, you should be able to:

1. **Prepare simple dry-cured and brine-cured foods.**

2. **Prepare simple smoked foods.**

3. **Prepare fresh, cured, and smoked sausages.**

jected to very high heat, such as when bacon is fried. Nitrosamines are known to cause cancer. Using only nitrites to cure foods usually avoids this problem because the nitrites break down quickly and are not usually a factor when the food is cooked. Nitrates, on the other hand, because they remain in meats longer, should not be used for curing bacon for this reason.

Some people feel that all use of nitrites and nitrates should be avoided because of the nitrosamine factor. However, if only nitrites and not nitrates are used in foods that will be exposed to extreme heat, the risk is low—much lower than the risk of botulism. So far, we know of no adequate substitute for these chemicals in curing pork and other meats.

Two special mixtures are employed that make it easy to add nitrites and nitrates in very low but sufficient concentration:

1. **Prague Powder #1**, or *curing salt*, is a blend of 6 percent sodium nitrite and 94 percent sodium chloride, or regular table salt. It is colored pink so that it will not be confused with regular salt, and thus it is often called **tinted curing mix** (TCM). It is also sold under various trade names, such as InstaCure I.

2. **Prague Powder #2** is similar to Prague Powder #1 except that it contains nitrates in addition to nitrites. It is used in curing products that have a long curing and drying period, as explained above. Prague Powder #2 is not used in any of the recipes in this chapter. Air-dried cured meats require advanced procedures that are beyond the scope of this book.

Fish and seafood are usually cured without the use of nitrites. Fish is almost always cured under refrigeration and the salt cure is sufficient to protect it, even when it is cold smoked (p. 828).

The quantity of nitrite to be added to meats depends on several factors, including the type of meat, the type of cure, and the length of curing time. For cooked sausage, the U.S. Department of Agriculture recommends 156 parts nitrite per million parts meat. This is equivalent to 1 ounce (30 g) nitrite per 400 pounds (192 kg) meat. To translate this to quantities similar to those used in this chapter, 10 pounds (4.5 kg) cooked sausage requires about 0.025 ounces (0.7 g) nitrite. This is the amount of nitrite contained in 0.4 ounces or 2 teaspoons (11 g or 10 mL) Prague Powder #1.

Keep in mind, however, that not all the nitrite specified in a recipe may be absorbed into the meat. In the case of the basic dry cures and brine cures (described below), part of the curing medium is discarded after the cure is complete. Therefore, enough nitrite must be used so the portion that is absorbed is adequate for the cure. The only exception is the case of sausages, in which all of the curing medium is mixed directly with the meat. The recipes in this book contain appropriate quantities of nitrite to cure the product.

Sugars

Ordinary white sugar (sucrose) and other forms of sugar, including corn syrup, honey, and maple syrup, are used in some cures. Sugars modify the flavor of the food and counteract some of the harsh flavor of the highly concentrated salt in the cure. Also, because salt extracts so much moisture, sugar adds to the perception of moistness in the cured product. Using less sweet forms of sugar, such as corn syrup and dextrose, provides the advantages of sugar without adding too much sweetness.

Herbs, Spices, and Other Flavorings

Nearly any spice or flavoring that can be used in cooking can be used in curing. Traditional recipes, of course, use traditional seasonings. Most of our most familiar cured sausages, for example, are of European origin and use such seasonings as garlic, pepper, coriander, caraway, nutmeg, and dry mustard. In addition, many chefs today are experimenting with unusual ingredients to give a modern accent to cured meats, poultry, fish, and sausages.

CURING METHODS

The two basic types of cures are **dry cures** and **brines**. With both of these methods, the food item remains in contact with the curing mixture, which contains salt plus any of the other ingredients discussed above, until the curing medium has penetrated the food uniformly. The difference between the methods is that in brines, the salt is dissolved in water, whereas in dry cures, it is not.

Dry Cures

In a dry cure, the cure ingredients (salt, plus seasonings and, in many cases, sugar and Prague Powder) are mixed together and packed or rubbed over the food product to coat it completely. The length of time required to dry-cure meats depends on their thickness. Lean meat 1 inch (2.5 cm) thick requires 3 to 8 hours, while a whole ham needs about 45 days. During a long cure, the food is repeatedly turned and rubbed with the cure mixture in order to maintain uniform contact. It is important that the entire surface area be coated.

The curing procedure for sausages could be considered a dry cure. However, in this case, the cure is mixed directly with the meat. Because no time is required for the cure to penetrate to the center of the meat, the curing process takes place very quickly, although the products may be air-dried or smoked for a longer period before being consumed.

Brine Cures

A brine is a solution of salt and other curing ingredients in water. The simplest way to use a brine is to immerse the meat in the brine and let it soak until the cure is complete. Compared with dry cures, brines are especially useful for poultry items, which are difficult to coat evenly with a dry cure because of their shape. Items that float, such as poultry, must be held down with a weight so they are completely submerged in the brine.

Simple brine soaking is used for small meat items, but because the brine takes time to penetrate to the center of large items such as hams, another method is used to speed the process. Brine is pumped or injected into the meat to make sure it penetrates evenly. After injection, the meat may be soaked in brine as well. Commercial operations use a variety of high-speed equipment for injecting brine. In addition, small pumps are available for brining by hand.

The length of time required for brining depends on the size and thickness of the item. Of course, meats that have been injected with brine need less time in the brine soak.

Fresh brine should be made for each batch of cured meats. Do not reuse brines because they are diluted and contaminated with juices from the first batch of meats.

SMOKING

Smoking has been used as a way of drying and preserving foods since prehistoric times. Smoking does have some preservative effects but, for modern cooking, it is more important for the flavors it gives to meats, poultry, and seafood. Even smoked cheeses and vegetables are enjoyed for their special flavors.

The first rule of smoking foods is *do not smoke meats, poultry, and fish that have not been cured.* The reason for this rule is a matter of food safety. During smoking, foods spend a period of time in the Food Danger Zone (p. 18)—that is, at a temperature that is favorable for the growth of bacteria. Without the preservative effects of curing, smoking could be unsafe. (This rule does not apply to *smoke roasting* and *barbecuing* [p. 71], which are more properly considered cooking methods rather than smoking methods because they take place at higher temperatures.)

After meats, poultry, and fish are cured, they should be allowed to dry slightly before being smoked. So that air can circulate all around the foods, place them on racks or hang them from hooks under refrigeration until the surface is dry to the touch. This preliminary drying allows the smoke to penetrate the foods more effectively.

The two basic types of smoking are cold smoking and hot smoking. In cold smoking, the temperature inside the smokehouse is kept at or below 85°F (30°C). At these temperatures, the foods take on the flavor of the smoke but are not cooked.

In hot smoking, the temperature inside the smokehouse may be as high as 165°F (74°C) for sausage and meats, or as high as 200°F (93°F) for fish and poultry. These temperatures are high enough to cook the foods being smoked. Higher temperatures are usually avoided because they result in excessive shrinkage. Foods may be hot smoked until they reach an internal temperature of 150° to 165°F (65° to 74°C) to ensure that they are fully cooked. Alternatively, they may be hot smoked for a shorter period and then poached until they reach this internal temperature. This second method is used when a less intense smoke flavor is desired. No matter which method is used, hot-smoked foods are always sold fully cooked.

A typical smoker consists of the following elements:

• An enclosed chamber for holding the foods to be smoked

• A source of smoke

• A means to circulate the smoke around the food and then to exhaust it

• A way of controlling the temperature inside the chamber

The smoke source consists of a receptacle for wood chips or sawdust plus a heating element, usually electric. If the smoker is to be used for cold smoking, the smoke generator should be outside the main chamber that holds the food. If the smoke generator is inside the food chamber, as in some less expensive smokers, the temperature will rise too high for cold smoking. This type of smoker is used only for hot smoking. Foods to be smoked are arranged on racks or hung from hangers with enough space between them so the smoke circulates freely around all surfaces. Commercially made smokers are safest to use, as improperly built smokers may present a fire hazard. If a smoker is used indoors, it is essential to provide for ventilation of the exhausted smoke to the outdoors.

Hickory is perhaps the most popular wood for smoking, but other hardwoods that may be used include oak, mesquite, and fruitwoods such as apple and cherry. Soft woods, like pine, are not used because they release bitter, tarry components when burned. It is important to use woods from a reliable source. Pressure-treated woods should never be used, as they contain toxic chemicals such as arsenic.

To summarize, the smoking process consists of the following steps:

1. Curing (dry cure or brine cure)

2. Air-drying

3. Smoking (hot smoking or cold smoking)

 ## Gravlax

Yield: 1 lb 14 oz (850 g) without skin

U.S.	Metric	Ingredients
2½ lb	1.2 kg	Salmon fillet, skin on
4 oz	125 g	Coarse salt
4 oz	1 mL	Sugar
¼ tsp	125 g	White pepper
2 oz	60 g	Fresh dill sprigs

Per 1 ounce:
Calories, 70; Protein, 8 g; Fat, 4 g (50% cal.); Cholesterol, 20 mg; Carbohydrates, 1 g; Fiber, 0 g; Sodium, 240 mg.

Figure 26.1 Slice gravlax and smoked salmon on the diagonal into paper-thin slices. Cut toward the tail end.

■ P r o c e d u r e

1. Pass your fingertips over the surface of the salmon fillet to locate any bones. Pull them out with needlenose pliers.

2. Mix together the salt, sugar, and pepper.

3. Select a stainless-steel, glass, ceramic, or other nonreactive pan to hold the salmon for curing. Sprinkle a little of the salt mixture on the bottom of the pan and lay the salmon on it skin side down. Cover the flesh side of the fillet completely with a layer of the salt mixture. Then top with the dill, again covering the fillet completely.

4. If you are doubling this recipe and curing 2 fillets, salt the second fillet in the same manner and invert it on top of the first so the dill is sandwiched between the fillets and the skin side of each fillet is toward the outside.

5. Cover the pan well and refrigerate for 1 day. Turn the fillet or fillets over and refrigerate for another day (for a total of 2 days). *Note:* Some instructions say to place a weight on the fish during the cure. This is optional. Weighting the fish produces a slightly drier, firmer finished product.

6. After 2 days, drain off any liquid that has accumulated in the pan. Carefully scrape all the dill and curing mixture from the fish.

7. To serve, cut on a sharp diagonal—that is, with the knife almost parallel to the table—into broad, paper-thin slices (Figure 26.1).

Smoked Salmon

Yield: 1 lb 14 oz (850 g) without skin

U.S.	Metric	Ingredients
2½ lb	1.2 kg	Salmon fillet, skin on
6 oz	180 g	Coarse salt
3 oz	90 g	Sugar
2 tsp	10 mL	Coarse black pepper
1 tsp	5 mL	Dry mustard
½ tsp	2 mL	Ground allspice
¼ tsp	1 mL	Cayenne
2 oz	60 g	Onion, chopped fine

Per 1 ounce:
Calories, 70; Protein, 8 g; Fat, 4 g (53% cal.); Cholesterol, 25 mg; Carbohydrates, 0 g; Fiber, 0 g; Sodium, 240 mg.

■ P r o c e d u r e

1. Pass your fingertips over the surface of the salmon fillet to locate any bones. Pull them out with needlenose pliers.

2. Mix together the salt, sugar, pepper, dry mustard, allspice, and cayenne.

3. Select a stainless-steel, glass, ceramic, or other nonreactive pan to hold the salmon for curing. Sprinkle a little of the salt mixture on the bottom of the pan and lay the salmon on it skin side down. Cover the flesh side of the fillet completely with a layer of the salt mixture. Then top with the chopped onion, distributing it evenly over the fillet.

4. If you are doubling this recipe and curing 2 fillets, salt the second fillet in the same manner and invert it on top of the first so the onion is sandwiched between the fillets and the skin side of each fillet is toward the outside.

5. Cover the pan well and refrigerate for 12–24 hours.

6. Remove the fillet from the pan and rinse off all the salt mixture and onion. Place on a rack set on a sheet pan, skin side down, and allow to dry, uncovered, in the refrigerator until a thin, dry skin (called a "pellicle") has formed on the surface of the flesh.

7. Cold smoke at 86°F (30°C).

8. To serve, cut on a sharp diagonal—that is, with the knife almost parallel to the table—into broad, paper-thin slices.

Smoked Trout

Yield: 10 fillets, 6–7 oz (180–200 g) each

U.S.	Metric	Ingredients
2 qt	2 L	Water
8 oz	250 g	Salt
2 oz	60 g	Light brown sugar
4	4	Bay leaves
2 tsp	10 mL	Black peppercorns
1 tsp	5 mL	Coriander seed
½ tsp	2 mL	Whole allspice
½ tsp	2 mL	Dry mustard
10	10	Trout fillets, about 8 oz (250 g) each

Per serving:
Calories, 320; Protein, 47 g; Fat, 12 g (36% cal.); Cholesterol, 135 mg; Carbohydrates, 2 g; Fiber, 0 g; Sodium, 3420 mg.

■ P r o c e d u r e

1. Prepare the brine: Combine the water, salt, sugar, bay leaves, peppercorns, coriander, allspice, and mustard in a pot. Bring to a simmer, stirring until the salt and sugar are dissolved.

2. Cool, then chill the brine.

3. Place the trout fillets in a stainless-steel, plastic, or other nonreactive pan in a single layer. Add enough cold brine to completely cover the fillets. Place a light weight on top of the fish to keep them submerged.

4. Refrigerate for 6–8 hours.

5. Remove from the brine and rinse in cold water. Blot dry.

6. Arrange on racks and allow to dry for several hours in the refrigerator.

7. Hot smoke at 185°F (85°C) until the internal temperature of the fish reaches 145°F (63°C), about 1–1½ hours. Cool, then refrigerate.

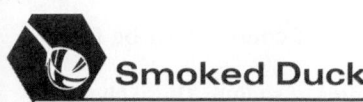

Smoked Duck

Yield: 2 smoked ducks

U.S.	Metric	Ingredients
1½ gal	6 L	Water
12 oz	360 g	Salt
6 oz	180 g	Sugar
3 oz	90 g	Prague Powder #1
3	3	Bay leaves
2 tsp	10 mL	Onion powder
2	2	Small ducks, about 4 lb (1.8 kg) each

■ P r o c e d u r e

1. Prepare the brine: Heat the water in a pot until it is warm. Add the salt, sugar, and Prague Powder and stir until they are dissolved. Add the bay leaves and onion powder.
2. Cool, then chill the brine.
3. Place the ducks in a stainless-steel, plastic, or other nonreactive container. Pour enough brine over them to cover them completely. Weight them to keep them submerged.
4. Allow to cure in the refrigerator for 2 days. (*Note:* Large ducks take 3–4 days to cure.)
5. Remove the ducks from the brine and rinse well.
6. Place on a rack and let dry in the refrigerator for at least 8 hours.
7. Hot smoke at 185° until the internal temperature of the duck reaches 165°F (74°F).

Per 1 duck, without skin:
Calories, 510; Protein, 79 g; Fat, 17 g (32% cal.); Cholesterol, 305 mg; Carbohydrates, 4 g; Fiber, 0 g; Sodium, 4330 mg.

V A R I A T I O N S

Smoked Turkey or Chicken
Brine the turkey or chicken as in the basic recipe. Turkey requires 4–6 days to cure in the brine, depending on the size. Chickens require 2–4 days, depending on their size.

SAUSAGES

A **sausage** is a mixture of ground meat, usually pork, and seasonings stuffed into a casing. The term sausage may also be used for the meat mixture itself, without the casing. Reduced to its simplest form, sausage meat may be nothing more than ground pork seasoned with salt.

Although there are hundreds or even thousands of kinds of sausages, the majority are based on the same few basic principles. These principles are simple enough that we can make a wide variety of sausages in the kitchen and not have to rely entirely on commercial products. Furthermore, it is not necessary to restrict ourselves to traditional sausage recipes. Many chefs are experimenting with ingredients and seasonings to add variety to the menu.

CATEGORIES OF SAUSAGES

Sausages can be classified into three basic groups:

Fresh sausages

Cured sausages

Smoked sausages

A **fresh sausage**, by USDA definition, is one that contains no nitrates or nitrites. It is basically a mixture of ground meat, seasonings, and flavorings. Although they are often raw, fresh sausages may contain cooked ingredients, or they may even be fully cooked before being sold. Any fresh raw sausage containing pork, of course, must be fully cooked before being served and eaten.

A cured sausage is one that contains nitrites or nitrates of sodium. These chemicals help prevent spoilage and food-borne disease, as explained in the first part of this chapter. Incidentally, they also keep the meat red or pink, even when cooked. Cured sausages may be sold raw or cooked, soft and moist like fresh sausages, semidried and firm, or dried and hard like salami. Pork salamis, which are Italian in origin, and similar cured, dried sausages are raw, but the curing, aging, and drying process renders them safe to eat. As explained on page 826, air-dried sausages that are intended to be eaten raw are made with nitrates in addition to nitrites for a longer lasting cure.

Smoked sausages may be hot smoked and, therefore, cooked, or cold smoked. Smoking may be light or heavy, depending on the sausage. Sausages, like other smoked meats, are cured before being smoked. The cure mixture is mixed directly with the sausage meat.

BASIC SAUSAGE INGREDIENTS

The basic ingredients of sausage meat are the following:

Lean pork

Pork fat, preferably hard fatback, ground with the meat

Salt

Spices, herbs, and other seasonings and flavorings

In the case of cured sausage, curing mixes containing nitrites or nitrates are added to the above list.

The Meat

Pork is the most commonly used meat in sausage-making, but other meats or mixtures of meat may be used. Beef, veal, lamb, chicken, turkey, duck, liver, rabbit, and venison all find their way into sausages. Mixtures of pork plus one or more of these meats are often used. More exotic sausages may include such ingredients as sweetbreads and brains.

Certified pork—that is, pork that is certified to be free of trichinosis—is used for sausages that are to be air-dried and eaten uncooked.

The Fat

Pork fat or other fat, such as the beef fat used in all-beef sausages, is an important ingredient. Because our impression of juiciness in any cooked meat is largely due to the meat's fat content, some fat is included in sausage mixtures. Without it, the texture of the cooked sausage would be very dry.

In most traditional sausages, fat makes up 25 to 50 percent of the total weight, with 33 percent fat being the norm. In other words, proportions of fat to lean range from 3 parts lean plus 1 part fat (the leanest sausages) to 1 part lean plus 1 part fat (rich, fatty sausages). Varying the proportions changes the character of the sausage.

Hard fatback is preferred over other fats for pork sausage. Softer fats are more likely to melt out of the sausage during cooking. A quick and easy way to make pork sausages without worrying about the ratio of fat to lean is to use whole pork butt. The ratio of fat to lean in this cut is very good for sausages.

In today's diet-conscious atmosphere, it may make sense to try to create low-fat sausages. But be advised that extra care is required when making sausages with less than 25 percent fat. Lean sausages should never be overcooked, as overcooking makes them dry. Keep the meat mixture cold to avoid damage to the texture of the meat and fat. With care, it is possible to make tasty sausages with a fat content as low as 10 or 15 percent. One should not expect, however, that the eating qualities of lean sausages will be the same as those of fattier sausages.

Cereal ingredients and fillers (rice, barley, bread crumbs, and so on) can be used to help reduce fat content. Because these starches absorb and retain moisture, they enhance the total moisture content of low-fat sausages.

Seasonings

Herbs, spices, and other flavorings account for the primary differences among sausages. Many, if not most, of the world's fresh sausages are made of nothing more than ground pork and seasonings. It is the seasonings that give them their characteristic flavor. A glance at the recipes in this section will confirm this.

Some of the major spices and herbs used in sausage making are

Allspice	Marjoram
Caraway seeds	Mustard
Cayenne or hot red pepper	Nutmeg
Cinnamon	Paprika
Cloves	Parsley
Coriander	Pepper, black and white
Cumin	Sage
Fennel seed	Tarragon
Ginger	Thyme
Mace	

Other important ingredients include

Garlic	Wine, white and red
Onion	Vinegar
Shallots	Eggs
Chives	

Standardized spice mixtures are often used to season sausages, pâtés, and similar items. One of the most common is **quatre épices** (French for "four spices"), a mixture that exists in many versions. It can usually be obtained commercially, or it can be home-made, using recipes such as those on page 839.

Cure Mixes

Sausages that are to be air-dried are cured with both nitrate and nitrite, as explained on page 826. For other cured sausages, only nitrite, usually in the form of Prague Powder #1, is used. Other ingredients, such as dextrose and additional salt, may be combined with the Prague Powder to make the cure mix. The cure mix may be incorporated into the sausage in one of two ways:

1. It may be mixed with the meat after it is diced. The diced meat is then chilled thoroughly before being ground.
2. It may be combined with the remaining spices and seasonings and mixed into the ground meat.

Refer to individual recipes for more detailed instructions on making and incorporating cure mixes.

Other Ingredients

A number of sausages are characterized by unusual or exotic ingredients. Some of these are traditional and time-honored, such as the black truffles included in some regional French sausages and the chestnuts or raisins in other specialty sausages.

Other unusual sausages are modern innovations by creative chefs. It is no longer uncommon, when reading today's restaurant menus, to come across sausages with such ingredients as sun-dried tomatoes or fresh vegetables like sweet bell peppers and spinach. In theory, there is no limit to what can be stuffed into sausage casings. The main requirement is that the ingredients complement or enhance one another, just as the meat, seasonings, and vegetable garnish on a dinner plate should complement one another.

CASINGS

Natural casings are made from the intestines of meat animals. *Sheep casings* are the smallest, ranging from ¾ inch (18 mm) to more than 1 inch (25 mm) in diameter. They are used for breakfast links, frankfurters, and similar sausages. *Hog casings* are medium-sized, about 1 to 1½ inches (3 to 4 cm) in diameter, depending on what part of the intestines they are taken from. They are used for many popular fresh sausages, such as Italian sausages and fresh bratwurst. *Beef casings* range in size from the so-called *beef round*, about 1¾ inches (45 mm) in diameter, through *beef middles*, 2½ inches (63 mm), to the large *beef bung*, more than 4 inches (100 mm) in diameter.

Natural casings are often sold packed in salt. Because of the preservative effect of the salt, the casings keep indefinitely as long as they are refrigerated. Natural casings are easy to use if they are handled correctly. Before being stuffed, they must be untangled, rinsed, and flushed, and examined for holes according to the following procedure.

Procedure for Preparing Natural Casings

1. Carefully remove the casings, one at a time, from the salt pack and unravel them. Because a single casing may be 12 feet (4 meters) long, it is easiest to do this on a large workbench. Separate the individual lengths and keep them separate in their own little stacks on the bench. When unraveling them, do not pull hard, because this may cause knotting.

   Unravel slightly more casing than you think you will need. It is easier to return unused casings to the salt pack than it is to separate and flush additional casings when you run out before you have stuffed your whole batch of meat.

2. Partially fill a large bowl with clean water and set it in a sink under the faucet. Take hold of the end of one casing and drop the rest of it into the bowl of water. Open the end of the casing and run cold water into it, enough to fill about 12 inches (30 cm) of it. Holding the casing at both ends of this "water sausage," allow the water to flush through the casing from one end to the other.

   This accomplishes two purposes. It rinses out the inside of the casing, and it identifies any holes that might be present. Pinpoint-size holes are no problem, but if a large hole is found, simply cut the casing in two at that point. Short pieces may be discarded for the sake of efficiency.

3. If you are making a small quantity of sausages and stuffing them immediately, each casing can be put on the stuffing horn as it is rinsed. If this is not the case, the casing must be stored for later use. Select a container with a cover and fill it about three-fourths full of cold water. Drop in the casing and let one end hang over the edge.

   Repeat with remaining casings. Fill the container to the top with cold water, cover, and refrigerate until needed. By letting the ends of the casings hang over the edge, you can remove one at a time from the container without tangling them. If the end of the casing dries out, simply cut it off.

Because the supply of natural casings is not nearly large enough to accommodate all the sausages produced, other types of casings have come into wide use. **Collagen casings** are molded from animal materials and are completely edible, like natural casings. Unlike natural casings, they are uniform in size, making portion control easier. Various types are manufactured for different uses. Some are used only for fresh sausages, as they are not strong enough to hold the weight of the sausages if they are hung for smoking. Other types are stronger and intended to be used for smoked sausages. Most collagen casings must be refrigerated to keep them from becoming dry and brittle. To use, dip them in water for a few seconds to soften them if they are dry, then put them on the sausage stuffing nozzle.

Synthetic fibrous casings are made from a plastic material and are not edible. They are widely used for salamis and luncheon meats, and the casing is peeled off before or after slicing. These casings are nonperishable and need no refrigeration. They must be soaked in water before using to make them flexible. Soaking time varies, and the manufacturer should specify the recommended time.

EQUIPMENT

Most fresh sausages can be made with no special equipment other than a meat grinder and a device for getting the meat into the casings.

The working parts of a meat grinder are a rotating blade and a selection of dies in various sizes. The size of the die determines the fineness of the grind. A screw forces the meat from the feed tube to the blade, and the blade chops the meat as it is forced through the holes of the die.

Before grinding meat, it is important to be sure of the following two points:

1. The equipment must be clean and sanitary. Make sure there is no trace of food from previous jobs hiding in the many nooks and crannies of the grinder, blades, and dies.

2. The equipment must be cold in order to avoid warming the meat. Refrigerate the grinder parts or set them in ice water before use.

The sausage stuffer is the second piece of equipment necessary for making sausages. The simplest stuffer resembles a funnel. The casings are pushed over the narrow end and the meat is pushed through the wide end by hand or with a wooden plunger. These are adequate for making a few pounds of sausage but are not suitable for larger batches.

Larger stuffers have detachable nozzles or horns for different casing sizes. The nozzle is attached to a cylindrical reservoir that holds the meat, which is pushed through by a piston. On smaller machines, the piston is simply pushed through by hand. These machines are suitable for small-scale production such as might be done in a small to medium-size restaurant. For large-scale commercial production, larger machines are used. The piston in a large machine is operated by means of a crank and a sequence of gears.

THE GRIND

The grind of the meat determines the texture of the sausage. We can divide sausage meat into two categories based on grind. Most common sausages are made simply of meat and fat ground to varying degrees of fineness or coarseness, mixed with seasonings, and stuffed into casings. We refer to these as **basic grind** sausages. Some sausages, on the other hand, including familiar ones like frankfurters, mortadella, and bologna, are made with meat and fat ground to a smooth purée and blended with a little liquid, such as water or milk. We refer to these as **emulsified** or **emulsion grind** sausages because of the added liquid content and the emulsion of the fat with the meat and liquid.

Basic Grind

The fineness or coarseness of the grind is an important characteristic of any sausage. For example, one identifying feature of Toulouse Sausages (p. 839) is their coarse texture. The meat is chopped by hand rather than ground. On the other hand, typical breakfast sausages have a fairly fine grind.

To grind meat, cut it into pieces small enough to fit easily into the feed tube of the grinder, then chill it well. Control the coarseness of the grind by selecting the proper die, as indicated in the recipe. In some cases, fine grinds are made by grinding the meat once through the large die and a second time through the fine die. As indicated in the procedure below, the meat, fat, and seasonings are mixed until uniformly blended after the meat is ground.

The meat mixture must be kept cold during grinding. When the mixture gets too warm, the fat becomes soft and begins to lose its structure. As a result, it may melt out too readily when the sausage is cooked, resulting in excessive shrinkage, poor texture, and dryness. If the kitchen is warm, return the meat to the refrigerator to chill it thoroughly after cutting it up and before grinding it. If it must be ground more than once, return it to the refrigerator between grindings.

Additional textural variation in basic grind sausages can be created by mixing chunks or dice of meat or other ingredients into a more finely ground forcemeat, as is often done in pâtés.

When following any sausage recipe, adhere closely to the grinding and processing directions in order to achieve the proper texture and character.

Emulsified Grind

In the finest-textured sausages, the meat is actually puréed to a smooth paste. Puréed raw meat is capable of absorbing a good deal of moisture, and water or milk is usually added to improve the texture. For sausages that include milk, a recipe may indicate either liquid milk or water plus dried milk solids. The dried milk is added at the same time as the spice mixture.

Because grinding meat to a smooth paste generates heat, water is added in the form of ice to keep the temperature low. If liquid milk is called for, freeze the milk into chunks.

Procedure for Making Fresh and Cured Basic Grind Sausages

1. Weigh the meats and fat. Cut them into chunks small enough to fit into the grinder.

2. If the sausages are to be cured, toss the cure mix with the diced meat at this point. Alternatively, combine the cure mix with the salt and spices in step 4.

3. Chill the meat well before proceeding.

4. Measure the salt and spices.

5. Grind the meat and fat, following the directions in the recipe to achieve the proper fineness or coarseness of grind.

6. Chill the meat well. Ideally, the meat should be chilled to 32° to 35°F (0° to 2°C) before mixing and stuffing.

7. Combine the meat, salt, and spices and mix thoroughly. This is best done by hand in a large tub or other container. It can also be done with a mixing machine using the paddle attachment.

    If the recipe calls for cold water or other liquid, mix the salt and spices with the water first, then mix this combination with the meat. This facilitates a better distribution of the spices than mixing them dry with the meat.

    Many recipes say to refrigerate the meat overnight after it is mixed to allow the meat to absorb the seasonings and the flavors to blend. However, it is easier to stuff the sausages immediately after mixing. If the salted meat mixture is allowed to stand, it becomes firmer and thus harder to force through the stuffer. Stuffing immediately allows the casings to be filled more uniformly and with fewer air bubbles. Besides, the meat can absorb the seasonings just as well in the casings as in the meat tub.

8. Test for seasonings. Do not taste the raw meat. Rather, make a small ball or patty and cook it in a small sauté pan or poach it in water. Then cool the meat slightly and taste. If more salt or other seasoning is needed, add it to the sausage mixture.

9. Place the meat in the stuffer, one handful at a time. Pack each handful firmly into the stuffer to eliminate air bubbles.

10. Slide the casings onto the nozzle. To help the casings slide on easily, moisten both them and the stuffer nozzle with water.

11. Stuff the sausages, following the directions for your equipment (see Figure 26.2). The sausages will pull the casings off the nozzle as the meat flows through it, but it is best to hold your hand at the end of the nozzle to help control the rate at which the casing is pulled from the nozzle. From time to time, as the casing is filled, it is necessary to push the bunched-up, unfilled casing toward the end of the nozzle so it will slide off more easily. Do not stuff the casings too tightly. If the meat is packed too tightly, it will be difficult to twist the sausage into links.

12. After all the meat is stuffed into casings, remove any air bubbles by pricking the casing and pressing the surface to expel the air.

13. Twist the sausage into links of uniform size.

Figure 26.2
Stuffing sausages.

(a) A small sausage stuffer fitted with a medium nozzle. This stuffer holds 5 lb (2.3 kg) meat at a time.

(b) Flush out the casings with fresh, cold water, while looking for holes.

(d) When stuffing the casings, use one hand to guide the casing as it slides off the nozzle.

(c) Slide the casings onto the proper size nozzle.

(e) Pinch and twist the sausage into links of the desired size.

Because a meat grinder is not capable of grinding sausage to this texture, the grinding procedure is done in two stages. First, grind the meat and fat separately using the fine die on the meat grinder. Keep the two separate and chill them after this grinding. Second, grind the meat to a smooth paste with a food chopper (buffalo chopper) or food processor. Place the lean meat in the bowl of the chopper and run it a few seconds. Then add the ice and continue to grind until smooth. Monitor the temperature carefully. Do not allow it to rise above 50°F (10°C). Add the fat and continue to grind to blend it in. Continue to monitor the temperature. Do not allow it to rise above 58°F (14°C).

Emulsified sausages are usually cooked in water, then chilled in cold water after stuffing. If they are to be smoked, they are smoked first and then cooked.

Procedure for Making Fresh and Cured Emulsified Sausages

1. Keeping the meat and fat separate, grind them with the fine die of a meat grinder, following steps 1 through 6 of the basic sausage-making procedure above. Chill well.

2. If indicated in the recipe, mix the seasonings with the lean meat. (Alternatively, add the seasonings at the same time as the ice in step 3.)

3. Place the lean meat in the bowl of a food chopper or food processor. Run the chopper a few turns, then add the ice. Continue to chop to a fine paste. Do not allow the temperature to rise above 50°F (10°C).

4. Add the fat and continue to grind to blend it in. Continue to monitor the temperature. Do not allow it to rise above 58°F (14°C).

5. Follow steps 8 through 12 in the procedure above to test the seasonings and stuff the casings.

SMOKING SAUSAGES

The procedure for smoking sausages is the same as for smoking other meats (see Figure 26.3). Refer to page 828 for basic information on smoking and follow the instructions in individual recipes. Note in particular the following points:

1. Only cured sausages should be smoked.

2. The sausages should be dried briefly before being smoked, like other smoked foods (see p. 828). Hang them so that air can circulate around them and allow to dry for about 1½ hours or as indicated in the recipe.

3. Hot smoke or cold smoke as indicated in the recipe. Air-dried sausages to be eaten raw are cold smoked. Sausages that are sold cooked are generally hot smoked. After smoking, they are usually poached to an internal temperature of 160° to 165°F (71° to 74°F), then cooled quickly in ice water and blotted dry.

Figure 26.3
Finished sausages before removing from the smoker

COOKING SAUSAGES

Although sausages are sometimes ingredients or components of more elaborate dishes, they are also popular as stand-alone menu items like other meats. Preparation of sausages before cooking is minimal. In most cases, sausages may be considered ready to cook—or, in the case of fully cooked sausages, ready to heat. Fresh raw sausages containing pork must be fully cooked before serving, like other fresh pork products. If a fresh sausage contains no pork, such as the lamb sausage on page 841, it may be served somewhat less done. Removing it from the heat when still pink inside helps retain juices.

Fully cooked sausages need only be heated through before serving. Cooking times, however, are nearly the same as for raw sausages. In other words, the time it takes for the heat to penetrate to the center is about the same.

The following cooking methods are most often used for sausages.

Simmering

Place sausages in a pan with enough salted water to cover. Bring to a simmer and simmer until completely cooked. Do not let the water boil. This is likely to make the sausages burst or shrink excessively.

Time depends on the thickness of the sausage. Sausages in hog casings take about 20 minutes to cook; smaller ones may take as little as 10 minutes, larger ones 30 minutes or more.

Raw sausages may be simmered until cooked through, then finished by one of the following methods.

Sautéing and Pan-Frying

Sausages are sautéed or pan-fried using the same techniques as for other meats. For many kinds of sausages, the browning that results makes them more appetizing than simmered ones.

If the sausages are not raw, it is necessary only to cook them until they are lightly browned and heated through. If they are raw, lower heat is necessary so they have time to become completely cooked by the time they are browned.

Sautéing and pan-frying are used not only for sausages in casings but also for patties and *crêpinettes*, which are sausage patties wrapped in caul fat (see p. 281). Do not press on the patties with the spatula while cooking. This forces out juices and makes them dry.

Braising

Because fresh raw sausages may require long cooking times, braising is often the preferred cooking method. The sausages are browned by sautéing them over moderate heat for up to 5 minutes, then finished using a moist-heat cooking method. Cooking with moisture may take any of several forms, including the four methods listed below. These methods are suitable not only for fresh sausages but also for fully cooked and smoked sausages that are served hot.

- Covering the pan to hold in steam.
- Adding a small amount of liquid (water, stock, wine, and so on), covering the pan, and cooking until done.
- Glazing—that is, adding a small amount of stock and continuing to cook. The pan may be covered or left uncovered at the beginning, but the last part of cooking takes place with the cover off. The sausages are basted with the stock as it reduces, giving them a glaze. Any stock remaining in the pan after the sausages are cooked will be reduced and thickened, and it may be served with the sausages as a sauce. This cooking method is especially suitable for patties and crêpinettes.
- Cooking the sausages in a casserole or stew after they are browned. Sauerkraut, bean dishes, and gumbos are examples.

Broiling and Grilling

Brush the sausages with oil to prevent sticking, and broil or grill as for other meats. Moderate heat is usually best. High heat may brown the sausages too much before they are fully cooked and is more likely to cause splitting.

ABOUT THE SAUSAGE RECIPES

Before proceeding to the sausage recipes that follow, please take note of the following points.

1. Refer to the general procedures for making sausages on pages 836–837. Some of these points are not repeated in each recipe.
2. Ratios of fat to lean are not specified in most of the recipes. Refer to the explanation of fat-lean ratios on page 832 and adjust the amount of fat in the recipes as desired.

Quatre Épices I

Yield: 1¼ oz (37 g)

U.S.	Metric	Ingredients
4 tbsp	25 g	Ground white or black pepper
2 tsp	4 g (10 mL)	Nutmeg
2 tsp	4 g (10 mL)	Ground cloves
2 tsp	4 g (10 mL)	Cinnamon

■ P r o c e d u r e

1. Combine the ingredients and mix well.
2. Store in a tightly sealed container.

Per 1 ounce:
Calories, 90; Protein, 3 g; Fat, 2 g (13% cal.); Cholesterol, 0 mg;
Carbohydrates, 19 g; Fiber, 8 g; Sodium, 10 mg.

 ## Quatre Épices II

Yield: 1¼ oz (34 g)

U.S.	Metric	Ingredients
10 tsp	20 g	Ground white pepper
3 tsp	6 g (15 mL)	Nutmeg
3 tsp	6 g (15 mL)	Ground ginger
1 tsp	2 g (5 mL)	Ground cloves

■ P r o c e d u r e

1. Combine the ingredients and mix well.
2. Store in a tightly sealed container.

Per 1 ounce:
Calories, 100; Protein, 3 g; Fat, 3 g (21% cal.); Cholesterol, 0 mg;
Carbohydrates, 18 g; Fiber, 7 g; Sodium, 5 mg.

 ## Pork Sausage

Yield: 6 lb (3 kg)

U.S.	Metric	Ingredients
6 lb	3 kg	Pork and pork fat
2 tbsp	30 g	Salt
2 tsp	4 g (10 mL)	Quatre épices
6 fl oz	200 mL	Water, cold

■ P r o c e d u r e

1. Cut the meat and fat into cubes small enough to fit into the grinder. Chill thoroughly.
2. Grind the meat once with the large die and again with the small die. If necessary, chill the meat between grindings.
3. Mix the salt and spices with the water. Add to the ground meat and mix thoroughly by hand.
4. Stuff into hog casings or sheep casings.

Per 1 ounce:
Calories, 70; Protein, 5 g; Fat, 5 g (69% cal.); Cholesterol, 20 mg;
Carbohydrates, 0 g; Fiber, 0 g; Sodium, 160 mg.

VARIATIONS

Toulouse Sausage
Use the ingredients specified in the recipe, but grind the meat coarsely. This can be done in three ways, with slightly different results for each method:

1. Chop the meat coarsely with a knife.
2. Grind only once using the large die of the grinder.
3. Grind very briefly in a food processor, just until achieving a coarse texture.

Stuff into hog casings.

Toulouse sausages should have a fat content of at least 33 percent—that is, 1 part fat to 2 parts lean.

Crêpinettes
Weigh out 3½-oz (100-g) portions of sausage meat. Shape it into oval patties. Cut squares of caul fat (p. 281) and wrap the sausage portions in the squares. Cook by pan-frying, glazing (see p. 838), or grilling.

Other ingredients are often mixed with the sausage meat. Classic additions include blanched, peeled pistachios (2–3 oz per lb sausage meat/125–175 g per kg); chopped, cooked chestnuts (4 oz per lb/250 g per kg); or fresh, diced truffle (whatever quantity the budget allows).

Other sausage mixtures, such as those in the other recipes in this section, may be used to make crêpinettes.

French Garlic Sausage

Yield: 7 lb (3.5 kg)

U.S.	Metric	Ingredients
6 lb	3 kg	Pork and pork fat
1 lb	500 g	Pork rind
2 tbsp	30 g	Salt
1½ tsp	3 g (7 mL)	Black pepper
2 tsp	8 g	Crushed garlic
½ tsp	2 mL	Ground sage
½ tsp	2 mL	Dried marjoram
½ tsp	2 mL	Dried thyme
4 fl oz	125 mL	Dry white wine

Per 1 ounce:
Calories, 70; Protein, 5 g; Fat, 5 g (69% cal.); Cholesterol, 20 mg;
Carbohydrates, 0 g; Fiber, 0 g; Sodium, 150 mg.

■ Procedure

1. Cut the meat and fat into cubes small enough to fit into the grinder. Chill thoroughly.
2. Simmer the pork rind in salted water at least 2 hours, until very tender. Chill thoroughly.
3. Grind the meat once with the large die and again with the medium die. If necessary, chill the meat between grindings.
4. Repeat this grinding procedure with the pork rind. Mix the ground pork rind with the ground meat.
5. Mix the salt and spices with the wine. Add to the ground meat and mix thoroughly by hand.
6. Stuff into hog casings.

Hot Italian Sausage

Yield: 6 lb (3 kg)

U.S.	Metric	Ingredients
6 lb	3 kg	Pork and pork fat
2 tbsp	30 g	Salt
2 tsp	10 mL	Black pepper
2 tsp	10 mL	Fennel seeds
4 tsp	20 mL	Paprika
2 tsp	10 mL	Crushed red pepper
1 tsp	5 mL	Ground coriander
2 tsp	10 mL	Sugar
6 fl oz	200 mL	Water, cold

Per 1 ounce:
Calories, 70; Protein, 5 g; Fat, 5 g (69% cal.); Cholesterol, 20 mg;
Carbohydrates, 0 g; Fiber, 0 g; Sodium, 160 mg.

■ Procedure

1. Cut the meat into cubes small enough to fit into the grinder. Chill the meat thoroughly.
2. Grind once with the medium die.
3. Mix the salt and spices with the cold water. Add to the ground meat and mix thoroughly by hand.
4. Stuff into hog casings.

VARIATIONS

Mild Italian Sausage
Omit the paprika, crushed red pepper, and coriander.

Spicy Garlic Sausage
Omit the fennel and coriander. Add 2 tsp (10 mL) dried oregano and 1–2 tsp (5–10 mL) chopped garlic.

Veal or Beef Sausage

Yield: 6 lb (3 kg)

U.S.	Metric	Ingredients
4 lb	2 kg	Pork and pork fat
2 lb	1 kg	Veal or beef, lean
2 tbsp	30 g	Salt
2 tsp	4 g (10 mL)	Quatre épices
6 fl oz	200 mL	Water, cold

Per 1 ounce:
Calories, 60; Protein, 5 g; Fat, 4 g (64% cal.); Cholesterol, 20 mg;
Carbohydrates, 0 g; Fiber, 0 g; Sodium, 170 mg.

■ Procedure

1. Cut the meat into cubes small enough to fit into the grinder. Chill the meat thoroughly.
2. Grind the meat once with the large or medium die for coarse sausage. For a finer texture, grind once more with the small die. If necessary, chill the meat between grindings.
3. Mix the salt and spices with the water. Add to the ground meat and mix thoroughly by hand.
4. Stuff into hog casings.

VARIATIONS

Instead of the meat ratios given in the main recipe, use 3 lb (1.5 kg) pork and pork fat and 3 lb (1.5 kg) veal or beef. These proportions make a somewhat leaner sausage with more of the flavor of the veal or beef.

Venison Sausage
Prepare as in the basic recipe or the first variation at left, substituting venison for the veal or beef. Add 4 juniper berries, crushed to a powder, to the spice mixture. Substitute chilled red wine for the cold water.

Fresh Bratwurst

Yield: 6 lb (3 kg)

U.S.	Metric	Ingredients
6 lb	3 kg	Pork and pork fat
2 tbsp	30 g	Salt
3 tsp	15 mL	White pepper
¼ tsp	1 mL	Mace
1 tsp	5 mL	Ground coriander
½ tsp	2 mL	Ground ginger
6 fl oz	200 mL	Water, cold

Per 1 ounce:
Calories, 70; Protein, 5 g; Fat, 5 g (69% cal.); Cholesterol, 20 mg; Carbohydrates, 0 g; Fiber, 0 g; Sodium, 160 mg.

■ P r o c e d u r e

1. Cut the meat and fat into cubes small enough to fit into the grinder. Chill thoroughly.
2. Grind the meat once with the large die and again with the small die. If necessary, chill the meat between grindings.
3. Mix the salt and spices with the water. Add to the ground meat and mix thoroughly by hand.
4. Stuff into hog casings.

V A R I A T I O N

Following the procedure on page 837, make an emulsified grind instead of a basic grind. Omit the water indicated in the recipe and add 12 oz (400 g) ice as indicated in the procedure.

Lamb Sausage

Yield: 6 lb (3 kg)

U.S.	Metric	Ingredients
6 lb	3 kg	Lamb shoulder (see note)
2 tbsp	30 g	Salt
4 tsp	20 mL	Chopped garlic
2 tbsp	30 mL	Paprika
1 tsp	5 mL	Cayenne
1 tsp	5 mL	Black pepper
2 tbsp	30 mL	Ground cumin
2 tsp	10 mL	Dried oregano
1 tsp	5 mL	Cinnamon
4 tbsp	60 mL	Chopped cilantro
6 fl oz	200 mL	Water, cold

Per 1 ounce:
Calories, 80; Protein, 5 g; Fat, 6 g (73% cal.); Cholesterol, 20 mg; Carbohydrates, 0 g; Fiber, 0 g; Sodium, 160 mg.

Note: Include some fat with the lean or, if desired, include some pork fat. If pork fat is used, the finished sausage must be cooked to the well-done stage. If all lamb is used, the sausage may be served slightly rare.

■ P r o c e d u r e

1. Cut the meat and fat into cubes small enough to fit into the grinder. Chill thoroughly.
2. Grind the meat once with the medium die.
3. Mix the salt and spices with the water. Add to the ground meat and mix thoroughly by hand.
4. Stuff into hog casings.

V A R I A T I O N S

For a simpler, more straightforward flavor, omit the oregano, cinnamon, and cilantro.

Herbed Lamb Sausage
The flavor of the sausages made by the main recipe is characteristic of the Middle East and parts of North Africa. For a lamb sausage of a more European or North American character, omit the paprika, cumin, oregano, cinnamon, and cilantro. Add 2 tsp (10 mL) dried thyme, 2 tsp (10 mL) dried rosemary, and 1 oz (30 g) chopped shallot.

Duck Sausage

Yield: 6 lb (3 kg)

U.S.	Metric	Ingredients
6 lb	3 kg	Boneless duck meat and fat
2 tbsp	30 g	Salt
2 tsp	10 mL	Quatre épices
6 oz	185 g	Pine nuts, toasted, or pistachios, blanched and peeled
6 oz	185 g	Marinated sun-dried tomatoes, drained and chopped
½ tsp	2 mL	Dried thyme

Per 1 ounce:
Calories, 160; Protein, 3 g; Fat, 17 g (91% cal.); Cholesterol, 25 mg; Carbohydrates, 1 g; Fiber, 0 g; Sodium, 160 mg.

■ P r o c e d u r e

1. Cut the meat and fat into cubes small enough to fit into the grinder. Chill thoroughly.
2. Grind the meat once with the medium die.
3. Mix the salt, spices, nuts, and sun-dried tomatoes. Add to the ground meat and mix thoroughly by hand.
4. Stuff into small hog casings.

Boudin Blanc (White Sausage)

Yield: 7 lb (3.6 kg)

U.S.	Metric	Ingredients
1 lb 8 oz	750 g	Chicken breast, boneless and skinless
2 lb	1 kg	Lean white pork
1 lb 8 oz	750 g	Pork fat
12 oz	375 g	Onion, chopped
1 pt	500 mL	Milk
8 oz	250 g	Fresh bread crumbs
4	4	Eggs
3 tbsp	45 mL	Salt
2 tsp	10 mL	White pepper
½ tsp	2 mL	Mace
1 oz	30 g	Parsley, chopped (optional)

Per 1 ounce:
Calories, 90; Protein, 4 g; Fat, 7 g (72% cal.); Cholesterol, 25 mg;
Carbohydrates, 2 g; Fiber, 0 g; Sodium, 210 mg.

■ **P r o c e d u r e**

1. Cut the chicken, pork, and fat into cubes small enough to fit into the grinder. Combine the chicken with the lean pork, but keep the pork fat separate.

2. Grind the meat once with the large die, then once with the small die. Chill.

3. Grind the fat once with the large die, then once with the small die. Chill.

4. Simmer the onions in the milk until they are tender. Pour this mixture over the bread crumbs in a bowl. Cool, then set in the freezer until partly frozen.

5. Place the ground meat in the bowl of a food chopper or food processor. Chop a few seconds, then add the partially frozen milk mixture. Grind until the mixture is uniformly blended.

6. Beat together the eggs, salt, pepper, mace, and parsley (if used). Add to the meat in the grinder and continue to grind to a smooth paste. Check the temperature to make sure it does not rise above 50°F (10°C). If necessary, chill before continuing.

7. Add the fat to the grinder and continue to grind until the mixture is smooth and uniform. Do not let the temperature rise above 58°F (14°C).

8. Stuff into hog casings.

9. Poach the sausages by simmering them slowly in water until cooked through, about 20 minutes. Drain and plunge into ice water to cool. Drain again and refrigerate.

V A R I A T I O N S

Other white meats, such as veal or rabbit, can be used instead of chicken.

Mortadella

Yield: 5 lb (2.4 kg)

U.S.	Metric	Ingredients
2 lb 8 oz	1.2 kg	Pork, lean
1 tsp	5 mL	Prague Powder #1
5 tsp	25 mL	Salt
1½ fl oz	45 mL	Dry white wine
1 lb 6 oz	660 g	Firm pork fat, such as fatback
		Garnish:
6 oz	180 g	Pork fatback
2 oz	60 g	Pistachios, peeled
14 oz	400 g	Ice
1½ tsp	7 mL	White pepper
1½ tsp	7 mL	Paprika
1 tsp	5 mL	Mace
1 tsp	5 mL	Quatre épices
1 tsp	5 mL	Ground coriander
¼ tsp	1 mL	Ground cloves
2 oz	60 g	Nonfat dry milk powder

Per 1 ounce:
Calories, 110; Protein, 4 g; Fat, 10 g (82% cal.); Cholesterol, 15 mg; Carbohydrates, 1 g; Fiber, 0 g; Sodium, 190 mg.

■ Procedure

1. Cut the pork into cubes small enough to fit into the grinder.
2. Toss the meat with the Prague Powder, salt, and wine and refrigerate for several hours or overnight.
3. Cut the pork fat into cubes. Refrigerate several hours or overnight.
4. Prepare the garnish. Cut the fatback into small dice. Blanch in boiling water for 2 minutes. Drain. Refrigerate.
5. Pick over the pistachios to be sure they are all peeled and in good condition.
6. Grind the lean pork using the small die of the grinder. Place it in a food chopper.
7. Grind the fat from step 3 (not the fat for the garnish) through the small die and set it aside. Refrigerate it if the kitchen is warm, even though you will be using it in a few minutes.
8. Start the food chopper and run a few seconds. Add the ice, the spices, and the milk powder and continue to chop the meat to a fine paste. Check the temperature of the meat. Do not let it rise above 50°F (10°C).
9. Add the ground fat and continue to run the chopper. Stop the machine from time to time and stir briefly by hand if necessary for even mixing. Process to a fine, uniform paste. Do not let the temperature rise above 58°F (14°C).
10. Remove the meat mixture from the chopper and place in a stainless-steel bowl set over ice. Add the garnish (diced pork and pistachios) and mix them into the meat purée.
11. Stuff into large beef casings or artificial casings.
12. Allow to dry for several hours in the refrigerator. This step is not essential, but it gives the sausage time to take on the desired pink color.
13. Poach the sausage in water over very low heat, using a thermometer to ensure that the temperature of the water stays at 165°F (74°C). Cook until the internal temperature of the sausage reaches 152°F (67°C).
14. Remove the sausage from the cooking water and cool it in 2 steps. First, place it in room-temperature water for 5–10 minutes. Next, place it a tub of cold running water until completely cooled.
15. Refrigerate.

V A R I A T I O N

Bologna
Omit the garnish of diced fat and pistachios. Omit the wine. After stuffing the casings and drying the sausage, hot smoke at 165°F (74°C) for 1 hour. Remove from the smoker and immediately poach as in the basic recipe.

Cajun-Style Sausage

Yield: 6 lb (3 kg)

U.S.	Metric	Ingredients
6 lb	3 kg	Pork and pork fat
1¼ tsp	6 mL	Prague Powder #1
2 tsp	10 mL	Salt
1 tsp	5 mL	Sugar
4 fl oz	125 mL	Water, cold
4 tsp	20 mL	Salt
4 tsp	20 mL	Crushed garlic
1 tbsp	15 mL	Black pepper
1 tsp	5 mL	Cayenne
1 tsp	5 mL	Ground bay leaf
½ tsp	2 mL	Ground cumin
1 tsp	5 mL	Chili powder
1 tbsp	15 mL	Paprika

Per 1 ounce:
Calories, 70; Protein, 5 g; Fat, 5 g (69% cal.); Cholesterol, 20 mg; Carbohydrates, 0 g; Fiber, 0 g; Sodium, 190 mg.

■ Procedure

1. Cut the pork and fat into cubes.
2. Mix together the Prague Powder, salt, and sugar.
3. Add this mixture and the water to the diced meat and fat and mix well. Refrigerate for several hours.
4. Grind the meat mixture using the large die.
5. Add the remaining ingredients to the meat and mix thoroughly.
6. Stuff into large hog casings
7. Hang the sausages in the refrigerator, if possible, or arrange on towel-covered sheet pans so they are not touching each other. Refrigerate for 24 hours to dry the sausages before smoking.
8. Cold smoke at 80°F (27°C) for 4 hours.
9. At this point, the sausages are still raw and should be treated the same way as fresh sausages. They may be sold this way but must be cooked (by poaching, sautéing, grilling, etc.) before being eaten. Alternatively, they may be poached to an internal temperature of 152°F (67°C) immediately after smoking.

VARIATION

Andouille

Prepare the sausage meat as in the basic recipe, but omit the seasonings added in step 5, substituting the seasonings and quantities listed below. Cold smoke for 12 hours. After smoking, again hang the sausages in the refrigerator, if possible, or arrange on towel-covered sheet pans so they are not touching each other. Allow to cure another 24 hours in the refrigerator.

4 tsp	20 mL	Salt
3 tbsp	50 mL	Crushed garlic
1 tsp	5 mL	Black pepper
1 tbsp	15 mL	Cayenne
¼ tsp	1 mL	Ground bay leaf
1 tsp	5 mL	Paprika
½ tsp	2 mL	Dried thyme
½ tsp	2 mL	Dried ground sage
½ tsp	2 mL	Mace
½ tsp	2 mL	Ground allspice

Smoked Garlic Sausage

Yield: 5 lb 12 oz (2750 g)

U.S.	Metric	Ingredients
6 lb	3 kg	Pork and pork fat
1¼ tsp	6 mL	Prague Powder #1
5 tsp	25 mL	Salt
1 tsp	5 mL	Sugar
1 tsp	5 mL	White pepper
1 tsp	5 mL	Quatre épices
2 tsp	10 mL	Crushed garlic
6 fl oz	180 mL	Dry white wine or water

Per 1 ounce:
Calories, 70; Protein, 5 g; Fat, 5 g (68% cal.); Cholesterol, 20 mg; Carbohydrates, 0 g; Fiber, 0 g; Sodium,170 mg.

■ Procedure

1. Cut the pork and fat into cubes.
2. Mix together the Prague Powder, salt, and sugar.
3. Add this mixture to the diced meat and fat and mix well. Refrigerate for several hours.
4. Grind the meat mixture using the medium die.
5. Add the remaining ingredients to the meat and mix thoroughly.
6. Stuff into large hog casings.
7. Hang the sausages in the refrigerator, if possible, or arrange on towel-covered sheet pans so they are not touching each other. Refrigerate for 24 hours to dry the sausages before smoking.
8. Hot smoke at 160°F (71°C) for 1½ hours, then poach in water at 165°F (74°C) until the internal temperature is 152°F (67°C).
9. Cool the sausages in cold water, then drain, dry, and refrigerate.

V A R I A T I O N S

For a darker color and heavier smoke flavor, leave the sausages in the hot smoke until their internal temperature is 152°F (67°C), and do not poach them. Spray them with cold water after removing them from the smoker to keep them from shriveling.

Cured Garlic Sausage
Dry the sausages for 24–48 hours (step 7). Omit the hot smoking and simply poach, cool, and refrigerate them as described in steps 8 and 9.

■ TERMS FOR REVIEW

charcutier	Prague Powder #2	hot smoking	quatre épices
charcuterie	curing salt	sausage	natural casing
sodium nitrite	tinted curing mix	fresh sausage	collagen casing
sodium nitrate	dry cure	cured sausage	basic grind
nitrosamine	brine cure	smoked sausage	emulsified grind
Prague Powder #1	cold smoking	certified pork	

■ QUESTIONS FOR DISCUSSION

1. Explain how salt helps preserve meats.
2. Nitrites and nitrites are both used to cure meats. Explain how their use differs. Against which food-borne disease are they important in protecting cured foods?
3. Explain why smoked meats are first cured.
4. Describe the basic differences between fresh, cured, and smoked sausages.
5. What are the four basic kinds of ingredients in sausage meat? List ways this basic formula can be changed to create different types of sausages.
6. Why should sausage meat be kept cold when it is being ground and processed?
7. Describe the procedure for preparing natural sausage casings for stuffing.

CHAPTER 27

Pâtés, Terrines, and Other Cold Foods

The techniques and procedures presented in this chapter belong to the culinary department known as **garde manger** (gard mawn zhay), a term whose basic meaning is "larder" or "food storage place." As explained in Chapter 21 (p. 673), this area, because of its cooler temperature, was traditionally used for the preparation of cold foods. Thus, the work carried out in the storage area, or garde manger, became known by the same name.

The art of garde manger includes the techniques of cold food decoration, cold platter design and presentation, and the design and planning of buffets. Garde manger is an intricate and complex discipline that is the subject of whole books and of extended courses of study.

This book is primarily concerned with à la carte cooking. Buffet service is beyond its scope. Nevertheless, à la carte restaurants have inherited from classical garde manger a number of special food preparations that can be served in single portions as well as on butler platters. Pâtés, terrines, galantines, and mousses are not only ideal for buffets, they are also popular in many restaurants. This chapter serves as an introduction to these preparations.

THE HANDLING AND SERVICE OF COLD DISHES

Because the dishes featured in this chapter are served cold, various factors relating to their handling and service require special consideration. These have to do with sanitation and presentation.

SANITATION AND STORAGE

Hot foods that have been handled in a sanitary manner and that are served at or above a temperature that kills microorganisms can usually be considered safe and sanitary to eat. Cold foods, on the other hand, present special problems because they have been stored and handled after cooking. During this time, they may be exposed to disease-causing organisms. Because these foods are not subjected to further cooking, the organisms will not be destroyed.

For this reason, it is particularly important to follow all the rules of safe food handling. Make sure tools, containers, and work surfaces are clean and sanitary. Keep ingredients refrigerated when they are not being worked on, and keep the finished product refrigerated until service time. Always observe the four-hour rule, as explained on page 26.

The length of time terrines and other cold foods can be stored in the refrigerator depends on the ingredients, the type of item, and the method of preparation. Uncut meat terrines sealed with a layer of fat (see p. 860) may keep as long as several weeks (although the quality may start to decline after a week or so), while seafood and vegetable terrines may keep no more than two or three days, or even less. Pâtés en croûte (see p. 857) do not keep as well as terrines because the pastry loses its freshness. Aspics should be kept covered or wrapped to prevent them from drying out.

PRESENTATION

Attractive plating or presentation of foods is, of course, always important, but it could be argued that it is even more important for cold foods than for hot foods. Foods presented hot and steaming, directly from the sauté pan or carving board, have an immediate appeal to the nose as well as the eye, but cold foods must rely more completely on visual impact to make their first impression.

Furthermore, because the urgency in getting the plate from the kitchen to the dining room before the food cools down is absent, the cook has more time to arrange cold foods on the plate. This does not mean, however, that the most elaborate or intricate presentation is the best. "Keep it simple" is a good rule of thumb. Food is not made more appetizing by excessive handling.

Arrangements should be kept neat, but this does not mean they must always be symmetrical or regular. As in the case of salads, a deliberate casualness in the arrangement can be appetizing when it suggests the dish has been freshly assembled with minimum handling and rushed to the table.

In the case of pâtés and terrines, careful handling is essential to the presentation. Slice these items carefully and plate each slice with the best side up. To make neat slices, use a sharp, thin-bladed slicing knife. Before each slice, wipe off any residue from the previous slice and dip the blade in hot water. Slice the pâté with a gentle sawing motion, using the full length of the blade. Don't force the knife straight down or make little jagged cuts; this will make the cut surface uneven rather than smooth.

If the cut end of the pâté has discolored somewhat from exposure to air, plate the first slice with this side down. In contrast to pâtés for buffet presentation, slices of pâté for à la carte service are often garnished with greens or other colorful items, which enliven the sometimes drab appearance of a plain meat pâté. In addition, greens and other vegetable garnish provide a pleasant flavor contrast to the somewhat rich, processed flavor of the pâté or terrine.

Tart or piquant garnishes and accompaniments, as well as tart sauces such as vinai-

---

After reading this chapter, you should be able to:

1. **Prepare and use aspic jellies.**

2. **Prepare and use classic chaud-froid and mayonnaise chaud-froid.**

3. **Prepare livers for use in forcemeats.**

4. **Prepare basic meat and poultry forcemeats.**

5. **Prepare pâtés and terrines using basic forcemeats.**

6. **Prepare galantines.**

7. **Prepare mousseline forcemeats and make terrines based on them.**

8. **Prepare specialty terrines and other molded dishes based on aspics and mousses.**

9. **Handle raw foie gras and prepare foie gras terrines.**

10. **Prepare baked liver terrines.**

11. **Prepare rillettes.**

grette and mayonnaise variations, help counter the richness of pâtés, which are often rather fatty. This is why sour pickles and mustard are classic accompaniments for these foods.

Consideration must be given to the serving temperature of cold foods such as aspics, pâtés, and terrines. A common error is to serve these items too cold. At refrigerator temperature, their flavors are masked. Furthermore, their textures are too firm; the fat in pâtés and the gelatin in aspics are firmly congealed. A little warmer temperature is necessary to enable them to melt pleasantly in the mouth.

To bring them to suitable serving temperature, remove individual portions from refrigeration and let stand at room temperature for about 5 or 10 minutes, but no longer. Remember the sanitation guidelines discussed earlier. This period is long enough to let them warm slightly but not long enough to give microorganisms time to start multiplying. Keep in mind, too, that this short period of tempering applies only to those portions to be served right away. Whole pâtés from which portions were cut, for example, should be returned immediately to refrigeration. Again, remember the four-hour rule.

ASPIC AND CHAUD-FROID

Aspic jelly, or *gelée* (zhuh lay), is clarified stock that contains enough gelatin that it solidifies when cold. The gelatin may be naturally extracted from bones or added from a package. Good stock naturally contains a certain amount of gelatin but, in most cases, it must be supplemented with additional unflavored packaged gelatin.

Aspic jelly may be nearly colorless (white aspic) or various shades of amber. Most often, however, it must be crystal clear. This is achieved by clarifying it like a consommé. White or light-colored aspic is used when the natural colors of the foods and decorations must show through. Amber or golden aspic enhances the brown color of foods such as roasted meats and poultry.

Aspic is used as a coating for foods and as a binding ingredient. When it is used as a coating, it has three main purposes:

1. To protect foods from the air, which would dry them out and discolor them.

2. To improve appearance and give shine.

3. To add flavor. This last purpose is, of course, best accomplished if the stock is of high quality.

As a binding ingredient, aspic is used in mousses, terrines, and aspic molds, as discussed later in this chapter. It is also the binding agent in chaud-froid sauce (see p. 850). *Note:* When aspic is used as a binding agent, it need not be perfectly clarified.

In addition, when congealed and chopped or cut into various shapes, aspic jelly is used as a garnish for platters or servings of pâtés, terrines, and other cold items.

PREPARING ASPIC JELLY

The best aspic is a well-made, naturally gelatinous stock. It has a superior texture and flavor, but it is time-consuming to make because a separate batch of stock must be made in addition to the normal stock production. Consequently, most aspics are made by reinforcing regular stock with gelatin. Aspic powders and mixes are available, but the flavor of aspic made from them does not compare with that made from stock. They can be useful in an emergency, however, or for pieces used purely for display or decoration.

Classic Aspic Jelly

Prepare classic aspic jelly as you would white or brown veal stock, but with the addition of products that release a good deal of gelatin, such as split calves' feet or pigs' feet, pork skin, and veal knuckle bones. If enough of these items are used, the stock will contain enough natural gelatin to be used as an aspic jelly.

Follow basic stock-making procedures, except do not brown the added feet and pork skin when making brown stock. When the stock is made, use the following procedure to convert it to aspic jelly.

Procedure for Preparing Classic Aspic Jelly

1. Test the stock for gelatin content. Ladle a small amount of cooled stock onto a small plate or saucer and refrigerate.

   - If the stock becomes firm, no additional gelatin is needed.

   - If it sets but is not firm enough, add about ½ oz or 2 tbsp (15 g) powdered gelatin per quart (liter) of stock, or 2 oz (60 g) per gallon (4 liters).

   - If it does not set at all (which is unlikely if the stock is properly made) but merely becomes thicker, add about 1 oz or 4 tbsp (30 g) powdered gelatin per quart (liter), or 4 oz (125 g) per gallon (4 liters). In this case, you will actually be making *regular aspic jelly* (see next section) rather than classic aspic jelly.

   Add the gelatin by first stirring it gradually into a little cold water, avoiding making lumps, and letting it soften. Then add the softened gelatin to the stock.

2. Clarify the stock as for consommé. For white aspic (made with white stock), omit the carrots in the mirepoix.

3. After the stock is clarified, remove all traces of fat. The aspic jelly is now ready to use.

Regular Aspic Jelly

This is normal meat, poultry, or fish stock reinforced with gelatin and clarified. Regular stock rarely has enough natural gelatin to enable it to be used as a jelly, so extra gelatin must be added. To test the stock for gelatin content and to convert it to aspic jelly, follow the same procedure as for classic aspic jelly, described above. However, note that if the stock contains very little gelatin and stays watery when chilled, more than 4 oz (125 g) gelatin may be needed per gallon (4 liters).

Aspic Powder

Aspic powder is unflavored gelatin mixed with a powdered stock base. To prepare it, follow the instructions on the container. Additional unflavored gelatin may be needed for some purposes.

Procedures for using aspic jelly are discussed following a brief consideration of a related topic, chaud-froid sauce.

CHAUD-FROID

Described in simplest terms, **chaud-froid sauce** is a white sauce containing enough gelatin that it sets like an aspic. The name *chaud-froid* is French for "hot-cold." The sauce is so called because the classic version is made hot but eaten cold.

Today, chaud-froid sauce is rarely used except for display pieces on buffets. Its main purpose there is to provide a smooth, uniformly white background for colored decorations. Because it is not eaten in these cases, it does not have to have a good flavor, and it may be made out of a simple béchamel sauce thickened with a roux made with white shortening.

Nevertheless, chaud-froid sauce finds occasional use in cold dishes—for example, as a component of some aspic molds and terrines. A brief discussion is warranted without going into the kind of detail found in books on garde manger.

Many kinds of white sauce may be used as a base for chaud-froid, including cream sauces, white stocks enriched with cream or cream and egg yolks, veloutés, and mayonnaise. There are also colored chaud-froid sauces, but they are not often used. Red sauce can be made with the addition of tomato paste and, sometimes, paprika. Green sauce is colored with spinach and watercress, puréed with some of the hot sauce, and strained. Brown chaud-froid can be made by combining glace de viande, tomato sauce, and aspic jelly in equal proportions.

Preparing Chaud-Froid Sauce

Two basic types of chaud-froid sauce are considered here, one based on white stock and cream, the other on mayonnaise. Both of these are of good eating quality and can be used for first-class cold foods. Heavier types based on roux-thickened sauces may be economical to make but are more appropriate for inedible display pieces.

Two recipes for chaud-froid are given here. *Classic chaud-froid* is essentially an aspic jelly with the addition of cream or a cream and egg yolk liaison. In fact, it can be made by combining aspic jelly and cream, but this mixture would have to be reinforced with extra gelatin because of the quantity of cream.

Mayonnaise chaud-froid, also called *mayonnaise collée*, which means something like "glued mayonnaise," is simply a mixture of aspic jelly and mayonnaise. It is easy to make and, if the two ingredients are of good quality, is a tasty and useful chaud-froid.

The basic proportion is equal parts aspic jelly and mayonnaise. The proportion can be varied to taste, however, from 1 part aspic and 2 parts mayonnaise to 1 part mayonnaise and 2 parts aspic jelly.

Using a commercially made mayonnaise is recommended. If you are using a homemade mayonnaise, it is best to prepare the chaud-froid at the last minute and use it at once. Reheating it to melt it could cause the mayonnaise to break. Commercial mayonnaise, on the other hand, can generally be melted without damage, but it is still best to use the sauce as soon it is made.

Classic Chaud-Froid

Yield: 2 qt (2 L)

U.S.	Metric	Ingredients
½–1 oz	15–30 g	Gelatin powder, unflavored (see note)
8 fl oz	250 mL	Heavy cream
1 qt	1 L	White stock (veal, chicken, or fish)
2–4	2–4	Egg yolks (optional)
1 pt 8 fl oz	750 mL	Heavy cream

Per 1 ounce:
Calories, 50; Protein, 1 g; Fat, 5 g (69% cal.); Cholesterol, 20 mg; Carbohydrates, 0 g; Fiber, 0 g; Sodium, 5 mg.

Note: If the stock is firmly set when cold, use the smaller quantity of gelatin. If the stock sets but is not firm when cool, use the larger quantity.

■ **P r o c e d u r e**

1. Soften the gelatin in the heavy cream.
2. Bring the stock to a simmer.
3. Add the gelatin mixture to the stock and heat until the gelatin is dissolved. Do not boil.
4. If the egg yolks are used, beat them with the remaining cream to make a liaison. Stir a little of the stock mixture into the liaison to temper it, then add the liaison to the hot stock. Heat the mixture carefully to cook the egg yolks, but do not let it simmer, or the yolks will curdle.
5. If the yolks are not used, simply temper the remaining cream with a little of the hot stock, then add it to the rest of the stock.
6. Strain through a cheesecloth.

Mayonnaise Chaud-Froid

Yield: 1 qt (1 L)

U.S.	Metric	Ingredients
1 pt	500 mL	Mayonnaise
1 pt	500 mL	Aspic jelly

Per 1 ounce:
Calories, 100; Protein, 0 g; Fat, 11 g (100% cal.); Cholesterol, 10 mg; Carbohydrates, 0 g; Fiber, 0 g; Sodium, 80 mg.

■ **P r o c e d u r e**

1. Stir the mayonnaise, if necessary, so it is smooth. If it has just been removed from the refrigerator, let it warm to cool room temperature. If it is too cold, the first drops of aspic may congeal as soon as they hit it, causing lumps.
2. Melt the aspic over a hot-water bath. Cool it to thicken slightly (see p. 852 for cooling aspic). It should be at about the same temperature as the mayonnaise or just slightly warmer.
3. Using a stirring whip (not a balloon whip, used for whipping in air), stir the aspic into the mayonnaise. Stir carefully to avoid making bubbles. If the gelatin begins to set before the mixing is complete, carefully remelt over the hot-water bath.
4. Set the chaud-froid over ice to thicken (see p. 852). When ready to use, it should be about the consistency of heavy cream. Use at once.

USING ASPIC JELLY AND CHAUD-FROID SAUCE

As discussed earlier, aspic and chaud-froid are used to enhance both the appearance and the flavor of cold foods. For best results, the aspic and chaud-froid, as well as the foods to be coated, should be prepared and handled in specific ways. The following sections offer general procedures for handling these products. Specific applications, such as recipes for aspic-based terrine molds, are included later in the chapter.

Aspic jelly must be cooled to just above congealing temperature before it is used to coat foods. If it is too warm, it will not have enough body to coat and will just run off.

Procedure for Cooling Aspic Jelly

The following procedure is used for chaud-froid as well as aspic jelly.

1. If the jelly is congealed, it must first be melted. Set the pan or container of jelly in a hot-water bath. Stir it gently from time to time until it is completely melted.
2. Place the warm aspic jelly in a stainless-steel bowl.
3. At all times, be careful not to make any bubbles. Bubbles in the jelly may get transferred to the surface of your food item and mar its appearance.
4. Select a ladle that fits the curve of the bowl. Set the bowl in crushed ice, pushing it in so that it sits in a well of ice. With the edge of the ladle against the inside of the bowl, rotate the bowl so the ladle continually scrapes the inside of the bowl. This method prevents the formation of lumps that occur when jelly touching the cold bowl solidifies too quickly.
5. Continue to rotate the bowl until the jelly is thick and syrupy but not yet set. The jelly is now ready for use. Remove from the ice bath and work quickly, because it will set very fast.
6. Remelt and recool the jelly as necessary.

Procedure for Coating Foods with Aspic Jelly

1. Chill the food to be coated. For best results, the surface of the item should be as smooth and as free of fat as possible.
2. Place the item on a wire rack over a tray or sheet pan. Excess aspic that falls onto the tray can be remelted and reused.
3. Cool the aspic jelly according to the procedure above.
4. Use the aspic as soon as it is ready. Various methods can be used to coat foods with aspic, depending on the size and shape of the item.
   - For smooth, regularly shaped items, use a large ladle and nap them with a single smooth stroke, as illustrated in Figure 27.1. Working too slowly may produce an uneven, bumpy coat.
   - Large items and items with steep sides or irregular shapes are harder to coat. Using a ladle, coat the sides first and then the top for best results.
   - For small items, it may be more convenient to use a kitchen spoon than a ladle.
   - A pastry brush can be used to coat small items. A brush is often used for small portions, such as canapés, that need only a light glaze rather than a perfectly smooth coating of aspic.
5. Chill the items until the jelly is thoroughly set.
6. Repeat with additional coats, if necessary, until the aspic is of the desired thickness.
7. To decorate, dip pieces of decoration in liquid aspic and place on the product in the desired pattern. Some items appropriate to use for decorating aspic are

Leek leaves	Black olives	Tomato peels
Fresh herbs, especially flat-leaf parsley and tarragon	Truffles, real or artificial	Carrots

As appropriate, cut the items for decoration into very thin slices and then into desired shapes. For most vegetable decorations, such as carrots and leek leaves, blanch to make them more limber and to intensify the color.

8. If decorations have been used, cover the decorated item with a final layer of aspic jelly to protect the design.

Figure 27.1
A smooth, regularly shaped item can be covered with an even layer of aspic using one stroke of the ladle.

Coating with Chaud-Froid

Apply chaud-froid sauce according to the same procedure as for aspic. Because most chaud-froid is thicker than aspic, it is usually kept a little warmer when poured.

If the first layer of chaud-froid is too transparent or not thick enough, apply one or two additional layers.

After the chaud-froid has chilled and set, apply decorations if desired. Finish with a layer of aspic for best appearance.

Procedure for Lining a Mold with Aspic Jelly

Many instructions for lining molds say to chill the mold, then pour in a little liquid aspic jelly and turn and tilt the mold until the bottom and sides are coated. This method works and is suitable for some purposes, but it does not produce a smooth, even layer of aspic.

It is not always necessary to line a mold with aspic. Many aspic molds are made by first pouring a thin layer of aspic into the bottom of the mold, chilling it, then adding layers of ingredients (vegetables, meats, mousses, and so on) and covering each layer with a little aspic. The mold is chilled after each layer is added to allow the aspic to set. As long as the layers of solid ingredients are not allowed to touch the sides of the mold, the liquid aspic will fill in these spaces and, in effect, line the mold.

If a mold must be lined with a perfectly even thickness of jelly, the following method is used (see Figure 27.2):

1. Press the mold into a bed of crushed ice so that the ice comes all the way to the top edge.

2. Fill the mold with cooled liquid aspic jelly. Leave the mold in place for 10 seconds. Immediately remove the mold from the ice and quickly dump out the jelly that is still liquid. If the layer of jelly remaining inside the mold is too thin, repeat. If it is too thick, remove it, clean the mold, and repeat the procedure, leaving the mold on ice for less time.

3. Decorate the inside of the mold as desired by dipping decorations in liquid aspic and arranging them in place. Chill. Then fill the mold with the selected food product.

Figure 27.2
Lining a mold with aspic jelly.

(a) Bury the mold up to the rim in crushed ice.

(b) Fill the mold with liquid aspic.

(c) After 10 seconds, quickly but smoothly pour out the aspic that is still liquid.

(d) An even layer of aspic jelly lines the mold, as can be seen by comparing it with an empty mold.

(e) At this point, you can decorate the mold by dipping vegetable cutouts in liquid aspic and carefully setting them in place in the mold.

SPECIAL FORCEMEAT DISHES

This section is concerned with classic meat and poultry dishes called **pâtés**, **terrines**, and **galantines**. Some terrines are based on vegetables and other items rather than meats, but these are the subject of a later section. The main ingredients of the items discussed here are a **forcemeat** and, usually but not always, a **garnish**.

A forcemeat may be defined as a mixture of seasoned, ground meats used as a stuffing or filling. The name comes from the French word *farce*, which means stuffing.

The garnish in a pâté or terrine is not just a decoration but a major ingredient that adds body, flavor, and nutritional value as well as appearance. Garnish usually consists of meats or other foods cut in dice, strips, or other shapes, or left whole if they are small. Classic pâté garnishes include:

Ham	Game
Veal	Fresh pork fatback
Chicken, duck, or turkey breast	Tongue
Chicken, duck, or goose livers	Pistachios
Foie gras	Truffles

TYPES OF FORCEMEATS

The following are the three basic types of forcemeats:

1. **Straight forcemeat (including country-style forcemeat).**
   This is a mixture of seasoned ground meats. As such, it is basically a form of sausage meat, except the grind is generally, but not always, finer. Consequently, many of the guidelines for making and handling sausage meat, discussed in Chapter 26, apply here as well. It may be helpful to read or to review pages 832–837 in conjunction with this discussion. Straight forcemeats are the basis of most traditional pâtés and terrines and are the major focus of this chapter.

   A *country-style forcemeat* is made the same way, except the grind is coarser. Most country-style forcemeats are made from pork and pork fat and contain some liver.

2. **Gratin forcemeat.**
   This type of forcemeat differs from a straight forcemeat in that a portion of the meat is seared, and thus partially cooked, and cooled before it is ground. Because the partial cooking eliminates some of the binding power of the meat protein, gratin forcemeats usually contain a starch binder called a *panada* (also called *panade*). This type of forcemeat is not used as often as straight or mousseline forcemeats and is not covered in this book.

3. **Mousseline forcemeat.**
   This type of forcemeat consists of white meat (usually poultry or veal) or seafood processed to a purée and combined with heavy cream and egg. See page 863 for a discussion.

STRAIGHT FORCEMEATS

A basic straight forcemeat consists of the following:

50 to 65 percent lean meat

35 to 50 percent fat

Seasonings

The many variations on this basic formula depend on the ingredients used and how they are combined.

Meat

Pork is the basic ingredient, but many other meats can be included in addition to or instead of pork, including veal, chicken, turkey, ham, duck, rabbit, and game of all kinds.

Liver

Chicken, goose, duck, or pork liver is often included in forcemeats. Liver gives flavor and also acts as a binder.

Fat

The classic proportion in forcemeats is equal parts fat and meat. Many forcemeats, however, contain less than 50 percent fat, especially in recent years, as people have become more attentive to nutrition and dietary considerations (see the discussion of the fat content of sausages on page 832). Nevertheless, a certain amount of fat is necessary for both moisture and flavor. A pâté with too little fat tastes dry. Hard fat, such as pork fatback, gives best results. Heavy cream is sometimes used to add fat as well as liquid to a forcemeat.

Note that this discussion of fat content refers only to the solid fat specifically added as a measured ingredient. There is, of course, some fat in the lean meat as well.

Other Ingredients

Eggs or egg whites may be added as a binder. Flour or other starches may be added for the same purpose. Extra binders are not absolutely necessary in a forcemeat made purely of meat and fat because the meat proteins are sufficient to bind the product when cooked. On the other hand, when brandy, cream, and other liquids are added to the forcemeat, extra binders may be needed or at least beneficial.

The Grind

Forcemeat may be ground coarse, medium, or fine. Country-style pâté, or **pâté de campagne** (cawm pah nyuh), is characterized by a coarse texture. Galantines, on the other hand, are usually made from finely ground forcemeats.

Preparing Straight Forcemeats

Many, if not most, pâté and terrine forcemeats contain some liver. Chicken livers or other poultry livers, both economical and widely available, are the most often used. For the best results, livers should be soaked in milk and then cleaned according to the following procedures. Pork liver and other larger livers can be cut into pieces and prepared in the same way.

Procedure for Preparing Poultry Livers for Forcemeats

1. Rinse the livers in cold water, drain, then soak for 24 hours in enough milk to cover.
2. Drain and rinse thoroughly in cold water. Drain again.
3. Remove all fat and connective tissue. At this point, the livers are ready to be used whole as garnish for pâtés and terrines. If they are to be added to forcemeats, continue with steps 4 and 5.
4. Blend in a blender until liquid.
5. Strain through a fine china cap or strainer to remove all traces of connective tissue.

The following recipe can be used with many garnishes to make a great variety of pâtés, terrines, and galantines. It can also be changed according to any of the variations listed by using different meats. Once the basic technique is understood, any kind of pâté can be produced.

The recipe should be viewed as a basic procedure that can be varied in ways other than those indicated following the recipe, just as sausage meat can be varied. The varieties and quantities of spices can be changed. In addition, the fineness of the grind can be varied to make pâtés of varying textures.

The proportion of fat can be increased or reduced, but remember that making the forcemeat too lean will reduce its eating quality. Although at first glance the recipe looks as if it calls for 50 percent fat, this is not the case, as the liver should be included as part of the meat. The proportion of fat is 44 percent. Taking the first column of ingredient quantities as an example, using 1 lb lean pork, 12 oz fat, and 4 oz liver lowers the proportion of fat to 38 percent (not counting, of course, the smaller amount of fat within the meats). Using 12 oz lean pork, 1 lb fat, and 4 oz liver raises the fat proportion to 50 percent.

 Basic Pork Forcemeat

Yield: 2 lb (900 g)

U.S.	Metric	Ingredients
14 oz	400 g	Lean pork
14 oz	400 g	Pork fat
		Marinade:
1½ oz	45 g	Shallots, minced
½ oz	15 g	Butter
2 fl oz	60 mL	White wine
2	2	Bay leaves
1 fl oz	30 mL	Brandy
2½ tsp	12 mL	Salt
½ tsp	2 mL	Pâté spice or quatre épices (see note)
¼ tsp	1 mL	White pepper
4 oz	100 g	Chicken livers, soaked, cleaned, and puréed (see p. 855)
2	2	Eggs (see step 7)

■ P r o c e d u r e

1. Before beginning, make sure all equipment and all ingredients are well chilled. Forcemeats must be kept cold at all times to prevent the fat from softening or melting.
2. Cut the meat and fat into small dice.
3. Sweat the minced shallots in the butter until soft. Add half of the white wine and reduce by half. Cool completely.
4. Combine the meat and fat with the shallots, the rest of the wine, the bay leaves, brandy, salt, spice mixture, and pepper. Toss to mix well. Cover and refrigerate overnight.
5. Remove the bay leaves. Grind the meat and fat twice through the fine blade of a meat grinder.
6. Combine the ground meats and liver purée.
7. Beat the eggs lightly and mix in thoroughly. (Note: The eggs are optional and are omitted in many pâtés.)
8. Make a quenelle (a small ball of forcemeat) and poach in simmering water. Cool. Taste and correct the seasonings in the forcemeat.
9. Keep the forcemeat chilled until ready for use.

Per 1 ounce:
Calories, 150; Protein, 3 g; Fat, 14 g (89% cal.); Cholesterol, 54 mg; Carbohydrates, 0 g; Fiber, 0 g; Sodium, 200 mg.

Note: Pâté spice may be purchased in various blends, or you may make your own blend to taste. Pâté spice usually contains black and white pepper, cloves, nutmeg, ginger, cayenne, bay leaf, thyme, and marjoram. Grind very fine and sift through a sieve. For quatre épices, see page 839.

V A R I A T I O N S

Omit the pork, fat, livers, and eggs in the basic recipe. Substitute the following ingredients and quantities. Vary seasonings to taste.

Veal Forcemeat

9 oz	250 g	Lean pork
9 oz	250 g	Lean veal
14 oz	400 g	Fresh pork fat
3	3	Eggs

Chicken Forcemeat I

9 oz	250 g	Lean pork
9 oz	250 g	Chicken meat
14 oz	400 g	Fresh pork fat
3	3	Eggs

Chicken Forcemeat II

1 lb 2 oz	500 g	Chicken meat
14 oz	400 g	Fresh pork fat
3	3	Eggs

Duck, Pheasant, or Game Forcemeat

7 oz	200 g	Lean pork, or a mixture of pork and veal
7 oz	200 g	Duck, pheasant, or game meat
14 oz	400 g	Fresh pork fat
4 oz	100 g	Livers, soaked, cleaned, and puréed
1	1	Egg

TERRINES AND PÂTÉS

Terrines and pâtés are baked forcemeats, often but not always containing one or more types of garnish. Strictly speaking, the difference between the two lies in how they are baked. By definition, a terrine is baked in an earthenware dish. The dish itself is also called a *terrine*, a word derived from the French *terre*, meaning "earth." Today, other materials besides earthenware, such as glass or metal, may be used for terrines. Terrines may be presented in their baking dish, or they may be unmolded.

A pâté is, by definition, baked in a crust. The word **pâté** (with an accent on the e) is derived from the word *pâte* (without the accent), meaning "pastry." Today, however, the word *pâté* is often used for terrines baked without a pastry crust. To avoid confusion, the term **pâté en croûte** is used to specify a pâté with a crust. In this book, the terms *terrine* and *pâté* are used in their traditional, literal senses.

It should be noted that many kinds of products are called *terrines* because they are prepared in terrine molds. The terrines discussed in this section are based on the straight forcemeats we have just considered. Other kinds of terrines are discussed in a later section.

Preparing Pâtés

The essential difference between a pâté and a terrine is the crust. Although a heavy pastry crust may not be suitable for all kinds of terrine mixtures, the typical baked forcemeat-type terrine under consideration here can usually be made with or without a crust.

This section concentrates on the specific procedures for making the pastry and finishing the assembled pâté. Making the meat filling is the same as for terrines and is not repeated here. To make a pâté en croûte, apply the following procedure to the Veal and Ham Terrine and to any of the variations following the basic recipe (see p. 861).

Pastries used to enclose pâtés are of various types, but the most commonly used are similar to pie pastries, but sturdier. A recipe for this type of *pâte à pâté*, or pâté pastry, is included here. Its advantage over many other types of pâté pastry is that it is relatively good to eat. Some authorities argue about whether the dough around a pâté is meant to be eaten. But because customers are not necessarily aware of this argument, it is best to use a pastry that is reasonably pleasant to eat.

Traditional English pâtés, or raised meat pies, use a hot-water pastry that can be modeled like clay and that is very sturdy when baked. Pastries used for display—that is, for show platters not intended to be eaten—are also made to be sturdy and easy to handle. These pastries are not considered here.

The procedure for assembling a pâté follows the pastry recipe (Figure 27.3).

Pâté Pastry (Pâte à Pâté)

Yield: 1 lb 12 oz (900 g)

U.S.	Metric	Ingredients	Procedure
1 lb	500 g	Flour	1. Place the flour in a large mixing bowl. Add the butter and lard. Rub them in until no lumps of fat remain.
4 oz	125 g	Butter	
3½ oz	100 g	Lard	
1	1	Eggs	2. Beat the eggs with the water and salt until the salt is dissolved.
3 fl oz	100 mL	Water, cold	3. Add the liquid to the flour mixture. Mix gently until it is completely absorbed.
1¼ tsp	7 mL	Salt	4. Gather the dough into a ball. On a work surface, knead the dough for a few minutes until it is smooth.
			5. Place the dough in a pan and cover with plastic film. Refrigerate until needed, or at least 4 hours.

Per 1 ounce:
Calories, 120; Protein, 2 g; Fat, 7 g (53% cal.); Cholesterol, 20 mg; Carbohydrates, 20 g; Fiber, 0 g; Sodium, 140 mg.

Figure 27.3
Making a pâté en croûte.

(a) Collapsible molds are used to make pâtés en croûte because they can be removed from the mold without damaging it. Assemble the mold and grease the inside well.

(b) Lightly roll the pastry into a rectangle, keeping it thick.

(c) Work the dough into a boat shape. Dust heavily with flour and fold the dough lengthwise to make a pocket.

(d) Roll the double thickness of dough into a rectangle the size of the mold. Open the pocket.

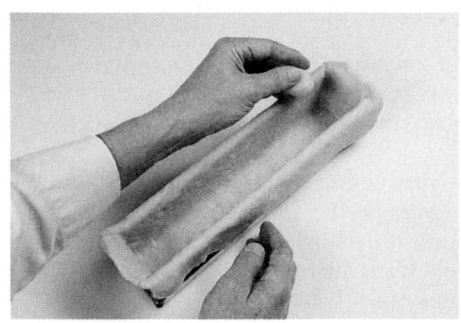

(e) Fit the dough into the mold. Carefully work it to fit snugly. A ball of dough dipped in flour helps fit the dough into the corners without tearing it.

(f) Partially fill the mold with forcemeat and arrange the garnish according to the instructions in the specific recipe.

(g) Finish filling the mold, mounding the forcemeat slightly.

(h) Fold the ends and then sides of the dough over the top of the forcemeat, trimming the dough so it meets in the middle. Eggwash the dough.

(i) Roll out and cut the top pastry and fit it in place, making sure it is sealed well to the dough below it. Eggwash. Make holes in the top and fit pastry tubes in them to serve as chimneys to allow the escape of steam and to prevent melted fat from bubbling over the top crust as the pâté bakes.

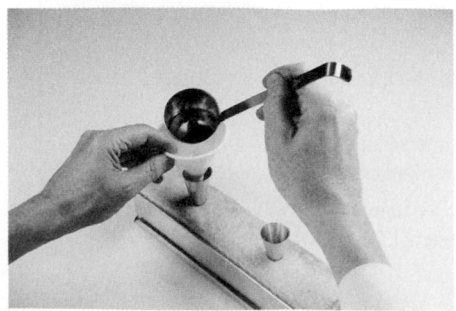

(j) After the pâté has baked and cooled, pour liquid aspic through the chimneys to fill the spaces left when the forcemeat shrank during baking.

Procedure for Lining and Filling Pâté Molds and Finishing Pâtés

1. Prepare the pastry in advance so it has plenty of time to rest. Remove it from refrigeration long enough ahead of time to allow it to warm up slightly.

2. Prepare the molds by greasing them well on the inside. The directions here pertain to standard rectangular pâté molds. These usually are hinged and collapsible so it is easy to remove the pâté without damaging it. If you are using bottomless molds, then also grease the sheet pans on which they are to set. For molds of other shapes, modify the pastry-molding procedure as necessary to fit the shape.

3. For best results, mold the pastry so it is of even thickness, has no seams, and fits the mold perfectly. First, work the pastry with the hands for a few seconds to make it pliable. Then shape it into a rectangle and roll it slightly with a rolling pin to flatten it, keeping it quite thick.

4. Make an indentation down the center of the dough with the fingers. Gradually make the dough into a sort of boat shape. Dust the inside of the dough shape well with flour (to keep the two layers of dough from sticking together) and fold the dough along the indentation to make a pocket.

5. Gently roll out the dough to make a rectangle the size of the mold. Be careful not to roll the dough too thin, which would make it fragile. Open up the pocket.

6. Fit the opened pocket into the mold. Carefully mold the pastry to the shape of the mold by pushing the dough with your fingers. Make sure there are no air bubbles between the dough and mold. A ball of dough dipped in flour is useful for pushing the dough into the corners of the mold without tearing it.

7. If the pâté is to be made without a top crust, leave a rim of dough about ¼ inch (5 mm) above the top of the mold. Crimp this rim to make a decorative border. If there is to be a top crust, leave a rim of half the width of the mold and let it hang over the sides. (For an alternative method, see step 10.)

8. The mold is now ready to fill. For display pieces, it is common practice to line the inside of the dough with thin sheets of fatback. For pâtés to be eaten, however, it is more appetizing to omit the fat lining. Fill the mold with the desired forcemeat and garnish as for terrines (see p. 860). Mound the filling slightly so the top crust, if used, will have an attractive domed shape. The dough should hold this shape even as the forcemeat shrinks and settles during baking.

   If the pâté is not to have a top crust, it is now ready for baking. Skip to step 12. Baking without a top crust is easier and allows you to make an attractive aspic glaze with decorations for the top.

9. Fold the rim of the dough from the sides of the mold over the top of the filling. If using a top crust:
   - Roll out a sheet of dough.
   - Lay the sheet of dough on top of the mold, trim it to size, and remove it.
   - Brush the edges of dough from the sides of the mold with egg wash.
   - Return the pastry top to the mold and fit it in place, gently sealing it to the egg-washed dough.

10. As an alternative method for fitting the top crust:
    - Leave a ¼-inch (5-mm) rim of dough, as in step 7.
    - Brush the inside of this rim with egg wash.
    - Roll out and cut a top crust slightly larger than the top of the mold. Place it on top of the filled mold.
    - Crimp or pinch the two layers of pastry together with the fingers to seal.

11. Decorate the top crust with pastry cutouts, if desired. Seal the cutouts to the crust with egg wash. Make one or two vent holes in the top crust to allow the steam to escape. Fit pastry tubes into these holes to form chimneys in order to keep juices from running over the top crust and spoiling its appearance.

12. To bake:
    - Preheat an oven to 400°F (200°C). Place the pâté on a sheet pan (if you are using a bottomless mold, it will, of course, already be on a sheet pan) and put it in the oven.
    - After 10 minutes, reduce the heat to 350°F (175°C). The higher initial temperature helps brown the pastry. Bake at this lower temperature until the internal temperature reaches 160° to 165°F (72°C).
    - For an average rectangular mold, the baking time will be about 1 to 2 hours. Small molds that make 1 to 4 portions will take 45 minutes or less. For very large molds, use a baking temperature of 325°F (160°C) so they cook evenly. Extend the baking time accordingly.

13. Remove the pâté from the oven. Let the pâté cool to room temperature in its mold. For a pâté made without a top crust, first let it cool until it is warm. Then let it finish cooling with a weight on top in order to give the pâté a firmer texture. The weight should be large enough to cover the meat but small enough so it doesn't touch the pastry rim. This can be accomplished by cutting a board to the proper size, laying it in place on the pâté, and placing the weights on the board. (Obviously, this cannot be done if there is a top crust.)

14. When the pâté is cool, prepare an aspic jelly. Melt the aspic and flavor it, if desired, with a little sherry, port, or Madeira wine. Cool it according to the procedure on page 852. Fill the pâté with the aspic.
    - If the pâté has a pastry top, pour the aspic through the vent hole or holes, using a funnel, until the pâté is completely full.
    - If the pâté has no top crust, fill it with enough aspic to completely cover the top of the meat.
    Refrigerate until the aspic is set.

15. Remove the pâté carefully from the mold.

16. Pâtés without a top crust may now be decorated and reglazed with aspic if desired. Decorate as desired (using the materials suggested on page 852) by dipping the decorations in liquid aspic and setting them in place. Chill briefly, then apply a little more aspic to glaze the top.

17. For storage, handling, and presentation, see page 848.

Preparing Forcemeat Terrines

Terrines, like pâtés, may be baked in molds of various shapes and sizes. Traditional oval molds, for example, have long been popular. For ease of portion control, however, rectangular molds are the most appropriate.

A terrine may be lined with thin sheets of fatback, although this is optional. The layer of fat does not contribute significantly, as is widely believed, to keeping the meat moist during baking; after all, the terrine mold itself is more moistureproof than the layer of fat. Although such a fat lining is traditional, today's diners are more likely to find a rim of fat unappetizing. Of course, the fat layer can be removed before serving. Alternatively, a sheet of caul fat, which is much thinner than a sheet of fatback, can be used to line the mold.

Procedure for Preparing Forcemeat Terrines

1. Prepare the desired forcemeat (see p. 856).

2. Prepare the selected garnish. Meat garnishes are usually cut into strips, which are laid lengthwise in the mold.

3. Marinate the garnish as desired. This step is optional but adds to the flavor.

4. Prepare the mold. Do not use a hinged or collapsible mold, which cannot be placed in a water bath. If desired, line the mold with thin sheets of fatback (sliced on a slicing machine) or with a sheet of caul fat, letting the excess hang over the sides. Make the sheets of fat sufficiently large so the amount of fat hanging over the sides can be folded over to cover the top completely. If the mold is not lined with fat, grease it well.

5. Place a layer of forcemeat in the bottom of the mold. If no garnish is used, simply fill the mold. Spread the forcemeat evenly and rap the mold sharply on the workbench to dislodge any air bubbles.

6. Arrange a layer of garnish on top of the forcemeat.

7. Continue adding forcemeat and garnish until they are all used. End with a layer of forcemeat on top. Two or three layers of garnish are usually sufficient.

8. If a fat lining has been used, fold the excess fat over the top of the forcemeat to cover it.

9. Cover the top with a sheet of aluminum foil. Cut a few holes in the foil to allow steam to escape.

10. Place the mold in a water bath for baking. Make sure the bath is deep enough to allow the hot water to come halfway up the sides of the mold. Bake at 350°F (175°C) until the internal temperature registers 165°F (74°C).

11. Remove the terrine from the water bath and place it on a rack to cool. When it has cooled somewhat but is still warm, finish cooling the pâté with a weight, as explained in the procedure for making pâtés. It should not be weighted when it is still hot because it is too fragile and may split or fracture, and the weight may force out too much juice. If a looser texture is desired, cool the terrine without weighting it.

12. When the terrine is completely cool, cover and refrigerate it.

13. The terrine may be sealed with a layer of fat or aspic. These protect the terrine from air and help preserve it.

    • To add a layer of fat, melt lard (or rendered duck fat or other fat appropriate to the terrine), then let stand until cool but still liquid. The terrine should be cool, about 50°F (10°C). Pour in enough fat to cover the meat completely. Let stand until the fat has congealed, then cover and refrigerate. The purpose of this fat is only to extend the keeping qualities of the terrine. It should be removed before serving.

    • Add aspic to a terrine in the same way as adding a layer of fat; see also the procedure for adding aspic to a pâté, page 859. Unlike melted fat, aspic extends the storage life of a terrine only a few days because the aspic itself dries out. On the other hand, aspic contributes to both flavor and appearance. If desired, apply decorations to the top of the terrine and add another layer of aspic to glaze.

Veal and Ham Terrine

Yield (approximate): 2 lb (1 kg)

U.S.	Metric	Ingredients
2 lb	1 kg	Veal Forcemeat (p. 856)
		Garnish:
4 oz	125 g	Veal, lean, trimmed
4 oz	125 g	Smoked ham
1 oz	30 g	Fresh pork fatback
2 fl oz	60 mL	Brandy
as needed	as needed	Fresh pork fatback or caul fat for lining molds (optional)

Per 1 ounce:
Calories, 170; Protein, 5 g; Fat, 15 g (83% cal.); Cholesterol, 50 mg; Carbohydrates, 0 g; Fiber, 0 g; Sodium, 250 mg.

■ P r o c e d u r e

1. Prepare the forcemeat according to the recipe on page 856. Refrigerate it until it is very cold.

2. Cut the veal, ham, and fatback for the garnish into strips about ¼ in. (6 mm) thick. Mix with the brandy and marinate in the refrigerator 1 hour or longer.

3. Have ready a 2-qt (2-L) rectangular terrine mold.

4. If using fatback to line the mold, have the fat very cold. Cut it on a slicer into broad, thin slices less than ⅛ in. (3 mm) thick. Line the mold with the slices, overlapping them by about ¼ in. (5 mm). Let the tops of the slices hang over the edges.

   If using caul fat, line the mold with a large sheet of caul, letting the edges hang over the edge of the mold.

   If not using caul or fat, grease the mold well.

5. Fill the terrine with alternating layers of forcemeat and garnish, beginning and ending with forcemeat and laying the strips of garnish lengthwise in the terrine. Press the meat firmly into the terrine so there are no air bubbles.

6. If using sheets of fat to line the mold, fold the overhanging fat over the top of the forcemeat to cover.

7. Cover with foil.

8. Set the terrine in a hot-water bath. Bake at 350°F (175°C) until the internal temperature is 165°F (74°C).

9. Remove from the oven and cool until just warm. Weight and continue to cool, following the basic procedure on page 860. Finish, if desired, with a layer of melted fat or aspic, as described in the basic procedure.

V A R I A T I O N S

Veal and Ham Terrine with Foie Gras
Prepare as in the basic recipe, but place a layer of sliced, cooked foie gras down the center of the terrine. Use slices of foie gras terrine (p. 873) or canned foie gras pâté. A row of sliced truffles may be placed on top of the foie gras layer.

Veal and Tongue Terrine
Use cooked, cured beef tongue in place of the ham.

Rabbit Terrine
Bone out a rabbit, keeping the loin meat in 2 long strips. Make a rabbit forcemeat by following the veal forcemeat recipe but substituting meat from the rabbit legs for all or part of the veal. Soak, clean, and liquefy the rabbit liver according to the procedure on page 855. Add it to the forcemeat. Omit the garnish from the basic recipe, instead using the rabbit loins marinated in the brandy. Fold the thin end of each loin back on itself so it is of uniform thickness. When filling the terrine, put half the forcemeat into the mold, lay the loins end to end down the center of the terrine, then fill with the remaining forcemeat.

   Optional step: Make a stock with the rabbit bones. Reduce the stock to a glaze, cool, and mix with the forcemeat.

   Optional step: Add a small quantity of nuts, such as skinned pistachios, to the forcemeat.

Game Terrine
Prepare as in the basic recipe, using Game Forcemeat (p. 856) and using strips of game meat instead of the veal and ham for garnish. Optional: Add a small quantity of green peppercorns, rinsed and drained, to the forcemeat.

Duck Terrine
Bone out a duck. Use the leg meat, any trimmings, and the liver for making Duck Forcemeat (p. 856). Flavor the forcemeat lightly with grated orange zest, using the zest of ½ orange for each 2 lb (1 kg) forcemeat. If desired, flavor the forcemeat with duck stock reduced to a glaze and cooled. Use the breast meat for garnish, omitting the veal and ham from the basic recipe but keeping the fatback. Cut the breast meat into strips and marinate in the brandy with the fatback strips.

Country Terrine
Use pork forcemeat, keeping the grind rather coarse. Chop the garnish coarsely and mix with the forcemeat.

GALANTINES

A galantine is a ground meat mixture—that is, a forcemeat—that is wrapped in the skin of the product it is made from, such as chicken or duck. A galantine is almost always poached although, in some instances, it is roasted.

A galantine is made by rolling up a forcemeat in a large piece of skin, giving it a cylindrical or sausage shape that yields round slices. Consequently, the name galantine is also given to forcemeats or other mixtures (such as mousselines) that are rolled into a sausage shape in a piece of parchment, plastic film, or other material.

A finished galantine is often displayed whole, decorated and glazed with aspic, with a few slices removed to show a cross section. For à la carte service, slices of galantine are served the same way as slices of pâté and terrine.

The following is a representative galatine recipe. The procedure is illustrated in Figure 27.4.

 ## Chicken Galantine

Yield: 3 lb (1.25 kg)

U.S.	Metric	Ingredients
1	1	Roasting chicken, about 5 lb (2.25 kg)
to taste	to taste	Salt
to taste	to taste	White pepper
4 fl oz	125 mL	Brandy
1 lb	450 g	Chicken Forcemeat I (p. 856), made with part of the leg meat (see step 3)
1	1	Liver from the chicken
		Garnish:
8 oz	225 g	Leg meat from the chicken (from step 4)
2 oz	60 g	Smoked ham
2 oz	60 g	Cured beef tongue, cooked
1 oz	30 g	Pimientos, rinsed and dried
1 oz	30 g	Truffles (optional)
2 oz	60 g	Pistachios, blanched and skinned
as needed	as needed	Chicken stock

Per 1 ounce:
Calories, 90; Protein, 5 g; Fat, 7 g (70% cal.); Cholesterol, 30 mg; Carbohydrates, 0 g; Fiber, 0 g; Sodium, 100 mg.

■ Procedure

1. One day in advance, prepare the chicken. Cut off the wings at the second joint. Slit the skin of the chicken along the backbone and carefully remove the skin in one piece. Remove the breasts, keeping them whole. Remove the meat from the legs and wings and reserve it for making the forcemeat.

2. Lay the skin flat, inside up, and trim it into a neat rectangle. Remove all fat and connective tissue. Place a piece of cheesecloth on a sheet pan and lay the skin in the center of it.

3. Butterfly the breast meat and pound it flat so the two breasts together make a rectangle. Place the flattened breast meat on the center of the skin. There should be at least 1–2 in. (2–5 cm) of skin showing around all sides of the breast meat rectangle. Sprinkle with salt, white pepper, and half of the brandy. Cover with plastic film and refrigerate overnight.

4. Trim all fat and connective tissue from the leg and wing meat and measure 9 oz (250 g) for making the forcemeat. Measure another 8 oz (225 g) leg meat for the garnish and mix it with the remaining brandy. Reserve any remaining meat for another use.

5. Use the carcass and giblets for making stock.

6. Prepare the forcemeat, grinding it very fine by using a food processor or by passing it 3 times through the fine blade of a grinder. Keep it cold at all times.

7. Soak, clean, and liquefy the livers according to the procedure on page 855. Mix the liver purée with the forcemeat.

8. Cut the chicken leg meat, ham, tongue, pimiento, and truffle into small dice.

9. Mix the diced garnish and the pistachios into the forcemeat until well combined.

10. Drain the brandy from the chicken skin and pat dry with a clean towel.

11. Form the forcemeat into a cylinder the length of the breast meat rectangle. Place the forcemeat on the breast meat and roll it up into the skin with the aid of the cheesecloth.

12. Roll the galantine in the cheesecloth and tie the ends. Then roll the galantine in a sheet of parchment, working to get the roll as smooth as possible. Tie the roll loosely at 2-in. (5-cm) intervals. (This method is used when the galantine must be completely smooth, with no tie marks. For a simpler method, tie the cheesecloth roll in 3 or 4 places and at the ends.)

13. Poach the galantine slowly in chicken stock until the internal temperature is 160°F (71°C). This will take about 45–60 minutes. Retie the galantine, which will have shrunk, then let it cool completely in the stock.

14. Remove from the stock, unwrap, and decorate as desired.

Figure 27.4 Making a chicken galantine.

(a) Place the flattened breast meat on the center of the skin so that there is an inch or two (3-5 cm) of skin showing around all sides.

(b) Shape the forcemeat into a cylinder and place it along one edge of the rectangle of chicken as shown.

(c) With the aid of the cheesecloth, roll up the forcemeat in the chicken skin. Do not roll the cheesecloth into the chicken.

(d) Tie the ends of the cheesecloth securely. Proceed as indicated in the recipe.

TERRINES BASED ON MOUSSELINES

The body of most fish terrines, as well as some vegetable terrines and other specialty items, consists of a mousseline forcemeat. They are made like traditional terrines, except that a mousseline forcemeat takes the place of the straight forcemeat.

A mousseline forcemeat consists of raw, puréed fish, poultry, or meat combined with heavy cream and, usually but not always, eggs or egg whites. Because they contain no starch or binder, and because of the large quantity of cream they contain, mousselines are the most delicate of forcemeats. The procedure for making a mousseline forcemeat is detailed in the basic recipe below.

Ingredient proportions in mousseline forcemeat depend on the qualities of the meat or fish being used. The albumin content of the egg white makes the mousseline firm when it is cooked. If the meat or fish you are using has a high albumin content, however, you may be able to reduce the quantity of egg white. In some cases, you may not need any egg. Similarly, the amount of cream depends on the firmness of the fish and on the intended use of the forcemeat. If it is to be the base of a terrine that will be sliced, too much cream will make it too delicate. On the other hand, for small timbale molds and similar items that don't need to be as firm, the quantity of cream can be increased beyond the amount indicated in the recipe below.

As for straight forcemeats, it is important to keep the ingredients cold at all times.

Basic Mousseline Forcemeat

Yield (approx): 1 lb 8 oz (750 g)

U.S.	Metric	Ingredients
1 lb	500 g	Chicken meat, lean veal, fish, or shellfish (see note)
2	2	Egg whites
12 fl oz	375 mL	Heavy cream
1 tsp, or to taste	5 mL, or to taste	Salt
to taste	to taste	White pepper
to taste	to taste	Cayenne
to taste	to taste	Nutmeg

Per 1 ounce:
Calories, 70; Protein, 5 g; Fat, 6 g (73% cal.); Cholesterol, 35 mg; Carbohydrates, 0 g; Fiber, 0 g; Sodium, 120 mg.

Note: Use lean, skinless chicken meat, lean veal, fillets from lean, white fish, or shellfish such as scallops, shrimp, or lobster.

■ Procedure

1. Dice the meat and place in the container of a food processor. Process until puréed.
2. Add the egg whites and process until well blended.
3. Force the purée through a sieve to remove sinews and other connective tissue.
4. Put the purée into a stainless-steel bowl nested in another bowl of crushed ice. Chill until the purée is very cold.
5. Gradually blend in the cream by hand.
6. Season with salt, white pepper, cayenne, and a dash of nutmeg
7. Test the seasoning and consistency by poaching, cooling, and tasting a small quenelle. Adjust as necessary.

The procedure for assembling and cooking a mousseline terrine is the same as for making a regular forcemeat terrine (see p. 860), except that the internal temperature, when done, is slightly lower, about 158° to 160°F (70°C).

Cooked vegetables, fish fillets, and other appropriate items are used as garnish. Two or more mousselines can be layered in the mold to make multicolored terrines. Alternatively, a mousseline forcemeat can be spread on the bottom and sides of the mold, which is then filled with a different mousseline plus garnish and topped with a layer of the first mousseline.

Terrine of Vegetables with Chicken Mousseline

Yield: 2 lb (1 kg)

U.S.	Metric	Ingredients
1 lb 8 oz	750 g	Chicken Mousseline Forcemeat (p. 863)
2 tbsp	7 g	Chopped parsley
1 tsp	1 g	Chopped fresh tarragon
½ oz	15 g	Glace de volaille, melted (optional)
2 oz	60 g	Zucchini, small, trimmed
2 oz	60 g	Red bell pepper, cored and seeded
2 oz	60 g	Carrots, trimmed and peeled
2 oz	60 g	Green beans, trimmed
2 oz	60 g	Shiitake mushroom caps

Per 1 ounce:
Calories, 60; Protein, 4 g; Fat, 5 g (67% cal.); Cholesterol, 25 mg; Carbohydrates, 1 g; Fiber, 0 g; Sodium, 90 mg.

■ Procedure

1. Mix the chicken mousseline with the chopped herbs and the glace de volaille, if used.

2. Cut the zucchini into strips about ¼–½ in. (1 cm) wide. Blanch 2 minutes in salted water, drain, and chill.

3. Char and peel the red pepper (see p. 529). Cut it into strips.

4. Cut the carrots into strips like the zucchini. Blanch 3 minutes, drain, and chill.

5. Blanch the green beans for 1–2 minutes, depending on their tenderness.

6. Cut the mushroom caps in half. Blanch for 30 seconds, drain, cool, and pat dry to remove extra moisture.

7. Butter well the bottom and sides of a 1½-qt (1.5-L) terrine mold.

8. Spread one-third of the mousseline on the bottom of the mold, being sure to eliminate air bubbles.

9. Arrange the carrot strips and beans lengthwise in the mold, pushing them partway into the mousseline. Keep the vegetables at least ¼ in. (5 mm) from the sides of the mold (see Figure 27.5).

10. Spread a thin layer of mousseline over the vegetables. Arrange the mushroom caps down the center of the mold, then cover with another thin layer of mousseline. About one-third of the mousseline should be left.

11. Arrange the pepper and zucchini strips lengthwise in the mold, adding a little more mousseline as necessary.

12. Top with the remaining mousseline, again spreading it carefully to avoid air bubbles. Rap the terrine sharply on the workbench to eliminate any remaining air bubbles. Smooth the top of the mousseline with a spatula.

13. Cover tightly with foil. Set in a hot-water bath and bake in an oven heated to 325°F (165°C) until set firm, about 1 hour and 15 minutes.

14. Cool thoroughly, then chill well in the refrigerator.

15. Unmold. Slice carefully with a knife dipped in hot water. Serve garnished with a few salad greens and an appropriate cold sauce.

VARIATIONS

Instead of the vegetables indicated, select your choice of seasonal vegetables.

For a more luxurious terrine, include thin slices of truffle with the garnish, or omit the parsley and add minced truffle to the mousseline.

Seafood Terrine with Vegetables
Use a fish or shellfish mousseline instead of the chicken mousseline. Reduce the number and quantity of vegetables. Add to the garnish some strips of smoked salmon.

Figure 27.5
Cross-section diagram of Terrine of Vegetables with Chicken Mousseline

TERRINES AND OTHER MOLDS WITH GELATIN

All the terrines we have discussed so far are traditional cooked terrines—that is, the raw forcemeat is cooked in the mold. There are many kinds of uncooked terrines as well. These are not cooked after assembly but are chilled until set. Any ingredients that require cooking are cooked before assembly. The terrines we discuss in this section rely on gelatin for their structure.

Preparing these items in terrine molds allows them to be cut into slices for serving, just as traditional forcemeat terrines are. They can also be made in molds of any other shape, including portion-size molds, which can simply be unmolded and garnished for serving. Cooked terrines, on the other hand, are best made in regularly shaped, symmetrical molds so they cook uniformly.

Most molds bound with gelatin fall into two general categories: those based on aspics and those based on mousses.

ASPIC MOLDS

Aspic-based terrines are simply glorified gelatin molds—that is, they consist of solid ingredients held together by gelatin in the form of aspic jelly.

The proportion of aspic to solids can vary greatly. At one extreme, there may be just enough aspic to hold the solid ingredients together, so that the aspic jelly itself is almost not evident. On the other hand, the aspic may predominate, with solid ingredients suspended in it at intervals. For this latter type to succeed, the aspic jelly must be of excellent quality, with good flavor, not too firm a texture, and sparkling clarity.

The majority of aspic terrines fall between these extremes.

The following procedure is applicable to the production of most aspic terrines and other aspic molds:

1. Either line the mold with aspic, following the procedure on page 853, or pour a layer of aspic into the bottom of the mold. Chill until firm.

2. Arrange a layer of garnish in the mold.

3. Add just enough aspic jelly to cover the solid garnish. Chill until firm.

4. Repeat steps 2 and 3 until the mold is full.

5. For best storage, leave the aspic in the mold, covered tightly with plastic film, until service time.

Terrines made by this method depend on a crystal-clear aspic jelly for their appearance and are often very elegant. Another approach is simply to combine the jelly with a mixture of ingredients and fill the terrine with this mixture. A clarified aspic may not be necessary for this method. Terrines made this way range from coarse, peasant-style dishes to more elaborate constructions such as the Lentil and Leek Terrine on page 868.

Headcheese and a number of other commercially made luncheon-meat loaves are examples of this type of terrine. Tripes à la Môde de Caen (p. 327), when properly made, can also be chilled until solid and unmolded because it contains enough natural gelatin from the calves' feet and other ingredients. Jambon Persillé or Parslied Ham (p. 866) is another example of a country-style aspic-based terrine made with unclarified jelly.

MOUSSES

A savory cold **mousse**, as used for the base of a terrine, is a preparation of puréed meat, poultry, fish, vegetable, or other food, bound with gelatin and usually lightened with the addition of partially whipped heavy cream. (It is true that the terms *mousse* and *mousseline* are often used more or less interchangeably, but we use them here in two distinct senses in order to avoid confusion.)

The gelatin used to bind or set the mousse may be added in the form of an aspic jelly or as powdered gelatin softened and dissolved in another liquid ingredient.

Because mousses, like aspics, are not cooked after assembly but merely chilled, they are often prepared not only in terrines but in decorative, irregularly shaped molds. The production of mousses is relatively simple. The procedure consists of four main steps:

1. Purée the main ingredient.
2. Add the aspic jelly or dissolved gelatin.
3. Fold in the lightly whipped cream and season to taste.
4. Pour into the prepared mold.

Molds are usually lined with aspic jelly and decorated according to the procedures on page 853. As with other kinds of terrines, garnish, if any, is either mixed with the mousse or arranged in the mold as the mousse is added.

Although this method is really little more than mixing together the ingredients in a given order, two precautions must be taken:

1. **Carry out the entire procedure, including the pouring of the mixture into the mold, quickly and in one continuous process.**

   If you stop partway through the procedure, the gelatin is likely to set, and you will have a lumpy, poorly mixed product.

2. **Do not overwhip the cream.**

   Whip it only until it forms soft mounds. When cream is overwhipped, it breaks and becomes grainy. This same effect can be caused by the extra beating the cream gets when it is being folded into the mousse mixture. A mousse made with over-whipped cream tastes dry and grainy, not smooth and creamy.

Mousses can also be made without gelatin or other binders. A soft mousse is simply a puréed or ground food with the addition of lightly whipped cream. Although these soft mousses are too soft to be used in terrines, they can be spooned into neat, oval quenelle shapes onto salad plates, garnished attractively, and served as elegant first courses.

 ## Jambon Persillé (Parslied Ham in Aspic)

Yield: approximately 2 lb (1 kg)

U.S.	Metric	Ingredients
2	2	Pig feet, split
1	1	Onion
1	1	Clove
		Sachet:
1	1	Garlic clove
1	1	Bay leaf
½ tsp	2 mL	Dried thyme
½ tsp	2 mL	Dried tarragon
12 fl oz	350 mL	White wine
as needed	as needed	White stock
1 lb 8 oz	750 g	Mild-cured ham, in 1 or more large pieces
½ cup	30 g	Chopped parsley
½ fl oz	15 mL	Wine vinegar
if needed	if needed	Salt
if needed	if needed	Pepper

Per 1 ounce:
Calories, 96; Protein, 10 g; Fat, 6 g (49% cal.); Cholesterol, 34 mg; Carbohydrates, 1 g; Fiber, 0 g; Sodium, 385 mg.

■ P r o c e d u r e

1. Put the pig feet, onion with the clove stuck in it, sachet, and wine in a heavy pot. Add enough white stock to cover. Simmer 2 hours, adding more stock or water as needed.

2. Add the ham to the pot. Add more stock as needed. Simmer until the ham is tender. Cooking time will vary greatly, depending on the ham.

3. Remove the ham. Trim off any fat and skin. Cut the ham into large dice. Remove any meat from the pig feet, chop it, and add it to the ham. (Skin from the feet may also be added, if desired.) Chill the meat.

4. Skim and strain the cooking liquid. The stock may be clarified if desired, but this is not necessary if a traditional rustic look is desired. The pig feet should have yielded sufficient gelatin, but test to make sure and add more gelatin if needed to make a strong aspic; see the procedure on page 850.

5. Melt the aspic (if it has congealed), and add the parsley and vinegar. Taste and add salt and pepper if necessary.

6. Select the desired molds; large salad bowls are traditional. Line the bottom of the mold with a thin layer of the parsley aspic. Chill until firm.

7. Combine the ham and aspic and pour into the mold. Chill until set.

8. To serve, unmold and slice. Serve unadorned or plated with salad greens and vinaigrette.

Terrine of Vegetables and Chicken in Aspic

Yield: approximately 2 lb 8 oz (1.1 kg)

U.S.	Metric	Ingredients
6 oz	175 g	Cooked chicken breast, boneless and skinless
2–4 oz	100 g	Mayonnaise Chaud-Froid (p. 851)
		Vegetable garnish AP:
4 oz	115 g	Carrots
2	2	Artichokes, medium
1	1	Lemon
8 oz	225 g	Spinach
4 oz	115 g	Tomatoes, whole, fresh
3 oz	90 g	Green beans
6 oz	175 g	Asparagus
1 pt (approximately)	500 mL (approximately)	Aspic jelly

Per 1 ounce:
Calories, 20; Protein, 2 g; Fat, 1 g (36% cal.); Cholesterol, 5 mg;
Carbohydrates, 2 g; Fiber, 1 g; Sodium, 20 mg.

■ P r o c e d u r e

1. If the chicken pieces are large, cut them in half lengthwise. They should be no more than about 2–2½ in. (5–6 cm) wide. Arrange them on a rack with the best side up. Coat them with a thin layer of chaud-froid. Chill until set.

2. Trim and peel the carrots. Cut into long batonnet shapes. Cook the carrots until tender but still firm. Chill.

3. Trim the artichokes down to the bases, rubbing with cut lemon to keep them from darkening. Cook in water with a little lemon juice until tender. Drain and chill. Cut crosswise into strips about ¼ in. (6 mm) thick.

4. Trim the stems from the spinach and rinse in several changes of water. Blanch, drain, rinse in cold water, and squeeze firmly to remove excess moisture. Chop coarsely.

5. Peel the tomatoes, cut them in half horizontally, and remove seeds and juice. Place them on a cutting board cut side down and slice vertically into slices about ¼ in. (6 mm) thick. Salt the slices lightly and let drain. Dry lightly on clean toweling.

6. Trim the green beans and cook until tender but still firm. Chill.

7. Remove the woody bottoms from the asparagus spears. Peel the lower ends of the spears. Cook until tender but still firm. Chill.

8. Melt and cool the aspic jelly according to the procedure on page 852.

9. Line a 1½ -qt (1.4-L) terrine mold with a layer of aspic according to the procedure on page 853, or ladle a ¼-in. (6-mm) layer of aspic onto the bottom of the mold. Chill until set.

10. Arrange the carrots and then the spinach in the mold. Add just enough aspic to cover. (See Figure 27.6. Note that this diagram shows only the relative positions of the ingredients. The actual proportion of vegetables is greater than shown.) Chill until set.

11. Arrange half of the chicken pieces down the center of the mold, chaud-froid side down. Place the artichokes and beans alongside the chicken. Add just enough aspic to cover. Chill until set.

12. Arrange the rest of the chicken, the tomato, and the asparagus in the mold. Add just enough aspic to cover. Chill overnight, until set firm.

13. For service, unmold and slice carefully with a sharp knife dipped in hot water. Serve with a vinaigrette.

V A R I A T I O N S

Substitute other appropriate vegetables in season. Other items, such as turkey, rabbit, fresh or smoked fish, and seafood, can be substituted for the chicken, or omit the protein item entirely and increase the quantity of vegetables.

Terrine of Vegetables with Foie Gras in Aspic
Substitute slices of foie gras terrine (p. 873) for the chicken. Omit the chaud-froid.

Figure 27.6
Cross-section diagram of Terrine of Vegetables and Chicken in Aspic

Lentil and Leek Terrine with Smoked Turkey and Prosciutto

Yield: approximately 2 lb (1 kg)

U.S.	Metric	Ingredients
5 oz	150 g	Lentils, preferably green Le Puy variety (see note)
2 oz	60 g	Carrots, cut brunoise
1	1	Onion, medium, whole, peeled
2	2	Cloves
1	1	Bay leaf
2 lb	1 kg	Leeks, small (see note)
6 oz	185 g	Smoked turkey
2 oz	60 g	Prosciutto, sliced tissue-thin
½ oz	15 g	Gelatin powder
5 fl oz	150 mL	Chicken stock
to taste	to taste	Salt

Per 1 ounce:
Calories, 40; Protein, 4 g; Fat, 1 g (11% cal.); Cholesterol, 5 mg; Carbohydrates, 5 g; Fiber, 1 g; Sodium, 60 mg.

Note: Green Le Puy lentils give the best results, as they retain their shape well and have the best appearance. The amount of leeks needed depends on the trimming yield, which can vary greatly. You will need enough trimmed, cooked leeks to cover the top and bottom of the terrine mold. Very small leeks are best because they cover the top and bottom of the terrine without filling it too much. Larger leeks can be cut in half lengthwise.

■ P r o c e d u r e

1. Soak the lentils several hours or overnight. Drain, combine with the carrots, the onion stuck with the cloves, and the bay leaf in a heavy pot. Add enough water to cover by several inches (more than 5 cm). Simmer until tender but still firm and whole. For presoaked green lentils, this takes less than 10 minutes. Drain in a fine strainer. Discard the onion, cloves, and bay leaf. Cool the lentils.

2. Trim the root ends and the coarse leaves from the leeks, leaving the lighter green parts attached so the leeks will be as long as possible. Wash carefully. Simmer or steam until tender. Chill.

3. Cut the turkey into long strips about ½ in. (12 mm) wide. Wrap each strip in a slice of prosciutto.

4. Soften the gelatin in the stock, then heat to dissolve it. Cool the aspic slightly. Because this is a very strong aspic, it should be kept slightly warm or it will solidify too quickly when mixed with the lentils.

5. Mix the aspic with the lentils. Add salt to taste. From this point, the terrine must be assembled quickly so it is finished before the aspic sets.

6. Line a 1¼-qt (1.25-L) terrine with plastic film to make unmolding easier. Cover the bottom of the terrine with a layer of leeks arranged lengthwise and end to end. Arrange them tightly against each other so there are no gaps (see Figure 27.7). If using large leeks, cut them in half lengthwise and arrange in the mold cut side up.

7. Fill the terrine with the lentils, alternating with the turkey strips. Arrange the strips lengthwise and at intervals so they are distributed evenly in the lentils.

8. Top with another layer of leeks, pressing them down firmly and leveling the top. If using large leeks, cut in half lengthwise and place them cut side down in the terrine.

9. Cover and chill overnight, until set firm.

10. Unmold and slice with a sharp knife dipped in hot water. Plate and garnish with a few salad greens. Serve with a vinaigrette, preferably one made with walnut or hazelnut oil.

V A R I A T I O N S

Various items can be used instead of the turkey and prosciutto, such as ham, duck breast cooked rare, or loin of rabbit.

Figure 27.7
Cross-section diagram of Lentil and Leek Terrine with Smoked Turkey and Prosciutto

Leeks

Smoked turkey wrapped in prosciutto

Lentils and aspic

Tricolor Vegetable Terrine

Yield: approximately 1 lb 12 oz (800 g)

U.S.	Metric	Ingredients
1 lb	450 g	Spinach
¼ oz	7 g	Shallot, minced
¼ oz	7 g	Butter
1 tsp	5 mL	Gelatin powder
1 fl oz	30 mL	Chicken stock, vegetable stock, or water, cold
to taste	to taste	Salt
2 fl oz	60 mL	Heavy cream
5 oz	150 g	Cauliflower, trimmed
2 oz	60 g	White turnips, peeled
1 tsp	5 mL	Gelatin powder
1 fl oz	30 mL	Chicken stock, vegetable stock, or water, cold
to taste	to taste	Salt
2 fl oz	60 mL	Heavy cream
7 oz	200 g	Carrots, trimmed and peeled
1 tsp	5 mL	Gelatin powder
1 fl oz	30 mL	Chicken stock, vegetable stock, or water, cold
to taste	to taste	Salt
2 fl oz	60 mL	Heavy cream

Per 1 ounce:
Calories, 30; Protein, 1 g; Fat, 3 g (65% cal.); Cholesterol, 10 mg; Carbohydrates, 2 g; Fiber, 1 g; Sodium, 20 mg.

■ **P r o c e d u r e**

1. Have ready a 1-qt (1-L) terrine mold. For ease of unmolding, line with plastic film.

2. Trim the stems from the spinach and wash it well in several changes of water. Cook in boiling, salted water until done, about 2 minutes, and drain. Rinse under cold water to cool. Drain. Squeeze dry.

3. Chop the spinach into fine pieces by hand or in a food processor.

4. Sweat the shallots in butter until soft. Add the spinach and cook slowly until quite dry. Cool thoroughly but do not chill.

5. Soften the gelatin in the stock, then heat until it is dissolved. Cool and stir into the spinach. Add salt to taste.

6. Quickly whip the cream until it forms soft peaks. Immediately fold it into the spinach mixture. Pour it into the mold and smooth with a spatula. Chill until set.

7. Steam the cauliflower and turnips until they are tender. Purée in a food processor. For the smoothest texture, force the purée through a sieve. Mix the vegetables together. Heat slowly in a large sauté pan to dry out the purée slightly. Cool thoroughly, but do not chill.

8. Repeat steps 5 and 6 to make the white mousse. Pour it into the mold on top of the green mousse. Chill.

9. Trim, cook, and purée the carrots in the same way, and dry the purée as above. Repeat steps 5 and 6 to make the orange mousse, and add it to the terrine (see Figure 27.8). Chill until set firm.

10. Unmold the terrine and slice to serve. Garnish as desired and serve with an appropriate cold sauce.

V A R I A T I O N S

Other vegetable purées may be substituted for those in the basic recipe.

For a low-fat version, omit the gelatin powder, stock, and heavy cream. In place of the stock and cream, use an equal quantity of a strong aspic. Mix the aspic with the vegetable purées.

Figure 27.8
Cross-section diagram of Tricolor Vegetable Terrine

Ham Mousse

Yield: 2 lb (1 kg)

U.S.	Metric	Ingredients
1 lb	500 g	Cooked, lean smoked ham
5 fl oz	150 mL	Chicken velouté
1 tbsp	15 mL	Madeira wine
to taste	to taste	White pepper
to taste	to taste	Dry mustard
to taste	to taste	Salt
¼ oz	7 g	Gelatin powder
4 fl oz	125 mL	Chicken stock, cold
8 fl oz	250 mL	Heavy cream

Per 1 ounce:
Calories, 50; Protein, 3 g; Fat, 4 g (69% cal.); Cholesterol, 20 mg; Carbohydrates, 1 g; Fiber, 0 g; Sodium, 190 mg.

■ P r o c e d u r e

1. Select a mold or molds totaling about 1 qt (1 L) in capacity. If desired, line the molds with aspic and decorate them according to the procedure on page 853. Keep chilled until needed.

2. Grind the ham until it is very fine.

3. Mix the velouté with the puréed ham. Add the Madeira and season to taste with white pepper, dry mustard, and salt. No salt may be needed if the ham is very salty.

4. Soften the gelatin in the stock. Heat the stock until the gelatin dissolves, then cool the liquid aspic, but do not let it set.

5. Whip the cream until it forms soft peaks.

6. Add the aspic jelly to the ham mixture and stir until well combined.

7. Quickly and thoroughly fold the cream into the ham mixture. Taste and adjust seasonings if necessary.

8. Fill the prepared molds. Chill several hours or overnight until set firm. Unmold just before serving.

V A R I A T I O N S

For a denser but less rich mousse, reduce the quantity of cream as desired.

Substitute prosciutto for one-eighth to one-fourth of the cooked ham.

Instead of velouté, substitute mayonnaise thinned with cream to the thickness of velouté.

Mousses of other meats, poultry, and fish may be prepared according to the same procedure, substituting an appropriate stock (such as fish stock for fish mousse) and using appropriate seasonings in place of the mustard and Madeira (for example, salmon mousse flavored with dill, cayenne, and white wine).

Mousse of Foie Gras

Yield: 1 lb (500 g)

U.S.	Metric	Ingredients
8 oz	250 g	Foie gras (see note)
4 fl oz	125 mL	Aspic jelly
4 fl oz	125 mL	Heavy cream
to taste	to taste	Salt
to taste	to taste	White pepper

Per 1 ounce:
Calories, 50; Protein, 3 g; Fat, 4 g (66% cal.); Cholesterol, 95 mg; Carbohydrates, 1 g; Fiber, 0 g; Sodium, 85 mg.

Note: See page 871 for a discussion of foie gras. Cooked, not raw foie gras is called for in this recipe. Terrine of Foie Gras (p. 873) may be used. If fresh foie gras products are not available, canned foie gras may be used.

■ P r o c e d u r e

1. Force the foie gras through a sieve to purée it.

2. Melt and cool the aspic according to the procedure on page 852. Add it to the foie gras, mixing it in thoroughly.

3. Whip the cream until it forms soft peaks. Quickly and thoroughly fold it into the foie gras.

4. While folding in the cream, taste and adjust the seasonings with salt and white pepper. It is best to do this while folding in the cream so there is no delay that would allow the gelatin to set too early and to avoid excess mixing, which may overwhip the cream.

5. Pour at once into a terrine or other mold. Cover tightly and chill at least 1 day.

6. This dish is very rich and should be served in small quantities, about 2 oz (60 g) per portion. Serve by dipping a spoon into hot water and drawing it across the surface of the terrine, as though scooping ice cream. Place the spoonful in the center of a plate and serve with melba toasts and raw vegetable garnish or salad greens.

FOIE GRAS, LIVER TERRINES, AND RILLETTES

The chapter concludes with three traditional terrines that require somewhat different techniques from those already discussed. It should be noted that, although these items are especially high in fat and cholesterol, they are as popular as they have ever been, even in these times of diet consciousness.

FOIE GRAS TERRINES

The most prized and, perhaps, the most famous ingredient for pâtés and terrines in classical cuisine is **foie gras** (fwah grah). This French term means "fat liver." Foie gras is the fatted liver of specially fed varieties of ducks and geese. Until recently, only canned or processed foie gras products were available in the United States. Now, however, the breed of duck that is raised to produce foie gras (called the *mullard* or *moulard*, a cross between the muscovy and white pekin ducks) is grown on American farms. Consequently, fresh, raw duck foie gras is now sold in this country. Its availability has created a great deal of enthusiasm among American cooks in spite of its high price.

The special feeding of the ducks makes the livers very large, more than 1 lb (500 g) as a rule, with a high fat content. A good-quality fresh foie gras is a pale yellowish-tan color with a smooth, velvety texture, almost the feel of butter. The liver has two lobes, one large and one small.

It is important to be aware that foie gras consists mostly of fat. Indeed, the rich flavor of the fat is the whole reason that foie gras is so highly prized. Any fat that cooks out during preparation is carefully saved and used for another purpose. Those who must avoid fats, especially animal fats, should probably steer clear of this delicacy. For the rest of us, the high price of foie gras helps protect our health by making overindulgence unlikely.

There are usually two grades of domestic duck foie gras. The A grade is larger, usually 1¼ lb (600 g) or more, with relatively few blemishes and blood spots. The B grade is smaller and has more blood spots and veins.

Preparing Foie Gras for Cooking

No matter how a raw foie gras is to be prepared, it should first be rinsed in cold water and examined closely for green spots. These are caused by bile; they must be cut or scraped away because the bile has a strong, bitter taste. Also, if there are any bits of external fat, remove them.

Next, the liver should be soaked. (This step is not required, but it does improve the product.) Place it in lightly salted ice-cold water or milk to cover. Let stand for up to 2 hours, no longer. Remove from the salted liquid and rinse in fresh, cold water.

For cold preparations such as terrines and mousses, the liver should first be deveined. To devein the foie gras, first let it come to room temperature. Its fat content makes a cold liver too brittle to devein without excessive breakage, which would result in more cooking loss. When the liver is at room temperature, even the heat of the hands melts the fat, so it is important to handle the liver lightly and to work quickly.

Begin by separating the two lobes and laying them, smooth side down, on a clean work surface. Carefully trim off any bloody spots. Grasping a lobe with your thumbs at the sides and fingers underneath in the center, very lightly bend the lobe lengthwise. The top, rough surface should open up slightly, revealing a heavy vein that runs lengthwise through the liver. (If it does not open up, help it along with a shallow incision with the point of a paring knife.) Carefully pull out this vein, along with any other heavy veins that are attached, all the while being careful to keep the liver as intact as possible. Repeat with the other lobe. The foie gras is now ready to be made into a terrine.

No matter how a foie gras is cooked, it is essential to avoid even the slightest overcooking. The liver is delicate, and the fat cooks out very quickly. Even a few seconds too long in a sauté pan can reduce a slice of foie gras to a few specks of connective tissue floating in a puddle of very expensive grease.

LIVER TERRINES

Liver terrines, often called *liver pâtés*, are popular, inexpensive appetizers—except, of course, for those made with foie gras. The classic liver terrine is a mixture of liquefied livers—that is, cleaned, soaked, blended, and strained according to the procedure on page 855—with eggs and seasonings, baked in a terrine until set. An example of this type of recipe can be found on page 874.

This kind of liver terrine generally contains flour as a stabilizer. Because the liver forcemeat is liquid, the flour improves the texture of the cooked product by helping bind the moisture. Heavy cream is also included in most recipes as a source of fat. Other sources of fat sometimes used in addition to or in place of the cream are ground pork fat, ground bacon, marrow, and rendered foie gras fat left over from making terrines.

Another type of liver terrine consists of a basic pork forcemeat with a liver content high enough so the flavor of the liver predominates. To make this type of terrine, make the forcemeat on page 856, but use 6 times the quantity of liver. The forcemeat will be quite soft. Follow the basic procedure for making forcemeat terrines (see p. 860), using whole, trimmed chicken livers marinated in brandy as the garnish.

A quick and simple substitute for these more elaborate terrines might be considered a type of rillettes (see the next section), as it consists of a seasoned mixture of cooked meat (liver, in this case) and fat. This is the type of chicken liver pâté found on delicatessen and coffee shop menus. To make this type of pâté, sauté some chicken livers, mash or purée them, and mix the purée with about one-eighth its weight in rendered chicken fat, pork fat, soft butter, or other fat, or else with one-fourth its weight in cream cheese. Season as desired, with salt, pepper, herbs, brandy or sherry, and/or sautéed minced onion.

RILLETTES

In France's Loire Valley, the first thing that customers are likely to be served in a typical neighborhood restaurant, whether they order it or not, is a crock of rillettes and some country bread to spread it on. Variations on this unpretentious dish have become widely popular and are served even in elegant North American restaurants.

Rillettes (ree yet) is a dish made of pork cooked slowly until it is very tender, then shredded, mixed with its own fat, seasoned, and packed into crocks or terrines.

Variations of the classic dish can be made by using other meats in addition to or instead of pork. Items rich in fat, such as duck and goose, are especially appropriate. Rillettes of lean meats, such as chicken, turkey, and rabbit, can be made, but some pork fat or other fat must be added to them when they are cooking.

Some chefs even serve rillettes made from fish, such as salmon or cod. The basic procedure is the same, except that the cooking time is, of course, much shorter. The cooked fish is shredded, mixed with just enough butter or other fat to give it a pleasant texture, and seasoned well.

A typical recipe for classic pork rillettes is on page 875. Follow the same basic procedure to make duck rillettes and other variations. A recipe for rillettes made with fish is on page 874.

Terrine of Foie Gras

Yield: variable, depending on size of liver

U.S.	Metric	Ingredients
1	1	Fresh, A-grade duck foie gras, about 1½ lb (700 g)
1 tsp	5 mL	Salt
¼ tsp	1 mL	White pepper
½–1 fl oz	15–30 mL	Choice of wine or liquor: port, Madeira, Sauternes, cognac, or Armagnac

Per 1 ounce:
Calories, 50; Protein, 6 g; Fat, 2 g (32% cal.); Cholesterol, 165 mg; Carbohydrates, 1 g; Fiber, 0 g; Sodium, 160 mg.

■ P r o c e d u r e

1. Soak, rinse, and devein the foie gras as described on page 871.

2. Place the liver in a bowl and season with salt and white pepper. Add the selected wine or liquor, using the smaller quantity for cognac or Armagnac; if using a sweet wine, use up to but not more than the larger quantity indicated. Turn the liver gently so that all sides are moistened.

3. Cover and refrigerate. Marinate for 24 hours.

4. Remove the livers from refrigeration about 1–2 hours before cooking time and let them come to room temperature. This is essential for the proper cooking of the terrine.

5. Pack the large lobe (or the pieces of the large lobe, if it broke during deveining) into the selected terrine, smooth side down. Top with the small lobe, smooth side up. Press the liver in firmly to eliminate air spaces. Cover with foil.

6. Place several folded kitchen towels on the bottom of a roasting pan or other pan used as a hot-water bath. (This helps insulate the terrine from strong bottom heat.) Place the terrine in the pan and add warm, not hot, water to come halfway up the sides of the terrine.

7. Place the terrine in an oven preheated to 200°–215°F (100°C). Bake until the proper doneness, as determined by an instant-read thermometer (see the following paragraph). This will take from 45 minutes to a little over 1 hour.

   The terrine is done when the thermometer reads 113°–130°F (45°–54°C). At the lower end of this range, the cooled terrine will be rather pink in the center, with a soft, creamy texture. At the higher end, the terrine will be firmer and less pink, but more fat will have cooked out, resulting in a lower yield. The right degree of doneness is a matter of personal preference.

8. Remove the terrine from the hot-water bath and set on a rack to cool. After about 10 minutes, weight it with a board that just fits inside the top of the terrine, or with another terrine, and several pounds of weights. When the terrine is almost cool but the fat is still liquid, pour off all the melted fat and juices. Separate and discard the juices. Reserve the fat. Put the weights back on the terrine and continue to cool.

9. When the terrine is cold, unmold it and remove and discard any bits of blood or juice on the bottom of the foie gras. Clean out the mold and put the foie gras back in it. Heat the reserved fat just until melted and pour it over the terrine. Refrigerate until cold, then cover tightly and refrigerate for 3–5 days so the flavors can develop.

10. To unmold, dip the terrine in warm water for a few seconds, then invert on a platter or cutting board. Slice with a sharp knife dipped in hot water before each slice. Serve with a little chopped aspic and toasted brioche, or with salad greens and a mild vinaigrette made with walnut oil.

Chicken Liver Terrine

Yield: 2 lb (1 kg)

U.S.	Metric	Ingredients
1 lb	50 g	Chicken livers
8 fl oz	250 mL	Heavy cream
5	5	Eggs, lightly beaten
2 oz	60 g	Flour
2 tsp	10 mL	Salt
½ tsp	2 mL	White pepper
1½ fl oz	50 mL	Brandy
as needed	as needed	Caul fat or thin slices of pork fatback for lining the mold (optional)

Per 1 ounce:
Calories, 60; Protein, 4 g; Fat, 4 g (57% cal.); Cholesterol, 105 mg; Carbohydrates, 2 g; Fiber, 0 g; Sodium, 170 mg.

■ P r o c e d u r e

1. Soak, rinse, liquefy, and strain the livers, following the procedure on page 855.

2. Mix in the remaining ingredients, except caul fat, until smooth. If necessary, strain to eliminate lumps.

3. If possible, cover and refrigerate this mixture overnight. This helps eliminate air bubbles that may have gotten in and allows the flour to absorb moisture.

4. Line a terrine mold with the caul or fatback, or grease it very generously with butter or lard.

5. Cover with foil. Bake in a water bath at 300°F (150°C) until set. The water in the water bath should come up to the same level as the liver mixture. Cooking time will depend on the size and shape of the terrine; approximate time is about 2 hours. Check it periodically after about 1½ hours so it does not overbake.

6. Remove from the water bath and cool on a rack. Refrigerate overnight or longer. Unmold and slice, or serve directly from the terrine.

V A R I A T I O N S

Substitute calf liver or pork liver for the chicken liver.

 ## Rillettes of Salmon, Haddock, or Finnan Haddie

Yield: 1 lb 4 oz (600 g)

U.S.	Metric	Ingredients
1 lb	500 g	Salmon, haddock, or finnan haddie, skinless and boneless
8 fl oz	250 mL	White wine
4 oz	125 g	Butter, unsalted
2 tsp	10 mL	Lemon juice
to taste	to taste	Salt
to taste	to taste	White pepper
to taste	to taste	Hot pepper sauce
as desired	as desired	Caviar, for garnish

Per 1 ounce:
Calories, 70; Protein, 59 g; Fat, 6 g (72% cal.); Cholesterol, 25 mg; Carbohydrates, 0 g; Fiber, 0 g; Sodium, 55 mg.

■ P r o c e d u r e

1. Combine the fish and wine in a saucepan or sauté pan. Poach the fish gently just until it is done. Because there is not enough wine to cover the fish, turn the fish over occasionally during cooking so it cooks evenly.

2. Drain the fish and cool completely.

3. Break the fish into small pieces, then mash with a fork until there are no lumps.

4. Soften the butter, then mix it with the fish until uniformly blended. Season to taste with lemon juice, salt, white pepper, and hot pepper sauce.

5. Pack the mixture into small ramekins or crocks for individual service. Chill.

6. Top each portion with a small spoonful of caviar just before serving. Use salmon caviar for salmon rillettes, or any desired caviar for haddock or finnan haddie rillettes.

7. For service, place the ramekin on a small plate lined with a folded napkin or a doily. Arrange slices of toast or bread on the underliner around the ramekin, or serve the toast on the side.

Rillettes of Pork

Yield: approximately 1 lb (500 g)

U.S.	Metric	Ingredients
2 lb	1 kg	Pork butt or shoulder, with fat but without skin and bones
1	1	Onion, small
2	2	Cloves
2	2	Bay leaves
pinch	pinch	Dried thyme
2 fl oz	60 mL	Water
1½ tsp	2 mL	Salt

Per 1 ounce:
Calories, 110; Protein, 9 g; Fat, 8 g (67% cal.);
Cholesterol, 35 mg; Carbohydrates, 2 g; Fiber, 0 g;
Sodium, 240 mg.

■ Procedure

1. Cut the meat, with all the fat, into large dice.

2. Cut off 1–2 oz (30–60 g) of the fat and render it slowly in a large, heavy pot. Add the meat and brown it lightly and gently over moderate heat.

3. Stick the onion with the cloves. Add the onion and the remaining ingredients. Cover and cook slowly in a low oven or on the range over very low heat, until the meat is very tender. This will take several hours. Check periodically to see if the meat has become dry. If it has, add 1–2 oz (30–60 mL) water.

4. Remove the bay leaves, onion, and cloves. Place the contents of the pot in a colander set over a large bowl. Press firmly on the meat and collect the fat and drippings in the bowl. Separate the fat and juices and reserve them separately.

5. Pound the meat with a large pestle or mallet, then shred it with two forks until the meat is a mass of fibers and no lumps. Alternatively, place the meat in the bowl of a mixer and mix with the paddle attachment at lowest speed until the meat is thoroughly shredded.

6. Add as much of the rendered fat as desired and mix it with the shredded meat. Taste and adjust the seasonings. It should be well seasoned because it is to be served cold. If the mixture seems dry, add some of the reserved juices to achieve the desired consistency. The mixture should be thick but spreadable, neither too dry nor too soft.

7. Pack into crocks or terrines and smooth the top. If the rillettes are to be kept for more than 1–2 days, seal the surface from the air by covering with a layer of melted fat. Refrigerate overnight or longer. Remove the layer of fat before serving.

8. Serve with crusty bread and sour pickles.

VARIATIONS

Rillettes of Duck, Goose, Rabbit, Turkey, or Chicken
Substitute any of the above meats for all or part of the pork. Lean meats should be cooked with additional pork fat to supply enough rendered fat to blend with the shredded meat.

■ TERMS FOR REVIEW

garde manger	forcemeat	pâté de campagne	mousseline forcemeat
aspic jelly	garnish (pâté)	pâté en croûte	mousse
aspic powder	pâté	pâte à pâté	foie gras
chaud-froid sauce	terrine	galantine	rillettes
mayonnaise chaud-froid			

■ QUESTIONS FOR DISCUSSION

1. Explain how to slice a meat terrine.

2. Why are mustards and vinaigrettes often served with pâtés and terrines?

3. What are three purposes of using aspic as a coating or glaze for cold foods?

4. Describe how to make mayonnaise chaud-froid.

5. Describe how to melt and cool aspic jelly.

6. What are the basic ingredients in a typical pork forcemeat?

7. How are raw livers prepared for use in forcemeats?

8. What is the purpose of pouring a layer of melted fat over a terrine after baking?

9. What is the difference between the terms mousseline and mousse, as used in this chapter?

10. What are the four basic steps in the production of a molded mousse? Why is it important to perform these steps quickly?

11. Why is it important not to overcook foie gras?

28

Food Presentation and Garnish

Until this point, most of the focus of this book has been on the preparation of food, from the selection of ingredients through mise en place and final cooking. We still have not reached our final goal, however. The point of learning and practicing procedures to prepare food of high quality is to ensure that the food is eaten and enjoyed.

In other words, our work isn't done until the food we have prepared is arranged on plates or platters and ready to be presented to the diner.

In traditional classical cuisine, until well after the middle of the twentieth century, the normal practice in fine dining establishments was to send the food on platters and in casseroles and other serving dishes to the dining room, where it would be transferred to dinner plates by the serving staff, sometimes after carving or portioning. The chefs who developed nouvelle cuisine, however, wanted to control the appearance of the food down to the last detail and so began to arrange food on dinner plates in the kitchen. Since that time, many styles of plating have come and gone, as chefs have devoted much attention to the appearance and arrangement of food on dinner plates.

Throughout this book, we stress making food look good as well as taste good. We talk about accurate, neat cutting of vegetables and fruits, about proper trimming of meats, poultry, and fish, about grill-marking steaks, about preserving color in cooked vegetables, and about attractive plating of salads. In this chapter, we continue the discussion of making food attractive.

HOT FOOD PRESENTATION

We eat for enjoyment as well as for nutrition and sustenance. Cooking is not just a trade but an art that appeals to our sense of taste, smell, and sight.

"The eye eats first" is a well-known saying. Our first impressions of a plate of food set our expectations. The sight of food stimulates our appetites, starts our digestive juices flowing, and makes us eager to dig in. Our meal becomes exciting and stimulating.

On the other hand, if the food looks carelessly served, tossed onto the plate in a sloppy manner, we assume it was cooked with the same lack of care. If the colors are pale and washed out, with no color accent, we expect the flavors to be bland and monotonous. If the size of the plate makes the steak *look* small (even if it's not), we go away unsatisfied.

Your job as a cook and a chef, then, is to get your customers interested in your food or, better yet, excited about it. You can't afford to turn them off before they even taste it. Your success depends on making your customers happy.

After reading this chapter, you should be able to

1. Explain why attractive food presentation is important.

2. Serve food that is attractively arranged on the plate or platter, with proper balance of color, shape, and texture.

3. Identify common terms from classical garniture that are still in general use today.

4. Garnish a banquet platter with attractive and appropriate vegetable accompaniments.

5. Plan and arrange attractive food platters for buffets.

FUNDAMENTALS OF PLATING

When a chef plans a new dish, appearance as well as flavor must be considered. Turn back to page 76 and look once again at the section called "Building Flavor Profiles." Remember that the senses of sight, taste, smell, and touch all come into play when we evaluate and enjoy food. How a dish looks is part of the identity of the dish, just like how it tastes, smells, and feels in the mouth.

In other words, how a dish looks is not something you think about only after you have prepared it. It is something you have in mind from the beginning of preparation. Remembering this helps you create natural-looking presentations, so the food looks like what it is rather than like an artificial construction with a complicated design.

THREE ESSENTIALS OF FOOD PRESENTATION

Making food look good requires careful attention to all kitchen tasks. The following three principles should be observed in order to create attractive food. Note that only one of them concerns arranging the food on the plate.

Good Preparation and Cooking Techniques

If vegetables are improperly cut during prep, the plate presentation will look improper. If meat is badly trimmed before cooking, a fancy plating design won't correct it. If a fish is overcooked and dry or a green vegetable is drab and mushy, it won't look good no matter what you do with it.

Professional Work Habits

Serving attractive food is largely a matter of being neat and careful and using common sense. This is an aspect of the professionalism we discussed in Chapter 1. Professionals take pride in their work and in the food they serve. They don't send a plate to the dining room with sauce accidentally dribbled across the rim and maybe a thumbprint or two for extra effect—not because their supervisors told them not to or because a rule in a textbook says so but because pride of workmanship prevents it.

Visual Sense

Beyond just being neat, effective food presentation depends on developing an understanding of techniques involving balance, arrangement, and garniture. These are the subjects of our next sections.

BALANCE

Balance is a term we used when talking about menu planning in Chapter 5. The rules of good menu balance also apply to plating. Select foods and garnishes that offer variety and contrast while avoiding combinations that are awkward or jarring.

Colors

Two or three colors on a plate are usually more interesting than just one. Visualize this combination: poached chicken breast with suprême sauce, mashed potatoes, and steamed cauliflower. Appetizing? Or how about fried chicken, French fries, and corn? Not quite as bad, but still a little monotonous.

Many hot foods, especially meats, poultry, and fish, have little color other than shades of brown, gold, or white. It helps to select vegetables or accompaniments that add color interest—one reason why green vegetables are so popular.

Garnish is often unnecessary, especially if the accompaniments have color, but it is very important in some cases. The classic combination of broiled steak (brown) and baked potato (brown and white) looks a little livelier with a few asparagus spears on the plate or even with the simple addition of a healthy sprig of watercress.

Shapes

Plan for variety of shape and form as well as of color. For example, you probably do not want to serve brussels sprouts with meatballs and new potatoes. Too many items of the same shape, in this case round, looks monotonous or even odd. Green beans and whipped potatoes might be better choices for accompaniment. Try for a variety of shapes that work together well.

Cutting vegetables into different shapes gives you great flexibility. Carrots, for example, which can be cut into dice, rounds, or sticks (batonnet, julienne, etc.), can be adapted to nearly any plate.

Textures

Textures are not strictly visual considerations, but they are important in plating as in menu planning (Chapter 5). Good balance requires a variety of textures on the plate. Perhaps the most common error is serving too many soft or puréed foods, such as baked salmon loaf with whipped potatoes and puréed squash.

Flavors

You can't see flavors, either, but this is one more factor you must consider when balancing colors, shapes, and textures on the plate. Consult the menu planning guidelines in Chapter 5.

PORTION SIZE

Portion sizes are important for presentation as well as for costing.

Match Portion Sizes and Plates

Select plates that are large enough to hold all the items without crowding. Too small a plate makes an overcrowded, jumbled, messy appearance.

On the other hand, too large a plate may make the portions look skimpy. If a plate does not look sufficiently full, customers may feel they are not getting good value.

Balance the Portion Sizes of the Items on the Plate

One item, generally a meat, poultry, or fish preparation, is usually considered the main item on the plate. It is the center of attention and is larger than the accompaniments.

Don't let the main item get lost amid excessive garnish and huge portions of vegetable and starch items.

Where there is no main item, as in some vegetable plates, strive for a logical balance of portions.

Arrangement on the Plate

Until recent years, plated main courses followed a standard pattern: meat or fish item at the front of the plate (closest to the diner), vegetable and starch items at the rear.

This arrangement is still the most commonly used because it is one of the simplest and most convenient. Nevertheless, many chefs are eager to display their creativity with imaginative plating presentations.

A style popular with today's chefs is to stack everything in one multilayered tower in the center of the plate. When used with restraint, this can make an effective and impressive plating. Often, however, it is carried to extremes, and customers are faced with the job of carefully deconstructing a towering pile of food and rearranging the items on the plate so they can begin eating. Some chefs like this style so much that they use it for nearly everything on the menu. Perhaps it works best for small dishes, such as some appetizers and the small portions of a tasting menu. It is important to keep the convenience and comfort of the diner in mind when plating.

Today's plating styles are many and varied. The following descriptions are examples of popular plating styles, and they serve as starting points for countless variations. The accompanying photos, as well as the remaining photos accompanying recipes throughout the text, show additional style variations and interpretations.

- The classic arrangement: main item in front, vegetables, starch items, and garnish at the rear.

- The main item alone in the center of the plate, sometimes with a sauce or simple garnish.

- The main item in the center, with vegetables distributed randomly around it, sometimes with a sauce underneath.

- The main item in the center, with neat piles of vegetables carefully arranged around it in a pattern.

- A starch or vegetable item heaped in the center; the main item sliced and leaning up against it; additional vegetables, garnish, and/or sauce on the plate around the center items.

- Main item, vegetable and starch accompaniments, and other garnish stacked neatly one atop the other in the center of the plate. Sauces or additional garnish may be placed around the outside.

- Vegetable in center of plate, sometimes with sauce; main item (in slices, medallions, small pieces, etc.) arranged around it toward the outside of the plate.

- Slices of the main item shingled on a bed of vegetables or a purée of vegetables or starch, with, perhaps, additional garnish to one side or around.

- Asymmetrical or random-looking arrangements that don't seem to follow any pattern. These often create the impression that the food was rushed to the dining room the instant it was cooked, without thought to the design. Of course, to be effective, these arrangements must be carefully thought out in advance.

The following guidelines will help you plate attractive, appealing food, no matter what plating style you are using.

1. **Keep food off the rim of the plate.**
   This guideline means, in part, selecting a plate large enough to hold the food without it hanging off the edge. In general, the rim should be thought of as the frame for the food presentation.

   Some chefs like to decorate this frame with a sprinkling of spice or chopped herbs or dots of a sauce. When tastefully done, this can enhance the appeal of the plate but, if overdone, it can make the plate look unattractive. Some restaurants got into the habit of throwing some badly chopped parsley over every plate that left the kitchen. Over the years, this practice has been so carelessly done, and—worse—so many customers have soiled their sleeves on sauced rims, that decorating the rim is falling out of fashion.

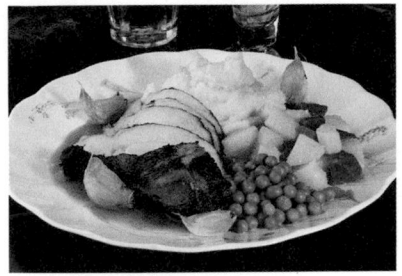

2. **Arrange the items for the convenience of the customer.**
   Put the best side of the meat forward. The customer should not have to turn the item around to start on it. The bony or fatty edge of the steak, the back side of the half-duckling, the boniest parts of the chicken pieces, and so on, should face away from the customer.

   Often the most imaginative platings are the most inconvenient. Tall, precarious towers of food are difficult to eat, and the customer may have to rearrange the food before eating.

3. **Keep space between items, unless, of course, they are stacked on one another.**
   Don't pile everything together in a jumbled heap. Each item should have its own identity. This is, of course, related also to selecting the right plate size.

   Even when items are stacked, this should be done neatly so that each item is identifiable.

4. **Maintain unity.**
   Basically, there is unity when the plate looks like one meal that happens to be made up of several items rather than like several unrelated items that just happen to be on the same plate.

   Create a center of attention and relate everything to it. The meat is generally the center of attention and is often placed front and center. Other items are placed around and behind it so as to balance it and keep the customer's eyes centered rather than pulled off the edge of the plate.

   Visual balance is similar to the balance of flavors discussed on page 77. In that discussion, we introduced the concept of primary flavors and supporting flavors. The primary flavors, you recall, are those of the main ingredients, and the supporting or secondary flavors are those of additional ingredients that are selected to enhance, harmonize with, or contrast with the primary flavors. Visual design works in a similar way. The main item on the plate is the primary design element. Other items, including side dishes and garnishes, are supporting design elements. Each item should enhance, harmonize with, or contrast with the main element and each other in a pleasing way.

5. **Make every component count.**
   Garnishes are not added just for color. Sometimes they are needed to balance a plate by providing an additional element. Two items on a plate often look unbalanced, but adding a simple sprig of parsley completes the picture.

   On the other hand, don't add unnecessary elements, especially unnecessary inedible garnishes. In many or even most cases, the food is attractive and colorful without garnish, and adding it clutters the plate and increases your food cost as well.

   In any case, it is usually best to add nothing to the plate that is not intended to be eaten. Before you place the parsley alongside the fish fillet or plant a bushy sprig of rosemary in the mashed potatoes, first consider if the plate needs an extra item.

If it does, then consider whether or not it wouldn't be better to add something edible to enhance the other foods with its taste and texture as well as its appearance.

6. **When using a sauce or gravy, add it attractively.**
Sauces are essential parts of many dishes, but sometimes ladling sauce all over an item hides colors and shapes. If the item is attractive by itself, let the customer see it. Ladle the sauce around or under it, or possibly covering only part of it, as with a band of sauce across the center. Always think of the sauce as part of the overall design of the plate.

7. **Keep it simple.**
As you have heard before, simplicity is more attractive than overworked, contrived arrangements and complicated designs. Unusual patterns are occasionally effective, but avoid making the food look too cute or too elaborate.

One of the simplest plating styles can also be one of the most attractive if it is carefully done—that is, placing only the meat or fish item and its sauce, if any, in the center of the plate, and serving vegetable accompaniments in separate dishes. This method is often used in restaurants to simplify service in the kitchen. However, it is usually best to use this method for only some of the menu items in order to avoid monotony.

TEMPERATURE

Serve hot foods hot, on hot plates.

Serve cold foods cold, on cold plates.

Your arrangement of beautiful food will not make much of a final impression if you forget this rule.

GARNISH

WHAT IS GARNISH?

The word **garnish** is derived from a French word meaning "to adorn" or "to furnish." In English, we use the word to mean "to decorate or embellish a food item by the addition of other items." The word is used also for the decorative items themselves.

This definition, at first, seems vague because it could include just about anything. To many people, the word *garnish* means a sprig of parsley haphazardly placed on the plate. Just as common is the practice in some restaurants of adopting a single garnish and using it routinely on every plate, from prime rib to batter-fried shrimp. No one garnish is appropriate for every plate, just as no one side dish is appropriate for every plate.

In fact, the term *garnish* has been used for a great variety of preparations and techniques in the history of classical and modern cuisines. Today, the use of parsley sprigs on every plate has become rare, and we are again using the word *garnish* in a more traditional way.

CLASSICAL GARNISH

In classical cooking, the terms *garnish* and **garniture** have been used the way we use the term *accompaniments*. In other words, garnishes are any items placed on the platter or plate or in the soup bowl in addition to the main item. It happens that these accompaniments also make the food look more attractive, but that is not the emphasis.

The classical French chef had a tremendous repertoire of simple and elaborate garnishes, and they all had specific names. A trained chef, or a well-informed diner, for that matter, knew that the word *Rachel* on the menu meant that the dish was served with artichoke bottoms filled with poached marrow and that *Portugaise* meant a garnish of stuffed tomatoes.

There were so many of these names, however, that no one could remember them all. So they were cataloged in handbooks to be used by chefs. *Le Répertoire de la Cuisine*, first published in 1914 and one of these handbooks, has 209 listings in the garnish section alone, not to mention nearly 7,000 other preparations, all with their own names. The garnishes may be as simple as the one called *Concorde* or as complex as the one called *Tortue*, quoted here to give you an idea of the complexity and elaborateness of classical garnish.

Concorde *(for large joints)*—Peas, glazed carrots, mashed potatoes.

Tortue *(for Entrées)*—Quenelles, mushroom heads, gherkins, garlic, collops of tongue and calves' brains, small fried eggs, heart-shaped croutons, crayfish, slices of truffles. Tortue sauce.

Classical Terms in the Modern Kitchen

Many of the classical names for garnishes are still used in modern kitchens, although they have lost the precise meanings they once had. You will encounter these terms frequently, so it is worthwhile learning them.

Remember that the following definitions are not the classical ones but simply the garnish or accompaniment generally indicated by the terms in today's kitchens.

Bouqetière: bouquet of vegetables

Printanière: spring vegetables

Jardinière: garden vegetables

Primeurs: first spring vegetables

These four terms refer to assortments of fresh vegetables, including carrots, turnips, peas, pearl onions, green beans, cauliflower, sometimes asparagus, and artichokes.

Clamart: peas

Crécy: carrots

Doria: cucumbers (cooked in butter)

Dubarry: cauliflower

Fermière: carrots, turnips, onions, and celery, cut into uniform slices

Florentine: spinach

Forestière: mushrooms

Judic: braised lettuce

Lyonnaise: onions

Niçoise: tomatoes concassé cooked with garlic

Parmentier: potatoes

Princesse: asparagus

Provençale: tomatoes with garlic, parsley, and, sometimes, mushrooms and/or olives

Vichy: carrots (especially Carrots Vichy, p. 554)

MODERN HOT PLATTER GARNISH

In classical cuisine, food was nearly always brought to the dining room on large platters and then served, rather than being plated in the kitchen, as is most often done today.

This practice is still sometimes used for banquet service, and nothing stimulates appetites as much as a succulent roast on a silver platter, sumptuously adorned with a colorful variety of vegetable garnishes.

The classical garnitures most often adapted to modern platter presentation are those called bouquetière, jardinière, and printanière. At one time, these were specific vegetable assortments cut in prescribed ways. Today the terms are taken in a more general way indicating colorful assortments of various fresh vegetables.

Platter garnish need not be elaborate or difficult to prepare. A simple assortment of colorful vegetables, carefully cut and properly cooked to retain color and texture, is appropriate to the most elegant presentation. Stuffed vegetables, such as tomato halves filled with peas, are a little fancier, but still easy to prepare. Borders of duchesse potatoes are also popular (see p. 590).

Many of the rules of proper plating apply to platter arrangement as well—for example, those that call for neatness, balance of color and shape, unity, and preserving the individuality of the items. Following are a few more guidelines that apply to hot platter presentation and garnish.

1. **Vegetables should be in easily served units.**
    In other words, don't heap green peas or mashed potatoes on one corner of the platter. More suitable are vegetables such as cauliflower, broccoli, boiled tomatoes, asparagus spears, whole green beans, mushroom caps, or anything that comes in large or easy-to-handle pieces. Small vegetables such as peas can be easily served if they are used to fill artichoke bottoms, tomato halves, or tartlet shells.

2. **Have the correct number of portions of each item.**
    Vegetables like brussels sprouts and tournéed carrots are easily portioned in the dining room if they are arranged in little portion-size piles.

3. **Arrange the garnishes around the platter to get the best effect from the different colors and shapes.**
    The meat, poultry, or fish is usually placed in the center of the platter, or in a row or rows, and the garnishes are arranged around it.

4. **Avoid being too elaborate.**
    While it is sometimes desirable to make ornate platters, simplicity is usually preferable to an overworked appearance. Let the attractiveness of the food speak for itself. The garnish should never dominate or hide the meat, which is the center of attention.

5. **Serve extra sauce or gravy in a sauceboat.**
    If it is appropriate, dress or nap the meat or fish items with some of the sauce, but don't drown the entire platter with it.

6. **Serve hot foods hot, on a hot platter.**
    Don't spend so much time arranging the food that it's cold by the time it reaches the dining room.

COLD FOOD PRESENTATION AND BUFFET SERVICE

The buffet is a popular and profitable form of food presentation found in nearly every kind of food service operation. There are at least three reasons for this popularity:

1. **Visual appeal.**
    An attractive presentation of foods has the effect of lavishness and ample quantity, and careful arrangement and garnish suggest quality as well.

2. **Efficiency.**
   The buffet allows the restaurant to serve a large number of people in a short time with relatively few service personnel.

3. **Adaptability.**
   Buffet service is adaptable to nearly every kind of food (except items that must be cooked to order, like broiled and deep-fried foods) and to all price ranges, occasions, restaurant styles, and local food customs.

BUFFET ARRANGEMENT AND APPEARANCE

The buffet's visual appeal is, perhaps, its greatest attraction for the customer. Eye appeal of food is always important, but perhaps nowhere more important than on a buffet, because the appearance sells the food. A buffet is not just food service—it is food display.

LAVISHNESS AND ABUNDANCE

Above all else, a buffet should look lavish and plentiful. The appearance of an abundance of food beautifully laid out is exciting and stimulating to the appetite. There are many ways to create this look.

1. **Color.**
   A variety of colors is as vital on a buffet as it is on a single plate. Plan menus and garnish so that you have enough color on the table.

2. **Height.**
   Flat foods on flat trays on flat tables are uninteresting to the eye.
   A centerpiece is an important feature, giving height and focus to the buffet. Ice carvings, tallow sculptures, and floral or fruit displays are some possibilities. These should be placed on a separate table behind the food table.
   Centerpieces on individual platters also add height. Large food items such as large cheeses and whole roasts being carved at the table are also effective. Multilevel tables, when available, are used to good effect.

3. **Full platters and bowls.**
   Replenish items as they become depleted. A nearly empty bowl isn't as appetizing as a full one.
   Arrange platters so they still have interest even when portions have been removed (more on this later).

4. **Proper spacing.**
   While you shouldn't crowd the items, don't spread them so far apart that the table looks half empty.

SIMPLICITY

This sounds like a contradiction to the lavishness principle, but it's not. You need to strike a good balance between the two. Lavishness is not the same as clutter.

1. **Overdesigned, overdecorated food scares people away from eating it.**
   How many times have you heard someone say, "Oh, it's so pretty I don't want to touch it"? Even if they don't say it, they'll think it.
   Too much design detracts from the food. Sometimes food is so overdecorated that it no longer looks like food. This completely defeats the purpose. The customer should at least be able to identify the food for what it is.

2. **Excessive garnish is quickly destroyed as customers take portions.**

ORDERLINESS

A buffet should look like it was planned, not like it just happened. Customers prefer food presentations that look carefully done, not just thrown together.

1. Simple arrangements are much easier to keep neat and orderly than are complicated designs.

2. Colors and shapes should look lively and varied, but make sure they go together and do not clash.

3. Keep the style consistent. If it's formal, then everything should be formal. If it's casual or rustic, then every part of the presentation should be casual or rustic. If it's a Mexican fiesta, don't include German sauerbraten just because your specialty happens to be sauerbraten.

    This is true not only of the food but of the dishes and serving pieces, too. Don't use ornate silver serving pieces for a country theme, for example.

MENU AND SERVING SEQUENCE

Practical reasons as well as visual appeal determine the order in which foods are arranged on the buffet. As far as possible, it is good to have items in the proper menu order (for example, appetizers first, main course afterward, desserts last) if only to avoid confusing the customers, who might otherwise wonder what the food is and how much they should take. But there are many reasons for changing the order. The following should be taken into account when arranging a buffet.

1. Hot foods are best served last. If served first, hot foods get cool while the guests make other selections from the cold foods. Also, it is more effective, visually, to place the decorative cold platters first and the less attractive chafing dishes last.

2. The more expensive foods are usually placed after the less expensive items. This gives you some control of food cost, as the guests' plates will be nearly full of other attractive foods by the time they get to the costly items.

3. Sauces and dressings should be placed next to the items with which they are to be served. Otherwise, the customer might not match them with the right foods.

4. A separate dessert table is often a good idea. This approach allows guests to make a separate trip for dessert without interfering with the main serving line. It is also possible, if the menu is large, to have a separate appetizer table.

5. Plates, of course, must be the first items on the table. Silverware, napkins, and other items not needed until the guest sits down to eat should be at the end of the buffet table or set in place on the dining tables.

THE COCKTAIL BUFFET—AN EXCEPTION

One kind of buffet doesn't conform to this menu order pattern. The cocktail buffet displays appetizers intended to accompany drinks and other refreshments at receptions, cocktail parties, and cocktail hours preceding banquets and dinners. There is no serving line—or, looking at it a different way, there is a separate line for each item.

1. Only appetizer-type foods are served: tasty, well-seasoned foods in small portions.

2. Stacks of small plates are placed beside each item rather than at the beginning of the table.

3. The table or tables must be easy to get to from all parts of the room and must not block traffic. Do not place them next to the entry because guests gather around them, blocking movement into and out of the room.

COLD PLATTER PRESENTATION

The cold platter is the mainstay of the buffet and offers the most opportunity for visual artistry. It also can be one of the most demanding forms of food presentation, particularly in the case of show platters, which require great precision, patience, and artistic sense.

Cold platters can range from a simple tray of cold cuts to elaborate constructions of pâtés, meats, poultry, or fish decorated with aspic, truffles, and vegetable flowers. In this chapter, we have space only for a discussion of general guidelines that you can apply both to formal buffet platters and to simple cold food arrangements. To learn more detailed, complex techniques, you will have to depend on your instructors, more advanced courses, and on-the-job experience. But this section should help you take the foods available in whatever kitchen you find yourself working and produce an attractive, appetizing buffet.

BASIC PRINCIPLES OF PLATTER PRESENTATION

1. The three elements of a buffet platter:

    *   Centerpiece or **grosse pièce** (gross pyess). This may be an uncut portion of the main food item, such as a pâté or a cold roast, decorated and displayed whole. It may be a separate but related item, such as a molded salmon mousse on a platter of poached slices of salmon in aspic. It may be something as simple as a bowl or **ravier** (rahv yay; an oval relish dish) of sauce or condiment. Or it may be strictly for decoration, such as a butter sculpture or a squash vase filled with vegetable flowers. Whether or not the grosse pièce is intended to be eaten, it should be made of edible materials.

    *   The slices or serving portions of the main food item, arranged artistically.

    *   The garnish, arranged artistically, in proportion to the cut slices.

2. The food should be easy to handle and serve, so one portion can be removed without ruining the arrangement.

3. A simple design is best. Simple arrangements are easier to serve, more appetizing than overworked food, and more likely to be still attractive when they are half demolished by the guests.

    Simple arrangements may be the hardest to produce. Everything has to be perfect because less decoration is available to divide the attention.

4. Attractive platter presentations may be made on silver or other metals, mirrors, china, plastic, wood, or many other materials, as long as they are presentable and suitable for use with food. Metal platters that might cause discoloration or metallic flavors are often covered with a thin layer of aspic before the food is placed on them.

5. Once a piece of food has touched the tray, do not remove it. Shiny silver or mirror trays are easily smudged, and you'll have to wash the tray and start over again. This shows the importance of good planning.

    Following this rule also helps eliminate overhandling of food, which is a bad sanitary practice.

6. Think of the platter as part of the whole buffet. It must look attractive and appropriate not only by itself but among the other presentations on the table. The arrangement should always be planned from the same angle from which it will be seen on the buffet.

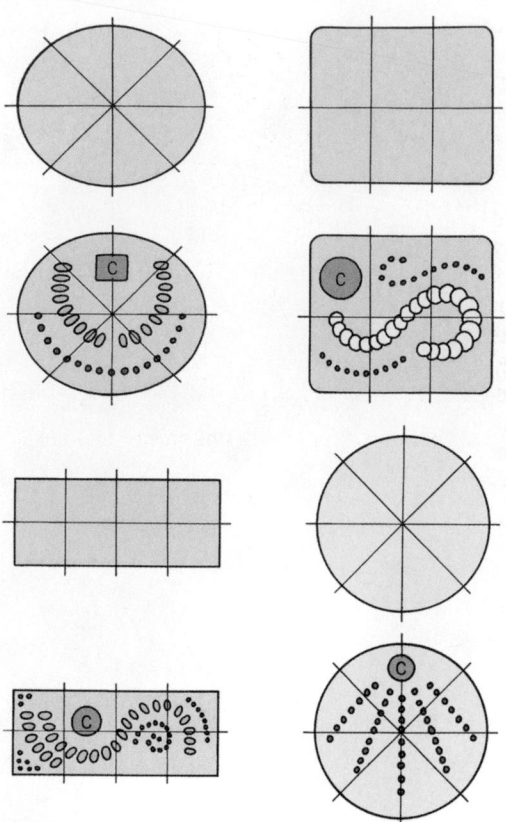

Figure 28.1
Begin your planning sketch of a buffet platter by
dividing the tray into six or eight sections. This helps
you lay out a balanced, symmetrical design. The
examples shown here indicate the placement of the
main items (usually slices of foods), the centerpiece
(labeled c), and the garnish (shown as tiny circles).

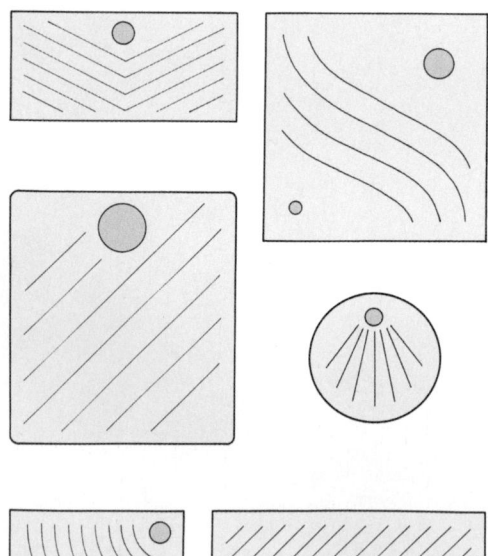

Figure 28.2
Arranging rows of foods in curves or angled lines
gives movement to the design.

DESIGNING THE PLATTER

1. **Plan ahead.**

   Making a sketch is a good idea. Otherwise, you might have half the food on the platter and suddenly realize you have to start over because everything doesn't fit the way you had hoped. The result is wasted time and excessive handling of food.

   One way to start a sketch is to divide the platter into six or eight equal parts, as in Figure 28.1. This helps you avoid lopsided or crooked arrangements by giving you equally spaced markers as guides. It is relatively easy, then, to sketch in a balanced, symmetrical layout, as the examples show.

2. **Plan for movement in your design.**

   This doesn't mean that you should mount the food on little wheels. It means that a good design makes the eye move across the platter, following the lines you have set up.

   Most food for platters consists of single small portions arranged in rows or lines. The trick is to put movement into those lines by curving or angling them, as shown in Figure 28.2. In general, curves and angles are said to have movement. Square corners do not.

3. **Give the design a focal point.**

   This is the function of the centerpiece, which emphasizes and strengthens the design by giving it direction and height. This may be done directly, by having the lines point at it, or more subtly, by having the lines angle toward it or sweep around it in graceful curves. Again, see Figures 28.1 and 28.2.

   Note that the centerpiece isn't always in the center, in spite of its name. Because of its height, it should be at the back or toward the side so it doesn't hide the food. Remember, you are designing the platter from the customer's point of view.

   It's not necessary for every platter on the buffet to have a centerpiece. Some of them should, however, or the buffet will lack height and be less interesting to the eye.

4. **Keep items in proportion.**

   The main items on the platter—the slices of meat, pâté, or whatever—should *look* like the main items. The centerpiece should not be so large or so tall that it totally dominates the platter. The garnish should enhance, not overwhelm, the main item in size, height, or quantity. The number of portions of garnish should be in proportion to the amount of the main item.

   The size of the platter should be in proportion to the amount of food. Don't select one that is so small as to become crowded or so large as to look almost empty even before the first guest has arrived.

   Keep enough space between items or between rows so the platter doesn't look jumbled or confused.

   Figure 28.1 indicates placement of garnish as well as of the main item. Note how the arrangement of garnish reflects or accents the pattern established by the sliced foods.

5. **Let the guest see the best side of everything.**

   Angle overlapping slices and wedge-shaped pieces toward the customer. Make sure the best side of each slice is face up.

CHEESE PLATTERS

Cheese trays are popular on both luncheon buffets as a main course item and on dinner buffets as a dessert item. Cheeses are presented much differently than the other cold buffet foods we have been talking about.

First, whole cheeses or cheeses in large pieces are generally more attractive than an arrangement of slices. This also helps the guest identify the varieties. Be sure to supply several knives so guests can cut their own portions.

Second, an assortment of fresh fruit is often included on a cheese tray. This adds a great deal to the appearance of a cheese presentation, and the flavors go well with cheese. The photograph on page 889 shows an example of a cheese and fruit presentation.

A NOTE ON SANITATION

Cold food for buffets presents a special sanitation problem. This is because the food spends a great deal of time out of refrigeration while it is being assembled and decorated and again while it sits on the buffet. For this reason, it is particularly important to follow all the rules of safe food handling. Keep foods refrigerated whenever they are not being worked on. Also, keep them chilled until the last minute before they are brought out for service.

For a buffet service that lasts a long time, it is a good idea to arrange each course or item on a number of small platters rather than on one big one. The replacements can then be kept refrigerated until needed.

One type of cheese and fruit presentation for buffet service.

HOT FOODS FOR BUFFETS

Everything we have learned about the preparation and holding of hot foods in quantity applies to hot foods for buffets. Hot items are nearly always served from chafing dishes, which may be ornate silver affairs or simple steam table pans kept warm over hot water. These foods cannot be elaborately decorated and garnished the way cold foods can. On the other hand, the bright, fresh, juicy appearance and good aroma of properly cooked hot food is generally sufficient to arouse appetites.

Hot foods for chafing dishes should be easily portioned (such as vegetables served with a kitchen spoon) or already portioned in the pan (braised pork chops, sliced baked ham, and poached fish fillets, for example). Items less suitable for buffets are those that must be cooked to order and served immediately, such as most broiled and deep-fried foods.

Whole roasts are popular items at buffets, carved to order by a member of the kitchen staff. Especially attractive are large roasts such as hams, turkeys, and large cuts of beef such as steamship round.

As previously noted, hot foods are best placed at the end of the buffet so they do not cool on the guests' plates before they are seated and so the decorated cold foods can steal the show.

■ TERMS FOR REVIEW

garnish	jardinière	fermière	parmentier
garniture	printanière	florentine	grosse pièce
classical garnish	clamart	forestière	ravier
bouquetière	dubarry	lyonnaise	

■ QUESTIONS FOR DISCUSSION

1. Discuss the idea of professionalism and how it applies to the presentation of food.

2. Following are several popular food combinations. Describe what plating problems they present, if any, and how you might efficiently and economically solve them.

   Fish and chips (deep-fried fillets and French fries)

   Prime rib of beef and baked potato

   Meat loaf, mashed potatoes, and gravy

   Open-faced hot turkey sandwich

   Beef stroganoff and egg noodles

   Chicken à la king in a patty shell

3. What is meant by plating food for the convenience of the customer, and how does this affect other rules of plating?

4. What is the difference between a cocktail buffet and a luncheon or dinner buffet?

5. Customers like to see a lot of food on a buffet. Is it correct to say, then, that the best way to please customers is to put out as much food as possible? Explain your answer.

6. When you are preparing a cold buffet platter, why is it a good idea to plan ahead by making a sketch? What would you include in the sketch? What do the terms *movement* and *focal point* mean in platter design?

29

CHAPTER

Bakeshop Production: Basic Principles and Ingredients

A t one time, it was common for food service establishments to produce their own breads, desserts, and other baked goods. Today, many operations find it more economical to buy these products from commercial bakeries. However, many owners and chefs have discovered that offering fresh, "home-baked" breads, cakes, and pastries attracts customers and increases profits. With little more than an oven and a mixer, many cooks turn out attractive baked items that set their operations apart from competitors.

For this reason, it is important for you to learn the fundamentals of baking, even if you intend to become a cook rather than a baker. These chapters will not make a professional baker out of you. A baker requires far more technical and specialized information than can be presented in this short space. But you will learn the basic methods for producing a wide variety of breads, desserts, and pastries with only the simplest of resources.

In this chapter, we introduce bakeshop production with a discussion of the basic processes and ingredients common to nearly all baked goods. This will give you the understanding necessary to proceed to actual production in the succeeding chapters.

After reading this chapter, you should be able to

1. Explain why it is important to weigh baking ingredients.

2. Use a baker's balance scale.

3. Calculate formulas based on baker's percentages.

4. Explain the factors that control the development of gluten in baked products.

5. Explain the changes that take place in a dough or batter as it bakes.

6. Prevent or retard the staling of baked items.

7. Describe the major ingredients of baked goods and their functions and characteristics.

BASIC PRINCIPLES OF BAKING

If you consider that most bakery products are made of the same few ingredients—flour, shortening, sugar, eggs, water or milk, and leavening—you should have no difficulty understanding the importance of accuracy in the bakeshop, where slight differences in proportions or procedures can mean great differences in the final product.

If you have begun your food service studies in a kitchen production laboratory, you have surely been told many times of the importance of measurement, not only for portion control and cost control but also for consistency in the quality of the final product. However, you have, no doubt, also learned that there is a great deal of margin for error and that it is possible (if not desirable) to cook many foods without measuring anything. Coming into the bakeshop, where measurement is absolutely essential, may be a bit of a shock to you after your kitchen experiences, but it should reinforce the habits of accuracy you may have let slip.

If, on the other hand, you are beginning your practical studies in the bakeshop, then you will do well to pay particular attention to the principles of measurement presented here. They will be valuable to you throughout your career.

FORMULAS AND MEASUREMENT

Bakers generally talk about *formulas* rather than *recipes*. If this sounds more like the chemistry lab than the kitchen, it is with good reason. The bakeshop is much like a chemistry laboratory both in the scientific accuracy of all the procedures and in the complex reactions that take place during mixing and baking.

MEASUREMENT

All ingredients must be weighed. Accuracy of measurement, as we have already said many times, is critical in the bakeshop. Measurement is by weight rather than by volume because weight is much more accurate. Unlike in recipes for the home baker, you will not see a professional baker's formula calling for 6 cups flour.

To demonstrate to yourself the importance of weighing rather than measuring by volume, measure 1 cup flour in two ways. (1) Sift some flour and lightly spoon it into a dry measure. Level the top and weigh the flour. (2) Scoop some unsifted flour into the

Digital professional scale
Courtesy of Cardinal Detecto

Procedure for Using a Baker's Balance Scale

The principle of using a baker's scale is simple: The scale must balance before setting the weights, and it must balance again after scaling. The example cited illustrates using a scale with U.S. units. The same procedure is used for metric scales.

1. Set the scale scoop or other container on the *left* side of the scale.

2. Balance the scale by placing counterweights on the *right* side and/or adjusting the ounce weight on the horizontal bar.

3. Set the scale for the desired weight by placing weights on the *right* side and/or by moving the ounce weight. For example, to set the scale for 1 pound 8 ounces, place a 1-pound weight on the *right* side and move the ounce weight to the *right* 8 ounces. If the ounce weight is already over 8 ounces, so that you cannot move it another 8, add 2 pounds to the right side of the scale and subtract 8 ounces by moving the ounce weight 8 places to the *left*. The result is still 1 pound 8 ounces.

4. Add the ingredient being scaled to the left side until the scale balances.

Balance scale
Courtesy of Cardinal Detecto

same measure and pack it lightly. Level the top and weigh the flour. Note the difference. No wonder home recipes can be so inconsistent!

The baker's term for weighing out ingredients is *scaling*.

The following ingredients may be measured by *volume* because they weigh *1 pound per pint or 1 kilogram per liter*:

Water	Milk	Eggs

Thus, if a formula calls for 2 pounds eggs, you may measure 2 pints (1 quart). (Liquid flavoring ingredients, such as vanilla extract, normally measured in very small quantities, may also be measured by volume; 1 tablespoon equals ½ ounce.) In the metric system, 1 milliliter water weighs 1 gram; 1 liter weighs 1 kilogram. All other liquid ingredients (such as corn syrup and molasses) and all dry ingredients are normally weighed.

BAKER'S PERCENTAGES

Bakers use a simple but versatile system of percentages for expressing their formulas. Bakers' percentages express the amount of each ingredient used as a percentage of the amount of flour used.

To put it differently, the percentage of each ingredient is its total weight divided by the weight of the flour and multiplied by 100 percent, or

$$\frac{\text{weight of ingredient}}{\text{weight of flour}} \times 100\% = \% \text{ of ingredient}$$

Thus, flour is always 100 percent. (If two kinds of flour are used, their total is 100 percent.) Any ingredient that weighs the same as the flour is also given as 100 percent. The following ingredients from a cake formula illustrate how these percentages are used. Both U.S. and metric examples are given. (Note that numbers may be rounded off for practical measuring.) Check the figures with the above equation to make sure you understand them.

Ingredient	Weight	Percentage
Cake flour	5 lb	100 %
Sugar	5 lb	100 %
Baking powder	4 oz	5 %
Salt	2 oz	2.5%
Emulsified shortening	2 lb 8 oz	50 %
Skim milk	3 lb	60 %
Egg whites	3 lb	60 %
	18 lb 14 oz	377.5%

Ingredient	Weight	Percentage
Cake flour	2500 g	100 %
Sugar	2500 g	100 %
Baking powder	125 g	5 %
Salt	60 g	2.5%
Emulsified shortening	1250 g	50 %
Skim milk	1500 g	60 %
Egg whites	1500 g	60 %
	9435 g	377.5%

The advantage of using baker's percentages is that the formula is easily adapted for any yield, and single ingredients may be varied without changing the whole formulation. Please remember that these numbers do not refer to the percentage of the total yield. They are simply a way of expressing *ingredient proportions*. The total of these percentage numbers will always be greater than 100 percent.

Procedure for Calculating the Weight of an Ingredient If the Weight of Flour Is Known

1. Change the ingredient percentage to decimal form by moving the decimal point two places to the left.

2. Multiply the weight of the flour by this decimal to get the weight of the ingredient.

   Example: A formula calls for 20 percent sugar and you are using 10 pounds flour. How much sugar do you need?

   $$20\% = 0.20$$

   $$10 \text{ lb} \times 0.20 = 2 \text{ lb sugar}$$

   Note: In the U.S. system, weights must normally be expressed all in one unit, either ounces or pounds, in order for the calculation to work, as explained in Chapter 5.

   Example (Metric): A formula calls for 20 percent sugar and you are using 5000 grams (5 kg) flour. How much sugar do you need?

   $$20\% = 0.20$$

   $$5000 \text{ g} \times 0.20 = 1000 \text{ g sugar}$$

Procedure for Converting a Formula to a New Yield

1. Change the total percentage to decimal form by moving the decimal point two places to the left.

2. Divide the desired yield by this decimal figure to get the weight of flour.

3. If necessary, round off this number to the next highest figure. This will allow for losses in mixing, makeup, and panning, and it will make calculations easier.

4. Use the weight of flour and remaining ingredient percentages to calculate the weights of the other ingredients, as in the previous procedure.

   Example: In the previous sample cake formula, how much flour is needed if you require 6 pounds (3000 grams) of cake batter?

   $$6 \text{ lb} = 96 \text{ oz}$$

   $$377.5\% = 3.775$$

   $$96 \text{ oz} \div 3.775 = 25.43 \text{ oz}$$

   or, rounded off, 26 oz (1 lb 10 oz)

   $$3000 \text{ g} \div 3.775 = 794.7 \text{ g}$$

   or, rounded off, 800 g

Clearly, the percentage system we have been discussing is used only when flour is a major ingredient, as in breads, cakes, and cookies. For these formulas, we use a written format different from our regular recipe format in this book.

In these formulas, the indicated yield is the total weight of the ingredients. This figure indicates the weight of the batter or dough. It is the figure we need to know for the purpose of scaling the dough or batter into loaves or pans. The finished weight of the baked goods will be less because moisture is lost during baking.

Also, please note that all yields, including percentage totals, are rounded off to the next lower whole number. This eliminates unimportant fractions and makes reading and calculating easier.

SELECTION OF INGREDIENTS

In addition to measuring, there is another basic rule of accuracy in the bakeshop: *Use the exact ingredients specified.*

As you will learn in this chapter, different flours, shortenings, and other ingredients do not function alike. Bakers' formulas are balanced for specific ingredients. Do not substitute bread flour for pastry flour or regular shortening for emulsified shortening, for example. They won't work the same way.

Occasionally, a substitution may be made, such as active dry yeast for compressed yeast (see p. 904), but not without adjusting the quantities or rebalancing the formula.

MIXING AND GLUTEN DEVELOPMENT

WHAT IS GLUTEN?

Gluten is a substance made up of proteins present in wheat flour; it gives structure and strength to baked goods.

In order for gluten to be developed, the proteins must first absorb water. Then, as the dough or batter is mixed or kneaded, the gluten forms long, elastic strands. As the dough or batter is leavened, these strands capture the gases in tiny pockets or cells, and we say the product rises. When the product is baked, the gluten, like all proteins (see p. 65), coagulates or solidifies and gives structure to the product.

HOW DOES THE BAKER CONTROL GLUTEN?

Flour is mostly starch, but its protein or gluten content, not its starch, concerns the baker most. Without gluten proteins to give structure, baked goods would not hold together.

The baker must be able to control the gluten, however. For example, we want French bread to be firm and chewy, which requires much gluten. On the other hand, we want cakes to be tender, which means we want very little gluten development.

Ingredient proportions and mixing methods are determined, in part, by how they affect the development of gluten. The baker has several methods for adjusting gluten development.

1. **Selection of flours.**
   Wheat flours are classified as *strong* or *weak*, depending on their protein content.

   Strong flours come from *hard wheat* and have a high protein content.

   Weak flours come from *soft wheat* and have a low protein content.

   Thus, we use strong flours for breads and weak flours for cakes.

   Only wheat flour develops gluten. To make bread from rye and other grains, the formula must be balanced with some high-gluten wheat flour, or the bread will be heavy.

2. **Shortening.**
   Any fat used in baking is called a **shortening** because it shortens gluten strands. It does this by surrounding the particles and lubricating them so they do not stick together. Thus, *fats are tenderizers*. A cookie or pastry that is very crumbly, due to high fat content, is said to be "short."

   You can see why French bread has little or no fat, while cakes contain a great deal.

3. **Liquid.**
   Because gluten proteins must absorb water before they can be developed, the amount of water in a formula can affect toughness or tenderness. Pie crusts and crisp cookies are made with very little liquid to keep them tender.

4. **Mixing methods.**
In general, the more a dough or batter is mixed, the more the gluten develops. Thus, bread doughs are mixed or kneaded for a long time to develop the gluten. Cakes, pie crusts, muffins, and other products that must be tender are mixed for a short time.

It is possible to overmix bread dough, however. Gluten strands stretch only so far. They break if the dough is overmixed.

THE BAKING PROCESS

The changes undergone by a dough or batter as it bakes are basically the same for all baked products, from breads to cookies and cakes. You should know what these changes are so you can learn how to control them.

The stages in the baking process take place as follows.

1. **Formation and expansion of gases.**
Some gases are already present in the dough, as in proofed bread dough and in sponge cake batters. As they are heated, the gases expand and leaven the product.

Some gases are not formed until heat is applied. Yeast and baking powder form gases rapidly when first placed in the oven. Steam is also formed as the moisture of the dough is heated.

Leavening and leavening agents are discussed in more detail beginning on page 903.

2. **Trapping of the gases in air cells.**
As the gases form and expand, they are trapped in a stretchable network formed by the proteins in the dough. These proteins are primarily gluten and, sometimes, egg protein.

Without gluten or egg protein, the gases would escape, and the product would not be leavened. Breads without enough gluten are heavy.

3. **Coagulation of proteins.**
Like all proteins, gluten and egg proteins coagulate or solidify when they reach high enough temperatures. This is the process that gives structure to baked goods.

Correct baking temperature is important. If the temperature is too high, coagulation will start too soon, before the expansion of gases has reached its peak. The product will have poor volume or a split crust. If the temperature is too low, the proteins will not coagulate soon enough, and the product may collapse.

4. **Gelatinization of starches.**
The starches absorb moisture, expand, and become firmer.

5. **Evaporation of some of the water.**
This takes place throughout the baking process.

6. **Melting of shortenings.**
Different shortenings melt—and release trapped gases—at different temperatures, so the proper shortening should be selected for each product.

As the fats melt, they surround the air cells and make the product more tender.

7. **Crust formation and browning.**
Browning occurs when sugars caramelize and starches and proteins undergo certain changes. This contributes to flavor. Milk, sugar, and egg increase browning.

A crust is formed as water evaporates from the surface and leaves it dry.

STALING

Staling is the change in texture and aroma of baked goods due to the change in structure and the loss of moisture by the starch granules. Stale baked goods have lost their fresh-baked aroma and are firmer, drier, and more crumbly than fresh products.

Prevention of staling is a major concern of the baker because most baked goods lose quality rapidly.

Staling can be slowed by these techniques.

1. **Protecting the product from air.**

   Wrapping bread in plastic and covering cakes with icing are two examples.

   Unfortunately, hard-crusted breads, which stale rapidly, should not be wrapped, or the crusts will become soft. These bread products should always be served fresh.

2. **Adding moisture retainers to the formula.**

   Fats and sugars are good moisture retainers, and products high in these ingredients keep best.

   Some of the best French bread has no fat at all, and if it is not served within hours of baking, it will begin to stale. For longer keeping, bakers often add a very small amount of fat and/or sugar to the formula.

3. **Freezing.**

   Baked goods frozen *before* they become stale maintain quality for longer periods. They should be served very soon after thawing. Frozen breads may be reheated with excellent results if they are to be served immediately.

   Refrigerating actually seems to speed staling rather than slowing it. Only baked goods that could develop health hazards, such as those with cream fillings, are refrigerated.

   Loss of crispness is caused by absorption of moisture, so it is, in a sense, the opposite of staling. This is a problem with low-moisture products such as cookies and pie crusts. The problem is usually solved by proper storage in airtight wraps or containers to protect the products from moisture in the air. Prebaked pie shells should be filled as close to service time as possible.

INGREDIENTS

The following introduction to baking ingredients is necessarily simplified. If you decide to pursue a career as a baker, you will need to learn a great deal of technical information. However, the basic information presented here is enough to enable you to produce a full range of baked items in a small bakeshop or restaurant kitchen.

FLOURS, MEALS, AND STARCHES

WHITE WHEAT FLOUR

White wheat flour is milled from wheat kernels after the outer covering, called bran, and the germ are removed. Wheat flour contains about 63 to 73 percent starch and 7 to 15 percent protein. The rest is moisture, fat, sugar, and minerals.

Wheat flour is the source of the protein called *gluten*, which you remember is one of the essential elements in baking. Bakers select flour on the basis of its gluten content. Flours high in protein are called *strong*, and those low in protein are called *weak*. (Note: Rye, barley, oats, and some other grains also contain gluten proteins, but these proteins do not develop into a gluten structure as do the proteins in wheat flour. Thus, for the baker, these other grains in effect do not contain gluten, but people with gluten intolerance may still have to avoid them in their diets.)

For our purposes, in the small bakeshop, we need to know about three kinds of wheat flour.

1. **Bread flour** is a strong flour used for making breads, hard rolls, and any product that requires high gluten. The best bread flours are called *patents*. *Straight* flours are also strong flours.

2. **Cake flour** is a weak or low-gluten flour made from soft wheat. It has a soft, smooth texture and a pure white color. Cake flour is used for cakes and other delicate baked goods that require low gluten content.

3. **Pastry flour** is lower in gluten than bread flour but higher than cake flour. It has the same creamy white color as bread flour, not the pure white of cake flour. Pastry flour is used for cookies, pie pastry, some sweet yeast doughs, biscuits, and muffins.

Being able to identify these three flours by sight and touch is an important skill because, sooner or later, someone will dump a bag of flour into the wrong bin, and you will need to recognize the problem.

Bread flour feels slightly coarse when rubbed between the fingers. If squeezed into a lump, it falls apart as soon as the hand is opened. Its color is creamy white.

Cake flour feels smooth and fine. It stays in a lump when squeezed in the palm of the hand. Its color is pure white.

Pastry flour feels like cake flour but has the creamy color of bread flour.

All-purpose flour, seen in retail markets, is not often found in bakeshops. This flour is formulated to be slightly weaker than bread flour so it can be used for pastries as well. A professional baker, however, prefers to use flours that are formulated for specific purposes because these give the best results.

WHOLE WHEAT FLOUR

Whole wheat flour is made by grinding the entire wheat kernel, including the bran and germ. The germ, which is the embryo of a new wheat plant, is high in fat, which can become rancid. This is why whole wheat flour does not keep as well as white flour.

Because it is made from wheat, whole wheat flour contains gluten, so it can be used alone in bread making. However, a bread made with 100 percent whole wheat will be heavy because the gluten strands are cut by the sharp edges of the bran flakes. Also, the fat from the wheat germ contributes slightly to the shortening action. This is why most whole wheat breads are strengthened with white bread flour.

Bran flour is flour to which bran flakes have been added. The bran may be coarse or fine, depending on specifications.

RYE FLOUR

Next to white and whole wheat, rye is the most popular flour in bread making. Because rye flour does not develop much gluten, breads made with it are heavy unless some hard wheat flour is added.

Rye flour is available in three shades, *light, medium,* and *dark. Rye meal* or **pumpernickel** is a coarse meal made from the whole rye grain. It looks something like oatmeal.

Rye blend is a mixture of rye flour and hard wheat flour.

OTHER FLOURS

Products milled from other grains are occasionally used to add variety to baked goods. These include cornmeal, buckwheat flour, soy flour, potato flour, oat flour, and barley flour. The term *meal* is used for products that are not as finely ground as flour.

All these products must normally be used in combination with wheat flour because they do not form gluten.

STARCHES

In addition to flours, other starch products are also used in the bakeshop. Unlike flour, they are used primarily to thicken puddings, pie fillings, and similar products. The principles of thickening with starches are covered in Chapter 8.

The most important starches in dessert production are as follows.

1. *Cornstarch* has a special property that makes it valuable for certain purposes. Products thickened with cornstarch set up almost like gelatin when cooled. For this reason, it is used to thicken cream pies and other products that must hold their shape.

2. *Waxy maize* and other *modified starches* also have valuable properties. They do not break down when frozen, so are used for products that are to be frozen. Also, they are clear when cooked, and give a brilliant, clear appearance to fruit pie fillings.

   Waxy maize does not set up firm like cornstarch but makes a soft paste, which has the same consistency hot and cold. Thus, it is not suitable for cream pie fillings.

3. *Instant starches* are precooked or pregelatinized, so they thicken cold liquids without further cooking. They are useful when heat will damage the flavor of the product, as in fresh fruit glazes (such as strawberry).

FATS

We have said that one of the main functions of fats in baking is to shorten gluten strands and tenderize the product. We can summarize the reasons for using fats in baked items as follows:

- To tenderize the product and soften the texture.
- To add moistness and richness.
- To increase keeping quality.
- To add flavor.
- To assist in leavening when used as creaming agents or when used to give flakiness to puff pastry, pie dough, and similar products.

SHORTENINGS

Any fat acts as a shortening in baking because it shortens gluten strands and tenderizes the product. However, we usually use the word *shortening* to mean any of a group of solid fats, usually white and tasteless, that are specially formulated for baking.

Because shortenings are used for many purposes, manufacturers have formulated different kinds of fats with different properties. Following are the three main types of shortening.

Regular Shortenings

These shortenings have a tough, waxy texture, and small particles of the fat tend to hold their shape in a dough or batter. This type of shortening does not melt until a high temperature is reached.

Regular shortening has good creaming ability. This means that a large quantity of air can be mixed into it to give a batter lightness and leavening power. Therefore, it is used in products mixed by the creaming method, such as certain cookies.

Because of its texture, this type of shortening is used for flaky products such as pie crusts and biscuits. It is also used in breads and many pastries. Unless another shortening is specified, regular shortening is generally used.

Emulsified Shortenings

These are soft shortenings that spread easily throughout a batter and quickly coat the particles of sugar and flour. Because of their easy spreading, they give a smoother and finer texture to cakes and make them moister.

Emulsified shortening is often used whenever the weight of sugar in a cake batter is greater than the weight of flour. Because this shortening spreads so well, a simpler mixing method can be used, as explained in Chapter 32. Such cakes are referred to as *high-ratio* cakes, so emulsified shortening is sometimes called *high-ratio shortening*.

In addition, emulsified shortening is used in certain icings because it can hold more sugar and liquid without curdling.

Puff Pastry Shortenings

Puff pastry shortenings are firm like regular shortening. They are especially formulated for puff pastry and other doughs that form layers, such as Danish pastry.

BUTTER AND MARGARINE

Shortenings are manufactured to have certain textures and hardness. Butter, on the other hand, is a natural product that doesn't have these advantages. It is hard and brittle when cold and soft at room temperature, and it melts easily. Consequently, doughs made with butter are hard to handle. Margarine is a little easier to handle, but it has many of the same disadvantages.

On the other hand, butter and margarine have two major advantages.

1. **Flavor.**
   Shortenings are intentionally flavorless, but butter has a highly desirable flavor.

2. **Melting qualities.**
   Butter melts in the mouth. Shortenings do not. After eating pastries or icings made with shortening, one can be left with an unpleasant film of shortening coating the mouth.

For these reasons, many bakers and pastry chefs feel that the advantages of butter outweigh its disadvantages for some purposes.

OILS

Oils are liquid fats. They are not often used as shortening in baking because they spread through a batter or dough too thoroughly and shorten too much. Their usefulness in the bakeshop is limited primarily to greasing pans and proofing bowls, to deep-frying doughnuts, and to serving as a wash for some kinds of rolls. A few quick breads and cakes use oil as a shortening.

LARD

Lard is the rendered fat of hogs. Because of its plastic quality, it was once highly valued for making flaky pie crusts. Since the development of modern shortenings, it is not often used in the bakeshop.

SUGARS

Sugars or sweetening agents are used for the following purposes in baking:

- To add sweetness and flavor.
- To create tenderness and fineness of texture by weakening the gluten structure.
- To give crust color.
- To increase keeping qualities by retaining moisture.
- To act as creaming agents with fats.

We customarily use the term *sugar* for regular refined sugars derived from sugar cane or beets. The chemical name for these sugars is **sucrose**. However, other sugars of different chemical structure are also used in the bakeshop. The following are the more important sugars.

REGULAR REFINED SUGARS, OR SUCROSE

Refined sugars are classified by the size of grains.

1. **Granulated sugar.**

   Regular granulated, also called *fine granulated* or *table* sugar, is the most familiar and the most commonly used.

   Very fine and *ultrafine* sugars are finer than regular granulated. They are prized for making cakes and cookies because they make a more uniform batter and can support higher quantities of fat.

   Sanding sugars are coarser and are used for coating doughnuts, cakes, and other products.

2. **Confectioners' or powdered sugars.**

   Confectioners' sugars are ground to a fine powder and mixed with a small amount of starch to prevent caking. They are classified by coarseness or fineness.

   10X is the finest sugar. It gives the smoothest textures in icings.

   6X is the standard confectioners' sugar. It is used in icings, toppings, and cream fillings.

   Coarser types (*4X* and *XX*) are used for dusting or for any purposes for which 6X and 10X are too fine.

MOLASSES AND BROWN SUGAR

Molasses is concentrated sugar cane juice. *Sulfured molasses* is a byproduct of sugar refining. It is the product that remains after most of the sugar has been extracted from cane juice. *Unsulfured molasses* is not a byproduct but a specially manufactured sugar product. Its taste is less bitter than that of sulfured molasses.

Molasses contains large amounts of sucrose, plus other sugars, acids, and impurities.

Brown sugar is mostly sucrose, but it also contains varying amounts of molasses and other impurities. The darker grades contain more molasses.

Because molasses and brown sugar contain *acids*, they can be used with baking soda to provide leavening (see p. 904).

Molasses retains moisture in baked goods and so prolongs freshness. However, crisp cookies made with molasses quickly become soft for the same reason.

CORN SYRUP

Corn syrup is a liquid sweetener consisting mainly of a sugar called *glucose*. It is made by converting cornstarch into simpler sugar compounds by the use of enzymes.

Corn syrup aids in retaining moisture and is used in some icings and in candy making.

GLUCOSE SYRUP

While corn syrup contains other sugars in addition to glucose, pure glucose syrup is also available. It resembles corn syrup but is colorless and nearly tasteless. If a recipe calls for glucose syrup and none is available, substitute light corn syrup.

HONEY

Honey is a natural sugar syrup consisting largely of glucose and fructose, plus other compounds that give it flavor. Honeys vary considerably in flavor and color, depending on their source. Flavor is the major reason for using honey, especially because it can be expensive.

Honey contains invert sugar, which means that it stays smooth and resists crystallizing. Like molasses, it contains *acid*, which enables it to be used with baking soda as a leavening.

MALT SYRUP

Malt syrup is used primarily in yeast breads. It serves as food for the yeast and adds flavor and crust color to the breads.

LIQUIDS

Gluten cannot be developed without moisture, so liquids are essential to the baking process.

Pie crusts provide a good illustration of how liquids function in baking. If too much water is incorporated in a pie dough, a lot of gluten develops and the crust is tough. If no water at all is used, no gluten develops and the crust does not hold together.

Some of the moisture in doughs and batters changes to steam during baking. This contributes to leavening.

WATER

Water is the basic liquid in baking, especially in breads.

Tap water is normally suitable for most baking purposes. However, in some localities, the water may be *hard*, meaning that it contains many dissolved minerals. These minerals interfere with proper gluten development. In these areas, the water may have to be treated for use in baking.

MILK AND CREAM

Milk products, as described in Chapter 25, are important in baking. These products include liquid whole and skim milk, buttermilk, and dry milk solids.

Milk contributes to the texture, flavor, nutritional value, keeping quality, and crust color of baked goods.

1. Whole milk contains fat, which must be calculated as part of the shortening in a dough. For this reason, whole and skim milk are not interchangeable in a formula unless adjustments are made for the fat.

2. Buttermilk, which is slightly acid, is often used in conjunction with baking soda as a leavening agent in quick breads.

3. Cream is not often used as a liquid in doughs and batters, except in a few specialty products. In these instances, it is used as a shortening as well as a liquid because of its fat content.

    Cream is more important in the production of fillings and toppings.

4. Dry milk is often used because of its convenience and low cost. In some formulas, it is not necessary to reconstitute it. The milk powder is included with the dry ingredients, and water is used as the liquid.

OTHER SOURCES OF LIQUIDS

Eggs, honey, molasses, and even butter (about 15 percent water) contribute moisture to a dough or batter. In many cookies, for example, eggs are the only liquid in the formula.

EGGS

FORMS

As we discussed in Chapter 24, eggs are purchased in the following forms:

1. Whole shell eggs.
2. Frozen: whites, yolks, whole, and whole with extra yolks.
3. Dried: whole, whites, yolks.

FUNCTIONS

Eggs perform the following functions in baking.

1. **Structure.**
    Like gluten protein, egg protein coagulates to give structure to baked products. This is especially important in high-ratio cakes, where the high sugar and fat content weakens the gluten.
    If used in large quantities, eggs make baked products tough or chewy unless balanced by high fat and sugar, which are tenderizers.

2. **Emulsification of fats.**
    Egg yolks contain natural emulsifiers, which help produce smooth batters. This contributes to volume and to texture.

3. **Leavening.**
    Beaten eggs incorporate air in tiny cells or bubbles. In a batter, this trapped air expands when heated and aids in leavening.

4. **Shortening action.**
    The fat in egg yolks acts as a shortening. This is an important function in products that are low in other fats.

5. **Moisture.**
    Whole eggs are about 70 percent water, egg whites about 86 percent water, and egg yolks about 49 percent water. This moisture must be calculated as part of the total liquid in a formula.

6. **Flavor.**

7. **Nutritional value.**

8. **Color.**
    Yolks impart a yellow color to doughs and batters. Also, eggs brown easily and contribute to crust color.

LEAVENING AGENTS

Leavening is the production or incorporation of gases in a baked product to increase volume and to produce shape and texture. These gases must be retained in the product until the structure is set enough (by the coagulation of gluten and egg protein) to hold its shape.

Exact measurement of leavening agents is important because small changes can produce major defects in baked products.

YEAST

Fermentation is the process by which yeast acts on carbohydrates and changes them into carbon dioxide gas and alcohol. This release of gas produces the leavening action in yeast products. The alcohol evaporates completely during and immediately after baking.

Yeast is a microscopic plant. As a living organism, it is sensitive to temperatures.

34°F (1°C)	Inactive; storage temperature.
60° to 70°F (15° to 20°C)	Slow action.
70° to 90°F (20° to 32°C)	Best growth; proofing temperature for bread doughs.
Above 100°F (38°C)	Reaction slows.
140°F (60°C)	Yeast is killed.

Yeast is available in three forms:

1. **Fresh yeast**, also called *compressed yeast*, is moist and perishable and is preferred by professional bakers. It is usually purchased in 1-lb (450-g) cakes.

2. **Active dry yeast** is a dry, granular form of yeast. Active dry yeast must be rehydrated in 4 times its weight of warm water [about 110°F (43°C)] before use. When using active dry yeast in a bread formula, use part of the water in the formula to dissolve the yeast. Do not add additional water.

3. **Instant dry yeast** is also a dry granular form of yeast, but it does not have to be dissolved in water before use. It can be added in its dry form because it absorbs water much more quickly than regular dry yeast. It also produces more gas than regular dry yeast, so less of it is needed. Instant dry yeast is sometimes called *rapid-rise* or *quick-rise yeast*.

In this book, when yeast is required in a formula, fresh yeast is specified. To substitute dry yeast, use the following guidelines.

To convert fresh yeast to regular active dry yeast, multiply the quantity by 0.5. For example, if the formula calls for 1½ ounces fresh yeast, multiply by 0.5 to get ¾ ounce active dry yeast.

To convert fresh yeast to instant dry yeast, multiply the quantity by 0.35. For example, if the formula calls for 40 g fresh yeast, multiply by 0.35 to get 14 g instant yeast.

Yeast contributes flavor in addition to leavening action.

CHEMICAL LEAVENERS

Chemical leaveners are those that release gases produced by chemical reactions.

Baking Soda

Baking soda is the chemical sodium bicarbonate. If *moisture* and an *acid* are present, soda releases carbon dioxide gas, which leavens the product.

Heat is not necessary for the reaction (although the gas is released faster at higher temperatures). For this reason, products leavened with soda must be baked at once, or the gases will escape and leavening power will be lost.

Acids that react with soda in a batter include honey, molasses, buttermilk, fruits, cocoa, and chocolate. Sometimes cream of tartar is used for the acid. The amount of soda used in a formula is generally the amount needed to balance the acid. If more leavening power is needed, baking powder, not more soda, is used.

Baking Powder

Baking powders are mixtures of baking soda plus an acid to react with it.

Because baking powders do not depend on acid ingredients for their leavening power in a formula, they are more versatile.

Single-acting baking powders require only moisture to be able to release gas. Like baking soda, they can be used only if the product is to be baked immediately after mixing.

Double-acting baking powders release some gas when cold, but they require heat for complete reaction. Thus, cake batters made with these can incorporate the leavening agent early in the mixing period and can stand for some time before being baked.

Do not include more baking powder than necessary in a formula because undesirable flavors may be created.

Baking Ammonia

Baking ammonia is the chemical ammonium carbonate. It decomposes during baking to form carbon dioxide gas and ammonia gas. Only heat and moisture are necessary for it to work. No acids are needed.

Because it decomposes completely, it leaves no residue that can affect flavor. However, it can be used only in small products, like cookies, which allow the ammonia gas to be completely driven off.

Baking ammonia releases gases quickly, so it is sometimes used in products like cream puffs where rapid leavening is desired.

AIR

Air is incorporated into a batter primarily by two methods, creaming and foaming. This air expands during baking and leavens the product.

1. **Creaming** is the process of beating fat and sugar together to incorporate air. It is an important technique in cake and cookie making. Some pound cakes and cookies are leavened almost entirely by this method.

2. **Foaming** is the process of beating eggs, with or without sugar, to incorporate air. Foams made with whole eggs are used to leaven sponge cakes, while angel food cakes, meringues, and soufflés are leavened with egg white foams.

STEAM

When water turns to steam, it expands to 1,600 times its original volume. Because all baked products contain some moisture, steam is an important leavening agent.

Puff pastry, cream puffs, popovers, and pie crusts use steam as their major or only leavening agent.

If the starting baking temperature for these products is high, steam is produced rapidly and leavening is greatest.

SALT, FLAVORINGS, AND SPICES

SALT

Salt plays an important role in baking. It is more than just a seasoning or flavor enhancer. It also has these functions:

1. Salt strengthens gluten structure and makes it more stretchable. Thus, it improves the texture of breads.

2. Salt inhibits yeast growth. It is, therefore, important for controlling fermentation in bread doughs and in preventing the growth of undesirable wild yeasts.

For these reasons, the quantity of salt in a formula must be carefully controlled.

CHOCOLATE AND COCOA

Chocolate and cocoa are derived from cocoa or cacao beans. When the beans are roasted and ground, the resulting product is called *chocolate liquor*, which contains a white or yellowish fat called *cocoa butter*.

Cocoa is the dry powder that remains after part of the cocoa butter is removed from chocolate liquor.

Dutch process cocoa is processed with an alkali. It is slightly darker, smoother in flavor, and more easily dissolved in liquids than regular cocoa.

Bitter or *unsweetened chocolate* is straight chocolate liquor. In some less expensive brands, some of the cocoa butter may be replaced by another fat.

Sweet chocolate is bitter chocolate with the addition of sugar in varying amounts. If the percentage of sugar is low, it is sometimes called *semisweet* or *bittersweet*.

Milk chocolate is sweet chocolate with the addition of milk solids. It is used primarily in candy making. (None of the recipes in this book call for milk chocolate.)

Cocoa and chocolate are high in starch. When cocoa is added to a cake formula, it is sometimes considered part of the flour proportion for this reason.

SPICES

Spices are discussed in detail in Chapter 4. The most important spices in the bakeshop are cinnamon, nutmeg, mace, cloves, ginger, caraway, cardamom, allspice, anise, and poppy seed.

Because spices are used in small quantities, it is not much more expensive to use the best quality, and the results are superior.

Spices should be measured by weight unless the quantity is so small that measuring spoons are necessary.

EXTRACTS AND EMULSIONS

Extracts are flavorful oils and other substances dissolved in alcohol. These include vanilla, lemon, and bitter almond.

Emulsions are flavorful oils mixed with water with the aid of emulsifiers such as vegetable gums. Lemon and orange are the most frequently used emulsions.

The flavorings of extracts and emulsions may be natural or artificial. Natural flavorings give the best results, but they are often expensive. Artificial flavorings must be used in moderation to avoid creating strong or undesirable flavors in baked items.

■ TERMS FOR REVIEW

gluten	pastry flour	confectioners' sugar	single- and double-acting
strong flour	whole wheat flour	leavening	baking powders
weak flour	pumpernickel	fermentation	creaming
shortening	rye blend	fresh yeast	foaming
staling	regular shortening	active dry yeast	extract
bread flour	emulsified shortening	instant dry yeast	emulsion
cake flour	sucrose	chemical leavener	

■ QUESTIONS FOR DISCUSSION

1. Below are ingredients for a white cake. The weight of the flour is given, and the proportions of other ingredients are indicated by percentages. Calculate the weights required for each.

Cake flour	3 lb or 1500 g (100%)
Baking powder	4%
Shortening	50%
Sugar	100%
Salt	1%
Milk	75%
Egg whites	33%
Vanilla	2%

2. Discuss four factors that affect the development of gluten in doughs and batters.

3. Why do some cakes fall if they are removed from the oven too soon?

4. Which kind of cake would you expect to have better keeping qualities—a sponge cake, which is low in fat, or a high-ratio cake?

5. Why is white wheat flour used in rye breads? in whole wheat breads? Some bakeries in Europe produce a kind of pumpernickel bread with 100 percent rye flour. What would you expect its texture to be like?

6. Describe how to distinguish among bread, pastry, and cake flours by touch and sight.

7. What is the difference between regular and emulsified shortenings?

8. Shortbread is a type of cookie made with flour, butter, and sugar, but no liquid. What would you expect its texture to be like? Why?

30

Yeast
Products

In its simplest form, bread is nothing more than a dough of flour and water, leavened by yeast and baked. In fact, some hard-crusted French breads contain only these ingredients, plus salt. Other kinds of bread contain additional ingredients, including sugar, shortening, milk, eggs, and flavorings. But flour, water, and yeast are still the basic building blocks of all breads.

Yet for something that seems so simple, bread can be one of the most exacting and complex products to make. Success in bread-making depends largely on your understanding two basic principles: gluten development, which we discussed in the previous chapter, and yeast fermentation, which we have touched on and which we study in greater detail here.

This chapter focuses on the production of many kinds of yeast products, including breads, dinner rolls, sweet rolls, Danish pastry, and croissants.

UNDERSTANDING YEAST PRODUCTS

YEAST PRODUCT TYPES

Although all yeast doughs are made according to essentially the same basic principles, it is useful to divide yeast products into categories such as the following.

REGULAR YEAST DOUGH PRODUCTS

Lean Dough Products

A **lean dough** is one that is low in fat and sugar.

- Hard-crusted breads and rolls, including French and Italian breads, kaiser rolls and other hard rolls, and pizza. These are the leanest of all bread products.

- Other white breads and dinner rolls. These have a higher fat and sugar content and, sometimes, also contain eggs and milk solids. Because they are slightly richer, they generally have soft crusts.

- Whole-grain breads. Whole wheat and rye breads are the most common. Many varieties of rye bread are produced with light or dark flours or with pumpernickel flour and with various flavorings, especially molasses and caraway seeds.

Rich Dough Products

There is no exact dividing line between rich and lean doughs but, in general, rich doughs contain higher proportions of fat, sugar, and, sometimes, eggs.

- Nonsweet breads and rolls, including rich dinner rolls and brioche. These have a high fat content but low enough sugar that they can be served as dinner breads. Brioche dough is especially rich, made with a high proportion of butter and eggs.

- Sweet rolls, including coffee cakes and many breakfast and tea rolls. These have high fat and sugar and, often, eggs. They are usually made with a sweet filling or topping.

ROLLED-IN YEAST DOUGH PRODUCTS

Rolled-in doughs are those in which a fat is incorporated into the dough in many layers by means of a rolling and folding procedure. The alternating layers of fat and dough give the baked product a flaky texture.

- Nonsweet rolled-in doughs: croissants.
- Sweet rolled-in doughs: Danish pastry.

MIXING METHODS

Mixing yeast doughs has three main purposes:

1. To combine all ingredients into a uniform, smooth dough.
2. To distribute the yeast evenly throughout the dough.
3. To develop gluten.

Three principal mixing methods are used for yeast doughs: the **straight dough method**, the **modified straight dough method**, and the **sponge method**.

STRAIGHT DOUGH METHOD

There is only one step in this method, as practiced by many bakers.

Some bakers dissolve the compressed yeast in some of the water before adding the remaining ingredients. Others omit this step. Active dry yeast, on the other hand, must be rehydrated before mixing.

The advantage of softening the yeast in water is that it helps ensure that the yeast is evenly distributed in the dough.

Procedure: Straight Dough Mixing Method

Combine all ingredients in the mixing bowl and mix.

MODIFIED STRAIGHT DOUGH METHOD FOR RICH DOUGHS

For rich sweet doughs, the method is modified to ensure even distribution of the fat and sugar.

Procedure: Modified Straight Dough Method

1. Soften the yeast in part of the water.
2. Combine the fat, sugar, salt, milk solids, and flavorings and mix until well combined, but do not whip until light.
3. Add the eggs gradually, as fast as they are absorbed.
4. Add the liquid and mix briefly.
5. Add the flour and yeast. Mix into a smooth dough.

Procedure: Sponge Method

1. Combine the liquid (or part of the liquid), the yeast, and part of the flour (and, sometimes, part of the sugar). Mix into a thick batter or soft dough. Let ferment until double in bulk.
2. Punch down and add the rest of the flour and remaining ingredients. Mix to a uniform, smooth dough.

SPONGE METHOD

Sponge doughs are prepared in two stages.

STEPS IN YEAST DOUGH PRODUCTION

The production of yeast breads involves 12 basic steps. These steps are applied to yeast products in general, with variations depending on the particular product.

1. Scaling ingredients
2. Mixing
3. Fermentation
4. Punching
5. Scaling
6. Rounding
7. Benching
8. Makeup and panning
9. Proofing
10. Baking
11. Cooling
12. Storing

As you can see, mixing of ingredients into a dough is only one part of a complex procedure.

SCALING INGREDIENTS

All ingredients must be weighed accurately. The only items that may be measured by volume are water, milk, and eggs, which may be scaled at 1 pint per pound (or 1 liter per kilogram).

MIXING

Use the *dough arm* attachment when using a vertical mixer. Mix for the specified time.

The first two purposes of mixing—combining the ingredients into a dough and distributing the yeast—are accomplished during the first part of mixing. The remaining time is necessary to develop the gluten. Overmixed and undermixed doughs have poor volume and texture. (Review "Gluten Development," p. 895.)

It is necessary for you to learn to tell by sight and feel when a dough is thoroughly mixed. This can be done only through experience and with the guidance of your instructor. A properly developed dough feels smooth and elastic. A lean dough should not be sticky.

Sometimes it is necessary to add a little more flour if the dough hasn't lost its stickiness after most of the mixing time has passed.

Rich doughs are generally undermixed slightly because greater tenderness is desired for these products.

Note: Mixing speeds and times given in bread formulas in this book are guidelines only. Small mixers might be damaged if they are run at too high a speed with a stiff dough. In such cases, use a lower speed and extend the mixing time as necessary. Depending on the mixer, developing a dough at first or slow speed requires about twice as much mixing time as at second speed. Follow the manufacturer's recommendations.

FERMENTATION

Fermentation is the process by which yeast acts on the sugars and starches in the dough to produce carbon dioxide gas and alcohol.

Procedure For Fermenting Yeast Doughs

1. Place the dough in a lightly oiled container and oil the surface to prevent a crust from forming. (This may not be necessary if humidity is high—about 75 percent.)
2. Cover the container lightly and let the dough rise at a temperature of about 80°F (27°C).
3. Fermentation is complete when the dough has doubled in volume. If fermentation is complete, a dent will remain after the hand is pressed into the top of the dough.

Gluten becomes smoother and more elastic during fermentation. An underfermented dough does not develop proper volume, and the texture will be coarse. A dough that ferments too long or at too high a temperature becomes sticky, hard to work, and slightly sour.

An underfermented dough is called a **young dough**. An overfermented dough is called an **old dough**.

Doughs with weak gluten, such as rye doughs and rich doughs, are usually underfermented or "taken to the bench young."

PUNCHING

Punching is *not* hitting the dough with your fist. It is a method of deflating the dough that *expels carbon dioxide*, *redistributes the yeast* for further growth, *relaxes the gluten*, and *equalizes the temperature* throughout the dough.

Procedure For Punching Yeast Doughs

Pull up the dough on all sides, fold over the center, and press down. Then turn the dough upside down in the bowl.

A second fermentation and punching may or may not take place, depending on the product.

SCALING

Using a baker's scale, divide the dough into pieces of uniform weight, according to the product being made.

During scaling, allowance is made for weight loss due to evaporation of moisture in the oven. This weight loss is approximately 10 to 13 percent of the weight of the dough. Allow an extra 1½ to 2 ounces of dough for each 1 pound of baked bread, or 50 to 65 grams per 500 grams.

ROUNDING

After scaling, the pieces of dough are shaped into smooth, round balls. This procedure forms a kind of skin by stretching the gluten on the outside of the dough into a smooth layer. Rounding simplifies later shaping of the dough and also helps retain gases produced by the yeast.

Your instructor will demonstrate rounding techniques. Machines are also available that divide and round portions of dough automatically. Figure 30.1 illustrates a piece of dough being rounded by hand.

Figure 30.1
To round a piece of dough, roll the dough on the bench with the palm of your hand. As you rotate the dough, use the edge of your hand to pinch the dough against the bench. This movement stretches the surface of the dough so it is completely smooth except for a seam at the bottom where it was pinched together.

BENCHING

Rounded portions of dough are allowed to rest on the bench for 10 to 15 minutes. This relaxes the gluten to make shaping the dough easier. Also, *fermentation* continues during this time.

MAKEUP AND PANNING

The dough is shaped into loaves or rolls and placed in pans or on baking sheets. For all loaves and rolls, the seam must be centered on the bottom to avoid splitting during baking.

Breads and rolls take a great many forms. A variety of shapes and techniques is presented in the next section.

PROOFING

Proofing is a continuation of the process of yeast *fermentation*, which increases the volume of the shaped dough. Bakers use different terms so they can distinguish between fermentation of the mixed dough and proofing of the made-up product before baking. Proofing temperatures are generally higher than fermentation temperatures.

Procedure For Proofing Yeast Dough Products

Place the panned products in a proof box at 80° to 85°F (27° to 30°C) and about 70 to 80 percent humidity, as indicated in the formula. Proof until double in bulk.

If a proof box is not available, come as close to these conditions as you can by covering the products to retain moisture and setting them in a warm place.

Underproofing results in poor volume and dense texture. Overproofing results in coarse texture and some loss of flavor.

Rich doughs are slightly underproofed because their weaker gluten structure will not withstand much stretching.

BAKING

As you recall from the previous chapter, many changes take place in a dough during baking. The most important changes are these:

1. **Oven spring**, which is the rapid rising in the oven due to production and expansion of trapped gases as a result of the oven heat. The yeast is very active at first but is killed when the temperature inside the dough reaches 140°F (60°C).

2. Coagulation of proteins and gelatinization of starches. In other words, the product becomes firm and holds its shape.

3. Formation and browning of the crust.

Load the ovens carefully, as proofed doughs are fragile until they become set by baking.

Oven temperatures must be adjusted for the product being baked. Rolls spaced apart are baked at a higher temperature than large loaves so they become browned in the short time it takes to bake them. In general, lean breads such as those popular in North America are baked at 400° to 425°F (200° to 220°C), while some French breads and rolls are baked at 425° to 475°F (220° to 245°C). Rich doughs and sweet doughs are baked at a lower temperature, 350° to 400°F (175° to 200°C) because their fat, sugar, and milk content makes the crust brown faster.

Hard-crusted breads are baked with steam injected into the oven during the first part of the baking period. This aids the formation of a thin, crisp crust.

Rye breads also benefit from baking with steam for the first ten minutes.

A break on the side of the loaf is caused by continued rising after the crust is formed. To allow for this final expansion, hard-crusted breads are cut or scored before baking by making shallow slashes on the top of the loaf with a sharp knife or razor.

Small rolls bake completely without a break, so they are usually not scored.

Baking times vary considerably, depending on the product. A golden-brown crust color is the normal indication of doneness. Loaves that are done sound hollow when thumped.

COOLING

After baking, bread must be removed from pans and cooled rapidly on racks to allow the escape of excess moisture and alcohol created during fermentation.

Rolls baked apart from each other on sheets may be left on them because they will get adequate air circulation.

If soft crusts are desired, breads may be brushed with melted shortening before cooling.

Do not cool in a draft, or crusts may crack.

STORING

Breads to be served within eight hours may be left on racks. For longer storage, wrap cooled breads in moistureproof bags to retard staling. Bread must be thoroughly cool before wrapping, or moisture will collect inside the bags.

Wrapping and freezing maintains quality for longer periods. Refrigeration, on the other hand, increases staling.

Hard-crusted breads should not be wrapped (unless frozen), or the crusts will soften.

Because of the complexity of bread production, many things can go wrong. To remedy common bread faults, check Table 30.1 for possible causes and correct your procedures.

Table 30.1
Bread Faults and Their Causes

Fault	Causes
Shape	
Poor volume	Too much salt Too little yeast Weak flour Under- or overmixing Improper fermentation or proofing Oven too hot
Too much volume	Too little salt Too much yeast Too much dough scaled Overproofing
Poor shape	Too much liquid Improper molding or makeup Improper proofing Too much steam in oven
Split or burst crust	Overmixing Underfermentation Improper molding—seam not on bottom Oven too hot Not enough steam in oven
Texture and crumb	
Too dense or close grained	Too little yeast Underproofing Too much salt Too little liquid
Too coarse or open	Too much yeast Too much liquid Incorrect mixing time Improper fermentation Overproofing Pan too large
Streaked crumb	Improper mixing procedure Poor molding or makeup techniques Too much flour used for dusting
Poor texture or crumbly	Fermentation time too long or too short Overproofing Baking temperature too low Flour too weak Too little salt
Gray crumb	Fermentation time too long or temperature too high
Crust	
Too dark	Too much sugar or milk Underfermentation (young dough) Oven temperature too high Baking time too long Insufficient steam at beginning of baking
Too pale	Too little sugar or milk Overfermentation (old dough) Overproofing Oven temperature too low Baking time too short Too much steam in oven
Too thick	Too little sugar or fat Overfermentation (old dough) Baked too long and/or at too low a temperature Too little steam
Blisters on crust	Too much liquid Improper fermentation Improper shaping of loaves
Flavor	
Flat taste	Too little salt
Poor flavor	Inferior, spoiled, or rancid ingredients Poor bakeshop sanitation Under- or overfermentation

DOUGH FORMULAS AND TECHNIQUES

BREAD AND ROLL FORMULAS

The basic yeast dough mixing and baking methods discussed earlier in this chapter apply to the following formulas. Therefore, the methods are not repeated in detail for each formula. The basic procedures are indicated, and you should refer to the first part of this chapter if you need to refresh your memory for details.

Makeup techniques for loaves, rolls, and other items are described and illustrated after this recipe section.

 Hard Rolls

Ingredients	U.S.		Metric	Percentage
Water	1 lb	8 oz	700 g	55%
Yeast, fresh		1.5 oz	45 g	3.5%
Bread flour	2 lb	12 oz	1250 g	100%
Salt		1 oz	30 g	2.25%
Sugar		1 oz	30 g	2.25%
Shortening		1 oz	30 g	2.25%
Egg whites		1 oz	30 g	2.25%
Yield:	*4 lb*	*9 oz*	*2115 g*	*167%*

Per 1 roll:
Calories, 90; Protein, 3 g; Fat, 1 g (10% cal.); Cholesterol, 0 mg;
Carbohydrates, 17 g; Fiber, 1 g; Sodium, 200 mg.

■ **P r o c e d u r e**

Mixing:
Straight dough method.

10 minutes, 2nd speed (see note, p. 912).
Fermentation:
About 1 hour at 80°F (27°C).
Scaling and makeup:
Rolls—1 lb (500 g) per dozen.

French-type loaf—18 oz (550 g) per loaf.

See makeup technique after recipe section.

Dock after proofing. Brush with water.
Baking:
425°F (220°C). Steam for first 10 minutes.

 Soft Rolls

Ingredients	U.S.		Metric	Percentage
Water	1 lb	8 oz	720 g	57%
Yeast, fresh		1.5 oz	44 g	3.5%
Bread flour	2 lb	10 oz	1250 g	100%
Salt		0.8 oz	24 g	2.25%
Sugar		4 oz	125 g	9%
Nonfat milk powder		2 oz	60 g	4.75%
Shortening		2 oz	60 g	4.75%
Butter or margarine		2 oz	60 g	4.75%
Yield:	*4 lb*	*14 oz*	*2343 g*	*186%*

Per 1 roll:
Calories, 120; Protein, 3 g; Fat, 2.5 g (20% cal.); Cholesterol, 0 mg;
Carbohydrates, 20 g; Fiber, 0.5 g; Sodium, 190 mg.

■ **P r o c e d u r e**

Mixing:
Straight dough method.

10–12 minutes at 2nd speed (see note, p. 912).
Fermentation:
1½ hours at 80°F (27°C).
Scaling and makeup:
16–20 oz (450–600 g) per dozen rolls.

See makeup techniques after recipe section.
Baking:
400°F (200°C).

French Bread

Ingredients	U.S.		Metric	Percentage
Water	1 lb	12 oz	875 g	58%
Yeast, fresh		1.5 oz	45 g	3%
Bread flour	3 lb		1500 g	100%
Salt		1 oz	30 g	2%
Yield:	*4 lb*	*14 oz*	*2450 g*	*163%*

Per 1 ounce:
Calories, 60; Protein, 2 g; Fat, 0.5 g (7% cal.); Cholesterol, 0 mg;
Carbohydrates, 13 g; Fiber, 0 g; Sodium, 140 mg.

■ **P r o c e d u r e**

Mixing:
Straight dough method. Dissolve yeast in water before adding flour and salt.

3 minutes at 2nd speed; rest 2 minutes; 3 minutes more at 2nd speed (see note, p. 912).

Fermentation:
1½ hours at 80°F (27°C).

Punch down.

1 hour at 80°F (27°C).

Scaling and makeup:
French loaves—12 oz (350 g).

Round loaves—18 oz (550 g).

Rolls—16–20 oz (450–600 g) per dozen.

See makeup techniques after recipe section.

Baking:
400°F (200°C). Steam for first 10 minutes.

White Pan Bread

Ingredients	U.S.		Metric	Percentage
Water	1 lb	8 oz	750 g	60%
Yeast, fresh		1.5 oz	45 g	3.75%
Bread flour	2 lb	8 oz	1250 g	100%
Salt		1 oz	30 g	2.5%
Sugar		1.5 oz	45 g	3.75%
Nonfat milk powder		2 oz	60 g	5%
Shortening		1.5 oz	45 g	3.75%
Yield:	*4 lb*	*7 oz*	*2225 g*	*178%*

Per 1 ounce:
Calories, 70; Protein, 2 g; Fat, 1 g (13% cal.); Cholesterol, 0 mg;
Carbohydrates, 13 g; Fiber, 0 g; Sodium, 160 mg.

■ **P r o c e d u r e**

Mixing:
Straight dough method.

10 minutes at 2nd speed (see note, p. 912).

Fermentation:
1 hour at 80°F (27°C).

Makeup:
Pan loaves. See makeup techniques after recipe section.

Baking:
400°F (200°C).

V A R I A T I O N

Whole Wheat Bread
Prepare basic White Pan Bread using

Bread flour	1 lb	500 g	40%
Whole wheat flour	1 lb 8 oz	750 g	60%

Rye Bread and Rolls

Ingredients	U.S.		Metric	Percentage
Water	1 lb	8 oz	750 g	60%
Yeast, fresh		1.5 oz	45 g	3.75%
Rye flour	1 lb		500 g	40%
Bread flour	1 lb	8 oz	750 g	60%
Salt		1 oz	30 g	2.5 %
Shortening		1 oz	30 g	2.5%
Molasses		1 oz	30 g	2.5%
Caraway seeds		0.5 oz	15 g	1.25%
Yield:	*4 lb*	*4 oz*	*2150 g*	*172%*

Per 1 ounce:
Calories, 60; Protein, 2 g; Fat, 1 g (14% cal.); Cholesterol, 0 mg; Carbohydrates, 12 g; Fiber, 2 g; Sodium, 160 mg.

■ **P r o c e d u r e**

Mixing:
Straight dough method. 5–6 minutes at 2nd speed (see note, p. 912).
Fermentation: 1 hour at 80°F (27°C).
Scaling and makeup:
1 lb (500 g) per pan loaf.
1 lb (500 g) per dozen rolls.
See makeup techniques after recipe section.
Baking:
400°F (200°C). Steam for first 10 minutes.

Focaccia

Ingredients	U.S.		Metric	Percentage
Water	1 lb	8 oz	750 g	60%
Yeast, fresh		1 oz	35 g	2.75%
Bread flour	2 lb	8 oz	1250 g	100%
Salt		0.7 oz (3½ tsp)	20 g	1.75%
Sugar		0.2 oz (1¼ tsp)	6 g	0.5%
Olive oil		2 oz	60 g	5%
Yield:	*4 lb*	*3 oz*	*2121 g*	*170%*

Per 1 ounce:
Calories, 70; Protein, 2 g; Fat, 1 g (13% cal.); Cholesterol, 0 mg; Carbohydrates, 12 g; Fiber, 1 g; Sodium, 115 mg.

■ **P r o c e d u r e**

Mixing:
Straight dough method.
8 minutes at first speed (see note, p. 912).
Fermentation:
1½ hours at 80°F (27°C) or 2 hours at 75°F (24°C).
Makeup:
Oil sheet pans with olive oil. Roll out dough to about ¾ in. (2 cm) thick and place in pans (see Figure 30.2). Brush tops generously with olive oil. After proofing, press dimples into the dough at approximately 3-in. (8-cm) intervals.
Baking:
425°F (220°C). Steam for first 10 minutes.

V A R I A T I O N S

Rosemary Focaccia
After pressing in the dimples, sprinkle the top with rosemary (preferably fresh) and coarse salt.

Olive Focaccia
Mix 30% (12 oz/375 g) chopped oil-cured black olives into the dough.

Figure 30.2 Focaccia.

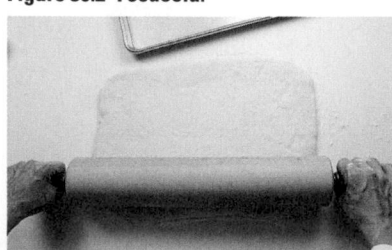

(a) Roll and stretch the dough into a rectangle large enough to fill the pan.

(b) Place the dough in the pan. Top with olive oil.

(c) With the fingertips, poke holes heavily at regular intervals.

(d) Top with the desired topping, such as fresh herbs and coarse salt.

Brioche

Ingredients	U.S.		Metric	Percentage
Milk		8 oz	250 g	20%
Yeast, fresh		2 oz	60 g	5%
Bread flour		8 oz	250 g	20%
Eggs	1 lb	4 oz	625 g	50%
Bread flour	2 lb		1000 g	80%
Sugar		2 oz	60 g	5%
Salt		0.5 oz	15 g	1.25%
Butter, softened	1 lb	8 oz	750 g	60%
Yield:	*6 lb*		*3010 g*	*241%*

Per 1 roll:
Calories, 160; Protein, 4 g; Fat, 10 g (56% cal.); Cholesterol, 60 mg; Carbohydrates, 14 g; Fiber, 0 g; Sodium, 190 mg.

V A R I A T I O N

To make the dough less sticky and less difficult to handle, reduce the butter to 35–50% (14–20 oz/450–625 g). This adjustment also reduces cost. However, the brioche will not be as rich and delicate.

■ P r o c e d u r e

Mixing:
Sponge method:
1. Scald milk and cool to lukewarm. Dissolve yeast. Add flour and mix to make a sponge. Let rise until double.
2. Gradually mix in eggs and then dry ingredients (using the paddle attachment) to make a soft dough.
3. Beat in butter, a little at a time, until completely absorbed and dough is smooth. Dough will be very soft and sticky.

Fermentation:
Cover with plastic film and place in retarder overnight.

Makeup:
1½ oz (50 g) per roll.

See makeup techniques after recipe section. Dough is very soft and is easiest to make up when chilled.

Egg wash after proofing.

Baking:
400°F (200°C).

 Sweet Roll Dough

Ingredients	U.S.		Metric	Percentage
Milk	1 lb		500 g	40%
Yeast, fresh		3 oz	100 g	7.5%
Butter/margarine/ shortening (see note)		8 oz	250 g	20%
Sugar		8 oz	250 g	20%
Salt		0.5 oz	15 g	1.25%
Eggs		6 oz	175 g	15%
Bread flour	2 lb		1000 g	80%
Cake flour		8 oz	250 g	20%
Yield:	*5 lb 1 oz*		*2540 g*	*203%*

Per 1 ounce:
Calories, 90; Protein, 2 g; Fat, 3 g (31% cal.): Cholesterol, 15 mg; Carbohydrates, 13 g; Fiber, 0.5 g; Sodium, 90 mg.

Note: Any of the fats listed may be used either alone or in combination.

■ P r o c e d u r e

Mixing:
Modified straight dough method:
1. Scald milk. Cool to lukewarm. Dissolve yeast in milk.
2. Mix fat, sugar, and salt until smooth, using paddle. Beat in eggs.
3. Add liquid and flour. With dough arm, mix 4 minutes at 2nd speed.

Fermentation:
1½ hours at 80°F (27°C).

Makeup:
See makeup techniques after recipe section.

Baking:
375°F (190°C).

V A R I A T I O N

Raised Doughnuts
Prepare basic sweet roll dough but reduce the fat and sugar by half. Mace, nutmeg, or other spices may be added.
  Scaling: 1½ oz (50 g) each.
    Give full proof.
  Frying: 360°F (182°C).
    Drain. Roll in cinnamon sugar or 6X sugar when cool.

ROLLED-IN DOUGHS: DANISH PASTRY AND CROISSANTS

Rolled-in doughs contain many layers of fat sandwiched between layers of dough. These layers create the flakiness you are familiar with in Danish pastry.

Two basic kinds of rolled-in yeast doughs are made in the bakeshop:

• sweet: Danish pastry   • nonsweet: croissants

Rolled-in doughs are mixed only slightly because the rolling-in procedure continues to develop the gluten.

Butter is the preferred fat for flavor and the melt-in-the-mouth quality of rolled-in doughs. Specially formulated shortenings are available when lower cost and greater ease of handling are more important considerations.

 ## Danish Pastry

Ingredients	U.S.	Metric	Percentage
Milk	1 lb	400 g	40%
Yeast, fresh	2.5 oz	65 g	6.25%
Butter	5 oz	125 g	12.5%
Sugar	6 oz	150 g	15%
Salt	0.5 oz	12 g	1.25%
Cardamom	1 tsp	2 g (5 mL)	0.2%
Eggs	8 oz	200 g	20%
Egg yolks	2 oz	50 g	5%
Bread flour	2 lb	800 g	80%
Cake flour	8 oz	200 g	20%
Butter	1 lb 4 oz	500 g	50%
Yield:	*6 lb 4 oz*	*2499 g*	*250%*

Per 1 ounce:
Calories, 110; Protein, 2 g: Fat, 6 g (53% cal.); Cholesterol, 35 mg; Carbohydrates, 10 g; Fiber, 0 g; Sodium, 120 mg.

■ P r o c e d u r e

Mixing:
Modified straight dough method:

1. Scald milk. Cool to lukewarm. Dissolve yeast in milk.
2. Mix butter, sugar, salt, and spice until smooth, using paddle. Beat in eggs and yolks.
3. Add liquid (from step 1) and flour. With dough arm, mix 3–4 minutes on 2nd speed.
4. Rest in retarder 20–30 minutes.
5. Roll in remaining butter and give 3 three-folds, as shown in Figure 30.3.

Makeup:
See makeup techniques after recipe section.

Proofing:
90°F (32°C) with little steam. Egg wash after proofing.

Baking:
375°F (190°C).

 ## Croissants

Ingredients	U.S.	Metric	Percentage
Milk	1 lb	450 g	57%
Yeast, fresh	1 oz	30 g	4%
Sugar	1 oz	30 g	4%
Salt	0.5 oz	15 g	2%
Butter, soft	3 oz	80 g	10%
Bread flour	1 lb 12 oz	800 g	100%
Butter	1 lb	450 g	57%
Yield:	*4 lb 1 oz*	*1855 g*	*234%*

Per 1 ounce:
Calories, 110; Protein, 2 g; Fat, 7 g (57% cal.); Cholesterol, 20 mg; Carbohydrates, 10 g; Fiber, 0 g; Sodium, 160 mg.

■ P r o c e d u r e

Mixing:
Straight dough method.

Scald milk, cool to lukewarm, and dissolve yeast. Add remaining ingredients except last 1 lb (450 g) butter. Mix into a smooth dough. Do not overmix.

Fermentation:
1 hour at 80°F (27°C).

Punch down, spread out on flat pan, and rest in retarder 30 minutes.

Roll in last amount of butter and give 3 three-folds (see Figure 30.3). Rest in retarder overnight.

Makeup:
See Figure 30.20 on page 929.

Proofing:
80°F (27°C). Egg wash after proofing.

Baking:
400°F (200°C).

Rolling-in Procedure for Danish and Croissant Dough

The rolling-in procedure has two parts.

1. **Enclosing the fat in the dough.**

   In the method illustrated in Figure 30.3, the fat is spotted on two-thirds of the dough and the dough is folded in thirds like a business letter. This results in five layers: three layers of dough and two layers of fat.

2. **Rolling out and folding the dough to increase the number of layers.**

   In these doughs, we use a *simple fold*, or *three-fold*, which means that we fold the dough in thirds. Each complete rolling and folding step is called a *turn*. We give the dough three turns, creating over 100 layers of dough and fat.

Figure 30.3 Rolling-in procedure for Danish and croissant dough.

(a, b) Roll the dough into a rectangle about 3 times as long as it is wide and ½ to ¾ in. (1 to 2 cm) thick. Smear the butter over two-thirds of the length of the dough, leaving a margin at the edges.

(c) Fold the unbuttered third over the center third.

(d) Fold the remaining third on top. Rest the dough in the retarder (under refrigeration) for 20 to 30 minutes to allow the gluten to relax.

(e) Place the dough on the bench at right angles to its position in step (d). Take this step before each rolling-out of the dough so the gluten is stretched in all directions, not just lengthwise. Roll the dough into a rectangle.

(f) Fold again into thirds by first folding the top third over the center. Be sure to brush off excess dusting flour from between the folds.

(g) Fold over the remaining third. You have now completed the first turn or fold. Incorporating the butter doesn't count as a turn. Press one finger in the dough near the end to make one indentation. This indicates "1 turn" to anyone who may have to take up where you left off, or to you if you have several batches going. Refrigerate the dough for 20 to 30 minutes to relax the gluten. Repeat the above rolling and folding procedures for a second and third turn, resting the dough between turns. Mark the number of turns in the dough with two or three fingers. After the third turn, rest the dough in the retarder for several hours or overnight. Cover it with plastic film to prevent crusting. The dough is then ready for makeup.

In Chapter 31, you will learn an even more complex rolling-in procedure used for puff pastry, which is leavened only by steam, not by yeast. This procedure produces over 1,000 layers!

FILLINGS AND TOPPINGS FOR SWEET DOUGH PRODUCTS AND DANISH

Cinnamon Sugar

Yield: about 1 lb (500 g)

U.S.	Metric	Ingredients
1 lb	500 g	Sugar
0.5 oz	15 g	Cinnamon

■ P r o c e d u r e

Stir together thoroughly.

Per 1 ounce:
Calories, 110; Protein, 0 g; Fat, 0 g (0% cal.); Cholesterol, 0 mg; Carbohydrates, 0 g; Fiber, 0 g; Sodium, 0 mg.

Streusel or Crumb Topping

Yield: 2 lb (1 kg)

U.S.	Metric	Ingredients
8 oz	250 g	Butter and/or shortening
5 oz	150 g	Granulated sugar
4 oz	120 g	Brown sugar
¼–1 tsp	2–5 mL	Cinnamon or mace
½ tsp	2 mL	Salt
1 lb	500 g	Pastry flour

■ P r o c e d u r e

Rub all ingredients together until crumbly.

V A R I A T I O N

Nut Streusel
Add 4 oz (125 g) finely chopped nuts to basic mixture.

Per 1 ounce:
Calories, 130; Protein, 1 g; Fat, 6 g (40% cal.); Cholesterol, 15 mg; Carbohydrates, 19 g; Fiber, 2 g; Sodium, 85 mg.

Clear Glaze for Coffee Cakes and Danish

Yield: 2 lb (1 kg)

U.S.	Metric	Ingredients
1 cup	250 mL	Water
1 lb	500 g	Light corn syrup
8 oz	250 g	Granulated sugar

■ P r o c e d u r e

1. Mix together and bring to a boil. Stir to ensure that the sugar is completely dissolved.
2. Brush on while hot.

Per 1 ounce:
Calories, 70; Protein, 0 g; Fat, 0 g (0% cal.); Cholesterol, 0 mg; Carbohydrates, 18 g; Fiber, 0 g; Sodium, 15 mg.

Date, Prune, or Apricot Filling

Yield: 3 lb (1.5 kg)

U.S.	Metric	Ingredients	Procedure
2 lb	1 kg	Dates, prunes (pitted), or dried apricots	1. Chop dried fruit very fine or pass through a grinder.
6 oz	200 g	Sugar	2. Combine all ingredients in a saucepan. Bring to a boil. Simmer and stir until thick and smooth, about 10 minutes.
1 pt	500 mL	Water	3. Cool before using.

Per 1 ounce:
Calories, 65; Protein, 0 g; Fat, 0 g (0% cal.); Cholesterol, 0 mg;
Carbohydrates, 17 g; Fiber, 1 g; Sodium, 0 mg.

Almond Filling

Yield: 3 lb (1500 g)

U.S.	Metric	Ingredients	Procedure
1 lb	500 g	Almond paste	1. With paddle attachment, mix almond paste and sugar at low speed until evenly mixed.
1 lb	500 g	Sugar	
8 oz	250 g	Butter and/or shortening	2. Mix in fat and flour until smooth.
4 oz	125 g	Pastry or cake flour	3. Beat in eggs, a little at a time, until smooth.
4 oz	125 g	Eggs	

Per 1 ounce:
Calories, 130; Protein, 1 g; Fat, 7 g (48% cal.); Cholesterol, 20 mg;
Carbohydrates, 16 g; Fiber, 1 g; Sodium, 45 mg.

Cheese Filling

Yield: Approximately 2 lb 3 oz (1125 g)

U.S.	Metric	Ingredients	Procedure
1 lb	500 g	Baker's cheese	1. Using the paddle attachment, cream the cheese, sugar, and salt until smooth.
5 oz	150 g	Sugar	
0.12 oz (⅝ tsp)	3 mL	Salt	
3 oz	100 g	Eggs	2. Add the eggs, butter, and vanilla. Blend in.
3 oz	100 g	Butter and/or shortening, soft	
1½ tsp	7 mL	Vanilla	
1.5 oz	50 g	Cake flour	3. Add the cake flour. Blend until just absorbed.
3–5 oz	100–150 g	Milk	4. Add the milk, a little at a time, adding just enough to bring the mixture to a smooth, spreadable consistency.
4 oz	125 g	Raisins (optional)	5. Stir in the raisins, if desired.

Per 1 ounce:
Calories, 60; Protein, 3 g; Fat, 2.5 g (38% cal.); Cholesterol, 20 mg;
Carbohydrates, 6 g; Fiber, 0 g; Sodium, 70 mg.

Figure 30.4 Rounding small rolls.

(a) Holding the palm of the hand fairly flat, roll the dough in a tight circle on the workbench. Do not use too much flour for dusting, as the dough must stick to the bench a little for the technique to work.

(b) As the ball of dough takes on a round shape, gradually cup your hand.

(c) The finished ball of dough should have a smooth surface, except for a slight pucker on the bottom.

MAKEUP TECHNIQUES

The object of yeast dough makeup techniques is to shape the dough into rolls or loaves that bake properly and have an attractive appearance. When you shape a roll or loaf correctly, you stretch the gluten strands on the surface into a kind of smooth skin. This tight gluten surface holds the item in shape. This is especially important for loaves and rolls that are baked freestanding, not in pans.

Units that are not made up correctly develop irregular shapes and splits and may flatten out on the pan.

Following are a few of the many makeup techniques for yeast doughs.

HARD ROLLS AND BREADS

Round Rolls

1. Scale the dough as indicated in the recipes, usually 1 pound (450 g) per dozen.
2. Round each unit as shown in Figure 30.4.
3. Place rolls 2 inches (5 cm) apart on sheet pans sprinkled with cornmeal.

Round Loaves

1. Flatten the rounded, benched dough into a circle. Fold the four sides over the center, then round again.
2. Place on sheet pans sprinkled with cornmeal.

Club Rolls

1. Make up as shown in Figure 30.5.
2. Place 2 inches (5 cm) apart on sheet pans sprinkled with cornmeal.

Crescent Rolls

1. Scale dough into 20-ounce (600-g) units.
2. After rounding and benching, flatten the dough and roll it out into a circle 12 inches (30 cm) across.
3. With a pastry wheel, cut the dough circle into 12 equal wedges or triangles. (Alternative method: For large quantities of dough, roll it out into a rectangle and cut like croissant dough. See Figure 30.19 on p. 929.)
4. Roll the triangles into crescents using the same technique as for croissants (see Figure 30.19 on p. 929).

    Note: If using soft roll dough, brush the dough with butter before cutting it into triangles. Do not use any fat with hard roll doughs.

Figure 30.5 Making club rolls.

(a) Flatten the piece of dough roughly into a rectangle.

(b) Begin to roll the dough by folding over the back edge of the rectangle. Press the seam firmly with your fingertips.

(c) Continue to roll the dough, always pressing the seam firmly after each turn. As you roll the dough, the front edge will appear to shrink. Stretch the front corners as shown by the arrows to keep the width uniform.

(d) When the roll is finished, seal the seam well so that you have a tight roll.

(e) Dock the proofed roll with a single slash to give the baked roll this appearance.

French-Type Loaves

1. Scale the dough into units weighing 12 to 18 ounces (350 to 500 g).
2. Make up as shown in Figure 30.6.

Figure 30.6
Making French-type loaves.

(a) Flatten the rounded, relaxed dough with your hands or with a rolling pin.

(b) Stretch the oval with the hands to lengthen it.

(c) Roll the dough tightly.

(d) Seal the seam well. If a longer, thinner loaf is required, relax the rolled units again for a few minutes. Flatten them with your palms and stretch the dough lightly to increase its length. Once again, roll tightly and seal the seam. Roll the loaf on the bench under your palms to make it even and to stretch it to the desired shape and length.

(e) Place the dough seam-side down on pans dusted with cornmeal. Proofing the loaves on special trough-shaped pans maintains their shape. Proof. Wash with water. Slash with diagonal cuts or with one lengthwise cut; this can be done before or after proofing.

SOFT ROLL DOUGHS

Tied or Knotted Rolls

1. Scale dough to 16 to 20 ounces (450 to 600 g) per dozen.
2. With the palm of the hand, roll each unit on the workbench into a strip or rope of dough.
3. Tie rolls as shown:

    Single-knot rolls: Figure 30.7

    Double-knot rolls: Figure 30.8

    Braided rolls: Figure 30.9

    Figure-eight rolls: Figure 30.10

4. Place 2 inches (5 cm) apart on greased baking sheets.
5. Egg wash after proofing.

Pan Rolls

1. Scale dough to 16 to 20 ounces (450 to 600 g) per dozen.
2. Make up as for round hard rolls.
3. Place on greased pans ½ inch (1 cm) apart.

Figure 30.7 Tying a single-knot roll

Figure 30.8
Tying a double-knot roll

Figure 30.9
Tying a braided roll

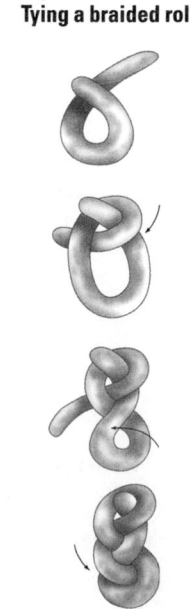

Figure 30.10
Tying a figure-eight roll

**Figure 30.11
Parker House rolls.**

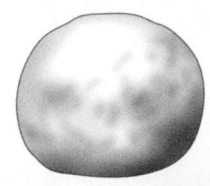

(a) Round the scaled piece of dough.

(b) Flatten the center of the dough with a thin rolling pin as shown.

(c) Fold the dough over and press down on the folded edge to make a crease.

(d) The baked roll has this shape.

Parker House Rolls

1. Scale dough to 16 to 20 ounces (450 to 600 g) per dozen.
2. Make up as shown in Figure 30.11.
3. Place on greased baking sheet ½ inch (1 cm) apart.

Cloverleaf Rolls

1. Scale dough to 16 to 20 ounces (450 to 600 g) per dozen.
2. Make up and pan as shown in Figure 30.12.

Butterflake Rolls

Make up as shown in Figure 30.13.

PAN LOAVES

Shaping dough into loaves to be baked in loaf pans is illustrated in Figure 30.14.

**Figure 30.12
Cloverleaf rolls.**

(a) Divide each piece of dough into 3 equal parts. Shape into balls. Place 3 balls in the bottom of each greased muffin tin.

(b) The baked roll has this appearance.

**Figure 30.13
Butterflake rolls.**

(a) Roll the dough into a thin rectangle. Brush with melted butter. Cut into strips 1 in. (2.5 cm) wide.

(b) Stack 6 strips. Cut into pieces 1½ in. (3.5 cm) long.

(c) Place the pieces on end in greased muffin tins. Proof.

(d) The baked rolls have this appearance.

**Figure 30.14
Pan loaves.**

(a) Start with the rounded, benched dough. Flatten it with the palms of the hands.

(b) Stretch it into a long rectangle.

(c, d) Fold into thirds.

(e) Roll the dough into a tight roll of the same length as the pan it is to be baked in. Seal the seam well and place the dough seam side down in the greased pan.

BRIOCHE

Brioche dough may be made into many shapes. The traditional shape is shown in Figure 30.15.

**Figure 30.15
Making brioche.**

(a) For a small brioche, roll the dough into a round piece.

(b) Using the edge of your hand, pinch off about one-fourth of the dough without detaching it. Roll the dough on the bench so that both parts are round.

(c) Place the dough in the tin, large end first. With your fingertips, press the small ball into the larger one as shown.

(d) For large brioche, separate the two parts of the dough. Place the large ball in the tin and make a hole in the center. Form the smaller ball into a pear shape and fit it into the hole.

(e) A baked large brioche.

SWEET DOUGH PRODUCTS

Note: Many sweet dough products may be glazed with Clear Glaze (p. 922) and/or iced with Flat Icing (p. 956) after baking. Flat icing is drizzled over the cooled products without covering them completely.

Cinnamon Rolls

1. Scale dough into 20-ounce (600-g) units. On a floured board, roll each piece of dough into a rectangle measuring 9 x 12 inches and about ¼ inch thick (23 x 30 x ½ cm).
2. Brush with butter and sprinkle with 2 ounces (60 g) cinnamon sugar.
3. Roll up like a jelly roll 12 inches (30 cm) long, as shown in the illustration.
4. Cut into 1-inch (2½-cm) rolls.
5. Place cut side down in greased muffin tins or on greased sheet pans. One full-size pan, 18 x 26 inches (46 x 66 cm), holds 48 rolls placed 6 by 8.

For variations on the basic cinnamon roll shape, see Figure 30.16.

**Figure 30.16
The filled dough roll is the starting point for a variety of sweet dough and Danish products.**

(a) Roll the dough into a rectangle. Brush with butter and sprinkle with cinnamon sugar, or spread with desired filling.

(b) Roll up like a jelly roll.

(c) For cinnamon rolls and similar products, cut off pieces 1 in. (2.5 cm) in length.

(d) For combs or bear claws, make the roll thinner and cut it into longer pieces. Flatten slightly and cut partway through each piece in 3 to 6 places as shown. Leave straight or bend into a curve to open the cuts.

(e) For figure-eight cinnamon rolls, cut the rolls almost through as shown. Open them and lay them flat on the baking sheet.

(f) To make a wreath-shaped coffee cake, join the ends of the dough roll to make a circle.

(g) Cut partway through the dough at 1-in. (2.5-cm) intervals as shown.

(h) Twist each segment outward to open the cuts.

Cinnamon Raisin Rolls

Prepare like cinnamon rolls, but add 2 ounces (60 g) raisins to the filling.

Caramel Rolls

1. Prepare like cinnamon rolls.
2. Before panning, spread the bottoms of the pans or muffin tins with the following mixture. Use about 1 ounce (30 g) of the mixture per roll.

> 2 lb (1 kg) brown sugar
>
> 8 oz (250 g) corn syrup
>
> 10 oz (300 g) butter
>
> 4 oz (125 mL) water

Cream the sugar, corn syrup, and butter. Beat in the water.

Quantities given are enough for 1 sheet pan of 48 rolls.

Caramel Nut Rolls or Pecan Rolls

Prepare like caramel rolls, but sprinkle the sugar-butter mixture in the pans with chopped nuts or pecan halves before placing the rolls in the pans.

Wreath Coffee Cake

1. Make a filled dough roll as for cinnamon rolls, but do not cut it into separate pieces. Other fillings, such as prune or date, may be used instead of butter and cinnamon sugar.
2. Shape the roll into a circle as shown in Figure 30.16f-h. Place on a greased baking sheet. Cut and shape as shown in the illustration.
3. Egg wash after proofing.

Filled Coffee Cake

1. Scale dough into 12-oz (350-g) units.
2. Roll each unit into a rectangle measuring 9 x 18 inches (23 x 46 cm).
3. Spread half of each rectangle with desired filling, using about 6 ounces (175 g) filling.
4. Fold the unspread half over the spread half to make a 9-inch (23-cm) square.
5. Place in greased 9-inch (23-cm) square pan.
6. Sprinkle with Streusel Topping (p. 922), about 4 ounces (125 g) per pan.
7. Proof and bake.

ROLLED-IN DOUGH PRODUCTS

Danish Rolls and Coffee Cakes

Most of the techniques given in the previous section for sweet dough products may be used for Danish pastry.

Two additional methods are illustrated in Figures 30.17 and 30.18.

Figure 30.17
Spiral Danish rolls.

(a) Roll the dough into a rectangle 16 in. (40 cm) wide and less than ¼ in. (0.5 cm) thick. (The length of the rectangle depends on the quantity of dough.) Brush the dough with melted butter. Sprinkle half of it with cinnamon sugar as shown.

(b) Fold the unsugared half over the sugared half. You now have a rectangle 8 in. (20 cm) wide. Roll the dough gently with a rolling pin to press the layers together.

(c) Cut the dough into strips ½ in. (1 cm) wide.

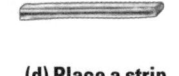

(d) Place a strip crosswise in front of you on the bench.

(e) With the palms of your hands on the ends of the strip, roll one end toward you and the other away from you so that the strip twists. Stretch the strip slightly as you twist it.

(f) Curl the strip into a spiral shape on the baking sheet. Tuck the end underneath and pinch it against the roll to seal it in place. If desired, press a hollow in the center of the roll and place a spoonful of filling (such as a fruit filling) in the center.

Figure 30.18 Danish pockets.

(a) Roll the dough to less than ¼ in. (0.5 cm) thick and cut into 5-in. (13-cm) squares. Place desired filling on the center of each square. Brush the corners lightly with water—this helps them seal when pressed together.

(b) Fold two opposite corners over the center. Press down firmly to seal them. (If desired, rolls may be left in this shape.)

(c) Fold the other two corners over the center and again press them firmly together.

Baked Danish dough products are frequently glazed with Clear Glaze (p. 922) and/or iced with Flat Icing (p. 956).

Croissants

The method for making up croissants is illustrated in Figure 30.19.

Figure 30.19 Making croissants.

(a) Roll the dough into a rectangle 10 in. (26 cm) wide and about ⅛ in. (3 mm) thick. (The length depends on the amount of dough used.)

(b) Cut into triangles as shown. Special roller cutters are available that do this quickly.

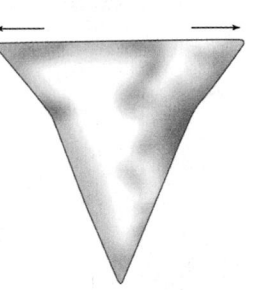

(c) Place a triangle on the bench in front of you. Stretch the back corners outward slightly, as shown by the arrows.

(d) Begin to roll the dough toward the point.

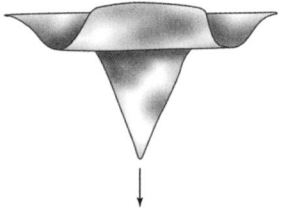

(e) Stretch the point of the triangle slightly as you roll it.

(f) Finish rolling the dough.

(g) Bend the roll into a crescent shape. The point of the triangle must be toward the inside of the crescent and tucked under the roll so that it won't pop up during baking.

■ TERMS FOR REVIEW

lean dough	modified straight dough	fermentation	proofing
rolled-in dough	method	young and old doughs	oven spring
straight dough method	sponge method	punching	

■ QUESTIONS FOR DISCUSSION

1. What are the three major purposes of mixing yeast doughs?

2. Explain the difference in procedure between the straight dough method and the sponge method. How is the straight dough method sometimes modified for sweet doughs, and why is this necessary?

3. What are the 12 steps in the production of yeast products? Explain each briefly.

4. Judging from what you know about fermentation of doughs, do you think it might be necessary for bakers to modify procedures from winter to summer? How?

5. As you know, butter is very hard when cold and melts easily at warm temperatures. What precautions do you think are necessary when using butter as the rolling-in fat for Danish pastry?

31

Quick Breads

Quick breads are the perfect solution for operations that want to offer their patrons fresh, homemade bread products but can't justify the labor cost of making yeast breads. Also, quick breads have the advantage of being easily made in almost unlimited varieties, using such ingredients as whole wheat flour, rye flour, cornmeal, bran, oatmeal, and many kinds of fruits, nuts, and spices.

As their name implies, quick breads are quick to make. Because they are leavened by chemical leaveners and steam, not by yeast, no fermentation time is necessary. And because they are usually tender products with little gluten development, mixing them takes just a few minutes.

Although prepared biscuit and muffin mixes are available, the only extra work required to make these products from scratch is the time to scale a few extra ingredients. With a careful and imaginative selection of ingredients and an understanding of basic mixing methods, you can create superior products.

You may already have studied two kinds of quick breads in the breakfast chapter: pancakes and waffles. In this chapter, we present two basic mixing methods and apply them to biscuits, muffins, quick loaf breads and coffee cakes, and corn breads. In addition, we discuss popovers, which are leavened by steam only.

MIXING AND PRODUCTION METHODS

After reading this chapter, you should be able to

1. **Prepare baking powder biscuits and variations.**

2. **Prepare muffins, loaf breads, coffee cakes, and corn breads.**

3. **Prepare popovers.**

TYPES OF DOUGH

Dough mixtures for quick breads are generally of two types:

1. *Soft doughs* are used for biscuits. These products are rolled out and cut into desired shapes. They are mixed by the biscuit method.

2. *Batters* may be either **pour batters**, which are liquid enough to pour, or **drop batters**, which are thicker and drop from a spoon in lumps.

Most quick-bread batters are mixed by the **muffin method**, except for drop biscuits, which are mixed by the **biscuit method**, and some rich cakelike muffins and coffee cakes, which are mixed by a cake-mixing method called the *creaming method*. The biscuit and muffin methods are presented in this chapter. The creaming method is presented in Chapter 32, along with other cake methods.

The muffins and loaf breads in this chapter should be thought of as breads rather than as tea cakes. They are lower in fat and sugar than some of the rich, cakelike muffins sometimes seen.

GLUTEN DEVELOPMENT IN QUICK BREADS

Only slight gluten development is desired in most quick breads. Tenderness is the desired quality, in contrast to the chewy quality of yeast breads. In addition, chemical leavening agents do not create the same kind of textures that yeast does and are not strong enough to create a light, tender product if the gluten is too strong.

1. Muffin, loaf bread, and pancake batters are mixed as little as possible, just until the dry ingredients are moistened. This, plus the presence of fat and sugar, keeps gluten development low.

   Overmixing muffins produces not only toughness but also irregular shapes and large, elongated holes inside the product. This latter condition is called **tunneling**.

2. Biscuit dough is often lightly kneaded, enough to develop some flakiness but not enough to toughen the product.

3. Popovers are the exception among quick breads. They are made with a thin batter and leavened by steam only. Large holes develop inside the product during baking, and the structure must be strong enough to hold without collapsing. Thus, bread flour is used, and the batter is mixed well to develop the gluten. The high percentage of egg in popovers also helps build structure.

THE BISCUIT METHOD

Procedure: Biscuit Method

1. Scale all ingredients accurately.
2. Sift the dry ingredients together into a mixing bowl.
3. Cut in the shortening, using the paddle attachment or the pastry knife attachment. If preferred, you may also cut in the fat by hand, using a pastry blender or your fingers. Continue until the mixture resembles coarse cornmeal.
4. Combine the liquid ingredients. Biscuits may be prepared in advance up to this point. Portions of each mixture may then be scaled and combined just before baking.
5. Add the liquid to the dry ingredients. Mix just until the ingredients are combined and a soft dough is formed. Do not overmix.
6. Bring the dough to the bench and knead it lightly by pressing it out and folding it in half. Rotate the dough 90 degrees after each fold.
7. Repeat this procedure about 10 to 20 times, or for about 30 seconds. The dough should be soft and slightly elastic but not sticky. Overkneading toughens the biscuits. The dough is now ready for makeup.

Variations on the basic procedure produce different characteristics in the finished product.

1. Using slightly more shortening and cutting it in less—until the pieces are the size of peas—produces a flakier biscuit.
2. Omitting the kneading step produces a tender, crustier biscuit, but with less volume.

MAKEUP OF BISCUITS

1. Roll the biscuit dough into a sheet about ½ inch (1 cm) thick, being careful to roll it evenly and to a uniform thickness.

    Biscuits approximately double in height during baking.

2. Cut into desired shapes.

    When using round hand cutters, cutting straight down produces the best shape after baking. Do not twist the cutter. Space the cuts closely to minimize scraps.

    Cutting into squares or triangles with a pastry cutter or knife eliminates scraps that would have to be rerolled. Roller cutters also eliminate or reduce scraps. Reworked scraps are tougher.

3. Place the biscuits ½ inch (1 cm) apart on baking sheet for crisp-crusted biscuits, or touching each other for softer biscuits. Bake as soon as possible.

    If desired, the tops may be brushed with egg wash or milk before baking to aid browning.

THE MUFFIN METHOD

This mixing method is used not only for muffins but also for pancakes, waffles, quick loaf breads, and coffee cakes. Loaf breads and coffee cakes are sometimes higher in fat and sugar than muffins, so they can withstand more mixing without toughening.

The muffin method is not as suitable for formulas high in fat and sugar, unlike the cake-mixing method called the creaming method, discussed in Chapter 32. Consequently, quick breads mixed by the muffin method are not as rich and cakelike as many of today's popular muffins, which are closer to cakes than to traditional muffins. Keep this fact in mind as you practice the muffin method with the recipes in this chapter.

Procedure: Muffin Method

1. Sift together the dry ingredients (see Figure 31.1).
2. Combine all liquid ingredients, including melted fat or oil.
3. Add the liquids to the dry ingredients and mix just until all the flour is moistened. The batter will look lumpy. Do not overmix.
4. Pan and bake immediately. The dry and liquid mixtures may be prepared in advance. Once they are combined, the batter should be baked without delay, or loss of volume may result. When portioning batter into muffin tins, be careful not to stir the mix and toughen it. Scoop the batter from the outside edge for best results.

Figure 31.1
The muffin method.

(a) Sift together the dry ingredients.

(b) Add the combined liquid ingredients to the dry ingredients and mix just until the flour is moistened.

(c) Pan and bake immediately. Scoop the batter from the outside edge to minimize additional mixing.

SUMMARY: BISCUIT AND MUFFIN METHODS

Biscuit Method

1. Combine dry ingredients and cut in fat.
2. Combine liquid ingredients.
3. Add liquid and dry ingredients and mix just until combined.
4. If required, knead very lightly.

Muffin Method

1. Combine dry ingredients.
2. Combine liquid ingredients, including melted fat.
3. Add liquid to dry ingredients and mix just until combined.

FORMULAS

 Biscuits

Ingredients	U.S.		Metric	Percentage
Bread flour	1 lb	4 oz	600 g	50%
Pastry flour	1 lb	4 oz	600 g	50%
Salt		0.75 oz	25 g	2%
Sugar		2 oz	60 g	5%
Baking powder		2.5 oz	75 g	6%
Shortening (regular) and/or butter		14 oz	425 g	35%
Milk	1 lb	10 oz	775 g	65%
Yield:	*5 lb*	*5 oz*	*2560 g*	*213%*

Per 1 biscuit:
Calories, 130; Protein, 2 g; Fat, 7 g (48% cal.); Cholesterol, 0 mg; Carbohydrates, 15 g; Fiber 1 g; Sodium, 260 mg.

■ **P r o c e d u r e**

Mixing and makeup:
Biscuit method.
Scaling:
Approximately 1 lb (500 g) per dozen 2-in. (5-cm) biscuits.
Baking:
425°F (220°C), about 15 minutes.

V A R I A T I O N S

Buttermilk Biscuits
Use buttermilk instead of regular milk.

Cheese Biscuits
Add 30% (12 oz/360 g) grated cheddar cheese to dry ingredients.

Currant Biscuits
Add 15% (6 oz/180 g) dried currants to dry ingredients. Increase sugar to 10% (4 oz/125 g). Sprinkle tops with cinnamon sugar before baking.

Herb Biscuits
Add 5% (2 oz/60 g) fresh chopped parsley to the dry ingredients.

 Banana Bread

Ingredients	U.S.		Metric	Percentage
Pastry flour	1 lb	8 oz	700 g	100%
Sugar		10 oz	275 g	40%
Baking powder		1.25 oz	35 g	5%
Baking soda		1 tsp	3.5 g (5 mL)	0.5%
Salt		2 tsp	9 g (10 mL)	1.25%
Chopped walnuts		6 oz	175 g	25%
Eggs		10 oz	275 g	40%
Ripe banana pulp, puréed	1 lb	8 oz	700 g	100%
Oil, melted shortening, or butter		8 oz	225 g	33%
Yield:	*5 lb*	*4 oz*	*2397 g*	*344%*

Per 1 ounce:
Calories, 90; Protein, 2 g; Fat, 4.5 g (41% cal.); Cholesterol, 15 mg; Carbohydrates, 12 g; Fiber, 1 g; Sodium, 120 mg.

■ **P r o c e d u r e**

Mixing:
Muffin method.
Scaling:
1 lb 10 oz (750 g) per loaf pan measuring 8½ x 4½ in. (22 x 11 cm).
Baking:
375°F (190°C), about 50 minutes.

Plain Muffins

Ingredients	U.S.		Metric	Percentage
Pastry flour	2 lb	8 oz	1200 g	100%
Sugar	1 lb	4 oz	600 g	50%
Baking powder		2.5 oz	72 g	6%
Salt		0.5 oz	15 g	1.25%
Eggs, beaten		12 oz	360 g	30%
Milk	1 lb	12 oz	840 g	70%
Vanilla extract		1 oz	30 g	2.5%
Melted butter or shortening	1 lb		480 g	40%
Yield:	*7 lb*	*8 oz*	*3591 g*	*299%*

■ P r o c e d u r e

Mixing:
Muffin method.

Scaling and panning:
Grease and flour muffin tins or use paper liners.

Scale batter with No. 16 scoop, 2 oz (60 g) per unit.

Baking:
400°F (200°C), about 20 minutes.

Per 1 muffin:
Calories, 170; Protein, 3 g; Fat, 7 g (36% cal.);
Cholesterol, 40 mg; Carbohydrates, 25 g; Fiber, 3 g;
Sodium, 230 mg.

V A R I A T I O N S

Raisin Spice Muffins
Add 20% raisins (8 oz/250 g), 2½ tsp (12 mL) cinnamon, and 1 tsp (5 mL) nutmeg to the dry ingredients.

Date Nut Muffins
Add 15% (6 oz/185 g) each chopped dates and chopped walnuts to the dry ingredients.

Blueberry Muffins
Gently fold 40% (1 lb/480 g) well-drained blueberries into the finished batter.

Whole Wheat Muffins
Use 70% (1 lb 12 oz/840 g) pastry flour and 30% (12 oz/ 360 g) whole wheat flour. Reduce baking powder to 4% (1½ oz/50 g) and add 0.75% (2 tsp/10 mL) baking soda. Add 10% (4 oz/120 g) molasses to the liquid ingredients.

Corn Muffins
Use 65% (1 lb 10 oz/800 g) pastry flour and 35% (14 oz/ 400 g) yellow cornmeal. (See also Corn Bread formula.)

Bran Muffins
Use 30% (12 oz/360 g) bran, 40% (1 lb/480 g) bread flour, and 30% (12 oz/360 g) pastry flour. Add 15% (6 oz/ 180 g) raisins to the dry ingredients. Add 15% (6 oz/180 g) molasses to the liquid ingredients.

Crumb Coffee Cake
Increase fat to 50% (1 lb 4 oz/600 g). Pour into greased, paper-lined sheet pan and spread smooth. Top with 80% (2 lb/1 kg) Streusel Topping (p. 922). Bake at 360°F (180°C), about 30 minutes.

Muffins, clockwise from top: blueberry, corn, bran

Popovers

Ingredients	U.S.		Metric	Percentage
Eggs	1 lb	4 oz	625 g	125%
Milk	2 lb		1000 g (1 L)	200%
Salt		0.25 oz (1¼ tsp)	8 g (6 mL)	1.5%
Melted butter or shortening		2 oz	60 g	12.5%
Bread flour	1 lb		500 g	100%
Yield:	*4 lb*	*6 oz*	*2193 g*	*439%*

Per 1 popover:
Calories, 70; Protein, 3 g; Fat, 3 g (38% cal.); Cholesterol, 60 mg;
Carbohydrates, 8 g; Fiber, 0 g; Sodium, 95 mg.

■ P r o c e d u r e

Mixing:

1. Beat eggs, milk, and salt together with whip attachment, until well blended. Add melted fat.

2. Replace whip with paddle. Mix in flour until completely smooth.

Scaling and panning:
Grease every other cup of muffin pans—popovers need room for expansion. Fill cups about two-thirds full, about 1½ oz (50 g) batter per unit.

Baking:
450°F (230°C) for 10 minutes. Reduce heat to 375°F (190°C) for 20–30 minutes.

Before removing them from oven, be sure popovers are dry and firm enough to avoid collapsing. Remove from pans immediately.

Corn Bread, Muffins, or Sticks

Ingredients	U.S.		Metric	Percentage
Pastry flour	1 lb	4 oz	600 g	50%
Cornmeal	1 lb	4 oz	600 g	50%
Sugar		6 oz	175 g	15%
Baking powder		2 oz	60 g	5%
Salt		0.75 oz	25 g	2%
Eggs, beaten		8 oz	250 g	20%
Milk	2 lb	2 oz	1000 g (1 L)	85%
Corn syrup		2 oz	60 g	5%
Melted butter or shortening		12 oz	350 g	30%
Yield:	6 lb	8 oz	3120 g	262%

■ P r o c e d u r e

Mixing:
Muffin method.
Scaling:
60 oz (1700 g) per half-size sheet pan
(13 x 18 in./33 x 46 cm).
24 oz (725 g) per 9-in. (23-cm) square pan or per dozen muffins.
10 oz (300 g) per dozen corn sticks.
Grease and flour pans well.
Baking:
400°F (200°C) for corn bread, 25–30 minutes. 425°F (220°C) for muffins or sticks, 15–20 minutes.

Per 1 muffin:
Calories, 160; Protein, 3 g; Fat, 7 g (39% cal.); Cholesterol, 35 mg; Carbohydrates, 22 g; Fiber, 2 g; Sodium, 290 mg.

Orange Nut Bread

Ingredients	U.S.		Metric	Percentage
Sugar		12 oz	350 g	50%
Grated orange zest		1 oz	30 g	4%
Pastry flour	1 lb	8 oz	700 g	100%
Nonfat dry milk		2 oz	60 g	8%
Baking powder		1 oz	30 g	4%
Baking soda		2 tsp	10 g	1.4%
Salt		2 tsp	10 g(10 mL)	1.4%
Chopped walnuts		12 oz	350 g	50%
Eggs		5 oz	150 g	20%
Orange juice		6 oz	175 g	25%
Water	1 lb		450 g	65%
Oil, melted butter, or shortening		6 oz	175 g	25%
Yield:	5 lb	5 oz	2490 g	344%

■ P r o c e d u r e

Mixing:
Muffin method.

Blend the sugar and orange zest thoroughly before adding remaining dry ingredients to ensure even distribution.
Scaling:
1 lb 10 oz (750 g) per loaf pan measuring 8½ x 4½ in. (22 x 11 cm).
Baking:
375°F (190°C), about 50 minutes.

Per 1 ounce:
Calories, 80; Protein, 2 g; Fat, 4 g (39% cal.); Cholesterol, 5 mg; Carbohydrates, 12 g; Fiber, 1 g; Sodium, 130 mg.

■ TERMS FOR REVIEW

pour batter	tunneling	muffin method
drop batter	biscuit method	

■ QUESTIONS FOR DISCUSSION

1. If you made a batch of muffins that came out of the oven with strange, knobby shapes, what would you expect was the reason?

2. What is the most important difference between the biscuit method and the muffin method?

3. Why do popovers require more mixing than other quick breads?

CHAPTER 32

Cakes and Icings

Cakes are the richest and sweetest of all the baked products we have studied so far. From the baker's point of view, producing cakes requires as much precision as producing breads, but for completely opposite reasons. Breads are lean products that require strong gluten development and careful control of yeast action during the long fermentation and proofing periods. Cakes, on the other hand, are high in both fat and sugar. The baker's job is to create a structure that will support these ingredients and yet keep it as light and delicate as possible. Fortunately, producing cakes in quantity is relatively easy if the baker has good, well-balanced formulas, scales ingredients accurately, and understands basic mixing methods well.

Cakes owe their popularity not only to their richness and sweetness but also to their versatility. They can be presented in many forms, from simple sheet cakes in cafeterias to elaborately decorated works of art for weddings and other important occasions. With only a few basic formulas and a variety of icings, the chef or baker can construct the perfect dessert for any occasion or purpose.

After reading this chapter, you should be able to

1. **Demonstrate the five basic cake mixing methods.**

2. **Describe the characteristics of high-fat cakes and low-fat cakes.**

3. **Prepare high-fat, or shortened, cakes and low-fat, or foam-type, cakes.**

4. **Prepare the six basic types of icings.**

5. **Assemble and ice layer cakes, small cakes, and sheet cakes.**

UNDERSTANDING CAKE-MAKING

BASIC MIXING METHODS

The mixing methods presented in this chapter are basic for most types of cakes prepared in the modern bakeshop. Each of these methods is used for particular types of formula.

High-fat or shortened cakes	Low-fat or foam-type cakes
Creaming method	Foaming or sponge method
Two-stage or blending method	Angel food method
	Chiffon method

We discuss these cake types in detail after you have had a chance to study the actual procedures.

CREAMING METHOD

The **creaming method,** also called the *conventional method,* was, for a long time, the standard method for mixing butter cakes. Recently, the development of emulsified or high-ratio shortenings has led to the development of simpler mixing methods for shortened cakes. But the creaming method is still used for many types of butter cakes.

Procedure: Creaming Method

1. Scale ingredients accurately. Have all ingredients at room temperature.

2. Place the butter or shortening in the mixing bowl. With the paddle attachment, beat slowly until the fat is smooth and creamy.

3. Add the sugar. Cream the mixture at moderate speed until the mixture is light and fluffy.

   Some bakers prefer to add the salt and flavorings with the sugar to ensure uniform distribution.

   If melted chocolate is used, it is added during creaming.

4. Add the eggs, a little at a time. After each addition, beat until the eggs are absorbed before adding more. The mixture should be light and fluffy after the eggs are beaten in.

5. Scrape down the sides of the bowl to ensure even mixing.

6. Add the sifted dry ingredients (including the spices, if they were not added in step 3), alternating with the liquids. This is done as follows:

   • Add one-fourth of the dry ingredients. Mix just until blended in.

   • Add one-third of the liquid. Mix just until blended in.

   • Repeat until all ingredients are used. Scrape down the sides of the bowl occasionally for even mixing.

   The reason for adding dry and liquids alternately is that the batter may not absorb all the liquid unless some of the flour is present.

   Cocoa, if used, is included with the flour.

TWO-STAGE METHOD

The **two-stage method,** also called the **blending method,** was developed for use with modern high-ratio shortenings (see Chapter 29). Although it is simpler than the creaming method, it produces a very smooth batter that bakes up into a fine-grained, moist cake. It is called *two-stage* because the liquids are added in two stages.

Procedure: Two-Stage Method

1. Scale ingredients accurately. Have all ingredients at room temperature.
2. Sift the flour, baking powder, soda, and salt into the mixing bowl and add the shortening. With the paddle attachment, mix at low speed for 2 minutes. Stop the machine, scrape down the bowl and beater, and mix again for 2 minutes.

   If melted chocolate is used, blend it in during this step.

   If cocoa is used, sift it with the flour in this step or with the sugar in step 3.
3. Sift the remaining dry ingredients into the bowl and add part of the water or milk. Blend at low speed for 3 to 5 minutes. Scrape down the sides of the bowl and the beater several times to ensure even mixing.
4. Combine the remaining liquids and lightly beaten eggs. With the mixer running, add this mixture to the batter in three parts. After each part, turn off the machine and scrape down the bowl.

   Continue mixing for a total of 5 minutes in this stage.

   The finished batter is normally quite liquid.

Variation

This variation combines steps 2 and 3 above into one step.

1. Scale ingredients as in the basic method.
2. Sift all dry ingredients into the mixing bowl. Add the shortening and part of the liquid. Mix on low speed for 7 to 8 minutes. Scrape down the sides of the bowl and the beater several times.
3. Continue with step 4 in the basic procedure.

FOAMING OR SPONGE METHOD

All egg-foam cakes are similar in that they contain little or no shortening and depend for most or all of their leavening on the air trapped in beaten eggs.

One mixing method is usually presented as the basic method for all foam cakes. However, because whole-egg foams and egg-yolk foams are handled differently than egg-white foams, we discuss two separate, although similar, methods: the **foaming method** and the **angel food method**. A third method, the **chiffon method**, is somewhat unusual. It combines an egg-white foam with a high-fat batter made with oil.

First, the method for sponge cakes:

Procedure: Foaming or Sponge Method

Figure 32.1

1. Scale ingredients accurately. Have all ingredients at room temperature.

   If butter is included, it must be melted.

   If liquid and butter are included, heat them together, just until the butter is melted.
2. Combine the eggs and sugar and warm to about 110°F (43°C). This may be done in one of two ways.
   - Stir the egg-sugar mixture over a hot-water bath.
   - Warm the sugar on a sheet pan in the oven (do not get it too hot) and gradually beat it into the eggs.

   The reason for this step is that the foam attains greater volume if warm.

(a) With a wire whip or the whip attachment of a mixer, beat the eggs until they are very thick and light.

3. With the whip attachment, beat the eggs at high speed until light and thick. This may take 10 to 15 minutes. This step is important. One of the most frequent causes of failure in the sponge method is not whipping the eggs and sugar enough. The foam must be very thick. When the beater is lifted from the bowl, the foam should fall slowly from it and make a ribbon that slowly sinks into the batter in the bowl (see Figure 32.1).
4. Fold in the sifted flour, being careful not to deflate the foam. Many bakers do this by hand.

   If other dry ingredients are used, such as cornstarch or baking powder, they are first sifted with the flour.
5. If melted butter or a butter-liquid mixture is being used, fold it in at this point. Be careful not to overmix, or the cake will be tough (because of developed gluten).
6. Immediately pan and bake the batter. Delays cause loss of volume.

(b) Fold in the sifted flour in three or four stages, until all the flour is blended in.

Variations

Some formulas contain water or some other liquid, but no butter (so you cannot heat the liquid and butter together, as in the basic procedure). In this case, the liquid is usually added after step 3 and before folding in the flour. Either whip it in a steady stream or stir it in, as indicated in the recipe.

In some formulas, the egg yolks and whites are separated. Use the yolks and part of the sugar to make the foam in steps 2 and 3. Use the remaining sugar to whip with the whites. Fold the egg-white foam into the batter after step 5.

ANGEL FOOD METHOD

Angel food cakes are based on egg-white foams and contain no fat. For success in beating egg whites, review the principles of egg foams in Chapter 23.

Procedure: Angel Food Method

1. Scale ingredients accurately. Have all ingredients at room temperature. You may warm the egg whites slightly for better volume.
2. Sift the flour with half the sugar. This step helps the flour mix more evenly with the foam.
3. Beat the egg whites, using the whip attachment, until they form soft peaks.

   Add salt and cream of tartar near the beginning of the beating process.
4. Gradually beat in the sugar that was not mixed with the flour. Continue to beat until the egg whites form soft, glossy peaks. Do not overbeat.
5. Fold in the flour-sugar mixture just until it is thoroughly absorbed, but no longer.
6. Pan and bake immediately.

CHIFFON METHOD

Chiffon cakes and angel food cakes are both based on egg-white foams. But here the similarities in the mixing methods end. In angel food cakes, a dry flour-sugar mixture is folded into the egg whites. In chiffon cakes, a batter containing flour, egg yolks, vegetable oil, and water is folded into the whites.

Whip egg whites for chiffon cakes until they are a little firmer than those for angel food cakes, but not until they are dry. Chiffon cakes contain baking powder, so they do not depend on the egg foam for all their leavening.

Procedure: Chiffon Method

1. Scale all ingredients accurately. Have all ingredients at room temperature. Use a good-quality, flavorless vegetable oil.
2. Sift the dry ingredients, including part of the sugar, into the mixing bowl.
3. Mixing with the paddle attachment at second speed, gradually add the oil, then the egg yolks, water, and liquid flavorings, all in a slow, steady stream. While adding the liquids, stop the machine several times and scrape down the bowl and the beater. Mix until smooth, but do not overmix.
4. Whip the egg whites until they form soft peaks. Add the cream of tartar and sugar in a stream and whip to firm, moist peaks.
5. Fold the whipped egg whites into the flour-liquid mixture.
6. Immediately deposit batter in ungreased tube pans (like angel food cakes) or in layer pans that have had the bottoms, but not the sides, greased and dusted (like sponge layers).

PREPARED MIXES

Many mixes are available that contain all ingredients except water and, sometimes, egg. These products also contain emulsifiers to ensure even blending of ingredients. To use them, follow the package instructions exactly.

Most mixes produce cakes with excellent volume, texture, and tenderness. Whether or not they also taste good is a matter of opinion. On the other hand, cakes made from scratch are not necessarily better. They are better only if they are carefully mixed and baked and are prepared using good, tested formulas and high-quality ingredients.

CAKE FORMULA TYPES

The proper mixing method for a particular formula depends on the balance of ingredients. A baker can look at the ingredients in a formula and know immediately which mixing method to use.

- If *fat is high*, use the creaming method or the two-stage method.

  The two-stage method may be used if the percentage of sugar is over 100 percent and if the fat is emulsified shortening.

  In other cases, the creaming method is used.

- If *fat is low* and *eggs and sugar are high*, use an egg-foam method.

HIGH-FAT CAKES

The creaming method's major disadvantage is the labor it requires. The two-stage method is quicker, but because the flour is mixed for a long time, two conditions are necessary to prevent the gluten from developing toughness:

1. Increased percentage of sugar (sugar is a tenderizer).

2. Emulsified shortening, which blends thoroughly to prevent toughness.

Cakes made by the two-stage method have good volume and lightness, a fine, velvety texture, and great tenderness. The texture of butter cakes made by the creaming method is coarser and the tenderness is generally somewhat less.

One factor seems to be neglected when cakes are rated, however—flavor. Shortening contributes no flavor to cakes, only texture. Butter, on the other hand, is highly prized for its flavor. It also influences texture because it melts in the mouth, while shortening does not. Thus, butter cakes are and always will be in demand. Therefore, the creaming method is important for you to know.

LOW-FAT CAKES

High-fat cakes depend on air incorporated by the creaming action of the fat and sugar for some of their leavening and much of their texture. Low-fat or no-fat cakes obviously cannot. They must depend on the foaming action of eggs.

Sponge cakes have a springy texture and are tougher than shortened cakes. This makes them valuable for many kinds of desserts that require much handling to assemble. For example, many European-style cakes or tortes are made by cutting sponge cake layers horizontally into thin layers and stacking them with a variety of rich fillings, creams, icings, and fruits.

Even if a high-ratio cake survived all this without breaking into crumbs, it would probably disintegrate when it absorbed moisture from the fillings. In addition, sponge layers in this kind of cake are usually moistened with a flavored sugar syrup to compensate for their lack of moisture.

The *fruit torte* (illustrated in the photograph) is an example of this type of cake. Genoise layers are split, moistened with dessert syrup (p. 1006), layered and iced with whipped cream, and topped with attractively arranged fruit pieces. The fruit is then coated with glaze (p. 957) to protect it and enhance its appearance.

Sponge sheets for jelly rolls and other rolled cakes are made without shortening, so they do not crack when rolled.

Flour for sponge cakes must be weak to avoid making the cake tough. Cornstarch is often added to cake flour for sponge cakes to weaken the flour further.

Fruit torte

SCALING AND PANNING

PAN PREPARATION

Prepare pans before mixing cake batters so cakes can be baked without delay as soon as they are mixed.

1. For high-fat cakes, the bottoms of layer pans must be greased, preferably with a commercial pan greasing preparation. If this is not available, dust the greased pan with flour and tap out the excess.

2. For sheet cakes, line the pan with greased parchment.

3. For angel food cakes, do not grease the pan. The batter must be able to cling to the sides in order to rise.

4. For sponge cake layers with a small percentage of fat, grease the bottoms but not the sides.

Procedure for Scaling Creaming-Method Batters

These batters are thick and do not pour easily. Scale cakes as follows:

1. Place the prepared cake pan on the left side of a balance scale. Balance the scale by placing another pan on the right side.
2. Set the scale for the desired weight.
3. Add batter to the left pan until the scale balances.
4. Remove the pan from the scale and spread the batter smooth with a spatula.
5. Repeat with remaining pans.
6. Give the pans several sharp raps on the bench to free large trapped air bubbles. Bake immediately.

Procedure for Scaling Two-Stage Batters

These batters are more liquid than creamed batters. They may be scaled like creamed batters or, for greater speed, they may be scaled as follows:

1. Place an empty volume measure on the left side of a balance scale. Balance the scale to zero.
2. Set the scale for the desired weight.
3. Pour batter into the measure until the scale balances.
4. Note the volume of batter in the measure.
5. Pour the measured batter into a prepared pan, quickly scraping out the measure to get all the batter.
6. Scale the remaining cakes with the volume measure, using the volume noted in step 4.
7. Give the pans several sharp raps on the bench to free large trapped air bubbles. Bake immediately.

Procedure for Scaling Foam Cakes

Foam cake batters should be handled as little as possible and baked immediately in order to avoid deflating the beaten eggs. Although they may be scaled like creamed batters, many bakers prefer to eyeball them in order to minimize handling.

1. Have all prepared pans lined up on the bench.
2. Scale the first pan as for creamed batters.
3. Quickly fill remaining pans to the same level as the first pan, judging the level by eye.
4. Spread the batter smooth and bake immediately.

See Table 32.1 for average scaling weights as well as baking temperatures and times.

BAKING AND COOLING

BAKING

Cake structure is fragile, so proper baking conditions are essential for high-quality products. The following guidelines will help you avoid cake failures.

1. Preheat the ovens. (But to conserve expensive energy, don't preheat longer than necessary.)

2. Make sure ovens and shelves are level.

Table 32.1
Average Cake Scaling Weights, Baking Temperatures, and Times

Pan Type and Size	Scaling Weight		Baking Temperature		Approximate Baking Time in Minutes
	U.S.	**Metric**	**U.S.**	**Metric**	
High-fat cakes					
Round layers					
6 in. (15 cm)	8–10 oz	230–285 g	375°F	190°C	18
8 in. (20 cm)	14–18 oz	400–510 g	375°F	190°C	25
10 in. (25 cm)	24–28 oz	680–800 g	360°F	180°C	35
12 in. (30 cm)	32–40 oz	900–1100 g	360°F	180°C	35
Sheets and square pans					
18 × 26 in. (46 × 66 cm)	7–8 lb	3.2–3.6 kg	360°F	180°C	35
18 × 13 in. (46 × 33 cm)	3½–4 lb	1.6–1.8 kg	360°F	180°C	35
9 × 9 in. (23 × 23 cm)	24 oz	680 g	360°F	180°C	30–35
Loaf (pound cake)					
2¼ × 3½ × 8 in. (6 × 9 × 20 cm)	16–18 oz	450–500 g	350°F	175°C	50–60
2¾ × 4½ × 8½ in. (7 × 11 × 22 cm)	24–27 oz	680–765 g	350°F	175°C	55–65
Cupcakes					
per dozen	18 oz	510 g	385°F	195°C	18–20
Foam-type cakes					
Round layers					
6 in. (15 cm)	5–6 oz	140–170 g	375°F	190°C	20
8 in. (20 cm)	10 oz	280 g	375°F	190°C	20
10 in. (25 cm)	16 oz	450 g	360°F	180°C	25–30
12 in. (30 cm)	24 oz	700 g	360°F	180°C	25–30
Sheets (for jelly roll or sponge roll)					
18 × 26 in., ½ in. thick (46 × 66 cm, 12 mm thick)	2½ lb	1.2 kg	375°F	190°C	15–20
18 × 26 in., ¼ in. thick (46 × 66 cm, 6 cm thick)	28 oz	800 g	400°F	200°C	7–10
Tube (angel food and chiffon)					
8 in. (20 cm)	12–14 oz	340–400 g	360°F	180°C	30
10 in. (25 cm)	24–32 oz	700–900 g	350°F	175°C	50
Cupcakes					
per dozen	10 oz	280 g	375°F	190°C	18–20

Note: The weights given are averages. Weights may be increased by 25 percent if thicker layers are desired. Baking times may then need to be increased slightly.

3. Do not let pans touch each other in oven. If pans touch, air circulation is inhibited and the cakes rise unevenly.

4. Bake at the correct temperature.
   Too hot an oven causes the cake to set unevenly or to set before it has fully risen. Crusts will be too dark.
   Too slow an oven causes poor volume and texture because the cake doesn't set fast enough and may fall.

5. Do not open the ovens or disturb the cakes until they have finished rising and are partially browned. Disturbing the cakes before they are set may cause them to fall.

6. If steam in the oven is available, use it for creamed and two-stage batters. These cakes bake with a flatter top if baked with steam because the steam delays the formation of the top crust.

7. Tests for doneness:
   - Shortened cakes shrink away from sides of pan slightly.

Table 32.2
Common Cake Faults and Their Causes

Fault	Causes
Volume and shape	
Poor volume	Too little flour
	Too much liquid
	Too little leavening
	Oven too hot
Uneven shape	Improper mixing
	Batter spread unevenly
	Uneven oven heat
	Oven racks not level
	Cake pans warped
Crust	
Too dark	Too much sugar
	Oven too hot
Too light	Too little sugar
	Oven not hot enough
Burst or cracked	Too much flour or flour too strong
	Too little liquid
	Improper mixing
	Oven too hot
Soggy	Underbaked
	Cooling in pans or with not enough ventilation
	Wrapping before cool
Texture	
Dense or heavy	Too little leavening
	Too much liquid
	Too much sugar
	Too much shortening
	Oven not hot enough
Coarse or irregular	Too much leavening
	Too little egg
	Improper mixing
Crumbly	Too much leavening
	Too much shortening
	Too much sugar
	Wrong kind of flour
	Improper mixing
Tough	Flour too strong
	Too much flour
	Too little sugar or shortening
	Overmixing
Poor flavor	
	Poor-quality ingredients
	Poor storage or sanitation
	Unbalanced formula

- Cakes are springy. The center of the top springs back when pressed slightly.
- A cake tester or pick inserted in the center of the cake comes out clean.

COOLING AND REMOVING FROM PANS

1. Cool layer cakes and sheet cakes 15 minutes in pans and turn out while slightly warm. They are too fragile to turn out when hot, and they may break.
2. Turn out layer cakes onto racks to finish cooling.
3. To turn out sheet cakes:
   - Sprinkle top lightly with granulated sugar.
   - Set an empty sheet pan on top, bottom side down.
   - Invert both pans.
   - Remove top pan.
   - Peel parchment off cake.
4. Cool angel food cakes upside down in pans. Support the edges of the pan so the top of the cake is off the bench. When cool, loosen the cake from the sides of the pan with a knife or spatula and pull out carefully.

COMMON CAKE FAULTS AND THEIR CAUSES

Errors in mixing, scaling, baking, and cooling cakes cause many kinds of defects and failures. For easy reference, these defects and their possible causes are summarized in the troubleshooting guide in Table 32.2.

ALTITUDE ADJUSTMENTS

At high altitudes, atmospheric pressure is much lower than at sea level. This factor must be taken into account in cake baking. Formulas must be adjusted to suit different baking conditions over 2,000 or 3,000 feet (600 or 900 meters) above sea level.

Although general guidelines can be given, the exact adjustments required vary for different kinds of cake. Many manufacturers of flour, shortening, and other bakery ingredients supply detailed information and adjusted formulas for any given locality.

In general, the following adjustments must be made above elevations of 2,000 or 3,000 feet (600 or 900 meters). See Table 32.3 for more specific adjustments.

Leavening

Leavening gases expand more when air pressure is lower, so baking powder and baking soda must be *decreased*.

Creaming and foaming procedures should also be reduced so that less air is incorporated.

Table 32.3
Approximate Formula Adjustment in Shortened Cakes at High Altitudes

Ingredient	Increase or Decrease	Percentage Adjustment		
		2500 Feet (750 m)	5000 Feet (1500 m)	7500 Feet (2300 m)
Baking powder	Decrease	20%	40%	60%
Flour	Increase	—	4%	9%
Eggs	Increase	2½%	9%	15%
Sugar	Decrease	3%	6%	9%
Fat	Decrease	—	—	9%
Liquid	Increase	9%	15%	22%

To make adjustments, multiply the percentage indicated by the amount of ingredient and add or subtract as indicated.

Example: To adjust 1 lb (16 oz) eggs for 7,500 feet:

$$0.15 \times 16 \text{ oz} = 2.4 \text{ oz}$$

$$16 \text{ oz} + 2.4 \text{ oz} = 18.4 \text{ oz}$$

Tougheners: Flour and Eggs

Cakes require firmer structure at high altitudes. Both eggs and flour must be increased to supply proteins for structure.

Tenderizers: Shortening and Sugar

Shortening and sugar must be decreased so that the structure of the cake is firmer.

Liquids

At high altitudes, water boils at a lower temperature and evaporates more easily. Liquids must be *increased* to prevent excess drying both during and after baking. This also helps compensate for the decrease in moisturizers (sugar and fat) and the increase in flour, which absorbs moisture.

Baking Temperatures

Increase baking temperatures about 25°F (14°C) above 3,500 feet.

Pan Greasing

High-fat cakes tend to stick at high altitudes. Grease pans more heavily. Remove baked cakes from pans as soon as possible.

Storing

Wrap or ice cakes as soon as they are cool to prevent drying.

CAKE FORMULAS

CREAMING METHOD

 ## Yellow Butter Cake

Ingredients	U.S.	Metric	Percentage
Butter	1 lb 8 oz	720 g	80%
Sugar	1 lb 10 oz	780 g	87%
Salt	0.25 oz (1¼ tsp)	7 g (6 mL)	1%
Eggs	15 oz	450 g	50%
Cake flour	1 lb 14 oz	900 g	100%
Baking powder	1.25 oz	35 g	4%
Milk	1 lb 14 oz	900 g	100%
Vanilla	0.5 oz	15 mL	1.5%
Yield:	*7 lb 14 oz*	*3810 g*	*423%*

Per 1 ounce:
Calories, 90; Protein, 1 g; Fat, 5 g (48% cal.); Cholesterol, 25 mg;
Carbohydrates, 11 g; Fiber, 0 g; Sodium, 80 mg.

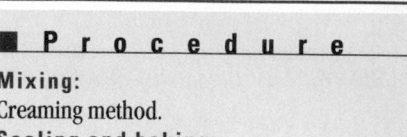

■ P r o c e d u r e

Mixing:
Creaming method.
Scaling and baking:
See Table 32.1.

 ## Brown Sugar Spice Cake

Ingredients	U.S.	Metric	Percentage
Butter	12 oz	400 g	80%
Brown sugar	15 oz	500 g	100%
Salt	0.25 oz	8 g	1.5%
Eggs	9 oz	300 g	60%
Cake flour	15 oz	500 g	100%
Baking powder	0.5 oz	15 g	3%
Baking soda	⅜ tsp	1.5 g (1.5 mL)	0.3%
Cinnamon	1½ tsp	2.5 g (7 mL)	0.5%
Ground cloves	¾ tsp	1.5 g (3 mL)	0.3%
Nutmeg	⅜ tsp	1 g (1.5 mL)	0.2%
Milk	15 oz	500 g	100%
Yield:	*4 lb 2 oz*	*2229 g*	*445%*

Per 1 ounce:
Calories, 90; Protein, 1 g; Fat, 5 g (46% cal.); Cholesterol, 30 mg;
Carbohydrates, 12 g; Fiber, 0 g; Sodium, 105 mg.

■ P r o c e d u r e

Mixing:
Creaming method.
Scaling and baking:
See Table 32.1.

V A R I A T I O N

Carrot Nut Cake
Reduce the milk to 90% (13.5 oz/450 g). Add
40% (6 oz/200 g) grated fresh carrots, 20% (3
oz/100 g) finely chopped walnuts, and 0.5% (1
tsp/3 g or 5 mL) grated orange zest after eggs
are beaten in. Omit cloves.

Chocolate Butter Cake

Ingredients	U.S.	Metric	Percentage
Butter	9 oz	280 g	75%
Sugar	15 oz	470 g	125%
Salt	0.2 oz (1 tsp)	6 g	1.5%
Unsweetened chocolate, melted	6 oz	188 g	50%
Eggs	8 oz	250 g	67%
Cake flour	12 oz	250 g	100%
Baking powder	0.5 oz	15 g	4%
Milk	14 oz	439 g	115%
Vanilla	0.25 oz (1½ tsp)	8 mL	2%
Yield:	*4 lb*	*1906 g*	*539%*

Per 1 ounce:
Calories, 90; Protein, 1 g; Fat, 5 g (46% cal.); Cholesterol, 25 mg;
Carbohydrates, 12 g; Fiber, 0.5 g; Sodium, 80 mg.

■ P r o c e d u r e

Mixing:
Creaming method. Blend in the melted chocolate after the fat and sugar are well creamed.
Scaling and baking:
See Table 32.1.

Old-Fashioned Pound Cake

Ingredients	U.S.	Metric	Percentage
Butter or butter and shortening combined (see note)	1 lb	500 g	100%
Sugar	1 lb	500 g	100%
Vanilla	2 tsp	10 mL	2%
Eggs	1 lb	500 g	100%
Cake flour	1 lb	500 g	100%
Yield:	*4 lb*	*2000 g*	*402%*

Per 1 ounce:
Calories, 110; Protein, 2 g; Fat, 7 g (51% cal.); Cholesterol, 45 mg;
Carbohydrates, 13 g; Fiber, 0 g; Sodium, 70 mg.

Note: If you are using unsalted butter or shortening, add 1.5% (¼ oz /1¼ tsp or 6 mL) salt during the first stage of mixing.

■ P r o c e d u r e

Mixing:
Creaming method. Add the eggs and the cake flour alternately to avoid curdling the mixture.
Scaling and baking:
See Table 32.1.

V A R I A T I O N S

Mace or grated lemon or orange zest may also be used to flavor pound cake.

Raisin Pound Cake
Add 25% (4 oz/125 g) raisins or dried currants that were soaked in boiling water and drained well.

Chocolate Pound Cake
Add 25% (4 oz/125 g) unsweetened chocolate to the butter and sugar after the creaming stage.

Marble Pound Cake
Fill pans one-third full of the basic yellow batter. Add a layer of Chocolate Pound Cake batter, then finish with the yellow batter. Run a spatula blade through the layers to marble them.

TWO-STAGE METHOD

 White Cake

Ingredients	U.S.		Metric	Percentage
Cake flour	1 lb	8 oz	700 g	100%
Baking powder		1.5 oz	45 g	6.25%
Salt		0.5 oz	15 g	2%
Emulsified shortening		12 oz	350 g	50%
Sugar	1 lb	14 oz	875 g	125%
Skim milk		12 oz	350 g	50%
Vanilla		2 tsp	10 mL	1.5%
Almond extract		1 tsp	5 mL	0.75%
Skim milk		12 oz	350 g	50%
Egg whites	1 lb		475 g	67%
Yield:	*6 lb*	*12 oz*	*3175 g*	*452%*

Per 1 ounce:
Calories, 90; Protein, 1 g; Fat, 3 g (33% cal.); Cholesterol, 0 mg;
Carbohydrates, 13 g; Fiber, 0 g; Sodium, 105 mg.

■ **P r o c e d u r e**

Mixing:
Two-stage method.
Scaling and baking:
See Table 32.1.

V A R I A T I O N S

Use water instead of milk and add 10% (2½ oz/70 g) nonfat dry milk powder to the dry ingredients.

Flavor with lemon extract or emulsion instead of vanilla and almond.

Yellow Cake
Reduce shortening to 45% (11 oz/325 g). Substitute whole eggs for egg whites, using the same total weight (67%). Use 2% vanilla (½ oz/15 g) and omit almond extract.

 Devil's Food Cake

Ingredients	U.S.		Metric	Percentage
Cake flour	1 lb	8 oz	700 g	100%
Cocoa		4 oz	125 g	17%
Salt		0.5 oz	15 g	2%
Baking powder		0.75 oz	20 g	3%
Baking soda		0.5 oz	15 g	2%
Emulsified shortening		14 oz	400 g	58%
Sugar	2 lb		925 g	133%
Skim milk	1 lb		475 g	67%
Vanilla		2 tsp	10 mL	1.5%
Skim milk		12 oz	350 g	50%
Eggs	1 lb		475 g	67%
Yield:	*7 lb*	*8 oz*	*3500 g*	*500%*

Per 1 ounce:
Calories, 90; Protein, 1 g; Fat, 4 g (39% cal.); Cholesterol, 15 mg;
Carbohydrates, 13 g; Fiber, 1 g; Sodium, 105 mg.

■ **P r o c e d u r e**

Mixing:
Two-stage method.
Scaling and baking:
See Table 32.1.

FOAMING METHODS

Sponge Cake (Genoise)

Ingredients	U.S.		Metric	Percentage
Eggs	2 lb	4 oz	1050 g	150%
Sugar	1 lb	8 oz	700 g	100%
Cake flour	1 lb	8 oz	700 g	100%
Butter, melted		8 oz	225 g	33%
Vanilla (or lemon flavor)		0.5 oz	15 mL	2%
Yield:	*5 lb 12 oz*		*2690 g*	*385%*

Per 1 ounce:
Calories, 90; Protein, 2 g; Fat, 3 g (31% cal.); Cholesterol, 55 mg;
Carbohydrates, 13 g; Fiber, 0 g; Sodium, 35 mg.

■ Procedure

Mixing:
Foaming method.
Scaling and baking:
See Table 32.1.

VARIATIONS

Chocolate Genoise
Substitute 4 oz (125 g) cocoa powder for 4 oz (125 g) flour. Use the vanilla, not the lemon flavor.

Sponge Roll or Jelly Roll
Prepare basic formula, but omit butter. Add the vanilla to the beaten eggs just before folding in the flour. Spread evenly in parchment-lined pans. When baked and cooled, trim the edges. Cut in half or into quarters. Spread each rectangle with desired filling (jelly, buttercream, etc.) and roll up so that the long side of the rectangle becomes the length of the roll. Ice or sprinkle with 6X sugar.

Milk and Butter Sponge

Ingredients	U.S.		Metric	Percentage
Sugar	1 lb	4 oz	625 g	125%
Eggs, whole		12 oz	375 g	75%
Egg yolks		4 oz	125 g	25%
Salt		0.25 oz (1¼ tsp)	7 g (6 mL)	1.5%
Cake flour	1 lb		500 g	100%
Baking powder		0.5 oz	15 g	3%
Skim milk		8 oz	250 g	50%
Butter		4 oz	125 g	25%
Vanilla		1 tbsp	15 mL	3%
Yield:	*4 lb*		*2037 g*	*407%*

Per 1 ounce:
Calories, 90; Protein, 2 g; Fat, 2.5 g (25% cal.); Cholesterol, 50 mg;
Carbohydrates, 15 g; Fiber, 0 g; Sodium, 90 mg.

■ Procedure

Mixing:
Sponge method. Heat the milk and butter until the butter is melted; fold into batter (step 5 in basic procedure).
Scaling and baking:
Cake layers; see Table 32.1.

Jelly Roll Sponge

Ingredients	U.S.	Metric	Percentage
Sugar	11 oz	325 g	100%
Eggs, Whole	10 oz	300 g	90%
Egg yolks	2 oz	65 g	20%
Salt	0.25 oz (1¼ tsp)	7 g (7 mL)	2%
Corn syrup	1.5 oz	45 g	14%
Water	1 oz	30 g	10%
Vanilla	1 tsp	5 mL	1.5%
Hot water	4 oz	125 g	36%
Cake flour	11 oz	325 g	100%
Baking powder	1 tsp	5 g (5 mL)	1.5%
Yield:	*2 lb 8 oz*	*1232 g*	*375%*

Procedure

Mixing:
Sponge method. Add the syrup, the first quantity of water, and the vanilla to the sugar and eggs in the first mixing stage. When the foam is completely whipped, stir in the second quantity of water.

Scaling and baking:
See Table 32.1. One recipe makes 1 sheet pan. Line the pans with greased paper. Immediately after baking, turn out of pan onto a sheet of parchment and remove the paper from the bottom of the cake. Spread with jelly and roll up tightly. When cool, dust with confectioners' sugar.

Per 1 ounce:
Calories, 80; Protein, 2 g; Fat, 1 g (12% cal.); Cholesterol, 50 mg; Carbohydrates, 15 g; Fiber, 0 g; Sodium, 40 mg.

Yellow Chiffon Cake

Ingredients	U.S.	Metric	Percentage
Cake flour	1 lb 4 oz	500 g	100%
Sugar	1 lb	400 g	80%
Salt	0.5 oz	12 g	2.5%
Baking powder	1 oz	25 g	5%
Vegetable oil	10 oz	250 g	50%
Egg yolks	10 oz	250 g	50%
Water	15 oz	375 g	75%
Vanilla	0.5 oz	12 mL	2.5%
Egg whites	1 lb 4 oz	500 g	100%
Sugar	10 oz	250 g	50%
Cream of tartar	1¼ tsp	2.5 g (5 mL)	0.5%
Yield:	*6 lb 7 oz*	*2576 g*	*515%*

Procedure

Mixing:
Chiffon method.
Scaling and baking:
Set Table 32.1.

VARIATION

Chocolate Chiffon Cake
Add 20% cocoa (4 oz/100 g); sift it with the flour. Increase the egg yolks to 60% (12 oz/300 g). Increase the water to 90% (1 lb 2 oz/450 g).

Per 1 ounce:
Calories, 90; Protein, 1 g; Fat, 3.5 g (38% cal.); Cholesterol, 35 mg; Carbohydrates, 12 g; Fiber, 0 g; Sodium, 95 mg.

Angel Food Cake

Ingredients	U.S.	Metric	Percentage
Egg whites	2 lb	1000 g	267%
Cream of tartar	0.25 oz (1 tbsp)	8 g (15 mL)	2%
Salt	1 tsp	5 g (5 mL)	1.5%
Sugar	1 lb	500 g	133%
Vanilla	2 tsp	10 mL	2.5%
Almond extract	1 tsp	5 mL	1.25%
Sugar	1 lb	500 g	133%
Cake flour	12 oz	375 g	100%
Yield:	*4 lb 12 oz*	*2403 g*	*640%*

Procedure

Mixing:
Angel food method.
Scaling and baking:
See Table 32.1.

VARIATION

Chocolate Angel Food Cake
Substitute 3 oz (90 g) cocoa for 3 oz (90 g) flour.

Per 1 ounce:
Calories, 70; Protein, 2 g; Fat, 0 g (0% cal.); Cholesterol, 0 mg; Carbohydrates, 16 g; Fiber, 0 g; Sodium, 50 mg.

ICINGS: PRODUCTION AND APPLICATION

PRODUCING AND HANDLING BASIC TYPES

Icings or frostings (the two terms mean the same thing) are sweet coatings for cakes and other baked goods. Icings have three main functions:

1. They improve the keeping qualities of the cake by forming a protective coating around it.
2. They contribute flavor and richness.
3. They improve appearance.

There are six basic kinds of icings:

Fondant	Fudge-type icing
Buttercream	Flat-type icing
Foam-type icing	Royal or decorator's icing

In addition, we consider two other preparations for cakes:

Glazes	Fillings

Use top-quality flavorings for icings so they enhance the cake rather than detract from it. Use moderation when adding flavorings and colors. Flavors should be light and delicate. Colors should be delicate, pastel shades—except chocolate, of course.

FONDANT

Fondant is a sugar syrup that is crystallized to a smooth, creamy white mass. It is familiar as the icing for napoleons, éclairs, petits fours, and some cakes. When applied, it sets up into a shiny, nonsticky coating.

Because it is difficult to make in the bakeshop, fondant is almost always purchased already prepared, either in ready-to-use moist form or in a dry form that requires only the addition of water.

BUTTERCREAM

Buttercream icings are light, smooth mixtures of fat and confectioners' sugar. They may also contain eggs to increase their smoothness or lightness. These popular icings are used for many kinds of cake. They are easily flavored and colored to suit a variety of purposes.

We consider three basic kinds of buttercream:

1. *Simple buttercreams* are made by creaming together fat and sugar to the desired consistency and lightness. A small quantity of egg whites may be whipped in.
    Decorator's buttercream is a simple buttercream used for making flowers and other cake decorations. It is creamed only a little because if too much air is beaten in, it would not be able to hold delicate shapes.
2. *Meringue-type buttercreams* are prepared by first beating egg whites and adding a boiling syrup or just sugar. Soft butter is then mixed into the meringue. This is a very light, smooth icing.

Guidelines for Using Fondant

1. Heat fondant over a warm water bath, stirring constantly, to thin the icing and make it pourable. *Do not heat over 100°F (38°C)*, or it will lose its shine.
2. If the fondant is still too thick, thin it with a little simple sugar syrup or water (simple syrup blends in more easily).
3. Add flavorings and colorings as desired.
4. To make *chocolate fondant*, stir melted bitter chocolate into warm fondant until the desired color and flavor are reached. Chocolate thickens the fondant, so the icing may require more thinning with sugar syrup.
5. Apply fondant by pouring it over the item or by dipping items into it.

3.   *French buttercreams* are similar to the meringue type, but the foam is made with egg yolks (and, sometimes, whole eggs) and boiling syrup. This is a very rich, light icing.

Butter, especially sweet, unsalted butter, is the preferred fat for buttercreams because of its flavor and melt-in-the-mouth quality. Icings made with shortening only can be unpleasant because the fat congeals and coats the inside of the mouth and does not melt. However, butter makes a less stable icing because it melts so easily. There are two ways around this problem:

1.   Use buttercreams in cool weather only.

2.   Blend a small quantity of emulsified shortening with the butter to stabilize it.

 ## Simple Buttercream

Yield: 3 lb 10 oz (1850 g)

U.S.	Metric	Ingredients
1 lb	500 g	Butter
8 oz	250 g	Shortening
2 lb	1 kg	Confectioners' sugar (10X)
2.5 oz	75 g	Egg whites, pasteurized
1 tsp	5 mL	Lemon juice
1 tbsp	15 mL	Vanilla

Per 1 ounce:
Calories, 150; Protein, 0 g; Fat, 10 g (58% cal.); Cholesterol, 15 mg; Carbohydrates, 16 g; Fiber, 0 g; Sodium, 65 mg.

■ P r o c e d u r e

1.   Cream together the butter, shortening, and sugar until well blended, using the paddle attachment.

2.   Add the egg whites, lemon juice, and vanilla. Blend in at medium speed. Then mix at high speed until light and fluffy.

V A R I A T I O N S

Decorator's Buttercream
Use 1 lb 8 oz (750 g) regular shortening, no butter. Omit lemon juice and vanilla. Reduce egg whites to 2 oz (60 g). Blend at low speed until smooth; do not whip.

Cream Cheese Icing
Substitute cream cheese for the butter and shortening. Omit egg whites. If necessary, thin the icing with cream or milk. If desired, flavor with grated lemon or orange zest instead of vanilla.

 ## Meringue-Type Buttercream

Yield: 5 lb 12 oz (2900 g)

U.S.	Metric	Ingredients
2 lb	1 kg	Sugar
8 fl oz	250 mL	Water
1 lb	500 g	Egg whites
2 lb	1 kg	Butter, soft
8 oz	250 g	Emulsified shortening
2 tsp	10 mL	Lemon juice
1 tbsp	15 mL	Vanilla

Per 1 ounce:
Calories, 130; Protein, 1 g; Fat, 10 g (67% cal.); Cholesterol, 20 mg; Carbohydrates, 10 g; Fiber, 0 g; Sodium, 90 mg.

■ P r o c e d u r e

1.   Combine the sugar and water in a saucepan. Bring to a boil, stirring to dissolve the sugar.

2.   Continue to boil until the syrup reaches a temperature of 240°F (115°C).

3.   While the syrup is boiling, beat the egg whites in a clean, grease-free bowl, using the whip attachment, until they form firm, moist peaks. Do not overbeat.

4.   As soon as the syrup reaches 240°F (115°C), pour it very slowly into the egg whites while the mixer is running at medium speed.

5.   Continue to beat until the meringue is cool and forms stiff peaks. (You have now made an Italian meringue. For more information, see Chapter 34.)

6.   With the mixer still running at medium speed, begin adding the butter, a little at a time. Add it just as fast as it can be absorbed by the meringue.

7.   When all the butter is beaten in, add the shortening in the same way.

8.   Beat in the lemon juice and vanilla.

French Buttercream

Yield: 5 lb 8 oz (2750 g)

U.S.	Metric	Ingredients
2 lb	1 kg	Sugar
8 fl oz	250 mL	Water
12 oz	375 g	Egg yolks
2 lb 8 oz	1.25 kg	Butter, soft
1 tbsp	15 mL	Vanilla

Per 1 ounce:
Calories, 150; Protein, 1 g; Fat, 12 g (71% cal.); Cholesterol, 80 mg; Carbohydrates, 10 g; Fiber, 0 g; Sodium, 110 mg.

■ Procedure

1. Combine the sugar and water in a saucepan. Bring to a boil, stirring to dissolve the sugar.
2. Continue to boil until the syrup reaches a temperature of 240°F (115°C).
3. While the syrup is boiling, beat the yolks with the whip attachment until they are thick and light.
4. As soon as the syrup reaches 240°F (115°C), pour it very slowly into the beaten yolks while the mixer is running at second speed.
5. Continue to beat until the mixture is cool and the yolks are very light and thick.
6. With the mixer still running, add the butter, a little at a time. Add it just as fast as it can be absorbed by the mixture.
7. Beat in the vanilla. If the icing is too soft, refrigerate until it is firm enough to spread.

V A R I A T I O N S

Flavored buttercreams are made by adding the desired flavoring to any of the basic buttercream recipes. In addition to the two variations given below, extracts and emulsions such as lemon, orange, and almond may be used.

Chocolate Buttercream
Add 4–5 oz (125–150 g) sweet chocolate, melted and cooled, to each 1 pound (500 g) buttercream.

Coffee Buttercream
For each 1 pound (500 g) buttercream, add 1½ tbsp (22 mL) instant coffee dissolved in 2 tsp (10 mL) hot water.

FOAM-TYPE ICING

Foam icings, sometimes called *boiled icings*, are simply meringues made with a boiling syrup. Some also contain stabilizing ingredients like gelatin.

Foam-type icings should be applied thickly to cakes and left in peaks and swirls.

These icings are not stable. They should be used the day they are prepared. Italian meringue, discussed in Chapter 34, is the simplest foam-type icing. Follow the recipe on page 1000 but add 8 ounces (250 g) corn syrup to the sugar and water for the boiled syrup. The meringue is usually flavored with vanilla.

FLAT ICING

Flat icings, also called *water icings*, are simply mixtures of 10X sugar, water, and, sometimes, corn syrup and flavoring. They are used mostly for coffee cakes, Danish pastry, and sweet rolls. Flat icings are warmed to 100°F (38°C) for application and are handled like fondant.

FUDGE-TYPE ICING

Fudge icings are rich cooked icings. Many are made somewhat like candy. Fudge icings are heavy and thick, and they may be flavored with a variety of ingredients. They are used on cupcakes, layer cakes, loaf cakes, and sheet cakes.

Fudge icings are stable and hold up well on cakes and in storage. Stored icings must be covered tightly to prevent drying and crusting.

To use stored fudge icing, warm it in a double boiler until soft enough to spread.

Fudge-type icings do not necessarily contain chocolate. Plain white fudge icings may be flavored with vanilla, almond, maple, coffee, or other desired flavoring.

Flat Icing

Yield: 2 lb 8 oz (1250 g)

U.S.	Metric	Ingredients
2 lb	1 kg	Confectioners' sugar (10X or 6X)
6 fl oz	180 g	Water, hot
2 fl oz	60 g	Corn syrup
1½ tsp	8 mL	Vanilla

■ P r o c e d u r e

1. Mix all ingredients together until smooth.
2. To use, place desired amount in a double boiler. Warm to 100°F (38°C) and apply to the product to be iced.

Per 1 ounce:
Calories, 90; Protein, 0 g; Fat, 0 g (0% cal.); Cholesterol, 0 mg; Carbohydrates, 24 g; Fiber, 0 g; Sodium, 0 mg.

Caramel Fudge Icing

Yield: 4 lb (2 kg)

U.S.	Metric	Ingredients
3 lb	1500 g	Brown sugar
1½ pt	750 mL	Milk
12 oz	375 g	Butter or shortening
¼ tsp	1 mL	Salt
1 tbsp	15 mL	Vanilla

■ P r o c e d u r e

1. Combine the sugar and milk in a saucepan. Bring to a boil, stirring to dissolve the sugar. Using a brush dipped in water, wash down the sides of the saucepan to prevent sugar crystals from forming. (See "Sugar Cooking," Chapter 35.)
2. Boil the mixture slowly, without stirring, until it reaches 240°F (115°C).
3. Pour the mixture into the bowl of a mixer. Add the butter and salt. Mix in with the paddle attachment.
4. Turn off the machine. Let the mixture cool to 110°F (43°C).
5. Add the vanilla and turn the machine on low speed. Beat the icing until it is smooth and creamy in texture. If it is too thick, thin it with a little cream or milk.
6. Spread on cooled cake while the icing is warm, or rewarm it in a double boiler.

Per 1 ounce:
Calories, 130; Protein, 0 g; Fat, 4.5 g (33% cal.); Cholesterol, 15 mg; Carbohydrates, 21 g; Fiber, 0 g; Sodium, 65 mg.

Quick White Fudge Icing

Yield: 5 lb 30 oz (2600 g)

U.S.	Metric	Ingredients
8 fl oz	250 mL	Water
4 oz	125 g	Butter
4 oz	125 g	Emulsified shortening
3 oz	90 g	Corn syrup
½ tsp	2 mL	Salt
4 lb	2 kg	Confectioners' sugar (10X or 6X)
1 tbsp	15 mL	Vanilla

■ P r o c e d u r e

1. Place the water, butter, shortening, syrup, and salt in a saucepan. Bring to a boil.

2. Sift the sugar into the bowl of a mixer.
3. Using the paddle attachment and with the machine running on low speed, add the boiling water mixture. Blend until smooth. Icing will become lighter the more it is mixed.
4. Blend in the vanilla.
5. Use while still warm, or rewarm in a double boiler. If necessary, thin with hot water.

Per 1 ounce:
Calories, 110; Protein, 0 g; Fat, 2.5 g (20% cal.); Cholesterol, 5 mg; Carbohydrates, 23 g; Fiber, 0 g; Sodium, 25 mg.

V A R I A T I O N

Quick Chocolate Fudge Icing
Omit the butter in the basic recipe. Beat in 12 oz (375 g) melted unsweetened chocolate after the boiling water has been added. Thin with more hot water as needed.

Cocoa Fudge Icing

Yield: 4 lb 12 oz (2375 g)

U.S.	Metric	Ingredients
2 lb	1 kg	Granulated sugar
10 oz	300 g	Corn syrup
8 fl oz	250 mL	Water
1 tsp	5 mL	Salt
8 oz	250 g	Butter or part butter and part emulsified shortening
1 lb	500 g	Confectioners' sugar (10X or 6X)
6 oz	175 g	Cocoa
to taste	to taste	Vanilla
as needed	as needed	Hot water

Per 1 ounce:
Calories, 110; Protein, 0 g; Fat, 2.5 g (20% cal.); Cholesterol, 5 mg; Carbohydrates, 22 g; Fiber, 1 g; Sodium, 60 mg.

Procedure

1. Combine the sugar, syrup, water, and salt in a saucepan. Bring to a boil, stirring to dissolve the sugar. Boil the mixture until it reaches 240°F (115°C). (See "Sugar Cooking," Chapter 35.)
2. While the sugar is cooking, mix the fat, sugar, and cocoa until evenly combined, using the paddle attachment of the mixer.
3. With the machine running at low speed, very slowly pour in the hot syrup.
4. Mix in the vanilla. Continue to beat until the icing is smooth, creamy, and spreadable. If necessary, thin with a little hot water.
5. Use while still warm, or rewarm in a double boiler.

VARIATION

Vanilla Fudge Icing
Use evaporated milk or light cream instead of water for the syrup. Omit cocoa. Adjust consistency with additional confectioners' sugar (to thicken) or water (to thin). Other flavorings may be used in place of vanilla, such as almond, maple, peppermint, or coffee.

ROYAL ICING

Royal icing, also called *decorating* or *decorator's icing*, is similar to flat icings except that it is much thicker and is made with egg whites, which make it hard and brittle when dry. It is used almost exclusively for decorative work.

To prepare royal icing:

1. Place the desired amount of 10X sugar in a mixing bowl. Add a small quantity of cream of tartar (for whiteness)—about ⅛ teaspoon per pound of sugar (1 g per kilogram).
2. Beat in egg white, a little at a time, until the sugar forms a smooth paste. You will need 2 to 3 ounces egg whites per pound of sugar (125 g per kilogram).
3. Keep unused icing covered with a damp cloth at all times to prevent hardening.

GLAZES

Glazes are thin, glossy, transparent coatings that give shine to baked products and help prevent drying.

The simplest glaze is a sugar syrup or diluted corn syrup brushed onto coffee cakes or Danish while the glaze is hot. See Chapter 30 for recipe (p. 922). Syrup glazes may contain gelatin or waxy maize starch. Fruit glazes, the most popular being apricot, are available commercially prepared. They are melted, thinned with a little water, and brushed on while hot.

Fruit glazes may also be made by melting apricot or other preserves and forcing them through a strainer.

One of the most common uses of glazes in cake-making is to coat the fruit arranged on the top of fruit tortes (see p. 943).

FILLINGS

Fillings are sometimes used instead of icings between cake layers. Fillings are also used in such products as jelly rolls, Danish, and other pastries.

1. **Fruit fillings.**
   Fruit fillings may be cooked or uncooked.

   Cooked fruit fillings are chopped or puréed fruits or fruit juices thickened with starch or eggs. They are prepared somewhat like pie fillings (see Chapter 34).

   Uncooked fruit fillings include jellies and preserves and dried fruits that have been ground and flavored (see recipes in Chapter 30). Fresh fruits, such as the strawberries in strawberry shortcake, are also used.

   Many ready-to-use fruit fillings are on the market.

2. **Cream fillings.**
   Cream fillings include pastry cream (recipes in Chapter 35) and various pudding-type preparations.

   Desserts with cream fillings should be assembled as close to service time as possible and kept refrigerated to avoid health hazards.

3. **Whipped cream.**
   Whipped cream is used as a dessert topping, filling, and frosting. See page 810 for instructions on whipping and handling heavy cream.

   Artificial whipped toppings resemble whipped cream in appearance. They should be used only if your customers actually like them.

ASSEMBLING AND ICING CAKES

SELECTION OF ICING

The flavor, texture, and color of the icing must be compatible with the cake.

1. **In general, use heavy frostings with heavy cakes and light frostings with light cakes.**
   For example, ice angel food cakes with a simple flat icing, fondant, or a light, fluffy boiled icing.

   High-ratio cakes go well with buttercreams and fudge-type icings.

   Shortened sponge layer cakes (genoise) are often combined with fruits or fruit fillings, light French or meringue-type buttercream, whipped cream, or flavored fondant.

2. **Use the best-quality flavorings, and use them sparingly. The flavor of the frosting should not be stronger than the cake.**
   Fudge-type icings may be flavored more strongly, as long as the flavor is of good quality.

3. **Use coloring sparingly. Light, pastel shades are more appetizing than loud colors.**
   Paste colors give the best results. Mix a little color with a small portion of the icing, then use this icing to color the rest.

SMALL CAKES

1. Cupcakes are iced by dipping the tops in a soft icing. Twist the cakes slightly and pull them out quickly in one smooth motion.

   Cupcakes may also be iced by spreading icing on with a spatula. Practice is necessary to develop speed and efficiency.

2. Petits fours are tiny cakes cut from sheet cakes. Select a cake that doesn't crumble easily. Carefully cut it into desired shapes. Remove all crumbs and place the cakes on a rack over a sheet pan. Ice by pouring fondant or flat icing over them to cover completely.

Procedure for Assembling Layer Cakes

1. Cool cake layers completely before assembling and icing.
2. Trim layers, if necessary.
   - Remove any ragged edges.
   - Slightly rounded tops are easily covered by icing, but excessively large bumps may have to be cut off.
   - If desired, layers may be split in half horizontally. This makes the cake higher and increases the proportion of filling to cake. See Figure 32.2.
3. Brush all crumbs from cakes. Loose crumbs make the icing process difficult.
4. Place the bottom layer upside down (to give a flat surface for the filling) on a cardboard cake circle of the same diameter. Place the cake in the center of a cake turntable.

   If a cake circle or turntable is not available, place the cake on a serving plate and slip sheets of waxed paper or parchment under the edges of the cake to keep the plate clean.
5. Spread filling on the bottom layer out to the edges. If the filling is different from the icing for the outside of the cake, be careful not to spread the filling over the edges.

   Use the proper amount of filling. If applied too heavily, it will ooze out when the top layer is set in place.
6. Place the top layer on the bottom layer, right side up.
7. Ice the cake:
   - If a thin or light icing is used, pour or spread the icing onto the center of the cake. Then spread it to the edges and down the sides with a spatula.
   - If a heavy icing is used, it may be necessary to spread the sides first, then place a good quantity of icing in the center of the top and push it to the edges with the spatula.

   Pushing the icing rather than pulling or dragging it with the spatula prevents pulling up crumbs and getting them mixed with the icing.

   Use enough icing to cover the entire cake generously, but not excessively, with an even layer.

   Smooth the icing with the spatula or leave it textured or swirled, as desired.

   The finished, iced cake should have a perfectly level top and perfectly straight, even sides.

Figure 32.2

Cake layers may be split in half horizontally, using a long-bladed, serrated knife.

SHEET CAKES

Sheet cakes are ideal for volume service because they require little labor to bake, ice, and decorate, and they keep well as long as they are uncut.

For special occasions, sheet cakes are sometimes decorated as a single unit with a design or picture in colored icing, a "Happy Special Occasion" message, and so on. It is more common, however, to ice them for individual service, as in the following procedure.

Procedure for Icing Sheet Cakes

1. Turn out the cake onto the bottom of another sheet pan or tray, as described on page 946. Cool the cake thoroughly.
2. Trim the edges evenly with a serrated knife.
3. Brush all crumbs from the cake.
4. Place a quantity of icing in the center of the cake. With a spatula, push the icing to the edges. Smooth the top with the spatula, giving the entire cake an even layer of icing.
5. With a long knife or spatula, mark the entire cake off into portions, as in Figure 32.3, by pressing the back of the knife lightly into the icing. Do not cut the cake.
6. Using a paper cone or pastry bag fitted with a star tube, pipe a rosette or swirl of icing onto the center of each marked-off portion, or select another decoration, as desired. Whatever decorations you use, keep them simple, and make them the same for every portion. The finished sheet cake will resemble that in Figure 32.4.
7. Hold for service. Cut as close as possible to service time to keep the cake from drying.

18 × 26 inch sheets

6 × 8 = 48 portions

8 × 8 = 64 portions

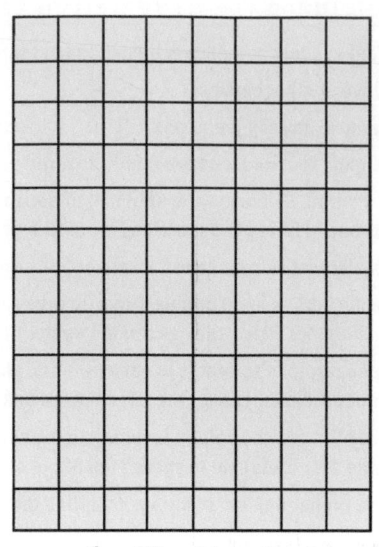

8 × 12 = 96 portions

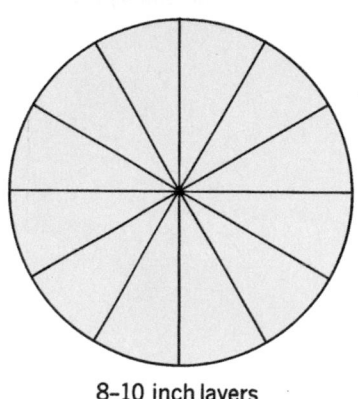

8–10 inch layers
12 portions

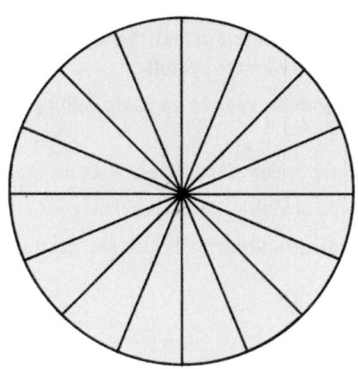

10–12 inch layers
16 portions

Figure 32.3
Cake-cutting guides for sheet cakes and round layer cakes. For sheets measuring 13 x 18 in. (33 x 46 cm), simply divide the above diagrams for full-sized sheet cakes in half.

Figure 32.4
A finished sheet cake marked off into portions and decorated so each portion is identical.

■ TERMS FOR REVIEW

creaming method	angel food method	fondant	fudge icing
two-stage method	chiffon method	buttercream	royal icing
blending method	high-fat cakes	foam icing	glaze
foaming method	low-fat cakes	flat icing	

■ QUESTIONS FOR DISCUSSION

1. Briefly list the steps in each of the four basic cake-mixing methods presented in this chapter.

2. What are the reasons, in the creaming method, for creaming the butter and sugar until the mixture is light and fluffy?

3. In both the creaming method and the two-stage method, scraping down the sides of the bowl is emphasized. Why is this necessary?

4. What might the finished product be like if you tried to mix a low-fat cake by the two-stage method? Explain.

5. Examine the following cake formulas and indicate which mixing method you would use for each.

6. What is the most important rule to consider when using fondant?

7. Compare the keeping qualities of simple buttercreams and meringue-type buttercreams.

8. List the steps in assembling and icing a three-layer cake.

Cake 1		
2 lb	Cake flour	1 kg
1 lb 2 oz	Emulsified shortening	525 g
1 oz	Salt	30 g
1.5 oz	Baking powder	45 g
2 lb 8 oz	Fine granulated sugar	1250 g
1 lb	Skim milk	500 g
1 lb 5 oz	Whole eggs	650 g
10 oz	Skim milk	300 g

Cake 2		
3 lb	Whole eggs	1.5 kg
1 lb	Egg yolks	500 g
2 lb 4 oz	Sugar	1125 g
2 lb	Cake flour	1 kg
6 oz	Cornstarch	175 g
6 oz	Melted butter	175 g

Cake 3		
1 lb	Butter	500 g
8 oz	Shortening	250 g
4 lb	Sugar	2 kg
1 oz	Vanilla	30 g
1 lb 4 oz	Whole eggs	625 g
3 lb 8 oz	Cake flour	1750 g
10 oz	Cocoa powder	300 g
1.5 oz	Baking soda	45 g
3 lb	Buttermilk	1.5 kg
1 lb 8 oz	Water	750 g

CHAPTER 33
Cookies

The word *cookie* means "small cake," and that's exactly what a cookie is. In fact, some cookies are made from cake batter. For some products, such as certain kinds of brownies, it's difficult to know whether to classify them as cakes or cookies.

Most cookie formulas, however, call for less liquid than cake formulas do. Cookie doughs range from soft to very stiff, unlike the thinner batters for cakes. This difference in moisture content means some differences in mixing methods, although the basic procedures are much like those for cakes.

The most apparent differences between cakes and cookies are in the makeup. Because most cookies are individually formed or shaped, a great deal of hand labor is involved. Learning correct methods and practicing diligently are essential for efficiency.

COOKIE CHARACTERISTICS AND THEIR CAUSES

Cookies come in an infinite variety of shapes, sizes, flavors, and textures. Characteristics that are desirable in some are not desirable in others. For example, we want some cookies to be crisp and others to be soft. We want some to hold their shape and others to spread during baking. In order to produce the characteristics we want and to correct faults, it is useful to know what causes these characteristics.

CRISPNESS

Cookies are crisp if they are very low in moisture. The following factors contribute to crispness:

1. Low proportion of liquid in the mix. Most crisp cookies are made from a stiff dough.
2. High sugar and fat content.
3. Evaporation of moisture during baking due to high temperatures and/or long baking.
4. Small size or thin shape, so the cookies dry quickly during baking.
5. Proper storage. Crisp cookies can become soft if they absorb moisture.

SOFTNESS

Softness is the opposite of crispness, so it has the opposite causes, as follows:
1. High proportion of liquid in mix.
2. Low sugar and fat.
3. Honey, molasses, or corn syrup included in formulas. These sugars are **hygroscopic**, which means they readily absorb moisture from the air or from their surroundings.
4. Underbaking.
5. Large size or thick shape. The cookies retain moisture.
6. Proper storage. Soft cookies can become stale and dry if not tightly covered or wrapped.

CHEWINESS

Moisture is necessary for chewiness, but other factors are also required. In other words, all chewy cookies are soft, but not all soft cookies are chewy.
1. High sugar and liquid content, but low fat content.
2. High proportion of eggs.
3. Strong flour, or gluten developed during mixing.

SPREAD

Spread is desirable in some cookies, while others must hold their shape. Several factors contribute to spread or lack of spread.
1. **Sugar.**
   High sugar content increases spread. Coarse granulated sugar increases spread, whereas fine sugar or confectioners' sugar reduces spread.
2. **Leavening.**
   High baking soda or baking ammonia content encourages spread. So does long creaming, which incorporates air.

After reading this chapter, you should be able to

1. **List the factors responsible for crispness, softness, chewiness, and spread in cookies.**
2. **Demonstrate the three basic cookie mixing methods.**
3. **Prepare the seven basic cookie types: dropped, bagged, rolled, molded, icebox, bar, and sheet.**
4. **Prepare pans for, bake, and cool cookies.**

3. **Temperature.**
Low oven temperature increases spread. High temperature decreases spread because the cookie sets up before it has a chance to spread too much.

4. **Liquid.**
A slack batter—that is, one with a high liquid content—spreads more than a stiff dough.

5. **Flour.**
Strong flour or activation of gluten decreases spread.

6. **Pan grease.**
Cookies spread more if baked on a heavily greased pan.

MIXING METHODS

Cookie-mixing methods are much like cake-mixing methods. The major difference is that less liquid is usually incorporated, so mixing is somewhat easier.

Less liquid means that gluten is less developed by the mixing. Also, a smooth, uniform mix is easier to obtain.

There are three basic cookie mixing methods:

1. One-stage
2. Creaming
3. Sponge

These methods are subject to many variations due to differences in formulas. The general procedures are as follows. Be sure, however, to follow the exact instructions when a formula indicates a variation in the procedure.

ONE-STAGE METHOD

The **one-stage method** is the counterpart of the blending or two-stage cake-mixing method, discussed in the previous chapter. Cake batters have more liquid, so it must be added in two or more stages in order to blend uniformly. Low-moisture cookies, on the other hand, can be mixed all in one stage.

CREAMING METHOD

The **creaming method** for cookies is nearly identical to the creaming method for cakes. Because cookies require less liquid, it is not necessary to add the liquid alternately with the flour. It can be added all at once.

SPONGE METHOD

The **sponge method** for cookies is essentially the same as the egg-foam methods for cakes. The procedure varies considerably, depending on the ingredients. Batches should be kept small because the batter is delicate.

Procedure for One-Stage Method

1. Scale ingredients accurately. Have all ingredients at room temperature.
2. Place all ingredients in mixer. With the paddle attachment, mix at low speed until uniformly blended. Scrape down the sides of the bowl as necessary.

Procedure for Creaming Method

1. Scale ingredients accurately. Have all ingredients at room temperature.
2. Place the fat, sugar, salt, and spices in the mixing bowl. With the paddle attachment, cream these ingredients at low speed.

   For light cookies, cream until the mix is light and fluffy, incorporating more air for leavening.

   For a dense, chewy cookie, cream only slightly.
3. Add the eggs and liquid, if any, and blend in at low speed.
4. Sift in the flour and leavening. Mix until just combined.

Procedure for Sponge Method

1. Scale all ingredients accurately. Have all ingredients at room temperature, or warm the eggs slightly for greater volume, as for sponge cakes.
2. Following the procedure given in the formula used, whip the eggs (whole, yolks, or whites) and the sugar to the proper stage: soft peaks for whites, thick and light for whole eggs or yolks.
3. Fold in the remaining ingredients as specified in the recipe. Be careful not to overmix or to deflate the eggs.

TYPES AND MAKEUP METHODS

We can classify cookie types by makeup method as well as by mixing method. Grouping by the makeup method is perhaps more useful from the point of view of production because mixing methods are relatively simple, whereas makeup procedures vary considerably.

In this section, we present basic procedures for producing seven cookie types:

1. Dropped
2. Bagged
3. Rolled
4. Molded
5. Icebox
6. Bar
7. Sheet

No matter what makeup method you use, follow one important rule: *Make all cookies of uniform size and thickness.* This is essential for even baking. Because baking times are so short, small cookies may burn before large ones are done.

DROPPED COOKIES

Dropped cookies are made from a soft dough or batter. They are fast and easy to make up. Many sponge or foam-type batters are made up as dropped cookies.

1. Select the proper size scoop for accurate portioning.

   A No. 30 scoop makes a large cookie, about 1 oz (30 g).
   A No. 40 scoop makes a medium cookie.
   Nos. 50, 60, or small scoops make small cookies.

2. Drop the cookies onto the prepared baking sheets. Allow enough space between cookies for spreading.

3. Rich cookies spread by themselves. However, if the formula requires it, flatten the mounds of batter slightly with a weight dipped in sugar.

BAGGED COOKIES

Bagged cookies, or pressed cookies, are also made from soft doughs. The dough must be soft enough to be forced through a pastry bag but stiff enough to hold its shape.

1. Fit a pastry bag with a tip of the desired size and shape. Fill the bag with the cookie dough. Review Figure 18.3 for tips on use of the pastry bag.

2. Press out cookies of desired shape and size directly onto prepared cookie sheets.

ROLLED COOKIES

Rolled cookies, which are cut from a stiff dough, are not often made in commercial food service because they require excessive labor. Also, scraps are always left over after cutting. When rerolled, these scraps make inferior, tough cookies.

1. Chill dough thoroughly.

2. Roll dough to ⅛ inch (3 mm) thick on a floured canvas or floured workbench. Use as little flour as possible for dusting because the flour can toughen the cookies.

3. Cut out cookies with cookie cutters and place on prepared baking sheets. Cut as close together as possible to reduce the quantity of scraps.

MOLDED COOKIES

The first part of the procedure for **molded cookies** (steps 1 and 2) is simply a fast and fairly accurate way of dividing the dough into equal portions. Each piece is then molded into the desired shape. This usually consists of simply flattening the pieces out with a weight. For some traditional cookies, special molds are used to flatten the dough and, at the same time, stamp it with a design.

The pieces may also be shaped by hand into crescents, fingers, or other shapes.

1. Roll the dough into long cylinders about 1 inch (2.5 cm) thick, or whatever size is required. (Refrigerate the dough if it is too soft to handle.)

2. With a knife or bench scraper, cut the roll into 1-ounce (30-g) pieces, or whatever size is required.

3. Place the pieces on prepared baking sheets, leaving 2 inches (5 cm) of space between them.

4. Flatten cookies with a weight (such as a can) dipped in granulated sugar after pressing each cookie.

    A fork is sometimes used for flattening the dough, as for peanut butter cookies.

5. Alternative method: After step 2, shape the dough by hand into desired shapes.

ICEBOX COOKIES

The **icebox method**, or *refrigerator method*, is ideal for operations that wish to have freshly baked cookies on hand at all times. The rolls of dough may be made up in advance and stored. Cookies can easily be cut and baked as needed.

1. Scale dough into pieces of uniform size, from 1½ pounds (700 g), if you are making small cookies, to 3 pounds (1400 g), for large cookies.

2. Form the dough into cylinders from 1 to 2 inches (2.5 to 5 cm) in diameter, depending on the size cookie desired.

    For accurate portioning, it is important to make all the cylinders of dough the same thickness and length.

3. Wrap the cylinders in parchment or waxed paper, place them on sheet pans, and refrigerate overnight.

4. Unwrap the dough and cut into slices of uniform thickness. The exact thickness required depends on the size of the cookie and how much the dough spreads during baking. The usual range is from ⅛ to ½ inch (3 to 12 mm).

    A slicing machine is recommended for ensuring even thickness. Doughs containing nuts or fruits should be sliced by hand with a knife.

5. Place the slices on prepared baking sheets, allowing 2 inches (5 cm) of space between cookies.

BAR COOKIES

Bar cookies are so called because the dough is shaped into long bars, which are baked and then cut. After cutting, they may be baked again, as in the case of biscotti, which means "twice baked." Do not confuse bar cookies with sheet cookies (see below), which are often called bars by consumers.

1. Scale the dough into 1¾-pound (800-g) units (1-pound units, or 500-g units, may be used for smaller cookies).

2. Shape the pieces of dough into cylinders the length of the sheet pans. Place three strips on each greased pan, spacing them well apart.

3. Flatten the dough with the fingers into strips about 3 to 4 inches wide and about ¼ inch thick (8 to 10 cm wide, 6 mm thick).

4. If required, brush with egg wash.

5. Bake as directed in the formula.

6. After baking, while cookies are still warm, cut each strip into bars about 1¾ inches (4.5 cm) wide.

SHEET COOKIES

Sheet cookies vary so much that it is nearly impossible to give a single procedure for all of them. Some of them are almost like sheet cakes, only denser and richer. They may even be iced like sheet cakes. Others consist of two or three layers added and baked in separate stages. The following procedure is a general guideline only.

1. Spread the cookie mixture into prepared sheet pans. Make sure the thickness is even.
2. If required, add topping or brush with an egg wash.
3. Bake as directed. Cool.
4. Apply icing or topping, if any.
5. Cut into individual squares or rectangles.

PANNING, BAKING, AND COOLING

PREPARING THE PANS

1. Use clean, unwarped pans.
2. Lining the sheets with parchment or silicone paper is fast, and it eliminates the necessity of greasing the pans.
3. A heavily greased pan increases the spread of the cookie. A greased and floured pan decreases spread.
4. Some high-fat cookies can be baked on ungreased pans.

BAKING

1. Most cookies are baked at a relatively high temperature for a short time.
2. Too low a temperature increases spreading and may produce hard, dry, pale cookies.
3. Too high a temperature decreases spreading and may burn the edges or bottoms.
4. Even one minute of overbaking can burn cookies, so watch them closely. The heat of the pan continues to bake the cookies even after they are removed from the oven.
5. Doneness is indicated by color. The edges and bottoms should just be turning a light golden color.
6. With some rich doughs, burnt bottoms may be a problem. In this case, double-pan the cookies by placing the sheet pan on a second pan of the same size.

COOLING

1. Remove the cookies from the pans while they are still warm, or they may stick.
2. If the cookies are very soft, do not remove them from the pans until they are cool enough and firm enough to handle. Cookies may be soft when hot but become crisp when cool.
3. Do not cool cookies too rapidly or in cold drafts, or they may crack.
4. Cool completely before storing.

Chocolate Chip Cookies

Ingredients	U.S.		Metric	Percentage
Butter and/or shortening	10 oz		300 g	50%
Granulated sugar	8 oz		240 g	40%
Brown sugar	8 oz		240 g	40%
Salt	0.25 oz (1½ tsp)		8 g (7 mL)	1.25%
Eggs	6 oz		175 g	30%
Vanilla	2 tsp		10 mL	1.5%
Pastry flour	1 lb 4 oz		600 g	100%
Baking soda	0.25 oz (1½ tsp)		8 g (7 mL)	1.25%
Chocolate chips	1 lb 4 oz		600 g	100%
Chopped walnuts or pecans	8 oz		240 g	40%
Yield:	*5 lb*		*2421 g*	*404%*

Per 1 ounce:
Calories, 130; Protein, 2 g; Fat, 7 g (47% cal.); Cholesterol, 15 mg;
Carbohydrates, 16 g; Fiber, 2 g; Sodium, 85 mg.

■ P r o c e d u r e

Mixing:
Creaming method. Blend in chocolate chips and nuts last.
Makeup:
Drop method. Use greased or parchment-lined baking sheets.
Baking:
375°F (190°C), 8–12 minutes, depending on size.

V A R I A T I O N S

Brown Sugar Nut Cookies
Omit granulated sugar and use 100% (1 lb 4 oz/600 g) brown sugar. Omit chocolate chips and increase nuts to 100% (1 lb 4 oz/600 g).

Oatmeal Raisin Cookies

Ingredients	U.S.		Metric	Percentage
Butter and/or shortening	8 oz		250 g	67%
Brown sugar	1 lb		500 g	133%
Salt	1 tsp		5 g (5 mL)	1.5%
Eggs	4 oz		125 g	33%
Vanilla	2 tsp		10 mL	3%
Milk	1 oz		30 g	8%
Pastry flour	12 oz		375 g	100%
Baking powder	0.5 oz (1 tbsp)		15 g	4%
Baking soda	0.25 oz (1½ tsp)		8 g	2%
Rolled oats (quick cooking)	10 oz		300 g	83%
Raisins (see note)	8 oz		250 g	67%
Yield:	*3 lb 11 oz*		*1858 g*	*500%*

■ P r o c e d u r e

Mixing:
Creaming method. Combine oats with other dry ingredients after they are sifted. Mix raisins into dough last.
Makeup:
Drop method. Use greased or parchment-lined baking sheets.
Baking:
375°F (190°C), 10–12 minutes, depending on size.

Per 1 ounce:
Calories, 110; Protein, 2 g; Fat, 4 g (31% cal.);
Cholesterol, 15 mg; Carbohydrates, 18 g; Fiber, 1 g;
Sodium, 135 mg.

Note: If raisins are hard and dry, soak them in hot water 30 minutes, drain, and dry well before adding to cookie dough.

Tea Cookies

Ingredients	U.S.	Metric	Percentage
Butter or half butter and half shortening	1 lb	500 g	67%
Granulated sugar	8 oz	250 g	33%
Confectioners' sugar	4 oz	125 g	17%
Eggs	6 oz	175 g	25%
Vanilla (or almond extract)	1½ tsp	8 mL	1%
Cake flour	1 lb 8 oz	750 g	100%
Yield:	*3 lb 10 oz*	*1823 g*	*243%*

Per 1 ounce:
Calories, 130; Protein, 1 g; Fat, 7 g (50% cal.); Cholesterol, 30 mg; Carbohydrates, 15 g; Fiber, 0 g; Sodium, 70 mg.

■ P r o c e d u r e

Mixing:
Creaming method.
Makeup:
Bagged method. Make small cookies, about 1 in. (2.5 cm) in diameter, using a star tube or plain tube. Bag out into ungreased or parchment-lined baking sheets.
Baking:
375°F (190°C), about 10 minutes.

V A R I A T I O N S

Almond Tea Cookies
Add 17% (4 oz/125 g) almond paste. Blend it thoroughly with the sugar before adding the butter.

Sandwich-Type Cookies
Select cookies with the same size and shape. Turn half of them over and dot the centers of the flat sides with small amount of jam or fudge icing. Sandwich with the remaining cookies.

Chocolate Tea Cookies
Substitute 6 oz (175 g) cocoa for 6 oz (175 g) flour.

Ladyfingers

Ingredients	U.S.	Metric	Percentage
Egg yolks	6 oz	180 g	60%
Sugar	3 oz	90 g	30%
Egg whites	9 oz	270 g	90%
Sugar	5 oz	150 g	50%
Lemon juice	½ tsp	1 mL	0.4%
Pastry flour	10 oz	300 g	100%
Yield:	*2 lb 1 oz*	*990 g*	*340%*
(enough for about 6 dozen ladyfingers)			

Per ladyfinger:
Calories, 35; Protein, 1 g; Fat, 1 g (24% cal.); Cholesterol, 30 mg; Carbohydrates, 6 g; Fiber, 1 g; Sodium, 5 mg.

■ P r o c e d u r e

Mixing:
Sponge method.
1. Beat egg yolks 1 minute at medium speed using whip attachment. With machine running, gradually add the first amount of sugar. Continue to whip until thick and light.
2. Whip the egg whites until they form soft peaks. Add the sugar and lemon juice and beat until stiff but still moist.
3. Sift the flour and fold into the yolks.
4. Fold the whites into the batter.

Makeup:
Bagged method. Use plain tube. Bag out strips measuring 3 inches x ¾ in. (7½ x 2 cm) onto pans that have been lined with parchment or greased and floured.
Baking:
375°F (190°C), about 10 minutes.

Coconut Macaroons (Meringue Type)

Ingredients	U.S.		Metric
Egg whites		8 oz	250 g
Cream or tartar		1 tsp	2 g (5 mL)
Sugar	1 lb	4 oz	625 g
Vanilla (or rum flavor)		0.5 oz	15 mL
Macaroon coconut	1 lb		500 g
Yield:	*2 lb 12 oz*		*1392 g*

Per 1 ounce:
Calories, 120; Protein, 1 g; Fat, 7 g (48% cal.); Cholesterol, 0 mg; Carbohydrates, 16 g; Fiber, 2 g; Sodium, 15 mg.

■ P r o c e d u r e

Mixing:
Sponge method.
1. Beat the egg whites and cream of tartar until they form soft peaks. Gradually beat in the sugar. Continue to beat until stiff and glossy.
2. Fold in the coconut.

Makeup:
Bagged method. Bag out with a star rube onto parchment-lined baking sheets.

Baking:
300°F (150°C), about 30 minutes.

Sugar Cookies

Ingredients	U.S.		Metric	Percentage
Butter and/or shortening	1 lb		500 g	40%
Sugar	1 lb	4 oz	625 g	50%
Salt		2 tsp	10 g (10 mL)	0.9%
Eggs		4 oz	125 g	10%
Milk		4 oz	125 g	10%
Vanilla		0.5 oz	15 mL	1.25%
Cake flour	2 lb	8 oz	1250 g	100%
Baking powder		1.25 oz	35 g	3%
Yield:	*5 lb*	*5 oz*	*2685 g*	*215%*

Per 1 ounce:
Calories, 120; Protein, 1 g; Fat, 4.5 g (36% cal.); Cholesterol, 15 mg; Carbohydrates, 17 g; Fiber, 0 g; Sodium, 150 mg.

■ P r o c e d u r e

Mixing:
Creaming method.

Makeup:
Rolled method. Before cutting the rolled-out dough, wash with milk and sprinkle with sugar. Use greased or parchment-lined baking sheets.

Baking:
375°F (190°C), 8–10 minutes.

V A R I A T I O N S

Lemon rind, extract, or emulsion may be used in place of vanilla.

Rolled Brown Sugar Cookies
Increase butter to 50% (1 lb 4 oz/625 g). Omit granulated sugar and use 60% (1 lb 8 oz/750 g) brown sugar.

Rolled Chocolate Cookies
Substitute 4 oz (125 g) cocoa for 4 oz (125 g) flour.

Shortbread Cookies

Ingredients	U.S.		Metric	Percentage
Butter	1 lb	8 oz	750 g	75%
Sugar	1 lb		500 g	50%
Salt		0.25 oz (1½ tsp)	8 g (7 mL)	0.75%
Egg yolks (see note)		8 oz	250 g	25%
Flavoring (optional; see note)				
Pastry flour	2 lb		1000 g	100%
Yield:	*5 lb*		*2508 g*	*250%*

Per 1 ounce:
Calories, 130; Protein, 2 g; Fat, 8 g (53% cal.); Cholesterol, 55 mg; Carbohydrates, 14 g; Fiber, 2 g; Sodium, 105 mg.

■ P r o c e d u r e

Mixing:
Creaming method.

Makeup:
Rolled method. Roll dough ¼ in. (½ cm) thick (this is thicker that most rolled cookies). Use greased or parchment-lined baking sheets.

Baking:
350°F (175°C), about 15 minutes.

Note: Traditional Scottish shortbread is made with butter, flour, and sugar—no eggs, flavoring, or liquid. Because the dough is crumbly, it is not rolled out but rather pressed into pans or molds and baked. For the recipe given here, you may make the cookies without added flavoring or flavor to taste with vanilla, almond, or lemon.

Cinnamon Cookies

Ingredients	U.S.		Metric	Percentage
Butter and/or shortening	1 lb		500 g	80%
Granulated sugar		8 oz	250 g	40%
Brown sugar		8 oz	250 g	40%
Salt		1 tsp	5 g (5 mL)	0.9%
Cinnamon		0.33 oz (1½ tbsp)	10 g	1.7%
Eggs		3 oz	90 g	15%
Milk		1 oz	30 g	5%
Pastry flour	1 lb	4 oz	625 g	100%
Yield:	*3 lb*	*8 oz*	*1760 g*	*282%*

Per 1 ounce:
Calories, 130; Protein, 1 g; Fat, 7 g (48% cal.); Cholesterol, 25 mg;
Carbohydrates, 16 g; Fiber, 1 g; Sodium, 110 mg.

■ **P r o c e d u r e**

Mixing:
Creaming method.
Makeup:
Molded method. Roll cut pieces in cinnamon sugar before placing on greased baking sheets and pressing flat.
Baking:
375°F (190°C), about 10 minutes.

V A R I A T I O N

Chocolate Cinnamon Cookies
Substitute 4 oz (125 g) cocoa for 4 oz (125 g) flour.

Raisin Spice Bars

Ingredients	U.S.		Metric	Percentage
Sugar	1 lb	8 oz	700 g	100%
Butter and/or shortening		8 oz	225 g	33%
Eggs		8 oz	225 g	33%
Molasses		4 oz	125 g	17%
Pastry flour	1 lb	8 oz	700 g	100%
Cinnamon		2 tsp	3 g (10 mL)	0.5%
Ground cloves		½ tsp	1 g (2 mL)	0.16%
Ground ginger		1 tsp	2 g (5 mL)	0.3%
Baking soda		¾ tsp	3 g (3 mL)	0.5%
Salt		1 tsp	5 g (5 mL)	0.75%
Raisins (see note)	1 lb		470 g	67%
Yield:	*5 lb*	*4 oz*	*2459 g*	*352%*

Per 1 ounce:
Calories, 100; Protein, 1 g; Fat, 2.5 g (21% cal.); Cholesterol, 15 mg;
Carbohydrates, 20 g; Fiber, 1 g; Sodium, 65 mg.

Note: If raisins are hard and dry, soak them in hot water 30 minutes, drain, and dry well before adding to the mix.

■ **P r o c e d u r e**

Mixing:
One-stage method.
Makeup:
Bar method. Eggwash with whole eggs or egg whites.
Baking:
350°F (175°C), about 15 minutes.

Peanut Butter Cookies

Ingredients	U.S.	Metric	Percentage
Butter and/or shortening	12 oz	375 g	75%
Brown sugar	8 oz	250 g	50%
Granulated sugar	8 oz	250 g	50%
Salt	1 tsp	5 g (5 mL)	1%
Peanut butter	12 oz	375 g	75%
Eggs	4 oz	125 g	25%
Pastry flour	1 lb	500 g	100%
Baking soda	1 tsp	5 g (5 mL)	1%
Yield:	*3 lb 12 oz*	*1885 g*	*377%*

Per 1 ounce:
Calories, 130; Protein, 2 g; Fat, 8 g (53% cal.); Cholesterol, 20 mg; Carbohydrates, 14 g; Fiber, 1 g; Sodium, 135 mg.

■ P r o c e d u r e

Mixing:
Creaming method. Cream peanut butter with the fat and sugar.
Makeup:
Molded method. Use a fork instead of a weight to flatten the cookies. Use greased or parchment-lined baking sheets.
Baking:
375°F (190°C), 8–12 minutes, depending on size.

Icebox Cookies

Ingredients	U.S.	Metric	Percentage
Butter and/or shortening	2 lb	1000 g	67%
Granulated sugar	1 lb	500 g	33%
Confectioners' sugar	1 lb	500 g	33%
Salt	0.5 oz	15 g	1%
Eggs	8 oz	250 g	17%
Vanilla	0.5 oz	15 mL	1%
Pastry flour	3 lb	1500 g	100%
Yield:	*7 lb 9 oz*	*3780 g*	*252%*

Per 1 ounce:
Calories, 120; Protein, 1 g; Fat, 6 g (44% cal.); Cholesterol, 25 mg; Carbohydrates, 16 g; Fiber, 1 g; Sodium, 110 mg.

■ P r o c e d u r e

Mixing:
Creaming method.
Makeup:
Icebox method. Scale dough strips to 1½ lb (750 g) each. Slice cookies ¼ in. (½ cm) thick. Bake on ungreased pans.
Baking:
375°F (190°C), about 12 minutes.

V A R I A T I O N S

To reduce spread, use all confectioners' sugar.

Butterscotch Icebox Cookies
In place of sugars in basic recipe, use 67% (2 lb/1 kg) brown sugar and use only butter. Increase eggs to 25% (12 oz/375 g). Add 1 tsp (5 g or 5 mL) baking soda to the flour.

Chocolate Icebox Cookies
Add 17% (8 oz/250 g) melted unsweetened chocolate to the creamed butter and sugar.

Nut Icebox Cookies
Add 25% (12 oz/375 g) finely chopped nuts to the sifted flour in the basic recipe or the Butterscotch or Chocolate Cookie recipes.

Brownies

Ingredients	U.S.		Metric	Percentage
Unsweetened chocolate	1 lb		450 g	100%
Butter	1 lb	8 oz	675 g	150%
Eggs	1 lb	8 oz	675 g	150%
Sugar	3 lb		1350 g	300%
Salt		0.25 oz (1½ tsp)	7 g (7 mL)	1.5%
Vanilla		1 oz	30 mL	6%
Cake flour	1 lb		450 g	100%
Chopped walnuts or pecans	1 lb		450 g	100%
Yield:	*9 lb*	*1 oz*	*4087 g*	*907%*

Per 1 brownie:
Calories, 190; Protein, 3 g; Fat, 12 g (54% cal.); Cholesterol, 45 mg; Carbohydrates, 20 g; Fiber, 1 g; Sodium, 95 mg.

■ P r o c e d u r e

Mixing:
Sponge method.
1. Melt chocolate and butter together in a double boiler. Stir so that the mixture is smooth. Let it cool to room temperature.
2. Blend the eggs, sugar, and salt until well mixed, but do not whip. Add the vanilla.
3. Blend in the chocolate mixture.
4. Sift the flour and fold it in.
5. Fold in the nuts.

Makeup:
Sheet method. Grease and flour the pans or line them with parchment. Quantity of basic recipe is enough for 1 full sheet pan, 18 × 26. in. (46 × 66 cm), 2 half-size sheet pans, 4 pans measuring 9 × 13 in. (23 × 33 cm), or 6 square pans measuring 9 in. (23 cm) per side.

If desired, batter may be sprinkled with an additional 50% (8 oz/255 g) chopped nuts after panning.

Baking:
325°F (165°C), about 60 minutes. For 2-in. (5-cm) square brownies, cut sheet pan 8 × 12 to yield 96 pieces.

V A R I A T I O N

Butterscotch Brownies or Blondies
Omit chocolate. Use brown sugar instead of granulated sugar. Increase flour to 1 lb 6 oz (600 g).

Almond Biscotti

Ingredients	U.S.	Metric	Percentage
Eggs	10 oz	300 g	35%
Sugar	1 lb 2 oz	550 g	65%
Salt	0.4 oz (2 tsp)	12 g (10 mL)	2%
Vanilla	0.3 oz (2 tsp)	8 mL	1%
Grated orange zest	0.1 oz (1¼ tsp)	3 g	0.5%
Pastry flour	1 lb 12 oz	850 g	100%
Baking powder	0.7 oz	20 g	2.5%
Blanched whole almonds	10 oz	300 g	35%
Yield:	*4 lb 3 oz*	*2047 g*	*241%*

Per 1 ounce:
Calories, 110; Protein, 3 g; Fat, 4.5 g (36% cal.); Cholesterol, 15 mg;
Carbohydrates, 15 g; Fiber, 2 g; Sodium, 110 mg.

■ P r o c e d u r e

Mixing:
Sponge method.
1. Combine the eggs, sugar, and salt. Stir over hot water to warm the mixture. Whip until thick and light.
2. Fold in the vanilla and orange zest.
3. Sift together the flour and baking powder. Fold in the egg mixture.
4. Mix in the almonds.

Makeup:
Bar method. Shape into logs about 2–2½ in. (6 cm) thick. Dust your hands and the workbench with flour. The dough will be soft, sticky, and difficult to handle, but the logs do not have to be perfectly shaped. Egg wash.

Baking:
325°F (160°C) about 30–40 minutes, until light golden.

Finishing:
Let cool slightly. Slice diagonally about ½ inch (12 mm) thick. Place slices cut side down on sheet pans. Bake at 275°F (135°C) until toasted and golden brown, about 30 minutes.

■ TERMS FOR REVIEW

spread	sponge method	rolled cookies	bar cookies
one-stage method	dropped cookies	molded cookies	sheet cookies
creaming method	bagged cookies	icebox cookies	

■ QUESTIONS FOR DISCUSSION

1. What makes cookies crisp, and how can you keep them crisp after they are baked?

2. If you baked some cookies that were unintentionally chewy, how would you correct them in the next batch?

3. Describe briefly the difference between the creaming method and the one-stage method.

4. Besides cost control, why are accurate scaling and uniform sizing important when making up cookies?

CHAPTER 34

Pies and Pastries

On the North American frontier, it was not uncommon for the pioneer housewife to bake 21 pies a week—one for every meal. Pies were so important to the settlers that in winter, when fruits were unavailable, cooks would bake pies for dessert out of whatever materials were available, such as potatoes, vinegar, and soda crackers.

Few of us today eat pie at every meal. Nevertheless, pies are still a favorite dessert. Most customers will order and pay a higher price for a piece of chocolate cream pie than for chocolate pudding, even if the pie filling is the same as the pudding and even if they leave the crust uneaten.

In this chapter, we present the preparation of pie crusts and fillings. In addition, we discuss how to make puff pastry, éclair paste, meringues, and fruit desserts.

PIES

PIE DOUGHS

Before you begin studying this section, it would be a good idea for you to review the section on gluten development in Chapter 29. Pie pastry is a simple product in terms of its ingredients: flour, shortening, water, and salt. Yet success or failure depends on how the shortening and flour are mixed and how the gluten is developed. The key to making pie dough is proper technique, and you will remember the techniques better if you understand why they work.

INGREDIENTS

Flour

Pastry flour is the best choice for pie doughs. It has enough gluten to produce the desired structure and flakiness, yet is low enough in gluten to yield a tender product, if handled properly.

If stronger flours are used, the percentage of shortening should be increased to provide more tenderness.

Fat

Regular hydrogenated shortening is the most popular fat for pie crusts because it has the right plastic consistency to produce a flaky crust. It is firm and moldable enough to make an easily worked dough. Emulsified shortening should not be used because it blends too quickly with the flour, making a flaky pastry difficult to achieve.

Butter contributes excellent flavor to pie pastry, but it is not frequently used in volume production for two reasons: It is expensive, and it melts very easily, making the dough difficult to work.

It is desirable, if costs permit, to blend a quantity of butter into the shortening used for pie crusts to improve flavor. The quantity of pie crust dumped in the garbage after customers have eaten out the filling is evidence that many people are not satisfied with the taste of pie crusts made with shortening.

If all butter is used in place of shortening, the percentage of fat in the formula should be increased by about one-fourth. (If 1 pound shortening is called for, use 1 pound 4 ounces butter. If 500 grams shortening are called for, use 625 grams butter.) The liquid should be reduced slightly, as butter contains moisture.

Lard is an excellent shortening for pies because it is firm and plastic. Some people dislike its flavor, however, so it is not widely used in food service.

Liquid

Water is necessary to develop some gluten in the flour and to give structure and flakiness to the dough. If too much water is used, the crust will become tough because of too much gluten development. If not enough water is used, the crust will fall apart.

Milk makes a rich dough that browns quickly. However, the crust is less crisp and the production cost is higher.

Whether water or milk is used, it must be added cold (40°F/4°C or colder) to maintain proper dough temperature.

Salt

Salt has some tenderizing and conditioning effect on the gluten. However, its main contribution is to flavor.

Salt must be dissolved in the liquid before being added to the mix to ensure even distribution.

After reading this chapter, you should be able to

1. **Prepare flaky pie dough and mealy pie dough.**

2. **Prepare crumb crusts and short, or cookie, crusts.**

3. **Assemble and bake pies.**

4. **Prepare the following pie fillings: fruit fillings using the cooked juice method, the cooked fruit method, and the old-fashioned method; custard or soft fillings; cream pie fillings; and chiffon fillings.**

5. **Prepare puff pastry dough and puff dough products.**

6. **Prepare éclair paste and éclair paste products.**

7. **Prepare standard meringues and meringue desserts.**

8. **Prepare fruit desserts.**

TEMPERATURE

Pie dough should be kept cool, about 60°F (15°C), during mixing and makeup for two reasons:

1. Shortening has the best consistency when cool. If it is warm, it blends too quickly with the flour. If it is very cold, it is too firm to be easily workable.

2. Gluten develops more slowly at cool temperatures than at warm temperatures.

PIE DOUGH TYPES

There are two basic types of pie dough: flaky and mealy.

The difference between the two is how the fat is blended with the flour. Complete mixing procedures are given later. First, it is important to understand the basic distinction between the two types.

Flaky Pie Dough

For **flaky pie dough**, the fat is cut or rubbed into the flour until the particles of shortening are about the size of peas or hazelnuts. That is, the flour is not completely blended with the fat, and the fat is left in pieces. (Many bakers distinguish between this crust, which they call *short-flake*, and *long-flake* crusts, in which the fat is left in pieces the size of walnuts and the flour is even less coated with shortening.)

When water is added, the flour absorbs water and develops some gluten. When the dough is rolled out, the lumps of fat and moistened flour are flattened and become flakes of dough separated by layers of fat.

Mealy Pie Dough

For **mealy pie dough**, the fat is blended into the flour more thoroughly, until the mixture looks like coarse cornmeal. Because the flour is more completely coated with fat:

- The crust is very short and tender because less gluten can develop.
- Less water is needed in the mix because the flour won't absorb as much as in flaky dough.
- The baked dough is less likely to absorb moisture from the filling and become soggy.

Mealy dough is used for bottom crusts in baked fruit pies and soft or custard-type pies because it resists sogginess. Flaky doughs are used for top crusts and for prebaked pie shells.

Trimmings

Reworked scraps or trimmings are tougher than freshly made dough. They may be combined with mealy dough and used for bottom crusts only.

MIXING PIE DOUGHS

Hand mixing is best for small quantities of dough, especially flaky dough, because it gives more control over the mixing. Quantities up to 10 pounds (5 kg) can be mixed almost as quickly by hand as by machine.

For machine mixing, use a pastry knife or paddle attachment and blend at low speed.

Procedures for rolling pie doughs and lining pie pans are discussed in the next section, "Assembly and Baking."

Flaky Pie Dough
Mealy Pie Dough

Ingredients	Flaky			Mealy		
	U.S.	Metric	Percentage	U.S.	Metric	Percentage
Pastry flour	2 lb 8 oz	1000 g	100%	2 lb 8 oz	1000 g	100%
Shortening	1 lb 12 oz	700 g	70%	1 lb 10 oz	650 g	65%
Salt	0.75 oz (4 tsp)	20 g	2%	0.75 oz (4 tsp)	20 g	2 %
Water	12 oz	300 g	30%	10 oz	250 g	25%
Yield:	*5 lb*	*2020 g*	*202%*	*4 lb 12 oz*	*1920 g*	*192%*

Per 1 ounce:
Calories, 130; Protein, 1 g; Fat, 10 g (65% cal.); Cholesterol, 0 mg;
Carbohydrates, 11 g; Fiber, 20 g; Sodium, 105 mg.

■ Procedure

Mixing:
1. Collect all equipment.
2. Collect and scale ingredients.
3. Dissolve salt in water. Set aside.
4. Place flour and shortening in mixing bowl.
5. Rub or cut shortening into flour to the proper degree:

   For mealy dough—until it resembles coarse cornmeal.

   For flaky dough—until fat particles are the size of peas or hazelnuts.
6. Add salt and water. Mix very gently, just until water is absorbed. Do not overwork the dough.
7. Place the dough in pans, cover with plastic film, and place in refrigerator or retarder for several hours.

OTHER PIE CRUSTS

Crumb Crusts

Graham cracker crusts are popular because they have an appealing flavor and are much easier to make than pastry crusts. For variation, vanilla or chocolate wafer crumbs or gingersnap crumbs may be used instead of graham cracker crumbs. Ground nuts may be added for special desserts.

Crumb crusts are used only for unbaked pies, such as cream pies and chiffon pies. Be sure the flavor of the crust is compatible with the filling. A lime chiffon pie with a chocolate crumb crust is not an appealing combination. Some cream fillings are so delicate they would be overwhelmed by a crust that is too flavorful.

Baking the crust makes a firmer, less crumbly crust and increases flavor.

Short-Dough Crusts

Short pastry is actually a kind of cookie dough. It is richer than regular pie pastry and contains butter, sugar, and eggs. Because short dough is difficult to handle, it is used primarily for small fruit tarts.

Graham Cracker Crust

Yield: 2 lb (900g)   Crusts for: 4 pies, 9 inches (23 cm) in diameter
5 pies 8 inches (20cm) in diameter

U.S.	Metric	Ingredients
1 lb	450 g	Graham cracker crumbs
8 oz	225 g	Sugar
8 oz	225 g	Butter, melted

Per 1 ounce
Calories, 140; Protein, 1 g: Fat, 7 g (45% cal); Cholesterol, 15 mg;
Carbohydrates, 18 g; Fiber, 0 g; Sodium, 140 mg.

■ P r o c e d u r e

1. Mix crumbs and sugar in mixing bowl.
2. Add butter and mix until evenly blended and crumbs are all moistened by the melted butter.
3. Scale the mixture into pie pans: 8 oz (225g) for 9-in. (23-cm) pans; 6 oz (175g) for 8-in. (20-cm) pans.
4. Spread mixture evenly on bottom and sides of pan. Press another pan on top to pack crumbs evenly.
5. Bake at 350°F (175°C) for 10 minutes.
6. Cool thoroughly before filling.

V A R I A T I O N S

Substitute chocolate or vanilla wafer crumbs or gingersnap crumbs for the cracker crumbs.

Short Dough

Ingredients	U.S	Metric	Percentage
Butter *or* butter and shortening	1 lb	500 g	67%
Sugar	6 oz	180 g	25%
Salt	0.12 oz (¼ tsp)	4 g	0.5%
Eggs	4.5 oz	140 g	19%
Pastry flour	1 lb 8 oz	750 g	100%
Yield	*3 lb 2 oz*	*1574 g*	*211%*

Per 1 ounce
Calories, 130; Protein, 2 g; Fat, 8 g (53% cal); Cholesterol, 30 mg;
Carbohydrates, 14 g; Fiber, 2 g; Sodium, 100 mg.

■ P r o c e d u r e

1. Using the paddle attachment, mix the butter, sugar, and salt at low speed until smooth and evenly blended.
2. Add the eggs and mix just until absorbed.
3. Sift the flour and add it to the mixture. Mix just until evenly blended.
4. Chill several hours before using.

Procedure for Making Small Fruit Tarts

1. Roll out chilled short dough on a floured surface until it is slightly less than ¼ inch (5 mm) thick.
2. With a round cutter about ½ inch (1 cm) larger than the top diameter of your individual tart shells, cut the dough into circles.
3. For each shell, fit a circle of dough into a tin and press it well against the bottom and sides. If you are using fluted tins, make sure the dough is thick enough on the sides so it won't break apart at the ridges.
4. Fit paper liners inside the shells and fill with dried beans to keep the dough from blistering or puffing while baking.
5. Bake at 400°F (200°C) for about 15 minutes or until the shells are fully baked. Remove the paper liners and the beans.
6. Cool the shells completely and remove them from the tins.
7. Fill the shells half full of vanilla pastry cream (see Chapter 35).
8. Arrange well-drained fresh, cooked, or canned fruits over the pastry cream.
9. Brush the top with apricot glaze, melted currant jelly, or other desired glaze (see Chapter 32).
10. Keep refrigerated until service.

ASSEMBLY AND BAKING

TYPES OF PIES

Pies may be classified into two groups based on method of assembling and baking.

1. **Baked pies.**
   Raw pie shells are filled and then baked. Fruit pies contain fruit fillings and usually have a top crust. Soft pies are those with custard-type fillings or, in other words, liquid fillings that become firm when their egg content coagulates. They are usually baked as single-crust pies.

2. **Unbaked pies.**
   Baked pie shells are filled with a prepared filling, chilled, and served when the filling is firm enough to slice. Cream pies are made with pudding or boiled custard-type fillings. Chiffon pies are made with fillings that are lightened by the addition of beaten egg whites and, sometimes, whipped cream. Gelatin or starch gives them a firm consistency.

Procedure for Rolling Pie Dough and Lining Pans

1. Scale the dough.

   8 ounces (225 g) for 9-inch (23-cm) bottom crusts   6 ounces (175 g) for 8-inch (20-cm) bottom crusts

   6 ounces (175 g) for 9-inch (23-cm) top crusts   5 ounces (150 g) for 8-inch (20-cm) top crusts

   Experienced bakers are able to roll crusts using less dough because less needs to be trimmed when the dough is rolled to a perfect circle of the exact size needed.

2. Dust the bench and rolling pin lightly with flour.

   Too much dusting flour toughens the dough. Use no more than needed to prevent sticking.

3. Roll out the dough.

   Flatten the dough lightly and roll it out to a uniform ⅛-inch (3-mm) thickness. Use even strokes and roll from the center outward in all directions. Lift the dough frequently to make sure it is not sticking. The finished dough should form a perfect circle.

4. Place the dough in a pan.

   To lift the dough without breaking it, roll it lightly around the rolling pin. Allow the dough to drop into the pan and press it into the corners without stretching it. Stretched dough shrinks during baking. There should be no air bubbles between the dough and the pan.

5. For single-crust pies, flute the edges, if desired, and trim off excess dough.

   Some bakers feel that fluted edges add to the appearance of the product. Others feel that fluting takes too much time and produces only a rim of heavy dough that customers leave on their plates.

6. For two-crust pies:

   Fill with cold filling, place the second crust on top, and seal the top and bottom crusts together at edges. Flute, if desired, and trim excess dough. Apply desired wash or glaze to top.

7. Bake as directed in the recipe.

THE SOGGY BOTTOM

A common pie fault is an underbaked bottom crust or a crust that soaks up moisture from the filling. Soggy bottoms can be avoided in several ways.

1. Use mealy dough for bottom crusts. Mealy dough absorbs less liquid than flaky dough.

2. Use high bottom heat, at least at the beginning of baking, to set the crust quickly. Bake the pies at the bottom of the oven.

3. Do not add hot fillings to unbaked crusts.

4. Use dark metal pie tins, which absorb heat. (If you use disposable aluminum pans, choose pans with the bottoms colored black.)

Procedure for Preparing Baked Pies

Note: For pies without a top crust, omit steps 3 through 7.

1. Line the pie pan with the pie dough as in the basic procedure (Figure 34.1).

2. Fill with *cooled* filling. See Table 34.1 for scaling instructions. Do not drop filling on the rim of the pie shell; this makes it hard to seal the rim to the top crust. To avoid spilling custard filling, place the empty shell on the rack in the oven and then pour in the filling.

3. Roll out the dough for the top crust.

4. Perforate the top crust to allow steam to escape during baking.

5. Moisten the rim of the bottom crust to help seal it to the top crust.

6. Fit the top crust in place. Seal the edges together firmly and trim excess dough. An easy way to do this is to press the rim with the tines of a fork. Alternatively, the rim may be fluted. An efficient way to trim excess dough is to rotate the pie tin while pressing on the edges with the palms of the hands.

Table 34.1
Scaling Instructions for Baked Pies

Pie Size		Weight of Filling	
U.S.	Metric	U.S.	Metric
8 in.	20 cm	26–30 oz	750–850 g
9 in.	23 cm	32–40 oz	900–1150 g
10 in.	25 cm	40–50 oz	1150–1400 g

Note: Weights are guidelines only. Exact weights may vary, depending on the filling and the depth of the pans.

7. Brush the top with the desired wash: milk, cream, eggs and milk, or water. Sprinkle with granulated sugar if desired.

8. Place the pie on the lower level of an oven preheated to 425° to 450°F (220° to 230°C). The high initial heat helps set the bottom crust to avoid soaking. Fruit pies are usually baked at this high heat until done. For custard pies, reduce the heat to 325° to 350°F (165° to 175°C) after 10 minutes to avoid overcooking and curdling the custard. Custard pies include those containing large quantities of egg, such as pumpkin pie and pecan pie.

Figure 34.1
Preparing baked pies.

(a) Line the pie pans with the pie dough.

(b) Fill with cooled fillings.

(c) Fit the top crusts in place.

(d) Seal the top crust to the rim and trim the dough from the edges.

Procedure for Preparing Unbaked Pies

1. Line a pie pan with pie dough as in the basic procedure.

2. Dock the crust well with a fork to prevent blistering.

3. Place another pan inside the first one so the dough is between two pans. This is called *double-panning.*

4. Place the pans upside down in an oven preheated at 450°F (230°C). Baking upside down helps keep the dough from shrinking down into the pan.

   Some bakers like to chill the crusts before baking to relax the gluten and help reduce shrinkage.

5. Bake at 450°F (230°C) for 10 to 15 minutes. The top pan may be removed during the last part of baking so the crust can brown.

6. Cool the baked crust completely.

7. Fill with cream or chiffon filling. Fill as close as possible to service time to prevent soaking the crust.

8. Chill the pie until it is set enough to slice.

FILLINGS

STARCHES FOR FILLINGS

Many kinds of pie filling, especially fruit fillings and cream fillings, depend on starch for their thick texture.

Types

Cornstarch is used for cream pies because it sets up into a firm gel that holds its shape when sliced. Cornstarch may also be used for fruit pies.

Waxy maize and other *modified starches* are best for fruit pies because they are clear when set and make a soft paste rather than a firm gel. Waxy maize should be used for pies that are to be frozen because it is not broken down by freezing.

Flour, tapioca, and other starches are used less frequently. Flour has less thickening power than other starches and makes the product cloudy.

Instant starch or *pregelatinized starch* needs no cooking because it has already been cooked. When used with certain fruit fillings, it eliminates the need to cook the filling before making up the pie. It has no advantage, however, if the filling contains such ingredients as raw fruit or eggs and so must be cooked.

Starches differ in thickening power, so follow the formulas exactly.

Cooking Starches

To avoid lumping, starches must be mixed with a cold liquid or sugar before being added to a hot liquid.

Sugar and *strong acids* reduce the thickening power of starch. When possible, all or part of the sugar and strong acids like lemon juice should be added *after the starch has thickened*.

FRUIT FILLINGS

Fruit pie fillings consist of fruits and fruit juices, sugar, spices, and a starch thickener.

Fruits for Pie Fillings

Fresh fruits make excellent pies if they are at their seasonal peak. Fresh apples are used extensively for high-quality pies. But the quality of fresh fruits can vary considerably, and fresh fruit pies require a lot of labor.

Frozen fruits are widely used for pies because they are consistent in quality and readily available.

Canned fruits can also be of high quality. Solid pack (with little juice) gives a higher yield of fruit per can than syrup or water pack.

Dried fruits must be rehydrated by soaking and, usually, simmering before they are made into pie fillings.

Fruits must have sufficient acid (tartness) to make flavorful fillings. If they lack natural acid, you may need to add lemon, orange, or pineapple juice to supply the acid.

Cooked Juice Method

The advantage of the cooked juice method is that only the juice is cooked. The fruit retains better shape and flavor because it is subjected to less heat and handling. This method is used when the fruit requires little or no cooking before filling the pie. Examples: cherry, peach, most frozen or canned fruits. Fresh berries can also be prepared by this method. Some of the berries are cooked or puréed to provide juice. The remaining berries are mixed with the finished gel.

Cooked Fruit Method

The cooked fruit method is used when the fruit requires cooking or there is not enough liquid for the cooked juice method. Examples: fresh apple, raisin, rhubarb.

Procedure: Cooked Juice Method

1. Drain the juice from the fruit.
2. Measure the juice and, if necessary, add water or other fruit juice to bring it to the desired volume.
3. Bring the juice to a boil.
4. Dissolve the starch in cold water and stir it into the boiling juice. Return the juice to the boil and cook until it is clear and thickened.
5. Add sugar, salt, and flavorings and stir until dissolved.
6. Pour the thickened juice over the drained fruit and mix gently. Be careful not to break or mash the fruit.
7. Cool.

Procedure: Cooked Fruit Method

1. Bring the fruit and its juice or water to a boil. Some sugar may be added to the fruit to draw out juices.
2. Dissolve the starch in cold water and stir it into the fruit. Return the fruit mixture to a boil and cook until it is clear and thickened. Stir while cooking.
3. Add sugar, salt, flavorings, and other ingredients and stir until dissolved.
4. Cool as quickly as possible.

Variation

Some fruits, such as fresh apples, may be cooked in butter rather than boiled in water for better flavor.

Old-Fashioned Method

This method is best suited to pies made with fresh apples or peaches. It is not as widely used in food service as the other methods because it is more difficult to control the thickening of the juices.

Procedure: Old-Fashioned Method

1. Mix the starch and spices with the sugar until uniformly blended.
2. Mix the fruit with the sugar mixture.
3. Fill the unbaked pie shell with the fruit.
4. Place lumps of butter on top of the filling.
5. Cover with a top crust or with Streusel (p. 922) and bake.

COOKED JUICE METHOD

 Apple Pie Filling (Canned Fruit)

Yield: about 9½ lb (4.5 kg).
         five 8-inch (20-cm) pies
         four 9-inch (23-cm) pies
         three 10 -inch (25-cm) pies

U.S.	Metric	Ingredients	
6 lb 8 oz	3 kg	Canned apples (1 No. 10 can)	
as needed	as needed	Water	
8 fl oz	250 mL	Water, cold	
3 oz	90 g	Cornstarch or modified starch	
1 lb 4 oz	575 g	Sugar	
¼ oz (1¼ tsp)	7 g (6 mL)	Salt	
¼ oz (4¼ tsp)	7 g (21 mL)	Cinnamon	
1 tsp	2 g (5 mL)	Nutmeg	
3 oz	90 g	Butter	

Per 1 ounce:
Calories, 30; Protein, 0 g; Fat, 0.5 g (14% cal.); Cholesterol, 0 mg; Carbohydrates, 7 g; Fiber, 0 g; Sodium, 25 mg.

■ P r o c e d u r e

1. Drain the apples and save the juice.
2. Add enough water to the juice to measure 1½ pt (750 mL).

3. Mix the cold water and starch
4. Bring the juice mixture to a boil.
5. Stir in the starch mixture and return to a boil.

6. Add the remaining ingredients (except the drained apples). Simmer until the sugar is dissolved.
7. Pour the syrup over the apples and mix gently. Cool completely.
8. Fill pie shells. Bake at 425°F (220°C) for about 30–40 minutes.

V A R I A T I O N S

Dutch Apple Pie Filling
Simmer 8 oz (250 g) raisins in water. Drain and add to Apple Pie Filling.

Cherry Pie Filling
Use 1 No. 10 can sour cherries instead of apples. Increase starch to 4 oz (125 g). Add 1½ fl oz (45 mL) lemon juice in step 6. Increase the sugar to 1 lb 12 oz (800 g). Omit cinnamon and nutmeg. Add almond extract to taste (optional). If desired, color with 2–3 drops red coloring.

Peach Pie Filling
Use 1 No. 10 can sliced peaches, preferably solid or heavy pack, instead of apples. Omit cinnamon and nutmeg.

Pineapple Pie Filling
Use 1 No. 10 can crushed pineapple instead of apples. Increase liquid in step 1 to 1 qt (1 L). Increase starch to 4 oz (125 g). Use 1 lb 8 oz (700 g) sugar and 8 oz (250 g) corn syrup. Omit cinnamon and nutmeg.

Apple Pie with Streusel Topping

Blueberry Pie Filling (Frozen Fruit)

Yield: *about 7 lb 8 oz (3375 g)*
Four 8-inch (20-cm) pies
Three 9-inch (23-cm) pies

Per 1 ounce:
Calories, 30; Protein, 0 g; Fat, 0 g (0% cal.); Cholesterol, 0 mg;
Carbohydrates, 8 g; Fiber, 1 g; Sodium, 20 g.

U.S.	Metric	Ingredients
5 lb	2250 g	Frozen unsweetened blueberries
as needed	as needed	Water
6 oz	175 g	Sugar
6 fl oz	190 mL	Water, cold
3 oz	90 g	Cornstarch or modified strach
14 oz	412 g	Sugar
¼ oz (1¼ tsp)	8 g (7 mL)	Salt
⅛ oz (2⅛ tsp)	4 g (10 mL)	Cinnamon
1.5 fl oz	45 mL	Lemon juice

■ Procedure

1. Thaw blueberries in original container without opening.
2. Drain the berries. Add enough water to the juice to measure 12 oz (250 mL). Stir in the sugar.
3. Mix the cold water and cornstarch.
4. Bring the juice mixture to a boil. Stir in the starch. Return to a boil to thicken.
5. Stir in the sugar, salt, cinnamon, and lemon juice. Stir over heat until the sugar is dissolved.
6. Pour the syrup over the drained blueberries. Mix gently. Cool completely.
7. Fill pie shells. Bake at 425°F (220°C) for about 30 minutes.

VARIATIONS

Apple Pie Filling

Use 5 lb (2.25 kg) frozen apples instead of blueberries. Reduce second quantity of sugar to 8 oz (225 g). Reduce starch to 1½ oz (45 g). Add ½ tsp (2 mL) nutmeg and 3 oz (87 g) butter in step 5.

Cherry Pie Filling

Use 5 lb (2.25 kg) frozen cherries instead of blueberries. Increase liquid in step 2 to 1 pt (500 mL). Decrease starch to 2½ oz (75 g). Reduce second quantity of sugar to 10 oz (285 g). Omit cinnamon and reduce lemon juice to ¾ fl oz (22 mL).

 ## Fresh Strawberry Pie Filling

Yield: *about 6 lb (2.75 kg)*
Three 8-inch (20-cm) pies
Two 10-inch (25-cm) pies

U.S.	Metric	Ingredients
4 lb 8 oz	2050 g	Fresh whole strawberries
8 fl oz	250 mL	Water, cold
14 oz	400 g	Sugar
2 oz	60 g	Cornstarch or modified starch
½ tsp	2 mL	Salt
1 fl oz	30 mL	Lemon juice

Per 1 ounce:
Calories, 25; Protein, 0 g; Fat, 0 g (0% cal.); Cholesterol, 0 mg;
Carbohydrates, 6 g; Fiber, 0 g; Sodium, 10 mg.

■ Procedure

1. Hull, wash and drain the berries. Set aside 3 lb 8 oz (1.6 kg) berries. These may be left whole if small or cut in halves or quarters if large.
2. Mash or purée the remaining 1 lb (450 g) berries. Mix with the water. (If a clear filling is desired, this mixture may be strained.)
3. Mix together the sugar, starch, and salt. Stir into the cold juice and water mixture until no lumps remain.
4. Bring to a boil, stirring constantly. Cook until thickened.
5. Remove from heat and stir in the lemon juice.
6. Cool to room temperature but do not chill.
7. Stir to eliminate lumps. Fold in the reserved berries.
8. Fill baked pie shells and chill (do not bake).

COOKED FRUIT METHOD

 ## Rhubarb Pie Filling

Yield: about 5 lb 8 oz (2.5 kg)
three 8-inch (20-cm) pies
two 10-inch (25-cm) pies

U.S.	Metric	Ingredients
3 lb 8 oz	1.6 kg	Fresh rhubarb
8 fl oz	250 mL	Water
8 oz	225 g	Sugar
4 fl oz	125 mL	Water
2.5 oz	75 g	Cornstarch
8 oz	225 g	Sugar
1 tsp	5 mL	Salt
1 oz	30 g	Butter

Per 1 ounce:
Calories, 30; Protein, 0 g; Fat, 5 g (14% cal.); Cholesterol, 0 mg;
Carbohydrates, 7 g; Fiber, 0 g; Sodium, 30 mg.

■ P r o c e d u r e

1. Cut the rhubarb into 1-in. (2½-cm) pieces.
2. Combine the rhubarb, water, and sugar in a saucepan. Bring to a boil and simmer 2 minutes.
3. Mix the water and starch. Stir into the rhubarb and boil until thick and clear.
4. Add the remaining ingredients. Stir gently until the sugar is dissolved and the butter is melted.
5. Cool completely.
6. Fill pie shells. Bake at 425°F (220°C), about 30–40 minutes.

V A R I A T I O N

Fresh Apple Pie Filling
Use 5 lb (2.25 kg) fresh peeled and sliced apples instead of rhubarb. Flavor with 1½ tsp (7 mL) cinnamon, ½ tsp (2 mL) nutmeg, and ½–1 fl oz (15–30 mL) lemon juice during step 4.

 ## Raisin Pie Filling

Yield: about 2 lb (1 kg)   One 9-inch (23-cm) pie

U.S.	Metric	Ingredients
13 oz	360 g	Raisins
13 fl oz	400 mL	Water
2 fl oz	50 mL	Water, cold
½ oz	15 g	Cornstarch or modified starch
4 oz	114 g	Sugar
½ tsp	2 mL	Salt
3½ tsp	18 mL	Lemon juice
½ tsp	2 mL	Grated lemon zest
⅛ tsp	1 mL	Cinnamon
0.6 oz	18 g	Butter

Per 1 ounce:
Calories 50, Protein, 0 g; Fat, 0 g; (0% cal.); Cholesterol, 0 mg. Carbohydrates, 12 g; Fiber, 5 g; Sodium, 35 mg.

■ P r o c e d u r e

1. Combine the raisins and water in a saucepan. Simmer 5 minutes.
2. Mix the water and starch. Stir into the raisins and simmer until thickened.
3. Add the remaining ingredients. Stir until sugar is dissolved and mixture is uniform.
4. Cool thoroughly.
5. Fill pie shells. Bake at 425°F (220°C) for about 30–40 minutes.

OLD-FASHIONED METHOD

 ## Old-Fashioned Apple Pie Filling

Yield: *about 11 lb (5 kg)*
six 8-inch (20-cm) pies
five 9-inch (23-cm) pies
four 10-inch (25-cm) pies

U.S.	Metric	Ingredients	
9 lb EP	4.1 kg EP	Fresh peeled, sliced apples	**■ P r o c e d u r e**
2 fl oz	60 mL	Lemon juice	1. Select firm, tart apples.
			2. Combine apple slices and lemon juice in a large mixing bowl and toss to coat apples with the juice.
2 lb	900 g	Sugar	3. Mix together the sugar, starch, salt, and spices.
3 oz	90 g	Cornstarch	4. Add to the apples and toss gently until well mixed.
¼ oz (1¼ tsp)	7 g (6 mL)	Salt	
¼ oz (4¼ tsp)	7 g (21 mL)	Cinnamon	
1 tsp	5 mL	Nutmeg	
3 oz	90 g	Butter	5. Fill pie shells. Dot the filling with butter before setting the top crusts in place. Bake at 400°F (200°C) for about 45 minutes.

Per 1 ounce:
Calories, 40; Protein, 0 g; Fat, 0.5 g (11% cal.); Cholesterol, 0 mg;
Carbohydrates, 9 g; Fiber, 0 g; Sodium, 20 mg.

CUSTARD OR SOFT FILLINGS

Custard, pumpkin, pecan, and similar pies are made with an uncooked liquid filling containing eggs. The eggs coagulate when the pie is baked, setting the filling.

The greatest difficulty in cooking soft pies is cooking the crust completely yet not overcooking the filling. Start the pie at the bottom of a hot oven (425° to 450°F/220° to 230°C) for first 10 minutes to set the crust. Then reduce the heat to 325° to 350°F (165° to 175°C) to cook the filling slowly.

To test for doneness:

1. Shake the pie very gently. If it is no longer liquid, it is done. The center will still be slightly soft but will continue cooking in its own heat after the pie is removed from the oven.

2. Insert a thin knife 1 inch (2.5 cm) from the center. It will come out clean if the pie is done.

Custard Pie Filling

Yield: **8 lb (3.6 kg)**
five 8-inch (20-cm) pies
four 9-inch (23-cm) pies
three 10-inch (25-cm) pies

U.S.	Metric	Ingredients
2 lb	900 kg	Eggs
1 lb	450 g	Sugar
1 tsp	5 mL	Salt
1 fl oz	30 mL	Vanilla
2½ qt	2.5 L	Milk (see note)
1–1½ tsp	5–7 mL	Nutmeg

Per 1 ounce:
Calories, 35; Protein, 2 g; Fat, 1.5 g (33% cal.); Cholesterol, 35 mg; Carbohydrates, 5 g; Fiber, 0 g; Sodium, 35 mg.

Note: For a richer custard, use part milk and part cream.

■ P r o c e d u r e

1. Beat the eggs lightly. Add sugar, salt, and vanilla. Blend until smooth. Do not whip air into the mixture.

2. Stir in the milk. Skim off any foam.
3. Pour into the unbaked pie shells.
4. Sprinkle tops with nutmeg.
5. Bake at 450°F (230°C) for 15 minutes. Reduce heat to 325°F (165°C) and bake until set, about 20–30 minutes more.

V A R I A T I O N

Coconut Custard Pie Filling
Use 10 oz (275 g) unsweetened, flaked coconut. Sprinkle coconut into pie shells before adding custard mixture. Coconut may be toasted lightly in oven before adding to pies, if desired. Omit nutmeg.

Pumpkin Pie Filling

Yield: about 4.25 lb (2 kg)   two 9-inch (23-cm) pies

U.S.	Metric	Ingredients
1 lb 10½ oz	750 g	Pumpkin purée, 1 No. 2½ can
1 oz	30 g	Pastry flour
2 tsp	10 mL	Cinnamon
¼ tsp	1 mL	Nutmeg
¼ tsp	1 mL	Ground ginger
⅛ tsp	0.5 mL	Ground cloves
⅝ tsp	3 mL	Salt
10 oz	290 g	Brown sugar
10 oz	300 g	Eggs
2 oz	60 g	Corn syrup or half corn syrup and half molasses
1 pt 4 oz	600 mL	Milk

■ P r o c e d u r e

1. Place pumpkin purée in the bowl of a mixer fitted with a whip attachment.
2. Sift together the flour, spices, and salt.
3. Add the flour mixture and sugar to the pumpkin. Mix at second speed until smooth and well blended.
4. Add the eggs and mix in. Scrape down the sides of the bowl.
5. Turn the machine to low speed. Gradually pour in the syrup-molasses mixture, then the milk. Mix until evenly blended.
6. Fill the pie shells. Bake at 450°F (230°C) for 15 minutes. Lower heat to 350°F (175°C) and bake until set, about 30–40 minutes more.

V A R I A T I O N S

Sweet Potato Pie Filling
Substitute canned sweet potatoes, drained and puréed, for the pumpkin.

Squash Pie Filling
Substitute puréed squash for the pumpkin.

Per 1 ounce:
Calories, 30; Protein, 1 g; Fat, 0.5 g (14% cal.); Cholesterol, 10 mg; Carbohydrates, 6 g; Fiber, 0 g; Sodium, 45 mg.

 ## Pecan Pie Filling

*Yield: 2 lb 8 oz (1640 g) filling plus 10 oz (285 g) pecans
two 9-inch (23-cm) pies*

U.S.	Metric	Ingredients
14 oz	400 g	Sugar (see note)
4 oz	120 g	Butter
½ tsp	2 mL	Salt
14 oz	400 g	Eggs
1 lb 8 oz (about 17 fl oz)	700 g	Dark corn syrup
½ fl oz	15 mL	Vanilla
10 oz	285 g	Pecans

■ P r o c e d u r e

1. Using the paddle attachment at low speed, blend the sugar, butter, and salt until evenly blended.
2. With the machine running, add the eggs, a little at a time, until they are all absorbed.
3. Add the syrup and vanilla. Mix until well blended.
4. To assemble pies, distribute pecans evenly in pie shells. Fill with syrup mixture.
5. Bake at 450°F (230°C) for 10 minutes. Reduce heat to 325°F (165°C). Bake about 40 minutes more, until set.

Per 1 ounce:
Calories, 120; Protein, 1 g; Fat, 5 g (38% cal.); Cholesterol, 35 mg; Carbohydrates, 17 g; Fiber, 0 g; Sodium, 70 mg.

Note: Brown sugar may be used if darker color and stronger flavor are desired.

CREAM PIE FILLINGS

Cream pie fillings are the same as puddings, which, in turn, are the same as basic pastry creams with added flavorings such as vanilla, chocolate, or coconut. Lemon filling is made by the same method, using water and lemon juice instead of milk.

The one difference between puddings and pie fillings that you should note is that *cream pie fillings are made with cornstarch* so slices hold their shape when cut. Puddings may be made with flour, cornstarch, or other starches.

Techniques and recipes for these fillings are included in Chapter 35, along with other basic creams and puddings.

CHIFFON PIES

Chiffon fillings are made by adding gelatin to a cream filling or to a thickened fruit and juice mixture and then folding in egg whites and/or whipped cream. The mixture is then poured into baked pie shells and allowed to set.

These preparations are the same as chiffon desserts, bavarians, and some mousses and cold soufflés. To avoid unnecessary repetition, techniques and recipes for these products are included in Chapter 35 with other puddings and creams.

PASTRIES, MERINGUES, AND FRUIT DESSERTS

In addition to pie dough, two other pastries have great importance in bakeshops and kitchens: *puff pastry*, used for such products as napoleons and turnovers, and *éclair* or *choux paste*, used for éclairs and cream puffs. These products are also used in the hot food kitchen and the pantry in the preparation of a number of hors d'oeuvres, entrées, and side dishes.

Meringues and fruit desserts are also covered in this section. Meringues are not only important as pie toppings but also can be formed, baked until crisp, and used in many of the same ways as pastry shells for desserts.

PUFF PASTRY

Puff pastry is one of the most remarkable products of the bakeshop. Although it includes no added leavening agent, it can rise to 8 times its original thickness when baked.

Puff pastry is a rolled-in dough, like Danish and croissant dough. This means it is made up of many layers of fat sandwiched in between layers of dough. Unlike Danish dough, however, puff pastry contains no yeast. Steam, created when the moisture in the dough layers is heated, is responsible for the spectacular rising power of puff pastry.

Puff pastry or puff dough is one of the most difficult of all bakery products to prepare. Because it consists of over 1,000 layers, many more than Danish dough, the rolling-in procedure requires a great deal of time and care.

As for so many other products, there are nearly as many versions of puff pastry as there are bakers. Both formulas and rolling-in techniques vary. The formula provided here contains no eggs, for example, although some bakers add them.

The folding-in technique used here differs somewhat from that used by European pastry chefs, although it is widely used by American bakers. (See Figure 34.2.)

Butter is the preferred fat for rolling in because of its flavor and melt-in-the-mouth quality. Special puff pastry shortening is also available. This shortening is much easier to work with than butter because it is not as hard when refrigerated and doesn't soften and melt as easily as butter at warm temperatures. It is also less expensive than butter.

However, puff pastry shortening can be unpleasant to eat because it tends to congeal and coat the inside of the mouth.

Skill at producing puff pastry requires careful attention to your instructor and diligent practice. Take special note of any alternative methods your instructor may present.

 ## Puff Pastry

Ingredients	U.S.		Metric	Percentage
Bread flour	1 lb	8 oz	750 g	75%
Cake flour		8 oz	250 g	25%
Butter, soft		4 oz	125 g	12.5%
Salt		0.5 oz	15 g	1.5%
Water, cold	1 lb	2 oz	562 g	56%
Butter	2 lb		1000 g	100%
Bread flour (see note)		4 oz	125 g	12.5%
Yield:	*5 lb*	*10 oz*	*2827 g*	*282%*

Per 1 ounce:
Calories, 120; Protein, 1 g; Fat 9 g (69% cal.); Cholesterol, 25 mg;
Carbohydrates, 8 g; Fiber, 0 g; Sodium, 150 mg.

Note: The purpose of the 4 oz (125 g) bread flour is to absorb some of the moisture of the butter. Omit if puff paste shortening is used instead of butter.

■ P r o c e d u r e

Mixing:
1. Place the first quantities of flour and butter in a mixing bowl. With a paddle attachment, mix at low speed until well blended.

2. Dissolve the salt in the cold water.

3. Add the salted water to the flour and mix at low speed until a soft dough is formed. Do not overmix.

4. Remove the dough from the mixer and let rest in the refrigerator for 20 minutes.

5. Cream the last quantities of butter and flour at low speed in the mixer until the mixture is about the same consistency as the dough, neither too hard nor too soft.

6. Roll the butter into the dough following the procedure shown in Figure 34.2. Give the dough 4 four-folds or 5 three-folds.

Figure 34.2
Rolling-in procedure for puff pastry.

(a) Dust the bench lightly with flour. Roll dough to a rectangle about 3 times as long as it is wide and about ½ in. (1–1.5 cm) thick. Make the corners as square as possible. Form the butter into a rectangle two-thirds the size of the dough, leaving room around the edges, and place on the dough as shown.

(b) Fold the third without fat over the center third.

(c) Fold the remaining third on top. Fold all ends and corners evenly and squarely. This procedure, enclosing the butter in the dough, does not count as one of the folds. The folding procedure starts with the next step.

(d) Turn the dough 90 degrees on the bench so the length becomes the width. This step must be taken before each rolling-out so the gluten is stretched in all directions, not just lengthwise. Failure to do this results in products that deform or shrink unevenly when they bake. Before rolling, beat the dough lightly as shown so the butter is evenly distributed. Roll the dough into a rectangle. Make sure the corners are square. Roll smoothly and evenly. Do not press down when rolling, or the layers may stick together and the product not rise properly.

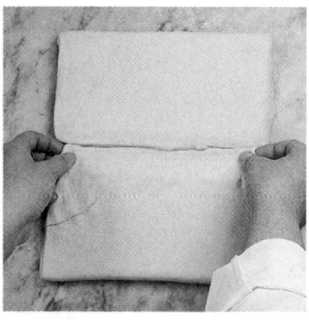

(e) Brush excess flour from the top of the dough.

(f) Fold the top edge of the dough to the center. Make sure the corners are square and even. Again brush off excess flour.

(g) Fold the bottom edge to the center.

(h) Fold the dough in half like closing a book. You have now given the dough *1 four-fold*. Refrigerate the dough for 15 to 20 minutes to relax the gluten. Do not refrigerate it too long, or the butter will become too hard. (If it does, let it soften a few minutes at room temperature before proceeding.)

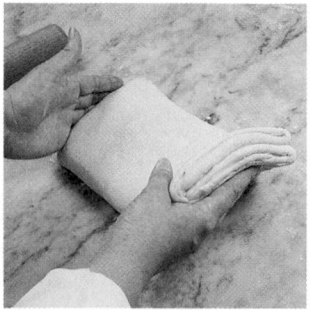

(i) Give the dough another *3 four-folds*, as in steps f to h. After another rest, the dough is ready to be rolled out and made up into the desired products. (Alternative method: Instead of giving the dough *4 four-folds*, you may give it *5 three-folds*.) See Figure 30.3 for the three-fold method.

BLITZ PUFF PASTRY

Blitz puff pastry is much easier and quicker to make than classic puff dough. (*Blitz* is German for "lightning.") It does not rise nearly as high as true puff pastry, so it is not suitable for patty shells and other products where a high, light pastry is desirable. However, it bakes up crisp and flaky and is perfectly suitable for napoleons and similar desserts that are layered with cream fillings.

Blitz puff paste, as you will see, is actually a flaky pie dough that is rolled and folded like regular puff dough.

Blitz Puff Pastry

Ingredients	U.S.	Metric	Percentage
Bread flour	1 lb	500 g	50%
Pastry flour	1 lb	500 g	50%
Butter, slightly softened	2 lb	1000 g	100%
Salt	0.5 oz	15 g	1.5%
Water, cold	1 lb	500 g	50%
Yield:	*5 lb*	*2515 g*	*250%*

Per 1 ounce:
Calories, 120; Protein, 1 g; Fat 9 g (69% cal.); Cholesterol, 25 mg; Carbohydrates, 8 g; Fiber, 1 g; Sodium, 160 mg.

■ Procedure

Mixing:
1. Sift the two flours together into a mixing bowl.
2. Cut the butter into the flour as for pie dough, but leave the fat in very large lumps, 1 in. (2½ cm) across.
3. Dissolve the salt in the water.
4. Add the water to the flour-butter mixture. Mix until the water is absorbed.
5. Let the dough rest for 15 minutes. Refrigerate if the bakeshop is warm.
6. Dust the bench with flour and roll out the dough into a rectangle. Give the dough three 4-folds.

VARIATION

Reduce the butter to 75% (1 lb 8 oz/750 g).

General Guidelines for Makeup of Puff Dough Products

1. The dough should be cool and firm when it is rolled and cut. If it is too soft, the layers may stick together at the cuts, preventing proper rising.
2. Cut with straight, firm, even cuts. Use a sharp cutting tool.
3. Avoid touching the cut edges with your fingers, which can make the layers stick together.
4. For best rising, place units upside down on baking sheets. Even sharp cutting tools may press the top layers of dough together. Baking upside down puts the stuck-together layers at the bottom.
5. Avoid letting egg wash run down the edges. Egg wash can cause the layers to stick together at the edges.
6. Rest made-up products for 30 minutes in a cool place or in the refrigerator before baking. This relaxes the gluten and reduces shrinkage.
7. Press trimmings together, keeping the layers in the same direction. After being rolled out and given another three-fold, they may be used again, although they will not rise as high.
8. Baking temperatures of 400° to 425°F (200° to 220°C) are best for most puff dough products. Cooler temperatures do not create enough steam in the products to leaven them well. Higher temperatures set the crust too quickly.

Procedure for Making Turnovers

See Figure 34.3.
1. Roll out puff pastry dough to ⅛ inch (3 mm) thick.
2. Cut the dough into 4-inch (10-cm) squares. Wash the edges of each with water.
3. Portion the desired filling into the center of each square.
4. Fold diagonally and press the edges together.
5. Puncture the tops with a knife in two or three places to allow steam to escape. Let rest 30 minutes.
6. Brush the tops with egg wash, if desired, or brush with milk or water and sprinkle with sugar.
7. Bake at 400°F (200°C) until crisp and brown.

Figure 34.3
Makeup of turnovers

(a) Cut the dough into 4-in. (10-cm) squares. Wash the edges with water and place filling in the center of each square.

(b) Fold over diagonally and press the edges together. Puncture two or three steam holes in top.

Procedure for Making Pinwheels

See Figure 34.4.

1. Roll out puff dough to ⅛ inch (3 mm) thick.

2. Cut the dough into 5-inch (12-cm) squares.

3. Wash the centers with water.

4. Cut diagonally from the corners to about 1 inch (2.5 cm) from the centers.

5. Fold every other corner into the centers and press in place.

6. Bake at 400°F (200°C).

7. Let cool. Spoon desired fruit filling into the centers. Dust lightly with confectioners' sugar. (Pinwheels may also be filled before baking if the filling is thick and not likely to burn.)

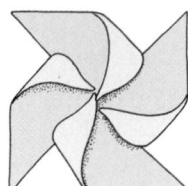

Figure 34.4 Makeup of pinwheels.
(a) Cut the dough into 5-in. (12-cm) squares. Wash the centers with water. Cut diagonally from the corners to 1 in. (2.5 cm) from center.

(b, c, d) Fold every other corner to the center and press down. Fill the center with fruit filling before or after baking.

Procedure for Making Patty Shells

See Figure 34.5.

1. Roll out puff dough to ⅛ inch (3 mm) thick.

2. Roll a second piece of dough to ¼ inch (6 mm) thick.

3. Cut out the same number of circles from each piece of dough with a round 3-inch (7.5-cm) cutter.

4. Using a 2-inch (5-cm) cutter, cut out the centers of the thick circles.

5. Wash the thin circles with water or egg wash and place a ring on top of each. Wash the top carefully with egg wash (do not drip wash down the edges). Let rest 30 minutes.

6. Place a sheet of greased parchment over the tops of the shells to prevent their toppling over while baking.

7. Bake at 400°F (200°C) until brown and crisp.

Figure 34.5
Makeup of patty shells.

(a) Roll 1 sheet of puff dough ⅛ in. (3 mm) thick and another sheet ¼ in. (6 mm) thick. Cut an equal number of 3-in. (7.5-cm) circles from each. Cut out the centers of the thick circles with a 2-in. (5-cm) cutter.

(b) Wash the thin circles with water or eggwash and place the thick circles on top.

Procedure for Making Cream Horns

See Figure 34.6.

1. Roll out puff dough into a sheet ⅛ inch (3 mm) thick and about 15 inches (38 cm) wide.

2. Cut out strips 1¼ inches (3 cm) wide by 15 inches (38 cm) long.

3. Wash the strips with water.

4. With the washed side out, roll the strips diagonally onto cream horn tubes, making a spiral. Overlap the edges by about ⅜ inch (1 cm). If you are using conical tubes, start at the small end.

5. Roll in granulated sugar and lay on baking sheets. The end of the dough strip should be on the bottom so it does not pop up during baking. Let rest 30 minutes.

6. Bake at 400°F (200°C) until brown and crisp.

7. Slip out the tubes while still warm.

8. Just before service, fill the horns from both ends with whipped cream or pastry cream, using a pastry bag with a star tip. Dust with confectioners' sugar.

Figure 34.6
Makeup of cream horns.

(a) Roll puff dough to ⅛ in. (3 mm) thick and cut it into strips 1¼ in. (3 cm) wide and 15 in. (38 cm) long. Wash the strips with water and press one end (washed side out) onto one end of a cream horn tube as shown.

(b) Roll the dough strip in a spiral by turning the tube. Overlap the edges by about ⅜ in. (1 cm). Do not stretch the dough.

(c) Roll completely and press the end in place to seal.

Procedure for Making Napoleons

1. Roll puff dough into a very thin sheet about the size of a sheet pan. Blitz puff paste or rerolled trimmings may be used.

2. Place on sheet pan and let rest 30 minutes.

3. Dock with a fork to prevent blistering.

4. Bake at 400°F (200°C) until brown and crisp.

5. Trim the edges of the pastry sheet and cut with a serrated knife into equal strips 4 inches (10 cm) wide. Set the best one aside for the top layer. (If one of the strips breaks, don't be upset. It can be used as the middle layer.)

6. Spread one rectangle with Vanilla Pastry Cream (p. 1009) or with a mixture of pastry cream and whipped cream.

7. Top with a second sheet of pastry.

8. Spread with another layer of pastry cream.

9. Place a third pastry rectangle on top, flattest side up.

10. Ice top with fondant (p. 953).

11. To decorate, pipe 4 strips of chocolate fondant lengthwise on the white fondant. Draw a spatula or the back of a knife across the top in opposite directions, 1 inch (2.5 cm) apart, as shown in Figure 34.7.

12. Cut into strips 2 inches (5 cm) wide.

Figure 34.7
Decorating napoleons.

(a) Spread the top of the assembled napoleon with white fondant. With a paper cone, pipe 4 strips of chocolate fondant.

(b) Draw a spatula or the back of a knife across the icing at 2-in. (5-cm) intervals.

(c) Draw the spatula in the opposite direction in the center of these 2-in. (5-cm) intervals as shown.

(d) Cut the napoleon into strips 2 in. (5 cm) wide.

ÉCLAIR PASTE

Éclairs and cream puffs are made from a dough called **éclair paste** or *choux paste*. The French name **pâte à choux** (pot a shoo) means "cabbage paste," referring to the fact that cream puffs look like little cabbages.

Unlike puff pastry, éclair paste is extremely easy to make. The dough itself can be prepared in just a few minutes. This is fortunate because for best baking results, the dough should not be prepared ahead of time.

In principle, éclair paste is similar to popover batter, even though one is a thick dough and the other a thin batter. Both products are leavened by steam, which expands the product rapidly and forms large holes in the center. The heat of the oven then coagulates the gluten and egg proteins to set the structure and make a firm product. A strong flour is necessary for sufficient structure.

Éclair paste must be firm enough to hold its shape when piped from a pastry bag. Occasionally, you may find a formula that produces too slack a dough. Correct such a formula by reducing the water or milk slightly.

Proper baking temperatures are important. Start at a high temperature (425° to 475°F/215° to 245°C) for the first 10 minutes to develop steam. Then reduce the heat to 375° to 425°F (190° to 215°C) to finish baking and set the structure. The products must be firm and dry before being removed from the oven. If they are removed too soon or cooled too quickly, they may collapse. Some bakers like to leave them in a turned-off oven with the door ajar. However, if the oven must be heated again for other products, this may not be the best idea, especially in these times of high energy costs. It may be better to bake the products thoroughly, remove them carefully from the oven, and let them cool slowly in a warm place.

Éclair Paste or Pâte à Choux

Ingredients	U.S.	Metric	Percentage
Water, milk, or half water and half milk	1 lb	500 g	133%
Butter or regular shortening	8 oz	250 g	67%
Salt	1 tsp	5 g (5 mL)	1.5%
Bread flour	12 oz	375 g	100%
Eggs	1 lb 4 oz	625 g	167%
Yield:	*3 lb 8 oz*	*1755 g*	*468%*

Per 1 ounce:
Calories, 70; Protein, 2 g; Fat, 4 g (56% cal.); Cholesterol, 35 mg;
Carbohydrates, 5 g; Fiber, 0 g; Sodium, 90 mg.

■ P r o c e d u r e

Mixing:
1. Combine liquid, butter, and salt in a heavy saucepan and bring to a boil.
2. Remove pan from heat and add the flour all at once. Stir quickly.
3. Return the pan to moderate heat and stir vigorously until the dough forms a ball and pulls away from the sides of the pan.
4. Transfer the dough to the bowl of a mixer. If you wish to mix by hand, leave it in the saucepan.
5. With the paddle attachment, mix at low speed until the dough has cooled slightly. It should be about 140°F (60°C)—still very warm, but not too hot to touch.
6. At medium speed, beat in the eggs, a little at a time. Add no more than one-fourth of the eggs at once, and wait until each is completely absorbed before adding the next. When all the eggs are absorbed, the paste is ready to use.

Procedure for Making Cream Puffs

1. Line sheet pans with silicone paper or butter them lightly.
2. Fit a large pastry bag with a plain tube. Fill the bag with the choux paste.
3. Pipe round mounds of dough about 1½ inches (4 cm) in diameter onto the lined baking sheets. If you prefer, you may drop the dough from a spoon (see Figure 34.8).
4. Bake at 425°F (215°C) for 10 minutes. Lower the heat to 375°F (190°C) until the puffs are well browned and very crisp.
5. Remove from oven and cool slowly in a warm place.
6. When cool, cut a slice from the top of each puff. Fill with whipped cream, Vanilla Pastry Cream (p. 1009), or desired filling, using a pastry bag with a star tube.
7. Replace the tops and dust with confectioners' sugar.
8. Fill the puffs as close to service as possible. If cream-filled puffs must be held, keep them refrigerated.
9. Unfilled and uncut puffs, if they are thoroughly dry, may be held in plastic bags in the refrigerator for 1 week. Recrisp in the oven for a few minutes before use.

Figure 34.8
For cream puffs or profiteroles, pipe choux paste into bulbs of desired size onto greased sheet pans, or onto pans that have been lined with parchment.

Procedure for Making Éclairs

1. Proceed as for cream puffs, except pipe the dough into strips about ¾ inch (2 cm) wide and 3 to 4 inches (8 to 10 cm) long (see Figure 34.9). Bake as for cream puffs.
2. Fill baked, cooled éclair shells with pastry cream. Two methods may be used:
   • Make a small hole in one end of the shell and fill using a pastry bag or a doughnut-filling pump.
   • Cut a slice lengthwise from the top and fill using a pastry bag.
3. Dip the tops of the éclairs in chocolate fondant (p. 953).
4. For service and holding, see cream puffs.

Variation: Frozen Éclairs or Profiteroles

1. Fill éclairs or small cream puffs (**profiteroles**) with ice cream. Keep frozen until service.
2. At service time, top with chocolate syrup.

Figure 34.9
For éclairs, pipe choux paste into fingers of desired size onto greased sheet pans, or onto pans that have been lined with parchment.

Procedure for Making French Crullers or French Doughnuts

1. Cut sheets of parchment paper to the same width as your deep fryer.
2. Using a pastry bag with a star tube, pipe choux paste onto the parchment in circles (doughnut shapes) about 2 inches (5 cm) across.
3. Slide the paper with the paste into a deep fryer heated to 375°F (190°C). Remove the paper as the doughnuts release and float free.
4. Fry the doughnuts on both sides until golden brown. French doughnuts must be completely fried, or they may collapse when cooling. Remove and drain on absorbent paper.
5. When cooled, drizzle fondant icing over the tops.

MERINGUES

Meringues are beaten egg whites sweetened with sugar. Their most frequent use in North America is for pie toppings and cake icings (known as boiled icing). They are also used to give volume and lightness to buttercream icings and to such preparations as dessert soufflés.

Another excellent use for meringues is to bake them in a slow oven until crisp. In this form, they can be used in place of cake layers or pastry shells to make light, elegant desserts. Chopped nuts may be folded into meringue before forming and baking to make these desserts more flavorful.

Basic rules for beating egg whites are discussed in Chapter 24, page 789. Please review this section before attempting to make any of the following preparations. We repeat one rule here because it is so important:

Make sure that all equipment is free of any trace of fat or grease, and that the egg whites have no trace of yolk in them. Even a small trace of fat will prevent the whites from foaming properly.

Soft meringues, used for pie topping, may be made with as little as 1 pound (500 g) sugar per pound (500 g) of egg whites. **Hard meringues**, baked until crisp, are made with up to twice as much sugar as egg whites.

BASIC MERINGUES

The stiffness to which meringues are beaten may vary, as long as they are not beaten until they are too stiff and dry. For most purposes, they are beaten until they form stiff, or nearly stiff, moist peaks.

1. **Common meringue** is made from egg whites at room temperature, beaten with sugar. It is the easiest to make, and it is reasonably stable due to the high percentage of sugar.
2. **Swiss meringue** is made from egg whites and sugar warmed over a double boiler while beating. Warming gives this meringue better volume and stability.
3. **Italian meringue** is made by beating a hot sugar syrup into the egg whites. This meringue is the most stable of the three because the egg whites are actually cooked by the heat of the syrup. When flavored with vanilla, this meringue is also known as boiled icing. It is also used in meringue-type buttercream icings.

Meringue

Ingredients	Common Meringue	Swiss Meringue	Italian Meringue
Egg whites	1 lb/500 g	1 lb/500 g	1 lb/500 g
Sugar	2 lb/1 kg	2 lb/1 kg	2 lb/1 kg
Water	—	—	8 fl oz/250 mL

Per 1 ounce:
Calories, 80; Protein, 1 g; Fat, 0 g (0% cal.); Cholesterol, 0 mg; Carbohydrates, 19 g; Fiber, 0 g; Sodium, 15 mg.

Note: For soft meringues to top pies, use half the amount of sugar.

Procedure for Making Common Meringue

1. With the whip attachment, beat the egg whites at high speed until they form soft peaks.
2. Gradually add the sugar with the machine running.
3. Continue to beat until the meringue forms stiff but moist peaks.

Procedure for Making Swiss Meringue

1. Place the egg whites and sugar in a stainless-steel bowl or the top of a double boiler. Beat with a wire whip over hot water until the mixture is warm (about 120°F/50°C).
2. Transfer the mixture to the bowl of a mixing machine and whip at high speed until stiff peaks form.

Procedure for Making Italian Meringue

1. Heat the sugar and water in a saucepan until the sugar dissolves and the mixture boils. Boil until a candy thermometer placed in the mixture registers 240°F (115°C).
2. While the syrup is cooking, beat the egg whites in a mixing machine until they form soft peaks.
3. With the machine running, very slowly beat the hot syrup into the egg whites.
4. Continue beating until the meringue forms firm peaks.

MERINGUE DESSERTS

Procedure for Making Pie Topping

1. Make common meringue or Swiss meringue using equal parts sugar and egg whites. Beat until just stiff.
2. Spread a generous amount (2–3 cups/500–700 mL) of meringue on still-warm pies. Mound it slightly and be sure to attach it to the edge of the crust all around. If this is not done, the meringue may slide around on the finished pie. Leave the meringue in ripples or peaks.
3. Bake at 400°F (200°C) until the surface is attractively browned.
4. Remove from oven and cool.

Procedure for Making Baked Meringue Shells

1. Beat common or Swiss meringue until stiff.
2. Using a pastry bag or a spoon, form the meringue into small nest shapes on a parchment-lined baking sheet.
3. Bake at 200° to 225°F (about 100°C) until crisp but not browned. This will take 1 to 3 hours.
4. Cool the shells and remove from the parchment. Be careful, as they may be fragile.
5. Use in place of pastry shells for fruit tarts, fill with whipped cream and fresh strawberries or raspberries, or fill with a scoop of ice cream and garnish with chocolate or raspberry sauce. Crisp meringues with ice cream make a dessert called meringue glacée (glah say).

Procedure for Making Japonaise Meringues

Japonaise (zhah po nez) meringues are used like cake layers. They may be filled and iced with light butter-cream, chocolate mousse, whipped cream, or similar light icings and creams.

1. Prepare 1 recipe (1 pound or 500 g egg whites plus 2 pounds or 1 kg sugar) Swiss meringue.
2. Quickly but carefully fold in 1 pound (500 g) finely chopped hazelnuts.
3. With a pastry bag, form circles of the desired diameter and about ½ inch (1.5 cm) thick on parchment-lined sheet pans, as shown in Figure 34.10.
4. Bake as for meringue shells.

Figure 34.10 To make meringue layers, mark a circle on a sheet of parchment and pipe the meringue in a spiral to fill the circle.

Procedure for Making Baked Alaska

1. Pack softened ice cream into a dome-shaped mold of the desired size. Freeze solid.
2. Prepare a layer of sponge cake the same size as the flat side of the mold and about ½ inch (1.5 cm) thick.
3. Unmold the frozen ice cream onto the cake layer so the cake forms a base for the ice cream.
4. With a spatula, cover the entire dessert with a thick layer of meringue. If desired, decorate with more meringue forced from a pastry bag.
5. Bake at 450°F (230°C) until the meringue is golden brown.
6. Serve immediately.

FRUIT DESSERTS

Fruit desserts are included here because many are similar to pies or pie fillings. Special favorites include cobblers, which are much like fruit pies made in large baking pans without a bottom crust; crisps, which are like cobblers, but with brown-sugar streusel topping instead of a pastry crust; and bettys, which have alternate layers of rich cake crumbs and fruit. Also, don't overlook fresh fruits for dessert, served plain, lightly sweetened, or with cream.

Fruit Cobbler

Yield: 1 pan, 12 x 20 inches (30 x 50 cm)   Portion: 48   Portion size: about 5 oz (150 g)

U.S.	Metric	Ingredients
12–15 lb	5.5–7 kg	Fruit pie filling (apple, cherry, blueberry, peach, etc.)
2 lb	1 kg	Flaky pie pastry

Per 1 serving:
Calories, 200; Protein, 1 g; Fat, 7 g (29% cal.); Cholesterol, 0 mg; Carbohydrates, 37 g; Fiber, 2 g; Sodium, 115 mg.

Note: If possible, use stainless-steel pans instead of aluminum pans. The acid of the fruit will react with aluminum and create an undesirable flavor.

■ Procedure

1. Place fruit filling in a baking pan measuring 12 × 20 in. (30 × 50 cm) (see note).
2. Roll out the pastry in a rectangle to fit the top of the baking pan. Place the pastry on the filling and seal the edge to the side of the pan. Pierce small holes in the pastry to allow steam to escape.
3. Bake at 425°F for about 30 minutes, until the top is browned.
4. Cut the dessert 6x8 to make 48 portions. Serve warm or cold.

Apple Betty

Yield: 1 pan, 12 x 20 inches (30 x 50 cm)   Portions: 48   Portion size: 4 oz (125 g)

U.S.	Metric	Ingredients
8 lb EP	4 kg EP	Apples, peeled and sliced
1 lb 8 oz	750 g	Sugar
1½ tsp	7 mL	Salt
1 tsp	5 mL	Nutmeg
1 tsp	15 mL	Grated lemon zest
2 fl oz	60 mL	Lemon juice
2 lb	1 kg	Yellow or white cake crumbs
8 oz	250 g	Melted butter

Per serving:
Calories, 200; Protein, 1 g; Fat, 7 g (30% cal); Cholesterol, 20 mg; Carbohydrates, 36 g; Fiber, 2 g; Sodium, 180 mg.

■ Procedure

1. Combine the apples, sugar, salt, nutmeg, lemon zest, and lemon juice in a bowl. Toss gently until well mixed.
2. Place one-third of the apple mixture in an even layer in a well-buttered baking pan measuring 12 × 20 in. (30 × 50 cm).
3. Top with one-third of the cake crumbs.
4. Continue until all the apples and crumbs have been used. You will have 3 layers of fruit and 3 layers of crumbs.
5. Pour the melted butter evenly over the top.
6. Bake at 350°F (175°C) for about 1 hour, until fruit is tender.

Apple Crisp

Yield: 1 pan, 12 x 20 inches (30 x 50 cm)   Portion: 48   Portion size: 4 oz (125 g)

U.S.	Metric	Ingredients
8 lb EP	4 kg EP	Apples, peeled and sliced
4 oz	125 g	Granulated sugar
2 fl oz	60 mL	Lemon juice
1 lb	500 g	Butter
1 lb 8 oz	750 g	Brown sugar
2 tsp	10 mL	Cinnamon
1 lb 8 oz	750 g	Pastry flour

■ P r o c e d u r e

1. Toss the apple gently with the granulated sugar and lemon juice.
2. Spread the apples evenly in a baking pan measuring 12 × 20 in. (30 × 50 cm) (see note).

3. Rub the butter, brown sugar, cinnamon, and flour together until well blended and crumbly.
4. Sprinkle evenly over the apples.
5. Bake at 350°F (175°C) for about 45 minutes, until the top is browned and the apples are tender.

V A R I A T I O N

Peach, Cherry, or Rhubarb Crisp
Substitute the indicated fruit for the apples. If rhubarb is used, increase the sugar in step 1 to 12 oz (350 g).

Per serving:
Calories, 180; Protein, 2 g; Fat, 8 g (37% cal.); Cholesterol, 20 mg; Carbohydrates, 28 g; Fiber, 2 g; Sodium, 85 mg.

Note: If possible, use stainless-steel pans instead of aluminum pans. The acid of the fruit will react with aluminum and create an undesirable flavor.

 Poached Pears

Portions: 24   Portion size: 2 pear halves

U.S.	Metric	Ingredients
2 qt	2 L	Water
3 lb	1.5 kg	Sugar
4 tsp	20 mL	Vanilla
24	24	Pears

■ P r o c e d u r e

1. Combine the water and sugar in a trunnion kettle or large saucepot. Bring to a boil. stirring until the sugar is dissolved.
2. Remove from heat and add the vanilla.

3. Peel the pears. Cut them in half and remove the cores with a melon ball cutter.
4. Add the pears to the syrup and simmer very slowly until just tender.
5. Let the pears cool in the syrup. When cool, refrigerate in the syrup until needed for service.

V A R I A T I O N S

Pears in Wine
Substitute red or white table wine for the water. Omit vanilla. Add 1 sliced lemon to the syrup. Peel the pears but leave them whole.

Poached Peaches
Substitute peaches for pears in basic recipe.

Peaches in Wine
Substitute peaches for pears in recipe for Pears in Wine.

Per serving:
Calories, 320; Protein, 1 g; Fat, 0.5 g (1% cal.); Cholesterol, 0 mg; Carbohydrates, 82 g; Fiber, 4 g; Sodium, 5 mg.

Raspberry or Cherry Gratin

Portions: 1

U.S.	Metric	Ingredients	Procedure
3 oz	90 g	Raspberries or sweet, pitted cherries	1. Select a shallow gratin dish or other heatproof dish large enough to hold the fruit in a shallow layer.
1	1	Genoise layer (see step 2)	2. Cut a thin slice of genoise, about ⅜ in. (1 cm) thick, to cover the bottom of the dish.
2 oz	60 g	Pastry cream	3. Arrange the fruit on top of the genoise.
1 oz	30 g	Whipped cream	4. Combine the pastry cream, whipped cream, and flavoring. Spread the mixture over the fruit to cover completely.
to taste	to taste	Optional flavoring: kirsch, orange liqueur, or raspberry or cherry brandy	
¼ oz	7 g	Sliced almonds	5. Mix the almonds and butter and sprinkle over the pastry cream. Dredge the top heavily with confectioners' sugar.
¼ oz	7 g	Melted butter	6. Place under a broiler or in the top of a hot oven for a few minutes to brown the top. Serve hot.
as needed	as needed	Confectioners' sugar	

Per serving:
Calories, 480; Protein, 7 g; Fat, 27 g (50% cal.); Cholesterol, 165 mg; Carbohydrates, 53 g; Fiber, 7 g; Sodium, 145 mg.

■ TERMS FOR REVIEW

flaky pie dough	cream pie	blitz puff pastry	hard meringue
mealy pie dough	chiffon pie	napoleon	common meringue
crumb crust	instant starch	éclair paste	Swiss meringue
short dough	cooked juice method	pâte à choux	Italian meringue
fruit pie	cooked fruit method	profiterole	meringue glacée
soft pie	puff pastry	soft meringue	Baked Alaska

■ QUESTIONS FOR DISCUSSION

1. Discuss the factors that affect tenderness, toughness, and flakiness in pie dough. Why should emulsified shortening not be used for pie dough?

2. What kind of crust or crusts would you use for a pumpkin pie? an apple pie? a banana cream pie?

3. What would happen to a flaky pie dough if you mixed it too long before adding the water? after adding the water?

4. How can you prevent shrinkage when baking pie shells?

5. What are the remedies for soggy or undercooked bottom pie crusts?

6. What starch would you use to thicken apple pie filling? chocolate pie filling? lemon pie filling? peach pie filling?

7. Why is lemon juice added to lemon pie filling after the starch has thickened the water? Wouldn't this thin the filling?

8. Why is it important to bake cream puffs and éclairs thoroughly and to cool them slowly?

9. Briefly describe the difference between common, Swiss, and Italian meringues.

35

CHAPTER

Creams, Custards, Puddings, Frozen Desserts, and Sauces

A quick glance at this last chapter may give you the impression that you will be overwhelmed with a great many recipes and techniques within a few pages. Among the subjects covered are custard sauces, pastry cream, puddings, custards, mousses, bavarians, soufflés, ice cream, and dessert sauces.

It's all much simpler than it seems. Once you have learned three basic preparations—vanilla custard sauce, pastry cream, and baked custard—you will have learned most of the rest. Vanilla custard sauce, also called *crème anglaise* (krem awng glezz) or *English cream*, is the basis for bavarians, ice cream, and some dessert sauces. Pastry cream, with a variety of flavorings, is also used for pie fillings and puddings and is the basis for some soufflés. Many baked puddings are baked custard with added starch or fruit ingredients.

There seems little point in giving you recipes for cream pie fillings in the pie section, a recipe for pastry cream filling for napoleons in the puff pastry section, and recipes for boiled puddings in the pudding section, and never tell you that they are all basically the same preparation. You are not just learning a collection of unrelated recipes; you are learning to cook and to understand what you are cooking.

After reading this chapter, you should be able to

1. **Cook sugar syrups to the seven stages of hardness.**

2. **Prepare crème anglaise, pastry cream, and baked custard.**

3. **Prepare starch-thickened puddings and baked puddings.**

4. **Prepare bavarians, chiffons, mousses, and dessert soufflés.**

5. **Assemble frozen desserts.**

6. **Prepare dessert sauces.**

SUGAR COOKING

Understanding sugar cooking is important in the preparation of desserts and confections because sugar syrups of various strengths are often required (see, for example, Italian Meringue, p. 1000).

BASIC PRINCIPLES

The principle of sugar cooking is fairly simple. A solution or syrup of sugar and water is boiled to evaporate part of the water. As the water is boiled off, the temperature of the syrup gradually rises. When all the water has evaporated, what you have left is melted sugar. The sugar then begins to caramelize or turn brown and change flavor. If heating continues, the sugar continues to darken and then burn.

A syrup cooked to a high temperature is harder when it is cooled than a syrup cooked to a lower temperature. For example, a syrup cooked to 240°F (115°C) forms a soft ball when cooled. A syrup cooked to 300°F (150°C) is hard and brittle when cooled.

One part water (by weight) is enough to dissolve and cook 3 to 4 parts sugar. There is no point in adding more water than is necessary because you just have to boil it off.

SIMPLE SYRUP

Simple syrup is a solution of equal weights of sugar and water. Combine equal weights of water and granulated sugar in a saucepan, stir, and bring to a boil to dissolve the sugar. Cool the syrup.

Dessert syrup is a flavored simple syrup used to moisten and flavor some cakes (see p. 943). (Many chefs use 2 or 3 parts water to 1 part sugar for a less sweet syrup.) Flavorings may be extracts, such as vanilla, or liquors, such as rum or kirsch. Add flavorings after the syrup has cooled because flavor may be lost if they are added to hot syrup. Syrups may also be flavored by boiling them with lemon or orange rind.

CRYSTALLIZATION

Graininess is a common fault in many candies and desserts. Graininess results when cooked sugar **crystallizes** or turns to tiny sugar crystals rather than staying dissolved in the syrup. If even one sugar crystal comes in contact with a cooked syrup, it can start a chain reaction that turns the whole thing into a mass of sugar crystals.

To avoid crystallization during the first stages of boiling, use one of the following techniques:

1. Wash down the sides of the saucepan with a brush dipped in water. This removes crystals that may seed the whole batch.

2. When first bringing the syrup to a boil, cover the pan and boil for several minutes. Condensed steam will wash down the sides of the pan. Uncover and finish cooking without stirring.

Sometimes an acid such as cream of tartar is added to a syrup before cooking. Acids change some of the sugar to *invert sugar*, which resists crystallizing. Corn syrup is sometimes added for the same reason.

STAGES OF SUGAR COOKING

Testing the temperature with a candy thermometer is the most accurate way to determine the desired doneness of a syrup.

In the old days, syrups were tested by dropping a little bit into a bowl of cold water and checking the hardness of the cooled sugar. The stages of doneness were given names that described their hardness. Table 35.1 lists these stages of sugar cooking.

Table 35.1 Stages of Doneness in Sugar Cooking		
	Temperature	
Stage	**°F**	**°C**
Thread	230	110
Soft ball	240	115
Firm ball	245	118
Hard ball	250–260	122–127
Small crack	265–270	130–132
Crack	275–280	135–138
Hard crack	290–310	143–155
Caramel	320–340	160–170

BASIC CUSTARDS AND CREAMS

The three preparations presented in this section are among the most basic and useful preparations in the bakeshop. All three can be classified as custards because they consist of a liquid thickened by the coagulation of eggs.

Crème anglaise, or vanilla custard sauce, is a stirred custard. It consists of milk, sugar, and egg yolks (and vanilla) stirred over very low heat until lightly thickened.

Pastry cream contains starch thickeners as well as eggs, resulting in a much thicker and more stable product. It is used as a cake and pastry filling, as a filling for cream pies, and as a pudding. With additional liquid, it is used as a custard sauce.

Baked custard, like vanilla custard sauce, consists of milk, sugar, eggs, and flavoring (usually whole eggs are used for greater thickening power). But, unlike the sauce, it is baked rather than stirred over heat so it sets and becomes firm. Baked custard is used as a pie filling, as a dessert by itself, and as a basis for many baked puddings.

All of these preparations are subject to a wide range of variations. Because they are based on eggs, it would be helpful for you to review the basic egg cooking principles discussed in Chapter 24.

CRÈME ANGLAISE

The following recipe gives the method for preparing vanilla custard sauce, or crème anglaise. Special care is necessary in preparing this sauce because the eggs can curdle easily if overcooked. The following guidelines will help you succeed.

1. Use clean, sanitized equipment and follow strict sanitation procedures. Egg mixtures are good breeding grounds for bacteria that cause food poisoning.

2. When combining the egg yolks and sugar, whip the mixture as soon as the sugar is added. Letting sugar and egg yolks stand together without mixing creates lumps that cannot be beaten out. Using a stainless-steel bowl for this step makes the cooking and stirring easier in step 5.

3. Heat the milk to scalding (just below simmering) before combining with the egg yolks. This makes the final cooking much shorter. To avoid scorching the milk, you can set the pan of milk in a pan of boiling water. This takes longer than using direct heat, but the pan can be left unattended for a few minutes while you perform other tasks.

4. *Slowly* beat the hot milk into the beaten eggs and sugar. This raises the temperature of the eggs gradually and helps prevent curdling.

5. Set the bowl containing the egg mixture in a pan of simmering water and stir constantly to prevent curdling.

6. To test for doneness, two methods are available. Keep in mind that this is a very light sauce, so you can't expect a lot of thickening.
    - Check the temperature with a thermometer. When it reaches 185°F (85°C), the sauce is cooked. Never let the temperature go above 190°F (87°C).
    - When the mixture lightly coats the back of a spoon instead of running off like milk, the sauce is cooked.

7. *Immediately* cool the sauce by setting the pan or bowl in ice water. Stir occasionally to cool it evenly.

8. If the sauce curdles, it is sometimes possible to save it. Immediately stir in 1 to 2 ounces (30–60 mL) cold milk, transfer the sauce to a blender, and blend at high speed.

Crème Anglaise (Vanilla Custard Sauce)

Yield: about 2½ pt (1.25 L)

U.S.	Metric	Ingredients	■ P r o c e d u r e
12	12	Egg yolks	1. Review the guidelines for preparing vanilla custard sauce preceding this recipe.
8 oz	250 g	Sugar	2. Combine the egg yolks and sugar in a stainless-steel bowl. Whip until thick and light.
1 qt	1 L	Milk	3. Scald the milk in a boiling-water bath or over direct heat.
			4. Very gradually pour the scalded milk into the egg yolk mixture while stirring constantly with the whip.
			5. Set the bowl over simmering water. Heat it slowly, stirring constantly, until it thickens enough to coat the back of a spoon (or until it reaches 185°F/85°C).
1 tbsp	15 mL	Vanilla	6. Immediately remove the bowl from the heat and set it in a pan of cool water. Stir in the vanilla. Stir the sauce occasionally as it cools.

Per 1 ounce:
Calories, 60; Protein, 2 g; Fat, 2.5 g (38 % cal.); Cholesterol, 65 mg; Carbohydrates, 7 g; Fiber, 0 g; Sodium, 15 mg.

V A R I A T I O N

Chocolate Crème Anglaise
Melt 6 oz (175 g) sweetened chocolate. Stir into the Crème Anglaise while it is still warm (not hot).

PASTRY CREAM

Although it requires more ingredients and steps, pastry cream is easier to make than custard because it is less likely to curdle. Pastry cream contains a starch thickening agent that stabilizes the eggs. It can actually be boiled without curdling. In fact, it *must* be brought to a boil, or the starch will not cook completely and the cream will have a raw, starchy taste.

Strict observance of all sanitation rules is essential when preparing pastry cream because of the danger of bacterial contamination. Use clean, sanitized equipment. Do not put your fingers in the cream, and do not taste it except with a clean spoon. Chill the finished cream rapidly in shallow pans. Keep the cream and all cream-filled products refrigerated at all times.

The procedure for preparing pastry cream is given in the following recipe. Note that the basic steps are similar to those for custard sauce. In this case, however, a starch is mixed with the eggs and half the sugar to make a smooth paste. (In some recipes with lower egg content, it is necessary to add a little cold milk to provide enough liquid to make a paste.) Meanwhile, the milk is scalded with the other half of the sugar (the sugar helps protect the milk from scorching on the bottom of the pan).

The egg mixture is then tempered with some of the hot milk, returned to the kettle, and brought to a boil. Some chefs prefer to add the cold paste gradually to the hot milk, but the tempering procedure given here seems to give better protection against lumping and curdling.

Pastry Cream Variations

Cream pie fillings and puddings are actually pastry cream flavored with various ingredients.

Cornstarch should be used as the thickening agent when the cream is to be used as a pie filling so the cut slices hold their shape. For other uses, either cornstarch or flour may be used. Remember that twice as much flour as cornstarch is required for the same thickening power. Other variations are possible, as you will see in the recipes. Sometimes whipped cream is folded into cold pastry cream to lighten it and make it creamier.

Lemon pie filling is also a variation of pastry cream. It is made with water instead of milk, and it is flavored with lemon juice and grated lemon rind.

 ## Vanilla Pastry Cream

Yield: about 2¼ qt (2.25 L)

U.S.	Metric	Ingredients
8 oz	250 g	Sugar
2 qt	2 L	Milk
8	8	Egg yolks
4	4	Whole eggs
5 oz	150 g	Cornstarch
8 oz	250 g	Sugar
4 oz	125 g	Butter
1 fl oz	30 mL	Vanilla

Per 1 ounce:
Calories, 70; Protein, 2 g; Fat, 3 g (38% cal.); Cholesterol, 45 mg; Carbohydrates, 9 g; Fiber, 0 g; Sodium 30 mg.

■ P r o c e d u r e

1. In a heavy saucepan or trunnion kettle, dissolve the sugar in the milk and bring just to a boil.
2. With a whip, beat the egg yolks and whole eggs in a stainless-steel bowl.
3. Sift the starch and sugar into the eggs. Beat with the whip until perfectly smooth.
4. Temper the egg mixture by slowly beating in the hot milk in a thin stream.
5. Return the mixture to the heat and bring to a boil, stirring constantly.
6. When the mixture comes to a boil and thickens, remove from the heat.
7. Stir in the butter and vanilla. Mix until the butter is melted and completely blended in.
8. Pour into a clean, sanitized hotel pan or other shallow pan. Dust lightly with sugar and cover with waxed paper to keep a crust from forming. Cool and chill as quickly as possible.
9. For filling pastries such as éclairs and napoleons, whip the chilled pastry cream until smooth before using.

V A R I A T I O N S

For a lighter pastry cream filling, fold whipped heavy cream into the chilled pastry cream. Quantities may be varied to taste. For every 2 qt (2 L) pastry cream, whip 1–2 cups (250–500 mL) heavy cream.

Chocolate Pastry Cream
Melt together 4 oz (125 g) sweetened chocolate and 4 oz (125 g) unsweetened chocolate. Stir into the hot pastry cream.

Coffee Pastry Cream
Add 4 tbsp (60 mL) instant coffee powder to the milk in step 1.

CREAM PIE FILLINGS
Quantities for four 8-inch (20-cm) pies

Vanilla Cream Pie Filling
This is the same as Vanilla Pastry Cream. Fill prebaked pie shells with cooled but not chilled filling.

Coconut Cream Pie Filling
Add 8 oz (250 g) toasted unsweetened coconut to Vanilla Pastry Cream.

Banana Cream Pie Filling
Using Vanilla Cream Pie Filling, pour half of the filling into the pie shells, cover with sliced bananas, and fill with remaining filling. (Bananas may be dipped in lemon juice to help prevent browning.)

Chocolate Cream Pie Filling I
This is the same as Chocolate Pastry Cream, above.

Chocolate Cream Pie Filling II
In step 1, use only 3½ pt (1.75 L) milk. Add 3 oz (90 g) cocoa to dry ingredients (sugar and cornstarch) in basic Vanilla Pastry Cream recipe. Add 8 fl oz (250 mL) cold milk to the eggs.

Butterscotch Cream Pie Filling
Combine 2 lb (900 g) brown sugar and 10 oz (300 g) butter in a saucepan over low heat. Heat and stir until butter is melted and ingredients are blended. Omit all the sugar from the basic Vanilla Pastry Cream recipe (steps 1 and 3). Increase the starch to 6 oz (175 g). As the mixture is nearing a boil in step 5, gradually stir in the brown sugar mixture. Finish as in basic recipe.

Lemon Pie Filling
Follow the procedure for Vanilla Pastry Cream, but make the following ingredient adjustments:
1. Use water instead of milk.
2. Increase sugar in step 1 to 1 lb (450 g).
3. Increase the cornstarch to 6 oz (175 g).
4. Add the grated zest of 2 lemons to the egg mixture.
5. Add 8 fl oz (250 mL) lemon juice to the finished, hot cream instead of the vanilla.

CREAM PUDDINGS

Vanilla Pudding
Coconut Pudding
Banana Cream Pudding
Chocolate Pudding I and II
Butterscotch Pudding

} For each of these puddings, prepare the corresponding pie filling but use only half the cornstarch.

BAKED CUSTARD

Baked custard is a mixture of eggs, milk, sugar, and flavorings that is baked until the eggs coagulate and the custard is set. A good custard holds a clean, sharp edge when cut.

The following recipe gives the procedure for making baked custard. Note these points in particular:

1. Scald the milk before beating it slowly into the eggs. This reduces cooking time and helps the product cook more evenly.

2. Remove any foam, which would mar the appearance of the finished product.

3. Bake at 325°F (165°C). High temperatures increase the risk of overcooking and curdling.

4. Bake in a water bath so the outside edges are not overcooked before the inside is set.

5. To test for doneness, insert a thin-bladed knife about 1 to 2 inches (3–5 cm) from the center. If it comes out clean, the custard is done. The center may not be completely set, but the custard will continue to cook in its own heat after removal from the oven.

Baked Custard

Portions: 12	*Portion size: 5 oz (150 g)*		
U.S.	**Metric**	**Ingredients**	
1 lb	500 g	Eggs	
8 oz	250 g	Sugar	
½ tsp	2 mL	Salt	
½ fl oz	15 mL	Vanilla	
2½ pt	1.25 L	Milk	

Per serving:
Calories, 190; Protein, 8 g; Fat, 7 g (33% cal.); Cholesterol, 175 mg; Carbohydrates, 24 g; Fiber, 0 g; Sodium, 190 mg.

■ P r o c e d u r e

1. Combine the eggs, sugar, salt, and vanilla in a mixing bowl. Mix until thoroughly blended, but do not whip.

2. Scald the milk in a double boiler or in a saucepan over low heat.

3. Gradually pour the milk into the egg mixture, stirring constantly.

4. Skim off all foam from the surface of the liquid.

5. Arrange custard cups in a shallow baking pan. (Butter the insides of the cups if the custards are to be unmolded.)

6. Carefully pour the custard mixture into the cups. If any bubbles form during this step, skim them off.

7. Set the baking pan on the oven shelf. Pour enough hot water into the pan around the cups so that the level of the water is about as high as the level of the custard mixture.

8. Bake at 325°F (165°C) until set, about 45 minutes.

9. Carefully remove from the oven and cool. Store, covered, in refrigerator.

V A R I A T I O N

Crème Caramel
Cook 12 oz (375 g) sugar and 2 fl oz (60 mL) water until it caramelizes (see the section on sugar cooking at the beginning of this chapter). Line the bottoms of the custard cups with the hot caramel. (Be sure the cups are clean and dry.) Fill with custard and bake as in basic recipe.

PUDDINGS

It is difficult to give a definition of pudding that includes everything called by that name. The term is used for such different dishes as chocolate pudding, blood sausages (blood puddings), and steak-and-kidney pudding. In this chapter, however, we consider only the more popular dessert puddings.

Two kinds of puddings, starch-thickened and baked, are the most frequently prepared in food service kitchens. These are the types we discuss here. A third type, steamed pudding, is less often served, and then mainly in cold weather, because steamed puddings are usually rather heavy and filling.

STARCH-THICKENED PUDDINGS

These are also called *boiled puddings* because they are boiled in order to cook the starch that thickens them.

1. **Cornstarch pudding or blancmange.**
   Cornstarch pudding consists of milk, sugar, and flavorings and is thickened with cornstarch (or, sometimes, another starch). If enough cornstarch is used, the hot mixture may be poured into molds, chilled, and unmolded for service.

2. **Cream puddings.**
   Cream puddings, as you learned in the previous section, are the same as pastry cream. Puddings are usually made with less starch, however, and may contain any of several flavoring ingredients, such as coconut or chocolate. Butterscotch pudding is given its flavor by using brown sugar instead of white sugar.

   If you look again at the recipe for Vanilla Pastry Cream (p. 1009), you will see that the only difference between cornstarch puddings and cream puddings is that the latter contain eggs. In fact, cream puddings may be made by stirring hot cornstarch pudding into beaten eggs, then heating the entire mixture to just below the simmer. Care must be taken to avoid curdling the eggs if this method is used.

   A basic recipe for cornstarch pudding follows. Recipes for cream puddings are included among the variations following the recipe for Vanilla Pastry Cream.

Blancmange, English Style

Portions: 12 Portion size: 4 oz (125 g)

U.S.	Metric	Ingredients	
			■ P r o c e d u r e
1 qt	1 L	Milk	1. Combine the milk, sugar, and salt in a heavy saucepan and bring to a simmer.
6 oz	190 g	Sugar	
¼ tsp	1 mL	Salt	
4 oz	125 g	Cornstarch	2. Mix the cornstarch and cold milk until perfectly smooth.
8 fl oz	250 mL	Milk, cold	3. Pouring in a thin stream, add about 1 cup (250 mL) hot milk to the cornstarch mixture.
			4. Stir this mixture back into the hot milk.
			5. Stir over low heat until the mixture thickens and comes to a boil.
1½ tsp	7 mL	Almond or vanilla extract	6. Remove from heat and add desired flavoring.
			7. Pour into ½-cup (125-mL) molds. Cool, then chill. Unmold for service.

Per Serving:
Calories, 150; Protein, 3 g; Fat, 3.5 g (20% cal.); Cholesterol, 15 mg; Carbohydrates, 28 g; Fiber, 0 g; Sodium, 100 mg.

Note: French blancmange is very different from English. The French style is made with almond milk and gelatin.

V A R I A T I O N S

Blancmange or cornstarch pudding may be flavored in any way that cream puddings are. See the variations following the Vanilla Pastry Cream recipe.

BAKED PUDDINGS

Baked puddings are custards that contain additional ingredients, usually in large quantities. Bread pudding, for example, is made by pouring a custard mixture over pieces of bread in a pan and baking it in the oven. Rice pudding, another popular item, is made of cooked rice and custard.

The procedure for making baked puddings is the same as for making baked custard. A water bath may not be necessary if the starch content of the pudding is high.

Soft pie fillings, such as pumpkin, could also be considered baked puddings.

Rice Pudding

Portions: 12   Portion size: 5 oz (150 g)

U.S.	Metric	Ingredients
8 oz	225 g	Rice (medium- or long-grain)
1½ qt	1.5 L	Milk
1 tsp	5 mL	Vanilla
¼ tsp	1 mL	Salt
1	1	Whole egg
2	2	Egg yolks
8 oz	250 g	Sugar
8 fl oz	250 mL	Light cream
as needed	as needed	Cinnamon

Per serving:
Calories, 270; Protein, 7 g; Fat, 9 g (30 % cal.); Cholesterol, 80 mg; Carbohydrates, 40 g; Fiber, 0 g; Sodium, 120 mg.

■ P r o c e d u r e

1. Wash the rice well. Drain.
2. Combine the rice, milk, vanilla, and salt in a heavy saucepan. Cover and simmer over very low heat until the rice is tender, about 30 minutes. Stir occasionally to be sure the mixture doesn't scorch on the bottom. Remove from heat when cooked.
3. Combine the egg, yolks, sugar, and cream in a mixing bowl. Mix until evenly combined.
4. Ladle some of the hot milk from the cooked rice into this mixture and mix well. Then very slowly stir the egg mixture back into the hot rice.
5. Pour into a buttered baking pan, 12 × 20 in. (30 × 50 cm). Sprinkle the top with cinnamon.
6. Bake in a water bath at 350°F (175°C) for 30–40 minutes, until set. Serve warm or chilled.

V A R I A T I O N S

Raising Rice Pudding
Add 8 oz (250 g) raisins to the cooked rice and milk mixture.

Bread and Butter Pudding

Portions: 12   Portion size: 6½ oz (200 g)

U.S.	Metric	Ingredients
1 lb	500 g	White bread, in thin slices
4 oz	125 g	Melted butter
1 lb	500 g	Eggs
8 oz	250 g	Sugar
½ tsp	2 mL	Salt
½ fl oz	15 mL	Vanilla
2½ pt	1.25 L	Milk
as needed	as needed	Cinnamon
as needed	as needed	Nutmeg

Per serving:
Calories, 350; Protein, 11 g; Fat, 16 g (41% cal.); Cholesterol, 190 mg; Carbohydrates, 41 g; Fiber, 1 g; Sodium, 440 mg.

■ P r o c e d u r e

1. Cut each slice of bread in half. Brush both sides of each piece with melted butter.
2. Arrange the bread overlapping in a buttered baking pan, 12 x 20 in. (30 x 50 cm).
3. Mix together the eggs, sugar, salt, and vanilla until thoroughly combined.
4. Gradually stir in the milk.
5. Pour the custard mixture over the bread slices in the pan. Let stand, refrigerated, for 1 hour or longer, so that the bread absorbs the custard mixture.
6. Sprinkle the top lightly with cinnamon and nutmeg.
7. Set the pan in a larger pan containing about 1 in. (3 cm) hot water.
8. Place in an oven preheated to 350°F (175°C). Bake about 1 hour, until set.
9. Serve warm or cold with whipped cream or light custard sauce, or dusted with confectioners' sugar.

V A R I A T I O N

Cabinet Pudding
Prepare in individual custard cups instead of a baking pan. Substitute diced sponge cake for the bread and omit the melted butter. Add about 1 tbsp (15 mL) raisins to each cup before pouring in the custard mix.

BAVARIANS, CHIFFONS, MOUSSES, AND SOUFFLÉS

All the preparations in this section have one thing in common: They all have a light, fluffy, or puffed texture created by the addition of whipped cream, beaten egg whites, or both.

Although these particular products may be new to you, you should have little trouble learning to prepare them if you have already studied the previous chapter and the first part of this chapter. Once you have learned to prepare crème anglaise, pastry cream, starch-thickened fruit fillings, meringues, and whipped cream and have learned to work with gelatin (read p. 717 if you have not yet studied gelatin), all you have to do is combine these products in different ways to make bavarians, chiffons, mousses, and soufflés.

Let's look at these four items separately to see what they are made of. Afterward, we examine the procedures for assembling them.

BAVARIANS

A **bavarian**, also known as bavarian cream or bavaroise, is made of three basic elements: crème anglaise (flavored as desired), gelatin, and whipped cream.

That's all there is to it. Gelatin is softened in cold liquid, stirred into the hot crème anglaise until dissolved, and chilled until almost set. Whipped cream is then folded in, and the mixture is poured into a mold until set. It is unmolded for service.

Accurate measuring of the gelatin is important. If not enough gelatin is used, the dessert will be too soft to hold its shape. If too much is used, it will be too firm and rubbery.

CHIFFONS

Chiffons are most popular as fillings for chiffon pies, but they may also be served more simply as puddings and chilled desserts.

The major difference between chiffons and bavarians is that beaten egg whites are used in place of or in addition to whipped cream. In other words, chiffons are made of a base plus gelatin plus beaten egg whites. (Some chiffons also contain whipped cream.)

Bases for chiffons include the following three main types.

1. **Thickened with starch.**
   The procedure is the same as for fruit pie fillings made by the cooked juice or cooked fruit method, except the fruit is finely chopped or puréed. Most fruit chiffons are made this way.

2. **Thickened with egg.**
   The procedure is the same as for custard sauce or crème anglaise. Many chocolate chiffons are made this way, as is pumpkin chiffon.

3. **Thickened with egg and starch.**
   The procedure is the same as for pastry cream. Lemon chiffon is usually made this way.

MOUSSES

There are so many varieties of mousse that it is impossible to give a rule for all of them. In general, we define a **mousse** as any soft or creamy dessert made light and fluffy by the addition of whipped cream, beaten egg whites, or both. Note that bavarians and chiffons both fit this description. In fact, they are often served as mousses, but with the gelatin reduced or left out so the mousse is softer.

Many kinds of base are used for mousses. The base may be nothing more than melted chocolate or puréed fresh fruit, or it may be more complex, like the bases for chiffons.

Some mousses contain both beaten egg whites and whipped cream. When this is the case, most chefs prefer to fold in the egg whites first, even though they may lose some volume. The reason is that if the cream is added first, there is more danger that it will be overbeaten and turn to butter during the folding and mixing procedure.

If egg whites are folded into a *hot* base, they will cook or coagulate, and the mousse will be firmer and more stable. Whipped cream should never be folded into hot mixtures, or it will melt and deflate.

DESSERT SOUFFLÉS

Soufflés are lightened with beaten egg whites, then baked. Baking causes the soufflé to rise like a cake because the air in the egg foam expands when heated.

To understand the structure of dessert soufflés, we can divide their preparation into four stages:

1. **Base.**
   Many kinds are used for dessert soufflés. Most are heavy, starch-thickened preparations, such as pastry cream or sweetened white sauce.

2. **Egg yolks.**
   When used, these are added to the base.

3. **Egg whites.**
   Whenever possible, egg whites should be whipped with some of the sugar. This makes dessert soufflés more stable than entrée soufflés.

4. **Baking.**
   Review the section on entrée soufflés (pp. 796–797) so you understand the general principles of baking soufflés.

SUMMARY AND COMPARISON

1. **Bavarian.**
   Base: custard sauce
   Gelatin
   Whipped cream

2. **Chiffon.**
   Base: Starch-thickened (fruit
       filling type)
       Egg-thickened (custard type)
       Egg- and starch-thickened
       (pastry cream type)
   Gelatin
   Egg whites
   (Optional whipped cream)

3. **Mousse.**
   Base: many varieties
   Little or no gelatin
   Egg whites and/or whipped cream

4. **Soufflé.**
   Base: many varieties, usually
       containing egg yolk
   Egg whites
   Baked

General Procedure

The following is a general procedure only. It is not a detailed method for one specific dessert but will give you a basic understanding that will help you tackle many recipes. These basic steps apply to most bavarians, chiffons, mousses, and soufflés.

1. Prepare the base.
2. If gelatin is used, soften it in cold liquid and stir it into the hot base until dissolved. Chill until almost set.
3. Fold in the beaten egg whites and/or whipped cream.
4. Chill (for bavarians, chiffons, and mousses) or bake (for soufflés).

Bavarian Cream

Portions: 24   Portion size: 3 oz (90 g)

U.S.	Metric	Ingredients
1½ oz	45 g	Gelatin (unflavored)
10 oz	300 mL	Cold water
		Crème anglaise:
12	12	Egg yolks
8 oz	250 g	Sugar
1 qt	1 L	Milk
1 tbsp	15 mL	Vanilla
1 qt	1 L	Heavy cream

Per Serving:
Calories, 240; Protein, 5 g; Fat, 19 g (70 % cal.); Cholesterol, 165 mg; Carbohydrates, 13 g; Fiber, 0 g; Sodium, 45 mg.

■ P r o c e d u r e

1. Soak the gelatin in cold water.

2. Prepare the crème anglaise; Whip the egg yolks and sugar until thick and light. Scald the milk and slowly stir it into the egg yolk mixture, beating constantly. Add vanilla. Cook over a hot-water bath, stirring constantly, until it just thickens slightly. (Review p. 1007) for details on making crème anglaise.)

3. When the sauce is still hot, add the softened gelatin. Stir until the gelatin is dissolved.

4. Cool in the refrigerator or over crushed ice, stirring occasionally to keep the mixture smooth.

5. While the custard sauce is cooling, whip the cream until it forms soft, not stiff, peaks. Do not overwhip.

6. When the custard sauce is very thick but not yet set, fold in the whipped cream.

7. Pour into molds or into serving dishes.

8. Chill until completely set. If prepared in molds, unmold for service.

V A R I A T I O N S

Chocolate Bavarian Cream
Add 12 oz (350 g) sweetened chocolate, chopped or grated, to the hot crème anglaise. Stir until completely melted and blended in.

Coffee Bavarian Cream
Add 3 tbsp (45 mL) instant coffee powder to the hot créme anglaise.

Strawberry Bavarian Cream
Reduce the milk to 1 pt (500 mL) and the sugar to 6 oz (175 g) when making the crème anglaise. Mash 1 lb (500 g) strawberries with 6 oz (175 g) sugar, or use 1½ lb (700 g) frozen, sweetened strawberries. Stir this purée into the custard sauce before adding the whipped cream.

Raspberry Bavarian Cream
Prepare like Strawberry Bavarian Cream, using raspberries.

Strawberry Chiffon Dessert or Pie Filling

Yield: **6 lb 8 oz (3 kg)**
six 8-inch (20-cm) pies
five 9-inch (23-cm) pies
four 10-inch (25-cm) pies

U.S.	Metric	Ingredients
4 lb	1800 g	Frozen sweetened strawberries (see note)
1 tsp	5 mL	Salt
1 oz	30 g	Cornstarch
4 fl oz	125 mL	Water
1 oz	30 g	Gelatin
8 fl oz	250 mL	Water, cold
1 fl oz	30 mL	Lemon juice
1 lb	450 g	Egg whites
12 oz	350 g	Sugar

Per 1 ounce:
Calories, 40; Protein, 1 g; Fat, 0 g (0% cal.); Cholesterol, 0 mg; Carbohydrates, 9 g; Fiber, 0 g; Sodium, 30 mg.

Note: To use fresh strawberries, slice or dice 3 lb (1.4 kg) fresh, hulled strawberries and mix with 1 lb (450 g) sugar. Let stand 2 hours in refrigerator. Drain and reserve juice. Proceed as in basic recipe.

■ P r o c e d u r e

1. Thaw and drain the strawberries, reserving the juice. Chop the strawberries coarsely.
2. Place the reserved juice and salt in a saucepan. Bring to a boil.
3. Dissolve the cornstarch in the water and stir into the strawberry juice. Cook until thick. Remove from heat.
4. Soften the gelatin in the water. Add to the hot, thickened fruit juice and stir until completely dissolved.
5. Stir in the lemon juice and the drained strawberries.
6. Chill the mixture until thickened but not set.
7. Beat the egg whites until they form soft peaks.
8. Gradually add the sugar and continue to beat until a thick, glossy meringue is formed.
9. Fold the meringue into the fruit mixture.
10. Portion into individual serving dishes or fill baked pie shells.
11. Chill until set.

V A R I A T I O N S

For a creamier chiffon, reduce egg whites to 12 oz (350 g). Whip 1 pt (500 mL) heavy cream and fold it in after the meringue.

Raspberry Chiffon Dessert or Pie Filling
Substitute raspberries for strawberries in basic recipe.

Pineapple Chiffon Dessert or Pie Filling
Use 3 lb (1.4 kg) crushed pineapple. Mix the drained juice with an additional 1 pt (500 mL) pineapple juice and add 8 oz (225 g) sugar.

Frozen Strawberry or Raspberry Mousse
Omit gelatin and second quantity of water from basic recipe or from raspberry variation. Reduce egg whites to 8 oz (225 g). Whip 1½ pt (750 mL) heavy cream and fold it in after the meringue. Pour into molds or other containers and freeze.

Chocolate Chiffon Dessert or Pie Filling

Yield: *7 lb (3.2 kg)*
six 8-inch (20-cm) pies
five 9-inch (23-cm) pies
four 10-inch (25-cm) pies

U.S.	Metric	Ingredients
10 oz	300 g	Unsweetened chocolate
1½ pt	750 mL	Water
1 lb	450 g	Egg yolks
1 lb	450 g	Sugar
1 oz	30 g	Gelatin
8 fl oz	250 mL	Water, cold
1 lb 4 oz	575 g	Egg whites
1 lb 8 oz	700 g	Sugar

Per 1 ounce:
Calories, 70; Protein, 2 g; Fat, 2.5 g (30% cal.); Cholesterol, 50 mg;
Carbohydrates, 11 g; Fiber, 0 g; Sodium, 10 mg.

■ **P r o c e d u r e**

1. Combine the chocolate and water in a heavy saucepan. Bring to a simmer, stirring constantly until smooth.

2. Beat the egg yolks and sugar together with the whip attachment until thick and light.

3. With the mixer running, gradually pour in the chocolate mixture.

4. Return the mixture to the saucepan and stir over very low heat until thickened. Remove from heat.

5. Soften the gelatin in the water. Add to the hot chocolate mixture and stir until the gelatin is completely dissolved.

6. Chill until thick but not set.

7. Beat the egg whites until they form soft peaks.

8. Gradually beat in the sugar. Continue beating until a firm, glossy meringue is formed.

9. Fold into the chocolate mixture.

10. Pour into serving dishes or into baked pie shells. Chill until set.

V A R I A T I O N

Chocolate Cream Chiffon Pie Filling
For a creamier chiffon, reduce the egg whites to 1 lb (450 g). Whip 1 pt (500 mL) heavy cream and fold it in after the meringue.

Lemon Chiffon Dessert or Pie Filling

Yield: 7 lb (3.2 kg)
six 8-inch (20-cm) pies
five 9-inch (23-cm) pies
four 10-inch (25-cm) pies

U.S.	Metric	Ingredients
1½ pt	750 mL	Water
8 oz	250 g	Sugar
12 oz	375 g	Egg yolks
4 fl oz	125 mL	Water, cold
3 oz	90 g	Cornstarch
8 oz	250 g	Sugar
		Grated zest of 4 lemons
1 oz	30 g	Gelatin
8 fl oz	250 mL	Water, cold
12 fl oz	350 mL	Lemon juice
1 lb	450 g	Egg whites
1 lb	450 g	Sugar

■ Procedure

1. Dissolve the sugar in the water and bring to a boil.

2. Beat together the egg yolks, water, cornstarch, sugar, and lemon zest until smooth.
3. Gradually beat in the boiling water in a thin stream.
4. Return the mixture to the heat and bring to a boil, beating constantly with a whip.
5. As soon as the mixture thickens and boils, remove it from the heat.

6. Soften the gelatin in the cold water.
7. Add the gelatin to the hot lemon mixture. Stir until it is dissolved.
8. Stir in the lemon juice.
9. Chill until thick but not set.

10. Beat the egg whites until they form soft peaks.
11. Gradually add the sugar and continue to beat until a thick, glossy meringue is formed.
12. Fold the meringue into the lemon mixture.
13. Pour into individual serving dishes or fill baked pie shells.
14. Chill until set.

Per 1 ounce:
Calories, 50; Protein, 1 g; Fat, 1 g (18% cal.); Cholesterol, 40 mg; Carbohydrates, 9 g; Fiber, 0 g; Sodium, 10 mg.

V A R I A T I O N S

Lime Chiffon Dessert or Pie Filling
Substitute lime juice and zest for the lemon.

Orange Chiffon Dessert or Pie Filling
Use orange juice instead of water in step 1 and omit the first 8 oz (250 g) sugar. Substitute orange zest for the lemon zest. Reduce the lemon juice to 4 fl oz (125 mL).

Frozen Lemon Mousse
Omit the gelatin and the water used to dissolve it. Decrease egg whites to 12 oz (350 g). Whip 1 qt (1 L) heavy cream and fold it in after meringue. Pour into molds or other containers and freeze.

Pumpkin Chiffon Dessert or Pie Filling

Yield: *7 lb 12 oz (3.4 kg)*
six 8-inch (20-cm) pies
five 9-inch (23-cm) pies
four 10-inch (25-cm) pies

U.S.	Metric	Ingredients
2½ lb	1.2 kg	Pumpkin purée
1 lb 4 oz	600 g	Brown sugar
12 oz	350 g	Milk
12 oz	350 g	Egg yolks, beaten
1 tsp	5 mL	Salt
4 tsp	20 mL	Cinnamon
2 tsp	10 mL	Nutmeg
1 tsp	5 mL	Ground ginger
1 oz	30 g	Gelatin
8 fl oz	250 mL	Water, cold
1 lb	450 g	Egg whites
1 lb	450 g	Granulated sugar

Per 1 ounce:
Calories, 50; Protein, 1 g; Fat, 1 g (18% cal.); Cholesterol, 35 mg;
Carbohydrates, 9 g; Fiber, 0 g; Sodium, 30 mg.

■ P r o c e d u r e

1. Combine the pumpkin, brown sugar, milk, egg yolks, salt, and spices. Mix until smooth and uniform.

2. Place in a double boiler. Cook, stirring frequently, until thickened or until the temperature of the mixture reaches 185°F (85°C). Remove from heat.

3. Soften the gelatin in the water.

4. Add it to the hot pumpkin mixture and stir until dissolved.

5. Chill until very thick but not set.

6. Beat egg whites until they form soft peaks.

7. Gradually add the granulated sugar and continue to beat until a thick meringue is formed.

8. Fold the meringue into the pumpkin mixture.

9. Portion into individual serving dishes or fill baked pie shells. Chill until set.

V A R I A T I O N

Pumpkin Cream Chiffon
Reduce the egg whites to 12 oz (350 g). Whip 1 pt (500 mL) heavy cream and fold it in after the meringue.

Vanilla Soufflé

Portions: 10   *Portion size: 4½ oz (125 g)*

U.S.	Metric	Ingredients
3 oz	90 g	Flour
3 oz	90 g	Butter
4 oz	125 g	Sugar
1 pt	500 mL	Milk
as needed	as needed	Butter
as needed	as needed	Sugar
8	8	Egg yolks
2 tsp	10 mL	Vanilla
8–10	8–10	Egg whites
2 oz	60 g	Sugar

Per serving;
Calories, 270; Protein, 8 g; Fat, 13 g (44% cal.);
Cholesterol, 195 mg; Carbohydrates, 29 g;
Fiber, 0 g; Sodium, 150 mg.

■ Procedure

1. Work the flour and butter together to form a smooth paste.

2. Dissolve the sugar in the milk and bring to a boil. Remove from the heat.

3. With a wire whip, beat in the flour paste. Beat vigorously to make sure there are no lumps.

4. Return the mixture to the heat and bring to a boil, beating constantly. Simmer for several minutes, until the mixture is very thick and no starchy taste remains.

5. Transfer the mixture to a mixing bowl. Cover and let cool for 5–10 minutes.

6. While the mixture is cooling, butter the soufflé dishes well and coat with sugar. For 1 recipe, use 1 dish, 10 in. (25 cm) in diameter; 2 dishes, 7 in. (18 cm) in diameter; or 10 single-portion dishes.

7. Quickly beat the egg yolks and vanilla into the milk mixture.

8. Beat the egg whites until they form soft peaks. Add the sugar and beat until the mixture forms firm, moist peaks.

9. Fold the egg whites into the soufflé base.

10. Pour the mixture into the prepared baking dishes and smooth the tops.

11. Bake at 375°F (190°C). Approximate baking times are 45–50 minutes for a 10-in. (25-cm) dish, 30–40 minutes for a 7-in. (18-cm) dish, and 15 minutes for single-portion dishes.

V A R I A T I O N

Chocolate Soufflé
Add 3 oz (90 g) melted unsweetened chocolate and 1 oz (30 g) melted sweet chocolate to the base after step 5.

Lemon Soufflé
Instead of vanilla, use the grated zest of 2 lemons for flavoring.

Liqueur Soufflé
Flavor with 2–3 fl oz (60–90 mL) liqueur, such as kirsch or Grand Marnier, added after step 5.

Coffee Soufflé
Flavor with 2 tbsp (30 mL) instant coffee powder, added to the milk in step 2.

Chocolate Mousse

Yield: about 2¾ lb (1.25 kg) or 2½ pt (1.25 L)   *Portions: 12*   *Portion size: 4½ fl oz (145 mL)*

U.S.	Metric	Ingredients	Procedure
1 lb	500 g	Bittersweet chocolate	■ **P r o c e d u r e**
4 oz	125 g	Butter	1. Melt the chocolate over hot water.
6 oz	180 g	Egg yolks	2. Remove from the heat and add the butter. Stir until the butter is melted and completely mixed in.
			3. Add the egg yolks, one at a time. Mix in each yolk completely before adding the next.
8 oz	250 g	Egg whites	4. Beat the egg whites until they form soft peaks. Add the sugar and beat until the egg whites form stiff but moist peaks. Do not overbeat.
2½ oz	75 g	Sugar	5. Fold the egg whites into the chocolate.
8 fl oz	250 mL	Heavy cream	6. Whip the heavy cream until it forms soft peaks. Fold it into the chocolate mixture.
			7. Spoon the mousse into serving dishes or use a pastry bag fitted with a star tube.
			8. Chill the mousse well before serving.

Per serving:
Calories, 380; Protein, 6 g; Fat, 29 g (64% cal.); Cholesterol, 220 mg; Carbohydrates, 30 g; Fiber, 2 g; Sodium, 120 mg.

Note: This mixture may also be used as a filling for cakes, pastries, and baked meringues. For another, very different chocolate mousse recipe, see the variation following the recipe for Chocolate Chiffon earlier in this chapter.

FROZEN DESSERTS

The popularity of ice cream needs no explanation. Whether a plain scoop of vanilla ice cream in a dish or an elaborate assemblage of fruits, syrups, toppings, and numerous flavors of ice cream and sherbet, frozen desserts appeal to just about everyone.

CLASSIFICATION

1. **Ice cream.**

   Ice cream is a smooth, frozen mixture of milk, cream, sugar, flavorings, and, sometimes, eggs. **Philadelphia-style ice cream** contains no eggs, while **French-style ice cream** contains egg yolks. The eggs add richness and help make a smoother product because of the emulsifying properties of the yolks.

   Ice milk is like ice cream, but with a lower butterfat content.

   Frozen yogurt contains yogurt in addition to the normal ingredients for ice cream or ice milk.

2. **Sherbet.**

   Sherbets and **ices** are made from fruit juices, water, and sugar. American sherbets usually contain milk or cream and, sometimes, egg whites. The egg whites increase smoothness and volume. Ices, also called *water ices*, contain only fruit juice, water, sugar, and, sometimes, egg whites. They do not contain milk products. The French word *sorbet* (sor bay) is sometimes used for these products. **Granité** (grah nee tay) is a coarse, crystalline ice made without egg white.

3. **Still-frozen dessert.**

   Ice cream and sherbet are churn-frozen, meaning that they are mixed constantly while being frozen. If they were not churned, they would freeze into solid blocks of ice. The churning keeps the ice crystals small and incorporates air into the ice cream.

   Frozen soufflés and *frozen mousses* are made like chilled mousses and bavarians—that is, whipped cream, beaten egg whites, or both are folded in to give them lightness. This allows them to be still-frozen in an ordinary freezer.

PRODUCTION AND QUALITY

Until recently, few establishments made their own ice cream because of the labor involved, the equipment required, and the convenience of commercially made products. Also, in some areas, strict health codes made it difficult for all but large producers to make ice cream. Today, more and more restaurants are making their own ice creams and sorbets.

A basic ice cream mix is simply a crème anglaise or custard sauce mixed with 1 or 2 parts heavy cream for every 4 parts milk used in the sauce. This base is flavored as desired with vanilla, melted chocolate, instant coffee, crushed strawberries, and so on. It is then chilled thoroughly, and then frozen according to the instructions for the equipment being used.

When the mix has frozen, it is transferred to containers and placed in a deep-freeze at below 0°F (–18°C) to harden. (Soft-frozen or soft-serve ice creams are served directly as they come from the churn freezer without being hardened.)

Whether you make ice cream or buy it, you should be aware of the following quality factors:

1. *Smoothness* is related to the size of the ice crystals in the product. Ice cream should be frozen rapidly and churned well during freezing so large crystals don't have a chance to form.

    Rapid hardening helps keep crystals small. So do eggs and emulsifiers or stabilizers added to the mix.

    Large crystals may form if the ice cream is not stored at a low enough temperature (below 0°F/–18°C).

2. Overrun is the increase in volume due to the incorporation of air when freezing ice cream. It is expressed as a percentage of the original volume of the mix. For example, if the ice cream doubles in volume, the amount of increase is equal to the original volume and the overrun is 100 percent.

    Some overrun is necessary to give a smooth, light texture. Ice cream with too much overrun is airy and foamy and lacks flavor. It was once thought that ice cream should have from 80 to 100 percent overrun and that less would make it heavy and pasty. This may be true for ice creams containing gums and other stabilizers. However, some high-quality manufacturers produce rich (and expensive) ice cream with as little as 20 percent overrun.

3. *Mouth feel* or *body* depends, in part, on smoothness and overrun as well as on other qualities. Good ice cream melts in the mouth to a smooth, not too heavy liquid. Some ice creams have so many stabilizers they never melt to a liquid. Unfortunately, many people have become so accustomed to these products that an ice cream that actually does melt strikes them as not rich enough.

STORAGE AND SERVICE

1. Store ice creams and sherbets at 0°F (–18°C) or lower. This low temperature helps prevent the formation of large ice crystals.

2. For service, temper frozen desserts at 8° to 15°F (–13° to –9°C) for 24 hours so they are soft enough to serve.

3. When serving, avoid packing the ice cream. The best method is to draw the scoop across the surface of the product so the product rolls into a ball in the scoop.

4. Use standard scoops for portioning ice cream. Normal portions for popular desserts are as follows:

Parfait	3 No. 30 scoops
Banana split	3 No. 30 scoops
À la mode topping for pie or cake	1 No. 20 scoop
Sundae	2 No. 20 scoops
Plain dish of ice cream	1 No. 10, 12, or 16 scoop

5. Measure syrups, toppings, and garnishes for portion control. For syrups, use pumps that dispense measured quantities, or use standard ladles.

POPULAR ICE CREAM DESSERTS

1. **Parfaits** are made by alternating layers of ice cream and fruit or syrup in a tall, narrow glass. They are usually named after the syrup or topping. For example: a *chocolate parfait* comprises three scoops of vanilla or chocolate ice cream alternating with layers of chocolate syrup and topped with whipped cream and shaved chocolate.

2. **Sundaes** or **coupes** consist of one or two scoops of ice cream or sherbet in a dish or glass and topped with syrups, fruits, toppings, and garnishes. They are quick to prepare, unlimited in variety, and as simple or as elegant as you could wish—served in an ordinary soda fountain glass, a silver cup, or a crystal champagne glass.

    Two sundaes have become classics:

    Peach Melba. Vanilla ice cream topped with a fresh, poached, or canned peach half, napped with sweetened raspberry purée (Melba sauce), and garnished with slivered almonds.

    Pear Belle Hélène. Vanilla ice cream topped with a poached or canned pear half, napped with chocolate sauce, and garnished with toasted sliced almonds.

3. **Bombes** are ice cream molds made by lining a chilled mold with softened ice cream, freezing it hard, and then filling the center with another flavor of ice cream or sherbet and freezing it again. (More than two flavors may be used.) The dessert is unmolded onto a cold platter for service and decorated as desired with whipped cream, fruits, and/or confections.

4. *Meringue glacée.* See discussion of meringues, page 1000.

5. *Baked Alaska.* See discussion of meringues, page 1001.

6. *Frozen éclairs* and *profiteroles.* See discussion of éclair pastries, page 998.

DESSERT SAUCES

Most dessert sauces fall into one of three categories.

1. **Custard sauces.**
    Vanilla custard sauce, or crème anglaise, is presented early in this chapter. It is among the most basic preparations in dessert cookery. Chocolate or other flavors may be added to create varieties. See recipe on page 1008.

2. **Fruit purées.**
    These are simply purées of fresh or cooked fruits, sweetened with sugar. Other flavorings and spices are sometimes added. Some fruit sauces are thickened with cornstarch or other starch.

    Raspberry sauce and strawberry sauce, two popular items, can be made by simply puréeing frozen sweetened berries or by puréeing fresh berries and adding sugar to taste. See also the recipe for Applesauce, page 198.

3. **Syrups.**
    This is a broad category that includes such products as chocolate sauce and caramel sauce. An understanding of sugar cooking is necessary to produce many of these sauces.

    The following recipes are popular examples of this category of sauce.

Chocolate Sauce

Yield: 1 qt (1 L)

U.S.	Metric	Ingredients
1 pt	500 mL	Water
2 lb	1 kg	Sugar
6 oz	190 g	Corn syrup
8 oz	250 g	Unsweetened chocolate, melted
2 oz	60 g	Butter

Per 1 ounce:
Calories, 170; Protein, 1 g; Fat, 5 g (24% cal.); Cholesterol, 5 mg;
Carbohydrates, 34 g; Fiber, 1 g; Sodium, 25 mg.

■ P r o c e d u r e

1. Combine the water, sugar, and syrup and bring to a boil, stirring to dissolve the sugar.
2. Boil 1 minute and remove from heat. Let cool 1–2 minutes.
3. Melt the chocolate and butter together over low heat. Stir until smooth.
4. Very slowly stir the hot syrup into the chocolate.
5. Place over moderate heat and bring to a boil. Boil for 4 minutes.
6. Remove from heat and cool.

Caramel Sauce

Yield: 1½ qt (1.5 L)

U.S.	Metric	Ingredients
1 lb	500 g	Sugar
4 oz	125 g	Water
1½ tsp	7 mL	Lemon juice
12 fl oz	375 mL	Heavy cream
8 fl oz	250 mL	Milk

Per 1 ounce:
Calories, 130; Protein, 1 g; Fat, 6 g (39% cal.); Cholesterol, 20 mg;
Carbohydrates, 20 g; Fiber, 0 g; Sodium, 10 mg.

■ P r o c e d u r e

1. Combine the sugar, water, and lemon juice in a heavy saucepan. Bring to a boil, stirring to dissolve the sugar.
2. When the sugar is dissolved, cover the pan and boil for 2 minutes.
3. Uncover and cook to the caramel stage (see pages 1006–1007). Toward the end of the cooking time, turn the heat very low to avoid burning the sugar or getting it too dark. It should be a golden color.
4. Remove from heat and cool 5 minutes.
5. Bring the heavy cream to a boil. Add a few ounces (50–100 mL) of the heavy cream to the caramel.
6. Stir and continue to add the cream slowly.
7. Return to the heat and stir until all the caramel is dissolved.
8. Let cool completely.
9. Stir the milk into the cooled caramel to thin it.

V A R I A T I O N S

Hot Caramel Sauce
Prepare as directed through step 7. Omit the milk.

Clear Caramel Sauce
Substitute 5–6 fl oz (150–175 mL) water for the heavy cream and omit the milk. If the sauce is too thick when cool, add more water.

■ TERMS FOR REVIEW

simple syrup	baked pudding	French-style ice cream	overrun
dessert syrup	bavarian	ice milk	parfait
crystallize	chiffon	sherbet	coupe
crème anglaise	mousse	ice	Peach Melba
pastry cream	ice cream	granité	bombe
blancmange	Philadelphia-style	still-frozen	
cream pudding	ice cream		

■ QUESTIONS FOR DISCUSSION

1. How can you avoid unwanted crystallization when cooking sugar syrups?

2. Light custard sauce and pastry cream both contain eggs. Why is it possible to boil pastry cream but not custard sauce?

3. Explain the importance of sanitation in the production of pastry cream. What specific steps should you take to ensure a safe product?

4. Light custard sauce, pastry cream, and baked custard are made with basic techniques that are also used for the following preparations. Identify which of the three techniques is used for each.

Coconut cream pie	French vanilla ice cream
Baked rice pudding	Pumpkin pie
Butterscotch pudding	Custard pie
Chocolate bavarian	Lemon meringue pie

5. Briefly describe the differences among bavarians, chiffons, mousses, and soufflés.

6. When making dessert soufflés, what is the advantage of beating the egg whites with part of the sugar?

7. What difficulty would you encounter, when making a bavarian or a chiffon, if you chilled the gelatin mixture too long before folding in the whipped cream or egg whites?

Metric Conversion Factors

Weight

1 ounce = 28.35 grams

1 gram = 0.035 ounce

1 pound = 454 grams

1 kilogram = 2.2 pounds

Volume

1 fluid ounce = 29.57 milliliters

1 milliliter = 0.034 ounce

1 cup = 237 milliliters

1 quart = 946 milliliters

1 liter = 33.8 fluid ounces

Length

1 inch = 25.4 millimeters

1 centimeter = 0.39 inch

1 meter = 39.4 inches

Temperature

To convert Fahrenheit to Celsius:

Subtract 32. Then multiply by $\frac{5}{9}$.

Example: Convert 140°F to Celsius.

$$140 - 32 = 108$$

$$108 \times \frac{5}{9} = 60°C$$

To convert Celsius to Fahrenheit:

Multiply by $\frac{9}{5}$. Then add 32.

Example: Convert 150°C to Fahrenheit.

$$150 \times \frac{9}{5} = 270$$

$$270 + 32 = 302°F$$

Note: The metric equivalents in the recipes in this book are rounded off. See page 102 for complete explanation.

Standard Can Sizes

Can Name	Volume		Approximate Weight[a]	
	U.S	Metric	U.S.	Metric
6 oz	5.75 fl oz	170 mL	6 oz	170 g
8 oz	8.3 fl oz	245 mL	8 oz	227 g
No. 1 picnic	10.5 fl oz	311 mL	10½ oz	298 g
No. 211 cylinder	12 fl oz	355 mL	12 oz	340 g
No. 300	13.5 fl oz	399 mL	14 oz	397 g
No. 303	15.6 fl oz	461 mL	16–17 oz	454–482 g
No. 2	20 fl oz	591 mL	1 lb 4 oz	567 g
No. 2½	28.5 fl oz	843 mL	1 lb 13 oz	822 g
No. 3 cylinder	46 fl oz	1360 mL	3 lb	1360 g
No. 5	56 fl oz	1656 mL	3 lb 8 oz	1588 g
No. 10	103.7 fl oz	3067 mL	6½–7 lb	2722–2948 g

[a] Because the density of foods varies, so does the net weight for any given size can.

Approximate Weight–Volume Equivalents of Dry Foods

The following equivalents are rough averages only. Actual weight per volume varies considerably. For accurate measurement, all ingredients should be weighed.

Bread flour, sifted
1 pound = 4 cups
1 cup = 4 ounces

Bread flour, unsifted
1 pound = 3⅓ cups
1 cup = 4.75 ounces

Cake flour, sifted
1 pound = 4¼ cups
1 cup = 3.75 ounces

Cake flour, unsifted
1 pound = 3½ cups
1 cup = 4.5 ounces

Granulated sugar
1 pound = 2¼ cups
1 cup = 7 ounces

Confectioners' sugar, sifted
1 pound = 4 cups
1 cup = 4 ounces

Confectioners' sugar, unsifted
1 pound = 3½ cups
1 cup = 4.5 ounces

Cornstarch, sifted
1 pound = 4 cups
1 cup = 4 ounces
1 ounce = 4 tablespoons = ¼ cup
1 tablespoon = 0.25 ounce

Cornstarch, unsifted
1 pound = 3½ cups
1 cup = 4.5 ounces
1 ounce = 3½ tablespoons
1 tablespoon = 0.29 ounce

Cocoa, unsifted
1 pound = 5 cups
1 cup = 3.2 ounces
1 ounce = 5 tablespoons
1 tablespoon = 0.2 ounce

Gelatin, unflavored
1 ounce = 3 tablespoons
¼ ounce = 2¼ teaspoons
1 tablespoon = ⅓ ounce
1 teaspoon = 0.11 ounce

Baking soda
Baking powder (phosphate type and sodium aluminum sulfate type)
1 ounces = 2 tablespoons
¼ ounce = 1½ teaspoons
1 tablespoon = ½ ounce
1 teaspoon = 0.17 ounce

Cream of tartar
1 ounce = 4 tablespoons
¼ ounce = 1 tablespoon
1 teaspoon = 0.08 ounce

Salt
1 ounce = 5 teaspoons
¼ ounce = 1¼ teaspoons
1 teaspoon = 0.2 ounce

Cinnamon
1 ounce = 17 teaspoons
¼ ounce = 4¼ teaspoons
1 teaspoon = 0.06 ounce

Ground spices (except cinnamon)
1 ounce = 14 teaspoons
¼ ounce = 3½ teaspoons
1 teaspoon = 0.07 ounce

Grated lemon zest
1 ounce = 4 tablespoons
1 teaspoon = 0.08 ounce

Dried beans
1 cup = 6.5 ounces
1 pound = 2½ cups (yields 6 cups cooked)

Rice, long-grain
1 cup = 7 ounces
1 pound = 2¼ cups (yields 8 cups cooked)

4

Kitchen Math Exercises: Metric Versions

This appendix includes metric sample calculations corresponding to the calculations in the text that use U.S. measures. Refer to the appropriate pages in the text for explanations.

Recipe Conversion, Pages 104–105

Beef Tenderloin Tips and Mushrooms à la Crème
Portions: 8
Portion size: 250 g

Butter	60 g
Onions	125 g
Flour	15 mL
Mushrooms	250 g
Beef tenderloin	1250 g
White wine	125 mL
Prepared mustard	10 mL
Brown sauce	750 mL
Heavy cream	250 mL
Salt	to taste
Pepper	to taste

To determine quantities for 18 portions, divide new yield by old yield to find conversion factor:

$$\frac{\text{new yield}}{\text{old yield}} = \frac{18}{8} = 2.25$$

Example 1

Ingredient	Quantity	Times	Conversion Factor	Equals	New Quantity (rounded off)
Butter	60 g	×	2.25	=	135 g
Onions	125 g	×	2.25	=	275 g
Flour	15 mL	×	2.25	=	35 mL
Mushrooms	250 g	×	2.25	=	575 g
Beef tenderloin	1250 g	×	2.25	=	2800 g
White wine	125 mL	×	2.25	=	275 mL
Prepared mustard	10 mL	×	2.25	=	23 mL
Brown sauce	750 mL	×	2.25	=	1700 mL
Heavy cream	250 mL	×	2.25	=	575 mL

To determine quantities for 40 portions at 175 grams each, first find the total yield of the old recipe. Multiply the portions by the portion size:

$$8 \text{ (portions)} \times 250 \text{ g} = 2000 \text{ g}$$

Do the same calculation for the desired yield:

$$40 \text{ (portions)} \times 175 \text{ g} = 7000 \text{ g}$$

Divide the desired yield by the old yield to find the conversion factor:

$$7000 \div 2000 = 3.5$$

Example 2

Ingredient	Quantity	Times	Conversion Factor	Equals	New Quantity (rounded off)
Butter	60 g	×	3.5	=	200 g
Onions	125 g	×	3.5	=	450 g
Flour	15 mL	×	3.5	=	50 mL
Mushrooms	250 g	×	3.5	=	875 g
Beef tenderloin	1250 g	×	3.5	=	4375 g
White wine	125 mL	×	3.5	=	450 mL
Prepared mustard	10 mL	×	3.5	=	35 mL
Brown sauce	750 mL	×	3.5	=	2625 mL
Heavy cream	250 mL	×	3.5	=	875 mL

Completed Raw Yield Test Form (Metric), Page 109

Item .... veal leg to scaloppine .... Test number .... 3 .... Date .... 6/5/2006 ....

Purveyor .... ABC Meats .... Price per kilogram ... $11.00 .... Total cost .... $148.50 ....

AP weight (1) ...... 13.5 kg .... Kg price (2) .... $11.00 .... Total cost (3) ...... $148.50 ....

Trim, salvage, and waste:

	Item	Weight	Value/kg	Total Value (kg x value)
(4)	fat	1.14 kg	$ 0.25	$ .29
(5)	bone	1.5 kg	$ 0.88	$1.32
(6)	ground veal	0.95 kg	$9.75	$9.26
(7)	stew meat	1.4 kg	$10.95	$15.33
(8)	unusable trim	0.4 kg	0	0
(9)	cutting loss	0.09 kg	0	0
(10)				

Total Weight (4 thru 10) (11) ____ 5.48 kg ____   Total Value (4 thru 10) (12) ____ $26.20 ____

Total yield of item (13) .... 8.02 kg ....

Net cost (3 minus 12) (14) ____ $122.30 ____

Cost per lb (14 divided by 13) (15) ____ $15.25 ____

Percentage of increase (15 divided by 2) (16) ____ 1.39 (139%) ____

Completed Cooked Yield Test Form (Metric), Page 111

Item .... roast fresh ham .... Test number .... 2 .... Date ...... 6/5/2006 ......

AP price per kg .... $7.75 ....

Cooking temperature .... 165°C ....

Net raw weight (1) ...... 5.5 kg ....   Net cost per kg (2) .... $8.73 ....

Total net cost (3) .... $48.02 ....

Weight as served (4) .... 3.75 kg ....

Cooked cost per lb (3 ÷ by 4) (5) ____ $12.81 ____

Shrinkage (1 – 4) (6) ____ 1.75 kg ____

Percentage of shrinkage (6 ÷ by 1) (7) ____ 32% ____

Total percentage of cost increase (5 ÷ by AP price per kg) (8) ____ 165% ____

Metric Example: Costing a Recipe, Page 112
Item: Baked Rice

Ingredient	Recipe Quantity	AP Quantity	Price	Total
Rice, long grain	2 kg	2 kg	$1.59/kg	$3.18
Butter	375 g	0.375 kg	4.25/kg	1.59
Onions	500 g	0.5 kg	0.79/kg	0.40
Chicken stock	4 L	4 L	0.30/L	1.20
Salt	30 g	0.03 kg	0.35/kg	0.01
			Total cost	$6.38
			Number of portions	50
			Cost per portion	$0.13

Eggs and Safety

Eggs and Egg-Based Products

Outbreaks of salmonellosis have been traced to clean, whole, uncracked-shell eggs contaminated with *Salmonella enteritidis*. Whole-shell eggs are now classified as potentially hazardous foods by the U.S. Food and Drug Administration (FDA).

The following guidelines, which treat eggs as potentially hazardous foods during storage, handling, preparation, and service, must be followed to prevent the possibility of food-borne illness:

- Store eggs at refrigerated temperatures of 45°F (7°C) or lower until time of use. Do not freeze eggs in shells.

- Cook eggs thoroughly until both the yolk and white are firm, not runny. Generally, eggs should be cooked to 145°F (63°C) or higher for at least 15 seconds.

- To hold cooked eggs for later service, cook them to 155°F (63°C) or higher for 15 seconds, then hold them at 135°F (57°C).

- Avoid pooling raw eggs for holding. Eggs may be pooled in small quantities for immediate cooking and serving.

- For lightly cooked egg items, such as custards, French toast, mousses, and meringues, pasteurized eggs should be used.

- Avoid raw egg menu items. Review menus, recipes, and preparation procedures using raw eggs. Pasteurized eggs may be substituted for Caesar salad, hollandaise and béarnaise sauces, eggnog, ice cream, and egg-fortified beverages.

- Pasteurized eggs require the same time and temperature handling as other potentially hazardous foods.

- Wash hands with hot, soapy water before and after handling eggs and egg products.

- Wash and sanitize utensils, equipment, and the work area after handling eggs and egg products.

- Do not reuse a container that has held a raw egg mixture. Use a clean, sanitized container for each batch.

Source: National Restaurant Association Educational Foundation, *ServSafe Coursebook, 3rd Edition*.

Bibliography

A

Amendola, Joseph. *The Baker's Manual for Quantity Baking and Pastry Making*, 5th ed. Hoboken, New Jersey: John Wiley & Sons, 2002.

Anderson, Jean. *The Food of Portugal*. New York: Morrow, 1986.

Anderson, Jean, and Hedy Wurz. *The New German Cookbook*. New York: HarperCollins, 1993.

Andoh, Elizabeth. *At Home with Japanese Cooking*. New York: Knopf, 1980.

B

Bayless, Rick. *Authentic Mexican*. New York: Morrow, 1987.

Bertolli, Paul, and Alice Waters. *Chez Panisse Cooking*. New York: Random House, 1988.

Bickel, Walter, ed. *Hering's Dictionary of Classical and Modern Cookery*. London: Virtue, 1991.

Bissel, Frances. *The Book of Food*. New York: Henry Holt, 1994.

Bocuse, Paul. *Paul Bocuse's French Cooking*. New York: Pantheon, 1977.

Boni, Ada. *Italian Regional Cooking*. New York: Bonanza, 1969.

Bugialli, Giuliano. *Classic Techniques of Italian Cooking*. New York: Simon & Schuster, 1982.

————. *The Fine Art of Italian Cooking*. New York: Times Books, 1977.

C

Casas, Penelope. *The Foods and Wines of Spain*. New York: Knopf, 1987.

Claiborne, Craig, and Virginia Lee. *The Chinese Cookbook*. Philadelphia: Lippincott, 1972.

Cordon Bleu, Le. *Kitchen Essentials*. Hoboken, New Jersey: John Wiley & Sons, 2001.

Cox, Beverly. *Cooking Techniques*. Boston: Little, Brown, 1981.

Culinary Institute of America. *Garde Manger: The Art and Craft of the Cold Kitchen*, 2nd ed. New Jersey: John Wiley & Sons, 2004.

————. *The Professional Chef*, 7th ed. Hoboken, New Jersey: John Wiley & Sons, 2002.

————. *The Professional Chef's Knife Kit*. Hoboken, New Jersey: John Wiley & Sons, 2000.

————. *Techniques of Healthy Cooking*, 2nd ed. Hoboken, New Jersey: John Wiley & Sons, 2000.

D

David, Elizabeth. *French Provincial Cooking*. Harmondsworth, England: Penguin, 1960.

————. *Italian Food*. Harmondsworth, England: Penguin, 1954.

Davidson, Alan. *The Oxford Companion to Food*. Oxford: Oxford University Press, 1999.

D'Ermo, Dominique. *The Modern Pastry Chef's Guide to Professional Baking*. New York: Harper & Row, 1962.

Dornenberg, Andrew, and Karen Page. *Culinary Artistry*. Hoboken, New Jersey: John Wiley & Sons, 1996.

E

Egan, Maureen, and Susan Davis Allen. *Healthful Quantity Baking*. Hoboken, New Jersey: John Wiley & Sons, 1992.

Escoffier, A. *The Escoffier Cook Book*. New York: Crown, 1969.

F

Feinstein, Andrew Hale, and John M. Stefanelli. *Purchasing: Selection and Procurement for the Hospitality Industry*, 6th ed. New Jersey: John Wiley & Sons, 2005.

Friberg, Bo. *The Professional Pastry Chef*, 4th ed. Hoboken, New Jersey: John Wiley & Sons, 2002.

G

Gisslen, Wayne. *Advanced Professional Cooking*. Hoboken, New Jersey: John Wiley & Sons, 1992.

————. *Professional Baking*, 4th ed. New Jersey: John Wiley & Sons, 2005.

Graham, Kevin. *Grains, Rice, and Beans*. New York: Artisan Books, 1995.

Grausman, Richard. *At Home with the French Classics*. New York: Workman, 1988.

H

Hazan, Marcella. *The Classic Italian Cookbook*. New York: Knopf, 1976.

————. *More Classic Italian Cooking*. New York: Knopf, 1978.

Hom, Ken. *Chinese Technique*. New York: Simon & Schuster, 1981.

K

Kapoor, Sandy. *Professional Healthy Cooking*. Hoboken, New Jersey: John Wiley & Sons, 1995.

Katsigris, Costas, and Chris Thomas. *Design and Equipment for Restaurants and Foodservice*, 2nd ed. New Jersey: John Wiley & Sons, 2005.

Kennedy, Diana. *The Cuisines of Mexico*, 2nd ed. New York: Harper & Row, 1986.

———. *Mexican Regional Cooking*. New York: Harper & Row, 1978.

Kinsella, John, and David T. Harvey. *Professional Charcuterie*. Hoboken, New Jersey: John Wiley & Sons, 1996.

Knight, John B., and Lendel H. Kotschevar. *Quantity Food Production, Planning, and Management*, 3rd ed. Hoboken, New Jersey: John Wiley & Sons, 2000.

L

Lang, George. *The Cuisine of Hungary*. New York: Bonanza, 1971.

Larousse, David Paul. *The Professional Garde Manger*. Hoboken, New Jersey: John Wiley & Sons, 1996.

———. *The Sauce Bible*. Hoboken, New Jersey: John Wiley & Sons, 1993.

Librairie Larousse. *Larousse Gastronomique*. New York: Clarkson Potter, 2001.

Loken, Joan K. *The HACCP Food Safety Manual*. Hoboken, New Jersey: John Wiley & Sons, 1995.

M

McClane, A.J. *The Encyclopedia of Fish*. New York: Holt, Rinehart & Winston, 1977.

McGee, Harold. *The Curious Cook*. San Francisco: North Point Press, 1990.

———. *On Food and Cooking*. New York: Scribner, 2004.

Madison, Deborah. *The Greens Cookbook*. New York: Broadway Books, 1987.

———. *Vegetarian Cooking for Everyone*. New York: Broadway Books, 1997.

Miller, Gloria Bley. *The Thousand Recipe Chinese Cookbook*. New York: Grosset & Dunlap, 1970.

Mizer, David A., Mary Porter, Beth Sonnier, and Karen Eich Drummond. *Food Preparation for the Professional*, 3rd ed. New York: Wiley, 2000.

N

National Association of Meat Processors. *Meat Buyers Guide*. Reston, Va., 1997.

National Restaurant Association Educational Foundation. *ServSafe Coursebook*, 3rd ed. Chicago, 2004.

P

Pauli, Eugen. *Classical Cooking the Modern Way: Recipes*, 3rd ed. Arno Schmidt, trans., and Margaret Schmidt, ed. Hoboken, New Jersey: John Wiley & Sons, 1997.

———. *Classical Cooking the Modern Way: Methods and Techniques*, 3rd ed. Arno Schmidt, trans., and Margaret Schmidt, ed. Hoboken, New Jersey: John Wiley & Sons, 1999.

Pepin, Jacques. *The Art of Cooking*. New York: Knopf, 1987.

———. *La Technique: The Fundamental Techniques of Cooking: An Illustrated Guide*. New York: Quadrangle/Times Books, 1976.

Peterson, James. *Fish and Shellfish*. New York: Morrow, 1996.

———. *Sauces,* 2nd ed. Hoboken, New Jersey: John Wiley & Sons, 1997.

———. *Splendid Soups: Recipes and Master Techniques for Making the World's Best Soups*. Hoboken, New Jersey: John Wiley & Sons, 2001.

S

Saulnier, L. *La Répertoire de la Cuisine*. Woodbury, N.Y.: Barron's, 1976.

Schmidt, Arno, and Inja Nam. *The Book of Hors d'Oeuvres and Canapés*. Hoboken, New Jersey: John Wiley & Sons, 1996.

Schneider, Elizabeth. *Uncommon Fruits and Vegetables: A Commonsense Guide*. New York: Harper & Row, 1986.

———. *Vegetables from Amaranth to Zucchini*. New York: William Morrow, 2001.

Sheraton, Mimi. *The German Cookbook*. New York: Random House, 1965.

Shugart, Grace, and Mary K. Molt. *Food for Fifty*, 9th ed. New York: Macmillan, 1992.

Somerville, Annie. *Field of Greens.* New York: Bantam, 1993.

Sonnenschmidt, Frederic H., and Jean F. Nicolas. *The Professional Chef's Art of Garde Manger*, 5th ed. Hoboken, New Jersey: John Wiley & Sons, 1993.

Sultan, William J. *Practical Baking*, 5th ed. Hoboken, New Jersey: John Wiley & Sons, 1990.

T

Torres, Marimar. *The Spanish Table*. Garden City, N.Y.: Doubleday, 1986.

Tsuji, Shizuo. *Japanese Cooking: A Simple Art*. Tokyo: Kodansha, 1980.

W

Waters, Alice. *Chez Panisse Vegetables*. New York: HarperCollins, 1996.

Willan, Anne. *La Varenne Pratique*. New York: Crown, 1989.

Glossary

Note: Phonetic guides are included for difficult French words, giving the approximate pronunciation using English sounds. Exact rendering is impossible in many cases because French has a number of sounds that don't exist in English.

A

Aboyeur (ah bwah yer) Kitchen worker who accepts and transmits orders from waiters, calls for orders to be finished, inspects finished dishes, and passes them to the dining room staff.

Adductor Muscle The muscle with which a mollusk closes its shell. In the case of American and Canadian scallops, this is usually the only part that is eaten.

Aerobic Requiring oxygen to live and grow; said of bacteria.

Aging Holding meats in coolers under controlled conditions to allow natural tenderizing to take place.

À la Carte (1) Referring to a menu on which each individual item is listed with a separate price. (2) Referring to cooking to order, as opposed to cooking ahead in large batches.

Al Dente Firm, not soft or mushy, to the bite. Said of vegetables and pasta.

Allemande (1) German style. (2) A sauce made of velouté (usually veal), a liaison, and lemon juice.

Allumette Cut into matchstick shapes; usually refers to potatoes.

Americano Espresso diluted with hot water.

Anadromous Referring to fish that live in salt water but spawn in fresh water.

Anaerobic Requiring an absence of oxygen to live and grow; said of bacteria.

Anthocyanins Red or purple pigments in vegetables and fruits.

Antipasto Italian hors d'oeuvre.

AP Weight As purchased; the weight of an item before trimming.

Arborio Rice A variety of short-grain rice from Italy.

Argenteuil (ar zhawn toy) Garnished with asparagus.

Artisan(al) Cheese A cheese produced primarily by hand, in small batches, with particular attention to the tradition of the cheesemaker's art and using as little mechanization as possible.

Aspic Jelly A clarified stock that contains enough gelatin to solidify when cold.

Aspic Powder Unflavored gelatin mixed with a powdered stock base.

AS Weight As served; the weight of an item as sold or served, after processing and/or cooking.

Au Gratin (oh gra tan) Having a browned or crusted top, often made by topping with bread crumbs, cheese, and/or a rich sauce and passing under the broiler or salamander.

Au Jus (oh zhoo) Served with its natural juices, usually unthickened pan drippings.

Au Sec (oh seck) Until dry.

Avgolemono Greek soup made of chicken stock, egg, and lemon juice.

B

Bacteria Microscopic organisms, some of which can cause disease, including food-borne disease.

Bain-Marie A container of hot water used for keeping foods hot.

Bake To cook foods by surrounding them with hot, dry air. Similar to roast, but the term *bake* usually applies to breads, pastries, vegetables, and fish.

Baked Alaska A dessert consisting of ice cream on a sponge cake base, covered with meringue and browned in the oven.

Barbecue To cook with dry heat created by the burning of hardwood or by the hot coals of this wood.

Bard To tie thin slices of fat, such as pork fatback, over meats with no natural fat cover to protect them while roasting.

Basic Grind Referring to sausages made simply by grinding meats to various stages of coarseness or fineness.

Basmati Rice A variety of long-grain rice from India.

Batonnet Cut into sticks, about ¼ × ¼ × 2⅓–3 inches (6 mm × 6 mm × 6–7.5 cm).

Batter Semiliquid mixture containing flour or other starch, used for the production of such products as cakes and breads and for coating products to be deep-fried.

Bavarian Cream A dessert made of custard sauce, gelatin, and whipped cream.

Bean Curd see Tofu.

Bean Paste see Miso.

Béarnaise (bare nez) A sauce made of butter and egg yolks and flavored with a reduction of vinegar, shallots, tarragon, and peppercorns.

Béchamel A sauce made by thickening milk with a roux.

Beignet Fritter.

Beurre Manié (burr mahn yay) A mixture of equal parts raw butter and flour mixed together into a smooth paste.

Beurre Noir (burr nwahr) Butter heated until it is dark brown, then flavored with vinegar.

Beurre Noisette (burr nwah zett) Whole butter heated until it is light brown.

Bisque A cream soup made from shellfish.

Bivalve A mollusk with a pair of hinged shells, such as clam and oyster.

Blanch To cook an item partially and briefly in boiling water or in hot fat. Usually a pre-preparation technique, as to loosen peels from vegetables, fruits, and nuts, to partially cook French fries or other foods before service, to prepare for freezing, or to remove undesirable flavors.

Blancmange (1) An English pudding thickened with cornstarch. (2) A French almond-flavored pudding containing gelatin and milk.

Blanquette A white stew made of white meat or poultry simmered without preliminary browning and served with a white sauce.

Boar Wild pig, or the meat from this animal.

Boeuf à la Mode A classic French dish of braised beef.

Boil To cook in water or other liquid that is bubbling rapidly, about 212°F (100°C) at sea level and at normal pressure.

Bombe A molded ice cream or sherbet dessert.

Bordelaise A brown sauce flavored with a reduction of red wine, shallots, pepper, and herbs and garnished with marrow.

Botulism A deadly food-borne intoxication usually associated with improperly canned foods.

Bouquet Garni A combination of fresh herbs tied together, used for flavoring.

Bouquetière (book tyair) Garnished with an assortment or bouquet of fresh vegetables, such as artichokes, carrots, turnips, green beans, peas, cauliflower, and potatoes.

Braise (1) To cook covered in a small amount of liquid, usually after preliminary browning. (2) To cook (certain vegetables) slowly in a small amount of liquid without preliminary browning.

Breve (bray vay) A mixture of espresso and steamed half-and-half.

Brine Cure A curing method in which the food is immersed in a solution (brine) made of the curing ingredients dissolved in water.

Brioche Rich yeast dough containing large amounts of eggs and butter, or the product made from this dough.

Broil To cook with radiant heat from above.

Broth A flavorful liquid obtained from the simmering of meats and/or vegetables.

Brunoise (broon wahz) (1) Cut into very small (⅛ inch/3 mm) dice. (2) Garnished with vegetables cut in this manner.

Bruschetta (broo sket ta) A slice of toasted Italian bread served as an appetizer, usually rubbed with garlic and moistened with olive oil, often served with additional toppings.

Bulgur A type of cracked wheat that has been partially cooked.

Buttercream An icing made of butter and/or shortening blended with confectioners' sugar or sugar syrup and, sometimes, other ingredients.

Butterflied Cut partially through and spread open to increase the surface area.

C

Calamari Italian for "squid" (plural).

Calorie The amount of heat needed to raise the temperature of 1 kg water by 1°C. Used as a measure of food energy. More correctly called a kilocalorie.

Canapé (can ah pay) Tiny open-faced sandwich, served as an hors d'oeuvre.

Capon A castrated male chicken.

Cappuccino Mixture of equal parts espresso and frothy, steamed milk.

Caramelization The browning of sugars caused by heat.

Carbohydrates Any of a group of compounds, including starches and sugars, that supply energy to the body.

Carême, Marie-Antoine Famous nineteenth-century French chef, often considered the founder of classical cuisine.

Carotenoids Yellow or orange pigments in vegetables and fruits.

Carpaccio Very thin slices of meat or fish, served raw.

Carry-over Cooking The rise in temperature inside roast meat after it is removed from the oven.

Catadromous Referring to fish that live in fresh water but spawn in the ocean.

Caul A fatty membrane that covers the stomach of a pig; used for wrapping meats for cooking and for lining terrines.

Caviar (1) The salted roe or eggs of sturgeon. (2) The salted roe of another fish, such as salmon or whitefish, if that fish is designated in the name, e.g. whitefish caviar.

Celsius Scale The metric system of temperature measurement, with 0°C set at the freezing point of water and 100°C set at the boiling point of water.

Centi- Prefix in the metric system meaning "one-hundredth."

Cephalopod A member of the class of mollusks that includes octopus and squid.

Certified Pork Pork that is guaranteed or certified to be free of trichinosis.

Chai A sweetened blend of spiced milk and tea.

Charcuterie (shar koo tree) The art of preparing fresh and cured pork products, including sausages and pâtés.

Charcutier (shar koo tyay) One who prepares and sells pork products, including sausages and pâtés.

Chasseur (sha sur) "Hunter style," usually referring to items served with a brown sauce containing mushrooms, tomato, and white wine.

Chaud-Froid An opaque sauce containing gelatin, used to coat certain cold foods.

Chef The person in charge of a kitchen or of a department of a kitchen.

Chèvre A cheese made from goat's milk.

Chiffon (1) A light, fluffy dessert or pie filling containing gelatin and beaten egg whites. (2) A type of cake made with an egg-white foam and with oil as a shortening.

Chiffonade Cut into fine shreds; usually said of leafy vegetables and herbs.

China Cap A cone-shaped strainer.

Chitterlings Pork intestines.

Chlorophyll Green pigment in vegetables and fruits.

Cholesterol A fatty substance found in foods derived from animal products and in the human body; it has been linked to heart disease.

Chop To cut into irregularly shaped pieces.

Choucroute (shoo kroot) Sauerkraut.

Choucroute Garni Sauerkraut cooked with sausage, pork, and, sometimes, poultry products. A specialty of Alsace, France.

Chowder A hearty American soup made from fish, shellfish, and/or vegetables, usually containing milk and potatoes.

Chutney Any of several types of spicy condiments or relishes.

Cilantro The fresh coriander plant, used as an herb.

Clamart Garnished with or containing peas.

Clarified Butter Purified butterfat, with water and milk solids removed.

Clearmeat A mixture of ground meat, egg whites, and flavoring ingredients, used to clarify consommés.

Club Sandwich A sandwich consisting of three slices of toast and filled with such ingredients as sliced chicken or turkey, lettuce, tomato, and bacon.

Coagulation The process by which proteins become firm, usually when heated.

Cocktail A type of appetizer generally made of seafood or fruit and often served with a tart or tangy sauce.

Cold Smoking A smoking method in which the foods are smoked at a low temperature, usually at or below 85°F (30°C), so that the food is not cooked during the smoking.

Collagen A type of connective tissue in meats that dissolves when cooked with moisture.

Collagen Casing An edible artificial sausage casing molded from animal materials.

Combi (Combination) Oven An oven that can operate in conventional, convection, and steamer modes.

Complementary Protein Protein supplied by foods that, if eaten together, supply all the amino acids necessary in the human diet.

Complete Protein A protein that supplies all the amino acids necessary in the human diet.

Compound Butter A mixture of raw butter and various flavoring ingredients.

Concasser To chop coarsely.

Conduction The transfer of heat from one item to something touching it or a cooler part of the first item.

Consommé A rich, flavorful seasoned stock or broth that has been clarified to make it perfectly clear and transparent.

Convection The transfer of heat by the movement of a liquid or gas.

Convection Oven An oven in which hot air is circulated by a fan.

Convenience Food Any food product that has been partially or completely prepared or processed by the manufacturer.

Coq au Vin (coke oh van) A French dish of chicken braised in wine.

Coral The roe or eggs of certain shellfish.

Coulis A vegetable or fruit purée, used as a sauce.

Coupe A dessert consisting of one or two scoops of ice cream or sherbet in a dish or glass, topped with syrups, fruits, toppings, and/or garnishes; a sundae.

Course A food or group of foods served at one time or intended to be eaten at the same time.

Court Bouillon (koor bwee yohn) Water containing seasonings, herbs, and, usually, an acid; used for cooking fish.

Couscous A type of granular pasta from North Africa, cooked like a grain.

Cream Soup A soup thickened with roux or another thickening agent and containing milk and/or cream.

Crècy (kray see) Garnished with or containing carrots.

Crème Anglaise (krem awng lezz) A light vanilla-flavored custard sauce made of milk, sugar, and egg yolks.

Crème Fraîche A thick, slightly aged heavy cream.

Crépinette A sausage patty wrapped in caul.

Critical Control Point (CCP) An action that can be taken to eliminate or minimize a food safety hazard.

Croissant A crescent-shaped roll made from a rich, rolled-in yeast dough.

Croquette (crow kett) Food that has been puréed or bound with a thick sauce, made into small shapes, breaded, and fried.

Cross-contamination The transfer of bacteria to food from another food or from equipment or work surfaces.

Crudité (croo dee tay) A raw vegetable served as a relish.

Crustacean A sea animal with a segmented shell and jointed legs, such as lobster and shrimp.

Curing Salt See Prague Powder #1.

Custard A liquid that is thickened or set firm by the coagulation of egg protein.

Cuttlefish A cephalopod similar to squid, but with a chalky interior bone and a squatter body shape.

Cycle Menu A menu that changes every day for a certain period, then repeats the same daily items in the same order.

D

Danish A rich, sweet, flaky yeast dough containing layers of rolled-in fat.

Deci- Prefix in the metric system meaning "one-tenth."

Deep-fry To cook submerged in hot fat.

Deglaze To swirl a liquid in a sauté pan or other pan to dissolve cooked particles or food remaining on the bottom.

Demi-glace A rich brown sauce that has been reduced by half.

Demitasse Literally, "half-cup." Strong, black coffee served in small cups after dinner.

Denature To change the structure of protein molecules by heat or by chemical means.

Doria Garnished with cucumbers cooked in butter.

Drawn With entrails removed.

Dressed (1) Poultry market form: killed, bled, and plucked. (2) Fish market form: viscera, scales, head, tail, and fins removed.

Drop Batter A batter that is too thick to pour but that drops from a spoon in lumps.

Dry Cure A curing method in which the curing ingredients are packed or rubbed over the food.

Dry-heat Cooking Method A method in which heat is conducted to foods without the use of moisture.

Dubarry Garnished with or containing cauliflower.

Duchesse Potatoes (doo shess) Potato purée mixed with butter and egg yolks.

Dumpling Any of a variety of small starch products made from soft dough or batter and cooked by simmering or steaming.

Duxelles A coarse paste or hash made of finely chopped mushrooms sautéed with shallots.

E

Elastin A type of connective tissue in meats that does not dissolve when cooked.

Emincer (em an say) To cut into very thin slices.

Empty Calorie Food A food that supplies few nutrients per calorie.

Emulsified Grind Referring to sausages made by processing the meat and fat to a purée, usually with the addition of water or another liquid.

Emulsion A uniform mixture of two unmixable liquids.

Entremetier (awn truh met yay) The cook who prepares vegetables, starches, soups, and eggs.

Epazote (ep ah so tay) A pungent herb, used in Mexican cooking.

EP Weight Edible portion; the weight of an item after all trimming and preparation is done.

Escoffier, Georges Auguste Great chef of the early twentieth century and the father of modern cookery.

Essential Fatty Acid A fatty acid that must be consumed in the diet because it can't be made by the body.

Espagnole A sauce made of brown stock and flavoring ingredients and thickened with a brown roux.

Espresso, Expresso Strong, dark coffee made from beans roasted until almost black, ground very fine, and brewed under steam pressure.

Étuver (ay too vay) To cook or steam an item in its own juices; to sweat.

Executive Chef The manager of a large kitchen or food production department.

Extended Meal Service Service of a meal at which customers eat at different times.

Expediter Kitchen worker who accepts and transmits orders from waiters, calls for orders to be finished, inspects finished dishes, and passes them to the dining room staff.

F

Facultative Able to live and grow with or without the presence of oxygen; said of bacteria.

Farmstead Cheese Cheese made entirely with milk from a farmer's own herd or flock, and made on the farm where the animals are raised.

Farro A grain that is the ancestor of modern wheat.

Fermentation The process by which yeast acts on carbohydrates to change them into carbon dioxide gas and alcohol.

Fermière (fair myair) Garnished with carrots, turnips, onions, and celery cut into uniform slices.

Fettuccine Flat egg noodles.

Fiber A group of indigestible carbohydrates found in grains, fruits, and vegetables.

Fillet, Filet (1) Meat: Boneless tenderloin. (2) Fish: Boneless side of fish.

Flavones White pigments in vegetables and fruits.

Flavor Profile The combination of flavors and aromas that make up the total taste impression of a dish.

Florentine Garnished with or containing spinach.

Flow of Food The path that food travels in a food service operation from receiving to serving.

Foie Gras (fwah grah) Liver of specially fattened geese and ducks.

Fondant A smooth, creamy white icing or candy consisting of very finely crystallized sugar syrup.

Fond Lié A sauce made by thickening brown stock with cornstarch or a similar starch.

Fondue, Swiss A dish consisting of melted Gruyère and Emmenthaler cheeses and white wine into which cubes of bread are dipped and eaten. From the French word meaning "melted."

Food Danger Zone The temperature range of 41° to 135°F (5° to 57°C), in which bacteria grow rapidly.

Forcemeat A seasoned mixture of ground meats and other foods, used as a filling or stuffing or as a base for terrines and pâtés.

Forestière Garnished with mushrooms.

Four-hour Rule The sanitary practice of permitting foods to remain in the food danger zone for a cumulative total of no more than four hours between receiving and serving.

Free-range Referring to animals, usually poultry, that are allowed to move relatively freely outdoors as they are raised for market.

French Dressing Salad dressing made of oil, vinegar, and seasonings.

French-style Ice Cream Ice cream containing egg yolks.

Fricassée A white stew in which the meat is cooked in fat without browning before liquid is added.

Frisée A variety of curly endive or chicory that is more tender and lighter in color than curly endive.

Frittata A flat, unfolded omelet.

Fry To cook in hot fat.

Fumet (foo may) A flavorful stock, usually fish stock.

G

Galantine A forcemeat wrapped in the skin of the animal from which it is made, such as a chicken or duck, or rolled into a cylinder without the skin.

Game Meat from animals and birds normally found in the wild; many game animals are now farm-raised.

Garde Manger (gard mawn zhay) (1) The cook in charge of cold food production, including salads and buffet items. (2) The department of a kitchen in which these foods are prepared.

Garni Garnished. Having had garnish added to it.

Garnish (1) Decorative edible item used to ornament or enhance the eye appeal of another food item. (2) To add such a decorative item to food.

Garniture (1) Garnish. (2) The act or process of garnishing.

Gastrique A mixture of caramelized sugar and vinegar, used to flavor sauces.

Gazpacho A cold Spanish soup made of puréed raw vegetables.

Gelatinization The process by which starch granules absorb water and swell in size.

Gelée Aspic jelly.

Genoise (zhen wahz) A French sponge cake.

Glace de Viande (glahss duh vee awnd) Meat glaze; a reduction of brown stock.

Glaze (1) A stock that is reduced until it coats the back of a spoon. (2) A shiny coating, such as a syrup, applied to a food. (3) To make a food shiny or glossy by coating it with a glaze or by browning it under a broiler or in a hot oven.

Gluten A substance made of proteins present in wheat flour that gives structure and strength to baked goods.

Glutinous Rice A type of short-grain rice that becomes sticky and chewy when cooked.

Goulash A Hungarian stew flavored with paprika.

Gram The basic unit of weight in the metric system; equal to about one-thirtieth of an ounce.

Granité (grah nee tay) A coarse, crystalline frozen dessert made of water, sugar, and fruit juice or other flavoring.

Gras Double (grah doo bl') A type of beef tripe that is smooth rather than honeycombed.

Green Meat Meat that has not had enough time after slaughter to develop tenderness and flavor.

Griddle To cook on a flat, solid cooking surface called a griddle.

Grill To cook on an open grid over a heat source.

Grillardin (gree ar dan) Broiler cook.

Gross Pièce (gross pyess) Centerpiece of a buffet platter.

Guinea A domestically raised relative of the pheasant.

H

HACCP Hazard Analysis Critical Control Point; a food safety system of self-inspection designed to highlight hazardous foods and to control food handling to avoid hazards.

Hare A game animal similar to rabbit, with dark red, lean meat.

Hash (1) To chop. (2) A dish made of chopped foods.

Hazard A potentially dangerous food condition due to contamination, growth of pathogens, survival of pathogens, or presence of toxins.

Herbs The leaves of certain plants, used in flavoring.

Hollandaise A sauce made of butter, egg yolks, and flavorings (especially lemon juice).

Hominy Corn that has been treated with lye.

Homogenized Milk Milk that has been processed so the cream doesn't separate out.

Hongroise (ong grwahz) Hungarian style.

Hot Smoking A smoking method in which the foods are smoked at a temperature high enough to cook or partially cook them.

Hygroscopic Readily absorbing moisture.

I

Induction Cooktop A type of cooktop that works by using magnetic energy to make pots hot without getting hot itself.

Infection Disease, including much food-borne disease, caused by bacteria in the body.

Intoxication Disease caused by poisons that bacteria produce while they are growing in food.

J

Jardinière (zhar din yair) Garnished with fresh garden vegetables, such as carrots, turnips, green beans, peas, and cauliflower.

Jasmine Rice A type of aromatic rice from Southeast Asia.

Judic Garnished with braised lettuce.

Julienne (1) Cut into small, thin strips, about $\frac{1}{8} \times \frac{1}{8} \times 2\frac{1}{2}$ inches (3 mm × 3 mm × 6.5 cm). (2) Garnished with foods cut in this manner.

Jus (zhoo) Unthickened juices from a roast.

Jus Lié Thickened juices from a roast.

K

Kasha Whole buckwheat groats.

Ketone Body A toxic compound that can form in the blood if fats are burned with no carbohydrates present.

Ketosis A condition in which the blood becomes unable to carry oxygen; sometimes the result of consuming insufficient carbohydrates.

Kilo- Prefix in the metric system meaning "one thousand."

L

Lacto-ovo-vegetarian Referring to a vegetarian diet that includes dairy products and eggs.

Lacto-vegetarian Referring to a vegetarian diet that includes milk and other dairy products.

Lard (1) The rendered fat of hogs. (2) To insert strips of fat into meats low in marbling.

Lasagne Broad, flat egg noodles, or a baked, layered casserole made with these noodles.

Latte Short for caffe latte. A mixture of one part espresso and two or more parts steamed milk.

Leading Sauce A basic sauce used in the production of other sauces. The five leading hot sauces are béchamel, velouté, espagnole, tomato, and hollandaise. Mayonnaise and vinaigrette are often considered leading cold sauces.

Leavening The production or incorporation of gases in a baked product to increase volume and to produce shape and texture.

Lemon Grass A tropical grass with the aroma of lemon, used for flavoring.

Liaison A binding agent, usually made of cream and egg yolks, used to thicken sauces and soups.

Lipid Any of a group of compounds that includes fats and cholesterol.

Liter The basic unit of volume in the metric system; equal to slightly more than 1 quart.

London Broil Flank steak or other cut of beef broiled rare and cut in thin slices.

Lyonnaise (lee oh nez) Containing or garnished with onions.

M

Macaroni Noodle product made of flour and water and dried.

Macchiato (mah kee ah toe) Espresso topped with a little frothed milk.

Mâche A small, tender leafy green with a delicate taste.

Magret The boneless breast of the moulard duck.

Maître d'Hôtel Butter (may truh doh tell) Compound butter containing parsley and lemon juice.

Marbling The fat deposited within muscle tissue.

Marinate To soak a food in a seasoned liquid.

Marsala A flavorful sweet to semidry wine from Sicily.

Mayonnaise A semisolid cold sauce or dressing consisting of oil and vinegar emulsified with egg yolks.

Mayonnaise Chaud-Froid A mixture of aspic jelly and mayonnaise, used like regular chaud-froid.

Meringue A foam made of beaten egg whites and sugar.

Meringue Glacée Baked meringue shells served with ice cream.

Mesclun A mixture of tender baby lettuces.

Meter The basic unit of length in the metric system; slightly longer than 1 yard.

Meunière Referring to fish prepared by dredging in flour and sautéing, served with brown butter, lemon juice, and parsley.

Microwave Radiation generated in special ovens and used to cook or heat foods.

Milli- Prefix in the metric system meaning "one-thousandth."

Mince To chop into very fine pieces.

Minestrone Italian vegetable soup.

Minimum Safe Internal Temperature The lowest temperature to which a food item must be heated and at which it must be held for a given time in order to be considered safe.

Mirepoix (meer pwah) A mixture of rough-cut or diced vegetables, herbs, and spices, used for flavoring.

Mise en Place (meez on plahss) French term meaning "everything in place." The setup for food production. All the preparations and organization that must be made before actual production can begin.

Miso A paste made of fermented soybeans, sometimes with the addition of other grains. Also called Bean Paste.

Mocha (moh kah) (1) A variety of Arabian coffee. (2) A mixture of espresso and hot chocolate or cocoa. (2) A flavoring made of coffee and chocolate.

Moist-heat Cooking Methods Methods in which heat is conducted to foods by water or other liquid or by steam.

Mollusk A soft-bodied sea animal, usually inside a pair of hinged shells, such as clam and oyster.

Monter au Beurre (mohn tay oh burr) To finish a sauce or soup by swirling in raw butter until it is melted.

Mornay A sauce made of béchamel and Gruyère cheese.

Moulard A breed of duck with a thick, meaty breast, raised for its large, fatty liver.

Mousse A soft, creamy food, either sweet or savory, made light by the addition of whipped cream, beaten egg whites, or both.

Mousseline Forcemeat A forcemeat made of puréed fish, poultry, or meat, heavy cream, and, usually, egg whites.

Mozzarella A mild unripened cheese, used in pizzas and many other Italian-style dishes.

N

Natural Casing A sausage casing made from the intestines of meat animals.

Navarin A brown lamb stew.

New England Boiled Dinner A dish consisting of simmered corned beef and simmered vegetables, served together.

Niçoise (nee swahz) (1) Prepared in the style of Nice, France. (2) Garnished with or containing tomato concassé cooked with garlic.

Nitrosamine A cancer-causing compound formed when meats containing sodium nitrate are subjected to high heat.

Nouvelle Cuisine A modern style of cooking that emphasizes lightness of sauces and seasonings, shortened cooking times, and new and sometimes startling combinations of foods.

Nutrient density The amount of nutrients per calorie in a food.

O

Offal Variety meats.

Oolong A greenish-brown, partially fermented tea.

Organic Grown or raised without chemical growth enhancers or medications or, for plants, without artificial fertilizers or pesticides.

Oven Spring The rapid rise of yeast goods in the oven due to production and expansion of trapped gases as a result of the oven heat.

Overrun The increase in volume of ice cream or frozen desserts due to the incorporation of air while freezing.

P

Pan Gravy A type of sauce made with the pan drippings of the meat or poultry it is served with.

Pan-Broil To cook uncovered in a sauté pan or skillet without fat.

Pan-Fry To cook in a moderate amount of fat in an uncovered pan.

Panino (1) Originally, a small Italian sandwich made with a dinner roll. (2) A grilled sandwich usually made in a device that grills both sides at once and compresses the sandwich.

Panko Coarse, Japanese-style breadcrumbs.

(en) Papillote (on poppy yote) Wrapped in paper or foil for cooking so that the food is steamed in its own moisture.

Parboil To cook partially in a boiling or simmering liquid.

Parcook To partially cook by any method.

Parfait A dessert consisting of alternating layers of ice cream and fruit or syrup in a tall, narrow glass.

Parmentier (par mawn tyay) Garnished with or containing potatoes.

Par Stock The inventory of goods that an operation must have on hand to continue operating between deliveries.

Pasta General term for any shape of macaroni product or egg noodles.

Pasteurized Heat-treated to kill bacteria that might cause disease or spoilage.

Pastry Cream A thick custard sauce containing eggs and starch.

Pâté A dish made of a baked forcemeat, usually in a crust.

Pâte à Choux (pot a shoo) A soft dough used for making éclairs and cream puffs. Also called *éclair paste*.

Pâte à Pâté Dough or pastry used to make a crust for pâté.

Pâté de Campagne A pâté or terrine characterized by a coarse texture.

Pâté en Croûte A pâté in a pastry crust.

Pathogen A bacteria that causes disease.

Pâtissier (pa tees syay) Pastry cook.

Peach Melba A sundae consisting of vanilla ice cream, a peach half, and Melba (raspberry) sauce.

Persillade (pear see yahd) A mixture of bread crumbs, parsley, and garlic, used to coat roast meat items, usually lamb.

Pesco-vegetarian Referring to a vegetarian diet that includes fish.

Philadelphia-style Ice Cream Ice cream containing no eggs.

Pigment Any substance that gives color to an item.

Pilaf Rice or other grain product that is first cooked in fat, then simmered in a stock or other liquid, usually with onions, seasonings, or other ingredients.

Pizza A thin sheet of lean bread dough baked with a topping.

Poach To cook gently in water or another liquid that is hot but not actually bubbling, about 160° to 180°F (71° to 82°C).

Poissonier (pwah so nyay) Fish cook.

Polenta Italian-style cornmeal.

Portion Control The measurement of portions to ensure that the correct amount of an item is served.

Potentially Hazardous Food A food that provides a good environment for the growth of hazardous bacteria.

Pot Roast A large cut of meat cooked by braising.

Poulette Allemande sauce flavored with mushrooms, parsley, and lemon juice.

Pour Batter A batter that is liquid enough to pour.

Poussin A young chicken weighing 1 pound (500 g) or less.

Pozole Whole-grain hominy.

Prague Powder #1 A blend of 6 percent sodium nitrite and 94 percent sodium chloride (table salt), used to cure meats; also called *curing salt* and *tinted curing mix*.

Prague Powder #2 A curing mixture similar to Prague Powder #1 but containing sodium nitrate in addition to sodium nitrite.

Primal Cut One of the primary divisions of meat quarters, foresaddles, hindsaddles, and carcasses as they are broken down into smaller cuts.

Primary Flavor The basic flavor of a main ingredient of a dish; one of the components of a flavor profile.

Primeur (pree mur) Garnished with fresh spring vegetables such as carrots, turnips, green beans, peas, cauliflower, and small potatoes.

Princesse Garnished with asparagus.

Printanière (pran tawn yair) Garnished with fresh spring vegetables such as carrots, turnips, pearl onions, peas, green beans, and asparagus.

Prix Fixe (pree fix) French term meaning "fixed price"; referring to a menu offering a complete meal, with a choice of courses, for one given price.

Process Cheese A product made by grinding and melting one or more cheeses, blending them with other ingredients, and pouring the mixture into molds to solidify.

Profiterole A tiny round pastry made from éclair paste; filled with savory fillings and served as an hors d'oeuvre, or filled with ice cream and served as a dessert.

Provençale (pro vawn sal) Garnished with or containing tomatoes, garlic, parsley, and, sometimes, mushrooms and olives.

Puff Pastry A light, flaky pastry made from a rolled-in dough and leavened by steam.

Pullman Loaf A long, rectangular loaf of bread.

Pumpernickel (1) Coarsely ground rye flour. (2) Bread made with this flour.

Purée (1) A food product that has been mashed or strained to a smooth pulp. (2) To make such a pulp by mashing or straining a food.

Q

Quail A small game bird, now domestically raised, usually weighing 6 ounces (175 g) or less.

Quatre Épices A spice mixture commonly used to season sausages and forcemeats; French for "four spices."

Quiche A savory tart or pie consisting of a custard baked in a pastry shell.

Quick Bread A bread leavened by chemical leaveners or steam rather than yeast.

R

Radiation The transfer of energy by waves, such as infrared or light waves.

Raft The coagulated clearmeat that forms when stock is clarified.

Ratatouille (ra ta twee) A Southern French vegetable stew of onions, tomatoes, zucchini, eggplant, and green bell peppers.

Ravier (rahv yay) Oval relish dish.

Ravioli Dumplings consisting of filled egg noodles.

Recipe A set of instructions for producing a certain dish.

Reduce To cook by simmering or boiling until quantity is decreased; often done to concentrate flavors.

Reduction (1) A liquid concentrated by cooking it to evaporate part of the water. (2) The process of making such a liquid.

Relish (1) A type of appetizer consisting of raw or pickled vegetables. (2) A mixture of chopped vegetables and sometimes fruits, at least one of which has been pickled in vinegar or a salt solution.

Ricotta An Italian-style cheese similar to cottage cheese but smoother, moister, and sweeter in flavor.

Rillettes (ree yet) A seasoned mixture of meat, such as pork, and fat, mashed to a paste; served as an appetizer.

Risotto A moist Italian dish of rice cooked in butter and stock.

Rissolé (riss oh lay) Browned. Often referring to potatoes cut in small shapes, parboiled, and browned in hot fat.

Roast To cook foods by surrounding them with hot, dry air, in an oven or on a spit over an open fire.

Roe Fish eggs.

Roesti Potatoes Boiled potatoes that are grated, formed into small cakes, and pan-fried until crisp.

Rolled-In Dough Dough in which a fat is incorporated into the dough in many layers by means of a rolling and folding procedure.

Roquefort A blue-veined cheese made in Roquefort, France, from sheep's milk.

Rotisserie An item of cooking equipment that slowly rotates meat or other foods in front of a heating element.

Rôtisseur (ro tee sur) Cook who prepares roasted, braised, and broiled meats.

Rough Prep The preliminary processing of ingredients to the point at which they can be used in cooking.

Roux A cooked mixture of equal parts flour and fat.

Royal Icing An icing made of confectioners' sugar and egg whites, used for decorating.

Russet Starchy potato often used for baking and deep-frying.

Rye Blend A mixture of rye flour and hard wheat flour.

S

Sachet (sa shay) A mixture of herbs and spices tied in a cheesecloth bag.

Salamander Small broiler used primarily for browning or glazing the tops of certain items.

Salmonella A widespread food-borne disease, spread by improper food handling and inadequate sanitation.

Sanitize To kill disease-causing bacteria, usually by heat or by chemical disinfectants.

Saturated Fat A fat that is normally solid at room temperature.

Sauce A flavorful liquid, usually thickened, used to season, flavor, and enhance other foods.

Saucier (so see ay) Sauce cook; prepares sauces and stews and sautés foods to order.

Sauerbraten A German dish consisting of beef marinated in and then cooked with vinegar and other ingredients.

Sausage A mixture of ground meat, usually pork, and seasonings, usually stuffed into casings.

Sausage, Cured A sausage that contains nitrites or nitrates.

Sausage, Fresh A sausage that contains no nitrites or nitrates.

Sauté To cook quickly in a small amount of fat.

Scampi A kind of shellfish similar to large shrimp. In the United States, the term is often used for large shrimp, especially if broiled with garlic butter.

Sear To brown the surface of a food quickly at high temperature.

Semolina A hard, high-protein flour often used for the best quality macaroni products.

Set Meal Service Service of a meal at which all the customers eat at one time.

Shirred Egg Egg baked in a shallow, buttered dish.

Short Having a high fat content, which makes the product (such as a cookie or pastry) crumbly and tender.

Shortening (1) Any fat used in baking to tenderize the product by shortening gluten strands. (2) A white, tasteless, solid fat formulated for baking or deep-frying.

Shred To cut into thin but irregular strips, either with the coarse blade of a grater or with a knife.

Sieve Size Size of individual pieces, usually of canned vegetables.

Simmer To cook in water or other liquid that is bubbling gently, about 185° to 200°F (85° to 93°C).

Sirniki Russian pan-fried cheesecakes.

Slurry A mixture of raw starch and cold liquid, used for thickening.

Small Sauce A sauce made by adding one or more ingredients to a leading sauce.

Smoke-Roast To cook with dry heat in the presence of wood smoke.

Sodium Nitrate A compound, $NaNO_3$, used to cure meats.

Sodium Nitrite A compound, $NaNO_2$, used to cure certain meats, especially air-dried meats.

Soft-shell Crab A just-molted crab whose new shell has not yet hardened.

Solanine A poisonous substance found in potatoes that have turned green.

Sorbet (sor bay) Sherbet, usually made without milk products.

Soufflé A light, fluffy baked egg dish consisting of a base (such as a heavy white sauce) mixed with egg yolks and flavoring ingredients into which beaten egg whites are folded just before baking. May be sweet or savory.

Sous Chef (soo shef) Cook who supervises food production and who reports to the executive chef.

Spaetzle Small dumplings or noodles made from a thin egg and flour batter.

Specialty Cheese Cheese in limited production, with particular attention to natural flavor and texture profiles.

Spelt A type of wheat grain similar to farro.

Spice Any part of a plant, other than the leaves, used in flavoring foods.

Squab Young, domestically raised pigeon.

Staling The change in texture and aroma of baked goods due to the loss of moisture by the starch granules.

Standard Breading Procedure The procedure for coating a food product with bread crumbs (or other crumbs or meal) by passing it through flour, then egg wash, then crumbs.

Standardized Recipe A set of instructions describing the way a particular establishment prepares a particular dish.

Staphylococcus, Staph A bacterium that causes food-borne disease by producing a toxin or poison in improperly stored foods.

Static Menu A menu that offers the same dishes every day.

Station Chef Cook in charge of a particular department in a kitchen or food production facility.

Steam To cook by direct contact with steam.

Stew (1) To simmer a food or foods in a small amount of liquid that is usually served with the food as a sauce. (2) A dish cooked by stewing, usually one in which the main ingredients are cut in small pieces.

Stock A clear, thin—that is, unthickened—liquid flavored with soluble substances extracted from meat, poultry, and fish, and their bones, and from vegetables and seasonings.

Streusel (stroy zel) A crumbly topping for baked goods, consisting of fat, sugar, and flour rubbed together.

Strong Flour Flour with a high protein or gluten content.

Supporting Flavor Flavors of seasoning and flavoring ingredients and other secondary ingredients of a dish; flavors that support and enhance the primary flavors.

Suprême Sauce A sauce made of chicken velouté and heavy cream.

Surimi A processed seafood product manufactured to resemble shellfish such as crab.

Sweat To cook in a small amount of fat over low heat, sometimes covered.

Sweetbreads The thymus glands of calves and young animals, used as food.

Swiss Steak Beef round steaks braised in brown sauce.

T

Table d'Hôte (tobble dote) (1) Referring to a fixed-price menu with no choices. (2) Referring to a menu on which prices are listed for complete meals rather than for each separate item.

Tang The portion of a metal knife blade that is inside the handle.

Tapa Any of a variety of Spanish-style appetizers, intended to be served with wine or other drinks.

Tasting Menu A type of fixed-price menu designed to showcase the chef's art by presenting a series of small courses.

Tatsoi A leafy vegetable or salad green related to mustard and watercress.

Tempeh A fermented soy product with a dense, meaty texture.

Temper To raise the temperature of a cold liquid gradually by slowly stirring in a hot liquid.

Teriyaki A grilled or pan-broiled food that is finished with a soy sauce-based glaze.

Textured Vegetable Protein (TVP) A high-protein product made from defatted soy flour, processed to give it a sponge-like texture; available unflavored or flavored to resemble various meats.

Tinted Curing Mix See Prague Powder #1.

Tofu A bland, white food made by coagulating soy milk. Also called Bean Curd.

Tomalley The liver of lobsters and some other shellfish.

Tournant (toor nawn) Cook who replaces other station cooks; relief cook or swing cook.

Tournedos (toor nuh doe) A small beef steak cut from the tenderloin.

Trans Fat A solid fat, usually manufactured by hydrogenation, which limits the body's ability to rid itself of cholesterol.

Treviso A red-leafed relative of radicchio and Belgian endive with elongated leaves.

Trichinosis A food-borne disease caused by a parasite, sometimes found in undercooked pork.

Tripe The muscular stomach lining of beef or other meat animals.

Truit au Bleu Poached trout that was alive until cooking time and that turns blue when cooked in court bouillon.

Trunnion Kettle A steam-jacketed kettle that can be tilted for emptying.

Truss To tie poultry into a compact shape for cooking.

Tunneling A condition of muffin products characterized by large, elongated holes; caused by overmixing.

TVP see Textured Vegetable Protein.

U

Univalve A mollusk with a single shell, such as abalone.

Unsaturated Fat A fat that is normally liquid at room temperature.

V

Variety Meats Various organs, glands, and other meats that don't form a part of the dressed carcass.

Vegan Referring to a vegetarian diet that omits all animal products, including dairy products and eggs.

Velouté A sauce made by thickening white stock with a roux.

Venison The meat of wild or farm-raised deer.

Vent To allow circulation or escape of a liquid or gas, such as by setting a pot of hot stock on blocks in a cold-water bath so that the cold water can circulate around the pot.

Viande (vee awnd) French for "meat."

Vichyssoise (vee she swahz) Cold purée of leek and potato soup with cream.

Vin Wine.

Vin Blanc White wine.

Vin Rouge Red wine.

Vinaigrette Dressing or sauce made of oil, vinegar, and flavoring ingredients.

Vitamin Any of a group of compounds that are present in foods in very small quantities and that are necessary for regulating body functions.

Volatile Evaporating quickly when heated.

W

Wash (1) To brush or coat a food item with a liquid such as egg wash or milk. (2) The liquid used in this procedure.

Waxy Potato A young potato high in sugar and low in starch.

Weak Flour Flour with a low protein or gluten content.

Welsh Rabbit A dish made of melted cheddar cheese and, usually, ale or beer. Sometimes called *Welsh rarebit*.

White Pekin The most common breed of domestic duck in the United States.

Whitewash A thin mixture or slurry of flour and cold water.

Winterized Oil Vegetable oil that stays clear and liquid when refrigerated.

Wrap A sandwich in which the filling is wrapped, like a Mexican burrito, in a large flour tortilla or similar flatbread.

Z

Zest The colored part of the peel of citrus fruits.

U.S.–U.K. Cooking Vocabulary

A

Aging (meat) Hanging.
All-Purpose Flour Plain flour.
Arugula Rocket.
Atholl Brose Scottish combination of oatmeal, honey, and whisky. Eaten for breakfast or used as a pastry filling.

B

Bake Includes oven cooking with steam.
Beef Tenderloin Fillet of beef.
Belgian Endive Chicory.
Beurre Manié Kneaded butter.
Boston Lettuce Round or cabbage lettuce.
Braid Plait.
Brassicas Vegetables of the cabbage family (includes broccoli and cauliflower).
Brine A preserving solution of water, salt, saltpeter, and aromatics, used for soaking meats such as tongue and brisket.
Broil Grill.
Brown Sugar (soft) Muscovado sugar.
Brown Sugar (unrefined) Demerara sugar.

C

Canning Jars Kilner jars.
Casserole Earthenware or cast-iron dish with one or two handles and a lid.
Celery Root Celeriac.
Channel Knife Canelle knife.
Cheesecloth Muslin.
Chicken Breasts (boneless, skinless) Suprêmes: boneless, skinless, chicken breasts.
Chickpea Flour Gram flour.
Cilantro Coriander.
Clarification Refers to the process of clearing stocks or to the mixture (raft).
Clotted Cream The resulting thick layer formed by heating heavy cream and then leaving it to cool.
Confectioners' or Powdered Sugar Icing sugar.
Cookies Biscuits.
Cornstarch Cornflour.
Croutes Small slices of bread; may be toasted.

D

Daikon Radish Mooli.
Dessert Pudding.
Doneness Degree of cooking.

E

Eggplant Aubergine.

F

Filet Mignon Fillet steak.
Fish Poacher Fish kettle.
Food Mill Mouli.

H

Hard Flour (high gluten) Strong flour.
Hard Fruits Apples, pears.

Heavy Cream Double cream.
Hotel Rack Best end of neck of lamb.

I

Italian Parsley Flat-leaf or continental parsley.

J

Jelly Roll Pan Swiss roll tin.
Joint (1) A piece of meat used for roasting, with or without the bone. (2) To cut up (as in poultry or meat).
Jus, Simple Gravy Roast gravy.

L

Legumes (dried) Pulses.
Liaison Thickener; mixture to thicken sauces.
Light Cream Single cream.

M

Malt Syrup Maltose, malt.
Meat Grinder Mincer.
Molasses Black treacle.

O

Offset Spatula Angled spatula; step palette knife.

P

Pastry Dough Paste.
Peanut Oil Groundnut oil.
Pit To stone.
Porcini Ceps.
Prosciutto Ham Parma ham.
Puff Pastry Puff.

R

Romaine Lettuce Cos lettuce.
Rutabaga Swede.

S

Salmon Roe Keta.
Sanding Sugar Nibbed sugar.
Scallion Green onion.
Season (condition a pan) Prove.
Sheet Pan Swiss roll tin.
Snow Peas Mangetout.
Strainer Sieve.

T

Tomato Paste Tomato purée.

V

Van Dyking English technique for serving fish whole, with the tail cut in the form of a V.
Very Fine Granulated Sugar Castor sugar.

W

Weak Flour Soft flour.
Whole Wheat Flour Whole meal flour.

Z

Zucchini (large) Marrow.
Zucchini Courgette.

French-English Cooking Vocabulary

A

Abaisser (ah bay say) To roll a dough to the desired thickness with the aid of a rolling pin.

Abats (ah bah) Offal; internal organs of butchered animals sold mainly by stores called triperies that specialize in this. White offal are sweetbreads, feet, brains. Red offal are heart, lungs, liver.

Abattis (ah bah tee) The feet, neck, head, wingtips, liver, gizzard, and heart of poultry.

Accommoder (ah koh mo day) To prepare and season a dish for cooking.

Acidifier (ah si di fee ay) To add lemon juice or vinegar to fruits, vegetables, and fish to prevent oxidation.

Aciduler (ah see dyoo lay) To make a preparation slightly acidic, tart, or tangy by adding a little lemon juice or vinegar.

Affuter (ah foo tay) To sharpen the cutting edge of a knife by using a steel or sharpening stone.

Aiguillette (ay gee yet) A long, narrow slice of meat cut from the breast of poultry (especially duck) and game birds.

Aiguiser (ay gee zay) See Affuter.

Allumettes (al loo met) (1) A type of savory petits fours (long rectangle of puff pastry) covered with cheese or filled with anchovies. (2) Very thin French fries; pommes allumettes.

Anglaise (on glez) (1) A mixture of whole eggs, oil, water, salt, and pepper, used to help coat food with flour and bread crumbs. (2) A dish cooked in boiling water (e.g., potatoes).

Aplatir (ah pla teer) To flatten a piece of meat or fish in order to make it more tender and to facilitate cooking.

Appareil (ah pa ray) A mixture of the principal elements of a final recipe (usually egg based).

Aromate (ah row mat) A condiment or vegetable with a characteristic smell or taste (spices and herbs). Often used in reference to a combination of flavoring vegetables, such as carrot, onion, leek, and celery.

Arroser (ah row zay) To baste; the wetting of meat or fish with a liquid or fat during or after cooking.

Aspic (a spik) A dish composed of meat, vegetables, and/or fish that is cooked, chilled, and molded in gelatin.

Assaisonner (ah say zo nay) To season; the addition of a preparation of certain ingredients that bring out the flavor of the food.

Attendrir (ah ton drear) (1) To allow a piece of meat to age under refrigeration for a few days to make it more tender. (2) To become stale.

Au Jus (oh zhu) Served with natural cooking juices.

B

Bain-marie (ban marie) A hot-water bath; a way of cooking or warming food by placing a container in a pot of very hot water. Used for preparations that must not cook over direct heat, for keeping delicate sauces hot, and for melting chocolate.

Ballotine (ball oh teen) A large piece of meat or a whole bird that is boned and stuffed.

Barder (bar day) To cover or wrap a piece of meat, poultry, and, occasionally, pastry with a very thin piece of pork fat for protection and basting during cooking. This prevents drying out.

Barquette (bar ket) A small, long oval pastry mold.

Basquaise (bas kez) In the Basque style; usually indicates the presence of red peppers in the dish.

Bâtonnet (ba tow nay) Small stick; refers to a type of vegetable cut.

Batterie (bat trie) Set; complete set of kitchen utensils.

Bavarois (ba var wha) Bavarian cream; a cold dessert made from crème anglaise, set with gelatin and whipped cream.

Béchamel (beh sha mel) White sauce made from milk and white roux.

Beignet (ben yay) Food dipped in a thin batter and deep-fried.

Bercy (bear see) A classic sauce with a white wine base, used for fish.

Beurre (burr) Butter.

Beurre Blanc (burr blahn) Butter-based sauce made from a reduction of dry white wine, vinegar, and shallots. Mainly served with poached or grilled fish.

Beurre Clarifié (burr cla ri fee ay) Clarified butter; butter that is gently melted in order to remove the impurities that float to the top and the whey that sinks to the bottom.

Beurre Composé (burr com po zay) Butter mixed with one or more ingredients, such as anchovy butter (butter and crushed anchovies).

Beurre Demi Sel (burr demi cell) Lightly salted butter containing up to 5 percent salt.

Beurre Fermier (burr fair miay) Farm-fresh butter.

Beurre Laitier (burr lay tee ay) Dairy-made butter.

Beurre Manié (burr man yay) Butter mixed with an equal amount of flour; used to thicken sauces.

Beurre Noisette (burr nwa set) Brown butter; butter that is cooked until colored a light brown (see Noisette).

Beurre Pasteurisé (burr pass ter ee zay) Factory-produced and -pasteurized butter.

Beurre en Pommade (burr on poh mahd) Softened (not melted) butter.

Beurrer (burr ray) (1) To lightly coat a container with butter in order to prevent sticking. (2) To add butter to a sauce or dough.

Beurre Salé (burr sa lay) Salted butter containing up to 10 percent salt.

Beurre Sec (burr sek) Dry butter; butter with a minimum water content. The percentage of water can vary from 5 to 8 percent, depending on the quality of butter.

Biscuit (beace quee) (1) A small cake or cookie. (2) A specific type of sponge cake, similar to genoise.

Bisque (bisk) Type of soup usually made from a shellfish base and thickened.

Blanc (blahn) (1) White. (2) A mixture of flour and cold water that is added to acidulated water (usually lemon juice) to prevent certain foods from discoloring during cooking.

Blanchir (blon sheer) To blanch. (1) To place vegetables or meats in cold water and then bring to a boil (or to plunge in boiling water) in order to precook, soften, or remove an excess of flavor (acidity, saltiness, or bitterness). (2) To whip sugar and eggs together until light in color. (3) To soak meat in cold water in order to remove excess blood, salt, and/or impurities.

Blondir (blon deer) To cook in fat in order to color lightly.

Bouchée (boo shay) A small round of puff pastry that can be filled with different mixtures.

Bouillir (boo year) To boil; to bring a liquid to the boiling point.

Boulangère (boo lawn zhare) Cooked with veal stock, onions, and potatoes; a style of meat preparation.

Bouquet Garni (boo kay gar nee) A mixture of herbs enclosed in the green portion of a leek used to flavor dishes during their cooking.

Braiser (bray zay) To braise; to cook a meat in a covered dish in or over gentle heat with a little liquid and, usually, on a bed of finely diced vegetables.

Brider (bree day) To truss; to tie a bird so that it keeps its shape during cooking.

Brochette (broe shet) (1) A skewer made of wood or bamboo. (2) Small pieces of food stuck on a long piece of metal or wood and grilled.

Broyer (broy yay) To crush or grind finely.

Brunoise (broon waz) Vegetables cut into very small regular cubes.

C

Cacao (ka ka oh) Cocoa.

Calvados (cal vaw dose) An alcoholic beverage distilled from cider, made exclusively in the Normandy region.

Canapé (can ah pay) Bite-sized slice of sandwich or other type of bread, toasted or not toasted, which is spread or garnished with various ingredients.

Canard (can arr) Duck or drake.

Caneton (can e tone) Male duckling.

Canette (can net) Female duckling.

Canneller (can nel lay) To channel, to flute, to groove.

Capre (capr) Caper.

Caraméliser (care a mel lee zay) To caramelize; to coat a mold with cooked sugar; to cook sugar until dark for use in other preparations (to coat or to make a sauce).

Cèpe (sepp) Bolete or porcini mushroom.

Champignon (shamp pin yon) Mushroom.

Champvallon (shamp val lawn) Preparation of lamb chops cooked in the oven with potatoes and onions.

Chantilly (shawn tee yee) Whipped cream to which sugar and vanilla have been added.

Chapelure (shap a lure) Dried bread crumbs made from both the crust and center of dried bread. Used for breading.

Charlotte (shar lott) (1) A dessert made in a special mold. (2) A savory preparation made in this mold.

Chaud-Froid (show fwah) A dish prepared hot but served cold and covered with a specific sauce (sauce chaud-froid, made from ⅓ velouté, ⅓ gelatin, and ⅓ cream).

Chemiser (shem ee zay) To line the interior of a mold before filling.

Chèvre (shevr) Goat.

Chiffonade (shi foe nod) Leafy herbs and greens that are finely shredded.

Chinois (shee nwah) China cap sieve; a fine conical strainer.

Chiqueter (sheek ah tay) To lightly score the cut edges of puff pastry to help ensure that it rises straight and evenly.

Cidre (seedr) Hard cider.

Ciseler (see ze lay) (1) To score; to make incisions in certain fish in order to facilitate cooking. (2) To finely mince; a manner of finely cutting onions, shallots, and garlic.

Citronner (see trone nay) (1) To rub foods with lemon to prevent them from discoloring. (2) To add lemon juice.

Clarifier (clare re fee ay) (1) To clarify; to clear a cloudy liquid by straining, heating, and gently simmering with egg whites. (2) Process of separating milk solids from butter.

Clouter (cloo tay) To stud; to pierce cured tongue with strips of truffle; to pierce an onion with a whole clove.

Coller (cole lay) To thicken or set using gelatin, as in making jelly or fruit mousse.

Concasser (cone cas say) To break up coarsely with a knife or mortar.

Concassé (de tomates) (cone cas say duh to maht) Peeled, seeded, and diced tomatoes.

Confit (cone fee) A food that is saturated with one of the following: vinegar (for vegetables); sugar (for fruits); alcohol (for fruits); fat (for poultry).

Consommé (cone so may) Clear bouillon made from meat, fish, or vegetables; served hot or cold.

Contiser (cone tee zay) To loosen the skin of fowl, game, and some fish in order to insert a thin slice of truffle.

Coquille (coe key) Shell.

Cordée (core day) Referring to a dough or potato purée that becomes elastic from overworking.

Coriandre (core ree andr) Cilantro (fresh), coriander.

Corne (corn) Plastic tool used for scraping the contents out of containers.

Corser (core say) To give strength or body to the flavor of a preparation.

Coucher (koo shay) (1) To lay; to place a rolled piece of dough on a baking sheet. (2) To spread; to spread a layer of cream or other garnish. (3) To pipe; to cover with a layer, using a piping bag.

Coulis (koo lee) A smooth purée of fruits or vegetables; used as a sauce.

Coupe (koop) Cup.

Couper (koo pay) To cut.

Court Bouillon (core bwee yone) A cooking liquid, composed of water, aromatic vegetables, and, sometimes, white wine vinegar, in which fish and certain meats are cooked.

Crécy (kreh see) Refers to dishes containing carrots. The name of an area known for its carrot production.

Crème Anglaise (krem on glez) A sweet sauce made from eggs, sugar, and milk that is cooked at 85°C (185°F).

Crème Fouettée (krem foo eh tay) Whipped cream; cream that has been whisked in order to incorporate air.

Crème Fraîche (krem fresh) A type of heavy cream.

Crème Pâtissière (krem pa tis see air) Pastry cream; milk thickened with flour or flan powder, used for pastry making.

Crémer (krem may) (1) To cream together sugar and butter. (2) To add cream.

Crème Renversée (krem ron vare say) Caramel flan; a mixture of sugar, milk, and eggs poured into a mold, usually lined with caramel, then gently cooked in the oven in a hot-water bath.

Crème de Riz (krem de ree) Cream of rice; a powder made from finely ground rice, used in pastry or to thicken sauces.

Crêpe (krep) Very thin pancake.

Crépine (kreh peen) Pork caul.

Crever (kreh vay) To blanch rice by placing it in cold water, then bringing to a boil for a few minutes. It is usually the first step in making rice desserts.

Croquette (kroh kett) A breaded, fried item consisting of a mixture of fruit, fish, or vegetables. Can be savory or sweet and in any shape.

Croustade (krew stod) (1) A crisp crust that is fried. (2) An empty pastry case.

Croûte (kroot) Crust; the brown outer covering of bread. A meat or fish en croûte is one that is wrapped in a crust.

Croûton (kroo tohn) A slice or piece of toasted bread.

Crudité (kroo dee tay) Raw vegetable, sliced or cut, served with a vinaigrette or mayonnaise as a first course.

Cuisson (kwees sohn) The cooking; the action and manner of cooking a food.

D

Dariole (dahr ree ole) A small thimble-shaped mold.

Darne (darn) Thick slice, containing the central bone, cut from round fish.

Daube (dobe) Stew of meat braised in red wine.

Décanter (day kahn tay) (1) To allow the impurities in a liquid to sink to the bottom so the liquid can be gently poured off, leaving the residue. (2) To separate meat from its cooking liquid in order to finish the sauce.

Décortiquer (day kor tee kay) To shell; to remove the outer covering from shellfish and crustaceans.

Découper (day koo pay) To cut; to cut using scissors, a knife, or pastry cutter.

Déglacer (day gla say) To deglaze; to dissolve with liquid the substance attached to the bottom of a pan.

Dégorger (day gor zhay) To degorge; to soak an ingredient in cold water in order to remove blood, salt, or impurities; to lightly salt vegetables in order to extract the maximum amount of water.

Dégraisser (day gray say) To degrease; to remove excess fat from the surface of a food or sauce.

Délayer (day lay yay) (1) To thin with water. (2) To dissolve in liquid.

Demi-glace (de mee glass) Meat, fish, or chicken stock, reduced to a concentrated form.

Démouler (day moo lay) To unmold; to carefully remove a preparation from the container in which it was placed to give it a specific form.

Dénerver (day nair vay) To remove the tendons from meat and fowl.

Dénoyauter (day noy oh tay) To pit; to remove the seed or pit of stone fruits and olives with a knife or pitter.

Dépouiller (day pwee yay) (1) To remove the skin that forms on the top of a sauce or soup. (2) To skin; to remove the skin of a small animal, fish, etc.

Dés (day) Cubes; small regular squares.

Désosser (day zohs say) To debone; to remove the bones from meat and fowl.

Dessécher (day se shay) To dry out; to remove moisture through heat.

Détailler (day tie yay) To cut up; to cut into pieces.

Détendre (day ton dr) To loosen (in consistency); to add a liquid to a preparation, such as a sauce.

Détrempe (day trompe) Dough made of flour and water, used for puff pastry.

Détremper (day trompe pay) To moisten with a liquid.

Dorer (doe ray) To brush with beaten egg or egg yolk in order to give a deep color and shine.

Dorure (doe ruhr) Egg wash; beaten egg or egg yolk, with water and/or salt added, used to color doughs just before cooking.

Douille (doo yeey) Pastry tip; a conical piece made of metal or plastic, used in decorating with a pastry bag.

Dresser (dres say) To dress; to arrange the prepared food on a plate or platter before serving.

Duchesse (dew shess) Mashed potatoes with the addition of egg yolks.

Dugléré (dew glay ray) A classic preparation for fish incorporating white wine and tomato; named for a nineteenth-century chef.

Duroc (dew rock) Classic preparation of small pieces of meat served with pan-fried potatoes, tomato sauce, and chasseur sauce. Named after the nineteenth-century chef Marshall Duroc.

Duxelles (duke sell) Finely chopped mushrooms cooked in butter with minced shallots; used as a garnish or filling.

E

Ébarber (eh bar bay) To debeard; to remove the fins and bones of fish; to remove the filaments from poached eggs.

Ébouillanter (eh boo yawn tay) To dip in boiling water; to scald.

Ébullition (eh boo lee see own) Boiling point; the appearance of bubbles in a hot liquid (98° to 100°C/208° to 212°F).

Écailler (eh kie yay) To scale; to remove the scales from fish.

Écailles (eh kie) Scales (of fish, snakes, etc.).

Écaler (eh kah lay) To shell (eggs); to remove the shell from soft- and hard-boiled eggs.

Écumer (eh kue may) To skim; to remove the foam from the surface of a boiling liquid.

Effiler (eh fee lay) To slice very thinly (e.g., almonds).

Égoutter (eh goo tay) To strain; to remove the cooking liquid by pouring into a strainer.

Émietter (eh myet tay) To crumble; to break into small pieces.

Émincer (eh man say) To cut into thin slices.

Émonder (eh moan day) To skin; to remove the skin from fruits and vegetables by heating.

En Croûte (on kroot) Wrapped in pastry.

En Robe (on robe) Coated or covered.

Enrober (on robe bay) To coat; to completely cover with various ingredients, such as chocolate or dough.

Entremet (on tre may) Literally, "between courses"; originally a course served between the roast and the dessert. Today it is a mousse-based cake.

Éplucher (eh ploo shay) To peel; to remove the skin or inedible part of fruits and vegetables.

Éponger (eh pone jay) To sponge; to remove excess liquid or fat by absorbing with a kitchen or paper towel.

Escaloper (eh scal oh pay) To cut scallops; to cut meat or fish on a bias.

Essence (ess sahns) Essence; concentrated extract, used as a flavoring (e.g., coffee essence).

Étuver (eh too vay) To stew, to cook slowly; to cook gently while covered with fat and a little water without changing the color of the ingredients.

Évider (eh vee day) To hollow, to gut; to hollow the center of an ingredient (poultry, fruit, vegetables).

F

Farce (farce) Forcemeat stuffing; a mixture of various ground ingredients (meat, herbs, vegetables), used to fill poultry, fish, vegetables, etc.

Farcir (far seer) To stuff; to fill poultry, fish, or meat with a forcemeat stuffing.

Fariner (far ee nay) To flour, to dredge; to sprinkle flour on fish or meat or to sprinkle a mold with flour and tap out the excess.

Fermière (fair mee yare) Farm-made or farm-raised.

Ficeler (fee se lay) To tie with string.

Filet (fee lay) Fillet.

Fines Herbes (feen zairb) Mix of edible aromatic plants used as seasoning (parsley, tarragon, chives).

Flamber (flom bay) Flambé. (1) To use a flame in order to remove the down from poultry. (2) To light alcohol in a preparation (e.g., crêpes suzette).

Flan (flahn) (1) Open pastry case or shell. (2) A custard tart.

Fleuron (flur rohn) Piece of puff pastry cut into crescent shapes, served as decoration with fish dishes.

Foie Gras (fwah grah) Fattened duck or goose liver.

Foncer (fone say) To line the bottom and sides of a mold or pan with dough.

Fond (fohn) Stock.

Fondant (fawn daunt) (1) A sugar icing used for glazing pastries. (2) Referring to something that melts in the mouth (literally, "melting").

Fondre (fone dr') (1) To melt; to turn a solid into liquid by heating (e.g., butter). (2) To cook, covered, certain vegetables in water and butter (e.g., mushrooms) until the liquid has completely evaporated, without changing the color of the ingredients.

Fondu (fone dew) Melted.

Fontaine (fone ten) A well; a deep impression made in flour in order to add other ingredients for making a dough.

Fraiser (fray zay) To mix a dough evenly by smearing it with the fleshy part of the palm of the hand.

Frémir (fray meer) To simmer; to bring a liquid just to the boiling point, the bubbles being barely perceptible.

Fricassée (free kah say) (1) A way of cutting a chicken into eight pieces. (2) A preparation in which meat or poultry is cut into pieces before being braised.

Frire (freer) To deep-fry.

Friture (free tur) (1) Deep fryer. (2) Deep-fried foods.

Fumet (few may) (1) Cooking aroma. (2) Sauce made from cooking juices. (3) Basic stock made from fish and used to make sauces.

Fusil (few zee) Sharpening steel; long, rounded metal tool, used to keep the cutting edge of a knife sharp.

G

Galantine (ga lawn teen) Cold poached meat that has been stuffed and larded, served with gelatin made from the poaching liquid.

Garniture (gar nee tur) Garnish; served as an accompaniment to a dish (usually vegetables).

Gastrique (ga streek) A caramel delazed with vinegar used as a base for a sweet and sour sauce (as with duck à l'orange).

Gaufrette (go frett) Waffle.

Gelée (jel lay) Gelatin, aspic; meat or fish stock that has been clarified, then set with gelatin. Used in various preparations en gelée to give shine to foods as well as to protect them from drying out.

Genoise (zhen wahz) Genoese sponge cake.

Glaçage (glah sahj) Glaze; mixture of ingredients with a syrupy consistency, sweet or savory, used to coat pastries, candies, and certain savory foods.

Glace (glahss) (1) Ice cream. (2) Glaze; stock reduced until thick and syrupy.

Glacé (glah say) (1) Glazed (usually refers to vegetables). (2) Frozen. (3) Served with ice cream (e.g., meringue glacé).

Glacer (glah say) To glaze; to cover or coat pastries with a glaze.

Goujonnettes (goo zhone nett) Strips of fish, breaded and deep-fried.

Graisser (gray say) To grease; to coat or cover with fat before baking or roasting in the oven.

Grandmère (grahn mare) A classic garniture made from bacon, sautéed button mushrooms, and glazed pearl onions.

Gratiner (gra tee nay) (1) To brown under the grill or salamander. (2) To glaze.

(à la) Grecque (ah la grek) Refers to a preparation of vegetables cooked in white wine.

Griller (gree yay) To grill; to cook on a grill.

H

Habiller (ah bee yay) To dress; to prepare an item, such as fish or meat, for cooking.

Hacher (ah shay) To chop; to reduce to small pieces with a knife.

Hareng (a rehng) Herring.

Haricot (are ree co) Bean.

Haricot Blanc (are ree co blahn) White bean.

Haricot Vert (are ree co vare) Green bean.

Historié (ee stow ree ay) Decorated.

Hollandaise (awl lawn daze) Hot emulsion sauce made from egg yolks and clarified butter and flavored with lemon juice.

Homard (oh mahr) Lobster.

Huile (weel) Oil.

Huile d'Olive (weel doe leave) Olive oil.

Huile d'Arachide (weel da rah sheed) Peanut oil.

Huile de Noix (weel de nwah) Walnut oil.

I

Imbiber (am bee bay) To imbibe; to wet or soak an element with stock or syrup.

Inciser (an see zay) To incise; to make small, shallow cuts in order to speed cooking.

Incorporer (an core po ray) To incorporate; to gradually mix ingredients together by gently mixing.

Infuser (an few zay) To place an element into simmering water and let sit so that the element flavors the water (e.g., tea).

J

Jambon (zhom bohn) Ham.

Jambonnette (zhom bo nett) Stuffed chicken leg made to resemble a small ham.

Jardinière (zhar dee nyair) Literally, "pertaining to a garden"; a mixture of carrots, turnips cut into sticks, green beans, and green peas. Cooked separately, then served together as an accompaniment.

Jarret (zhah ray) Knuckle or shank of meat.

Jet (zhett) A dash of liquid, a squirt.

Joue (zhoo) Cheek (beef or pork).

Julienne (zhoo lee yen) Cut into very fine strips.

Jus (zhoo) Juice; liquid made from pressing a fruit or vegetable or from the cooking of a meat.

L

Lait (lay) Milk.

Langoustine (lawn goo steen) Dublin Bay prawn.

Lard (lahr) Solid fat from pork. Lard gras contains fat only, while lard maigre (bacon) contains meat as well.

Larder (lahr day) To lard; to insert strips of pork fat into lean meats, using a larding needle, in order to prevent the meat from drying out during cooking.

Lardon (lahr doan) A small piece or strip of slab bacon.

Légume (leh gyoom) Vegetable.

Lentille (lawn teey) Lentil.

Levain (le vanh) Starter dough; a dough made from live yeast and flour, used to make breads.

Lever (le vay) To rise; to leave a dough to rise (as with brioche, bread, croissants).

Lever les Filets (le vay lay fee lay) To fillet; to remove the fillets of a fish using a knife.

Levure (le vure) Yeast.

Levure Chimique (le vure she meek) Baking powder; odorless and flavorless rising agent made from bicarbonate of soda and cream of tartar.

Liaison (lee ay zonh) Thickener; element or mixture used to thicken a liquid or sauce.

Lier (lee ay) To thicken; to change the consistency of a liquid by adding a roux, starch, egg, flour, or beurre manié.

Lotte (lot) Monkfish.

M

Macédoine (mass e dwan) A mixture of vegetables or fruit, cut into small cubes.

Macérer (mass e ray) To macerate; to soak an element in alcohol in order to flavor it (usually done for pastry).

Magret (mah gray) The breast meat of a fattened duck.

Manchonner (mahn show nay) To remove the meat that covers the end of a bone, such as a chicken leg or a rack of meat, in order to achieve a clean presentation.

Mandoline (man do leen) A slicer with several blades, allowing various cuts and thicknesses of fruits and vegetables.

Mange Tout (manj too) Chinese pea pods or snow peas.

Manier (man yay) To knead.

Mariner (mar ee nay) To marinate; to soak a piece of meat or fish in a liquid and aromatics in order to tenderize, flavor, and preserve. Can also be used to tame the flavor of strong-flavored game.

Médaillon (may die yohn) Medallion; round slice of meat, fowl, fish, or crustacean, served hot or cold.

Meringue (me rang) Mixture of beaten egg whites and sugar.

Meringue Glacée (me rang gla say) Vacherin.

Mie de Pain (mee de pan) Fresh bread crumbs.

Mijoter (mee joo tay) To simmer; to cook over gentle heat.

Mirepoix (meer pwah) (1) Vegetables cut into cubes, the size depending on the length of cooking. (2) A certain blend of aromatic vegetables (onions, carrots, and celery).

Monder (moan day) To skin; to remove the skin of certain fruits or vegetables (e.g., peaches, tomatoes) by plunging into boiling water.

Monter (moan tay) (1) To mount; to whisk (egg whites, cream) in order to incorporate air and increase the volume. (2) To add butter to a sauce in small pieces.

Morille (mow reey) Morel mushroom.

Mouiller (moo yay) To wet; to add a liquid to a preparation before cooking.

Mouler (moo lay) To mold; to fill a mold before or after cooking.

Moulu (moo loo) Milled; ground.

N

Napper (nap pay) To coat; to cover a food, savory, or sweet with a light layer of sauce, aspic, or jelly.

Navarin (na va rahn) Brown lamb stew containing tomato.

Nem (nem) Vietnamese-style spring roll.

Noircir (nwahr seer) To blacken; to darken when exposed to air (said of certain fruits and vegetables).

Noisette (nwah set) A hazelnut. See also Beurre Noisette.

O

Oeuf (euf) Egg.

Oie (wah) Goose.

Graisse d'Oie (gress dwah) Goose fat.

Os (ohss) Bone.

Ôter (oh tay) To remove.

Ouvrir (oov rear) To open.

P

Paner (pan ay) To coat a food with fresh or dry bread crumbs after dipping in an anglaise (see Anglaise) and then cook.

Panier (pan yay) Basket. (1) A frying basket, used with a deep fryer in order to easily plunge foods into and remove them from the hot oil. (2) A steam basket, used for placing foods to be steamed. (3) Nestling baskets; a frying tool in the form of two ladle-shaped baskets, one slightly smaller than the other, used to form nests of shredded potatoes with which to decorate certain platters.

Papillote (pa pee yote) (1) Buttered or oiled paper, used to wrap fruits, meats, fish, etc. for cooking. (2) Paper frill used to decorate the ends of bones of certain poultry and meats.

Parer (pah ray) To trim; to remove the nerves or excess fat from meat or fish, or to remove the damaged or inedible portions of fruit and vegetables before cooking or serving.

Parfait (par fay) A frozen dessert made of a sweet egg-yolk foam and whipped cream.

Parfumer (par few may) To flavor.

Passer (pas say) To strain, generally using a strainer or china cap sieve.

Pâte (pat) Dough or batter.

Pâté (pat tay) Chopped meat, poultry, fish, etc., cooked in a dough. Today considered almost synonymous with *terrine*.

Pâtissier (pat tee see ay) Pastry chef.

Pâton (pat tohn) Large square piece of dough (puff pastry, bread) before cooking.

Paupiette (po pee yet) Thin piece of meat or fish that is stuffed, rolled, tied, and cooked.

Pavé (pa vay) Thick cross-section slices of fish fillets.

Paysanne (pay yee zahn) Vegetables cut into small, thin triangles or squares.

Persillade (pear see yahd) A mixture of parsley and chopped garlic.

Pétrir (pe trear) To knead; to work a dough.

Piler (pee lay) To grind (e.g., with a mortar and pestle); to make a powder by crushing with a mortar and pestle.

Pilon (pee lohn) (1) A pestle; a tool used for crushing and grinding. (2) The drumstick of a chicken leg.

Piment (pee mon) Chile pepper.

Pincée (pan say) A pinch; small quantity of a dry ingredient measured by pinching with the thumb and index finger.

Pincer (pan say) To pinch; to use a pastry crimper to crimp the edges of dough before cooking.

Pintade (pan todd) Guinea fowl.

Piquer (pee kay) (1) To pick; to lard a piece of meat, using a larding needle, in order to keep the meat from drying out during cooking. (2) To make small holes in dough, using a fork, to prevent it from rising too much.

Pluche (ploosh) Sprig; small leaves picked off the stems (e.g., sprig of chervil).

Pocher (po shay) To poach; to cook in barely simmering water.

Poêler (po e lay) To pan-fry; to cook an element in a frying pan over high heat with minimal oil.

Pointe (pwahnt) Point (of a knife). (1) A small quantity measured using the point of a knife (e.g., point of ground vanilla). (2) The tip of something (e.g., tip of asparagus).

Poivron (pwahv rohn) Sweet bell pepper.

Poulet (poo lay) Chicken.

Pousser (poos say) To rise (literally, "to push"). (1) To leave a yeast dough to increase in volume. (2) To feed meat into a meat grinder.

Poussin (poos san) Cornish game hen.

Praline (prah leen) Caramelized sugar with almonds or hazelnuts, ground to a smooth paste, used to flavor and decorate pastries.

Primeur (pree mer) Early vegetable or fruit.

Profiterole (pro feet er role) Choux ball filled with sweet or savory filling. The best known is a dessert filled with vanilla ice cream and served with chocolate sauce.

Provençale (pro von sal) Provence style; refers to dishes containing one or all of the following: olive oil, tomatoes, garlic, bell peppers, and olives.

Q

Quadriller (ca dree yay) (1) To mark squares or diamonds on meat, using a grill. (2) To mark squares using a knife.

Quatre Épices (catr eh peace) Four spices; a mixture of ground pepper, cinnamon, nutmeg, and cloves. Often used to flavor meat stuffings.

Quenelle (kuh nel) (1) Dumpling made of meat, poultry, or fish purée, mixed with egg white and cream. Usually molded with two spoons into an egg shape. (2) Oval three-sided shape made using two large spoons.

Quiche (keesh) Savory tart with a creamy egg base (e.g., quiche Lorraine: bacon and cheese custard tart).

R

Rafraîchir (rah fray sheer) To refresh, to cool, to chill; to quickly cool in cold water a food that has been blanched.

Raidir (ray deer) To seize or sear (esp. in boiling fat); to precook without coloring.

Râper (ra pay) To grate; to reduce to thin slices or powder using a grating tool (e.g., with cheese).

Rassis (ras see) Stale, not fresh.

Ratatouille (ra tah too yee) Dish made from red bell peppers, onions, tomatoes, zucchini, eggplant, and, often, olives.

Rectifier (reck tee fee yay) To rectify; to correct the seasoning of a dish.

Réduire (ray dweer) To reduce; to heat a liquid or to reduce it in volume by boiling.

Relever (re le vay) To reinforce flavor through the use of spices.

Remonter (re moan tay) To remount; to repair a sauce or a cream that has separated in order to return it to its proper appearance and texture.

Revenir (faire) (re ve near fehr) To quickly color a food in hot fat or oil.

Rissoler (rees so lay) To cook a food in hot fat or oil until well colored.

Rondelle (ron dell) Small, round slice.

Roux (roo) A cooked mixture of equal amounts of flour and fat (usually butter). The three types of roux—white, blond, and brown—vary in color depending on how long they cook.

S

Sabayon (sa ba yohn) A thick, frothy sauce, either sweet or savory, that is made from whisking egg yolks and liquid over low heat. Similar to the Italian zabaglione.

Saisir (say zeer) To seize; to quickly color over very high heat at the start of cooking.

Salamandre (sal ah mandr) A salamander or broiler; the upper heating element in an oven or a professional appliance, used to brown foods.

Saupoudrer (so poo dray) To sprinkle; to evenly distribute a powder over the surface of a dish or dessert.

Sauter (so tay) To sauté (literally, "to jump"); to cook over high heat, stirring constantly to prevent sticking.

Singer (san jay) To sprinkle with flour at the start of cooking in order to eventually give a certain consistency to the sauce.

Siroper (seer oh pay) To add syrup to a pastry. See Imbiber.

Sorbet (soar bay) Flavored water ice; frozen confection made from fruit juice or pulp and sugar syrup.

Sous Chef (soo shef) Second to the chef.

Suer (soo ay) To sweat; to gently cook vegetables in a little fat, without coloring them, in order to bring out their flavor.

Suprême (soo prem) (1) The breast part of the fowl. (2) A fillet of fish.

Suprême Sauce (soo prem sauce) Classic sauce made from a velouté enriched with cream.

T

Tailler (tie yay) To cut in a precise fashion.

Tamis (ta mee) Drum sieve.

Tamiser (ta mee zay) To sift; to press through a fine drum sieve.

Tapenade (ta peh nahd) Purée of black olives, anchovies, and olive oil.

Terrine (tare reen) (1) A deep rectangular mold traditionally made of white porcelain, used to cook seasoned ground meats, fish, or poultry. (2) The food cooked in such a mold.

Timbale (tam ball) (1) A mold in the shape of a large thimble. (2) Type of dough shaped as a container, baked, and filled with various foods.

Tourer (tour ray) To turn; to roll and fold butter into a dough (e.g., for puff pastry, croissants).

Tourner (tour nay) To turn. (1) To give certain vegetables a regular long shape, using a knife. (2) To mix ingredients together by mixing in a circular motion.

Travailler (tra vie yay) To work; to knead, mix, soften.

Tremper (trom pay) To soak; to dip; to wet.

Truffer (troo fay) To add chopped truffles to a dish, stuffing, or foie gras. To slide a thin slice of truffle under the skin of poultry.

Turban (toor bahn) (1) A type of ring mold. (2) Food prepared in such a mold.

V

Vallée d'Auge (val lay dozh) In the style of a region of Normandy; indicates a dish prepared with cider, apples, and cream.

Vanner (van nay) To mix a cream or sauce as it cools in order to prevent lumps or the formation of a skin on the surface.

Vapeur (va purr) Steam.

Velouté (ve loo tay) A thickened sauce made from a white stock and a roux.

Vinaigre (vee negre) Vinegar.

Vinaigrette (vee ne gret) A sauce made of vinegar, oil, and seasonings.

Volaille (voe lye) Poultry.

> **Blanc de Volaille** (blahn duh voe lye) Chicken breast.
>
> **Cuisse de Volaille** (kweese duh voe lye) Chicken leg.

Z

Zester (zes tay) To zest; to remove the colored part of the skin of a citrus fruit (e.g., orange, lemon).

Subject Index

Acid:
- and bacterial growth, 18
- and connective tissue, 65
- in consommé production, 211
- and curdling of milk, 809
- and egg foams, 789
- and fiber, 506
- in marinades, 141
- in stock, 151
- and vegetable pigments, 508-510

Aging, of meat, 261-262
Allergen, 24
Amaranth, 620
Amino acid, 657-658
Ammonia, baking, 905
Amuse bouche, 765-766
Antelope, 283
Antipasto, 764
AP (as purchased) measurement, 100, 108
Appetizers, see Hors d'oeuvres
Arrowroot, 164
Aspic, 849-850, 852-853, 865-867

Bacon, 804-805
Bacteria, 16-19, 20-21
Baked Alaska, 1001
Baking, 70-71
- bread, 914
- cake, 944-946
- cookies, 968
- fish, 458-463
- potatoes, 592-597
- poultry, 366-375
- vegetables, 565-562
Baking ammonia, 905
Baking powder, 904
Baking soda, 904
- and vegetable cooking, 507, 510
- effect of on fiber, 65
Barbecue, 71
Barding, 258, 273
Barley, 620
Base (stock), 159
Basting, 289, 376
Batch cooking, 539
Batonnet, 134
Batter (for frying), 144, 576
Bavarian cream, 1013-1015
Bean thread, 638
Beans, dried, see Legumes
Beef:
- cooking methods, 272, 273
- cuts, 264-265, 268
- grades, 261
- tenderloin, preparing, 317
- See also Meat
Beef recipes, see Recipe Index
Beurre blanc, 178-180
Beurre manié, 164
Beurre noir, 177
Beurre noisette, 177
Biscuits, 933, 934, 935
Bison, 283
Bisque, 207, 237
Blanch and chill method, 539
Blanching, 69, 140-141
Blancmange, 1011
Blanquette, 326, 331, 403
Boar, 283, 298, 322
Boiling, 68-69
- pasta, 638-639
- potatoes, 585-591
- rice, 621-622
- vegetables, 544-555
Bones, in meat, 267-270

Bones, in stock, 150, 152, 153, 156
Boulanger, M., 4
Bouquet garni, 152
Brains, 280
Braising, 70
- fish, 458
- meat, 331-348
- poultry, 410-422
- sausages, 838
- vegetables, 559-565
Bread:
- faults of, 915
- for sandwiches, 736
- mixing and production methods, 910-914, 924-926
- quick, 931-937
- storage, 736, 914
- types, 910
Bread recipes, see Recipe Index
Breading, 142-143
Breakfast preparation, 785-805
Broilers, 46
Broiling and grilling, 71-72
- fish, 464-470
- meat, 305-312
- poultry, 376-378
- sausage, 838
- vegetables, 573-574
Broth, 185, 209-210
Brunoise, 134
Bruschetta, 764, 780
Buckwheat, 620
Buffalo, 283
Buffet service, 884-889, 719-720
Bulgur, 619
Butter, 810
- clarified, 177, 178
- compound, 178, 179
- in baking, 900
- in sandwiches, 737
- in sauces, 161, 167, 177-183
Buttercream, 953-955

Cake, 939-960
- altitude adjustments, 946-947
- assembling and icing, 958-959
- baking and cooling, 944-946
- cutting, 960
- faults of, 946
- icings for, 953-957
- mixing methods, 940-942
- scaling and panning, 943-944
- types, 942-943
Cake recipes, see Recipe Index
Calamari, 446
Calorie, 118
Canapé, 756-760
Can sizes, 1026
Caramelization, 64
Carbohydrate:
- as nutrient, 119, 120, 125
- effect of heat on, 64
- in meat, 258-259
Carême, Marie-Antoine, 4-5
Caribou, 283
Carpaccio, fish, 498, 503
Carving, poultry, 369, 371
Casing, sausage, 834
Caterina de Medici, 8-9
Caul, 281
Caviar, 765
Cereal, breakfast, 804
Chaud-froid, 850-852, 853
Cheese, 811-818
- artisan, 814-816
- composition, 811-812

cooking with, 816-818
- in sandwiches, 738
- on buffets, 888, 889
- pastry filling, 923
- storage and service, 816
- varieties, 812-816
Cheese recipes, see Recipe Index
Chef, 9, 10
Chemical poisoning, 16, 24-25
Chicken, 352-363
- braising, 410-421
- broiling and grilling, 376-380
- cutting, 360-363
- deep-frying, 383-384, 386, 394
- free range, 352
- roasting and baking, 366-374
- sautéing and pan-frying, 383-398
- simmering and poaching, 399-407
Chicken recipes, see Recipe Index
Chiffon, 1013, 1016-1019
Chiffonade, 139
Chiffon cake, see Cake
Chitterlings, 281
Chocolate, 905-906
Cholesterol, 121
Chowder, see Soup
Chutney, 187, 192, 193, 202
Clam, 442-444
Clam recipes, see Recipe Index
Coagulation, 65, 258
- in baking, 896
- egg, 788-789
Cobbler, 1001
Cocktail, 760
Coffee, 819-821
Conduction, 66
Confit, duck, 422
Connective tissue, 65
- in fish. 428
- in meat, 259-260, 272-273
- in poultry, 352, 353
Consommé, 206, 210-214
Convection, 44, 66-67
Convenience foods, 144-146, 159
Cookie, 963-975
- characteristics, 964-965
- mixing methods, 965
- panning, baking and cooling, 968
- types and makeup methods, 966-968
Cookie recipes, see Recipe Index
Cooking methods. See also Baking; Boiling; Braising; Broiling, Deep-frying; Griddling; Grilling; Pan-broiling; Pan-frying; Poaching; Roasting; Sautéing; Simmering; Steaming
- dry-heat, 70-75
- moist-heat, 68-70
Corn (grain), 619
Corn syrup, 901
Cornstarch, 164
Court bouillon, 482-483, 484
Couscous, 619
Crab, 451-454
Crab recipes, see Recipe Index.
Crayfish or crawfish, 454
Cream, 808-809
- in baking, 902
- in sauces, 167, 186
- in soup, 221
Crème anglaise, 1007-1008
Crêpe, 770
Crêpinette, 281, 839
Critical Control Point, 33, 34
Croissant, 910, 920, 929
Croquette, 575, 604, 605

Cross-contamination, 25, 28
Crudité, 760
Cryovac, 262
Cuisson, 483
Cured foods, 825-831
Custard, 799, 1007-1008, 1010
Cutting loss, 110
Cutting techniques, basic, 134-140
Cuttlefish, 446

Dairy products, 807-818. See also Butter; Cheese; Cream; Milk
- in vegetarian diet, 656, 658, 661
Danish pastry, 910, 920-929
Deep fryers, 47-48
Deep-frying, 73
- fish, 479-481
- potatoes, 602-605
- poultry, 383-384, 386, 394
- preparation for, 142-144
- vegetables, 575-578
Deglaze, 167, 313
Demi-glace, 168, 169, 175
Dessert, frozen, 1021-1023
Dessert, fruit, 1001-1003. See also Pie
Dessert recipes, see Recipe Index
Dice, 134
Dips, 761-763
Doughnut, 919, 999
Dressing, salad, see Salad dressing
Dressing and stuffing, for poultry, 423-424
Dry rub, 142, 298-299
Duck, 353, 355, 356
- wild, 357
Duck recipes, see Recipe Index
Dumplings, 651-652

Éclair paste, 997-999
Egg, 786-799
- in baking, 903
- in breading, 142-143
- composition, 786
- in consommé production, 211
- cooking, 790-799
- custard, 799
- deviled, 775
- foam, 789, 941, 999-1001
- grades and quality, 787
- market forms, 787
- in salad dressing, 721
- in sauces, 165-166
- size, 787
- soufflé, 796-797, 798, 1014, 1020
- substitutes, 788
- in vegetarian diet, 656, 661
Egg recipes, see Recipe Index
Elastin, 260
Elk, 283, 312
Emu, 357-358, 381
Emulsion:
- in salad dressing, 722, 726-729
- in sauces, 165, 180
EP (edible portion) measurement, 100, 108
Equipment, 41-61
- cleaning and sanitizing, 30-31, 42
- cooking (stationary), 43-49
- for sandwich-making, 740-741
- hand tools, 57-61
- holding and storage, 52-53
- knives, 57-58
- limitations, 93
- measuring, 56-57
- pot, pans, and containers, 53-56

processing, 50-52
and recipe conversion, 106
for sausage making, 834-835
Escabeche, 467
Escargot, 454
Escoffier, Georges-Auguste, 5
Espagnole sauce, 168, 169, 174
Extract, 906

Farro, 620, 634
Fat:
effect of heat on, 65
in baking, 899-900
in forcemeat, 855
in game, 282
in meat, 258
as nutrient, 119-121, 125
in roux, 161-162
in sausage, 832
smoke point, 65
Fatty acid, 121
Feet (meat), 281
Fiber, 64-65, 506-507
Fish, 427-503
baking, 458-463
broiling and grilling, 464-470
in canapés, 759
composition and structure, 428
cooking methods, 429, 458-493
cutting and filleting, 429-431
deep-frying, 479-481
doneness, 428
fat and lean, 428-429
freshness, 439
handling and storage, 439-440
inspection, 439
market forms, 429
mixed cooking techniques, 492-498
poaching and simmering, 482-491
in sandwiches, 738
sautéing and pan-frying, 470-478
served raw, 498-503
steaming, 489, 492-493
varieties and characteristics, 432-438
Fish recipes, see Recipe Index
Flavor profile, building, 76-78
Flavoring, 78-84
for simmered meats, 324
in baking, 905-906
in salad dressing, 721-722
vegetables, 579
Flour:
dredging with, 144
in pie doughs, 978
in sauces, 162
strength, 895
types, 897-898
Flow of food, 33
Foie gras, 870, 871, 873
Fondant, 953
Fond lié, 174
Food cost, 107-114
Food Danger Zone, 18, 26, 27, 28, 130
Forcemeat, 854-856
Formulas, baking, 892-895
Four-hour rule, 26
French toast, 802-803
Fricassée, 331, 342, 410, 416
Fritter, 575, 576, 577
Frog legs, 454
Frosting (Icing), 953-957
Fruit, 677, 680-684
in pie, 984
Fruit dessert, 1001-1003
Fumet, 158
Fungus, 16, 22
Fusion cuisine, 8

Galantine, 862-863
Game, 281-284
Game birds, 357-358
Game and game bird recipes, see Recipe Index
Garde manger, 673, 847
Garnish, 882-885
for canapés, 758-760
for pâtés and terrines, 854
for salad, 684-685
for soup, 208-209
Gastrique, 174
Gelatin, 717-719
aspic, 849-850
in stock, 150
Gelatinization, 64, 161
in baking, 896

Glaze (icing):
for cake, 957
for pastry, 922
Glaze (reduced stocks), 158-159
Glazing:
fish, 484
vegetables, 554
Gloves, disposable, 26
Glucose, 901
Gluten, 895-896, 897-898, 902
in éclair paste, 997
in pie doughs, 978
in quick breads, 932
Gnocchi, 652
Goose, 355, 356
Grain, 617-634
cooking, 621
in vegetarian diet, 659
storing and handling, 620-621
types, 617-620
Grain recipes, see Recipe Index
Gravlax, 829
Gravy, 183-184, 290, 292
Griddles, 47
Griddling, 72, 313
Grilling, 71-72
fish, 464-470
meat, 305-312
poultry, 376-382
sausage, 838
vegetables, 573-574
Grills, 46-47
Grinder, 51
Grits, 619, 633
Guinea, 355, 356

HACCP, 16, 33-34, 97
Hare, 294
Hazard, chemical, 24-25
Hazard, food, 16
Hazard, physical, 24, 25
HDL, 122
Heart, 280
Heat, effects of on food, 64-66
Herbs, 80-84, 137
in stock, 152
Hollandaise, see Sauce, Sauce recipes
Hominy, 619
Honey, 901-902
Hors d'oeuvre, 755-782
adapted from other recipes, 763-764
canapés, 756-760
cocktails, 760
dips, 761-763
relishes, 760-761
serving, 756
Hors d'oeuvre recipes, see Recipe Index
Hygiene, 25-26

Ice cream, 1021-1023
Icing, 953-957
Icing recipes, see Recipe Index
Insect control, 32
Inspection, of meat, 260
Inspection, of seafood, 439
Intestines, 281

Julienne, 134
Jus, 184, 185-186, 290, 291-292
Jus lié, 174

Kamut, 620
Kasha, 620, 634
Kidneys, 279, 312
Knife:
handling and using, 133-140
sharpening, 133
types of, 57-58

La Varenne, 6
Lag phase, 18
Lamb:
cooking methods, 272, 273
cuts, 266, 269
grades, 261
leg of, carving, 295
leg of, trimming, 295
rack of, preparing, 297
Lamb recipes, see Recipe Index
Langouste, langoustine, 450
Lard, 900
Larding, 273-274
LDL, 122
Leavening, 903-905
Legumes, 608-617
cooking, 610

in vegetarian diet, 659
types, 608-610
Lettuce, see Salad
Liaison (egg yolk and cream), 165, 167
in soup, 221, 222
Liver, 278, 321
Lobster, 447-450
Lobster recipes, See Recipe Index

Macaroni, see Pasta
Magret, 356
Maillard reaction, 65
Malt syrup, 902
Margarine, 811
in baked goods, 900
in sauces, 161
in sandwiches, 737
Marinade, 748
Marinating, 141-142
of game, 282
of poultry, 376
Mayonnaise, 726-728
in chaud-froid, 851
for sandwiches, 737
Measurement, 99-102, 105, 114, 1027
in baking, 892-894
equipment for, 56-57
metric, 101-102, 1026
Meat. See also, Beef; Game; Lamb; Pork; Variety meats; and Veal
aging, 261-262
bone structure, 267
breakfast, 804-805
in canapés, 760
composition, 258-259
cooking methods, 271-275, 288-348
cuts, 262-271
doneness, 275-278
game and specialty, 281-284
inspection and grading, 260-261
in salad, 677
in sandwiches, 737
in sausage, 832
selection, 270-271
specifications, 271
in stock, 150-151
storage, 284-285
structure, 259-260
Medici, Caterina de, 8-9
Menu, 87-95
à la carte and table d'hôte, 89-90
accuracy, 94-95
and cost control, 94
classical, 90-91
modern, 91-92
planning 112-113
prix fixe, 90
static and cycle, 89
tasting, 90
types, 89-90
variety and balance in, 92-93
Meringue, 999-1001
Mesclun, 679
Metric system, 101-102, 1026
Meunière, 177, 470-472
Microbiology, 16-23
Microwave, 46, 67, 74-75
Milk, 808-809
in baking, 902
Millet, 620
Minerals, 65, 120, 122
Minimum Safe Internal Temperature, 29
Mirepoix, 137
in consommé production, 211
for roast meats, 289-290
in stock, 151, 152
Mise en place, 129-146, 512-534
Miso, 660
Mixers, 50
Molasses, 901
Moose, 283
Mousse, dessert, 1013, 1014, 1016, 1018, 1021
Mousse, savory, 865-866, 870
Mousse recipes, see Recipe Index
Mousseline, 863-864, 854
MSG, 83
Muffin, 933-934, 936-937
Mushrooms, 534-536
Mussels, 444-445
Mussel recipes, see Recipe Index

Nitrates and nitrites, 826-827
Noodles, See Pasta
Nutrient density, 118
Nutrition, 117-127

in vegetarian diet, 656-658

Oats, 620
Octopus, 446
Oil:
flavored, 188, 200
in baking, 900
in salad dressing, 720-721
Omelet, 794-796
Organic, 352, 512
Organization, kitchen, 8-11
Ostrich, 357-358, 381
Ovens, 44-46
Oxtails, 219, 280, 335
Oysters, 441-442
Oyster recipes, see Recipe Index

Pan-broiling, 71-72
meat, 305-307
Pancakes, 800-802
Pan-frying, 72
fish, 470-478
meat, 313-323
potatoes, 598-601
poultry, 383-397
sausage, 838
vegetables, 556-557
Pan gravy, 183-184, 290, 292
Panino, 740, 749, 750
Papillote, 69, 495
Parasite, 16, 19, 23
Partridge, 357, 419
Pasta, 635-650
cooking, 638-639
kinds, characteristics, and quality factors, 635-638
shapes, 636, 637
Pasta and pasta sauce recipes, see Recipe Index
Pastry, 992-999
cream horns, 996
danish, 910, 920-929
éclairs and cream puffs, 997-999
napoleon, 997
patty shells, 996
pinwheels, 996
puff, 992-997
turnovers, 995
Pastry bag, 591
Pastry cream, 1008-1009
Pastry recipes, see Recipe Index
Pâté, 857-859
chicken liver, 778
pastry for, 857
Pâté and terrine recipes, See recipe index
Pâte à choux, 997-999
Pathogen, 16
Pepper, black, white, and green, 82
Pepper, red, 82-83
Persillade, 296
Pest control, 32
Pheasant, 357, 415
Phytochemicals, 122
Pie, 978-992
assembly and baking 982-983
chiffon, 992, 1013, 1014, 1016-1019
filling, 984-992
fruit tarts, 981
Pie dough, 978-981
ingredients, 978
types, 979
Pie dough recipes, see Recipe Index
Pie filling:
cream, 992, 1009
custard or soft, 990-991
fruit, 984-989
Pie filling recipes, see Recipe Index
Pigments, in vegetables, 508-510
Pilaf, 623, 624, 625
Pizza, 739, 752-753
Plating, 878-882
Poaching, 68, 69
eggs, 790-791
fish, 482-491
poultry, 399, 401
Point, Fernand, 7
Polenta, 619, 632-633
Popover, 932, 936
Pork:
aging, 261
cooking methods, 272, 273
cuts, 266, 270
doneness, 275-276
grades, 261
yield grades, 260
Pork recipes, see Recipe Index

Portion control, 100-101
  in salad bars, 720
  in sandwiches, 740
Portion cost, 112
Potatoes, 508-509, 530, 581-605
  baking, 592-597
  boiling and steaming, 585-591
  deep-frying, 602-605
  duchesse, 590-591
  market forms, 584-585
  purée, 588
  quality, 584
  in salad, 676, 702, 704, 705
  sautéing and pan-frying, 598-601
  storing and handling, 584
  types, 582-584
Potato recipes, see Recipe Index
Potentially hazardous foods, 18
Pots, pans, and containers, 53-56
Poultry, 351-424. See also Chicken;
  Duck; Game birds; Turkey
    composition and structure, 352-
      353
    cooking methods, 366-411
    doneness, 358
    handling and storage, 358, 359-363
    in sandwiches, 737
    inspection and grading, 354
    market forms, 354-358
    simmering and poaching, 399-409
    trussing, 359
Poussin, 356
Pozole, 619
Prague powder, 827
Presentation, see Garnish; Plating
Professionalism, 11-13
Protein:
  as nutrient, 120, 121
  complementary, 121, 657-658
  effect of heat on, 65
  in meat, 258
  in vegetarian diet, 656-658
Pudding, 1009, 1010-1021. See also
  Bavarian cream; Chiffon; Custard;
  Mousse
Pudding recipes, see Recipe Index

Quail, 357
Quail recipes, see Recipe Index
Quatre épices, 833, 839
Quenelle, 393
Quiche, 799
Quinoa, 620

Rabbit, 283-284, 305, 344
Rabbit recipes, see Recipe Index
Radiation, 67
Radicchio, 679
Rangetops, 43-44
Ratites, 357
Ravioli, 641, 645
Recipe, 95-112
  baking formulas, 892-895
  conversion, 103-107
  instructional, 97
  standardized, 96-97
  uses and limitations, 95-96
Reduction, 158, 165-166
Relish, 187, 192
Remouillage, 157
Rice, 618-619
  cooking, 621-628
  pilaf, 623, 624, 625
  risotto, 623-624, 626-627
  wild, 619-620
Rice and grain recipes, see Recipe Index
Rice stick, 638, 650
Rillettes, 872, 874-875
Risotto, 623-624, 626-627
Roasting, 70-71
  meat, 288-305
  poultry, 366-375
Rock lobster, 449-450
Rock shrimp, 450
Rodent control, 32
Rotisseries, 47
Roux, 161-164

Sachet, 152
Safety, 35-38, 42
Salad, 673-732
  arrangement and presentation,
    684-685
  bound, 702-705
  composed, 708-716
  fruit, 706-707
  gelatin, 717-719

green, 687-690
  ingredients, 675-684
  quantity production, 686
  types, 674-675
  vegetable, grain, legume, and pasta,
    690-701
Salad bar, 719-720
Salad dressing, 685, 720-732
Salad and salad dressing recipes, see
  Recipe Index
Salamanders, 46, 71
Salsa, 187, 191, 199
Salt, 82
  in baking, 905
  curing, 826
  in stock, 151-152
Sandwiches, 735-753
  basic ingredients, 736-738
  production, 740-752
  types, 738-739
Sandwich recipes, see Recipe Index
Sanitation, 16-34, 182
  and eggs, 788, 1030
  for cold foods, 848, 889
  and pastry cream, 1008
Sauce, 159-202
  Asian, 187, 193-196
  béchamel, 168, 171
  butter, 177-183
  dessert, 1007-1008, 1023-1024
  espagnole, 168, 169, 174
  families, 167-170
  finishing, 166-167
  flavored oil, 188, 200
  fond lié, 168, 174
  for broiled meat, 307
  functions of, 160
  hollandaise, 168, 169, 170, 180-183
  integral, 183
  leading, 160, 167-169
  small, 168-169
  standards of quality for, 170
  structure of, 160-161
  tomato, 168, 169, 176-177
  velouté, 168, 169, 172
Sauce recipes, see Recipe Index
Sausage, 831-845
  breakfast, 805
  casings, 834
  categories, 831-832
  cooking, 837-838
  ingredients, 832-833
  smoking, 837
Sausage recipes, see Recipe Index
Sautéing, 72
  fish, 470-477
  meat, 313-323
  potatoes, 598-601
  poultry, 383-398
  sausage, 838
  vegetables, 556-559
Scale, 56, 99, 893
Scallop, 445
Scallop recipes, see Recipe Index
Scaloppine, veal, cutting, 316
Scampi, 450
Scoops, 56, 57
Seasoning, 78-84
  broiled meat, 306
  for meat, 288
  poultry, 366
  in salad dressing, 721-722
  of sauces, 167
  in sausage, 833
  vegetables, 579
Seviche, 498, 502
Sherbet, 1021
Shortening, 899-900
Shrimp, 450-451
Shrimp recipes, see Recipe Index
Simmering, 68-69
  eggs, 790
  fish, 482-491
  meat, 324-330
  poultry, 399-409
  sausage, 838
Skillet, tilting, 48
Slicers, 51
Smoke-roasting, 71, 298, 374, 462
Smoking, 828-831, 837
Snails, 454
Solanine, 584
Sorbet, 1021
Soufflé:
  dessert, 1014, 1020
  frozen, 1021
  savory 796-797, 798

Soup, 205-255
  bisque, 207, 237
  broth, 209-210
  chowder, 207, 238-240
  clear, 206, 209-220
  consommé, 206, 210-214
  cream, 206, 221-228
  low-fat, 207
  purée, 206-207, 229-236
  service of, 207-209
  specialty and national, 207, 241-
    255
  thick, 206-207
  vegetarian, 207
Soup recipes, see Recipe Index
Spaetzle, 651
Spaghetti, see Pasta
Spelt, 620
Spice, 80-84
  in baking, 906
  in cured foods, 833
  in stock, 152
Spreads:
  for canapés, 758
  for sandwiches, 736-737
Squab, 355, 356
Squab recipes, see Recipe Index
Squid, 446
Staling, 896-897
Standard Breading Procedure, 142-143
Starch:
  in baking, 899
  instant, 165, 899, 984
  as nutrient, 119
  in pie filling, 984
  as thickening agent, 161-165
  in vegetables, 5
Steamer, 45, 49
Steaming, 69
  fish, 489, 492-493
  potatoes, 585-591
  vegetables, 544-555
Steam kettle, 48-49
Steam table, 53
Stewing, 70, 324
Stir-frying, 313-314, 395, 559
Stock, 150-159
  brown or espagnole, 156-157, 168,
    174
  dashi, 195
  fish, 158
  ingredients for, 150-153
  in sauces, 160
  vegetable, 153, 155
  white, 154-155
Storage, 26-28, 114
  of bread, 736, 914
  of butter, 810
  of cheese, 816
  of convenience foods, 145
  of eggs, 787
  of fish and seafood, 439-440, 442,
    444, 445, 449, 451, 452
  of ice cream, 1022
  of meat, 284-285
  of potatoes, 584
  of poultry, 358
  of rice, 620
  of vegetables, 540
Streusel, 922
Stuffing and dressing, for poultry, 423-
  424
Sugar:
  in baking, 900-902
  cooking, 1006-1007
  as nutrient, 119
Surimi, 454
Sushi, 499, 500-501
Sweetbreads, 277-278, 322, 346
Syrup, cooking, 1006-1007

Taillevent, 6
Tandoori chicken, 381
Tapas, 764-765
Tartare, seafood, 498-499
Tea, 822-823
Tempeh, 660
Temperature, and bacterial growth, 18
Tempering, 165
Tempura, 481
Teriyaki, 396
Terrine, 857-861, 863-869, 871-874
Terrine and pâté recipes, see Recipe In-
  dex
Textured vegetable protein (TVP), 660
Thickening agents, 161-165
Tofu, 659-660, 664, 668

Tomato concassé, 533
Tongue, 280
Tourné, 138
Toxin:
  chemical, 24-25
  plant, 22
  seafood, 24
Trans fat, 122
Tripe, 281, 327
Triticale, 620
Truit au bleu, 482
Turkey, 355, 356
  braising, 410
  carving, 371
  quantity service, 371
  roasting, 366-367, 370
  sautéing, 383, 387
  simmering and poaching, 399, 409
Turkey recipes, see Recipe Index

Variety meats, 278-281
Veal:
  aging, 261
  cooking methods, 272, 273
  cuts, 265, 269
  doneness, 275
  grades, 261
  scaloppine, 316
Veal recipes, see Recipe Index
Vegetable, 506-605
  baking, 565-572
  boiling and steaming, 544-555
  braising, 559-565
  broiling and grilling, 573-574
  in canapés, 759
  classifying, 514
  color changes, 508-510
  deep-frying, 575-578
  doneness, 507
  dried, 538, 585, 608-610
  evaluating, 514-534
  flavor changes, 507-508
  general cooking rules, 511
  handling, 512-513
  mise en place, 512-534
  nutrient loss, 510-511
  processed, 536-538, 540
  puréeing, 545
  quality standards, 512
  quantity cooking, 539
  in salad, 676, 690-701
  in sandwiches, 738
  sautéing and pan-frying, 556-559
  storage, 540
  texture changes, 506-507
Vegetable recipes, see Recipe Index
Vegetarian diet, 656-671
  menus for, 658-662
  nutrition, 656-658
  types, 656
Venison, 282, 304, 312, 322
Vinaigrette, 723-726
Vinegar, 721
Virus, 16, 19, 22
Vitamin, 65-66, 120, 121-122

Waffles, 800-801
Water:
  in baking, 902
  as food component, 66
  as nutrient, 122
Waters, Alice, 7
Waxy maize, 164, 899
Wheat, 619
Whitewash, 164

Yeast, 903-904
Yeast dough products, 909-929
Yield grading, 260
Yogurt, 809

Zest, citrus, 140

Recipe Index

Aioli, 201, 728
Albufera Sauce, 173
Allemande Sauce, 173
Allumette Potatoes (Shoestring or Matchstick Potatoes), 603
Almond Biscotti, 975
Almond Filling, 923
Almond Tea Cookies, 970
Amandine, 546
American French or Tomato French Dressing, 725
Ancho Mashed Potatoes, 589
Ancho Sauce, 191
Anchovy Butter, 179
Anchovy Sauce, 173
Andouille, 844
Anna Potatoes, 597
Apple and Parsnip Soup with Floating Calvados Cream, 234
Apple Betty, 1001
Apple Crisp, 1002
Apple Pie Filling (Canned Fruit), 986
Apple Pie Filling, 987
Apple Slices with Curried Chicken and Mango, 769
Applesauce, 198
Arroz a la Mexicana, 629
Arroz con Pollo (Spanish Rice with Chicken), 421
Arroz Verde, 629
Artichokes Clamart, 553
Artichokes Gribiche, 553
Arugula, Citrus, and Fennel Salad, 707
Aurora Sauce, 173
Avocado Dressing, 723

Babaganouj, 762
Bacon Cheese Dip, 761
Bacon, Lettuce, and Tomato Sandwich (BLT), 743
Baked Acorn Squash, 566
Baked Beans, New England Style, 611
Baked Chicken Parmesan, 367
Baked Chicken, 367
Baked Clams Oreganata, 461
Baked Cod Fillets Portugaise, 459
Baked Custard, 1010
Baked Fish à la Ménagère, 460
Baked Fish with Tomatoes and Mushrooms, 460
Baked Herbed Chicken, 367
Baked Lasagne, 644
Baked Meatballs, 303
Baked Oysters with Balsamic Vinegar, Arugula, and Pine Nuts, 463
Baked Pork Chops with Prune Stuffing, 301
Baked Potatoes, 592
Baked Rosemary Chicken, 367
Baked Stuffed Mackerel, 461
Ballotine de Poulet Grandmère (Stuffed Boneless Chicken Legs with Mushrooms, Onion, and Bacon), 418
Balsamic Vinaigrette, 723
Banana Bread, 935
Banana Cream Pie Filling, 1009
Banana Bread Pudding, 1009
Barbecue Sauce, 198
Barbecued Pork or Beef Sandwich, 745
Barbecued Spareribs, 299
Barley Pilaf, 625
Barley with Wild Mushrooms and Ham, 629
Basic Bread Dressing, 424
Basic Brown Stock, 157
Basic Flavored Gelatin with Fruit, 719

Basic Fried Rice, 628
Basic Mousseline Forcemeat, 863
Basic Pork Forcemeat, 856
Basic Vinaigrette, 723
Basic White Stock, 155
Basil Oil, 200
Basque-Style Pepper Salad, 692
Bavarian Cream, 1015
Béarnaise Sauce, 183
Béchamel Sauce, 171
Beef:
    Baked Meatballs, 303
    Barbecued Pork or Beef Sandwich, 745
    Beef Fajitas, 309
    Beef Pot Pie, 336
    Beef Pot Roast, 334
    Beef Stew with Carrots, 337
    Beef Stew with Red Wine, 336
    Beef Stew, 336
    Beef Teriyaki Skewers, 771
    Boeuf à la Mode, 337
    Boeuf Bourguignon, 336
    Boiled Beef, 325
    Braised Beef Jardinière, 334
    Braised Beef with Ancho Chiles, 340
    Braised Oxtails, 335
    Braised Short Ribs, 335
    Broiled Strip Loin Steak Maître d'Hôtel, 307
    California Burger, 742
    California Cheeseburger Deluxe, 742
    California Cheeseburger, 742
    Carbonnade à la Flamande, 348
    Cheeseburger (plain), 742
    Cheeseburger with Bacon, 742
    Chile con Carne, 339
    Chili with Beans, 339
    Entrecôte Sauté Bordelaise, 319
    Grilled Chopped Beef "Steaks" with Marjoram, 311
    Home-Style All-Beef Meatloaf, 303
    Home-Style Meatloaf, 303
    Hungarian Goulash, 344
    Italian-Style Meatloaf, 303
    London Broil, 308
    New England Boiled Dinner, 325
    Pacific Rim Salad with Beef, 696
    Poached Beef Tenderloin with Beef Short Rib Ravioli in Morel Consommé, 330
    Roast Beef Gravy, 292
    Roast Beef with Gravy, 291
    Roast Rib of Beef au Jus, 291
    Salisbury Steak, 303
    Sauerbraten with Sour Cream Gravy, 345
    Sauerbraten, 345
    Simmered Fresh Beef Brisket, 325
    Sirloin Steak with Red Wine and Shallot Sauce, 319
    Stir-Fried Beef with Green Peppers, 323
    Swedish Meatballs, 346
    Swiss Steaks in Red Wine Sauce, 335
    Swiss Steaks in Tomato Sauce, 335
    Swiss Steaks with Sour Cream, 335
    Swiss Steaks, 335
    Teriyaki-Style London Broil, 308
    Texas Red, 339
    Texas Short Ribs, 339
    Tournedos Béarnaise, 317
    Tournedos Bordelaise, 317

    Tournedos Chasseur, 317
    Tournedos Rossini, 317
    Tournedos Vert-Pré, 317
Beef Broth, 210
Beef Noodle Soup, 217
Beer Batter, 576
Bell Pepper and Tomato Coulis, 189
Bell Pepper Coulis, 189
Bercy Sauce, 173, 175
Berny Potatoes, 604
Beurre Blanc, 180
Beurre Rouge, 180
Bigarade Sauce, 175
Biscuits, 935
Black Bean Cakes with Salsa, 612
Black Bean Quesadillas, 778
Blancmange, English Style, 1011
Blanquette of Lamb, 326
Blanquette of Pork, 326
Blanquette of Veal, 326
Blitz Puff Pastry, 995
Blue Cheese Dip, 761
Blue Cheese Dressing, 728
Blue Cheese or Roquefort Dressing, 723
Blueberry Muffins, 936
Blueberry Pie Filling (Frozen Fruit), 987
Boeuf à la Mode, 337
Boeuf Bourguignon, 336
Boiled and Steamed Rice, 623
Boiled Beef, 325
"Boiled" Fowl, 400
Boiled Potatoes (Pommes Natures), 586
"Boiled" Shellfish (Lobster, Crab, Shrimp), 485
Bologna, 843
Bordelaise Sauce, 175
Borscht, 243
Boudin Blanc (White Sausage), 842
Bouillon Potatoes, 587
Boulangère Potatoes, 596
Bourride of Monkfish, 490
Braised Beef Jardinière, 334
Braised Beef with Ancho Chiles, 340
Braised Celery Hearts, 562
Braised Celery Root, 562
Braised Celery with Brown Sauce, 562
Braised Celery, 562
Braised Duckling with Cabbage, 412
Braised Duckling with Sauerkraut, 412
Braised Green or White Cabbage, 560
Braised Lamb Shanks, 335
Braised Lamb Shoulder, 334
Braised Lettuce, 562
Braised Oxtails, 335
Braised Pork Loin with Olives, 241
Braised Red Cabbage, 560
Braised Short Ribs, 335
Braised Sweetbreads, 346
Bran Muffins, 936
Brandade de Morue (France), 779
Bread and Butter Pudding, 1012
Breaded Pork Cutlets, 315
Breaded Veal Cutlets, 315
Brioche, 919
Broccoli Mornay, 548
Broccoli with Cheddar Cheese Sauce, 548
Broccoli, Prosciutto, and Sunflower Salad, 700
Broiled Chicken, 377
Broiled Fish Fillets or Steaks with Garlic Butter, 469
Broiled Fish Steaks Maître d'Hotel 465,
Broiled Lamb Chops, 307
Broiled Lamb Kidneys with Bacon, 312
Broiled Lobster, 468

Broiled Mako Shark Steaks with Browned Garlic Vinaigrette, 466
Broiled Poussin or Cornish Hens with Mustard Crust, 378
Broiled Rock Cornish Game Hen, 377
Broiled Rock Lobster Tail, 468
Broiled Salmon in Escabeche, 467
Broiled Scallops, 469
Broiled Shrimp, Scampi Style, 469
Broiled Smoked Pork Chop with Flageolet Beans and Wilted Arugula, 309
Broiled Strip Loin Steak Maître d'Hôtel, 307
Broiled Tarragon Chicken, 377
Broiled Tomato Slices, 573
Brown Lamb Stew, 336
Brown Rice, Barley, Farro, or Cracked Wheat with Pecans and Poblanos, 630
Brown Sauce, 174
Brown Sugar Nut Cookies, 969
Brown Veal Stew with White Wine, 336
Brown Veal Stew, 336
Brownies, 974
Brunswick Soup, 217
Bruschetta with Parmesan Cheese, 780
Bruschetta with Tomato and Basil, 780
Bruschetta with White Beans and Prosciutto, 780
Bruschetta, 780
Brussels Sprouts Paysanne, 552
Buckwheat Pancakes, 802
Buckwheat Pasta, 640
Bulgur Pilaf with Lemon, 628
Butter:
    Anchovy, 179
    Curry, 179
    Escargot, 179
    Garlic, 179
    Herb, 179
    Maître d'Hôtel, 179
    Mustard, 179
    Scallion, 179
    Shallot, 179
    Shrimp, 179
    Snail, 179
Buttered Vegetables, 546
Buttermilk Batter, 576
Buttermilk Biscuits, 935
Buttermilk Pancakes, 801
Butternut Squash Soup with Caramelized Apples, 232
Butterscotch Brownies or Blondies, 974
Butterscotch Cream Pie Filling, 1009
Butterscotch Icebox Cookies, 973
Butterscotch Pudding, 1009

Cabinet Pudding, 1012
Caesar Dressing, 729
Caesar Salad (Method 1), 689
Caesar Salad (Method 2), 689
Cajun-Style Sausage, 844
Caldo Verde, 251
Calf's Liver Lyonnaise, 321
California Burger, 742
California Cheeseburger Deluxe, 742
California Cheeseburger, 742
Caramel Fudge Icing, 956
Caramel Sauce, 1024
Carbonnade à la Flamande, 348
Carnitas, 328
Carrot Celery Salad, 695
Carrot Coleslaw, 691
Carrot Pineapple Salad, 695
Carrot Purée with Orange and Cumin, 563
Carrot Raisin Salad, 695

Carrot Salad, 695
Carrots with Orange and Cumin, 563
Cauliflower au Gratin, 549
Cauliflower Pakoras, 782
Celery Leaf Fritters, 576
Celery Salad, 695
Chantilly Dressing, 728
Charcutière Sauce, 175
Chasseur Sauce, 175
Château Potatoes, 599
Cheddar Cheese Dip, 761
Cheddar Cheese Sauce, 171
Cheese and Chili Dip, 761
Cheese Biscuits, 935
Cheese Filling, 923
Cheese Soufflé, 798
Cheese Straws, 818
Cheese Wafers, 818
Cheeseburger (plain), 742
Cheeseburger with Bacon, 742
Chef's Salad, 708
Cherry Pie Filling, 986
Cherry Pie Filling, 987
Chervil Oil, 200
Chestnut Dressing, 424
Chicken:
 "Boiled" Fowl, 400
 Arroz con Pollo (Spanish Rice with Chicken), 421
 Baked Chicken Parmesan, 367
 Baked Chicken, 367
 Baked Herbed Chicken, 367
 Baked Rosemary Chicken, 367
 Ballotine de Poulet Grandmère (Stuffed Boneless Chicken Legs with Mushrooms, Onion, and Bacon), 418
 Broiled Chicken, 377
 Broiled Poussin or Cornish Hens with Mustard Crust, 378
 Broiled Rock Cornish Game Hen, 377
 Broiled Tarragon Chicken, 377
 Chicken Bercy, 411
 Chicken Blanquette à l'Ancienne (Ancient Style), 403
 Chicken Blanquette Argenteuil, 403
 Chicken Blanquette Brunoise, 403
 Chicken Blanquette I, 403
 Chicken Blanquette II, 403
 Chicken Breast Salad with Walnuts and Blue Cheese, 712
 Chicken Breasts Parmesan, 397
 Chicken Chasseur, 411
 Chicken en Cocotte with Côte du Rhône, 417
 Chicken Forcemeat, 856
 Chicken Fricassée à l'Indienne, 410
 Chicken Fricassée with Tarragon, 410
 Chicken Fricassée, 410
 Chicken Galantine, 862
 Chicken Hongroise, 411
 Chicken or Turkey Pot Pie, 402
 Chicken or Turkey Salad, 703
 Chicken or Turkey Stew, 402
 Chicken Paillard with Grilled Vegetables, 377
 Chicken Pojarski Princesse, 393
 Chicken Portugaise, 411
 Chicken Satay, 771
 Chicken Stew with Sorrel, 405
 Chicken Stir-Fry with Walnuts 395,
 Chicken Teriyaki, 396
 Coq au Vin 420,
 Country-Style Fried Chicken, 384
 Deep-Fried Chicken, 386
 Fricassée à l'Ancienne, 410
 Fricassée Argenteuil, 410
 Fricassée Brunoise, 410
 Fricassée de Volaille Vallée d'Auge (Fricassée of Chicken with Apples and Cider), 416
 Fried Chicken Maryland, 387
 Goujons of Chicken in Salad with Sesame Seeds, 394
 Grilled Chicken Aioli Sandwich with Tomato and Avocado, 751
 Grilled Chicken Caesar, 689
 Grilled Chicken Marinated in Yogurt and Spices, 380
 Grilled Chicken with Garlic and Ginger, 380
 Grilled Chicken, Oriental Style, 380
 Grilled Spiced Cornish Hen, 379
 Mole Poblano de Polo or de Guajolote, 409

Oyako Donburi, 406
Pan-Fried Chicken 384,
Paprika Chicken, 413
Poached Chicken Breast Florentine, 401
Poached Chicken Breast Princesse, 401
Pollo con Peperoni all'Abruzzese, 338
Poulet Sauté au Vinaigre (Lyonnaise-Style Chicken with Tomatoes and Vinegar), 414
Poulet Sauté Basquaise (Basque-Style Chicken), 414
Red-Cooked Chicken, 407
Roast Capons and Large Chickens, 370
Roast Chicken with Cream Gravy, 368
Roast Chicken with Gravy, 368
Roast Chicken with Natural Gravy, 368
Roast Herbed Chicken, 368
Sautéed Boneless Breast of Chicken with Mushroom Sauce, 385
Sautéed Chicken Breasts with Lemon Grass and Three Peppers, 392
Sautéed Chicken with Tomatoes and Mushrooms, 391
Simmered Chicken or Turkey, 400
Smoked Chicken Forcemeat I, 856
Smoked Chicken Purses with Sun-Dried Tomatoes, 770
Smoked Chicken, 831
Smoke-Roasted Spiced Chicken Breasts with Fruit Salsa, 374
Southwestern Grilled Chicken, 380
Spicy Barbecue-Style Grilled Chicken 380
Stuffed Chicken Breasts Doria, 404
Vietnamese Stir-Fried Chicken with Chile, 398
Chicken and Andouille Gumbo, 244
Chicken and Celery Consommé, 214
Chicken and Leek Soup, 252
Chicken Liver Pâté, 778
Chicken Liver Terrine, 874
Chicken Noodle Soup, 217
Chicken or Beef Noodle Soup with Vegetables, 217
Chicken Tomato Bouillon with Pesto, 218
Chicken Tomato Bouillon with Rice, 218
Chicken Vegetable Rice Soup, 215
Chickpeas in Spicy Tomato Sauce, 617
Chicory and Smoked Chicken Salad with Mustard Vinaigrette, 713
Chiffonade Dressing, 723
Chile con Carne, 339
Chiles Rellenos, 578
Chili Barbecue Sauce, 199
Chili Marinade, 748
Chili with Beans, 339
Chilled Leek and Potato Soup with Shrimp and Fennel Salad, 236
Chilled Melon and Mint Soup, 255
Chilled Tomato and Basil Soup, 247
Chimichurri Sauce, 191
Chinese Hot and Sour Soup, 246
Chipotle Cream Sauce, 190
Chirashizushi (Scatter Sushi), 500
Chocolate Bavarian Cream, 1015
Chocolate Buttercream, 955
Chocolate Chiffon Dessert or Pie Filling, 1017
Chocolate Chip Cookies, 969
Chocolate Cinnamon Cookies, 972
Chocolate Cream Chiffon Pie Filling, 1017
Chocolate Cream Pie Filling I, 1009
Chocolate Cream Pie Filling II, 1009
Chocolate Crème Anglaise, 1008
Chocolate Icebox Cookies, 973
Chocolate Mousse, 1021
Chocolate Pastry Cream, 1009
Chocolate Pudding I and II, 1009
Chocolate Sauce, 1008
Chocolate Soufflé, 1020
Chocolate Tea Cookies, 970
Choron Sauce, 183
Chowder, Corn and Crab with Basil, 239
Chowder, Corn, 238
Chowder, Manhattan Clam, 240
Chowder, New England Clam, 240
Chowder, New England Fish, 240

Chowder, Potato, 238
Chutney:
 Lime and Ginger, 202
 Pineapple, 193
 Tomato Raisin, 192
Cilantro Oil, 200
Cinnamon Cookies, 972
Cinnamon Oil, 200
Cinnamon Raisin French Toast, 803
Cinnamon Sugar, 922
Cipolline in Agrodolce, 555
Clams Casino, 470
Classic Chaud-Froid, 851
Clear Caramel Sauce, 1024
Clear Glaze for Coffee Cakes and Danish, 922
Clear Vegetable Soup, 215
Club Sandwich, 743
Cocktail Sauce, 201
Cocoa Fudge Icing, 957
Coconut Cream Pie Filling, 1009
Coconut Custard Pie Filling, 990
Coconut Macaroons (Meringue Type), 971
Coconut Pudding, 1009
Cod Cakes, 480
Coffee Bavarian Cream, 1015
Coffee Buttercream, 955
Coffee Pastry Cream, 1009
Coffee Soufflé, 1020
Colcannon, 587
Cold Borscht, 243
Cold Chicken Tomato Bouillon, 218
Cold Cream Soup, 223
Cold Jellied Consommé, 213
Coleslaw with Fruit, 691
Collards with Ham, 552
Compote of Carrots and Onions, 551
Consommé, 212
 Brunoise, 213
 Chicken and Celery, 213
 Chicken and Celery, 214
 Chicken, 213
 Cold Jellied, 213
 Double, 213
 Julienne, 213
 Madrilène, 213
 Paysanne, 213
 with Pearl Tapioca, 213
 au Porto, 213
 Printanière, 213
 au Sherry, 213
 Vermicelli, 213
Cooked Salad Dressing, 730
Cookies:
 Almond Biscotti, 975
 Almond Tea Cookies, 970
 Brown Sugar Nut Cookies, 969
 Brownies, 974
 Butterscotch Brownies or Blondies, 974
 Butterscotch Icebox Cookies, 973
 Chocolate Chip Cookies, 969
 Chocolate Cinnamon Cookies, 972
 Chocolate Icebox Cookies, 973
 Chocolate Tea Cookies, 970
 Cinnamon Cookies, 972
 Coconut Macaroons (Meringue Type), 971
 Icebox Cookies, 973
 Ladyfingers, 973
 Nut Icebox Cookies, 973
 Oatmeal Raisin Cookies, 969
 Peanut Butter Cookies, 973
 Raisin Spice Bars, 972
 Rolled Brown Sugar Cookies, 971
 Rolled Chocolate Cookies, 971
 Sandwich-Type Cookies, 970
 Shortbread Cookies, 971
 Sugar Cookies, 971
 Tea Cookies, 970
Coq au Vin 420,
Corn and Crab Chowder with Basil, 239
Corn and Poblanos In Cream, 558
Corn Bread Dressing, 424
Corn Bread, Muffins, or Sticks, 937
Corn Chowder, 238
Corn Muffins, 936
Corn with Poblanos, 558
Cornmeal-Crusted Soft-Shell Crabs with Cornmeal Pancakes and Roasted Tomatoes, 475
Costolette alla Milanese, 323
Costolette di Vitello Ripiene alla Valdostana, 323
Côte de Veau Grandmère, 319
Country Terrine, 861

Country-Style Fried Chicken, 384
Court Bouillon for Fish, 484
Crab Beignets with Lime and Ginger Chutney, 774
Crab Cakes with Roasted Pepper Rémoulade, 474
Crab or Lobster Salad, 705
Crab, Shrimp, or Lobster Louis, 705
Cracked Wheat Pilaf, 625
Cranberry Beans with Asparagus, 616
Cream Cheese Icing, 954
Cream of Asparagus Soup, 223, 224
Cream of Broccoli Soup, 223, 224, 225
Cream of Carrot Soup, 223, 224
Cream of Cauliflower Soup, 223, 224
Cream of Celery Soup, 223, 224
Cream of Chicken Soup, 223, 224
Cream of Corn Soup, 223, 224
Cream of Cucumber Soup, 223, 224
Cream of Mushroom Soup, 223
Cream of Pea Soup, 223, 224
Cream of Spinach Soup, 223, 224
Cream of Tomato Soup, 226
Cream of Watercress Soup, 223, 224
Cream Sauce, 171
Creamed Mushrooms, 558
Creamed Potatoes, 586
Creamed Spinach, 547
Creamed Vegetables, 547
Crème Anglaise (Vanilla Custard Sauce), 1008
Crème Caramel, 1010
Creole Sauce, 176
Crêpes, 770
Crépinettes, 839
Crispy Duck, 408
Croissants, 920
Crumb Coffee Cake, 936
Cucumber Raita, 193
Cucumber Roundels with Smoked Trout Pâté, 773
Cucumber Salad with Dill and Yogurt, 693
Cumin Oil, 200
Cured Garlic Sausage, 845
Currant Biscuits, 935
Curried Rice Salad with Shrimp, 705
Curry Butter, 179
Curry Oil, 200
Curry Paste, 194, 195
Curry Sauce, 173
Custard Pie Filling, 990

Danish Pastry, 920
Dashi, 195
Date Nut Muffins, 936
Date, Prune, or Apricot Filling, 923
Daube d'Agneau Provençale, 342
Dauphine Potatoes, 604
Decorator's Buttercream, 954
Deep-Fried Calamari with Spicy Tomato Sauce and Aioli, 480
Deep-Fried Chicken, 386
Demi-glace, 175
Deviled Eggs, 775
Deviled Sauce, 175
Diable Sauce, 175
Dilled Shrimp Salad, 705
Dillkött på Lamm, 329
Dillkött, 329
Double Consommé. 213
Duchesse Potatoes, 590
Duck Confit, 422
Duck Sausage, 841
Duck Terrine, 861
Duck, Pheasant, or Game Forcemeat, 856
Duckling in Paprika, 373
Dutch Apple Pie Filling, 986
Duxelles, 558

Éclair Paste, 998
Ecuadorian Quinoa and Peanut Soup, 247
Egg Rolls or Spring Rolls, 776
Egg Salad, 703
Eggplant Caviar, 768
Eggplant Parmigiana, 557
Eggplant, Roasted Pepper, and Fontina Panino, 750
Eggplant, Sichuan Style, 564
Eggplants Bayaldi, 570
Eggs Benedict, 791
Eggs Bombay, 791
Eggs Florentine, 791
Elote con Queso, 571
Empanadas with Roasted Poblanos and Cheese, 781

Emulsified French Dressing, 729
Entrecôte Sauté Bordelaise, 319
Escalope of Salmon with Sorrel, 473
Escargot Butter, 179
Espagnole Sauce, 174
Essence of Celery Consommé, 213

Falafel, 671
Falafel and Roasted Vegetables in Pita, 747
Farrotto with Pecorino Cheese, 634
Fat-Free Roasted Garlic Vinaigrette, 726
Fat-Free Vinaigrette, 726
Fettuccine Alfredo, 642
Fettuccine with Gorgonzola, 642
Fettuccine with Seafood, 642
Fettuccine with Vegetables I (Fettuccine Primavera), 642
Fettuccine with Vegetables II, 642
Fettucine with Chiles and Grilled Chicken, 647
Feuilleté Chorizo, 773
Fig Compote, 202
Fillet of Lamb with Mint and Cilantro Jus, 321
Fillets of Fish Doré, 472
Fillets of Sole Meunière, 472
Fish:
    Baked Cod Fillets Portugaise, 459
    Baked Fish à la Menagère, 460
    Baked Fish with Tomatoes and Mushrooms, 460
    Baked Stuffed Mackerel, 461
    Bourride of Monkfish, 490
    Broiled Fish Fillets or Steaks with Garlic Butter, 469
    Broiled Fish Steaks Maître d'Hotel 465,
    Broiled Mako Shark Steaks with Browned Garlic Vinaigrette, 466
    Broiled Salmon in Escabeche, 467
    Chirashizushi (Scatter Sushi), 500
    Cod Cakes, 480
    Court Bouillon for Fish, 484
    Escalope of Salmon with Sorrel, 473
    Fillets of Fish Doré, 472
    Fillets of Sole Meunière, 472
    Fish Sauté Amandine, 472
    Fish Sauté Grenobloise, 472
    Fisherman's Stew, 497
    Fried Breaded Fish Fillets, 479
    Glazed Poached Fish, 487
    Gravlax, 829
    Grilled Mahi-mahi with Fruit Salsa, 466
    Grilled Tuna with Sauce Vierge and Spinach, 465
    Mackerel en Papillote, 495
    Nigirizushi (Finger Sushi), 500
    Pan-Fried Catfish with Shrimp Etouffée, 478
    Peppered Haddock with Garlic Whipped Potatoes and Parsley Sauce, 475
    Peppered Haddock with Purée of Flageolet Beans, 475
    Pesce con Salsa Verde, 489
    Poached Fingers of Salmon and Turbot with Saffron and Julienne of Vegetables, 488
    Poached Fish Bonne Femme, 487
    Poached Fish Dugléré, 487
    Poached Fish Florentine, 487
    Poached Fish Mornay, 487
    Poached Fish Steaks, 485
    Poached Salmon with Lentils in Cream, 488
    Poached Whole Fish, 485
    Roasted Monkfish Wrapped in Prosciutto, 463
    Salmon or Tuna Cakes, 480
    Salmon or Tuna Casserole, 498
    Salmon with an Almond Crust, 474
    Seafood ala Nage, 487
    Seafood Casserole au Gratin, 498
    Seafood Curry, 496
    Seafood Newburg, 496
    Skate with Caper Butter, 477
    Smoked Salmon, 830
    Smoked Trout, 830
    Smoke-Roasted Salmon Fillet with Pepper Salad, 462
    Sole Fillets Steamed in Beaujolais, 489
    Sole Vin Blanc (Poached Fillets of Sole in White Wine Sauce), 486

Southwestern Grilled Salmon Sandwich, 748
Steamed Sea Bass with Garlic and Ginger, 496
Tartar of Sea Bass and Salmon, 499
Tekka-maki (Tuna Roll), 500
Trout Meunière, 472
Zuppa di Pesce, 491
Fish Fumet, 158
Fisherman's Stew, 497
Flageolet Beans with Wilted Arugula, 613
Flaky Pie Dough, 980
Flat Icing, 956
Flavored Oils, 200
Focaccia, 918
Fond Lié, 174
Foyot Sauce, 183
French Bread, 917
French Buttercream, 955
French Fries, 603
French Garlic Sausage, 840
French Onion Soup Gratinée, 241
French Potato Salad, 705
Fresh Apple Pie Filling, 988
Fresh Bratwurst, 841
Fresh Egg Pasta, 640
Fresh Sauerkraut, 561
Fresh Strawberry Pie Filling, 987
Fresh Tomato Coulis with Garlic, 177
Fricassée à l'Ancienne, 410
Fricassée Argenteuil, 410
Fricassée Brunoise, 410
Fricassée de Volaille Vallée d'Auge (Fricassée of Chicken with Apples and Cider), 416
Fricassee of Turkey Wings. 410
Fried Breaded Fish Fillets, 479
Fried Breaded Scallops, 479
Fried Breaded Shrimp, 479
Fried Chicken Maryland, 387
Fried Chicken Wings, 768
Fried Oysters or Clams, 479
Fried Pork Balls, 328
Frijoles de la Olla, 611
Frijoles Refritos, 611
Frozen Lemon Mousse, 1018
Frozen Strawberry or Raspberry Mousse, 1016
Fruit Cobbler, 1001
Fruit Fritters, 577
Fruit Salad Dressing, 731
Fruit Salsa, 199
Fruit-Glazed Ham, 302

Game:
    Game Chili, 339
    Game Forcemeat, 856
    Game Terrine, 861
    Grilled Loin of Elk, 312
    Grilled Venison with Lime Butter, 312
    Leg of Venison Grand Veneur, 304
    Loin or Rack of Venison Grand Veneur, 304
    Medallions of Boar Poîvrade with Cassis, 322
    Medallions of Venison Poîvrade with Cassis, 322
    Rabbit with Mustard, 344
    Red Wine Marinade for Game, 304
    Roast Loin of Rabbit with Risotto, 305
    Smoke-Roasted Shoulder of Boar, 298
    Venison Sausage, 840
    See also Game birds
Game birds:
    Grilled Ostrich or Emu with Adobo Spices, 381
    Grilled Quail Marinated in Soy Barbecue Sauce, 381
    Pheasant en Cocotte, 415
    Quail Baked with Prosciutto and Herbs, 375
    Quail with Balsamic Glaze, 389
    Quail with Creole Spices, 390
    Salmis of Partridge, Pheasant, Squab, Wild Duck, or Guinea Hen, 419
Garden Salad 690 Coleslaw, 691
Garden Slaw, 691
Garlic Butter, 179
Garlic Cheese Dip, 761
Garlic Mashed Potatoes, 589
Garlic Oil, 200
Gazpacho, 254
Giblet Dressing, 424

Ginger Oil, 200
Gingered Squash, 566
Glazed Carrots (Carrots Vichy), 554
Glazed Ham with Cider Sauce, 302
Glazed Poached Fish, 487
Glazed Root Vegetables, 554
Glazed Sweet Potatoes, 568
Goujons of Chicken in Salad with Sesame Seeds, 394
Graham Cracker Crust, 981
Gratin Dauphinoise I, 594
Gratin Dauphinoise II, 595
Gratin of Corn and Poblanos, 558
Gratin of Fennel, 565
Gravlax, 829
Green Beans Basquaise, 549
Green Beans with Pecans and Browned Shallots, 551
Green Beans with Roasted Peppers and Bacon, 551
Green Beans with Sesame Dressing, 550
Green Curry Paste, 195
Grilled Cheese and Bacon Sandwich, 744
Grilled Cheese Sandwich, 744
Grilled Ham and Swiss Sandwich, 744
Grilled Chicken Aioli Sandwich with Tomato and Avocado, 751
Grilled Chicken Caesar, 689
Grilled Chicken Marinated in Yogurt and Spices, 380
Grilled Chicken with Garlic and Ginger, 380
Grilled Chicken, Oriental Style, 380
Grilled Chopped Beef "Steaks" with Marjoram. 311
Grilled Chopped Lamb "Steaks" with Rosemary and Pine Nuts, 311
Grilled Loin of Elk, 312
Grilled Mahi-mahi with Fruit Salsa, 466
Grilled Marinated Pork Tenderloin with Sweet Potato Purée and Warm Chipotle Salsa, 310
Grilled Ostrich or Emu with Adobo Spices, 381
Grilled Portobello and Boursin Sandwich, 751
Grilled Portobello and Tomato Sandwich, 751
Grilled Quail Marinated In Soy Barbecue Sauce, 381
Grilled Spiced Cornish Hen, 379
Grilled Spiced Squab with Couscous and Fig Compote, 379
Grilled Spiced Turkey Burger, 382
Grilled Tuna with Sauce Vierge and Spinach, 465
Grilled Vegetable Kebabs, 574
Grilled Vegetable Medley, 574
Grilled Vegetable Sandwich with Goat Cheese and Sun-Dried Tomatoes, 750
Grilled Venison with Lime Butter, 312
Grits with Cheddar Cheese, 633
Guacamole, 763
Gulyas, 243

Ham Mousse, 870
Ham with Brown Cider Sauce, 302
Hard Rolls, 916
Hashed Brown Potatoes, 598
Heirloom Tomato Salad, 697
Herb Biscuits, 935
Herb Butter, 179
Herb Cream Sauce, 190
Herb Sauce, 173
Herbed Broiled Tomatoes, 573
Herbed Butter Sauce, 180
Herbed Lamb Sausage, 841
Herbed Vegetables, 546
Herbed Vinaigrette, 723
Herb-Roasted Squab, 373
Hollandaise Sauce, 182
Hollandaise, 546
Home Fries or American Fries, 599
Home-Style All-Beef Meatloaf, 303
Home-Style Meatloaf, 303
Honey Cream Dressing, 731
Honey Lemon Dressing, 731
Honey Lime Dressing, 731
Hoppin' John, 615
Horseradish Oil, 200
Horseradish Sauce, 173
Horseradish Sauce, 201
Hot Caramel Sauce, 1024
Hot German Potato Salad, 705
Hot Italian Sausage, 840
Huevos Rancheros, 793

Hummus (Chickpea Dip), 762
Hungarian Goulash (Veal, Beef, or Pork), 344
Hungarian Potatoes, 587
Hungarian Sauce, 173

Icebox Cookies, 973
Indonesian Peanut Sauce, 195
Insalata Caprese, 697
Irish Lamb Stew, 327
Italian Chickpea and Rice Soup, 252
Italian Dressing, 723
Italian Sauce, 175
Italian-Style Meatloaf, 303
Ivory Sauce, 173

Jambon Persillé (Parslied Ham in Aspic), 866
Japanese Clear Soup with Shrimp, 250
Jellied Fruit Salad, 718
Jus, Mushroom, 188
Jus Lié, 174, 292

Kappa-maid (Cucumber Roll), 500
Kasha Pilaf with Egg, 634

Ladyfingers, 970
Lamb:
    Blanquette of Lamb, 326
    Braised Lamb Shanks, 335
    Braised Lamb Shoulder, 334
    Broiled Lamb Chops, 307
    Broiled Lamb Kidneys with Bacon, 312
    Brown Lamb Stew, 336
    Daube d'Agneau Provençale, 342
    Dillkött på Lamm, 329
    Fillet of Lamb with Mint and Cilantro Jus, 321
    Grilled Chopped Lamb "Steaks" with Rosemary and Pine Nuts, 311
    Herbed Lamb Sausage, 841
    Irish Lamb Stew, 327
    Lamb Curry, 347
    Lamb Medaillons with Thyne and Garlic Cream, 320
    Lamb Sausage, 841
    Lamb Tagine with Chickpeas, 329
    Moussaka, 572
    Navarin of Lamb, 336
    Rack of Lamb Persillé, 296
    Roast Boneless Shoulder of Lamb, 294
    Roast Leg of Lamb Boulangère, 294
    Roast Leg of Lamb, 294
    Roast Rack of Lamb aux Primeurs, 296
    Roast Rack of Lamb, 296
    Roast Stuffed Shoulder of Lamb, 294
    Shish Kebab, 311
Lecsó (Hungary), 564
Leg of Venison Grand Veneur, 304
Lemon Chiffon Dessert or Pie Filling, 1018
Lemon Oil, 200
Lemon Pie Filling, 1009
Lemon Soufflé, 1020
Lemon Vinaigrette, 723
Lentil and Leek Terrine with Smoked Turkey and Prosciutto, 868
Lentil Salad, 700
Lentils in Cream, 613
Lightly Saffroned Mussel Soup, 251
Lime and Ginger Chutney, 202
Lime Chiffon Dessert or Pie Filling, 1018
Linguine with White Clam Sauce, 643
Liqueur Soufflé, 1020
Lobster a l'Americaine, 493
Lobster Bisque, 237
Lobster Newburg, 493
Loin or Rack of Venison Grand Veneur, 304
Lombatine di Maiale alla Napoletana, 338
London Broil, 308
Lorette Potatoes, 604
Louis Dressing, 728
Low-Fat Buttermilk Yogurt Dressing, 732
Lyonnaise Hashed Browns, 598
Lyonnaise Potatoes, 599
Lyonnaise Sauce, 175

Macaire Potatoes, 593
Macaroni and Cheese, 646
Macedoine of Vegetables Mayonnaise, 703

Mackerel en Papillote, 495
Madeira Sauce, 175
Maître d'Hôtel Butter, 179
Maltaise Sauce, 183
Manhattan Clam Chowder, 240
Marchand de Vin Sauce, 175
Mashed or Whipped Potatoes, 589
Mashed Rutabagas or Yellow Turnips, 547
Masoor Dal (Red Lentils with Spices), 615
Mayonnaise Chaud-Froid, 851
Mayonnaise, 728
Mealy Pie Dough, 980
Meat Sauce, 639
Medallions of Boar Poîvrade with Cassis, 322
Medallions of Venison Poîvrade with Cassis, 322
Meringue, 1000
Meringue-Type Buttercream, 954
Michigan Baked Beans, 611
Mignonette Sauce, 202
Mild Italian Sausage, 840
Minestrone, 253
Miniature Gougére Puffs, 775
Miso Soup, 250
Mixed Bean Salad with Olives and Tomatoes, 698
Mixed Cabbage Slaw, 691
Mixed Green Salad 688 Spinach Salad ,688
Mixed Vegetable Salad with Pasta, 697
Mixed Vegetables with Herbs, 550
Mole Poblano de Pollo or de Guajolote, 409
Monte Cristo Sandwich, 745
Mornay Sauce for Glazing or Gratinée-ing, 171
Mornay Sauce, 171
Mortadella, 843
Moules Marinière (Steamed Mussels), 494
Moussaka, 572
Mousse of Foie Gras, 870
Mousseline Sauce, 183
Mushroom Barley Soup, 216
Mushroom Dressing, 424
Mushroom Jus, 188
Mushroom Quiche, 799
Mushroom Sauce, 173, 175
Mushroom Soufflé, 798
Mushrooms á la Grecque, 694
Mushrooms Stuffed with Tapenade, 774
Mussels In Cream, 494
Mussels, Steamed, 494
Mustard Butter, 179
Mustard Sauce, 171
Mustard Vinaigrette, 723

Nantua Sauce, 171
Navarin of Lamb, 336
Navy Bean Soup, 234
New England Boiled Dinner, 325
New England Clam Chowder, 240
New England Fish, 240
New Potatoes, 586
Nigirizushi (Finger Sushi), 500
Nonpuréed Bean Soups, 231
Noodle Bowl with Stir-Fried Vegetables, Tofu, and Peanuts, 664
Normandy Sauce, 173
Nuoc Cham (Vietnamese Dipping Sauce), 193
Nut Icebox Cookies, 973
Nut Streusel, 922

Oatmeal Raisin Cookies, 969
Old-Fashioned Apple Pie Filling, 989
Olive Focaccia, 918
Onion Quiche, 799
Onion Rings, 576
Orange Chiffon Dessert or Pie Filling, 1018
Orange Nut Bread, 937
Orange Oil, 200
Oregano Oil, 200
Oriental Vinaigrette, 725
Oriental-Style Shrimp Soup with Egg Flowers, 220
Orzo Pilaf, 625
Oven Roast Potatoes, 593
Oxtail Soup, 219
Oyako Donburi, 406
Oysters Casino, 470

Pacific Rim Salad with Beef, 696

Paella ,631
Pan-Fried Catfish with Shrimp Etouffée, 478
Pan-Fried Chicken 384,
Pan-Fried Eggplant Creole, 557
Pan-Fried Eggplant with Tomato Sauce, 557
Panzanella, 699
Paprika Chicken, 413
Paprika Oil, 200
Parisienne and Noisette Potatoes, 599
Parmesan Broiled Tomatoes, 573
Parsley Oil, 200
Parsley Potatoes, 586
Pasta and pasta sauce:
    Baked Lasagne, 644
    Buckwheat Pasta, 640
    Fettuccine Alfredo, 642
    Fettuccine with Gorgonzola, 642
    Fettuccine with Seafood, 642
    Fettuccine with Vegetables I (Fettuccine Primavera), 642
    Fettuccine with Vegetables II, 642
    Fettucine with Chiles and Grilled Chicken, 647
    Fresh Egg Pasta, 640
    Linguine with White Clam Sauce, 643
    Macaroni and Cheese, 646
    Meat Sauce, 639
    Other Colored Pastas, 640
    Pesto (Fresh Basil Sauce), 644
    Pizzoccheri, 648
    Ravioli with Cheese Filling, 641
    Rice Sticks, Singapore Style, 650
    Rigatoni or Penne with Sausage and Clams, 646
    Rigatoni or Penne with Sausage, Pepper, and
    Spaghettini Puttanesca, 643
    Spinach Pasta, 640
    Tomato Cream Sauce, 639
    Tomato Sauce for Pasta, 639
    Tomato Sauce with Ham and Rosemary, 639
    Tomato Sauce with Sausage and Eggplant, 639
    Tomato Sauce with Sausage, 639
    Tomatoes, 646
    Vegetable Ravioli In Lemon Grass Broth, 645
    Whole Wheat Maltagliate with Porcini and Peas, 649
    Whole Wheat Pasta, 640
Pasta e Fagioli, 614
Pâté Pastry (Pâte á Pâté), 857
Pea Fritters with Sesame, 577
Peach Pie Filling, 986
Peach, Cherry, or Rhubarb Crisp, 1002
Peaches In Wine, 1002
Peanut Butter Cookies, 973
Pearl Balls, 328
Pears in Wine, 1002
Peas à la Française, 562
Peas, Carrots, and Pearl Onions with Tarragon Butter, 546
Pecan Pie Filling, 991
Peppered Haddock with Garlic Whipped Potatoes and Parsley Sauce, 475
Peppered Haddock with Purée of Flageolet Beans, 475
Perigueux Sauce, 175
Persillade, 296
Pesce con Salsa Verde, 489
Pesto (Fresh Basil Sauce), 644
Pheasant en Cocotte, 415
Pho Bo, 245
Picadillo, 328
Pie fillings:
    Apple Pie Filling (Canned Fruit), 986
    Apple Pie Filling, 987
    Banana Cream Pie Filling, 1009
    Blueberry Pie Filling (Frozen Fruit), 987
    Butterscotch Cream Pie Filling, 1009
    Cherry Pie Filling, 986
    Cherry Pie Filling, 987
    Chocolate Chiffon Dessert or Pie Filling, 1017
    Chocolate Cream Chiffon Pie Filling, 1017
    Chocolate Cream Pie Filling I, 1009
    Chocolate Cream Pie Filling II, 1009
    Coconut Cream Pie Filling, 1009

Coconut Custard Pie Filling, 990
Custard Pie Filling, 990
Dutch Apple Pie Filling, 986
Fresh Apple Pie Filling, 988
Fresh Strawberry Pie Filling, 987
Lemon Chiffon Dessert or Pie Filling, 1018
Lemon Pie Filling, 1009
Lime Chiffon Dessert or Pie Filling, 1018
Old-Fashioned Apple Pie Filling, 989
Orange Chiffon Dessert or Pie Filling, 1018
Peach Pie Filling, 986
Pecan Pie Filling, 991
Pineapple Chiffon Dessert or Pie Filling, 1016
Pineapple Pie Filling, 986
Pumpkin Chiffon Dessert or Pie Filling, 1019
Pumpkin Pie Filling, 991
Raisin Pie Filling, 988
Raspberry Chiffon Dessert or Pie Filling, 1016
Rhubarb Pie Filling, 988
Squash Pie Filling, 991
Strawberry Chiffon Dessert or Pie Filling, 1016
Sweet Potato Pie Filling, 991
Vanilla Cream Pie Filling, 1009
Pineapple Chiffon Dessert or Pie Filling, 1016
Pineapple Chutney, 193
Pineapple Pie Filling, 986
Pinto Bean Enchiladas, 666
Piquant Vegetable Soup with Chickpeas, 216
Piquant Vegetable Soup with Roasted Garlic, 216
Piquante Dressing, 723
Piquante Sauce, 175
Pizza Margherita, 752
Pizza Marinara, 752
Pizzoccheri, 648
Plain Muffins, 936
Poached Beef Tenderloin with Beef Short Rib Ravioli in Morel Consommé, 330
Poached Chicken Breast Florentine, 401
Poached Chicken Breast Princesse, 401
Poached Fingers of Salmon and Turbot with Saffron and Julienne of Vegetables, 488
Poached Fish Bonne Femme, 487
Poached Fish Dugléré, 487
Poached Fish Florentine, 487
Poached Fish Mornay, 487
Poached Fish Steaks, 485
Poached Peaches, 1002
Poached Pears, 1002
Poached Salmon with Lentils in Cream, 488
Poached Whole Fish, 485
Poîvrade Sauce, 175
Polenta al Burro e Formaggio, 632
Polenta con Salsicce, 632
Polenta con Sugo di Pomodoro, 632
Polenta Fritta or Grigliata, 632
Polenta Grassa, 632
Polenta Pasticciata, 632
Polenta, 632
Pollo con Peperoni all'Abruzzese, 338
Polonaise, 546
Pont-Neuf Potatoes, 603
Ponzu Sauce, 196
Popovers, 936
Pork:
    Baked Pork Chops with Prune Stuffing, 301
    Barbecued Pork or Beef Sandwich, 745
    Barbecued Spareribs, 299
    Basic Pork Forcemeat, 856
    Blanquette of Pork, 326
    Braised Pork Loin with Olives, 241
    Breaded Pork Cutlets, 315
    Broiled Lamb Kidneys with Bacon, 312
    Broiled Smoked Pork Chop with Flageolet Beans and Wilted Arugula, 309
    Carnitas, 328
    Crépinettes, 839
    French Garlic Sausage, 840
    Fried Pork Balls, 328
    Fruit-Glazed Ham, 302

Glazed Ham with Cider Sauce, 302
Grilled Marinated Pork Tenderloin with Sweet Potato Purée and Warm Chipotle Salsa, 310
Ham with Brown Cider Sauce, 302
Hot Italian Sausage, 840
Hungarian Goulash, 344
Irish Lamb Stew, 327
Lombatine di Maiale alla Napoletana, 338
Mild Italian Sausage, 840
Pearl Balls, 328
Picadillo, 328
Pork Chops Charcutière, 318
Pork Chops Piquante, 318
Pork Chops Robert, 318
Pork Fricassée, 342
Pork Fricassée, 410
Pork Sausage, 839
Rillettes of Pork, 875
Roast Loin of Pork with Ginger, 300
Roast Loin of Pork with Sage and Apples, 293
Roast Pork Tenderloin with Leeks and Whole Grain Mustard, 300
Shish Kebab, 311
Shortcut Picadillo, 328
Shredded Pork (Carnitas), 328
Simmered Pork Shoulder with Cabbage, 325
Smoke-Roasted Pork Shoulder, 298
Spicy Garlic Sausage, 840
Thai Green Curry of Pork with Vegetables, 318
Toulouse Sausage, 839
Wontons, 328
Port Wine Sauce, 175, 198
Portugaise (Portuguese) Sauce, 176
Pot Pie:
    Beef, 336
    Chicken or Turkey, 402
Pot Roast, Beef, 334
Potage Crécy, 230
Potage Cressonière (Watercress Soup, 233
Potage Parmentier, 230
Potage Solferino, 230
Potatoes:
    Allumette Potatoes (Shoestring or Matchstick Potatoes), 603
    Ancho Mashed Potatoes, 589
    Anna Potatoes, 597
    Baked Potatoes, 592
    Berny Potatoes, 604
    Boiled Potatoes (Pommes Natures), 586
    Bouillon Potatoes, 587
    Boulangère Potatoes, 596
    Château Potatoes, 599
    Colcannon, 587
    Creamed Potatoes, 586
    Dauphine Potatoes, 604
    Duchesse Potatoes, 590
    French Fries, 603
    Garlic Mashed Potatoes, 589
    Gratin Dauphinoise I, 594
    Gratin Dauphinoise II, 595
    Hashed Brown Potatoes, 598
    Home Fries or American Fries, 599
    Hungarian Potatoes, 587
    Lorette Potatoes, 604
    Lyonnaise Hashed Browns, 598
    Lyonnaise Potatoes, 599
    Macaire Potatoes, 593
    Mashed or Whipped Potatoes, 589
    New Potatoes, 586
    Oven Roast Potatoes, 593
    Parisienne and Noisette Potatoes, 599
    Parsley Potatoes, 586
    Pont-Neuf Potatoes, 603
    Potato and Eggplant Stew with Cilantro, 588
    Potato Chips, 603
    Potato Croquettes with Peppers, 605
    Potato Croquettes, 604
    Potato Dumplings, 651
    Potato Gnocchi with Tomato Sauce, 652
    Potato Pancakes, 600
    Potato Salad, 704
    Potatoes au Gratin, 596
    Potatoes O'Brien, 599
    Potatoes with Chick Peas and Chiles, 601
    Rissolé or Cocotte Potatoes, 599

Roasted New Potatoes with Herbs and Garlic, 594
Roesti Potatoes, 598
Savoyarde Potatoes, 595
Scalloped Potatoes with Cheese, 595
Scalloped Potatoes with Ham, 595
Scalloped Potatoes with Onions, 595
Scalloped Potatoes, 595
Steakhouse Fries, 603
Steamed Potatoes (Pommes Vapeurs), 586
Straw Potatoes, 603
Stuffed Baked Potatoes, 593
Voisin Potatoes, 597
Waffle or Gaufrette Potatoes, 603
Potato and Leek Soup with Sorrel, 235
Potato Chowder, 238
Poulet Sauté au Vinaigre (Lyonnaise-Style Chicken with Tomatoes and Vinegar), 414
Poulet Sauté Basquaise (Basque-Style Chicken), 414
Poulette Sauce, 173
Prosciutto and Melon Balls, 769
Prosciutto, Blue Cheese, and Walnut Parcels, 772
Provençale Vegetables Confit, 569
Puff Pastry, 993
Pumpkin Chiffon Dessert or Pie Filling, 1019
Pumpkin Cream Chiffon, 1019
Pumpkin Pie Filling, 991
Purée Dubarry, 230
Purée Mongole, 231
Purée of Black Bean Soup, 231
Purée of Carrot Soup, 230
Purée of Cauliflower Soup, 230
Purée of Celery or Celery Root Soup, 230
Purée of Flageolet Beans with Garlic, 613
Purée of Green Pea Soup with Mint Cream, 229
Purée of Jerusalem Artichoke Soup, 230
Purée of Kidney Bean Soup, 231
Purée of Lentil Soup, 231
Purée of Mixed Vegetable Soup, 230
Purée of Potato and Leek Soup, 230
Purée of Potato Soup, 230
Purée of Split Pea Soup, 231
Purée of Spring Vegetable Soup, 233
Purée of Turnip Soup, 230
Purée of Watercress Soup, 230
Purée of White Bean Soup, 231
Purée of Yellow Split Pea Soup, 231
Puréed Butternut Squash, 547
Puréed Squash, 566

Quail Baked with Prosciutto and Herbs, 375
Quail with Balsamic Glaze, 389
Quail with Creole Spices, 390
Quail, Grilled, Marinated in Soy Barbecue Sauce, 381
Quatre épices I, 839
Quatre épices II, 839
Quiche au Fromage (Cheese Tart), 799
Quiche Lorraine, 799
Quick Chocolate Fudge Icing, 956
Quick White Fudge Icing, 956
Quinoa Salad with Bell Peppers, 699

Rabbit Terrine, 861
Rabbit with Mustard, 344
Rack of Lamb Persillé, 296
Raifort Sauce, 201
Raised Doughnuts, 919
Raisin Pie Filling, 988
Raisin Rice Pudding, 1012
Raisin Spice Bars, 972
Raisin Spice Muffins, 936
Ranch Dressing, 728
Raspberry Bavarian Cream, 1015
Raspberry Chiffon Dessert or Pie Filling, 1016
Raspberry or Cherry Gratin, 1003
Ratatouille, 563
Ravioli with Cheese Filling, 641
Red Curry Paste, 194
Red Lentil and Apricot Soup, 249
Red Rice, Spinach with Tofu Dressing, and Eggplant Dengaku, 668
Red Wine Butter Sauce for Fish, 180
Red Wine Marinade for Game, 304
Red-Cooked Chicken, 407

Reduced-Fat Vinaigrette, 726
Relish, Vegetable Caper, 192
Rémoulade Sauce, 200
Reuben Sandwich, 744
Rhubarb Pie Filling, 988
Rice and grains:
    Arroz ala Mexicana, 629
    Arroz Verde, 629
    Barley Pilaf, 625
    Barley with Wild Mushrooms and Ham, 629
    Basic Fried Rice, 628
    Boiled and Steamed Rice, 623
    Brown Rice, Barley, Farro, or Cracked Wheat with Pecans and Poblanos, 630
    Bulgur Pilaf with Lemon, 628
    Cracked Wheat Pilaf, 625
    Farrotto with Pecorino Cheese, 634
    Grits with Cheddar Cheese, 633
    Kasha Pilaf with Egg, 634
    Orzo Pilaf, 625
    Paella, 631
    Polenta al Burro e Formaggio, 632
    Polenta con Salsicce, 632
    Polenta con Sugo di Pomodoro, 632
    Polenta Fritta or Grigliata, 632
    Polenta Grassa, 632
    Polenta Pasticciata, 632
    Polenta, 632
    Red Rice, Spinach with Tofu Dressing, and Eggplant Dengaku, 668
    Rice and Shrimp Salad, 705
    Rice Pilaf, 625
    Rice Pudding, 1012
    Risi Bisi, 626
    Risotto alla Parmigiana, 626
    Risotto Milanaise, 626
    Risotto with Mushrooms, 626
    Spanish Rice, 625
    Sushi, 500
    Tomato Pilaf, 625
    Turkish Pilaf, 625
    Wheatberries with Pecans and Poblanos, 630
Rice Sticks, Singapore Style, 650
Rigatoni or Penne with Sausage and Clams, 646
Rigatoni or Penne with Sausage, Pepper, and
Rillettes of Duck, Goose, Rabbit, Turkey, or Chicken, 875
Rillettes of Pork, 875
Rillettes of Salmon, Haddock, or Finnan Haddie, 874
Risi Bisi, 626
Risotto alla Parmigiana, 626
Risotto Milanaise, 626
Risotto with Mushrooms, 626
Rissolé or Cocotte Potatoes, 599
Roast Beef Gravy, 292
Roast Beef with Gravy, 291
Roast Boneless Shoulder of Lamb, 294
Roast Capons and Large Chickens, 370
Roast Chicken with Cream Gravy, 368
Roast Chicken with Gravy, 368
Roast Chicken with Natural Gravy, 368
Roast Duckling with Caramelized Apples, 372
Roast Herbed Chicken, 368
Roast Leg of Lamb Boulangère, 294
Roast Leg of Lamb, 294
Roast Loin of Pork with Ginger, 300
Roast Loin of Pork with Sage and Apples, 293
Roast Loin of Rabbit with Risotto, 305
Roast Loin or Rack of Veal with Sage and Apples, 293
Roast Pork Tenderloin with Leeks and Whole Grain Mustard, 300
Roast Rack of Lamb aux Primeurs, 296
Roast Rack of Lamb, 296
Roast Rib of Beef au Jus, 291
Roast Stuffed Shoulder of Lamb, 294
Roast Turkey with Giblet Gravy, 370
Roast Turkey, Chicken, or Capon with Cream Gravy, 370
Roasted Beet Salad with Gorgonzola, 710
Roasted Garlic Soup with Black Olive Crostini, 242
Roasted Garlic, 567
Roasted Monkfish Wrapped in Prosciutto, 463
Roasted New Potatoes with Herbs and Garlic, 594

Roasted Onions, 567
Roasted Summer Vegetables, 567
Roasted Winter Vegetables, 567
Robert Sauce, 175
Roesti Potatoes, 598
Rohkostsalatteller, 709
Rolled Brown Sugar Cookies, 971
Rolled Chocolate Cookies, 971
Romesco, 762
Rosemary Focaccia, 918
Rosemary Oil, 200
Russian Dressing, 728
Rye Bread and Rolls, 918

Sage Oil, 200
Salad:
    Arugula, Citrus, and Fennel Salad, 707
    Basic Flavored Gelatin with Fruit, 719
    Basque-Style Pepper Salad, 692
    Broccoli, Prosciutto, and Sunflower Salad, 700
    Caesar Salad (Method 1), 689
    Caesar Salad (Method 2), 689
    Carrot Celery Salad, 695
    Carrot Coleslaw, 691
    Carrot Pineapple Salad, 695
    Carrot Raisin Salad, 695
    Carrot Salad, 695
    Celery Salad, 695
    Chef's Salad, 708
    Chicken Breast Salad with Walnuts and Blue Cheese, 712
    Chicken or Turkey Salad, 703
    Chicory and Smoked Chicken Salad with Mustard Vinaigrette, 713
    Coleslaw with Fruit, 691
    Crab or Lobster Salad, 705
    Crab, Shrimp, or Lobster Louis, 705
    Cucumber Salad with Dill and Yogurt, 693
    Curried Rice Salad with Shrimp, 705
    Dilled Shrimp Salad, 705
    Egg Salad, 703
    French Potato Salad, 705
    Garden Salad 690 Coleslaw, 691
    Garden Slaw, 691
    Grilled Chicken Caesar, 689
    Heirloom Tomato Salad, 697
    Hot German Potato Salad, 705
    Insalata Caprese, 697
    Jellied Fruit Salad, 718
    Lentil Salad, 700
    Macedoine of Vegetables Mayonnaise, 703
    Mixed Bean Salad with Olives and Tomatoes, 698
    Mixed Cabbage Slaw, 691
    Mixed Green Salad 688 Spinach Salad, 688
    Mixed Vegetable Salad with Pasta, 697
    Mushrooms á la Grecque, 694
    Pacific Rim Salad with Beef, 696
    Panzanella, 699
    Potato Salad, 704
    Quinoa Salad with Bell Peppers, 699
    Rice and Shrimp Salad, 705
    Roasted Beet Salad with Gorgonzola, 710
    Rohkostsalatteller, 709
    Salad of Belgian Endive, Scallops, and Walnuts, 714
    Salad of Mixed Cabbage and Apples, 692
    Salad of Seared Sea Scallops with Oriental Vinaigrette, 713
    Salade Niçoise, 711
    Stuffed Tomatoes Chinoise, 715
    Tabouli, 701
    Taco Salad, 716
    Thai Papaya and Mango Salad, 707
    Tuna or Salmon Salad, 703
    Vegetable Chopped Salad with Kidney Beans and Provolone, 698
    Waldorf Salad, 706
    Warm Goat Cheese Salad, 714
    Wheatberry Salad with Mint, 701
    White Bean Salad, 693
Salisbury Steak, 303
Salmis of Partridge 419,
Salmon or Tuna Cakes, 480
Salmon or Tuna Casserole, 498

Salmon Soufflé, 798
Salmon with an Almond Crust, 474
Salsa, Fruit, 199
Salsa Cruda, 191
Salsa Roja, 190
Salsa Verde Cocida, 190
Saltimbocca alla Romana, 348
Sandwich-Type Cookies, 970
Sauce:
    Aioli, 201
    Albufera, 173
    Allemande, 173
    Ancho, 191
    Anchovy, 173
    Applesauce, 198
    Aurora, 173
    Barbecue, 198
    Béarnaise, 183
    Béchamel, 171
    Bell Pepper and Tomato Coulis, 189
    Bell Pepper Coulis, 189
    Bercy, 175
    Beurre Blanc, 180
    Beurre Rouge, 180
    Bigarade, 175
    Bordelaise, 175
    Brown, 174
    Charcutière, 175
    Chasseur, 175
    Cheddar Cheese, 171
    Chili Barbecue, 199
    Chimichurri, 191
    Chipotle Cream, 190
    Choron, 183
    Cocktail, 201
    Cream, 171
    Creole, 175
    Cucumber Raita, 193
    Curry, 173
    Demi-glace, 175
    Deviled, 175
    Diable, 175
    Espagnole, 174
    Flavored Oils, 200
    Fond Lié, 174
    Foyot, 183
    Fresh Tomato Coulis with Garlic, 177
    Fruit Salsa, 199
    Herb Cream, 190
    Herb, 173
    Herbed Butter Sauce, 180
    Hollandaise, 182
    Horseradish, 173
    Horseradish, 201
    Hungarian, 173
    Indonesian Peanut, 195
    Italian, 175
    Ivory, 173
    Jus Lié, 174
    Lyonnaise, 175
    Madeira, 175
    Maltaise, 183
    Marchand de Vin, 175
    Mignonette, 202
    Mornay, 171
    Mousseline, 183
    Mushroom, 173
    Nantua, 171
    Normandy, 173
    Nuoc Cham (Vietnamese Dipping Sauce), 193
    Perigueux, 175
    Piquante, 175
    Poivrade, 175
    Ponzu, 196
    Port Wine, 175
    Port Wine, 198
    Portuguese (Portuguese), 176
    Poulette, 173
    Raifort, 201
    Red Wine Butter Sauce for Fish, 180
    Rémoulade, 200
    Robert, 175
    Salsa Cruda, 191
    Salsa Roja, 190
    Salsa Verde Cocida, 190
    Sauce Gribiche, 724
    Sauce Vierge, 197
    Sesame Miso, 196
    Shrimp, 173
    Soubise, 171
    Soy Barbecue, 199
    Spanish, 176
    Suprême, 172
    Sweet Corn and Chile Purée, 189
    Tartar, 200

Thai Green Curry, 194
Thai Red Curry, 194
Tomato (Vegetarian), 176
Tomato Broth for Chiles Rellenos, 190
Tomato, 176
Tomatoed Soubise, 171
Velouté, 172
Venetian, 173
White Bean Purée, 189
White Wine Cream Sauce for Fish, 197
White Wine, 172
Wine Merchant, 175
Yakitori, 196
Yogurt Sour Cream, 197
Sauerbraten, 345
Sauerbraten with Sour Cream Gravy, 345
Sauerkraut, 561
Sausage:
    Andouille, 844
    Bologna, 843
    Boudin Blanc (White Sausage), 842
    Cajun-Style Sausage, 844
    Crépinettes, 839
    Cured Garlic Sausage, 845
    Duck Sausage, 841
    French Garlic Sausage, 840
    Fresh Bratwurst, 841
    Herbed Lamb Sausage, 841
    Hot Italian Sausage, 840
    Lamb Sausage, 841
    Mild Italian Sausage, 840
    Mortadella, 843
    Pork Sausage, 839
    Smoked Garlic Sausage, 845
    Spicy Garlic Sausage, 840
    Toulouse Sausage, 839
    Veal or Beef Sausage, 840
    Venison Sausage, 840
Sausage Dressing, 424
Sautéed Boneless Breast of Chicken with Mushroom Sauce, 385
Sautéed Chicken Breasts with Lemon Grass and Three Peppers, 392
Sautéed Chicken with Tomatoes and Mushrooms, 391
Sautéed Mushrooms, 558
Sautéed Scallops with Tomato, Garlic, and Parsley, 473
Sautéed Shrimp, 473
Sautéed Soft-Shell Crabs, 472
Sautéed Veal Sweetbreads with Shiitake Mushrooms and Port Wine Sauce, 322
Savoyarde Potatoes, 595
Scallion Butter, 179
Scallop Seviche, 502
Scalloped Potatoes with Cheese, 595
Scalloped Potatoes with Ham, 595
Scalloped Potatoes with Onions, 595
Scalloped Potatoes, 595
Schnitzel à la Holstein, 315
Scotch Broth, 253
Seafood ala Nage, 487
Seafood Casserole au Gratin, 498
Seafood Curry, 496
Seafood Gumbo, 244
Seafood Newburg, 496
Seafood Quiche, 799
Seafood Terrine with Vegetables, 864
Sesame Miso Dressing, 550
Sesame Miso Sauce, 196
Shallot Butter, 179
Shallot Oil, 200
Shish Kebab, 311
Short Dough, 981
Shortbread Cookies, 971
Shortcut Picadillo, 328
Shredded Pork (Carnitas), 328
Shredded Zucchini with Shallots, 557
Shrimp a l'Americaine or Shrimp Newburg, 493
Shrimp and Cucumber in Thai Red Curry, 477
Shrimp and Vegetable Tempura, 481
Shrimp Bisque, 237
Shrimp Brochettes, 469
Shrimp Butter, 179
Shrimp Sauce, 173
Simmered Chicken or Turkey, 400
Simmered Fresh Beef Brisket, 325
Simmered Pork Shoulder with Cabbage, 325
Simple Buttercream, 954
Sirloin Steak with Red Wine and Shallot Sauce, 319
Sirniki (Russian Fried Cheese Cakes), 817

Skate with Caper Butter, 477
Smoked Chicken Purses with Sun-Dried Tomatoes, 770
Smoked Duck, 831
Smoked Garlic Sausage, 845
Smoked Ham and Taleggio Panino, 749
Smoked Salmon and Trout Logs on Pumpernickel, 772
Smoked Salmon Rolls, 767
Smoked Salmon, 830
Smoked Trout, 830
Smoked Turkey or Chicken, 831
Smoke-Roasted Pork Shoulder, 298
Smoke-Roasted Salmon Fillet with Pepper Salad, 462
Smoke-Roasted Shoulder of Boar, 298
Smoke-Roasted Spiced Chicken Breasts with Fruit Salsa, 374
Snail Butter, 179
Soft Rolls, 916
Sole Fillets Steamed in Beaujolais, 489
Sole Vin Blanc (Poached Fillets of Sole in White Wine Sauce), 486
Soubise Sauce, 171
Soufflés:
    Cheese Soufflé, 798
    Chocolate Soufflé, 1020
    Coffee Soufflé, 1020
    Lemon Soufflé, 1020
    Liqueur Soufflé, 1020
    Mushroom Soufflé, 798
    Other Vegetable Soufflés, 798
    Salmon Soufflé, 798
    Spinach and Ham Soufflé, 798
    Spinach Soufflé, 798
    Vanilla Soufflé, 1020
Soups:
    Apple and Parsnip Soup with Floating Calvados Cream, 234
    Beef Broth, 210
    Beef Noodle Soup, 217
    Borscht, 243
    Brunswick Stew, 217
    Butternut Squash Soup with Caramelized Apples, 232
    Caldo Verde, 251
    Chicken and Andouille Gumbo, 244
    Chicken and Celery Consommé, 214
    Chicken and Leek Soup, 252
    Chicken Consommé, 213
    Chicken Noodle Soup, 217
    Chicken or Beef Noodle Soup with Vegetables, 217
    Chicken Tomato Bouillon with Pesto, 218
    Chicken Tomato Bouillon with Rice, 218
    Chicken Vegetable Rice Soup, 215
    Chilled Leek and Potato Soup with Shrimp and Fennel Salad, 236
    Chilled Melon and Mint Soup, 255
    Chilled Tomato and Basil Soup, 247
    Chinese Hot and Sour Soup, 246
    Clear Vegetable Soup, 215
    Cold Borscht, 243
    Cold Chicken Tomato Bouillon, 218
    Cold Cream Soup, 223
    Cold Jellied Consommé, 213
    Consommé au Porto, 213
    Consommé au Sherry, 213
    Consommé Brunoise, 213
    Consommé Julienne, 213
    Consommé Madrilène, 213
    Consommé Paysanne, 213
    Consommé Printanière, 213
    Consommé Vermicelli, 213
    Consommé with Pearl Tapioca, 213
    Consommé, 212
    Corn and Crab Chowder with Basil, 239
    Corn Chowder, 238
    Cream of Asparagus Soup, 223, 224
    Cream of Broccoli Soup, 223, 224, 225
    Cream of Carrot Soup, 223, 224
    Cream of Cauliflower Soup, 223, 224
    Cream of Celery Soup, 223, 224
    Cream of Chicken Soup, 223, 224
    Cream of Corn Soup, 223, 224
    Cream of Cucumber Soup, 223, 224
    Cream of Mushroom Soup, 223
    Cream of Pea Soup, 223, 224
    Cream of Spinach Soup, 223, 224
    Cream of Tomato Soup, 226

    Cream of Watercress Soup, 223, 224
    Double Consommé. 213
    Ecuadorian Quinoa and Peanut Soup, 247
    Essence of Celery Consommé, 213
    French Onion Soup Gratinée, 241
    Gazpacho, 254
    Gulyas, 243
    Italian Chickpea and Rice Soup, 252
    Japanese Clear Soup with Shrimp, 250
    Lightly Saffroned Mussel Soup, 251
    Lobster Bisque, 237
    Manhattan Clam Chowder, 240
    Minestrone, 253
    Miso Soup, 250
    Mushroom Barley Soup, 216
    Navy Bean Soup, 234
    New England Clam Chowder, 240
    New England Fish, 240
    Nonpuréed Bean Soups, 231
    Oriental-Style Shrimp Soup with Egg Flowers, 220
    Oxtail Soup, 219
    Pho Bo, 245
    Piquant Vegetable Soup with Chickpeas, 216
    Piquant Vegetable Soup with Roasted Garlic, 216
    Potage Crécy, 230
    Potage Cressonière (Watercress Soup), 233
    Potage Parmentier, 230
    Potage Solferino, 230
    Potato and Leek Soup with Sorrel, 235
    Potato Chowder, 238
    Purée Dubarry, 230
    Purée Mongole, 231
    Purée of Black Bean Soup, 231
    Purée of Carrot Soup, 230
    Purée of Cauliflower Soup, 230
    Purée of Celery or Celery Root Soup, 230
    Purée of Green Pea Soup with Mint Cream, 229
    Purée of Jerusalem Artichoke Soup, 230
    Purée of Kidney Bean Soup, 231
    Purée of Lentil Soup, 231
    Purée of Mixed Vegetable Soup, 230
    Purée of Potato and Leek Soup, 230
    Purée of Potato Soup, 230
    Purée of Split Pea Soup, 231
    Purée of Spring Vegetable Soup, 233
    Purée of Turnip Soup, 230
    Purée of Watercress Soup, 230
    Purée of White Bean Soup, 231
    Purée of Yellow Split Pea Soup, 231
    Red Lentil and Apricot Soup, 249
    Roasted Garlic Soup with Black Olive Crostini, 242
    Scotch Broth, 253
    Seafood Gumbo, 244
    Shrimp Bisque, 237
    Spicy Black Bean Soup, 235
    Summer Vegetable and Smoked Tomato Soup, 249
    Tortilla Soup, 248
    Vegetable Beef Barley Soup, 215
    Vegetable Beef Soup, 215
    Vegetable Rice Soup, 215
    Velouté Agnes Sorel, 252
    Vichyssoise, 236
    Viennese-Style Vegetable Broth, 242
    Vietnamese Beef and Rice Noodle Soup, 245
    Watercress Soup, 233
    Wild Rice and Mushroom Soup, 227
    Wisconsin Cheddar and Broccoli Soup, 228
    Zuppa di Ceci e Riso, 252
Sour Cream Avocado Dip, 763
Sour Cream Fruit Salad Dressing, 730
Southwestern Corn and Pinto Bean Gratin, 569
Southwestern Grilled Chicken, 380
Southwestern Grilled Salmon Sandwich, 748
Soy Barbecue Sauce, 199
Spaetzle, 651
Spaghettini Puttanesca, 643

Spanish Rice, 625
Spanish Sauce, 176
Spice Rub I, 298
Spice Rub II, 299
Spicy Barbecue-Style Grilled Chicken 380
Spicy Black Bean Soup, 235
Spicy Garlic Sausage, 840
Spicy Meat Empanadas, 781
Spicy Shrimp or Scallop Sauté, 476
Spinach and Ham Soufflé, 798
Spinach Boreks, 766
Spinach Pasta, 640
Spinach Quiche, 799
Spinach Soufflé, 798
Spinach Timbales, 568
Spinaci alla Piemontese, 555
Spinaci alla Romana, 555
Squash Pie Filling, 991
Steakhouse Fries, 603
Steamed Mussels (without wine), 494
Steamed Potatoes (Pommes Vapeurs), 586
Steamed Sea Bass with Garlic and Ginger, 496
Stew, Beef with Red Wine, 336
Stew, Beef, 336
Stew, Brown Lamb, 336
Stew, Brown Veal with White Wine, 336
Stew, Brown Veal, 336
Stew, Chicken or Turkey, 402
Stew, Chicken with Sorrel, 405
Stew, Fisherman's, 497
Stew, Irish Lamb, 327
Stir-Fried Beef with Green Peppers, 323
Stir-Fried Mixed Vegetables, 559
Stock:
    Basic Brown, 157
    Basic White, 155
    Dashi, 195
    Fish, 158
    Vegetable, 155
Straw Potatoes, 603
Strawberry Bavarian Cream, 1015
Strawberry Chiffon Dessert or Pie Filling, 1016
Streusel or Crumb Topping, 922
Stuffed Baked Potatoes, 593
Stuffed Chicken Breasts Doria, 404
Stuffed Mushrooms with Cheese, 767
Stuffed Tomatoes Chinoise, 715
Submarine Sandwich, 743
Sugar Cookies, 971
Summer Squash, Spinach, and Leek Frittata, 797
Summer Vegetable and Smoked Tomato Soup, 249
Suprême Sauce, 172
Sushi Rice, 500
Swedish Meatballs, 346
Sweet Corn and Chile Purée, 189
Sweet Potato Pie Filling, 991
Sweet Roll Dough, 919
Swiss Fondue, 818
Swiss Steaks, 335
Swiss Steaks in Red Wine Sauce, 335
Swiss Steaks in Tomato Sauce, 335
Swiss Steaks with Sour Cream, 335

Tabouli, 701
Taco Salad, 716
Tahini Yogurt Dressing, 747
Tangerine-Marinated Breast of Duck, 391
Tartar of Sea Bass and Salmon, 499
Tartar Sauce, 200
Tea Cookies, 970
Tea-Smoked Duck, 408
Tekka-maki (Tuna Roll), 500
Tendon, 406
Teriyaki-Style London Broil, 308
Terrines and pâtés:
    Chicken Galantine, 862
    Chicken Liver Terrine, 874
    Country Terrine, 861
    Duck Terrine, 861
    Game Terrine, 861
    Jambon Persillé (Parslied Ham in Aspic), 866
    Lentil and Leek Terrine with Smoked Turkey and Prosciutto, 868
    Rabbit Terrine, 861
    Seafood Terrine with Vegetables, 864
    Terrine of Foie Gras, 873
    Terrine of Vegetables and Chicken in Aspic, 867

Terrine of Vegetables with Chicken Mousseline, 864
Terrine of Vegetables with Foie Gras in Aspic, 867
Tricolor Vegetable Terrine, 869
Veal and Ham Terrine with Foie Gras, 861
Veal and Ham Terrine, 861
Veal and Tongue Terrine, 861
Texas Red, 339
Texas Short Ribs, 339
Thai Green Curry of Pork with Vegetables, 318
Thai Green Curry Sauce, 194
Thai Papaya and Mango Salad, 707
Thai Red Curry Sauce, 194
Thousand Island Dressing, 728
Three-Bean Chili with Tostaditas, 667
Thyme Oil, 200
Tomato and Zucchini Tian, 571
Tomato Broth for Chiles Rellenos, 190
Tomato Cream Sauce, 639
Tomato Pilaf, 625
Tomato Raisin Chutney, 192
Tomato Sauce (Vegetarian), 176
Tomato Sauce for Pasta, 639
Tomato Sauce with Ham and Rosemary, 639
Tomato Sauce with Sausage and Eggplant, 639
Tomato Sauce with Sausage, 639
Tomato Sauce, 176
Tomatoed Soubise Sauce, 171
Tomatoes, 646
Tortilla Soup, 248
Toulouse Sausage, 839
Tournedos Béarnaise, 317
Tournedos Bordelaise, 317
Tournedos Chasseur, 317
Tournedos Rossini, 317
Tournedos Vert-Pré, 317
Traditional Falafel in Pita, 747
Tricolor Vegetable Terrine, 869
Tripes à la Mode de Caen, 327
Trout Meunière, 472
Tuna Carpaccio with Sheep's-Milk Cheese, 503
Tuna or Salmon Salad, 703
Turkey:
    Chicken or Turkey Pot Pie, 402
    Chicken or Turkey Stew, 402
    Fricassee of Turkey Wings, 410
    Grilled Spiced Turkey Burger, 382
    Mole Poblano de Pollo or de Guajolote, 409
    Roast Turkey with Giblet Gravy, 370
    Roast Turkey, Chicken, or Capon with Cream Gravy, 370
    Simmered Chicken or Turkey, 400
    Smoked Turkey, 831
    Turkey BLT Wrap, 746
    Turkey Scaloppine with Shiitake Mushrooms and Roasted Shallots, 388
Turkish Pilaf, 625

Vanilla Cream Pie Filling, 1009
Vanilla Fudge Icing, 957
Vanilla Pastry Cream, 1009
Vanilla Pudding, 1009
Vanilla Soufflé, 1020
Veal:
    Blanquette of Veal, 326
    Breaded Veal Cutlets, 315
    Brown Veal Stew with White Wine, 336
    Brown Veal Stew, 336
    Costolette alla Milanese, 323
    Costolette di Vitello Ripiene alla Valdostana, 323

Côte de Veau Grandmère, 319
Dillkött, 329
Hungarian Goulash, 344
Roast Loin or Rack of Veal with Sage and Apples, 293
Saltimbocca alla Romana, 348
Sautéed Veal Sweetbreads with Shiitake Mushrooms and Port Wine Sauce, 322
Schnitzel à la Holstein, 315
Veal and Ham Terrine with Foie Gras, 861
Veal and Ham Terrine, 861
Veal and Tongue Terrine, 861
Veal Chops with Bacon, Mushrooms, and Onions, 319
Veal Chops, 318
Veal Cordon Bleu, 315
Veal Curry with Mangoes and Cashews, 347
Veal Cutlet Sauté Gruyère, 315
Veal Cutlet, Viennese Style, 315
Veal Forcemeat, 856
Veal Fricassée, 342
Veal Fricassée, 410
Veal Parmigiana, 315
Veal Sausage, 840
Veal Scaloppine à la Crème, 316
Veal Scaloppine alla Marsala, 316
Veal Scaloppine with Mushrooms and Cream, 316
Veal Scaloppine with Sherry, 316
Veal Scaloppine, with Lemon, 316
Veal Shank with Orange, 343
Wiener Schnitzel, 315
Vegan Vegetable and Split Pea Curry, 663
Vegetable:
    Amandine, 546
    Artichokes Clamart, 553
    Artichokes Gribiche, 553
    Baked Acorn Squash, 566
    Braised Celery Hearts, 562
    Braised Celery Root, 562
    Braised Celery with Brown Sauce, 562
    Braised Celery, 562
    Braised Green or White Cabbage, 560
    Braised Lettuce, 562
    Braised Red Cabbage, 560
    Broccoli Mornay, 548
    Broccoli with Cheddar Cheese Sauce, 548
    Broiled Tomato Slices, 573
    Brussels Sprouts Paysanne, 552
    Buttered Vegetables, 546
    Carrot Purée with Orange and Cumin, 563
    Carrots with Orange and Cumin, 563
    Cauliflower au Gratin, 549
    Cauliflower Pakoras, 782
    Celery Leaf Fritters, 576
    Chiles Rellenos, 578
    Cipolline in Agrodolce, 555
    Collards with Ham, 552
    Compote of Carrots and Onions, 551
    Corn and Poblanos In Cream, 558
    Corn with Poblanos, 558
    Creamed Mushrooms, 558
    Creamed Spinach, 547
    Creamed Vegetables, 547
    Duxelles, 558
    Eggplant Caviar, 768
    Eggplant Parmigiana, 557
    Eggplant, Roasted Pepper, and Fontina Panino, 750
    Eggplant, Sichuan Style, 564
    Eggplants Bayaldi, 570
    Elote con Queso, 571

Fettuccine with Vegetables I (Fettuccine Primavera), 642
Fettuccine with Vegetables II, 642
Fresh Sauerkraut, 561
Gingered Squash, 566
Glazed Carrots (Carrots Vichy), 554
Glazed Root Vegetables, 554
Glazed Sweet Potatoes, 568
Gratin of Corn and Poblanos, 558
Gratin of Fennel, 565
Green Beans Basquaise, 549
Green Beans with Pecans and Browned Shallots, 551
Green Beans with Roasted Peppers and Bacon, 551
Green Beans with Sesame Dressing, 550
Grilled Portobello and Boursin Sandwich, 751
Grilled Portobello and Tomato Sandwich, 751
Grilled Vegetable Kebabs, 574
Grilled Vegetable Medley, 574
Grilled Vegetable Sandwich with Goat Cheese and Sun-Dried Tomatoes, 750
Herbed Broiled Tomatoes, 573
Herbed Vegetables, 546
Hollandaise, 546
Lecsó (Hungary), 564
Mashed Rutabagas or Yellow Turnips, 547
Mixed Vegetables with Herbs, 550
Moussaka, 572
Mushrooms Stuffed with Tapenade, 774
Noodle Bowl with Stir-Fried Vegetables, Tofu, and Peanuts, 664
Onion Rings, 576
Pan-Fried Eggplant Creole, 557
Pan-Fried Eggplant with Tomato Sauce, 557
Parmesan Broiled Tomatoes, 573
Pea Fritters with Sesame, 577
Peas ala Française, 562
Peas, Carrots, and Pearl Onions with Tarragon Butter, 546
Polonaise, 546
Provençale Vegetables Confit, 569
Puréed Butternut Squash, 547
Puréed Squash, 566
Ratatouille, 563
Red Rice, Spinach with Tofu Dressing, and Eggplant Dengaku, 668
Roasted Garlic, 567
Roasted Onions, 567
Roasted Summer Vegetables, 567
Roasted Winter Vegetables, 567
Sauerkraut, 561
Sautéed Mushrooms, 558
Sesame Miso Dressing, 550
Shredded Zucchini with Shallots, 557
Southwestern Corn and Pinto Bean Gratin, 569
Spinach TImbales, 568
Spinaci alla Piemontese, 555
Spinaci alla Romana, 555
Stir-Fried Mixed Vegetables, 559
Three-Bean Chili with Tostaditas, 667
Tomato and Zucchini Tian, 571
Tuna Carpaccio with Sheep's-Milk Cheese, 503
Vegan Vegetable and Split Pea Curry, 663
Vegetable Caper Relish, 192
Vegetable Chopped Salad with Kidney Beans and Provolone, 698
Vegetable Fritters, 577
Vegetable Ravioli In Lemon Grass

Broth, 645
Vegetable Tagliatelle, 548
Vietnamese Vegetable Pancake, 669
Winter Vegetable Gratin with Feta Cheese and Bulgur Pilaf, 670
Yellow Split Pea and Vegetable Curry with Spiced Rice and Cucumber Raita, 663
Zucchini and Eggplant Lasagne, 665
Zucchini Sauté Provençale, 557
Zucchini with Cream, 557
Zucchini with Tomatoes, 557
Vegetable Beef Barley Soup, 215
Vegetable Beef Soup, 215
Vegetable Rice Soup, 215
Vegetable Stock, 155
Vegetarian Dashi, 195
Vegetarian Pinto Beans, 611
Vegetarian Wrap with White Beans, 746
Velouté Agnes Sorel, 252
Velouté Sauce, 173
Venetian Sauce, 173
Venison Sausage, 840
Vichyssoise, 236
Viennese-Style Vegetable Broth, 242
Vietnamese Beef and Rice Noodle Soup, 245
Vietnamese Stir-Fried Chicken with Chile, 398
Vietnamese Vegetable Pancake, 669
Voisin Potatoes, 597

Waffle or Gaufrette Potatoes, 603
Waffles, 801
Waldorf Salad, 706
Walnut Herb Vinaigrette, 724
Warm Goat Cheese Salad, 714
Watercress Soup, 233
Welsh Rabbit, 817
Wheatberries with Pecans and Poblanos, 630
Wheatberry Salad with Mint, 701
White Bean Purée, 189
White Bean Salad, 693
White Beans, Bretonne Style, 612
White Pan Bread, 917
White Wine Cream Sauce for Fish, 197
White Wine Sauce, 172
Whole Wheat Bread, 917
Whole Wheat Maltagliate with Porcini and Peas, 649
Whole Wheat Muffins, 936
Whole Wheat Pasta, 640
Wiener Schnitzel, 315
Wild Rice and Mushroom Soup, 227
Wine Merchant Sauce, 175
Winter Vegetable Gratin with Feta Cheese and Bulgur Pilaf, 670
Wisconsin Cheddar and Broccoli Soup, 228
Wontons, 328

Yakitori Sauce, 196
Yellow Split Pea and Vegetable Curry with Spiced Rice and Cucumber Raita, 663
Yogurt Fruit Salad Dressing, 730
Yogurt Sour Cream Sauce, 197

Zucchini and Eggplant Lasagne, 665
Zucchini Sauté Provençale, 557
Zucchini with Cream, 557
Zucchini with Tomatoes, 557
Zuppa di Ceci e Riso, 252
Zuppa di Cozze, 491
Zuppa di Frutti di Mare, 491
Zuppa di Pesce, 491
Zuppa di Vongole, 491